GREAT BOOKS OF THE WESTERN WORLD

GREAT BOOKS
OF THE WESTERN WORLD

ROBERT MAYNARD HUTCHINS, *EDITOR IN CHIEF*

19.

THOMAS AQUINAS: I

GREAT BOOKS
OF THE WESTERN WORLD

ROBERT MAYNARD HUTCHINS, EDITOR IN CHIEF

19.

THOMAS AQUINAS: I

THE
SUMMA THEOLOGICA

OF SAINT THOMAS AQUINAS

Translated by Fathers of the English Dominican Province

Revised by Daniel J. Sullivan

VOLUME I

William Benton, *Publisher*

ENCYCLOPÆDIA BRITANNICA, INC.

CHICAGO · LONDON · TORONTO

The text of this edition is derived from the translation of *The Summa Theo-logica* by Fathers of the English Dominican Province by arrangement with BURNS, OATES & WASHBOURNE LTD., London, and BENZIGER BROTHERS, INC., New York.

The bibliographical footnotes and bibliography in this edition are derived from the Piana Edition of the *Summa Theologiae* published by the Dominican Fathers in Ottawa by arrangement with the Institute of Medieval Studies Albert le Grand of the University of Montreal. Copyright, 1941, by COLLEGE DOMINICAIN D'OTTAWA.

THE UNIVERSITY OF CHICAGO

The Great Books
is published with the editorial advice of the faculties
of The University of Chicago

BIOGRAPHICAL NOTE

St. Thomas Aquinas, c. 1225-1274

At the end of 1224 or the beginning of 1225 Thomas was born at Roccasecca, near Naples, in the ancestral castle of the counts of Aquino. He was the seventh and youngest son of Landulfo, the head of one of the most illustrious families of Southern Italy and nephew to Frederick Barbarossa. His mother, Countess Teodora Carracciolo, was a descendent of the Normans who wrested Sicily from the Saracens. Landulfo and his sons were closely involved in the struggle between Frederick II and the pope, and in 1229 they besieged and plundered the papal stronghold of Monte Cassino. In connection with the peace settlement of the following year, Thomas, who was then in his fifth year, was sent to the Abbey as an oblate with the hope that he would one day become its abbot. His stay there lasted for nine years, during which he received his preliminary education. In 1239 the emperor again attacked Monte Cassino, and Thomas returned to his family.

To continue his education Thomas attended the University of Naples, where he followed the course in liberal arts. While there he became acquainted with the Dominicans, who had opened a school of theology as part of the university. In 1244 Thomas, against the wishes of his family, took the habit of the Dominicans and set out for Paris with the master-general to study theology. His father had recently died, and his mother, in an effort to alter Thomas' decision, sent her two elder sons from the imperial army to seize him and hold him prisoner. He did not obtain his release until the following year after the Dominicans had appealed to both the pope and the emperor and his family had discovered that nothing could shake his determination.

Arriving in Paris in 1245, Thomas began his theology at the Dominican convent. His master there was Albert the Great, who was beginning to be known as the champion of Aristotle, whose complete works, recovered from Arabic sources, were coming into general use at the University of Paris. When Albert was appointed to organize a Dominican house of studies at Cologne in 1248, he took Thomas with him as his particular student. After four years more of study, Thomas received his baccalaureate and, on the recommendation of his master, was sent back to Paris to teach and to prepare for becoming a master in theology.

In 1252 Thomas entered upon the teaching career to which he was to devote the rest of his life and which was to involve him in every great intellectual conflict of the time. Beginning as a bachelor, he lectured upon the Scriptures and the basic theological text-book of the day, the *Sentences* of Peter Lombard. He enjoyed great popularity as a teacher. One of his students later recorded that "he introduced new articles into his lectures, founded a new and clear method of scientific investigation and synthesis, and developed new proofs in his argumentation." Although the university required that a master in theology be at least thirty-four years old, Thomas, after a papal dispensation, was given his degree in 1256, when little more than thirty-one, and appointed to fill one of the two chairs allowed the Dominicans at the university.

Almost immediately after entering upon his university career, Thomas was called upon to defend the right of the new religious orders to teach at the university. Thomas and his friend Bonaventure became respectively the spokesmen for the Dominicans and the Franciscans against the charges made by the secular clerics of the university. Besides providing written refutation of their accusations, Thomas showed by his own teaching that the religious orders had all the necessary qualifications. As part of his work at this period he held during the three academic years between 1256 and 1259 the two hundred and fifty-three scholastic disputations which constitute his treatise *De veritate*. It was also at this time that he began, perhaps at the request of the famous missionary, Raymond of Peñafort, the *Summa contra Gentiles*.

In 1259, after three years of theological teaching as a master at Paris, Thomas returned to Italy. He remained there nine years, residing first at the papal curia at Anagni and Orvieto, then at the Dominican convent in Rome, and again with the pope at Viterbo. Offers to make him archbishop of Naples or abbot of Monte

Cassino were turned down so that he might continue his teaching. He commented on the Scriptures, lectured on canon law, at the request of the pope compiled the *Catena Aurea* of the glosses on the Gospels, and wrote a work aiming at the reconciliation of the Greek church with Rome. On the institution of the feast of Corpus Christi, he was chosen to provide its liturgical office, for which he wrote the hymns, *Pange lingua gloriosi corporis mysterium, Sacris solemniis juncta sint gaudia,* and the *Verbum supernum prodiens.* Also with papal encouragement Thomas then began his exposition of the works of Aristotle. At the papal curia he met his confrère, William of Moerbeke, who at the suggestion of Thomas began a new translation of Aristotle direct from the Greek. Aided by a good text, free of the corruptions that characterized the versions taken from the Arabic, Thomas between 1265 and 1269 commented on the *Physics, Metaphysics, On the Soul, Ethics, Politics,* and the *Posterior Analytics.*

At the beginning of 1269 Thomas was suddenly called back to Paris, where the conflict over Aristotle was coming to a climax. His activity in large part consisted, on the one hand, in refuting the Latin Averroists of the Faculty of Arts who were presenting an Aristotelianism seemingly incompatible with Christianity, and, on the other, in combatting the Augustinians of the Theological Faculty who tended to look with disfavor upon the use of Aristotle in theology. Against the Averroists, Thomas wrote two treatises, *De aeternitate mundi* and *De unitate intellectus,* to prove that their work was not sound philosophically. He also continued his exposition of the text of Aristotle. He had occasion to answer both Augustinians and Averroists while expounding his theological doctrine through

Scriptural commentaries, the many disputations he held at this time, and particularly the *Summa Theologica,* which he had begun in Italy in 1267.

Thomas was recalled to Italy by his superiors in 1272 and charged with reorganizing all the theological courses of his order. Allowed the choice of location for his work, he returned to Naples. There at the university he lectured on the Psalms and St. Paul, commented on Aristotle's *On the Heavens* and *On Generation and Corruption,* and worked on the third part of the *Summa.* He also continued to write special treatises at the requests of his friends, as he had done throughout his life. At the very beginning of his career he had written for his fellow students the *De ente et essentia;* for the king of Cyprus he composed the *De regimine principum;* in the Platonic tradition he had commented on treatises of Boethius and the *Liber de causis,* which he showed was not a work of Aristotle; as his life drew to its close he composed numerous minor works on theology, including the *Compendium theologiae.*

The writing career of Thomas came suddenly to an end on December 6, 1273. While saying mass that morning a great change came over him, and afterwards he ceased to write or dictate. Urged by his companion to complete the *Summa,* he replied: "I can do no more; such things have been revealed to me that all I have written seems as straw, and I now await the end of my life." Early the following year he was appointed by Pope Gregory X to attend the General Council of Lyons. Overcome by illness shortly after his departure from Naples, he retired to the Cistercian monastery of Fossanova. There he commented on the *Song of Solomon* at the request of the monks, and died, March 7, 1274.

GENERAL CONTENTS, VOL. I

vii

GENERAL CONTENTS, VOL. I

CONTENTS, VOLUME I

BIBLIOGRAPHY OF FOOTNOTE REFERENCES

ABBREVIATIONS

DZ—DENZINGER, H., and BANNWART, C., *Enchiridion Symbolorum Definitionum et Declarationum de Rebus Fidei et Morum*, 16th–17th edition by J. P. Umberg, Freiburg, 1928.

MA—MANSI, J. D., *Sacrorum Conciliorum Nova et Amplissima Collectio*, 54 vols., Paris and

Leipsig, 1901–1927.

PG—MIGNE, J. P., *Patrologiae Cursus Completus*, Series Graeca, 166 vols., Paris, 1857–1866.

PL—MIGNE, J. P., *Patrologiae Cursus Completus*, Series Latina, 217 vols. text, 4 vols. indices, Paris, 1844–1855.

SOURCES

ABELARD, *Opera*, PL 178.

Acta Sanctorum, ed. I. Bollandus, and others [BL], 60 vols., Paris, 1863–1870 and 6 vols., Brussels, 1883–1925.

AGATHO, Epistola I, *Ad Augustos Imperatores*, PL 87, 1161–1214.

——, Epistola III, *Epistola Agathonis et Romanae Synodi*, PL 87, 1215–1248.

ALAN OF LILLE, *Theologicae Regulae*, PL 210, 621–684.

ALBERT THE GREAT, *Opera*, ed. A. Borgnet [BO], 38 vols., Paris, 1890–1899.

——, *De quindecim Problematibus*, ed. P. Mandonett [MD] in *Siger de Brabant et l'Averroisme Latin*, Louvain, 1908.

ALCHER OF CLAIRVAUX (PSEUDO-AUGUSTINE), *De Spiritu et Anima*, PL 40, 779–832.

ALCUIN, *Opera*, PL 100–101.

ALEXANDER, *Epistola Alexandri de Ariana Haeresi*, PG 18, 547–582.

ALEXANDER III, Epistola DCCXLIV, *Ad Willelmum Archiepiscopum Senonensem*, PL 200, 685.

ALEXANDER OF APHRODISIAS, *De Intellectu et Intellecto* in G. Théry [TH], *Alexandre d'Aphrodise* (Bibliothèque Thomiste, VII), Kain, 1926.

——, *Praeter Commentaria Scripta Minora: De Anima Liber cum Mantissa*, ed. I. Bruns (Supplementum Aristotle [SA], Vol. II. P. 1), Berlin, 1887.

ALEXANDER OF HALES, *Summa Theologica*, 3 vols., Quarrachi [QR], Florence, 1924–1930.

——, *Summa Theologica*, 4 vols., Lyons, A. Koburger, 1515–1516.

ALFARABI, *Al Farabi's philosophische Abhandlungen*, aus dem Arabischen übersetzt von F. Dieterici [DI], Leinden, 1892.

——, *De Intellectu*, in Avicenna, *Opera*, Venice, 1508.

——, *De Intellectu et Intellecto*, ed. E. Gilson [GI], in Archives d'histoire doctrinale et littéraire du moyen-âge, IV, 1929.

ALGAZEL, *Metaphysica*, ed. J. T. Muckle [MK], Toronto, 1933.

AMBROSE, *Opera*, PL 14–17.

PSEUDO-AMBROSE, Epistola I, *Ad Virgines Sacras*, PL 17, 813–821.

AMBROSIASTER, *Commentaria in Duodecim Epistolas Beati Pauli*, PL 17, 45–536.

——, *Quaestiones Veteris et Novi Testamenti*, PL 35, 2213–2416.

ANONYMOUS, *Presbyterum et Diaconorum Achaiae Epistola de Martyrio Sancti Andreae Apostoli*, PG, 2, 1217–1248.

ANONYMOUS (PSEUDO-HUGH OF ST. VICTOR), *Summa Sententiarum septem Tractatibus Distincta*, PL 176, 41–174.

ANSELM, *Opera*, PL 158–159.

APULEIUS, *De Deo Socratis Liber*, Firmin-Didot [DD], Paris, 1842.

ARISTOTLE, *Aristotelis Opera*, ex recensione I. Bekkeri, edidit Academia Regia Borussica, 5 vols., Berlin, 1831.

——, *The Works of Aristotle*, ed. W. D. Ross, 11 vols., Oxford, 1928–1931.

——, **For *The Works of Aristotle*, see volumes 8 and 9 of this set.**

[ARNIM, H. VON] *Stoicorum Veterum Fragmenta*, 4 vols., Leipsig, 1921–1924.

ATHANASIUS, *Opera*, PG 25–28.

PSEUDO-ATHANASIUS, *Symbolum*, MA II, 1353–1356; DZ no. 39–40.

AUGUSTINE, *Opera*, PL 32–46.

——, **For *The Confessions, The City of God*, and *On Christian Doctrine*, see volume 18 of this set.**

PSEUDO-AUGUSTINE, *Hypomnesticon contra Pelagianos et Caelestianos vulgo Libri Hypognosticon*, PL 45, 1611–1664.

AVERROES, *Commentaria in Opera Aristotelis*, 12 vols., Venice, 1562–1576.

AVICEBRON, *Fons Vitae*, ed. C. BAEUMKER [BK], (Beiträge zur Geschichte der Philos. und Theol. des Mittelalters, I, 2–4), Münster, 1892–1895.

AVICENNA, *Opera*, trans. by Dominic Gundissalinus, Venice, 1508.

BARONIUS, C., and others, *Annales Ecclesiastici*, ed. A. Theiner, 37 vols., Paris and Freiburg, Surtz., 1864–1883.

BASIL, *Opera*, PG 29–32.

BEDE, *Opera*, PL 90–95.

BEDE (?), *Sententiae sive Axiomata Philosophica ex Aristotele et alia Praestantibus Collecta*, PL 90, 965–1090.

BENEDICT, *Regula, cum Commentariis*, PL 66, 215–932.

BERNARD, *Opera*, PL 182–185.

BOËTHIUS, *Opera*, PL 63–64.

BONAVENTURE, *Opera*, 10 vols., Quarrachi [QR], 1882–1902.

[BREMOND, A.] *Bullarium Ordinis FF, Praedicatorum*, 8 vols., Rome, 1729–1740.

CAESAR, *Commentarii de Bello Gallico*, Firmin-Didot [DD], Paris, 1879.

CAIUS ROMANUS, *Fragmenta ex Dialogo sive Disputatione adversus Proclum*, PG 10, 25–26.

CANDIDUS ARIANUS, *Liber de Generatione Divina*, PL 8, 1013–1020.

CASSIANUS, *Collationum XXIV Collectio in tres Partes Divisa*, PL 49, 477–1328.

———, *De Coenobiorum Institutis Libri duodecim*, PL 49, 53–476.

CASSIODORUS, *De Anima*, PL 70, 1279–1308.

———, *In Psalterium Expositio*, PL 70, 25–1056.

CASSIODORUS (?), *Expositio in Cantica Canticorum*, PL 70, 1055–1106.

CHALCIDIUS, *Timaeus ex Platonis Dialogo translatus et in eundem Commentarius (Fragmenta Philosophorum Graecorum*, Firmin-Didot [DD] Vol. II), Paris, 1862.

CICERO, *Oeuvres Complètes*, Firmin-Didot [DD], Paris, 1881.

PSEUDO-CLEMENT OF ROME, *De Actibus, Peregrinationibus et Praedicationibus S. Petri*, PG 2, 469–604.

CORNELIUS (CYPRIANUS?), Epistola X, *Ad Antonianum*, PL 3, 787–820.

[CORSSEN, P.] *Monarchianische Prologe zu den vier Evangelien*, Leipsig, 1896.

COSTA-BEN-LUCA, *De Differentia Animae et Spiritus*, ed. C. S. Barach [BH], Innsbruck, 1878.

CYPRIAN, *De Oratione Dominica Liber*, PL 4, 535–562.

———, Epistola LXX, *Ad Januarium*, PL 3, 1073–1082; cf. PL 4, 421.

———, *Liber de Habitu Virginum*, PL 4, 451–478.

CYPRIAN (CORNELIUS?), Epistola LII, *Ad Antonianum, De Cornelio et Novatiano*, PL 4, 355; cf. PL 3, 787–820.

CYRIL OF ALEXANDRIA, *Opera*, PG 68–77.

DECIUS AUSONIUS, *Epigrammata, Idyllia, Epistolae, etc.*, PL 19, 817–958.

Decretales Gregorii in *Corpus Iuris Canonici*, ed. Richter and Friedberg [RF], Leipsig, 1922.

[DENIFLE, H. and CHATELAIN, E.] *Chartularium Universitatis Parisiensis*, 4 vols, Paris, 1889–1897.

DIDYMUS OF ALEXANDRIA, *Liber de Spiritu Sancto*, trans. Jerome, PG 39, 1029–1110.

[DIELS, H.] *Die Fragmente der Vorsokratiker*, 3 vols., Berlin, 1910–1912.

———, *Doxographia Graeci*, Berlin and Leipsig, 1929.

Digesta, ed. T. Mommsen, rev. P. Krueger [KR]

in *Corpus Iuris Civilis*, 15th edition, Vol. I, Berlin, 1928.

DIOGENES LAËRTIUS, *De Clarorum Philosophorum Vitis*, Firmin-Didot [DD], Paris, 1878.

DIONYSIUS OF ALEXANDRIA, *Interpretatio in S. Evangelii secundum Lucam* PG 10, 1589–1596.

DIONYSIUS THE PSEUDO-AREOPAGITE, *Opera*, PG 3–4.

EADMER, *Liber de Sancti Anselmi Similitudinibus*, PL 159, 605–708.

EPIPHANIUS, *Adversus Octoginta Haereses Panarium*, PG 41, 173–42, 774.

———, *Epistola ad Ioannem*, PG 43, 379–392.

EUCLID, *Geometria*, tr. Boëthius, PL 63, 1307–1364.

———, For *The Thirteen Books of Euclid's Elements*, see volume 11 of this set.

EUSEBIUS, *Historia Ecclesiastica*, PG 20, 9–906.

EUSTRATIUS, *In Ethica Nicomachea Commentaria*, ed. G. Heylbut (*Commentaria in Aristotelem Graeca* (CG), XX), Berlin, 1892.

FRONTINUS, *Strategematicon Libri quatuor*, Firmin-Didot [DD], Paris, 1878.

FULGENTIUS (PSEUDO-AUGUSTINE), *De Fide ad Petrum*, PL 65, 671–708.

——— *Liber de duplici Praedestinatione Dei*, PL 65, 153–178.

GALEN, *Opera Omnia*, ed. D. C. Gottlob Kühn [KU], 20 vols., Leipsig, 1821–1833.

GENNADIUS (PSEUDO-AUGUSTINE), *Liber de Ecclesiasticis Dogmatibus*, PL 58, 979–1000.

GERHOHUS, Epistola VII, *Ad Adamum Abbatem Eberacensem*, PL 193, 496–500.

———, Epistola VIII, *Ad Eberhardum Archiepiscopum Salzburgensem*, PL 193, 500–514.

GILBERT DE LA PORRÉE, *Commentaria in Librum De Trinitate* (Boëthius), PL 64, 1255–1300.

———, *Commentaria in Librum de Praedicatione trium Personarum*, (Boëthius), PL 64, 1302–1310.

———, *Liber de Sex Principiis*, PL 188, 1257–1270.

Glossa in Decretum Gratiani (Decretum Gratiani Emendatum et Notationibus Illustratum una cum Glossis), 2 vols., Venice, 1595.

Glossa (Glossa ordin. and Glossa interl.) cum expositione Lyre Litterali et morali, necnon additionibus et relicis, 6 v., Basel, 1506–1508.

GRATIAN, *Decretum Magistri Gratiani in Corpus Iuris Canonici*, ed. Richter and Friedberg [RF], Leipsig, 1922.

GREGORY NAZIANZEN, *Opera*, PG 35–38.

GREGORY OF NYSSA, *Opera*, PG 44–46.

GREGORY OF TOURS, *Historiae Ecclesiasticae Francorum Libri Decem*, PL 71, 161–572.

GREGORY THE GREAT, *Opera*, PL 75–79.

GUNDISSALINUS, *De Anima*, ed. J. T. Muckle [MK] (Medieval Studies, II), New York-London, 1940.

HAYMO, *Opera*, PL 116–117.

PSEUDO-HERMES TRISMEGISTUS, *Liber XXIV Philosophorum*, ed. Baeumker [BK], in Abhandlungen aus dem Gebiete der Philosophie und ihrer Geschichte, Freiburg, 1913.

HESYCHIUS, *Commentarius in Leviticum*, PG 93, 787–1180.

HILARY, *Opera*, PL 9–10.

HILDEBERT, *Versus de Excidio Troiae*, PL 171, 1447–1453.

HUGH OF ST. CHER, *Opera Omnia in Universum Vetus, et Novum Testamentum*, 8 vols., Venice, 1754.

HUGH OF ST. VICTOR, *Opera*, PL 175–177.

PSEUDO-HUGH OF ST. VICTOR, *Summa Sententiarum septem Tractatibus Distincta*, PL 176, 41–174.

INNOCENT I, Epistola II, *Ad Victricium Episcopum Rotomagensem*, PL 20, 469–481.

———, Epistola XVII, *Ad Rufinum, Eusebium, etc.*, PL 20, 526–537.

IRENAEUS, *Contra Haereses Libri Quinque*, PG 7, 433–1224.

ISAAC ISRAELI, *Liber de Definicionibus* ed. Muckle in Archives d'histoire doctrinale et littéraire du moyen-âge [AHDLM], XII–XIII, 1937–1938.

ISIDORE, *Opera*, PL 81–84.

JEROME, *Opera*, PL 22–30.

JOHN CHRYSOSTOM, *Opera*, PG 47–64.

PSEUDO-JOHN CHRYSOSTOM, *Opus, Imperfectum in Matthaeum*, PG 56, 611–946.

JOHN DAMASCENE, *Opera*, PG 94–96.

JOHN OF SALISBURY, *Vita Sancti Thomae Cantuariensis*, PL 190, 195–208.

JOSEPHUS, *Works*, trans. by H. Thackeray and R. Marcus, Loeb Classical Library, Cambridge, Mass., 1926.

JULIAN OF TOLEDO, *Prognosticon Futuri Saeculi Libri tres*, PL 96, 453–524.

JULIANUS POMERIUS, *De Vita Contemplativa Libri tres*, PL 59, 415–520.

JUSTINIAN, *Codex Justinianus*, ed. Paul Krueger [KR], in *Corpus Iuris Civilis*, 9th edition, Vol. II, Berlin, 1915.

———, *Digesta*, ed. T. Mommsen, rev. P. Krueger [KR] in *Corpus Iuris Civilis*, 15th edition, Vol. I, Berlin, 1928.

Koran, trans. by G. Sale [SL], London, 1863.

LANFRANC, *De Corpore et Sanguine Domini adversus Berengarium Turonensem*, PL 150, 407–442.

———, *In Omnes Pauli Epistolas Commentarii cum Glossula Interiecta*, PL 150, 101–406.

LEO THE GREAT, *Epistles and Sermons*, PL 54.

Liber de Causis, ed. O Bardenhewer [BA], Freiburg i. B., 1882.

MACROBIUS, *Commentarius ex Cicerone in Somnum Scipionis*, Firmin-Didot [DD], Paris, 1875.

MAIMONIDES, *Guide for the Perplexed*, trans. by M. Friedlander [FR], London, 1928.

MAXIMUS, *Commentaria in S. Dionysii Areopagitae Librum de Caelesti Hierarchia*, PG 4, 29–114.

——— *Commentaria in Librum de Ecclesiastica Hierarchia*, PG 4, 115–184.

MAXIMUS OF TURIN, *Sermones in tres Classes Distributi*, PL 57, 529–760.

MOMBRITIUS, B., *Sanctuarium seu Vitae Sanctorum*, 2 vols., Paris, 1910.

NEMESIUS EMESENUS (PSEUDO-GREGORY OF NYSSA), *De Natura Hominis*, PG 40, 503–818.

NESTOR, *Blasphemarium Capitula XII*, trans. by M. Mercator, PL 48, 907–923.

NESTOR, Epistola II, *Ad Cyrillum*, PG 77, 49–58; Cf. Mercator's translation, PL 48, 818–827.

ORIGEN, *Opera*, PG 11–17.

OVID, *Oeuvres complètes*, Firmin-Didot [DD], Paris, 1881.

PASCHASIUS DIACONUS, *De Spiritu Sancto Libri Duo*, PL 62, 9–40.

PAUL THE DEACON, *Liber Exhortationis, Vulgo De Salutaribus Documentis ad Hencricum Comitem*, PL 99, 197–282; item, PL 40, 1047–1078.

PELAGIUS, *Commentarius in Evangelium secundum Marcum*, PL 30, 609–668.

———, Epistola I, *Ad Demetriadem*, PL 30, 16–47.

———, *Libellus Fidei Pelagii ad Innocentium*, PL 45, 1716–1718.

PETER DAMIAN, *De Novissimis et Antichristo*, PL 145, 837–842.

PETER THE EATER, *Historia Scholastica*, PL 198, 1053–1722.

PETER LOMBARD, *Glosses*, PL 191, 55–192, 520.

——— *Liber IV Sententiarum*, 2 vols., Quaracchi [QR], 1916.

PETER OF POITIERS, *Sententiarum Libri Quinque*, PL 211, 783–1280.

PHILIP THE CHANCELLOR, *Summa Quaestionum Theologicarum* (*Summa de Bono*), MS. Tolosae 192, 171 ff.

PLATO, *The Dialogues of Plato*, 5 vols., trans. by B. Jowett, Oxford, 1871.

———, for *The Dialogues of Plato*, see volume 7 of this set.

PLOTINUS, *Ennéades*, ed. and trans. by E. Bréhier, 6 vols. (édition Budé [BU]), Paris, 1924–1938.

———, for the *Ennéads*, see volume 17 of this set.

PORPHYRY, *Isagoge*, ed. A. Busse (Commentaria in Aristotelem Graeca [CG], vol. IV, part 1), Berlin, 1887.

PRAEPOSITINUS, *Summa*, MS. Turone, 142 ff. 53–127.

PROCLUS, *Institutio Theologica*, ed. F. Dubner, Firmin-Didot [DD], Paris, 1855.

PROSPER OF AQUITAINE, *Sententiarum ex Operibus S. Aug. Delibatarum Liber Unus*, PL 51, 427–496.

PTOLEMY, *Liber Ptholemei quattuor tractatuum* (*Quadripartitum*) *cum Centiloquio*, Venice, 1484.

———, *Syntaxis Mathematica* (*Almagest*), 2 vols., ed. J. L. Heiberg [HB], Leipsig, 1898–1903.

———, for *The Almagest*, see volume 16 of this set.

RAYMOND OF PENNAFORT, *Summa*, Verona, 1744.

RHABANUS MAURUS, *Opera*, PL 107–112.

RICHARD OF ST. VICTOR, *Opera*, PL 196.

ROBERT GROSSETESTE, *An unedited text by Robert Grosseteste on the subject-matter of theology* (*Hexaëmeron*), ed. G. B. Phelan in Revue néo-scholastique de philosophie [RNP], XXXVI (Mélanges de Wulf), 1934.

———, *Die philosophischen Werke des Robert Grosseteste*, ed. L. Baur [BR], in Beiträge zur Geschichte der Philosophie des Mittelalters, Band IX, Münster, 1912.

ROBERT KILWARDBY, *De Natura Theologiae*, ed. F. Stegmüller, Münster, 1935.

RUFINUS, *Orationum Gregorii Naziazeni novem in-*

terpretatio, ed. A. Engelbrecht (Corpus script. eccles. lat. [CV] t. 46), Vindob., 1910.

RUPERT, *De Gloria et Honore Filii Hominis super Matthaeum*, PL 168, 1307–1634.

——, *De Trinitate*, PL 167, 199–1828.

SALLUST, *Conjuration de Catilina—Guerre de Jugurtha*, ed. and trans. by J. Roman (éditions Budé [BU]), Paris, 1924.

SEDULIUS SCOTUS, *Collectanea in Omnes B. Pauli Epistolas*, PL 103, 9–270.

SENECA, *Works*, Firmin-Didot [DD], Paris, 1887.

SIMPLICIUS, *In Aristotelis Categorias Commentarium*, ed. C. Kalbfleisch (Commentaria in Aristotelem Graeca [CG], VIII), Berlin, 1907.

SIRICIUS, Epistola VII, *Ad Diversos Episcopos Missa adversus Iovinianum Haereticum*, PL 13, 1168–1172.

SOCRATES SCHOLASTICUS, *Historia Ecclesiastica*, PG 67, 29–842.

STOBAEUS, *Eglogarum Physicarum et Ethicarum Libri Duo*, ed. T. Gaisford, Oxford, 1850.

TERTULLIAN, *Adversus Valentinianos Liber*, PL 2, 557–632.

THEMISTIUS, *In Libros Aristotelis de Anima Paraphrasis*, ed. R. Heinze (Commentaria in Aristotelem Graeca [CG] V, 3), Berlin, 1899.

THEODORE OF MOPSUESTIA, *Ex Epistola ad Domnum Fragmenta*, PG 66, 1011–1014.

——, *Fragmenta ex Libris de Incarnatione Filii Dei*, PG 66, 969–994.

THEODORE THE NESTORIAN, *Epistolae ad Ioannem, Antiochenum Episcopum*, PG 83, 1483–1486.

——, *Haereticarum Fabularum Compendium*, PG 83, 335–556.

THEODOTUS OF ANCYRA, *Homiliae*, PG 77, 1349–1432.

THEOPHANES, *Chronographia Annorum DXXVIII*, PG 108, 55–1164.

THEOPHILUS OF ALEXANDRIA, *Epistola Altera Paschalis Anni 402 Ad Totius Aegypti Episcopos*, trans. by Jerome, PL 22, 792–812.

[THIEL, A.] *Epistolae Romanorum Pontificum Genuinae et Quae ad Eos Scriptae Sunt a S. Hilaro usque ad Pelagium II*, Brunsbergae, 1868.

THOMAS AQUINAS, *Opera Omnia*, ed. E. Fretté and P. Maré, 34 vols., Paris, 1872–1880.

——, *Summa Theologiae*, cura et studio Instituti Studiorum Medievalium Ottaviensis, 5 vols., Ottawa, 1941–1945.

——, *Opuscula Omnia*, ed. P. Mandonnet, 5 vols., Paris, 1927.

TICHONIUS AFER, *Liber de Septem Regulis*, PL 18, 15–66.

VALERIUS MAXIMUS, *Factorum et Dictorum Memorabilium Libri novem*, Firmin-Didot [DD], Paris, 1841.

VARRO, *De Lingua Latina ad Ciceronem*, Firmin-Didot [DD], Paris, 1875.

VEGETIUS RENATUS, *Institutorum Rei Militaris*, Firmin-Didot [DD], Paris, 1878.

VIGILIUS TAPSENSIS, *Contra Arianos etc. Dialogus*, PL 62, 179–238.

VIGILIUS TAPSENSIS (PS.-AUGUSTINE), *Contra Felicianum et Arianum De Unitate Trinitatis ad Optatum Liber*, PL 62, 333–352; Cf. PL 42, 1157–1172.

Vitae Patrum sive Historiae Eremetricae Libri Decem, PL 73, 89–74, 240.

VOLUSIANUS, Inter Epistolas Augustini Epistola CXXXV, *Ad Augustinum Episcopum*, PL 33, 512–514.

WILLIAM OF AUXERRE, *Summa Aurea*, MS. Paris, Bibl. Nat., lat. 15.746, 330 ff.

WILLIAM OF PARIS (WILLIAM OF AUVERGNE), *Works*, 2 vols., Venice, 1591; 2 vols., Paris, 1674.

WILLIAM OF ST. THIERRY, *Tractatus de Natura et Dignitate Amoris*, PL 184, 379–408.

WILLIAM OF SHYRESWOOD, *Introductiones in Logicam*, ed. Grabmann, Munich, 1937.

SECONDARY WORKS

BAEUMKER, C. *Witelo, ein Philosoph und Naturforscher des XII. Jahrhunderts* (Beiträge zur Geschichte der Philosophie und Theologie des Mittelalters, III, 2), Münster, 1908.

BERGERON, M., *La Structure du concept latin de Personne*, in Etudes d'histoire littéraire et doctrinale du XIII siècle [EHLD], II, Ottawa, 1932.

BRUNET, P. and MIELI, A., *Histoire des Sciences-Antiquité*, Paris, 1935.

CAPELLE, G. C., *Amaury de Bène (Autour du décret de 1210*, III [Bibliothèque Thomiste, vol. XVI]), Paris, 1932.

CHENU, M. D., *Grammaire et théologie au XIIe et XIIIe siècles*, Archives d'histoire doctrinale et littéraire du moyen-âge [AHDLM], X-XI, 1935–1936.

——, *La psychologie de la foi dans la théologie du XIIIe siècle*, Etudes d'histoire littéraire et doctrinale du XIIIe siècle [EHLD], deuxième série, Paris and Ottawa, 1932.

CHENU, M.D., *Les réponses de S. Thomas et de Kilwardby à la consultation de Jean de Verceil (1271)*, Mélanges Mandonnet, I, (Bibliothèque Thomiste, XIII) Paris, 1930.

——, *Notes de Lexicographie philosophique médiévale—Antiqui, Moderni*, Revue des sciences philosophiques et théologiques [RSPT], XVII, 1928.

DESTREZ, J., *La lettre de Saint Thomas d'Aquin dite lettre au Lecieur de Venise*, Mél. Mandonnet, I (Bibliothèque Thomiste, XIII), Paris, 1930.

DEVAUX, R., *Note conjointe sur un texte retrouvé de David de Dinant*, Revue des sciences philosophiques et théologiques [RSPT], XXII, 1933.

[DTC] *Dictionnaire de théologie catholique*, ed. A. Vacant, and others, Paris, 1923–1939.

DUCANGE D., DUFRESNE, C., *Glossarium ad Scriptores Mediae et Infimae Latinatis*, Venice, 1736–1740.

Duhem, P., *Le Système du Monde*, 5 vols., Paris, 1913–1917.

Geyer, B., *Die Übersetzungen der Aristotelischen Metaphysik bei Albertus Magnus und Thomas von Aquin*, Philosophisches Jahrb. [PJ], XXX, 1917

Gilson, E., *La Philosophie de saint Bonaventure*, Paris, 1924.

——, *L'Esprit de la philosophie médiévale*, 2 vols., Paris, 1932.

——, *Les sources gréco-arabes de l'augustinisme avicennisant*, Archives d'histoire doctrinale et littéraire de moyen-âge [AHDLM], IV, 1929.

——, *Pourquoi saint Thomas a critiqué saint Augustin*, Archives d'histoire doctrinale et littéraire du moyen-âge [AHDLM], I, 1926.

Glorieux, P., "*Contra Geraldinos.*" *L'enchaînement des polémiques*. Recherches de théologie ancienne et médiévale [RTAM], VII, 1935.

——, *Le "Contra Impugnantes" de s. Thomas. Ses sources—son plan*. Mélanges Mandonnet, I, (Bibliothèque Thomiste, XIII), Paris, 1930

——, *Les polémiques "contra Geraldinos." Les pièces du dossier*, Recherches de théologie ancienne et médiévale [RTAM], VI, 1934.

Grabmann, M., *Forschungen über die Lateinischen Aristotelesübersetzungen des XIII. Jahrhunderts* (Beiträge zur Geschichte der Philosophie des Mittelalters, XVII, 5–6), Münster, 1916.

Grundmann, H., *Studien über Joachim von Floris* (Beiträge zur Kulturgeschichte des Mittelalters und der Renaissance), Leipsig and Berlin, 1927.

Kleineidam, E., *Das Problem der hylemorphen Zusammensetzung der geistigen Substanzen im 13. Jahrhundert, behandelt bis Thomas von Aquin*, Breslau, 1930.

Kors, J. B., *La Justice primitive et le Péché originel d'après S. Thomas*, (Bibliothéque Thomiste, II), Le Saulchoir, 1922.

Lagrange, M. J., *Evangile selon saint Marc*, Paris, 1929.

Lebon, J., *Le Monophysisme sévérien*, Louvain, 1909.

Lottin, O., *La composition hylémorphique des substances spirituelles*, Revue néo-scolastique de philosophie [RNP], XXXIV, 1932, pp. 21–41.

——, *La nature du péché d'ignorance*, Revue thomiste [RT], XXXVII, 1932

——, *La pluralité des formes substantielles avant s. Thomas d'Aquin*, Revue néo-scolastique de philosophie [RNP] XXXIV, 1932, pp. 449–467.

——, *La syndérèse chez les premiers maîtres franciscains de Paris*, Revue néo-scolastique de philosophie [RNP], XXIV, 1927

——, *La théorie des vertus cardinales de 1230 à 1250*, Mélanges Mandonnet, II (Bibliothéque Thomiste, XIV), Paris, 1930

——, *La théorie du libre-arbitre depuis saint Anselme jusqu'à saint Thomas d'Aquin*, Saint Maximin, 1929.

——, *Le droit naturel chez s. Thomas d'Aquin et ses prédécesseurs*, 2ème édition, Bruges, 1931.

——, *Les dons du Saint-Esprit chez les théologiens depuis P. Lombard jusqu'à S. Thomas d'Aquin*,

Recherches de théologie ancienne et médiévale [RTAM], 1929, I.

Lottin, O., *Les premiers définitions et classifications des vertus au moyen-âge*, Revue des sciences philosoph. et théologiques [RSPT], XVIII, 1929.

——, *Les premiers linéaments du traité de la syndérèse au moyen-âge*, Revue néo-scolastique de philosophie [RNP], XXVIII, 1926.

——, *L'identité de l'âme et des facultés pendant la première moitié de XIIIe siècle*, Revue néo-scolastique de philosophie, XXXIV (Mélanges de Wulf, février 1934).

Luyckx, B., *Die Erkenntnislehre Bonaventuras* (Beiträge zur Geschichte der Philosophie und Theologie des Mittelalters, XXIII, 3–4) Münster, 1923.

Manser, G. M., *Johann von Rupella*, Jahrbuch für Philosophie und speculative Theologie [JPST], XXVI, 1912.

Martin, J., *Priscillianus oder Justantius?* Historisches Jahrbuch, XLVII, 1927.

Motte, A. M., *Une fausse accusation contre Abélard et Arnaud de Brescia*, Revue des sciences philosophiques et théologiques [RSPT], XXII, 1933.

Muckle, J T. *Isaac Israeli's Definition of Truth*, Archives d'histoire doctrinale et littéraire du moyen-âge [AHDLM], VIII, 1933.

Parent, J. M. *La Notion de Dogma au XIIIe siècle*, in Etudes d'histoire littéraire et doctrinale du XIIIe siècle [EHLD], première série, Paris and Ottawa, 1932.

Pegis, A. C., *St. Thomas and the Greeks*, Milwaukee, 1939.

——, *St. Thomas and the Problem of the Soul in the Thirteenth Century*, Toronto, 1934.

Pergamo, B., *La Dottrina della "Gratia Unionis" in Allexandro d'Hales*, Studi Francescani, XXIV, 1932.

Prantl, C., *Geschichte der Logik im Abendlande*, 4 vols., Leipsig, 1855.

Rousselot, P., *Pour l'histoire du problème de l'amour au moyen-âge* (Beiträge zur Geschichte der Philosophie und Theologie des Mittelalters, VI, 6), Münster, 1908.

Sarton, G., *Introduction to the History of Science*, 2 vols., Baltimore, 1927–1931.

Schmaus, M., *Die Texte der Trinitatslehre in den Sententiae des Simon von Tournai*, Rech. de théologie ancienne et médiévale [RTAM] IV, 1932

Simonin, H. D and Meersseman, S., *De Sacramentorum Efficentia apud Theologos Ord. Praed.*, Rome, 1936.

Thorndike, L., *A History of Magic and Experimental Science during the First Thirteen Centuries of our Era*, 2 vols., New York, 1929.

[TJE] *The Jewish Encyclopaedia*, 12 vols., ed I Singer, New York, 1901–1906.

[UJE] *The Universal Jewish Encyclopaedia*, 10 vols., ed. I. Landmann, L. Rittenberg, and others, New York, 1939–1943

Von Lieshout, H., *La théorie plotinienne de la vertu*, Fribourg, Switz., 1926.

PROLOGUE

BECAUSE the teacher of catholic truth ought to teach not only those who have advanced along the road but also to instruct beginners (according to the saying of the Apostle: *As unto little ones in Christ, I gave you milk to drink, not meat*—I Cor. 3. 1, 2), we purpose in this book to treat of whatever belongs to the Christian religion in a way that is suited to the instruction of beginners.

We have considered that students in this doctrine have not seldom been hampered by what they have found written by other authors, partly on account of the multiplication of useless questions, articles, and arguments, partly also because those things that are necessary for them to know are not taught according to the order of the subject-matter, but according as the plan of the book might require, or the occasion of disputation offer, partly, too, because frequent repetition brought weariness and confusion to the minds of the readers.

Endeavouring to avoid these and other like faults, we shall try, with confidence in the help of God, to set forth whatever is included in sacred doctrine as briefly and clearly as the matter itself may allow.

FIRST PART

❖❖❖❖❖❖❖❖❖❖❖

TREATISE ON GOD

QUESTION I
THE NATURE AND EXTENT OF SACRED
DOCTRINE

(In Ten Articles)

To place our purpose within proper limits, it is necessary first to investigate the nature and extent of this sacred doctrine. Concerning this there are ten points of inquiry.

(1) On the necessity of this doctrine? (2) Whether it is a science? (3) Whether it is one or many? (4) Whether it is speculative or practical? (5) How it is compared with other sciences? (6) Whether it is a wisdom? (7) What is its subject-matter? (8) Whether it is a matter of argument? (9) Whether it rightly employs metaphors and similes? (10) Whether the Sacred Scripture of this doctrine may be expounded in different senses?

ARTICLE 1. *Whether, besides Philosophy, any further Doctrine is required?*

We proceed thus to the First Article: It seems that, besides philosophical doctrine we have no need of any further knowledge.

Objection 1. For man should not seek to know what is above reason: *Seek not the things that are too high for thee* (Ecclus. 3. 22). But those things which fall under reason are fully treated of in the philosophical sciences. Therefore any other knowledge besides philosophical science is superfluous.

Obj. 2. Further, knowledge can be concerned only with being, for nothing can be known except truth, and truth is convertible with being. But philosophical science treats of all being, even God Himself, so that there is a part of philosophy called theology, or the divine science, as Aristotle has proved.[1] Therefore, besides philosophical

[GENERAL NOTE. Unless otherwise indicated, the reference to Articles is within the same question, and the reference to Questions is in the same part of the *Summa*.]

[1] *Metaphysics*, VI, I (1026ᵃ19).

doctrine, there is no need of any further knowledge.

On the contrary, It is written (II Tim. 3. 16): *All Scripture inspired of God is profitable to teach, to reprove, to correct, to instruct in justice.* Now Scripture inspired of God is no part of the philosophical sciences, which have been built up by human reason. Therefore it is useful that besides philosophical doctrine there should be other knowledge that is, inspired of God.

I answer that, It was necessary for man's salvation that there should be a knowledge revealed by God, besides the philosophical sciences built up by human reason. First, indeed, because man is directed to God as to an end that surpasses the grasp of his reason: *The eye hath not seen, O God, besides Thee, what things Thou hast prepared for them that wait for Thee* (Isa. 64. 4). But the end must first be known by men who are to direct their thoughts and actions to the end. Hence it was necessary for the salvation of man that certain truths which exceed human reason should be made known to him by divine revelation.

Even as regards those truths about God which human reason can discover, it was necessary that man should be taught by a divine revelation, because the truth about God such as reason could discover would only be known by a few, and that after a long time, and with the admixture of many errors. But man's whole salvation, which is in God, depends upon the knowledge of this truth. Therefore, in order that the salvation of men might be brought about more fitly and more surely, it was necessary that they should be taught divine truths by divine revelation.

It was therefore necessary that, besides the philosophical sciences discovered by reason there should be a sacred science obtained through revelation.

Reply Obj. 1. Although those things which are higher than man's knowledge may not be sought for by man through his reason, nevertheless, once they are revealed by God they must be accepted by faith. Hence the sacred text continues, *For many things are shown to thee above the understanding of man* (Ecclus. 3. 25). And sacred doctrine consists in things of this kind.

Reply Obj. 2. Sciences are differentiated according to the different natures of knowable things. For the astronomer and the physicist both may prove the same conclusion—that the earth, for instance, is round; the astronomer by means of mathematics (that is, by abstracting from matter), but the physicist by means of matter itself. Hence there is no reason why those things which are dealt with in the philosophical sciences, so far as they can be known by natural reason, may not also be taught us by another science so far as they fall within revelation. Hence theology which pertains to sacred doctrine differs in genus from that theology which is part of philosophy.

ARTICLE 2. *Whether Sacred Doctrine Is a Science?*

We proceed thus to the Second Article: It seems that sacred doctrine is not a science.

Objection 1. For every science proceeds from self-evident principles. But sacred doctrine proceeds from articles of faith which are not self-evident, since they are not admitted by all: *For all men have not faith* (II Thess. 3. 2). Therefore sacred doctrine is not a science.

Obj. 2. Further, science is not of singulars. But sacred science treats of singulars, such as the deeds of Abraham, Isaac, and Jacob, and such like. Therefore sacred doctrine is not a science.

On the contrary, Augustine says (*De Trin.* XIV),[1] "to this science alone belongs that whereby saving faith is begotten, nourished, protected, and strengthened." But this can be said of no science except sacred doctrine. Therefore sacred doctrine is a science.

I answer that, Sacred doctrine is a science. We must bear in mind that there are two kinds of sciences. There are some which proceed from a principle known by the natural light of the intellect, such as arithmetic and geometry and the like. There are some which proceed from principles known by the light of a higher science. Thus the science of perspective proceeds from principles established by geometry, and music from principles established by arithmetic. And in this way sacred doctrine is a science, because it proceeds from principles established by the light of a higher science, namely, the science of God and the blessed. Hence, just as the musician

accepts on authority the principles taught him by the mathematician, so sacred science believes the principles revealed to it by God.

Reply Obj. 1. The principles of any science are either in themselves self-evident, or reducible to the knowledge of a higher science. And such, as we have said, are the principles of sacred doctrine.

Reply Obj. 2. Singulars are not treated of in sacred doctrine because it is concerned with them principally, but they are introduced rather both as examples to be followed in our lives (as in moral sciences), and in order to establish the authority of those men through whom the divine revelation, on which this sacred scripture or doctrine is based, has come down to us.

ARTICLE 3. *Whether Sacred Doctrine Is One Science?*

We proceed thus to the Third Article: It seems that sacred doctrine is not one science.

Objection 1. For according to the Philosopher[2] "that science is one which treats only of one class of subjects." But the creator and the creature, both of whom are treated of in sacred doctrine, cannot be grouped together under one class of subjects. Therefore sacred doctrine is not one science.

Obj. 2. Further, in sacred doctrine we treat of angels, corporeal creatures, and human morality. But these belong to separate philosophical sciences. Therefore sacred doctrine cannot be one science.

On the contrary, Holy Scripture speaks of it as one science: *Wisdom gave him the knowledge* [*scientiam*] *of holy things* (Wisd. 10. 10).

I answer that, Sacred doctrine is one science. The unity of a power and habit is to be gauged by its object, not indeed, in its material aspect, but as regards the formal aspect under which it is an object. For example, man, ass, stone, agree in the one formal aspect of being coloured; and colour is the formal object of sight. Therefore, because Sacred Scripture considers things according as they are divinely revealed, as we have said (A. 2), whatever has been divinely revealed shares in the one formal aspect of the object of this science, and therefore is included under sacred doctrine as under one science.

Reply Obj. 1. Sacred doctrine does not treat of God and creatures equally, but of God primarily; and of creatures only so far as they are referable to God as their beginning or end. Hence the unity of this science is not impaired.

Reply Obj. 2. Nothing prevents inferior pow-

---

[1] Chap. 7 (PL 42, 1037).   [2] *Posterior Analytics,* I, 28 (87ᵃ38).

ers or habits from being differentiated by something which falls under a higher power or habit as well, because the higher power or habit regards the object under a more universal formal aspect, just as the object of the common sense is whatever affects the senses, including whatever is visible or audible. Hence the common sense, although one power, extends to all the objects of the five senses. Similarly, those things which are the subject-matter of different philosophical sciences can yet be treated of by this one single sacred science under one aspect, namely, in so far as they can be included in revelation. So in this way sacred doctrine bears, as it were, the stamp of the divine knowledge, which is one and simple, yet extends to everything.

ARTICLE 4. *Whether Sacred Doctrine Is a Practical Science?*

We proceed thus to the Fourth Article: It seems that sacred doctrine is a practical science.

Objection 1. For "a practical science is that which ends in action," according to the Philosopher.[1] But sacred doctrine is ordered to action: *Be ye doers of the word, and not hearers only* (Jas. 1. 22). Therefore sacred doctrine is a practical science.

Obj. 2. Further, sacred doctrine is divided into the Old and the New Law. But law pertains to moral science, which is a practical science. Therefore sacred doctrine is a practical science.

On the contrary, Every practical science is concerned with human operations, as for example moral science is concerned with human acts, and architecture with buildings. But sacred doctrine is chiefly concerned with God, of whom rather is man the handiwork. Therefore it is not a practical but a speculative science.

I answer that, Sacred doctrine, although it is one, as we have said (A. 3), extends to things which belong to different philosophical sciences, because it considers in each the same formal aspect, namely so far as they can be known in the divine light. Hence, although among the philosophical sciences one is speculative and another practical, nevertheless sacred doctrine includes both, just as God, by one and the same knowledge, knows both Himself and His works.

Still, it is speculative rather than practical, because it is more concerned with divine things than with human acts, though it does treat even of these latter, according as man is ordered by them to the perfect knowledge of God, in which eternal Happiness consists. This is a sufficient *answer to the Objections.*

[1] *Metaphysics,* II, 1 (993^{b}21).

ARTICLE 5. *Whether Sacred Doctrine Is Nobler Than Other Sciences?*

We proceed thus to the Fifth Article: It seems that sacred doctrine is not nobler than other sciences.

Objection 1. For the nobility of a science depends on the certitude it establishes. But other sciences, the principles of which cannot be doubted, seem to be more certain than sacred doctrine, for its principles—namely, articles of faith—can be doubted. Therefore other sciences seem to be nobler.

Obj. 2. Further, it is the sign of a lower science to depend upon a higher, as music depends upon arithmetic. But sacred doctrine receives from the philosophical sciences. For Jerome observes, in his Epistle to Magnus,[2] that "the ancient doctors so enriched their books with the doctrines and opinions of the philosophers, that thou knowest not what more to admire in them, their profane erudition or their scriptural learning." Therefore sacred doctrine is inferior to other sciences.

On the contrary, Other sciences are called the handmaidens of this one: *Wisdom sent her maids to invite to the tower* (Prov. 9. 3).

I answer that, Since this science is partly speculative and partly practical, it transcends all others whether speculative or practical. Now one speculative science is said to be nobler than another either by reason of its greater certitude or by reason of the higher worth of its subject-matter. In both these respects this science surpasses other speculative sciences: in point of greater certitude, because other sciences derive their certitude from the natural light of human reason, which can err, while this derives its certitude from the light of the divine knowledge, which cannot be deceived; in point of the higher worth of its subject-matter, because this science treats chiefly of those things which by their sublimity transcend human reason, while other sciences consider only those things which are within reason's grasp.

Of the practical sciences, that one is nobler which is ordered to a further end, as political science is nobler than military science, for the good of the army is directed to the good of the state. But the end of this science, in so far as it is practical, is eternal happiness, to which as to an ultimate end the purposes of every practical science are ordered. Hence it is clear that from every standpoint it is nobler than other sciences.

Reply Obj. 1. It may well happen that what is

[2] *Epist.* LXX (PL 22, 668).

in itself the more certain may seem to us the less certain on account of the weakness of our intellect, "which is dazzled by the clearest objects of nature; as the owl is dazzled by the light of the sun."[1] Hence the fact that some happen to doubt about articles of faith is not due to the uncertain nature of the truths, but to the weakness of the human intellect. Yet the slenderest knowledge that may be obtained of the highest things is more desirable than the most certain knowledge obtained of lesser things, as is said in the treatise *On the Parts of Animals*.[2]

Reply Obj. 2. This science can in a sense take from the philosophical sciences, not as though it stood in need of them, but only in order to make its teaching clearer. For it takes its principles not from other sciences, but immediately from God, by revelation. Therefore it does not take from the other sciences as from the higher, but makes use of them as of the lesser, and as handmaidens; just as the master sciences make use of the sciences that supply their materials, as political of military science. That it thus uses them is not due to its own defect or insufficiency, but to the defect of our intellect, which is more easily led by what is known through natural reason (from which proceed the other sciences), to that which is above reason, such as are the teachings of this science.

ARTICLE 6. *Whether This Doctrine Is a Wisdom?*

We proceed thus to the Sixth Article: It seems that this doctrine is not a wisdom.

Objection 1. For no doctrine which borrows its principles is worthy of the name of wisdom, seeing that the wise man directs, and is not directed.[3] But this doctrine borrows its principles, as is clear from what we have said (A. 2). Therefore this science is not wisdom.

Obj. 2. Further, it is a part of wisdom to prove the principles of other sciences. Hence it is called the chief of sciences, as is clear in the *Ethics*.[4] But this doctrine does not prove the principles of other sciences. Therefore it is not the same as wisdom.

Obj. 3. Further, this doctrine is acquired by study, but wisdom is acquired by God's inspiration. And so it is numbered among the gifts of the Holy Spirit (Isa. 11. 2). Therefore this doctrine is not the same as wisdom.

On the contrary, It is written (Deut. 4. 6):

This is your wisdom and understanding in the sight of nations.

I answer that, This doctrine is wisdom above all human wisdoms, not merely in any one order, but absolutely. For since it is the part of a wise man to order and to judge, and since lesser matters should be judged in the light of some higher cause, he is said to be wise in any one order who considers the highest cause in that order. Thus in the order of building he who plans the form of the house is called wise and architect, in relation to the inferior labourers who trim the wood and make ready the stones: *As a wise architect I have laid the foundation* (I Cor. 3. 10). Again, in the order of all human life, the prudent man is called wise, because he orders his acts to a fitting end: *Wisdom is prudence to a man* (Prov. 10. 23). Therefore he who considers absolutely the highest cause of the whole universe, namely God, is most of all called wise. Hence wisdom is said to be the knowledge of divine things, as Augustine says (*De Trin.* XII, 14).[5] But sacred doctrine most especially treats of God viewed as the highest cause—not just in so far as He can be known through creatures, which the philosophers knew—*That which is known of God is manifest in them* (Rom. 1. 19)—but also in so far as He is known to Himself alone and revealed to others. Hence sacred doctrine is especially called wisdom.

Reply Obj. 1. Sacred doctrine derives its principles not from any human knowledge, but from the divine knowledge, through which, as through the highest wisdom, all our knowledge is ordered.

Reply Obj. 2. The principles of other sciences either are self-evident and cannot be proved, or are proved by natural reason through some other science. But the knowledge proper to this science comes through revelation, and not through natural reason. Therefore it has no concern to prove the principles of other sciences, but only to judge of them. Whatsoever is found in other sciences contrary to any truth of this science, must be condemned as false: *Destroying counsels and every height that exalteth itself against the knowledge of God* (II Cor. 10. 4, 5).

Reply Obj. 3. Since judgment pertains to wisdom, according to a twofold manner of judging there is a twofold wisdom. A man may judge in one way by inclination, as whoever has the habit of a virtue judges rightly of what concerns that virtue by his very inclination towards it. Hence the virtuous man, as we read in the *Ethics*,[6] is the measure and rule of human acts. In another way,

---

[1] Aristotle, *Metaphysics*, II, 1 (993ᵇ9).
[2] Aristotle, I, 5 (644ᵇ31).
[3] Aristotle, *Metaphysics*, I, 2 (982ᵃ28).
[4] Aristotle, VI, 7 (1141ᵃ20).
[5] PL 42, 1009.　　[6] Aristotle, X, 5 (1176ᵃ17).

by knowledge, just as a man learned in moral science might be able to judge rightly about virtuous acts, though he had not the virtue. The first manner of judging divine things belongs to that wisdom which is set down among the gifts of the Holy Ghost: *The spiritual man judgeth all things* (I Cor. 2. 15). And Dionysius says (*Div. Nom.* ii):[1] "Hierotheus is taught not by mere learning, but by experience of divine things." The second manner of judging belongs to this doctrine, since it is acquired by study, though its principles are obtained by revelation.

ARTICLE 7. *Whether God Is the Subject of This Science?*

We proceed thus to the Seventh Article: It seems that God is not the subject of this science.

Objection 1. For in every science what its subject is is presupposed, as the philosopher says.[2] But this science does not presuppose what God is, for Damascene says (*De Fide Orth*, 1, 4):[3] "It is impossible to say of God what He is." Therefore God is not the subject of this science.

Obj. 2. Further, whatever conclusions are reached in any science must be included in the subject of the science. But in Holy Writ we reach conclusions not only concerning God, but concerning many other things, such as creatures and human morality. Therefore God is not the subject of this science.

On the contrary, The subject of the science is that of which it principally treats. But in this science the treatment is mainly about God, for it is called theology as treating of God. Therefore God is the subject of this science.

I answer that, God is the subject of this science. The relation between a science and its subject is the same as that between a habit or power and its object. Now properly speaking the object of a power or habit is the thing under the aspect of which all things are referred to that power or habit, as man and stone are referred to the power of sight in that they are coloured. Hence coloured things are the proper objects of sight. But in sacred science all things are treated of under the aspect of God, either because they are God Himself, or because they are ordered to God as their beginning and end. Hence it follows that God is truly the subject of this science. This is clear also from the principles of this science, namely, the articles of faith, for faith is about God. The subject of the principles and of the whole science must be the same, since the whole

science is contained virtually in its principles.

Some, however, looking to what is treated of in this science, and not to the aspect under which it is treated, have asserted the subject of this science to be something other than God—that is, either things and signs,[4] or the works of salvation,[5] or the whole Christ, that is, the head and members.[6] For we treat of all these things, in this science, but only so far as they are ordered to God.

Reply Obj. 1. Although we cannot know of God what He is, nevertheless in this doctrine we make use of His effects, either of nature or of grace, in place of a definition, in regard to whatever is treated of in this doctrine concerning God, even as in some philosophical sciences we demonstrate something about a cause from its effect, by taking the effect in place of a definition of the cause.

Reply Obj. 2. Whatever other conclusions are reached in this sacred science are comprehended under God, not as parts or species or accidents, but as in some way ordered to Him.

ARTICLE 8. *Whether Sacred Doctrine Is a Matter of Argument?*

We proceed thus to the Eighth Article: It seems this doctrine is not a matter of argument.

Objection 1. For Ambrose says (*De Fide*, 1):[7] "Put arguments aside where faith is sought." But in this doctrine faith especially is sought: *But these things are written that you may believe* (John 20. 31). Therefore sacred doctrine is not a matter of argument.

Obj. 2. Further, if it is a matter of argument, the argument is either from authority or from reason. If it is from authority, it seems unbefitting its dignity, for the proof from authority is the weakest form of proof according to Boethius.[8] But if from reason, this is unbefitting its end, because, according to Gregory (*Homil.* 26),[9] "faith has no merit in those things of which human reason brings its own experience." Therefore sacred doctrine is not a matter of argument.

On the contrary, The Scripture says that a

---

[1] Sect. 9 (PG 3, 648).
[2] *Posterior Analytics*, 1, 1 (71ª13).
[3] PG 94, 797.

[4] Peter Lombard, *Sent.*, 1, d. 1, 1 (QR 1, 14); cf. Augustine, *Christian Doctrine*, 1, 2 (PL 34, 19).
[5] Hugh of St. Victor, *De Sacram.*, Prol., chap. 2 (PL 176, 183).
[6] Robert of Mélun, quoted in Alexander of Hales, *Summa* (QR 1, 6, note 4); Robert Grosseteste, *Hexaëm.* (text quoted by Phelan, *Mélanges De Wulf*, p. 176); Robert Kilwardby, *De Na.. Theol.*, p. 17; cf. *Glossa Lombardi, In Ps., Praef.* (PL 191, 59).
[7] Chap. 13 (PL 16, 570).
[8] *In Top. Cicer.* 1 (PL 64, 1166); *De Differ. Top.* III (PL 64, 1199).
[9] PL 76, 1197.

bishop should *embrace that faithful word which is according to doctrine, that he may be able to exhort in sound doctrine and to convince the gainsayers* (Tit. 1. 9).

I answer that, As other sciences do not argue in proof of their principles, but argue from their principles to demonstrate other truths in these sciences, so this doctrine does not argue in proof of its principles, which are the articles of faith, but from them it goes on to prove something else, as the Apostle from the resurrection of Christ argues in proof of the general resurrection (I Cor. 15.).

However, it is to be borne in mind, in regard to the philosophical sciences, that the inferior sciences neither prove their principles nor dispute with those who deny them, but leave this to a higher science. But the highest of them, namely, metaphysics, can dispute with one who denies its principles only if the opponent will make some concession. But if he concede nothing, it can have no dispute with him, though it can answer his objections. Hence Sacred Scripture, since it has no science above itself, can dispute with one who denies its principles only if the opponent admits some at least of the truths obtained through divine revelation. Thus we can argue with heretics from texts in Holy Writ, and against those who deny one article of faith we can argue from another. But if our opponent believes nothing of divine revelation, there is no longer any means of proving the articles of faith by reasoning, but only of answering his objections—if he has any—against faith. Since faith rests upon infallible truth, and since the contrary of a truth can never be demonstrated, it is clear that proofs brought against faith cannot be demonstrations, but are arguments that can be answered.

Reply Obj. 1. Although arguments from human reason cannot avail to prove what must be received on faith, nevertheless this doctrine argues from articles of faith to other truths.

Reply Obj. 2. To argue from authority is most proper to this doctrine, since its principles are obtained by revelation, and thus we must believe the authority of those to whom the revelation has been made. Nor does this take away from the dignity of this doctrine, for although the argument from authority based on human reason is the weakest, yet the argument from authority based on divine revelation is the strongest.

But sacred doctrine makes use even of human reason, not, indeed, to prove faith (for thereby the merit of faith would come to an end), but to make clear other things that are put forward in this doctrine. Since therefore grace does not destroy nature, but perfects it, natural reason should minister to faith as the natural bent of the will ministers to charity. And so the Apostle says: *Bringing into captivity every understanding unto the obedience of Christ* (II Cor. 10. 5). Hence sacred doctrine makes use also of the authority of philosophers in those questions in which they were able to know the truth by natural reason, as Paul quotes a saying of Aratus: *As some also of your own poets said; For we are also His offspring* (Acts 17. 28).

Nevertheless, sacred doctrine makes use of these authorities as extrinsic and probable arguments. But it properly uses the authority of the canonical Scriptures as a necessary argument, and the authority of the doctors of the Church as one that may properly be used, though merely as probable. For our faith rests upon the revelation made to the apostles and prophets, who wrote the canonical books, and not on the revelations (if any such there are) made to other doctors. Hence Augustine says (*Epist. ad Hieron.*):[1] "Only those books of Scripture which are called canonical have I learnt to hold in such honour as to believe their authors have not erred in any way in writing them. But other authors I so read as not to deem anything in their works to be true merely on account of their having so thought and written, whatever may have been their holiness and learning."

ARTICLE 9. *Whether Holy Scripture Should Use Metaphors?*

We proceed thus to the Ninth Article: It seems that Holy Scripture should not use metaphors.

Objection 1. For that which is proper to the lowest science seems not to be appropriate to this science, which holds the highest place of all, as we have said (A. 5). But to proceed by the aid of various likenesses and figures is proper to poetry, the least of all the sciences. Therefore it is not fitting that this science should make use of such likenesses.

Obj. 2. Further, this doctrine seems to be ordered to the manifestation of truth. Hence a reward is held out to those who manifest it: *They that explain me shall have life everlasting* (Ecclus. 24. 31). But by such likenesses truth is obscured. Therefore to put forward divine truths by likening them to corporeal things does not befit this science.

Obj. 3. Further, the higher creatures are, the nearer they approach to the divine likeness. If therefore any creature be taken to represent

[1] *Epist.* LXXXII, Chap. 1 (PL 33, 277).

God, this representation ought chiefly to be taken from the higher creatures, and not from the lower. Yet this is often found in the Scriptures.

On the contrary, It is written (Osee 12. 10): *I have multiplied visions, and I have used similitudes by the ministry of the prophets.* But to put forward anything by means of similitudes is to use metaphors. Therefore this sacred science may use metaphors.

I answer that, It is befitting Holy Writ to put forward divine and spiritual truths under the likenesses of material things. For God provides for everything according to the capacity of its nature. Now it is natural to man to attain to intellectual truths through sensible things, because all our knowledge originates from sense. Hence in Holy Writ spiritual truths are fittingly taught under the metaphors of material things. This is what Dionysius says (*Cælest. Hierarch.* i):[1] "We cannot be enlightened by the divine rays except they be hidden within the covering of many sacred veils."

It is also befitting Holy Writ, which is proposed to all without distinction of persons—*To the wise and to the unwise I am a debtor* (Rom. 1. 14)—that spiritual truths be expounded by means of likenesses taken from corporeal things, in order that thereby even the simple who are unable by themselves to grasp intellectual things may be able to understand it.

Reply Obj. 1. Poetry makes use of metaphors to produce a representation, for it is natural to man to be pleased with representations. But sacred doctrine makes use of metaphors as both necessary and useful, as we have said.

Reply Obj. 2. The ray of divine revelation is not extinguished by the sensible imagery in which it is veiled, as Dionysius says (*Cælest Hierarch.* i).[2] And its truth so far remains that it does not allow the minds of those to whom the revelation has been made to rest in the likenesses, but raises them to the knowledge of intelligible things. And through those to whom the revelation has been made others also may receive instruction in these matters. Hence those things that are taught metaphorically in one part of Scripture, in other parts are taught more openly. The very hiding of truth in figures is useful for the exercise of thoughtful minds, and as a defence against the ridicule of the impious, according to the words *Give not that which is holy to dogs* (Matt. 7. 6).

Reply Obj. 3. As Dionysius says, (*loc. cit.*)[3] it is more fitting that divine truths should be expounded under the figure of less noble than of

[1] Sect. 2 (PG 3, 121).   [2] Sect. 2 (PG 3, 121).
[3] PG 3, 136.

nobler bodies, and this for three reasons. First, because in this way men's minds are the better freed from error. For then it is clear that these things are not literal descriptions of divine truths, which might have been open to doubt had they been expressed under the figure of nobler bodies, especially for those who did not know how to think of anything nobler than bodies. Secondly, because this is more befitting the knowledge of God that we have in this life. For what He is not is clearer to us than what He is. Therefore likenesses drawn from things farthest away from God form within us a truer estimate that God is above whatsoever we may say or think of Him. Thirdly, because thereby divine truths are the better hidden from the unworthy.

ARTICLE 10. *Whether in Holy Scripture a Word May Have Several Senses?*

We proceed thus to the Tenth Article: It seems that in Holy Writ a word cannot have several senses, historical or literal, allegorical, tropological or moral, and anagogical.

Objection 1. For many different senses in one text produce confusion and deception and destroy all force of argument. Hence no proof, but only fallacies, can be deduced from a multiplicity of propositions. But Holy Writ ought to be able to state the truth without any fallacy. Therefore there cannot be several senses to a word in Holy Writ.

Obj. 2. Further, Augustine says (*De util. cred.* iii)[4] that "the Old Testament has a fourfold division namely, according to history, etiology, analogy, and allegory." Now these four seem altogether different from the four divisions mentioned in the first objection. Therefore it does not seem fitting to explain the same word of Holy Writ according to the four different senses mentioned above.

Obj. 3. Further, besides these senses, there is the parabolical, which is not one of these four.

On the contrary, Gregory says (*Moral.* xx, 1):[5] "Holy Writ by the manner of its speech transcends every science, because in one and the same sentence, while it describes a fact, it reveals a mystery."

I answer that, The author of Holy Writ is God, in whose power it is to signify His meaning not by words only (as man also can do), but also by things themselves. So, whereas in every other science things are signified by words, this science has the property that the things signified by the words have themselves also a meaning. Therefore that first meaning whereby words signify

[4] PL 42, 68.   [5] PL 76, 135.

things belongs to the first sense, the historical or literal. That meaning whereby things signified by words have themselves also a meaning is called the spiritual sense, which is based on the literal, and presupposes it.

Now this spiritual sense has a threefold division. For as the Apostle says (Heb. 10. 1) the Old Law is a figure of the New Law, and Dionysius says[1] the New Law itself is a figure of future glory. Again, in the New Law, whatever our Head has done is a type of what we ought to do. Therefore, so far as the things of the Old Law signify the things of the New Law, there is the allegorical sense. But so far as the things done in Christ, or so far as the things which signify Christ, are types of what we ought to do, there is the moral sense. But so far as they signify what relates to eternal glory, there is the anagogical sense.

Since the literal sense is that which the author intends, and since the author of Holy Writ is God, Who by one act comprehends all things by His intellect, it is not unfitting, as Augustine says[2] if, even according to the literal sense, one word in Holy Writ should have several senses.

Reply Obj. 1. The multiplicity of these senses does not produce equivocation or any other kind of multiplicity, seeing that these senses are not multiplied because one word signifies several things, but because the things signified by the words can be themselves types of other things. Thus in Holy Writ no confusion results, for all the senses are founded on one—the literal—from which alone can any argument be drawn, and not from those intended in allegory, as Augustine says (*Epist.* xciii).[3] Nevertheless, nothing of Holy Scripture perishes on account of this, since nothing necessary to faith is contained under the spiritual sense which is not elsewhere put forward by the Scripture in its literal sense.

Reply Obj. 2. These three—history, etiology, analogy—are grouped under the literal sense. For it is called history, as Augustine expounds[4] whenever anything is simply related; it is called etiology when its cause is assigned, as when Our Lord gave the reason why Moses allowed the putting away of wives—namely, on account of the hardness of men's hearts (Matt. 19. 8); it is called analogy whenever the truth of one text of Scripture is shown not to contradict the truth of another. Of these four, allegory alone stands for the three spiritual senses. Thus Hugh of S. Victor (*Sacram.* 1, 4)[5] includes the anagogical under the allegorical sense, laying down three senses only—the historical, the allegorical, and the tropological.

Reply Obj. 3. The parabolical sense is contained in the literal, for by words things are signified properly and figuratively. Nor is the figure itself, but that which is figured, the literal sense. When Scripture speaks of God's arm, the literal sense is not that God has such a member, but only what is signified by this member, namely, operative power. Hence it is plain that nothing false can ever underlie the literal sense of Holy Writ.

QUESTION II

THE EXISTENCE OF GOD

(*In Three Articles*)

BECAUSE the chief aim of sacred doctrine is to teach the knowledge of God, not only as He is in Himself, but also as He is the beginning of things and their end, and especially of rational creatures, as is clear from what has been already said (Q. I, A. 7), therefore, in our endeavour to expound this science, we shall treat: (1) Of God. (2) Of the rational creature's movement towards God (Part II). (3) Of Christ, Who as man, is our way to God (Part III).

In treating of God there will be a threefold division:—

For we shall consider (1) whatever concerns the Divine Essence. (2) Whatever concerns the distinctions of Persons (Q. XXVII). (3) Whatever concerns the procession of creatures from Him (Q. XLIV).

Concerning the Divine Essence, we must consider:—

(1) Whether God exists? (2) The manner of His existence, or, rather, what is not the manner of His existence (Q. III). (3) Whatever concerns His operations—namely, His knowledge (Q. XIV), will (Q. XIX), power (Q. XXV).

Concerning the first, there are three points of inquiry:—

(1) Whether the proposition "God exists" is self-evident? (2) Whether it is demonstrable? (3) Whether God exists?

ARTICLE 1. *Whether the Existence of God Is Self-Evident?*

We proceed thus to the First Article: It seems that the existence of God is self-evident.

Objection 1. Now those things are said to be self-evident to us the knowledge of which is nat-

---

[1] *De Eccl. Hier.*, v, 2 (PG 3, 501).
[2] *Confessions*, XII, 42 (PL 32, 844).
[3] Chap. 8 (PL 33, 334).
[4] *De Util. Cred.*, 3 (PL 42, 68).

[5] PL 176, 184; Cf. *De Scriptur. et Scriptor. Sacris.*, III (PL 175, 11).

urally in us, as we can see in regard to first principles. But as Damascene says (*De Fid. Orth.* i, 1, 3),[1] "the knowledge of God is naturally implanted in all." Therefore the existence of God is self-evident.

Obj. 2. Further, those things are said to be self-evident which are known as soon as the terms are known, which the Philosopher says[2] is true of the first principles of demonstration. Thus, when the nature of a whole and of a part is known, it is at once known that every whole is greater than its part. But as soon as the meaning of the word "God" is understood, it is at once seen that God exists. For by this word is signified that thing than which nothing greater can be conceived. But that which exists actually and in the intellect is greater than that which exists only in the intellect. Therefore, since as soon as the word "God" is understood it exists in the intellect, it also follows that it exists actually. Therefore the proposition "God exists" is self-evident.

Obj. 3. Further, the existence of truth is self-evident. For whoever denies the existence of truth grants that truth does not exist. And, if truth does not exist, then the proposition "Truth does not exist" is true. And if there is anything true, there must be truth. But God is truth itself: *I am the way, the truth, and the life* (John 14.6). Therefore "God exists" is self-evident.

On the contrary, No one can think the opposite of what is self-evident, as the Philosopher states[3] concerning the first principles of demonstration. But the opposite of the proposition "God is" can be thought, for, *The fool said in his heart, There is no God* (Ps. 52.1). Therefore, that God exists is not self-evident.

I answer that, A thing can be self-evident in either of two ways. On the one hand, self-evident in itself, though not to us, on the other, self-evident in itself, and to us. A proposition is self-evident because the predicate is included in the notion of the subject, as "Man is an animal," for animal is contained in the essence of man. If, therefore the essence of the predicate and subject be known to all, the proposition will be self-evident to all as is clear with regard to the first principles of demonstration, the terms of which are common things that no one is ignorant of, such as being and non-being, whole and part, and the like. If, however, there are some to whom the essence of the predicate and subject is unknown, the proposition will be self-evident in itself, but not to those who do not know the meaning of the

predicate and subject of the proposition. Therefore, it happens, as Boëthius says (*Hebdom.*)[4] that "there are some concepts of the mind self-evident only to the learned, as that incorporeal substances are not in space." Therefore I say that this proposition, "God exists," of itself is self-evident, for the predicate is the same as the subject, because God is His own existence as will be hereafter shown (Q. III, A. 4). Now because we do not know the essence of God, the proposition is not self-evident to us, but needs to be demonstrated by things that are more known to us, though less known in their nature—namely, by effects.

Reply Obj. 1. To know that God exists in a general and confused way is implanted in us by nature, since God is man's Happiness. For man naturally desires happiness, and what is naturally desired by man must be naturally known to him. This, however, is not to know absolutely that God exists, just as to know that someone is approaching is not the same as to know that Peter is approaching, even though it is Peter who is approaching. For there are many who imagine that man's perfect good which is Happiness, consists in riches, and others in pleasures, and others in something else.

Reply Obj. 2. Perhaps not everyone who hears this word "God" understands it to signify something than which nothing greater can be thought, seeing that some have believed God to be a body.[5] Yet, granted that everyone understands that by this word "God" is signified something than which nothing greater can be thought, nevertheless, it does not therefore follow that he understands that what the word signifies exists actually, but only that it exists in the intellect. Nor can it be argued that it actually exists, unless it be admitted that there actually exists something than which nothing greater can be thought. And this is what is not admitted by those who hold that God does not exist.

Reply Obj. 3. The existence of truth in general is self-evident, but the existence of a First Truth is not self-evident to us.

ARTICLE 2. *Whether It Can Be Demonstrated That God Exists?*

We proceed thus to the Second Article: It seems that the existence of God cannot be demonstrated.

---

[1] PG 94, 789, 793.   [2] *Posterior Analytics,* 1, 3.
[3] *Metaphysics,* IV, 3 (1005^{b}11); also *Posterior Analytics,* 1, 10 (76^{b}23).

[4] PL 64, 1311.
[5] Cf. St. Thomas, *Contra Gentiles,* 1, 20. See also Augustine, *City of God,* VIII, 2 (PL 41, 226); chap. 5 (PL 41, 230); *De Haeres.,* 46, 50, 86 (PL 42, 35, 39, 46); *De Gen. ad Litt.,* X, 25 (PL 34, 427); Maimonides, *Guide,* 1, 53 (FR 42). Aristotle, *Physics,* 1, 4 (187^{a}12).

Objection 1. For it is an article of faith that God exists. But what is of faith cannot be demonstrated, because a demonstration produces knowledge, while faith is of the unseen (Heb. 11. 1). Therefore it cannot be demonstrated that God exists.

Obj. 2. Further, essence is the middle term of demonstration. But we cannot know in what God's essence consists, but solely in what it does not consist, as Damascene says (*De Fid. Orth.* i, 4).[1] Therefore we cannot demonstrate that God exists.

Obj. 3. Further, if the existence of God were demonstrated, this could only be from His effects. But His effects are not proportionate to Him, since He is infinite and His effects are finite, and between the finite and infinite there is no proportion. Therefore, since a cause cannot be demonstrated by an effect not proportionate to it, it seems that the existence of God cannot be demonstrated.

On the contrary, The Apostle says: *The invisible things of Him are clearly seen, being understood by the things that are made* (Rom. 1. 20). But this would not be unless the existence of God could be demonstrated through the things that are made. For the first thing we must know of anything is whether it exists.

I answer that, Demonstration can be made in two ways. One is through the cause, and is called *propterquid,* and this is to argue from what is prior absolutely. The other is through the effect, and is called a demonstration *quia.* This is to argue from what is prior relatively only to us. When an effect is better known to us than its cause, from the effect we proceed to the knowledge of the cause. And from every effect the existence of its proper cause can be demonstrated, so long as its effects are better known to us, because since every effect depends upon its cause, if the effect exists, the cause must pre-exist. Hence the existence of God, in so far as it is not self-evident to us, can be demonstrated from those of His effects which are known to us.

Reply Obj. 1. The existence of God and other like truths about God which can be known by natural reason, are not articles of faith, but are preambles to the articles. For faith presupposes natural knowledge, even as grace presupposes nature, and perfection supposes something that can be perfected. Nevertheless, there is nothing to prevent a man who cannot grasp a proof accepting, as a matter of faith, something which in itself is capable of being known and demonstrated.

Reply Obj. 2. When the existence of a cause is

[1] PG 94, 800.

demonstrated from an effect, this effect takes the place of the definition of the cause in proof of the cause's existence. This is especially the case in regard to God, because, in order to prove the existence of anything, it is necessary to accept as a middle term the meaning of the name, and not its essence, for the question of its essence follows on the question of its existence. Now the names given to God are derived from His effects, as we will show later (Q. XIII, A. 1). Consequently, in demonstrating the existence of God from His effects, we may take for the middle term the meaning of the word "God."

Reply Obj. 3. From effects not proportionate to the cause no perfect knowledge of that cause can be obtained. Yet from every effect the existence of the cause can be clearly demonstrated, and so we can demonstrate the existence of God from His effects, though from them we cannot perfectly know God as He is in His essence.

ARTICLE 3. *Whether God Exists?*

We proceed thus to the Third Article: It seems that God does not exist.

Objection 1. For if one of two contraries were infinite, the other would be altogether destroyed. But the word "God" means that He is infinite goodness. If, therefore, God existed, there would be no evil discoverable. But there is evil in the world. Therefore God does not exist.

Obj. 2. Further, what can be accomplished by a few principles is not effected by many. But it seems that everything we see in the world can be accounted for by other principles, supposing God did not exist. For all natural things can be reduced to one principle, which is nature, and all voluntary things can be reduced to one principle, which is human reason, or will. Therefore there is no need to suppose God's existence.

On the contrary, It is said in the person of God: *I am Who am* (Exod. 3. 14).

I answer that, The existence of God can be proved in five ways.

The first and more manifest way is the argument from motion. It is certain, and evident to our senses, that in this world some things are in motion. Now whatever is in motion is put in motion by another, for nothing can be in motion unless it is in potency to that towards which it is in motion. But a thing moves in so far as it is in act. For motion is nothing else than the reduction of something from potency to act. But nothing can be reduced from potency to act except by something in a state of act. Thus that which is actually hot, as fire, makes wood, which is potentially hot, to be actually hot, and thereby moves and changes it. Now it is not possible that the same thing should be at once in act and potency in the same respect, but only in different respects. For what is actually hot cannot simultaneously be potentially hot, though it is simultaneously potentially cold. It is therefore impossible that in the same respect and in the same way a thing should be both mover and moved, that is, that it should move itself. Therefore, whatever is moved must be moved by another. If that by which it is moved be itself moved, then this also must be moved by another, and that by another again. But this cannot go on to infinity, because then there would be no first mover, and, consequently, no other mover, seeing that subsequent movers move only because as they are moved by the first mover, just as the staff moves only because it is moved by the hand. Therefore it is necessary to arrive at a first mover which is moved by no other. And this everyone understands to be God.

The second way is from the notion of efficient cause. In the world of sense we find there is an order of efficient causes. There is no case known (nor indeed, is it possible) in which a thing is found to be the efficient cause of itself, because in that case it would be prior to itself, which is impossible. Now in efficient causes it is not possible to go on to infinity, because in all efficient causes following in order, the first is the cause of the intermediate cause, and the intermediate is the cause of the ultimate cause, whether the intermediate cause be several, or one only. Now to take away the cause is to take away the effect. Therefore, if there be no first cause among efficient causes, there will be no ultimate, nor any intermediate cause. But if in efficient causes it is possible to go on to infinity, there will be no first efficient cause, neither will there be an ultimate effect, nor any intermediate efficient causes, all of which is plainly false. Therefore it is necessary to admit a first efficient cause, to which everyone gives the name of God.

The third way is taken from possibility and necessity, and runs thus. We find in nature things that are possible to be and not to be, since they are found to be generated, and to be corrupted, and consequently they are possible to be and not to be. But it is impossible for these always to exist, for that which is possible not to be at some time is not. Therefore, if everything is possible not to be, then at one time there could have been nothing in existence. Now if this were true, even now there would be nothing in existence, because that which does not exist only begins to exist by something already existing. Therefore, if at one

time nothing was in existence, it would have been impossible for anything to have begun to exist; and thus even now nothing would be in existence—which is clearly false. Therefore, not all beings are merely possible, but there must exist something the existence of which is necessary. But every necessary thing either has its necessity caused by another, or not. Now it is impossible to go on to infinity in necessary things which have their necessity caused by another, as has been already proved in regard to efficient causes. Therefore we must admit the existence of some being having of itself its own necessity, and not receiving it from another, but rather causing in others their necessity. This all men speak of as God.

The fourth way is taken from the gradation to be found in things. Among beings there are some more and some less good, true, noble, and the like. But "more" and "less" are predicated of different things, according as they resemble in their different ways something which is the maximum, as a thing is said to be hotter according as it more nearly resembles that which is hottest. There is then, something which is truest, something best, something noblest, and, consequently, something which is most being; for those things that are greatest in truth are greatest in being, as it is written in the *Metaphysics*.[1] Now the maximum in any genus is the cause of all in that genus; as fire, which is the maximum of heat, is the cause of all hot things as is said in the same book.[2] Therefore there must also be something which is to all beings the cause of their being, goodness, and every other perfection. And this we call God.

The fifth way is taken from the governance of things. We see that things which lack knowledge, such as natural bodies, act for an end, and this is evident from their acting always, or nearly always, in the same way, so as to obtain the best result. Hence it is plain that they achieve their end not by chance, but by design. Now whatever lacks knowledge cannot move towards an end, unless it be directed by some being endowed with knowledge and intelligence, as the arrow is directed by the archer. Therefore some intelligent being exists by whom all natural things are ordered to their end; and this being we call God.

Reply Obj. 1. As Augustine says (*Enchir.* xi):[3] "Since God is the highest good, He would not allow any evil to exist in His works, unless His omnipotence and goodness were such as to bring good even out of evil." This is part of the infinite goodness of God, that He should allow evil to exist, and out of it produce good.

[1] Aristotle, II, 1 (993^{b}30).   [2] II, 1 (993^{b}25).
[3] PL, 40, 236.

Reply Obj. 2. Since nature works for a determinate end under the direction of a higher agent, whatever is done by nature must be traced back to God, as to its first cause. So also whatever is done voluntarily must also be traced back to some higher cause other than human reason or will, since these can change and fail. For all things that are changeable and capable of defect must be traced back to an immovable and self-necessary first principle, as was shown in the body of the Article.

QUESTION III

OF THE SIMPLICITY OF GOD
(In Eight Articles)

WHEN the existence of a thing has been ascertained there remains the further question of the manner of its existence, in order that we may know what it is. Now, because we cannot know what God is, but rather what He is not, we have no means for considering how God is, but rather how He is not.

Therefore, we must consider (1) How He is not. (2) How He is known by us. (Q. XII) (3) How He is named. (Q. XIII).

Now it can be shown how God is not, by denying of Him whatever is unfitting to Him—namely, composition, motion, and the like. Therefore (1) we must discuss His simplicity, whereby we deny composition in Him; and because whatever is simple in material things is imperfect and a part of something else, we shall discuss (2) His perfection. (Q. IV) (3) His infinity. (Q. VII) (4) His immutability. (Q. IX) (5) His unity. (Q. XI).

Concerning His simplicity, there are eight points of inquiry: (1) Whether God is a body? (2) Whether He is composed of matter and form? (3) Whether in Him there is composition of quiddity, essence or nature, and subject? (4) Whether He is composed of essence and existence? (5) Whether He is composed of genus and difference? (6) Whether He is composed of subject and accident? (7) Whether He is in any way composite, or wholly simple? (8) Whether He enters into composition with other things?

ARTICLE 1. *Whether God Is a Body?*

We proceed thus to the First Article: It seems that God is a body.

Objection 1. For a body is that which has three dimensions. But Holy Scripture attributes three dimensions to God, for it is written: *He is higher than Heaven, and what wilt thou do? He is deeper than Hell, and how wilt thou know? The measure of Him is longer than the earth and broader than the sea* (Job 11.8, 9). Therefore God is a body.

Obj. 2. Further, everything that has figure is a body, since figure is a quality of quantity. But God seems to have figure, for it is written: *Let us make man to our image and likeness* (Gen 1. 26). Now a figure is called an image, according to the text: *Who being the brightness of His glory and the figure i.e.,* the image *of His substance* (Heb. 1.3). Therefore God is a body.

Obj. 3. Further, whatever has corporeal parts is a body. Now Scripture attributes corporeal parts to God. *Hast thou an arm like God?* (Job 40.4); and *The eyes of the Lord are upon the just* (Ps. 33.16); and *The right hand of the Lord hath wrought strength* (Ps. 117.16). Therefore God is a body.

Obj. 4. Further, posture belongs only to bodies. But something which supposes posture is said of God in the Scriptures: *I saw the Lord sitting* (Isa. 6. 1), and *He standeth up to judge* (Isa. 3.13). Therefore God is a body.

Obj. 5. Further, only bodies or things corporeal can be a local term from which or to which. But in the Scriptures God is spoken of as a local term to which, according to the words, *Come ye to Him and be enlightened* (Ps. 23.6), and as a term from which: *All they that depart from Thee shall be written in the earth* (Jer. 17. 13). Therefore God is a body.

On the contrary, It is written in the Gospel of St. John (4. 24): *God is a spirit.*

I answer that, It is absolutely true that God is not a body; and this can be shown in three ways. First, because no body is in motion unless it be put in motion, as is evident from induction. Now it has been already proved (Q. II, A. 3), that God is the First Mover unmoved. Therefore it is clear that God is not a body.

Secondly, because the first being must of necessity be in act, and in no way in potency. For although in one and the same thing that passes from potency to act, the potency is prior in time to the act, nevertheless, absolutely speaking, act is prior to potency. For whatever is in potency can be reduced to act only by some being in act. Now it has been already proved that God is the First Being. It is therefore impossible that in God there should be anything in potency. But every body is in potency, because the continuous, as such, is divisible to infinity. It is therefore impossible that God should be a body.

Thirdly, because God is the most noble of beings as is clear from what was said above (Q. II, A. 3). Now it is impossible for a body to be the most noble of beings, for a body must be either animate or inanimate, and an animate body is manifestly nobler than any inanimate body. But an animate body is not animate in so far as it is a body. Otherwise all bodies would be animate. Therefore its animation depends upon some other thing, as our body depends for its animation on the soul. Hence that by which a body becomes animated must be nobler than the body. Therefore it is impossible that God should be a body.

Reply Obj. 1. As we have said above (Q. 1, A. 9.), Holy Writ puts before us spiritual and divine things under the likenesses of corporeal things. Hence, when it attributes to God the three dimensions under the likeness of corporeal quantity, it designates His virtual quantity; thus, by depth, it signifies His power of knowing hidden things; by height, the excellence of His power over all things; by length, the duration of His being; by breadth, His act of love for all. Or, as Dionysius says (*Div. Nom.* ix.),[1] by the depth of God is meant the incomprehensibility of His essence, by length, the procession of His all-pervading power, by breadth, His overspreading all things, since, namely, all things lie under His protection.

Reply Obj. 2. Man is said to be after the image of God not as regards his body, but as regards that whereby he excels other animals. Hence, when it is said, *Let us make man to our image and likeness,* it is added, *And let him have dominion over the fishes of the sea* (Gen. 1. 26). Now man excels all animals by his reason and intelligence. Hence it is according to his intelligence and reason, which are incorporeal, that man is said to be according to the image of God.

Reply Obj. 3. Corporeal parts are attributed to God in Scripture on account of His actions, and this is owing to a certain likeness. For instance the act of the eye is to see; hence the eye attributed to God signifies His power of seeing intellectually, not sensibly, and so on with the other parts.

Reply Obj. 4. Whatever pertains to posture, also, is only attributed to God by some sort of likeness. He is spoken of as sitting, on account of His unchangeableness and dominion, and as standing, on account of His power of overcoming whatever withstands Him.

Reply Obj. 5. We draw near to God by no corporeal steps, since He is everywhere, but by the affections of our mind, and in the same way we withdraw from Him. Thus, to draw near or to withdraw signifies merely spiritual affections based on the likeness of local motion.

[1] Sect. 9 (PG 3, 913).

ARTICLE 2. *Whether God Is Composed of Matter and Form?*

We proceed thus to the Second Article: It seems that God is composed of matter and form.

Objection 1. For whatever has a soul is composed of matter and form, since the soul is the form of the body. But Scripture attributes a soul to God, for it is mentioned in Hebrews (10. 38), where God says: *But My just man liveth by faith; but if he withdraw himself, he shall not please My soul.* Therefore God is composed of matter and form.

Obj. 2. Further, anger, joy, and the like are passions of the composite as is said in the book on the *Soul.*[2] But these are attributed to God in Scripture: *The Lord was exceeding angry with His people* (Ps. 105. 40). Therefore God is composed of matter and form.

Obj. 3. Further, matter is the principle of individuation. But God seems to be individual, for He is not predicated of many. Therefore He is composed of matter and form.

On the contrary, Whatever is composed of matter and form is a body; for dimensive quantity is what first inheres in matter. But God is not a body as proved in the preceding Article. Therefore He is not composed of matter and form.

I answer that, It is impossible that matter should exist in God. First, because matter is that which is in potency. But we have shown (Q. II, A. 3) that God is pure act, without any potentiality. Hence it is impossible that God should be composed of matter and form.

Secondly, because everything composed of matter and form is perfect and good through its form. Therefore its goodness is participated, according as matter participates the form. Now the first good and the best—namely God—is not a participated good, because the essential good is prior to the participated good. Hence it is impossible that God should be composed of matter and form.

Thirdly, because every agent acts by its form. Hence the manner in which it has its form is the manner in which it is an agent. Therefore whatever is primarily and essentially an agent must be primarily and essentially form. Now God is the first agent, since He is the first efficient cause as we have shown (Q. II, A. 3). He is therefore of His essence a form, and not composed of matter and form.

Reply Obj. 1. A soul is attributed to God because His acts resemble the acts of a soul; for,

[2] Aristotle, I, I (403ᵃ3).

that we will anything, is due to our soul. Hence what is pleasing to His will is said to be pleasing to His soul.

Reply Obj. 2. Anger and the like are attributed to God on account of a likeness of effect. Thus, because to punish is properly the act of an angry man, God's punishment is metaphorically spoken of as His anger.

Reply Obj. 3. Forms which can be received in matter are individualized by matter, which cannot be in another since it is the first underlying subject; but form of itself, unless something else prevents it, can be received by many. But that form which cannot be received in matter, but is self-subsisting, is individualized precisely because it cannot be received in another; and such a form is God. Hence it does not follow that matter exists in God.

ARTICLE 3. *Whether God Is the Same As His Essence or Nature?*

We proceed thus to the Third Article: It seems that God is not the same as His essence or nature.

Objection 1. For nothing is in itself. But the essence or nature of God, which is the Godhead, is said to be in God. Therefore it seems that God is not the same as His essence or nature.

Obj. 2. Further, the effect is likened to its cause, for every agent produces its like. But in created things the suppositum is not identical with its nature, for a man is not the same as his humanity. Therefore God is not the same as His Godhead.

On the contrary, It is said of God that He is life, and not only that He is living: *I am the way, the truth, and the life* (John 14. 6). Now the relation between Godhead and God is the same as the relation between life and a living thing. Therefore God is His very Godhead.

I answer that, God is the same as His essence or nature. To understand this, it must be noted that in things composed of matter and form, the nature or essence must differ from the suppositum, because the essence or nature comprises in itself only what is included in the definition of the species; as, humanity comprises in itself all that is included in the definition of man, for it is by this that man is man, and it is this that humanity signifies, that, namely, whereby man is man. Now individual matter, with all its individualizing accidents, is not included in the definition of the species. One of the elements in this defect in imitation is that what is one and simple can be represented only by many things. And so there comes about in these effects com-

position, which renders suppositum distinct from nature in them. For this flesh, these bones, this blackness or whiteness, etc., are not included in the definition of a man. Therefore this flesh, these bones, and the accidents designating this matter, are not included in humanity; and yet they are included in the thing which is a man. Hence the thing which is a man has something in it which humanity does not have. Consequently humanity and a man are not wholly the same, but humanity is taken to mean the formal part of a man, because the principles by which a thing is defined are as the formal constituent in relation to the individualizing matter.

On the other hand, in things not composed of matter and form, in which individualization is not due to individual matter—that is to say, to *this* matter—the very forms being individualized of themselves,—it is necessary that the forms themselves should be subsisting supposita. Therefore suppositum and nature do not differ in them as we have shown above (A. 2.). Since God then is not composed of matter and form, He must be His own Godhead, His own Life, and whatever else is thus predicated of Him.

Reply Obj. 1. We can speak of simple things only as though they were like the composite things from which we derive our knowledge. Therefore, in speaking of God, we use concrete nouns to signify His subsistence, because with us only those things subsist which are composite; and we use abstract nouns to signify His simplicity. In saying therefore that Godhead, or life, or the like are in God, it must be ascribed to the diversity which lies in the way our intellect receives, and not to any diversity in reality.

Reply Obj. 2. The effects of God do not imitate Him perfectly, but only as far as they are able.

ARTICLE 4. *Whether Essence and Being Are the Same in God?*

We proceed thus to the Fourth Article: It seems that essence and being (*esse*) are not the same in God.

Objection 1. For if this is so, then the divine being has nothing added to it. Now being to which no addition is made is being in general which is predicated of all things. Therefore it follows that God is being in general, predicable of everything. But this is false: *For men gave the incommunicable name to stones and wood* (Wisd. 14. 21). Therefore God's being is not His essence.

Obj. 2. Further, we can know *whether* God exists as said above (Q. 11, A. 2), but we cannot know *what* He is. Therefore God's being is not the same as His essence—that is, as His quiddity or nature.

On the contrary, Hilary says (*Trin.* vii) :[1] "In God existence is not an accidental quality, but subsisting truth." Therefore what subsists in God is His own being.

I answer that, God is not only His own essence, as shown in the preceding article, but also His own being. This may be shown in several ways. First, whatever a thing has besides its essence must be caused either by the principles of that essence (like an accident properly consequent upon the species—as the faculty of laughing is proper to a man—and caused by the essential principles of the species), or by some exterior agent,—as heat is caused in water by fire. Therefore, if the being itself of a thing differs from its essence, the being of that thing must be caused either by some exterior agent or by its essential principles. Now it is impossible for a thing's being to be caused by its essential principles, for nothing can be the sufficient cause of its own being, if its being is caused. Therefore that thing whose being differs from its essence must have its being caused by another. But this cannot be said of God, because we call God the first efficient cause. Therefore it is impossible that in God His being should differ from His essence.

Secondly, being is the actuality of every form or nature; for goodness or humanity are spoken of as actual only because they are spoken of as being. Therefore being must be compared to essence, if the latter is distinct from the former, as act to potency. Therefore, since in God there is no potentiality, as shown above (A. 1), it follows that in Him essence does not differ from His being. Therefore His essence is His being.

Thirdly, because just as that which has fire but is not itself fire is on fire by participation, so that which has being but is not being, is a being by participation. But God is His own essence, as shown above (A. 3); if, therefore, He is not His own being He will be not essential, but participated being. He will not therefore be the first being—which is absurd. Therefore God is His own being, and not merely His own essence.

Reply Obj. 1. A thing that has nothing added to it can be understood in two ways. Either its notion precludes any addition; thus, for example, it is of the notion of an irrational animal to be without reason. Or we may understand a thing to have nothing added to it because its notion does not require that anything should be added to it; thus animal in general is without reason,

because it is not of the notion of animal in general to have reason; but neither is it to lack reason. And so the divine being has nothing added to it in the first sense but, being in general has nothing added to it in the second sense.

Reply Obj. 2. "To be" can mean either of two things. It may mean the act of being, or it may mean the composition of a proposition effected by the mind in joining a predicate to a subject. Taking "to be" in the first sense, we cannot understand God's being nor His essence, but only in the second sense. We know that this proposition which we form about God when we say "God is," is true; and this we know from His effects (Q. 11, A. 2).

ARTICLE 5. *Whether God Is Contained in a Genus?*

We proceed thus to the Fifth Article: It seems that God is contained in a genus.

Objection 1. For a substance is a being that subsists of itself. But this is especially true of God. Therefore God is in the genus of substance.

Obj. 2. Further, nothing can be measured save by something of its own genus; as length is measured by length and numbers by number. But God is the measure of all substances, as the Commentator shows (*Metaph.* x).[2] Therefore God is in the genus of substance.

On the contrary, In the intellect, genus is prior to what it contains. But nothing is prior to God either really or in the intellect. Therefore God is not in any genus.

I answer that, A thing can be in a genus in two ways: either absolutely and properly, as a species contained under a genus; or as being reducible to it, as principles and privations. For example, a point and unity are reduced to the genus of quantity, as its principles, while blindness and all other privations are reduced to the genus of habit. But in neither way is God in a genus.

That He cannot be a species of any genus may be shown in three ways. First, because a species is constituted of genus and difference. Now that from which the difference constituting the species is derived is always related to that from which the genus is derived, as act is related to potency. For animal is derived from sensitive nature by concretion, as it were, for that is animal which has a sensitive nature. Rational on the other hand, is derived from intellectual nature, because that is rational which has an intellectual nature, and intelligence is compared to sense, as

[1] PL 10, 208.   [2] Comm. 7 (viii, 257A).

act is to potency. The same is shown in other things. Hence since in God potency is not added to act, it is impossible that He should be in any genus as a species.

Secondly, since the being of God is His essence as we have shown (A. 4), if God were in any genus, He would have to be in the genus "being," because, since genus is predicated essentially it refers to the essence of a thing. But the Philosopher has shown[1] that being cannot be a genus, for every genus has differences distinct from its generic essence. Now no difference can be found which would be outside being, for non-being cannot be a difference. It follows then that God is not in a genus.

Thirdly, because all in one genus agree in the quiddity or essence of the genus which is predicated of them essentially, but they differ in their being. For the being of man and of horse is not the same, as also of this man and that man; thus in every member of a genus, being and quiddity —that is, essence—must differ. But in God they do not differ, as shown in the preceding article. Therefore it is plain that God is not in a genus as a species.

From this it is also plain that He has no genus nor difference, nor can there be any definition of Him; nor, save through His effects, a demonstration of Him, for a definition is from genus and difference; and the mean of a demonstration is a definition.

That God is not in a genus as reducible to it as its principle, is clear from this, that a principle reducible to any genus does not extend beyond that genus; as a point is the principle of continuous quantity alone, and unity, of discontinuous quantity. But God is the principle of all being as we shall indicate below (Q. XLIV, A. I). Therefore He is not contained in any genus as its principle.

Reply Obj. 1. The word substance signifies not only what is being of itself—for being cannot of itself be a genus, as shown in the body of the article; but, it also signifies an essence in which it is appropriate to be in this way—namely, being of itself; this being, however, is not its essence. Thus it is clear that God is not in the genus of substance.

Reply Obj. 2. This objection turns upon proportionate measure, which must be homogeneous with what is measured. Now, God is not a measure proportionate to anything. Still, He is called the measure of all things, in the sense that everything has being only according as it approaches Him.

[1] *Metaphysics*, III, 3 (998ᵇ22).

ARTICLE 6. *Whether in God There Are Any Accidents?*

We proceed thus to the Sixth Article: It seems that there are accidents in God.

Objection 1. For substance cannot be an accident, as Aristotle says.[2] Therefore that which is an accident in one, cannot, in another, be a substance. Thus it is proved that heat cannot be the substantial form of fire, because it is an accident in other things. But wisdom, virtue, and the like, which are accidents in us, are attributed to God. Therefore in God there are accidents.

Obj. 2. Further, in every genus there is one first. But there are many genera of accidents. If, therefore, the first members of these genera are not in God, there will be many first beings other than God—which is unfitting.

On the contrary, Every accident is in a subject. But God cannot be a subject, for "a simple form cannot be a subject," as Boethius says (*De Trinit.*).[3] Therefore in God there cannot be any accident.

I answer that, From all we have said, it is clear there can be no accident in God. First, because a subject is compared to its accidents as potency to act; for a subject is in some way in act by its accidents. But there can be no potency in God, as was shown (Q. II, A. 3). Secondly, because God is His existence; and as Boëthius says (*De Hebdom.*),[4] although every essence may have something superadded to it, this cannot apply to absolute being; thus what is hot can have something outside of heat added to it, as whiteness, although heat itself can have nothing else than heat. Thirdly, because what is essential is prior to what is accidental. Hence as God is absolute primal being, there can be nothing accidental in Him. Neither can He have any essential accidents (as the capability of laughing is an essential accident of man), because such accidents are caused by the principles of the subject. Now there can be nothing caused in God, since He is the first cause. Hence it follows that there is no accident in God.

Reply Obj. 1. Virtue and wisdom are not said of God and of us univocally. Hence it does not follow that there are accidents in God as there are in us.

Reply Obj. 2. Since substance is prior to its accidents, the principles of accidents are reducible to the principles of the substance as to that which is prior. God, however, is not first as if contained in the genus of substance, but He is

[2] *Physics*, I, 3 (186ᵇ4).   [3] Chap. 2 (PL 64, 1250).
[4] PL 64, 1311.

first in respect to all being, outside of every genus.

ARTICLE 7. *Whether God Is Altogether Simple?*

We proceed thus to the Seventh Article: It seems that God is not altogether simple.

Objection 1. For whatever is from God must imitate Him. Thus from the first being are all beings; and from the first good is all good. But in the things which are from God, nothing is altogether simple. Therefore neither is God altogether simple.

Obj. 2. Further, whatever is best must be attributed to God. But with us that which is composite is better than that which is simple; thus, compounds are better than simple elements, and animals than plants. Therefore it cannot be said that God is altogether simple.

On the contrary, Augustine says (*De Trin.* iv, 6)[1] that God is truly and absolutely simple.

I answer that, The absolute simplicity of God may be shown in many ways. First, from the previous articles of this question. For there is neither composition of quantitative parts in God, since He is not a body; nor composition of form and matter; nor does His nature differ from His suppositum; nor His essence from His being; neither is there in Him composition of genus and difference, nor of subject and accident. Therefore, it is clear that God is in no way composite, but is altogether simple.

Secondly, because every composite is posterior to its component parts, and is dependent on them; but God is the first being, as shown above (Q. II, A. 3).

Thirdly, because every composite has a cause, for things in themselves different cannot unite unless something causes them to unite. But God is uncaused, as shown above (*loc. cit.*), since He is the first efficient cause.

Fourthly, because in every composite there must be potency and act; but this does not apply to God; for either one of the parts is act in respect to another, or at least all the parts are as though in potency with respect to the whole.

Fifthly, because every composite is something which does not accord with any of its parts. And this is evident in a whole made up of dissimilar parts; for no part of a man is a man, nor any of the parts of the foot, a foot. But in wholes made up of similar parts, although something which is said of the whole may be said of a part (as a part of the air is air, and a part of water, water), nevertheless certain things are said of the whole which do not accord with any of the parts; for instance, if the whole volume of water is two cubits, no part of it can be two cubits. Thus in every composite there is something which is not it itself. But, even if this could be said of whatever has a form, namely, that it has something which is not it itself, as in a white object there is something which does not belong to the notion of white, nevertheless in the form itself there is nothing besides itself. And so, since God is form itself, or rather being itself, He can be in no way composite. Hilary touches on this argument, when he says (*De Trin.* vii):[2] "God, Who is strength, is not made up of things that are weak; nor is He Who is light, composed of things that are dim."

Reply Obj. 1. Whatever is from God imitates Him, as caused things imitate the first cause. But it is of the very notion of a thing caused to be in some sort composite, because at least its being differs from its essence, as will be shown below, (Q. L, A. 2).

Reply Obj. 2. With us composite things are better than simple things because the perfection of created goodness cannot be found in one simple thing, but in many things. But the perfection of divine goodness is found in one simple thing as we will show below (Q. IV, A. 2, Ans. 1).

ARTICLE 8. *Whether God Enters into the Composition of Other Things?*

We proceed thus to the Eighth Article: It seems that God enters into the composition of other things.

Objection 1. For Dionysius says (*Cæl. Hier.* iv):[3] "The being of all things is that which is above being—the Godhead." But the being of all things enters into the composition of everything. Therefore God enters into the composition of other things.

Obj. 2. Further, God is a form; for Augustine says (*De Verb. Dom.*)[4] that the word of God, which is God, is an uncreated form. But a form is part of a composite. Therefore God is part of some composite.

Obj. 3. Further, whatever things exist in no way differing from each other, are the same. But God and prime matter exist, and in no way differ from each other. Therefore they are completely the same. But prime matter enters into the composition of things. Therefore also does God. Proof of the minor—whatever things differ, they differ by some differences, and therefore must be composite. But God and prime matter are alto-

---

[1] PL 42, 928.

[2] PL 10, 223.   [3] Sect. 1 (PG 3, 177).

[4] *Serm.*, CXVII, 2 (PL 38, 662).

gether simple. Therefore they in no way differ from each other.

On the contrary, Dionysius says (*Div. Nom.* ii):[1] "There can be no touching Him (that is, God), nor any other union with Him by mingling part with part."

Further, the first cause rules all things without commingling with them, as the Philosopher says (*Liber de Causis*).[2]

I answer that, On this point there have been three errors. Some have affirmed that God is the world-soul, as is clear from Augustine.[3] This is practically the same as the opinion of those who assert that God is the soul of the highest heaven.[4] Again, others have said that God is the formal principle of all things; and this was the theory of the Almaricians.[5] The third error is that of David of Dinant,[6] who most foolishly taught that God was prime matter. Now all these contain manifest untruth, since it is not possible for God to enter into the composition of anything, either as a formal or a material principle.

First, because as we said above (Q. II, A. 3) God is the first efficient cause. Now the efficient cause is not identical numerically with the form of the thing made, but only specifically; for man begets man. But matter can be neither numerically nor specifically identical with an efficient cause, for the former is merely potential, while the latter is actual.

Secondly, because, since God is the first efficient cause, to act belongs to Him primarily and essentially. But that which enters into composition with anything does not act primarily and essentially, but rather the composite so acts; for the hand does not act, but the man by his hand, and, fire warms by heat. Hence God cannot be part of a composite.

Thirdly, because no part of a composite can be absolutely first among beings—not even matter, nor form, though they are the primal parts of every composite. For matter is in potency, and potency is absolutely posterior to act, as is clear from the foregoing (Q. III, A. I), while a form which is part of a composite is a participated form, and as that which participates is posterior to that which is essential, so likewise is that which is participated; as fire in ignited objects is posterior to fire that is essentially

such. Now it has been proved that God is the absolutely first being (Q. II, A. 3).

Reply Obj. 1. The Godhead is called the being of all things, as their effecting and exemplar cause, but not as being their essence.

Reply Obj. 2. The Word is an exemplar form, but not a form that is part of a composite.

Reply Obj. 3. Simple things do not differ by added differences,—for this is the property of composites. Thus man and horse differ by their differences, rational and irrational, which differences, however, do not differ from each other by other differences. Hence, to be quite accurate, it is better to say that they are, not different, but diverse. Hence, according to the Philosopher,[7] things which are diverse are absolutely distinct, but things which are different differ by something. Therefore, strictly speaking, prime matter and God do not differ, but are by their very being diverse. Hence it does not follow they are the same.

QUESTION IV

THE PERFECTION OF GOD

(*In Three Articles*)

HAVING considered the divine simplicity, we treat next of God's perfection. Now because everything in so far as it is perfect is called good, we shall speak first of the divine perfection; secondly of the divine goodness (Q. V).

Concerning the first there are three points of inquiry:—

(1) Whether God is perfect? (2) Whether God is perfect universally, as having in Himself the perfections of all things? (3) Whether creatures can be said to be like God?

ARTICLE I. *Whether God Is Perfect?*

We proceed thus to the First Article: It seems that to be perfect does not belong to God.

Objection 1. For we say a thing is perfect if it is completely made. But it does not befit God to be made. Therefore He is not perfect.

Obj. 2. Further, God is the first beginning of things. But the beginnings of things seem to be imperfect, as seed is the beginning of animal and vegetable life. Therefore God is imperfect.

Obj. 3. Further, as shown above (Q. III, A. 4), God's essence is being itself. But being itself seems most imperfect, since it is most general and receptive of all addition. Therefore God is imperfect.

On the contrary, It is written: *Be you perfect as also your heavenly Father is perfect* (Matt. 5. 48).

---

[1] Sect. 5 (PG 3, 643).
[2] Sect. 19 (BA 181.7).
[3] *City of God,* VII, 6 (PL 41, 199).
[4] Cf. Thomas, *Contra Gent.,* I, 27; cf. Averroes, *In Meta.,* XII, Comm. 41 (VIII, 325 B).
[5] See Cappelle, *Amaury de Bène* (p. 42–50).
[6] See De Vaux, RSPT (1933), p. 243–245.
[7] *Metaphysics,* X, 3 (1054[b]24).

I answer that, As the Philosopher relates[1] some ancient philosophers, namely, the Pythagoreans, and Leucippus, did not attribute "best" and "most perfect" to the first principle. The reason was that the ancient philosophers considered only a material principle, and a first material principle is most imperfect. For since matter as such is in potency, the first material principle must be potential in the highest degree, and thus most imperfect. Now God is the first principle, not material, but in the order of efficient cause, which must be most perfect. For just as matter, as such, is in potency, an agent, as such, is in act. Hence, the first active principle must be most actual, and therefore most perfect; for a thing is said to be perfect according as it is in act, because we call that perfect which lacks nothing of the mode of its perfection.

Reply Obj. 1. As Gregory says (*Moral.* v, 36):[2] "Though our lips can only stammer, we yet chant the high things of God." For that which is not made is improperly called perfect. Nevertheless because created things are then called perfect when from potency they are brought into act, this word "perfect" signifies whatever is not wanting in act, whether this be by way of perfection or not.

Reply Obj. 2. The material principle which with us is found to be imperfect, cannot be absolutely first, but must be preceded by something perfect. For seed, though it is the principle of animal life reproduced through seed, has previous to it the animal or plant from which it came. Because, previous to that which is in potency must be that which is in act; since a being in potency can only be reduced to act by some being in act.

Reply Obj. 3. Being itself is the most perfect of all things, for it is compared to all things as act; for nothing has actuality except so far as it exists. Hence being itself is the actuality of all things, even of forms themselves. Therefore it is not compared to other things as the receiver is to the received, but rather as the received to the receiver. When therefore I speak of the being of man, or horse, or anything else, being itself is considered as formal, and as something received, and not as that to which being belongs.

ARTICLE 2. *Whether the Perfections of All Things Are in God?*

We proceed thus to the Second Article: It seems that the perfections of all things are not in God.

Objection 1. For God is simple, as shown above (Q. III, A. 7), but the perfections of things are many and diverse. Therefore the perfections of all things are not in God.

Obj. 2. Further, opposites cannot exist in the same being. Now the perfections of things are opposed to each other, for each species is perfected by its specific difference. But the differences by which genera are divided, and species constituted are opposed to each other. Therefore, because opposites cannot be at the same time in the same subject, it seems that the perfections of all things are not in God.

Obj. 3. Further, a living thing is more perfect than what merely exists; and a knowing thing than what merely lives. Therefore, to live is more perfect than to be and to know than to live. But the essence of God is being itself. Therefore He has not the perfections of life, and knowledge, and other similar perfections.

On the contrary, Dionysius says (*Div. Nom.* v)[3] that "God in His one existence prepossesses all things."

I answer that, The perfections of all things are in God. Hence He is spoken of as universally perfect, because "He does not lack (says the Commentator, *Metaph.* v)[4] any excellence which may be found in any genus." This may be seen from two considerations.

First, because whatever perfection exists in an effect must be found in the effecting cause: either according to the same nature, if it is a univocal agent—as when man reproduces man; or in a more eminent manner, if it is an equivocal agent—thus in the sun is the likeness of whatever is generated by the sun's power. Now it is plain that the effect pre-exists virtually in the efficient cause; and although to pre-exist in the potentiality of a material cause is to pre-exist in a more imperfect way, since matter as such is imperfect, and an agent as such is perfect, still to pre-exist virtually in the efficient cause is to pre-exist not in a more imperfect, but in a more perfect way. Since therefore God is the first effecting cause of things, the perfections of all things must pre-exist in God in a more eminent way. Dionysius implies the same line of argument by saying of God (*Div. Nom.* v):[5] "It is not that He is this and not that, but that He is all, as the cause of all."

Secondly; from what has been already proved, God is being itself, of itself subsistent (Q. III, A. 4). Consequently, He must contain within Himself the whole perfection of being. For it is

---

[1] *Metaphysics*, XII, 7 (1072ᵇ30).
[2] PL 75, 715.

[3] Sect. 9 (PG 3, 825).   [4] Comm. 21 (VIII, 131, C).
[5] Sect. 8 (PG 3, 824).

clear that if some hot thing has not the whole perfection of heat, this is because heat is not participated in its full perfection; but if this heat were self-subsisting, nothing of the excellence of heat would be wanting to it. Since therefore God is subsisting being itself, nothing of the perfection of being can be wanting to Him. Now all perfections relate to the perfection of being, for things are perfect, according as they have being after some fashion. It follows therefore that the perfection of no one thing is wanting to God. This line of argument, too, is implied by Dionysius (loc. cit.), when he says that, "God exists not in any single mode, but embraces all being within Himself, absolutely, without limitation, uniformly"; and afterwards he adds that, "He is the very existence to subsisting things." [1]

Reply Obj. 1. Even as the sun as Dionysius remarks (loc. cit.), "while remaining one and shining uniformly, contains within itself first and uniformly the substances of sensible things, and many and diverse qualities, even more should all things in a kind of natural unity pre-exist in the cause of all things"; and thus things diverse and in themselves opposed to each other pre-exist in God as one, without injury to His simplicity.

This suffices for the Reply to the Second Objection.

Reply Obj. 3. The same Dionysius says (loc. cit.) that, although being is more perfect than life, and life than wisdom, if they are considered as distinguished in idea; nevertheless, a living thing is more perfect than what merely exists, because living things also exist, and knowing things both exist and live. Although therefore being does not include life and wisdom, because that which participates in being need not participate in every mode of being, nevertheless God's being includes in itself life and wisdom, because nothing of the perfection of being can be wanting to Him who is subsisting being itself.

ARTICLE 3. Whether Any Creature Can Be Like God?

We proceed thus to the Third Article: It seems that no creature can be like God.

Objection 1. For it is written (Ps. 85. 8): There is none among the gods like unto Thee, O Lord. But of all creatures the most excellent are those which are called by participation gods. Therefore still less can other creatures be said to be like to God.

Obj. 2. Further, likeness is a kind of comparison. But there can be no comparison between

[1] I, 4 (PG 3, 817).

things in a different genus. Therefore neither can there be any likeness. Thus we do not say that sweetness is like whiteness. But no creature is in the same genus as God, since God is in no genus, as shown above (Q. III, A. 5). Therefore no creature is like God.

Obj. 3. Further, we speak of those things as like which agree in form. But nothing can agree with God in form; for, save in God alone, essence and being itself differ. Therefore no creature can be like to God.

Obj. 4. Further, among like things there is mutual likeness; for like is similar to like. If therefore any creature is like God, God will be like some creature, which is against what is said by Isaias: To whom have you likened God? (40. 18).

On the contrary, It is written: Let us make man to our image and likeness (Gen. 1. 26), and: When He shall appear we shall be like to Him (I John 3. 2).

I answer that, Since likeness is based upon agreement or communication in form, it varies according to the many modes of communication in form. Some things are said to be like which communicate in the same form according to the same notion, and according to the same measure, and these are said to be not merely like, but equal in their likeness; as two things equally white are said to be alike in whiteness. And this is the most perfect likeness. In another way, we speak of things as alike which communicate in form according to the same notion, though not according to the same measure, but according to more or less, as something less white is said to be like another thing more white. And this is imperfect likeness. In a third way some things are said to be alike which communicate in the same form, but not according to the same aspect, as we see in non-univocal agents. For since every agent reproduces itself so far as it is an agent, and everything acts according to the manner of its form, the effect must in some way resemble the form of the agent. If therefore the agent is contained in the same species as its effect, there will be a likeness in form between that which makes and that which is made, according to the same aspect of the species; as man reproduces man. If however the agent and its effect are not contained in the same species, there will be a likeness, but not according to the aspect of the same species; as things generated by the sun's power may be in some sort spoken of as like the sun, not as though they received the form of the sun in its specific likeness, but in its generic likeness.

Therefore if there is an agent not contained

in any genus, its effects will still more distantly reproduce the form of the agent, not, that is, so as to participate in the likeness of the agent's form according to the same specific or generic aspect, but only according to some sort of analogy; as being is common to all. In this way the things that are from God, so far as they are beings, are like God as the first and universal principle of all being.

Reply Obj. 1. As Dionysius says (*Div. Nom.* ix),[1] when Holy Writ declares that nothing is like God, "it does not mean to deny all likeness to Him. For, the same things can be like and unlike to God: like, according as they imitate Him, as far as He, Who is not perfectly imitable, can be imitated; unlike according as they fall short of their cause," not merely in intensity and lessening, as that which is less white falls short of that which is more white, but because they are not in agreement, specifically or generically.

Reply Obj. 2. God is not related to creatures as though belonging to a different genus, but as that which is outside genus, and as the principle of all genera.

Reply Obj. 3. Likeness of creatures to God is not affirmed on account of agreement in form according to the aspect of the same genus or species, but solely according to analogy, according as namely, God is being by essence, while other things are beings by participation.

Reply Obj. 4. Although it may be admitted that creatures are in some sort like God, it must in no way be admitted that God is like creatures; because, as Dionysius says (*Div. Nom.* ix):[2] "A mutual likeness may be found between things of the same order, but not between a cause and that which is caused." For, we say that a statue is like a man, but not conversely; so also a creature can be spoken of as in some sort like God, but not that God is like a creature.

QUESTION V
OF THE GOOD IN GENERAL
(*In Six Articles*)

WE next consider goodness:—

First, of the good in general. Secondly, the goodness of God (Q. VI).

Under the first head there are six points of inquiry:—

(1) Whether good and being are the same really? (2) Granted that they differ only in idea, which is prior in thought? (3) Granted that being is prior, whether every being is good? (4) To what cause should goodness be reduced? (5) Whether the nature of good consists in mode,

species, and order? (6) In what way the good is divided into the virtuous, the useful, and the pleasant?

ARTICLE 1. *Whether the Good Differs Really from Being?*

We proceed thus to the First Article: It seems that the good differs really from being.

Objection 1. For Boethius says (*De Hebdom.*):[3] "I perceive that in nature the fact that things are good is one thing; that they are is another." Therefore good and being really differ.

Obj. 2. Further, nothing can be its own form. But that is called good which has the form of being, according to the commentary on *De Causis*.[4] Therefore good differs really from being.

Obj. 3. Further, good can be more or less. But being cannot be more or less. Therefore good differs really from being.

On the contrary, Augustine says[5] that, "in so far as we exist we are good."

I answer that, Good and being are really the same, and differ only according to reason, which is clear from the following argument. The essence of good consists in this, that it is in some way desirable. Hence the Philosopher says[6] "The good is what all desire." Now it is clear that a thing is desirable only in so far as it is perfect; for all desire their own perfection. But everything is perfect so far as it is in act. Therefore it is clear that a thing is good so far as it is being; for it is being is the actuality of all things, as is clear from the foregoing (Q. III, A. 4; Q. IV, A. 1). Hence it is clear that good and being are the same really. But good presents the aspect of desirableness, which being does not present.

Reply Obj. 1. Although good and being are the same really, nevertheless since they differ in reason they are not said of a thing absolutely in the same way. Since being properly signifies that something is, in act, and act is properly ordered to potentiality, a thing is, in consequence, called being absolutely according as it is primarily distinguished from that which is only in potency; and this is each thing's substantial being. Hence by its substantial being, anything whatsoever is called being absolutely; but by any act added to this it is said to have being relatively. Thus to be white implies relative being, for to be white does not take a thing out of potential being absolutely, since it comes to a thing already existing actually. But good signifies the notion of perfection

---

[1] Sect. 7 (PG 3, 916).   [2] Sect. 6 (PG 3, 913).

[3] PL 64, 1312.
[4] Sect. 19 (BA 181).
[5] *Christian Doctrine*, I, 32 (PL 34, 32).
[6] *Ethics*, I, 1 (1094ᵃ3).

which is desirable, and consequently signifies the notion of something ultimate. Hence that which has ultimate perfection is said to be good absolutely; but that which has not the ultimate perfection it ought to have (although, in so far as it is at all actual, it has some perfection), is not said to be perfect absolutely nor good absolutely, but only relatively. In this way, therefore, viewed in its first (that is, substantial) being a thing is said to be good relatively (that is, in so far as it has being), but viewed in its complete actuality, a thing is said to be relatively, and to be good absolutely. Hence the saying of Boëthius (*loc. cit.*), "that things are good is one thing, that they are is another," is to be referred to a thing's being good, and having being absolutely. Because, regarded in its first act, a thing is being absolutely, and regarded in its complete actuality, it is good absolutely—in such sort that even in its first act it is in some sort good, and even in its complete actuality it is in some sort being.

Reply Obj. 2. Good is a form so far as absolute good signifies complete actuality.

Reply Obj. 3. Again, good is spoken of as more or less according to a thing's superadded actuality, for example, as to knowledge or virtue.

ARTICLE 2. *Whether Good Is Prior in Idea to Being?*

We proceed thus to the Second Article: It seems that good is prior in idea to being.

Objection 1. For names are arranged according to the arrangement of the things signified by the names. But Dionysius (*Div. Nom.* iii)[1] assigned the first place, amongst other names of God, to His goodness rather than to His being. Therefore in idea good is prior to being.

Obj. 2. Further, that which extends to more things is prior according to reason. But good extends to more things than being, because, as Dionysius notes (*loc. cit.* v),[2] "the good extends to things both existing and non-existing; but existence extends to existing things alone." Therefore good is prior in idea to being.

Obj. 3. Further, what is the more universal is prior in idea. But good seems to be more universal than being, since the good has the aspect of desirable, while for some non-being is desirable; for it is said of Judas: *It were better for him, if that man had not been born* (Matt. 26. 24). Therefore good is prior in idea to being.

Obj. 4. Further, not only is being desirable, but life, knowledge, and many other things besides. Thus it seems that being is a particular desirable thing, and goodness a universal one. Therefore, absolutely, goodness is prior in idea to being.

On the contrary, It is said by Aristotle[3] that "the first of created things is being."

I answer that, being is prior in idea to good. For the meaning signified by the name of a thing is that which the intellect conceives of the thing and intends by the word that stands for it. Therefore, that is prior in idea, which is first conceived by the intellect. Now the first thing conceived by the intellect is being, because everything is knowable only in so far as it is in act as it says in the *Metaphysics*.[4] Hence, being is the proper object of the intellect, and is that which is primarily intelligible, as sound is that which is primarily audible. Therefore being is prior in idea to good.

Reply Obj. 1. Dionysius discusses the Divine Names (*Div. Nom.* i, iii)[5] as implying some causal relation in God; for we name God, as he says, from creatures, as a cause from its effects. But the good, since it has the aspect of desirable, implies the relation of a final cause, the causality of which is first, since an agent does not act except for some end, and by an agent matter is moved to its form. Hence the end is called the cause of causes. Thus good, as a cause, is prior to being, as is the end to the form. Therefore among the names signifying the divine causality, good precedes being. Again, according to the Platonists, who, through not distinguishing matter from privation, said that matter was non-being,[6] the good is more extensively participated than being; for prime matter participates in goodness as tending to it, for all seek their like; but it does not participate in being, since it is held to be non-being. Therefore Dionysius says that "goodness extends to non-existence" (*loc. cit. Obj.* 2).

Reply Obj. 2. The same solution is applied to this objection. Or it may be said that goodness extends to existing and non-existing things not so far as it can be predicated of them, but so far as it can cause them—provided that by non-existence we understand not absolutely those things which do not exist at all, but those which are potential, and not actual. For good has the nature of end, in which not only actual things rest, but also towards which even those things which are not in act, but merely in potency tend.

---

[3] *Lib. de Causis,* 4 (BA 166.19).

[4] Aristotle, IX, 9 (1051ª31).

[5] Sect. 7 (PG 3, 596).

[6] Aristotle, *Physics,* I, 9 (192ª2); see Albert the Great, *Physics,* I, 3, 16 (BO III, 856).

---

[1] Sect. 1 (PG 3, 680).

[2] PG 3, 816.

Now being implies the relation of a formal cause only, either inherent or exemplar; and its causality does not extend save to those things which are actual.

Reply Obj. 3. Non-being is desirable not of itself, but only accidentally—that is, in so far as the removal of an evil, which can only be removed by non-being, is desirable. Now the removal of an evil cannot be desirable except so far as this evil deprives a thing of some being. Therefore being is desirable of itself, and non-being only accidentally, in so far as one seeks some being of which one cannot bear to be deprived; thus even non-being can be spoken of as relatively good.

Reply Obj. 4. Life, knowledge, and the like, are desired only so far as they are actual. Hence in each one of them some sort of being is desired. And thus nothing can be desired except being, and consequently nothing is good except being.

ARTICLE 3. *Whether Every Being Is Good?*

We proceed thus to the Third Article: It seems that not every being is good.

Objection 1. For good is something superadded to being, as is clear from A. 1. But whatever is added to something beyond being limits it; as substance, quantity, quality, etc. Therefore good limits being. Therefore not every being is good.

Obj. 2. Further, no evil is good: *Woe to you that call evil good, and good evil* (Isa. 5. 20). But some being is called evil. Therefore not every being is good.

Obj. 3. Further, goodness has the aspect of desirability. Now prime matter does not have the aspect of desirability, but rather that which desires. Therefore prime matter does not have the aspect of good. Therefore not every being is good.

Obj. 4. Further, the Philosopher notes[1] that in mathematics the good does not exist. But mathematics are beings of a sort; otherwise there would be no knowledge of them. Therefore not every being is good.

On the contrary, Every being that is not God is God's creature. Now every creature of God is good (I Tim. 4. 4): and God is the greatest good. Therefore every being is good.

I answer that, Every being, as being, is good. For every being, as being, is in act and is in some way perfect, since every act is a sort of perfection, and perfection implies desirability and goodness, as is clear from A. 1. Hence it follows that every being as such is good.

Reply Obj. 1. Substance, quantity, quality,

and everything included in them, limit being by applying it to some quiddity or nature. Now in this sense, good does not add anything to being beyond the aspect of desirability and perfection, which is also proper to being in whatever kind of nature it may be. Hence good does not limit being.

Reply Obj. 2. No being can be spoken of as evil, in so far as it is being, but only so far as it lacks being. Thus a man is said to be evil because he lacks the being of virtue; and an eye is said to be evil because it lacks the power to see well.

Reply Obj. 3. As prime matter has only potential being, so is it only potentially good. Although, according to the Platonists,[2] prime matter may be said to be a non-being on account of the privation attaching to it, nevertheless, it does participate to a certain extent in good, namely, by its relation to, or aptitude for, good. Consequently, to be desirable does not belong to it, but rather to desire.

Reply Obj. 4. Mathematical things do not subsist separated according to being, because if they subsisted there would be good in them, the good namely of their very being. But mathematical things are separate according to reason only, according as they are abstracted from motion and matter; and thus they are abstracted from the notion of end, which has the character of a mover. Nor is it unfitting that there should be in some logical being neither good nor the aspect of good, since the idea of being is prior to the idea of good, as was said in the preceding article.

ARTICLE 4. *Whether Good Has the Aspect of a Final Cause?*

We proceed thus to the Fourth Article: It seems that good has not the aspect of a final cause, but rather of the other causes.

Objection 1. For, as Dionysius says (*Div. Nom.* iv),[3] "Goodness is praised as beauty." But beauty has the aspect of a formal cause. Therefore goodness has the aspect of a formal cause.

Obj. 2. Further, goodness is self-giving, according to Dionysius who says (*loc. cit.*)[4] that goodness is "that whereby all things subsist, and are." But to be self-giving implies the aspect of an efficient cause. Therefore goodness has the aspect of an efficient cause.

Obj. 3. Further, Augustine says[5] that "we are,

---

[1] *Metaphysics*, III, 2 (996^{b}1).

[2] See Aristotle, *Physics*, I, 9 (192^{a}2).
[3] Sect. 7 (PG 3, 701).
[4] Chap. 4, Sect. 20 (PG 3, 720); see also sections 1 & 4.
[5] *Christian Doctrine*, I, 32 (PL 34, 32).

because God is good." But we are from God as from an efficient cause. Therefore goodness implies the aspect of an efficient cause.

On the contrary, The Philosopher says[1] that "that is to be considered as the end and the good of other things for the sake of which something is." Therefore good has the aspect of a final cause.

I answer that, Since good is that which all things desire, and since this has the aspect of an end, it is clear that good implies the aspect of an end. Nevertheless the notion of good presupposes the notion of an efficient cause, and also of a formal cause. For we see that what is first in causing is last in the thing caused. Fire, for instance, heats first of all before bringing in the form of fire, though the heat in the fire follows from the substantial form. Now in causing, good and the end, which move the agent to act, come first; second, the action of the agent moving to the form; third, the form comes. Hence in that which is caused the converse ought to take place, so that there should be first, the form whereby it is a being; secondly, we consider in it its effecting power, whereby it is perfect in being, for a thing is perfect when it can reproduce its like, as the Philosopher says;[2] thirdly, there follows the aspect of good which is the basic principle in a being of perfection.

Reply Obj. 1. Beauty and good in a subject are the same, for they are based upon the same thing, namely, the form; and consequently good is praised as beauty. But they differ logically, for good properly relates to the appetite (good being what all things desire), and therefore it has the aspect of an end (for the appetite is a kind of movement towards a thing). On the other hand, beauty relates to the knowing power, for beautiful things are those which please when seen. Hence beauty consists in due proportion, for the senses delight in things duly proportioned, as in what is after their own kind—because even sense is a sort of reason, just as is every knowing power. Now, since knowledge is by assimilation, and likeness relates to form, beauty properly belongs to the nature of a formal cause.

Reply Obj. 2. Good is described as self-giving in the sense that an end is said to move.

Reply Obj. 3. He who has a will is said to be good, so far as he has a good will, because it is by our will that we employ whatever powers we may have. Hence a man is said to be good, not by his good understanding, but by his good will.

[1] *Physics,* II, 3 (195ᵃ23).
[2] *Meteorology,* IV, 3 (380ᵃ12).

Now the will relates to the end as to its proper object. Thus the saying, "we are because God is good" has reference to the final cause.

ARTICLE 5. *Whether the Notion of Good Consists in Mode, Species, and Order?*

We proceed thus to the Fifth Article: It seems that the notion of good does not consist in mode, species, and order.

Objection 1. For good and being differ logically, as we said above (A. 1). But mode, species, and order seem to belong to the notion of being, for it is written: *Thou hast ordered all things in measure, and number, and weight* (Wisd. 11. 21). And to these three can be reduced species, mode, and order, as Augustine says (*Gen. ad lit.* iv, 3).[3] "Measure marks the mode of everything, number gives it its species, and weight gives it rest and stability." Therefore the notion of good does not consist in mode, species, and order.

Obj. 2. Further, mode, species, and order are themselves goods. Therefore if the notion of good consists in mode, species, and order, then every mode must have its own mode, species, and order. The same would be the case with species and order in endless succession.

Obj. 3. Further, evil is the privation of mode, species, and order. But evil is not the total absence of good. Therefore the notion of good does not consist in mode, species, and order.

Obj. 4. Further, that in which the nature of good consists cannot be spoken of as evil. Yet we can speak of an evil mode, species, and order. Therefore the notion of good does not consist in mode, species, and order.

Obj. 5. Further, mode, species, and order are caused by weight, number, and measure, as appears from the quotation from Augustine. But not every good thing has weight, number, and measure; for Ambrose says (*Hexam.* i, 9):[4] "It is of the nature of light not to have been created in number, weight, and measure." Therefore the notion of good does not consist in mode, species, and order.

On the contrary, Augustine says (*De Nat. Boni,* iii):[5] These three—mode, species, order—as common good things, are in everything God has made; thus, where these three abound the things are very good; where they are less, the things are less good; where they do not exist at all, there can be nothing good." But this would not be unless the notion of good consisted in them. Therefore the notion of goodness consists in mode, species, and order.

I answer that, Everything is said to be good

[3] PL 34, 299.   [4] PL 14, 154.   [5] PL 42, 553.

so far as it is perfect, for in that way it is desirable (as shown above, AA. 1, 3). Now a thing is said to be perfect if it lacks nothing according to the mode of its perfection. But since everything is what it is by its form (and since the form presupposes certain things, and from the form certain things necessarily follow), in order for a thing to be perfect and good it must have a form, together with all that precedes and follows upon that form. Now the form presupposes determination or commensuration of its principles, whether material or efficient, and this is signified by the mode; hence it is said that "the measure marks the mode." But the form itself is signified by the species, for everything is placed in its species by its form. Hence the number is said to give the species, for "definitions signifying species are like numbers," according to the Philosopher;[1] for as a unit added to or taken from a number, changes its species, so a difference added to or taken from a definition, changes its species. Further, upon the form follows an inclination to the end, or to an action, or something of the sort; for everything, in so far as it is in act, acts and tends towards that which is in accordance with its form, and this pertains to weight and order. Hence the notion of good, so far as it consists in perfection, consists also in mode, species, and order.

Reply Obj. 1. These three only follow upon being in so far as it is perfect, and according to this perfection is it good.

Reply Obj. 2. Mode, species, and order, are said to be good, and to be beings, not as though they themselves were subsistences, but because it is through them that other things are both beings and good. Hence they have no need of other things whereby they are good, for they are spoken of as good, not as though formally constituted so by something else, but as formally constituting others good; thus whiteness is not said to be a being as though it were by anything else, but because by it something else has accidental being, as a thing that is white.

Reply Obj. 3. Every being is consequent upon some form. Hence, according to every being of a thing is its mode, species, order. Thus, a man has a mode, species, and order, as a man; and another mode, species, and order, as he is white, virtuous, learned, and so on, according to everything predicated of him. But evil deprives a thing of some sort of being, as blindness deprives us of that being which is sight; yet it does not destroy every mode, species, and order, but only such as follow upon the being of sight.

[1] *Metaphysics*, VIII, 3 (1043[b]34).

Reply Obj. 4. Augustine says (*De Nat. Boni*, xxii),[2] "Every mode, as mode, is good" (and the same can be said of species and order). "But an evil mode, species, and order are so called as being less than they ought to be, or as not belonging to that to which they ought to belong. Therefore they are called evil, because they are out of place and incongruous."

Reply Obj. 5. The nature of light is spoken of as being without number, weight, and measure not absolutely, but in comparison with corporeal things, because the power of light extends to all corporeal things, since it is an active quality of the first body that causes change, that is, the heavens.

ARTICLE 6. *Whether Good Is Rightly Divided into the Fitting, the Useful, and the Pleasant?*

We proceed thus to the Sixth Article: It seems that good is not rightly divided into the fitting, the useful, and the pleasant.

Objection 1. For goodness is divided by the ten predicaments, as the Philosopher says.[3] But the fitting, the useful, and the pleasant can be found under one predicament. Therefore goodness is not rightly divided by them.

Obj. 2. Further, every division is made by opposites. But these three do not seem to be opposites, for the fitting is pleasing, and no wickedness is useful; but this ought to be the case if the division were made by opposites, for then the virtuous and the useful would be opposed as Tully also says (*De Offic.* ii).[4] Therefore this division is incorrect.

Obj. 3. Further, where one thing is on account of another, there is only one thing. But the useful is not good except so far as it is pleasing and fitting. Therefore the useful ought not to be divided against the pleasant and the virtuous.

On the contrary, Ambrose makes use of this division of good (*De Offic.* i, 9).[5]

I answer that, This division properly concerns the good of man. But if we consider the nature of good from a higher and more general point of view, we shall find that this division properly concerns good as such. For everything is good so far as it is desirable, and is a term of the movement of the appetite, the term of whose movement can be seen from a consideration of the movement of a natural body. Now the movement of a natural body is terminated by the end absolutely, and relatively by the means through which it comes to the end, where the movement ceases; so a thing is called a term of the move-

[2] PL 42, 558.   [3] *Ethics*, 1, 6 (1096[a]19).
[4] Chap. 3 (DD IV, 465).   [5] PL 16, 35.

ment so far as it terminates any part of that movement. Now the ultimate term of movement can be taken in two ways, either as the thing itself towards which it tends, for example, a place or form; or a state of rest in that thing. Thus, in the movement of the appetite, the thing desired that terminates the movement of the appetite relatively, as a means by which something tends towards another, is called the useful; but that sought after as the last thing terminating completely the movement of the appetite, as a thing towards which for its own sake the appetite tends, is called the fitting, for the fitting is that which is desired for its own sake; but that which terminates the movement of the appetite in the form of rest in the thing desired is called the pleasant.

Reply Obj. 1. Goodness, so far as it is identical with being, is divided by the ten predicaments. But this division belongs to it according to its own notion.

Reply Obj. 2. This division is not by opposite things, but by opposite aspects. Now those things are called pleasing which have no other aspect under which they are desirable except the pleasant, although sometimes they are hurtful and unfitting. But the useful applies to such as have nothing desirable in themselves, but are desired only as helpful to something further, as the taking of bitter medicine, while the fitting is predicated of such as are desirable in themselves.

Reply Obj. 3. Good is not divided into these three as something univocal to be predicated equally of them all, but as something analogical to be predicated of them according to priority and posteriority. Hence it is predicated chiefly of the fitting, then of the pleasant, and lastly of the useful.

QUESTION VI
THE GOODNESS OF GOD
(In Four Articles)

WE next consider the goodness of God, under which head there are four points of inquiry: (1) Whether to be good belongs to God? (2) Whether God is the supreme good? (3) Whether He alone is good through His essence? (4) Whether all things are good by the divine goodness?

ARTICLE 1. *Whether To Be Good Belongs to God?*

We proceed thus to the First Article: It seems that to be good does not belong to God.

Objection 1. For the notion of good consists in mode, species, and order. But these do not seem to belong to God, since God is boundless,

and is not ordered to anything. Therefore to be good does not belong to God.

Obj. 2. Further, the good is what all things desire. But all things do not desire God, because all things do not know Him, and nothing is desired unless it is known. Therefore to be good does not belong to God.

On the contrary, It is written (Lam. 3. 25): *The Lord is good to them that hope in Him, to the soul that seeketh Him.*

I answer that, To be good belongs especially to God. For a thing is good according to its desirableness. Now everything seeks after its own perfection. And the perfection and form of an effect consist in a certain likeness to the agent, since every agent makes its like. Hence the agent itself is desirable and has the nature of good. But the very thing which is desirable in it is the participation of its likeness. Therefore, since God is the first effecting cause of all things, it is manifest that the aspect of good and of desirableness belong to Him; and hence Dionysius (*Div. Nom.* iv)[1] attributes good to God as to the first efficient cause, saying that, "God is called good as by Whom all things subsist."

Reply Obj. 1. To have mode, species, and order, belongs to the notion of caused good; but good is in God as in its cause, and hence it pertains to Him to impose mode, species, and order on others. Therefore these three things are in God as in their cause.

Reply Obj. 2. All things, by desiring their own perfection, desire God Himself, since the perfections of all things are so many likenesses of the divine being, as appears from what is said above (Q. IV, A. 3). And so of those things which desire God, some know Him as He is Himself, and this is proper to the rational creature; others know some participation of His goodness, and this extends even to sensible knowledge; others have a natural desire without knowledge, as being directed to their ends by a higher intelligence.

ARTICLE 2. *Whether God Is the Supreme Good?*

We proceed thus to the Second Article: It seems that God is not the supreme good.

Objection 1. For the supreme good adds something to good; otherwise it would belong to every good. But everything which is an addition to anything else is a composite thing. Therefore the supreme good is composite. But God is supremely simple, as was shown above (Q. III, A. 7). Therefore God is not the supreme good.

Obj. 2. Further, "Good is what all desire," as the Philosopher says.[2] Now what all desire is

[1] PG, 3, 700.   [2] *Ethics*, I, 1 (1094ᵃ3).

nothing but God, Who is the end of all things. Therefore there is no other good but God. This appears also from what is said (Luke 18.19): *None is good but God alone.* But we use the word supreme in comparison with others, as, for instance, supreme heat is used in comparison with all other heats. Therefore God cannot be called the supreme good.

Obj. 3. Further, supreme implies comparison. But things not in the same genus are not comparable; as, sweetness is not properly called greater or less than a line. Therefore, since God is not in the same genus as other good things, as appears above (QQ. III, A. 5; IV, A. 3) it seems that God cannot be called the supreme good in relation to others.

On the contrary, Augustine says (*De Trin.* ii)[1] that the Trinity of the divine persons "is the supreme good, discerned by purified minds."

I answer that, God is the supreme good absolutely, and not only as existing in any genus or order of things. For good is attributed to God, as was said in the preceding article, inasmuch as all desired perfections flow from Him as from the first cause. They do not, however, flow from Him as from a univocal agent, as shown above (Q. IV, A, 3), but as from an agent which does not agree with its effects either in species or genus. Now the likeness of an effect in the univocal cause is found uniformly; but in the equivocal cause it is found more excellently, as, heat is in the sun in a more excellent way than it is in fire. Therefore as good is in God as in the first, but not the univocal, cause of all things, it must be in Him in a most excellent way. And therefore He is called the supreme good.

Reply Obj. 1. The supreme good does not add to good any absolute thing, but only a relation. Now a relation by which something is said of God in relation to creatures is not really in God, but in the creature, for it is in God in our idea only, as what is knowable is called so with relation to knowledge not because it depends on knowledge, but because knowledge depends on it. Thus it is not necessary that there should be composition in the supreme good, but only that other things are deficient in comparison with it.

Reply Obj. 2. When we say that good is what all desire, it is not to be understood that every kind of good thing is desired by all, but that whatever is desired has the aspect of good. And when it is said, *None is good but God alone,* this is to be understood of essential goodness, as will be explained in the next article.

Reply Obj. 3. Things not of the same genus

are in no way comparable to each other if indeed they are in different genera. Now we say that God is not in the same genus with other good things. Not that He is in any other genus, but that He is outside genus, and is the principle of every genus. And thus He is compared to others by excess, and it is this kind of comparison the supreme good implies.

ARTICLE 3. *Whether To Be Essentially Good Belongs to God Alone?*

We proceed thus to the Third Article: It seems that to be essentially good does not belong to God alone.

Objection 1. For as "one" is convertible with "being," so is "good," as we said above (Q. V, A. 1). But every being is one through its own essence, as appears from the Philosopher;[2] therefore every being is good through its own essence.

Obj. 2. Further, if good is what all things desire, since being itself is desired by all, then the being of each thing is its good. But everything is a being through its own essence; therefore every being is good through its own essence.

Obj. 3. Further, everything is good by its own goodness. Therefore if there is anything which is not good through its own essence it is necessary to say that its goodness is not its own essence. Therefore its goodness, since it is a being, must be good; and if it is good by some other goodness, the same question applies to that goodness also; therefore we must either proceed to infinity, or come to some goodness which is not good by any other goodness. Therefore the first supposition holds good. Therefore everything is good through its own essence.

On the contrary, Boëthius says (*De Hebdom.*),[3] that all things but God are good by participation. Therefore they are not good essentially.

I answer that, God alone is good through His own essence. For everything is called good according to its perfection. Now perfection of a thing is threefold: first, according to the constitution of its own being; secondly, in respect of any accidents being added as necessary for its perfect operation; thirdly, perfection consists in the attaining to something else as the end. Thus, for instance, the first perfection of fire consists in its being, which it has through its own substantial form; its secondary perfection consists in heat, lightness and dryness, and the like; its third perfection is to rest in its own place.

This triple perfection belongs to no creature

[1] Bk. I (PL 42, 822).
[2] *Metaphysics,* IV, 2 (1003^{b}32).
[3] PL 64, 1313.

by its own essence; it belongs to God only, in Whom alone essence is His being; in Whom there are no accidents, since whatever belongs to others accidentally belongs to Him essentially, as to be powerful, wise, and the like, as appears from what is stated above (Q. III, A. 6); and He is not directed to anything else as to an end, but is Himself the last end of all things. Hence it is manifest that God alone has every kind of perfection by His own essence; therefore He Himself alone is good by His own essence.

Reply Obj. 1. "One" does not include the notion of perfection, but of indivision only, which belongs to everything according to its own essence. Now the essences of simple things are undivided both in act and in potency, but the essences of composite things are undivided only according to act; and therefore everything must be one by its own essence, but not good by its own essence, as was shown above.

Reply Obj. 2. Although everything is good in that it has being, yet the essence of a creature is not itself being and therefore it does not follow that a creature is good through its essence.

Reply Obj. 3. The goodness of a creature is not its very essence, but something superadded; it is either its being, or some added perfection, or the order to its end. Still, the goodness itself thus added is good, just as it is being. But it is called being because by it something has being, not because it itself has being through something else; hence it is called good because by it something is good, and not because it itself has some other goodness whereby it is good.

ARTICLE 4. *Whether All Things Are Good by the Divine Goodness?*

We proceed thus to the Fourth Article: It seems that all things are good by the divine goodness.

Objection 1. For Augustine says (*De Trin.* viii),[1] "This and that are good; take away this and that, and see good itself if thou canst; and so thou shalt see God, good not by any other good, but the good of every good." But everything is good by its own good; therefore everything is good by that very good which is God.

Obj. 2. Further, as Boethius says (*De Hebdom.*),[2] all things are called good according as they are ordered to God, and this is by reason of the divine goodness; therefore all things are good by the divine goodness.

On the contrary, All things are good in so far as they have being. But they are not called beings through the divine being, but through their

own being; therefore all things are not good by the divine goodness but by their own goodness.

I answer that, As regards relative things, we may admit extrinsic denomination; for example, a thing is denominated "placed" from "place," and "measured" from "measure." But as regards absolute things opinions differ. Plato held the species of all things to be separate, and that individuals were denominated by them as participating in the separate species; for instance, that Socrates is called man according to the separate idea of man.[3] Now just as he laid down separate ideas of man and horse which he called absolute man and absolute horse,[4] so likewise he laid down separate ideas of being and of one, and these he called absolute being and absolute oneness,[5] and by participation of these everything was called being or one. And what was thus absolute being and absolute one, he said was the supreme good.[6] And because good is convertible with being, as one is also, he called God the absolute good,[7] from whom all things are called good by way of participation.[8]

Although this opinion appears to be unreasonable in affirming separate species of natural things as subsisting of themselves—as Aristotle argues in many ways[9]—still, it is absolutely true that there is first something which is essentially being and essentially good, which we call God, as appears from what is shown above (Q. II, A. 3), and Aristotle agrees with this.[10]

Hence from the first being, essentially being, and good, everything can be called good and a being, since it participates in it by way of a certain assimilation, although it is far removed and defective, as appears from the above (Q. IV, A. 3). Everything is therefore called good from the divine goodness as from the first exemplary, effecting, and final principle of all goodness. Nevertheless, everything is called good by reason of the likeness of the divine goodness belonging to it, which is formally its own goodness, by which it is denominated good. And so of all things there is one goodness, and yet many goodnesses.

This is a sufficient *Reply to the Objections.*

[3] Cf. Aristotle, *Metaphysics*, I, 6 (987ᵇ7); Augustine, *83 Questions*, Q. 46 (PL 40, 30).
[4] Aristotle, *Metaphysics*, III, 2 (997ᵇ8),
[5] Aristotle, *Metaphysics*, III, 4 (999ᵇ26).
[6] Cf. Aristotle, *Ethics*, I, 6 (1096ᵃ23); Macrobius, *In Somn. Scip.*, I, 2 (DD 12b).
[7] Augustine, *City of God*, VIII, 8 (PL 41, 233); cf. Plato, *Republic* (508).
[8] Cf. Augustine, *De Trin.*, VIII, 3 (PL 42, 949); Albert the Great, *In Ethic.* I, Tr. 5, Chap. 13 (BO vii, 76).
[9] *Metaphysics*, I, 9 (990ᵃ33); VII, 6–8 (1031ᵃ15); *Ethics*, I, 6 (1096ᵃ11).
[10] *Metaphysics*, II, 1 (993ᵇ24); see above, Q. II, A. 3.

[1] Chap. 3 (PL 42, 949).   [2] PL 64, 1312.

QUESTION VII
The infinity of god
(In Four Articles)

After considering the divine perfection we must consider the divine infinity, and God's existence in things (Q. VIII); for God is everywhere, and in all things, since He is boundless and infinite.

Concerning the first, there are four points of inquiry: (1) Whether God is infinite? (2) Whether anything besides Him is infinite in essence? (3) Whether anything can be infinite in magnitude? (4) Whether an infinite multitude can exist?

Article 1. *Whether God Is Infinite?*

We proceed thus to the First Article: It seems that God is not infinite.

Objection 1. For everything infinite is imperfect, because it has parts and matter, as is said in the *Physics*.[1] But God is most perfect. Therefore He is not infinite.

Obj. 2. Further, according to the Philosopher[2] finite and infinite belong to quantity. But there is no quantity in God, for He is not a body, as was shown above (Q. III, A. 1). Therefore it does not belong to Him to be infinite.

Obj. 3. Further, what is here in such a way as not to be elsewhere, is finite according to place. Therefore that which is a thing in such a way as not to be another thing is finite according to substance. But God is this, and not another; for He is not a stone or wood. Therefore God is not infinite in substance.

On the contrary, Damascene says (*De Fide Orth.* i, 4)[3] that, "God is infinite and eternal, and boundless."

I answer that, All the ancient philosophers attribute infinity to the first principle, as is said in the *Physics*[4] and "this with reason";[5] for they considered that things flow forth infinitely from the first principle. But because some erred concerning the nature of the first principle, as a consequence they erred also concerning its infinity. For as they asserted that matter was the first principle,[6] consequently they attributed to the first principle a material infinity, to the effect that some infinite body was the first principle of things.

We must consider therefore that a thing is called infinite because it is not finite. Now mat-

[1] Aristotle, III, 6 (207a27).
[2] *Physics*, I, 2 (185b2).
[3] PG 94, 800.   [4] Aristotle, III, 4 (203a1).
[5] Aristotle, *Ibid.* (203b4).
[6] *Metaphysics*, I, 3, where Aristotle names Thales, Anaximines, Heraclitus, etc.

ter is in a way made finite by form, and the form by matter. Matter indeed is made finite by form, because matter, before it receives its form, is in potency to many forms, but on receiving a form, it is terminated by that one. Again, form is made finite by matter, because form, considered in itself, is common to many, but when received in matter, the form is determined to this one particular thing. Now matter is perfected by the form by which it is made finite; therefore infinite as attributed to matter, has the nature of something imperfect, for it is as it were formless matter. On the other hand form is not made perfect by matter, but rather its fulness is contracted by matter; and hence the infinite, viewed on the part of the form not determined by matter, has the nature of something perfect. Now being is the most formal of all things, as appears from what is shown above (Q. IV, A. 1, Ans. 3). Since therefore the divine being is not a being received in anything, but He is His own subsistent being as was shown above (Q. III, A. 4), it is clear that God Himself is infinite and perfect.

From this appears the *Reply to the First Objection*.

Reply Obj. 2. Quantity is terminated as it were by its form, which can be seen in the fact that a figure which consists in the termination of quantity, is a kind of form in respect to quantity. Hence the infinite of quantity is the infinite of matter, and such a kind of infinite cannot be attributed to God, as was said above in this article.

Reply Obj. 3. The fact that the being of God is self-subsisting, not received in any other, and is thus called infinite, shows Him to be distinguished from all other beings, and all others to be apart from Him. In the same way, if there were such a thing as a self-subsisting whiteness, the very fact that it did not exist in anything else would make it distinct from every other whiteness existing in a subject.

Article 2. *Whether Anything but God Can Be Essentially Infinite?*

We proceed thus to the Second Article: It seems that something else besides God can be essentially infinite.

Objection 1. For the power of anything is proportioned to its essence. Now if the essence of God is infinite, His power must also be infinite. Therefore He can produce an infinite effect, since the extent of a power is known by its effect.

Obj. 2. Further, whatever has infinite power has an infinite essence. Now the created intellect has an infinite power, for it apprehends the universal, which can extend itself to an infinity of singular things. Therefore every created intellectual substance is infinite.

Obj. 3. Further, prime matter is something other than God, as was shown above (Q. III, A. 8). But prime matter is infinite. Therefore something besides God can be infinite.

On the contrary, The infinite cannot have a beginning, as said in the *Physics.*[1] But everything outside God is from God as from its first principle. Therefore besides God nothing can be infinite.

I answer that, Things other than God can be relatively infinite, but not absolutely infinite. For with regard to infinite as applied to matter, it is manifest that everything actually existing possesses a form, and thus its matter is determined by form. But because matter, considered as existing under some substantial form, remains in potency to many accidental forms, what is absolutely finite can be relatively infinite; as, for example, wood is finite according to its own form, but still it is relatively infinite, since it is in potentiality to an infinite number of shapes.

But if we speak of the infinite in reference to form, it is manifest that those things the forms of which are in matter are absolutely finite, and in no way infinite. If however any created forms are not received into matter, but are self-subsisting, as some think is the case with the angels,[2] these will be relatively infinite, in so far as such kinds of forms are not terminated, nor contracted by any matter. But because a created form thus subsisting has being, and yet is not its own being, it is necessary that its being is received and contracted to a determinate nature. Hence it cannot be absolutely infinite.

Reply Obj. 1. It is against the nature of a made thing for its essence to be its being, because subsisting being is not a created being; hence it is against the nature of a made thing to be absolutely infinite. Therefore, as God, although He has infinite power, cannot make a thing to be not made (for this would imply that two contradictories exist at the same time), so likewise He cannot make anything to be absolutely infinite.

Reply Obj. 2. The fact that the power of the intellect extends itself in a way to infinite things is because the intellect is a form not in matter, but either wholly separated from matter, as is the angelic substance, or at least an intellectual power, which is not the act of any organ, in the intellectual soul joined to a body.

Reply Obj. 3. Prime matter does not exist by itself in nature, since it is not being in act, but in potency only; hence it is something concreated rather than created. Nevertheless, prime matter even as regards potency is not absolutely infinite, but relatively, because its potency extends only to natural forms.

ARTICLE 3. *Whether an Actually Infinite Magnitude Can Exist?*

We proceed thus to the Third Article: It seems that there can be something actually infinite in magnitude.

Objection 1. For in the mathematical sciences there is no error, since "there is no lie in things abstract," as the Philosopher says.[3] But the mathematical sciences use the infinite in magnitude; thus, the geometrician in his demonstrations says, "Let this line be infinite." Therefore it is not impossible for a thing to be infinite in magnitude.

Obj. 2. Further, what is not against the nature of anything, can agree with it. Now to be infinite is not against the nature of magnitude, but rather both the finite and the infinite seem to be passions of quantity. Therefore it is not impossible for some magnitude to be infinite.

Obj. 3. Further, magnitude is infinitely divisible, for the continuous is defined, "that which is infinitely divisible," as is clear from the *Physics.*[4] But contraries are concerned about one and the same thing. Since therefore addition is opposed to division, and increase is opposed to diminution, it appears that magnitude can be increased to infinity. Therefore it is possible for magnitude to be infinite.

Obj. 4. Further, movement and time have quantity and continuity derived from the magnitude over which movement passes, as is said in the *Physics.*[5] But it is not against the nature of time and movement to be infinite, since every determinate (signatum) indivisible in time and circular movement is both a beginning and an end. Therefore neither is it against the nature of magnitude to be infinite.

On the contrary, Every body has a surface. But every body which has a surface is finite, because surface is the term of a finite body. Therefore all bodies are finite. The same applies both to surface and to a line. Therefore nothing is infinite in magnitude.

I answer that, It is one thing to be infinite in essence, and another to be infinite in magni-

---

[1] Aristotle, III, 4 (203b7).
[2] See below, Q. L. A. 2.
[3] *Physics,* II, 2 (193b35).
[4] Aristotle, III, 1 (200b20).
[5] Aristotle, IV, 11 (219a12).

tude. For granted that a body exists infinite in magnitude, as fire or air, yet this would not be infinite in essence, because its essence would be terminated in a species by its form, and confined to something individual by matter. And so assuming from what has been said before (A. 2), that no creature is infinite in essence, it still remains to inquire whether any creature can be infinite in magnitude.

We must therefore observe that a body, which is a complete magnitude, can be considered in two ways: mathematically, in respect to its quantity only, and naturally, as regards its matter and form.

Now it is manifest that a natural body cannot be actually infinite. For every natural body has some determined substantial form. Since therefore the accidents follow upon the substantial form, it is necessary that determinate accidents should follow upon a determinate form, and among these accidents is quantity. So every natural body has a greater or smaller determinate quantity. Hence it is impossible for a natural body to be infinite. The same appears from movement; because every natural body has some natural movement. But an infinite body could not have any natural movement. Neither direct, because nothing moves naturally by a direct movement unless it is out of its place, and this could not happen to an infinite body, for it would occupy every place, and thus every place would be indifferently its own place. Neither could it move circularly; since circular motion requires that one part of the body is necessarily transferred to a place occupied by another part, and this could not happen as regards an infinite circular body; for if two lines be drawn from the centre, the farther they extend from the centre, the farther they are from each other; therefore, if a body were infinite, the lines would be infinitely distant from each other, and thus one could never reach the place belonging to any other.

The same applies to a mathematical body. For if we imagine a mathematical body actually existing, we must imagine it under some form, because nothing is actual except by its form; hence, since the form of quantity as such is figure, such a body must have some figure, and so would be finite, for figure is confined by a term or boundary.

Reply Obj. 1. A geometrician does not need to assume a line actually infinite, but takes some actually finite line, from which he subtracts whatever he finds necessary, which line he calls infinite.

Reply Obj. 2. Although the infinite is not against the nature of magnitude in general, still it is against the nature of any species of it; thus, for instance, it is against the nature of a bicubical or tricubical magnitude, whether circular or triangular, and so on. Now what is not possible in any species cannot exist in the genus; hence there cannot be any infinite magnitude, since no species of magnitude is infinite.

Reply Obj. 3. The infinite which pertains to quantity, as was shown above (A. 1, Ans. 2), belongs to matter. Now by division of the whole we approach to matter, since parts have the aspect of matter; but by addition we approach to the whole which has the aspect of a form. Therefore the infinite is not in the addition of magnitude, but only in division.

Reply Obj. 4. Movement and time are whole not actually but successively; hence they have potency mixed with act. But magnitude is an actual whole; therefore the infinite in quantity refers to matter, and does not agree with the totality of magnitude; yet it agrees with the totality of time or movement, for it is proper to matter to be in potency.

ARTICLE 4. *Whether an Infinite Multitude of Things Can Exist?*

We proceed thus to the Fourth Article: It seems that an actually infinite multitude is possible.

Objection 1. For it is not impossible for what is in potency to be reduced to act. But number can be multiplied to infinity. Therefore it is possible for an infinite multitude actually to exist.

Obj. 2. Further, it is possible for any individual of any species to be made actual. But the species of figures are infinite. Therefore an infinite number of actual figures is possible.

Obj. 3. Further, things not opposed to each other do not obstruct each other. But supposing a multitude of things to exist, there can still be many others not opposed to them. Therefore it is not impossible for others also to coexist with them, and so on to infinity; therefore an actual infinite number of things is possible.

On the contrary, It is written, *Thou hast ordered all things in measure, and number, and weight* (Wisd. 11. 21).

I answer that, A twofold opinion exists on this subject. Some, as Avicenna and Algazel,[1] said that "it is impossible for an actually in-

---

[1] Cf. Averroes, *Dest. Dest.,* disp. 1 (IX, 20 A, F; Cf. IX. 18 M).

finite multitude to exist absolutely, but an accidentally infinite multitude is not impossible. A multitude is said to be infinite absolutely when an infinite multitude is necessary that something may exist." Now this is impossible, because it would entail something dependent on an infinity for its existence, and hence its generation could never come to be, because it is impossible to pass through an infinite medium.

A multitude is said to be accidentally infinite when its existence as such is not necessary, but accidental. This can be shown, for example, in the work of an artisan, which requires a certain multitude of itself; namely, art in the soul, the movement of the hand, and a hammer; and supposing that such things were infinitely multiplied, the work of hammering would never be finished, since it would depend on an infinite number of causes. But the multitude of hammers which one may use according as one may be broken and another used, is an accidental multitude; for it happens by accident that many hammers are used, and it matters little whether one or two, or many are used, or an infinite number, if the work is carried on for an infinite time. In this way they said that there can be an accidentally infinite multitude.

This, however, is impossible, since every kind of multitude must belong to a species of multitude. Now the species of multitude are to be reckoned by the species of numbers. But no species of number is infinite; for every number is multitude measured by one. Hence it is impossible for there to be an actually infinite multitude, either absolute or accidental. Likewise multitude in nature is created, and everything created is comprehended under some clear intention of the Creator, for no agent acts aimlessly. Hence everything created must be comprehended in a certain number. Therefore it is impossible for an actually infinite multitude to exist, even accidentally.

But a potentially infinite multitude is possible, because the increase of multitude follows upon the division of magnitude, since the more a thing is divided, the greater number of things result. Hence, as the infinite is to be found potentially in the division of the continuous, because we thus approach matter, as was shown in the preceding article, by the same reason the infinite can be also found potentially in the addition of multitude.

Reply Obj. 1. Whatever is in potency is reduced to act according to its mode of being; for instance, a day is reduced to act successively, and not all at once. Likewise the infinite in multitude is reduced to act successively, and not all at once, because every multitude can be succeeded by another multitude to infinity.

Reply Obj. 2. Species of figures are infinite by infinitude of number. Now there are various species of figures, such as trilateral, quadrilateral and so on; and as an infinitely numerable multitude is not all at once reduced to act, so neither is the multitude of figures.

Reply Obj. 3. Although the supposition of some things does not preclude the supposition of others, still the supposition of an infinite number is opposed to any single species of multitude. Hence it is not possible for an actually infinite multitude to exist.

QUESTION VIII
THE BEING OF GOD IN THINGS
(In Four Articles)

SINCE it apparently belongs to the infinite to be present everywhere, and in all things, we now consider whether this belongs to God; and concerning this there arise four points of inquiry: (1) Whether God is in all things? (2) Whether God is everywhere? (3) Whether God is everywhere by essence, power, and presence? (4) Whether to be everywhere belongs to God alone?

ARTICLE 1. *Whether God Is in All Things?*

We proceed thus to the First Article: It seems that God is not in all things.

Objection 1. For what is above all things is not in all things. But God is above all, according to the (Psalm 112. 4), *The Lord is high above all nations,* etc. Therefore God is not in all things.

Obj. 2. Further, what is in anything is contained by it. Now God is not contained by things, but rather He contains them. Therefore God is not in things, but things are rather in Him. Hence Augustine says (*Octog. Tri. Quæst. qu.* 20),[1] that "in Him things are, rather than He is in any place."

Obj. 3. Further, the more powerful an agent is, the more extended is its action. But God is the most powerful of all agents. Therefore His action can extend to things which are far removed from Him, nor is it necessary that He should be in all things.

Obj. 4. Further, the demons are things. But God is not in the demons, for there is no *fellowship between light and darkness* (II Cor. 6. 14). Therefore God is not in all things.

[1] PL 40, 15.

On the contrary, A thing is wherever it operates. But God operates in all things, according to Isa. 26. 12, *Lord . . . Thou hast wrought all our works in* [Vulg., *for*] *us*. Therefore God is in all things.

I answer that, God is in all things; not, indeed, as part of their essence, nor as an accident, but as an agent is present to that upon which it works. For an agent must be joined to that wherein it acts immediately, and touch it by its power; hence it is proved in the *Physics*[1] that the thing moved and the mover must be together. Now since God is being itself by His own essence, created being must be His proper effect; just as to ignite is the proper effect of fire. Now God causes this effect in things not only when they first begin to be, but as long as they are preserved in being; as for instance light is caused in the air by the sun as long as the air remains illuminated. Therefore as long as a thing has being, God must be present to it, according to its mode of being. But being is innermost in each thing and most deeply inherent in all things since it is formal in respect of everything found in a thing, as was shown above (Q. IV, A. I, Ans. 3). Hence it must be that God is in all things, and most intimately.

Reply Obj. 1. God is above all things by the excellence of His nature; nevertheless, He is in all things as the cause of the being of all things, as was shown above in this article.

Reply Obj. 2. Although corporeal things are said to be in another as in that which contains them, nevertheless spiritual things contain those things in which they are, as the soul contains the body. Hence also God is in things as containing them; nevertheless by a certain likeness to corporeal things, it is said that all things are in God, since they are contained by Him.

Reply Obj. 3. No action of an agent, however powerful it may be, acts at a distance except through a medium. But it belongs to the very great power of God that He acts immediately in all things. Hence nothing is distant from Him, as though it did not have God in itself. But things are said to be distant from God by the unlikeness to Him in nature or grace, as also He is above all by the excellence of His own nature.

Reply Obj. 4. In the demons there is their nature which is from God, and also the deformity of sin which is not from Him; therefore, it is not to be absolutely conceded that God is in the demons, except with the addition,

[1] Aristotle, VII, 2 (243ª4).

in so far as they are beings. But in things not deformed in their nature, we must say absolutely that God is in them.

ARTICLE 2. *Whether God Is Everywhere?*

We proceed thus to the Second Article: It seems that God is not everywhere.

Objection 1. For to be everywhere means to be in every place. But to be in every place does not belong to God, to Whom it does not belong to be in a place; for incorporeal things, as Boëthius says (*De Hebdom.*),[2] are not in a place. Therefore God is not everywhere.

Obj. 2. Further, the relation of time to succession is the same as the relation of place to permanence. But one indivisible part of action or movement cannot exist in different times; therefore neither can one indivisible part in the genus of permanent things be in every place. Now the divine being is not successive, but permanent. Therefore God is not in many places; and thus He is not everywhere.

Obj. 3. Further, what is wholly in any one place is not in part elsewhere. But if God is in any one place He is wholly there, for He has no parts. No part of Him then is elsewhere, and therefore God is not everywhere.

On the contrary, It is written, *I fill heaven and earth* (Jer. 23. 24).

I answer that, Since place is a thing, to be in place can be understood in a twofold sense: either by way of other things—that is, as one thing is said to be in another no matter how, and thus the accidents of a place are in place; or by a way proper to place, and thus things placed are in place.

Now in both these senses in some way God is in every place, and this is to be everywhere. First, as He is in all things as giving them being, power, and operation, so He is in every place as giving it being and power to be in a place. Again, things placed are in place in so far as they fill a place: and God fills every place; not, indeed, as a body, for a body is said to fill place in so far as it excludes the presence of another body; but by God being in a place, others are not thereby excluded from it; rather indeed, He Himself fills every place by the very fact that He gives being to the things that fill every place.

Reply Obj. 1. Incorporeal things are in place not by contact of dimensive quantity, as bodies are, but by contact of power.

Reply Obj. 2. The indivisible is twofold. One is the term of the continuous, as a point in per-

[2] PL 64, 1311.

manent things, and as a moment in succession; and this kind of the indivisible in permanent things, since it has a determinate site, cannot be in many parts of place, or in many places; likewise the indivisible of action or movement, since it has a determinate order in movement or action, cannot be in many parts of time. Another kind of the indivisible is outside of the whole genus of the continuous; and in this way incorporeal substances, like God, angel, and soul, are called indivisible. Such a kind of indivisible does not belong to the continuous, as a part of it, but as touching it by its power; hence, according as its power can extend itself to one or to many, to a small thing, or to a great one, in this way it is in one or in many places, and in a small or large place.

Reply Obj. 3. A whole is so called with reference to its parts. Now part is twofold: namely, a part of the essence, as the form and the matter are called parts of the composite, while genus and difference are called parts of species. There is also a part of quantity, into which any quantity is divided. What therefore is whole in any place by totality of quantity, cannot be outside of that place, because the quantity of anything placed is commensurate to the quantity of the place, and hence there is no totality of quantity without totality of place. But totality of essence is not commensurate to the totality of place. Hence it is not necessary for that which is whole by totality of essence in a thing not to be at all outside of it. This appears also in accidental forms, which have accidental quantity; as an example, whiteness is whole in each part of the surface if we speak of its totality of essence, because it is found to exist in every part of the surface according to the perfect notion of its species. But if its totality be considered according to quantity which it has accidentally, then it is not whole in every part of the surface. On the other hand incorporeal substances have no totality either of themselves or accidentally, except in reference to the perfect notion of their essence. Hence, as the soul is whole in every part of the body, so is God whole in all things and in each one.

ARTICLE 3. *Whether God Is Everywhere by Essence, Presence, and Power?*

We proceed thus to the Third Article: It seems that the mode of God's existence in all things is not properly described by way of essence, presence and power.[1]

Objection 1. For what is by essence in any-

thing is in it essentially. But God is not essentially in things, for He does not belong to the essence of anything. Therefore it ought not to be said that God is in things by essence, presence, and power.

Obj. 2. Further, to be present to anything means not to be absent from it. Now this is the meaning of God being in things by His essence, that He is not absent from anything. Therefore the presence of God in all things by essence and presence means the same thing. Therefore it is superfluous to say that God is present in things by His essence, presence, and power.

Obj. 3. Further, as God by His power is the principle of all things, so He is the same likewise by His knowledge and will. But it is not said that He is in things by knowledge and will. Therefore neither is He present by His power.

Obj. 4. Further, as grace is a perfection added to the substance of a thing, so many other perfections are likewise added. Therefore if God is said to be in certain persons in a special way by grace, it seems that according to every perfection there ought to be a special mode of God's being in things.

On the contrary, A gloss on the Canticle of Canticles, 5, says that, "God by a common mode is in all things by His presence, power, and substance; still He is said to be present more familiarly in some by grace."[2]

I answer that, God is said to be in a thing in two ways: in one way after the manner of an efficient cause, and thus He is in all things created by Him; in another way He is in things as the object of operation is in the operator, and this is proper to the operations of the soul, according as the thing known is in the one who knows, and the thing desired in the one desiring. In this second way God is especially in the rational creature who knows and loves Him actually or habitually. And because the rational creature possesses this by grace, as will be shown later (Part I-II, Q. CIX, AA. 1, 3). He is said to be thus in the saints by grace.

But how He is in other things created by Him may be considered from human affairs. A king, for example, is said to be in the whole kingdom by his power, although he is not everywhere present. Again a thing is said to be by its presence in other things which are subject to its inspection, as things in a house are said to be present to someone, who nevertheless may not be in substance in every part of the house. Lastly a thing is said to be by way of substance

---

[1] Cf. Peter Lombard, *Sent.*, I, d. 37, chap. I (QR I, 229).

[2] Cf. *Glossa ordin.*, (III, 364 A); Peter Lombard, *loc. cit.*; cf. also Gregory, *Moral.*, II, 12 (PL 75, 565).

or essence in that place in which its substance may be. Now there were some (the Manichees)[1] who said that spiritual and incorporeal things were subject to the divine power, but that visible and corporeal things were subject to the power of a contrary principle. Therefore against these it is necessary to say that God is in all things by His power.

But others,[2] though they believed that all things were subject to the divine power, still did not allow that divine providence extended to these inferior bodies, and in the person of these it is said, *He walketh about the poles of the heavens; and He doth not consider our things* (Job 22. 14). Against these it is necessary to say that God is in all things by His presence.

Further, others said[3] that, although all things are subject to God's providence, still all things are not immediately created by God, but that He immediately created the first creatures, and these created the others. Against these it is necessary to say that He is in all things by His essence.

Therefore, God is in all things by His power, since all things are subject to His power; He is by His presence in all things, since all things are bare and open to His eyes; He is in all things by His essence, because He is present to all as the cause of their being, as we have said. (A. 2).

Reply Obj. 1. God is said to be in all things by essence, not indeed by the essence of the things themselves, as if He were of their essence, but by His own essence, because His substance is present to all things as the cause of their being, as we have said. (A. 1).

Reply Obj. 2. A thing can be said to be present to another when in its sight, though the thing may be distant in substance, as was shown in this article; and therefore two modes of presence are necessary, namely, by essence, and by presence.

Reply Obj. 3. Knowledge and will require that the thing known should be in the one who knows, and the thing willed in the one who wills. Hence by knowledge and will things are more truly in God than God in things. But power is the principle of acting on another; hence by power the agent is related and applied to an external thing, and thus by power an agent may be said to be present to another.

Reply Obj. 4. No other perfection, except

grace, added to substance renders God present in anything as the object known and loved; therefore only grace constitutes a special mode of God's being in things. There is, however, another special mode of God's being in man by union, which will be treated of in its own place (Part III, Q. 11).

ARTICLE 4. *Whether To Be Everywhere Is Proper to God?*

We proceed thus to the Fourth Article: It seems that to be everywhere is not proper to God.

Objection 1. For the universal, according to the Philosopher,[4] is "everywhere, and always"; first matter also, since it is in all bodies, is everywhere. But neither of these is God, as appears from what is said above (Q. III, AA 5, 8). Therefore to be everywhere does not belong to God alone.

Obj. 2. Further, number is in things numbered. But the whole universe is constituted in number, as appears from the Book of Wisdom (11. 21). Therefore there is some number which is in the whole universe, and is thus everywhere.

Obj. 3. Further, the universe is a kind of a whole perfect body.[5] But the whole universe is everywhere, because there is no place outside of it. Therefore to be everywhere does not belong to God alone.

Obj. 4. Further, if any body were infinite, no place would exist outside of it, and so it would be everywhere. Therefore to be everywhere does not appear to belong to God alone.

Obj. 5. Further, the soul, as Augustine says (*De Trin.* vi, 6),[6] is "whole in the whole body, and whole in every one of its parts." Therefore if there was only one animal in the world, its soul would be everywhere; and thus to be everywhere does not belong to God alone.

Obj. 6. Further, as Augustine says (*Ep.* cxxxvii),[7] "The soul feels where it sees, and lives where it feels, and is where it lives." But the soul sees as it were everywhere, for in a succession of glances it comprehends the entire space of the heavens in its sight. Therefore the soul is everywhere.

On the contrary, Ambrose says (*De Spir. Sanct.* i, 7)[8]: "Who dares to call the Holy Ghost a creature, Who in all things, and everywhere, and always is, which assuredly belongs to the divinity alone?"

---

[1] Cf. Augustine, *De Haeres.*, XLVI (PL 42, 35).
[2] See below, Q. XXII, A 2.
[3] See below, Q. XLV, A 5.
[4] *Posterior Analytics*, I, 31 (87ᵇ33).
[5] Aristotle, *Heavens*, I, I (268ᵇ8).
[6] PL 42, 929.   [7] Chap. 2 (PL 33, 518).
[8] PL 16, 753.

I answer that, To be everywhere primarily and per se is proper to God. Now to be everywhere primarily is said of that which in its whole self is everywhere; for if a thing were everywhere according to its parts in different places, it would not be primarily everywhere, since what belongs to anything according to its parts does not belong to it primarily; thus if a man has white teeth, whiteness belongs primarily not to the man but to his teeth. But a thing is everywhere per se when it does not pertain to it to be everywhere accidentally, that is, merely on some supposition; as a grain of millet would be everywhere supposing that no other body existed. It pertains therefore to a thing to be everywhere per se when, on any supposition, it must be everywhere; and this properly belongs to God alone. For whatever number of places be supposed, even if an infinite number be supposed besides what already exist, it would be necessary that God should be in all of them, for nothing can exist except by Him. Therefore to be everywhere primarily and per se belongs to God, and is proper to Him, because whatever number of places be supposed to exist, God must be in all of them, not as to a part of Him, but as to His very self.

Reply Obj. 1. The universal and primary matter are indeed everywhere, but not according to the same being.

Reply Obj. 2. Number, since it is an accident, does not of itself exist in place, but accidentally; neither is the whole but only part of it in each of the things numbered. Hence it does not follow that it is primarily and per se everywhere.

Reply Obj. 3. The whole body of the universe is everywhere, but not primarily, since it is not wholly in each place, but according to its parts; nor again is it everywhere per se, because, supposing that other places existed besides itself, it would not be in them.

Reply Obj. 4. If an infinite body existed, it would be everywhere, but according to its parts.

Reply Obj. 5. Were there one animal only, its soul would be everywhere, primarily indeed, but accidentally.

Reply Obj. 6. When it is said that the soul sees anywhere, this can be taken in two senses. In one sense the adverb "anywhere" determines the act of seeing on the part of the object; and in this sense it is true that while it sees the heavens, it sees in the heavens, and in the same way it feels in the heavens. But it does not follow that it lives or exists in the heavens, be-

cause to live and to exist do not import an act passing to an exterior object. In another sense it can be understood according as the adverb determines the act of the seer, as proceeding from the seer; and thus it is true that where the soul feels and sees, there it is, and there it lives according to this mode of speaking. And thus it does not follow that it is everywhere.

QUESTION IX

The immutability of God

(*In Two Articles*)

We next consider God's immutability, and His eternity which follows on immutability (q. x).

On the immutability of God there are two points of inquiry: (1) Whether God is altogether immutable? (2) Whether to be immutable belongs to God alone?

Article 1. *Whether God Is Altogether Immutable?*

We proceed thus to the First Article: It seems that God is not altogether immutable.

Objection 1. For whatever moves itself is in some way mutable. But, as Augustine says (*Gen. ad. lit.* viii, 20),[1] "The Creator Spirit moves Himself neither by time, nor by place." Therefore God is in some way mutable.

Obj. 2. Further, it is said of Wisdom, that *it is more mobile than all things active*—(Vulg. *mobilior.*) (Wisd. 7. 24). But God is wisdom itself. Therefore God is movable.

Obj. 3. Further, to approach and to recede signify movement. But these are said of God in Scripture, *Draw nigh to God, and He will draw nigh to you* (James 4. 8). Therefore God is mutable.

On the contrary, It is written, *I am the Lord, and I change not* (Mal. 3. 6).

I answer that, From what precedes, it is shown that God is altogether immutable. First, because it was shown above (q. ii, a. 3) that there is some first being, whom we call God, and that this first being must be pure act, without the admixture of any potency, for the reason that, absolutely, potency is posterior to act (q. iii, a. 1). Now everything which is in any way changed is in some way in potency. Hence it is evident that it is impossible for God to be in any way changeable.

Secondly, because everything which is moved remains as it was in part, and passes away in part, as what is moved from whiteness to blackness, remains as to substance; thus in

[1] PL 34, 388.

everything which is moved, there is some kind of composition to be found. But it has been shown above (Q. III, A. 7.) that in God there is no composition, for He is altogether simple. Hence it is manifest that God cannot be moved.

Thirdly, because everything which is moved acquires something by its movement, and attains to what it had not attained previously. But since God is infinite, comprehending in Himself all the plenitude of perfection of all being, He cannot acquire anything new, nor extend Himself to anything to which He was not extended previously. Hence movement in no way belongs to Him. So, some of the ancients,[1] constrained, as it were, by truth itself, decided that the first principle was immovable.

Reply Obj. 1. Augustine there speaks in a similar way to Plato, who said[2] that the first mover moves Himself, calling every operation a movement, even as the acts of understanding, and willing, and loving, are called movements. Therefore because God understands and loves Himself, in that respect they said that God moves Himself, not, however, as movement and change belong to a thing existing in potency, as we now speak of change and movement.

Reply Obj. 2. Wisdom is called movable by way of likeness, according as it diffuses its likeness even to the outermost of things; for nothing can exist which does not proceed from the divine wisdom by way of some kind of imitation, as from the first effecting and formal principle, as also artificial things proceed from the wisdom of the maker. And so in the same way, since the likeness of the divine wisdom proceeds in degrees from the highest things, which participate more fully of its likeness, to the lowest things which participate of it in a lesser degree, there is said to be a kind of procession and movement of the divine wisdom to things, as when we say that the sun proceeds to the earth, because the ray of light touches the earth. In this way Dionysius (*Cæl. Hier.* i)[3] expounds the matter, that every procession of the divine manifestation comes to us from the movement of the Father of light.

Reply Obj. 3. These things are said of God in Scripture metaphorically. For as the sun is said to enter a house or to go out according as its rays reach the house, so God is said to approach to us or to recede from us when we receive the influx of His goodness, or fall away from Him.

ARTICLE 2. *Whether To Be Immutable Belongs to God Alone?*

We proceed thus to the Second Article: It seems that to be immutable does not belong to God alone.

Objection 1. For the Philosopher says[4] that "matter is in everything which is moved." But, according to some,[5] certain created substances, as angels and souls, have not matter. Therefore to be immutable does not belong to God alone.

Obj. 2. Further, everything that is moved, is moved on account of some end. What therefore has already attained its ultimate end, is not moved. But some creatures have already attained to their ultimate end, as for example all the blessed. Therefore some creatures are immovable.

Obj. 3. Further, everything which is mutable, is variable. But forms are invariable; for it is said (*Sex Princip.* i)[6] that "form is essence consisting of the simple and invariable." Therefore it does not belong to God alone to be immutable.

On the contrary, Augustine says (*De Nat. Boni,* i),[7] "God alone is immutable; and whatever things He has made, being from nothing, are mutable."

I answer that, God alone is altogether immutable, while, every creature is in some way mutable. We must realize therefore that a mutable thing can be called so in two ways: by a power in itself, and by a power possessed by another. For all creatures before they existed, were possible, not by any created power, since no creature is eternal, but by the divine power alone, in so far as God could produce them into being. Thus, as the production of a thing into being depends on the will of God, so likewise it depends on His will that things should be preserved in being; for He does not preserve them otherwise than by ever giving them being. Hence if He took away His action from them, all things would be reduced to nothing, as appears from Augustine (*Gen. ad. lit.* iv, 12).[8] Therefore as it was in the Creator's power to produce them as things before they existed in themselves, so likewise it is in the Creator's

---

[1] Parmenides, and Melissus, according to Aristotle, *Physics,* I, 2 (184ᵇ16).

[2] Aristotle, *Metaphysics,* XII, 6 (1071ᵇ37); cf. Plato, *Timaeus* (30, 34); *Phaedrus* (245).—See also Averroes, *In Phys.,* VIII, 40 (IV, 380 B).

[3] PG 3, 120.

[4] *Metaphysics,* II, 2 (994ᵇ26).

[5] Cf. St. Thomas, below, Q. L, A. 2; William of Paris (Wm. of Auvergne), *De Univ.,* II–II, chap. 8 (II, 802); John of Rochelle, *Summa de An.,* chaps. 11, 23; Albertus Magnus, *Sent.,* II, d. 3, A. 7 (BO XXVII, 68).

[6] Gilbert de la Porrée (PL 188, 1257).

[7] PL 34, 305.   [8] PL 34, 305.

power when they exist in themselves to bring them to nothing. In this way therefore, by the power of another—namely, of God—they are mutable, since they are producible from nothing by Him, and are by Him reducible from being to non-being.

If, however, a thing is called mutable by a power existing in itself, thus also in some manner every creature is mutable. For every creature has a twofold power, active and passive; and I call that power passive which enables anything to attain its perfection either in being, or in attaining to its end. Now if the mutability of a thing be considered according to its power for being, in that way all creatures are not mutable, but those only in which what is possible in them is consistent with non-being. Hence, in the inferior bodies there is mutability both as regards substantial being, since their matter can exist with privation of their substantial form, and also as regards their accidental being, supposing the subject to coexist with privation of accident; as, for example, this subject "man" can exist with "not-whiteness," and can therefore be changed from white to not-white. But supposing the accident to be such as to follow on the essential principles of the subject, then the privation of such an accident cannot coexist with the subject. Hence the subject cannot be changed as regards that kind of accident; as, for example, snow cannot be made black. Now in the celestial bodies matter is not consistent with privation of form, because the form perfects the whole potentiality of the matter; therefore these bodies are not mutable as to substantial being, but only as to being in place, because the subject is consistent with privation of this or that place. On the other hand incorporeal substances, being subsistent forms which, although with respect to their own being are as potency to act, are not consistent with the privation of this act, because being is consequent upon form, and nothing is corrupted unless it lose its form. Hence in the form itself there is no potency to non-being, and so these kinds of substances are immutable and invariable as regards their being. Therefore Dionysius says (*Div. Nom.* iv),[1] that "intellectual created substances are pure from generation and from every variation, as also are incorporeal and immaterial substances." Still, there remains in them a twofold mutability: one as regards their potency to their end, and in that way there is in them a mutability according to choice from good to evil, as Damascene says (*De Fide*, ii, 3, 4)[2]; the other as regards place, since by their finite power they attain to certain places which they did not reach before—which cannot be said of God, who by His infinity fills all places, as was shown above (Q. VIII, A. 2).

Thus in every creature there is a potency to change either as regards substantial being as in the case of corruptible bodies, or as regards being in place only, as in the case of the celestial bodies, or as regards the order to their end, and the application of their powers to divers objects, as is the case with the angels; and universally all creatures generally are mutable by the power of the Creator, in Whose power is their being and non-being. Hence since God is in none of these ways mutable, it belongs to Him alone to be altogether immutable.

Reply Obj. 1. This objection proceeds from mutability as regards substantial or accidental being; for philosophers treated of such movement.

Reply Obj. 2. The good angels, besides their natural endowment of immutability of being, have also immutability of choice by divine power; nevertheless there remains in them mutability as regards place.

Reply Obj. 3. Forms are called invariable because they cannot be subjects of variation; but they are subject to variation because by them their subject is variable. Hence it is clear that they vary in so far as they are; for they are not called beings as though they were the subject of being, but because through them something has being. And thus the answers to the objections are clear.

QUESTION X

THE ETERNITY OF GOD

(*In Six Articles*)

WE must now consider the eternity of God, concerning which arise six points of inquiry: (1) What is eternity? (2) Whether God is eternal? (3) Whether to be eternal belongs to God alone? (4) Whether eternity differs from time? (5) The difference of æviternity and of time. (6) Whether there is only one æviternity, as there is one time, and one eternity?

ARTICLE 1. *Whether This Is a Good Definition of Eternity, "The Simultaneously-Whole and Perfect Possession of Interminable Life?"*

We proceed thus to the First Article: It seems that the definition of eternity given by

---

[1] Sect. 1 (PG 3, 693).

[2] PG 94, 868.

Boethius (*De Consol.* v)[1] is not a good one: "Eternity is the simultaneously-whole and perfect possession of interminable life."

Objection 1. For the word interminable is a negative one. But negation only belongs to what is defective, and this does not belong to eternity. Therefore in the definition of eternity the word interminable ought not to be found.

Obj. 2. Further, eternity signifies a certain kind of duration. But duration regards being rather than life. Therefore the word life ought not to come into the definition of eternity, but rather the word being.

Obj. 3. Further, a whole is what has parts. But this does not apply to eternity, which is simple. Therefore it is improperly said to be "whole."

Obj. 4. Many days cannot exist all at once, nor can many times. But in eternity days and times are in the plural, for it is said, *His going forth is from the beginning, from the days of eternity* (Mic. 5. 2); and also it is said, *According to the revelation of the mystery hidden from eternity* (Rom. 16. 25). Therefore eternity is not simultaneously whole.

Obj. 5. Further, the whole and the perfect are the same thing. Supposing, therefore, that it is whole, it is superfluously described as perfect.

Obj. 6. Further, duration does not pertain to possession. But eternity is a kind of duration. Therefore eternity is not possession.

I answer that, As we attain to the knowledge of simple things by way of compound things, so we must reach to the knowledge of eternity by means of time, which is nothing but "the numbering of movement by before and after."[2] For since succession occurs in every movement, and one part comes after another, the fact that we consider before and after in movement makes us apprehend time, which is nothing else but the measure of before and after in movement. Now in a thing which lacks movement, and which is always the same, there is no before and after. As therefore the nature of time consists in the numbering of before and after in movement, so likewise in the apprehension of the uniformity of what is altogether outside of movement consists the nature of eternity.

Further, "those things are said to be measured by time which have a beginning and an end in time," as is said in the *Physics*,[3] because in everything which is moved there is a begin-

ning and there is an end. But as whatever is wholly immutable can have no succession, so it has no beginning, and no end.

Thus eternity is known from two sources: first, because what is eternal is interminable—that is, lacks beginning and end (that is, no term either way); secondly, because eternity lacks succession, being simultaneously whole.

Reply Obj. 1. Simple things are usually defined by way of negation, as for instance "a point is that which has no parts." Yet this is not to be taken as if the negation belonged to their essence, but because our intellect which first apprehends composite things cannot attain to the knowledge of simple things except by removing the composition.

Reply Obj. 2. What is truly eternal is not only being, but also living; and life extends to operation, which is not true of being. Now the protraction of duration seems to belong to operation rather than to being; hence time is the numbering of movement.

Reply Obj. 3. Eternity is called whole, not because it has parts, but because it is wanting in nothing.

Reply Obj. 4. As God, although incorporeal, is named in Scripture metaphorically by corporeal names, so eternity though simultaneously whole, is called by names implying time and succession.

Reply Obj. 5. Two things are to be considered in time: time itself, which is successive; and the "now" of time, which is imperfect. Hence the expression "simultaneously whole" is used to remove the idea of time, and the word "perfect" is used to exclude the "now" of time.

Reply Obj. 6. Whatever is possessed, is held firmly and calmly; therefore to designate the immutability and permanence of eternity, we use the word "possession."

ARTICLE 2. *Whether God Is Eternal?*

We proceed thus to the Second Article: It seems that God is not eternal.

Objection 1. For nothing made can be predicated of God. But eternity is a thing made, for Boethius says (*De Trin.* iv)[4] that, "The now that flows away makes time, the now that stands still makes eternity"; and Augustine says (*Octog. Tri. Quæst. qu.* 23)[5] that "God is the author of eternity." Therefore God is not eternal.

Obj. 2. Further, what is before eternity and after eternity is not measured by eternity. But,

---

[1] Bk. v, 6 (PL 63, 858); cf. III, 2 (PL 63, 724).
[2] Aristotle, *Physics*, IV, 11 (220ᵃ25).
[3] Aristotle, IV, 12 (221ᵇ28).

[4] PL 64, 1253.   [5] PL 40, 16.

as Aristotle says,[1] "God is before eternity and He is after eternity"; for it is written that *the Lord shall reign for eternity, and beyond* (Douay,—*for ever and ever*). (Exod. 15. 18). Therefore to be eternal does not belong to God.

Obj. 3. Further, eternity is a kind of measure. But to be measured does not belong to God. Therefore it does not belong to Him to be eternal.

Obj. 4. Further, in eternity there is no present, past, nor future, since it is simultaneously whole, as was said in the preceding article. But words denoting present, past, and future time are applied to God in Scripture. Therefore God is not eternal.

On the contrary, Athanasius says in his Creed:[2] The Father is eternal, the Son is eternal, the Holy Ghost is eternal.

I answer that, The notion of eternity follows immutability, as the notion of time follows movement, as appears from the preceding article. Hence, as God is supremely immutable, it supremely belongs to Him to be eternal. Nor is He eternal only, but He is His own eternity; but no other being is its own duration, as no other is its own being. Now God is His own uniform being, and hence, as He is His own essence, so He is His own eternity.

Reply Obj. 1. The "now" that stands still, is said to make eternity according to our apprehension. As the apprehension of time is caused in us by the fact that we apprehend the flow of the "now," so the apprehension of eternity is caused in us by our apprehending the "now" standing still. When Augustine says that "God is the author of eternity," this is to be understood of participated eternity. For God communicates His eternity to some in the same way as He communicates His immutability.

Reply Obj. 2. From this appears the answer to the second objection. For God is said to be before eternity according as it is shared by immaterial substances. Hence, also, in the same book, it is said that intelligence "is equal to eternity." In the words of Exodus, *The Lord shall reign for eternity, and beyond,* eternity stands for age, as another rendering has it. Thus, it is said that the Lord will reign beyond eternity because He endures beyond every age, that is, beyond every kind of given duration. For age is nothing more than the period of each thing, as is said in the book on the *Heavens*.[3] Or to reign beyond eternity can be taken to

mean that if any other thing were conceived to exist for ever, as the movement of the heavens according to some philosophers,[4] then God would still reign beyond, since His reign is simultaneously whole.

Reply Obj. 3. Eternity is nothing else but God Himself. Hence God is not called eternal as if He were in any way measured, but the notion of measurement is there taken according to the apprehension of our mind alone.

Reply Obj. 4. Words denoting different times are applied to God, because His eternity includes all times and not as if He Himself were altered through present, past, and future.

ARTICLE 3. *Whether To Be Eternal Is Proper to God?*

We proceed thus to the Third Article: It seems that it is proper to God alone to be eternal.

Objection 1. For it is written, that *those who instruct many to justice,* shall be as *stars unto perpetual eternities* (Douay,—*for all eternity*). (Dan. 12. 3). Now if God alone were eternal, there could not be many eternities. Therefore God alone is not the only eternal.

Obj. 2. Further, it is written, *Depart, ye cursed, into eternal* (Douay,—*everlasting*) *fire* (Matt. 25. 41). Therefore God is not the only eternal.

Obj. 3. Further, every necessary thing is eternal. But there are many necessary things; as, for instance, all principles of demonstration, and all demonstrative propositions. Therefore God is not the only eternal.

On the contrary, Augustine says[5] (*De Fide ad Petrum,* vi) that "God is the only one who has no beginning." Now whatever has a beginning is not eternal. Therefore God alone is eternal.

I answer that, Eternity truly and properly is in God alone, because eternity follows on immutability, as appears from the first article. But God alone is altogether immutable, as was shown above (Q. IX, A. 1). Accordingly, however, as some receive immutability from Him, they share in His eternity.

Thus some receive immutability from God in the way of never ceasing to exist; in that sense it is said of the earth, that *it standeth for ever* (Eccl. 1. 4). And in this way eternity can be attributed to the angels, according to the Psalm (75. 5): *Thou enlightenest wonderfully from the everlasting hills.* Again some things are called eternal in Scripture because of the

---

[1] *Lib. de Causis,* II (BA 165.4).
[2] See the Creed "*Quicumque*" (MA II, 1354; DZ 39).
[3] Aristotle, I, 9 (279ᵃ23).

[4] See below, Q. XLVI, A. 1, Ans. 3, 5.
[5] Cf. Jerome, *Epist.* XV *ad Damasum* (PL 22, 357).

length of their duration, although they are in nature corruptible; thus (Ps. 75. 5) the hills are called eternal, and we read *of the fruits of the eternal hills* (Deut. 33. 15). Some again, share more fully than others in the nature of eternity, since they possess unchangeableness either in being or further still in operation, like the angels, and the blessed, who enjoy the Word, because as regards that vision of the Word, no changing thoughts exist in the Saints, as Augustine says (*De Trin.* xv).[1] Hence those who see God are said to have eternal life, according to that text, *This is eternal life, that they may know Thee the only true God,* etc. (John 17. 3).

Reply Obj. 1. There are said to be many eternities according as many share in eternity by the contemplation of God.

Reply Obj. 2. The fire of hell is called eternal only because it never ends. Still, there is change in the pains of the lost, according to the words, *To extreme heat they will pass from snowy waters* (Job 24. 19). Hence in hell true eternity does not exist, but rather time, according to the text of the Psalm, *Their time will be for ever* (Ps. 80. 16).

Reply Obj. 3. Necessary means a certain mode of truth, and truth, according to the Philosopher[2] is in the intellect. Therefore in this sense the true and necessary are eternal, because they are in the eternal intellect, which is the divine intellect alone. Hence it does not follow that anything beside God is eternal.

ARTICLE 4. *Whether Eternity Differs from Time?*

We proceed thus to the Fourth Article: It seems that eternity does not differ from time.

Objection 1. For two measures of duration cannot exist together unless one is part of the other. For instance two days or two hours cannot be together; nevertheless, we may say that a day and an hour are together, considering hour as part of a day. But eternity and time, each of which imports a certain measure of duration, exist together. Since therefore eternity is not a part of time, because eternity exceeds time, and includes it, it seems that time is a part of eternity, and is not a different thing from eternity.

Obj. 2. Further, according to the Philosopher[3] the "now" of time remains the same in the whole of time. But the nature of eternity seems to be that it is the same indivisible thing in the whole space of time. Therefore eternity is the "now" of time. But the "now" of time is not different, according to substance, from time. Therefore eternity is not different from time according to substance.

Obj. 3. Further, as the measure of the first movement is the measure of every movement, as said in the *Physics,*[4] it thus appears that the measure of the first being is that of every being. But eternity is the measure of the first being— that is, of the divine being. Therefore eternity is the measure of every being. But the being of things corruptible is measured by time. Time therefore is either eternity, or is a part of eternity.

On the contrary, Eternity is simultaneously whole. But time has a before and an after. Therefore time and eternity are not the same thing.

I answer that, It is manifest that time and eternity are not the same. Some[5] have founded the nature of this difference on the fact that eternity lacks beginning and end, whereas time has a beginning and an end. This, however, is an accidental and not an absolute difference, because, granted that time always was and always will be, according to the idea of those[6] who think the movement of the heavens goes on for ever, there would yet remain a difference between eternity and time, as Boëthius says (*De Consol.* v),[7] arising from the fact that eternity is simultaneously whole, which cannot be applied to time; for eternity is the measure of a permanent being, while time is the measure of movement.

Supposing, however, that this difference be considered on the part of the things measured, and not as regards the measures, then there is another reason for it, since that alone is measured by time which has beginning and end in time as the fourth book of the *Physics* says.[8] Hence, if the movement of the heavens lasted always, time would not be its measure as regards the whole of its duration, since the infinite is not measurable; but it would measure any revolution whatsoever which has beginning and end in time.

Another reason for the same can be taken from these measures in themselves, if we consider the end and the beginning as potentialities, because, granted also that time always

---

1 Chap. 16 (PL 42, 1079).
2 *Metaphysics,* VI, 4 (1027[b]27).
3 *Physics,* IV, 11 (219[b]11); Cf. IV, 13 (222[a]15).

4 Aristotle, IV, 14 (223[b]18).
5 Alexander of Hales, *Summa Theol.,* I, 65 (QR I, 100).
6 See Q. XLVI, A. 1, Ans. 3, 5.
7 PL 63, 858.   8 Aristotle, 12 (221[b]28).

goes on, yet it is possible to note in time both the beginning and the end, by considering its parts; thus we speak of the beginning and the end of a day, or of a year, which cannot be applied to eternity.

Still these differences follow upon the essential and primary difference, from the fact that eternity is simultaneously whole, but that time is not so.

Reply Obj. 1. Such a reason would be a valid one if time and eternity were the same kind of measure; but this is seen not to be the case when we consider those things of which time and eternity are the measure.

Reply Obj. 2. The "now" of time is the same as regards its subject in the whole course of time, but it differs in aspect; for since time corresponds to movement, its "now" corresponds to what is movable, and the thing movable has the same one subject in all time, but differs in aspect as being here and there; and such alternation is movement. Likewise the flow of the "now" as alternating in aspect, is time. But eternity remains the same according to both subject and aspect. And hence eternity is not the same as the "now" of time.

Reply Obj. 3. As eternity is the proper measure of being itself, so time is the proper measure of movement; and hence, according as any being recedes from permanence of being, and undergoes change, it recedes from eternity, and is subject to time. Therefore the being of things corruptible, because it is changeable, is not measured by eternity, but by time; for time measures not only things actually changed, but also things changeable. Hence it not only measures movement, but it also measures repose, which belongs to whatever is naturally movable, but is not actually in motion.

ARTICLE 5. *The Difference of Æviternity and Time.*

We proceed thus to the Fifth Article: It seems that æviternity is the same as time.

Obj. 1. For Augustine says (*Gen. ad. lit*, viii, 20, 22),[1] that "God moves the spiritual creature through time." But æviternity is said to be the measure of spiritual substances. Therefore time is the same as æviternity.

Obj. 2. Further, it is of the nature of time to have before and after; but it is of the nature of eternity to be simultaneously whole, as was shown above in the first article. Now æviternity is not eternity, for it is written (Ecclus. 1. 1), that eternal *Wisdom is before age.* Therefore

[1] PL 34, 388, 389.

it is not simultaneously whole but has before and after; and thus it is the same as time.

Obj. 3. Further, if there is no before and after in æviternity, it follows that in æviternal things there is no difference between being, having been, or going to be. Since then it is impossible for æviternal things not to have been, it follows that it is impossible for them not to be in the future, which is false, since God can reduce them to nothing.

Obj. 4. Further, since the duration of æviternal things is infinite as to subsequent duration, if æviternity is simultaneously whole, it follows that some creature is actually infinite, which is impossible. Therefore æviternity does not differ from time.

On the contrary, Boëthius says (*De. Consol.* iii, 9),[2] "Who commandest time to separate out from æviternity."

I answer that, Æviternity differs from time and from eternity as the mean between them both. This difference is explained by some[3] to consist in the fact that eternity has neither beginning nor end, æviternity, a beginning but no end, and time both beginning and end. This difference, however, is an accidental one, as was shown above in the preceding article, because even if æviternal things had always been, and would always be, as some think,[4] and even if they might sometimes fail to be, which is possible to God to allow, even granted this, æviternity would still be distinguished from eternity, and from time.

Others[5] assign the difference between these three to consist in the fact that eternity has no before and after, but that time has both, together with newness and oldness, and that æviternity has before and after without newness and oldness. This theory, however, involves a contradiction, which appears manifestly if newness and oldness be referred to the measure itself. For since before and after of duration cannot exist together, if æviternity has before and after it must follow that with the receding of the first part of æviternity the after part of æviternity must newly appear, and thus innovation would occur in æviternity itself, as it does in time. And if they be referred to the things measured, even then an incongruity would follow. For a thing which exists in time "grows old with time," because it has a changeable existence, and from the changeableness of

[2] PL 63, 758.

[3] Alexander of Hales, *Summa Theol.* 1, 65 (QR I, 100).

[4] See below, Q. XLVI, A. 1, Ans. 3, 5.

[5] Bonaventure, *In Sent.*, 11, d. 2, Pt. 1, A. 1, Q. 3 (QR 11, 62).

a thing measured there follows before and after in the measure, as is clear from the *Physics*.[1] Therefore the fact that an æviternal thing is neither subject to newness nor oldness comes from its changelessness; and consequently its measure does not contain before and after.

We say then that since eternity is the measure of a permanent being, in so far as anything recedes from permanence of being it recedes from eternity. Now some things recede from permanence of being, so that their being is subject to change, or consists in change; and these things are measured by time, as are all movements, and also the being of all things corruptible. But others recede less from permanence of being, because their being neither consists in change, nor is the subject of change; nevertheless they have change annexed to them either actually, or potentially. This appears in the heavenly bodies, the substantial being of which is unchangeable; and yet along with unchangeable being they have changeableness of place. The same applies to the angels, who have an unchangeable being with changeableness as regards choice, which pertains to their nature; moreover they have changeableness of intelligence, of affections, and of places, in their own degree. Therefore these are measured by æviternity, which is a mean between eternity and time. But the being that eternity measures is not changeable, nor is it joined to change. In this way time has before and after; æviternity in itself has no before and after, but they can be joined to it; while eternity has neither before nor after, nor is it at all compatible with such.

Reply Obj. 1. Spiritual creatures as regards successive affections and intelligences, are measured by time. Hence also Augustine says (*ibid.*), that to be moved through time is to be moved by affections. But as regards their natural being they are measured by æviternity; as regards the vision of glory, however, they have a share of eternity.

Reply Obj. 2. Æviternity is simultaneously whole; yet it is not eternity, because before and after are compatible with it.

Reply Obj. 3. In the very being of an angel considered absolutely, there is no difference of past and future, but only as regards added changes. Now to say that an angel was, or is, or will be, is to be taken in a different sense according to the acceptation of our intellect, which considers the angelic being by comparison with different parts of time. But when we say that an angel is, or was, we suppose something the supposition of whose opposite is incompatible with the divine power. But when we say he will be, we do not as yet suppose anything. Hence, since the being and non-being of an angel (considered absolutely is subject to the divine power), God can make the being of an angel not future; but He cannot cause him not to be while he is, or not to have been after he has been.

Reply Obj. 4. The duration of æviternity is infinite, since it is not limited by time. Hence, there is no incongruity in saying that a creature is infinite in so far as it is not limited by any other creature.

ARTICLE 6. *Whether There Is Only One Æviternity?*

We proceed thus to the Sixth Article: It seems that there is not only one æviternity.

Objection 1. For it is written in the apocryphal books of Esdras: *Majesty and power of ages are with Thee, O Lord.*

Obj. 2. Further, different genera have different measures. But some æviternal things belong to the corporeal genus, as for instance the heavenly bodies, and others are spiritual substances, as for instance the angels. Therefore there is not only one æviternity.

Obj. 3. Further, since æviternity is a term of duration, where there is one æviternity, there is also one duration. But not all æviternal things have one duration, for some begin to exist after others, as appears in the case especially of human souls. Therefore there is not only one æviternity.

Obj. 4. Further, things not dependent on each other do not seem to have one measure of duration; for there appears to be one time for all temporal things, since the first movement, which is first measured by time, is in some way the cause of all movement. But æviternal things do not depend on each other, for one angel is not the cause of another angel. Therefore there is not only one æviternity.

On the contrary, Æviternity is more simple than time, and is nearer to eternity. But time is one only. Therefore much more is æviternity one only.

I answer that, A twofold opinion exists on this subject. Some[2] say there is only one æviternity, others[3] that there are many æviternities. Which of these is true, must be considered

---

[1] Aristotle, IV, 12 (221ª31).

[2] Alexander of Hales, *Summa Theol.*, I, 66 (QR I, 102).

[3] Bonaventure, *In Sent.*, Bk. II, dist. II, P. I, A. 1, Q. 2 (QR II, 60).

from the cause of the unity of time; for we rise from corporeal things to the knowledge of spiritual things.

Now some[1] say that there is only one time for temporal things, since there is one number for all things numbered; for "time is a number," according to the Philosopher.[2] This, however, is not a sufficient reason, because "time is not a number" as abstracted from the thing numbered, but as "existing in the thing numbered"; otherwise it would not be continuous; for ten ells of cloth are continuous not by reason of the number, but by reason of the thing numbered. Now number as it exists in the thing numbered is not the same for all, but is different for different things.

Hence, others assert[3] that the unity of eternity which is the principle of all duration is the cause of the unity of time. Thus all durations are one in the light of their principle, but are many in the light of the diversity of things receiving duration from the influx of the first principle. On the other hand others[4] assign prime matter as the cause why time is one, as it is the first subject of movement, the measure of which is time. Neither of these reasons, however, is sufficient, since things which are one in principle, or in subject, especially if distant, are not one absolutely, but relatively.

Therefore the reason of the unity of time is the oneness of the first movement by which, since it is most simple, all other movements are measured, as is said in the *Metaphysics*.[5] Therefore time is referred to that movement, not only as a measure is to the thing measured, but also as accident is to subject, and thus receives unity from it. But to other movements it is compared only as the measure is to the thing measured. Hence it is not multiplied according to their multitude, because by one separate measure many things can be measured.

This being established, we must observe that a twofold opinion existed concerning spiritual substances. Some said that all proceeded from God in a certain equality, as Origen said (*Peri Archon.* i)[6]; or at least many of them, as some others thought.[7] Others said that all spiritual

---

[1] Themistius, in Averroes, *In Phys.*, IV, comm. 132 (IV, 203 L); cf. St. Thomas, *In Sent.*, II, d. 2, Q. 1, A. 2.

[2] *Physics*, IV, 12 (220^{b}8).

[3] Alexander of Hales, *Summa Theol.*, I, 66 (QR I, 102).

[4] Bonaventure, *In Sent.*, II, 1, A. 1, Q. 2 (QR II, 59). Cf. also Avicenna, *Suffic.*, II, 11 (fol. 44 v).

[5] Aristotle, X, 1 (1053^{a}8); cf. *Physics*, IV, 14 (223^{a}29; ^{b}18); Averroes, *In Phys.*, IV, 132 (IV, 2031); Albert the Great, *In Phys.*, IV, 3, 17 (BO III, 340).

[6] Chap. 8 (PG 11, 176).

[7] See below, Q. L, A. 4.

substances proceeded from God in a certain degree and order; and Dionysius (*Cæl. Hier.* x)[8] seems to have thought so, when he said that among spiritual substances there are the first, the middle, and the last, even in one order of angels. Now according to the first opinion, it must be said that there are many æviternities, as there are many æviternal things of first degree. But according to the second opinion, it would be necessary to say that there is one æviternity only, because since each thing is measured by the most simple element of its genus as is said in the *Metaphysics*,[9] it must be that the being of all æviternal things should be measured by the being of the first æviternal thing, which is all the more simple the nearer it is to the first. Therefore because the second opinion is the truer, as will be shown later (Q. XLVII, A. 2; Q. LI, A. 4), we concede at present that there is only one æviternity.

Reply Obj. 1. Æviternity is sometimes taken for age, that is, the period of a thing's duration; and thus we say many æviternities when we mean ages.

Reply Obj. 2. Although the heavenly bodies and spiritual things differ in the genus of their nature, still they agree in having a changeless being, and are thus measured by æviternity.

Reply Obj. 3. All temporal things did not begin together; nevertheless there is one time for all of them, by reason of the first thing measured by time; and thus all æviternal things have one æviternity by reason of the first, though all did not begin together.

Reply Obj. 4. For things to be measured by one it is not necessary that the one should be the cause of all, but that it be more simple than the rest.

QUESTION XI
THE UNITY OF GOD
(In Four Articles)

AFTER the foregoing, we consider the divine unity, concerning which there are four points of inquiry: (1) Whether "one" adds anything to "being"? (2) Whether "one" and "many" are opposed to each other? (3) Whether God is one? (4) Whether He is in the highest degree one?

ARTICLE 1. *Whether One Adds Anything to Being?*

We proceed thus to the First Article: It seems that one adds something to being.

[8] Sect. 3 (PG 3, 273).   [9] Aristotle, X, 1 (1052^{b}33)

Objection 1. For everything is in a determinate genus by addition to being, which is common to all genera. But one is in a determinate genus, for it is the principle of number, which is a species of quantity. Therefore one adds something to being.

Obj. 2. Further, what divides a thing common to all is an addition to it. But being is divided by one and by many. Therefore one is an addition to being.

Obj. 3. Further, if one is not an addition to being, one and being must have the same meaning. But it would be useless to call being being; therefore it would be equally so to call being one. Now this is false. Therefore one is an addition to being.

On the contrary, Dionysius says (*Div. Nom.* v, *ult.*)[1]: "Nothing which exists is not in some way one," which would be false if one were an addition to being, in the sense of limiting it. Therefore one is not an addition to being.

I answer that, One does not add any reality to being but, only the negation of division for one means undivided, being. From this very fact it is evident that one is convertible with being. Now every being is either simple or composite. But what is simple is undivided, both actually and potentially. But what is composite does not have being while its parts are divided, but after they make up and compose it. Hence it is manifest that the being of anything consists in indivision; and hence it is that everything guards its unity as it guards its being.

Reply Obj. 1. Some, thinking that the one convertible with being is the same as the one which is the principle of number, were divided into contrary opinions. Pythagoras and Plato,[2] seeing that the one convertible with being did not add any reality to being, but signified the substance of being as undivided, thought that the same applied to the one which is the principle of number. And because number is composed of unities, they thought that "numbers were the substances of all things." Avicenna,[3] however, on the contrary, considering that one which is the principle of number added a reality to the substance of being (otherwise number made of unities would not be a species of quantity), thought that the one convertible with being added a reality to the substance of beings, just as white adds to man. This, how-

ever, is manifestly false, because each thing is one by its substance. For if a thing were one by anything else, since this again would be one, supposing it were again one by another thing, we should be driven on to infinity. Hence we must adhere to the former statement. Therefore we must say that the one which is convertible with being does not add a reality to being, but that the one which is the principle of number does add something to being, belonging to the genus of quantity.

Reply Obj. 2. There is nothing to prevent a thing which in one way is divided from being another way undivided, as what is divided in number may be undivided in species; thus it may be that a thing is in one way one, and in another way many. Still, if it is absolutely undivided, either because it is undivided according to what belongs to the essence of the thing, though it may be divided as regards what is outside the essence of the thing, as what is one in subject and many as to accidents; or because it is undivided actually, and divided potentially, as what is one in the whole, and is many in parts; in such a case a thing will be one absolutely, and many relatively. On the other hand, if it be undivided relatively, and divided absolutely, as if it were divided in essence and undivided in notion or in principle or cause, it will be many absolutely, and one relatively; as what are many in number and one in species, or one in principle. Hence in that way, being is divided by one and by many, as it were by one absolutely, and by many relatively. For multitude itself would not be contained under being unless it were in some way contained under one. Thus Dionysius says (*Div. Nom., cap. ult.*)[4] that "there is no kind of multitude that is not in a way one. But what are many in their parts, are one in their whole; and what are many in accidents are one in subject; and what are many in number are one in species; and what are many in species are one in genus; and what are many in processions are one in principle."

Reply Obj. 3. It does not follow that it is futile to say being is one, since one adds something to being according to reason.

ARTICLE 2. *Whether One and Many Are Opposed?*

We proceed thus to the Second Article: It seems that one and many are not opposed.

Objection 1. For no opposite thing is predicated of its opposite. But every multitude is

---

[1] Sect. 2 (PG 3, 977).

[2] Cf. Aristotle, *Metaphysics,* I, 5 (987[a]13); I, 6 (987[b]23); Albert the Great, *In Meta.,* I, IV, 13 (BO VI, 83). Plato, *Republic* (478).

[3] *Metaph.,* III, 3 (79r); Averroes, *Dest. Dest.,* disp. III (IX, 55G).

[4] Sect. 2 (PG 3, 980).

in a certain way one, as appears from the preceding article. Therefore one is not opposed to multitude.

Obj. 2. Further, no opposite thing is constituted by its opposite. But multitude is constituted by one. Therefore it is not opposed to multitude.

Obj. 3. Further, one thing is opposed to one thing. But few is opposed to many. Therefore one is not opposed to many.

Obj. 4. Further, if one is opposed to multitude, it is opposed as the undivided is to the divided, and is thus opposed to it as privation is to habit. But this appears to be incongruous, because it would follow that one comes after multitude, and is defined by it; whereas, on the contrary, multitude is defined by one. Hence there would be a vicious circle in the definition, which is inadmissible. Therefore one and many are not opposed.

On the contrary, Things which are opposed in idea are themselves opposed to each other. But the notion of one consists in indivisibility, and the notion of multitude contains division. Therefore one and many are opposed to each other.

I answer that, One is opposed to many, but in various ways. The one which is the principle of number is opposed to multitude which is number as the measure is to the thing measured. For "one has the nature of a primary measure, and number is multitude measured by one," as is clear from the *Metaphysics*.[1] But the one which is convertible with being is opposed to multitude by way of privation; as the undivided is to the thing divided.

Reply Obj. 1. No privation entirely takes away the being of a thing, since "privation is negation in the subject," according to the Philosopher.[2] Nevertheless every privation takes away some being; and so in being, by reason of its universality, the privation of being has its foundation in being, which is not the case in privations of special forms, as of sight, or of whiteness, and the like. And what applies to being applies also to one and to good, which are convertible with being, for the privation of good is founded in some good; likewise the removal of unity is founded in some one thing. Hence it happens that multitude is some one thing, and evil is some good thing, and nonbeing is some kind of being. Nevertheless, opposite is not predicated of opposite, since one is absolute and the other is relative; for what is

relative being (as being in potency) is nonbeing absolutely, that is, in act; or what is absolute being in the genus of substance, is nonbeing relatively as regards some accidental being. In the same way, what is relatively good is absolutely bad, or contrariwise; likewise, what is absolutely one is relatively many, and contrariwise.

Reply Obj. 2. A whole is twofold. In one sense it is homogeneous, composed of like parts. In another sense it is heterogeneous, composed of dissimilar parts. Now in every homogeneous whole, the whole is made up of parts having the form of the whole, as, for instance, every part of water is water; and such is the constitution of a continuous thing made up of its parts. In every heterogeneous whole, however, every part lacks the form of the whole, as, for instance, no part of a house is a house, nor is any part of a man a man. Now multitude is such a kind of whole. Therefore since its part has not the form of the multitude, the latter is composed of unities, as a house is composed of not houses; not, indeed, as if unities constituted multitude so far as they are undivided, in which way they are opposed to multitude, but so far as they have being, as also the parts of a house make up the house by the fact that they are beings, not by the fact that they are not houses.

Reply Obj. 3. Many is taken in two ways: absolutely, and in that sense it is opposed to one, in another way as importing some kind of excess, in which sense it is opposed to few. Hence in the first sense two are many, but not in the second sense.

Reply Obj. 4. One is opposed to many privatively, in so far as the notion of many involves division. Hence division must be prior to unity not absolutely, but according to the nature of our apprehension. For we apprehend simple things by composite things; and hence we define a point to be, "what has no part," or "the beginning of a line." Multitude also, in idea, follows on one, because we do not understand divided things to convey the idea of multitude except by the fact that we attribute unity to every part. Hence one is placed in the definition of multitude, but multitude is not placed in the definition of one. But division is understood from the very negation of being, so what first comes to the intellect is being; secondly, that this being is not that being, and thus we apprehend division as a consequence; thirdly, comes the notion of one; fourthly, the notion of multitude.

---

[1] Aristotle, X, 1 (1052ᵇ18); X, 6 (1057ᵃ3).
[2] *Categories*, 10 (12ᵇ26); *Metaphysics*, IV, 2 (1004ᵃ15).

ARTICLE 3. *Whether God Is One?*

We proceed thus to the Third Article: It seems that God is not one.

Objection 1. For it is written, *For there be many gods and many lords* (I Cor. 8. 5).

Obj. 2. Further, one, as the principle of number, cannot be predicated of God, since quantity is not predicated of God; likewise, neither can one which is convertible with being be predicated of God, because it imports privation, and every privation is an imperfection, which cannot apply to God. Therefore God is not one.

On the contrary, It is written, *Hear, O Israel, the Lord our God is one Lord* (Deut. 6. 4).

I answer that, It can be shown from three sources that God is one. First from His simplicity. For it is manifest that the reason why any singular thing is this particular thing is because it cannot be communicated to many; for that by which Socrates is a man can be communicated to many, while what makes him this particular man is only communicable to one. Therefore, if Socrates were a man by what makes him to be this particular man, as there cannot be many Socrates, so there could not in that way be many men. Now this belongs to God alone, for God Himself is His own nature, as was shown above (Q. III, A. 3). Therefore, in the very same way God is God, and He is this God. It is impossible therefore that many Gods should exist.

Secondly, this is proved from the infinity of His perfection. For it was shown above (Q. IV, A. 2) that God comprehends in Himself the whole perfection of being. If then many gods existed, they would necessarily differ from each other. Something therefore would belong to one which did not belong to another. And if this were a privation, one of them would not be absolutely perfect; but if a perfection, one of them would be without it. So it is impossible for many gods to exist. Hence also the ancient philosophers, constrained as it were by truth itself, when they asserted an infinite principle asserted likewise that there was only one such principle.

Thirdly, this is shown from the unity of the world. For all things that exist are seen to be ordered to each other since some serve others. But things that are diverse do not agree in one order unless they are ordered thereto by some one being. For many things are reduced into one order by one better than by many, because one is the *per se* cause of one, and many are only the accidental cause of one, in so far as they are in some way one. Since therefore what is first is most perfect, and is so *per se* and not accidentally, it must be that the first which reduces all into one order should be only one. And this one is God.

Reply Obj. 1. Gods are called many by the error of some who worshipped many deities, thinking as they did that the planets and other stars were gods, and also the separate parts of the world. Hence the Apostle adds: *Our God is one,* etc.

Reply Obj. 2. *One* which is the principle of number is not predicated of God, but only of things which have being in matter. For one the principle of number belongs to the genus of mathematical things, which have being in matter, but are abstracted from matter according to reason. But one which is convertible with being is a metaphysical entity, and does not depend on matter in its being. And although in God there is no privation, still, according to the mode of our apprehension, He is known to us by way only of privation and remotion. Thus there is no reason why a certain kind of privation should not be predicated of God; for instance, that He is incorporeal, and infinite. And in the same way it is said of God that He is one.

ARTICLE 4. *Whether God Is Supremely One?*

We proceed thus to the Fourth Article: It seems that God is not supremely one.

Objection 1. For one is so called from the privation of division. But privation cannot be greater or less. Therefore God is not more one than other things which are called one.

Obj. 2. Further, nothing seems to be more indivisible than what is actually and potentially indivisible; such as a point, and unity. But a thing is said to be more one according as it is indivisible. Therefore God is not more one than unity is one and a point is one.

Obj. 3. Further, what is essentially good is supremely good. Therefore, what is essentially one is supremely one. But every being is essentially one, as the Philosopher says.[1] Therefore every being is supremely one; and therefore God is not one more than any other being is one.

On the contrary, Bernard says (*De Consid.* v):[2] "Among all things called one, the unity of the Divine Trinity holds the first place."

I answer that, Since one is an undivided being, if anything is supremely one it must be

[1] *Metaphysics,* IV. 2 (1003ᵇ32).
[2] Chap. 8 (PL 182, 799).

supremely being, and supremely undivided. Now both of these belong to God. For He is supremely being, since His being is not determined by any nature to which it is adjoined; for He is being itself, subsistent, undetermined in every way. But He is supremely undivided since He is divided neither actually nor potentially by any mode of division, for He is altogether simple, as was shown above (Q. III, A. 7). Hence it is manifest that God is one in the supreme degree.

Reply Obj. 1. Although privation considered in itself is not susceptive of more or less, still according as its opposite is subject to more and less, privation also can be considered itself in the light of more and less. Therefore, according as a thing is more divided or divisible, or less, or not at all, in that degree it is called more, or less, or supremely, one.

Reply Obj. 2. A point and unity which is the principle of number are not supremely being, since they have being only in some subject. Hence neither of them can be supremely one. For as a subject cannot be supremely one because of the difference within it of accident and subject, so neither can an accident.

Reply Obj. 3. Although every being is one by its substance, still every such substance is not equally the cause of unity; for the substance of some things is composed of many things but others not.

QUESTION XII
How GOD IS KNOWN BY US
(In Thirteen Articles)

SINCE up to now we have considered God as He is in Himself, we now go on to consider in what manner He is in our knowledge, that is, how He is known by creatures. Concerning this there are thirteen points of inquiry. (1) Whether any created intellect can see the essence of God? (2) Whether the essence of God is seen by the intellect through any created species? (3) Whether the essence of God can be seen by the corporeal eye? (4) Whether any created intellectual substance is sufficient by its own natural powers to see the essence of God? (5) Whether the created intellect needs any created light in order to see the essence of God? (6) Whether of those who see God, one sees Him more perfectly than another? (7) Whether any created intellect can comprehend the essence of God? (8) Whether the created intellect seeing the essence of God knows all things in it? (9) Whether what is there known is known by

any likenesses? (10) Whether the created intellect knows all at once what it sees in God? (11) Whether in the state of this life any man can see the essence of God? (12) Whether by natural reason we can know God in this life? (13) Whether there is in this life any knowledge of God through grace above the knowledge of natural reason?

ARTICLE 1. *Whether Any Created Intellect Can See the Essence of God?*

We proceed thus to the First Article: It seems that no created intellect can see the essence of God.

Objection 1. For Chrysostom (*Hom.* xiv, *in Joan*)[1] commenting on John 1. 18, *No man hath seen God at any time,* says: "Not prophets only, but neither angels nor archangels have seen God. For how can a creature see what is increatable?" Dionysius also says (*Div. Nom.* i),[2] speaking of God: "Neither is there sense, nor phantasm, nor opinion, nor reason, nor knowledge of Him."

Obj. 2. Further, everything infinite, as such, is unknown. But God is infinite, as was shown above (Q. VII, A. 1). Therefore in Himself He is unknown.

Obj. 3. Further, the created intellect knows only existing things. For what falls first under the apprehension of the intellect is being. Now God is not something existing, but He is rather "super-existence," as Dionysius says (*Div. Nom.* iv).[3] Therefore God is not intelligible; but above all intellect.

Obj. 4. Further, there must be some proportion between the knower and the known, since the known is the perfection of the knower. But no proportion exists between the created intellect and God, for there is an infinite distance between them. Therefore the created intellect cannot see the essence of God.

On the contrary, It is written: *We shall see Him as He is* (I John 3. 2).

I answer that, Since everything is knowable according as it is in act, God, Who is pure act without any admixture of potency, is in Himself supremely knowable. But what is supremely knowable in itself, is not knowable to some other intellect, on account of the excess of the intelligible object above the intellect; as, for example, the sun, which is supremely visible, cannot be seen by the bat by reason of its excess of light.

---

[1] PG 59, 98.
[2] Sect. 5 (PG 3, 593).
[3] Sect. 3 (PG 3, 593).

Therefore some[1] who considered this, held that no created intellect can see the essence of God. This opinion, however, it not tenable. For as the ultimate happiness of man consists in the use of his highest function, which is the operation of the intellect, the created intellect could never see God, it would either never attain to happiness or its happiness would consist in something else beside God, which is opposed to faith. For the ultimate perfection of the rational creature is to be found in that which is the principle of its being, since a thing is perfect so far as it attains to its principle. Further, the same opinion is also against reason. For there resides in every man a natural desire to know the cause of any effect which he sees, and from this wonder arises in men. But if the intellect of the rational creature could not reach so far as to the first cause of things, the natural desire would remain void.

Hence it must be absolutely granted that the blessed see the essence of God.

Reply Obj. 1. Both of these authorities speak of the vision of comprehension. Hence Dionysius premises immediately before the words cited, "He is universally to all incomprehensible," etc. Chrysostom, likewise after the words quoted, says: "He says this of the most certain vision of the Father, which is such a perfect consideration and comprehension as the Father has of the Son."

Reply Obj. 2. The infinity of matter not made perfect by form is unknown in itself, because all knowledge comes by the form; but the infinity of the form not limited by matter is in itself supremely known. God is Infinite in this way, and not in the first way, as appears from what was said above (Q. VII, A. 1).

Reply Obj. 3. God is not said to be not existing as if He did not exist at all, but because He exists above all that exists, since He is His own existence. Hence it does not follow that He cannot be known at all, but that He exceeds every kind of knowledge, which means that He is not comprehended.

Reply Obj. 4. Proportion is twofold. In one sense it means a certain relation of one quantity to another, according as double, treble, and equal are species of proportion. In another sense every relation of one thing to another is called proportion. And in this sense there can be a proportion of the creature to God, in so far as it is related to Him as the effect to its cause, and as potency to act; and in this way

the created intellect can be proportioned to know God.

ARTICLE 2. *Whether the Essence of God Is Seen by the Created Intellect Through Some Likeness?*

We proceed thus to the Second Article: It seems that the essence of God is seen through some likeness by the created intellect.

Objection 1. For it is written: *We know that when He shall appear, we shall be like to Him, and* (Vulg., *because*) *we shall see Him as He is* (I John 3. 2).

Obj. 2. Further, Augustine says (*De Trin.*):[2] "When we know God, some likeness of God is made in us."

Obj. 3. Further, the intellect in act is the intelligible in act, as sense in act is the sensible in act. But this comes about only in so far as sense is informed with the likeness of the sensible thing, and the intellect with the likeness of the thing understood. Therefore, if God is seen by the created intellect in act, it must be that He is seen by some likeness.

On the contrary, Augustine says (*De Trin.* xv),[3] that when the Apostle says, *We see through a glass and in an enigma* (Douay,— *in a dark manner*), "by the terms 'glass' and 'enigma' certain likenesses are signified by him, which are accommodated to the understanding of God." But to see the essence of God is not an enigmatic nor a speculative vision, but is, on the contrary, of an opposite kind. Therefore the divine essence is not seen through likenesses.

I answer that, Two things are required both for sensible and for intellectual vision—namely, power of sight, and union of the thing seen with the sight. For vision is made actual only when the thing seen is in a certain way in the seer. Now in corporeal things it is clear that the thing seen cannot be by its essence in the seer, but only by its likeness; as the likeness of a stone is in the eye, by which the vision is made actual, but the substance of the stone is not there. But if the principle of the visual power and the thing seen were one and the same thing, it would necessarily follow that the seer would receive both the visual power and the form by which it sees from that one same thing.

Now it is manifest both that God is the author of the intellectual power, and that He can be seen by the intellect. And since the intellectual power of the creature is not the essence

---

[1] Amalric of Benes. (Cf. Capelle, *Amaury de Bène*, p. 105); cf. Denifle, *Chartularium*, 128 (I, 170).

[2] IX, 11 (PL 42, 969).   [3] Chap. 9 (PL 42, 1069).

of God, it follows that it is some kind of participated likeness of Him who is the first intellect. Hence also the intellectual power of the creature is called an intelligible light, as though derived from the first light, whether this be understood of the natural power, or of some perfection superadded of grace or of glory. Therefore, in order to see God, there must be some likeness of God on the part of the seeing power whereby the intellect is made capable of seeing God.

But on the part of the object seen, which must necessarily be united to the seer, the essence of God cannot be seen by any created likeness. First, because, as Dionysius says (*Div. Nom.* i),[1] "by the likenesses of the inferior order of things, the superior can in no way be known"; just as by the species of a body the essence of an incorporeal thing cannot be known. Much less therefore can the essence of God be seen by any created species whatever. Secondly, because the essence of God is His own very being, as was shown above (Q. III, A. 4), which cannot be said of any created form; and so no created form can be the likeness representing the essence of God to the seer. Thirdly, because the divine essence is uncircumscribed, and contains in itself supereminently whatever can be signified or understood by the created intellect. Now this cannot in any way be represented by any created species; for every created form is determined according to some aspect of wisdom, or of power, or of being itself, or of some like thing. Hence to say that God is seen by some likeness, is to say that the divine essence is not seen at all, which is erroneous.

Therefore it must be said that to see the essence of God there is required some likeness in the seeing power, namely, the light of divine glory strengthening the intellect to see God, which is spoken of in the Psalm (35. 10), *In Thy light we shall see light*. The essence of God, however, cannot be seen by any created likeness representing the divine essence itself as it is in itself.

Reply Obj. 1. That authority speaks of the likeness which is caused by participation of the light of glory.

Reply Obj. 2. Augustine speaks of the knowledge of God here on earth.

Reply Obj. 3. The divine essence is existence itself. Hence as other intelligible forms which are not their own being are united to the intellect by means of some being by which the intellect itself is informed, and made in act, so the divine essence is united to the created intellect as the thing actually understood, by itself making the intellect in act.

ARTICLE 3. *Whether the Essence of God Can Be Seen with the Bodily Eye?*

We proceed thus to the Third Article: It seems that the essence of God can be seen by the corporeal eye.

Objection 1. For it is written (Job 19. 26): *In my flesh I shall see . . . God*, and (*ibid.* 42. 5), *With the hearing of the ear I have heard Thee, but now my eye seeth Thee.*

Obj. 2. Further, Augustine says[2] "Those eyes [namely of the glorified] will therefore have a greater power of sight, not so much to see more keenly, as some report of the sight of serpents or of eagles (for whatever acuteness of vision is possessed by these creatures, they can see only corporeal things) but to see even incorporeal things." Now whoever can see incorporeal things can be raised up to see God. Therefore the glorified eye can see God.

Obj. 3. Further, God can be seen by man through a vision of the imagination. For it is written: *I saw the Lord sitting upon a throne*, etc. (Isa. 6. 1). But an imaginary vision has its origin in sense, "for the imagination is moved by sense to act," as it is stated in the book on the *Soul*.[3] Therefore God can be seen by a vision of sense.

On the contrary, Augustine says (*De Vid. Deum, Ep.* cxlvii)[4]: "No one has ever seen God as He is, either in this life, nor in the angelic life, as visible things are seen by corporeal vision."

I answer that, It is impossible for God to be seen by the sense of sight, or by any other sense, or power of the sensitive part. For every such kind of power is the act of a corporeal organ, as will be shown later (Q. LXXVIII, A. 1). Now act is proportioned to that of which it is the act. Hence no power of that kind can go beyond corporeal things. For God is incorporeal, as was shown above (Q. III, A. 1). Hence He cannot be seen by the sense or the imagination, but only by the intellect.

Reply Obj. 1. The words, *In my flesh I shall see God my Saviour*, do not mean that God will be seen with the eye of flesh, but that man existing in the flesh after the resurrection will see God. Likewise the words, *Now my eye seeth*

---

[1] Sect. 3 (PG 3, 588).

[2] *City of God*, XXII, 29 (PL 41, 799).
[3] Aristotle, III, 3 (429ª1).
[4] Chap. 11 (PL 33, 609).

Thee, are to be understood of the mind's eye, as the Apostle says: *May* He *give unto you the spirit of wisdom . . . in the knowledge of Him,* that *the eyes of your heart* may be *enlightened* (Eph. 1. 17, 18).

Reply Obj. 2. Augustine speaks as one inquiring, and conditionally. This appears from what he says previously: "Therefore they will have an altogether different power [namely the glorified eyes], if they shall see that incorporeal nature"; and afterwards he explains this, saying: "It is very credible that we shall so see the mundane bodies of the new heaven and the new earth as to see most clearly God everywhere present, governing all corporeal things, not as we now see the invisible things of God as understood by what is made, but as when we see men among whom we live, living and exercising the functions of human life, we do not believe they live, but see it." Hence it is evident how the glorified eyes will see God, as now our eyes see the life of another. But life is not seen with the corporeal eye, as a thing in itself visible, but as the accidental object of the sense; which indeed is not known by sense, but at once, together with sense, by some other knowing power. But that the divine presence is known by the intellect immediately on the sight of, and through, corporeal things, happens from two causes—namely, from the clearness of the intellect, and from the refulgence of the divine brightness in the renewed body.

Reply Obj. 3. The essence of God is not seen in a vision of the imagination; but the imagination produces some form representing God according to some mode of likeness, as in divine Scripture divine things are metaphorically described by means of sensible things.

ARTICLE 4. *Whether Any Created Intellect by its Natural Powers Can See the Divine Essence?*

We proceed thus to the Fourth Article: It seems that a created intellect can see the divine essence by its own natural power.

Objection 1. For Dionysius says (*Div. Nom.* iv)[1]: An angel "is a pure mirror, most clear, receiving, if it is right to say so, the whole beauty of God." But if a reflection is seen, the original thing is seen. Therefore, since an angel by his natural power understands himself, it seems that by his own natural power he understands the divine essence.

Obj. 2. Further, what is supremely visible is made less visible to us by reason of our defec-

[1] Sect. 22 (PG 3, 724).

tive corporeal or intellectual sight. But the angelic intellect has no such defect. Therefore, since God is supremely intelligible in Himself, it seems that in like manner He is supremely so to an angel. Therefore, if he can understand other intelligible things by his own natural power, much more can he understand God.

Obj. 3. Further, corporeal sense cannot be raised up to understand incorporeal substance, which is above its nature. Therefore if to see the essence of God is above the nature of every created intellect, it follows that no created intellect can reach up to see the essence of God at all. But this is false, as appears from what is said above (A. 1). Therefore it seems that it is natural for a created intellect to see the divine essence.

On the contrary, It is written: *The grace of God is life everlasting* (Rom. 6. 23). But life everlasting consists in the vision of the divine essence, according to the words: *This is eternal life, that they may know Thee the only true God,* etc. (John 17. 3). Therefore, to see the essence of God belongs to the created intellect by grace, and not by nature.

I answer that, It is impossible for any created intellect to see the essence of God by its own natural power. For knowledge occurs according as the thing known is in the knower. But the thing known is in the knower according to the mode of the knower. Hence the knowledge of every knower is according to the mode of its own nature. If therefore the mode of anything's being exceeds the mode of the nature of the knower, it must result that the knowledge of that thing is above the nature of the knower.

Now the mode of being of things is manifold. For there are some things whose natures have being only in this one individual matter, as for instance, all bodies. But there are others whose natures subsist of themselves, not residing in matter at all, which, however, are not their own being, but receive it; and these are the incorporeal beings, called angels. But to God alone does it belong to be His own subsistent being.

Therefore, what has being only in individual matter we know naturally, since our soul, by which we know, is the form of some certain matter. Now our soul possesses two cognitive powers. One is the act of a corporeal organ, which naturally knows things existing in individual matter; hence sense knows only the singular. But there is another kind of cognitive power in the soul, called the intellect, and this is not the act of any corporeal organ. Therefore the intellect naturally knows natures which have being only in individual matter; not however as they are in individual matter, but according as they are abstracted from it by the consideration of the intellect. Hence it follows that through the intellect we can understand things of this kind as universal, and this is beyond the power of sense. Now the angelic intellect naturally knows natures not existing in matter; but this is beyond the natural power of the intellect of our soul in the state of its present life, united as it is to the body.

It follows therefore that to know self-subsistent being is natural to the divine intellect alone, and that it is beyond the natural power of any created intellect; for no creature is its own being but rather has participated being. Therefore the created intellect cannot see the essence of God unless God by His grace unites Himself to the created intellect, as an object made intelligible to it.

Reply Obj. 1. This mode of knowing God is natural to an angel—namely, to know Him by His own likeness refulgent in the angel himself. But to know God by any created likeness is not to know the essence of God, as was shown above (A. 2). Hence it does not follow that an angel can know the essence of God by his own power.

Reply Obj. 2. The angelic intellect is not defective if defect be taken to mean privation, as if it were without anything which it ought to have. But if defect be taken negatively, in that sense every creature is defective when compared with God, since it does not possess the excellence which is in God.

Reply Obj. 3. The sense of sight, as being altogether material, cannot be raised up to anything immaterial. But our intellect, or the angelic intellect, because it is elevated above matter in its own nature, can be raised up above its own nature to a higher level by grace. The mark of this is that sight cannot in any way know in the abstract what it knows in the concrete; for in no way can it perceive a nature except as this one particular nature, although our intellect is able to consider by abstraction what it knows in the concrete. Now although it knows things which have a form residing in matter, still it resolves the composite into both of these elements, and it considers the form separately by itself. Likewise, also, the intellect of an angel, although it naturally knows the concrete being in any nature, still it is able to separate that being by its intellect, since it knows that the thing itself is one thing, and its

being is another. Since therefore the created intellect is naturally capable of apprehending the concrete form, and the concrete being by abstraction, by way of a kind of resolution, it can by grace be raised up to know separate subsisting substance and separate subsisting being.

ARTICLE 5. *Whether the Created Intellect Needs Any Created Light in order to See the Essence of God?*

We proceed thus to the Fifth Article: It seems that the created intellect does not need any created light in order to see the essence of God.

Objection 1. For what is of itself clear in sensible things does not require any other light in order to be seen. Therefore the same applies to intelligible things. Now God is intelligible light. Therefore He is not seen by the means of any created light.

Obj. 2. Further, if God is seen through a medium, He is not seen in His essence. But if seen by any created light He is seen through a medium. Therefore He is not seen in His essence.

Obj. 3. Further, what is created can be natural to some creature. Therefore, if the essence of God is seen through any created light, such a light can be made natural to some other creature; and thus, that creature would not need any other light to see God, which is impossible. Therefore it is not necessary that every creature should require a superadded light in order to see the essence of God.

On the contrary, It is written: *In Thy light we shall see light* (Ps. 35. 10).

I answer that, Everything which is raised up to what exceeds its nature must be prepared by some disposition above its nature; as, for example, if air is to receive the form of fire, it must be prepared by some disposition for such a form. But when any created intellect sees the essence of God, the essence of God itself becomes the intelligible form of the intellect. Hence it is necessary that some supernatural disposition should be added to the intellect in order that it may be raised up to such a great and sublime height. Now since the natural power of the created intellect does not avail to enable it to see the essence of God, as was shown in the preceding article, it is necessary that the power of understanding should be increased further by divine grace. Now this increase of the intellectual powers is called the illumination of the intellect, as we also call the intelligible itself by the name of light or illumination. And this is the light spoken of in the Apocalypse (21. 23). *The glory of God hath enlightened it*—namely, the society of the blessed who see God. By this light the blessed are made "deiform"—that is, like to God, according to the saying: *When He shall appear we shall be like to Him, and* [Vulg., *because*] *we shall see Him as He is* (I John 3. 2).

Reply Obj. 1. The created light is necessary to see the essence of God, not in order to make the essence of God intelligible, which is of itself intelligible, but in order to enable the intellect to understand in the same way as a habit makes a power abler to act. In the same way corporeal light is necessary as regards external sight, since it makes the medium transparent, in act, so that it may be moved by colour.

Reply Obj. 2. This light is required to see the divine essence, not as a likeness in which God is seen, but as a perfection of the intellect, strengthening it to see God. Therefore it may be said that this light is to be described not as a medium in which God is seen, but as one under which He is seen; and such a medium does not take away the immediate vision of God.

Reply Obj. 3. The disposition to the form of fire can be natural only to what has the form of fire. Hence the light of glory cannot be natural to a creature unless the creature has a divine nature, which is impossible. But by this light the rational creature is made deiform, as is said in this article.

ARTICLE 6. *Whether of Those Who See the Essence of God, One Sees More Perfectly Than Another?*

We proceed thus to the Sixth Article: It seems that of those who see the essence of God, one does not see more perfectly than another.

Objection 1. For it is written (I John 3. 2): *We shall see Him as He is.* But He is only in one way. Therefore He will be seen by all in one way only; and therefore He will not be seen more perfectly by one and less perfectly by another.

Obj. 2. Further, as Augustine says (*Octog. Trium Quest., qu.* xxxii)[1] that one person cannot understand one and the same thing more perfectly than another. But all who see the essence of God understand the divine essence, for God is seen by the intellect and not by sense, as was shown above (A. 3). Therefore, of those who see the divine essence, one does not see more clearly than another.

[1] PL 40, 22

Obj. 3. Further, That anything be seen more perfectly than another can happen in two ways: either on the part of the visible object, or on the part of the visual power of the seer. On the part of the object, it may so happen because the object is received more perfectly in the seer, that is, according to the greater perfection of the likeness; but this does not apply to the present question, for God is present to the intellect seeing Him not by way of a likeness, but by His essence. It follows then that if one sees Him more perfectly than another, this happens according to the difference of the intellectual power; thus it follows too that the one whose intellectual power is the higher will see Him the more clearly, and this is incongruous, since equality with angels is promised to men in the state of happiness.

On the contrary, Eternal life consists in the vision of God, according to John 17. 3: *This is eternal life, that they may know Thee the only true God,* etc. Therefore, if all saw the essence of God equally in eternal life, all would be equal; the contrary to which is declared by the Apostle: *Star differs from star in glory* (I Cor. 15. 41).

I answer that, Of those who see the essence of God, one sees Him more perfectly than another. This, indeed, does not take place as if one had a more perfect likeness of God than another, since that vision will not spring from any likeness; but it will take place because one intellect will have a greater power or faculty to see God than another. The faculty of seeing God, however, does not belong to the created intellect naturally, but is given to it by the light of glory, which establishes the intellect in a kind of deiformity, as appears from what is said above in the preceding article.

Hence the intellect which participates more of the light of glory will see God the more perfectly. And he will have a fuller participation of the light of glory who has more charity, because where there is the greater charity, there is the more desire, and desire in a certain way makes the one desiring apt and prepared to receive the thing desired. Hence he who possesses the more charity will see God the more perfectly, and will be the more happy.

Reply Obj. 1. In the words, *We shall see Him as He is,* the conjunction "as" determines the mode of vision on the part of the thing seen, so that the meaning is, we shall see Him to be as He is, because we shall see His being, which is His essence. But it does not determine the mode of vision on the part of the one seeing, as if the meaning was that the mode of seeing God will be as perfect as is the perfect mode of God's being.

Thus appears the answer to the *Second Objection.* For when it is said that one intellect does not understand one and the same thing better than another, this would be true if referred to the mode of the thing understood, for whoever understands it otherwise than it really is does not truly understand it, but not if referred to the mode of understanding, for the understanding of one is more perfect than the understanding of another.

Reply Obj. 3. The diversity of seeing will not arise on the part of the object seen, for the same object will be presented to all—namely, the essence of God; nor will it arise from the diverse participation of the object by different likenesses; but it will arise on the part of the diverse power of the intellect, not, indeed, the natural power, but the glorified faculty as we have said in the body of the article.

ARTICLE 7. *Whether Those Who See the Essence of God Comprehend Him?*

We proceed thus to the Seventh Article: It seems that those who see the essence of God comprehend Him.

Objection 1. For the Apostle says (Phil. 3. 12): *But I follow after, if I may by any means comprehend* (Douay, *apprehend*). But the Apostle did not follow in vain; for he said (I Cor. 9. 26): *I . . . so run, not as at an uncertainty.* Therefore he comprehended. And in the same way others also, whom he invites to do the same, saying: *So run that you may comprehend.*

Obj. 2. Further, Augustine says (*De Vid. Deum,* Ep. cxlvii):[1] "That is comprehended which is so seen as a whole, that nothing of it is hidden from the seer." But if God is seen in His essence, He is seen whole, and nothing of Him is hidden from the seer, since God is simple. Therefore, whoever sees His essence, comprehends Him.

Obj. 3. Further, if we say that He is seen as a whole, but not wholly, it may be contrarily urged that wholly refers either to the mode of the seer, or to the mode of the thing seen. But he who sees the essence of God, sees Him wholly if the mode of the thing seen is considered, since he sees Him as He is as we have said (A. 6, ANS. 1); also, likewise, he sees Him wholly if the mode of the seer be meant, since the intellect will with its full power see the di-

[1] Chap. 9 (PL 33, 606).

vine essence. Therefore all who see the essence of God see Him wholly. Therefore they comprehend Him.

On the contrary, It is written: *O most mighty, great, and powerful, the Lord of hosts is Thy Name. Great in counsel, and incomprehensible in thought* (Jer. 32. 18, 19). Therefore He cannot be comprehended.

I answer that, It is impossible for any created intellect to comprehend God; yet "for the mind to attain to God in some degree is great happiness," as Augustine says.[2]

In proof of this we must consider that what is comprehended is perfectly known, and that is perfectly known which is known so far as it can be known. Thus, if anything which is capable of scientific demonstration is held only by an opinion resting on a probable proof, it is not comprehended; as, for instance, if anyone knows by scientific demonstration that a triangle has three angles equal to two right angles, he comprehends that truth. But if anyone accepts it as a probable opinion because wise men or most men teach it, he cannot be said to comprehend the thing itself, because he does not attain to that perfect mode of knowledge of which it is capable.

But no created intellect can attain to that perfect mode of the knowledge of the divine intellect of which it is capable. Which appears thus. Everything is knowable according as it is being in act. But God, whose being is infinite, as was shown above (Q. VII, A. 1) is infinitely knowable. Now no created intellect can know God infinitely. For the created intellect knows the divine essence more or less perfectly in proportion as it receives a greater or lesser light of glory. Since therefore the created light of glory received into any created intellect cannot be infinite, it is impossible for any created intellect to know God in an infinite degree. Hence it is impossible that it should comprehend God.

Reply Obj. 1. Comprehension is twofold. In one sense it is taken strictly and properly, according as something is included in the one comprehending; and thus in no way is God comprehended either by intellect, or in any other way, since He is infinite and cannot be included in any finite being, so that no finite being can contain Him infinitely, in the degree of His own infinity. In this sense we now take comprehension. But in another sense comprehension is taken more largely as opposed to non-attainment; for he who attains to anyone is said to comprehend him when he attains to him. And in

[2] *Serm. ad Popul.,* CXVII, 3 (PL 38, 663).

this sense God is comprehended by the blessed, according to the words, *I held him, and I will not let him go* (Cant. 3. 4); in this sense also are to be understood the words quoted from the Apostle concerning comprehension. And in this way *comprehension* is one of the three endowments of the soul, corresponding to hope, as vision corresponds to faith, and fruition corresponds to charity. For even among ourselves not everything seen is held or possessed, since things either appear sometimes afar off, or they are not in our power of attainment. Neither, again, do we always enjoy what we possess; either because we find no pleasure in them, or because such things are not the ultimate end of our desire, so as to satisfy and quell it. But the blessed possess these three things in God, because they see Him, and in seeing Him, possess Him as present, having the power to see Him always; and possessing Him, they enjoy Him as the ultimate fulfilment of desire.

Reply Obj. 2. God is called incomprehensible not because anything of Him is not seen, but because He is not seen as perfectly as He is capable of being seen; thus when any demonstrable proposition is known by a probable reason only, it does not follow that any part of it is unknown, either the subject, or the predicate, or the composition, but that the whole is not as perfectly known as it is capable of being known. Hence Augustine (*loc. cit.*), in his definition of comprehension, says the whole is comprehended when it is seen in such a way that nothing of it is hidden from the seer, or when its boundaries can be completely viewed or traced; for the boundaries of a thing are said to be completely surveyed when the end according to that mode of knowledge of it is attained.

Reply Obj. 3. The word "wholly" denotes a mode of the object; not that the whole object does not come under knowledge, but that the mode of the object is not the mode of the one who knows. Therefore, he who sees God's essence sees in Him that He exists infinitely, and is infinitely knowable; nevertheless, this infinite mode does not extend to enable the knower to know infinitely; thus, for instance, a person can know with probability that a proposition is demonstrable, although he himself does not know it as demonstrated.

ARTICLE 8. *Whether Those Who See the Essence of God See All in God?*

We proceed thus to the Eighth Article: It seems that those who see the essence of God see all things in God.

Objection 1. For Gregory says (*Dialog*, iv)[1]: "What do they not see, who see Him Who sees all things?" But God sees all things. Therefore, those who see God see all things.

Obj. 2. Further, whoever sees a mirror sees what is reflected in the mirror. But all actual or possible things shine forth in God as in a mirror for He knows all things, in Himself. Therefore, whoever sees God, sees all the things that are, and all the things that can be.

Obj. 3. Further, whoever understands the greater can understand the least, as is said in the book on the *Soul*.[2] But all that God does, or can do, are less than His essence. Therefore, whoever understands God, can understand all that God does or can do.

Obj. 4. Further, the rational creature naturally desires to know all things. Therefore, if in seeing God it does not know all things, its natural desire will not rest satisfied; thus, in seeing God it will not be fully happy, which is incongruous. Therefore, he who sees God knows all things.

On the contrary, The angels see the essence of God, and yet do not know all things. For, as Dionysius says (*Cæl. Hier.* vii)[3] that the inferior angels are cleansed from ignorance by the superior angels. Also they are ignorant of future contingent things and of secret thoughts, for this knowledge belongs to God alone. Therefore, whosoever sees the essence of God, does not know all things.

I answer that, The created intellect, in seeing the divine essence, does not see in it all that God does or can do. For it is manifest that things are seen in God as they are in Him. But all other things are in God as effects are in the power of their cause. Therefore all things are seen in God as an effect is seen in its cause. Now it is clear that the more perfectly a cause is seen, the more of its effects can be seen in it. For whoever has a lofty understanding, as soon as one demonstrative principle is put before him gathers the knowledge of many conclusions; but this is beyond one of a weaker intellect, for he needs things to be explained to him separately. And so an intellect can know all the effects of a cause and the reasons for those effects in the cause itself, if it comprehends the cause wholly. Now no created intellect can comprehend God wholly, as shown above (A. 7). Therefore no created intellect in seeing God can know all that God does or can do, for this would be to comprehend His power;

[1] Chap. 33 (PL 77, 376).
[2] Aristotle, III, 4 (429[b]3).
[3] Sect. 3 (PG 3, 208).

but of what God does or can do, the more any intellect knows them, the more perfectly it sees God.

Reply Obj. 1. Gregory speaks as regards the object being sufficient, namely, God, who in Himself sufficiently contains and shows forth all things; but it does not follow that whoever sees God knows all things, for he does not perfectly comprehend Him.

Reply Obj. 2. It is not necessary that whoever sees a mirror should see all that is in the mirror, unless his glance comprehends the mirror.

Reply Obj. 3. Although it is more to see God than to see all things else, still it is a greater thing to see Him so that all things are known in Him than to see Him in such a way that not all things, but fewer or more, are known in Him. For it has been shown in this article that the more things are known in God according as He is seen more or less perfectly.

Reply Obj. 4. The natural desire of the rational creature is to know everything that belongs to the perfection of the intellect, namely, the species and genera of things and their types, and these everyone who sees the divine essence will see in God. But to know other singular beings, their thoughts, and their deeds, does not belong to the perfection of the created intellect nor does its natural desire go out to these things; neither, again, does it desire to know things that do not as yet exist, but which God can call into being. Yet if God alone were seen, Who is the fount and principle of all being and of all truth, He would so fill the natural desire of knowledge that nothing else would be desired, and the seer would be completely happy. Hence Augustine says[1]: "Unhappy the man who knoweth all these (that is, all creatures) and knoweth not Thee! but happy whoso knoweth Thee although he know not these. And whoso knoweth both Thee and them is not the happier for them, but for Thee alone."

ARTICLE 9. *Whether What Is Seen in God by Those Who See the Divine Essence Is Seen Through Any Likeness?*

We proceed thus to the Ninth Article: It seems that what is seen in God by those who see the divine essence is seen by means of some likeness.

Objection 1. For every kind of knowledge comes about by the knower being assimilated to the object known. For thus the intellect in act becomes the actual thing understood, and the

sense in act becomes the actual sensible, in so far as it is informed by its likeness, as the eye by the likeness of colour. Therefore, if the intellect of one who sees the divine essence understands any creatures in God, it must be informed by their likenesses.

Obj. 2. Further, what we have seen, we keep in memory. But Paul, seeing the essence of God whilst in ecstasy, when he had ceased to see the divine essence, as Augustine says (*Gen. ad lit.* xii, 28, 34),[2] remembered many of the things he had seen in the rapture; hence he said: I have *heard secret words which it is not granted to man to utter* (II Cor. 12. 4). Therefore it must be said that certain likenesses of what he remembered remained in his mind; and in the same way, when he actually saw the essence of God he had certain likenesses or species of what he actually saw in it.

On the contrary, A mirror and what is in it are seen by means of one species. But all things are seen in God as in an intelligible mirror. Therefore, if God Himself is not seen by any likeness but by His own essence, neither are the things seen in Him seen by any likenesses or species.

I answer that, Those who see the divine essence see what they see in God not by any species, but by the divine essence itself united to their intellect. For each thing is known in so far as its likeness is in the one who knows. Now this takes place in two ways. For since things which are like one and the same thing are like each other, the knowing power can be assimilated to any knowable object in two ways. In one way it is assimilated by the object itself, when it is directly informed by its likeness, and then the object is known in itself. In another way when informed by a species which resembles the object; and in this way the knowledge is not of the thing in itself, but of the thing in its likeness. For the knowledge of a man in himself differs from the knowledge of him in his image. Hence to know things thus by their likeness in the one who knows is to know them in themselves or in their own nature; but to know them by their likenesses pre-existing in God is to see them in God. Now there is a difference between these two kinds of knowledge. Hence, according to the knowledge by which things are known by those who see the essence of God, they are seen in God Himself not by any other likenesses but by the divine essence alone present to the intellect, by which also God Himself is seen.

---

[1] *Confessions,* v, 7 (PL 32, 708).

[2] PL 34, 478, 483; *Epist.* CXLVII, 13 (PL 33, 611).

Reply Obj. 1. The created intellect of one who sees God is assimilated to the things that are seen in God in so far as it is united to the divine essence, in which the likenesses of all things pre-exist.

Reply Obj. 2. Some of the knowing powers can form other species from those first conceived; thus the imagination from the preconceived species of a mountain and of gold can form the species of a golden mountain; and the intellect, from the preconceived species of genus and difference forms the notion of species: in like manner from the likeness of an image we can form in ourselves the likeness of the original of the image. Thus Paul, or any other person who sees God, by the very vision of the divine essence can form in himself the likenesses of the things that are seen in the divine essence, which remained in Paul even when he had ceased to see the essence of God. Still this kind of vision whereby things are seen by this species conceived in this way is not the same as that by which things are seen in God.

ARTICLE 10. *Whether Those Who See the Essence of God See All They See In It at the Same Time?*

We proceed thus to the Tenth Article: It seems that those who see the essence of God do not see all they see in Him at one and the same time.

Objection 1. For, according to the Philosopher:[1] "It may happen that many things are known, but only one is understood." But what is seen in God, is understood, for God is seen by the intellect. Therefore those who see God do not see all in Him at the same time.

Obj. 2. Further, Augustine says (*Gen. ad lit.* viii, 22, 23),[2] "God moves the spiritual creature according to time"—that is, by understanding and affection. But the spiritual creature is the angel, who sees God. Therefore those who see God understand and are affected successively, for time means succession.

On the contrary, Augustine says (*De Trin.* xv, 16):[3] "Our thoughts will not be unstable, going to and fro from one thing to another, but we shall see all we know all at once in one glance."

I answer that, What is seen in the Word is seen not successively but at the same time. In proof of this we must consider that we ourselves cannot know many things all at once, since we understand many things by various species.

But our intellect cannot be actually informed by diverse species at the same time, so as to understand by them, just as one body cannot bear different shapes simultaneously. Hence, when many things can be understood by one species, they are understood at the same time; as the parts of a whole are understood successively, and not all at the same time, if each one is understood by its own species; but if all are understood under the one species of the whole, they are understood simultaneously. Now it was shown above (A. 9) that things seen in God are not seen singly by their own likenesses, but all are seen by the one essence of God. Hence they are seen simultaneously and not successively.

Reply Obj. 1. We understand one thing only when we understand by one species; but many things understood by one species are understood simultaneously, as in the species of man we understand animal and rational, and in the species of house we understand the wall and the roof.

Reply Obj. 2. As regards their natural knowledge, by which they know things by various species infused in them, the angels do not know all things simultaneously, and thus they are moved, in understanding, according to time; but according as they see things in God, they see all at the same time.

ARTICLE 11. *Whether Anyone in This Life Can See the Essence of God?*

We proceed thus to the Eleventh Article: It seems that one can in this life see the divine essence.

Objection 1. For Jacob said: *I have seen God face to face* (Gen. 32. 30). But to see Him face to face is to see His essence, as appears from the words: *We see now in a glass and in a dark manner, but then face to face* (I Cor. 13. 12). Therefore God can be seen in this life in His essence.

Obj. 2. Further, the Lord said of Moses: *I speak to him mouth to mouth, and plainly, and not by riddles and figures doth he see the Lord* (Num. 12. 8); but this is to see God in His essence. Therefore it is possible to see the essence of God in this life.

Obj. 3. Further, that in which we know all other things, and by which we judge of other things is known in itself to us. But even now we know all things in God, for Augustine says:[4] "If we both see that what you say is true, and we both see that what I say is true; where, I

---

[1] *Topics*, II, 10 (114ᵇ34).
[2] PL 34, 388, 389.   [3] PL 42, 1079.

[4] *Confessions*, XII, 35 (PL 32, 840).

ask, do we see this? neither I in thee, nor thou in me; but both of us in the very incommutable truth itself above our minds." He also says (*De Vera Relig.* xxx)[1] that we judge of all things according to the divine truth; and (*De Trin.* xii)[2] that, "it is the duty of reason to judge of these corporeal things according to the incorporeal and eternal types, which unless they were above the mind, could not be truly unchangeable." Therefore even in this life we see God Himself.

Obj. 4. Further, according to Augustine(*Gen. ad lit.* xii, 24, 25),[3] those things that are in the soul by their essence are seen by intellectual vision. But intellectual vision is of intelligible things, not by likenesses, but by their very essences, as he also says (*ibid.*). Therefore, since God is in our soul by His essence, it follows that He is seen by us in His essence.

On the contrary, It is written, *Man shall not see Me, and live* (Exod. 33. 20), and a gloss upon this says:[4] "In this mortal life God can be seen by certain images, but not by the species itself of His own nature."

I answer that, God cannot be seen in His essence by a mere human being, unless he be separated from this mortal life. The reason is, because, as was said above (A. 4), the mode of knowledge follows the mode of the nature of the knowing thing. But our soul, as long as we live in this life, has its being in corporeal matter; hence naturally it knows only what has a form in matter, or what can be known in this way. Now it is evident that the divine essence cannot be known through the natures of material things. For it was shown above (AA. 2, 9) that the knowledge of God by means of any created likeness is not the vision of His essence. Hence it is impossible for the soul of man in this life to see the essence of God. This can be seen in the fact that the more our soul is abstracted from corporeal things, the more it is capable of receiving abstract intelligible things. Hence in dreams and withdrawals from the bodily senses divine revelations and foresight of future events are perceived the more clearly. It is not possible, therefore, that the soul in this mortal life should be raised up to the uttermost of intelligible things, that is, to the divine essence.

Reply Obj. 1. According to Dionysius (*Cæl. Hier.* iv),[5] "a man is said in the Scriptures to see God in the sense that certain figures are formed in the senses or imagination, according to some likeness representing in part the divinity." So when Jacob says, *I have seen God face to face,* this does not mean the divine essence, but some figure representing God. And this is to be referred to some high mode of prophecy, so that God seems to speak, though in an imaginary vision, as will later be explained (Part II-II., Q. CLXXIV, A. 3) in treating of the degrees of prophecy. We may also say that Jacob spoke thus to designate some exalted intellectual contemplation, above the ordinary state.

Reply Obj. 2. As God works miracles in corporeal things, so also He does supernatural wonders above the common order, raising the minds of some living in the flesh beyond the use of sense, even up to the vision of His own essence, as Augustine says (*Gen. ad lit.* xii, 26, 27, 28)[6] of Moses, the teacher of the Jews,[7] and of Paul, the teacher of the Gentiles. This will be treated more fully in the question of ecstasy (Part II-II., Q. CLXXV, AA. 3, 4, 5, 6).

Reply Obj. 3. All things are said to be seen in God, and all things are judged in Him, because by the participation of His light we know and judge all things; for the light of natural reason itself is a participation of the divine light, as likewise we are said to see and judge of sensible things in the sun, that is, by the sun's light. Hence Augustine says (*Soliloq.* i, 8),[8] "The lessons of instruction can only be seen as it were by their own sun," namely God. As therefore in order to see something sensibly it is not necessary to see the substance of the sun, so in like manner to see something intelligibly it is not necessary to see the essence of God.

Reply Obj. 4. Intellectual vision is of the things which are in the soul by their essence, as intelligible things are in the intellect. And thus God is in the souls of the blessed; not in this way is He in our soul, but by presence, essence, and power.

ARTICLE 12. *Whether We Can Know God in This Life by Natural Reason?*

We proceed thus to the Twelfth Article: It seems that by natural reason we cannot know God in this life.

Objection 1. For Boëthius says (*De Consol.* v)[9] that "reason does not grasp simple form." But God is a supremely simple form, as was

---

[1] PL 34, 146; Chap. 31 (PL 34, 147).
[2] Chap. 2 (PL 42, 999).
[3] PL 34, 474; Chap. 31 (PL 34, 479).
[4] *Glossa ordin.* (I. 203B).   [5] Sect. 3 (PG 3, 180).

[6] PL 34, 476–478.
[7] Letter CXLVII, chap. 13 (PL 33, 610).
[8] PL 32, 877.
[9] Sect. 4 (PL 63, 847).

shown above (Q. III. A. 7). Therefore natural reason cannot attain to know Him.

Obj. 2. Further, the soul understands nothing by natural reason without phantasms as is said in the book on the *Soul*.[1] But there cannot be a phantasm of God in us, since He is incorporeal. Therefore we cannot know God by natural knowledge.

Obj. 3. Further, the knowledge of natural reason belongs to both good and evil, since they have a common nature. But the knowledge of God belongs only to the good; for Augustine says (*De Trin.* i)[2] "This weak eye of the human mind is not fixed on that excellent light unless purified by the justice of faith." Therefore God cannot be known by natural reason.

On the contrary, It is written (Rom. 1. 19), *That which is known of God,* namely, what can be known of God by natural reason, *is manifest in them.*

I answer that, Our natural knowledge takes its beginning from sense. Hence our natural knowledge can go as far as it can be led by sensible things. But our mind cannot be led by sense so far as to see the essence of God, because the sensible effects of God do not equal the power of God as their cause. Hence from the knowledge of sensible things the whole power of God cannot be known; nor therefore can His essence be seen. But because they are His effects and depend on their cause, we can be led from them so far as to know of God whether He exists, and to know of Him what must necessarily belong to Him as the first cause of all things, exceeding all things caused by Him.

Hence we know of His relationship with creatures that He is the cause of them all; also that creatures differ from Him, since He is not in any way part of what is caused by Him; and that creatures are not removed from Him by reason of any defect on His part, but because He superexceeds them all.

Reply Obj. 1. Reason cannot reach up to simple form so as to know what it is; but it can know whether it is.

Reply Obj. 2. God is known by natural knowledge through the phantasms of His effects.

Reply Obj. 3. As the knowledge of God's essence is by grace, it belongs only to the good; but the knowledge of Him by natural reason can belong to both good and bad; and hence Augustine says (*Retract.* i),[3] retracting what he had said before:[4] "I do not approve what I said in prayer, 'God who willest that only the pure should know truth.' For it can be answered that many who are not pure can know many truths," that is, by natural reason.

ARTICLE 13. *Whether By Grace a Higher Knowledge of God Can Be Obtained Than by Natural Reason?*

We proceed thus to the Thirteenth Article: It seems that by grace a higher knowledge of God is not obtained than by natural reason.

Objection 1. For Dionysius says (*De Mystica Theol.* i),[5] that whoever is the more united to God in this life is united to Him as to one entirely unknown. He says the same of Moses, who nevertheless obtained a certain excellence by the knowledge conferred by grace. But to be united to God while not knowing of Him "what He is," comes about also by natural reason. Therefore God is not more known to us by grace than by natural reason.

Obj. 2. Further, we can acquire the knowledge of divine things by natural reason only through phantasms, and the same applies to the knowledge given by grace. For Dionysius says (*Cæl. Hier.* i)[6] that "it is impossible for the divine ray to shine upon us except as screened round about by the many coloured sacred veils." Therefore we cannot know God more fully by grace than by natural reason.

Obj. 3. Further, our intellect adheres to God by the grace of faith. But faith does not seem to be knowledge; for Gregory says (*Homil.* xxvi, *in Ev.*)[7] that "things not seen are of faith, and not of knowledge." Therefore there is not given to us a more excellent knowledge of God by grace.

On the contrary, The Apostle says that *God hath revealed to us by His Spirit,* what *none of the princes of this world knew* (I Cor. 2. 10), namely, the philosophers, as the gloss expounds.[8]

I answer that, We have a more perfect knowledge of God by grace than by natural reason. Which appears thus. The knowledge which we have by natural reason requires two things: phantasms received from the sensible objects, and the natural intelligible light, by whose power we abstract from them intelligible concepts.

Now in both of these human knowledge is assisted by the revelation of grace. For the intel-

---

[1] Aristotle, III, 7 (431ª16).
[2] Chap. 2 (PL 42, 822).　　[3] I, 4 (PL 32, 589).
[4] *Solil.*, I, 1 (PL 32, 870).
[5] Sect. 3 (PG 3, 1001).　　[6] Sect. 2 (PG 3, 121).
[7] Bk. II (PL 76, 1202).　　[8] *Glossa interl.*, (VI, 36r).

lect's natural light is strengthened by the infusion of gratuitous light. And sometimes also the phantasms in the human imagination are divinely formed, so as to express divine things better than those do which we receive from sensible things, as appears in prophetic visions; while sometimes sensible things, or even voices, are divinely formed to express some thing divine, as in the Baptism, the Holy Ghost was seen in the shape of a dove, and the voice of the Father was heard, *This is My beloved Son* (Matt. 3. 17).

Reply Obj. 1. Although by the revelation of grace in this life we cannot know of God "what He is," and thus are united to Him as to one unknown, still we know Him more fully according as many and more excellent of His effects are demonstrated to us, and according as we attribute to Him some things known by divine revelation, to which natural reason cannot reach, as, for instance, that God is Three and One.

Reply Obj. 2. From the phantasms either received from sense in the natural order, or divinely formed in the imagination, we have so much the more excellent intellectual knowledge, the stronger the intelligible light is in man; and thus through the revelation given by the phantasms a fuller knowledge is received by the infusion of the divine light.

Reply Obj. 3. Faith is a kind of knowledge, in so far as the intellect is determined by faith to some knowable object. But this determination to one thing does not proceed from the vision of the believer, but from the vision of Him who is believed. Thus, as far as faith falls short of vision, it falls short of the knowledge which belongs to science, for science determines the intellect to one thing by the vision and understanding of first principles.

QUESTION XIII
THE NAMES OF GOD
(*In Twelve Articles*)

AFTER the consideration of those things which belong to the divine knowledge, we now proceed to the consideration of the divine names. For everything is named by us according to our knowledge of it.

Under this head, there are twelve points for inquiry. (1) Whether God can be named by us? (2) Whether any names applied to God are predicated of Him substantially? (3) Whether any names applied to God are said of Him literally, or are all to be taken metaphorically? (4)

Whether many names applied to God are synonymous? (5) Whether some names are applied to God and to creatures univocally or equivocally? (6) Whether, supposing they are applied analogically, they are applied first to God or to creatures? (7) Whether any names are applicable to God from time? (8) Whether this name "God" is a name of nature, or of the operation? (9) Whether this name "God" is a communicable name? (10) Whether it is taken univocally or equivocally as signifying God by nature, by participation, and by opinion? (11) Whether this name, "Who is," is the supremely appropriate name of God? (12) Whether affirmative propositions can be formed about God?

ARTICLE 1. *Whether Any Name Is Suitable to God?*

We proceed thus to the First Article: It seems that no name is suitable to God.

Objection 1. For Dionysius says (*Div. Nom.* i)[1] that, "Of Him there is neither name, nor can one be found of Him"; and it is written: *What is His name, and what is the name of His Son, if thou knowest?* (Prov. 30. 4).

Obj. 2. Further, every name is either abstract or concrete. But concrete names do not belong to God, since He is simple, nor do abstract names belong to Him, since they do not signify any perfect subsisting thing. Therefore no name can be said of God.

Obj. 3. Further, nouns are taken to signify substance with quality; verbs and participles signify substance with time; pronouns the same with demonstration or relation. But none of these can be applied to God, for He has no quality, nor accident, nor time; moreover, He cannot be felt, so as to be pointed out; nor can He be described by relation, since relations serve to recall a thing mentioned before by nouns, participles, or demonstrative pronouns. Therefore God cannot in any way be named by us.

On the contrary, It is written (Exod. 15. 3): *The Lord is a man of war, Almighty is His name.*

I answer that, Since according to the Philosopher,[2] words are signs of ideas, and ideas the likeness of things, it is evident that words relate to the meaning of things signified through the medium of the intellectual conception. It follows therefore that we can give a name to anything in as far as it can be known by our intellect. Now it was shown above (Q. XII, AA.

[1] Sect. 5 (PG 3, 593).
[2] *Interpretation,* 1 (16ᵃ3).

11, 12) that in this life we cannot see the essence of God; but we know God from creatures as their principle, and also by way of excellence and remotion. In this way therefore He can be named by us from creatures, yet not so that the name which signifies Him expresses the divine essence in itself, as for instance the name "man" expresses by its meaning the essence of man in himself, since it signifies the definition of man by declaring his essence. For the notion expressed by the name is the definition.

Reply Obj. 1. The reason why God has no name, or is said to be above being named, is because His essence is above all that we understand about God and signify in word.

Reply Obj. 2. Because we know and name God from creatures, the names we attribute to God signify what belongs to material creatures, of which the knowledge is natural to us as we have said before (Q. XII, A. 4). And because in creatures of this kind what is perfect and subsistent is composite, whereas their form is not a complete subsisting thing, but rather is that whereby a thing is, hence it follows that all names used by us to signify a complete subsisting thing must have a concrete meaning according as they belong to composite things. But names given to signify simple forms signify a thing not as subsisting, but as that by which a thing is; as, for instance, whiteness signifies that by which a thing is white. And as God is simple, and subsisting, we attribute to Him abstract names to signify His simplicity, and concrete names to signify His subsistence and perfection, although both these kinds of names fail to express His mode of being, since our intellect does not know Him in this life as He is.

Reply Obj. 3. To signify substance with quality is to signify the suppositum with a nature or determined form in which it subsists. Hence, as some things are said of God in a concrete sense to signify His subsistence and perfection, so likewise nouns are applied to God signifying substance with quality. Further, verbs and participles which signify time are applied to Him because His eternity includes all time. For just as we can apprehend and signify simple subsistences only by way of composite things, so we can understand and express simple eternity only by way of temporal things, because our intellect has a natural affinity to composite and temporal things. But demonstrative pronouns are applied to God as pointing out what is understood, not what is sensed. For we can only describe Him as far as we understand Him. Thus, according as nouns, participles and demonstrative pronouns are applicable to God, so far can He be signified by relative pronouns.

ARTICLE 2. *Whether Any Name Can Be Applied to God Substantially?*

We proceed thus to the Second Article: It seems that no name can be applied to God substantially.

Objection 1. For Damascene says (*De Fid. Orth.* i, 9):[1] "Everything said of God signifies not His substance, but rather shows forth what He is not; or expresses some relation, or something following from His nature or operation."

Obj. 2. Further, Dionysius says (*Div. Nom.* i)[2]: "You will find a chorus of all the holy doctors addressed to the end of distinguishing clearly and praiseworthily the divine processions in the denominations of God." Thus the names applied by the holy doctors in praising God are distinguished according to the divine processions themselves. But what expresses the procession of anything does not signify anything pertaining to its essence. Therefore the names applied to God are not said of Him substantially.

Obj. 3. Further, a thing is named by us according as we understand it. But God is not understood by us in this life in His substance. Therefore neither is any name we can use applied substantially to God.

On the contrary, Augustine says (*De Trin.* vi)[3]: "The being of God is the being strong, or the being wise, or whatever else we may say of that simplicity whereby His substance is signified." Therefore all names of this kind signify the divine substance.

I answer that, Negative names applied to God or signifying His relation to creatures manifestly do not at all signify His substance, but rather express the distance of the creature from Him, or His relation to something else, or rather, the relation of creatures to Himself.

But as regards absolute and affirmative names of God, such as good, wise, and the like, various and many opinions have been given. For some have said that all such names, although they are applied to God affirmatively, nevertheless have been brought into use more to express some remotion from God rather than to place anything in Him. Hence they assert that when we say that God lives, we mean that God is not like an inanimate thing, and the same in like manner applies to other names;

---

[1] PG 94, 833.
[2] Sect. 4 (PG 3, 589).
[3] Chap. 4 (PL 42, 927).

and this was taught by Rabbi Moses.[1] Others[2] say that these names applied to God signify His relationship towards creatures; thus in the words, "God is good," we mean, God is the cause of goodness in things; and the same rule applies to other names.

Both of these opinions, however, seem to be untrue for three reasons. First because in neither of them can a reason be assigned why some names more than others are applied to God. For He is assuredly the cause of bodies in the same way as He is the cause of good things; therefore if the words "God is good," signified no more than, "God is the cause of good things," it might in like manner be said that God is a body, since He is the cause of bodies. So also to say that He is a body, takes away the notion that He is being in potency only as is prime matter. Secondly, because it would follow that all names applied to God would be said of Him by way of being taken in a secondary sense, as healthy is secondarily said of medicine, because it signifies only the cause of health in the animal which primarily is called healthy. Thirdly, because this is against the intention of those who speak of God. For in saying that God lives, they assuredly mean more than to say that He is the cause of our life, or that He differs from inanimate bodies.

Therefore we must hold a different doctrine —namely, that these names signify the divine substance and are predicated substantially of God, although they fall short of a full representation of Him. Which is proved thus. For these names express God so far as our intellects know Him. Now since our intellect knows God from creatures, it knows Him as far as creatures represent Him. Now it was shown above (Q. IV, A. 2) that God possesses beforehand in Himself all the perfections of creatures, being Himself absolutely and universally perfect. Hence every creature represents Him, and is like Him so far as it possesses some perfection; yet it represents Him not as something of the same species or genus, but as the excelling principle of whose form the effects fall short, although they derive some kind of likeness to it, even as the forms of inferior bodies represent the power of the sun. This was explained above (Q. IV, A. 3), in treating of the divine perfection. Therefore these names signify the divine substance, but in an imperfect manner, even as creatures represent it imperfectly.

[1] *Guide*, I, 58 (FR 82).
[2] Alan of Lille, *Theol. Reg.*, REG. 21, 26 (PL 210, 631, 633).

So when we say, "God is good," the meaning is not, "God is the cause of goodness," or "God is not evil," but the meaning is, "Whatever good we attribute to creatures pre-exists in God," and in a higher way. Hence it does not follow that God is good because He causes goodness, but rather, on the contrary, He pours out goodness in things because He is good, according to what Augustine says,[3] "Because He is good, we are."

Reply Obj. 1. Damascene says that these names do not signify what God is, since by none of these names is perfectly expressed what He is, but each one signifies Him in an imperfect manner, even as creatures represent Him imperfectly.

Reply Obj. 2. In the signification of names, that from which the name is derived is different sometimes from what it is intended to signify, as for instance this name "stone" (*lapis*) is imposed from the fact that it hurts the foot (*lædit pedem*); but it is not imposed to signify that which hurts the foot, but rather to signify a certain kind of body; otherwise everything that hurts the foot would be a stone. So we must say that these kinds of divine names are imposed from the divine processions; for as according to the diverse processions of their perfections, creatures are the representations of God, although in an imperfect manner, so likewise our intellect knows and names God according to each kind of procession. But nevertheless these names are not imposed to signify the processions themselves, as if when we say "God lives," the senses were, "life proceeds from Him," but to signify the principle itself of things, in so far as life pre-exists in Him, although it pre-exists in Him in a more eminent way than can be understood or signified.

Reply Obj. 3. We cannot know the essence of God in this life, as He really is in Himself; but we know Him according as He is represented in the perfections of creatures; and thus the names imposed by us signify Him in that manner only.

ARTICLE 3. *Whether Any Name Can Be Applied to God Properly?*

We proceed thus to the Third Article: It seems that no name is applied properly to God.

Objection 1. For all names which we apply to God are taken from creatures, as was explained above (A. 1). But the names of creatures are applied to God metaphorically, as when we say, God is a stone, or a lion, or the like. Therefore

[3] *Christian Doctrine*, I, 32 (PL 34, 32).

names are applied to God in a metaphorical sense.

Obj. 2. Further, no name can be applied literally to anything if it should be withheld from it rather than given to it. But all such names as good, wise, and the like, are more truly withheld from God than given to Him, as appears from what Dionysius says (*Cæl. Hier.* ii).[1] Therefore none of these names belong to God in their proper sense.

Obj. 3. Further, corporeal names are applied to God in a metaphorical sense only, since He is incorporeal. But all such names imply some kind of corporeal condition, for their meaning is bound up with time and composition and like corporeal conditions. Therefore all these names are applied to God in a metaphorical sense.

On the contrary, Ambrose says (*De Fide,* ii),[2] "Some names there are which express evidently the property of the divinity, and some which express the clear truth of the divine majesty, but others there are which are applied to God figuratively by way of similitude." Therefore not all names are applied to God in a metaphorical sense, but there are some which are said of Him in their proper sense.

I answer that, According to the preceding article, our knowledge of God is derived from the perfections which flow from Him to creatures, which perfections are in God in a more eminent way than in creatures. Now our intellect apprehends them as they are in creatures, and as it apprehends them it signifies them by names. Therefore as to the names applied to God, there are two things to be considered—namely, the perfections which they signify, such as goodness, life, and the like, and their mode of signification. As regards what is signified by these names, they belong properly to God, and more properly than they belong to creatures, and are applied primarily to Him. But as regards their mode of signification, they do not properly and strictly apply to God, for their mode of signification applies to creatures.

Reply Obj. 1. There are some names which signify these perfections flowing from God to creatures in such a way that the imperfect way in which creatures receive the divine perfection is part of the very signification of the name itself, as *stone* signifies a material being, and names of this kind can be applied to God only in a metaphorical sense. Other names, however, express these perfections absolutely, without any such mode of participation being part of their signification, as the words *being, good, living,* and the like, and such names can be properly applied to God.

Reply Obj. 2. Such names as these, as Dionysius shows, are denied of God for the reason that what the name signifies does not belong to Him in the ordinary sense of its signification, but in a more eminent way. Hence Dionysius says also that God is "above all substance and all life."

Reply Obj. 3. These names which are applied to God properly imply corporeal conditions not in the thing signified, but as regards their mode of signification; but those which are applied to God metaphorically imply and mean a corporeal condition in the thing signified.

ARTICLE 4. *Whether Names Applied to God Are Synonymous?*

We proceed thus to the Fourth Article: It seems that these names applied to God are synonymous names.

Objection 1. For synonymous names are those which mean exactly the same. But these names applied to God mean entirely the same thing in God; for the goodness of God is His essence, and likewise it is His wisdom. Therefore these names are entirely synonymous.

Obj. 2. Further, if it be said these names signify one and the same thing in reality, but differ in idea, it can be objected that an idea to which no reality corresponds is an empty idea. Therefore if these ideas are many, and the thing is one, it seems also that these ideas are ideas to no purpose.

Obj. 3. Further, a thing which is one in reality and in idea, is more one than what is one in reality and many in idea. But God is supremely one. Therefore it seems that He is not one in reality and many in idea, and thus the names applied to God do not signify different ideas; and thus they are synonymous.

On the contrary, All synonyms united with each other are redundant, as when we say,"vesture clothing." Therefore if all names applied to God are synonymous, we cannot properly say "good God," or the like, and yet it is written, *O most mighty, great and powerful, the Lord of hosts is Thy name* (Jer. 32. 18).

I answer that, These names spoken of God are not synonymous. This would be easy to understand if we said that these names are used to remove or to express the relation of cause to creatures; for thus it would follow that there are different ideas as regards the diverse things denied of God, or as regards diverse effects connoted. But even according to what was said

---

[1] Sect. 3 (PG 3, 141).   [2] Prologue (PL 16, 583).

above (A. 2), that these names signify the divine substance, although in an imperfect manner, it is also clear from what has been said (AA. 1, 2) that they have diverse meanings. For the notion signified by the name is the conception in the intellect of the thing signified by the name. But our intellect, since it knows God from creatures, in order to understand God, forms conceptions proportional to the perfections flowing from God to creatures, which perfections pre-exist in God unitedly and simply, while in creatures they are received divided and multiplied. As, therefore, to the different perfections of creatures there corresponds one simple principle represented by different perfections of creatures in a various and manifold manner, so also to the various and multiplied conceptions of our intellect there corresponds one altogether simple principle, according to these conceptions. Therefore, although the names applied to God signify one thing, still because they signify that thing under many and different aspects they are not synonymous.

Thus appears the solution of the *First Objection,* since synonymous terms signify one thing under one aspect; for words which signify different aspects of one thing, do not signify primarily and absolutely one thing, because the term only signifies the thing through the medium of the intellectual conception, as was said above.

Reply Obj. 2. The many aspects of these names are not empty and worthless, for there corresponds to all of them one simple reality represented by them in a manifold and imperfect manner.

Reply Obj. 3. The perfect unity of God requires that what are manifold and divided in others should exist in Him simply and unitedly. Thus it comes about that He is one in reality, and yet many in idea, because our intellect apprehends Him in a manifold manner, just as things represent Him in a manifold way.

ARTICLE. 5. *Whether What Is Said of God and of Creatures Is Univocally Predicated of Them?*

We proceed thus to the Fifth Article: It seems that what is said of God and creatures is said of them univocally.

Objection 1. For every equivocal term is reduced to the univocal, as many are reduced to one; for if the name dog be said equivocally of the barking dog, and of the dogfish, it must be said of some univocally—namely, of all barking dogs; otherwise we proceed to infinity. Now there are some univocal agents which agree with

their effects in name and definition, as man generates man; and there are some agents which are equivocal, as the sun which causes heat, although the sun is hot only in an equivocal sense. Therefore it seems that the first agent to which all other agents are reduced is an univocal agent; and thus what is said of God and creatures is predicated univocally.

Obj. 2. Further, there is no likeness among equivocal things. Therefore as creatures have a certain likeness to God, according to the word of Genesis (1. 26), *Let us make man to our image and likeness,* it seems that something can be said of God and creatures univocally.

Obj. 3. Further, "measure is homogeneous" with the thing measured as is said in the *Metaphysics.*[1] But God is the first measure of all beings, as it says in the same place. Therefore God is homogeneous with creatures, and thus a word may be applied univocally to God and to creatures.

On the contrary, Whatever is predicated of various things under the same name but not in the same meaning is predicated equivocally. But no name belongs to God in the same meaning that it belongs to creatures; for instance, wisdom in creatures is a quality, but not in God. Now a different genus changes a nature, since the genus is part of the definition; and the same applies to other things. Therefore whatever is said of God and of creatures is predicated equivocally.

2. *Further,* God is more distant from creatures than any creatures are from each other. But the distance of some creatures makes any univocal predication of them impossible, as in the case of those things which are not in the same genus. Therefore much less can anything be predicated univocally of God and creatures. And so only equivocal predication can be applied to them.

I answer that, Univocal predication is impossible between God and creatures. The reason of this is that every effect which is not an adequate result of the power of the efficient cause receives the likeness of the agent not in its full degree, but in a measure that falls short, so that what is divided and multiplied in the effects resides in the agent simply, and in the same manner; as for example the sun by the exercise of its one power produces manifold and various forms in all inferior things. In the same way, as said in the preceding article, all perfections of things which exist in creatures divided and multiplied pre-exist in God unitedly. Thus, when

---

[1] Aristotle, x, 1 (1053ᵃ24).

any term expressing perfection is applied to a creature, it signifies that perfection distinct in idea from other perfections; as, for instance, by this term *wise* applied to a man, we signify some perfection distinct from a man's essence, and distinct from his power and being, and from all similar things; but when we apply it to God, we do not mean to signify anything distinct from His essence, or power, or being. Thus also this term *wise* applied to man in some degree circumscribes and comprehends the thing signified; but this is not the case when it is applied to God, but it leaves the thing signified as incomprehended, and as exceeding the signification of the name. Hence it is evident that this term *wise* is not applied in the same aspect to God and to man. The same applies to other terms. Hence no name is predicated univocally of God and of creatures.

Neither, on the other hand, are names applied to God and creatures in a purely equivocal sense, as some have said.[1] Because if that were so, it follows that from creatures nothing could be known or demonstrated about God at all, for the reasoning would always fall into the fallacy of equivocation. Such a view is as much against philosophy which proves many things about God as it is against what the Apostle says: *The invisible things of God are clearly seen being understood by the things that are made* (Rom. 1. 20).

Therefore it must be said that these names are said of God and creatures according to analogy, that is, according to proportion. Now names are thus used in two ways: either according as many things are proportionate to one, as for example *healthy* is predicated of medicine and urine in so far as each has an order and proportion to the health of the animal, of which the latter is the sign and the former the cause, or according as one thing is proportionate to another; thus *healthy* is said of medicine and animal, since medicine is the cause of health in the animal. And in this way some things are said of God and creatures analogically, and not in a purely equivocal nor in a purely univocal sense. For we can name God only from creatures (A. 1). Thus, whatever is said of God and creatures, is said according to the relation of a creature to God as its principle and cause, wherein all perfections of things pre-exist excellently.

Now this mode of community is a mean between pure equivocation and simple univocation. For in those things which are spoken of

analogically neither is there one notion, as there is in univocal things, nor totally diverse notions as in equivocal things; but a term which is thus used in a multiple sense signifies different proportions to some one thing; thus *healthy* applied to urine signifies the sign of animal health, and applied to medicine signifies the cause of the same health.

Reply Obj. 1. Although in predication the equivocal must be reduced to the univocal, still in actions the non-univocal agent must precede the univocal agent. For the non-univocal agent is the universal cause of the whole species, as for instance the sun is the cause of the generation of all men. But the univocal agent is not the universal efficient cause of the whole species (otherwise it would be the cause of itself, since it is contained in the species), but is a particular cause of this individual which it places under the species by way of participation. Therefore the universal cause of the whole species is not an univocal agent, and the universal cause comes before the particular cause. But this universal agent while it is not univocal, nevertheless is not altogether equivocal, otherwise it could not produce its own likeness; but it can be called an analogical agent, just as in predications all univocal terms are reduced to one first non-univocal analogical term, which is being.

Reply Obj. 2. The likeness of the creature to God is imperfect, for it does not represent one and the same generic thing (Q. IV, A. 3).

Reply Obj. 3. God is not the measure proportioned to things measured; hence it is not necessary that God and creatures should be in the same genus.

The arguments adduced *in the contrary,* prove indeed that these names are not predicated univocally of God and creatures, yet they do not prove that they are predicated equivocally.

ARTICLE 6. *Whether Names Are Predicated Primarily of Creatures Rather Than of God?*

We proceed thus to the Sixth Article: It seems that names are predicated primarily of creatures rather than of God.

Objection 1. For we name anything accordingly as we know it, since names, as the Philosopher says,[2] are signs of ideas. But we know creatures before we know God. Therefore the names imposed by us are predicated primarily of creatures rather than of God.

Obj. 2. Further, Dionysius says (*Div. Nom.* i)[3] that we name God from creatures. But

---

[1] Maimonides, *Guide,* I, 59 (FR 84); Averroes, *In Meta.,* XII, comm. 51 (VIII, 337B).

[2] *Interpretation,* 1 (16ª3).   [3] Sect. 6 (PG 3, 596).

names transferred from creatures to God are said primarily of creatures rather than of God, as lion, stone, and the like. Therefore all names applied to God and creatures are applied primarily to creatures rather than to God.

Obj. 3. Further, all names applied in common to God and creatures, "are applied to God as the cause of all things," as Dionysius says (*De Myst. Theol.*).[1] But what is said of anything through its cause is applied to it secondarily; for "healthy" is primarily said of animal rather than of medicine, which is the cause of health. Therefore these names are said primarily of creatures rather than of God.

On the contrary, It is written, *I bow my knees to the Father of our Lord Jesus Christ, of Whom all paternity in heaven and earth is named* (Eph. 3. 14, 15); and the same applies to the other names applied to God and creatures. Therefore these names are applied primarily to God rather than to creatures.

I answer that, In all names which are said of many in an analogical sense, they must all be said with reference to one thing, and therefore this one thing must be placed in the definition of them all. And since "the nature expressed by the name is the definition," as the Philosopher says,[2] such a name must be said primarily of that which is put in the definition of such other things, and secondarily to these others according to the order in which they approach more or less to that first. Thus, for instance, healthy applied to animals comes into the definition of healthy applied to medicine, which is called healthy as being the cause of health in the animal, and also into the definition of healthy which is applied to urine, which is called healthy in so far as it is the sign of the animal's health.

Thus, all names which are said metaphorically of God, are said of creatures primarily rather than of God, because when said of God they mean only likenesses to such creatures. For as smiling said of a field means only that the field in the beauty of its flowering is like to the beauty of the human smile according to the likeness of proportion, so the name of lion said of God means only that God manifests strength in His works, as a lion in his. Thus it is clear that as they are said of God the signification of names can be defined only from what is said of creatures.

But to other names not said of God in a metaphorical sense, the same rule would apply if they were spoken of God as the cause only, as

some have supposed.[3] For when it is said, "God is good," it would then only mean, "God is the cause of the creature's goodness"; thus the term good applied to God would include in its meaning the creature's goodness. Hence good would apply primarily to creatures rather than God. But as was shown above (A. 2), these names are applied to God not as the cause only, but also essentially. For the words, "God is good," or "wise," signify not only that He is the cause of wisdom or goodness, but that these pre-exist in Him in a more excellent way. Hence as regards the thing which the name signifies, these names are applied primarily to God rather than to creatures, because these perfections flow from God to creatures; but as regards the imposition of the names, they are primarily applied by us to creatures, which we know first. Hence they have a mode of signification which belongs to creatures, as said above (A. 3).

Reply Obj. 1. This objection refers to the imposition of the name.

Reply Obj. 2. The same rule does not apply to metaphorical and to other names, as said above.

Reply Obj. 3. This objection would be valid if these names were said of God only as cause, and not also essentially, for instance as healthy is applied to medicine.

ARTICLE 7. *Whether Names Which Imply Relation to Creatures Are Predicated of God Temporally?*

We proceed thus to the Seventh Article: It seems that names which imply relation to creatures are not predicated of God temporally.

Objection 1. For all such names signify the divine substance, as is universally held. Hence also Ambrose says (*De Fide,* i)[4] that "this name 'Lord' is a name of power," which is the divine substance; and Creation signifies the action of God, which is His essence. Now the divine substance is not temporal, but eternal. Therefore these names are not applied to God temporally, but eternally.

Obj. 2. Further, that to which something applies temporally can be described as made; for what is white temporally is made white. But to be made does not apply to God. Therefore nothing can be predicated of God temporally.

Obj. 3. Further, if any names are applied to God temporally as implying relation to creatures, the same rule holds good of all things that imply relation to creatures. But some

---

[1] 1, 2 (PG 3, 1000).
[2] *Metaphysics,* IV, 7 (1012ᵃ23).
[3] Alan of Lille, *Theol. Reg.,* reg. 21, 26 (PL 210, 631, 633).   [4] PL 16, 553.

names implying relation to creatures are spoken of God from eternity; for from eternity He knew and loved the creature, according to the word: *I have loved thee with an everlasting love* (Jer. 31. 3). Therefore also other names implying relation to creatures, such as Lord and Creator, are applied to God from eternity.

Obj. 4. Further, names of this kind signify relation. Therefore that relation must be something in God or in the creature only. But it cannot be that it is something in the creature only, for in that case God would be called "Lord" from the opposite relation which is in creatures; and nothing is named from its opposite. Therefore the relation must be something in God. But nothing temporal can be in God, for He is above time. Therefore these names are not said of God temporally.

Obj. 5. Further, a thing is called relative from relation; for instance lord from lordship, and as white from whiteness. Therefore if the relation of lordship is not really in God, but only in idea, it follows that God is not really Lord, which is plainly false.

Obj. 6. Further, in relative things which are not simultaneous in nature, one can exist without the other; as "a thing knowable can exist without the knowledge of it," as the Philosopher says.[1] But relative things which are said of God and creatures are not simultaneous in nature. Therefore a relation can be predicated of God to the creature even without the existence of the creature; and thus these names, "Lord" and "Creator," are said of God from eternity, and not temporally.

On the contrary, Augustine says (*De Trin.* v, 18),[2] that this relative appellation "Lord" belongs to God temporally.

I answer that, Certain names which import relation to creatures are said of God temporally, and not from eternity.

To see this we must learn that some have said[3] that relation is not a thing of nature, but of reason only. But this is plainly seen to be false from the very fact that things themselves have a natural order and relation to one another. Nevertheless it is necessary to know that since relation requires two extremes, it happens in three ways that a relation is real or logical. Sometimes from both extremes it is a thing of reason only, as when mutual order or relation can be between things only in the apprehension of reason; as when we say the same thing is

the same as itself. For reason apprehending one thing twice regards it as two; thus it apprehends a certain relation of the same thing to itself. And the same applies to relations between being and non-being which reason forms in so far as it apprehends, non-being as an extreme. The same is true of all relations that follow upon an act of reason, as genus and species, and the like.

Now there are other relations which are things of nature as regards both extremes, as when for instance a relation exists between two things according to some reality that belongs to both, as is clear of all relations consequent upon quantity, such as great and small, double and half, and the like; for quantity exists in both extremes. And the same applies to relations consequent upon action and passion, as moving power and the moveable thing, father and son, and the like.

Again, sometimes a relation in one extreme may be a thing of nature, while in the other extreme it is a thing of reason only; and this happens whenever two extremes are not of one order; as for example sense and science refer respectively to sensible things and to knowable things which, in so far as they are realities existing in nature, are outside the order of sensible and intelligible existence. Therefore in science and in sense a real relation exists, according as they are ordered to the knowing or to the sensing of things; but the things looked at in themselves are outside this order, and hence in them there is no real relation to science and sense, but according to reason only in so far as the intellect apprehends them as terms of the relations of science and sense. Hence, the Philosopher says[4] that they are called relative, not because they are related to other things, but because "others are related to them." Likewise for instance, "on the right" is not applied to a column unless it stands as regards an animal on the right side, which relation is not really in the column but in the animal.

Since therefore God is outside the whole order of creation, and all creatures are ordered to Him, and not conversely, it is manifest that creatures are really related to God Himself; in God however there is no real relation to creatures, but a relation according to reason only, in so far as creatures are referred to Him. Thus there is nothing to prevent these names which import relation to the creature from being predicated of God temporally, not by reason of any change in Him, but by reason of the change of the creature; as a column is on the right of an

---

[1] *Categories*, 7 (7ᵇ30).   [2] Chap. 16 (PL 42, 922).
[3] Unnamed in Averroes, *In Meta.*, XII, comm. 19 (VIII, 306B). Cf. also St. Thomas, *De Pot.*, Q. VIII, A. 2.

[4] *Metaphysics*, v, 15 (1021ᵃ29).

animal without change in itself, but by the shifting of the animal.

Reply Obj. 1. Some relative names are imposed to signify the relative relations themselves, as master and servant, father and son, and the like, and these are called relative according to being (*secundum esse*). But others are imposed to signify the things from which follow certain relations such as the mover and the thing moved, the head and the thing that has a head, and the like; and these are called relative according to appellation (*secundum dici*). Thus, there must be considered the same twofold difference in divine names. For some signify the relation itself to the creature, as "Lord," and these do not signify the divine substance directly, but indirectly, in so far as they presuppose the divine substance; as dominion presupposes power, which is the divine substance. Others signify the divine essence directly, and consequently the corresponding relations, as "Saviour," "Creator," and the like; and these signify the action of God, which is His essence. Yet both names are said of God temporally as to the relation they imply, either principally or consequently, but not as signifying the essence, either directly or indirectly.

Reply Obj. 2. As relations applied to God temporally are not in God except according to reason, so, to become, or to be made are not said of God except according to reason, with no change in Him, as for instance when we say, *Lord, Thou art become* [Douay, *hast been*] *our refuge* (Ps. 89. 1).

Reply Obj. 3. The operation of the intellect and will is in the operator, and therefore names signifying relations following upon the action of the intellect or will are applied to God from eternity; but those following upon the actions proceeding according to our mode of thinking to external effects are applied to God temporally, as "Saviour," "Creator," and the like.

Reply Obj. 4. Relations signified by these names which are said of God temporally are in God according to reason only, but the opposite relations in creatures are real. Nor is it incongruous that God should be denominated from relations really existing in the thing, yet so that the opposite relations in God should also be understood by us at the same time, in the sense that God is spoken of relatively to the creature, in so far as the creature is referred to Him; thus the Philosopher says[1] that the object is said to be knowable relatively because knowledge refers to it.

[1] *Metaphysics.* v. 15 (1021ᵃ30).

Reply Obj. 5. Since God is related to the creature for the reason that the creature is related to Him, and since the relation of subjection is real in the creature, it follows that God is Lord not according to reason only, but in reality; for He is called Lord according to the manner in which the creature is subject to Him.

Reply Obj. 6. To know whether relations are simultaneous by nature or otherwise, it is not necessary to consider the order of things to which they belong but the meaning of the relations themselves. For if one in its idea includes another, and *vice versa*, then they are simultaneous by nature; as for instance double and half, father and son, and the like. But if one in its idea includes another, and not *vice versa*, they are not simultaneous by nature. And this is the way science and the knowable thing are related; for the knowable thing is spoken of according to potency, and the science according to habit, or act. Hence the knowable thing in its mode of signification exists before science, but if the same thing is considered in act, then it is simultaneous with science in act; for the thing known is nothing unless it is known. Thus, though God is prior to the creature, still because the signification of Lord includes the idea of a servant and *vice versa*, these two relative terms, "Lord" and "servant," are simultaneous by nature. Hence God was not "Lord" until He had a creature subject to Himself.

ARTICLE 8. *Whether This Name God Is a Name of the Nature?*

We proceed thus to the Eighth Article: It seems that this name, God, is not a name of the nature.

Objection 1. For Damascene says (*De Fid. Orth.* i)[2] that "God (Θεός) is so called from θεεῖν which means to take care of, and to cherish all things; or from αἴθειν, that is, to burn, for our God is a consuming fire; or from θεᾶσθαι, which means to consider all things." But all these names belong to operation. Therefore this name God signifies His operation and not His nature.

Obj. 2. Further, a thing is named by us as we know it. But the divine nature is unknown to us. Therefore this name God does not signify the divine nature.

On the contrary, Ambrose says (*De Fide*, i)[3] that God is a name of a nature.

I answer that, That by which a name is imposed and what the name signifies are not always the same thing. For as we know the sub-

[2] Chap. 9 (PG 94. 835).　　　　[3] Chap. 1 (PL 16, 553).

stance of a thing from its properties and operations, so we name the substance of a thing sometimes from its operation, or its property; for
example, we name the substance of a stone from
its act, as for instance that it hurts the foot
(*lædit pedem*); but still this name is not meant
to signify the particular action, but the stone's
substance. The things, on the other hand, known
to us in themselves, such as heat, cold, whiteness, and the like, are not named from other
things. Hence as regards such things the meaning of the name and its source are the same.

Because therefore God is not known to us in
His nature, but is made known to us from His
operations or effects, we can name Him from
these, as said in A. 1. Hence this name God is a
name of operation so far as relates to the source
of its meaning. For this name is imposed from
His universal providence over all things, since
all who speak of God intend to name God as exercising providence over all; hence Dionysius
says (*Div. Nom.* xii),[1] "The Deity watches
over all with perfect providence and goodness."
But taken from this operation, this name God
is imposed to signify the divine nature.

Reply Obj. 1. All that Damascene says refers
to providence, which is the source of the signification of the name God.

Reply Obj. 2. We can name a thing according
to the knowledge we have of its nature from its
properties and effects. Hence because we can
know what the substance of stone is in itself
from its property, this name "stone" signifies the
nature of stone as it is in itself; for it signifies
the definition of stone, by which we know what
it is, for "the nature which the name signifies is
the definition," as is said in the *Metaphysics*.[2]
Now from the divine effects we cannot know
the divine nature as it is in itself, so as to know
what it is, but only by way of eminence, and by
way of causality and of negation as stated above
(Q. XII, A. 12). Thus the name God signifies the
divine nature, for this name was imposed to
signify something existing above all things, the
principle of all things, and removed from all
things; for those who name God intend to signify all this.

ARTICLE 9. *Whether This Name* God *Is Communicable?*

We proceed thus to the Ninth Article: It
seems that this name *God* is communicable.

Objection 1. For whosoever shares in the
thing signified by a name shares in the name itself. But this name God as we have said above

[1] Sect. 2 (PG 3, 969).   [2] Aristotle, IV, 7 (1012ᵃ23).

(A. 8) signifies the divine nature, which is communicable to others, according to the words,
He hath given us great [Vulg., *most great*] *and
precious promises, that by these we* [Vulg.,
ye] *may be made partakers of the divine nature*
(II Pet. 1. 4). Therefore this name *God* can be
communicated to others.

Obj. 2. Further, only proper names are not
communicable. Now this name God is not a
proper, but an appellative noun, which appears
from the fact that it has a plural, according to
the text, *I have said, You are gods* (Ps. 81. 6).
Therefore this name God is communicable.

Obj. 3. Further, this name God comes from
operation, as explained (A. 8). But other names
given to God from His operations or effects are
communicable, such as good, wise, and the like.
Therefore this name God is communicable.

On the contrary, It is written: *They gave the
incommunicable name to wood and stones*
(Wisd. 14. 21), in reference to the divine name.
Therefore this name God is incommunicable.

I answer that, A name is communicable in
two ways, properly, and by likeness. It is properly communicable in the sense that its whole
signification can be given to many; by likeness
it is communicable according to some part of
the signification of the name. For instance this
name "lion" is properly communicated to all
things of the same nature as lion; by likeness
it is communicable to those who participate in
something lion-like, as for instance by courage,
or strength, and those who thus participate are
called lions metaphorically.

To know, however, what names are properly
communicable, we must consider that every
form existing in the singular suppositum, by
which it is individualized, is common to many
either in reality, or at least according to reason; as human nature is common to many in
reality, and in idea; but the nature of the sun is
not common to many in reality, but only in
idea; for the nature of the sun can be understood as existing in many supposita, and the
reason is because the mind understands the nature of every species by abstraction from the
singular. Hence to be in one singular suppositum
or in many is outside the idea of the nature of
the species. So, given the idea of the nature of
a species, it can be understood as existing in
many. But the singular, from the fact that it is
singular, is divided off from all others. Hence
every name imposed to signify any singular
thing is incommunicable both in reality and
idea, for the plurality of this individual thing
cannot fall within the apprehension. Hence no

name signifying any individual thing is properly communicable to many, but only by way of likeness; as for instance a person can be called Achilles metaphorically, because he may possess something of the properties of Achilles, such as strength.

On the other hand, forms which are individualized not by any suppositum, but by themselves, because they are subsisting forms, if understood as they are in themselves could not be communicated either in reality or in idea, but only perhaps by way of likeness, as was said of individuals. But because we are unable to understand simple self-subsisting forms as they really are, but understand them after the mode of composite things having forms in matter, therefore, as was said in the first article (Ans. 2), we give them concrete names signifying a nature existing in some suppositum. Hence, so far as concerns names, the same rules apply to names we impose to signify the nature of composite things as to names given by us to signify simple subsisting natures.

Since, then, this name God is given to signify the divine nature as stated above (A. 8), and since the divine nature cannot be multiplied as shown above (Q. XI, A. 3), it follows that this name God is incommunicable in reality, but communicable in opinion, just in the same way as this name "sun" would be communicable according to the opinion of those who say there are many suns. Therefore, it is written: *You served them who by nature are not gods* (Gal. 4. 8), and a gloss adds,[1] Gods not in nature, "but in human opinion." Nevertheless this name God is communicable not in its whole signification, but in some part of it by way of likeness, so that those are called gods who share in divinity by likeness, according to the text, *I have said, You are gods* (Ps. 81. 6).

But if any name were given to signify God not as to His nature but as to His suppositum, according as He is considered as "this something," that name would be in every way incommunicable; as, for instance, perhaps the name Tetragrammaton among the Hebrews; and this is like giving a name to the sun as signifying this individual thing.

Reply Obj. 1. The divine nature is only communicable according to the participation of some likeness.

Reply Obj. 2. This name God is an appellative name, and not a proper name, for it signifies the divine nature in the possessor, although God Himself in reality is neither universal nor particular. For names do not follow upon the mode of being which is in things, but upon the mode of being as it is in our knowledge. And yet it is incommunicable according to the truth of the thing, as was said above concerning the name sun.

Reply Obj. 3. These names good, wise, and the like, are imposed from the perfections proceeding from God to creatures; but they do not signify the divine nature, but rather signify the perfections themselves absolutely, and therefore they are in truth communicable to many. But this name God is given to God from His own proper operation, which we experience continually, to signify the divine nature.

ARTICLE 10. *Whether This Name* God *Is Applied to God Univocally, by Nature, by Participation, and According to Opinion?*

We proceed thus to the Tenth Article: It seems that this name God is applied to God univocally by nature, by participation, and according to opinion.

Objection 1. For where a diverse signification exists, there is no contradiction of affirmation and negation; for equivocation prevents contradiction. But a Catholic who says: "An idol is not God," contradicts a pagan who says: "An idol is God." Therefore God in both senses is spoken of univocally.

Obj. 2. Further, as an idol is God in opinion, and not in truth, so the enjoyment of carnal pleasures is called happiness in opinion, and not in truth. But this name happiness is applied univocally to this supposed happiness, and also to true happiness. Therefore also this name God is applied univocally to the true God and to God also in opinion.

Obj. 3. Further, names are called univocal because they contain one notion. Now when a Catholic says: "There is one God," he understands by the name of God an omnipotent being, and one venerated above all, while the heathen understands the same when he says: "An idol is God." Therefore this name God is applied univocally to both.

On the contrary, That which is in the intellect is the likeness of what is in the thing as is said in *Interpretation*.[2] But the word animal applied to a true animal and to a picture of one is equivocal. Therefore this name God applied to the true God and to God in opinion is applied equivocally.

Further, No one can signify what he does not

---

[1] *Glossa Lombardi* (PL 192, 139); cf. *Glossa interl.*, (VI, 84v).

[2] Aristotle, 1 (16ª5).

know. But the gentile does not know the divine nature. So when he says an idol is God, he does not signify the true Deity. On the other hand, a Catholic signifies the true Deity when he says there is one God. Therefore this name God is not applied univocally, but equivocally to the true God, and to God according to opinion.

I answer that, This name God in the three above significations is taken neither univocally nor equivocally, but analogically. This is apparent for this reason. Univocal terms mean absolutely the same thing, but equivocal terms absolutely different things; but in analogical terms a word taken in one signification must be placed in the definition of the same word taken in other senses; as, for instance, being which is applied to substance is placed in the definition of being as applied to accident; and healthy applied to animal is placed in the definition of healthy as applied to urine and medicine. For urine is the sign of health in the animal, and medicine is the cause of health.

The same applies to the question at issue. For this name God, as signifying the true God, includes the idea of God when it is used to denote God in opinion, or participation. For when we name anyone god by participation, we understand by the name of god something having likeness to the true God. Likewise, when we call an idol god, by this name god we understand that we are signifying something which men think is God; thus it is manifest that the name has different meanings, but that one of them is comprised in the other significations. Hence it is manifestly said analogically.

Reply Obj. 1. The multiplication of names does not depend on the predication of the name, but on the meaning; for this name man, of whomsoever it is predicated, whether truly or falsely, is predicated in one sense. But it would be multiplied if by the name man we meant to signify different things; for instance, if one meant to signify by this name man what man really is, and another meant to signify by the same name a stone, or something else. Hence it is evident that a Catholic saying that an idol is not God contradicts the pagan asserting that it is God, because each of them uses this name God to signify the true God. For when the pagan says an idol is God, he does not use this name as meaning God in opinion, for he would then speak the truth, as also Catholics sometimes use the name in that sense, as in the Psalm, *All the gods of the Gentiles are demons* (Ps. 95. 5).

The same remark applies to the *second and*

third Objections. For those reasons proceed from the different predication of the name, and not from its various significations.

Reply Obj. 4. The term animal applied to a true and a pictured animal is not purely equivocal for the Philosopher[1] takes equivocal names in a wide sense, including analogous names; because being also, which is predicated analogically, is sometimes said to be predicated equivocally of different predicaments.

Reply Obj. 5. Neither a Catholic nor a pagan knows the very nature of God as it is in itself, but each one knows it according to some idea of causality, or excellence, or remotion (Q. XII, A. 12). So the Gentile can take this name God in the same way when he says an idol is God as the Catholic does in saying an idol is not God. But if anyone should be quite ignorant of God altogether, he could not even name Him, unless, perhaps, as we use names the meaning of which we know not.

ARTICLE 11. *Whether This Name, He Who Is, Is the Most Proper Name of God?*

We proceed thus to the Eleventh Article: It seems that this name HE WHO IS is not the most proper name of God.

Objection 1. For this name God is an incommunicable name, as we have said (A. 9). But this name HE WHO IS, is not an incommunicable name. Therefore this name HE WHO IS is not the most proper name of God.

Obj. 2. Further, Dionysius says (*Div. Nom.* iii)[2] that "the name of good excellently manifests all the processions of God." But it especially belongs to God to be the universal principle of all things. Therefore this name good is supremely proper to God, and not this name HE WHO IS.

Obj. 3. Further, every divine name seems to imply relation to creatures, for God is known to us only through creatures. But this name HE WHO IS imports no relation to creatures. Therefore this name HE WHO IS is not the most applicable to God.

On the contrary, It is written that when Moses asked, *If they should say to me, What is His name? what shall I say to them?* the Lord answered him, *Thus shalt thou say to them,* HE WHO IS *hath sent me to you* (Exod. 3. 13. 14). Therefore this name, HE WHO IS, most properly belongs to God.

I answer that, This name, HE WHO IS, is most properly applied to God, for three reasons.

First, because of its signification. For it does

---

[1] *Categories,* 1 (1ᵃ1).   [2] Sect. 1 (PG 3, 680).

not signify form, but being itself. Hence since the being of God is His essence itself, which can be said of no other (Q. III, A. 4), it is clear that among other names this one specially names God, for everything is denominated by its form.

Secondly, on account of its universality. For all other names are either less universal, or, if convertible with it, add something above it at least in idea, hence in a certain way they inform and determine it. Now our intellect cannot know the essence of God itself in this life, as it is in itself, but whatever mode it applies in determining what it understands about God, it falls short of the mode of what God is in Himself. Therefore the less determinate the names are, and the more universal and absolute they are, the more properly are they applied to God. Hence Damascene says (De Fid. Orth. i)[1] that, "HE WHO IS, is the principal of all names applied to God; for comprehending all in itself, it contains being itself as an infinite and indeterminate sea of substance." Now by any other name some mode of substance is determined, whereas this name HE WHO IS determines no mode of being, but is indeterminate to all; and therefore it denominates the "infinite sea of substance."

Thirdly, from its consignification, for it signifies being in the present, and this above all properly applies to God, "whose being knows not past or future," as Augustine says (De Trin. v).[2]

Reply Obj. 1. This name HE WHO IS is the name of God more properly than this name God both as regards its source, namely, being, and as regards the mode of signification and consignification, as said above. But as regards the meaning intended by the name, this name God is more proper, as it is imposed to signify the divine nature; and still more proper is the Tetragrammaton, imposed to signify the substance of God itself, incommunicable and, if one may so speak, singular.

Reply Obj. 2. This name "good" is the principal name of God in so far as He is a cause, but not absolutely; for being, considered absolutely, comes before the idea of cause.

Reply Obj. 3. It is not necessary that all the divine names should import relation to creatures, but it suffices that they be imposed from some perfections flowing from God to creatures. Among these the first is being itself, from which comes this name, HE WHO IS.

---

[1] Chap. 9 (PG 94, 836).
[2] Cf. Peter Lombard, *Sent.*, I, d. 8, chap. 1 (QR I, 58); cf. Isidore, *Etym.*, VII, 1 (PL 82, 261).

ARTICLE 12. *Whether Affirmative Propositions Can Be Formed about God?*

We proceed thus to the Twelfth Article: It seems that affirmative propositions cannot be formed about God.

Objection 1. For Dionysius says (*Cæl Hier.* ii)[3] that "negations about God are true; but affirmations are vague."

Obj. 2. Further, Boethius says (*De Trin.* ii),[4] that "a simple form cannot be a subject." But God is the most absolutely simple form, as shown (Q. III, A. 7); therefore He cannot be a subject. But everything about which an affirmative proposition is made is taken as a subject. Therefore an affirmative proposition cannot be formed about God.

Obj. 3. Further, every intellect is false which understands a thing otherwise than as it is. But God has being without any composition as shown above (Q. III, A. 7). Therefore since every affirming intellect understands something as composite, it follows that a true affirmative proposition about God cannot be made.

On the contrary, What is of faith cannot be false. But some affirmative propositions are of faith, as that God is Three and One, and that He is omnipotent. Therefore affirmative propositions can be formed truly about God.

I answer that, Affirmative propositions can be formed truly about God. To prove this we must know that in every true affirmative proposition the predicate and the subject signify in some way the same thing in reality, and different things according to reason. And this appears to be the case both in propositions which have an accidental predicate, and in those which have a substantial predicate. For it is manifest that "man" and "white" are the same in subject, and different in idea; for the notion of man is one thing, and that of whiteness is another. The same applies when I say, "man is an animal," since the same thing which is man is truly animal; for in the same suppositum there is sensible nature by reason of which he is called animal, and the rational nature by reason of which he is called man; hence here again predicate and subject are the same as to suppositum, but different as to idea. But in propositions where one same thing is predicated of itself, the same rule in some way applies, since the intellect draws to the *suppositum* what it places in the subject; and what it places in the predicate it draws to the nature of the form existing in the *suppositum*, according to the

---

[3] Sect. 3 (PG 3, 140).   [4] PL 64, 1250.

saying that predicates are taken formally, and subjects materially. To this diversity in idea corresponds the plurality of predicate and subject, while the intellect signifies the identity of the thing by the composition itself.

God, however, considered in Himself, is altogether one and simple, yet our intellect knows Him by different conceptions because it cannot see Him as He is in Himself. Nevertheless, although it understands Him under different conceptions, it knows that all its conceptions correspond to one and the same thing absolutely. Therefore the plurality of predicate and subject represents the plurality of idea and the intellect represents the unity by composition.

Reply Obj. 1. Dionysius says that the affirmations about God are vague or, according to another translation, "incongruous," in so far as no name can be applied to God according to its mode of signification.

Reply Obj. 2. Our intellect cannot comprehend simple subsisting forms, as they are in themselves; but it apprehends them according after the manner of composite things in which there is something taken as subject and something that is inherent. Therefore it apprehends the simple form under the aspect of a subject, and attributes something to it.

Reply Obj. 3. This proposition, "The intellect understanding anything otherwise than it is, is false," can be taken in two senses, according as this adverb "otherwise" determines the word "understanding" on the part of the thing understood, or on the part of the one who understands. Taken as referring to the thing understood, the proposition is true, and the meaning is: Any intellect which understands that the thing is otherwise than it is, is false. But this does not hold in the present case, because our intellect, when forming a proposition about God, does not affirm that He is composite, but that He is simple. But taken as referring to the one who understands, the proposition is false. For the mode of the intellect in understanding is different from the mode of the thing in being. For it is clear that our intellect understands material things existing below itself in an immaterial manner; not that it understands them to be immaterial things, but its manner of understanding is immaterial. Likewise, when it understands simple things which are above itself, it understands them according to its own mode, which is in a composite manner, yet not so as to understand them to be composite things. And thus our intellect is not false in forming a composed proposition about God.

QUESTION XIV
OF GOD'S KNOWLEDGE
(*In Sixteen Articles*)

HAVING considered what belongs to the divine substance, we have now to treat of God's operation. And since one kind of operation remains in the operator, and another kind of operation proceeds to the exterior effect, we treat first of knowledge and of will (Q. XIX) (for understanding is in the intelligent agent, and will is in the one who wills); and afterwards of the power of God which is considered as the principle of the divine operation as proceeding to the exterior effect (Q. XXV). Now because to understand is in a certain way to live, after treating of the divine knowledge, we consider the divine life (Q. XVIII). And as knowledge concerns truth, we consider truth (Q. XVI) and falsehood (Q. XVII). Further, as everything known is in the knower, and the types of things as existing in the knowledge of God are called ideas, to the consideration of knowledge will be added the treatment of ideas (Q. XV).

Concerning knowledge, there are sixteen points for inquiry: (1) Whether there is knowledge in God? (2) Whether God understands Himself? (3) Whether He comprehends Himself? (4) Whether His understanding is His substance? (5) Whether He understands other things besides Himself? (6) Whether He has a proper knowledge of them? (7) Whether the knowledge of God is discursive? (8) Whether the knowledge of God is the cause of things? (9) Whether God has knowledge of non-existing things? (10) Whether He has knowledge of evil? (11) Whether He has knowledge of individual things? (12) Whether He knows the infinite? (13) Whether He knows future contingent things? (14) Whether He knows enunciable things? (15) Whether the knowledge of God is variable? (16) Whether God has speculative or practical knowledge of things?

ARTICLE 1. *Whether There Is Knowledge in God?*

We proceed thus to the First Article: It seems that there is not knowledge (*scientia*) in God.

Objection 1. For knowledge is a habit, and habit does not belong to God, since it is the mean between potency and act. Therefore knowledge is not in God.

Obj. 2. Further, since science is about conclusions, it is a kind of knowledge caused by something else; namely, by the knowledge of principles. But nothing is caused in God. Therefore science is not in God.

Obj. 3. Further, all knowledge is universal, or particular. But in God there is no universal nor particular (Q. XIII, A. 9, ANS. 2). Therefore in God there is not knowledge.

On the contrary, The Apostle says, *O the depth of the riches of the wisdom and of the knowledge of God* (Rom. 11. 33).

I answer that, In God there exists the most perfect knowledge. To prove this, we must note that knowing beings are distinguished from non-knowing beings in that the latter possess only their own form, while the knowing being is naturally adapted to have also the form of some other thing; for the species of the thing known is in the knower. Hence it is manifest that the nature of a non-knowing thing is more contracted and limited, while the nature of knowing things has a greater amplitude and extension; therefore the Philosopher says[1] that "the soul is in a certain way all things." Now the contraction of the form comes from the matter. Hence, as we have said above (Q. VII, A. 1, 2) forms according as they are the more immaterial, approach more nearly to a kind of infinity. Therefore it is clear that the immateriality of a thing is the reason why it is cognitive, and the mode of knowledge is according to the mode of immateriality. Hence, it is said in the *Soul*[2] that plants do not know because of their materiality. But sense is cognitive because it can receive species without matter, and the intellect is still further cognitive, because it is more "separated from matter and unmixed," as said in the *Soul*.[3] Since therefore God is in the highest degree of immateriality, as stated above (Q. VII, A. 1), it follows that He occupies the highest place in knowledge.

Reply Obj. 1. Because perfections flowing from God to creatures exist in a higher state in God Himself (Q. IV, A. 2), whenever a name taken from any created perfection is attributed to God, there must be separated from its signification anything that belongs to that imperfect mode proper to creatures. Hence knowledge is not a quality in God, nor a habit, but substance and pure act.

Reply Obj. 2. Whatever is divided and multiplied in creatures exists in God simply and unitedly (Q. XIII, A. 4). Now man has different kinds of knowledge, according to the different things known. He has understanding as regards the knowledge of principles; he has science as regards knowledge of conclusions; he has wisdom, according as he knows the highest cause; he has counsel or prudence, according as he knows what is to be done. But God knows all these by one simple act of knowledge, as will be shown (A. 7). Hence the simple knowledge of God can be named by all these names, in such a way, however, that there must be removed from each of them, so far as they enter into the divine predication, everything that savours of imperfection; and everything that expresses perfection is to be retained in them. Hence it is said, *With Him is wisdom and strength, He hath counsel and understanding* (Job 12. 13).

Reply Obj. 3. Knowledge is according to the mode of the one who knows, for the thing known is in the knower according to the mode of the knower. Now since the mode of the divine essence is higher than that of creatures, divine knowledge does not exist in God after the mode of created knowledge, so as to be universal or particular, or habitual, or in potency, or existing according to any such mode.

ARTICLE 2. *Whether God Understands Himself?*

We proceed thus to the Second Article: It seems that God does not understand Himself.

Objection 1. For it is said by the Philosopher,[4] "Every knower who knows his own essence, returns completely to his own essence." But God does not go out from His own essence, nor is He moved in any way; thus He cannot return to His own essence. Therefore He does not know His own essence.

Obj. 2. Further, to understand is in a certain way to suffer and to be moved, as the Philosopher says,[5] and knowledge also is a kind of assimilation to the object known; and the thing known is the perfection of the knower. But nothing is moved, or suffers, or is made perfect by itself, "nor," as Hilary says (*De Trin.* iii),[6] "is a thing its own likeness." Therefore God does not understand Himself.

Obj. 3. Further, we are like God chiefly in our intellect, because we are the image of God in our mind, as Augustine says (*Gen. ad. lit.* vi).[7] But our intellect understands itself, only as it understands other things, as is said in the *Soul*.[8] Therefore God does not understand Himself, unless perhaps by understanding other things.

---

[1] *Soul*, III, 8 (431[b]21).   [2] II, 12 (424[a]32).
[3] Aristotle, III, 4 (429[a]18; [b]5).

[4] *Lib. de Causis*, 14 (BA 177.6).
[5] *Soul*, III, 4, 7 (429[b]24; 431[a]6).   [6] Chap. 23 (PL 10, 92).
[7] Chap. 12 (PL 34, 347).   [8] Aristotle, III, 4 (430[a]2).

On the contrary, It is written: *The things that are of God no man knoweth, but the Spirit of God* (I Cor. 2. 11).

I answer that, God understands Himself through Himself. In proof of this it must be known that although in operations which pass to an external effect the object of the operation, which is taken as the term, is something outside the operator, nevertheless in operations that remain in the operator, the object signified as the term of operation, is in the operator; and according as it is in the operator, the operation is actual. Hence the Philosopher says,[1] that the sensible in act is sense in act, and the intelligible in act is intellect in act. For the reason why we actually feel or know a thing is because our intellect or sense is actually informed by the sensible or intelligible species. And because of this only, it follows that sense or intellect is distinct from the sensible or intelligible object, since both are in potency.

Since therefore God has nothing in Him of potentiality, but is pure act, His intellect and the thing understood are the same, so that He neither lacks the intelligible species, as is the case with our intellect when it understands in potency; nor is the intelligible species other than the substance of the divine intellect, as happens in our intellect when it understands actually; but the intelligible species itself is the divine intellect itself, and thus God understands Himself through Himself.

Reply Obj. 1. Return to its own essence means only that a thing subsists in itself. For in so far as the form perfects the matter by giving it being, it is in a certain way diffused in it; and it returns to itself in so far as it has being in itself. Therefore those knowing powers which are not subsisting but are the acts of organs, do not know themselves, as is clear in each of the senses; but those knowing powers which are self-subsisting, know themselves; hence it is said in *De Causis*[2] that, "whoever knows his essence returns to it." Now it supremely belongs to God to be self-subsisting. Hence according to this mode of speaking, He supremely returns to His own essence, and knows Himself.

Reply Obj. 2. To be moved and to suffer are taken equivocally, according as to understand is described as a kind of movement or passion, as stated in the treatise in the *Soul*.[3] For to understand is not a movement that is an act of something imperfect passing from one thing to another, but it is an act, existing in the agent itself, of something perfect. Likewise that the intellect is perfected by the intelligible thing, or is assimilated to it, belongs to an intellect which is sometimes in potency; because the fact that it is in potency makes it differ from the intelligible object and assimilates it to it through the intelligible species, which is the likeness of the thing understood, and makes it to be perfected by it, as potency is perfected by act. On the other hand the divine intellect, which is no way in potency, is not perfected by the intelligible object, nor is it assimilated to it, but is its own perfection, and its own intelligible object.

Reply Obj. 3. Natural being does not belong to primary matter, which is a potentiality, unless it is reduced to act by a form. Now our possible intellect has the same relation to intelligible things as primary matter has to natural things; for it is in potency as regards intelligible things just as primary matter is to natural things. Hence our possible intellect can be exercised concerning intelligible things only so far as it is perfected by the intelligible species of something; and in that way it understands itself by an intelligible species as it understands other things; for it is manifest that by knowing the intelligible object it understands also its own act of understanding, and by this act knows the intellectual power. But God is a pure act in the order of existing things as well as in the order of intelligible things; therefore He understands Himself through Himself.

ARTICLE 3. *Whether God Comprehends Himself?*

We proceed thus to the *Third Article:* It seems that God does not comprehend Himself.

Objection 1. For Augustine says (*Octog. Tri. Quæst.* xv),[4] that "whatever comprehends itself is finite as regards itself." But God is in all ways infinite. Therefore He does not comprehend Himself.

Obj. 2. If it be said that God is infinite to us and finite to Himself, it can be urged to the contrary that everything in God is truer than it is in us. If therefore God is finite to Himself but infinite to us, then God is more truly finite than infinite, which is against what was laid down above (Q. VII, A. 1). Therefore God does not comprehend Himself.

On the contrary, Augustine says (*ibid.*), "Everything that understands itself comprehends itself." But God understands Himself. Therefore He comprehends Himself.

[1] *Soul,* III, 2, 4 (426ª16; 430ª3).
[2] Sect. 14 (BA 177.6).
[3] III, 4, 7 (429b24; 431ª6).   [4] PL 40, 15.

I answer that, God perfectly comprehends Himself, which appears in this way. A thing is said to be comprehended when the end of the knowledge of it is attained, and this is accomplished when it is known as perfectly as it is knowable; as, for instance, a demonstrable proposition is comprehended when known by demonstration, but not, however, when it is known by some probable reason. Now it is manifest that God knows Himself as perfectly as He is perfectly knowable. For everything is knowable according to the mode of its own actuality, since a thing is not known according as it is in potency, but in so far as it is in act, as said in the *Metaphysics*.[1] Now the power of God in knowing is as great as His actuality in existing, because it is from the fact that He is in act and free from all matter and potency, that God is cognitive, as shown above (AA. 1 and 2). Hence it is manifest that He knows Himself as much as He is knowable, and for that reason He perfectly comprehends Himself.

Reply Obj. 1. The strict meaning of comprehension signifies that one thing holds and includes another, and in this sense everything comprehended is finite, as also is everything included in another. But God is not said to be comprehended by Himself in this sense, as if His intellect were something apart from Himself, and as if it held and included Himself; for these ways of speaking are to be taken by way of negation. For just as God is said to be in Himself because He is not contained by anything outside of Himself, so He is said to be comprehended by Himself because nothing in Himself is hidden from Himself. For Augustine says,[2] "The whole is comprehended when seen, if it is seen in such a way that nothing of it is hidden from the seer."

Reply Obj. 2. When it is said that God is finite to Himself, this is to be understood according to a certain likeness of proportion, because He has the same relation in not exceeding His intellect as anything finite has in not exceeding finite intellect. But God is not to be called finite to Himself in this sense, as if He understood Himself to be something finite.

ARTICLE 4. *Whether the Act of God's Intellect Is His Substance?*

We proceed thus to the Fourth Article: It seems that the act of God's intellect is not His substance.

Objection 1. For to understand is an opera-

tion. But an operation signifies something proceeding from the operator. Therefore the act of God's intellect is not His substance.

Obj. 2. Further, When anyone understands himself to understand, this is to understand something that is neither great nor chiefly understood, but secondary and accessory. If therefore God be his own act of understanding, His act of understanding will be as when we understand our act of understanding, and thus God's act of understanding will not be something great.

Obj. 3. Further, every act of understanding means understanding something. When therefore God understands Himself, if He Himself is not distinct from this act of understanding, He understands that He understands, and that He understands that He understands Himself, and so on to infinity. Therefore the act of God's intellect is not His substance.

On the contrary, Augustine says (*De Trin.* vii),[3] "In God to be is the same as to be wise." But to be wise is the same thing as to understand. Therefore in God to be is the same thing as to understand. But God's being is His substance, as shown above (Q. III, A. 4). Therefore the act of God's intellect is His substance.

I answer that, It must be said that the act of God's intellect is His substance. For if His act of understanding were other than His substance, then something else, as the Philosopher says,[4] in the *Metaphysics,* would be the act and perfection of the divine substance, to which the divine substance would be related as potency is to act, which is altogether impossible, because the act of understanding is the perfection and act of the one understanding.

Let us now consider how this is. As was laid down above (A. 2), to understand is not an act passing to anything extrinsic; for it remains in the operator as his own act and perfection; as being is the perfection of the one existing. For just as being follows on the form, so in like manner to understand follows on the intelligible species. Now in God there is no form which is something other than His being, as shown above (Q. III, A. 4). Hence as His essence itself is also His intelligible species, it necessarily follows that His act of understanding must be His essence and His being.

Thus it follows from all the foregoing that in God, intellect, and what is understood, and the intelligible species, and His act of understanding are entirely one and the same. Hence, when

---

[1] Aristotle, IX, 9 (1051ᵃ31).
[2] *Epist.*, CXLVII, 9 (PL 33, 606).

[3] Chap. 2 (PL 42, 927); Bk VI, chap 4 (PL 42, 936).
[4] XII, 9 (1074ᵇ18).

God is said to be understanding, no kind of multiplicity is attached to His substance.

Reply Obj. 1. To understand is not an operation proceeding out of the operator, but remaining in him.

Reply Obj. 2. When that act of understanding which is not subsistent is understood, something not great is understood, as when we understand our act of understanding; and so this cannot be likened to the act of the divine understanding, which is subsistent.

Thus appears the *Reply to Obj.* 3. For the act of divine understanding subsists in itself, and belongs to its very self and is not another's. Hence it need not proceed to infinity.

ARTICLE 5. *Whether God Knows Things Other Than Himself?*

We proceed thus to the Fifth Article: It seems that God does not know things other than Himself.

Objection 1. For all other things but God are outside of God. But Augustine says (*Octog. Tri. Quæst., qu.* xlvi)[1] that "God does not see anything out of Himself." Therefore He does not know things other than Himself.

Obj. 2. Further, the thing understood is the perfection of the one who understands. If therefore God understands other things besides Himself, something else will be the perfection of God, and will be nobler than He, which is impossible.

Obj. 3. Further, the act of understanding itself has its species from the intelligible object, as is every other act from its own object. Hence the intellectual act is so much the nobler according as what is understood is nobler. But God is His own act of understanding, as appears from what was said before (A. 4) If therefore God understands anything other than Himself, then God Himself is specified by something else than Himself, which is impossible. Therefore He does not understand things other than Himself.

On the contrary, It is written: *All things are naked and open to His eyes* (Heb. 4. 13).

I answer that, God necessarily knows things other than Himself. For it is manifest that He perfectly understands Himself; otherwise His being would not be perfect, since His being is His act of understanding. Now if anything is perfectly known, it follows of necessity that its power is perfectly known. But the power of anything can be perfectly known only by knowing to what its power extends. Since therefore

the divine power extends to other things by the very fact that it is the first effecting cause of all things, as is clear from what we have said (Q. II, A. 3), God must necessarily know things other than Himself. And this appears still more plainly if we add that the very being of the first efficient cause—namely, God—is His own act of understanding. Hence whatever effects pre-exist in God, as in the first cause, must be in His act of understanding, and all things must be in Him according to an intelligible mode: for everything which is in another, is in it according to the mode of that in which it is.

Now in order to know how God knows things other than Himself, we must consider that a thing is known in two ways: in itself, and in another. A thing is known in itself when it is known by the proper species adequate to the knowable object, as when the eye sees a man through the image of a man. A thing is seen in another through the species of that which contains it, as when a part is seen in the whole by the species of the whole, or when a man is seen in a mirror by the species in the mirror, or by any other mode by which one thing is seen in another.

So we say that God sees Himself in Himself, because He sees Himself through His essence; and He sees other things not in themselves, but in Himself, because His essence contains the likeness of things other than Himself.

Reply Obj. 1. The passage of Augustine in which it is said that God sees nothing outside Himself is not to be taken in such a way as if God saw nothing outside Himself, but in the sense that what is outside Himself He does not see except in Himself, as above explained.

Reply Obj. 2. The thing understood is a perfection of the one understanding not by its substance, but by its species, according to which it is in the intellect, as its form and perfection, as is said in the book on the *Soul*,[2] for "a stone is not in the soul, but its species." Now those things which are other than God are understood by God in so far as the essence of God contains their species as above explained; hence it does not follow that there is any perfection of the divine intellect other than the divine essence.

Reply Obj. 3. The intellectual act is not specified by what is understood in another, but by the principal thing understood in which other things are understood. For the intellectual act is specified by its object in so far as the intelligible form is the principle of the intellectual operation, since every operation is specified by

[2] Aristotle, III, 8 (431[b]29).

the form which is its principle of operation, as heating by heat. Hence the intellectual operation is specified by that intelligible form which makes the intellect in act. And this is the species of the principal thing understood, which in God is nothing but His own essence in which all species of things are comprehended. Hence it does not follow that the divine act of understanding, or rather God Himself, is specified by anything else than the divine essence itself.

ARTICLE 6. *Whether God Knows Things Other Than Himself by Proper Knowledge?*

We proceed thus to the Sixth Article: It seems that God does not know things other than Himself by proper knowledge.

Objection 1. For, as was shown (A. 5), God knows things other than Himself according as they are in Himself. But other things are in Him as in their common and universal first cause, and are known by God as in their first and universal cause. This is to know them by general, and not by proper knowledge. Therefore God knows things besides Himself by general, and not by proper knowledge.

Obj. 2. Further, the created essence is as distant from the divine essence, as the divine essence is distant from the created essence. But the divine essence cannot be known by the created essence, as said above (Q. XII, A. 2). Therefore neither can the created essence be known by the divine essence. Thus as God knows only by His essence, it follows that He does not know what the creature is in its essence, so as to know "what it is," which is to have proper knowledge of it.

Obj. 3. Further, proper knowledge of a thing can come only through its proper notion. But as God knows all things by His essence, it seems that He does not know each thing by its proper notion, for one thing cannot be the proper notion of many and diverse things. Therefore God has not a proper knowledge of things, but a general knowledge; for to know things otherwise than by their proper notion is to have only a general knowledge of them.

On the contrary, To have a proper knowledge of things is to know them not only in general, but as they are distinct from each other. Now God knows things in that manner. Hence it is written that He reaches *even to the division of the soul and the spirit, of the joints also and the marrow, and is a discerner of the thoughts and intents of the heart; neither is there any creature invisible in His sight* (Heb. 4. 12, 13).

I answer that, Some have erred on this point,

saying that God knows things other than Himself only in general, that is, only as beings.[1] For just as fire, if it knew itself as the principle of heat, would know the nature of heat, and all things else in so far as they are hot, so God, through knowing Himself as the principle of being, knows the nature of being, and all other things in so far as they are beings.

But this cannot be. For to know a thing in general and not in particular, is to have an imperfect knowledge of it. Hence our intellect, when it is reduced from potency to act, acquires first a universal and confused knowledge of things, before it has a proper knowledge of them, as proceeding from the imperfect to the perfect, as is clear from the *Physics*.[2] If therefore the knowledge of God regarding things other than Himself is only universal and not special, it would follow that His act of understanding would not be absolutely perfect; therefore neither would His being be perfect; and this is against what was said above (Q. IV, A. 1). We must therefore hold that God knows things other than Himself with a proper knowledge—not only in so far as being is common to them, but in so far as one is distinguished from the other.

In proof of this we may observe that some wishing to show that God knows many things by one, bring forward examples, as, for instance, that if the centre knew itself, it would know all lines that proceed from the centre[3]; or if light knew itself, it would know all colours.[4] Now these examples although they are similar in part, namely, as regards universal causality, nevertheless they fail in this respect, that multitude and diversity are caused by the one universal principle not as regards that which is the principle of distinction, but only as regards that in which they communicate. For the diversity of colours is not caused by the light only, but by the different disposition of the diaphanous medium which receives it; and likewise, the diversity of the lines is caused by their different position. Hence it is that this kind of diversity and multitude cannot be known in its principle by proper knowledge, but only in a general way. In God, however, it is otherwise. For it was shown above (Q. IV, A. 2) that whatever perfection exists in any creature, wholly pre-exists

---

[1] Unnamed in Averroes, *In Meta.*, XII, comm. 51 (VIII, 337A). St. Thomas wrongly attributed this opinion to Averroes. Cf. *In Sent.*, I, d. 35, Q. I, A. 3.
[2] Aristotle, I, I (184ᵃ22).
[3] Cf. Alexander of Hales, *Summa Theol.*, PT. I, n. 166 (QR I, 249).
[4] Cf. Dionysius, *De Div. Nom.*, VII, 2 (PG 3, 870).

and is contained in God in an excelling manner. Now not only what is common to creatures—namely being—belongs to their perfection, but also what makes them distinguished from each other; as living and understanding, and the like, whereby living beings are distinguished from the non-living, and the intelligent from the non-intelligent. Likewise every form by which each thing is constituted in its own species, is a perfection; and thus all things pre-exist in God not only as regards what is common to all, but also as regards what distinguishes one thing from another. And therefore as God contains all perfections in Himself, the essence of God is compared to all essences of things not as the common to the proper, as unity is to numbers, or as the centre (of a circle) to the (radiating) lines, but as perfect acts to imperfect; as if I were to compare man to animal or six, a perfect number, to the imperfect numbers contained under it. Now it is manifest that by a perfect act imperfect acts can be known not only in general, but also by proper knowledge; thus, for example, whoever knows a man, knows an animal by proper knowledge, and whoever knows the number six, knows the number three also by proper knowledge.

As therefore the essence of God contains in itself all the perfection contained in the essence of any other thing, and far more, God can know in Himself all of them with proper knowledge. For the nature proper to each thing consists in some degree of participation in the divine perfection. Now God could not be said to know Himself perfectly unless He knew all the ways in which His own perfection can be shared by others. Neither could He know the very nature of being perfectly unless He knew all modes of being. Hence it is manifest that God knows all things with proper knowledge, in their distinction from each other.

Reply Obj. 1. So to know a thing as it is in the knower, may be understood in two ways. In one way this adverb "so," imports the mode of knowledge on the part of the thing known; and in that sense it is false. For the knower does not always know the thing known according to the being it has in the knower; for the eye does not know a stone according to the being it has in the eye, but by the species of the stone which is in the eye, the eye knows the stone according to its being outside the eye. And if any knower has a knowledge of the thing known according to the being it has in the knower, the knower nevertheless knows it according to its being outside the knower; thus the intellect knows a stone according to the intelligible being it has in the intellect, in so far as it knows that it understands, while nevertheless it knows what a stone is in its own nature. If however the adverb "so" be understood to import the mode (of knowledge) on the part of the knower, in that sense it is true that only the knower has knowledge of the thing known as it is in the knower; for the more perfectly the thing known is in the knower, the more perfect is the mode of knowledge.

We must say therefore that God not only knows that things are in Himself, but by the fact that they are in Him, He knows them in their own nature and all the more perfectly the more perfectly each one is in Him.

Reply Obj. 2. The essence of the creature is compared to the essence of God as the imperfect to the perfect act. Therefore the essence of the creature cannot sufficiently lead us to the knowledge of the divine essence, but rather the converse.

Reply Obj. 3. The same thing cannot be taken in an equal manner as the notion of different things. But the divine essence excels all creatures. Hence it can be taken as the proper notion of each thing according to the diverse ways in which diverse creatures participate in, and imitate it.

ARTICLE 7. *Whether the Knowledge of God Is Discursive?*

We proceed thus to the Seventh Article: It seems that the knowledge of God is discursive.

Objection 1. For the knowledge of God is not habitual knowledge, but actual knowledge. Now the Philosopher says:[1] "The habit of knowledge may regard many things at once; but actual understanding regards only one thing at a time." Therefore as God knows many things, Himself and others, as shown above (AA. 2, 5), it seems that He does not understand all at once, but discourses from one to another.

Obj. 2. Further, discursive knowledge is to know the effect through its cause. But God knows other things through Himself, as an effect through its cause. Therefore His knowledge is discursive.

Obj. 3. Further, God knows each creature more perfectly than we know it. But we know the effects in their created causes, and thus we go discursively from causes to things caused. Therefore it seems that the same applies to God.

On the contrary, Augustine says (*De Trin.*

[1] *Topics,* II, 10 (114^{b}34).

xv),[1] "God does not see all things in their particularity or separately, as if He saw alternately here and there; but He sees all things together at once."

I answer that, In the divine knowledge there is no discursion, which appears as follows. In our knowledge there is a twofold discursion; one is according to succession only, as when we have actually understood anything, we turn ourselves to understand something else, while the other mode of discursion is according to causality, as when through principles we arrive at the knowledge of conclusions. The first kind of discursion cannot belong to God. For many things, which we understand in succession if each is considered in itself, we understand simultaneously if we see them in some one thing; if, for instance, we understand the parts in the whole, or see different things in a mirror. Now God sees all things in one thing, which is Himself. Therefore God sees all things together, and not successively as we have held (A. 5). Likewise the second mode of discursion cannot be applied to God. First, because this second mode of discursion presupposes the first mode; for whosoever proceeds from principles to conclusions does not consider both at once. Secondly, because to discourse thus is to proceed from the known to the unknown. Hence it is manifest that when the first is known, the second is still unknown, and thus the second is known not in the first, but from the first. Now the term of discursive reasoning is attained when the second is seen in the first, by resolving the effects into their causes; and then the discursion ceases. Hence as God sees His effects in Himself as in their cause, His knowledge is not discursive.

Reply Obj. 1. Although there is only one act of understanding in itself, nevertheless many things may be understood in some one thing, as shown above.

Reply Obj. 2. God does not know through the cause as though he knew the cause first and then previously unknown effects, but He knows the effects in the cause; and hence His knowledge is not discursive, as was shown above.

Reply Obj. 3. God sees the effects of created causes in the causes themselves much better than we can, but still not in such a manner that the knowledge of the effects is caused in Him by the knowledge of the created causes, as is the case with us; and hence His knowledge is not discursive.

[1] Chap. 14 (PL 42, 1077).

ARTICLE 8. *Whether the Knowledge of God Is the Cause of Things?*

We proceed thus to the Eighth Article: It seems that the knowledge of God is not the cause of things.

Objection 1. For Origen says, on Rom. 8. 30, *Whom He called, them He also justified,* etc.: "A thing will happen not because God knows it as future, but because it is future it is on that account known by God before it is made.[2]

Obj. 2. Further, given the cause, the effect follows. But the knowledge of God is eternal. Therefore if the knowledge of God is the cause of things created, it seems that creatures are eternal.

Obj. 3. Further, The thing known is prior to knowledge, and is its measure, as the Philosopher says.[3] But what is posterior and measured cannot be a cause. Therefore the knowledge of God is not the cause of things.

On the contrary, Augustine says (*De Trin.* xv),[4] "Not because they are, does God know all creatures spiritual and temporal, but because He knows them, therefore they are."

I answer that, The knowledge of God is the cause of things. For the knowledge of God is to all creatures what the knowledge of the artificer is to things made by his art. Now the knowledge of the artificer is the cause of the things made by his art from the fact that the artificer works by his intellect. Hence the form of the intellect must be the principle of operation, as heat is the principle of heating. Nevertheless, we must observe that a natural form, being a form that remains in that to which it gives being, denotes a principle of action according only as it has an inclination to an effect; and likewise, the intelligible form does not denote a principle of action in so far as it resides in the one who understands unless there is added to it the inclination to an effect, which inclination is through the will. For since the intelligible form has a relation to opposite things (since the same knowledge relates to opposites), it would not produce a determinate effect unless it were determined to one thing by the appetite, as the Philosopher says.[5] Now it is manifest that God causes things by His intellect, since His being is His act of understanding, and so His knowledge must be the cause of things, in so far as His will is joined to it. Hence the

[2] Bk. VII (PG 14, 1126).
[3] *Metaphysics,* X, 1 (1053ª33).
[4] Chap. 13 (PL 42, 1076); VI, 10 (PL 42, 931).
[5] *Metaphysics,* IX, 5 (1048ª11).

knowledge of God as the cause of things is usually called the knowledge of approbation.

Reply Obj. 1. Origen spoke in reference to that aspect of knowledge to which the idea of causality does not belong unless the will is joined to it, as is said above.

But when he says the reason why God foreknows some things is because they are future, this must be understood according to the cause of consequence, and not according to the cause of being. For if things are in the future, it follows that God knows them, but not that the futurity of things is the cause why God knows them.

Reply Obj. 2. The knowledge of God is the cause of things according as things are in His knowledge. Now that things should be eternal was not in the knowledge of God; hence although the knowledge of God is eternal, it does not follow that creatures are eternal.

Reply Obj. 3. Natural things are midway between the knowledge of God and our knowledge, for we receive knowledge from natural things, of which God is the cause by His knowledge. Hence, as the natural things of knowledge are prior to our knowledge, and are its measure, so, the knowledge of God is prior to natural things, and is the measure of them; as, for instance, a house is midway between the knowledge of the builder who made it and the knowledge of the one who gathers his knowledge of the house from the house already built.

ARTICLE 9. *Whether God Has Knowledge of Things That Are Not?*

We proceed thus to the Ninth Article: It seems that God has knowledge of beings only.

Objection 1. For the knowledge of God is of true things. But truth and being are convertible terms. Therefore the knowledge of God is not of things that are not.

Obj. 2. Further, knowledge requires likeness between the knower and the thing known. But those things that are not cannot have any likeness to God, Who is being itself. Therefore what is not cannot be known by God.

Obj. 3. Further, the knowledge of God is the cause of what is known by Him. But it is not the cause of things that are not, because a thing that is not has no cause. Therefore God has no knowledge of things that are not.

On the contrary, The Apostle says: *Who . . . calleth those things that are not as those that are* (Rom. 4. 17).

I answer that, God knows all things whatsoever that in any way are. Now it is possible that

things that are not absolutely should be in a certain sense. For things absolutely are which are in act, while things which are not in act are in the power either of God Himself or of a creature, whether in active power, or passive; whether in power of thought or of imagination, or of any other manner of meaning whatsoever. Whatever therefore can be made, or thought, or said by the creature, as also whatever He Himself can do, all are known to God, although they are not actual. And in so far it can be said that He has knowledge even of things that are not.

Now a certain difference is to be noted in the consideration of those things that are not actual. For though some of them may not be in act now, still they were, or they will be, and God is said to know all these with the knowledge of vision; for since God's act of understanding, which is His being, is measured by eternity, and since eternity is without succession, comprehending all time, the present glance of God extends over all time, and to all things which exist in any time, as to subjects present to Him. But there are other things in God's power, or the creature's, which nevertheless are not, nor will be, nor were; and as regards these He is said to have the knowledge, not of vision, but of simple intelligence. This is so called because the things we see around us have distinct being outside the seer.

Reply Obj. 1. Those things that are not actual are true in so far as they are in potency, for it is true that they are in potency; and as such they are known by God.

Reply Obj. 2. Since God is being itself everything exists in so far as it participates in the likeness of God, just as everything is hot in so far as it participates in heat. So also, things in potency are known by God, although they are not in act.

Reply Obj. 3. The knowledge of God when it is joined to His will is the cause of things. Hence it is not necessary that whatever God knows, is, or was, or will be, but only what He wills to be, or permits to be. Further, it is in the knowledge of God not that they are, but that they are possible.

ARTICLE 10. *Whether God Knows Evil Things?*

We proceed thus to the Tenth Article: It seems that God does not know evil things.

Objection 1. For the Philosopher says[1] that the intellect which is not in potency does not know privation. But evil is "the privation of

[1] *Soul,* III, 6 (430[b]23).

good," as Augustine says.[1] Therefore, as the intellect of God is never in potency but is always in act, as is clear from the foregoing (A. 2), it seems that God does not know evil things.

Obj. 2. Further, all knowledge is either the cause of the thing known, or is caused by it. But the knowledge of God is not the cause of evil, nor is it caused by evil. Therefore God does not know evil things.

Obj. 3. Further, everything known is known either by its likeness, or by its opposite. But whatever God knows, He knows through His essence, as is clear from the foregoing (AA. 2, 5). Now the divine essence neither is the likeness of evil, nor is evil contrary to it, for to the divine essence there is no contrary, as Augustine says.[2] Therefore God does not know evil things.

Obj. 4. Further, what is known through another and not through itself is imperfectly known. But evil is not known by God through itself, because otherwise evil would be in God, for the thing known must be in the knower. Therefore if evil is known through another, namely, through good, it would be known by Him imperfectly, which cannot be, for the knowledge of God is not imperfect. Therefore God does not know evil things.

On the contrary, It is written (Prov. 15. 11), *Hell and destruction are before God* (Vulg., the Lord).

I answer that, Whoever knows a thing perfectly must know all that can happen to it. Now there are some good things to which corruption by evil may happen. Hence God would not know good things perfectly unless He also knew evil things. Now a thing is knowable in the degree in which it is; hence, since this is the being of evil that it is the privation of good, by the very fact that God knows good things He knows evil things also, just as by light is known darkness. Hence Dionysius says (*Div. Nom.* vii)[3]: "God through Himself receives the vision of darkness, not otherwise seeing darkness except through light."

Reply Obj. 1. The saying of the Philosopher must be understood as meaning that the intellect which is not in potency does not know privation by privation existing in it; and this agrees with what he had said previously, that a point and every indivisible thing are known by privation of division. This is because simple and indivisible forms are in our intellect not ac-

tually, but only in potency; for were they actually in our intellect, they would not be known by privation. It is thus that simple things are known by separate substances. God therefore knows evil not by privation existing in Himself, but by the opposite good.

Reply Obj. 2. The knowledge of God is not the cause of evil, but is the cause of the good by which evil is known.

Reply Obj. 3. Although evil is not opposed to the divine essence, which is not corruptible by evil, it is opposed to the effects of God, which He knows by His essence; and knowing them, He knows the opposite evils.

Reply Obj. 4. To know a thing by something else only belongs to imperfect knowledge if that thing is of itself knowable; but evil is not of itself knowable, because the very notion of evil means the privation of good. Therefore evil can neither be defined nor known except by good.

ARTICLE 11. *Whether God Knows Singular Things?*.

We proceed thus to the Eleventh Article: It seems that God does not know singular things.

Objection 1. For the divine intellect is more immaterial than the human intellect. Now the human intellect by reason of its immateriality does not know singular things, but as the Philosopher says,[4] "Reason has to do with universals, sense with singular things." Therefore God does not know singular things.

Obj. 2. Further, in us those powers alone know the singular which receive the species not abstracted from material conditions. But in God things are in the highest degree abstracted from all materiality. Therefore God does not know singular things.

Obj. 3. Further, all knowledge is through some likeness. But the likeness of singular things in so far as they are singular does not seem to be in God; for the principle of singularity is matter, which, since it is being in potency only, is altogether unlike God, Who is pure act. Therefore God cannot know singular things.

On the contrary, It is written (Prov. 16. 2), *All the ways of a man are open to His eyes.*

I answer that, God knows singular things. For all perfections found in creatures pre-exist in God in a higher way, as is clear from the foregoing (Q. IV, A. 2). Now to know singular things is part of our perfection. Hence God must know singular things. Even the Philosopher considers it incongruous that anything

---

[1] *Confessions,* III, 12 (PL 32, 688).
[2] *City of God,* XII, 2 (PL 41, 350).
[3] Sect. 2 (PG 3, 869).
[4] *Soul,* II, 5 (417b22).

known by us should be unknown to God; and thus against Empedocles he argues[1] that "God would be most ignorant if He did not know discord." Now the perfections which are divided among inferior beings exist simply and unitedly in God; hence, although by one power we know the universal and immaterial, and by another we know singular and material things, nevertheless God knows both by His simple intellect.

Now some, wishing to show how this can be, said that God knows singular things by universal causes.[2] For nothing exists in any singular thing that does not arise from some universal cause. They give the example of an astrologer who knows all the universal movements of the heavens, and can thence foretell all eclipses that are to come. This, however, is not enough, for singular things from universal causes attain to certain forms and powers which, however they may be joined together, are not individualized except by individual matter. Hence he who knows Socrates because he is white, or because he is the son of Sophroniscus, or because of something of that kind, would not know him in so far as he is this particular man. Hence according to the foregoing mode, God would not know singular things in their singularity.

On the other hand, others have said[3] that God knows singular things by the application of universal causes to particular effects. But this means nothing, because no one can apply a thing to another unless he first knows that thing; hence the said application cannot be the reason of knowing the particular, for it presupposes the knowledge of singular things.

Therefore it must be said otherwise, that, since God is the cause of things by His knowledge, as stated above (A. 8), His knowledge extends as far as His causality extends. Hence as the active power of God extends not only to forms, which are the source of universality, but also to matter, as we shall prove further on (Q. XLIV, A. 2), the knowledge of God must extend to singular things, which are individualized by matter. For since He knows things other than Himself by His essence, as being the likeness of things, or as their active principle, His essence must be the sufficing principle of knowing all things made by Him, not only in the universal, but also in the singular. The same would apply

to the knowledge of the artificer, if it were productive of the whole thing, and not only of the form.

Reply Obj. 1. Our intellect abstracts the intelligible species from the individualizing principles; hence the intelligible species in our intellect cannot be the likeness of the individual principles, and on that account our intellect does not know the singular. But the intelligible species in the divine intellect, which is the essence of God, is immaterial not by abstraction but of itself, being the principle of all the principles which enter into the composition of things, whether principles of the species or principles of the individual. Hence by it God knows not only universal, but also singular things.

Reply Obj. 2. Although as regards the species in the divine intellect, its being has no material conditions like the species received in the imagination and sense, yet its power extends to both immaterial and material things.

Reply Obj. 3. Although matter as regards its potentiality recedes from likeness to God, yet, even in so far as it has being in this way, it retains a certain likeness to the divine being.

ARTICLE 12. *Whether God Can Know Infinite Things?*

We proceed thus to the Twelfth Article: It seems that God cannot know infinite things.

Objection 1. For the infinite, as such, is unknown; since the infinite is that which, "to those who measure it, leaves always something more to be measured," as the Philosopher says.[4] Moreover, Augustine says[5] that "whatever is comprehended by knowledge is bounded by the comprehension of the knower." Now infinite things have no boundary. Therefore they cannot be comprehended by the knowledge of God.

Obj. 2. Further, if we say that things infinite in themselves are finite in God's knowledge, against this it may be urged that the essence of the infinite is that it is untraversable, and the finite that it is traversable, as said in the *Physics*.[6] But the infinite is not traversable either by the finite or by the infinite, as is proved in *Physics*.[7] Therefore the infinite cannot be bounded by the finite, nor even by the infinite. And so the infinite cannot be finite in God's knowledge, which is infinite.

Obj. 3. Further, the knowledge of God is the measure of what is known. But it is contrary to

---

[1] *Soul*, I, 5 (410ᵇ4); *Metaphysics*, III, 4 (1000ᵇ3).

[2] Cf. Averroes, *Dest. Dest.*, disp. VI (IX,85F); cf. also Algazel, *Metaph.*, tr. III, sent. 5 (MK 71.16); Avicenna, *Metaph.*, VIII, 6 (100rb).

[3] Cf. Averroes, *Dest. Dest.*, disp. 6 (IX, 85M).

[4] *Physics*, III, 6 (207ᵃ7).

[5] *City of God*, XII, 18 (PL 41, 368).

[6] Aristotle, III, 4 (204ᵃ3).

[7] Aristotle, VI, 7 (238ᵇ17).

the notion of the infinite that it be measured. Therefore infinite things cannot be known by God.

On the contrary, Augustine says,[1] "Although we cannot number the infinite, nevertheless it can be comprehended by Him whose knowledge has no bounds."

I answer that, Since God knows not only things which are in act but also things in the power of Himself or created things, as shown above (A. 9), and as these must be infinite, it must be held that He knows infinite things. Although the knowledge of vision which is only of things that are, or will be, or were, is not of infinite things, as some say,[2] (for we do not say that the world existed from eternity, nor that generation and movement will go on for ever, so that individuals be infinitely multiplied), yet, if we consider more attentively, we must hold that God knows infinite things even by the knowledge of vision. For God knows even the thoughts and affections of hearts, which will be multiplied to infinity as rational creatures endure for ever.

The reason of this is to be found in the fact that the knowledge of every knower is measured by the mode of the form which is the principle of knowledge. For the sensible species in sense is the likeness of only one individual thing, and can give the knowledge of only one individual. But the intelligible species of our intellect is the likeness of the thing as regards the nature of the species, which can be shared in by infinite particulars. Hence our intellect by the intelligible species of man in a certain way knows infinite men—not however as distinguished from each other, but as communicating in the nature of the species; and the reason is because the intelligible species of our intellect is the likeness of man not as to the individual principles, but as to the principles of the species. On the other hand, the divine essence, whereby the divine intellect understands, is a sufficing likeness of all things that are, or can be, not only as regards the common principles, but also as regards the principles proper to each one, as shown above (A. 11). Hence it follows that the knowledge of God extends to infinite things, even as distinct from each other.

Reply Obj. 1. "The idea of the infinite pertains to quantity," as the Philosopher says.[3] But the idea of quantity implies the order of parts. Therefore to know the infinite according to the

mode of the infinite is to know part after part; and in this way the infinite cannot be known, for whatever quantity of parts be taken, there will always remain something else outside. But God does not know the infinite or infinite things as if He enumerated part after part, since He knows all things simultaneously, and not successively, as said above (A. 7). Hence there is nothing to prevent Him from knowing infinite things.

Reply Obj. 2. Transition imports a certain succession of parts, and hence it is that the infinite cannot be traversed by the finite, nor by the infinite. But equality suffices for comprehension, because that is said to be comprehended which has nothing outside the comprehender. Hence, it is not against the idea of the infinite to be comprehended by the infinite. And so, what is infinite in itself can be called finite to the knowledge of God as comprehended; but not as if it were traversable.

Reply Obj. 3. The knowledge of God is the measure of things, not quantitatively, for the infinite does not have this kind of measure, but because it measures the essence and truth of things. For everything has truth of nature according to the degree in which it imitates the knowledge of God, as the thing made by art agrees with the art. Granted, however, an actually infinite number of things, for instance, an infinitude of men, or an infinitude in continuous quantity, as an infinitude of air, as some of the ancients held,[4] yet it is manifest that these would have a determinate and finite being, because their being would be limited to some determinate nature. Hence they would be measurable as regards the knowledge of God.

ARTICLE 13. *Whether the Knowledge of God Is of Future Contingent Things?*

We proceed thus to the Thirteenth Article: It seems that the knowledge of God is not of future contingent things.

Objection 1. For from a necessary cause proceeds a necessary effect. But the knowledge of God is the cause of things known, as said above (A. 8). Since therefore that knowledge is necessary, what He knows must also be necessary. Therefore the knowledge of God is not of contingent things.

Obj. 2. Further, every conditional proposition of which the antecedent is absolutely necessary must have an absolutely necessary consequent. For the antecedent is to the consequent

---

[1] *City of God,* XII, 18 (PL 41, 368).
[2] Avicenna and Algazel; cf. above, Q. VII, A. 4; below, Q. XLVI, A. 2, Reply obj. 8.   [3] *Physics,* I, 2 (185[a]33).
[4] Anaximenes and Diogenes; cf. Aristotle, *Physics,* III, 4 (203[a]18); *Metaphysics,* I, 3 (984[a]5).

as principles are to the conclusion, and from necessary principles only a necessary conclusion can follow, as is proved in *Posterior Analytics*.[1] But this is a true conditional proposition, "If God knew that this thing will be, it will be,"[2] for the knowledge of God is only of true things. Now the antecedent conditional of this is absolutely necessary, because it is eternal, and because it is signified as past. Therefore the consequent is also absolutely necessary. Therefore whatever God knows, is necessary; and so the knowledge of God is not of contingent things.

Obj. 3. Further, everything known by God must necessarily be, because even what we ourselves know must necessarily be; and, of course, the knowledge of God is much more certain than ours. But no future contingent thing must necessarily be. Therefore no contingent future thing is known by God.

On the contrary, It is written (Ps. 32. 15), *He Who hath made the hearts of every one of them; Who understandeth all their works,* that is, of men. Now the works of men are contingent, since they are subject to free choice. Therefore God knows future contingent things.

I answer that, Since as was shown above (A. 9), God knows all things, not only things actual but also things in the power of Him and the creature; and since some of these are future contingent to us, it follows that God knows future contingent things.

In evidence of this, we must consider that a contingent thing can be considered in two ways. First, in itself, in so far as it is now in act, and in this sense it is not considered as future, but as present; neither is it considered as contingent to one of two terms, but as determined to one; and on account of this it can infallibly yield certain knowledge, for instance to the sense of sight, as when I see that Socrates is sitting down. In another way a contingent thing can be considered as it is in its cause; and in this way it is considered as future, and as a contingent thing not yet determined to one, because a contingent cause has relation to opposite things; and in this sense a contingent thing is not subject to any certain knowledge. Hence, whoever knows a contingent effect in its cause only, has merely a conjectural knowledge of it. Now God knows all contingent things not only as they

are in their causes, but also as each one of them is actually in itself.

And although contingent things become actual successively, nevertheless God knows contingent things not successively, as they are in their own being, as we do, but simultaneously. The reason is because His knowledge is measured by eternity, as is also His being; and eternity being simultaneously whole comprises all time, as said above (Q. X, A. 2). Hence, all things that are in time are present to God from eternity, not only because He has the types of things present within Him, as some say,[3] but because His glance is carried from eternity over all things as they are in their presentness.

Hence it is manifest that contingent things are infallibly known by God, since they are subject to the divine sight in their presentness; yet they are future contingent things in relation to their own causes.

Reply Obj. 1. Although the supreme cause is necessary, the effect may be contingent by reason of the proximate contingent cause, just as the germination of a plant is contingent by reason of the proximate contingent cause, although the movement of the sun which is the first cause, is necessary. So likewise things known by God are contingent on account of their proximate causes, although the knowledge of God, which is the first cause, is necessary.

Reply Obj. 2. Some[4] say that this antecedent, "God knew this contingent to be future," is not necessary, but contingent, because, although it is past, still it imports relation to the future. This however does not remove necessity from it, for whatever has had relation to the future, must have had it, although the future sometimes does not follow.

On the other hand some say[5] that this antecedent is contingent, because it is a composite of necessary and contingent, as this saying is contingent, "Socrates is a white man." But this also is to no purpose, for when we say, "God knew this contingent to be future," contingent is used here only as the matter of the word, and not as the chief part of the proposition. Hence its contingency or necessity has no reference to the necessity or contingency of the proposition, or to its being true or false. For it may be just as true that I said a man is an ass, as that I said Socrates runs, or God is; and the same applies to necessary and contingent.

[1] Aristotle, I, 6 (75ª 4).

[2] Cf. Anselm, *De Concord. Praesc. cum Lib. Arb.*, Q. I (PL 158, 509); cf. also Augustine, *City of God*, V, 9; XI, 21 (PL 41, 148, 334); *De Lib. Arb.*, III, 4 (PL 32, 1276); Boethius, *De Consol.*, V, 3, 6 (PL 63, 840, 860); Peter Lombard, *Sent.*, I, d. 38, chap. 2 (QR I, 244).

[3] Avicenna. Cf. *Meta.*, VIII, 6 (100rb).

[4] Bonaventure, *In Sent.*, I, d. 38, A. 2, Q. 2 (QR I, 678); Albert the Great, *In Sent.*, I, d. 38, A. 4 (BO XXVI, 290).

[5] Robert Grosseteste, *De Lib. Arb.*, chap. 6 (BR 170.8).

Hence it must be said that this antecedent is absolutely necessary. Nor does it follow, as some say,[1] that the consequent is absolutely necessary, because the antecedent is the remote cause of the consequent, which is contingent by reason of the proximate cause. But this is to no purpose. For the conditional would be false were its antecedent the remote necessary cause and the consequent a contingent effect; as, for example, if I said, "if the sun moves, the grass will grow."

Therefore we must reply otherwise that when the antecedent contains anything belonging to an act of the soul, the consequent must be taken not as it is in itself, but as it is in the soul; for the being of a thing in itself is different from the being of a thing in the soul. For example, when I say, "If the soul understands something, that something is immaterial," this to to be understood that it is immaterial as it is in the intellect, not as it is in itself. Likewise if I say, "If God knew anything, it will be," the consequent must be understood as it is subject to the divine knowledge, that is, as it is in its presentiality. And thus it is necessary, as also is the antecedent; "for everything that is, while it is, must necessarily be," as the Philosopher says in *Interpretation*.[2]

Reply Obj. 3. Things reduced to act in time are known by us successively in time, but by God are known in eternity, which is above time. Hence to us they cannot be certain, since as we know future contingent things as such but, they are certain to God alone, whose understanding is in eternity above time; just as he who goes along the road does not see those who come after him, although he who sees the whole road from a height sees at once all travelling by the way. Hence what is known by us must be necessary, even as it is in itself; for what is future contingent in itself cannot be known by us. But what is known by God must be necessary according to the mode in which they are subject to the divine knowledge, as already stated (ANS. 1), but not absolutely as considered in their own causes. Hence also this proposition, "Everything known by God must necessarily be," is usually distinguished,[3] for this may refer to the thing, or to the saying. If

it refers to the thing, it is divided, and false, for the sense is, "Everything which God knows is necessary," If understood of the saying it is composite and true, for the sense is, "This proposition, 'that which is known by God is' is necessary."

Now some[4] urge an objection and say that this distinction holds good with regard to forms that are separable from the subject; thus if I said, "It is possible for a white thing to be black," it is false as applied to the saying, and true as applied to the thing, for a thing which is white, can become black; but this saying, "a white thing is black," can never be true. But in forms that are inseparable from the subject, this distinction does not hold, for instance, if I said, "A black crow can be white"; for in both senses it is false. Now to be known by God is inseparable from the thing, for what is known by God cannot be not known. This objection, however, would hold if these words "that which is known" implied any disposition inherent to the subject; but since they import an act of the knower, something can be attributed to the thing known, in itself (even if it always be known), which is not attributed to it in so far as it stands under actual knowledge; thus material being is attributed to a stone in itself, which is not attributed to it according as it is known.

ARTICLE 14. *Whether God Knows Enunciable Things?*

We proceed thus to the Fourteenth Article: It seems that God does not know enunciable things.

Objection 1. For to know enunciable things belongs to our intellect as it composes and divides. But in the divine intellect there is no composition. Therefore God does not know enunciable things.

Obj. 2. Further, every kind of knowledge is made through some likeness. But in God there is no likeness of enunciable things, since He is altogether simple. Therefore God does not know enunciable things.

On the contrary, It is written: *The Lord knoweth the thoughts of men* (Ps. 93. 11). But enunciable things are contained in the thoughts of men. Therefore God knows enunciable things.

I answer that, Since it is in the power of our intellect to form enunciations, and since God

---

[1] Alexander of Hales, *Summa Theol.*, I, 171, 184 (QR I, 255, 270); Alan of Lille, *Theol. Reg.*, REG. 66 (PL 210, 653).

[2] Aristotle, 9 (19ᵃ23).

[3] See William of Shyreswood, *Introd. in Logicam* (Grabmann, p. 89); Wm. of Auxerre, *Summa Aurea*, 1, 9, chap. 2 (fol. 21vb); Albert the Great, *In Prior. An.*, 1, 4, 16 (BO 1, 562).

[4] Cf. Alexander of Hales, *Summa Theol.* I, 185 (QR I, 271); cf. also St. Thomas, *In Sent.*, I, d. 38, Q. 1, A. 5, obj. 5; *De ver.*, Q. II, A. 12, obj. 4.

knows whatever is in His own power or in that of creatures, as said above (A. 9), it follows of necessity that God knows all enunciations that can be formed.

Now just as He knows material things immaterially, and composite things simply, so likewise He knows enunciable things not after the manner of enunciable things, as if in His intellect there were composition or division of enunciations, but He knows each thing by simple intelligence, by understanding the essence of each thing, as if we by the very fact that we understand what man is, were to understand all that can be predicated of man. This, however, does not happen in our intellect, which discourses from one thing to another, because the intelligible species represents one thing in such a way as not to represent another. Hence when we understand what man is, we do not from this understand other things which belong to him, but we understand them one by one, according to a certain succession. On this account the things we understand separately we must reduce to one by way of composition or division, by forming an enunciation. Now the species of the divine intellect, which is God's essence, suffices to represent all things. Hence by understanding His essence, God knows the essences of all things, and also whatever can happen to them.

Reply Obj. 1. This objection would avail if God knew enunciable things after the manner of enunciable things.

Reply Obj. 2. Enunciatory composition signifies some being of a thing; and thus God by His being, which is His essence, is the likeness of all those things which are signified by enunciable things.

ARTICLE 15. *Whether the Knowledge of God Is Variable?*

We proceed thus to the Fifteenth Article: It seems that the knowledge of God is variable.

Objection 1. For knowledge is related to what is knowable. But whatever imports relation to the creature is applied to God from time, and varies according to the variation of creatures. Therefore the knowledge of God is variable according to the variation of creatures.

Obj. 2. Further, whatever God can make, He can know. But God can make more than He does. Therefore He can know more than He knows. Thus His knowledge can vary according to increase and diminution.

Obj. 3. Further, God knew that Christ would be born. But He does not know now that Christ will be born, because Christ is not to be born in the future. Therefore God does not know everything He once knew; and thus the knowledge of God is variable.

On the contrary, It is said, that in God *there is no change nor shadow of alteration* (James 1. 17).

I answer that, Since the knowledge of God is His substance, as is clear from the foregoing (A. 4), just as His substance is altogether immutable, as shown above (Q. IX, A. 1), so His knowledge likewise must be altogether invariable.

Reply Obj. 1. "Lord," "Creator," and the like, import relations to creatures in so far as they are in themselves. But the knowledge of God imports relation to creatures in so far as they are in God, because everything is actually understood according as it is in the one who understands. Now created things are in God in an invariable manner, while they exist variably in themselves. We may also say that "Lord," "Creator," and the like, import the relations consequent upon the acts which are understood as terminating in the creatures themselves, as they are in themselves; and thus these relations are attributed to God variously, according to the variation of creatures. But knowledge and love, and the like, import relations consequent upon the acts which are understood to be in God, and therefore these are predicated of God in an invariable manner.

Reply Obj. 2. God knows also what He can make, and does not make. Hence from the fact that He can make more than He makes, it does not follow that He can know more than He knows, unless this be referred to the knowledge of vision, according to which He is said to know those things which are in act in some period of time. But from the fact that He knows some things might be which are not, or that some things might not be which are, it does not follow that His knowledge is variable, but rather that He knows the variability of things. If, however, anything existed which God did not previously know, and afterwards knew, then His knowledge would be variable. But this could not be; for whatever is, or can be in any period of time, is known by God in His eternity. Therefore from the fact that a thing exists in some period of time, it follows that it is known by God from eternity. Therefore it cannot be granted that God can know more than He knows, because such a proposition implies that first of all He did not know, and then afterwards knew.

Reply Obj. 3. The Nominalists[1] of old said that it was the same thing to say Christ is born and will be born, and was born, because the same thing is signified by these three—namely, the nativity of Christ. Therefore it follows, they said, that whatever God knew, He knows; because now He knows that Christ is born, which means the same thing as that Christ will be born. This opinion, however, is false; both because the diversity in the parts of a sentence causes a diversity of enunciations, and because it would follow that a proposition which is true once would be always true, which is contrary to what the Philosopher lays down[2] when he says that this sentence, "Socrates sits," is true when he is sitting, and false when he rises up. Therefore, it must be conceded that this proposition is not true, "Whatever God knew He knows," if referred to enunciable propositions. But because of this, it does not follow that the knowledge of God is variable. For as it is without variation in the divine knowledge that God knows one and the same thing sometime to be, and sometime not to be, so it is without variation in the divine knowledge that God knows an enunciable proposition is sometime true, and sometime false. The knowledge of God, however, would be variable if He knew enunciable things by way of enunciation, by composition and division, as occurs in our intellect. Hence our knowledge varies either as regards truth and falsity, for example, if when a thing suffers change we retained the same opinion about it; or as regards diverse opinions, as if we first thought that anyone was sitting, and afterwards thought that he was not sitting; neither of which can be in God.

ARTICLE 16. *Whether God Has a Speculative Knowledge of Things?*

We proceed thus to the Sixteenth Article: It seems that God has not a speculative knowledge of things.

Objection 1. For the knowledge of God is the cause of things, as shown above (A. 8). But speculative knowledge is not the cause of the things known. Therefore the knowledge of God is not speculative.

Obj. 2. Further, speculative knowledge comes by abstraction from things, which does not belong to the divine knowledge. Therefore the knowledge of God is not speculative.

[1] Cf. Abelard, *Introd. ad Theol.*, III, 5 (PL 178, 1102); Lombard, *Sent.*, I, d. 41, chap. 3 (QR I, 258); cf. Chenu, AHDLM (1936). pp. 5–28.
[2] *Categories*, 5 (4ᵃ23).

On the contrary, Whatever is the more excellent must be attributed to God. But speculative knowledge is more excellent than practical knowledge, as the Philosopher says in the beginning of the *Metaphysics*.[3] Therefore God has a speculative knowledge of things.

I answer that, Some knowledge is speculative only, some is practical only, and some is partly speculative and partly practical. In proof of this it must be observed that knowledge can be called speculative in three ways. First, on the part of the things known, which are not operable by the knower; such is the knowledge of man about natural or divine things. Secondly, as regards the manner of knowing—as, for instance, if a builder consider a house by defining and dividing, and considering what belongs to it in general, for this is to consider operable things in a speculative manner, and not as they are operable; for operable means the application of form to matter, and not the resolution of the composite into its universal formal principles. Thirdly, as regards the end; "for the practical intellect differs in its end from the speculative," as the Philosopher says.[4] For the practical intellect is ordered to the end of the operation, whereas the end of the speculative intellect is the consideration of truth. Hence if a builder should consider how a house can be made, not ordering this to the end of operation, but only to know (how to do it), this would be only a speculative consideration as regards the end, although it concerns an operable thing. Therefore knowledge which is speculative by reason of the thing itself known, is merely speculative. But that which is speculative either in its mode or as to its end is partly speculative and partly practical; and when it is ordered to an operative end it is simply practical.

In accordance with this, therefore, it must be said that God has of Himself a speculative knowledge only, for He Himself is not operable.

But of all other things He has both speculative and practical knowledge. He has speculative knowledge as regards the mode, for whatever we know speculatively in things by defining and dividing, God knows all this much more perfectly.

Now of things which He can make, but does not make at any time, He has not a practical knowledge, accordingly as knowledge is called practical from the end. But He has a practical knowledge of what He makes in some period of time. And, as regards evil things, although they are not operable by Him, yet they fall under

[3] I, 1 (982ᵃ1).   [4] *Soul*, III, 10 (433ᵃ14).

His practical knowledge, like good things, in so far as He permits, or impedes, or directs them; as also sicknesses fall under the practical knowledge of the physician in so far as he cures them by his art.

Reply Obj. 1. The knowledge of God is the cause, not indeed of Himself, but of other things. He is actually the cause of some, that is, of things that come to be in some period of time; and He is virtually the cause of others, that is, of things which He can make, and which nevertheless are never made.

Reply Obj. 2. The fact that knowledge is derived from things known does not essentially belong to speculative knowledge, but only accidentally in so far as it is human.

In answer to what is objected *on the contrary*, we must say that perfect knowledge of operable things is obtainable only if they are known in so far as they are operable. Therefore, since the knowledge of God is in every way perfect, He must know what is operable by Him, in so far as they are of this kind, and not only in so far as they are speculative. Nevertheless this does not impair the nobility of His speculative knowledge, since He sees all things other than Himself in Himself, and He knows Himself speculatively; and so in the speculative knowledge of Himself, He possesses both speculative and practical knowledge of all other things.

QUESTION XV
OF IDEAS
(In Three Articles)

AFTER considering the knowledge of God, it remains to consider ideas. And about this there are three points of inquiry: (1) Whether there are ideas? (2) Whether they are many, or one only? (3) Whether there are ideas of all things known by God?

ARTICLE 1. *Whether There Are Ideas?*

We proceed thus to the First Article: It seems that there are no ideas.

Objection 1. For Dionysius says (*Div. Nom.* vii),[1] that God does not know things by ideas. But ideas are for nothing else except that things may be known through them. Therefore there are no ideas.

Obj. 2. Further, God knows all things in Himself, as has been already said (Q. XIV, A. 5). But He does not know Himself through an idea; neither therefore other things.

[1] Sect. 2 (PG 3, 868).

Obj. 3. Further, an idea is considered to be the principle of knowledge and operation. But the divine essence is a sufficient principle of knowing and effecting all things. It is not therefore necessary to suppose ideas.

On the contrary, Augustine says (*Octog. Tri. Quæst., qu.* xlvi),[2] "Such is the power inherent in ideas that no one can be wise unless they are understood."

I answer that, It is necessary to place ideas in the divine mind. For the Greek word Ἰδέα is in Latin *Forma.* Hence by ideas are understood the forms of things, existing apart from the things themselves. Now the form of anything existing apart from the thing itself can be for one of two ends: either to be the type of that of which it is called the form, or to be the principle of the knowledge of that thing, according as the forms of things knowable are said to be in the knower. In either case we must suppose ideas, as is clear for the following reason.

In all things not generated by chance, the form must be the end of any generation whatsoever. But an agent does not act on account of the form except in so far as the likeness of the form is in the agent, as may happen in two ways. For in some agents the form of the thing to be made pre-exists according to its natural being, as in those that act by their nature; as a man generates a man, or fire generates fire. But in other agents (the form of the thing to be made pre-exists) according to intelligible being, as in those that act by the intellect; and thus the likeness of a house pre-exists in the mind of the builder. And this may be called the idea of the house, since the builder intends to build his house like to the form conceived in his mind.

As then the world was not made by chance, but by God acting by His intellect, as will appear later (Q. XX, A. 4; Q. XLIV, A. 3), there must exist in the divine mind a form to the likeness of which the world was made. And in this the notion of an idea consists.

Reply Obj. 1. God does not understand things according to an idea existing outside Himself. Thus Aristotle[3] rejects the opinion of Plato, who held that ideas existed of themselves, and not in the intellect.

Reply Obj. 2. Although God knows Himself and all else by His own essence, yet His essence is the operative principle of all things, except of

[2] PL 40, 29.
[3] *Metaphysics,* III, 2; VII, 6 (997b6; 1031b6); cf. Averroes, *In Meta.,* XII, 18 (VIII, 305D); *De Gener.* II, 52 (V, 384G).

Himself. It has therefore the nature of an idea with respect to other things, though not with respect to Himself.

Reply Obj. 3. God is the likeness of all things according to His essence. Therefore an idea in God is identical with His essence.

ARTICLE 2. *Whether Ideas Are Many?*

We proceed thus to the Second Article: It seems that ideas are not many.

Objection 1. For an idea in God is His essence. But God's essence is one only. Therefore there is only one idea.

Obj. 2. Further, as the idea is the principle of knowing and operating, so are art and wisdom. But in God there are not several arts or wisdoms. Therefore in Him there is no plurality of ideas.

Obj. 3. Further, if it be said that ideas are multiplied according to their relations to different creatures, it may be argued on the contrary that the plurality of ideas is eternal. If, then, ideas are many, but creatures temporal, then the temporal must be the cause of the eternal.

Obj. 4. Further, these relations are either real in creatures only, or in God also. If in creatures only, since creatures are not from eternity, the plurality of ideas cannot be from eternity, if ideas are multiplied only according to these relations. But if they are real in God, it follows that there is a real plurality in God other than the plurality of Persons, and this is against the teaching of Damascene (*De Fide Orthod.* i, 10),[1] who says, in God all things are one, except ingenerability, generation, and procession. Ideas therefore are not many.

On the contrary, Augustine says (*Octog. Tri. Quæst., qu.* xlvi),[2] "Ideas are certain principal forms, or permanent and immutable types of things, they themselves not being formed. Thus they are eternal, and existing always in the same manner, as being contained in the divine intelligence. Whilst, however, they themselves neither come into being nor decay, yet we say that in accordance with them everything is formed that can arise or decay, and all that actually does so."

I answer that, It must necessarily be held that ideas are many. In proof of which it is to be considered that in every effect the ultimate end is the proper intention of the principal agent, as the order of an army (is the proper intention) of the general. Now the highest good existing in things is the good of the order of the universe, as the Philosopher clearly teaches in the

Metaphysics.[3] Therefore the order of the universe is properly intended by God, and is not the accidental result of a succession of agents, as has been supposed by those[4] who have taught that God created only the first creature, and that this creature created the second creature, and so on, until this great multitude of beings was produced. According to this opinion God would have the idea of the first created thing alone; but if the order itself of the universe was created by Him immediately, and intended by Him, He must have the idea of the order of the universe. Now there cannot be an idea of any whole unless particular ideas are had of those parts of which the whole is made; just as a builder cannot conceive the species of a house unless he has the notion of each of its parts. So, then, it must be that in the divine mind there are the proper notions of all things. Hence Augustine says (*Octog. Tri Quæst., qu.* xlvi),[5] "that each thing was created by God according to the idea proper to it," from which it follows that in the divine mind ideas are many.

Now it can easily be seen how this is not contrary to the simplicity of God, if we consider that the idea of a work is in the mind of the operator as that which is understood, and not as the species by which he understands, which is a form that makes the intellect in act. For the form of the house in the mind of the builder is something understood by him, to the likeness of which he forms the house in matter. Now, it is not against the simplicity of the divine mind that it understand many things, though it would be against its simplicity were His understanding to be formed by many species. Hence many ideas exist in the divine mind, as understood by it.

And this can be seen in this way. Since God knows His own essence perfectly, He knows it according to every mode in which it can be known. Now it can be known not only as it is in itself, but as it can be participated in by creatures according to some degree of likeness. But every creature has its own proper species, according to which it participates in some degree in likeness to the divine essence. So far, therefore, as God knows His essence as capable of such imitation by any creature, He knows it as the particular type and idea of that creature; and in like manner as regards other creatures. So it is clear that God understands many particular types of many things, and these are many ideas.

[1] PG 94, 837.   [2] PL 40, 30.

[3] XII, 10 (1075ᵃ13).   [4] See below, Q. XLV, A. 5.
[5] PL 40, 30.

Reply Obj. 1. The divine essence is not called an idea in so far as it is that essence, but only in so far as it is the likeness or type of this or that thing. Hence ideas are said to be many, according as many types are understood through the self-same essence.

Reply Obj. 2. By wisdom and art we signify that by which God understands; but by idea, that which God understands. For God by one act of understanding understands many things, and not only according to what they are in themselves, but also according as they are understood, and this is to understand the several types of things. In the same way, an artist is said to understand a house when he understands the form of the house in matter. But if he understands the form of a house, as devised by himself, from the fact that he understands that he understands it, he thereby understands the type or the idea of the house. Now not only does God understand many things by His essence, but He also understands that He understands many things by His essence. And this means that He understands the several types of things, or that many ideas are in His intellect as understood by Him.

Reply Obj. 3. Such relations, whereby ideas are multiplied, are caused not by the things themselves, but by the divine intellect comparing its own essence with these things.

Reply Obj. 4. Relations multiplying ideas do not exist in created things, but in God. Yet they are not real relations, such as those by which the Persons are distinguished, but relations understood by God.

ARTICLE 3. *Whether There Are Ideas of All Things That God Knows?*

We proceed thus to the Third Article: It seems that there are not ideas in God of all things that He knows.

Objection 1. For the idea of evil is not in God; since it would follow that evil was in Him. But evil things are known by God. Therefore there are not ideas of all things that God knows.

Obj. 2. Further, God knows things that neither are, nor will be, nor have been, as has been said above (A. 9). But of such things there are no ideas, since, as Dionysius says (*Div. Nom.* v):[1] "Acts of the divine will are the determining and effective types of things." Therefore there are not in God ideas of all things known by him.

Obj. 3. Further, God knows prime matter, of

which there can be no idea, since it has no form. Hence the same conclusion.

Obj. 4. Further, it is certain that God knows not only species, but also genera, singulars, and accidents. But there are no ideas of these, according to Plato's teaching, who first taught ideas, as Augustine says (*Octog. Tri. Quæst., qu.* xlvi).[2] Therefore there are not ideas in God of all things known by Him.

On the contrary, Ideas are types existing in the divine mind, as is clear from Augustine (*ibid.*). But God has the proper types of all things that He knows, and therefore He has ideas of all things known by Him.

I answer that, As ideas, according to Plato,[3] are principles of the knowledge of things and of their generation, an idea has this twofold office, as it exists in the mind of God. So far as the idea is the principle of the making of things, it may be called an exemplar, and belongs to practical knowledge. But so far as it is a principle of knowledge, it is properly called a type, and may belong to speculative knowledge also. As an exemplar, therefore, it has respect to everything made by God in any period of time; but as a knowing principle it has respect to all things known by God, even though they never come to be in time, and to all things that He knows according to their proper type, in so far as they are known by Him in a speculative manner.

Reply Obj. 1. Evil is known by God not through its own type, but through the type of good. Evil, therefore, has no idea in God, neither in so far as an idea is an exemplar nor as a type.

Reply Obj. 2. God has no practical knowledge, except virtually, of things which neither are, nor will be, nor have been. Hence, with respect to these there is no idea in God in so far as idea signifies an exemplar, but only in so far as it denotes a type.

Reply Obj. 3. Plato is said by some[4] to have considered matter as not created, and therefore he posited not an idea of matter but a concause with matter. Since, however, we hold matter to be created by God, though not apart from form, matter has its idea in God; but not

---

[1] Sect. 8 (PG 3, 824).   [2] PL 40, 29.

[3] For ideas as principles in knowing, cf. below, Q. LXXXIV, A. 4; as principles in generation, cf. Aristotle, *Metaphysics,* I, 9 (991^{b}3); cf. *Phaedo* (100); *Timaeus,* (51); See also Seneca, *Epist.,* LXV (DD 639); Dionysius, *De Div., Nom.* v, 8 (PG 3, 823); Augustine, *Octo. Tri. Quæst.,* Q. XLVI (PL 40, 30).
[4] Unnamed commentators, in Chalcidius, *In Timaeum,* Chap. 248 (DD 245). Cf. Lombard, *Sent.,* II, d. 1, chap. 1. (QR I, 307).

apart from the idea of the composite, for matter in itself can neither have being, nor be known.

Reply Obj. 4. Genus can have no idea apart from the idea of species, in so far as idea denotes an exemplar, for genus cannot exist except in some species. The same is the case with those accidents that inseparably accompany their subject, for these come into being along with their subject. But accidents which are added to the subject have their special idea. For an architect produces through the form of the house all the accidents that originally accompany it, while those that are superadded to the house when completed, such as painting, or any other such thing, are produced through some other form. Now individual things, according to Plato,[1] have no other idea than that of the species; both because particular things are individualized by matter, which, as some say, he held to be uncreated and the concause with the idea, and because the intention of nature is for the species, and produces individuals only that in them the species may be preserved. However, divine providence extends not merely to species; but to individuals, as will be shown later (Q. XXII, A. 2).

QUESTION XVI
OF TRUTH
(In Eight Articles)

SINCE knowledge is of things that are true, after the consideration of the knowledge of God, we must inquire concerning truth. About this there are eight points of inquiry: (1) Whether truth resides in the thing, or only in the intellect? (2) Whether it resides only in the intellect composing and dividing? (3) On the comparison of the true to being (4) On the comparison of the true to the good. (5) Whether God is truth? (6) Whether all things are true by one truth, or by many? (7) On the eternity of truth. (8) On the unchangeableness of truth.

ARTICLE 1. *Whether Truth Is Only in the Intellect?*

We proceed thus to the First Article: It seems that truth is not only in the intellect, but rather in things.

Objection 1. For Augustine (*Soliloq.* ii, 5)[2] condemns this definition of truth, "That is true which is seen," since it would follow that stones hidden in the bosom of the earth would not be

true stones, as they are not seen. He also condemns the following, "That is true which is as it appears to the knower, who is willing and able to know," for according to this it would follow that nothing would be true unless someone could know it. Therefore he defines truth thus: "That is true which is." It seems, then, that truth resides in things, and not in the intellect.

Obj. 2. Further, whatever is true, is true by reason of truth. If, then, truth is only in the intellect, nothing will be true except in so far as it is understood. But this is the error of the ancient philosophers,[3] who said that whatever seems to be true is so. Consequently contradictories can be true at the same time, since contradictories seem to be true as seen by different persons at the same time.

Obj. 3. Further, "that on account of which a thing is so is itself more so," as is evident from the Philosopher.[4] But "it is from the fact that a thing is or is not, that our thought or word is true or false," as the Philosopher teaches.[5] Therefore truth resides rather in things than in the intellect.

On the contrary, The Philosopher says,[6] "The true and the false are not in things, but in the intellect."

I answer that, As the good denotes that towards which the appetite tends, so the true denotes that towards which the intellect tends. Now there is this difference between the appetite and the intellect, or any knowledge whatsoever, that knowledge is according as the thing known is in the knower, whilst appetite is according as the desirer tends towards the thing desired. Thus the term of the appetite, namely good, is in the thing desirable, and the term of knowledge, namely true, is in the intellect itself.

Now as good exists in a thing so far as that thing is related to the appetite—and hence the aspect of goodness passes on from the desirable thing to the appetite, according as the appetite is called good if the thing desired is good, so, since the true is in the intellect in so far as it is conformed to the thing understood, the aspect of the true must pass from the intellect to the thing understood, so that also the thing understood is said to be true in so far as it has some relation to the intellect.

Now a thing understood may be in relation to an intellect either essentially or accidentally. It is related essentially to an intellect on which

---

[1] Cf. Aristotle, *Metaphysics*, I, 9 (990[b]29).
[2] PL 32, 888.

[3] Democritus and Pythagoras, in Aristotle, *Soul*, I, 2 (404[a]28); *Metaphysics*, IV, 5 (1009[a]8).
[4] *Posterior Analytics*, I, 2 (72[a]29).
[5] *Categories*, 5 (4[b]8).
[6] *Metaphysics*, VI, 4 (1027[b]25).

it depends as regards its being, but accidentally to an intellect by which it is knowable; even as we may say that a house is related essentially to the intellect of the architect, but accidentally to the intellect upon which it does not depend.

Now we do not judge of a thing by what is in it accidentally, but by what is in it essentially. Hence, everything is said to be true absolutely in so far as it is related to the intellect from which it depends; and thus it is that artificial things are said to be true as being related to our intellect. For a house is said to be true that expresses the likeness of the form in the architect's mind, and words are said to be true so far as they are the signs of truth in the intellect. In the same way natural things are said to be true in so far as they express the likeness of the species that are in the divine mind. For a stone is called true, because it expresses the nature proper to a stone, according to the preconception in the divine intellect. Thus, then, truth is principally in the intellect, and secondarily in things according as they are related to the intellect as their principle.

Consequently there are various definitions of truth. Augustine says (*De Vera Relig.* xxxvi),[1] "Truth is that whereby is made manifest that which is"; and Hilary says[2] that "Truth makes being clear and evident," and this pertains to truth according as it is in the intellect. As to the truth of things in so far as they are related to the intellect, we have Augustine's definition (*loc. cit.*), "Truth is a supreme likeness, without any unlikeness, to a principle"; also Anselm's definition (*De Verit.*),[3] "Truth is rightness, perceptible by the mind alone"; for that is right which is in accordance with the principle; also Avicenna's definition (*Metaph.* viii, 6),[4] "The truth of each thing is a property of the being which is immutably attached to it." The definition that "Truth is the squaring of thought and thing" is applicable to it under either aspect.[5]

Reply Obj. 1. Augustine is speaking about the truth of things, and excludes from the notion of this truth relation to our intellect, for what is accidental is excluded from every definition.

Reply Obj. 2. The ancient philosophers held[6] that the species of natural things did not proceed from any intellect, but were produced by chance. But as they saw that truth implies relation to intellect, they were compelled to base the truth of things on their relation to our intellect. From this, conclusions result that are inadmissible, and which the Philosopher refutes.[7] Such, however, do not follow, if we say that the truth of things consists in their relation to the divine intellect.

Reply Obj. 3. Although the truth of our intellect is caused by the thing, yet it is not necessary that the character of truth should be there primarily, any more than that the character of health should be primarily in medicine, rather than in the animal; for the power of medicine, and not its health, is the cause of health, for here the agent is not univocal. In the same way the being of the thing, not its truth, is the cause of truth in the intellect. Hence the Philosopher says that "a thought or word is true from the fact that a thing is, not because a thing is true."

ARTICLE 2. *Whether Truth Resides Only in the Intellect Composing and Dividing?*

We proceed thus to the Second Article: It seems that truth does not reside only in the intellect composing and dividing.

Objection 1. For the Philosopher[8] says that "just as the senses are always true as regards their proper sensible objects, so is the intellect as regards what a thing is." Now composition and division are neither in the senses nor in the intellect knowing what a thing is. Therefore truth does not reside only in the intellect composing and dividing.

Obj. 2. Further, Isaac says in his book *On Definitions* that truth is the equation (adequatio) of thought and thing.[9] Now just as the intellect with regard to complex things can be equated to things, so also with regard to the understanding of simple things; and this is true also of sense sensing a thing as it is. Therefore truth does not reside only in the intellect composing and dividing.

On the contrary, the Philosopher says[10] that "with regard to simple things and what a thing is, truth is found neither in the intellect nor in things."

I answer that, As stated before, truth resides, in its primary aspect, in the intellect. Now since

---

[1] PL 34, 151.

[2] Cf. *De Trin.* v (PL 10, 131); cited by Philip the Chancellor, *Summa de Bono* (fol. 1 vb); also Alexander of Hales, *Summa Theol.*, 1, 88 (QR 1, 141).

[3] Chap. XI (PL 158, 480).   [4] 100r.

[5] See below, A. 2, Ans. 2.   [6] See below, Q. XXII, A. 2.

[7] *Metaphysics*, IV, 5, 6 (1009ª6; 1011ª3).

[8] *Soul*, III, 6 (430ᵇ27).

[9] Cf. Muckle, AHDLM (1933) pp. 5-8; Avicenna, *Meta.*, I, 9 (74r). For this definition in Averroes, cf. Editors of *Summa* of Alexander of Hales, pt. 1, n. 89 (QR 1, 142, n.).

[10] *Metaphysics*, VI,4 (1027ᵇ27).

everything is true according as it has the form proper to its nature, the intellect, in so far as it is knowing, must be true so far as it has the likeness of the thing known, which is its form in so far as it is knowing. For this reason truth is defined by the conformity of intellect and thing, and hence to know this conformity is to know truth. But in no way can sense know this. For although sight has the likeness of a visible thing, yet it does not know the comparison which exists between the thing seen and that which itself apprehends concerning it. But the intellect can know its own conformity with the intelligible thing; yet it does not apprehend it by knowing of a thing "what a thing is." When, however, it judges that a thing corresponds to the form which it apprehends about that thing, then first it knows and expresses truth. This it does by composing and dividing, for in every proposition it either applies to, or removes from the thing signified by the subject, some form signified by the predicate; and this clearly shows that the sense is true of any thing, as is also the intellect, when it knows "what a thing is," but it does not thereby know or affirm truth. This is in like manner the case with complex or non-complex terms. Truth therefore may be in the senses, or in the intellect knowing "what a thing is," as in anything that is true; yet not as the thing known in the knower, which is implied by the word "truth," for the perfection of the intellect is truth as known. Therefore, properly speaking, truth resides in the intellect composing and dividing, and not in the senses, nor in the intellect knowing "what a thing is."

And thus the Objections given are solved.

ARTICLE 3. *Whether the True and Being Are Convertible Terms?*

We proceed thus to the Third Article: It seems that the true and being are not convertible terms.

Objection 1. For the true resides properly in the intellect, as stated (A. 1); but being is properly in things. Therefore they are not convertible.

Obj. 2. Further, that which extends to being and not-being is not convertible with being. But the true extends to being and not-being; for it is true that what is, is, and that what is not, is not. Therefore the true and being are not convertible.

Obj. 3. Further, things which stand to each other in order of priority and posteriority seem not to be convertible. But the true appears to be prior to being, for being is not understood except under the aspect of the true. Therefore it seems they are not convertible.

On the contrary, the Philosopher says[1] that there is the same disposition of things in being and in truth.

I answer that, As good has the aspect of what is desirable, so truth is related to knowledge. Now everything, in as far as it has being, is to that extent knowable. Therefore it is said in the book on the *Soul*[2] that "the soul is in some manner all things," through the senses and the intellect. And therefore, as good is convertible with being, so is the true. But as good adds to being the notion of desirable, so the true adds relation to the intellect.

Reply Obj. 1. The true resides in things and in the intellect, as said before (A. 1). But the true that is in things is convertible with being as to substance, while the true that is in the intellect is convertible with being as that which manifests with what is manifested; for this belongs to the nature of truth, as has been said already (*ibid.*). It may, however, be said that being also is in things and in the intellect, as is the true; although truth is primarily in the intellect, while being is primarily in things; and this is so because truth and being differ in idea.

Reply Obj. 2. Not-being has nothing in itself by which it can be known, yet it is known in so far as the intellect renders it knowable. Hence the true is based on being, in so far as not-being is a kind of logical being, apprehended, that is, by reason.

Reply Obj. 3. When it is said that being cannot be apprehended except under the notion of the true, this can be understood in two ways. In the one way so as to mean that being is not apprehended unless the idea of the true follows apprehension of being; and this is true. In the other way, so as to mean that being cannot be apprehended unless the idea of the true be apprehended also; and this is false. But the true cannot be apprehended unless the idea of being be apprehended also, since being is included in the idea of the true. The case is the same if we compare the intelligible thing with being. For being cannot be understood unless being is intelligible. Yet being can be understood while its intelligibility is not understood. Similarly, being when understood is true, yet the true is not understood by understanding being.

[1] *Metaphysics,* II, 1 (993^{b}30).
[2] III, 8 (431^{b}21).

ARTICLE 4. *Whether Good Is Logically Prior to the True?*

We proceed thus to the Fourth Article: It seems that good is logically prior to the true.

Objection 1. For what is more universal is logically prior, as is evident from the *Physics*.[1] But the good is more universal than the true, since the true is a kind of good, namely, of the intellect. Therefore the good is logically prior to the true.

Obj. 2. Further, good is in things, but the true in the intellect composing and dividing, as said before (A. 2). But that which is in things is prior to that which is in the intellect. Therefore good is logically prior to the true.

Obj. 3. Further, truth is a species of virtue, as is clear from the *Ethics*.[2] But virtue is included under good, since, as Augustine says (*De Lib. Arbit.* ii, 19),[3] it is a good quality of the mind. Therefore the good is prior to the true.

On the contrary, What is in more things is prior logically. But the true is in some things in which good is not, as, for instance, in mathematics. Therefore the true is prior to good.

I answer that, Although the good and the true are convertible with being, as to suppositum, yet they differ logically. And in this manner the true, speaking absolutely, is prior to good, as appears from two reasons. First, because the true is more closely related to being, which is prior, than is good. For the true regards being itself absolutely and immediately, while the nature of good follows being in so far as being is in some way perfect; for thus it is desirable. Secondly, it is evident from the fact that knowledge naturally precedes appetite. Hence, since the true regards knowledge, but the good regards the appetite, the true must be prior in idea to the good.

Reply Obj. 1. The will and the intellect mutually include one another, for the intellect understands the will, and the will wills the intellect to understand. So then, among things directed to the object of the will, are comprised also those that belong to the intellect, and conversely. And so in the order of things desirable, good stands as the universal, and the true as the particular; but in the order of intelligible things the converse is the case. From the fact, then, that the true is a kind of good, it follows that the good is prior in the order of things desirable, but not that it is prior absolutely.

Reply Obj. 2. A thing is prior logically in so far as it is prior to the intellect. Now the intellect apprehends primarily being itself; secondly, it apprehends that it understands being; and thirdly, it apprehends that it desires being. Hence the idea of being is first, that of truth second, and the idea of good third, though good is in things.

Reply Obj. 3. The virtue which is called truth is not truth in general, but a certain kind of truth according to which man shows himself in deed and word as he really is. But truth as applied to life is used in a particular sense, in so far as a man fulfils in his life that to which he is ordained by the divine intellect, as it has been said that truth exists in others things (A. 1). But the truth of justice is found in man as he fulfils his duty to his neighbour, as ordained by law. Hence we cannot argue from these particular truths to truth in general.

ARTICLE 5. *Whether God Is Truth?*

We proceed thus to the Fifth Article: It seems that God is not truth.

Objection 1. For truth consists in the intellect composing and dividing. But in God there is not composition and division. Therefore in Him there is not truth.

Obj. 2. Further, truth, according to Augustine (*De Vera Relig.* xxxvi),[4] is a "likeness to the principle." But in God there is no likeness to a principle. Therefore in God there is not truth.

Obj. 3. Further, whatever is said of God, is said of Him as of the first cause of all things; thus the being of God is the cause of all being, and His goodness the cause of all good. If therefore there is truth in God, all truth will be from Him. But it is true that someone sins. Therefore this will be from God, which is evidently false.

On the contrary, Our Lord says, *I am the Way, the Truth and the Life* (John 14. 6).

I answer that, As said above (A. 1), truth is found in the intellect according as it apprehends a thing as it is, and in things according as they have being conformable to an intellect. This is to the greatest degree found in God. For His being is not only conformed to His intellect, but it is the very act of His intellect, and His act of understanding is the measure and cause of every other being and of every other intellect, and He Himself is His own being and act of understanding. And so it follows not only that truth is in Him, but that He is truth itself, and the supreme and first truth.

---

[1] Aristotle, I, 5 (189^{a}5).
[2] Aristotle, IV, 7 (1127^{a}29).
[3] PL 32, 1267.
[4] PL 34, 152.

Reply Obj. 1. Although in the divine intellect there is neither composition nor division, yet in His simple act of intelligence He judges of all things and knows all things complex. And thus there is truth in His intellect.

Reply Obj. 2. The truth of our intellect is according to its conformity with its principle, that is to say, to the things from which it receives knowledge. The truth also of things is according to their conformity with their principle, namely, the divine intellect. Now this cannot be said, properly speaking, of divine truth, unless perhaps in so far as truth is appropriated to the Son, Who has a principle. But if we speak of divine truth in its essence, we cannot understand this unless the affirmative must be resolved into the negative, as when one says: "the Father is of Himself, because He is not from another." Similarly, the divine truth can be called "a likeness to the principle," inasmuch as His being is not different from His intellect.

Reply Obj. 3. Not-being, and privation, have no truth of themselves, but only in the apprehension of the intellect. Now all apprehension of the intellect is from God. Hence all the truth that exists in the statement,—"that a person commits fornication is true," is entirely from God. But to argue, "Therefore that this person fornicates is from God," is a fallacy of Accident.

ARTICLE 6. *Whether There Is Only One Truth, According to Which All Things Are True?*

We proceed thus to the Sixth Article: It seems that there is only one truth, according to which all things are true.

Objection 1. For according to Augustine (*De Trin.* xv, 1),[1] nothing is greater than the mind of man, except God. Now truth is greater than the mind of man; otherwise the mind would be the judge of truth, while in fact it judges all things according to truth, and not according to its own measure. Therefore God alone is truth. Therefore there is no other truth but God.

Obj. 2. Further, Anselm says (*De Verit.* xiv),[2] that, just as the relation of time is to temporal things, so that of truth is to true things. But there is only one time for all temporal things. Therefore there is only one truth, by which all things are true.

On the contrary, it is written (Ps. 11. 2), *Truths are decayed from among the children of men.*

I answer that, In one sense truth, by which all things are true, is one, and in another sense it is not. In proof of which we must consider that when anything is predicated of many things univocally, it is found in each of them according to its proper nature; as animal is found in each species of animal. But when anything is said of many things analogically, it is found in only one of them according to its proper nature, and from this one the rest are denominated. So health is predicated of animal, of urine, and of medicine; not that health is only in the animal, but from the health of the animal medicine is called healthy in so far as it is the cause of health, and urine is called healthy in so far as it indicates health. And although health is neither in medicine nor in urine, yet in either there is something by which the one causes, and the other indicates health.

Now we have said (A. 1) that truth resides primarily in the intellect, and secondarily in things, according as they are related to the divine intellect. If therefore we speak of truth as it exists in the intellect, according to its proper nature, then are there many truths in many created intellects, and even in one and the same intellect, according to the number of things known. Hence a gloss on Ps. 11. 2, *Truths are decayed from among the children of men,* says[3]: "As from one man's face many likenesses are reflected in a mirror, so many truths are reflected from the one divine truth." But if we speak of truth as it is in things, then all things are true by one primary truth; to which each one is assimilated according to its own entity. And thus, although the essences or forms of things are many, yet the truth of the divine intellect is one, according to which all things are said to be true.

Reply Obj. 1. The soul does not judge of all things according to any kind of truth, but according to the primary truth, in so far as it is reflected in the soul, as in a mirror, by reason of the first principles of the understanding. It follows, therefore, that the primary truth is greater than the soul. And yet, even created truth, which resides in our intellect, is greater than the soul, not absolutely, but relatively, in so far as it is its perfection, even as science may be said to be greater than the soul. Yet it is true that nothing subsisting is greater than the rational mind, except God.

Reply Obj. 2. The saying of Anselm is correct in so far as things are said to be true by their relation to the divine intellect.

---

[1] PL 42, 1057.
[2] PL 158, 484.
[3] *Glossa* Lombardi (PL 191, 155); cf. *Glossa interl.* (III, 102h); Augustine, *Enarr. in Ps.* 11.2 (PL 36, 138).

ARTICLE 7. *Whether Created Truth Is Eternal?*

We proceed thus to the Seventh Article: It seems that created truth is eternal.

Objection 1. For Augustine says (*De Lib. Arbit.* ii, 8),[1] Nothing is more eternal than the nature of a circle, and that two added to three make five. But the truth of these is a created truth. Therefore created truth is eternal.

Obj. 2. Further, that which is always, is eternal. But universals are always and everywhere. Therefore they are eternal. So therefore is truth, which is the most universal.

Obj. 3. Further, it was always true that what is true in the present was to be in the future. But as the truth of a proposition regarding the present is a created truth, so is that of a proposition regarding the future. Therefore some created truth is eternal.

Obj. 4. Further, all that is without beginning and end is eternal. But the truth of enunciations is without beginning and end; for if their truth had a beginning, since it was not before, it was true that truth was not, and true, of course, by reason of truth so that truth was before it began to be. Similarly, if it be asserted that truth has an end, it follows that it is after it has ceased to be, for it will still be true that truth is not. Therefore truth is eternal.

On the contrary, God alone is eternal, as laid down before (Q. X, A. 3).

I answer that, The truth of enunciations is no other than the truth of the intellect. For an enunciation resides in the intellect, and in speech. Now according as it is in the intellect it has truth of itself; but according as it is in speech, it is called enunciable truth, according as it signifies some truth of the intellect, not on account of any truth existing in the enunciation, as though in a subject. Thus urine is called healthy not from any health within it but from the health of an animal which it indicates. In like manner it has been already said that things are called true from the truth of the intellect. Hence, if no intellect were eternal, no truth would be eternal. Now because only the divine intellect is eternal, in it alone truth has eternity. Nor does it follow from this that anything else but God is eternal, since the truth of the divine intellect is God himself, as shown already (A. 5).

Reply Obj. 1. The nature of a circle, and the fact that two and three make five, have eternity in the mind of God.

Reply Obj. 2. That something is always and

[1] PL 32, 1257; *Soliloq.*, II, 19 (PL 32, 901).

everywhere, can be understood in two ways. In one way, as having in itself the power of extending to all time and to all places, as it belongs to God to be everywhere and always. In the other way as not having in itself determination to any place or time, as prime matter is said to be one not because it has one form, as man is one by the unity of one form, but by the absence of all distinguishing form. In this manner all universals are said to be everywhere and always, in so far as universals abstract from here and now. It does not, however, follow from this that they are eternal, except in an intellect, if one exists that is eternal.

Reply Obj. 3. That which now is, was future, before it (actually) was, because it was in its cause that it would be. Hence, if the cause were removed, that thing's coming to be was not future. But the first cause is alone eternal. Hence it does not follow that it was always true that what now is would be, except in so far as its future being was in the sempiternal cause; and God alone is such a cause.

Reply Obj. 4. Because our intellect is not eternal, neither is the truth of enunciable propositions which are formed by us eternal, but it had a beginning in time. Now before such truth existed, it was not true to say that such a truth did exist, except by reason of the divine intellect, in which alone truth is eternal. But it is true now to say that that truth did not then exist, and this is true only by reason of the truth that is now in our intellect, and not by reason of any truth in the things. For this is truth concerning non-being, and non-being has no truth of itself, but only so far as our intellect apprehends it. Hence it is true to say that truth did not exist, in so far as we apprehend its non-being as preceding its being.

ARTICLE 8. *Whether Truth Is Immutable?*

We proceed thus to the Eighth Article: It seems that truth is immutable.

Objection 1. For Augustine says (*De Lib. Arbit.* ii, 12),[2] that truth and mind do not rank as equals, otherwise truth would be mutable, as the mind is.

Obj. 2. Further, what remains after every change is immutable; as prime matter is unbegotten and incorruptible, since it remains after all generation and corruption. But truth remains after all change, for after every change it is true to say that a thing is, or is not. Therefore, truth is immutable.

Obj. 3. Further, if the truth of an enuncia-

[2] PL 32, 1259.

tion changes, it changes mostly with the changing of the thing. But it does not thus change. For truth, according to Anselm (*De Verit.* vii),[1] "is a certain rightness" in so far as a thing answers to that which is in the divine mind concerning it. But this proposition "Socrates sits," receives from the divine mind the signification that Socrates does sit, and it has the same signification even though he does not sit. Therefore the truth of the proposition in no way changes.

Obj. 4. Further, where there is the same cause, there is the same effect. But the same thing is the cause of the truth of the three propositions, "Socrates sits, will sit, sat." Therefore the truth of each is the same. But one or other of these must be the true one. Therefore the truth of these propositions remains immutable, and for the same reason, that of any other.

On the contrary, It is written (Ps. 11. 2), *Truths are decayed from among the children of men.*

I answer that, Truth, properly speaking, is only in the intellect, as said before (A. 1), but things are called true in virtue of the truth residing in an intellect. Hence the mutability of truth must be regarded from the point of view of the intellect, the truth of which consists in its conformity to the thing understood. Now this conformity may vary in two ways, even as any other likeness, through change in one of the two extremes. Hence in one way truth varies on the part of the intellect from the fact that a change of opinion occurs about a thing which in itself has not changed, and in another way when the thing is changed but not the opinion; and in either way there can be a change from true to false.

If, then, there is an intellect wherein there can be no alternation of opinions, and the knowledge of which nothing can escape, in this intellect there is immutable truth. Now such is the divine intellect, as is clear from what has been said before (Q. XIV, A. 15). Hence the truth of the divine intellect is immutable. But the truth of our intellect is mutable; not because it is itself the subject of change, but in so far as our intellect changes from truth to falsity, for thus forms may be called mutable. But the truth of the divine intellect is that according to which natural things are said to be true, and this is altogether immutable.

Reply Obj. 1. Augustine is speaking of divine truth.

Reply Obj. 2. The true and being are convertible terms. Hence just as being is not gen-

erated nor corrupted of itself, but accidentally, in so far as this being or that is corrupted or generated, as is said in *Physics*,[2] so does truth change, not so as that no truth remains, but because that truth does not remain which was before.

Reply Obj. 3. A proposition not only has truth, as other things are said to have it, in so far, that is, as they fulfil that which is ordained for them by the divine intellect, but it is said to have truth in a special way, in so far as it signifies the truth of the intellect, which consists in the conformity of the intellect with a thing. When this is taken away, the truth of an opinion changes, and consequently the truth of the proposition. So therefore this proposition, "Socrates sits," is true as long as he is sitting, both with the truth of the thing, in so far as the expression is significative, and with the truth of signification, in so far as it signifies a true opinion. When Socrates rises, the first truth remains, but the second is changed.

Reply Obj. 4. The sitting of Socrates, which is the cause of the truth of the proposition, "Socrates sits," has not the same meaning when Socrates sits, after he sits, and before he sits. Hence the truth which results, varies, and is variously signified by these propositions concerning present, past, or future. Thus it does not follow, though one of the three propositions is true, that the same truth remains invariable.

QUESTION XVII
OF FALSITY
(In Four Articles)

WE next consider falsity. About this four points of inquiry arise: (1) Whether falsity exists in things? (2) Whether it exists in the sense? (3) Whether it exists in the intellect? (4) Concerning the opposition of the true and the false.

ARTICLE 1. *Whether Falsity Exists in Things?*

We proceed thus to the First Article: It appears that falsity does not exist in things.

Objection 1. For Augustine says (*Soliloq.* ii, 8),[3] "If the true is that which is, it will be concluded that the false exists nowhere, whatever reason may appear to the contrary."

Obj. 2. Further, false is derived from *fallere* (to deceive). But things do not deceive; "for," as Augustine says (*De vera relig.* 36),[4] "they show nothing but their own species." Therefore the false is not found in things.

[1] PL 158, 475; Chap. 10 (PL 158, 478).
[2] Aristotle, I, 8 (191b17).
[3] PL 32, 892.   [4] PL 34, 152.

Obj. 3. Further, the true is said to exist in things by conformity to the divine intellect, as stated above (Q. XVI, A. 1). But everything, in so far as it exists, imitates God. Therefore everything is true without admixture of falsity; and thus nothing is false.

On the contrary, Augustine says (*ibid.* 34): "Every body is a true body and a false unity"; for it imitates unity without being unity. But everything imitates the divine unity, yet falls short of it. Therefore in all things falsity exists.

I answer that, Since true and false are opposed, and since opposites stand in relation to the same thing, we must seek falsity where primarily we find truth, that is to say, in the intellect. Now, in things, neither truth nor falsity exists, except in relation to the intellect. And since every thing is denominated absolutely by what belongs to it *per se,* but is denominated relatively by what belongs to it accidentally, a thing indeed may be called false absolutely when compared with the intellect on which it depends, and to which it is compared *per se,* but may be called false only relatively as directed to another intellect, to which it is compared accidentally.

Now natural things depend on the divine intellect, as artificial things on the human. Therefore artificial things are said to be false absolutely and in themselves, in so far as they fall short of the form of the art and so a craftsman is said to produce a false work if it falls short of the operation of his art. In things that depend on God, falseness cannot be found, in so far as they are compared with the divine intellect, since whatever takes place in things proceeds from the ordinance of that intellect, unless perhaps in the case of voluntary agents only, who have it in their power to withdraw themselves from what is so ordained, wherein consists the evil of sin. Thus sins themselves are called untruths and lies in the Scriptures, according to the words of the text, *Why do you love vanity, and seek after lying?* (Ps. 4. 3), as on the other hand virtuous deeds are called the truth of life as being obedient to the order of the divine intellect. Thus it is said, *He that doth truth, cometh to the light* (John 3. 21).

But in relation to our intellect, natural things which are compared thereto accidentally can be called false not absolutely, but relatively, and that in two ways. In one way according to the thing signified, and thus a thing is said to be false as being signified or represented by word or thought that is false. In this respect anything can be said to be false as regards any quality not possessed by it, as if we should say that a diameter is a false commensurable thing, as the Philosopher says.[1] So, too, Augustine says (*Soliloq.* ii, 10):[2] "The true tragedian is a false Hector," even as, on the contrary, anything can be called true, in regard to that which belongs to it. In another way a thing can be called false, by way of cause—and thus a thing is said to be false that naturally begets a false opinion. And because it is innate in us to judge of things by external appearances, since our knowledge takes its rise from sense, which principally and naturally deals with external accidents, therefore those external accidents, which resemble things other than themselves are said to be false with respect to those things; thus gall is falsely honey and tin, false silver. Regarding this, Augustine says (*ibid.* 6) that we call those things false that appear to our apprehension like the true; and the Philosopher says (*loc. cit.*): Things are called false "that are naturally apt to appear such as they are not, or what they are not." In this way "a man is called false as delighting in false opinions or words, and not because he can invent them; for in this way many wise and learned persons might be called false," as stated in the *Metaphysics.*[3]

Reply Obj. 1. A thing compared with the intellect is said to be true in respect to what it is and false in respect to what it is not. Hence, "The true tragedian is a false Hector," as stated in *Soliloq.* ii (*loc. cit.*). As, therefore, in things that are is found a certain non-being, so in things that are is found a degree of falseness.

Reply Obj. 2. Things do not deceive by their own nature, but by accident. For they give occasion to falsity by the likeness they bear to things which they actually are not.

Reply Obj. 3. Things are said to be false, not as compared with the divine intellect, in which case they would be false absolutely, but as compared with our intellect; and thus they are false only relatively.

To the argument which is urged on the contrary, likeness or defective representation does not involve the idea of falsity except in so far as it gives occasion to false opinion. Hence a thing is not always said to be false because it resembles another thing, but only when the resemblance is such as naturally to produce a false opinion, not in any one case, but in the majority of instances.

[1] *Metaphysics,* V, 29 (1024^{b}19).

[2] PL 32, 893.

[3] Aristotle, V, 29 (1025^{a}2).

ARTICLE 2. *Whether There Is Falsity in the Senses?*

We proceed thus to the Second Article: It seems that falsity is not in the senses.

Objection 1. For Augustine says (*De vera relig.* 33):[1] "If all the bodily senses report as they are affected, I do not know what more we can require from them." Thus it seems that we are not deceived by the senses; and therefore that falsity is not in them.

Obj. 2. Further, the Philosopher says[2] that falsity is not proper to the senses, but to the imagination.

Obj. 3. Further, in non-complex things there is neither true nor false, but in complex things only. But to compose and divide do not belong to the senses. Therefore in the senses there is no falsity.

On the contrary, Augustine says (*Soliloq.* ii, 6),[3] "It appears that the senses entrap us into error by their deceptive similitudes."

I answer that, Falsity is not to be sought in the senses except as truth is in them. Now truth is not in them in such a way as that the senses know truth, but in so far as they apprehend sensible things truly, as said above (Q. XVI, A. 2), and this takes place through the senses apprehending things as they are, and hence it happens that falsity exists in the senses through their apprehending or judging things to be otherwise than they really are.

The knowledge of things by the senses is in proportion to the existence of their likeness in the senses; and the likeness of a thing can exist in the senses in three ways. In the first way, primarily and per se, as in sight there is the likeness of colours, and of other sensible objects proper to it. Secondly, per se, though not primarily; as in sight there is the likeness of shape, size, and of other sensible objects common to more than one sense.

Thirdly, neither primarily nor per se, but accidentally, as in sight, there is the likeness of a man, not as man, but in so far as it is accidental to the coloured object to be a man.

Sense, then, has no false knowledge about its proper objects, except accidentally and rarely, and then, because of the unsound organ it does not receive the sensible form rightly; just as other passive subjects because of their indisposition receive defectively the impressions of the agent. Hence, for instance, it happens that on account of an unhealthy tongue sweet seems bitter to a sick person. But as to common objects of sense, and accidental objects, even a rightly disposed sense may have a false judgment, because it is referred to them not directly, but accidentally, or as a consequence of being directed to other things.

Reply Obj. 1. The affection of sense is its sensation itself. Hence, from the fact that sense reports as it is affected, it follows that we are not deceived in the judgment by which we judge that we experience sensation. Since, however, sense is sometimes affected otherwise than the thing is, it follows that it sometimes reports the thing to us otherwise than it is; and thus we are deceived by sense about the thing, but not about the fact of sensation.

Reply Obj. 2. Falsity is said not to be proper to sense, since sense is not deceived as to its proper object. Hence in another translation[4] it is said more plainly, "Sense, about its proper object, is never false." Falsity is attributed to the imagination, as it represents the likeness of something even in its absence. Hence, when anyone perceives the likeness of a thing as if it were the thing itself, falsity results from such an apprehension; and for this reason the Philosopher says[5] that shadows, pictures, and dreams are said to be false in so far as they convey the likeness of things that are not present in substance.

Reply Obj. 3. This argument proves that the false is not in the sense as in that which knows the true and the false.

ARTICLE 3. *Whether Falsity Is in the Intellect?*

We proceed thus to the Third Article: It seems that falsity is not in the intellect.

Objection 1. For Augustine says (QQ. LXXXIII, 32),[6] "Everyone who is deceived understands not that in which he is deceived." But falsity is said to exist in any knowledge in so far as we are deceived by it. Therefore falsity does not exist in the intellect.

Obj. 2. Further, the Philosopher says[7] that "the intellect is always right." Therefore there is no falsity in the intellect.

On the contrary, It is said in the book on the *Soul*[8] that "where there is composition of things understood, there is truth and falsehood." But such composition is in the intellect. There-

---

[1] PL 34, 149.
[2] *Metaphysics,* IV, 5 (1010b2), according to the Arabic-Latin translation; see text in Averroes, *In Meta.,* IV, comm. 24 (VIII, 91H).   [3] PL 32, 890.

[4] See Geyer, PJ (1917), p. 406.
[5] *Metaphysics,* V, 29 (1024b23).   [6] PL 40, 22.
[7] *Soul,* III, 10 (433a26).   [8] Aristotle, III, 6 (430a27).

fore truth and falsehood exist in the intellect.

I answer that, Just as a thing has being by its proper form, so the knowing power has knowledge by the likeness of the thing known. Hence, as natural things cannot fall short of the being that belongs to them by their form, but may fall short of accidental or consequent qualities, even as a man may fail to possess two feet, but not fail to be a man, so the knowing power cannot fail in knowledge of the thing with the likeness of which it is informed, but may fail with regard to something consequent upon that form, or accidental to it. For it has been said (A. 2), that sight is not deceived in its proper sensible, but about common sensibles that are consequent to that object, or about accidental objects of sense.

Now as the sense is directly informed by the likeness of its proper sensible, so is the intellect by the likeness of the essence of a thing. Hence the intellect is not deceived about the essence of a thing, as neither the sense about its proper sensible. But in composing and dividing the intellect may be deceived, by attributing to the thing of which it understands the quiddity something which is not consequent upon it, or is opposed to it. For the intellect is in the same position as regards judging of such kind of things as sense is as to judging of common, or accidental, sensibles. There is, however, this difference, as before mentioned regarding truth (Q. XVI, A. 2), that falsity can exist in the intellect not only because the knowledge of the intellect is false, but because the intellect is conscious of that knowledge, as it is conscious of truth; in sense however falsity does not exist as known, as stated above (A. 2).

But because falsity of the intellect is concerned per se only with the composition of the intellect, falsity occurs also accidentally in that operation of the intellect whereby it knows the essence of a thing, in so far as composition of the intellect is mixed up in it. This can take place in two ways. In one way, by the intellect applying to one thing the definition proper to another, as that of a circle to a man. Hence the definition of one thing is false of another. In another way, by composing a definition of parts which cannot be joined together. For thus the definition is not only false of the thing, but false in itself. A definition such as "a reasonable four-footed animal" would be of this kind, and the intellect false in making it, for such a statement as "some reasonable animals are four-footed" is false in itself. For this reason the intellect cannot be false in its knowledge of simple

quiddities, but it is either true, or it understands nothing at all.

Reply Obj. 1. Because the quiddity of a thing is the proper object of the intellect, we are properly said to understand a thing when we reduce it to its essence, and judge of it thereby, as takes place in demonstrations, in which there is no falsity. In this sense Augustine's words must be understood, "that he who is deceived, understands not that wherein he is deceived," and not in the sense that no one is ever deceived in any operation of the intellect.

Reply Obj. 2. The intellect is always right as regards first principles, since it is not deceived about them for the same reason that it is not deceived about what a thing is. For self-known principles are such as are known as soon as the terms are understood, from the fact that the predicate is contained in the definition of the subject.

ARTICLE 4. *Whether True and False Are Contraries?*

We proceed thus to the Fourth Article: It seems that true and false are not contraries.

Objection 1. For true and false are opposed as that which is to that which is not; for "truth," as Augustine says (*Soliloq.* ii, 5),[1] "is that which is." But that which is and that which is are not opposed as contraries. Therefore true and false are not contrary things.

Obj. 2. Further, one of two contraries is not in the other. But falsity is in truth, because, as Augustine says, (*Soliloq.* ii, 10),[2] "A tragedian would not be a false Hector, if he were not a true tragedian." Therefore true and false are not contraries.

Obj. 3. Further, in God there is no contrariety, for nothing is contrary to the Divine Substance, as Augustine says.[3] But falsity is opposed to God, for an idol is called in Scripture a lie, *They have laid hold on lying* (Jer. 8. 5), that is to say, "an idol," as a gloss says.[4] Therefore false and true are not contraries.

On the contrary, The Philosopher says,[5] that a false opinion is contrary to a true one.

I answer that, True and false are opposed as contraries, and not, as some have said,[6] as affirmation and negation. In proof of which it must be considered that negation neither asserts any-

[1] PL 32, 889.
[2] PL 32, 893.
[3] *City of God,* XII, 2 (PL 41, 350).
[4] *Glossa interl.,* (IV, 123v).
[5] *Interpretation,* 14 (23ᵇ35).
[6] Cf. Alexander of Hales, *Summa Theol.,* I, 101 (QR 1, 159).

thing nor determines any subject, and can therefore be said of being as of non-being, for instance not-seeing or not-sitting. But although privation asserts nothing, it determines its subject, for it is negation in a subject, as stated in the *Metaphysics*;[1] for blindness is not said except of one "whose nature it is to see." Contraries, however, both assert something and determine the subject, for black is a species of colour. Falsity asserts something, for a thing is false, as the Philosopher says,[2] because "something is said or seems to be something that it is not, or not to be what it is." For as truth implies an adequate receiving of a thing, so falsity implies the contrary. Hence it is clear that true and false are contraries.

Reply Obj. 1. What is in things is the truth of the thing; but what is as apprehended, is the truth of the intellect, wherein truth primarily resides. Hence the false is that which is not as apprehended. To apprehend being, and non-being, implies contrariety; for, as the Philosopher proves,[3] the contrary of this statement good is good is, good is not good.

Reply Obj. 2. Falsity is not founded in the truth which is contrary to it, just as evil is not founded in the good which is contrary to it, but in that which is its proper subject. This happens in either case because true and good are universals, and convertible with being. Hence, as every privation is founded in a subject, that is, a being, so every evil is founded in some good, and every falsity in some truth.

Reply Obj. 3. Because contraries and opposites by way of privation are by nature about one and the same thing, therefore there is nothing contrary to God, considered in Himself, either with respect to His goodness or His truth, for in His intellect there can be nothing false. But in our apprehension of Him contraries exist, for the false opinion concerning Him is contrary to the true. So idols are called lies, opposed to the divine truth, in so far as the false opinion concerning them is contrary to the true opinion of the divine unity.

QUESTION XVIII

THE LIFE OF GOD

(In Four Articles)

SINCE to understand belongs to living beings, after considering the divine knowledge and intellect, we must consider the divine life. About this, four points of inquiry arise: (1) To whom does it belong to live? (2) What is life? (3) Whether life is properly attributed to God? (4) Whether all things in God are life?

ARTICLE 1. *Whether To Live Belongs to All Natural Things?*

We proceed thus to the First Article: It seems that to live belongs to all natural things.

Objection 1. For the Philosopher says[4] that "Movement is like a kind of life possessed by all things existing in nature." But all natural things participate in movement. Therefore all natural things share in life.

Obj. 2. Further, plants are said to live in so far as they have in themselves a principle of movement of growth and decay. But local movement is naturally more perfect than, and prior to, movement of growth and decay, as the Philosopher shows.[5] Since, then, all natural bodies have in themselves some principle of local movement, it seems that all natural bodies live.

Obj. 3. Further, amongst natural bodies the elements are the less perfect. Yet life is attributed to them, for we speak of "living waters." Much more, therefore, have other natural bodies life.

On the contrary, Dionysius says (*Div. Nom.* vi, 1)[6] that "The last echo of life is heard in the plants," whereby it is inferred that their life is life in its lowest degree. But inanimate bodies are below plants. Therefore they have not life.

I answer that, We can gather to what things life belongs and to what it does not from such things as manifestly possess life. Now life manifestly belongs to animals, for it is said in the book on *Plants*[7] that "in animals life is manifest." We must, therefore, distinguish living from non-living things by comparing them to that by reason of which animals are said to live, and this it is in which life is manifested first and remains last. We say then that an animal begins to live when it begins to move of itself, and as long as such movement appears in it, so long is it considered to be alive. When it no longer has any movement of itself, but is only moved by another power, then its life is said to fail, and the animal to be dead. From this it is clear that those things are properly called living that move themselves by some kind of movement, whether it be movement properly so called, as the act of an imperfect thing, that is,

---

[1] Aristotle, IV, 2 (1004ª15); cf. v, 22 (1022ª26).
[2] *Metaphysics*, IV, 7 (1011ᵇ26).
[3] *Interpretation*, 14 (23ᵇ35).

[4] *Physics*, VIII, 1 (250ᵇ14).
[5] *Ibid.*, VIII, 7 (260ª28). [6] PG 3, 856.
[7] Aristotle, I, 1 (815ª10).

of a thing in potency, is called movement; or movement in a more general sense, as when said of the act of a perfect thing, as understanding and feeling are called movement according to the book on the *Soul*.[1] Accordingly all things are said to be alive that determine themselves to movement or operation of any kind; but those things that cannot by their nature do so, cannot be called living, unless by some likeness.

Reply Obj. 1. These words of the Philosopher may be understood either of the first movement, namely, that of the celestial bodies, or of movement in its general sense. In either way is movement called the life, as it were, of natural bodies, speaking by a likeness, and not attributing it to them as their property. The movement of the heavens is in the universe of corporeal natures as the movement of the heart, whereby life is preserved, is in animals. Similarly also every natural movement in respect to natural things has a certain likeness to the operations of life. Hence, if the whole corporeal universe were one animal, so that its movement came from an intrinsic moving force, as some have held, in that case movement would really be the life of all natural bodies.

Reply Obj. 2. Movement does not belong to bodies, whether heavy or light, except in so far as they are displaced from their natural conditions, as being out of their proper place; for when they are in the place that is proper and natural to them, then they are at rest. Plants and other living things move with vital movement in accordance with the disposition of their nature, but not by approaching thereto, or by receding from it, for in so far as they recede from such movement, so far do they recede from their natural disposition. And furthermore, "Heavy and light bodies are moved by an extrinsic mover, either generating them and giving them form, or removing obstacles from their way," as it is stated in the *Physics*.[2] They do not therefore move themselves, as do living bodies.

Reply Obj. 3. Waters are called living that have a continuous current, for standing waters that are not connected with a continually flowing source are called dead, as in cisterns and ponds. This is merely a likeness, in so far as the movement they are seen to possess makes them look as if they were alive. Yet this is not life in them in its real sense, since this movement of theirs is not from themselves but from the cause that generates them. The same is the case

with the movement of other heavy and light bodies.

ARTICLE 2. *Whether Life Is an Operation?*

We proceed thus to the Second Article: It seems that life is an operation.

Objection 1. For nothing is divided except into parts of the same genus. But life is divided by certain operations, as is clear from the Philosopher[3] who distinguishes four kinds of life, namely the use of food, sensation, local movement, and understanding. Therefore life is an operation.

Obj. 2. Further, the active life is said to be different from the contemplative. But the contemplative is only distinguished from the active by certain operations. Therefore life is an operation.

Obj. 3. Further, to know God is an operation. But this is life, as is clear from the words of John 18. 3, *Now this is eternal life, that they may know Thee, the only true God.* Therefore life is an operation.

On the contrary, The Philosopher says[4] "In living things to live is to be."

I answer that, As is clear from what has been said (Q. XVII, A. 3), our intellect, which knows the quiddity of a thing as its proper object, takes from the sense, of which the proper objects are external accidents. Hence from external appearances we come to the knowledge of the essence of things. And because we name a thing in accordance with our knowledge of it, as is clear from what has already been said (Q. XIII, A. 1), so from external properties names are often imposed to signify essences. Hence such names are sometimes taken strictly to denote the essence itself, the signification of which is their principal purpose; but sometimes, and less strictly, to denote the properties by reason of which they are imposed. And so we see that the word "body" is used to denote a genus of substances from the fact of their possessing three dimensions, and is sometimes taken to denote the dimensions themselves, in which sense body is said to be a species of quantity.

The same must be said of life. The name is given from a certain external appearance, namely, self-movement, yet not precisely to signify this, but rather a substance to which self-movement and the application of itself to any kind of operation, belong naturally. To live, accordingly, is nothing else than to be in this or that nature; and life signifies this, though in the ab-

---

[1] Aristotle, III, 7 (431ᵃ6); cf. I, 4 (408ᵇ6).
[2] Aristotle, VIII, 4 (255ᵇ35).

[3] *Soul*, II, 2 (413ᵃ22).
[4] *Ibid.*, II, 4 (415ᵇ13).

stract, just as the word running denotes to run in the abstract.

Hence living is not an accidental but an essential predicate. Sometimes, however, life is used less properly for the operations from which its name is taken, and thus the Philosopher says[1] that "to live is principally to sense or to understand."

Reply Obj. 1. The Philosopher here takes to live to mean an operation of life. Or it would be better to say that sensation and intelligence and the like are sometimes taken for the operations, sometimes for the being itself of the operator. For he says[2] that to be is "to sense or to understand"—in other words, to have a nature capable of sensation or understanding. Thus, then, he distinguishes life by the four operations mentioned. For in this lower world there are four kinds of living things. It is the nature of some to be capable of nothing more than taking nourishment, and, as a consequence, of growing and generating. Others are able, in addition, to sense, as we see in the case of shellfish and other animals without movement. Others have the further power of moving from place to place, as perfect animals, such as quadrupeds, and birds, and so on. Others, as man, have the still higher faculty of understanding.

Reply Obj. 2. By vital operations are meant those whose principles are within the operator, and in virtue of which the operator produces such operations of itself. It happens that there exist in men not merely such natural principles of certain operations as are their natural powers, but something over and above these, such as habits inclining them like a second nature to particular kinds of operations, so that the operations become sources of pleasure. Thus, as by a kind of likeness, any kind of work in which a man takes delight, so that his bent is towards it, his time spent in it, and his whole life ordered with a view to it, is said to be the life of that man. Hence some are said to lead a life of self-indulgence, others a life of virtue. In this way the contemplative life is distinguished from the active, and thus to know God is said to be life eternal.

From this the *Reply to the third objection* is clear.

ARTICLE 3. *Whether Life Is Properly Attributed to God?*

We proceed thus to the Third Article: It seems that life is not properly attributed to God.

Objection 1. For things are said to live according as they move themselves, as previously stated (AA. 1, 2). But to be moved does not belong to God. Neither therefore does life.

Obj. 2. Further, in all living things we must suppose some principle of living. Hence it is said by the Philosopher[3] that "the soul is the cause and principle of the living body." But God has no principle. Therefore life cannot be attributed to Him.

Obj. 3. Further, the principle of life in the living things that exist among us is the vegetative soul. But this exists only in corporeal things. Therefore life cannot be attributed to incorporeal things.

On the contrary, It is said (Ps. 83. 3): *My heart and my flesh have rejoiced in the living God.*

I answer that, Life is in the highest degree properly in God. In proof of this it must be considered that since a thing is said to live in so far as it operates of itself and not as moved by another, the more perfectly this is found in anything, the more perfect is the life of that thing. In things that move and are moved a threefold order is found. In the first place the end moves the agent; and the principal agent is that which acts through its form, and sometimes it does so through some instrument that acts by virtue not of its own form, but of the principal agent, and does no more than execute the action. Accordingly there are things that move themselves not in respect of any form or end naturally inherent in them, but only in respect of the executing of the movement, the form by which they act, and the end of the action being alike determined for them by their nature. Of this kind are plants, which move themselves according to the form given to them by nature, with regard to growth and decay.

Other things have self-movement in a higher degree, that is, not only with regard to executing the movement, but even as regards the form which is the principle of movement, which form they acquire of themselves. Of this kind are animals, in which the principle of movement is not a naturally implanted form, but one received through sense. Hence the more perfect is their sense, the more perfect is their power of self-movement. Such as have only the sense of touch, as shellfish, move only with the motion of expansion and contraction; and thus their movement hardly exceeds that of plants. But such as have the sensitive power in perfection, so as to recognize not only what is joined to and

---

[1] *Ethics,* IX, 9 (1170ᵃ18).   [2] *Ibid.,* IX, 9 (1170ᵃ33).   [3] *Soul,* II, 4 (415ᵇ8).

touches them, but also objects apart from themselves, can move themselves to a distance by progressive movement.

Yet although animals of the latter kind receive through sense the form that is the principle of their movement, nevertheless they cannot of themselves propose to themselves the end of their operation, or movement; for this has been implanted in them by nature, and by natural instinct they are moved to any action through the form apprehended by sense. Hence such animals as move themselves in respect to an end they themselves propose are superior to these. This can only be done by reason and intellect, whose province it is to know the proportion between the end and the means to that end, and to order the one to the other. Hence a more perfect degree of life is that of intelligent beings, for their power of self-movement is more perfect. This is shown by the fact that in one and the same man the intellectual power moves the sensitive powers, and these by their command move the organs which carry out the movement. Thus in the arts we see that the art of using a ship, that is, the art of navigation, rules the art of ship-designing; and this in its turn rules the art that is only concerned with preparing the material for the ship.

But although our intellect moves itself to some things, yet others are supplied by nature, as for example first principles, which it cannot doubt, and the last end, which it cannot will. Hence, although with respect to some things it moves itself, yet with regard to other things it must be moved by another. Therefore that being whose act of understanding is its very nature, and which, in what it naturally possesses, is not determined by another, must have life in the most perfect degree. Such is God; and hence in Him principally is life. From this the Philosopher concludes[1] after showing God to be intelligent, that God has life most perfect and eternal, since His intellect is most perfect and always in act.

Reply Obj. 1. As stated in the *Metaphysics*,[2] action is two-fold. Actions of one kind pass out to external matter, as to heat or to cut, whilst actions of the other kind remain in the agent, as to understand, to sense, and to will. The difference between them is this, that the former action is the perfection not of the agent that moves, but of the thing moved, while the latter action is the perfection of the agent. Hence, because movement is an act of the thing in move-

ment, the latter action, in so far as it is in the act of the operator, is called its movement, by this likeness, that as movement is an act of the thing moved, so an act of this kind is the act of the agent, although movement is an act of the imperfect, that is, of what is in potency, while this kind of act is an act of the perfect, that is to say, of what is in act as stated in the book on the *Soul*.[3] In the sense, therefore, in which understanding is movement, that which understands itself is said to move itself. It is in this sense that Plato also taught that God moves Himself,[4] not in the sense in which movement is an act of the imperfect.

Reply Obj. 2. As God is His own very being and understanding, so is He His own life; and therefore He so lives that He has no principle of life.

Reply Obj. 3. Life in this lower world is bestowed on a corruptible nature that needs generation to preserve the species and nourishment to preserve the individual. For this reason life is not found here below apart from a vegetative soul; but this does not hold good with incorruptible things.

ARTICLE 4. *Whether All Things Are Life in God?*

We proceed thus to the Fourth Article: It seems that not all things are life in God.

Objection 1. For it is said (Acts 17. 28), *In Him we live, and move, and be.* But not all things in God are movement. Therefore not all things are life in Him.

Obj. 2. Further, all things are in God as their first exemplar. But things typified ought to conform to the exemplar. Since, then, not all things have life in themselves, it seems that not all things are life in God.

Obj. 3. Further, as Augustine says (*De vera relig.* 29),[5] a living substance is better than a substance that does not live. If, therefore, things which in themselves have not life, are life in God, it seems that things exist more truly in God than in themselves. But this appears to be false; since in themselves they are in act, but in God in potency.

Obj. 4. Further, just as good things and things made in time are known by God, so are bad things, and things that God can make, but that never will be made. If, therefore, all things are life in God, in so far as they are known by Him, it seems that even bad things and things that

---

[1] *Metaphysics*, XII, 7 (1072b27).
[2] Aristotle, IX, 8 (1050a22).
[3] Aristotle, III, 7 (431a6).
[4] See above, Q. IX, A. 1, ANS. 1.
[5] PL 34, 145.

will never be made are life in God, as known by Him, and this appears inadmissible.

On the contrary (John 1. 3, 4), It is said, *What was made, in Him was life.* But all things were made, except God. Therefore all things are life in God.

I answer that, In God to live is to understand, as before stated (A. 3). In God intellect, the thing understood, and the act of understanding, are one and the same. Hence whatever is in God as understood is the very living or life of God. Now, therefore, since all things that have been made by God are in Him as things understood, it follows that all things in Him are the divine life itself.

Reply Obj. 1. Creatures are said to be in God in a twofold sense. In one way, so far as they are held together and preserved by the divine power, even as we say that things that are in our power are in us. And creatures are thus said to be in God, even as they exist in their own natures. In this sense we must understand the words of the Apostle when he says, *In Him we live, and move, and be,* since our being, living, and moving are themselves caused by God. In another sense things are said to be in God as in Him who knows them, in which sense they are in God through their proper ideas, which in God are not distinct from the divine essence. Hence things as they are in God are the divine essence. And since the divine essence is life and not movement, it follows that things in God in this manner of speaking are not movement, but life.

Reply Obj. 2 The thing typified must be like the type according to the form, not the mode of being. For sometimes the form has being of another kind in the exemplar from that which it has in the thing typified. Thus the form of a house has in the mind of the architect immaterial and intelligible being, but in the house that exists outside his soul, material and sensible being. Hence the ideas of things, though not living in themselves, are life in the divine mind, as having a divine being in that mind.

Reply Obj. 3. If form only, and not matter, belonged to natural things, then in all respects natural things would exist more truly in the divine mind, by the ideas of them, than in themselves. For which reason, in fact, Plato held[1] that the separate man was the true man; and that material man is man only by participation. But since matter enters into the being of natural things, we must say that those things have being absolutely in the divine mind more

[1] Cf. Augustine, *Epist.,* III (PL 33, 64); *Epist.,* CXVIII, 3 (PL 33, 441); cf. also Aristotle, *Metaphysics,* I, 6 (987^{b}7).

truly than in themselves, because in that mind they have an uncreated being, but in themselves a created being, while to be this particular being, a man, or a horse, for example, is realized more truly in its own nature than in the divine mind, because it belongs to the truth of man to be material, which, as existing in the divine mind, he is not. Even so a house has nobler being in the architect's mind than in matter; yet a material house is called a house more truly than the one which exists in the mind, since the former is a house in act, the latter only in potency.

Reply Obj. 4. Although bad things are in God's knowledge as being comprehended under that knowledge, yet they are not in God as created by Him, or preserved by Him, or as having their type in Him. They are known by God through the types of good things. Hence it cannot be said that bad things are life in God. Those things that are not in time may be called life in God in so far as life means understanding only, and in so far as they are understood by God, but not in so far as life implies a principle of operation.

QUESTION XIX
THE WILL OF GOD
(*In Twelve Articles*)

AFTER considering the things belonging to the divine knowledge, we consider what belongs to the divine will. The first consideration is about the divine will itself; the second about what belongs absolutely to His will (Q. XX); the third about what belongs to the intellect in relation to His will (Q. XXII). About His will itself there are twelve points of inquiry: (1) Whether there is will in God? (2) Whether God wills things apart from Himself? (3) Whether whatever God wills, He wills necessarily? (4) Whether the will of God is the cause of things? (5) Whether any cause can be assigned to the divine will? (6) Whether the divine will is always fulfilled? (7) Whether the will of God is mutable? (8) Whether the will of God imposes necessity on the things willed? (9) Whether there is in God the will of evil things? (10) Whether God has free choice? (11) Whether the will of sign is distinguished in God? (12) Whether five signs of will are rightly assigned to the divine will?

ARTICLE 1. *Whether There Is Will in God?*

We proceed thus to the First Article: It seems that there is not will in God.

Objection 1. For the object of will is the end and the good. But we cannot assign to God any end. Therefore there is not will in God.

Obj. 2. Further, will is a kind of appetite. But appetite, as it is directed to things not possessed, implies imperfection, which does not belong to God. Therefore there is not will in God.

Obj. 3. Further, according to the Philosopher,[1] "the will moves, and is moved." But God is the first mover, Himself unmoved, as proved in the *Physics*.[2] Therefore there is not will in God.

On the contrary, The Apostle says (Rom. 12. 2): *That you may prove what is the will of God.*

I answer that, There is will in God, as there is intellect, since will follows upon intellect. For as natural things have actual being by their form, so the intellect is actually intelligent by its intelligible form. Now everything has this disposition towards its natural form, that when it has it not it tends towards it, and when it has it, it is at rest in it. It is the same with every natural perfection, which is a natural good. This disposition to good in things without knowledge is called natural appetite. Hence also intellectual natures have a like disposition to good as apprehended through its intelligible form, so as to rest in it when possessed, and when not possessed to seek to possess it, both of which pertain to the will. Hence in every intellectual being there is will, just as in every sensible being there is animal appetite. And so there must be will in God, since there is intellect in Him. And as His act of understanding is His own being, so is His will.

Reply Obj. 1. Although nothing apart from God is His end, yet He Himself is the end with respect to all things made by Him. And this by His essence, for by His essence He is good, as shown above (Q. VI, A. 3), for the end has the aspect of good.

Reply Obj. 2. Will in us belongs to the appetitive part, which, although named from appetite, has not for its only act the seeking what it does not possess, but also the loving and delighting in what it does possess. In this respect will is said to be in God, as having always good which is its object, since, as already said (add), it is not distinct from His essence.

Reply Obj. 3. A will the principal object of which is a good outside itself must be moved by another; but the object of the divine will is His goodness, which is His essence. Hence, since

the will of God is His essence, it is not moved by another than itself, but by itself alone, in the same sense as understanding and willing are said to be movement. This is what Plato meant when he said that the first mover moves itself.[3]

ARTICLE 2. *Whether God Wills Things Apart from Himself?*

We proceed thus to the Second Article: It seems that God does not will things apart from Himself.

Objection 1. For the divine will is the divine being. But God is not other than Himself. Therefore He does not will things other than Himself.

Obj. 2. Further, the willed moves the willer, as the thing desired the appetite, as stated in the book on the *Soul*.[4] If, therefore, God wills anything apart from Himself, His will must be moved by another, which is impossible.

Obj. 3. Further, if what is willed suffices the willer, he seeks nothing beyond it. But His own goodness suffices God, and completely satisfies His will. Therefore God does not will anything apart from Himself.

Obj. 4. Further, acts of the will are multiplied in proportion to the number of things willed. If, therefore, God wills Himself and things apart from Himself, it follows that the act of His will is manifold, and consequently His being, which is His will. But this is impossible. Therefore God does not will things apart from Himself.

On the contrary, The Apostle says (I Thess. 4. 3): *This is the will of God, your sanctification.*

I answer that, God wills not only Himself, but other things apart from Himself. This is clear from the comparison which we made above (A. 1). For natural things have a natural inclination not only towards their own proper good, to acquire it if not possessed, and, if possessed, to rest therein, but also to spread abroad their own good amongst others, so far as possible. Hence we see that every agent, in so far as it is perfect and in act, produces its like. It pertains, therefore, to the nature of the will to communicate as far as possible to others the good possessed; and especially does this pertain to the divine will, from which all perfection is derived in some kind of likeness. Hence, if natural things, in so far as they are perfect, communicate their good to others, much more does it pertain to the divine will to communicate by

---

[1] *Soul*, III, 10 (433b16).
[2] Aristotle, VIII, 6 (258b10).

[3] See above, Q. IX, A. 9, Ans. 1.
[4] Aristotle, III, 10 (433b17).

likeness its own good to others as much as is possible. Thus, then, He wills both Himself to be, and other things to be; but Himself as the end, and other things as ordered to that end, in so far as it befits the divine goodness that other things should be partakers therein.

Reply Obj. 1. The divine will is God's own being essentially, yet they differ in aspect, according to the different ways of understanding them and expressing them, as is clear from what has been already said (Q. XIII, A. 4). For when we say that God exists, no relation to any other thing is implied, as we do imply when we say that God wills. Therefore, although He is not anything other than Himself, yet He does will things other than Himself.

Reply Obj. 2. In things willed for the sake of the end, the whole reason for our being moved is the end, and this it is that moves the will, as most clearly appears in things willed only for the sake of the end. He who wills to take a bitter draught, in doing so wills nothing else than health, and this alone moves his will. It is different with one who takes a draught that is sweet, which anyone may will to do, not only for the sake of health, but also for its own sake. Hence, although God wills things apart from Himself only for the sake of the end, which is His own goodness as we have said, it does not follow that anything else moves His will, except His goodness. So, as He understands things apart from Himself by understanding His own essence, so He wills things apart from Himself by willing His own goodness.

Reply Obj. 3. From the fact that His own goodness suffices the divine will, it does not follow that it wills nothing else, but rather that it wills nothing except by reason of its goodness. Thus, too, the divine intellect, though its perfection consists in its very knowledge of the divine essence, yet in that essence knows other things.

Reply Obj. 4. As the divine intellect is one, as seeing the many only in the one, in the same way the divine will is one and simple, as willing the many only through the one, that is, through its own goodness.

ARTICLE 3. *Whether Whatever God Wills He Wills Necessarily?*

We proceed thus to the Third Article: It seems that whatever God wills He wills necessarily.

Objection 1. For everything eternal is necessary. But whatever God wills He wills from eternity, for otherwise His will would be mu-

table. Therefore whatever He wills, He wills necessarily.

Obj. 2. Further, God wills things apart from Himself since He wills His own goodness. Now God wills His own goodness necessarily. Therefore He wills things apart from Himself necessarily.

Obj. 3. Further, whatever is natural to God is necessary, for God is of Himself necessary being, and the principle of all necessity, as above shown (Q. II, A. 3). But it is natural to Him to will whatever He wills, since in God there can be nothing besides His nature as stated in the *Metaphysics*.[1] Therefore whatever He wills, He wills necessarily.

Obj. 4. Further, being that is not necessary and being that is possible not to be are one and the same thing. If, therefore, God does not necessarily will a thing that He wills, it is possible for Him not to will it, and therefore possible for Him to will what He does not will. And so the divine will is contingent upon one or the other of two things, and imperfect, since everything contingent is imperfect and mutable.

Obj. 5. Further, on the part of that which is indifferent to one or the other of two things, no action results unless it is inclined to one or the other by some other power, as the Commentator says on the second book of the *Physics*.[2] If, then, the Will of God is indifferent with regard to anything, it follows that His determination to act comes from another; and thus He has some cause prior to Himself.

Obj. 6. Further, whatever God knows, He knows necessarily. But as the divine knowledge is His essence, so is the divine will. Therefore whatever God wills He wills necessarily.

On the contrary, The Apostle says (Eph. 1. 11): *Who worketh all things according to the counsel of His will.* Now, what we work according to the counsel of the will, we do not will necessarily. Therefore God does not will necessarily whatever He wills.

I answer that, There are two ways in which a thing is said to be necessary, namely, absolutely, and by supposition. We judge a thing to be absolutely necessary from the relation of the terms, as when the predicate forms part of the definition of the subject; thus it is necessary that man is an animal. It is the same when the subject forms part of the notion of the predicate; thus it is necessary that a number must be odd or even. In this way it is not necessary that Socrates sits, and so it is not necessary abso-

---

[1] Aristotle, v, 5 (1015b15).
[2] Averroes, comm. 48 (IV, 68K).

lutely, though it may be so by supposition; for, granted that he is sitting, he must necessarily sit, as long as he is sitting.

Accordingly as to things willed by God, we must observe that He wills something of absolute necessity, but this is not true of all that He wills. For the divine will has a necessary relation to the divine goodness, since that is its proper object. Hence God wills His own goodness necessarily, even as we will our own happiness necessarily, and as any other power has necessary relation to its proper and principal object, for instance the sight to colour, since it tends to it by its own nature. But God wills things apart from Himself in so far as they are ordered to His own goodness as their end. Now in willing an end we do not necessarily will things that lead to it, unless they are such that the end cannot be attained without them; as, for example, we will to take food to preserve life, or to take ship in order to cross the sea. But we do not necessarily will things without which the end is attainable, such as a horse for a journey which we can take on foot, for we can make the journey without one. The same applies to other means. Hence, since the goodness of God is perfect, and can exist without other things since no perfection can accrue to Him from them, it follows that His willing things apart from Himself is not absolutely necessary. Yet it can be necessary by supposition, for supposing that He wills a thing, then He is unable not to will it, as His will cannot change.

Reply Obj. 1. From the fact that God wills from eternity whatever He wills, it does not follow that He wills it necessarily, except by supposition.

Reply Obj. 2. Although God necessarily wills His own goodness, He does not necessarily will things willed on account of His goodness, for it can exist without other things.

Reply Obj. 3. It is not natural to God to will any of those other things that He does not will necessarily; and yet it is not unnatural or contrary to His nature, but voluntary.

Reply Obj. 4. Sometimes a necessary cause has a non-necessary relation to an effect, owing to a deficiency in the effect, and not in the cause. Even so, the sun's power has a non-necessary relation to some contingent events on this earth, owing to a defect not in the solar power, but in the effect that proceeds not necessarily from the cause. In the same way, that God does not necessarily will some of the things that He wills does not result from defect in the divine will, but from a defect belonging to the

nature of the thing willed, namely, that the perfect goodness of God can be without it; and such defect accompanies all created good.

Reply Obj. 5. A naturally contingent cause must be determined to the effect by some external power. The divine will, which by its nature is necessary, determines itself to will things to which it has no necessary relation.

Reply Obj. 6. As the divine being is necessary of itself, so is the divine will and the divine knowledge; but the divine knowledge has a necessary relation to the thing known; not however the divine will to the thing willed. The reason for this is that knowledge is of things as they exist in the knower, but the will is directed to things as they exist in themselves. Since then all other things have necessary existence according as they exist in God, but no absolute necessity so as to be necessary in themselves, in so far as they exist in themselves, it follows that God knows necessarily whatever He knows, but does not will necessarily whatever He wills.

ARTICLE 4. *Whether the Will of God Is the Cause of Things?*

We proceed thus to the Fourth Article: It seems that the will of God is not the cause of things.

Objection 1. For Dionysius says (*Div. Nom.* iv, 1):[1] "As our sun, not by reason nor by preelection, but by its very being, enlightens all things that can participate in its light, so the divine good by its very essence pours the rays of its goodness upon everything that exists." But every voluntary agent acts by reason and preelection. Therefore God does not act by will, and so His will is not the cause of things.

Obj. 2. Further, The first in any order is that which is essentially so; thus in the order of burning things, that comes first which is fire by its essence. But God is the first agent. Therefore He acts by His essence; and that is His nature. He acts then by nature, and not by will. Therefore the divine will is not the cause of things.

Obj. 3. Further, whatever is the cause of anything through being such a thing, is the cause by nature, and not by will. For fire is the cause of heat as being itself hot, while an architect is the cause of a house because he wills to build it. Now Augustine says,[2] "Because God is good, we exist." Therefore God is the cause of things by His nature, and not by His will.

Obj. 4. Further, Of one thing there is one

[1] PG 3, 693.
[2] *Christian Doctrine*, I, 32 (PL 34, 32).

cause. But the cause of created things is the knowledge of God, as we said before (Q. XIV, A. 8). Therefore the will of God cannot be considered the cause of things.

On the contrary, It is said (Wis. 11. 26), *How could anything endure, if Thou wouldst not?*

I answer that, We must hold that the will of God is the cause of things, and that He acts by the will, and not, as some have supposed, by a necessity of His nature.

This can be shown in three ways: First, from the order itself of active causes. Since "intellect and nature" act for an end, as proved in the *Physics,*[1] the natural agent must have the end and the necessary means predetermined for it by some higher intellect; as, for example, the end and definite movement is predetermined for the arrow by the archer. Hence the intellectual and voluntary agent must precede the agent that acts by nature. Hence, since God is first in the order of agents, He must act by intellect and will.

This is shown, secondly, from the character of a natural agent, of which the property is to produce one effect; for nature operates in one and the same way, unless it be prevented. This is because the nature of the act is according to the nature of the agent, and hence as long as it has that nature, its acts will be in accordance with that nature, for every natural agent has a determinate being. Since, then, the Divine Being is undetermined, and contains in Himself the full perfection of being, it cannot be that He acts by a necessity of His nature, unless He were to cause something undetermined and infinite in being; and that this is impossible has been already shown (Q. VII, A. 2). He does not, therefore, act by a necessity of His nature, but determined effects proceed from His own infinite perfection according to the determination of His will and intellect.

Thirdly, it is shown by the relation of effects to their cause. For effects proceed from the agent that causes them, in so far as they pre-exist in the agent, since every agent produces its like. Now effects pre-exist in their cause after the mode of the cause. Therefore since the Divine Being is His own intellect, effects pre-exist in Him after the mode of intellect, and therefore proceed from Him after the same mode. Consequently, they proceed from Him after the mode of will, for His inclination to doing what His intellect has conceived pertains to the will.

[1] Aristotle, II, 5 (196ᵇ21).

Therefore the will of God is the cause of things.

Reply Obj. 1. Dionysius in these words does not intend to exclude election from God absolutely, but only in a certain sense, in so far, that is, as He communicates His goodness not merely to certain beings, but to all, and as election implies a certain distinction.

Reply Obj. 2. Because the essence of God is His intellect and will, from the fact of His acting by His essence it follows that He acts after the mode of intellect and will.

Reply Obj. 3. Good is the object of the will. The words, therefore, "Because God is good, we exist," are true in so far as His goodness is the reason of His willing all other things, as said before (A. 2).

Reply Obj. 4. Even in us the cause of one and the same effect is knowledge as directing it, whereby the form of the work is conceived, and will as commanding it, since the form as it is in the intellect only is not determined to exist or not to exist in the effect except by the will. Hence, the speculative intellect has nothing to say to operation. But the power is cause, as executing the effect, since it denotes the immediate principle of operation. But in God all these things are one.

ARTICLE 5. *Whether Any Cause Can Be Assigned to the Divine Will?*

We proceed thus to the Fifth Article: It seems that some cause can be assigned to the divine will.

Objection 1. For Augustine says (QQ. LXXXIII, 46).[2] "Who would venture to say that God made all things irrationally?" But to a voluntary agent, what is the reason of operating is also the cause of willing. Therefore the will of God has some cause.

Obj. 2. Further, in things made by one who wills to make them, and whose will is influenced by no cause, there can be no cause assigned except the will of him who wills. But the will of God is the cause of all things, as has been already shown (A. 4). If, then, there is no cause of His will, we cannot seek in any natural things any cause except the divine will alone. Thus all science would be in vain, since science seeks to assign causes to effects. This seems inadmissible, and therefore we must assign some cause to the divine will.

Obj. 3. Further, what is done by the one who wills on account of no cause, depends absolutely on his will. If, therefore, the will of God has no cause, it follows that all things made de-

[2] PL 40, 30.

pend simply on His will, and have no other cause. But this also is not admissible.

On the contrary, Augustine says (QQ. LXXXIII, 28):[1] "Every efficient cause is greater than the thing effected." But nothing is greater than the will of God. We must not then seek for a cause of it.

I answer that, In no way has the will of God a cause. In proof of this we must consider that since the will follows from the intellect there is a cause of the will in the person that wills, in the same way as there is a cause of the understanding in the person that understands. The case with the understanding is this, that if the premiss and its conclusion are understood separately from each other, the understanding the premiss is the cause that the conclusion is known. If the understanding perceive the conclusion in the premiss itself, apprehending both the one and the other at the same glance, in this case the knowing of the conclusion would not be caused by understanding the premisses, since a thing cannot be its own cause; and yet, it would be true that the thinker would understand the premisses to be the cause of the conclusion. It is the same with the will, with respect to which the end stands in the same relation to the means to the end as do the premisses to the conclusion with regard to the understanding.

Hence, if anyone in one act wills an end, and in another act the means to that end, his willing the end will be the cause of his willing the means. This cannot be the case if in one act he wills both end and means, for a thing cannot be its own cause. Yet it will be true to say that he wills to order to the end, the means to the end.

Now as God by one act understands all things in His essence, so by one act He wills all things in His goodness. Hence, as in God to understand the cause is not the cause of His understanding the effect, for He understands the effect in the cause, so, in Him, to will an end is not the cause of His willing the means, yet He wills the ordering of the means to the end. Therefore He wills this to be as means to that, but does not will this on account of that.

Reply Obj. 1. The will of God is reasonable not because anything is to God a cause of willing, but in so far as He wills one thing to be on account of another.

Reply Obj. 2. Since God wills effects to proceed from causes that are fixed, for the preservation of order in the universe, it is not superfluous to seek for causes secondary to the divine

will. It would, however, be superfluous to do so if such were sought after as primary, and not as dependent on the will of God. In this sense Augustine says (*De Trin.* iii, 2):[2] "Philosophers in their vanity have thought fit to attribute contingent effects to other causes, being utterly unable to perceive the cause that is above all others, the will of God."

Reply Obj. 3. Since God wills effects to be on account of causes, all effects that presuppose some other effect do not depend solely on the will of God, but on something else besides; but the first effect depends on the divine will alone. Thus, for example, we may say that God willed man to have hands to serve his intellect by their work, and intellect, that he might be man, and willed him to be man that he might enjoy Him, or for the completion of the universe. But this cannot be reduced to other created secondary ends. Hence such things depend on the simple will of God, but the others on the order of other causes.

ARTICLE 6. *Whether the Will of God Is Always Fulfilled?*

We proceed thus to the Sixth Article: It seems that the will of God is not always fulfilled.

Objection 1. For the Apostle says (I Tim. 2. 4): *God will have all men to be saved, and to come to the knowledge of the truth* But this does not happen. Therefore the will of God is not always fulfilled.

Obj. 2. Further, as knowledge is to truth, so is the will to good. Now God knows all truth. Therefore He wills all good. But not all good actually exists, for much more good might exist. Therefore the will of God is not always fulfilled.

Obj. 3. Further, since the will of God is the first cause, it does not exclude mediate causes as we have said (A. 5). But the effect of a first cause may be hindered by a defect of a secondary cause, as the effect of the moving power may be hindered by weakness of the limb. Therefore the effect of the divine will may be hindered by a defect of the secondary causes. The will of God, therefore, is not always fulfilled.

On the contrary, It is said (Ps. 113. 11): *God hath done all things, whatsoever He would.*

I answer that, The will of God must always be fulfilled. In proof of this we must consider that since an effect is conformed to the agent according to its form. the rule is the same with

[1] PL 40, 18.   [2] PL 42, 871.

active causes as with formal causes. The rule in forms is this, that although a thing may fall short of any particular form, it cannot fall short of the universal form. For though a thing may fail to be, for example, a man or a living being, yet it cannot fail to be a being. Hence the same must happen in active causes. Something may fall outside the order of any particular active cause, but not outside the order of the universal cause, under which all particular causes are included; and if any particular cause fails of its effect, this is because of the hindrance of some other particular cause, which is included in the order of the universal cause. Therefore an effect cannot possibly escape the order of the universal cause. Even in corporeal things this is clearly seen. For it may happen that a star is hindered from producing its effects, yet whatever effect does result, in corporeal things, from this hindrance of a corporeal cause, must be referred through mediate causes to the universal influence of the first heaven.

Since, then, the will of God is the universal cause of all things, it is impossible that the divine will should not produce its effect. Hence that which seems to depart from the divine will in one order, is brought back to it in another order, as does the sinner, who by sin falls away from the divine will as much as lies in him, yet falls back into the order of that will when by its justice he is punished.

Reply Obj. 1. The words of the Apostle, *God will have all men to be saved*, etc., can be understood in three ways. First, by a restricted application, in which case they would mean, as Augustine says (*Enchir.* 103),[1] "God wills all men to be saved that are saved, not because there is no man whom He does not wish saved, but because there is no man saved whose salvation He does not will."

Secondly, they can be understood as applying to every class of individuals, not to every individual of each class, in which case they mean that God wills some men of every class and condition to be saved, males and females, Jews and Gentiles, great and small, but not all of every condition.

Thirdly, according to Damascene (*De Fide Orth.* ii, 29)[2] they are understood of the antecedent will of God, not of the consequent will. This distinction must not be taken as applying to the divine will itself, in which there is nothing antecedent nor consequent, but to the things willed.

[1] PL 40, 280.
[2] PG 94, 968.

To understand this we must consider that everything, in so far as it is good, is willed by God. A thing taken in its primary sense, and absolutely considered, may be good or evil, and yet when some additional circumstances are taken into account, by a consequent consideration may be changed into the contrary. Thus that a man should live is good, and that a man should be killed is evil, absolutely considered. But if in a particular case we add that a man is a murderer or dangerous to society, to kill him is a good, that he live is an evil. Hence it may be said of a just judge, that antecedently he wills all men to live, but consequently wills the murderer to be hanged. In the same way God antecedently wills all men to be saved, but consequently wills some to be damned, as His justice exacts. Nor do we will absolutely what we will antecedently, but rather we will it in a qualified manner; for the will is directed to things as they are in themselves, and in themselves they exist under particular qualifications. Hence we will a thing absolutely according as we will it when all particular circumstances are considered, and this is what is meant by willing consequently. Thus it may be said that a just judge wills absolutely the hanging of a murderer, but in a qualified manner he would will him to live, in so far namely, as he is a man. Such a qualified will may be called a willingness (*velleitas*) rather than an absolute will. Thus it is clear that whatever God wills absolutely takes place, although what He wills antecedently may not take place.

Reply Obj. 2. An act of the cognitive power is according as the thing known is in the knower, while an act of the appetitive power is directed to things as they exist in themselves. But all that can have the nature of being and truth exists virtually in God, though it does not all exist in created things. Therefore God knows all truth, but does not will all good, except in so far as He wills Himself, in Whom all good virtually exists.

Reply Obj. 3. A first cause can be hindered in its effect by deficiency in the secondary cause, when it is not the universal first cause, including within itself all causes, for then the effect could in no way escape its order. And thus it is with the will of God, as said above.

ARTICLE 7. *Whether the Will of God Is Changeable?*

We proceed thus to the Seventh Article: It seems that the Will of God is changeable.

Objection 1. For the Lord says (Gen. 6. 7): *It repenteth Me that I have made man.* But whoever repents of what he has done, has a changeable will. Therefore God has a changeable will.

Obj. 2. Further, it is said in the person of the Lord: *I will speak against a nation and against a kingdom, to root out, and to pull down, and to destroy it; but if that nation shall repent of its evil, I also will repent of the evil that I have thought to do to them* (Jer. 18. 7, 8). Therefore God has a changeable will.

Obj. 3. Further, whatever God does, He does voluntarily. But God does not always do the same thing, for at one time He ordered the law to be observed and at another time forbade it. Therefore He has a changeable will.

Obj. 4. Further, God does not will of necessity what He wills, as said before (A. 3). Therefore He can both will and not will the same thing. But whatever is in potency to opposites, is changeable; as that which can be and not be is changeable according to substance, and that which can exist in a place or not in that place, is changeable according to place. Therefore God is changeable as regards His will.

On the contrary, It is said: *God is not as a man, that He should lie, nor as the son of man, that He should be changed* (Num. 23. 19).

I answer that, The will of God is entirely unchangeable. On this point we must consider that to change the will is one thing, to will that certain things should be changed is another. It is possible to will a thing to be done now and its contrary afterwards, and yet for the will to remain permanently the same; but the will would be changed if one should begin to will what before he had not willed, or cease to will what he had willed before. This cannot happen unless we presuppose change either in the knowledge or in the disposition of the substance of the one who wills. For since the will regards good, a man may in two ways begin to will a thing. In one way when that thing begins to be good for him, and this does not take place without a change in him. Thus when the cold weather begins, it becomes good to sit by the fire, though it was not so before. In another way when he knows for the first time that a thing is good for him, though he did not know it before; hence we take counsel in order to know what is good for us. Now it has already been shown that both the substance of God and His knowledge are entirely unchangeable (QQ. IX, A. 1; XIV, A.

15). Therefore His will must be entirely unchangeable.

Reply Obj. 1. These words of the Lord are to be understood metaphorically, and according to our likeness. For when we repent, we destroy what we have made, although we may even do so without change of will, as, for example, when a man wills to make a thing, at the same time intending to destroy it later. Therefore God is said to have repented by way of comparison with our mode of acting, in so far as by the deluge He destroyed from the face of the earth man whom He had made.

Reply Obj. 2. The will of God, as it is the first and universal cause, does not exclude mediate causes that have power to produce certain effects. Since however all mediate causes are inferior in power to the first cause, there are many things in the divine power, knowledge and will that are not included in the order of inferior causes. Thus in the case of the raising of Lazarus, one who looked only at inferior causes might have said: "Lazarus will not rise again"; but looking at the divine first cause could have said: "Lazarus will rise again." And God wills both: that is, that in the order of the inferior cause a thing shall happen, but that in the order of the higher cause it shall not happen; or He may will conversely. We may say, then, that God sometimes declares that a thing shall happen according as it falls under the order of inferior causes, as of nature, or merit, which yet does not happen as not being in the designs of the divine and higher cause. Thus He foretold to Ezechias: *Take order with thy house, for thou shalt die, and not live* (Isa. 38, 1). Yet this did not take place, since from eternity it was otherwise disposed in the divine knowledge and will, which is unchangeable. Hence Gregory says (*Moral.* xvi, 10):[1] "The sentence of God changes, but not His counsel"—that is to say, the counsel of His will. When therefore He says, *I also will repent,* His words must be understood metaphorically. For men seem to repent, when they do not fulfil what they have threatened.

Reply Obj. 3. It does not follow from this argument that God has a will that changes, but that He sometimes wills that things should change.

Reply Obj. 4. Although God's willing a thing is not by absolute necessity, yet it is necessary by supposition, on account of the unchangeableness of the divine will, as has been said above (A. 3).

[1] PL 75, 1127.

ARTICLE 8. *Whether the Will of God Imposes Necessity on the Things Willed?*

We proceed thus to the Eighth Article: It seems that the will of God imposes necessity on the things willed.

Objection 1. For Augustine says (*Enchir.* 103):[1] "No one is saved, except whom God has willed to be saved. He must therefore be asked to will it; for if He wills it, it must necessarily be."

Obj. 2. Further, every cause that cannot be hindered produces its effect necessarily, because, as the Philosopher says:[2] Nature always works in the same way, "if there is nothing to hinder it." But the will of God cannot be hindered. For the Apostle says (Rom. 9. 19): *Who resisteth His will?* Therefore the will of God imposes necessity on the things willed.

Obj. 3. Further, whatever is necessary by its antecedent cause is necessary absolutely; it is thus necessary that animals should die, being composed of contrary elements. Now things created by God are related to the divine will as to an antecedent cause, whereby they have necessity. For the conditional statement is true that if God wills a thing, it comes to pass, and every true conditional statement is necessary. It follows therefore that all that God wills is necessary absolutely.

On the contrary, All good things that are made God wills to be made. If therefore His will imposes necessity on things willed, it follows that all good happens of necessity, and thus there is an end of free choice, counsel, and all other such things.

I answer that, The divine will imposes necessity on some things willed but not on all. The reason of this some have chosen to assign to intermediate causes, holding that what God produces by necessary causes is necessary, and what He produces by contingent causes contingent.

This does not seem to be a sufficient explanation, for two reasons. First, because the effect of a first cause is contingent on account of the secondary cause, from the fact that the effect of the first cause is hindered by deficiency in the second cause, as the sun's power is hindered by a defect in the plant. But no defect of a secondary cause can hinder God's will from producing its effect. Secondly, because if the distinction between the contingent and the necessary is to be referred only to secondary

[1] PL 40, 280.
[2] *Physics,* II, 8 (199[b]18).

causes, it follows that this is outside the divine intention and will, which is inadmissible.

It is better therefore to say that this happens on account of the efficacy of the divine will. For when a cause is efficacious to act, the effect follows upon the cause not only as to the thing done, but also as to its manner of being done or of being. Thus from defect of active power in the seed it may happen that a child is born unlike its father in accidental points that belong to its manner of being. Since then the divine will is perfectly efficacious, it follows not only that things are done which God wills to be done, but also that they are done in the way that He wills. Now God wills some things to be done necessarily, some contingently, that there might be an order in things, for the building up of the universe. Therefore to some effects He has attached necessary causes, that cannot fail, but to others defectible and contingent causes, from which arise contingent effects. Hence it is not because the proximate causes are contingent that the effects willed by God happen contingently, but because it is His will that they should happen contingently, God has prepared contingent causes for them.

Reply Obj. 1. By the words of Augustine we must understand a necessity in things willed by God that is not absolute, but conditional. For the conditional statement that if God wills a thing it must necessarily be, is necessarily true.

Reply Obj. 2. From the very fact that nothing resists the divine will, it follows that not only those things happen that God wills to happen, but that they happen necessarily or contingently according to His will.

Reply Obj. 3. Consequents have necessity from their antecedents according to the mode of the antecedents. Hence things effected by the divine will have that kind of necessity that God wills them to have, either absolute or conditional. Not all things, therefore, are absolute necessities.

ARTICLE 9. *Whether God Wills Evils?*

We proceed thus to the Ninth Article: It seems that God wills evils.

Objection 1. For every good that exists, God wills. But it is a good that evil should exist. For Augustine says (*Enchir.* 96):[3] "Although evil in so far as it is evil is not a good, yet it is good that not only good things should exist, but also evil things." Therefore God wills evil things.

Obj. 2. Further, Dionysius says (*Div. Nom.*

[3] PL 40, 276.

iv, 19):[1] "Evil would conduce to the perfection of everything," that is, the universe. And Augustine says (*Enchir.* 10, 11):[2] "Out of all things is built up the admirable beauty of the universe, wherein even that which is called evil, properly ordered and disposed, commends the good the more evidently in that good is more pleasing and praiseworthy when contrasted with evil." But God wills all that pertains to the perfection and beauty of the universe, for this is what God desires above all things in His creatures. Therefore God wills evil.

Obj. 3. Further, that evil should exist, and should not exist, are contradictory opposites. But God does not will that evil should not exist; otherwise, since various evils do exist, God's will would not always be fulfilled. Therefore God wills that evil should exist.

On the contrary, Augustine says (QQ. LXXXIII, 3):[3] "No wise man is the cause of another man becoming worse. Now God surpasses all men in wisdom. Much less therefore is God the cause of man becoming worse; and when He is said to be the cause of a thing, He is said to will it." Therefore it is not by God's will that man becomes worse. Now it is clear that every evil makes a thing worse. Therefore God does not will evil things.

I answer that, Since the notion of good is the notion of desirability, as said before (Q. V, A. 1), and since evil is opposed to good, it is impossible that any evil, as such, should be sought for by the appetite, either natural, or animal, or by the intellectual appetite which is the will. Nevertheless evil may be sought accidentally, so far as it accompanies a good, as appears in each of the appetites. For a natural agent does not intend privation or corruption, but the form to which is joined the privation of some other form, and the generation of one thing, which implies the corruption of another. For when a lion kills a stag, his object is food, to which is joined the killing of the animal. Similarly the fornicator intends the pleasure, to which is joined the deformity of sin.

Now the evil that accompanies one good, is the privation of another good. Never therefore would evil be sought after, not even accidentally, unless the good that accompanies the evil were more desired than the good of which the evil is the privation. Now God wills no good more than He wills His own goodness; yet He wills one good more than another. Hence He in no way wills the evil of sin, which is the privation of order towards the divine good. The evil of natural defect, or of punishment, He does will, by willing the good to which such evils are attached. Thus in willing justice He wills punishment; and in willing the preservation of the natural order, He wills some things to be naturally corrupted.

Reply Obj. 1. Some have said[4] that although God does not will evil, yet He wills that evil should be or be done, because, although evil is not a good, yet it is good that evil should be or be done. This they said because things evil in themselves are ordered to some good; and this order they thought was expressed in the words "that evil should be" or "be done." This, however, is not correct, since evil is not of itself ordered to good, but accidentally. For it is beside the intention of the sinner that any good should follow from his sin, as it was beside the intention of tyrants that the patience of the martyrs should shine forth from all their persecutions. It cannot therefore be said that such an ordering to good is implied in the statement that it is a good thing that evil should be or be done, since nothing is judged by that which appertains to it accidentally, but by that which belongs to it per se.

Reply Obj. 2. Evil does not operate towards the perfection and beauty of the universe, except accidentally, as said above (ANS. 1). Therefore Dionysius in saying that "evil would conduce to the perfection of the universe," draws a conclusion by reduction to an absurdity.

Reply Obj. 3. The statements that evil should exist, and that evil should not exist, are opposed as contradictories; yet the statements that anyone wills evil to be and that he wills it not to be, are not so opposed, since either is affirmative. God therefore neither wills evil to be done, nor wills it not to be done, but wills to permit evil to be done; and this is a good.

ARTICLE 10. *Whether God Has Free Choice?*

We proceed thus to the Tenth Article: It seems that God has not free choice.

Objection 1. For Jerome says, in a homily on the prodigal son:[5] "God alone is He who is not liable to sin, nor can be liable; all others, as having free choice, can be inclined to either side."

---

[1] PG 3, 717.
[2] PL 40, 236.
[3] PL 40, 11.

[4] Hugh of St. Victor, *De Sacram.*, I, IV, 13 (PL 176, 239); Ps. Hugh of St. Victor, *Summa Sent.*, I, 13 (PL 176, 66); cf. Peter Lombard, *Sent.*, I, d. 46, chap. 3 (QR I, 280).
[5] *Epist.*, XXI, *ad Damas* (PL 22, 393).

Obj. 2. Further, free choice is a power of the reason and will, by which good and evil are chosen. But God does not will evil, as has been said (A. 9). Therefore there is not free choice in God.

On the contrary, Ambrose says (*De Fide,* ii, 6):[1] "The Holy Spirit divideth unto each one as He will, namely, according to the free choice of the will, not in obedience to necessity."

I answer that, We have free choice with respect to what we do not will of necessity, nor by natural instinct. For that we will to be happy does not appertain to free choice, but to natural instinct. Hence other animals, that are moved to act by natural instinct, are not said to be moved by free choice. Since then God necessarily wills His own goodness, but other things not necessarily, as shown above (A. 3), He has free choice with respect to what He does not necessarily will.

Reply Obj. 1. Jerome seems to deny free choice to God not absolutely, but only as regards the inclination to sin.

Reply Obj. 2. Since the evil of sin consists in turning away from the divine goodness, by which God wills all things, as above shown (*loc. cit.*), it is manifestly impossible for Him to will the evil of sin; yet He can make choice of one of two opposites, since He can will a thing to be, or not to be. In the same way we ourselves, without sin, can will to sit down, and not will to sit down.

ARTICLE 11. *Whether the Will of Sign Is To Be Distinguished in God?*

We proceed thus to the Eleventh Article: It seems that the will of sign is not to be distinguished in God.

Objection 1. For as the will of God is the cause of things, so is His knowledge. But no signs are ascribed to the divine knowledge. Therefore no signs ought to be ascribed to the divine will.

Obj. 2. Further, every sign that is not in agreement with the mind of him who expresses himself, is false. If therefore the signs ascribed to the divine will are not in agreement with that will, they are false. But if they do agree, they are superfluous. No signs therefore must be ascribed to the divine will.

On the contrary, The will of God is one, since it is the very essence of God. Yet sometimes it is spoken of as many, as in the words of Ps. 110. 2: *Great are the works of the Lord, sought out according to all His wills.* Therefore,

[1] PL 16, 592.

sometimes the sign must be taken for the will.

I answer that, Some things are said of God in their proper sense, others by metaphor, as appears from what has been said before (Q. XIII, A. 3). When certain human passions are predicated of the Godhead metaphorically, this is done because of a likeness in the effect. Hence a thing that is in us a sign of some passion, is signified metaphorically in God under the name of that passion. Thus with us it is usual for an angry man to punish, so that punishment becomes a sign of anger. Therefore punishment itself is signified by the word anger, when anger is attributed to God. In the same way, what is usually with us a sign of will is sometimes metaphorically called will in God, just as when anyone lays down a precept, it is a sign that he wishes that precept obeyed. Hence, a divine precept is sometimes called by metaphor the will of God, as in the words: *Thy will be done on earth, as it is in heaven* (Matt. 6. 10). There is, however, this difference between will and anger, that anger is never attributed to God properly, since in its primary meaning it includes passion, whereas will is attributed to Him properly. Therefore in God there are distinguished will in its proper sense, and will as attributed to Him by metaphor. Will in its proper sense is called the will of good pleasure (*voluntas bene placiti*) and will metaphorically taken is the will of sign, from the fact that the sign itself of will is called will.

Reply Obj. 1. Knowledge is not the cause of a thing being done, unless through the will. For we do not put into act what we know unless we will to do so. Accordingly sign is not attributed to knowledge, but to will.

Reply Obj. 2. Signs of will are called divine wills not as being signs that God wills anything, but because what in us is the usual sign of our will is called the divine will in God. Thus punishment is not a sign that there is anger in God, but it is called anger in Him, from the fact that it is a sign of anger in ourselves.

ARTICLE 12. *Whether Five Signs of Will Are Rightly Attributed to the Divine Will?*

We proceed thus to the Twelfth Article: It seems that five signs of will—namely, prohibition, precept, counsel, operation, and permission—are not rightly attributed to the divine will.

Objection 1. For the same things that God bids us do by His precept or counsel, these He sometimes operates in us, and the same things that He prohibits, these He sometimes permits.

They ought not therefore to be enumerated as distinct.

Obj. 2. Further, God works nothing unless He wills it, as the Scripture says (Wis. 11. 26). But the will of sign is distinct from the will of good pleasure. Therefore operation ought not to be comprehended in the will of sign.

Obj. 3. Further, operation and permission pertain to all creatures in common, since God works in them all, and permits some action in them all. But precept, counsel, and prohibition belong to rational creatures only. Therefore they do not come rightly under one division, not being of one order.

Obj. 4. Further, evil happens in more ways than good, since good happens in one way, but evil "in all kinds of ways," as declared by the Philosopher,[1] and Dionysius (*Div. Nom.* iv, 30).[2] It is not right therefore to attribute one sign only in the case of evil—namely, prohibition—and two—namely, counsel and precept—in the case of good.

I answer that, By these signs we name the signs of will by which we are accustomed to show that we will something. A man may show that he wills something either by himself or by means of another. He may show it by himself, by doing something either directly, or indirectly and accidentally. He shows it directly when he works in his own person; in that way the sign of his will is his own working. He shows it indirectly, by not hindering the doing of a thing; for "what removes an impediment is called an accidental mover," as it is said in the *Physics.*[3] In this respect the sign is called permission. He declares his will by means of another when he orders another to perform a work, either by insisting upon it as necessary by precept, and by prohibiting its contrary, or by persuasion, which is a part of counsel.

Since in these ways the will of man makes itself known, the same five are sometimes denominated with regard to the divine will, as the sign of that will. That precept, counsel, and prohibition are called the will of God is clear from the words of Matt. 6. 10: *Thy will be done on earth as it is in heaven.* That permission and operation are called the will of God is clear from Augustine (*Enchir.* 95),[4] who says: "Nothing is done, unless the Almighty wills it to be done, either by permitting it, or by actually doing it."

Or it may be said that permission and operation refer to present time, permission being with respect to evil, operation with regard to good. While as to future time, prohibition is in respect to evil, precept to good that is necessary and counsel to good that is beyond what duty requires.

Reply Obj. 1. There is nothing to prevent anyone declaring his will about the same matter in different ways; thus we find many words that mean the same thing. Hence there is no reason why the same thing should not be the subject of precept, operation, and counsel, or of prohibition or permission.

Reply Obj. 2. As God may by metaphor be said to will what by His will, properly speaking, He wills not, so He may by metaphor be said to will what He does, properly speaking, will. Hence there is nothing to prevent the same thing being the object of the will of good pleasure, and of the will of sign. But operation is always the same as the will of good pleasure, while precept and counsel are not; both because the former regards the present, and the two latter the future, and because the former is of itself the effect of the will, the latter its effect as fulfilled by means of another, as we have said (in the body of the Article).

Reply Obj. 3. Rational creatures are masters of their own acts, and for this reason certain special signs of the divine will are ascribed to their acts, in so far as God ordains rational creatures to act voluntarily and of themselves. Other creatures act only as moved by the divine operation; therefore only operation and permission are concerned with these.

Reply Obj. 4. All evil of sin, though happening in many ways, agrees in being out of harmony with the divine will. Hence with regard to evil, only one sign is ascribed, that of prohibition. On the other hand, good stands in various ways to the divine goodness, since there are goods without which we cannot attain to the enjoyment of that goodness, and these are the subject of precept; and there are others by which we attain to it more perfectly, and these are the subject of counsel. Or it may be said that counsel is not only concerned with the obtaining of greater good, but also with the avoiding of lesser evils.

QUESTION XX
GOD'S LOVE
(*In Four Articles*)

WE next consider those things that pertain absolutely to the will of God. In the appetitive

---

[1] *Ethics,* II, 6 (1106ᵇ35).

[2] PG 3, 729.

[3] Aristotle, VIII, 4 (255ᵇ24).   [4] PL 40, 276.

part of the soul there are found in ourselves both the passions of the soul, as joy, love, and the like; and the habits of the moral virtues, as justice, fortitude, and the like. Hence we shall first consider the love of God, and secondly His justice and mercy (Q. XXI). About the first there are four points of inquiry: (1) Whether love exists in God? (2) Whether He loves all things? (3) Whether He loves one thing more than another? (4) Whether He loves more the better things?

ARTICLE 1. *Whether Love Exists in God?*

We proceed thus to the First Article: It seems that love does not exist in God.

Objection 1. For in God there are no passions. Now love is a passion. Therefore love is not in God.

Obj. 2. Further, love, anger, sorrow, and the like, are divided against one another. But sorrow and anger are not attributed to God, unless by metaphor. Therefore neither is love attributed to Him.

Obj. 3. Further, Dionysius says (*Div. Nom.* iv):[1] "Love is a uniting and binding force." But this cannot take place in God, since He is simple. Therefore love does not exist in God.

On the contrary, It is written: *God is love* (I John 4. 16).

I answer that, We must assert that in God there is love, because love is the first movement of the will and of every appetitive power. For since the acts of the will and of every appetitive power tend towards good and evil as to their proper objects, and since good is essentially and especially the object of the will and the appetite, while evil is only the object secondarily and indirectly, as opposed to good, it follows that the acts of the will and appetite that look towards good must naturally be prior to those that look towards evil; thus, for instance, joy is prior to sorrow, love to hate, because what exists of itself is always prior to that which exists through another.

Again, the more universal is naturally prior to what is less so. Hence the intellect is first ordered to universal truth, and in the second place to particular and special truths. Now there are certain acts of the will and appetite that regard good under some special condition, as joy and delight regard good present and possessed, whereas desire and hope regard good not as yet possessed. Love, however, regards good in general, whether possessed or not. Hence love is naturally the first act of the will and appetite,

for which reason all the other appetitive movements presuppose love as their first root. For nobody desires anything nor rejoices in anything except as a good that is loved; nor is there hate except of something as opposed to the thing loved. Similarly, it is clear that sorrow, and other things like it, must be referred to love as to their first principle. Hence, in whomsoever there is will and appetite, there must also be love, since if the first is wanting, all that follows is also wanting. Now it has been shown that will is in God (Q. XIX, A. 1), and hence we must attribute love to Him.

Reply Obj. 1. The knowing power does not move except through the medium of the appetitive; and just as in ourselves the universal reason moves through the medium of the particular reason, as stated in the book on the *Soul*,[2] so in ourselves the intellectual appetite, which is called the will, moves through the medium of the sensitive appetite. Hence, in us the sensitive appetite is the proximate moving force of our bodies. Some bodily change therefore always accompanies an act of the sensitive appetite, and this change affects especially the heart, which is the first principle of movement in animals. Therefore acts of the sensitive appetite, since they have joined to them some bodily change, are called passions, but acts of the will are not so called. Love, therefore, and joy and delight are passions, in so far as they denote acts of the sensitive appetite; but in so far as they denote acts of the intellective appetite, they are not passions. It is in this latter sense that they are in God. Hence the Philosopher says:[3] "God rejoices by an operation that is one and simple," and for the same reason He loves without passion.

Reply Obj. 2. In the passions of the sensitive appetite there may be distinguished a certain material element—namely, the bodily change—and a certain formal element, which is on the part of the appetite. Thus in anger, as the Philosopher says,[4] the material element is the rising of the blood about the heart or something of this kind, but the formal, the appetite for vengeance. Again, as regards the formal element of certain passions a certain imperfection is implied, as in desire, which is of the good we have not, and in sorrow, which is about the evil we have. This applies also to anger, which supposes sorrow. Certain other passions, however, as love and joy, imply no imperfection.

[1] Sect. 15 (PG 3, 713).
[2] Aristotle, III, 11 (434ª20).
[3] *Ethics*, VII, 14 (1154ᵇ26).
[4] *Soul*, I, 1 (403ª30).

Since therefore none of these can be attributed to God on their material side, as has been said (*ad* 1), neither can those that even on their formal side imply imperfection be attributed to Him, except metaphorically, from likeness of effects, as already shown (QQ. III, A. 2, ANS. 2 and XIX, A. 11). However, those that do not imply imperfection, such as love and joy, can be properly predicated of God, though without attributing passion to Him, as said before (ANS. 1).

Reply Obj. 3. An act of love always tends towards two things: to the good that one wills, and to the person for whom one wills it, since to love a person is to wish that person good. Hence, in so far as we love ourselves, we wish ourselves good, and, so far as possible, union with that good. So love is called the unitive force, even in God, yet without implying composition; for the good that He wills for Himself is no other than Himself, Who is good by His essence, as above shown (Q. VI, A. 3). And by the fact that anyone loves another, he wills good to that other. Thus he puts the other, as it were, in the place of himself, and regards the good done to him as done to himself. And for this reason love is called a binding force, since it attaches another to ourselves, and refers his good to our own. And in this way also the divine love is a binding force, since God wills good to others; yet it implies no composition in God.

ARTICLE 2. *Whether God Loves All Things?*

We proceed thus to the Second Article: It seems that God does not love all things.

Objection 1. For according to Dionysius (*Div. Nom.* iv, 1),[1] love places the lover outside himself, and carries him over in a certain way into the object of his love. But it is not admissible to say that God is placed outside of Himself, and passes into other things. Therefore it is inadmissible to say that God loves things other than Himself.

Obj. 2. Further, the love of God is eternal. But things apart from God are not from eternity, except in God. Therefore God does not love anything except as it exists in Himself. But as existing in Him, it is no other than Himself. Therefore God does not love things other than Himself.

Obj. 3. Further, love is twofold—the love, namely, of desire, and the love of friendship. Now God does not love irrational creatures with the love of desire, since He needs no creature outside Himself. Nor with the love of friend-

ship, since there can be no friendship with irrational creatures, as the Philosopher shows.[2] Therefore God does not love all things.

Obj. 4. Further, it is written (Ps. 5. 7): *Thou hatest all the workers of iniquity.* Now nothing is at the same time hated and loved. Therefore God does not love all things.

On the contrary, It is said (Wisd. 11. 25): *Thou lovest all things that are, and hatest none of the things which Thou hast made.*

I answer that, God loves all existing things. For all existing things, in so far as they exist, are good, since the being of a thing is itself a good, and likewise, whatever perfection it possesses. Now it has been shown above (Q. XIX, A. 4) that God's will is the cause of all things. It must be, therefore, that a thing has being, or any kind of good, only in so far as it is willed by God. To every existing thing, then, God wills some good. Hence, since to love anything is nothing else than to will good to that thing, it is manifest that God loves everything that exists. Yet not as we love. Because since our will is not the cause of the goodness of things, but is moved by it as by its object, our love, whereby we will good to anything, is not the cause of its goodness; but conversely its goodness, whether real or imaginary, calls forth our love, by which we will that it should preserve the good it has, and receive besides the good it has not, and to this end we direct our actions. But the love of God infuses and creates goodness.

Reply Obj. 1. A lover is placed outside himself and made to pass into the object of his love in so far as he wills good to the beloved, and works for that good by his forethought even as he works for his own. Hence Dionysius says (*loc. cit.*): "On behalf of the truth we must make bold to say even this, that He Himself, the cause of all things, by the abundance of His loving goodness, is placed outside Himself by His providence for all existing things."

Reply Obj. 2. Although creatures have not existed from eternity, except in God, yet because they have been in Him from eternity, God has known them eternally in their proper natures, and for that reason has loved them, even as we, by the likenesses of things within us, know things existing in themselves.

Reply Obj. 3. Friendship cannot exist except towards rational creatures, who are capable of returning love, and communicating one with another in the various works of life, and who may fare well or ill, according to the changes of fortune and happiness, even as to them is benev-

---

[1] Sect. 13 (PG 3, 712).

[2] *Ethics*, VIII, 2 (1155[b]27).

olence properly speaking exercised. But irrational creatures cannot attain to loving God, nor to any share in the intellectual and blessed life that He lives. Properly speaking, therefore, God does not love irrational creatures with the love of friendship, but as it were with the love of desire, in so far as He orders them to rational creatures, and even to Himself. Yet this is not because He stands in need of them, but only on account of His goodness, and of the services they render to us. For we can desire a thing for others as well as for ourselves.

Reply Obj. 4. Nothing prevents one and the same thing being loved under one aspect, while it is hated under another. God loves sinners in so far as they are natures; for they both are, and are from Him. In so far as they are sinners, they are not, but fall away from being; and this in them is not from God. Hence under this aspect, they are hated by Him.

ARTICLE 3. *Whether God Loves All Things Equally?*

We proceed thus to the Third Article: It seems that God loves all things equally.

Objection 1. For it is said: *He hath equally care of all* (Wisd. 6. 8). But God's providence over things comes from the love with which He loves them. Therefore He loves all things equally.

Obj. 2. Further, the love of God is His essence. But God's essence does not admit of more and less; neither therefore does His love. He does not therefore love some things more than others.

Obj. 3. Further, as God's love extends to created things, so do His knowledge and will extend. But God is not said to know some things more than others, nor to will one thing more than another. Neither therefore does He love some things more than others.

On the contrary, Augustine says (*Tract. in Joan.* cx):[1] "God loves all things that He has made, and amongst them rational creatures more, and of these especially those who are members of His only-begotten Son; and much more than all, His only-begotten Son Himself."

I answer that, Since to love a thing is to will it good, anything may be loved more, or less, in a twofold way. In one way on the part of the act of the will itself, which is more or less intense. In this way God does not love some things more than others, because He loves all things by an act of the will that is one, simple, and always the same. In another way on the part of the good itself that a person wills for the

[1] PL 35, 1924.

beloved. In this way we are said to love that one more than another for whom we will a greater good, though our will is not more intense. In this way we must say that God loves some things more than others. For since God's love is the cause of goodness in things, as has been said (A. 2), no one thing would be better than another if God did not will greater good for one than for another.

Reply Obj. 1. God is said to have equally care of all not because by His care He deals out equal good to all, but because He administers all things with a like wisdom and goodness.

Reply. Obj. 2. This argument is based on the intensity of love on the part of the act of the will, which is the divine essence. But the good that God wills for His creatures, is not the divine essence. Therefore nothing prevents its increase or decrease.

Reply Obj. 3. To understand and to will denote the act alone, and do not include in their meaning objects from the diversity of which God may be said to know or will more or less, as has been said with respect to God's love.

ARTICLE 4. *Whether God Always Loves More the Better Things?*

We proceed thus to the Fourth Article: It seems that God does not always love more the better things.

Objection 1. For it is manifest that Christ is better than the whole human race, being God and man. But God loved the human race more than He loved Christ, for it is said: *He spared not His own Son, but delivered Him up for us all* (Rom. 8. 32). Therefore God does not always love more the better things.

Obj. 2. Further, an angel is better than a man. Hence it is said of man: *Thou hast made him a little less than the angels* (Ps. 8. 6). But God loved men more than He loved the angels, for it is said: *Nowhere doth He take hold of the angels, but of the seed of Abraham He taketh hold* (Heb. 2. 16). Therefore God does not always love more the better things.

Obj. 3. Further, Peter was better than John, since he loved Christ more. Hence the Lord knowing this to be true, asked Peter, saying: *"Simon, son of John, lovest thou Me more than these?"* Yet Christ loved John more than He loved Peter. For as Augustine says,[2] commenting on the words, *Simon, son of John, lovest thou Me?* "By this very mark is John distinguished from the other disciples, not that He loved him only, but that He loved him more

[2] *In Joann.,* tract. cxxiv (PL 35, 1971).

than the rest." Therefore God does not always love more the better things.

Obj. 4. Further, the innocent man is better than the repentant, since repentance is, as Jerome says,[1] "a second plank after shipwreck." But God loves the penitent more than the innocent, since He rejoices over him the more. For it is said; *I say to you that there shall be joy in heaven upon one sinner that doth penance, more than upon ninety-nine just who need not penance* (Luke 15. 7). Therefore God does not always love more the better things.

Obj. 5. Further, the just man who is foreknown is better than the predestined sinner. Now God loves more the predestined sinner, since He wills for him a greater good, life eternal. Therefore God does not always love more the better things.

On the contrary, Everything loves what is like it, as appears from (Ecclus. 13. 19): *Every beast loveth its like.* Now the better a thing is, the more like is it to God. Therefore the better things are more loved by God.

I answer that, We must say from what has been said before, that God loves more the better things. For it has been shown (A. 3), that God's loving one thing more than another is nothing else than His willing for that thing a greater good; for God's will is the cause of goodness in things, and the reason why some things are better than others, is that God wills for them a greater good. Hence it follows that He loves more the better things.

Reply Obj. 1. God loves Christ not only more than He loves the whole human race, but more than He loves the entire created universe, because He willed for Him the greater good in giving Him *a name that is above all names,* (Philipp. 2. 9) in so far as He was true God. Nor did anything of His excellence diminish when God delivered Him up to death for the salvation of the human race; rather did He become thereby a glorious victor: *The government was placed upon His shoulder,* according to Isa. 9. 6.

Reply Obj. 2. God loves the human nature assumed by the Word of God in the person of Christ more than He loves all the angels, for that nature is better, especially by reason of the union with the Godhead. But speaking of human nature in general, and comparing it with the angelic, the two are found equal, in the order of grace and of glory, since according to Apoc. 21. 17, *the measure of a man and of an angel* is the same. Yet so that, in this respect,

some angels are found more to be preferred than some men, and some men more to be preferred than some angels. But as to natural condition an angel is better than a man. God therefore did not assume human nature because He loved man, absolutely speaking, more, but because the needs of man were greater; just as the master of a house may give some costly delicacy to a sick servant that he does not give to his own son in sound health.

Reply Obj. 3. This doubt concerning Peter and John has been solved in various ways. Augustine (*loc. cit.*) interprets it mystically, and says that the active life, signified by Peter, loves God more than the contemplative signified by John, because the former is more conscious of the miseries of this present life, and therefore the more ardently desires to be freed from them, and depart to God. God, he says, loves more the contemplative life, since He preserves it longer. For it does not end. as the active life does, with the life of the body.

Some say[2] that Peter loved Christ more in His members, and therefore was loved more by Christ also, for which reason He gave him the care of the Church; but that John loved Christ more in Himself, and so was loved more by Him, on which account Christ commended His mother to his care. Others say[3] that it is uncertain which of them loved Christ more with the love of charity, and uncertain also which of them God loved more and ordained to a greater degree of glory in eternal life. Peter is said to have loved more, in regard to a certain promptness and fervour, but John to have been more loved, with respect to certain marks of familiarity which Christ showed to him rather than to others, on account of his youth and purity. But others say[4] that Christ loved Peter more, from his more excellent gift of charity, but John more, from his gifts of intellect. Hence, absolutely speaking, Peter was the better and the more beloved; but, in a certain sense, John was the better, and was loved the more. However, it may seem presumptuous to pass judgment on these matters, since *the Lord* and no other *is the weigher of spirits* (Prov. 16. 2).

Reply Obj. 4. The penitent and the innocent are related as exceeding and exceeded. For whether innocent or penitent, those are the better and the better loved who have most grace.

---

[1] *In Isa.*,II, 3 (PL 24, 66).

[2] Albert the Great, *In Sent.*, III, d. 31, A. 12 (BO XXVIII, 593). Cf. Bonaventure, *In Sent.*, III, d. 32, Q. 6 (QR III, 707).

[3] Albert and Bonaventure (cf. preceding note) attribute this position to Bernard. Cf. Bernard, *Serm.* XXIX (PL 183, 622).

[4] Cf. Albert the Great, *Enarr. in Joann.*, (BO XXIV, 13).

Other things being equal, innocence is the nobler thing and the more beloved. God is said to rejoice more over the penitent than over the innocent because often penitents rise from sin more cautious, humble, and fervent. Hence Gregory commenting on these words (*Hom.* xxxiv *in Ev.*)[1] says that, "In battle the general loves the soldier who after flight returns and bravely pursues the enemy more than him who has never fled, but has never done a brave deed."

Or it may be answered that gifts of grace, equal in themselves, are more as conferred on the penitent, who deserved punishment, than as conferred on the innocent, to whom no punishment was due; just as a hundred marks are a greater gift to a poor man than to a king.

Reply Obj. 5. Since God's will is the cause of goodness in things, the goodness of one who is loved by God is to be weighed according to the time when some good is to be given to him by the divine goodness. According therefore to the time when there is to be given by the divine will to the predestined sinner a greater good, the sinner is the better, although according to some other time he is the worse; because even according to some time he is neither good nor bad.

QUESTION XXI
THE JUSTICE AND MERCY OF GOD
(In Four Articles)

AFTER considering the divine love, we must treat of God's justice and mercy. Under this head there are four points of inquiry: (1) Whether there is justice in God? (2) Whether His justice can be called truth? (3) Whether there is mercy in God? (4) Whether in every work of God there are justice and mercy?

ARTICLE 1. *Whether There Is Justice in God?*

We proceed thus to the First Article: It seems that there is not justice in God.

Objection 1. For justice is divided against temperance. But temperance does not exist in God. Neither therefore does justice.

Obj. 2. Further, he who does whatsoever he wills and pleases does not work according to justice. But, as the Apostle says: *God worketh all things according to the counsel of his will* (Ephes. 1. 11). Therefore justice cannot be attributed to Him.

Obj. 3. Further, the act of justice is to render what is due. But God is no man's debtor. Therefore justice does not belong to God.

[1] Bk. II (PL 76, 1248).

Obj. 4. Further, whatever is in God, is His essence. But justice cannot belong to this. For Boethius says (*De Hebdom.*):[2] "Good regards the essence; justice the act." Therefore justice does not belong to God.

On the contrary, It is said (Ps. 10. 8): *The Lord is just, and hath loved justice.*

I answer that, There are two kinds of justice. The one consists in mutual giving and receiving, as in buying and selling, and other kinds of intercourse and exchange. This the Philosopher[3] calls commutative justice, that directs exchange and the intercourse of business. This does not belong to God, since, as the Apostle says: *Who hath first given to Him, and recompense shall be made him?* (Rom. 11. 35). The other consists in distribution, and is called distributive justice, whereby a ruler or a steward gives to each what his rank deserves. As then the proper order displayed in ruling a family or any kind of multitude evinces justice of this kind in the ruler, so the order of the universe, which is seen both in things of nature and in things of will, shows forth the justice of God. Hence Dionysius says (*Div. Nom.* viii, 7):[4] "We must see that God is truly just, in seeing how He gives to all existing things what is proper to the condition of each, and preserves the nature of each one in the order and with the powers that properly belong to it."

Reply Obj. 1. Certain of the moral virtues are concerned with the passions, as temperance with concupiscence, fortitude with fear and daring, meekness with anger. Such virtues as these can only metaphorically be attributed to God, since, as stated above (Q. XX, A. 11), in God there are no passions, nor a sensitive appetite, which is, as the Philosopher says,[5] those virtues exist as in a subject. On the other hand, certain moral virtues are concerned with operations, as for example, giving and spending, such as justice, liberality, and magnificence; and these reside not in the sensitive part, but in the will. Hence, there is nothing to prevent our attributing these virtues to God; although not in civil matters, but in such acts as are not unbecoming to Him. For, as the Philosopher says,[6] it would be absurd to praise God for His political virtues.

Reply Obj. 2. Since good as perceived by the intellect is the object of the will, it is impossible for God to will anything but what His wisdom approves. This is, as it were, His law of justice, in accordance with which His will is right and

[2] PL 64, 1314.   [3] *Ethics*, V, 4 (1131b25).
[4] PG 3, 896.   [5] *Ethics*, III, 10 (1117b24).
[6] *Ibid.*, X, 8 (1178b10).

just. Hence, what He does according to His will He does justly, as we do justly what we do according to law. But whereas law comes to us from some higher power God is a law unto Himself.

Reply Obj. 3. To each one is due what is his own. Now that which is ordered to a man is said to be his own. Thus the master owns the slave, and not conversely, for that is free which is its own cause. In the word "due," therefore, is implied a certain order of exigence or necessity of the thing to which it is ordered. Now a twofold order has to be considered in things: the one, whereby one created thing is ordered to another, as the parts to the whole, accident to substance, and all things whatsoever to their end; the other, whereby all created things are ordered to God. Thus in the divine operations the word "due" may be regarded in two ways, as due either to God, or to creatures, and in either way God renders what is due. It is due to God that there should be fulfilled in things what His will and wisdom require, and what manifests His goodness. In this respect God's justice regards what befits Him, since as He renders to Himself what is due to Himself. It is also due to a created thing that it should possess what is ordered to it; thus it is due to man to have hands, and that other animals should serve him. Thus also God exercises justice, when He gives to each thing what is due to it by its nature and condition. This meaning of "due" however is derived from the former, since what is due to each thing is what is ordered to it according to the order of the divine wisdom. And although God in this way gives each thing its due, yet He Himself is not the debtor, since He is not ordered to other things, but rather other things to Him. Justice, therefore, in God is sometimes spoken of as the fitting accompaniment of His goodness; sometimes as the reward of merit. Anselm touches on either view where he says (*Proslog.* 10):[1] "When Thou dost punish the wicked, it is just, since it agrees with their deserts; and when Thou dost spare the wicked, it is just, since it befits Thy goodness."

Reply Obj. 4. Although justice regards act, this does not prevent its being the essence of God, since even that which is of the essence of a thing may be the principle of action. But good does not always regard act, since a thing is called good not merely with respect to act, but also as regards perfection in its essence. For this reason it is said (*ibid.*), that the good is related to the just as the general to the special.

[1] PL 158, 233.

ARTICLE 2. *Whether the Justice of God Is Truth?*

We proceed thus to the Second Article: It seems that the justice of God is not truth.

Objection 1. For justice resides in the will, since, as Anselm says (*Dial. Verit.* 12),[2] it is a "rectitude of the will," whereas truth resides "in the intellect," as the Philosopher says.[3] Therefore justice does not pertain to truth.

Obj. 2. Further, according to the Philosopher[4] truth is a virtue distinct from justice. Truth therefore does not pertain to the notion of justice.

On the contrary, It is said (Ps. 84. 11): *Mercy and truth have met each other,* where truth stands for justice.

I answer that, Truth consists in the squaring of intellect and thing, as said above (Q. XVI, A. 1). Now the intellect that is the cause of the thing is related to it as its rule and measure, while the converse is the case with the intellect that receives its knowledge from things. When therefore things are the measure and rule of the intellect, truth consists in the squaring of the intellect to the thing, as happens in ourselves. For according as a thing is, or is not, our opinions or our words about it are true or false. But when the intellect is the rule or measure of things, truth consists in the squaring of the thing to the intellect; just as an artist is said to make a true work when it is in accordance with his art.

Now as artificial things are related to the art, so are works of justice related to the law with which they accord. Therefore God's justice, which establishes things in the order conformable to the rule of His wisdom, which is His law, is suitably called truth. Thus we also in human affairs speak of the truth of justice.

Reply Obj. 1. Justice, as to the law that regulates, is in the reason or intellect; but as to the command whereby our actions are regulated according to the law, it is in the will.

Reply Obj. 2. The truth of which the Philosopher is speaking in this passage is that virtue whereby a man shows himself in word and deed such as he really is. Thus it consists in the conformity of the sign with the thing signified, and not in that of the effect with its cause and rule, as has been said regarding the truth of justice.

[2] PL 158, 482.
[3] *Metaphysics,* VI, 4 (1027^{b}27); *Ethics,* VI, 2 (1139^{a}27).
[4] *Ethics,* IV, 7 (1127^{a}34).

ARTICLE 3. *Whether Mercy Belongs to God?*

We proceed thus to the Third Article: It seems that mercy does not belong to God.

Objection 1. "For mercy is a kind of sorrow," as Damascene says (*De Fide Orth.* ii, 14).[1] But there is no sorrow in God, and therefore there is no mercy in Him.

Obj. 2. Further, mercy is a relaxation of justice. But God cannot remit what pertains to His justice. For it is said (II Tim. 2. 13): *If we believe not, He continueth faithful: He cannot deny Himself.* But "He would deny Himself," as a gloss says,[2] "if He should deny His words." Therefore mercy does not belong to God.

On the contrary, It is said (Ps. 110. 4): *He is a merciful and gracious Lord.*

I answer that, Mercy is especially to be attributed to God, as seen in its effect, but not as an affection of passion. In proof of this it must be considered that a person is said to be merciful (*misericors*), as being, so to speak, sorrowful at heart (*miserum cor*), being affected with sorrow at the misery of another as though it were his own. Hence it follows that he endeavours to dispel the misery of this other as if it were his, and this is the effect of mercy. To sorrow, therefore, over the misery of others belongs not to God, but it does most properly belong to Him to dispel that misery, whatever be the defect we call by that name. Now defects are not removed except by the perfection of some kind of goodness, and the primary source of goodness is God, as shown above (Q. VI, A. 4). It must, however, be considered that to bestow perfections pertains not only to the divine goodness, but also to His justice, liberality, and mercy, yet under different aspects. The communicating of perfections, absolutely considered, pertains to goodness, as shown above (Q. VI, A. 1, Ans. 4); in so far as perfections are given to things according to their proportion, it pertains to justice, as has been already said (A. 1); in so far as God does not bestow them for His own use, but only on account of His goodness, it pertains to liberality; in so far as perfections given to things by God expel all defect, it pertains to mercy.

Reply Obj. 1. This argument is based on mercy regarded as an affection of passion.

Reply Obj. 2. God acts mercifully, not indeed by going against His justice, but by doing some-

thing above justice; thus a man who pays another two hundred pieces of money, though owing him only one hundred, does nothing against justice, but acts liberally or mercifully. The case is the same with one who pardons an offence committed against him, for in remitting it he may be said to bestow a gift. Hence the Apostle calls remission a forgiving: *Forgive one another, as Christ has forgiven you* (Eph. 4. 32). Hence it is clear that mercy does not destroy justice, but in a sense is the fulness of justice. And thus it is said: *Mercy exalteth itself above judgment* (Jas. 2. 13).

ARTICLE 4. *Whether in Every Work of God There Are Mercy and Justice?*

We proceed thus to the Fourth Article: It seems that not in every work of God are mercy and justice.

Objection 1. For some works of God are attributed to mercy, as the justification of the ungodly, and others to justice, as the damnation of the wicked. Hence it is said: *Judgment without mercy to him that hath not done mercy* (Jas. 2. 13). Therefore not in every work of God do mercy and justice appear.

Obj. 2. Further, the Apostle attributes the conversion of the Jews to justice and truth, but that of the nations to mercy (Rom. 15). Therefore not in every work of God are justice and mercy.

Obj. 3. Further, many just persons are afflicted in this world, which is unjust. Therefore not in every work of God are justice and mercy.

Obj. 4. Further, it is the part of justice to render what is due, but of mercy to relieve misery. Thus both justice and mercy presuppose something in their works, whereas creation presupposes nothing. Therefore in creation neither mercy nor justice is found.

On the contrary, It is said (Ps. 24. 10): *All the ways of the Lord are mercy and truth.*

I answer that, Mercy and truth are necessarily found in all God's work, if mercy be taken to mean the removal of any kind of defect. Not every defect, however, can properly be called a misery, but only defect in a rational nature whose lot is to be happy; for misery is opposed to happiness.

For this necessity there is a reason, because since a debt paid according to the divine justice is one due either to God, or to some creature, neither the one nor the other can be lacking in any work of God, because God can do nothing that is not in accord with His wisdom and goodness: and it is in this sense, as we have said, that

---

[1] PG 94, 932.

[2] *Glossa interl.,* (VI, 125r); *Glossa* Lombardi (PL 192, 370).

anything is due to God. Likewise, whatever is done by Him in created things, is done according to a fitting order and proportion, in which consists the notion of justice. Thus justice must exist in all God's works.

Now the work of divine justice always presupposes the work of mercy, and is founded upon it. For nothing is due to creatures except for something pre-existing in them, or foreknown. Again, if this is due to a creature, it must be due on account of something that precedes. And since we cannot go on to infinity, we must come to something that depends only on the goodness of the divine will—which is the ultimate end. We may say, for instance, that to possess hands is due to man on account of his rational soul, and his rational soul is due to him that he may be man, and his being man is on account of the divine goodness. So in every work of God, as to its primary root, there appears mercy. In all that follows, the power of mercy remains, and works indeed with even greater force, just as the influence of the first cause is more intense than that of second causes. For this reason does God out of the abundance of His goodness bestow upon creatures what is due to them more bountifully than is proportionate to their deserts, since less would suffice for preserving the order of justice than what the divine goodness confers; because between creatures and God's goodness there can be no proportion.

Reply Obj. 1. Certain works are attributed to justice, and certain others to mercy, because in some justice appears more forcibly and in others mercy. Even in the damnation of the reprobate mercy is seen, which, though it does not totally remit, yet somewhat alleviates, in punishing short of what is deserved.

In the justification of the wicked justice is seen when God remits sins on account of love, though He Himself has mercifully infused that love. So we read of Magdalen: *Many sins are forgiven her, because she hath loved much* (Luke 7. 47).

Reply Obj. 2. God's justice and mercy appear both in the conversion of the Jews and of the Nations. But an aspect of justice appears in the conversion of the Jews which is not seen in the conversion of the Nations, such as, for example, that the Jews were saved on account of the promises made to the fathers.

Reply Obj. 3. Justice and mercy appear in the punishment of the just in this world, since by afflictions lesser faults are cleansed in them, and they are the more raised up from earthly affec-

tions to God. As to this Gregory says: (*Moral.* xxvi, 13):[1] "The evils that press on us in this world force us to go to God."

Reply Obj. 4. Although creation presupposes nothing in the universe, yet it does presuppose something in the knowledge of God. In this way too the idea of justice is preserved in creation, by the production of beings in a manner that accords with the divine wisdom and goodness. And the idea of mercy, also, is preserved in the change of creatures from non-being to being.

QUESTION XXII

THE PROVIDENCE OF GOD

(In Four Articles)

HAVING considered those things that relate to the will absolutely, we must now proceed to those things which have relation to both the intellect and the will, namely providence, in respect to all things; also predestination and reprobation and all that is connected with these in respect especially of man as regards his eternal salvation (Q. XXIII). For in the science of morals, after the moral virtues themselves, comes the consideration of prudence, to which providence would seem to belong. Concerning God's providence there are four points of inquiry: (1) Whether providence is suitably assigned to God? (2) Whether everything comes under divine providence? (3) Whether divine providence is immediately concerned with all things? (4) Whether divine providence imposes any necessity upon things foreseen?

ARTICLE 1. *Whether Providence Can Suitably Be Attributed to God?*

We proceed thus to the First Article: It seems that providence is not suitably assigned to God.

Objection 1. For providence, according to Tully (*De Invent.* ii),[2] is a part of prudence. But prudence, since, according to the Philosopher,[3] "it gives good counsel," cannot belong to God, Who never has any doubt for which He should take counsel. Therefore providence cannot belong to God.

Obj. 2. Further, whatever is in God, is eternal. But providence is not anything eternal, for "it is concerned with existing things" that are not eternal, according to Damascene (*De Fide Orthod.* ii, 29).[4] Therefore there is no providence in God.

[1] PL 76, 360.   [2] *Rhet.*, II, 53 (DD I, 165).
[3] *Ethics*, VI, 5 (1140[a]26).   [4] PG 94, 964.

Obj. 3. Further, there is nothing composite in God. But providence seems to be something composite, because it includes both the intellect and the will. Therefore providence is not in God.

On the contrary, It is said (Wisd. 14. 3): *But Thou, Father, governeth all things by providence.* (Vulg., *But Thy providence, O Father, governeth it.*)

I answer that, It is necessary to attribute providence to God. For all the good that is in things has been created by God, as was shown above (Q. VI, A. 4). In things good is found not only as regards their substance, but also as regards their order towards an end and especially their last end, which, as was said above, is the divine goodness (Q. XXI, A. 4). This good of order existing in things created is itself created by God. Since, however, God is the cause of things by His intellect, and thus it must be that the type of every effect should pre-exist in Him, as is clear from what has gone before (Q. XIX, Q. XV, A. 2; A. 4), it is necessary that the type of the order of things towards their end should pre-exist in the divine mind, and the type of things ordered towards an end is, properly speaking, providence. For providence is the chief part of prudence, to which two other parts are directed —namely, remembrance of the past, and understanding of the present, according as from the remembrance of what is past and the understanding of what is present, we gather how to provide for the future. Now it belongs to prudence, according to the Philosopher,[1] "to order other things towards an end," whether in regard to oneself—as for instance, a man is said to be prudent, who orders well his acts towards the end of life—or in regard to others subject to him, in a family, city, or kingdom; in which sense it is said (Matt. 24. 45), *a faithful and wise servant, whom his lord hath appointed over his family.* In this way prudence or providence may suitably be attributed to God. For in God Himself there can be nothing ordered towards an end, since He is the last end. This type of the order in things towards an end is therefore in God called providence. Hence Boethius says (*De Consol.* iv, 6)[2] that "Providence is the divine type itself, seated in the Supreme Ruler, which disposeth all things," which disposition may refer either to the type of the order of things towards an end, or to the type of the order of parts in the whole.

Reply Obj. 1. According to the Philosopher,[3]

Prudence is what, strictly speaking, "commands all that *'eubulia'* has rightly counselled and *'synesis'* rightly judged." And so, though to take counsel may not be fitting to God, from the fact that counsel is an inquiry into matters that are doubtful, nevertheless to give a command as to the ordering of things towards an end, the right reason of which He possesses, does belong to God, according to Ps. 148. 6: *He hath made a decree, and it shall not pass away.* In this manner both prudence and providence belong to God. Although at the same time it may be said that the very reason of things to be done is called counsel in God; not because of any inquiry necessitated, but from the certitude of the knowledge, to which those who take counsel come by inquiry. Hence it is said: *Who worketh all things according to the counsel of His will* (Eph. 1. 11).

Reply Obj. 2. Two things pertain to the care of providence—namely, the plan of order, which is called providence and disposition; and the execution of order, which is termed government. Of these, the first is eternal, and the second is temporal.

Reply Obj. 3. Providence resides in the intellect, but presupposes the act of willing the end. Nobody gives a precept about things done for an end unless he wills that end. Hence prudence presupposes the moral virtues, by means of which desire is directed towards good, as the Philosopher says.[4] Even if Providence has to do with the divine will and intellect equally, this would not affect the divine simplicity, since in God both the will and intellect are one and the same thing, as we have said above (Q. XIX, A. 1, A. 4, Ans. 2).

ARTICLE 2. *Whether Everything Is Subject to the Providence of God?*

We proceed thus to the Second Article: It seems that everything is not subject to divine providence.

Objection 1. For nothing foreseen can happen by chance. If then everything was foreseen by God, nothing would happen by chance. And thus chance and luck would disappear, which is against common opinion.

Obj. 2. Further, a wise provider excludes defect and evil, as far as he can, from those over whom he has a care. But we see many evils existing. Either, then, God cannot hinder these, and thus is not omnipotent, or else He does not have care for everything.

Obj. 3. Further, whatever happens of neces-

---

[1] *Ethics*, VI, 12 (1144ᵃ8). [2] PL 63, 816.
[3] *Ethics*, VI, 9, 10 (1142ᵇ31; 1143ᵃ8).
[4] *Ibid.*, VI, 13 (1144ᵇ32).

sity does not require providence or prudence. Hence, according to the Philosopher:[1] "Prudence is the right reason of things contingent concerning which there is counsel and choice." Since, then, many things happen from necessity, everything cannot be subject to providence.

Obj. 4. Further, whatsoever is left to itself cannot be subject to the providence of a governor. But men are left to themselves by God, in accordance with the words: *God made man from the beginning, and left him in the hand of his own counsel* (Ecclus. 15. 14). And particularly in reference to the wicked: *I let them go according to the desires of their heart* (Ps. 80. 13). Everything, therefore, cannot be subject to divine providence.

Obj. 5. Further, the Apostle says (I Cor. 9. 9): *God doth not care for oxen* (Vulg.,—*Doth God take care for oxen?*), and we may say the same of other irrational creatures. Thus everything cannot be under the care of divine providence.

On the contrary, It is said of Divine Wisdom: *She reacheth from end to end mightily, and ordereth all things sweetly* (Wisd. 8. 1).

I answer that, Certain persons totally denied the existence of providence, as Democritus and the Epicureans,[2] maintaining that the world was made by chance. Others[3] taught that incorruptible things only were subject to providence, and corruptible things not in their individual selves, but only according to their species; for in this respect they are incorruptible. They are represented as saying (Job 22. 14): *The clouds are His covert; and He doth not consider our things; and He walketh about the poles of heaven.* Rabbi Moses,[4] however, excluded men from the generality of things corruptible, on account of the excellence of the intellect which they possess, but in reference to all else that suffers corruption he adhered to the opinion of the others.

We must say, however, that all things are subject to divine providence, not only in general, but even in their own individual selves. This is made evident thus. For since every agent acts for an end, the ordering of effects towards that end extends as far as the causality of the first agent extends. From this it happens that in the works of an agent something takes place

which has no reference towards the end, because the effect comes from a cause other than and outside the intention of the agent. But the causality of God, Who is the first agent, extends to all being, not only as to the principles of species, but also as to the individualizing principles; not only of things incorruptible, but also of things corruptible. Hence all things that exist in whatever manner are necessarily directed by God towards some end, as the Apostle says: *Those things that are of God are well ordered*[5] (Rom. 13. 1). Since, therefore, as the providence of God is nothing less than the type of the order of things towards an end, as we have said, it necessarily follows that all things, as in so far as they participate being, must likewise be subject to divine providence.

It has also been shown (Q. XIV, A. 11) that God knows all things, both universal and particular. And since His knowledge may be compared to the thing as the knowledge of art to the objects of art as was said above (Q. XIV, A. 8), all things must of necessity come under His ordering, just as all things wrought by art are subject to the ordering of that art.

Reply Obj. 1. There is a difference between universal and particular causes. A thing can escape the order of a particular cause, but not the order of a universal cause. For nothing escapes the order of a particular cause except through the intervention and hindrance of some other particular cause; as, for instance, wood may be prevented from burning by the action of water. Since, then, all particular causes are included under the universal cause, it could not be that any effect should take place outside the range of that universal cause. So far then as an effect escapes the order of a particular cause, it is said to be casual or fortuitous in respect to that cause; but if we regard the universal cause, outside whose range no effect can happen, it is said to be foreseen. Thus, for instance, the meeting of two servants, although to them it appears a chance circumstance, has been fully foreseen by their master, who has purposely sent them to meet at the one place, in such a way that the one knows not about the other.

Reply Obj. 2. It is otherwise with one who has care of a particular thing and one whose providence is universal, because a particular provider excludes all defects from what is subject to his care as far as he can, whereas one

---

[1] *Ethics*, VI, 5, 7, 13 (1140ᵃ35; 1141ᵇ9; 1144ᵇ27).
[2] Cf. Nemesius, *De Nat. Hom.*, chap. 44 (PG 40, 795); Augustine, *City of God*, XVIII, 41 (PL 41, 601); Maimonides, *Guide*, III, 17 (FR, 282).
[3] Aristotle and Averroes, according to St. Thomas, *In Sent.* I, d. 39, Q. 2, A. 2; cf. Maimonides, *Guide*, III, 17 (FR 282); Averroes. *In Meta.*, XII, 52 (VIII, 337M).
[4] Maimonides, *Guide*, III, 17 (FR 286).

[5] Vulg.,—*Those powers that are, are ordained of God;— Quœ autem sunt, a Deo ordinatœ sunt.* St. Thomas often quotes this passage, and invariably reads: *Quœ a Deo sunt, ordinata sunt.*

who provides universally allows some defect to remain, lest the good of the whole should be hindered. Hence, corruption and defects in natural things are said to be contrary to some particular nature; yet they are in keeping with the plan of universal nature, since the defect in one thing yields to the good of another, or even to the universal good; for the corruption of one is the generation of another, by which means the species is conserved. Since God, then, provides universally for all being, it belongs to His providence to permit certain defects in particular effects, that the perfect good of the universe may not be hindered, for if all evil were prevented much good would be absent from the universe. A lion would cease to live if there were no slaying of animals, and there would be no patience of martyrs if there were no tyrannical persecution. Thus Augustine says (*Enchir.* ii):[1] "Almighty God would in no way permit evil to exist in His works, unless He were so almighty and so good as to produce good even from evil." It would appear that it was on account of these two arguments to which we have just replied that some were persuaded to consider corruptible things—for example, casual and evil things—as removed from the care of divine providence.

Reply Obj. 3. Man is not the author of nature but he uses natural things in applying art and virtue to his own use. Hence human providence does not reach to that which takes place in nature from necessity; but divine providence extends thus far, since God is the author of nature. Apparently it was this argument that moved those who withdrew the course of nature from the care of divine providence, attributing it rather to the necessity of matter, as Democritus, and other Naturalists among the ancients.[2]

Reply Obj. 4. When it is said that God left man to himself, this does not mean that man is exempt from divine providence but merely that he has not a prefixed operating force determined to only the one effect, as in the case of natural things which are only acted upon as though directed by another towards an end, and do not act of themselves, as if they directed themselves towards an end, like rational creatures, through free choice, by which they take counsel and choose. Hence it is pointedly said: *In the hand of his own counsel.* But since the very act of free choice is traced to God as to a cause, it necessarily follows that everything

happening from the exercise of free choice must be subject to divine providence. For human providence is included under the providence of God, as a particular under a universal cause. God, however, extends His providence over the just in a certain more excellent way than over the wicked, since, He prevents anything happening which would impede their final salvation. For *to them that love God, all things work together unto good* (Rom. 8. 28). But from the fact that He does not restrain the wicked from the evil of sin, He is said to abandon them—not that He altogether withdraws His providence from them, for otherwise they would return to nothing, if they were not preserved by His providence. This was the reason that had weight with Tully,[3] who withdrew from the care of divine providence human affairs concerning which we take counsel.

Reply Obj. 5. Since a rational creature has, through free choice, control over its actions, as was said above (Q. XIX, A. 10), it is subject to divine providence in a special manner, so that something is imputed to it as a fault, or as a merit; and there is given it accordingly something by way of punishment or reward. In this way the Apostle withdraws oxen from the care of God; not, however, that individual irrational creatures escape the care of divine providence, as was the opinion of the Rabbi Moses (*loc. cit.*).

ARTICLE 3. *Whether God Has Immediate Providence over Everything?*

We proceed thus to the Third Article: It seems that God has not immediate providence over all things.

Objection 1. For whatever is contained in the notion of dignity must be attributed to God. But it belongs to the dignity of a king that he should have ministers, through whose mediation he provides for his subjects. Therefore much less has God Himself immediate providence over all things.

Obj. 2. Further, it belongs to providence to order all things to an end. Now the end of everything is its perfection and its good. But it pertains to every cause to direct its effect to good; hence every agent cause is a cause of the working out of providence. If therefore God were to have immediate providence over all things, all secondary causes would be withdrawn.

Obj. 3. Further, Augustine says (*Enchir.* 17),[4]

[1] PL 40, 236.

[2] Cf. Aristotle. *Metaphysics*, I, 3 (983b7); I, 4 (985b5).

[3] *De Divinat.*, II, 5 (DD IV, 218).

[4] PL 40, 239.

that "It is better to be ignorant of some things than to know them," for example, vile things; and the Philosopher says the same.[1] But whatever is better must be assigned to God. Therefore He has not immediate providence over vile and evil things.

On the contrary, It is said (Job 34. 13): *What other hath He appointed over the earth? or whom hath He set over the world which He made?* On which passage Gregory says (*Moral.* xxiv, 20):[2] *Himself He ruleth the world which He Himself hath made.*

I answer that, Two things belong to providence—namely, the plan of the order of things foreordained towards an end, and the execution of this order, which is called government. As regards the first of these, God has immediate providence over everything, because he has in His intellect the types of everything, even the smallest, and whatsoever causes He assigns to certain effects, He gives them the power to produce those effects. Hence it must be that He has beforehand in idea the order of those effects in Himself. As to the second, there are certain intermediaries of God's providence, for He governs things inferior by superior, not on account of any defect in His power, but by reason of the abundance of His goodness, so that the dignity of causality is imparted even to creatures.

Thus Plato's opinion, as narrated by Gregory of Nyssa (*De provid.* viii, 3),[3] is excluded. He taught a threefold providence. First, one which belongs to the supreme God, Who first and foremost has provision over spiritual things, and thus over the whole world as regards genus, species, and universal causes. The second providence, which is over the individuals of all that can be generated and corrupted, he attributed to the gods who circulate in the heavens; that is, certain separate substances, which move corporeal things in a circular direction. The third providence, over human affairs, he assigned to demons, whom the Platonic philosophers placed between us and the gods, as Augustine tells us.[4]

Reply Obj. 1. It pertains to a king's dignity to have ministers who execute his providence. But the fact that he has not the plan of those things which are done by them arises from a deficiency in himself. For every operative science is the more perfect the more it considers the particular things with which its action is concerned.

Reply Obj. 2. God's immediate provision over everything does not exclude the action of secondary causes, which are the executors of His order, as was said above.

Reply Obj. 3. It is better for us not to know evil and vile things, because by them we are impeded in our knowledge of what is better and higher, for we cannot understand many things simultaneously, and because the thought of evil sometimes perverts the will towards evil. This does not hold with God, Who sees everything simultaneously at one glance, and whose will cannot turn in the direction of evil.

ARTICLE 4. *Whether Providence Imposes Any Necessity on Things Foreseen?*

We proceed thus to the Fourth Article: It seems that divine providence imposes necessity upon things foreseen.

Objection 1. For every effect that has a *per se* cause, either present or past, which it necessarily follows, happens from necessity, as the Philosopher proves.[5] But the providence of God, since it is eternal, pre-exists, and the effect flows from it of necessity, for divine providence cannot be frustrated. Therefore divine providence imposes a necessity upon things foreseen.

Obj. 2. Further, every provider makes his work as stable as he can, lest it should fail. But God is most powerful. Therefore He assigns the stability of necessity to things provided.

Obj. 3. Further, Boëthius says (*De Consol.* iv, 6):[6] "Fate from the immutable source of providence binds together human acts and fortunes by the indissoluble connection of causes." It seems therefore that providence imposes necessity upon things foreseen.

On the contrary, Dionysius says that (*Div. Nom.* iv, 33)[7] "to corrupt nature is not the work of providence." But it is in the nature of some things to be contingent. Divine providence does not therefore impose any necessity upon things so as to destroy their contingency.

I answer that, Divine providence imposes necessity upon some things, not upon all, as some have believed.[8] For to providence it belongs to order things towards an end. Now after the divine goodness, which is an end separate from all things, the principal good in things themselves is the perfection of the universe, which would not be, were not all grades of be-

---

[1] *Metaphysics,* XII, 9 (1074[b]32).
[2] PL 76, 314.
[3] See Nemesius, *De Nat. Hom.,* chap. 44 (PG 40, 794).
[4] *City of God,* IX, 1, 2; VIII, 14 (PL 41, 257; 238).

[5] *Metaphysics,* VI, 3 (1027[a]30).
[6] PL 63, 817.
[7] PG 3, 733.
[8] The Stoics; cf. Nemesius, *De Nat. Hom.,* chap. 37 (PG 40, 752).

ing found in things. Hence it pertains to divine providence to produce every grade of being. And thus it has prepared for some things necessary causes, so that they happen of necessity. for others contingent causes, that they may happen by contingency, according to the condition of their proximate causes.

Reply Obj. 1. The effect of divine providence is not only that things should happen somehow, but that they should happen either by necessity or by contingency. Therefore whatsoever divine providence ordains to happen infallibly and of necessity happens infallibly and of necessity, and that happens from contingency, which the plan of divine providence conceives to happen from contingency.

Reply Obj. 2. The order of divine providence is unchangeable and certain, so far as all things which are provided for by Him happen as they have been provided for, whether from necessity or from contingency.

Reply Obj. 3. That indissolubility and unchangeableness of which Boëthius speaks pertain to the certainty of providence, which does not fail to produce its effect, and that in the way of happening that He provided for; but they do not pertain to the necessity of the effects. We must remember that *necessary* and *contingent* are properly consequent upon being as such. Hence the mode both of necessity and of contingency falls under the provision of God, who provides universally for all being, not under the provision of causes that provide only for some particular order of things.

QUESTION XXIII
Of predestination
(*In Eight Articles*)

After the consideration of divine providence, we must treat of predestination and the book of life (Q. XXIV). Concerning predestination there are eight points of inquiry: (1) Whether predestination is suitably attributed to God? (2) What is predestination, and whether it places anything in the predestined? (3) Whether to God belongs the reprobation of some men? (4) On the comparison of predestination to election; whether, that is to say, the predestined are chosen? (5) Whether merits are the cause or reason of predestination, or reprobation, or election? (6) Of the certainty of predestination; whether the predestined will infallibly be saved? (7) Whether the number of the predestined is certain? (8) Whether predestination can be furthered by the prayers of the saints?

Article 1. *Whether Men Are Predestined by God?*

We proceed thus to the First Article: It seems that men are not predestined by God.

Objection 1. For Damascene says (*De Fide Orthod.* ii, 30):[1] "It must be borne in mind that God foreknows but does not predetermine everything, since He foreknows all that is in us, but does not predetermine it all." But human merit and demerit are in us, since we are the masters of our own acts by free choice. All that pertains therefore to merit or demerit is not predestined by God, and thus man's predestination is done away.

Obj. 2. Further, all creatures are ordered to their end by divine providence, as was said above (Q. XXII, AA. 1, 2). But other creatures are not said to be predestined by God. Therefore neither are men.

Obj. 3. Further, the angels are capable of happiness as well as men. But predestination is not suitable to angels, since in them there never was any unhappiness (*miseria*); for predestination, as Augustine says (*De prædest. sanct.* 17),[2] is the purpose to take pity (*miserendi*). Therefore men are not predestined.

Obj. 4. Further, the benefits God confers upon men are revealed by the Holy Ghost to holy men according to the saying of the Apostle (I Cor. 2. 12): *Now we have received not the spirit of this world, but the Spirit that is of God: that we may know the things that are given us from God.* Therefore if man were predestined by God, since predestination is a benefit from God, his predestination would be made known to each predestined, which is clearly false.

On the contrary, It is written (Rom. 8. 30): *Whom He predestined, them He also called.*

I answer that, It is fitting that God should predestine men. For all things are subject to His providence, as was shown above (Q. XXII, A. 2). Now it belongs to providence to order things towards their end, as was also said (Q. XXII, A. 1). The end towards which created things are ordered by God is twofold: one which exceeds all proportion and power of created nature, and this end is life eternal, that consists in seeing God which is above the nature of every creature, as shown above (Q. XII, 4). The other end, however, is proportionate to created nature, to which end created being can attain according to

[1] PG 94, 972.
[2] PL 44, 985; also, Chap. 3 (965); chap. 6 (969); cf. also *De Div. Quaest. ad Simplic.*, I, 2 (PL 40, 115); *Cont. Duas Epist. Pelag.*, II, 9 (PL 44, 586).

the power of its nature. Now if a thing cannot attain to something by the power of its nature, it must be conveyed there by another; thus, an arrow is sent by the archer towards a mark. Hence, properly speaking, a rational creature, capable of eternal life, is led towards it, conveyed, as it were, by God. The plan of that direction pre-exists in God, just as in Him is the type of the order of all things towards an end, which we said to be providence (Q. XXII, A. I). Now the type in the mind of the doer of something to be done is a kind of pre-existence in him of the thing to be done. Hence the type of this direction of a rational creature towards the end of life eternal is called predestination. For to destine, is to send. Thus it is clear that predestination, as regards its objects, is a part of providence.

Reply Obj. I. Damascene calls predetermination an imposition of necessity, after the manner of natural things which are predetermined towards one end. This is clear from his adding: "He does not will malice, nor does He compel virtue." Hence predestination is not excluded by him.

Reply Obj. 2. Irrational creatures are not capable of that end which exceeds the power of human nature. And so they cannot be properly said to be predestined, although improperly the term is used in respect of any other end.

Reply Obj. 3. Predestination applies to angels, just as it does to men, although they have never been unhappy. For movement does not take its species from the term from which, but from the term to which. Because it matters nothing, in respect of the notion of making white, whether he who is made white was before black, sallow, or ruddy. Likewise it matters nothing in respect of the notion of predestination whether one is predestined to life eternal from the state of misery or not. Although it may be said that every conferring of good above that which is due pertains to mercy, as was shown previously (Q. XXI, AA. 3, ad 2. A. 4).

Reply Obj. 4. Even if by a special privilege their predestination were revealed to some, it is not fitting that it should be revealed to everyone; because, if so, those who were not predestined would despair, and security would beget negligence in the predestined.

ARTICLE 2. *Whether Predestination Places Anything in the Predestined?*

We proceed thus to the Second Article: It seems that predestination does place something in the predestined.

Objection I. For every action of itself brings in passion. If therefore predestination is action in God, predestination must be passion in the predestined.

Obj. 2. Further, Origen says[1] on the text, *He who was predestined*, etc. (Rom. I. 4): "Predestination is of one who is not; destination, of one who is." And Augustine says (*De Præd. Sanct.*):[2] "What is predestination but the destination of one who is?" Therefore predestination is only of one who actually exists, and it thus places something in the predestined.

Obj. 3. Further, preparation is something in the thing prepared. But predestination is "the preparation of God's benefits" as Augustine says (*De Præd. Sanct.* ii, 14).[3] Therefore predestination is something in the predestined.

Obj. 4. Further, nothing temporal enters into the definition of eternity. But grace, which is something temporal, is found in the definition of predestination. For predestination is said to be[4] the "preparation of grace in the present and of glory in the future." Therefore predestination is not anything eternal. So it must be that it is in the predestined, and not in God, for whatever is in Him is eternal.

On the contrary, Augustine says (*ibid.*) that predestination is "the foreknowledge of God's benefits." But foreknowledge is not in the things foreknown, but in the person who foreknows them. Therefore, predestination is in the one who predestines, and not in the predestined.

I answer that, Predestination is not anything in the predestined but only in the person who predestines. We have said above (A. I) that predestination is a part of providence. Now providence is not anything in the things provided for, but is a type in the mind of the provider, as was proved above (Q. XXII, A. I.). But the execution of providence which is called government is in a passive way in the thing governed, and in an active way in the governor. Hence it is clear that predestination is a kind of type of the ordering of some persons towards eternal salvation, existing in the divine mind. The execution, however, of this order is in a passive way in the predestined, but actively in God. The execution of predestination is the calling and magnification, according to the Apostle (Rom. 8. 30): *Whom He predestined, them He also called; and whom He called, them He also magnified* (Vulg., *justified*).

[1] Bk. I (PG 14, 849).
[2] Cf. *De Div. Quaest. ad Simplic.*, Bk. I, Q. 2 (PL 40, 114).
[3] Cf. *De Dono Persev.*, chap. 14 (PL 45, 1014).
[4] Cf. Peter Lombard, *Sent.*, I, d. 40, chap. 2 (QR I, 251).

Reply Obj. 1. Actions passing out to external matter of themselves bring in passion—for example, the actions of warming and cutting; but not actions remaining in the agent, as understanding and willing, as said above (QQ. XIV, A. 2; XVIII, A. 3, Ans. 1). Predestination is an action of this latter class. Therefore, it does not put anything in the predestined. But its execution, which passes out to external things, places an effect in them.

Reply Obj. 2. Destination sometimes denotes a real sending of someone to a given end, and in this way destination can only be said of someone actually existing. It is taken, however, in another sense for a mission which a person conceives in the mind, and in this manner we are said to destine a thing which we firmly propose in our mind. In this latter way it is said that Eleazar *determined not to do any unlawful things for the love of life* (II Mac. 6. 20). Thus destination can be of a thing which does not exist. Predestination, however, by reason of the antecedent character it implies, can be attributed to a thing which does not actually exist, in whatever way destination is accepted.

Reply Obj. 3. Preparation is twofold: of the patient in respect to passion, and this is in the thing prepared; and of the agent to action, and this is in the agent. Such a preparation is predestination, according as an agent by intellect is said to prepare itself to act in so far as it preconceives the idea of what is to be done. Thus, God from all eternity prepared by predestination, conceiving the idea of the order of some towards salvation.

Reply Obj. 4. Grace does not come into the definition of predestination as something belonging to its essence, but in so far as predestination implies a relation to grace, as of cause to effect, and of act to its object. Hence it does not follow that predestination is anything temporal.

ARTICLE 3. *Whether God Reprobates Any Man?*

We proceed thus to the Third Article: It seems that God reprobates no man.

Objection 1. For nobody reprobates what he loves. But God loves every man, according to (Wisd. 11. 25): *Thou lovest all things that are, and Thou hatest none of the things Thou hast made.* Therefore God reprobates no man.

Obj. 2. Further, if God reprobates any man, it would be necessary for reprobation to have the same relation to the reprobate as predestination has to the predestined. But predestination is the cause of the salvation of the predestined. Therefore reprobation will likewise be the cause of the loss of the reprobate. But this is false. For it is said (Osee 13. 9): *Destruction is thy own, O Israel; Thy help is only in Me.* God does not, then, reprobate any man.

Obj. 3. Further, to no one ought anything to be imputed which he cannot avoid. But if God reprobates anyone, that one must perish. For it is said (Eccl. 7. 14): *Consider the works of God, that no man can correct whom He hath despised.* Therefore it could not be imputed to any man, were he to perish. But this is false. Therefore God does not reprobate anyone.

On the contrary, It is said (Malach. 1. 2, 3): *I have loved Jacob, but have hated Esau.*

I answer that, God does reprobate some. For it was said above (A. 1) that predestination is a part of providence. To providence, however, it belongs to permit certain defects in those things which are subject to providence, as was said above (Q. XXII, A. 2). Thus, as men are ordained to eternal life through the providence of God, it likewise is part of that providence to permit some to fall away from that end; this is called reprobation.

Thus, as predestination is a part of providence, in regard to those divinely ordained to eternal salvation, so reprobation is a part of providence in regard to those who turn aside from that end. Hence reprobation implies not only foreknowledge, but also something more, as does providence, as was said above (Q. XXII, A. 1, Ans. 3). Therefore, as predestination includes the will to confer grace and glory, so also reprobation includes the will to permit a person to fall into sin, and to impose the punishment of damnation on account of that sin.

Reply Obj. 1. God loves all men and all creatures, in so far as He wishes them all some good, but He does not wish every good to them all. So far, therefore, as He does not wish this particular good—namely, eternal life—He is said to hate or reprobate them.

Reply Obj. 2. Reprobation differs in its causality from predestination. This latter is the cause both of what is expected in the future life by the predestined—namely, glory—and of what is received in this life—namely, grace. Reprobation, however, is not the cause of what is in the present—namely, sin, but it is the cause of abandonment by God. It is the cause, however, of what is assigned in the future—namely, eternal punishment. But guilt proceeds from the free choice of the person who is reprobated and deserted by grace. In this way the word of the prophet is true—namely, *Destruction is thy own, O Israel.*

Reply Obj. 3. Reprobation by God does not take anything away from the power of the person reprobated. Hence, when it is said that the reprobated cannot obtain grace, this must not be understood as implying absolute impossibility, but only conditional impossibility; as was said above (Q. XIX, A. 8, Ans. 1), that the predestined must necessarily be saved, yet by a conditional necessity, which does not do away with the liberty of choice. Hence, although anyone reprobated by God cannot acquire grace, nevertheless that he falls into this or that particular sin comes from his free choice. And so it is rightly imputed to him as guilt.

ARTICLE 4. *Whether the Predestined Are Chosen by God?*

We proceed thus to the Fourth Article: It seems that the predestined are not chosen by God.

Objection 1. For Dionysius says (*Div. Nom.* iv, 1)[1] that as the corporeal sun sends his rays upon all without selection, so does God His goodness. But the goodness of God is communicated to some in an especial manner through a participation of grace and glory. Therefore God without any selection communicates His grace and glory; and this belongs to predestination.

Obj. 2. Further, election is of things that exist. But predestination from all eternity is also of things which do not exist. Therefore, some are predestined without election.

Obj. 3. Further, election implies some discrimination. Now *God wills all men to be saved* (I Tim. 2. 4). Therefore, predestination which ordains men beforehand towards eternal salvation, is without election.

On the contrary, It is said (Ephes. 1. 4): *He chose us in Him before the foundation of the world.*

I answer that, Predestination presupposes election in the order of reason, and election presupposes love. The reason of this is that predestination, as stated above (A. 1), is a part of providence. Now providence, as also prudence, is the plan existing in the intellect directing the ordering of some things towards an end, as was proved above (Q. XXII, A. 1). But nothing is directed towards an end unless the will for that end already exists. Hence the predestination of some to eternal salvation presupposes, in the order of reason, that God wills their salvation,

and to this belong both election and love:— love, in so far as He wills them this particular good of eternal salvation, since to love is to wish good to anyone, as stated above (Q. XX, AA. 2, 3); election, in so far as He wills this good to some in preference to others, since He reprobates some, as stated above (A. 3).

Election and love, however, are differently ordered in God, and in ourselves, because in us the will in loving does not cause good, but we are incited to love by the good which already exists; and therefore we choose someone to love, and so election in us precedes love. In God, however, it is the reverse. For His will, by which in loving He wishes good to someone, is the cause of that good possessed by some in preference to others. Thus it is clear that love precedes election in the order of reason, and election precedes predestination. And so all the predestinate are objects of election and love.

Reply Obj. 1. If the communication of the divine goodness in general be considered, God communicates His goodness without election, since there is nothing which does not in some way share in His goodness, as we said above (Q. VI, A. 4). But if we consider the communication of this or that particular good, He does not allot it without election, since He gives certain goods to some men, which He does not give to others. Thus in the conferring of grace and glory election is implied.

Reply Obj. 2. When the will of the person choosing is stirred up to make a choice by the good already pre-existing in the thing, the choice must be of those things which already exist, as happens in our choice. In God it is otherwise, as was said above (Q. XX, A. 2). Thus, as Augustine says:[2] "Those are chosen by God, who do not exist; yet He does not err in His choice."

Reply Obj. 3. God wills all men to be saved by His antecedent will, which is to will not absolutely but relatively as we have said above (Q. XIX, A. 6); and not by His consequent will, which is to will absolutely.

ARTICLE 5. *Whether the Foreknowledge of Merits Is the Cause of Predestination?*

We proceed thus to the Fifth Article: It seems that foreknowledge of merits is the cause of predestination.

Objection 1. For the Apostle says (Rom. 8. 29): *Whom He foreknew, He also predestinated.* Again a gloss of Ambrose on Rom. 9. 15: *I will have mercy upon whom I will have mercy*

---

[1] PG 3, 693.

[2] *Serm. ad Popul.*, XXVI, 4 (PL 38, 173).

says: "I will give mercy to him who, I foresee, will turn to Me with his whole heart."[1] Therefore it seems the foreknowledge of merits is the case of predestination.

Obj. 2. Further, Divine predestination includes the divine will, which can not be irrational, since predestination is the purpose to have mercy, as Augustine says (*De Præd. Sanct.*).[2] But there can be no other reason for predestination than the foreknowledge of merits. Therefore it must be the cause or reason of predestination.

Obj. 3. Further, *There is no injustice in God* (Rom. 9. 14). Now it would seem unjust that unequal things be given to equals. But all men are equal as regards both nature and original sin, and inequality in them arises from the merits or demerits of their own actions. Therefore God does not prepare unequal things for men by predestining and reprobating, unless through the foreknowledge of their merits and demerits.

On the contrary, The Apostle says (Tit. 3. 5): *Not by the works of justice which we have done, but according to His mercy He saved us.* But as He saved us, so He predestined that we should be saved. Therefore, foreknowledge of merits is not the cause or reason of predestination.

I answer that, Since predestination includes will, as was said above (AA. 3, 4), the reason of predestination must be sought for in the same way as was the reason of the will of God. Now it was shown above (Q. XIX, A. 5) that we cannot assign any cause of the divine will on the part of the act of willing; but a reason can be found on the part of the things willed, in so far as God wills one thing on account of something else. Therefore nobody has been so insane as to say that merit is the cause of divine predestination as regards the act of the predestinator. But the question is this, whether, as regards the effect, predestination has any cause; or what comes to the same thing, whether God pre-ordained that He would give the effect of predestination to anyone on account of any merits.

Accordingly there were some who held that the effect of predestination was pre-ordained for some on account of pre-existing merits in a former life. This was the opinion of Origen,[3]

who thought that the souls of men were created in the beginning, and according to the diversity of their works different states were assigned to them in this world when united to the body. The Apostle, however, rebuts this opinion where he says (Rom. 9. 11, 12): *For when they were not yet born, nor had done any good or evil, . . . not of works, but of Him that calleth, it was said to her: The elder shall serve the younger.*

Others said that pre-existing merits in this life are the reason and cause of the effect of predestination. For the Pelagians taught[4] that the beginning of doing well came from us, and the completion from God, so that it came about that the effect of predestination was granted to one and not to another because the one made a beginning by preparing, whereas the other did not. But against this we have the saying of the Apostle (II Cor. 3. 5), that *we are not sufficient to think anything of ourselves as of ourselves.* Now no principle of action can be found previous to the act of thinking. Therefore it cannot be said that anything begun in us can be the reason of the effect of predestination.

And so others said[5] that merits following the effect of predestination are the reason of predestination, giving us to understand that God gives grace to a person, and pre-ordains that He will give it, because He knows beforehand that He will make good use of that grace, as if a king were to give a horse to a soldier because he knows he will make good use of it. But these seem to have drawn a distinction between that which flows from grace, and that which flows from free choice, as if the same thing cannot come from both. It is, however, manifest that what is of grace is the effect of predestination; and this cannot be considered as the reason of predestination, since it is contained in the notion of predestination. Therefore, if anything else in us be the reason of predestination, it will be outside the effect of predestination. Now there is no distinction between what flows from free choice and what is of predestination, as there is no distinction between what flows from a secondary cause and from a first cause. For the providence of God produces effects through the operation of secondary causes, as was above shown (Q. XXII, A. 3). Therefore, that which flows from free choice is also of predestination.

We must say, therefore, that the effect of predestination may be considered in a twofold

---

[1] *Glossa ordin.*, (VI, 21E); Ambrose, *In Rom.*, IX, 15 (PL 17, 142).

[2] Chaps. 3, 6, 17 (PL 44, 965, 969, 985); cf. *De Div. Quaest. ad Simplic.*, I, 2 (PL 40, 115); *Cont. Duas Epist. Pelag.*, II, 9 (PL 44, 586).

[3] *Peri Archon.*, I, 6 (PG 11, 166); cf. Augustine, *Serm. ad Popul.*, CLXV, 5 (PL 38, 905); Peter Lombard, *Sent.*, I, d. 41, chap. 2 (QR I, 257).

[4] See II Council of Carthage, 416; can. 5 (MA III, 322; DZ 105).

[5] Cf. St. Thomas, *In Rom.*, IX, 3; cf. also *Glossa ordin.*, on Rom. IX, 5 (VI, 21E); Peter Lombard, *Sent.*, I, d. 41, chap. 2 (QR I, 254).

light. In one way, in particular; and thus there is no reason why one effect of predestination should not be the reason or cause of another, a subsequent effect being the reason of a previous effect, as its final cause, and the previous effect being the reason of the subsequent as its meritorious cause, which is reduced to the disposition of the matter. Thus we might say that God preordained to give glory on account of merit, and that He preordained to give grace to merit glory.

In another way, the effect of predestination may be considered in general. Thus, it is impossible that the whole of the effect of predestination in general should have any cause as coming from us, because whatsoever is in man ordering him towards salvation is included wholly under the effect of predestination, even the preparation for grace. For neither does this happen otherwise than by divine help, according to the prophet Jeremias (Lam. 5. 21): *Convert us, O Lord, to Thee, and we shall be converted.* Yet predestination has in this way, in regard to its effect, the goodness of God for its reason, towards which the whole effect of predestination is ordered as to an end, and from which it proceeds, as from its first moving principle.

Reply Obj. 1. The use of grace foreknown by God is not the cause of conferring grace, except after the manner of a final cause; as was explained above.

Reply Obj. 2. Predestination has its reason in the goodness of God as regards its effects in general. Considered in its particular effects, however, one effect is the reason of another, as already stated.

Reply Obj. 3. The reason for the predestination of some and reprobation of others must be sought for in the goodness of God. Thus He is said to have made all things through His goodness, so that the divine goodness might be represented in things. Now it is necessary that God's goodness, which in itself is one and undivided, should be manifested in many ways in His creation, because creatures in themselves cannot attain to the simplicity of God. Thus it is that for the completion of the universe there are required different grades of being, some of which hold a high and some a low place in the universe. That this multiformity of grades may be preserved in things, God allows some evils, lest many good things should never happen, as was said above (Q. II, A. 3, Ans. I; Q. XXII, A. 2).

Let us then consider the whole of the human race, as we consider the whole universe. God wills to manifest His goodness in men: in respect to those whom He predestines, by means of His mercy, in sparing them; and in respect of others, whom he reprobates, by means of His justice, in punishing them. This is the reason why God elects some and rejects others. To this the Apostle refers, saying (Rom. 9. 22, 23): *What if God, willing to show His wrath* (that is, the vengeance of His justice), *and to make His power known, endured* (that is, permitted) *with much patience vessels of wrath, fitted for destruction; that He might show the riches of His glory on the vessels of mercy, which He hath prepared unto glory* (Rom. 9. 22, 23); and (II Tim. 2. 20): *But in a great house there are not only vessels of gold and silver; but also of wood and of earth; and some, indeed, unto honour, but some unto dishonour.*

Yet why He chooses some for glory and reprobates others has no reason except the divine will. Hence Augustine says (*Tract.* xxvi *in Joan.*):[1] "Why He draws one, and another He draws not, seek not to judge, if thou dost not wish to err." Thus too, in the things of nature, a reason can be assigned, since prime matter is altogether uniform, why one part of it was fashioned by God from the beginning under the form of fire, another under the form of earth, that there might be a diversity of species in things of nature. Yet why this particular part of matter is under this particular form, and that under another, depends upon the simple will of God; as from the simple will of the artificer it depends that this stone is in this part of the wall, and that in another, although the plan requires that some stones should be in this place, and some in that place.

Neither on this account can there be said to be injustice in God if He prepares unequal lots for not unequal things. This would be altogether contrary to the notion of justice if the effect of predestination were granted as a debt, and not from grace. In things which are given from grace a person can give more or less, just as he pleases (provided he deprives nobody of his due), without any infringement of justice. This is what the master of the house said: *Take what is thine, and go thy way. Is it not lawful for me to do what I will?* (Matt. 20. 14, 15).

ARTICLE 6. *Whether Predestination Is Certain?*

We proceed thus to the Sixth Article: It seems that predestination is not certain.

Objection 1. Because on the words *Hold fast that which thou hast, that no one take thy crown* (Apoc. 3. 11), Augustine says (*De Corr.*

[1] PL 35, 1607.

et Grat. 13):[1] "Another will not receive, unless this one were to lose it." Hence the crown which is the effect of predestination can be both acquired and lost. Therefore predestination is not certain.

Obj. 2. Further, granted what is possible, nothing impossible follows. But it is possible that one predestined—for example, Peter—may sin and then be killed. But if this were so, it would follow that the effect of predestination would be thwarted. This, then, is not impossible. Therefore predestination is not certain.

Obj. 3. Further, whatever God could do in the past, He can do now. But He could have not predestined whom He has predestined. Therefore now He is able not to predestine him. Therefore predestination is not certain.

On the contrary, A gloss on Rom. 8. 29: *Whom He foreknew, He also predestinated,* says[2]: "Predestination is the foreknowledge and preparation of the benefits of God, by which whosoever are freed will most certainly be freed."

I answer that, Predestination most certainly and infallibly takes effect; yet it does not impose any necessity, so that, namely, its effect should take place from necessity. For it was said above (A. 1), that predestination is a part of providence. But not all things subject to providence are necessary, some things happening from contingency, according to the condition of the proximate causes, which divine providence has ordered for such effects. Yet the order of providence is infallible, as was shown above (Q. XXII, A. 4). So also the order of predestination is certain; yet free choice from which the effect of predestination has its contingency, is not taken away. Moreover all that has been said about the divine knowledge and will (QQ. XIV, A. 13, and XIX, A. 8) must also be taken into consideration, since they do not take away contingency from things, although they themselves are most certain and infallible.

Reply Obj. 1. The crown may be said to belong to a person in two ways: first, by God's predestination, and thus no one loses his crown; secondly, by the merit of grace, for what we merit, in a certain way is ours, and thus anyone can lose his crown by mortal sin. Another person receives that crown thus lost, since he takes the former's place. For God does not permit some to fall without raising others, according to Job 34. 24: *He shall break in pieces many and*

innumerable, *and make others to stand in their stead.* Thus men are substituted in the place of the fallen angels, and the Gentiles in that of the Jews. He who is substituted for another in the state of grace also receives the crown of the fallen in that in eternal life he will rejoice at the good the other has done, in which life he will rejoice at all good whether done by himself or by others.

Reply Obj. 2. Although it is possible for one who is predestined considered in himself to die in mortal sin, yet it is not possible, supposed, as in fact it is supposed, that he is predestined. Hence it does not follow that predestination can fall short of its effect.

Reply Obj. 3. Since predestination includes the divine will as stated above (Q. XIX, A. 3), and the fact that God wills any created thing is necessary on the supposition that He so wills, on account of the immutability of the divine will, but is not necessary absolutely, so the same must be said of predestination. Therefore we ought not to say that God is able not to predestine one whom He has predestined, taking it in a composite sense, though, absolutely speaking, God can predestine or not. But in this way the certainty of predestination is not taken away.

ARTICLE 7. *Whether the Number of the Predestined Is Certain?*

We proceed thus to the Seventh Article: It seems that the number of the predestined is not certain.

Objection 1. For a number to which an addition can be made is not certain. But there can be an addition to the number of the predestined as it seems, for it is written (Deut. 1. 11): *The Lord God adds to this number many thousands,* and a gloss adds,[3] "fixed by God, who knows those who belong to Him." Therefore the number of the predestined is not certain.

Obj. 2. Further, no reason can be assigned why God preordains to salvation one number of men more than another. But nothing is arranged by God without a reason. Therefore the number to be saved preordained by God cannot be certain.

Obj. 3. Further, the operations of God are more perfect than those of nature. But in the works of nature good is found in the majority of things, defect and evil in the minority. If, then, the number of the saved were fixed by God at a certain figure, there would be more saved than lost. Yet the contrary follows from

[1] PL 44, 940.

[2] *Glossa ordin.,* (VI, 19F); *Glossa* Lombardi (PL 191, 1449); cf. Augustine, *De Dono Persev.,* XIV (PL 45, 1014).

[3] *Glossa ordin.,* (I, 330B).

Matt. 7. 13, 14: *For wide is the gate, and broad the way that leadeth to destruction, and many there are who go in thereat. How narrow is the gate, and strait is the way that leadeth to life; and few there are that find it!* Therefore the number of those preordained by God to be saved is not certain.

On the contrary, Augustine says (*De Corr. et Grat.* 13):[1] "The number of the predestined is certain, and can neither be increased nor diminished."

I answer that, The number of the predestined is certain. Some have said[2] that it was formally, but not materially certain, as if we were to say that it was certain that a hundred or a thousand would be saved, not however these or those individuals. But this takes away the certainty of predestination, of which we spoke above (A. 6). Therefore we must say that to God the number of the predestined is certain, not only formally, but also materially.

It must, however, be observed that the number of the predestined is said to be certain to God not only by reason of His knowledge, because, that is to say, He knows how many will be saved (for in this way the number of drops of rain and the sands of the sea are certain to God), but by reason of His deliberate choice and determination.

For the further evidence of this we must remember that every agent intends to make something finite, as is clear from what has been said above when we treated of the infinite (Q. VII, A. 4). Now whoever intends some definite measure in his effect thinks out some definite number in the essential parts, which are by their very nature required for the perfection of the whole. For of those things which are required not principally, but only on account of something else, he does not select any definite number *per se,* but he accepts and uses them in such numbers as are necessary on account of that other thing. For instance, a builder thinks out the definite measurements of a house, and also the definite number of rooms which he wishes to make in the house, and definite measurements of the walls and the roof; he does not, however, select a definite number of stones, but accepts and uses just so many as are sufficient for the required measurements of the wall.

So also must we consider concerning God in regard to the whole universe, which is His effect. For He preordained the measurements of the whole of the universe, and what number would befit the essential parts of that universe —that is to say, which have in some way been ordained in perpetuity; how many spheres, how many stars, how many elements, and how many species of things. Individuals, however, which undergo corruption, are not ordained as it were chiefly for the good of the universe, but in a secondary way, in so far as the good of the species is preserved through them. Hence, although God knows the number of all the individuals, the number of oxen, flies, and the like is not preordained by God *per se,* but divine providence produces just so many as are sufficient for the preservation of the species.

Now of all creatures the rational creature is chiefly ordained for the good of the universe, being as such incorruptible; more especially those who attain to eternal happiness, since they more immediately reach the ultimate end. Hence the number of the predestined is certain to God not only by way of knowledge, but also by way of a principal preordination.

It is not exactly the same thing in the case of the number of the reprobate, who would seem to be preordained by God for the good of the elect, in whose regard *all things work together unto good* (Rom. 8. 28). Concerning the number of all the predestined, some say[3] that so many men will be saved as angels fell; some,[4] so many as there were angels left; others,[5] as many as the number of angels who fell, added to that of all the angels created by God. It is, however, better to say that, "to God alone is known the number for whom is reserved eternal happiness."[6]

Reply Obj. 1. These words of Deuteronomy must be taken as applied to those who are marked out by God beforehand in respect to present justice. For their number is increased and diminished, but not the number of the predestined.

Reply Obj. 2. The reason of the quantity of any one part must be judged from the proportion of that part to the whole. Thus in God the reason why He has made so many stars, or so many species of things, or predestined so many, is according to the proportion of the principal parts to the good of the whole universe.

---

[1] PL 44, 940.

[2] Cf. St. Thomas, *De Ver.*, VI. 4; Albert the Great, *In Sent.*, I, d. 40, A. 11 (BO XXVI, 319).

[3] Augustine, *Enchir.*, 29, 62 (PL 40, 246, 261); *City of God,* XXII, 1 (PL 41, 751); Isidore, *Sent.*, I, 10 (PL 83, 556).

[4] Peter Lombard, *Sent.* II, d. IX, chap. 7 (QR I, 350); Gregory the Great, *In Evang.*, II, hom. 34 (PL 76, 1252); *Moral.*, XXXI, 49 (PL 76, 628).

[5] See DTC, art. *Anges.* (I, 1206).

[6] From the *secret* prayer in the missal, *pro vivis et defunctis,* for the living and the dead.

Reply Obj. 3. The good that is proportionate to the common state of nature is to be found in the majority and is wanting in the minority. The good that exceeds the common state of nature is to be found in the minority, and is wanting in the majority. Thus it is clear that the majority of men have a sufficient knowledge for the guidance of life, and those who have not this knowledge are said to be half-witted or foolish; but they who attain to a profound knowledge of things intelligible are a very small minority in respect to the rest. Since their eternal happiness, consisting in the vision of God, exceeds the common state of nature, and especially in so far as this is deprived of grace through the corruption of original sin, those who are saved are in the minority. In this especially, however, appears the mercy of God, that He has chosen some for that salvation, from which very many in accordance with the common course and tendency of nature fall short.

ARTICLE 8. *Whether Predestination Can Be Furthered by the Prayers of the Saints?*

We proceed thus to the Eighth Article: It seems that predestination cannot be furthered by the prayers of the saints.

Objection 1. For nothing eternal can be interfered with by anything temporal; and in consequence nothing temporal can help towards making something else eternal. But predestination is eternal. Therefore, since the prayers of the saints are temporal, they cannot so help as to cause anyone to become predestined. Predestination therefore is not furthered by the prayers of the saints.

Obj. 2. Further, as there is no need of counsel except on account of defective knowledge, so there is no need of help except through defective power. But neither of these things can be said of God when He predestines. Whence it is said: *Who hath helped the Spirit of the Lord?* (Vulg., *Who hath known the mind of the Lord?*) *Or who hath been His counsellor?* (Rom. 11. 34). Therefore predestination cannot be furthered by the prayers of the saints.

Obj. 3. Further, if a thing can be helped, it can also be hindered. But predestination cannot be hindered by anything. Therefore it cannot be furthered by anything.

On the contrary, It is said that *Isaac besought the Lord for his wife because she was barren; and He heard Him and made Rebecca to conceive* (Gen. 25. 21). But from that conception Jacob was born, and he was predestined. Now his predestination would not have happened if he had never been born. Therefore predestination can be furthered by the prayers of the saints.

I answer that, Concerning this question, there were different errors. Some,[1] regarding the certainty of divine predestination, said that prayers were superfluous, as also anything else done to attain salvation, because whether these things were done or not, the predestined would attain, and the reprobate would not attain, eternal salvation. But against this opinion are all the warnings of Holy Scripture, exhorting us to prayer and other good works.

Others declared[2] that the divine predestination was altered through prayer. This is stated to have been the opinion of the Egyptians, who thought that the divine ordination, which they called fate, could be interfered with by certain sacrifices and prayers. Against this also is the authority of Scripture. For it is said: *But the triumpher in Israel will not spare and will not be moved to repentance* (I Kings 15. 29); and that *the gifts and the calling of God are without repentance* (Rom. 11. 29).

Therefore we must say otherwise that in predestination two things are to be considered —namely, the divine preordination, and its effect. As regards the former, in no way can predestination be furthered by the prayers of the saints. For it is not due to their prayers that anyone is predestined by God. As regards the latter, predestination is said to be helped by the prayers of the saints, and by other good works, because providence, of which predestination is a part, does not do away with secondary causes but so provides effects that the order of secondary causes falls also under providence. So, as natural effects are provided by God in such a way that natural causes are directed to bring about those natural effects, without which those effects would not happen, so the salvation of a person is predestined by God in such a way that whatever helps that person towards salvation falls under the order of predestination; whether it be one's own prayers, or those of another, or other good works, and the like, without which one would not attain to salvation. And so, the predestined must strive after good works and prayer because through these means predestination is most certainly fulfilled. For this reason it is said: *Labour the more that by good works*

---

[1] *De Ver.,* Q. VI, A 6: "And this was said to have been the opinion of Epicurus." See the fragment of Epicurus cited by Nemesius, *De Nat. Hom.,* Chap. 44 (PG40, 796).

[2] Nemesius, *De Nat. Hom.,* Chap. 36 (PG 40, 746). See below, Q. CXVI, A. 3.

you may make sure your calling and election (II Pet. 1. 10).

Reply Obj. 1. This argument shows that predestination is not furthered by the prayers of the saints as regards the preordination.

Reply Obj. 2. One is said to be helped by another in two ways. In one way, in so far as he receives power from him, and to be helped thus belongs to the weak; but this cannot be said of God, and thus we are to understand, *Who hath helped the Spirit of the Lord?* In another way one is said to be helped by a person through whom he carries out his work, as a master through a servant. In this way God is helped by us, in so far as we execute His orders, according to I Cor. 3. 9: *We are God's coadjutors.* Nor is this on account of any defect in the power of God, but because He employs intermediary causes, in order that the beauty of order may be served in things, and also that He may communicate to creatures the dignity of causality.

Reply Obj. 3. Secondary causes cannot escape the order of the first universal cause, as has been said above (Q. XIX, A. 6); indeed, they execute that order. And therefore predestination can be furthered by creatures, but it cannot be impeded by them.

QUESTION XXIV
THE BOOK OF LIFE
(*In Three Articles*)

WE now consider the book of life, concerning which there are three points of inquiry: (1) What is the book of life? (2) Of what life is it the book? (3) Whether anyone can be blotted out of the book of life?

ARTICLE 1. *Whether the Book of Life Is the Same As Predestination?*

We proceed thus to the First Article: It seems that the book of life is not the same thing as predestination.

Objection 1. For it is said, *All these things are the book of life* (Ecclus. 24. 32)—that is, the Old and New Testament according to a gloss.[1] This, however, is not predestination. Therefore the book of life is not predestination.

Obj. 2. Further, Augustine says[2] that the book of life is "a certain divine energy, by which it happens that to each one his good or evil works are recalled to memory." But divine energy belongs, it seems, not to predestination,

but rather to divine power. Therefore the book of life is not the same thing as predestination.

Obj. 3. Further, Reprobation is opposed to predestination. So, if the book of life were the same as predestination, there should also be a book of death, as there is a book of life.

On the contrary, It is said in a gloss upon Ps. 68. 29,[3] *Let them be blotted out of the book of the living:* "This book is the knowledge of God, by which He hath predestined to life those whom He foreknew."

I answer that, The book of life is in God taken in a metaphorical sense, according to a comparison with human affairs. For it is usual among men that they who are chosen for any office should be inscribed in a book; as, for instance, soldiers, or counsellors, who formerly were called conscript Fathers. Now it is clear from the preceding (Q. XXIII, A. 4) that all the predestined are chosen by God to possess eternal life. This conscription, therefore, of the predestined is called the book of life.

A thing is said metaphorically to be written upon the mind of anyone when it is firmly held in the memory, according to Prov. (3. 3): *Forget not My law, and let thy heart keep My commandments,* and further on, *Write them in the tables of thy heart.* For things are written down in material books to help the memory. Hence, the knowledge of God, by which He firmly remembers that He has predestined some to eternal life, is called the book of life. For as the writing in a book is the sign of things to be done, so the knowledge of God is a sign in Him of those who are to be brought to eternal life, according to II Tim. 2. 19: *The sure foundation of God standeth firm, having this seal; the Lord knoweth who are His.*

Reply Obj. 1. The book of life may be understood in two senses. In one sense as the inscription of those who are chosen to life; thus we now speak of the book of life. In another sense the inscription of those things which lead us to life may be called the book of life; and this also is twofold, either as of things to be done, and thus the Old and New Testaments are called a book of life; or of things already done, and thus that divine energy by which it happens that to each one his deeds will be recalled to memory is spoken of as the book of life. Thus that also may be called the book of war, whether it contains the names inscribed of those chosen for military service, or treats of

---

[1] *Glossa interl.*, (III, 412v).
[2] *City of God*, XX, 14 (PL 41, 680).

[3] *Glossa ordin.*, (III, 182F); *Glossa Lombardi* (PL 191, 639). Augustine, *Ennar. in Ps.*, 68, Serm. 2; v, 29 (PL 36, 862).

the art of warfare, or relates the deeds of soldiers.

Hence the solution of the *Second Objection* is clear.

Reply Obj. 3. It is the custom to inscribe not those who are rejected, but those who are chosen. Hence there is no book of death corresponding to reprobation, as the book of life to predestination.

Reply Obj. 4. Predestination and the book of life are different aspects of the same thing. For this latter implies the knowledge of predestination, as also is made clear from the gloss quoted above.

ARTICLE 2. *Whether the Book of Life Regards Only the Life of Glory of the Predestined?*

We proceed thus to the Second Article: It seems that the book of life does not only regard the life of glory of the predestined.

Objection 1. For the book of life is the knowledge of life. But God, through His own life, knows all other life. Therefore the book of life is so called especially in regard to divine life, and not only in regard to the life of the predestined.

Obj. 2. Further, as the life of glory comes from God, so also does the life of nature. Therefore, if the knowledge of the life of glory is called the book of life, so also should the knowledge of the life of nature be so called.

Obj. 3. Further, some are chosen to the life of grace who are not chosen to the life of glory, as is clear from what is said: *Have not I chosen you twelve, and one of you is a devil?* (John 6. 71). But the book of life is the inscription of the divine election, as stated above (A. 1). Therefore it applies also to the life of grace.

On the contrary, The book of life is the knowledge of predestination, as stated above (A. 1). But predestination does not regard the life of grace, except so far as it is ordered to glory; for those are not predestined who have grace and yet fail to obtain glory. The book of life therefore is only so called in regard to the life of glory.

I answer that, The book of life, as stated above (A. 1), implies a conscription or a knowledge of those chosen to life. Now a man is chosen for something which does not belong to him by nature; and again that to which a man is chosen has the aspect of an end. For a soldier is not chosen or inscribed merely to put on armour, but to fight, since this is the proper duty to which military service is directed. But the life of glory is an end above nature, as said

above (Q. XII, A. 4; Q. XXIII, A. 1). Therefore, strictly speaking, the book of life regards the life of glory.

Reply Obj. 1. The divine life, even considered as a life of glory, is natural to God; hence in His regard there is no election, and in consequence no book of life; for we do not say that anyone is chosen to possess the power of sense, or any of those things that are consequent on nature.

From this we gather the *Reply* to the *Second Objection.* For there is no election, nor a book of life as regards the life of nature.

Reply Obj. 3. The life of grace has the aspect not of an end, but of something directed towards an end. Hence nobody is said to be chosen to the life of grace except so far as the life of grace is directed to glory. For this reason those who, possessing grace, fail to obtain glory, are not said to be chosen absolutely, but relatively. Likewise they are not said to be written in the book of life absolutely, but relatively; that is to say, that it is in the ordination and knowledge of God that they are to have some relation to eternal life, according to their participation in grace.

ARTICLE 3. *Whether Anyone May Be Blotted out of the Book of Life?*

We proceed thus to the Third Article: It seems that no one may be blotted out of the book of life.

Objection 1. For Augustine says[1]: "God's foreknowledge, which cannot be deceived, is the book of life." But nothing can be taken away from the foreknowledge of God, nor from predestination. Therefore neither can anyone be blotted out from the book of life.

Obj. 2. Further, whatever is in a thing is in it according to the disposition of that thing. But the book of life is something eternal and immutable. Therefore whatsoever is written in it is there not in a temporary way, but immovably and indelibly.

Obj. 3. Further, blotting out is the contrary to inscription. But nobody can be written a second time in the book of life. Neither therefore can he be blotted out.

On the contrary, It is said, *Let them be blotted out from the book of the living.* (Ps. 68. 29).

I answer that, Some have said that none could be really blotted out of the book of life, but only in the opinion of men. For it is customary in the Scriptures to say that something is done

[1] *City of God,* xx, 15 (PL 41, 681).

when it becomes known. Thus some are said to be written in the book of life because men think they are written therein, on account of the present justice they see in them; but when it becomes evident, either in this world or in the next, that they have fallen from that justice, they are then said to be blotted out. And thus a gloss explains the passage: *Let them be blotted out of the book of the living.*[1]

But because not to be blotted out of the book of life is placed among the rewards of the just, according to the text, *He that shall overcome, shall thus be clothed in white garments, and I will not blot his name out of the book of life* (Apoc. 3. 5) (and what is promised to holy men, is not merely something in the opinion of men), it can therefore be said that to be blotted out, and not blotted out, of the book of life is not only to be referred to the opinion of man, but to reality. For the book of life is the inscription of those ordained to eternal life, to which one is ordered from two sources: namely, from predestination, which ordering never fails, and from grace; for whoever has grace, by this very fact becomes fitted for eternal life. This ordering fails sometimes, because some are ordered, by possessing grace, to obtain eternal life, yet they fail to obtain it through mortal sin. Therefore those who are ordained to possess eternal life through divine predestination are written down in the book of life absolutely, because they are written therein to have eternal life in itself; such are never blotted out from the book of life. Those, however, who are ordained to eternal life not through the divine predestination, but through grace, are said to be written in the book of life not absolutely, but relatively, for they are written therein not to have eternal life in itself, but in its cause only. These latter are blotted out of the book of life, though this blotting out must not be referred to God as if God foreknew a thing, and afterwards knew it not, but to the thing known, namely, because God knows one is first ordained to eternal life, and afterwards not ordained when he falls from grace.

Reply Obj. 1. The act of blotting out, as we have said, does not refer to the book of life as regards God's foreknowledge, as if in God there were any change, but as regards the things foreknown, which can change.

Reply Obj. 2. Although things are immutably in God, yet in themselves they are subject to change. To this it is that the blotting out of the book of life refers.

Reply Obj. 3. The way in which one is said to be blotted out of the book of life is that in which one is said to be written therein anew; either in the opinion of men, or because he begins again to have relation towards eternal life through grace, which also is included in the knowledge of God, although not anew.

QUESTION XXV
THE POWER OF GOD
(In Six Articles)

AFTER considering the divine foreknowledge and will, and other things pertaining thereto, it remains for us to consider the power of God. About this are six points of inquiry: (1) Whether there is power in God? (2) Whether His power is infinite? (3) Whether He is almighty? (4) Whether He could make the past not to have been? (5) Whether He could do what He does not, or not do what He does? (6) Whether what He makes He could make better?

ARTICLE 1. *Whether There Is Power in God?*

We proceed thus to the First Article: It seems that power is not in God.

Objection 1. For as prime matter is to power, so God, who is the first agent, is to act. But prime matter, considered in itself, is devoid of all act. Therefore, the first agent—namely, God—is devoid of power.

Obj. 2. Further, according to the Philosopher,[2] better than every power is its act. For form is better than matter, and action than active power, since it is its end. But nothing is better than what is in God, because whatsoever is in God, is God, as was shown above (Q. III, A. 3). Therefore, there is no power in God.

Obj. 3. Further, Power is the principle of operation. But the divine power is God's essence, since there is nothing accidental in God, and of the essence of God there is no principle. Therefore there is no power in God.

Obj. 4. Further, it was shown above (QQ. XIV, A. 8; XIX, A. 4) that God's knowledge and will are the cause of things. But cause and principle are the same. We ought not, therefore, to assign power to God, but only knowledge and will.

On the contrary, It is said: *Thou art mighty, O Lord, and Thy truth is round about Thee* (Ps. 68. 9).

I answer that, Power is twofold—namely,

---

[1] *Glossa ordin.*, super Ps. 68. 29 (III, 182F); *Glossa* Lombardi (PL 191, 639); Augustine, *Enarr. in Ps.*, (PL 36; 862).

[2] *Metaphysics*, IX, 9 (1051ª4).

passive, which exists in no way in God; and active, which we must assign to Him in the highest degree. For it is manifest that everything according as it is in act and is perfect is the active principle of something, while a thing is acted upon according as it is deficient and imperfect. Now it was shown above (QQ. III, A. 1; IV, AA. 1, 2), that God is pure act, absolutely and in all ways perfect, nor in Him does any imperfection find place. Hence it most fittingly belongs to Him to be an active principle, and in no way to be acted upon. On the other hand, the notion of active principle is consistent with active power. For active power is the principle of acting upon something else, whereas passive power is the principle of being acted upon by something else, as the Philosopher says.[1] It remains, therefore, that in God there is active power in the highest degree.

Reply Obj. 1. Active power is not divided against act, but is founded upon it, for everything acts according as it is actual; but passive power is divided against act, for a thing is acted upon according as it is in potency. Hence this potency is not in God, but only active power.

Reply Obj. 2. Whenever act is distinct from power, act must be nobler than power. But God's action is not distinct from His power, for both are His divine essence, because neither is His being distinct from His essence. Hence it does not follow that there should be anything in God nobler than His power.

Reply Obj. 3. In creatures, power is the principle not only of action, but likewise of effect. Thus in God the idea of power is retained in so far as it is the principle of an effect; not, however, as it is a principle of action, for this is the divine essence itself; unless perhaps, after our manner of understanding, in so far as the divine essence, which contains beforehand in itself all perfection that exists in created things, can be understood either under the notion of action, or under that of power just as also it is understood under the notion of a *suppositum* possessing nature, and under that of nature. Accordingly the notion of power is retained in God in so far as it is the principle of an effect.

Reply Obj. 4. Power is predicated of God not as something really distinct from His knowledge and will, but as differing from them according to reason; in so far, that is, as power implies a notion of a principle putting into execution what the will commands, and what knowledge directs, which three things in God are identi-

[1] *Metaphysics*, V, 12 (1019ᵃ19).

fied. Or we may say that the knowledge or will of God, according as it is the effecting principle, has the notion of power contained in it. Hence the consideration of the knowledge and will of God precedes the consideration of His power as the cause precedes the operation and effect.

ARTICLE 2. *Whether the Power of God Is Infinite?*

We proceed thus to the Second Article: It seems that the power of God is not infinite.

Objection 1. For everything that is infinite is imperfect according to the Philosopher.[2] But the power of God is not imperfect. Therefore it is not infinite.

Obj. 2. Further, every power is made known by its effect; otherwise it would be without effect. If, then, the power of God were infinite, it could produce an infinite effect, but this is impossible.

Obj. 3. Further, the Philosopher proves[3] that if the power of any corporeal thing were infinite, it would cause instantaneous movement. God, however, does not cause instantaneous movement, but moves the spiritual creature in time, and the corporeal creature in place and time, as Augustine says.[4] Therefore, His power is not infinite.

On the contrary, Hilary says (*De Trin.* viii, 24),[5] that "God's power is immeasurable. He is the living mighty One." Now everything that is immeasurable is infinite. Therefore the power of God is infinite.

I answer that, As stated above (A. 1), active power exists in God according to the measure in which He is actual. Now His being is infinite, since it is not limited by anything that receives it, as is clear from what has been said, when we discussed the infinity of the divine essence (Q. VII, A. 1). Hence it is necessary that the active power in God should be infinite. For in every agent it is found that the more perfectly an agent has the form by which it acts, the greater its power in acting. For instance, the hotter a thing is, the greater power it has to give heat; and it would have infinite power to give heat, were its own heat infinite. Hence, since the divine essence, through which God acts, is infinite, as was shown above (*loc. cit.*), it follows that His power likewise is infinite.

Reply Obj. 1. The Philosopher is here speaking of an infinity in regard to matter not lim-

[2] *Physics*, III, 6 (207ᵃ7).　　[3] *Ibid.*, VIII, 10 (266ᵃ31).
[4] *Gen. ad lit.*, VIII, 20, 22 (PL 34, 388; 389).
[5] PL 10, 253.

ited by any form, which is the kind of infinity that belongs to quantity. But the divine essence is not infinite in this way, as was shown above (*loc. cit.*), and consequently neither is His power. It does not follow, therefore, that it is imperfect.

Reply Obj. 2. The power of a univocal agent is wholly manifested in its effect. The generative power of man, for example, is not able to do more than beget man. But the power of a non-univocal agent does not wholly manifest itself in the production of its effect; as, for example, the power of the sun does not wholly manifest itself in the production of an animal generated from putrefaction. Now it is clear that God is not a univocal agent. For nothing agrees with Him either in species or in genus, as was shown above (Q. III, A. 5). Hence it follows that His effect is always less than His power. It is not necessary, therefore, that the infinite power of God should be manifested so as to produce an infinite effect. Yet even if it were to produce no effect, the power of God would not be in vain, because a thing is in vain which is ordered towards an end to which it does not attain. But the power of God is not ordered toward its effect as towards an end; rather, it is the end of the effect produced by it.

Reply Obj. 3. The Philosopher proves[1] that "if a body had infinite power, it would move without time." And he shows[2] that the power of the mover of heaven is infinite, because it can move in an infinite time. It remains, therefore, according to his meaning, that the infinite power of a body, if such existed, would move without time; not, however, the power of an incorporeal mover. The reason of this is that one body moving another is a univocal agent; hence it follows that the whole power of the agent is made known in its motion. Since then the greater the power of a moving body, the more quickly does it move, it is necessary that if its power were infinite it would move beyond comparison faster, and this is to move without time. An incorporeal mover, however, is not a univocal agent; hence it is not necessary that the whole of its power should be manifested in motion, so as to move without time; and especially since it moves in accordance with the disposition of its will.

ARTICLE 3. *Whether God Is Omnipotent?*

We proceed thus to the Third Article: It seems that God is not omnipotent.

[1] *Physics*, VIII, 10 (266ᵃ29).
[2] *Ibid.*, VIII, 10 (267ᵇ24).

Objection 1. For to be moved and to be acted upon belong to everything. But this is impossible with God, for He is immovable, as was said above (Q. II, A. 3; Q. IX, A. 1). Therefore He is not omnipotent.

Obj. 2. Further, sin is an act of some kind. But God cannot sin, nor *deny Himself,* as it is said II Tim. 2. 13. Therefore He is not omnipotent.

Obj. 3. Further, it is said of God that "He manifests His omnipotence especially by sparing and having mercy."[3] Therefore the greatest act possible to the divine power is to spare and have mercy. There are things much greater, however, than sparing and having mercy; for example, to create another world, and the like. Therefore God is not omnipotent.

Obj. 4. Further, upon the text, *God hath made foolish the wisdom of this world* (I Cor. 1. 20), a gloss says:[4] "God hath made the wisdom of this world foolish, (Vulg., *Hath not God*, etc.) by showing those things to be possible which it judges to be impossible." Hence it would seem that nothing is to be judged possible or impossible in reference to inferior causes, as the wisdom of this world judges them; but in reference to the divine power. If God, then, were omnipotent, all things would be possible; nothing, therefore, impossible. But if we take away the impossible, then we destroy also the necessary; for what necessarily exists is impossible not to exist. Therefore there would be nothing at all that is necessary in things if God were omnipotent. But this is an impossibility. Therefore God is not omnipotent.

On the contrary, It is said: *No word shall be impossible with God* (Luke 1. 37).

I answer that, All confess that God is omnipotent; but it seems difficult to explain in what His omnipotence consists; for there may be a doubt as to what is comprehended under the distribution of the word "all" when we say that God can do all things. If, however, we consider the matter rightly, since power is said in reference to possible things, this phrase, "God can do all things," is rightly understood to mean that God can do all things that are possible and for this reason He is said to be omnipotent. Now according to the Philosopher,[5] a thing is said to be possible in two ways. First in relation to some power; thus whatever is subject to human power is said to be possible to man. Now God cannot be said to be omnipotent

[3] *Collect*, tenth Sunday after Pentecost.
[4] *Glossa ordin.*, (VI, 34E).
[5] *Metaphysics*, V, 12 (1019ᵇ34).

through being able to do all things that are possible to created nature, for the divine power extends farther than that. If, however, we were to say that God is omnipotent because He can do all things that are possible to His power, there would be a vicious circle in the explanation of omnipotence. For this would be saying nothing else but that God is omnipotent, because He can do all that He is able to do.

It remains, therefore, that God is called omnipotent because he can do all things that are possible absolutely; which is the second way of saying a thing is possible. For a thing is said to be possible or impossible absolutely according to the relation in which the very terms stand to one another: possible if the predicate is not incompatible with the subject, as that Socrates sits; and absolutely impossible when the predicate is altogether incompatible with the subject, as, for instance, that a man is a donkey.

It must, however, be remembered that since every agent produces an effect like itself, to each active power there corresponds a thing possible as its proper object according to the nature of that act on which its active power is founded; for instance, the power of giving warmth is related as to its proper object to the being capable of being warmed. The divine being, however, upon which the nature of power in God is founded, is infinite, and is not limited to any genus of being, but possesses beforehand within itself the perfection of all being. Hence, whatever can have the nature of being is numbered among the absolutely possible things in respect of which God is called omnipotent.

Now nothing is opposed to the notion of being except non-being. Therefore that which implies being and non-being at the same time is incompatible with the notion of an absolutely possible thing, within the scope of the divine omnipotence. For such cannot come under the divine omnipotence, not because of any defect in the power of God, but because it has not the nature of a feasible or possible thing. Therefore, everything that does not imply a contradiction is numbered amongst those possible things, in respect of which God is called omnipotent; but whatever implies contradiction does not come within the scope of divine omnipotence, because it cannot have the aspect of possibility. Hence it is better to say that such things cannot be done, than that God cannot do them. Nor is this contrary to the word of the angel, saying (Luke 1. 37): *No word shall be impossible with God.* For whatever implies a contradiction cannot be a word, because no intellect can possibly conceive such a thing.

Reply Obj. 1. God is said to be omnipotent in respect to His active power, not to passive power, as was shown above (A. 1). Hence the fact that He is immovable or cannot be acted upon is not contrary to His omnipotence.

Reply Obj. 2. To sin is to fall short of a perfect action; hence to be able to sin is to be able to fall short in action, which is contrary to omnipotence. Therefore God cannot sin, because He is omnipotence. Nevertheless, the Philosopher says[1] that "God can deliberately do what is evil." But this must be understood either on a condition, the antecedent of which is impossible—as, for instance, if we were to say that God can do evil things if He will. For there is no reason why a conditional proposition should not be true, though both the antecedent and consequent are impossible, as if one were to say: "If man is a donkey, he has four feet." Or he may be understood to mean that God can do some things which now seem to be evil, which, however, if He did them, would then be good. Or he is, perhaps, speaking after the common opinion of the gentiles, who thought that men became gods, like Jupiter or Mercury.

Reply Obj. 3. God's omnipotence is particularly shown in sparing and having mercy, because in this is it made manifest that God has supreme power, that He freely forgives sins. For it is not for one who is bound by laws of a superior to forgive sins of his own free will. Or, because by sparing and having mercy upon men, He leads them on to the participation of an infinite good, which is the ultimate effect of the divine power. Or because, as was said above (Q. XXI, A. 4), the effect of the divine mercy is the foundation of all the divine works. For nothing is due to anyone except on account of something already given him freely by God. In this way the divine omnipotence is particularly made manifest, because to it pertains the first foundation of all good things.

Reply Obj. 4. The absolute possible is not called so in reference either to higher causes, or to inferior causes, but in reference to itself. But the possible in reference to some power is named possible in reference to its proximate cause. Hence those things which it belongs to God alone to do immediately—as, for example, to create, to justify, and the like—are said to be possible in reference to a higher cause. Those things, however, which are of such kind as to be done by inferior causes are said to be possible in

[1] *Topics*, IV, 5 (126ª34).

reference to those inferior causes. For according to the condition of the proximate cause the effect has contingency or necessity, as was shown above (Q. XIV, A. 13, Ans. 1). Thus is it that the wisdom of the world is deemed foolish, because what is impossible to nature it judges to be impossible to God. So it is clear that the omnipotence of God does not take away from things their impossibility and necessity.

ARTICLE 4. *Whether God Can Make the Past Not To Have Been?*

We proceed thus to the Fourth Article: It seems that God can make the past not to have been.

Objection 1. For what is impossible in itself is more impossible than that which is only impossible accidentally. But God can do what is impossible in itself, as to give sight to the blind, or to raise the dead. Therefore, and much more can He do what is only impossible accidentally. Now for the past not to have been is impossible accidentally; thus for Socrates not to be running is accidentally impossible, from the fact that his running is a thing of the past. Therefore God can make the past not to have been.

Obj. 2. Further, what God could do, He can do now, since His power is not lessened. But God could have effected, before Socrates ran, that he should not run. Therefore, when he has run, God could effect that he did not run.

Obj. 3. Further, charity is a more excellent virtue than virginity. But God can supply charity that is lost; therefore also lost virginity. Therefore He can so effect that what was corrupt should not have been corrupt.

On the contrary, Jerome says (*Ep. 22 ad Eustoch.*):[1] "Although God can do all things, He cannot make a thing that is corrupt not to have been corrupted." Therefore, for the same reason, He cannot effect that anything else which is past should not have been.

I answer that, As was said above (A. 3; Q. VII, A. 2, Ans. 1), there does not fall under the scope of God's omnipotence anything that implies a contradiction. Now that the past should not have been implies a contradiction. For as it implies a contradiction to say that Socrates is sitting, and is not sitting, so does it to say that he sat, and did not sit. But to say that he did sit is to say that it happened in the past. To say that he did not sit, is to say that it did not happen. Hence, that the past should not have been does not come under the scope of divine power. This is what Augustine means when he says (*Contra*

Faust. XXV, 5):[2] "Whosoever says, If God is almighty, let Him make what is done as if it were not done, does not see that this is to say: If God is almighty let Him effect that what is true, by the very fact that it is true, be false"; and the Philosopher says:[3] "Of this one thing alone is God deprived—namely, to make undone the things that have been done."

Reply Obj. 1. Although it is impossible accidentally for the past not to have been, if one considers the past thing itself, as, for instance, the running of Socrates, nevertheless, if the past thing is considered as past, that it should not have been is impossible, not only in itself, but absolutely since it implies a contradiction. Thus, it is more impossible than the raising of the dead, which does not imply a contradiction, because this is reckoned impossible in reference to some power, that is to say, some natural power; for such impossible things do come beneath the scope of divine power.

Reply Obj. 2. As God, in accordance with the perfection of the divine power, can do all things, and yet some things are not subject to His power because they fall short of being possible, so, also, if we regard the immutability of the divine power, whatever God could do He can do now. Some things, however, at one time had the nature of possibility, whilst they were yet to be done, which now fall short of the nature of possibility when they have been done. So is God said not to be able to do them because they themselves cannot be done.

Reply Obj. 3. God can remove all corruption of the mind and body from a woman who has fallen, but the fact that she had been corrupt cannot be removed from her; as also is it impossible that the fact of having sinned or of having lost charity thereby can be removed from the sinner.

ARTICLE 5. *Whether God Can Do What He Does Not?*

We proceed thus to the Fifth Article: It seems that God cannot do other than what He does.

Objection 1. For God cannot do what He has not foreknown and preordained that He would do. But He neither foreknew nor preordained that He would do anything except what He does. Therefore He cannot do except what He does.

Obj. 2. Further, God can only do what ought to be done and what it is just to do. But God is not bound to do what He does not; nor is it just that He should do what He does not. Therefore He cannot do except what he does.

Obj. 3. Further, God cannot do anything that is not good and befitting things made. But it is not good for things made nor befitting them to be otherwise than as they are. Therefore God cannot do except what He does.

On the contrary, It is said: *Thinkest thou that I cannot ask My Father, and He will give Me presently more than twelve legions of angels?* (Matt. 26. 53). But He neither asked for them, nor did His Father show them to refute the Jews. Therefore God can do what He does not.

I answer that, In this matter certain persons erred in two ways. Some[1] laid it down that God acts from a necessity of nature in such way that as from the action of natural things nothing else can happen beyond what actually takes place— as, for instance, from the seed of man, a man must come, and from that of an olive, an olive, so from the divine operation there could not result other things, nor another order of things, than that which now is. But we showed above (Q. XIX, A. 3) that God does not act as though from a necessity of nature, but that His will is the cause of all things; nor is that will naturally and from necessity determined to those things. Hence in no way at all is the present course of events produced by God from any necessity, so that other things could not happen.

Others, however, said[2] that the divine power is restricted to this present course of events through the order of the divine wisdom and justice, without which God does nothing. But since the power of God, which is His essence, is nothing else but His wisdom, it can indeed be fittingly said that there is nothing in the divine power which is not in the order of the divine wisdom; for the divine wisdom includes the whole potency of the divine power. Yet the order placed in creation by divine wisdom, in which order the notion of His justice consists, as said above (Q. XXI, A. 4), does not so square so strictly with the divine wisdom that the divine wisdom should be restricted to this present order of things. Now it is clear that the whole idea of order which a wise man puts into things made by him is taken from their end. So, when the end is proportionate to the things made for

that end, the wisdom of the maker is restricted to some definite order. But the divine goodness is an end exceeding beyond all proportion things created. And so the divine wisdom is not so restricted to any particular order that no other course of events could happen. Therefore we must simply say that God can do other things than those He has done.

Reply Obj. 1. In ourselves, in whom power and essence are distinct from will and intellect, and again intellect from wisdom, and will from justice, there can be something in the power which is not in the just will nor in the wise intellect. But in God, power, essence, will, intellect, wisdom and justice, are one and the same. Hence, there can be nothing in the divine power which cannot also be in His just will or in His wise intellect. Then, because His will cannot be determined from necessity to this or that order of things, except upon supposition, as was said above (Q. XIX, A. 3), neither are the wisdom and justice of God restricted to this present order, as was shown above; and so nothing prevents there being something in the divine power which He does not will, and which is not included in the order which He has placed in things. Again, because power is considered as executing, the will as commanding, and the intellect and wisdom as directing, what is attributed to His power considered in itself, God is said to be able to do in accordance with His absolute power. Of such a kind is everything which has the nature of being, as was said above (A. 3). What is, however, attributed to the divine power according as it carries into execution the command of a just will, God is said to be able to do by His power as ordained. In this manner, we must say that God can do other things by His absolute power than those He has foreknown and preordained Himself to do. But it could not happen that He should do anything which He had not foreknown, and had not preordained that He would do, because His actual doing is subject to His foreknowledge and preordination, though His being able, which is from His nature, is not so. For God does things because He wills so to do; yet the power to do them does not come from His will, but from His nature.

Reply Obj. 2. God does not owe anything to anybody, unless to Himself. Hence, when it is said that God can only do what He ought, nothing else is meant by this than that God can do nothing but what is befitting to Himself, and just. But these words "befitting" and "just" may be understood in two ways: one, in direct

[1] Referred to in Averroes, *Destruct. Destruct.*, disp. 3 (IX, 44L) and Maimonides, *Guide*, II, 20 (FR 189); cf. Avicenna, *Meta.*, IX, 4 (104v); St. Thomas, *De Potentia*, Q. III, A. 4.

[2] Peter Abelard, *Introd. ad Theol.*, III, 5 (PL 178, 1093); cf. Albert the Great, *In Sent.*, I, d. 44, A. 2 (BO XXVI, 391); St. Thomas, *De Pot.*, Q. 1, A. 5.

connection with the verb "is," and thus they would be restricted to the present order of things, and would concern His power. Then what is said in the objection is false, for the sense is that God can do nothing except what is now fitting and just. If, however, they be joined directly with the verb "can" (which has the effect of extending the meaning), and then secondly with "is," the present will be signified, but in a confused way. The sentence would then be true in this sense: "God cannot do anything except that which, if He did it, would be suitable and just."

Reply Obj. 3. Although this order of things be restricted to what now exists, the divine power and wisdom are not thus restricted. Hence, although no other order would be suitable and good to the things which now are, yet God can do other things and impose upon them another order.

ARTICLE 6. *Whether God Can Do Better Than What He Does?*

We proceed thus to the Sixth Article: It seems that God cannot do better than He does.

Objection 1. For whatever God does, He does in a most powerful and wise way. But a thing is so much the better done as it is more powerfully and wisely done. Therefore God cannot do anything better than He does.

Obj. 2. Further, Augustine thus argues (*Contra Maximin.* ii, 7):[1] "If God could, but would not, beget a Son His equal, He would have been envious." For the same reason, if God could have made better things than He has done, but was not willing so to do, He would have been envious. But envy is far removed from God. Therefore God makes everything best. He cannot therefore make anything better than He does.

Obj. 3. Further, what is most good and the best of all cannot be bettered, because nothing is better than the best. But as Augustine says (*Enchir.* 10),[2] "each thing that God has made is good, and, taken all together they are very good, because in them all consists the wondrous beauty of the universe." Therefore the good in the universe could not be made better by God.

Obj. 4. Further, Christ as man is full of grace and truth, and has the Spirit without measure; and so He cannot be better. Again created Happiness is described as the highest good, and thus could not be better. And the Blessed Virgin Mary is raised above all the choirs of angels, and so cannot be better than she is. God cannot

therefore make all things better than He has made them.

On the contrary, It is said (Eph. 3. 20) : *God is able to do all things more abundantly than we desire or understand.*

I answer that, The goodness of anything is twofold. One is of its essence; thus, for instance, to be rational pertains to the essence of man. As regards this good, God cannot make a thing better than it is itself, although He can make another thing better than it, even as He cannot make the number four greater than it is because if it were greater it would no longer be four, but another number. For the addition of a substantial difference in definitions is after the manner of the addition of unity in numbers.[3] Another kind of goodness is that which is over and above the essence; thus, the good of a man is to be virtuous or wise. As regards this kind of goodness, God can make better the things He has made. Absolutely speaking, however, God can make something else better than each thing made by Him.

Reply Obj. 1. When it is said that God can make a thing better than He makes it, if "better" is taken as a noun, this proposition is true. For He can always make something else better than each individual thing, and He can make the same thing in one way better than it is, and in another way not, as was explained above. If, however, "better" is taken as an adverb, implying the manner of the making, in this way God cannot make anything better than He makes it, because He cannot make it from greater wisdom and goodness. But if it implies the manner of the thing made, He can make something better, because He can give to things made by Him a better manner of being as regards the accidents, although not as regards essential things.

Reply Obj. 2. It is of the nature of a son that he should be equal to his father, when he comes to maturity. But it is not of the nature of anything created that it should be better than it was made by God. Hence the comparison fails.

Reply Obj. 3. The universe, the things that exist now being supposed, cannot be better, on account of the most noble order given to these things by God, in which the good of the universe consists. For if any one thing were bettered, the proportion of order would be destroyed, just as if one string were stretched more than it ought to be, the melody of the harp would be destroyed. Yet God could make other things, or add something to those things

---

[1] PL 42, 762.   [2] PL 40, 236.   [3] Aristotle, *Metaphysics*, VIII, 3 (1044ᵃ1).

that are made, and then that universe would be better.

Reply Obj. 4. The humanity of Christ, from the fact that it is united to God, and created Happiness from the fact that it is the enjoyment of God, and the Blessed Virgin from the fact that she is the mother of God, have all a certain infinite dignity from the infinite good, which is God. And on this account there cannot be anything better than these, just as there cannot be anything better than God.

QUESTION XXVI
Of the divine happiness
(*In Four Articles*)

AFTER considering all that pertains to the unity of the divine essence, we come to treat of the divine happiness. Concerning this, there are four points of inquiry: (1) Whether happiness belongs to God? (2) In regard to what is God called happy? Does this regard His act of intellect? (3) Whether He is essentially the Happiness of each of the blessed? (4) Whether all other happiness is included in the divine happiness?

ARTICLE 1. *Whether Happiness Belongs to God? We proceed thus to the First Article:* It seems that happiness does not belong to God.

Objection 1. For happiness according to Boethius (*De consol.* iv, 2)[1] "is a state made perfect by the aggregation of all good things." But aggregation of goods has no place in God, nor has composition. Therefore happiness does not belong to God.

Obj. 2. Further, Happiness or felicity, is "the reward of virtue," according to the Philosopher.[2] But reward does not apply to God, as neither does merit. Therefore neither does happiness.

On the contrary, The Apostle says: *Which in His times He shall show, who is the Blessed and only Mighty, the King of Kings and Lord of Lords* (I Tim. 6. 15).

I answer that, Happiness belongs to God in a very special manner. For nothing else is understood to be meant by the term happiness than the perfect good of an intellectual nature, which is capable of knowing that it has a sufficiency of the good which it possesses, and to which it belongs that good or ill may befall, and which can control its own actions. All of these things belong in a most excellent manner to God—namely, to be perfect, and to possess intelli-

gence. Hence happiness belongs to God in the highest degree.

Reply Obj. 1. Aggregation of good is in God after the manner not of composition, but of simplicity; for those things which in creatures are manifold, pre-exist in God, as was said above (QQ. IV, A. 2, ANS. 1; XIII, A. 4), in simplicity and unity.

Reply Obj. 2. It belongs as an accident to happiness or felicity to be the reward of virtue, in so far as anyone attains to happiness; even as to be the term of generation belongs accidentally to a being, so far as it passes from potency to act. As, then, God has being, though not begotten, so He has happiness, although not acquired by merit.

ARTICLE 2. *Whether God Is Called Happy in Respect of His Intellect?*

We proceed thus to the Second Article: It seems that God is not called happy in respect of His intellect.

Objection 1. For happiness is the highest good. But good is said to be in God in regard to His essence, because good has reference to being which is according to essence, according to Boëthius (*De Hebdom.*).[3] Therefore happiness also is said to be in God in regard to His essence, and not to His intellect.

Obj. 2. Further, Happiness has the notion of end. Now the end is the object of the will, as also is the good. Therefore happiness is said to be in God with reference to His will, and not with reference to His intellect.

On the contrary, Gregory says (*Moral.* xxxii, 6):[4] "He is full of glory, Who whilst He rejoices in Himself, needs not further praise." To be full of glory, however, is the same as to be happy. Therefore, since we enjoy God in respect of our intellect, because "vision is the whole of the reward," as Augustine says,[5] it would seem that happiness is said to be in God in respect of His intellect.

I answer that, Happiness, as stated above (A. 1), is the perfect good of an intellectual nature. Thus it is that, as everything desires its perfection, intellectual nature desires naturally to be happy. Now that which is most perfect in any intellectual nature is the intellectual operation, by which in some sense it grasps everything. Hence the happiness of every intellectual nature consists in understanding. Now in God, to be and to understand are really one and the

---

[1] PL 63, 724.   [2] *Ethics,* I, 9 (1099[b]16).

[3] PL 64, 1314.   [4] PL 76, 639.
[5] *Enarr. in Ps.,* 90., 16 (PL37, 1170); *De Trin.,* I, 9 (PL42, 833).

same thing, differing only in the manner of our understanding them. Happiness must therefore be assigned to God in respect of His intellect, as also to the blessed, who are called happy (*beati*) by reason of the assimilation to His happiness (*beatitudo*).

Reply Obj. 1. This argument proves that God is happy according to His essence, not that happiness pertains to Him under the aspect of His essence, but rather under the aspect of His intellect.

Reply Obj. 2. Since happiness is a good, it is the object of the will; now the object is understood as prior to the act of a power. Hence according to our mode of understanding, divine happiness precedes the act of the will at rest in it. This cannot be other than the act of the intellect, and thus happiness is to be found in an act of the intellect.

ARTICLE. 3. *Whether God Is the Happiness of Each of the Blessed?*

We proceed thus to the Third Article:—It seems that God is the Happiness of each of the blessed.

Objection 1. For God is the supreme good, as was said above (Q. VI, A. 2). But it is impossible that there should be many supreme goods, as also is clear from what has been said above (Q. XI, A. 3). Therefore, since it is of the notion of Happiness that it should be the supreme good, it seems that Happiness is nothing else but God Himself.

Obj. 2. Further, Happiness is the last end of the rational nature. But to be the last end of the rational nature belongs only to God. Therefore the Happiness of each of the blessed is God alone.

On the contrary, The Happiness of one is greater than that of another, according to I Cor. 15. 41: *Star differeth from star in glory.* But nothing is greater than God. Therefore Happiness is something different from God.

I answer that, The Happiness of an intellectual nature consists in an act of the intellect. In this we may consider two things—namely, the object of the act, which is the thing understood; and the act itself, which is to understand. If, then, Happiness be considered on the side of the object, God is the only Happiness; for everyone is happy from this sole fact, that he understands God, in accordance with the saying of Augustine:[1] "Happy is he who knoweth Thee, though he know nought else." But as regards the act of understanding, Happiness is a cre-

[1] *Confessions,* V, 7 (PL 32, 708).

ated thing in beatified creatures; but in God, even in this way, it is an uncreated thing.

Reply Obj. 1. Happiness, as regards its object, is the supreme good absolutely, but as regards its act, in beatified creatures it is their supreme good not absolutely, but in that kind of goods which a creature can participate.

Reply Obj. 2. "End is twofold namely, objective and subjective," as the Philosopher says,[2] namely, the thing itself and its use. Thus to a miser the end is money, and its acquisition. Accordingly God is indeed the last end of a rational creature, as the thing itself, but created Happiness is the end, as the use, or rather enjoyment, of the thing.

ARTICLE 4. *Whether All Happiness Is Included in the Happiness of God?*

We proceed thus to the Fourth Article: It seems that the divine happiness does not embrace all happinesses.

Objection 1. For there are some false happinesses. But nothing false can be in God. Therefore the divine happiness does not embrace all happiness.

Obj. 2. Further, a certain happiness, according to some, consists in things corporeal, as in pleasure, riches, and such like. Now none of these have to do with God, since He is incorporeal. Therefore His happiness does not embrace all happiness.

On the contrary, Happiness is a certain perfection. But the divine perfection embraces all other perfection, as was shown above (Q. IV, A. 2.). Therefore the divine happiness embraces all happiness.

I answer that, Whatever is desirable in whatsoever happiness, whether true or false, pre-exists wholly and in a more eminent degree in the divine happiness. As to contemplative happiness, God possesses a continual and most certain contemplation of Himself and of all things else; and as to that which is active, he has the governance of the whole universe. As to earthly happiness, which consists in pleasure, riches, power, dignity, and fame, according to Boethius (*De Consol.* iii, 2),[3] He possesses joy in Himself and all things else for His delight; instead of riches He has that complete self-sufficiency which is promised by riches; in place of power, He has omnipotence; for dignities, the government of all things; and in place of fame, He possesses the admiration of all creatures.

Reply Obj. 1. A certain kind of happiness is

[2] *Soul,* II, 4 (415^{b}20).
[3] PL 63, 724.

false according as it falls short of the notion of true happiness; and thus it is not in God. But whatever semblance it has, howsoever slight, of happiness, the whole of it pre-exists in the divine happiness.

Reply Obj. 2. The good that exists in things corporeal in a corporeal manner is also in God. Spiritually according to the mode of His being.

We have now spoken enough concerning what pertains to the unity of the divine essence.

TREATISE ON THE TRINITY

QUESTION XXVII

THE PROCESSION OF THE DIVINE PERSONS

(In Five Articles)

HAVING considered what pertains to the unity of the divine essence, it remains to treat of what pertains to the Trinity of the persons in God. And because the divine Persons are distinguished from each other according to the relations of origin, the order of doctrine leads us to consider firstly the question of origin or procession; secondly, the relations of origin (Q. XXVIII); thirdly, the persons (Q. XXIX).

Concerning procession there are five points of inquiry:

(1) Whether there is procession in God? (2) Whether any procession in God can be called generation? (3) Whether there can be any other procession in God besides generation? (4) Whether that other procession can be called generation? (5) Whether there are more than two processions in God?

ARTICLE 1. *Whether There is Procession in God?*

We proceed thus to the First Article: It would seem that there cannot be any procession in God.

Objection 1. For procession signifies outward movement. But in God there is nothing subject to motion, nor anything extraneous. Therefore neither is there procession in God.

Obj. 2. Further, everything which proceeds differs from that from which it proceeds. But in God there is no diversity, but supreme simplicity. Therefore in God there is no procession.

Obj. 3. Further, to proceed from another seems to be against the nature of the first principle. But God is the first principle, as shown above (Q. II, A. 3). Therefore in God there is no procession.

On the contrary, Our Lord says, *From God I proceeded* (John 8. 42).

I answer that, Divine Scripture uses, in relation to God, names which pertain to procession.

This procession has been differently understood. Some have understood it in the sense of an effect proceeding from its cause. And this is the way in which Arius took it,[1] saying that the Son proceeds from the Father as His primary creature, and that the Holy Ghost proceeds from the Father and the Son as the creature of both. In this sense neither the Son nor the Holy Ghost would be true God, and this is contrary to what is said of the Son, *That . . . we may be in His true Son. This is the true God* (I John 5. 20). Of the Holy Ghost it is also said, *Know you not that your members are the temple of the Holy Ghost?* (I Cor. 6. 19.) Now, to have a temple is God's prerogative.

Others take this procession to mean the cause proceeding to the effect, as moving it, or impressing its own likeness on it, in which sense it was understood by Sabellius,[2] who said that God the Father is called Son in assuming flesh from the Virgin, and that the Father also is called Holy Ghost in sanctifying the rational creature, and moving it to life. The words of the Lord contradict such a meaning, when He speaks of Himself, *The Son cannot of Himself do anything* (John 5. 19); and many other passages show the same, whereby we know that the Father is not the Son.

Careful examination shows that both of these opinions take procession as meaning an outward act; hence neither of them affirms procession as existing in God Himself. But since procession always supposes action, and as there is an outward procession corresponding to the act tending to external matter, so there must be an inward procession corresponding to the act remaining within the agent. This appears most conspicuously in the intellect, the action of which namely, to understand, remains in the intelligent agent. For whenever we understand, by the very fact of understanding there proceeds something within us, which is a conception of the thing understood, a conception issuing from our intellectual power and proceeding from our knowledge of that thing. This conception is signified by the spoken word, and it is

[1] See Augustine, *De Haeres*, 49 (PL 42, 39).
[2] *Ibid.*, sect. 41 (42, 32).

153

called the word of the heart signified by the word of the voice.

As God is above all things, we should understand what is said of God not according to the mode of the lowest creatures, namely bodies, but from the likeness of the highest creatures, the intellectual substances; although even the likenesses derived from these fall short in the representation of divine objects. Procession, therefore, is not to be understood from what it is in bodies, either according to local movement, or by way of a cause proceeding forth to its exterior effect, as, for instance, like heat from the agent to the thing made hot. Rather it is to be understood by way of an intelligible emanation, for example, of the intelligible word which proceeds from the speaker, yet remains in him. In that sense the Catholic Faith understands procession as existing in God.

Reply Obj. 1. This objection comes from the idea of procession in the sense of local motion, or of an action tending to external matter, or to an exterior effect; which kind of procession does not exist in God, as we have explained.

Reply Obj. 2. Whatever proceeds by way of outward procession is necessarily distinct from the source from which it proceeds, whereas whatever proceeds within by an intelligible procession is not necessarily distinct; indeed, the more perfectly it proceeds, the more closely it is one with the source from which it proceeds. For it is clear that the more a thing is understood, the more closely is the intellectual conception joined and united to the intelligent agent, since the intellect by the very act of understanding is made one with the object understood. Thus, as the divine act of understanding is the very supreme perfection of God (Q. XIV, A. 1), the divine Word is of necessity perfectly one with the source whence He proceeds, without any kind of diversity.

Reply Obj. 3. To proceed from a principle so as to be something outside and distinct from that principle is irreconcilable with the notion of a first principle; but an intimate and uniform procession by way of an intelligible act is included in the notion of a first principle. For when we call the builder the principle of the house, in the notion of such a principle is included the conception of his art; and it would be included in the notion of the first principle were the builder the first principle. God, Who is the first principle of all things, may be compared to things created as the artificer to artificial things.

ARTICLE 2. *Whether Any Procession in God Can Be Called Generation?*

We proceed thus to the Second Article: It would seem that the procession which is in God cannot be called generation.

Objection 1. For generation is change from non-being to being, and is opposed to corruption, while matter is the subject of both. Nothing of all this belongs to God. Therefore generation cannot exist in God.

Obj. 2. Further, procession exists in God according to an intelligible mode, as above explained (A. 1). But such a procession is not called generation in us. Therefore neither is it to be called so in God.

Obj. 3. Further, anything that is generated derives being from its generator. Therefore such being is a received being. But no received being can be a self-subsistence. Therefore, since the divine being is self-subsisting (Q. III, A. 4), it follows that no generated being can be the divine being. Therefore there is no generation in God.

On the contrary, It is said (Ps. 2. 7): *This day have I begotten Thee.*

I answer that, The procession of the Word in God is called generation. In proof of this we must observe that generation has a twofold meaning: one common to everything subject to generation and corruption, in which sense generation is nothing but change from non-being to being. In another sense it is proper and belongs to living things, in which sense it signifies the origin of a living being from a conjoined living principle; and this is properly called birth. Not everything of that kind, however, is called begotten, but, strictly speaking, only what proceeds by way of likeness. Hence the hair or a hair has not the aspect of generation and of sonship, but only that has which proceeds by way of likeness. Nor will any likeness suffice; for a worm which is generated from animals has not the aspect of generation and sonship, although it has a generic likeness; for the notion of this kind of generation requires that there should be a procession by way of likeness in the same specific nature, as a man proceeds from a man, and a horse from a horse. So in living things, which proceed from potential to actual life, such as men and animals, generation includes both these kinds of generation. But if there is a being whose life does not proceed from potency to act, procession (if found in such a being) excludes entirely the first kind of generation; but it may have that kind of generation which belongs to living things.

So in this manner the procession of the Word in God is generation. For He proceeds by way of intelligible action, which is a vital operation: from a conjoined principle (as above described); by way of likeness because the conception of the intellect is a likeness of the thing understood; and exists in the same nature, because in God the act of understanding and His being are the same, as shown above (Q. XIV, A. 4). Hence the procession of the Word in God is called generation, and the Word Himself proceeding is called the Son.

Reply Obj 1. This objection is based on the idea of generation in the first sense, importing the issuing forth from potency to act, in which sense it is not found in God.

Reply Obj. 2. The act of human understanding in ourselves is not the substance itself of the intellect; hence the word which proceeds within us by intelligible operation is not of the same nature as the source from which it proceeds; so the notion of generation cannot be properly and fully applied to it. But the divine act of intelligence is the very substance itself of the one who understands (Q. XIV, A. 4). The World proceeding therefore proceeds as subsisting in the same nature, and so is properly called begotten, and Son. Hence Scripture employs terms which denote generation of living things in order to signify the procession of the divine Wisdom, namely, conception and birth, as is declared in the person of the divine Wisdom, *The depths were not as yet, and I was already conceived; before the hills, I was brought forth* (Prov. 8. 24). In our way of understanding we use the word "conception" in order to signify that in the word of our intellect is found the likeness of the thing understood, although there be no identity of nature.

Reply Obj. 3. Not everything received from another has existence in another subject; otherwise we could not say that the whole substance of created being comes from God, since there is no subject that could receive the whole substance. So, then, what is generated in God receives its being from the generator, not as though that being were received into matter or into a subject (which would conflict with the divine subsistence); but when we speak of His being as received, we mean that He Who proceeds receives divine being from another; not, however, as if He were other from the divine nature. For in the perfection itself of the divine being are contained both the Word intelligibly proceeding and the principle of the Word, with whatever belongs to His perfection (Q. IV, A. 2).

ARTICLE 3. *Whether Any Other Procession Exists in God Besides That of the Word?*

We proceed thus to the Third Article: It would seem that no other procession exists in God besides the generation of the Word.

Objection 1. Because, for whatever reason we admit another procession, we should be led to admit yet another, and so on to infinity, which cannot be. Therefore we must stop at the first, and hold that there exists only one procession in God.

Obj. 2. Further, every nature possesses but one mode of communication of that nature, because operations derive unity and diversity from their terms. But procession in God is only by way of communication of the divine nature. Therefore, as there is only one divine nature (Q. XI, A. 3), it follows that only one procession exists in God.

Obj. 3. Further, if any other procession but the intelligible procession of the Word existed in God, it could only be the procession of love, which is by the operation of the will. But such a procession could not be other than the intelligible procession of the intellect, since the will in God is the same as His intellect (Q. XIX, A. 1). Therefore in God there is no other procession but the procession of the Word.

On the contrary, The Holy Ghost proceeds from the Father (John 15. 26), and He is distinct from the Son, according to the words, *I will ask My Father, and He will give you another Paraclete* (John 14. 16). Therefore in God another procession exists besides the procession of the Word.

I answer that, There are two processions in God: the procession of the Word, and another.

In evidence of this we must observe that procession exists in God only according to an action which does not tend to anything external, but remains in the agent itself. Such action in an intellectual nature is that of the intellect, and of the will. The procession of the Word is by way of an intelligible action. The operation of the will within ourselves involves also another procession, that of love, whereby the thing loved is in the lover; just as, by the conception of the word, the thing spoken of or understood is in the intelligent agent. Hence, besides the procession of the Word in God, there exists in Him another procession called the procession of love.

Reply Obj. 1. There is no need to go on to infinity in the divine processions, for the procession which is accomplished within the agent in an intellectual nature terminates in the procession of the will.

Reply Obj. 2. All that exists in God, is God (Q. III, AA. 3, 4), but the same does not apply to others. Therefore the divine nature is communicated by every procession which is not outward, and this does not apply to other natures.

Reply Obj. 3. Though will and intellect are not diverse in God, nevertheless the nature of will and intellect requires the processions which are according to the action of each of them to exist in a certain order. For the procession of love occurs in order as regards the procession of the Word, since nothing can be loved by the will unless it is conceived in the intellect. So as there exists a certain order of the Word to the principle from which He proceeds, although in God the substance of the intellect and its conception are the same; so, although in God the will and the intellect are the same, still since love requires by its very nature that it proceed only from the conception of the intellect, there is a distinction of order between the procession of love and the procession of the Word in God.

ARTICLE 4. *Whether the Procession of Love in God Is Generation?*

We proceed thus to the Fourth Article: It would seem that the procession of love in God is generation.

Objection 1. For what proceeds by way of likeness of nature among living things is said to be generated and born. But what proceeds in God by way of love proceeds in the likeness of nature; otherwise it would be extraneous to the divine nature, and would be an external procession. Therefore what proceeds in God by way of love proceeds as generated and born.

Obj. 2. Further, as likeness is of the nature of the word, so does it belong to love. Hence it is said, that *every beast loves its like* (Ecclus. 13 19). Therefore if the Word is begotten and born by way of likeness, it seems becoming that love should proceed by way of generation.

Obj. 3. Further, what is not in any of its species is not in the genus. So if there is a procession of love in God, there ought to be some special name besides this common name of procession. But no other name is applicable but generation. Therefore the procession of love in God is generation.

On the contrary, Were this true, it would follow that the Holy Ghost Who proceeds as love would proceed as begotten, which is against the statement of Athanasius:[1] "The Holy Ghost is from the Father and the Son, not made, nor begotten, but proceeding."

I answer that, The procession of love in God ought not to be called generation. In evidence of this we must consider that the intellect and the will differ in this respect, that the intellect is put in act by the thing understood being according to its own likeness in the intellect, whereas the will is put in act not by any likeness of the thing willed within it, but by its having a certain inclination to the thing willed. Thus the procession of the intellect is by way of likeness, and is called generation, because every generator begets its own like; but the procession of the will is not by way of likeness, but is rather by way of impulse and movement towards an object.

So what proceeds in God by way of love, does not proceed as begotten, or as son, but proceeds rather as spirit; which name expresses a certain vital movement and impulse, according as anyone is described as moved or impelled by love to perform an action.

Reply Obj. 1. All that exists in God is one with the divine nature. Hence the proper notion of this or that procession, by which one procession is distinguished from another, cannot be on the part of this unity, but the proper notion of this or that procession must be taken from the order of one procession to another, which order is derived from the notion of will and intellect. Hence, each procession in God takes its name from the proper notion of will and intellect, the name being imposed to signify what its nature really is; and so it is that the Person proceeding as love receives the divine nature, but is not said to be born.

Reply Obj. 2. Likeness belongs in a different way to the word and to love. It belongs to word as being the likeness of the thing understood, as the thing generated is the likeness of the generator; but it belongs to love, not as though love itself were a likeness, but because likeness is the principle of loving. Thus it does not follow that love is begotten, but that the one begotten is the principle of love.

Reply Obj. 3. We can name God only from creatures (Q. XIII, A. 1). As in creatures generation is the only principle of communication of nature, procession in God has no proper or special name except that of generation. Hence the procession which is not generation has remained without a special name; but it can be called spiration, as it is the procession of the Spirit.

[1] Cf. The Creed *"Quicumque"* (MA II, 1354; DZ 39).

ARTICLE 5. *Whether There Are More Than Two Processions in God?*

We proceed thus to the Fifth Article: It would seem that there are more than two processions in God.

Objection 1. As knowledge and will are attributed to God, so is power. Therefore, if two processions exist in God, according to intellect and will, it seems that there must also be a third procession according to power.

Obj. 2. Further, goodness seems to be the greatest principle of procession, since goodness is said to be self-giving.[1] Therefore there must be a procession of goodness in God.

Obj. 3. Further, in God there is greater power of fecundity than in us. But in us there is not only one procession of the word, but there are many: for in us from one word proceeds another, and also from one love proceeds another. Therefore in God there are more than two processions.

On the contrary, In God there are not more than two who proceed—the Son and the Holy Ghost. Therefore there are in Him but two processions.

I answer that, The divine processions can be derived only from the actions which remain within the agent. In a nature which is intellectual, and in the divine nature these actions are two, to understand and to will. For to sense, which also appears to be an operation within the one sensing, is outside the intellectual nature, nor is it wholly removed from the genus of external actions; for the act of sensation is perfected by the action of the sensible upon sense. It follows that no other procession is possible in God but the procession of the Word, and of Love.

Reply Obj. 1. Power is the principle whereby one thing acts on another. Hence it is that external action points to power. Thus the divine power does not imply the procession of a divine person, but is indicated by the procession of creatures.

Reply Obj. 2. As Boëthius says (*De Hebdom.*),[2] goodness belongs to the essence and not to the operation, unless perhaps considered as the object of the will. Thus, as the divine processions must be denominated from certain actions, no other processions can be understood in God according to goodness and the like attributes except those of the Word and of love, according as God understands and loves His own essence, truth, and goodness.

[1] Cf. Dionysius, *De Div. Nom.,* IV, 20 (PG 3, 720).
[2] PL 64, 1314.

Reply Obj. 3. As above explained (QQ. XIV, A. 7, and XIX, A. 5), God understands all things by one simple act; and by one act also He wills all things. Hence there cannot exist in Him a procession of Word from Word, nor of Love from Love, for there is in Him only one perfect Word, and one perfect Love. And in this is manifested His perfect fecundity.

QUESTION XXVIII
THE DIVINE RELATIONS
(*In Four Articles*)

THE divine relations are next to be considered, in four points of inquiry: (1) Whether there are real relations in God? (2) Whether those relations are the divine essence itself, or are joined to it extrinsically? (3) Whether in God there can be several relations really distinct from each other? (4) The number of these relations.

ARTICLE 1. *Whether There Are Real Relations in God?*

We proceed thus to the First Article: It would seem that there are no real relations in God.

Objection 1. For Boëthius says (*De Trin.* IV),[3] "All possible predicaments used as regards the Godhead refer to the substance; for nothing can be predicated relatively." But whatever really exists in God can be predicated of Him. Therefore no real relation exists in God.

Obj. 2. Further, Boëthius says (*ibid.*) that, "Relation in the Trinity of the Father to the Son, and of both to the Holy Ghost, is the relation of the same to the same." But a relation of this kind is only a logical one; for every real relation requires and implies in reality two terms. Therefore the divine relations are not real relations, but are of the reason only.

Obj. 3. Further, the relation of paternity is the relation of a principle. But to say that God is the principle of creatures does not import any real relation, but only a logical one. Therefore paternity in God is not a real relation; and the same applies for the same reason to the other relations in God.

Obj. 4. Further, the divine generation is according to the procession of an intelligible word. But the relations following upon the operation of the intellect are logical relations. Therefore paternity and filiation in God, consequent upon generation, are only logical relations.

On the contrary, The Father is denominated only from paternity, and the Son only from filiation. Therefore, if no real paternity or filiation

[3] PL 64, 1253.

existed in God, it would follow that God is not really Father or Son, but only in our manner of understanding; and this is the Sabellian heresy.

I answer that, Relations exist in God really. In proof of this we may consider that only in things spoken of as having relation is found something which is only in reason and not in reality. This is not found in any other genus, since other genera, such as quantity and quality, according to their proper notion, signify something inherent in a subject. But relation in its own proper notion signifies only what refers to another. Such relation to another exists sometimes in the nature of things, as in those things which by their own very nature are ordered to each other, and have an inclination to each other, and such relations are necessarily real relations; as in a heavy body is found an inclination and order to the centre, and hence there exists in the heavy body a certain relation in regard to the centre; and the same applies to other things. Sometimes, however, this respect to another, signified by relation, is to be found only in the apprehension of reason comparing one thing to another, and this is a logical relation only; as, for instance, when reason compares man to animal as the species to the genus.

But when something proceeds from a principle of the same nature, then both the one proceeding and the source of procession agree in the same order; and then they have real relations to each other. Therefore as the divine processions are in the identity of the same nature, as above explained (Q. XXVII, A. 3, Ans. 2), these relations, which are considered according to the divine processions, are necessarily real relations.

Reply Obj. 1. Relationship is not predicated of God according to its proper notion, that is to say, in so far as its proper notion denotes comparison to that in which relation is inherent, but only as denoting respect to another. Nevertheless Boëthius did not wish to exclude relation in God but he wished to show that it was not to be predicated of Him as regards the mode of inherence in Himself in the strict notion of relation, but rather by way of relation to another.

Reply Obj. 2. The relation signified by the term "the same" is a logical relation only, if in regard to absolutely the same thing, because such a relation can exist only in a certain order observed by reason as regards the order of anything to itself, according to some two considerations of it. The case is otherwise, however, when things are called the same, not numerically, but generically or specifically. Thus Boëthius likens the divine relations to a relation of identity, not

in every respect, but only as regards the fact that the substance is not diversified by these relations, as neither is it by relation of identity.

Reply Obj. 3. As the creature proceeds from God in diversity of nature, God is outside the order of the whole creation, nor does any relation to the creature arise from His nature; for He does not produce the creature by necessity of His nature but by His intellect and will, as is above explained (QQ. XIV, A. 8, and XIX, A. 4). Therefore there is no real relation in God to the creature, whereas in creatures there is a real relation to God, because creatures are contained under the divine order, and their very nature entails dependence on God. On the other hand, the divine processions are in the same nature. Hence no parallel exists.

Reply Obj. 4. Relations which result in the things understood from the intellectual operation alone are logical relations only, since reason observes them as existing between two things understood. Those relations, however, which follow the operation of the intellect, and which exist between the word intellectually proceeding and the source whence it proceeds, are not logical relations only, but are real relations, since the intellect and the reason are real things, and are really related to that which proceeds from them intelligibly, just as a corporeal thing is related to that which proceeds from it corporeally. Thus paternity and filiation are real relations in God.

ARTICLE 2. *Whether Relation in God Is the Same as His Essence?*

We proceed thus to the Second Article: It would seem that the divine relation is not the same as the divine essence.

Objection 1. For Augustine says (*De Trin.* v, 5)[1] that "not all that is said of God is said of His substance, for we say some things relatively, as Father in respect of the Son: but such things do not refer to the substance." Therefore the relation is not the divine essence.

Obj. 2. Further, Augustine says (*De Trin.* viii)[2] that, "every relative expression is something besides the relation expressed, as master is a man, and slave is a man." Therefore, if relations exist in God, there must be something else besides relation in God. This can only be His essence. Therefore essence differs from relation.

Obj. 3. Further, the being of relation is the being referred to another, as the Philosopher says.[3] So if relation is the divine essence, it fol-

[1] PL 42, 914.   [2] PL 42, 935.
[3] *Categories,* 7 (8ᵃ39).

lows that the being of the divine essence is itself a relation to something else; but this is contrary to the perfection of the divine being, which is supremely absolute and self-subsisting (Q. III, A. 4). Therefore relation is not the divine essence.

On the contrary, Everything which is not the divine essence is a creature. But relation really belongs to God; and if it is not the divine essence, it is a creature, and it cannot claim the adoration of latria, contrary to what is sung in the Preface:[1] "Let us adore the distinction of the Persons, and the equality of their Majesty."

I answer that, It is reported that Gilbert de la Porrée[2] erred on this point, but revoked his error later at the council of Rheims.[3] For he said that the divine relations are assistant, or externally affixed.

To perceive the error here expressed, we must consider that in each of the nine genera of accidents there are two things to be considered. One is the being belonging to each one of them considered as an accident; and it commonly applies to each of them to be inherent in a subject, for the being of an accident is to inhere. The other thing to be considered in each one is the proper notion of each one of these genera. In the genera apart from that of relation, as in quantity and quality, even the proper notion of the genus itself is derived from a relation to the subject; for quantity is called the measure of substance, and quality is the disposition of substance. But the true notion of relation is not taken from its respect to that in which it is, but from its respect to something outside.

So if we consider even in creatures, relations as such, in that aspect they are said to be "assistant," and not intrinsically affixed, for they signify as it were a respect which affects the thing related according as it tends from that thing to something else; but if relation is considered as an accident, it inheres in a subject, and has an accidental being in it. Gilbert de la Porrée considered relation in the former mode only.

Now whatever has an accidental being in creatures, when considered as transferred to God, has a substantial being, for there is nothing which is as an accident in a subject in God, but whatever is in God is His essence. So, as regards that aspect by which relation has an accidental being in creatures, relation really existing in God has the being of the divine essence,

[1] Preface of the Most Holy Trinity.
[2] *In De Trin.* (PL 64,1292); *In De Praedicat. trium Pers.* (PL 64,1309).
[3] Cf. Bernard, *In Cant.*, Serm. LXXX (PL 183, 1170).

in no way distinct from it. But in so far as relation implies respect to something else, no reference to the essence is signified, but rather to its opposite term.

Thus it is manifest that relation really existing in God is really the same as His essence, and only differs according to mode of intelligibility, according as in relation is meant that regard to its opposite which is not expressed in the name of essence. Thus it is clear that in God relation and essence do not differ from each other, but are one and the same.

Reply Obj. 1. These words of Augustine do not imply that paternity or any other relation which is in God is not in its very being the same as the divine essence, but that it is not predicated under the mode of substance, as existing in Him to Whom it is applied, but as a relation. So there are said to be two predicaments only in God, since other predicaments import relation to that of which they are spoken, both in their generic and in their specific nature. But nothing that exists in God can have any relation to that wherein it exists, or of whom it is spoken, except the relation of identity; and this by reason of God's supreme simplicity.

Reply Obj. 2. As the relation which exists in creatures involves not only a regard to another, but also something absolute, so the same applies to God, yet not in the same way. What is found in the creature above and beyond what is contained in the meaning of relation is something else besides that relation; but in God there is no distinction, but both are one and the same; and this is not perfectly expressed by the word "relation," as if it were comprehended in the ordinary meaning of that term. For it was above explained (Q. XIII, A. 2), in treating of the divine names, that more is contained in the perfection of the divine essence than can be signified by any name. Hence it does not follow that there exists in God anything besides relation in reality, but only in the various names imposed by us.

Reply Obj. 3. If the divine perfection contained only what is signified by names that indicate relation, it would follow that it is imperfect, being thus related to something else; as in the same way, if nothing more were contained in it than what is signified by the word wisdom, it would not in that case be a subsistence. But as the perfection of the divine essence is greater than can be included in any name, it does not follow, if a relative term or any other name applied to God signify something imperfect, that the divine essence is in any way imperfect; for the divine essence comprehends within itself the perfection of every genus (Q. IV, A. 2).

ARTICLE 3. *Whether the Relations in God Are Really Distinguished from Each Other?*

We proceed thus to the Third Article: It would seem that the divine relations are not really distinguished from each other.

Objection 1. For things which are identified with the same, are identified with each other. But every relation in God is really the same as the divine essence. Therefore the relations are not really distinguished from each other.

Obj. 2. Further, as paternity and filiation are by name distinguished from the divine essence, so likewise are goodness and power. But this kind of distinction does not make any real distinction of the divine goodness and power. Therefore neither does it make any real distinction of paternity and filiation.

Obj. 3. Further, in God there is no real distinction but that of origin. But one relation does not seem to arise from another. Therefore the relations are not really distinguished from each other.

On the contrary, Boëthius says (*De Trin.*)[1] that "in God the substance contains the unity, and relation multiplies the trinity." Therefore, if the relations were not really distinguished from each other, there would be no real trinity in God, but only a trinity of reason, which is the error of Sabellius.[2]

I answer that, The attributing of anything to another involves the attribution likewise of whatever is contained in its notion. So when "man" is attributed to anyone, a rational nature is likewise attributed to him. The notion of relation, however, necessarily means respect of one to another, according as one is relatively opposed to another. So as in God there is a real relation (A. 1) there must also be a real opposition. The very notion of relative opposition includes distinction. Hence, there must be real distinction in God, not, indeed, according to that which is absolute—namely, essence, wherein there is supreme unity and simplicity—but according to that which is relative.

Reply Obj. 1. According to the Philosopher[3] this argument holds, that whatever things are identified with the same thing are identified with each other, if the identity be real and logical, as, for instance, a tunic and a garment but not if they differ logically. Hence in the same place he

says that although action is the same as motion, and likewise passion, still it does not follow that action and passion are the same because action implies reference as of something *from which* there is motion in the thing moved, whereas passion implies reference as of something *which is from* another. Likewise, although paternity, just as filiation, is really the same as the divine essence, nevertheless these two in their own proper notion and definitions import opposite respects. Hence they are distinguished from each other.

Reply Obj. 2. Power and goodness do not import any opposition in their respective notions, and hence there is no parallel argument.

Reply Obj. 3. Although relations, properly speaking, do not arise or proceed from each other, nevertheless they are considered as opposed according to the procession of one from another.

ARTICLE 4. *Whether in God There Are Only Four Real Relations—Paternity, Filiation, Spiration, and Procession?*

We proceed thus to the Fourth Article: It would seem that in God there are not only four real relations—paternity, filiation, spiration, and procession.

Objection 1. For it must be observed that in God there exist the relations of the intelligent agent to the thing understood, and of the one willing to the thing willed, which seem to be real relations not comprised under those above named. Therefore there are not only four real relations in God.

Obj. 2. Further, real relations in God are understood as coming from the intelligible procession of the Word. But intelligible relations are infinitely multiplied, as Avicenna says.[4] Therefore in God there exists an infinite number of real relations.

Obj. 3. Further, ideas in God are eternal (Q. XV, A. 2), and are only distinguished from each other by reason of their relation to things, as above stated (Q. XV, A. 2). Therefore in God there are many more eternal relations.

Obj. 4. Further, equality, and likeness, and identity are relations, and they are in God from eternity. Therefore several more relations are eternal in God than the above named.

Obj. 5. Further, it may also *on the contrary* be said that there are fewer relations in God than those above named. For, according to the Philosopher,[5] "It is the same way from Athens

---

[1] Chap. 6 (PL 64, 1255).
[2] See Augustine, *De Haeres.*, sect. 41 (PL 42, 32).
[3] *Physics*, III, 3 (202ᵃ13).

[4] *Meta.*, III, 10 (83va).
[5] *Physics*, III, 3 (202ᵇ13).

to Thebes, as from Thebes to Athens." By the same way of reasoning there is the same relation from the Father to the Son, that of paternity, and from the Son to the Father, that of filiation; and thus there are not four relations in God.

I answer that, According to the Philosopher,[1] every relation is based either on quantity, as double and half, or on action and passion, as the doer and the deed, the father and the son, the master and the servant, and the like. Now as there is no quantity in God, for He is great without quantity, as Augustine says,[2] it follows that a real relation in God can be based only on action. Such relations are not based on the actions of God according to any extrinsic procession, since the relations of God to creatures are not real in Him (A. 1, Ans. 3, Q. XIII, A. 7). Hence, it follows that real relations in God can be understood only in regard to those actions according to which there are internal, and not external, processions in God.

These processions are two only, as above expounded (Q. XXVII, A. 5), one derived from the action of the intellect, the procession of the Word, and the other from the action of the will, the procession of love. In respect of each of these processions two opposite relations arise. One of these is the relation of the person proceeding from the principle; the other is the relation of the principle Himself. The procession of the Word is called generation in the proper sense of the term, whereby it is applied to living things. Now the relation of the principle of generation in perfect living beings is called paternity, and the relation of the one proceeding from the principle is called filiation. But the procession of Love has no proper name of its own (Q. XXVII, A. 4), and so neither have the ensuing relations a proper name of their own. The relation of the principle of this procession is called spiration and the relation of the person proceeding is called procession, although these two names belong to the processions or origins themselves, and not to the relations.

Reply Obj. 1. In those things in which there is a difference between the intellect and its object and the will and its object, there can be a real relation, both of knowledge to the thing known and of the willer to the thing willed. In God, however, the intellect and what is understood are one and the same, because by understanding Himself God understands all other things; and the same applies to His will and what He wills. Hence it follows that in God

these kinds of relations are not real, as neither is the relation of a thing to itself. Nevertheless, the relation to the word is a real relation, because the word is understood as proceeding by an intelligible action and not as a thing understood. For when we understand a stone that which the intellect conceives from the thing understood is called the word.

Reply Obj. 2. Intelligible relations in ourselves are infinitely multiplied because a man understands a stone by one act, and by another act understands that he understands the stone, and again by another, understands that he understands this; thus the acts of understanding are infinitely multiplied, and consequently also the relations understood. This does not apply to God, since He understands all things by one act alone.

Reply Obj. 3. Ideal relations exist as understood by God. Hence it does not follow from their plurality that there are many relations in God, but that God knows many relations.

Reply Obj. 4. Equality and likeness in God are not real relations but are only logical relations (Q. XLII, A. 1, Ans. 1).

Reply Obj. 5. The way from one term to another and conversely is the same; nevertheless the mutual relations are not the same. Hence, we cannot conclude that the relation of the father to the son is the same as that of the son to the father; but we could conclude this of something absolute, if there were such between them.

QUESTION XXIX
THE DIVINE PERSONS
(In Four Articles)

HAVING taken up first what have appeared necessary notions concerning the processions and the relations, we must now approach the subject of the persons.

First, we shall consider the persons absolutely, and then comparatively as regards each other (Q. XXXIX). We must consider the persons absolutely first in common, and then singly. (Q. XXXIII).

The general consideration of the persons seemingly involves four points: (1) The signification of this word person; (2) the number of the persons (Q. XXX); (3) what is involved in the number of the persons, or is opposed thereto, as diversity, and likeness, and the like (Q. XXXI); (4) what belongs to our knowledge of the persons (Q. XXXII).

Four subjects of inquiry are comprised in the

---

[1] *Metaphysics,* v, 15 (1020ᵇ26).
[2] *Contra Epist. Manich.,* 15 (PL 42, 184).

first point: (1) The definition of person. (2) The comparison of person to essence, subsistence, and hypostasis. (3) Whether the name of person is becoming to God? (4) What does it signify in Him?

ARTICLE 1. *The Definition of "Person"*

We proceed thus to the First Article: It would seem that the definition of person given by Boëthius (*De Duab. Nat.*)[1] is insufficient—that is, "a person is an individual substance of a rational nature."

Objection 1. For nothing singular can be subject to definition. But person signifies something singular. Therefore person is improperly defined.

Obj. 2. Further, substance as placed above in the definition of person is either first substance or second substance. If it is the former, the word individual is superfluous, because first substance is individual substance; if it stands for second substance, the word individual is false, for there is contradiction of terms, since second substances are the genera or species. Therefore this definition is incorrect.

Obj. 3. Further, an intentional term must not be included in the definition of a thing. For to define a man as "a species of animal" would not be a correct definition, since man is the name of a thing, and species is a name of an intention. Therefore, since person is the name of a thing (for it signifies a substance of a rational nature), the word individual which is an intentional name comes improperly into the definition.

Obj. 4. Further, "Nature is the principle of motion and rest in those things in which it is essentially, and not accidentally," as Aristotle says.[2] But person exists in things immovable, as in God, and in the angels. Therefore the word nature ought not to enter into the definition of person, but the word should rather be essence.

Obj. 5. Further, the separated soul is an individual substance of the rational nature, but it is not a person. Therefore person is not properly defined as above.

I answer that, Although the universal and particular are found in every genus, nevertheless, in a certain special way, the individual is found in the genus of substance. For substance is individualized by itself, whereas the accidents are individualized by the subject, which is the substance, for this particular whiteness is called "this" because it exists in this particular subject.

And so it is reasonable that the individuals of the genus substance should have a special name of their own; for they are called *hypostases*,[3] or first substances.

Further still, in a more special and perfect way, the particular and the individual are found in rational substances which have dominion over their own actions, and which are not only made to act, like others, but which can act of themselves; for actions belong to singulars. Therefore also the singulars of the rational nature have also a special name even among other substances, and this name is person.

Thus the term "individual substance" is placed in the definition of person as signifying the singular in the genus of substance and the term "rational nature" is added, as signifying the singular in rational substances.

Reply Obj. 1. Although this or that singular may not be definable, yet what belongs to the common notion of singularity can be defined; and so the Philosopher[4] gives a definition of first substance, and in this way Boëthius defines person.

Reply Obj. 2. In the opinion of some,[5] the term substance in the definition of person stands for first substance, which is the hypostasis; nor is the term individual superfluously added, for by the name of hypostasis or first substance the idea of universality and of part is excluded. For we do not say that man in general is an hypostasis, nor that the hand is, since it is only a part. But where "individual" is added, the notion of being able to be assumed is excluded from person; for the human nature in Christ is not a person, since it is assumed by a greater—that is, by the Word of God. It is, however, better to say that substance is here taken in a general sense, as divided into first and second, and when "individual" is added, it is restricted to first substance.

Reply Obj. 3. Substantial differences being unknown to us, or at least unnamed by us, it is sometimes necessary to use accidental differences in the place of substantial; as, for example, we may say that fire is a simple, hot, and dry body, for proper accidents are the effects of substantial forms, and make them known. Likewise, terms expressive of intention can be used in defining things if used to signify things which are unnamed. And so the term "individual" is

---

[1] Chap. 3 (PL 64, 1343).
[2] *Physics,* II, 1 (192b21).

[3] Cf. Boëthius, *De Duabus Nat.,* 3 (PL 64, 1344).
[4] *Categories,* 5 (2a11).
[5] Richard of St. Victor, *De Trin.,* IV, 4 (PL 196, 932); chap. 20 (943); Also, Alexander of Hales, *Summa Theol.,* II, 387 (QR 1, 571).

placed in the definition of person to signify the mode of subsistence which belongs to particular substances.

Reply Obj. 4. According to the Philosopher[1] the word nature was first used to signify the "generation of living things," which is called nativity. And because this kind of generation comes from an intrinsic principle, this term is extended to signify the "intrinsic principle of any kind of movement." In this sense he defines "nature."[2] And since this kind of principle is either formal or material, both matter and form are commonly called nature. And as the essence of anything is completed by the form, so the essence of anything, signified by the definition, is commonly called nature. And here nature is taken in that sense. Hence Boëthius says (*loc. cit.*) that, "nature is the specific difference giving its form to each thing," for the specific difference completes the definition, and is derived from the proper form of a thing. So in the definition of person, which means the singular in a determined genus, it is more correct to use the term nature than essence, because the latter is taken from being, which is most common.

Reply Obj. 5. The soul is a part of the human species, and so, although it may exist in a separate state, yet since it ever retains its nature of unibility, it cannot be called an individual substance, which is the hypostasis or first substance, as neither can the hand nor any other part of man; thus neither the definition nor the name of person belongs to it.

ARTICLE 2. *Whether "Person" is the Same as Hypostasis, Subsistence, and Essence?*

We proceed thus to the Second Article: It would seem that person is the same as hypostasis, subsistence, and essence.

Objection 1. For Boëthius says (*De Duab. Nat.*)[3] that "the Greeks called the individual substance of the rational nature by the name hypostasis." But this with us signifies person. Therefore person is altogether the same as hypostasis.

Obj. 2. Further, just as we say there are three persons in God, so we say there are three subsistences in God, which implies that person and subsistence have the same meaning. Therefore person and subsistence mean the same.

Obj. 3. Further, Boëthius says (*Com. Præd.*)[4] that οὐσία, which is the same as essence, sig-

nifies a being composed of matter and form. Now, that which is composed of matter and form is the individual substance called *hypostasis* and *person*. Therefore all the aforesaid names seem to have the same meaning.

Obj. 4. *On the contrary,* Boëthius says (*De Duab. Nat.*)[5] that "genera and species only subsist; whereas individuals are not only subsistent, but also substand." But subsistences are so called from subsisting, as substance or hypostasis is so called from substanding. Therefore, since genera and species are not hypostases or persons, the latter are not the same as subsistences.

Obj. 5. Further, Boëthius says[6] that matter is called hypostasis, and form is called ὀυσιῶσις —that is, subsistence. But neither form nor matter can be called person. Therefore person differs from the others.

I answer that, According to the Philosopher[7] substance is spoken of in two ways. In one sense it means the quiddity of a thing, signified by its definition, and thus we say that the definition means the substance of a thing; in this sense substance is called by the Greek οὐσία, which we may call essence. In another sense substance means a subject or suppositum, which subsists in the genus of substance. To this, taken in a general sense, can be applied a name expressive of an intention; and thus it is called the suppositum. It is also called by three names signifying a reality—that is, "a thing of nature," "subsistence," and "hypostasis," according to a threefold consideration of the substance thus named. For, as it exists in itself and not in another, it is called subsistence; as we say that those things subsist which exist in themselves, and not in another. As it underlies some common nature, it is called a thing of nature; as, for instance, this particular man is a human natural thing. As it underlies the accidents, it is called hypostasis, or substance. What these three names signify in common to the whole genus of substances, this name person signifies in the genus of rational substances.

Reply Obj. 1. Among the Greeks, the term hypostasis, taken in the proper meaning of the word, signifies any individual of the genus substance; but in the usual way of speaking, it means the individual of the rational nature, by reason of the excellence of that nature.

Reply Obj. 2. As we say three persons plurally

---

[1] *Metaphysics,* v, 4 (1014^{b}16).
[2] *Physics,* II, 1 (192^{b}14).
[3] Chap. 3 (PL 64, 184).
[4] *In Cat. Arist.,* Bk. I, chap. *De subst.* (PL 64, 184).

[5] Chap. 3 (PL 64, 1344).
[6] *In Cat. Arist.,* (*loc. cit.*); cf. Albert the Great, *Sent.,* I, d. XXIII, A. 4 (BO XXV, 591).
[7] *Metaphysics,* v, 8 (1017^{b}23).

in God, and three subsistences, so the Greeks say three hypostases. But because the word substance, which, properly speaking, corresponds in meaning to hypostasis, is used among us in an equivocal sense, since it sometimes means essence, and sometimes means hypostasis, in order to avoid any occasion of error, it was thought preferable to use subsistence for hypostasis, rather than substance.

Reply Obj. 3. Strictly speaking, the essence is what is expressed by the definition. Now, the definition comprises the principles of the species but not the individual principles. Hence in things composed of matter and form, the essence signifies not only the form, nor only the matter, but what is composed of matter and the common form, as the principles of the species. But what is composed of this matter and this form has the nature of hypostasis and person. For soul, flesh, and bone belong to the notion of man; but this soul, this flesh, and this bone belong to the notion of this man. Therefore hypostasis and person add the individual principles to the notion of essence; nor are these identified with the essence in things composed of matter and form, as we said above when treating of divine simplicity (Q. III, A. 3).

Reply Obj. 4. Boëthius says[1] that genera and species subsist, inasmuch as it belongs to some individual things to subsist, from the fact that they belong to genera and species comprehended in the predicament of substance, but not because the species and genera themselves subsist (except in the opinion of Plato, who asserted that the species of things subsisted separately from singular things). To substand, however, belongs to the same individual things in relation to the accidents, which are outside the notion of genera and species.

Reply Obj. 5. The individual composed of matter and form substands in relation to accident from the very nature of matter. Hence Boëthius says (*De Trin.*):[2] "A simple form cannot be a subject." Its self-subsistence is derived from the nature of its form, which does not supervene to the things subsisting, but gives actual being to the matter, and thus it is able to subsist as an individual. On this account, therefore, he ascribes hypostasis to matter, and ὀυσίωσις, or subsistence, to the form. because the matter is the principle of substanding, and the form is the principle of subsisting.

<hr />

[1] *In Porphyrium*, Bk. 1. "*Mox de generibus,*" etc. (PL 64, 85).
[2] Chap. 2 (PL 64, 1250).

ARTICLE 3. *Whether the Word "Person" Should Be Said of God?*

We proceed thus to the Third Article: It would seem that the name person should not be said of God.

Objection 1. For Dionysius says (*Div. Nom.* i):[3] "No one should ever dare to say or think anything of the supersubstantial and hidden Divinity beyond what has been divinely expressed to us by the sacred oracles." But the name person is not expressed to us in the Old or New Testament. Therefore person is not to be applied to God.

Obj. 2. Further, Boëthius says (*De Duab. Nat.*):[4] "The word person seems to be taken from those persons who represented men in comedies and tragedies. For person comes from sounding through (*personando*), since a greater volume of sound is produced through the cavity in the mask. These 'persons' or masks the Greeks called πρόσωπα, as they were placed on the face and covered the features before the eyes." This, however, can apply to God only in a metaphorical sense. Therefore the word person is only applied to God metaphorically.

Obj. 3. Further, every person is a hypostasis. But the word hypostasis does not apply to God, since, as Boëthius says (*ibid.*), it signifies what is the subject of accidents, which do not exist in God. Jerome also says (*Ep. ad Damas.*)[5] that, "in this word hypostasis, poison lurks in honey." Therefore the word person should not be said of God.

Obj. 4. Further, if a definition is denied of anything, the thing defined is also denied of it. But the definition of person, as given above (A. 1), does not apply to God. Both because reason implies a discursive knowledge, which does not apply to God, as we proved above (Q. XIV, A. 7), and thus God cannot be said to have a rational nature. And also because God cannot be called an individual substance, since the principle of individuation is matter, while God is immaterial; nor is He the subject of accidents, so as to be called a substance. Therefore the word person ought not to be attributed to God.

On the contrary, In the Creed of Athanasius we say:[6] "One is the person of the Father, another of the Son, another of the Holy Ghost."

I answer that, Person signifies what is most perfect in all nature—that is, a subsistent in-

<hr />

[3] Chap. 1. Sect. 1 (PG 3, 588).
[4] Chap. 3 (PL 64, 1344).
[5] *Epist.*, xv (PL 22, 357).
[6] Cf. Creed "*Quicumque*" (MA II, 1354; DZ 39).

dividual of a rational nature. Hence, since everything that is perfect must be attributed to God; because His essence contains every perfection, this name person is fittingly applied to God; not, however, as it is applied to creatures, but in a more excellent way; as other names also, which, while giving them to creatures, we attribute to God, as we showed above when treating of the names of God (Q. XIII, A. 2).

Reply Obj. 1. Although the word person is not found applied to God in Scripture, either in the Old or New Testament, nevertheless what the word signifies is found to be affirmed of God in many places of Scripture; as for instance that He is the supreme self-subsisting being, and the most perfectly intelligent being. If we could speak of God only in the very terms themselves of Scripture, it would follow that no one could speak about God in any but the original language of the Old or New Testament. The urgency of confuting heretics made it necessary to find new words to express the ancient faith about God. Nor is such a kind of novelty to be shunned, since it is by no means profane, for it does not lead us astray from the sense of Scripture, though the Apostle warns us to avoid *profane novelties of words* (I Tim. 6. 20).

Reply Obj. 2. Although this name person may not belong to God as regards the origin of the term, nevertheless it especially belongs to God as to its meaning. For as famous men were represented in comedies and tragedies, the name person was given to signify those who held high dignity. Hence, those who held high rank in the Church came to be called persons. Thence by some [1] the definition of person is given as "hypostasis distinct by reason of dignity." And because subsistence in a rational nature is of high dignity, therefore every individual of the rational nature is called a person, as we have said (A. 1). Now the dignity of the divine nature excels every other dignity, and thus the name person pre-eminently belongs to God.

Reply Obj. 3. The word hypostasis does not apply to God as regards its source of origin, since He does not underlie accidents; but it applies to Him in so far as it is imposed to signify the subsistence. Jerome said that "poison lurks in this word" because before it was fully known by the Latins the heretics used this term to deceive the simple, to make people profess many essences as they profess several hypostases, since the word substance, which corresponds to hypostasis in Greek, is commonly taken amongst us to mean essence.

[1] Alan of Lille, *Theol. Reg.*, 32 (PL 210, 637).

Reply Obj. 4. It may be said that God has a rational nature, if reason be taken to mean not discursive thought, but, in a general sense, an intelligent nature. But God cannot be called an individual in the sense that individuality comes from matter, but only in the sense which implies incommunicability. Substance can be applied to God in the sense of signifying self-subsistence. There are some,[2] however, who say that the definition of Boëthius, quoted above (A. 1), is not a definition of person in the sense we use when speaking of persons in God. Therefore Richard of St. Victor amends this definition by adding that Person in God is "the incommunicable existence of the divine nature."

ARTICLE 4. *Whether This Word "Person" Signifies Relation?*

We proceed thus to the Fourth Article: It would seem that this word person, as applied to God, does not signify relation, but substance.

Objection 1. For Augustine says (*De Trin.* vii, 6):[3] "When we speak of the person of the Father, we mean nothing else but the substance, for person is said in regard to Himself, and not in regard to the Son."

Obj. 2. Further, the interrogation "What?" refers to the essence. But, as Augustine says:[4] When we say there are three who bear witness in heaven, the Father, the Word, and the Holy Ghost, and it is asked, Three what? the answer is, Three persons. Therefore person signifies essence.

Obj. 3. According to the Philosopher[5] the meaning of a word is its definition. But the definition of person is this: "The individual substance of the rational nature," as above stated (A.1). Therefore person signifies substance.

Obj. 4. Further, person in men and angels does not signify relation, but something absolute. Therefore, if in God it signified relation, it would bear an equivocal meaning in God, in man, and in angels.

On the contrary, Boëthius says (*De Trin.*)[6] that "every word that refers to the persons signifies relation." But no word belongs to person more strictly than the very word person itself. Therefore this word person signifies relation.

I answer that, A difficulty arises concerning the meaning of this word person in God[7] from

[2] Richard of St. Victor, *De Trin.*, IV. 21 (PL 196, 945).
[3] PL 42, 943.
[4] *De Trin.*, VII, 4 (PL 42, 940).
[5] *Metaphysics*, IV, 7 (1012ᵃ23).
[6] Chap. 6 (PL 64, 1254).
[7] Cf. Richard Fishacre, *In Sent.*, I, d. 25, in Bergeron, EHLD II, p. 149.

the fact that it is predicated plurally of the Three in contrast to the nature of the names belonging to the essence; nor does it in itself refer to another, as do the words which express relation.

Hence some[1] have thought that this word person of itself expresses absolutely the divine essence, as this name God and this word Wise, but that to meet heretical attack, it was ordained by conciliar decree that it was to be taken in a relative sense, and especially in the plural, or with the addition of a distinguishing adjective; as when we say, "Three persons," or, "one is the person of the Father, another of the Son," etc. Used, however, in the singular, it may be either absolute or relative. But this does not seem to be a satisfactory explanation; for, if this word person by force of its own signification expresses the divine essence only, it follows that since we speak of three persons, so far from the heretics being silenced, they had still more reason to argue. Seeing this, others[2] maintained that this word person in God signifies both the essence and the relation. Some of these said[3] that it signifies directly the essence, and relation indirectly, forasmuch as *person* means as it were *by itself one (per se una)*; and unity belongs to the essence. And what is *by itself* implies relation indirectly; for the Father is understood to exist *by Himself*, as by relation distinct from the Son. Others, however, said,[4] on the contrary, that it signifies relation directly, and essence indirectly, because in the definition of "person" the term nature is mentioned indirectly; and these come nearer to the truth.

To determine the question, we must consider that something may be included in the meaning of a less common term which is not included in the more common term; as rational is included in the meaning of man, and not in the meaning of animal. So that it is one thing to ask the meaning of the word animal, and another to ask its meaning when the animal in question is a man. Also, it is one thing to ask the meaning of this word person in general, and another to ask the meaning of person as applied to God. For person in general signifies the individual substance of a rational nature as we have said (A. 1). The individual is what is in itself is undivided, but is distinct from others. Therefore person in any nature signifies what is distinct in

that nature; thus in human nature it signifies this flesh, these bones, and this soul, which are the individuating principles of a man, and which though not belonging to the meaning of person, nevertheless do belong to the meaning of a human person.

Now distinction in God is only by relation of origin, as stated above (Q. XXVIII, A. 3), while relation in God is not as an accident in a subject, but is the divine essence itself, and so it is subsistent, for the divine essence subsists. Therefore, as the Godhead is God, so the divine paternity is God the Father, Who is a divine person. Therefore a divine person signifies a relation as subsisting.

And this is to signify relation by way of substance, and such a relation is a hypostasis subsisting in the divine nature, although that which subsists in the divine nature is the divine nature itself. Thus it is true to say that the name person signifies relation directly, and the essence indirectly; not, however, the relation as such, but as expressed by way of a hypostasis. So likewise it signifies directly the essence, and indirectly the relation, since the essence is the same as the hypostasis; but in God the hypostasis is expressed as distinct by the relation, and thus relation, as such, enters into the notion of the person indirectly.

Thus we can say that this signification of the word person was not clearly perceived before it was attacked by heretics. Hence, this word person was used just as any other absolute term. But afterwards it was applied to express relation, as it lent itself to that signification, so that this word person means relation not only by use and custom, according to the first opinion, but also by force of its own signification.

Reply Obj. 1. This word person is said in respect to itself, not to another, since it signifies relation not as such, but by way of a substance —which is a hypostasis. In that sense Augustine says that it signifies the essence, since in God essence is the same as the hypostasis, because in God what He is, and that by which He is are the same.

Reply Obj. 2. The term "what" refers sometimes to the nature expressed by the definition, as when we ask, What is man? and we answer, A mortal rational animal. Sometimes it refers to the suppositum, as when we ask, What swims in the sea? and answer, A fish. So to those who ask, Three what? we answer, Three persons.

Reply Obj. 3. In God the individual—that is, distinct and incommunicable substance—includes the idea of relation, as above explained.

---

[1] Augustine, *De Trin.*, VII, 5 (PL 42, 943); *Summa Sent.*, (anon.), tr. I, chap. 9 (PL 176, 56).

[2] Peter Lombard, *Sent.*, I, d. 25, chap. 2 (QR I, 159).

[3] Simon of Tournai, *Sent.*, in Schmaus, RTAM (1932) p. 62.

[4] William of Auxerre, *Summa Aurea*, Pt. I, tr. 6, chap. 3 (fol. 11a).

Reply Obj. 4. The different sense of the less common term does not produce equivocation in the more common. Although a horse and an ass have their own proper definitions, nevertheless they agree univocally in animal, because the common definition of animal applies to both. So it does not follow that although relation is contained in the signification of divine person but not in that of an angelic or of a human person, that the word person is used in an equivocal sense. Though neither is it applied univocally, since nothing can be said univocally of God and creatures (Q. XIII, A. 5).

QUESTION XXX
THE PLURALITY OF PERSONS IN GOD
(*In Four Articles*)

WE are now led to consider the plurality of the persons; about which there are four points of inquiry: (1) Whether there are several persons in God? (2) How many are they? (3) What the numeral terms signify in God? (4) The community of the term person.

ARTICLE 1. *Whether There Are Several Persons in God?*

We proceed thus to the First Article: It would seem that there are not several persons in God.

Objection 1. For person is the individual substance of a rational nature. If then there are several persons in God, there must be several substances, which appears to be heretical.

Obj. 2. Further, Plurality of absolute properties does not make a distinction of persons, either in God, or in ourselves. Much less therefore is this effected by a plurality of relations. But in God there is no plurality but of relations (Q. XXVIII, A. 3). Therefore there cannot be several persons in God.

Obj. 3. Further, Boëthius says of God (*De Trin.* III),[1] that "this is truly one which has no number." But plurality implies number. Therefore there are not several persons in God.

Obj. 4. Further, where number is, there is whole and part. Thus, if in God there exist a number of persons, there must be whole and part in God, which is inconsistent with the divine simplicity.

On the contrary, Athanasius says:[2] "One is the person of the Father, another of the Son, another of the Holy Ghost." Therefore the Father, and the Son, and the Holy Ghost are several persons.

---

[1] PL 64, 1251.
[2] Creed "*Quicumque*," (MA II, 1354; DZ 39).

I answer that, It follows from what precedes that there are several persons in God. For it was shown above (Q. XXIX, A. 4) that this word person signifies in God a relation as subsisting in the divine nature. It was also established (Q. XXVIII, AA. 1, 3, 4) that there are several real relations in God; and hence it follows that there are also several realities subsistent in the divine nature, which means that there are several persons in God.

Reply Obj. 1. The definition of person includes substance, not as meaning the essence, but the suppositum which is made clear by the addition of the term individual. To signify the substance thus understood, the Greeks use the name hypostasis. So, as we say "Three persons," they say "Three hypostases." We are not, however, accustomed to say Three substances, lest we be understood to mean three essences or natures, by reason of the equivocal signification of the term.

Reply Obj. 2. The absolute properties in God, such as goodness and wisdom, are not opposed to one another; and hence, neither are they really distinguished from each other. Therefore, although they subsist, nevertheless they are not several subsistent realities—that is, several persons. But the absolute properties in creatures do not subsist, although they are really distinguished from each other, as whiteness and sweetness; on the other hand, the relative properties in God subsist, and are really distinguished from each other (Q. XXVIII, A. 3; Q. XXIX, A. 4). Hence the plurality of such properties suffices for the plurality of persons in God.

Reply Obj. 3. The supreme unity and simplicity of God exclude every kind of plurality of absolute things, but not plurality of relations, which are predicated of something as having relation to something else, and thus the relations do not import composition in that of which they are predicated, as Boëthius teaches in the same book.

Reply Obj. 4. Number is twofold, namely, simple or absolute, as two and three and four, and number as existing in things numbered, as two men and two horses. So, if number in God is taken absolutely or abstractly, there is nothing to prevent whole and part from being in Him, and thus number in Him is only in our way of understanding, because number regarded apart from things numbered exists only in the intellect. But if number be taken as it is in the things numbered, in that sense, as existing in creatures, one is part of two, and two of three as one man is part of two men and two of three; but in this way it does not apply to God, because the Father is of the same magnitude as the whole Trinity, as we shall show further on (Q. XLII, A. 4, Ans. 3).

ARTICLE 2. *Whether There Are More Than Three Persons in God?*

We proceed thus to the Second Article: It would seem that there are more than three persons in God.

Objection 1. For the plurality of persons in God arises from the plurality of the relative properties as stated above (A. 1). But there are four relations in God as stated above (Q. XXVIII, A. 4), paternity, sonship, common spiration, and procession. Therefore there are four persons in God.

Obj. 2. The nature of God does not differ from His will more than from His intellect. But in God, one person proceeds from the will as Love, and another proceeds from His nature as Son. Therefore another proceeds from His intellect as Word, besides the one Who proceeds from His nature as Son; thus again it follows that there are not only three persons in God.

Obj. 3. Further, the more perfect a creature is, the more interior operations it has; as a man has understanding and will beyond other animals. But God infinitely excels every creature. Therefore in God not only is there a person proceeding from the will and another from the intellect, but also in an infinite number of ways. Therefore there are an infinite number of persons in God.

Obj. 4. Further, it is from the infinite goodness of the Father that He communicates Himself infinitely in the production of a divine person. But there is infinite goodness also in the Holy Ghost. Therefore the Holy Ghost produces a divine person, and that person another, and so to infinity.

Obj. 5. Further, everything within a determinate number is measured, for number is a measure. But the divine persons are immense, as we say in the Creed of Athanasius[1]: "The Father is immense, the Son is immense, the Holy Ghost is immense." Therefore the persons are not contained within the number three.

On the contrary, It is said: *There are three who bear witness in heaven, the Father, the Word, and the Holy Ghost* (I John 5. 7). To those who ask, "Three what?" we, answer, with Augustine (*De Trin.* vii, 4),[2] "Three persons." Therefore there are but three persons in God.

[1] MA II, 1354; DZ 39.
[2] PL 42, 940.

I answer that, As was explained above, there can be only three persons in God. For it was shown above (A. 1) that the several persons are the several subsisting relations really distinct from each other. But a real distinction between the divine relations can come only from relative opposition. Therefore two opposite relations must refer to two persons, and if any relations are not opposite, they must belong to the same person. Since then paternity and sonship are opposite relations, they belong necessarily to two persons. Therefore the subsisting paternity is the person of the Father, and the subsisting sonship is the person of the Son. The other two relations are not opposed to either of these, but they are opposed to each other. Therefore these two cannot belong to one person. Hence either one of them must belong to both of the aforesaid persons, or one must belong to one person, and the other to the other. Now, procession cannot belong to the Father and the Son, or to either of them; for thus it would follow that the procession of the intellect, which in God is generation, from which paternity and sonship are derived, would issue from the procession of love, from which spiration and procession are derived, if the person generating and the person generated proceeded from the person spirating; and this is against what was laid down above (Q. XXVII, A. 3, Ans. 3). We must consequently admit that spiration belongs to the person of the Father, and to the person of the Son since it has no relative opposition either to paternity or to sonship; and consequently that procession belongs to the other person who is called the person of the Holy Ghost, who proceeds by way of love, as above explained (Q. XXVII, A. 4). Therefore only three persons exist in God, the Father, the Son, and the Holy Ghost.

Reply Obj. 1. Although there are four relations in God, one of them, spiration, is not separated from the person of the Father and of the Son, but belongs to both; thus, although it is a relation, it is not called a property, because it does not belong to only one person, nor is it a personal relation—that is, constituting a person. The three relations—paternity, sonship, and procession—are called personal properties, constituting as it were the persons; for paternity is the person of the Father, sonship is the person of the Son, procession is the person of the Holy Ghost proceeding.

Reply Obj. 2. That which proceeds by way of intellect, as word, proceeds according to likeness, as also that which proceeds by way of nature; thus, as above explained (Q. XXVII, A. 2; Q. XXVIII, A. 4), the procession of the divine Word is the same as generation by way of nature. But love, as such, does not proceed as the likeness of that from which it proceeds, although in God love is co-essential as being divine. And therefore the procession of love is not called generation in God.

Reply Obj. 3. As man is more perfect than other animals, he has more intrinsic operations than other animals, because his perfection is something composite. Hence the angels, who are more perfect and more simple, have fewer intrinsic operations than man, for they have no imagination, or feeling, or the like. In God there exists only one real operation—that is, His essence. How there are in Him two processions was above explained (Q. XXVII, AA. 3, 5).

Reply Obj. 4. This argument would prove if the Holy Ghost possessed another goodness apart from the goodness of the Father; for then if the Father produced a divine person by His goodness, the Holy Ghost also would do so. But the Father and the Holy Ghost have one and the same goodness. Nor is there any distinction between them except by the personal relations. So goodness belongs to the Holy Ghost, as derived from another, and it belongs to the Father as the principle of its communication to another. The opposition of relation does not allow the relation of the Holy Ghost to be joined with the relation of principle of another divine person, because He Himself proceeds from the other persons who are in God.

Reply Obj. 5. A determinate number if taken as a simple number existing in the intellect only, is measured by one. But when we speak of a number of things in the persons in God, the notion of measure has no place, because the magnitude of the three persons is the same (Q. XLII, AA. 1, 4), and the same is not measured by the same.

ARTICLE 3. *Whether the Numeral Terms Denote Anything Real in God?*

We proceed thus to the Third Article: It would seem that the numeral terms denote something real in God.

Objection 1. For the divine unity is the divine essence. But every number is unity repeated. Therefore every numeral term in God signifies the essence; and therefore it denotes something real in God.

Obj. 2. Further, whatever is said of God and of creatures belongs to God in a more eminent manner than to creatures. But the numeral terms denote something real in creatures. Therefore much more so in God.

Obj. 3. Further, if the numeral terms do not denote anything real in God, and are introduced simply in a removing sense, as plurality removes unity, and unity plurality, it follows that a vicious circle results, confusing the intellect and obscuring the truth; and this ought not to be. Therefore it must be said that the numeral terms denote something real in God.

On the contrary, Hilary says (*De Trin.* iv):[1] "If we admit companionship"—that is, plurality —"we exclude the idea of oneness and of solitude"; and Ambrose says (*De Fide.* i)[2] that when we say one God, unity excludes plurality of gods, and does not imply quantity in God. Hence we see that these terms are applied to God in order to remove something, and not to denote anything positive.

I answer that, The Master (*Sent.* i. D. 24)[3] considers that the numeral terms do not denote anything positive in God, but only take away something. Others, however, assert the contrary.[4]

In order to resolve this point, we may observe that all plurality follows on some division. Now division is twofold. One is material, and is division of the continuous; from this results number, which is a species of quantity. Number in this sense is found only in material things which have quantity. The other kind of division is called formal, and is effected by opposite or diverse forms, and this kind of division results in a multitude, which does not belong to a genus, but is transcendental in the sense in which being is divided by one and by many. This kind of multitude only is found in immaterial things.

Some, considering only that multitude which is a species of discrete quantity, and seeing that such kind of quantity has no place in God, asserted that the numeral terms do not denote anything real in God, but remove something from Him.[5] Others,[6] considering the same kind of multitude, said that as knowledge exists in God according to the proper sense of the word, but not in the sense of its genus (as in God there is no such thing as a quality), so number exists in God in the proper sense of number, but not in the sense of its genus, which is quantity.

[1] PL 10, 111.

[2] Chap. 2 (PL 16, 555).

[3] Peter Lombard (QR 1, 153).

[4] Bonaventure (*In Sent.*, 1, d. 24, A. 2, Q. 1, concl.—QR 1, 426) says that this opinion was generally rejected at Paris.

[5] Peter Lombard, *Sent.*, 1, d. 24 (QR 1, 154).

[6] The general opinion at Paris.

But we say that numeral terms predicated of God are not derived from number which is a species of quantity, for in that sense they could bear only a metaphorical sense in God, like other corporeal properties, such as length, breadth, and the like, but that they are taken from multitude in a transcendent sense. Now multitude so understood has relation to the many of which it is predicated as one convertible with being is related to being, which kind of oneness does not add anything to being except a negation of division, as we saw when treating of the divine unity (Q. XI, A. I); for one signifies undivided being. So, of whatever we say "one," we imply its undivided reality; thus, for instance, "one" applied to man signifies the undivided nature or substance of a man. In the same way, when we speak of many things, multitude in this latter sense points to those things as being each undivided in itself. But number if taken as a species of quantity denotes an accident added to being, as also does one which is the principle of that number.

Therefore the numeral terms in God signify the things of which they are said, and beyond this they add negation only, as stated (*loc. cit.*), in which respect the Master was right (*loc. cit.*). So when we say the essence is one, the term one signifies the essence undivided; and when we say the person is one, it signifies the person undivided; and when we say the persons are many, we signify those persons, and their individual undividedness; for it is of the very notion of multitude that it should be composed of units.

Reply Obj. 1. One, as it is a transcendental, is more general than substance and relation. And so likewise is multitude. Hence in God it may mean both substance and relation, according to the context. Still, the very signification of such names adds a negation of division, beyond substance and relation, as was explained above.

Reply Obj. 2. Multitude, which denotes something real in creatures, is a species of quantity, and cannot be used when speaking of God; unlike transcendental multitude, which adds only indivision to those of which it is predicated. Such a kind of multitude is applicable to God.

Reply Obj. 3. One does not exclude multitude, but division, which logically precedes one or multitude. Multitude does not remove unity, but division from each of the individuals which compose the multitude. This was explained when we treated of the divine unity (Q. XI, A. 2, Ans. 4).

It must be observed, nevertheless, that the authorities brought in on the opposite side do not sufficiently prove the point advanced. Although the idea of solitude is excluded by plurality, and the plurality of gods by unity, it does not follow that these terms express this signification alone. For blackness is excluded by whiteness; yet nevertheless the term whiteness does not signify the mere exclusion of blackness.

ARTICLE 4. *Whether This Term "Person" Can Be Common to the Three Persons?*

We proceed thus to the Fourth Article: It would seem that this term person cannot be common to the three persons.

Objection 1. For nothing is common to the three persons but the essence. But this term person does not signify the essence directly. Therefore it is not common to all three.

Obj. 2. Further, the common is the opposite to the incommunicable. But the very meaning of person is that it is incommunicable, as appears from the definition given by Richard of St. Victor (Q. XXIX, A. 3, Ans. 4). Therefore this term person is not common to all the three persons.

Obj. 3. Further, if the name person is common to the three, it is common either really or logically. But it is not so really; otherwise the three persons would be one person. Nor again is it so logically; otherwise person would be a universal. But in God there is neither universal nor particular, neither genus nor species, as we proved above (Q. III, A. 5). Therefore this term person is not common to the three.

On the contrary, Augustine says (*De Trin.* vii, 4)[1] that when as ask, "Three what?" we say, "Three persons," because what a person is, is common to them.

I answer that, The very mode of expression itself shows that this term person is common to the three when we say three persons; for when we say three men we show that man is common to the three. Now it is clear that this is not community of a real thing, as if one essence were common to the three; otherwise there would be only one person of the three, as also one essence.

What is meant by such a community has been variously determined by those who have examined the subject. Some[2] have called it a community of negation, because the definition of person contains the word incommunicable. Others[3] thought it to be a community of intention, as the definition of person contains the word individual; as we say that to be a species is com-

---

[1] PL 42, 940.
[2] William of Auxerre, *Summa Aurea*, 1, 6, 2 (fol. 10c).
[3] See Alexander of Hales, *S.T.*, 11, 389 (QR 1, 573).

mon to horse and ox. Both of these explanations, however, are excluded by the fact that person is not a name of exclusion nor of intention, but the name of a reality.

We must therefore say that even in human things this name person is common by a community of notion not as genus or species, but as a vague individual thing. The names of genera and species, as man or animal, are given to signify the common natures themselves, but not the intentions of those common natures, signified by the terms genus or species. The vague individual thing, as "some man," signifies the common nature with the determinate mode of being of singular things—that is, something self-subsisting distinct from others. But the name of a designated singular thing signifies that which distinguishes the determinate thing; as the name Socrates signifies this flesh and this bone. But there is this difference—that the term "some man" signifies the nature, or the individual on the part of its nature, with the mode of existence of singular things, while this name person is not given to signify the individual on the part of the nature, but the subsistent reality in that nature. Now this is common in idea to the divine persons, that each of them subsists distinctly from the others in the divine nature. Thus this name person is common in idea to the three divine persons.

Reply Obj. 1. This argument is founded on a real community.

Reply Obj. 2. Although person is incommunicable, yet the mode itself of incommunicable existence can be common to many.

Reply Obj. 3. Although this community is logical and not real, yet it does not follow that in God there is universal or particular, or genus, or species; both because neither in human affairs is the community of person the same as community of genus or species, and because the divine persons have one being, whereas genus and species and every other universal are predicated of many which differ in being.

QUESTION XXXI
Of what belongs to the unity or plurality in God
(In Four Articles)

We now consider what belongs to the unity or plurality in God, which gives rise to four points of inquiry: (1) Concerning the word Trinity. (2) Whether we can say that the Son is other than the Father? (3) Whether an exclusive term, which seems to exclude otherness, can be joined to an essential name in God? (4) Whether it can be joined to a personal term?

Article 1. *Whether There Is Trinity in God?*

We proceed thus to the First Article: It seems there is not trinity in God.

Objection 1. For every name in God signifies substance or relation. But this name Trinity does not signify the substance; otherwise it would be predicated of each one of the persons. Nor does it signify relation, for it does not express a name that refers to another. Therefore the word Trinity is not to be applied to God.

Obj. 2. Further, this word trinity is a collective term, since it signifies multitude. But such a word does not apply to God, since the unity of a collective name is the least of unities, while in God there exists the greatest possible unity. Therefore this word trinity does not apply to God.

Obj. 3. Further, every triple is threefold. But in God there is no triplicity, since triplicity is a kind of inequality. Therefore neither is there trinity in God.

Obj. 4. Further, all that exists in God exists in the unity of the divine essence, because God is His own essence. Therefore, if Trinity exists in God, it exists in the unity of the divine essence; and thus in God there would be three essential unities, which is heresy.

Obj. 5. Further, in all that is said of God, the concrete is predicated of the abstract; for Deity is God and paternity is the Father. But the Trinity cannot be called triple; otherwise there would be nine realities in God, which is erroneous. Therefore the word trinity is not to be applied to God.

On the contrary, Athanasius says:[1] "Unity in Trinity, and Trinity in Unity is to be revered."

I answer that, The name Trinity in God signifies the determinate number of persons. And so the plurality of persons in God requires that we should use the word trinity, because what is indeterminately signified by plurality is signified by trinity in a determinate manner.

Reply Obj. 1. In its etymological sense, this word Trinity seems to signify the one essence of the three persons, according as trinity may mean trine-unity. But in the strict meaning of the term it rather signifies the number of persons of one essence. And on this account we cannot say that the Father is the Trinity, as He is not three persons. Yet it does not mean the relations themselves of the Persons, but rather the number of persons related to each other. And hence

[1] Creed *"Quicumque"* (MA II, 1355, DZ 39).

it is that the word in itself does not express regard to another.

Reply Obj. 2. Two things are implied in a collective term, plurality of the supposita, and a unity of some kind, namely of some order. For people is a multitude of men comprehended under a certain order. In the first sense, this word trinity is like other collective words; but in the second sense it differs from them, because in the divine Trinity not only is there unity of order, but also with this there is unity of essence.

Reply Obj. 3. Trinity is taken in an absolute sense, for it signifies the threefold number of persons. Triplicity signifies a proportion of inequality; for it is a species of unequal proportion, according to Boëthius (*Arithm.* i, 23).[1] Therefore in God there is not triplicity, but Trinity.

Reply Obj. 4. In the divine Trinity is to be understood both number and the persons numbered. So when we say, "Trinity in Unity," we do not place number in the unity of the essence, as if we meant three times one, but we place the Persons numbered in the unity of nature, just as the supposita of a nature are said to exist in that nature. On the other hand, we say "Unity in Trinity," meaning that the nature is in its supposita.

Reply Obj. 5. When we say, "Trinity is triple," by reason of the number implied we signify the multiplication of that number by itself, since the word triple imports a distinction in the supposita of which it is spoken. Therefore it cannot be said that the Trinity is triple; otherwise it follows that, if the Trinity be triple, there would be three supposita of the Trinity; as when we say, "God is triple," it follows that there are three supposita of the Godhead.

ARTICLE 2. *Whether the Son Is Other Than the Father?*

We proceed thus to the Second Article: It would seem that the Son is not other than the Father.

Objection 1. For "other" is a relative term implying diversity of substance. If, then, the Son is other than the Father, He must be different from the Father, which is contrary to what Augustine says (*De Trin.* vii),[2] that when we speak of three persons, we do not mean to imply diversity.

Obj. 2. Further, whosoever are other from one another, differ in some way from one another. Therefore, if the Son is other than the Father, it

follows that He differs from the Father, which is against what Ambrose says (*De Fide* i),[3] that "the Father and the Son are one in Godhead; nor is there any difference in substance between them, nor any diversity."

Obj. 3. Further, the term alien is taken from *alius* (other). But the Son is not alien from the Father, for Hilary says (*De Trin.* vii)[4] that in the divine persons "there is nothing diverse, nothing alien, nothing separable." Therefore the Son is not other than the Father.

Obj. 4. Further, the terms "other person" and "other thing" (*alius et aliud*) have the same meaning, differing only in gender. So if the Son is another person from the Father, it follows that the Son is a thing apart from the Father.

On the contrary, Augustine says:[5] "There is one essence of the Father and Son and Holy Ghost, in which the Father is not one thing, the Son another, and the Holy Ghost another; although the Father is one person, the Son another, and the Holy Ghost another."

I answer that, Since as Jerome remarks,[6] a "heresy arises from words wrongly used," when we speak of the Trinity we must proceed with care and with befitting modesty; because, as Augustine says (*De Trin.* i, 3),[7] "nowhere is error more harmful, the quest more toilsome, the finding more fruitful." Now, in treating of the Trinity we must beware of two opposite errors, and proceed cautiously between them—namely, the error of Arius,[8] who placed a Trinity of substance with the Trinity of persons, and the error of Sabellius,[9] who placed unity of person with the unity of essence.

Thus, to avoid the error of Arius we must shun the use of the terms diversity and difference in God, lest we take away the unity of essence; we may, however, use the term "distinction" on account of the relative opposition. Hence, whenever we find terms of diversity or difference of Persons used in an authentic work, these terms of diversity or difference are taken to mean distinction. But lest the simplicity and singleness of the divine essence be taken away, the terms "separation" and "division," which belong to the parts of a whole, are to be avoided; and lest equality be taken away, we avoid the use of the term "disparity"; and lest we remove likeness, we avoid the terms "alien" and "dis-

---

[1] PL 63, 1101.
[2] Chap. 4 (PL 42, 940).

[3] Chap. 2 (PL 16, 555).
[4] PL 10, 233.
[5] Fulgentius, *De Fide ad Petrum*, 1 (PL 65, 674).
[6] See Peter Lombard, *Sent.*, IV, XIII, 2 (QR II, 818).
[7] PL 42, 822.
[8] See Augustine, *De Haeres*, 49 (PL 42, 39).
[9] *Ibid.*, 41 (PL 42, 32).

crepant." For Ambrose says (*De Fide*, i)[1] that "in the Father and the Son there is no discrepancy, but one Godhead"; and according to Hilary, as quoted above, "in God there is nothing alien, nothing separable."

To avoid the heresy of Sabellius, we must shun the term "singularity," lest we take away the communicability of the divine essence. Hence Hilary says (*De Trin.* vii):[2] "It is sacrilege to assert that the Father and the Son are separate in Godhead." We must avoid the adjective "only" (*unici*) lest we take away the number of persons. Hence Hilary says in the same book that we exclude from God "the idea of singularity or uniqueness. Nevertheless, we can say the only Son," for in God there is no plurality of Sons. Yet, we do not say "the only God," for Deity is common to many. We avoid the word "confused" lest we take away from the Persons the order of their nature. Hence Ambrose says (*loc. cit.*): "What is one is not confused; and there is no multiplicity where there is no difference." The word "solitary" is also to be avoided, lest we take away the society of the three persons; for, as Hilary says (*De Trin.* iv),[3] "We confess neither a solitary nor a diverse God."

This word "other" (*alius*), however, in the masculine sense, means only a distinction of suppositum; and hence we can properly say that "The Son is other than the Father," because He is another suppositum of the divine nature, as He is another person and another hypostasis.

Reply Obj. 1. "Other," being like the name of a particular thing, refers to the suppositum; and so, a distinct substance in the sense of hypostasis or person suffices to its notion. But diversity requires a distinct substance in the sense of essence. Thus we cannot say that the Son is diverse from the Father, although He is another.

Reply Obj. 2. "Difference" implies distinction of form. There is one form only in God, as appears from the text, *Who, when He was in the form of God* (Phil. 2. 6). Therefore the term "difference" does not properly apply to God, as appears from the authority quoted. Yet, Damascene (*De Fide Orthod.* iii, 5)[4] employs the term difference in the divine persons as meaning that the relative property is signified by way of form. Hence he says that the "hypostases do not differ from each other in substance, but according to determinate properties." But "difference" is taken for "distinction," as above stated.

Reply Obj. 3. The term "alien" means what is extraneous and dissimilar, which is not expressed by the term "other" (*alius*); and therefore we say that the Son is other than the Father, but not that He is anything alien.

Reply Obj. 4. The neuter gender is formless; the masculine however is formed and distinct, and so is the feminine. So the common essence is properly and aptly expressed by the neuter gender, but by the masculine and feminine is expressed the determined subject in the common nature. Hence also in human affairs, if we ask, Who is this man? we answer, Socrates, which is the name of the suppositum. But if we ask, What is he? we reply, A rational and mortal animal. So, because in God distinction is by the persons and not by the essence, we say that the Father is other than the Son, but not something else; while conversely we say that they are one thing, but not one person.

ARTICLE 3. *Whether the Exclusive Word "Alone" Should Be Added to an Essential Term in God?*

We proceed thus to the Third Article: It would seem that the exclusive word "alone" (*solus*) is not to be added to an essential term in God.

Objection 1. For, according to the Philosopher,[5] "He is alone who is not with another." But God is with the angels and the souls of the saints. Therefore we cannot say that God is alone.

Obj. 2. Further, whatever is joined to the essential term in God can be predicated of every person *per se,* and of all the persons together; for, as we can properly say that God is wise, we can say the Father is a wise God, and the Trinity is a wise God. But Augustine says (*De Trin.* vi, 9):[6] "We must consider the opinion that the Father is not true God alone." Therefore God cannot be said to be alone.

Obj. 3. Further, if this expression "alone" is joined to an essential term, it would be so joined as regards either the personal predicate or the essential predicate. But it cannot be the former, as it is false to say, "God alone is Father," since man also is a father; nor again, can it be applied as regards the latter, for, if this saying were true, "God alone creates," it would follow that "the Father alone creates," as whatever is said of God can be said of the Father; and it would be false, as the Son also creates. Therefore this ex-

---

[1] Chap. 2 (PL 16, 555).   [2] PL 10, 233.
[3] PL 10, 111.   [4] PG 94, 1000.

[5] *Sophistical Refutations*, 22 (178ᵃ30).
[6] PL 42, 930.

pression "alone" cannot be joined to an essential term in God.

On the contrary, It is said, *To the King of ages, immortal, invisible, the only God* (I Tim. I. 17).

I answer that, This term "alone" can be taken as a categorematical term, or as a syncategorematical term. A categorematical term is one which ascribes absolutely the thing signified to a given suppositum; as, for instance, white to man, as when we say a white man. If the term "alone" is taken in this sense, it cannot in any way be joined to any term in God; for it would mean solitude in the term to which it is joined, and it would follow that God was solitary, against what is above stated (A. 2). A syncategorematical term imports the order of the predicate to the subject, as this expression "every one" or "no one"; and likewise the term "alone," as excluding every other suppositum from the predicate. Thus, when we say, "Socrates alone writes," we do not mean that Socrates is solitary, but that he has no companion in writing, though many others may be with him. In this way nothing prevents the term "alone" being joined to any essential term in God, as excluding the predicate from all things but God; as if we said, "God alone is eternal," because nothing but God is eternal.

Reply Obj 1. Although the angels and the souls of the saints are always with God, nevertheless, if plurality of persons did not exist in God He would be alone or solitary. For solitude is not removed by association with anything that is extraneous in nature; thus anyone is said to be alone in a garden, though many plants and animals are with him in the garden. Likewise, God would be alone or solitary, though angels and men were with Him, supposing that many persons were not within Him. Therefore the society of angels and of souls does not take away absolute solitude from God; much less does it remove respective solitude, in reference to a predicate.

Reply Obj. 2. This expression "alone," properly speaking, does not affect the predicate, which is taken formally, for it refers to the suppositum, as excluding any other suppositum from the one to which it is joined. But the adverb "only," being exclusive, can be applied either to subject or predicate. For we can say, "Only Socrates"—that is, no one else—"runs"; and "Socrates runs only"—that is, he does nothing else. Hence it is not properly said that the Father is God alone, or the Trinity is God alone, unless some implied meaning be assumed in the

predicate, as, for instance, "The Trinity is God Who alone is God." In that sense it can be true to say that "the Father is that God who alone is God," if the relative be referred to the predicate, and not to the suppositum. So, when Augustine says that the Father is not God alone, but that the Trinity is God alone, he speaks in an expository manner, as he might explain the words, "To the King of ages, invisible, the only God," as applying not to the Father, but to the Trinity alone.

Reply Obj. 3. In both ways can the term "alone" be joined to an essential term. For this proposition, "God alone is Father," can mean two things, because the word "Father" can signify the person of the Father, and then it is true, for no man is that person; or it can signify the relation only, and thus it is false, because the relation of paternity is found also in others, though not in a univocal sense. Likewise it is true to say "God alone creates"; nor, does it follow, "therefore the Father alone creates," because, as logicians say, an exclusive diction so fixes the term to which it is joined that what is said exclusively of that term cannot be said exclusively of an individual contained in that term; for instance, from the premiss, "Man alone is a mortal rational animal," we cannot conclude, "therefore Socrates alone is such."

ARTICLE 4. *Whether an Exclusive Diction Can Be Joined to the Personal Term?*

We proceed thus to the Fourth Article: It would seem that an exclusive diction can be joined to the personal term, even though the predicate is common.

Objection 1. For our Lord speaking to the Father, said: *That they may know Thee, the only true God* (John 17. 3). Therefore the Father alone is true God.

Obj. 2. Further, He said: *No one knows the Son but the Father* (Matt. 11. 27), which means that the Father alone knows the Son. But to know the Son is common (to the Persons). Therefore the same conclusion follows.

Obj. 3. Further, an exclusive diction does not exclude what enters into the understanding of the term to which it is joined. Hence it does not exclude the part, nor the universal; for it does not follow that if we say "Socrates alone is white," that therefore "his hand is not white", or that "man is not white." But one person is in the comprehension of another, as the Father is in the comprehension of the Son; and conversely. Therefore, when we say, "The Father alone is God," we do not exclude the Son, nor the Holy Ghost. And so such a mode of speaking is true.

Obj. 4. Further, the Church sings: "Thou alone art Most High, O Jesus Christ."[1]

On the contrary, This proposition "The Father alone is God," includes two assertions—namely, that the Father is God, and that no other besides the Father is God. But this second proposition is false, for the Son is another from the Father, and He is God. Therefore this is false, "The Father alone is God"; and the same of the like sayings.

I answer that, When we say, "The Father alone is God," such a proposition can be taken in several senses. If "alone" means solitude in the Father, it is false in a categorematical sense; but if taken in a syncategorematical sense it can again be understood in several ways. For if it exclude (all others) from the form of the subject, it is true, the sense being "the Father alone is God"—that is, "He who with no other is the Father, is God." In this way Augustine expounds when he says (*De Trin.* vi, 7):[2] "We say the Father alone not because He is separate from the Son or from the Holy Ghost but because they are not the Father together with Him." This, however, is not the usual way of speaking, unless we understand another implication, as though we said "He who alone is called the Father is God." But in the strict sense the exclusion affects the predicate. And thus the proposition is false if it excludes another in the masculine sense, but true if it excludes it in the neuter sense, because the Son is another person than the Father, but not another thing; and the same applies to the Holy Ghost. But because this term "alone," properly speaking, refers to the subject, as we have said (A. 3, Ans. 2), it tends to exclude another Person rather than other things. Hence such a way of speaking is not to be taken too literally, but it should be reverently expounded whenever we find it in an authentic work.

Reply Obj. 1. When we say, "Thee the only true God," we do not understand it as referring to the person of the Father, but to the whole Trinity, as Augustine expounds (*De Trin.* vi, 9).[3] Or, if understood of the person of the Father, the other persons are not excluded by reason of the unity of essence, in so far as the word "only" excludes another thing, as above explained.

The same Reply can be given to *Obj.* 2. For an essential term applied to the Father does not exclude the Son or the Holy Ghost, by reason of the unity of essence. Hence we must understand that in the authority quoted the term "no one" (*nemo*) is not the same as "no man," (*nullus homo*) which the word itself would seem to signify[4] (for the person of the Father could not be expected), but is taken according to the usual way of speaking in a distributive sense, to mean any rational nature.

Reply Obj. 3. The exclusive diction does not exclude what enters into the understanding of the term to which it is adjoined if they do not differ in suppositum, as part and universal. But the Son differs in suppositum from the Father; and so there is no parity.

Reply Obj. 4. We do not say absolutely that the Son alone is Most High, but that He alone is Most High "with the Holy Ghost, in the glory of God the Father."

QUESTION XXXII
The knowledge of the divine persons
(In Four Articles)

We proceed to inquire concerning the knowledge of the divine persons, and this involves four points of inquiry: (1) Whether the divine persons can be known by natural reason? (2) Whether notions are to be attributed to the divine persons? (3) The number of the notions? (4) Whether we may lawfully have various contrary opinions of these notions?

Article 1. *Whether the Trinity of the Divine Persons Can Be Known by Natural Reason?*

We proceed thus to the First Article: It would seem that the trinity of the divine persons can be known by natural reason.

Objection 1. For philosophers came to the knowledge of God not otherwise than by natural reason. Now we find that they said many things about the trinity of persons,[5] for Aristotle says[6] "Through this number"—namely, three—"we bring ourselves to acknowledge the greatness of one God, surpassing all things created." And Augustine says:[7] "I have read in their works, that is, in the books of the Platonists, not in so many words, but enforced by many and various reasons, that in the beginning was the

---

[1] From the Mass, *Gloria in Excelsis.*
[2] PL 42, 929.
[3] PL 42, 930.

[4] *Nemo = non-homo,* that is, no man.
[5] See DTC., art. "*Platonisme des Pères.*" (XII, 2322).
[6] *Heavens,* I, 1 (268ª13).
[7] *Confessions,* VII, 13 (PL 32, 740).

Word, and the Word was with God, and the Word was God," and so on, in which passage the distinction of persons is laid down. We read, moreover, in a gloss[1] on Rom. 1 and Exod. 8 that the magicians of Pharaoh failed in the third sign—that is, as regards knowledge of a third person—that is, of the Holy Ghost—and thus it is clear that they knew at least two persons. Likewise Trismegistus says:[2] "The monad begot a monad, and reflected upon itself its own ardour." By these words the generation of the Son and the procession of the Holy Ghost seem to be indicated. Therefore knowledge of the divine persons can be obtained by natural reason.

Obj. 2. Further, Richard of St. Victor says (*De Trin.* i, 4):[3] "I believe without doubt that probable and even necessary arguments can be found for any explanation of the truth." So even to prove the Trinity of Persons some[4] have brought forward a reason from the infinite goodness of God, who communicates Himself infinitely in the procession of the divine persons, while some[5] are moved by the consideration that "no good thing can be joyfully possessed without partnership." Augustine proceeds (*De Trin.* IX, 4)[6] to prove the trinity of persons by the procession of the word and of love in our own mind, and we have followed him in this (Q. XXVII, AA. 1, 3). Therefore the trinity of persons can be known by natural reason.

Obj. 3. Further, it seems to be superfluous to teach what cannot be known by natural reason. But it ought not to be said that the divine tradition of the Trinity is superfluous. Therefore the trinity of persons can be known by natural reason.

On the contrary, Hilary says (*De Trin.* i),[7] "Let not man think to reach the sacrament of generation by his own mind." And Ambrose says (*De Fide* i, 10),[8] "It is impossible to know the secret of generation. The mind fails, the voice is silent." But the trinity of the divine persons

is distinguished by origin of generation and procession (Q. XXX, A. 2). Since, therefore, man cannot know, and with his understanding grasp that for which no necessary reason can be given, it follows that the trinity of persons cannot be known by reason.

I answer that, It is impossible to attain to the knowledge of the Trinity of divine Persons by natural reason. For, as above explained (Q. XII, AA. 4, 11, 12), man cannot obtain the knowledge of God by natural reason except from creatures. Now creatures lead us to the knowledge of God, as effects do to their cause. Accordingly, by natural reason we can know of God that only which of necessity belongs to Him as the principle of all things, and we have cited this fundamental principle in treating of God as above (Q. XII, A. 12). Now, the creative power of God is common to the whole Trinity, and hence it belongs to the unity of the essence, and not to the distinction of the persons. Therefore, by natural reason we can know what belongs to the unity of the essence, but not what belongs to the distinction of the Persons. Whoever, then, tries to prove the Trinity of Persons by natural reason detracts from faith in two ways. First, as regards the dignity of faith itself, which consists in its being concerned with invisible things, that exceed human reason; hence the Apostle says that *faith is of things that appear not* (Heb. 11. 1), and the same Apostle says also, *We speak wisdom among the perfect, but not the wisdom of this world, nor of the princes of this world; but we speak the wisdom of God in a mystery which is hidden* (I Cor. 2. 6, 7). Secondly, as regards the utility of drawing others to the faith. For when anyone in the endeavour to prove the faith brings forward reasons which are not cogent, he falls under the ridicule of the unbelievers, since they suppose that we stand upon such reasons, and that we believe on such grounds.

Therefore, we must not attempt to prove what is of faith, except by authority alone, to those who receive the authority; and as regards others it suffices to prove that what faith teaches is not impossible. Hence it is said by Dionysius (*Div. Nom.* ii):[9] "Whoever wholly resists the word, is far off from our philosophy; but if he regards the truth of the word—that is, the sacred word, we too follow this rule."

Reply Obj. 1. The philosophers did not know the mystery of the Trinity of the Divine Persons by its proper attributes, such as paternity, sonship, and procession, according to the

[1] *Glossa ordin.,* on Exod. 8.19 (1, 140E); cf. Isidore, *Quaest. in Vet. Test., In Exod.,* chap. 14, or 8.19 (PL 83, 293); see also Augustine, *Epist.,* LV, chap. 16 (PL 33, 219). [2] Pseudo Hermes Trismegistus, *Liber viginti quattuor phil.,* prop. 1 (BK 31). [3] PL 196, 892. [4] Alexander of Hales, *S.T.,* PT. I, n. 295 (QR 1, 414); Bonaventure, *Itinerarium,* chap. 6 (QR V, 310); cf. DTC, art. "*Fils de Dieu*" (V, 2465). [5] Richard of St. Victor, *De Trin.,* III, 3 (PL 196, 917); cf. Alexander of Hales, *S.T.,* PT. I, n. 76 (QR 1, 122); also Bonaventure, *In Sent.,* I, d. ii, Q. 2 (QR 1, 53). [6] PL 42, 963. [7] PL 10, 58. [8] PL 16, 566. [9] PG 3, 640.

Apostle's words, *We speak the wisdom of God which none of the princes of the world knew* (I Cor. 2. 6)—that is, the philosophers, according to the Gloss.[1] Nevertheless, they knew some of the essential attributes appropriated to the persons, as power to the Father, wisdom to the Son, goodness to the Holy Ghost, as will later on appear (Q. XXXIX, A. 7). So, when Aristotle said, "By this number," etc., we must not take it as if he affirmed a threefold number in God, but that he wished to say that the ancients used the threefold number in their sacrifices and prayers on account of some perfection residing in the number three. In the Platonic books[2] also we find, *In the beginning was the word*, not as meaning the Person begotten in God, but as meaning the ideal type whereby God made all things, and which is appropriated to the Son. And although they knew these were appropriated to the three persons, yet they are said to have failed in the third sign—that is, in the knowledge of the third person, because they deviated from the goodness appropriated to the Holy Ghost, in that knowing God *they did not glorify Him as God* (Rom. 1); or, because the Platonists asserted the existence of one Primal Being whom they also declared to be the "Father" of the universe,[3] they consequently maintained the existence of another substance beneath him, which they called "mind"[4] or the "paternal intellect,"[5] containing the idea of all things, as Macrobius relates (*Som. Scrip.*).[6] They did not, however, assert the existence of a third separate substance which might correspond to the Holy Ghost. So also we do not assert that the Father and the Son differ in substance, which was the error of Origen and Arius, who in this followed the Platonists.[7] When Trismegistus says, "Monad begot monad," etc., this does not refer to the generation of the Son, or to the procession of the Holy Ghost, but to the production of the world. For one God produced one world by reason of His love for Himself.

Reply Obj. 2. Reason may be employed in two ways to establish a point: first for the purpose of furnishing sufficient proof of some principle, as in natural science, where sufficient proof can be brought to show that the movement of the heavens is always of uniform velocity. Reason is employed in another way, not as furnishing a sufficient proof of a principle, but as confirming an already established principle, by showing the congruity of its results, as in astrology the theory of eccentrics and epicycles is considered as established because thereby the sensible appearances of the heavenly movements can be explained; not, however, as if this reason were sufficient, since some other theory might explain them. In the first way we can prove that God is one, and the like. In the second way, reasons avail to prove the Trinity; because, that is, when assumed to be true, such reasons confirm it. We must not, however, think that the trinity of persons is adequately proved by such reasons. This becomes evident when we consider each point, for the infinite goodness of God is manifested also in creation, because to produce from nothing is an act of infinite power. For if God communicates Himself by His infinite goodness, it is not necessary that an infinite effect should proceed from God, but that according to its own mode it should receive the divine goodness. Likewise, when it is said that joyous possession of good requires partnership, this holds in the case of one not having perfect goodness; hence it needs to share some other's good, in order to have the goodness of complete happiness. Nor is the likeness of our intellect an adequate proof in the case of God, since the intellect is not in God, and ourselves univocally. Hence, Augustine says (*Tract.* XXVI, *in Joan*)[8] that by faith we arrive at knowledge, and not conversely.

Reply Obj. 3. There are two reasons why the knowledge of the divine persons was necessary for us. It was necessary for the right opinion of creation. The fact of saying that God made all things by His Word excludes the error of those who say that God produced things by necessity. When we say that in Him there is a procession of love, we show that God produced creatures not because He needed them, nor because of any other extrinsic reason, but on account of the love of His own goodness. So Moses, (Gen. 1. 1, 3, 4), when he had said, *In the beginning God created heaven and earth*, added, *God said, Let there be light*, to manifest the divine Word; and then said, *God saw the light that it was good*, to show the proof of the divine love. The same is also found in the other works of creation. In another way, and chiefly, that we may think rightly concerning the salvation of the

---

[1] *Glossa Interl.*, (VI, 36r); *Glossa* Lombardi (PL 191, 1548).
[2] See Augustine, *Confessions*, VII, 13 (PL 32, 740).
[3] Macrobius, *In Somn. Scipion.*, I, 14 (DD 45b).
[4] *Ibid.*, I, 2 (DD 12b).
[5] Not in Macrobius; see Albert the Great, *Meta.*, I, 4, 12 (BO VI, 82); *De Quindecim Problem.*, I (MD 34).
[6] Bk. I, chap. 2 (DD 12b); chap. 5 (DD 21a).
[7] See Jerome, *Epist.*, LXXXIV, 1 (PL 22, 746).
[8] PL 35, 1618.

human race, accomplished by the Incarnate Son, and by the gift of the Holy Ghost.

ARTICLE 2. *Whether There Are Notions in God?*

We proceed thus to the Second Article: It seems that in God there are no notions.

Objection 1. For Dionysius says (*Div. Nom.* i):[1] "We must not dare to say anything of God but what is taught to us by the Holy Scripture." But Holy Scripture does not say anything concerning notions. Therefore there are none in God.

Obj. 2. Further, all that exists in God concerns the unity of the essence or the trinity of the persons. But the notions do not concern the unity of the essence, nor the trinity of the persons, for neither can what belongs to the essence be predicated of the notions; for instance, we do not say that paternity is wise or creates. Nor can what belongs to the persons be so predicated; for example, we do not say that paternity begets, nor that sonship is begotten. Therefore there do not exist notions in God.

Obj. 3. Further, we are not to presuppose any abstract notions as principles of knowing simple things, for they are known of themselves. But the divine persons are supremely simple. Therefore we are not to suppose any notions in God.

On the contrary, Damascene says (*De Fide Orthod.* iii, 5):[2] "We recognize difference of hypostases that is, of persons, in the three properties; i.e., in the paternal, the filial, and the processional." Therefore we must admit properties and notions in God.

I answer that, Prepositinus, considering the simplicity of the persons, said[3] that in God there were no properties or notions, and wherever they were mentioned, he propounded the abstract for the concrete. For as we are accustomed to say, "I beseech your kindness"—that is, you who are kind—so when we speak of paternity in God, we mean God the Father.

But, as was shown above (Q. III, A. 3, ANS. I; Q. XIII, A. I, ANS. 2), the use of concrete and abstract names in God is not in any way against the divine simplicity, since we always name a thing as we understand it. Now, our intellect cannot attain to the absolute simplicity of the divine essence considered in itself, and therefore, our human intellect apprehends and names divine things according to its own mode, that is in so far as they are found in sensible things from which its knowledge is derived. In these things we use abstract terms to signify simple

forms, and to signify subsistent things we use concrete terms. Hence also we signify divine things, as above stated, (*loc. cit.*), by abstract names, to express their simplicity; but, to express their subsistence and completeness, we use concrete names.

But not only must essential names be signified in the abstract and in the concrete, as when we say Deity and God, or wisdom and wise, but the same applies to the personal names, so that we may say paternity and Father.

Two chief motives for this can be cited. The first arises from the obstinacy of heretics. For since we confess the Father, the Son, and the Holy Ghost to be one God and three persons, to those who ask: "Whereby are They one God? and whereby are they three persons?" as we answer that they are one in essence or deity, so there must also be some abstract terms whereby we may answer that the persons are distinguished; and these are the properties or notions signified by an abstract term, as paternity and sonship. Therefore the divine essence is signified as "What", and the person as "Who", and the property as "Whereby."

The second motive is because one person in God is related to two Persons—namely, the person of the Father to the person of the Son and to the person of the Holy Ghost. This is not, however, by one relation; otherwise it would follow that the Son also and the Holy Ghost would be related to the Father by one and the same relation. Thus, since relation alone multiplies the Trinity, it would follow that the Son and the Holy Ghost would not be two persons. Nor can it be said with Prepositinus that as God is related in one way to creatures, while creatures are related to Him in divers ways, so the Father is related by one relation to the Son and to the Holy Ghost, but these two persons are related to the Father by two relations. For, since the specific idea of a relation is that it refers to another, it must be said that two relations are not specifically different if but one opposite relation corresponds to them. For the relation of lord and father must differ according to the difference of sonship and servitude. Now, all creatures are related to God as His creatures by one specific relation. But the Son and the Holy Ghost are not related to the Father by one and the same kind of relation. Hence there is no parity.

Further, in God there is no need to admit any real relation to the creature (Q. XXVIII, A. I, ANS. 3), while there is no reason against our admitting in God many logical relations. But in

[1] Sect. 1, 2 (PG 3, 588).   [2] PG 94, 1000.
[3] *Summa* (fol. 67rb).

the Father there must be a real relation to the Son and to the Holy Ghost. Hence, corresponding to the two relations of the Son and of the Holy Ghost, whereby they are related to the Father, we must understand two relations in the Father, whereby He is related to the Son and to the Holy Ghost. Hence, since there is only one Person of the Father, it is necessary that the relations should be separately signified in the abstract; and these are what we mean by properties and notions.

Reply Obj. 1. Although the notions are not mentioned in Holy Scripture, yet the persons are mentioned, comprising the idea of notions, as the abstract is contained in the concrete.

Reply Obj. 2. In God the notions have their significance not after the manner of realities, but by way of certain ideas whereby the persons are known, although in God these notions or relations are real, as stated above (Q. XXVIII, A. 1) Therefore whatever has order to any essential or personal act cannot be applied to the notions, since this is against their mode of signification. Hence we cannot say that paternity begets, or creates, or is wise, or is intelligent. The essentials, however, which are not ordered to any act, but simply remove created conditions from God, can be predicated of the notions; for we can say that paternity is eternal, or immense, or such like. So also on account of the real identity, substantive terms, whether personal or essential, can be predicated of the notions; for we can say that paternity is God, and that paternity is the Father.

Reply Obj. 3. Although the persons are simple, still without prejudice to their simplicity, the proper ideas of the persons can be abstractly signified, as above explained.

ARTICLE 3. *Whether There Are Five Notions?*

We proceed thus to the Third Article: It would seem that there are not five notions.

Objection 1. For the notions proper to the persons are the relations whereby they are distinguished from each other. But the relations in God are only four (Q. XXVIII, A. 4). Therefore the notions are only four in number.

Obj. 2. Further, as there is only one essence in God, He is called one God, and because in Him there are three persons, He is called the Triune God. Therefore, if in God there are five notions, He may be called quinary; which cannot be allowed.

Obj. 3. Further, if there are five notions for the three persons in God, there must be in some one person two or more notions, as in the Person

of the Father there is innascibility and paternity, and common spiration. Either these three notions really differ, or not. If they really differ, it follows that the person of the Father is composed of several things. But if they differ only logically, it follows that one of them can be predicated of another, so that we can say that as the divine goodness is the same as the divine wisdom by reason of the common reality, so common spiration is paternity, which is not to be admitted. Therefore there are not five notions.

Obj. 4. *On the contrary,* It seems that there are more, because, as the Father is from no one, and from this is derived the notion of innascibility, so from the Holy Ghost no other person proceeds. And in this respect there ought to be a sixth notion.

Obj. 5. Further, as the Father and the Son are the common origin of the Holy Ghost, so it is common to the Son and the Holy Ghost to proceed from the Father. Therefore as one notion is common to the Father and the Son, so there ought to be one notion common to the Son and to the Holy Ghost.

I answer that, A notion is the proper idea whereby we know a divine Person. Now the divine persons are multiplied by reason of their origin; and origin includes the idea of someone from whom another comes, and of someone that comes from another, and by these two modes a person can be known. Therefore the Person of the Father cannot be known by the fact that He is from another but by the fact that He is from no one; and thus the notion that belongs to Him is called innascibility. As the source of another, He can be known in two ways, because as the Son is from Him, the Father is known by the notion of paternity; and as the Holy Ghost is from Him, He is known by the notion of common spiration. The Son can be known as begotten by another, and thus He is known by sonship; and also by another person proceeding from Him, the Holy Ghost, and thus He is known in the same way as the Father is known, by common spiration. The Holy Ghost can be known by the fact that He is from another, or from others; thus He is known by procession, but not by the fact that another is from Him, as no divine Person proceeds from Him.

Therefore there are Five notions in God: innascibility, paternity, sonship, common spiration, and procession. Of these only four are relations, for innascibility is not a relation, except by reduction, as will appear later (Q. XXXIII, A. 4, ANS. 3). Four only are properties. For common spiration is not a property, because it belongs to two persons. Three are personal notions—that is, constituting persons, paternity, sonship, and procession. Common spiration and innascibility are called notions of Persons, but not personal notions, as we shall explain further on (Q. XL, A. 1, Ans. 1).

Reply Obj. 1. Besides the four relations, another notion must be admitted, as above explained.

Reply Obj. 2. The divine essence is signified as a reality, and likewise the persons are signified as realities; but the notions are signified as ideas making the persons known. Therefore, although God is one by unity of essence, and triune by trinity of persons, nevertheless He is not quinary by the five notions.

Reply Obj. 3. Since the real plurality in God is founded only on relative opposition, the several properties of one Person, as they are not relatively opposed to each other, do not really differ. Nor again are they predicated of each other, because they are different ideas of the persons; just as we do not say that the attribute of power is the attribute of knowledge, although we do say that knowledge is power.

Reply Obj. 4. Since Person implies dignity, as stated above (Q. XIX, A. 3), we cannot derive a notion of the Holy Spirit from the fact that no person is from Him. For this does not belong to His dignity, as it belongs to the authority of the Father that He is from no one.

Reply Obj. 5. The Son and the Holy Ghost do not agree in one special mode of existence derived from the Father, as the Father and the Son agree in one special mode of producing the Holy Ghost. But the principle on which a notion is based must be something special; thus no parity of reasoning exists.

ARTICLE 4. *Whether It is Lawful To Have Various Contrary Opinions of Notions?*

We proceed thus to the Fourth Article: It would seem that it is not lawful to have various contrary opinions of the notions:

Objection 1. For Augustine says (*De Trin.* i, 3):[1] "No error is more dangerous" than any as regards the Trinity, to which mystery the notions assuredly belong. But contrary opinions must be in some way erroneous. Therefore it is not right to have contrary opinions of the notions.

Obj. 2. Further, the persons are known by the notions as we have said (AA. 2, 3). But no contrary opinion concerning the persons is to be

[1] PL 42, 822.

allowed. Therefore neither can there be about the notions.

On the contrary, The notions are not articles of faith. Therefore different opinions of the notions are permissible.

I answer that, Anything is of faith in two ways: directly, where any truth comes to us principally as divinely delivered, as the trinity and unity of God, the Incarnation of the Son, and the like; and concerning these truths a false opinion of itself involves heresy, especially if it be held obstinately. A thing is of faith indirectly if the denial of it involves as a consequence something against faith; as for instance if anyone said that Samuel was not the son of Elcana, for it follows that the divine Scripture would be false. Concerning such things anyone may have a false opinion without danger of heresy before the matter has been considered or settled as involving consequences against faith, and particularly if no obstinacy be shown; but when it is manifest, and especially if the Church has decided that consequences follow against faith, then the error cannot be free from heresy. For this reason many things are now considered as heretical which were formerly not so considered as their consequences are now more manifest.

So we must decide that anyone may entertain contrary opinions about the notions if he does not mean to uphold anything at variance with faith. If, however, anyone should entertain a false opinion of the notions, thinking that consequences against the faith would follow, he would slip into heresy.

By what has been said all *the objections* may be solved.

QUESTION XXXIII
OF THE PERSON OF THE FATHER
(*In Four Articles*)

WE now consider the persons singly; and first, the Person of the Father, concerning Whom there are four points of inquiry: (1) Whether the Father is the Principle? (2) Whether the Person of the Father is properly signified by this name "Father"? (3) Whether "Father" in God is said personally before it is said essentially? (4) Whether it belongs to the Father alone to be unbegotten?

ARTICLE 1. *Whether It Belongs to the Father To Be the Principle?*

We proceed thus to the First Article: It would seem that the Father cannot be called the principle of the Son, or of the Holy Ghost.

Objection 1. For principle and cause are the same, according to the Philosopher.[1] But we do not say that the Father is the cause of the Son. Therefore we must not say that He is the principle of the Son.

Obj. 2. Further, a principle is so called in relation to the thing principled. So if the Father is the principle of the Son, it follows that the Son is a person principled, and is therefore created; which appears false.

Obj. 3. Further, the word principle is taken from priority. But in God "there is no before and after," as Athanasius says.[2] Therefore in speaking of God we ought not to use the term principle.

On the contrary, Augustine says (*De Trin.* iv, 20),[3] "The Father is the Principle of the whole Deity."

I answer that, The word "principle" signifies only that from which another proceeds: For anything from which something proceeds in any way we call a principle, and conversely. As the Father then is the one from which another proceeds, it follows that the Father is a principle.

Reply Obj. 1. The Greeks use the words cause and principle indifferently, when speaking of God, but the Latin Doctors do not use the word cause, but only principle. The reason is because principle is a wider term than cause, just as cause is more common than element. For the first term of a thing, as also the first part, is called the principle, but not the cause. Now the wider a term is, the more suitable it is to use as regards God (Q. XIII, A. 11), because the more special terms are the more they determine the mode adapted to the creature. Hence this term cause seems to mean diversity of substance, and dependence of one from another, which is not implied in the word principle. For in all kinds of causes there is always to be found between the cause and the effect a distance of perfection or of power, whereas we use the term principle even in things which have no such difference, but have only a certain order to each other; as when we say that a point is the principle of a line, or also when we say that the fore part of a line is the principle of a line.

Reply Obj. 2. It is the custom with the Greeks to say that the Son and the Holy Ghost are principled. This is not, however, the custom with our Doctors because, although we attribute to the Father something of authority by reason of His being the principle, still we do not attribute

any kind of subjection or inferiority to the Son, or to the Holy Ghost, to avoid any occasion of error. In this way, Hilary says (*De Trin.* ix):[4] "By authority of the Giver, the Father is the greater; nevertheless the Son is not less to Whom oneness of being is given."

Reply Obj. 3. Although this word principle, as regards its derivation, seems to be taken from priority, still it does not signify priority, but origin. For what a term signifies, and the reason why it was imposed, are not the same thing, as stated above (Q. XIII, A. 2, Ans. 2; A. 8).

ARTICLE 2. *Whether This Name "Father" Is Properly the Name of a Divine Person?*

We proceed thus to the Second Article: It would seem that this name "Father" is not properly the name of a divine person.

Objection 1. For the name Father signifies relation. Moreover person is an individual substance. Therefore this name Father is not properly a name signifying a Person.

Obj. 2. Further, a begetter is more common than father, for every father begets; but it is not so conversely. But a more common term is more properly applied to God, as stated above (Q. XIII, A. 11). Therefore the more proper name of the divine person is begetter and genitor than Father.

Obj. 3. Further, a metaphorical term cannot be the proper name of anyone. But the word is by us metaphorically called begotten, or offspring; and consequently, he to whom the word applies is metaphorically called father. Therefore the principle of the Word in God is not properly called Father.

Obj. 4. Further, everything which is said properly of God is said of God first before creatures. But generation appears to apply to creatures before God, because generation seems to be truer when the one who proceeds is distinct from the one from whom it proceeds, not only by relation but also by essence. Therefore the name Father taken from generation does not seem to be the proper name of any divine person.

On the contrary, It is said (Ps. 88 27): *He shall cry out to me: Thou art my Father.*

I answer that, The proper name of any person signifies that whereby the person is distinguished from all other persons. For as body and soul belong to the notion of man, so to the comprehension of this particular man belong "this soul and this body" as it is stated in the *Metaphysics;*[5] and by these is this man distinguished from all

---

[1] *Metaphysics,* IV, 2 (1003ᵇ24).
[2] Creed (MA II, 1354; DZ 39).
[3] PL 42, 908.
[4] PL 10, 325.
[5] Aristotle, VII, 11 (1037ᵃ9).

other men. Now it is paternity which distinguishes the person of the Father from all the other persons. Hence this name Father, whereby paternity is signified, is the proper name of the person of the Father.

Reply Obj. 1. Among us relation is not a subsisting person. So this name father among us does not signify a person, but the relation of a person. In God, however, it is not so, as some wrongly thought, for in God the relation signified by the name Father is a subsisting person. Hence, as above explained (Q. XXIX, A. 4), this name *person* in God signifies a relation subsisting in the divine nature.

Reply Obj. 2. According to the Philosopher[1] a thing is denominated chiefly by its perfection, and by its end. Now generation signifies something in process of being made, while paternity signifies the complement of generation; and therefore the name Father is more expressive as regards the divine person than genitor or begetter.

Reply Obj. 3. In human nature the word is not a subsistence, and hence is not properly called begotten or son. But the divine Word is something subsistent in the divine nature, and hence He is properly and not metaphorically called Son, and His principle is called Father.

Reply Obj. 4. The terms generation and paternity, like the other terms properly applied to God, are said of God before creatures as regards the thing signified, but not as regards the mode of signification. Hence also the Apostle says, *I bend my knee to the Father of my Lord Jesus Christ, from whom all paternity in heaven and on earth is named* (Eph. 3. 14). This is explained thus. It is manifest that generation receives its species from the term which is the form of the thing generated; and the nearer it is to the form of the generator, the truer and more perfect is the generation, just as univocal generation is more perfect than non-univocal, for it belongs to the essence of a generator to generate what is like itself in form. Hence the very fact that in the divine generation the form of the Begetter and Begotten is numerically the same, while in creatures it is not numerically, but only specifically, the same, shows that generation, and consequently paternity, is applied to God before creatures. Hence the very fact that in God a distinction exists of the Begotten from the Begetter as regards relation only belongs to the truth of the divine generation and paternity.

[1] *Soul*, II, 4 (416^b23).

ARTICLE 3. *Whether This Name "Father" Is Applied to God, Firstly As a Personal Name?*

We proceed thus to the Third Article: It would seem that this name Father is not applied to God firstly as a personal name.

Objection 1. For in the intellect the common precedes the proper. But this name Father as a personal name is proper to the person of the Father; and taken in an essential sense it is common to the whole Trinity, for we say "Our Father" to the whole Trinity. Therefore Father comes first as an essential name before its personal sense.

Obj. 2. Further, in things of which the notion is the same there is no predication of before and after. But paternity and sonship seem to be of the same nature, according as a divine person is Father of the Son, and the whole Trinity is our Father, or the creature's; since, according to Basil (*Hom.* xv, *De Fide*),[2] "to receive is common to the creature and to the Son." Therefore "Father" in God is not taken as an essential name before it is taken personally.

Obj. 3. Further, it is not possible to compare things which have not a common notion. But the Son is compared to the creature by reason of sonship or generation, according to Col. 1. 15: *Who is the image of the invisible God, the firstborn of every creature.* Therefore paternity taken in a personal sense is not prior to, but has the same notion as, paternity taken essentially.

On the contrary, The eternal comes before the temporal. But God is the Father of the Son from eternity, while He is Father of the creature in time. Therefore paternity in God is taken in a personal sense as regards the Son before it is so taken as regards the creature.

I answer that, A name is applied to that wherein is perfectly contained its whole meaning before it is applied to that which only partially contains it; for the latter bears the name by reason of a kind of likeness to that which answers perfectly to the meaning of the name, since all imperfect things are taken from perfect things. Hence this name lion is applied first to the animal containing the whole nature of a lion, and which is properly so called, before it is applied to a man who shows something of a lion's nature, as boldness, or strength, or the like, and of whom it is said by way of likeness.

Now it is manifest from the foregoing (QQ. XXVII, A. 2; XXVIII, A. 4), that the perfect idea of paternity and filiation is to be found in God the Father and in God the Son, because one is

[2] PG 31, 468.

the nature and glory of the Father and the Son. But in the creature, sonship is found in relation to God not in a perfect manner, since the Creator and the creature have not the one nature, but by way of a certain likeness, which is the more perfect the nearer we approach to the true idea of sonship. For God is called the Father of some creatures by reason only of a trace, for instance of irrational creatures, according to Job 38. 28: *Who is the father of the rain? or who begot the drops of dew?* Of some, namely, the rational creature (He is the Father), by reason of the likeness of image, according to Deut. 32. 6: *Is He not thy Father, who possessed, and made, and created thee?* And of others He is the Father by likeness of grace, and these are also called adoptive sons, as ordained to the heritage of eternal glory by the gift of grace which they have received, according to Rom. 8. 16, 17: *The Spirit Himself gives testimony to our spirit that we are the sons of God; and if sons, heirs also.* Lastly, He is the Father of others by likeness of glory, because they have obtained possession of the heritage of glory, according to Rom. 5. 2: *We glory in the hope of the glory of the sons of God.* Therefore it is plain that "paternity" is applied to God first, as expressing the relation of one Person to another Person, before it expresses the relation of God to creatures.

Reply Obj. 1. Common terms taken absolutely, in the order of our intellect, come before proper terms because they are included in the understanding of proper terms, but not conversely. For in the comprehension of the person of the Father, God is understood, but not conversely. But common terms which express relation to the creature come after proper terms which express personal relations, because the person proceeding in God proceeds as the principle of the production of creatures. For as the word conceived in the mind of the artist is first understood to proceed from the artist before the thing made, which is produced in likeness to the word conceived in the mind, so the Son proceeds from the Father before the creature, to which the name of sonship is applied as it participates in the likeness of the Son, as is clear from the words of Rom. 8. 29: *Whom He foreknew and predestined to be made conformable to the image of His Son.*

Reply Obj. 2. "To receive" is said to be common to the creature and to the Son not in a univocal sense but according to a certain remote likeness whereby He is called the First Born of creatures. Hence the authority quoted adds: *That He may be the First Born among many*

brethren (Rom. 8. 29), after saying that *some were conformed to the image of the Son of God.* But the Son of God naturally possesses a position of singularity above others, in having by nature what He receives, as Basil also declares (*ibid.*); hence He is called the only begotten (John 1. 18): *The only begotten Who is in the bosom of the Father, He hath declared unto us.*

From this appears the *Reply* to *Obj.* 3.

ARTICLE 4. *Whether It Is Proper to the Father To Be Unbegotten?*

We proceed thus to the Fourth Article: It would seem that it is not proper to the Father to be unbegotten.

Objection 1. For every property supposes something in that of which it is the property. But "unbegotten" supposes nothing in the Father; it only removes something. Therefore it does not signify a property of the Father.

Obj. 2. Further, "Unbegotten" is taken either in a privative, or in a negative, sense. If in a negative sense, then whatever is not begotten can be called unbegotten. But the Holy Ghost is not begotten; neither is the divine essence. Therefore to be unbegotten belongs also to them; thus it is not proper to the Father. But if it be taken in a privative sense, since every privation signifies imperfection in the thing which is the subject of privation, it follows that the Person of the Father is imperfect, which cannot be.

Obj. 3. Further, in God, "unbegotten" does not signify relation, for it is not used relatively. Therefore it signifies substance. Therefore unbegotten and begotten differ in substance. But the Son, Who is begotten, does not differ from the Father in substance. Therefore the Father ought not to be called unbegotten.

Obj. 4. Further, property means what belongs to one alone. Since, then, there are more than one in God proceeding from another, there is nothing to prevent several not receiving their being from another. Therefore the Father is not alone unbegotten.

Obj. 5. Further, as the Father is the principle of the person begotten, so is He of the person proceeding. So if by reason of His opposition to the person begotten it is proper to the Father to be unbegotten, it follows that it is proper to Him also to be unproceeding.

On the contrary, Hilary says (*De Trin.* iv):[1] "One is from one—that is, the Begotten is from the Unbegotten—namely, by the property in each one respectively of innascibility and origin.'

[1] PL 10, 120.

I answer that, As in creatures there exist a first and a secondary principle, so also in the divine Persons, in Whom there is no before or after, is found the principle not from a principle, Who is the Father; and the principle from a principle, Who is the Son.

Now in things created a first principle is known in two ways. In one way as the first *principle* by reason of its having a relation to what proceeds from itself; in another way, because it is a *first* principle by reason of its not being from another. Thus therefore the Father is known both by paternity and by common spiration in relation to the persons proceeding from Himself. But as the principle not from a principle He is known by the fact that He is not from another, and this belongs to the property of innascibility, signified by this word "unbegotten."

Reply Obj. 1. There are some who say[1] that innascibility, signified by the word "unbegotten," as a property of the Father is not a negative term only, but either that it means both these things together—namely, that the Father "is from no one, and that He is the principle of others"; or that it means "universal authority," or also "His plenitude as the source of all." This, however, does not seem true, because thus innascibility would not be a property distinct from paternity and spiration but would include them as the proper is included in the common. For source and authority signify in God nothing but the principle of origin. We must therefore say with Augustine (*De Trin.* v, 7)[2] that *unbegotten* means the negation of passive generation. For he says that "unbegotten has the same meaning as 'not a son.'" Nor does it follow that "unbegotten" is not the proper notion of the Father; for primary and simple things are made known by negations, as, for instance, a point is defined as what has no part.

Reply Obj. 2. "Unbegotten" is taken sometimes in a negative sense only, and in that sense Jerome says[3] that "the Holy Ghost is unbegotten —that is, He is not begotten." Otherwise "unbegotten" may be taken in a kind of privative sense, but not as implying any imperfection. For privation can be taken in many ways. In one way when a thing has not what naturally belongs to another, even though it is not of its own nature to have it; as, for instance, if a stone be called a dead thing, as wanting life, which naturally belongs to some other things. In another sense,

privation is so called when something has not what naturally belongs to some members of its genus; as for instance when a mole is called blind. In a third sense privation means the absence of what something ought to have, in which sense, privation implies an imperfection. In this sense, "unbegotten" is not attributed to the Father as a privation, but it may be so attributed in the second sense, meaning that a certain suppositum of the divine nature is not begotten, while some suppositum of the same nature is begotten. In this sense the term "unbegotten" can be applied also to the Holy Ghost. Hence to consider it as a term proper to the Father alone, it must be further understood that the name "unbegotten" belongs to a divine person as the principle of another person, so that it be understood to imply negation in the genus of principle taken personally in God. Or that there be understood in the term "unbegotten" that He is not in any way derived from another, and not only that He is not from another by way only of generation. In this sense the term "unbegotten" does not belong at all to the Holy Ghost, Who is from another by procession, as a subsisting person; nor does it belong to the divine essence, of which it may be said that it is in the Son or in the Holy Ghost from another— namely, from the Father.

Reply Obj. 3. According to Damascene (*De Fide Orthod.* ii, 8),[4] "unbegotten in one sense signifies the same as uncreated"; and thus it applies to the substance, for in this way the created substance differs from the uncreated. In another sense it signifies "what is not begotten," and in this sense it is a relative term; just as negation is reduced to the genus of affirmation, as "not man" is reduced to the genus of substance, and "not white" to the genus of quality. Hence, since "begotten" implies relation in God, "unbegotten" belongs also to relation. Thus it does not follow that the Father unbegotten is substantially distinguished from the Son begotten, but only by relation; that is, as the relation of Son is denied of the Father.

Reply Obj. 4. In every genus there must be something first; so in the divine nature there must be some one principle which is not from another, and which we call "unbegotten." To admit two innascibles is to suppose the existence of two Gods, and two divine natures. Hence Hilary says (*De Synod.*):[5] "As there is one God, so there cannot be two innascibles." And this especially because, if two innascibles did

---

[1] Cf. William of Auxerre, *Summa Aurea*, I, 8, 5 (fol. 16va).
[2] PL 42, 916.
[3] Cf. Peter Lombard, *Sent.*, I, XIII, 4 (QR I, 89).
[4] PG 94, 817.
[5] PL 10 521.

exist, one would not be from the other, and they would not be distinguished by relative opposition; therefore they would have to be distinguished from each other by diversity of nature.

Reply Obj. 5. The property of the Father whereby He is not from another is rather signified by the removal of the nativity of the Son than by the removal of the procession of the Holy Ghost; both because the procession of the Holy Ghost has no special name, as stated above (Q. XXVII, A. 4, ANS. 3), and because also in the order of nature it presupposes the generation of the Son. Hence, when it is removed from the Father that He is begotten, although He is the principle of generation, it follows as a consequence that He does not proceed by the procession of the Holy Ghost, because the Holy Ghost is not the principle of generation but proceeds from the person begotten.

QUESTION XXXIV
OF THE PERSON OF THE SON
(*In Three Articles*)

WE next consider the person of the Son. Three names are attributed to the Son—namely, Son, Word, and Image. The idea of Son is gathered from the idea of Father. Hence it remains for us to consider Word and Image.

Concerning Word there are three points of inquiry: (1) Whether Word is an essential term in God, or a personal term? (2) Whether it is the proper name of the Son? (3) Whether in the name of Word is expressed relation to creatures?

ARTICLE 1. *Whether Word in God Is a Personal Name?*

We proceed thus to the First Article: It would seem that Word in God is not a personal name.

Objection 1. For personal names are applied to God in a proper sense, as Father and Son. But "Word is applied to God metaphorically," as Origen says[1] on (John 1. 1), *In the beginning was the Word*. Therefore Word is not a personal name in God.

Obj. 2. Further, according to Augustine (*De Trin.* ix, 10),[2] "The Word is knowledge with love"; and according to Anselm (*Monol.*),[3] to speak is to the Supreme Spirit nothing but to see by thought. But knowledge and thought, and sight, are essential terms in God. Therefore Word is not a personal term in God.

Obj. 3. Further, it is essential to word to be spoken. But, according to Anselm (*ibid.* lxii), as the Father is intelligent, the Son intelligent, and the Holy Ghost intelligent, so the Father speaks, the Son speaks, and the Holy Ghost speaks; and likewise, each one of them is spoken. Therefore, the name Word is used as an essential term in God, and not in a personal sense.

Obj. 4. Further, no divine person is made. But the Word of God is something made. For it is said, *Fire, hail, snow, ice, the storms which do His Word* (Ps. 148. 8). Therefore the Word is not a personal name in God.

On the contrary, Augustine says (*De Trin.* vii, 2):[4] "As the Son is related to the Father, so also is the Word to Him Whose Word He is." But Son is a personal name, since it is said relatively. Therefore so also is Word.

I answer that, The name of Word in God, if taken in its proper sense, is a personal name, and in no way an essential name.

To see how this is true, we must know that our own word taken in its proper sense has a threefold meaning, while in a fourth sense it is taken improperly or figuratively. The clearest and most common sense is when it is said of the word spoken by the voice; and this proceeds from an interior source as regards two things found in the exterior word—that is, the vocal sound itself, and the signification of the sound. For, according to the Philosopher,[5] vocal sound signifies the concept of the intellect. Again the vocal sound proceeds from the signification or the imagination, as stated in the book on the *Soul.*[6] The vocal sound, which has no signification, cannot be called a word: hence the exterior vocal sound is called a word because it signifies the interior concept of the mind. Thus, therefore first and chiefly, the interior concept of the mind is called a word; secondarily, the vocal sound itself, signifying the interior concept, is so called; and thirdly, the imagination of the vocal sound is called a word. Damascene mentions these three kinds of words (*De Fide Orthod.* i, 13),[7] saying that "word is called the natural movement of the intellect, whereby it is moved, and understands, and thinks, as light and splendour," which is the first kind. "Again," he says, "the word is what is not pronounced by a vocal word, but is uttered in the heart," which is the third kind. "Again," also, "the word is the angel"—that is, the messenger "of intelligence," which is the second kind. Word is also used in a

---

[1] PG 14, 59.   [2] PL 42, 969.
[3] Chap. 63 (PL 158, 208).

[4] PL 42, 936.   [5] *Interpretation,* 1 (16ᵃ3).
[6] Aristotle, II, 8 (420ᵇ32).   [7] PG 94, 857.

fourth way figuratively for that which is signi-fied or effected by a word; thus we are accus-tomed to say, "this is the word I have said to you," or "which the king has commanded," al-luding to some deed signified by the word either by way of assertion or of command.

Now word is taken properly in God as signify-ing the concept of the intellect. Hence Augus-tine says (*De Trin.* xv, 10):[1] "Whoever can un-derstand the word not only before it is sounded, but also before thought has clothed it with imag-inary sound, can already see some likeness of that Word of Whom it is said: *In the beginning was the Word.*" The concept itself of the heart has the nature of proceeding from something other than itself—namely, from the knowledge of the one conceiving. Hence Word, according as we use the term properly of God, signifies something proceeding from another, which be-longs to the nature of personal terms in God, since the divine persons are distinguished by origin (Q. XXVII, Introd.; Q. XXXII, A. 3). Hence the term "Word," according as we use the term properly of God, is to be taken as said not essen-tially, but personally only.

Reply Obj. 1. The Arians, who sprang from Origen,[2] declared that the Son differed in sub-stance from the Father. Hence, they endeav-oured to maintain that when the Son of God is called the Word this is not to be understood in a proper sense, lest the idea of the Word proceed-ing should compel them to confess that the Son of God is of the same substance as the Father. For the interior word proceeds in such a manner from the one who pronounces it as to remain within him. But supposing Word to be said metaphorically of God, we must still admit Word in its proper sense. For if a thing be called a word metaphorically, this can only be by rea-son of some manifestation; either it makes something manifest as a word, or it is manifested by a word. If manifested by a word, there must exist a word whereby it is manifested. If it is called a word because it exteriorly manifests, what it exteriorly manifests cannot be called word except in as far as it signifies the interior concept of the mind, which anyone may also manifest by exterior signs. Therefore, although Word may be sometimes said of God metaphor-ically, nevertheless we must also admit Word in the proper sense, which is said personally.

Reply Obj. 2. Nothing belonging to the intel-lect can be applied to God personally except word alone, for word alone signifies that which

emanates from another. For what the intellect forms in its conception is the word. Now, the intellect itself, according as it is put in act by the intelligible species, is considered absolutely; likewise the act of understanding which is to the intellect in act what being is to being in act, since the act of understanding does not signify an act going out from the intelligent agent, but an act remaining in the agent. Therefore when we say that word is knowledge, the term knowl-edge does not mean the act of a knowing intel-lect, or any one of its habits, but stands for what the intellect conceives by knowing. Hence also Augustine says (*De Trin.* vii, 2)[3] that the Word is "begotten wisdom," for it is nothing but the concept of the Wise One; and in the same way It can be called "begotten knowledge." Thus also can be explained how to speak is in God to see by thought, since the Word is conceived by the gaze of the divine thought. Still the term thought does not properly apply to the Word of God. For Augustine says (*De Trin.* xv, 16)[4]: "Therefore do we speak of the Word of God, and not of the Thought of God, lest we believe that in God there is something unstable, now as-suming the form of Word, now putting off that form and remaining latent and as it were form-less." For thought consists properly in the search after truth, and this has no place in God. But when the intellect attains to the form of truth, it does not think, but perfectly contemplates the truth. Hence Anselm (*loc. cit.*) takes thought in an improper sense for contempla-tion.

Reply Obj. 3. As, properly speaking, Word in God is said personally, and not essentially, so likewise is "to speak." Hence, as the Word is not common to the Father, Son, and Holy Ghost, so it is not true that the Father, Son, and Holy Ghost are one speaker. So Augustine says (*De Trin.* vii, 1):[5] "That co-eternal Word is under-stood as not alone in God." On the other hand, "to be spoken" belongs to each Person, for not only is the word spoken, but also the thing un-derstood or signified by the word. Therefore in this manner to one person alone in God does it belong to be spoken in the same way as a word is spoken; but in the way whereby a thing is spoken as being understood in the word, it be-longs to each Person to be spoken. For the Father, by understanding Himself, the Son, and the Holy Ghost, and all other things comprised in this knowledge, conceives the Word, so that thus the whole Trinity is spoken in the Word,

---

[1] PL 42, 1071.
[2] *In Joann.*, II (PG 14, 109).

[3] PL 42, 936.   [4] PL 42, 1079.
[5] PL 42, 933.

and likewise also all creatures; just as the intellect of a man by the word he conceives in the act of understanding a stone, speaks a stone. Anselm took the term speak improperly for the act of understanding, whereas they differ from each other; for "to understand" means only the relation of the intelligent agent to the thing understood, in which relation no notion of origin is conveyed, but only a certain informing of our intellect, according as our intellect is put in act by the form of the thing understood. In God, however, it means complete identity, because in God the intellect and the thing understood are altogether the same, as was proved above (Q. XIV, AA. 2, 4). But to speak means chiefly the relation to the word conceived, for to speak is nothing but to utter a word. But by means of the word it signifies a relation to the thing understood which in the word uttered is manifested to the one who understands. Thus, only the Person who utters the Word is speaker in God, although each Person understands and is understood, and consequently is spoken by the Word.

Reply Obj. 4. The term word is taken there figuratively, as the thing signified or effected by word is called word. For thus creatures are said to do the word of God, as executing any effect to which they are ordained by the word conceived of the divine wisdom; just as anyone is said to do the word of the king when he does the work to which he is appointed by the king's word.

ARTICLE 2. *Whether "Word" Is Proper Name of the Son?*

We proceed thus to the Second Article: It would seem that Word is not the proper name of the Son.

Objection 1. For the Son is a subsisting person in God. But word does not signify a subsisting thing, as appears in ourselves. Therefore word cannot be the proper name of the person of the Son.

Obj. 2. Further, the word proceeds from the speaker by being uttered. Therefore if the Son is properly the word, He proceeds from the Father by way only of utterance, which is the heresy of Valentine, as appears from Augustine (*De Hæres.* xi).[1]

Obj. 3. Further, every proper name of a person signifies some property of that person. Therefore, if the Word is the Son's proper name, it signifies some property of His; and thus there will be several more properties in God than those above mentioned.

[1] PL 42, 28.

Obj. 4. Further, Whoever understands conceives a word in the act of understanding. But the Son understands. Therefore some word belongs to the Son, and consequently to be Word is not proper to the Son.

Obj. 5. Further, it is said of the Son (Heb. 1. 3): *Bearing all things by the word of His power,* from which Basil infers (*Cont. Eunom.* v, 11)[2] that the Holy Ghost is the Son's Word. Therefore to be Word is not proper to the Son.

On the contrary, Augustine says (*De Trin.* vi. 2):[3] "By Word we understand the Son alone."

I answer that, Word, said of God in its proper sense, is used personally, and is the proper name of the person of the Son. For it signifies an emanation of the intellect: and the person Who proceeds in God, by way of emanation of the intellect is called the Son; and this procession is called generation, as we have shown above (Q. XXVII, A. 2). Hence it follows that the Son alone is properly called Word in God.

Reply Obj. 1. To be and to understand are not the same in us. Hence that which in us has intelligible being does not belong to our nature. But in God to be and to understand are one and the same; hence the Word of God is not an accident in Him, or an effect of His, but belongs to His very nature. And therefore it must be something subsistent, for whatever is in the nature of God subsists; and so Damascene says (*De Fide Orthod.* i, 18)[4] that "the Word of God is substantial and has a hypostatic being; but other words [as our own] are powers of the soul."

Reply Obj. 2. The error of Valentine was condemned, not, as the Arians pretended, because he asserted that the Son was born by being uttered, as Hilary relates (*De Trin.* vi),[5] but on account of the different mode of utterance proposed by its author, as appears from Augustine (*De Hæres, loc. cit.*).

Reply Obj. 3. In the term Word the same property is signified as in the name Son. Hence Augustine says (*De Trin.* vii, 2):[6] "Word and Son express the same." For the Son's nativity, which is His personal property, is signified by different names which are attributed to the Son to express His perfection in various ways. To show that He is of the same nature as the Father, He is called the Son; to show that He is coeternal, He is called the Splendour; to show that He is altogether like, He is called the Image; to show that He is begotten immaterially, He is

[2] PG 29, 732.   [3] PL 42, 925.
[4] Chap. 13 (PG 94, 857).
[5] PL 10, 162.
[6] PL 42, 936.

called the Word. All these truths cannot be expressed by only one name.

Reply Obj. 4. To be intelligent belongs to the Son in the same way as it belongs to Him to be God, since to understand is said of God essentially, as stated above, (A. 1, Ans. 2, 3). Now the Son is God begotten, and not God begetting; and hence He is intelligent not as producing a Word, but as the Word proceeding, because in God the Word proceeding does not differ really from the divine intellect, but is distinguished from the principle of the Word only by relation.

Reply Obj. 5. When it is said of the Son, "Bearing all things by the word of His power," *word* is taken figuratively for the effect of the Word. Hence a gloss says[1] that "word" is here taken to mean command, since by the effect of the power of the Word things are kept in being, as also by the effect of the power of the Word things are brought into being. Basil speaks improperly and figuratively in applying Word to the Holy Ghost, in the sense that everything that makes a person known may be called his word, and so in that way the Holy Ghost may be called the Son's Word, because He manifests the Son.

ARTICLE 3. *Whether the Name "Word" Signifies Relation to Creatures?*

We proceed thus to the Third Article: It would seem that the name Word does not signify relation to creatures.

Objection 1. For every name that connotes some effect in creatures is said of God essentially. But Word is not said essentially, but personally, as we have stated (A. 1). Therefore Word does not signify relation to creatures.

Obj. 2. Further, whatever signifies relation to creatures is said of God in time; as Lord and Creator. But Word is said of God from eternity. Therefore it does not signify relation to the creature.

Obj. 3. Further, Word signifies relation to the source whence it proceeds. Therefore if it signifies relation to the creature, it follows that the Word proceeds from the creature.

Obj. 4. Further, Ideas are many according to their various relations to creatures. Therefore if Word signifies relation to creatures, it follows that in God there is not one Word only, but many.

Obj. 5. Further, if Word signifies relation to the creature, this can only be because creatures

[1] *Glossa interl.*, on Heb. 1.3 (VI, 134r); *Glossa* Lombardi, on Heb. 1.3 (PL 192, 406).

are known by God. But God does not know beings only; He knows also non-beings. Therefore in the Word are implied relations to non-beings, which appears to be false.

On the contrary, Augustine says (QQ. lxxxiii, qu. 63),[2] that the name Word "signifies not only relation to the Father, but also relation to those beings which are made through the Word, by His operative power."

I answer that, Word implies relation to creatures. For God by knowing Himself knows every creature. Now the word conceived in the mind is representative of everything that is actually understood. Hence there are in ourselves different words for the different things which we understand. But because God by one act understands Himself and all things, His unique Word is expressive not only of the Father, but of all creatures.

And as the knowledge of God is only cognitive as regards God, whereas as regards creatures, it is both cognitive and operative, so the Word of God is only expressive of what is in God the Father, but is both expressive and operative of creatures; and therefore it is said (Ps. 32. 9): *He spake, and they were made,* because in the Word is implied the operative idea of what God makes.

Reply Obj. 1. The nature is also included indirectly in the name of the person, for person is an individual substance of a rational nature. Therefore the name of a divine person as regards the personal relation does not imply relation to the creature, but it is implied in what belongs to the nature. Yet there is nothing to prevent its implying relation to creatures so far as the essence is included in its meaning; for as it properly belongs to the Son to be the Son, so it properly belongs to Him to be God begotten, or the Creator begotten. And in this way the name Word implies relation to creatures.

Reply Obj. 2. Since the relations result from actions, some names import the relation of God to creatures, which relation follows on the action of God which passes into some exterior effect, as to create and to govern; and the like are applied to God in time. But others import a relation which follows from an action which does not pass into an exterior effect, but which remains in the agent—as to know and to will; such are not applied to God in time. And this kind of relation to creatures is implied in the name of the Word. Nor is it true that the names which imply relation of God to creatures are applied to Him in time, but only those names are

[2] PL 40, 54.

applied in time which imply relation following on the action of God passing into exterior effect.

Reply Obj. 3. Creatures are known to God not by a knowledge derived from the creatures themselves, but by His own essence. Hence it is not necessary that the Word should proceed from creatures, although the Word is expressive of creatures.

Reply Obj. 4. The name of Idea is imposed chiefly to signify relation to creatures and therefore it is applied in a plural sense to God, and it is not said personally. But the name of Word is imposed chiefly to signify relation to the speaker, and consequently, relation to creatures, since God, by understanding Himself, understands every creature. And so there is only one Word in God, and that a personal one.

Reply Obj. 5. God's knowledge of non-beings and God's Word about non-beings are the same because the Word of God contains no less than does the knowledge of God, as Augustine says (*De Trin.* xv, 14).[1] Nevertheless the Word is expressive and operative of beings, but of non-beings is expressive and manifestive.

QUESTION XXXV
OF THE IMAGE
(*In Two Articles*)

WE next inquire concerning the Image, about which there are two points of inquiry: (1) Whether Image in God is said personally? (2) Whether this name belongs to the Son alone?

ARTICLE 1. *Whether Image in God Is Said Personally?*

We proceed thus to the First Article: It would seem that image is not said personally of God.

Objection 1. For Augustine (Fulgentius—*De Fide ad Petrum* i)[2] says, "The Godhead of the Holy Trinity and the Image to which man is made are one." Therefore Image is said of God essentially, and not personally.

Obj. 2. Further, Hilary says (*De Synod.*):[3] "An image is a like species of that which it represents." But species or form is said of God essentially. Therefore so also is Image.

Obj. 3. Further, Image is derived from imitation, which implies before and after. But in the divine persons there is no before and after. Therefore Image cannot be a personal name in God.

On the contrary, Augustine says (*De Trin.* vii, 1):[4] "What is more absurd than to say that an image is referred to itself?" Therefore Image in God is said as a relation, and is thus a personal name.

I answer that, The idea of Image includes likeness. Still, not any kind of likeness suffices for the notion of image, but only likeness of species, or at least of some specific sign. In corporeal things the specific sign consists chiefly in the figure. For we see that the species of different animals are of different figures, but not of different colours. Hence if the colour of anything is depicted on a wall, this is not called an image unless the figure is likewise depicted. Further, neither the likeness of species nor of figure is enough for an image, which requires also the idea of origin; because, as Augustine says (QQ. LXXXIII, qu. 74):[5] "One egg is not the image of another, because it is not derived from it." Therefore for a true image it is required that one proceeds from another like to it in species, or at least in specific sign. Now whatever imports procession or origin in God, belongs to the persons. Hence the name Image is a personal name.

Reply Obj. 1. Image, properly speaking, means whatever proceeds forth in likeness to another. That to the likeness of which anything proceeds is properly speaking called the exemplar, and is improperly called the image. Nevertheless Augustine (Fulgentius) uses the name of Image in this sense when he says that the divine nature of the Holy Trinity is the Image to whom man was made.

Reply Obj. 2. Species, as mentioned by Hilary in the definition of image, means the form derived from one thing to another. In this sense image is said to be the species of anything, as that which is assimilated to anything is called its form because it has a like form.

Reply Obj. 3. Imitation in the divine Persons does not signify posteriority, but only assimilation.

ARTICLE 2. *Whether the Name of Image Is Proper to the Son?*

We proceed thus to the Second Article: It would seem that the name of Image is not proper to the Son.

Objection 1. Because, as Damascene says (*De Fide Orthod.* i, 13),[6] The Holy Ghost is "the Image of the Son." Therefore Image does not belong to the Son alone.

Obj. 2. Further, the notion of an image implies likeness plus derivation as Augustine says

[1] PL 42, 1076.   [2] PL 65, 674.
[3] PL 10, 490.   [4] PL 42, 934.
[5] PL 40, 86.
[6] PG 94, 856.

(QQ. LXXXIII, qu. 74).[1] But this belongs to the Holy Ghost, Who proceeds from another by way of likeness. Therefore the Holy Ghost is an Image; and so to be Image does not belong to the Son alone.

Obj. 3. Further, man is also called the image of God, according to I Cor. 11. 7, *The man ought not to cover his head, for he is the image and the glory of God.* Therefore Image is not proper to the Son.

On the contrary, Augustine says (*De Trin.* vi, 2):[2] "The Son alone is the Image of the Father."

I answer that, The Greek Doctors commonly say[3] that the Holy Ghost is the Image both of the Father and of the Son; but the Latin Doctors attribute the name Image to the Son alone.[4] For it is not found in the canonical Scripture except as applied to the Son, as in the words, *Who is the Image of the invisible God, the firstborn of creatures* (Col. 1. 15); and again: *Who being the brightness of His glory, and the figure of His substance* (Heb. 1. 3).

Some explain this[5] by the fact that the Son agrees with the Father not in nature only, but also in the notion of principle, whereas the Holy Ghost agrees neither with the Son, nor with the Father in any notion. This, however, does not seem to suffice. Because as it is not by reason of the relations that we consider either equality or inequality in God, as Augustine says (*De Trin.* v, 6),[6] so neither (by reason thereof do we consider) that likeness which is required for the notion of image. Hence others say[7] that the Holy Ghost cannot be called the Image of the Son, because there cannot be an image of an image; nor of the Father, because again the image must be immediately related to that of which it is the image, and the Holy Ghost is related to the Father through the Son; nor again is He the Image of the Father and the Son because then there would be one image of two, which is impossible.

Hence it follows that the Holy Ghost is in no way an Image. But this is no proof, for the Father and the Son are one principle of the Holy Ghost, as we shall explain further on (Q. XXXVI, A. 4). Hence there is nothing to prevent there being one Image of the Father and of the Son, since they are one; for even man is one image of the whole Trinity.

Therefore we must explain the matter otherwise by saying that, as the Holy Ghost, although by His procession He receives the nature of the Father as the Son also receives it, nevertheless is not said to be born, so, although He receives the likeness of the Father He is not called the Image. Because the Son proceeds as word, the notion of which implies the being of like species with that from which it proceeds, while this does not belong to the notion of love, although it may belong to that love which is the Holy Ghost, since He is the divine love.

Reply Obj. 1. Damascene and the other Greek Doctors commonly employ the term image as meaning a perfect likeness.

Reply Obj. 2. Although the Holy Ghost is like the Father and the Son, still it does not follow that He is the Image, as above explained.

Reply Obj. 3. The image of a thing may be found in something in two ways. In one way it is found in something of the same specific nature, as the image of the king is found in his son. In another way it is found in something of a different nature, as the king's image on the coin. In the first sense the Son is the Image of the Father; in the second sense man is called the image of God; and therefore in order to express the imperfect character of the image in man, man is not simply called the image, but "to the image," by which is expressed a certain movement of tendency to perfection. But it cannot be said that the Son of God is "to the image," because He is the perfect Image of the Father.

QUESTION XXXVI

OF THE PERSON OF THE HOLY GHOST

(*In Four Articles*)

WE now proceed to treat of what belongs to the person of the Holy Ghost, Who is called not only the Holy Ghost, but also Love and Gift of God. Concerning the Holy Ghost there are four points of treatment: (1) Whether this Name, Holy Ghost, is the proper name of a divine Person? (2) Whether that divine person Who is called the Holy Ghost proceeds from the Father and the Son? (3) Whether He proceeds from

---

[1] PL 40, 86.

[2] PL 42, 925.

[3] Cf. St. Thomas, *Contra Errores Graec.*, chap. 10, where he names Athanasius, *Epist.* 1 *ad Seraph.*, (PG 26, 587); Basil, *Contra Eunom.*, v (PG 29, 747); John Damascene, *De Fide Orth.*, i, 13 (PG 94, 855).

[4] Cf. St. Thomas, *loc. cit.*, where he names Augustine, *De Trin.*, vi, 2 (PL 42, 933); Richard of St. Victor, *De Trin.*, vi, 11 (PL 196, 975).

[5] Richard of St. Victor, *loc. cit.*; Alexander of Hales, *S.T.*, pt. ii, n. 418 (QR 1, 609); Bonaventure, *In Sent.*, iv, d. 31, pt. ii, A. 1, Q. 2 (QR ii, 542); see DTC., art. "*Fils de Dieu*" (v, 2474).

[6] *Contra Maxim. Haeret.*, ii, 14, 18 (PL 42, 775, 786); *De Trin.*, v, 6 (PL 42, 914).

[7] Rupertus, *De Trin.*, ii, 2 (PL 167, 248); cf. DTC., *loc. cit.*; cf. also Alexander of Hales, *S.T.* ii, 418 (QR 1, 609).

the Father through the Son? (4) Whether the Father and the Son are one principle of the Holy Ghost?

ARTICLE 1. *Whether This Name, "Holy Ghost," Is the Proper Name of a Divine Person?*

We proceed thus to the First Article: It would seem that this name, "Holy Ghost," is not the proper name of a divine person.

Objection 1. For no name which is common to the three persons is the proper name of any one person. But this name of "Holy Ghost"[1] is common to the three persons; for Hilary (*De Trin.* viii)[2] shows that the *Spirit of God* sometimes means the Father, as in the words of Isaias (61. 1): *The Spirit of the Lord is upon me;* and sometimes the Son, as when the Son says: *In the Spirit of God I cast out devils* (Matt. 12. 28), showing that He cast out devils by the power of His nature; and that sometimes it means the Holy Ghost, as in the words of Joel (2. 28): *I will pour out of My Spirit over all flesh.* Therefore this name Holy Ghost is not the proper name of a divine person.

Obj. 2. Further, the names of the divine persons are relative terms, as Boëthius says (*De Trin.*).[3] But this name Holy Ghost is not a relative term. Therefore this name is not the proper name of a divine Person.

Obj. 3. Further, because the Son is the name of a divine Person He cannot be called the Son of this one or of that. But the spirit is spoken of as of this or that man, as appears in the words, *The Lord said to Moses, I will take of thy spirit and will give to them* (Num. 11. 17), and also, *The Spirit of Elias rested upon Eliseus* (IV Kings 2. 15). Therefore Holy Ghost does not seem to be the proper name of a divine Person.

On the contrary, It is said (I John 5. 7): *There are three who bear witness in heaven, the Father, the Word, and the Holy Ghost.* As Augustine says (*De Trin.* vii, 4),[4] when we ask,

Three what? we say, Three persons. Therefore the Holy Ghost is the name of a divine person.

I answer that, While there are two processions in God, one of these, the procession of love, has no proper name of its own, as stated above (Q. XXVII, A. 4, ANS. 3). Hence the relations also which follow from this procession are without a name (Q. XXVIII, A. 4), for which reason the Person proceeding in that manner has not a proper name. But as some names are accommodated by the usual mode of speaking to signify these relations, as when we use the names of procession and spiration, which in the proper sense more fittingly signify the notional acts than the relations, so to signify the divine Person, Who proceeds by way of love, this name Holy Ghost is, from the usage of scriptural speech, accommodated to Him. The appropriateness of this name may be shown in two ways. First, from the fact that the person who is called Holy Ghost has something in common with the other Persons. For, as Augustine says (*De Trin.* xv, 19; v, 11),[5] because the Holy Ghost "is common to both, He Himself is called that properly which both are called in common. For the Father also is a spirit, and the Son is a spirit; and the Father is holy, and the Son is holy." Secondly, from the proper signification of the name. For the name spirit in things corporeal seems to signify impulse and motion; for we call the breath and the wind by the term spirit. Now it is a property of love to move and impel the will of the lover towards the thing loved. Further, holiness is attributed to whatever is ordered to God. Therefore because the divine person proceeds by way of the love whereby God is loved, that person is most properly named The Holy Ghost.

Reply Obj. 1. The expression Holy Spirit, if taken as two words, is applicable to the whole Trinity. Because by "spirit" the immateriality of the divine substance is signified, for corporeal spirit is invisible, and has but little matter; hence we apply this term to all immaterial and invisible substances. And by adding the word "holy" we signify the purity of divine goodness. But if Holy Spirit be taken as one word, it is thus that the expression, in the usage of the Church, is accommodated to signify one of the three persons, the one who proceeds by way of love, for the reason above explained.

Reply Obj. 2. Although this name Holy Ghost does not indicate a relation, still it takes the place of a relative term, since it is accommodated to signify a Person distinct from the oth-

---

[1] It should be borne in mind that the word "ghost" is the old English equivalent for the Latin *spiritus*, whether in the sense of breath or blast, or in the sense of spirit as an immaterial substance. Thus we read in the former sense (Hampole, Psalter, x. 7), "The Gost of Storms" (*spiritus procellarum*), and in the latter, "Trubled gost is sacrifice of God" (Prose Psalter, A.D. 1325), and "Oure wrestlynge is ... against the spiritual wicked gostes of the ayre" (More, "Comfort against Tribulation"); and in our modern expression of "giving up the ghost." As applied to God, and not specially to the third Holy Person, we have an example from Maunder, "Jhesu Criste was the worde and the goste of Good." (See Oxford Dictionary.)

[2] PL 10, 253.

[3] Chap. 5 (PL 64, 1254).

[4] PL 42, 940; also, chap. 6 (943) and v, 9 (918).

[5] PL 42, 943, 918.

ers by relation only. Yet this name may be understood as including a relation, if we understand the Holy Spirit as being breathed (*spiratus*).

Reply Obj. 3. In the name Son we understand that relation only which is of something from a principle, in relation to that principle; but in the name Father we understand the relation of principle, and likewise in the name of Spirit since it implies a moving power. But to no creature does it belong to be a principle as regards a divine person, but rather the reverse. Therefore we can say "our Father," and "our Spirit," but we cannot say "our Son."

ARTICLE 2. *Whether the Holy Ghost Proceeds from the Son?*

We proceed thus to the Second Article: It would seem that the Holy Ghost does not proceed from the Son.

Objection 1. For as Dionysius says (*Div. Nom.* i).[1] "We must not dare to say anything concerning the substantial Divinity except what has been divinely expressed to us by the sacred oracles." But in the Sacred Scripture we are not told that the Holy Ghost proceeds from the Son, but only that He proceeds from the Father, as appears from John 15. 26: *The Spirit of truth, Who proceeds from the Father.* Therefore the Holy Ghost does not proceed from the Son.

Obj. 2. Further, in the creed of the council of Constantinople (Can. vii)[2] we read: "We believe in the Holy Ghost, the Lord and Lifegiver, Who proceeds from the Father; with the Father and the Son to be adored and glorified." Therefore it should not be added in our Creed that the Holy Ghost proceeds from the Son, and those who added such a thing appear to be worthy of anathema.

Obj. 3. Further, Damascene says (*De Fide Orthod.* i):[3] "We say that the Holy Ghost is from the Father, and we name Him the Spirit of the Father; but we do not say that the Holy Ghost is from the Son, yet we name Him the Spirit of the Son." Therefore the Holy Ghost does not proceed from the Son.

Obj. 4. Further, nothing proceeds from that in which it rests. But the Holy Ghost rests in the Son; for it is said in the legend of St. Andrew:[4] "Peace be to you and to all who believe in the one God the Father, and in His only Son

our Lord Jesus Christ, and in the one Holy Ghost proceeding from the Father, and abiding in the Son." Therefore the Holy Ghost does not proceed from the Son.

Obj. 5. Further, the Son proceeds as the Word. But our breath (*spiritus*) does not seem to proceed in ourselves from our word. Therefore the Holy Ghost does not proceed from the Son.

Obj. 6. Further, the Holy Ghost proceeds perfectly from the Father. Therefore it is superfluous to say that He proceeds from the Son.

Obj. 7. Further, "the actual and the possible do not differ in things perpetual,"[5] and much less so in God. But it is possible for the Holy Ghost to be distinguished from the Son, even if He did not proceed from Him. For Anselm says (*De Process. spir. Sancti*):[6] "The Son and the Holy Ghost have their Being from the Father, but each in a different way, one by Birth, the other by Procession, so that they are thus distinct from one another." And further on he adds: "For even if for no other reason were the Son and the Holy Spirit distinct, this alone would suffice." Therefore the Holy Spirit is distinct from the Son, without proceeding from Him.

On the contrary, Athanasius says:[7] "The Holy Ghost is from the Father and the Son; not made, nor created, nor begotten, but proceeding."

I answer that, It must be said that the Holy Ghost is from the Son. For if He were not from Him, He could in no wise be personally distinguished from Him, as appears from what has been said above (QQ. XXVIII, A. 3; XXX, A. 2). For it cannot be said that the divine Persons are distinguished from each other in any absolute sense; for it would follow that there would not be one essence of the three persons, since everything that is spoken of God in an absolute sense pertains to the unity of essence. Therefore it must be said that the divine persons are distinguished from each other only by the relations.

Now the relations cannot distinguish the persons except according as they are opposite relations, which appears from the fact that the Father has two relations, by one of which He is related to the Son, and by the other to the Holy Ghost; but these are not opposite relations, and therefore they do not make two persons, but belong only to the one person of the Father. If therefore in the Son and the Holy Ghost there were two relations only, whereby each of them were related to the Father, these relations would

---

[1] Sect. 1 (PG 3, 588); sect. 2 (588).
[2] MA III, 565; DZ 86.
[3] Chap. 8 (PG 94, 832).
[4] *Acta S. Andr.*, (PG 2, 1217).

[5] Aristotle, *Physics*, III, 4 (203^{b}30).
[6] Chap. 4 (PL 158, 292).
[7] Creed "*Quicumque*" (MA 1354; DZ 39).

not be opposite to each other, as neither would be the two relations whereby the Father is related to them. Hence, as the person of the Father is one, it would follow that the person of the Son and of the Holy Ghost would be one, having two relations opposed to the two relations of the Father. But this is heretical since it takes away the Faith in the Trinity. Therefore the Son and the Holy Ghost must be related to each other by opposite relations. Now there cannot be in God any relations opposed to each other, except relations of origin, as proved above (Q. XXVIII, A. 4). And opposite relations of origin are to be understood as of a principle, and of what is from the principle. Therefore we must conclude that it is necessary to say that either the Son is from the Holy Ghost, which no one says, or that the Holy Ghost is from the Son, as we confess.

Furthermore, the notion of the procession of each one agrees with this conclusion. For it was said above (QQ. XXVII, AA. 2, 4; XXVIII, A. 4), that the Son proceeds by way of the intellect as Word, and the Holy Ghost by way of the will as Love. Now love must proceed from a word. For we do not love anything unless we apprehend it by a mental conception. Hence also in this way it is manifest that the Holy Ghost proceeds from the Son.

We derive a knowledge of the same truth from the very order of nature itself. For we nowhere find that several things proceed from one without order except in those which differ only by their matter, as for instance one smith produces many knives distinct from each other materially, with no order to each other; but in things in which there is not only a material distinction we always find that some order exists in the multitude produced. Hence also in the order of creatures produced, the beauty of the divine wisdom is displayed. So if from the one Person of the Father, two persons proceed, the Son and the Holy Ghost, there must be some order between them. Nor can any other be assigned except the order of their nature, whereby one is from the other. Therefore it cannot be said that the Son and the Holy Ghost proceed from the Father in such a way as that neither of them proceeds from the other, unless we admit in them a material distinction; which is impossible.

Hence also the Greeks themselves recognize that the procession of the Holy Ghost has some order to the Son. For they grant that the Holy Ghost is the Spirit *of the Son;* and that He is from the Father *through the Son.* Some of them are said also to concede that *He is from the*

Son, or that He *flows from the Son,* but not that He proceeds; which seems to come from ignorance or obstinacy. For a just consideration of the truth will convince anyone that the word procession is the one most commonly applied to all that denotes origin of any kind. For we use the term to describe any kind of origin, as when we say that a line proceeds from a point, a ray from the sun, a stream from a spring, and likewise in everything else. Hence, granted that the Holy Ghost originates in any way from the Son, we can conclude that the Holy Ghost proceeds from the Son.

Reply Obj. 1. We ought not to say about God anything which is not found in Holy Scripture either explicitly or implicitly. But although we do not find it verbally expressed in Holy Scripture that the Holy Ghost proceeds from the Son, still we do find it in the sense of Scripture, especially where the Son says, speaking of the Holy Ghost, *He will glorify Me, because He shall receive of Mine* (John 16. 14). It is also a rule of Holy Scripture that whatever is said of the Father, applies to the Son, even though there is added an exclusive term; except only as regards what belongs to the opposite relations, whereby the Father and the Son are distinguished from each other. For when the Lord says, *No one knoweth the Son, but the Father,* the idea of the Son knowing Himself is not excluded. So therefore when we say that the Holy Ghost proceeds from the Father, even though it be added that He proceeds from the Father alone, the Son would not thereby be excluded, because as regards being the principle of the Holy Ghost, the Father and the Son are not opposed to each other, but only as regards the fact that one is the Father, and the other is the Son.

Reply Obj. 2. In every council of the Church a creed has been drawn up to meet some prevalent error condemned in the council at that time. Hence subsequent councils are not to be described as making a new creed, but what was implicitly contained in the first creed was explained by some addition directed against rising heresies. Hence in the decision of the council of Chalcedon[1] it is declared that those who were congregated together in the council of Constantinople handed down the doctrine about the Holy Ghost, not implying that there was anything wanting in the doctrine of their predecessors who had gathered together at Nicæa, but explaining against the heretics what those fathers had understood of the matter. Therefore, because at the time of the ancient councils the

[1] Actio v (MA VII, 111).

error of those who said that the Holy Ghost did not proceed from the Son had not arisen it was not necessary to make any explicit declaration on that point; but, later on, when certain errors rose up, in another council[1] assembled in the west, the matter was explicitly defined by the authority of the Roman Pontiff, by whose authority also the ancient councils were summoned and confirmed. Nevertheless the truth was contained implicitly in the belief that the Holy Ghost proceeds from the Father.

Reply Obj. 3. The Nestorians were the first to introduce the error that the Holy Ghost did not proceed from the Son, as appears in a Nestorian creed condemned in the council of Ephesus.[2] This error was embraced by Theodoric the Nestorian,[3] and several others after him, among whom was also Damascene.[4] Hence, in that point his opinion is not to be held. Although, too, it has been asserted by some that while Damascene did not confess that the Holy Ghost was from the Son, neither do those words of his express a denial thereof.

Reply Obj. 4. When the Holy Ghost is said to rest or abide in the Son, it does not mean that He does not proceed from Him, for the Son also is said to abide in the Father, although He proceeds from the Father. Also the Holy Ghost is said to rest in the Son as the love of the lover rests in the beloved; or in reference to the human nature of Christ, by reason of what is written: *On whom thou shalt see the Spirit descending and remaining upon Him, He it is who baptizes* (John 1. 33).

Reply Obj. 5. The Word in God is not taken after the likeness of the vocal word, from which the breath (*spiritus*) does not proceed, for it would then be only metaphorical, but after the likeness of the mental word, from which proceeds love.

Reply Obj. 6. For the reason that the Holy Ghost proceeds from the Father perfectly, not only is it not superfluous to say He proceeds from the Son, but rather it is absolutely necessary. Because one power belongs to the Father and the Son, and because whatever is from the Father, must be from the Son unless it be opposed to the property of sonship; for the Son is not from Himself, although He is from the Father.

Reply Obj. 7. The Holy Ghost is distinguished personally from the Son, since the origin of the one is distinguished from the origin of the other; but the difference itself of origin comes from the fact that the Son is only from the Father, while the Holy Ghost is from the Father and the Son; for otherwise the processions would not be distinguished from each other, as explained above, and in Q. XXVII.

ARTICLE 3. *Whether the Holy Ghost Proceeds from the Father through the Son?*

We proceed thus to the Third Article: It would seem that the Holy Ghost does not proceed from the Father through the Son.

Objection 1. For whatever proceeds from one through another does not proceed immediately. Therefore, if the Holy Ghost proceeds from the Father through the Son He does not proceed immediately from the Father; which seems to be unfitting.

Obj. 2. Further, if the Holy Ghost proceeds from the Father through the Son, He does not proceed from the Son except on account of the Father. But whatever causes a thing to be such is itself even more so. Therefore He proceeds more from the Father than from the Son.

Obj. 3. Further, the Son has His being by generation. Therefore if the Holy Ghost is from the Father through the Son, it follows that the Son is first generated and afterwards the Holy Ghost proceeds; and thus the procession of the Holy Ghost is not eternal, which is heretical.

Obj. 4. Further, when anyone acts through another, the same may be said conversely. For as we say that the king acts through the bailiff, so it can be said conversely that the bailiff acts through the king. But we can never say that the Son spirates the Holy Ghost through the Father. Therefore it can never be said that the Father spirates the Holy Ghost through the Son.

On the contrary, Hilary says (*De Trin.* xii):[5] "Keep me, I pray, in this expression of my faith, that I may ever possess the Father—namely, Thyself: that I may adore Thy Son together with Thee: and that I may deserve Thy Holy Spirit, Who is through Thy Only Begotten."

I answer that, In every sentence in which one is said to act through another, this preposition "through" points out, in what is covered by it, some cause or principle of that act. But since action is a mean between the agent and the thing done, sometimes that which is covered by the preposition "through" is the cause of the action, as proceeding from the agent; and in that case it is the cause of why the agent acts, whether it be a final cause or a formal cause, whether it be

---

[1] Council of Rome, under Pope Damasus.
[2] *Actio* VI (MA IV, 1347).
[3] *Epist.*, CLXXI (PG 83, 1484).
[4] *De Fide Orth.*, I, 8 (PG 94, 832).
[5] PL 10, 471.

effective or motive. It is a final cause when we say, for instance, that the artisan works through love of gain. It is a formal cause when we say that he works through his art. It is a moving cause when we say that he works through the command of another. Sometimes, however, that which is covered by this preposition "through" is the cause of the action regarded as determined to the thing done; as, for instance, when we say, the artisan acts through the mallet, for this does not mean that the mallet is the cause of the artisan acting, but that it is the cause of the thing made proceeding from the artisan, and that it has this effect from the artisan. This is why it is sometimes said that this preposition "through" sometimes denotes direct authority, as when we say, the king works through the bailiff; and sometimes indirect authority, as when we say, the bailiff works through the king.

Therefore, because the Son receives from the Father that the Holy Ghost proceeds from Him, it can be said that the Father spirates the Holy Ghost through the Son, or that the Holy Ghost proceeds from the Father through the Son, which has the same meaning.

Reply Obj. 1. In every action two things are to be considered, the suppositum acting, and the power whereby it acts; as, for instance, fire heats through heat. So if we consider in the Father and the Son the power whereby they spirate the Holy Ghost, there is no mean, for this is one and the same power. But if we consider the persons themselves spirating, then, as the Holy Ghost proceeds in common from the Father and from the Son, the Holy Ghost proceeds from the Father immediately, as from Him, and mediately, as from the Son; and thus He is said to proceed from the Father through the Son. So also did Abel proceed immediately from Adam, since Adam was his father, and mediately, as Eve was his mother, who proceeded from Adam; although, indeed, this example of a material procession is inept to signify the immaterial procession of the divine persons.

Reply Obj. 2. If the Son received from the Father a numerically distinct power for the spiration of the Holy Ghost, it would follow that He would be a secondary and instrumental cause; and thus the Holy Ghost would proceed more from the Father than from the Son, whereas, on the contrary, the same spirative power belongs to the Father and to the Son. And therefore the Holy Ghost proceeds equally from both, although sometimes He is said to proceed principally or properly from the Father, because the Son has this power from the Father.

Reply Obj. 3. As the begetting of the Son is coeternal with the begetter (and hence the Father does not exist before begetting the Son), so the procession of the Holy Ghost is coeternal with His principle. Hence, the Son was not begotten before the Holy Ghost proceeded. But each of the operations is eternal.

Reply Obj. 4. When anyone is said to work through anything, the converse proposition is not always true. For we do not say that the mallet works through the carpenter; but we can say that the bailiff acts through the king, because it is the bailiff's place to act, since he is master of his own act, but it is not the mallet's place to act, but only to be made to act, and hence it is used only as an instrument. The bailiff is, however, said to act through the king, although this preposition "through" denotes a medium, for the more a suppositum is prior in action, so much the more is its power immediate as regards the effect, because the power of the first cause joins the second cause to its effect. Hence also first principles are said to be immediate in the demonstrative sciences. Therefore, so far as the bailiff is a medium according to the order of the subject's acting, the king is said to work through the bailiff; but according to the order of powers, the bailiff is said to act through the king, since the power of the king gives the bailiff's action its effect. Now there is no order of power between Father and Son, but only order of supposita. And hence we say that the Father spirates through the Son; and not conversely.

ARTICLE 4. *Whether the Father and the Son Are One Principle of the Holy Ghost?*

We proceed thus to the Fourth Article: It would seem that the Father and the Son are not one principle of the Holy Ghost.

Objection 1. For the Holy Ghost does not proceed from the Father and the Son as they are one; not as they are one in nature, for the Holy Ghost would in that way proceed from Himself, as He is one in nature with Them; nor again in so far as they are united in any one property, for it is clear that one property cannot belong to two subjects. Therefore the Holy Ghost proceeds from the Father and the Son as distinct from one another. Therefore the Father and the Son are not one principle of the Holy Ghost.

Obj. 2. Further, in this proposition "the Father and the Son are one principle of the Holy Ghost," we do not designate personal unity, because in that case the Father and the Son would be one person; nor again do we designate the unity of property, because if one property were the reason of the Father and the Son being one principle of the Holy Ghost, similarly, on account of His two properties, the Father would be two principles of the Son and of the Holy Ghost, which cannot be admitted. Therefore the Father and the Son are not one principle of the Holy Ghost.

Obj. 3. Further, the Son is not one with the Father more than is the Holy Ghost. But the Holy Ghost and the Father are not one principle as regards any other divine person. Therefore neither are the Father and the Son.

Obj. 4. Further, if the Father and the Son are one principle of the Holy Ghost, this one is either the Father or it is not the Father. But we cannot assert either of these positions because if the one is the Father it follows that the Son is the Father; and if the one is not the Father, it follows that the Father is not the Father. Therefore we cannot say that the Father and the Son are one principle of the Holy Ghost.

Obj. 5. Further, if the Father and the Son are one principle of the Holy Ghost, it seems necessary to say, conversely, that the one principle of the Holy Ghost is the Father and the Son. But this seems to be false; for this word "principle" stands either for the person of the Father or for the person of the Son, and in either sense it is false. Therefore this proposition also is false, that the Father and the Son are one principle of the Holy Ghost.

Obj. 6. Further, unity in substance makes identity. So if the Father and the Son are the one principle of the Holy Ghost, it follows that they are the same principle, which is denied by many. Therefore we cannot grant that the Father and the Son are one principle of the Holy Ghost.

Obj. 7. Further, the Father, Son, and Holy Ghost are called one Creator, because they are the one principle of the creature. But the Father and the Son are not one, but two Spirators, as many assert;[1] and this agrees also with what Hilary says (*De Trin.* ii)[2] that the Holy Ghost "is to be confessed as proceeding from Father and Son as authors." Therefore the Father and the Son are not one principle of the Holy Ghost.

On the contrary, Augustine says (*De Trin.* v,

14)[3] that "the Father and the Son are not two principles, but one principle of the Holy Ghost."

I answer that, The Father and the Son are in everything one, wherever there is no distinction between them of opposite relation. Hence since there is no relative opposition between them as the principle of the Holy Ghost it follows that the Father and the Son are one principle of the Holy Ghost.

Some, however, assert[4] that this proposition is incorrect: "The Father and the Son are one principle of the Holy Ghost," because, they declare, since the word principle in the singular number does not signify person, but property, it must be taken as an adjective; and since an adjective cannot be modified by another adjective, it cannot properly be said that the Father and the Son are one principle of the Holy Ghost unless "one" be taken as an adverb, so that the meaning should be: They are one principle—that is, in one and the same way. But then it might be equally right to say that the Father is two principles of the Son and of the Holy Ghost —namely, in two ways.

Therefore we must say that, although this word principle signifies a property, it does so after the manner of a noun, as do the words father and son even in things created. Hence it takes its number from the form that it signifies, like other nouns. Therefore, as the Father and the Son are one God by reason of the unity of the form that is signified by this word *God,* so they are one principle of the Holy Ghost by reason of the unity of the property that is signified in this word principle.

Reply Obj. 1. If we consider the spirative power, the Holy Ghost proceeds from the Father and the Son as they are one in the spirative power, which in a certain way signifies the nature with the property, as we shall see later (Q. XLI, A. 5). Nor is there any reason against one property being in two supposita that possess one nature. But if we consider the supposita of the spiration, then we may say that the Holy Ghost proceeds from the Father and the Son, as distinct; for He proceeds from them as the uniting love of both.

Reply Obj. 2. In the proposition "the Father and the Son are one principle of the Holy Ghost", one property is designated which is the form signified by the term. It does not however follow that by reason of the several properties the Father can be called several principles, for

---

[1] Cf. Alexander of Hales, *S.T.* II, 493 (QR I, 695); cf. also Bonaventure, *In Sent.*, I, d. 29, A. 2, Q. 2 (QR I, 515); Albert, *In Sent.*, I, d. 29, A. 5 (BO XXVI, 9); St. Thomas, *In Sent.*, Bk. I, XI, Q. I, A. 4.
[2] PL 10, 69.

[3] PL 42, 921.
[4] Alan of Lille, *Theol. Reg.*, 51 (PL 210, 644). Cf. Wm. of Auxerre, *Summa Aurea*, I, 8, 6 (fol. 17va).

this would imply in Him a plurality of supposita.

Reply Obj. 3. It is not by reason of relative properties that we speak of likeness or unlikeness in God, but by reason of the essence. Hence, as the Father is not more like to Himself than He is to the Son, so likewise neither is the Son more like to the Father than is the Holy Ghost.

Reply Obj. 4. These two propositions, "The Father and the Son are one principle which is the Father," or, "one principle which is not the Father," are not contradictory opposites; and hence it is not necessary to assert one or other of them. For when we say the Father and the Son are one principle, this word principle has not determinate supposition but rather it stands indeterminately for two persons together. Hence there is a fallacy of figure of speech as the argument concludes from the indeterminate to the determinate.

Reply Obj. 5. This proposition is also true:— "The one principle of the Holy Ghost is the Father and the Son," because the word "principle" does not stand for one person only, but indistinctly for the two persons as above explained.

Reply Obj. 6. There is no reason against saying that the Father and the Son are the same principle, because the word "principle" stands confusedly and indistinctly for the two Persons together.

Reply Obj. 7. Some say[1] that although the Father and the Son are one principle of the Holy Ghost, there are two spirators, by reason of the distinction of supposita, as also there are two spirating, because acts refer to supposita. Yet this does not hold good as to the name "Creator," because the Holy Ghost proceeds from the Father and the Son as from two distinct persons, as above explained; but the creature proceeds from the three persons not as distinct persons, but as one in essence. It seems, however, better to say that because spirating is an adjective, and spirator a noun, we can say that the Father and the Son are two spirating, by reason of the plurality of the supposita, but not two spirators by reason of the one spiration. For adjectival words derive their number from the supposita, but nouns from themselves, according to the form signified. As to what Hilary says, that the Holy Ghost is "from the Father and the Son as His authors," this is to be explained in the sense that the noun here stands for the adjective.

[1] Cf. p. 196, footnote 1, above.

QUESTION XXXVII

Of the name of the Holy Ghost—Love

(*In Two Articles*)

WE now inquire concerning the name Love, on which arise two points for consideration: (1) Whether it is the proper name of the Holy Ghost? (2) Whether the Father and the Son love each other by the Holy Ghost?

ARTICLE 1. *Whether "Love" is the Proper Name of the Holy Ghost?*

We proceed thus to the First Article: It would seem that Love is not the proper name of the Holy Ghost.

Objection 1. For Augustine says (*De Trin.* xv, 17)[2]: "As the Father, Son, and Holy Ghost are called Wisdom, and are not three Wisdoms, but one, I know not why the Father, Son, and Holy Ghost should not be called Charity, and all together one Charity." But no name which is predicated in the singular of each person and of all together, is a proper name of a person. Therefore this name, Love, is not the proper name of the Holy Ghost.

Obj. 2. Further, the Holy Ghost is a subsisting person, but love is not used to signify a subsisting person, but rather an action passing from the lover to the beloved. Therefore Love is not the proper name of the Holy Ghost.

Obj. 3. Further, Love is the bond between lovers, for as Dionysius says (*Div. Nom.* iv):[3] Love is "a unitive force." But a bond is a medium between what it joins together, not something proceeding from them. Therefore, since the Holy Ghost proceeds from the Father and the Son, as was shown above (Q. XXXVI, A. 2), it seems that He is not the Love or bond of the Father and the Son.

Obj. 4. Further, Love belongs to every lover. But the Holy Ghost is a a lover; therefore He has love. So if the Holy Ghost is Love, He must be love of love, and spirit from spirit; which is not admissible.

On the contrary, Gregory says (*Hom.* xxx, *in Pentecost.*):[4] "The Holy Ghost Himself is Love."

I answer that, The name Love in God can be taken essentially and personally. If taken personally it is the proper name of the Holy Ghost, just as Word is the proper name of the Son.

[2] PL 42, 1081.
[3] Sect. 15 (PG 3, 713).
[4] PL 76, 1220.

To see this we must know that since, as shown above (Q. XXVII, AA. 1, 3, 5), there are two processions in God, one by way of the intellect, which is the procession of the Word, and another by way of the will, which is the procession of Love, because the former is the more known to us we have been able to apply more suitable names to express our various considerations as regards that procession, but not as regards the procession of the will. Hence, we are obliged to employ circumlocution as regards the person Who proceeds, and the relations following from this procession, which are called procession and spiration, as stated above (Q. XXVIII, A. 4), and yet express the origin rather than the relation, in the proper sense of the term.

Nevertheless we must consider them in a like way in respect to each procession. For just as when a thing is understood by anyone there results in the one who understands a conception of the object understood, which conception we call word, so when anyone loves an object, a certain impression results, so to speak, of the thing loved in the affection of the lover, by reason of which the object loved is said to be in the lover, as also the thing understood is in the one who understands; so that when anyone understands and loves himself he is in himself, not only by real identity, but also as the thing understood is in the one who understands, and the thing loved is in the lover. As regards the intellect, however, words have been found to describe the mutual relation of the one who understands to the thing understood, as appears in the word "to understand"; and other words are used to express the procession of the intellectual conception—namely, "to speak," and "word." Hence in God, "to understand" is applied only essentially, because it does not imply relation to the Word that proceeds; but Word is said personally, because it signifies what proceeds; and the term "to speak" is a notional term as signifying the relation of the principle of the Word to the Word Himself. One the other hand, on the part of the will, with the exception of the words "dilection" and "love," which express the relation of the lover to the thing loved, there are no other terms in use which express the relation of the impression or affection of the object loved produced in the lover by the fact that he loves—to the principle of that impression, or *vice versa*. And therefore, on account of the poverty of our vocabulary, we express these relations by the words "love" and "dilection"; just as if we were to call the Word "intelligence conceived," or "wisdom begotten."

It follows that so far as love or dilection means only the relation of the lover to the thing loved, "love" and "to love" are said of the essence, as "understanding" and "to understand"; but, on the other hand, so far as these words are used to express the relation to its principle of what proceeds by way of love, and *vice versa*, so that by "love" is understood "the love proceeding," and by "to love" is understood "the spiration of the love proceeding," in that sense "love" is the name of the person, and "to love" is a notional term, as "to speak" and "to beget."

Reply Obj. 1. Augustine is there speaking of charity as it means the divine essence, as was said above (here and Q. XXIV, A. 2 Ans. 4).

Reply Obj. 2. Although to understand, and to will, and to love signify actions passing on to their objects, nevertheless they are actions that remain in the agents, as stated above (Q. XIV, A. 2), yet in such a way that in the agent itself they signify a certain relation to their object. Hence, love also in ourselves is something that remains in the lover, and the word of the heart is something remaining in the speaker, yet with a relation to the thing expressed by word, or loved. But in God, in whom there is nothing accidental, there is more than this, because both Word and Love are subsistent. Therefore, when we say that the Holy Ghost is the Love of the Father for the Son, or for something else, we do not mean anything that passes into another, but only the relation of love to the thing loved; as also in the Word is signified the relation of the Word to the thing expressed by the Word.

Reply Obj. 3. The Holy Ghost is said to be the bond of the Father and Son, in so far as He is Love, because, since the Father loves Himself and the Son with one Love, and conversely, there is expressed in the Holy Ghost, as Love, the relation of the Father to the Son, and conversely, as that of the lover to the beloved. But from the fact that the Father and the Son mutually love one another, it necessarily follows that this mutual Love, the Holy Ghost, proceeds from both. As regards origin, therefore, the Holy Ghost is not the medium, but the third person in the Trinity; but as regards the aforesaid relation He is the bond between the two persons, as proceeding from both.

Reply Obj. 4. As it does not belong to the Son, though He understands, to produce a word, for it belongs to Him to understand as the word proceeding, so, although the Holy Ghost loves, taking Love as an essential term, still it does not belong to Him to spirate love, which is to take love as a notional term; because He loves essentially as love proceeding, but not as the one from which love proceeds.

ARTICLE 2. *Whether the Father and the Son Love Each Other by the Holy Ghost?*

We proceed thus to the Second Article: It would seem that the Father and the Son do not love each other by the Holy Ghost.

Objection 1. For Augustine (*De Trin.* vii, 1)[1] proves that the Father is not wise by the Wisdom begotten. But as the Son is Wisdom begotten, so the Holy Ghost is the Love proceeding, as explained above (A. 1). Therefore the Father and the Son do not love each other by the Love proceeding—that is, by the Holy Ghost.

Obj. 2. Further, in the proposition, "The Father and the Son love each other by the Holy Ghost," this word "love" is to be taken either essentially or notionally. But it cannot be true if taken essentially, because in the same way we might say that "the Father understands by the Son"; nor, again, if it is taken notionally, for then, in like manner, it might be said that "the Father and the Son spirate by the Holy Ghost," or "that the Father generates by the Son." Therefore in no way is this proposition true: "The Father and the Son love each other by the Holy Ghost."

Obj. 3. Further, by the same love the Father loves the Son, and Himself, and us. But the Father does not love Himself by the Holy Ghost; for no notional act is reflected back on the principle of the act, since it cannot be said that the Father begets Himself, or that He spirates Himself. Therefore, neither can it be said that He loves Himself by the Holy Ghost, if "to love" is taken in a notional sense. Again, the love with which He loves us is not the Holy Ghost, because it expresses a relation to creatures, and this belongs to the essence. Therefore this also is false: "The Father loves the Son by the Holy Ghost."

On the contrary, Augustine says (*De Trin.* vi, 5):[2] "The Holy Ghost is He whereby the Begotten is loved by the one begetting and loves His Begetter."

I answer that, A difficulty about this question is offered, that when we say, "the Father loves the Son by the Holy Ghost," since the ablative is construed as denoting a cause, it seems to mean that the Holy Ghost is the principle of

love to the Father and the Son; which cannot be admitted.

In view of this difficulty some have held[3] that it is false that "the Father and the Son love each other by the Holy Ghost"; and they add that it was retracted by Augustine when he retracted its equivalent to the effect that the Father is wise by the Wisdom begotten.[4] Others say[5] that the proposition is improper and ought to be expounded, thus: "the Father loves the Son by the Holy Ghost—that is, by His essential Love," which is appropriated to the Holy Ghost. Others further say[6] that this ablative should be construed as signifying a sign, so that it means, "the Holy Ghost is the sign that the Father loves the Son," since the Holy Ghost proceeds from them both, as Love. Others, again, say[7] that this ablative must be construed as signifying the relation of formal cause, because the Holy Ghost is the love whereby the Father and the Son formally love each other. Others, again, say[8] that it should be construed as signifying the relation of a formal effect; and these approach nearer to the truth.

To make the matter clear, we must consider that since a thing is commonly denominated from its forms, as white from whiteness, and man from humanity, everything from which anything is denominated, in this particular respect stands to that thing in the relation of form. So when I say, "this man is clothed with a garment," the ablative is to be construed as having relation to the formal cause, although the garment is not the form. Now it may happen that a thing may be denominated from that which proceeds from it, not only as an agent is from its action, but also as from the term itself of the action—that is, the effect, when the effect itself is included in the comprehension of the action. For we say that fire warms by heating, although heating is not the heat which is the form of the fire, but is an action proceeding from the fire; and we say that a tree flowers with the flower, although the flower is not the tree's form, but is the effect proceeding from the form.

In this way, therefore, we must say that since in God "to love" is taken in two ways, essen-

---

[3] Peter of Poitiers, *Sent.*, I, 21 (PL 211, 872).

[4] *Retract.*, I, 26 (PL 32, 625).

[5] Cf. Alexander of Hales, *Summa Theol.*, II, 460 (QR I, 657).

[6] Simon of Tournai, *Sent.*, I, 21 (Schmaus, RTAM (1932), p. 297).

[7] Wm. of Auxerre, *Summa Aurea*, I, 8, 7 (fol. 18rb).

[8] See opusculum *"Quomodo Spiritus Sanctus"* among the works of Richard of St. Victor (PL 196, 1011). Cf. Bonaventure, *In Sent.*, I, dist. XXXII, A. 1, Q. 2 (QR I, 560, *nota* 7).

---

[1] PL 42, 933.

[2] PL 42, 928.

tially and notionally, when it is taken essentially, it means that the Father and the Son love each other not by the Holy Ghost, but by their essence. Hence Augustine says (*De Trin.* xv, 7):[1] "Who dares to say that the Father loves neither Himself, nor the Son, nor the Holy Ghost, except by the Holy Ghost?" The opinions first quoted are to be taken in this sense. But when the term Love is taken in a notional sense it means nothing else than "to spirate love;" just as to speak is to produce a word, and to flower is to produce flowers. As therefore we say that a tree flowers by its flower, so do we say that the Father, by the Word or the Son, speaks Himself, and His creatures, and that the Father and the Son love each other and us, by the Holy Ghost, or by Love proceeding.

Reply Obj. 1. To be wise or intelligent is taken only essentially in God. Therefore we cannot say that the Father is wise or intelligent by the Son. But to love is taken not only essentially, but also in a notional sense; and in this way we can say that the Father and the Son love each other by the Holy Ghost, as was above explained.

Reply Obj. 2. When the comprehension of an action implies a determined effect, the principle of the action may be denominated both from the action, and from the effect; so we can say, for instance, that a tree flowers by its flowering and by its flower. When, however, the idea of an action does not include a determined effect, then in that case, the principle of the action cannot be denominated from the effect, but only from the action. For we do not say that the tree produces the flower by the flower, but by the production of the flower. So when we say, "spirates" or "begets," this means only a notional act. Hence we cannot say that the Father spirates by the Holy Ghost, or begets by the Son. But we can say that the Father speaks by the Word, as by the Person proceeding, "and speaks by the speaking," as by a notional act; because "to speak" signifies a determinate person proceeding, since "to speak" means to produce word. Likewise to love, taken in a notional sense, means to produce love; and so it can be said that the Father loves the Son by the Holy Ghost, as by the person proceeding, and by Love itself as a notional act.

Reply Obj. 3. The Father loves not only the Son but also Himself and us, by the Holy Ghost; because, as above explained, (A. 1) to love, taken in a notional sense, not only means the production of a divine person, but also the per-

son produced by way of love, which has relation to the thing loved. Hence, as the Father speaks Himself and every creature by His begotten Word, in so far as the Word "begotten" adequately represents the Father and every creature, so He loves Himself and every creature by the Holy Ghost, in so far as the Holy Ghost proceeds as the love of the primal goodness whereby the Father loves Himself and every creature. Thus it is evident that relation to the creature is implied both in the Word and in the proceeding Love, as it were in a secondary way, since the divine truth and goodness are a principle of understanding and loving all creatures.

QUESTION XXXVIII
OF THE NAME OF THE HOLY GHOST AS "GIFT"
(*In Two Articles*)

THERE now follows the consideration of the Gift, concerning which there are two points of inquiry: (1) Whether "Gift" can be a personal name? (2) Whether it is the proper name of the Holy Ghost?

ARTICLE I. *Whether "Gift" Is a Personal name?*

We proceed thus to the First Article: It would seem that "Gift" is not a personal name.

Objection 1. For every personal name expresses a distinction in God. But the name of Gift does not express a distinction in God, for Augustine says (*De Trin.* xv, 19)[2] that the Holy Ghost "is so given as God's Gift, that He also gives Himself as God." Therefore Gift is not a personal name.

Obj. 2. Further, no personal name belongs to the divine essence. But the divine essence is the Gift which the Father gives to the Son, as Hilary says (*De Trin.* ix).[3] Therefore Gift is not a personal name.

Obj. 3. Further, according to Damascene (*De Fide Orthod.* iv)[4] "there is no subjection nor service in the divine persons." But gift implies a subjection both as regards him to whom it is given and as regards him by whom it is given. Therefore Gift is not a personal name.

Obj. 4. Further Gift implies relation to the creature, and it thus seems to be said of God in time. But personal names are said of God from eternity; as Father, and Son. Therefore Gift is not a personal name.

On the contrary, Augustine says (*De Trin.* xv, 19):[5] "As the body of flesh is nothing but

---

[1] PL 42, 1065.

[2] PL 42, 1086. [3] PL 10, 325.
[4] Chap. 21 (PG 94, 1085). [5] PL 42, 1086.

flesh, so the gift of the Holy Ghost is nothing but the Holy Ghost." But the Holy Ghost is a personal name; so also therefore is Gift.

I answer that, The word "gift" implies an aptitude for being given. And what is given has an aptitude or relation both to the giver and to that to which it is given. For it would not be given by anyone unless it was his to give, and it is given to someone to be his. Now a divine person is said to belong to another either by origin, as the Son belongs to the Father, or as possessed by another. But we are said to possess what we can freely use or enjoy as we please; and in this way a divine person cannot be possessed except by a rational creature united to God. Other creatures can be moved by a divine person, not, however, in such a way as to be able to enjoy the divine person, and to use its effect. The rational creature does sometimes attain to this, as when it is made partaker of the divine Word and of the Love proceeding, so as freely to know God truly and to love God rightly. Hence the rational creature alone can possess the divine person. Nevertheless in order that it may possess Him in this manner, its own power avails nothing. Hence this must be given it from above; for that is said to be given to us which we have from another source. Thus a divine person can be given, and can be a gift.

Reply Obj. 1. The name Gift implies a personal distinction in so far as gift implies something belonging to another through its origin. Nevertheless, the Holy Ghost gives Himself, since He is His own, and can use or rather enjoy Himself; as also a free man belongs to himself. And as Augustine says (*In Jo. Tract.* xxix):[1] "What is more yours than yourself?" Or we might say, and more fittingly, that a gift must belong in a way to the giver. But the phrase, "this is this one's," can be understood in several senses. In one way it means identity, as Augustine says (*ibid.*); and in that sense "gift" is the same as "the giver," but not the same as the one to whom it is given. The Holy Ghost gives Himself in that sense. In another sense, a thing is another's as a possession, or as a slave; and in that sense gift is essentially distinct from the giver, and the gift of God so taken is a created thing. In a third sense "this is this one's" through its origin only; and in this sense the Son is the Father's, and the Holy Ghost belongs to both. Therefore, so far as gift in this way signifies the possession of the giver, it is personally distinguished from the giver, and is a personal name.

[1] PL 35, 1629.

Reply Obj. 2. The divine essence is the Father's gift in the first sense, as being the Father's by way of identity.

Reply Obj. 3. Gift as a personal name in God does not imply subjection, but only origin, in relation to the giver; but in relation to the one to whom it is given, it implies a free use, or enjoyment, as above explained.

Reply Obj. 4. Gift is not so called from being actually given, but from its aptitude to be given. Hence the divine person is called Gift from eternity, although He is given in time. Nor does it follow that it is an essential name because it implies relation to the creature, but that it includes something essential in its meaning; just as the essence is included in the comprehension of person, as stated above (Q. XXXIV, A. 31).

ARTICLE 2. *Whether "Gift" Is the Proper Name of the Holy Ghost?*

We proceed thus to the Second Article: It would seem that Gift is not the proper name of the Holy Ghost.

Objection 1. For the name Gift comes from being given. But, as Isaias says, *A Son is given to us* (9. 6). Therefore to be Gift belongs to the Son, as well as to the Holy Ghost.

Obj. 2. Further, every proper name of a person signifies a property. But this word Gift does not signify a property of the Holy Ghost. Therefore Gift is not a proper name of the Holy Ghost.

Obj. 3. Further, the Holy Ghost can be called the spirit of a man, but He cannot be called the gift of any man, but "God's Gift" only. Therefore Gift is not the proper name of the Holy Ghost.

On the contrary, Augustine says (*De Trin.* iv, 20):[2] "As 'to be born' is, for the Son, to be from the Father, so, for the Holy Ghost, 'to be the Gift of God' is to proceed from Father and Son." But the Holy Ghost receives His proper name from the fact that He proceeds from Father and Son. Therefore Gift is the proper name of the Holy Ghost.

I answer that, Gift, taken personally in God, is the proper name of the Holy Ghost.

In proof of this we must know that a gift is properly an "unreturnable giving," as Aristotle says[3] that is, a thing which is not given with the intention of a return—and it thus implies a free giving. Now, the reason of free giving is love, since we give something to anyone freely because we wish good to him. So what we first

[2] PL 42, 908.
[3] *Topics,* IV, 4 (125ᵃ18).

give him is the love whereby we wish him well. Hence it is manifest that love has the nature of a first gift, through which all free gifts are given. So since the Holy Ghost proceeds as love, as stated above (Q. XXVII, A. 4; Q. XXXVII, A. I), He proceeds as the first gift. Hence Augustine says (*De Trin.* xv, 19):[1] "By the gift, which is the Holy Ghost, many particular gifts are portioned out to the members of Christ."

Reply Obj. 1. As the Son is properly called the Image because He proceeds by way of a word, whose nature it is to be the likeness of its principle, (although the Holy Ghost also is like to the Father), so also, because the Holy Ghost proceeds from the Father as love He is properly called Gift, although the Son, too, is given. For that the Son is given, is from the Father's love, according to the words, *God so loved the world, as to give His only begotten Son* (John 3. 16).

Reply Obj. 2. The name Gift involves the idea of belonging to the Giver through its origin; and thus it implies the property of the origin of the Holy Ghost—that is, His procession.

Reply Obj. 3. Before a gift is given, it belongs only to the giver; but when it is given, it is his to whom it is given. Therefore, because Gift does not imply the actual giving, it cannot be called a gift of man, but the Gift of God giving. When, however, it has been given, then it is the spirit of man, or a gift bestowed on man.

QUESTION XXXIX
OF THE PERSONS IN RELATION TO THE ESSENCE
(*In Eight Articles*)

SINCE we have considered those things which belong to the divine persons absolutely, we next treat of what concerns the person in relation to the essence, to the properties (Q. XL), and to the notional acts (Q. XLI); and of the comparison of these with each other (Q. XLII).

As regards the first of these, there are eight points of inquiry: (1) Whether the essence in God is the same as the person? (2) Whether we should say that the three persons are of one essence? (3) Whether essential names should be predicated of the persons in the plural, or in the singular? (4) Whether notional adjectives, or verbs, or participles, can be predicated of the essential names taken in a concrete sense? (5) Whether the same can be predicated of essential names taken in the abstract? (6) Whether the names of the persons can be predicated of concrete essential names? (7) Whether essen-

[1] PL 42, 1084.

tial attributes can be appropriated to the persons? (8) Which attributes should be appropriated to each person?

ARTICLE 1. *Whether in God the Essence Is the Same As the Person?*

We proceed thus to the First Article: It would seem that in God the essence is not the same as person.

Objection 1. For whenever essence is the same as person or suppositum, there can be only one suppositum of one nature, as is clear in the case of all separate substances. For in those things which are really one and the same, one cannot be multiplied apart from the other. But in God there is one essence and three persons, as is clear from what is above expounded (Q. XXVIII, A. 3; Q. XXX, A. 2). Therefore essence is not the same as person.

Ob. 2. Further, simultaneous affirmation and negation of the same things in the same respect cannot be true. But affirmation and negation are true of essence and of person. For person is distinct, while essence is not. Therefore person and essence are not the same.

Obj. 3. Further, nothing can be subject to itself. But person is subject to essence, and hence it is called suppositum or hypostasis. Therefore person is not the same as essence.

On the contrary, Augustine says (*De Trin.* vi, 6):[2] "When we say the person of the Father we mean nothing else but the substance of the Father."

I answer that, The truth of this question is quite clear if we consider the divine simplicity. For it was shown above (Q. III, A. 3) that the divine simplicity requires that in God essence is the same as suppositum, which in intellectual substances is nothing else than person.

But a difficulty seems to arise from the fact that while the divine persons are multiplied, the essence nevertheless retains its unity. And because, as Boëthius says (*De Trin.* 6),[3] "relation multiplies the Trinity of persons," some have thought that in God essence and person differ, since they held the relations to be "assistant" (*assistentes*), considering only in the relations the idea of reference to another, and not the relations as realities.

But as it was shown above (Q. XXVIII, A. 2) in creatures relations are accidental, while in God they are the divine essence itself. From this it follows that in God essence is not really distinct from person, and yet that the persons are

[2] PL 42, 943.
[3] PL 64, 1255.

really distinguished from each other. For person, as above stated (Q. XXIX, A. 4), signifies relation as subsisting in the divine nature. But relation as referred to the essence does not differ from it really, but only in our way of thinking, while as referred to an opposite relation, it has a real distinction by virtue of that opposition. Thus there are one essence and three persons.

Reply Obj. 1. There cannot be a distinction of suppositum in creatures by means of relations, but only by essential principles, because in creatures relations are not subsistent. But in God relations are subsistent, and so by reason of the opposition between them they distinguish the supposita; and yet the essence is not distinguished, because the relations themselves are not distinguished from each other so far as they are really the same as the essence.

Obj. 2. As essence and person in God differ in our way of thinking, it follows that something can be denied of the one and affirmed of the other. And therefore, when we suppose the one, we need not suppose the other.

Obj. 3. Divine things are named by us after the way of created things, as above explained (Q. XIII, A. 1 Ans. 2, 3). And since created natures are individualized by matter which is the subject of the specific nature, it follows that individuals are called subjects, supposita, or hypostases. So the divine persons are named supposita or hypostases, but not as if there really existed any real supposition or subjection.

ARTICLE 2. *Whether It Must Be Said That the Three Persons Are of One Essence?*

We proceed thus to the Second Article: It would seem not right to say that the three persons are of one essence.

Objection 1. For Hilary says (*De Synod.*)[1] that the Father, Son, and Holy Ghost "are indeed three by substance, but one in harmony." But the substance of God is His essence. Therefore the three persons are not of one essence.

Obj. 2. Further, nothing is to be affirmed of God except what can be confirmed by the authority of Holy Writ, as appears from Dionysius (*Div. Nom.* i).[2] Now Holy Writ never says that the Father, Son, and Holy Ghost are of one essence. Therefore this should not be asserted.

Obj. 3. Further, the divine nature is the same as the divine essence. It suffices therefore to say that the three persons are of one nature.

Obj. 4. Further, it is not usual to say that the person is of the essence, but rather that the essence is of the person. Therefore is does not seem fitting to say that the three persons are of one essence.

Obj. 5. Further, Augustine says (*De Trin.* vii, 6)[3] that "we do not say that the three persons are *from one essence,* lest we should seem to indicate a distinction between the essence and the persons in God." But prepositions which imply transition denote the oblique case. Therefore it is equally wrong to say that the three persons are "of one essence."

Obj. 6. Further, nothing should be said of God which can be occasion of error. Now, to say that the three persons are of one essence or substance furnishes occasion of error. For, as Hilary says (*De Synod.*):[4] "One substance predicated of the Father and the Son signifies either one subsistent, with two denominations; or one substance divided into two imperfect substances; or a third prior substance taken and assumed by the other two." Therefore it must not be said that the three persons are of one substance.

On the contrary, Augustine says (*Contra Maxim.* iii)[5] that "the word ὁμοούσιον, which the Council of Nicæa adopted against the Arians, means that the three persons are of one essence."

I answer that, As above explained (Q. XIII, A. 1, ANS. 2; A. 3), divine things are named by our intellect not as they really are in themselves, for in that way it knows them not, but in a way that belongs to things created. And as in sensible things from which the intellect derives its knowledge the nature of the species is made individual by the matter, and thus the nature is as the form, and the individual is the suppositum of the form, so also in God the essence is taken as the form of the three persons, according to our mode of signification. Now in creatures we say that every form belongs to that whereof it is the form; as the health and beauty of a man belongs to the man. But we do not say of that which has a form that it belongs to the form, unless some adjective qualifies the form; as when we say: "That woman is of a handsome figure," or: "This man is of perfect virtue." In like manner, as in God the persons are multiplied and the essence is not multiplied, we speak of one essence of the three persons, and three persons of the one essence, provided that these genitives be understood as designating the form.

1 PL 10, 503.
2 Sect. 2 (PG 3, 588).

3 PL 42, 945.   4 PL 10, 526.
5 Chap. 14 (PL 42, 772); *Contra Serm. Arian.*, chap. 36 (PL 42, 707).

Reply Obj. 1. Substance is here taken for the hypostasis, and not for the essence.

Reply Obj. 2. Although we may not find it declared in Holy Writ in so many words that the three persons are of one essence, nevertheless we find it so stated as regards the meaning; for instance, *I and the Father are one* (John 10. 30), and *I am in the Father, and the Father in Me* (*ibid.* 38); and there are many other texts of the same meaning.

Reply Obj. 3. Because "nature" designates the principle of action, while "essence" comes from being (*essendo*), things may be said to be of one nature which agree in some action, as all things which give heat, but only those things can be said to be "of one essence" which have one being. So the divine unity is better described by saying that the three persons are "of one essence," than by saying they are "of one nature."

Reply Obj. 4. Form, in the absolute sense, is usually designated as belonging to that of which it is the form, as we say "the virtue of Peter." On the other hand the thing having form is not usually designated as belonging to the form except when we wish to qualify or designate the form. In this case two genitives are required, one signifying the form, and the other signifying the determination of the form, as, for instance, when we say, "Peter is of great virtue" (*magnæ virtutis*), or else one genitive must have the force of two, as, for instance, "he is a man of blood"—that is, he is a man who sheds much blood (*multi sanguinis*). So, because the divine essence is signified as a form as regards the person, it may properly be said that the essence is of the person, but we cannot say the converse, unless we add some term to designate the essence; as, for instance, the Father is a person of the divine essence, or, the three persons are of one essence.

Reply Obj. 5. The preposition "from" or "out of" does not designate the relation of a formal cause, but rather the relation of an efficient or material cause, which causes are in all cases distinguished from those things of which they are the causes. For nothing is its own matter, nor its own active principle. Yet a thing may be its own form, as appears in all immaterial things. So, when we say, "three persons of one essence," taking essence as having the relation of form, we do not mean that essence is different from person, which we should mean if we said, "three persons from the same essence."

Reply Obj. 6. As Hilary says (*De Synod.*):[1] "It would be prejudicial to holy things, if we

[1] PL 10, 538, 527.

had to do away with them, just because some do not think them holy. So if some misunderstand ὁμοούσιον, what is that to me, if I understand it rightly?" . . . "The oneness of substance does not result from likeness, or from union or from community of possession, but from one substance being proper to both Father and Son."

ARTICLE 3. *Whether Essential Names Should Be Predicated in the Singular of the Three Persons?*

We proceed thus to the Third Article: It would seem that essential names, as the name "God," should not be predicated in the singular of the three persons, but in the plural.

Objection 1. For as man signifies one that has humanity, so God signifies one that has Godhead. But the three persons are three who have Godhead. Therefore the three persons are three Gods.

Obj. 2. Further, Gen. 1. 1, where it is said, *In the beginning God created heaven and earth,* the Hebrew original has *Elohim,* which may be rendered *Gods* or *Judges;* and this word is used on account of the plurality of persons. Therefore the three persons are several Gods, and not one God.

Obj. 3. Further, this word "thing," when it is said absolutely, seems to belong to substance. But it is predicated of the three persons in the plural. For Augustine says:[2] "The things that are the objects of our future glory are the Father, Son, and Holy Ghost." Therefore other essential names can be predicated in the plural of the three persons.

Obj. 4. Further, as this word God signifies a being who has Deity, so also this word person signifies a being subsisting in an intellectual nature. But we say there are three persons. So for the same reason we can say there are three Gods.

On the contrary, It is said (Deut. 6. 4): *Hear, O Israel, the Lord thy God is one God.*

I answer that, Some essential names signify the essence after the manner of nouns, while others signify it after the manner of adjectives. Those which signify it as nouns are predicated of the three persons in the singular only, and not in the plural. Those which signify the essence as adjectives are predicated of the three persons in the plural.

The reason of this is that nouns (substantives) signify something by way of substance, while adjectives signify something by way of accident, which adheres to a subject. Now just as substance has being of itself, so also it has of itself unity or multitude; hence the singularity

[2] *Christian Doctrine,* I, 5 (PL 34, 21).

or plurality of a substantive name depends upon the form signified by the name. But as accidents have their being in a subject, so they have unity or plurality from their subject, and therefore the singularity and plurality of adjectives depends upon their supposita.

In creatures, one form does not exist in several supposita except by unity of order, as the form of an ordered multitude. So if the names signifying such a form are nouns, they are predicated of many in the singular, but otherwise if they are adjectives. For we say that many men are a college, or an army, or a people, but we say that many men are collegians. Now in God the divine essence is signified by way of a form, as above explained (A. 2), which, indeed, is simple and supremely one, as shown above (QQ. III, A. 7; XI, A. 4). So, names which signify the divine essence in a substantive manner are predicated of the three persons in the singular, and not in the plural. This, then, is the reason why we say that Socrates, Plato, and Cicero are three men, whereas we do not say the Father, Son, and Holy Ghost are three Gods, but one God; because in the three supposita of human nature there are three humanities, but in the three divine Persons there is but one divine essence.

On the other hand, the names which signify essence in an adjectival manner are predicated of the three persons plurally, by reason of the plurality of supposita. For we say there are three existent or three wise beings, or three eternal, uncreated, and immense beings, if these terms are understood in an adjectival sense. But if taken in a substantive sense, we say one uncreated, immense, eternal being, as Athanasius declares.[1]

Reply Obj. 1. Though the name God signifies a being having Godhead, nevertheless the mode of signification is different. For the name God is used substantively, but "having Godhead" is used adjectivally. Consequently, although there are "three having Godhead," it does not follow that there are three Gods.

Reply Obj. 2. Various languages have diverse modes of expression. So as by reason of the plurality of supposita the Greeks said three hypostases, so also in Hebrew *Elohim* is in the plural. We, however, do not apply the plural either to God or to substance, lest plurality be referred to the substance.

Reply Obj. 3. This word "thing" is one of the transcendentals. And hence, so far as it is referred to relation, it is predicated of God in the

[1] Creed "*Quicumque*," (MA II, 1354; DZ 39).

plural; but so far as it is referred to the substance, it is predicated in the singular. So Augustine says, in the passage quoted, that the same Trinity is a thing supreme.

Reply Obj. 4. The form signified by the word person is not essence or nature, but personality. So, as there are three personalities—that is, three personal properties in the Father, Son, and Holy Ghost—it is predicated of the three, not in the singular, but in the plural.

ARTICLE 4. *Whether the Concrete Essential Names Can Stand for the Person?*

We proceed thus to the Fourth Article: It would seem that the concrete, essential names cannot stand for the person, so that we can truly say "God begot God."

Objection 1. For, as the logicians say, "a singular term signifies what it stands for."[2] But this name *God* seems to be a singular term, for it cannot be predicated in the plural, as above explained (A. 3). Therefore, since it signifies the essence, it stands for essence, and not for person.

Obj. 2. Further, a term in the subject is not restricted by a term in the predicate, as to its signification, but only as to the time signified in the predicate. But when I say, "God creates," this name "God" stands for the essence. So when we say "God begot," this term *God* cannot, by reason of the notional predicate, stand for person.

Obj. 3. Further, if this be true, "God begot," because the Father generates, for the same reason this is true, "God does not beget," because the Son does not beget. Therefore there is God who begets, and there is God who does not beget; and thus it follows that there are two Gods.

Obj. 4. Further, if "God begot God," He begot either God, that is Himself, or another God. But He did not beget God, that is Himself; for, as Augustine says (*De Trin.* i, 1),[3] "nothing begets itself." Neither did He beget another God, as there is only one God. Therefore it is false to say, "God begot God."

Obj. 5. Further, if God begot God, He begot either God who is the Father, or God who is not the Father. If God who is the Father, then God the Father was begotten. If God who is not the Father, then there is a God who is not God the Father, which is false. Therefore it cannot be said that "God begot God."

On the contrary, In the Creed it is said, "God of God."[4]

[2] Peter of Spain, *Summulae Logicae,* VII, 3. See Prantl, *Gesch. der Logik,* chap. 17.   [3] PL, 42, 820.
[4] Nicaean Creed (MA II, 666; DZ 54).

I answer that, Some have said[1] that "this name God and the like, properly according to their nature, stand for the essence, but by reason of some notional adjunct are made to stand for the Person." This opinion apparently arose from considering the divine simplicity, which requires that in God, He Who possesses and what is possessed be the same. So He Who possesses Godhead, which is signified by the name God, is the same as Godhead.

But when we consider the proper way of expressing ourselves, the mode of signification must be considered no less than the thing signified. Hence as this word God signifies the divine essence as in Him Who possesses it, just as the name man signifies humanity in a suppositum, others more truly have said[2] that "this word God, from its mode of signification, can, in its proper sense, stand for person," as does the word man.

So this word God sometimes stands for the essence, as when we say "God creates," because this predicate belongs to the subject by reason of the form signified—that is, Godhead. But sometimes it stands for the person, either for only one, as when we say God begets, or for two, as when we say, God spirates; or for three, as when it is said: *To the King of ages, immortal, invisible, the only God,* etc. (I Tim. i. 17).

Reply Obj. 1. Although this name God agrees with singular terms as regards the form signified not being multiplied, nevertheless it agrees also with general terms so far as the form signified is to be found in several supposita. So it need not always stand for the essence it signifies.

Reply Obj. 2. This holds good against those who say that the word God does not naturally stand for person.

Reply Obj. 3. The word God stands for the person in a different way from that in which this word man does; for since the form signified by this word man—that is, humanity—is really divided among its different supposita, it stands of itself for the person, even if there is nothing added determining it to the person—that is, to a distinct suppositum. The unity or community of the human nature, however, is not a reality, but is only in the consideration of the mind. Hence this term man does not stand for the common nature, unless this is required by something

added, as when we say, man is a species, but the form signified by the name God—that is, the divine essence—is really one and common. So of itself it stands for the common nature, but by some adjunct it may be restricted so as to stand for the person. So, when we say, "God generates," by reason of the notional act this name God stands for the person of the Father. But when we say, "God does not generate," there is no addition to determine this name to the person of the Son, and hence the phrase means that generation is contrary to the divine nature. If, however, something be added belonging to the person of the Son, this proposition, for instance, "God begotten does not beget," is true. Consequently, it does not follow that there exists a "God generator," and a "God not generator," unless there be added something pertaining to the persons; as, for instance, if we were to say, "the Father is God the generator," and "the Son is God the non-generator"; and so it does not follow that there are many Gods, for the Father and the Son are one God, as was said above (A. 3).

Reply Obj. 4. This is false, "the Father begot God, that is Himself," because the word Himself, as a reciprocal term, refers to the same suppositum. Nor is this contrary to what Augustine says[3] that God the Father begot another self (*alterum se*), since the word "*se*" is either in the ablative case, and then it means "He begot another from Himself," or it indicates a simple relation, and thus points to identity of nature. This is, however, either an improper or an emphatic way of speaking, so that it would really mean, "He begot another most like to Himself." Likewise also it is false to say, "He begot another God," because although the Son is another than the Father, as above explained (Q. XXXI, A. 2), nevertheless it cannot be said that He is "another God," because this adjective "another" would be understood to apply to the noun God; and thus the meaning would be that there is a distinction of Godhead. Yet this proposition "He begot another God" is tolerated by some,[4] provided that another be taken as a noun, and the word God be construed in apposition with it. This, however, is an improper way of speaking, and to be avoided, for fear of giving occasion to error.

Reply Obj. 5. To say, "God begot God Who is God the Father," is wrong, because since the word Father is construed in apposition to God, the word God is restricted to the person of the Father, so that it would mean, "He begot God,

---

[1] Gilbert de la Porrée, *In De Praedicat. Trium Pers.,* (PL 64, 1310); cf. Wm. of Auxerre, *Summa Aurea,* pt. I, tr. 4, chap. 4 (fol. 5d); Alexander of Hales, *S.T.* II, 357 (QR I, 535).

[2] Alan of Lille, *Theol. Reg.,* 24 (PL 210, 632); 32 (636); also, Wm. of Auxerre, *Summa Aurea,* II, 4, 4 (fol. 6a).

[3] *Epist.,* CLXX (PL 33, 749).

[4] Wm. of Auxerre, *Summa Aurea,* I, 4, 4 (fol. 5d).

Who is Himself the Father," and then the Father would be spoken of as begotten, which is false. Therefore the negative of this proposition is true, "He begot God Who is not God the Father. If, however, we understand these words not to be in apposition, and require something to be added, then, on the contrary, the affirmative proposition is true, and the negative is false; so that the meaning would be "He begot God Who is God Who is the Father." Such a rendering, however, appears to be forced, so that it is better to say simply that the affirmative proposition is false, and the negative is true.

Yet Prepositinus said[1] that both the negative and affirmative are false, because this relative "Who" in the affirmative proposition can be referred to the suppositum, while in the negative it denotes both the thing signified and the suppositum. Hence, in the affirmative the sense is that to be God the Father is befitting to the person of the Son, and in the negative the sense is that "to be God the Father," is to be removed from the Son's divinity as well as from His personality. This, however, appears to be irrational, since, according to the Philosopher,[2] what is open to affirmation, is open also to negation.

ARTICLE 5. *Whether Abstract Essential Names Can Stand for the Person?*

We proceed thus to the Fifth Article: It would seem that abstract essential names can stand for the person, so that this proposition is true, Essence begets essence.

Objection 1. For Augustine says (*De Trin.* vii, 2):[3] "The Father and the Son are one Wisdom, because they are one essence; and taken singly Wisdom is from Wisdom, as essence from essence."

Obj. 2. Further, generation or corruption in ourselves implies generation or corruption of what is within us. But the Son is generated. Therefore since the divine essence is in the Son, it seems that the divine essence is generated.

Obj. 3. Further, God and the divine essence are the same, as is clear from what is above explained (Q. III, A. 3). But, as was shown, it is true to say that "God begets God." Therefore this is also true:—"Essence begets essence."

Obj. 4. Further, a predicate can stand for that of which it is predicated. But the Father is the divine essence. Therefore essence can stand for the person of the Father. Thus the essence begets.

Obj. 5. Further, the essence is "a thing begetting," because the essence is the Father Who is begetting. Therefore if the essence is not begetting, the essence will be "a thing begetting" and "not begetting," which cannot be.

Obj. 6. Further, Augustine says (*De Trin.* iv, 20):[4] "The Father is the principle of the whole Godhead." But He is principle only by begetting or spirating. Therefore the Father begets or spirates the Godhead.

On the contrary, Augustine says (*De Trin.* i, 1):[5] "Nothing begets itself." But if the essence begets the essence, it begets itself only, since nothing exists in God as distinguished from the divine essence. Therefore the essence does not beget the essence.

I answer that, Concerning this, the abbot Joachim erred[6] in asserting that as we can say "God begot God," so we can say, "Essence begot essence," considering that, by reason of the divine simplicity God is nothing else but the divine essence.

In this he was wrong, because if we wish to express ourselves correctly, we must take into account not only the thing which is signified, but also the mode of its signification, as above stated (A. 4). Now although God is really the same as Godhead, nevertheless the mode of signification is not in each case the same. For since this word God signifies the divine essence in Him that possesses it, from its mode of signification it can of its own nature stand for person. Thus the things which properly belong to the persons can be predicated of this word God, as, for instance, we can say "God is begotten" or "is Begetter," as above explained (A. 4). The word essence, however, in its mode of signification, cannot stand for Person, because it signifies the essence as an abstract form. Consequently, what properly belongs to the persons whereby they are distinguished from each other cannot be attributed to the essence. For that would imply distinction in the divine essence in the same way as there exists distinction in the suposita.

Reply Obj. 1. To express unity of essence and of person, the holy Doctors have sometimes expressed themselves with greater emphasis than the property of terms allows. And so instead of enlarging upon such expressions we should rather explain them: thus, for instance, abstract names should be explained by concrete names. or even by personal names; as when we find "essence from essence," or "wisdom from wis-

---

[1] *Summa* (fol. 55vb).
[2] *Interpretation*, 6 (17ª30).
[3] PL 42, 820.

[4] PL 42, 908.
[5] PL 42, 820.
[6] Cf. *Decretal. Gregor.*, IX, I, tit. I, chap. 2 (RF II, 6).

dom" we should take the sense to be, the Son, Who is essence and wisdom, is from the Father Who is essence and wisdom. Nevertheless, as regards these abstract names a certain order should be observed, because what belongs to act is more nearly allied to the persons because acts belong to supposita. So "nature from nature," and "wisdom from wisdom" are less improper than "essence from essence."

Reply Obj. 2. In creatures the one generated has not the same nature numerically as the generator, but another nature, numerically distinct, which begins to exist in it anew by generation, and ceases to exist by corruption, and so it is generated and corrupted accidentally; but God begotten has the same nature numerically as the begetter. So the divine nature in the Son is not begotten either per se or accidentally.

Reply Obj. 3. Although God and the divine essence are really the same, nevertheless, on account of their different mode of signification, we must speak in a different way about each of them.

Reply Obj. 4. The divine essence is predicated of the Father by mode of identity by reason of the divine simplicity; yet it does not follow that it can stand for the Father because its mode of signification is different. This objection would hold good as regards things which are predicated of another as the universal of a particular.

Reply Obj. 5. The difference between substantive and adjectival names consists in this, that the former carry their suppositum with them, while the latter do not, but add the thing signified to the noun. Hence logicians say[1] that the noun stands in the place of but the adjective does not stand for but joins. Therefore substantive personal terms can be predicated of the essence because they are really the same; nor does it follow that a personal property makes a distinct essence, but it belongs to the suppositum implied in the substantive name. But notional and personal adjectives cannot be predicated of the essence unless we add some noun. We cannot say that the essence is begetting; yet we can say that the essence is a thing begetting, or that it is God begetting, if "thing and "God" stand for person, but not if they stand for essence. Consequently, there exists no contradiction in saying that "essence is a thing begetting," and "a thing not begetting," because in the first case "thing" stands for person, and in the second it stands for the essence.

Reply Obj. 6. So far as Godhead is one in several supposita, it agrees in a certain degree with the form of a collective term. So when we say, the Father is the principle of the whole Godhead, the term Godhead can be taken for all the persons together, since it is the principle in all the divine persons. Nor does it follow that He is His own principle, as for example one of the people may be called the ruler of the people without being ruler of himself. We may also say that He is the principle of the whole Godhead, not as generating or spirating it, but as communicating it by generation and spiration.

ARTICLE 6. *Whether the Persons Can be Predicated of the Essential Terms?*

We proceed thus to the Sixth Article: It would seem that the persons cannot be predicated of the concrete essential names, so that we can say for instance, God is three persons, or, God is the Trinity.

Objection 1. For it is false to say, man is every man, because it cannot be verified as regards any suppositum. For neither Socrates, nor Plato, nor anyone else is every man. In the same way this proposition, God is the Trinity, cannot be verified of any one of the supposita of the divine nature. For the Father is not the Trinity, nor is the Son, nor is the Holy Ghost. So to say, God is the Trinity, is false.

Obj. 2. Further, the lower is not predicated of the higher except by accidental predication; as for instance when I say, animal is man, for it is accidental to animal to be man. But this name God as regards the three persons is as a general term to inferior terms, as Damascene says (*De Fide Orthod.* iii, 4).[2] Therefore it seems that the names of the persons cannot be predicated of this name God, except in an accidental sense.

On the contrary, Augustine says,[3] in his sermon on Faith, We believe that one God is one divinely named Trinity.

I answer that, As above explained (A. 5, Ans. 5), although adjectival terms, whether personal or notional, cannot be predicated of the essence, nevertheless substantive terms can be so predicated, owing to the real identity of essence and person. The divine essence is not only really the same as one person, but it is really the same as the three persons. And so, one person, and two, and three, can be predicated of the essence as if we were to say, The essence is the Father, and the Son, and the Holy Ghost. And because this word God can of itself stand for the essence, as above explained (A. 4, Ans. 3), hence, just as it is

---

[1] Peter of Spain, *Summulae Logicae*, VII, I, I; see Prantl, *Gesch. der Logik*, 17, 200 (III, 51).

[2] PG 94, 997.
[3] Cf. Fulgentius, PL 65, 673.

true to say, The essence is the three persons, so likewise it is true to say, God is the three persons.

Reply Obj. 1. As above explained (A. 4, Ans. 3) this term man can of itself stand for person, whereas an addition is required for it to stand for the universal human nature. So it is false to say, Man is every man, because it cannot be verified of any suppositum. On the contrary, this word God can of itself stand for the divine essence. So, although to say of any of the supposita of the divine nature, God is the Trinity, is untrue, nevertheless it is true of the divine essence. This was denied by Gilbert de la Porrée[1] because he did not take note of this distinction.

Reply Obj. 2. When we say, God, or the divine essence, is the Father the predication is one of identity, and not of the lower in regard to a higher species, because in God there is no universal and singular. Hence, as this proposition, The Father is God, is of itself true, so this proposition, God is the Father, is true of itself, and not in any accidental way.

Article 7. *Whether the Essential Names Should Be Appropriated to the Persons?*

We proceed thus to the Seventh Article: It would seem that the essential names should not be appropriated to the persons.

Objection 1. For whatever might verge on error in faith should be avoided in the treatment of divine things; for, as Jerome says,[2] "careless words involve risk of heresy." But to appropriate to any one person the names which are common to the three persons may verge on error in faith, for it may be supposed either that such belong only to the person to whom they are appropriated, or that they belong to Him in a fuller degree than to the others. Therefore the essential attributes should not be appropriated to the persons.

Obj. 2. Further, the essential attributes expressed in the abstract signify by mode of form. But one person is not as a form to another, since a form is not distinguished in suppositum from that of which it is the form. Therefore the essential attributes, especially when expressed in the abstract, are not to be appropriated to the persons.

Obj. 3. Further, what is proper is prior to the appropriated, for what is proper is included in the idea of the appropriated. But the essential attributes, in our way of understanding, are prior to the persons; as what is common is prior to what is proper. Therefore the essential attributes are not to be appropriated to the persons.

On the contrary, The Apostle says: *Christ the power of God and the wisdom of God* (I Cor. 1. 24).

I answer that, For the manifestation of our faith it is fitting that the essential attributes should be appropriated to the persons. For although the trinity of persons cannot be proved by demonstration, as was above expounded (Q. XXXII, A. 1), nevertheless it is fitting that it be declared by things which are more known to us. Now the essential attributes of God are more clear to us from the standpoint of reason than the personal properties, because we can derive certain knowledge of the essential attributes from creatures which are sources of knowledge to us, such as we cannot obtain regarding the personal properties, as was above explained (*ibid.*). As, therefore, we make use of the likeness of the trace or image found in creatures for the manifestation of the divine persons, so also in the same manner do we make use of the essential attributes. And such a manifestation of the divine persons by the use of the essential attributes is called "appropriation."

The divine person can be manifested in a twofold manner by the essential attributes. In one way by likeness, and thus the things which belong to the intellect are appropriated to the Son, Who proceeds by way of intellect, as Word. In another way by unlikeness; as power is appropriated to the Father, as Augustine says,[3] because fathers by reason of old age are sometimes feeble, lest anything of the kind be imagined of God.

Reply Obj. 1. The essential attributes are not appropriated to the persons as if they exclusively belonged to them, but in order to make the persons manifest by way of likeness, or unlikeness, as above explained. So, no error in faith can arise, but rather manifestation of the truth.

Reply Obj. 2. If the essential attributes were appropriated to the persons as exclusively belonging to each of them, then it would follow that one person would be as a form as regards another; which Augustine altogether repudiates (*De Trin.* vii, 1),[4] showing that the Father is wise, not by the wisdom begotten by Him, as though only the Son were Wisdom, so that the Father and the Son together only can be called wise, but not the Father without the Son. But

---

[1] *De Trin.*, (PL 64, 1311).
[2] Peter Lombard, *Sent.*, IV, 13, 2 (QR II, 818).
[3] Cf. Hugh of St. Victor, *De Sacram.*, I, II, 8 (PL 176, 209).
[4] PL 42, 933.

the Son is called the Wisdom of the Father because He is Wisdom from the Father Who is Wisdom. For each of them is of Himself Wisdom, and both together are one Wisdom. Hence the Father is not wise by the wisdom begotten by Him, but by the wisdom which is His own essence.

Reply Obj. 3. Although the essential attribute is in its proper concept prior to person, according to our way of understanding, nevertheless, so far as it is appropriated, there is nothing to prevent the personal property from being prior to that which is appropriated. Thus colour is posterior to body considered as body, but is naturally prior to white body, considered as white.

ARTICLE 8. *Whether the Essential Attributes Are Appropriated to the Persons in a Fitting Manner by the Holy Doctors?*

We proceed thus to the Eighth Article: It would seem that the essential attributes are appropriated to the persons unfittingly by the holy doctors.

Objection 1. For Hilary says (*De Trin.* ii),[1] "Eternity is in the Father, the species is in the Image; and use is in the Gift." In these words he designates three names proper to the persons: the name of the Father, the name Image proper to the Son (Q. XXXV, A. 2), and the name Bounty or Gift, which is proper to the Holy Ghost (Q. XXXVIII, A. 2). He also designates three appropriated terms. For he appropriates eternity to the Father, species to the Son, and use to the Holy Ghost. This he does apparently without reason. For eternity imports duration of being; species, the principle of being; and use belongs to the operation. But essence and operation are not found to be appropriated to any person. Therefore the above terms are not fittingly appropriated to the persons.

Obj. 2. Further, Augustine says:[2] "Unity is in the Father, equality in the Son, and in the Holy Ghost is the concord of equality and unity." This does not, however, seem fitting, because one person does not receive formal denomination from what is appropriated to another. For the Father is not wise by the wisdom begotten, as above explained (A. 7, ANS. 2; Q. XXXVII, A. 2, ANS. 1). But, as he adds, "All these three are one by the Father, all are equal by the Son, and all united by the Holy Ghost." The above, therefore, are not fittingly appropriated to the Persons.

Obj. 3. Further, according to Augustine,[3] to the Father is attributed power, to the Son wisdom, to the Holy Ghost goodness. Nor does this seem fitting; for strength is part of power, whereas strength is found to be appropriated to the Son, according to the text, *Christ the strength* (Douay, *power*) *of God* (I Cor. 1. 24). So it is likewise appropriated to the Holy Ghost, according to the words, *strength* (Douay, *virtue*) *came out from Him and healed all* (Luke 6. 19). Therefore power should not be appropriated to the Father.

Obj. 4. Likewise Augustine says (*De Trin.* vi, 10):[4] "What the Apostle says, *From Him, and by Him, and in Him,* is not to be taken in a confused sense." And (*Contra Maxim.* ii.)[5] "'from Him' refers to the Father, 'by Him' to the Son, 'in Him' to the Holy Ghost." This, however, seems to be incorrectly said; for the words "in Him" seem to imply the relation of final cause, which is first among the causes. Therefore this relation of cause should be appropriated to the Father, Who is the principle from no principle.

Obj. 5. Likewise, Truth is appropriated to the Son, according to John 14. 6, *I am the Way, the Truth, and the Life;* and likewise the book of life, according to Ps. 39. 9, *In the beginning of the book it is written of Me,* where a gloss observes,[6] "that is, with the Father Who is My head"; also this word "Who is," because on the text of Isaias, *Behold I go to the Gentiles* (65. 1), a gloss adds,[7] "The Son speaks Who said to Moses, I am Who am."

But it seems that these are proper to the Son, and are not appropriated. For truth, according to Augustine (*De Vera Relig.* 36),[8] is "the supreme likeness of the principle without any unlikeness." So it seems that it properly belongs to the Son, Who has a principle. Also the book of life seems to be proper to the Son, as signifying "a thing from another," for every book is written by someone. This also, "Who is," appears to be proper to the Son, because if when it was said to Moses, *I am Who am,* the Trinity spoke, then Moses could have said, "He Who is the Father, Son, and Holy Ghost sent me to you"; so also he could have said further, "He Who is the Father, and the Son, and the Holy Ghost sent me to you," pointing out a certain Person. This, however, is false, because no person is Father, Son, and Holy Ghost. Therefore it cannot be common to the Trinity, but is proper to the Son.

---

[1] PL 10, 51.
[2] *Christian Doctrine,* I, 5 (PL 34, 21).
[3] Cf. Hugh of St. Victor, *De Sacram.* I, II, 6 (PL 176, 208).
[4] PL 42, 932.   [5] Chap. 23 (PL 42, 800).
[6] *Glossa ordin.* (III, 143[b]).   [7] *Glossa interl.* (IV, 1041[r]).
[8] PL 34, 152.

I answer that, Our intellect, which is led to the knowledge of God from creatures, must consider God according to the mode derived from creatures. In considering any creature four points present themselves to us in due order. First, the thing itself taken absolutely is considered as a being. Secondly, it is considered as one. Thirdly, its intrinsic power of operation and causality is considered. The fourth point of consideration embraces its relation to its effects. Hence this fourfold consideration comes to our mind in reference to God.

According to the first point of consideration, whereby we consider God absolutely in His being, the appropriation mentioned by Hilary applies, according to which eternity is appropriated to the Father, species to the Son, use to the Holy Ghost. For eternity in so far as it means a being without a principle, has a likeness to the property of the Father, Who is a principle without a principle. Species or beauty has a likeness to the property of the Son. For beauty includes three conditions: integrity or perfection, since those things which are impaired are by the very fact ugly; due proportion or harmony; and lastly, brightness, or clarity, whence things are called beautiful which have an elegant colour.

The first of these has a likeness to the property of the Son, since as Son He has in Himself truly and perfectly the nature of the Father. To suggest this, Augustine says in his explanation (*De Trin.* vi, 10):[1] "Where—that is, in the Son —there is supreme and primal life," etc.

The second agrees with the Son's property, since He is the express Image of the Father. Hence we see that an image is said to be beautiful if it perfectly represents even an ugly thing. This is indicated by Augustine when he says (*ibid.*), "Where there exists wondrous proportion and primal equality," etc.

The third agrees with the property of the Son as the Word, "which is the light and splendour of the intellect," as Damascene says (*De Fide Orthod.*).[2] Augustine alludes to the same when he says (*ibid.*): "As the perfect Word, not wanting in anything, and, so to speak, the art of the omnipotent God," etc.

"Use" has a likeness to the property of the Holy Ghost; provided that "use" be taken in a wide sense, as including also the sense of "to enjoy," according as "to use is to employ something at the beck of the will, and to enjoy means to use joyfully," as Augustine says (*De Trin.* x,

11).[3] So "use," whereby the Father and the Son enjoy each other, agrees with the property of the Holy Ghost, as Love. This is what Augustine says (*De Trin.* vi, 10):[4] "That love, that delectation, that felicity or beatitude, is called use by him (Hilary)." But the use by which we enjoy, is likened to the property of the Holy Ghost as the Gift, and Augustine points to this when he says (*ibid.*): "In the Trinity, the Holy Ghost, the sweetness of the Begetter and the Begotten, pours out upon us mere creatures His immense bounty and wealth." Thus it is clear how eternity, species, and use are attributed or appropriated to the persons, but not essence or operation; because, being common, there is nothing in their notion to liken them to the properties of the Persons.

The second consideration of God regards Him as "one." In that view Augustine[5] appropriates "unity to the Father, equality to the Son, concord or union to the Holy Ghost." It is manifest that these three imply unity, but in different ways. For unity is said absolutely, as it does not presuppose anything else; and for this reason it is appropriated to the Father, to Whom any other person is not presupposed, since He is the principle without a principle. Equality implies unity in relation to another, for that is equal which has the same quantity as another. So equality is appropriated to the Son, Who is the principle from a principle. Union implies the unity of two, and is therefore appropriated to the Holy Ghost, since He proceeds from two. And from this we can understand what Augustine means when he says (*loc. cit.*) that "The Three are one, by reason of the Father; They are equal by reason of the Son; and are united by reason of the Holy Ghost." For it is clear that we trace a thing back to that in which we find it first, just as in this lower world we attribute life to the vegetative soul, because therein we find the first trace of life. Now, unity is perceived at once in the person of the Father, even if by an impossible hypothesis, the other persons were removed. So the other persons derive their unity from the Father. But if the other persons be removed, we do not find equality in the Father, but we find it as soon as we suppose the Son. So, all are equal by reason of the Son, not as if the Son were the principle of equality in the Father, but that, without the Son equal to the Father, the Father could not be called equal; because His equality is considered first in

1 PL 42, 931.
2 Bk. I, chap. 13 (PG 94, 857).
3 PL 42, 982.
4 PL 42, 932.
5 *Christian Doctrine,* I, 5 (PL 34, 21).

regard to the Son, for that the Holy Ghost is equal to the Father, is also from the Son. Likewise, if the Holy Ghost, Who is the union of the two, be excluded, we cannot understand the oneness of the union between the Father and the Son. So all are connected by reason of the Holy Ghost, because given the Holy Ghost, we find the reason for the union among the divine Persons, from which the Father and the Son are said to be united.

According to the third consideration, which brings before us the adequate power of God in the sphere of causality, there is said to be a third kind of appropriation: of power, wisdom, and goodness.[1] This kind of appropriation is made both by reason of likeness as regards what exists in the divine persons, and by reason of unlikeness if we consider what is in creatures. For power has the nature of a principle, and so it has a likeness to the heavenly Father, Who is the principle of the whole Godhead. But in an earthly father it is wanting sometimes by reason of old age. Wisdom has likeness to the heavenly Son, as the Word, for a word is nothing but the concept of wisdom. In an earthly son this is sometimes absent by reason of lack of years. Goodness, as the nature and object of love, has likeness to the Holy Ghost, Who is Love; but seems contrary to the earthly spirit, which often implies a certain violent impulse, according to Isaias 25. 4: *The spirit of the strong is as a blast beating on the wall.* Strength is appropriated to the Son and to the Holy Ghost, not as denoting the power itself of a thing, but as sometimes used to express that which proceeds from power; for instance, we say that the strong work done by an agent is its strength.

According to the fourth consideration, that is, God's relation to His effects, there arises appropriation of the expression "from Whom," "by Whom," and "in Whom." For this preposition "from" (*ex*) sometimes implies a certain relation of the material cause, which has no place in God; and sometimes it expresses the relation of the efficient cause, which can be applied to God by reason of His active power; hence it is appropriated to the Father in the same way as power. The preposition "by" (*per*) sometimes designates an intermediate cause; thus we may say that a smith works by a hammer. Hence the word by is not always appropriated to the Son, but belongs to the Son properly and strictly, according to the text, *All things were made by Him* (John 1. 3); not that the Son is an instru-

[1] Cf. Hugh of St. Victor, *De Sacram.*, I, II, 6 (PL 176, 208).

ment, but as the principle from a principle. Sometimes it designates the relation of a form "by" which an agent works; thus we say that an artificer works by his art. Hence, as wisdom and art are appropriated to the Son, so also is the expression "by Whom." The preposition "in" strictly denotes the relation of one containing. Now, God contains things in two ways: in one way by their likeness; thus things are said to be in God, as existing in His knowledge. In this sense the expression "in Him" should be appropriated to the Son. In another sense things are contained in God because He in His goodness preserves and governs them, by guiding them to a fitting end; and in this sense the expression "in Him" is appropriated to the Holy Ghost, as likewise is "goodness." Nor need the relation of the final cause (though the first of causes) be appropriated to the Father, Who is the principle without a principle, because the divine persons, of Whom the Father is the principle, do not proceed from Him as towards an end, since each of Them is the last end; but They proceed by a natural procession, which seems more to belong to the nature of a natural power.

Regarding the other points of inquiry, we can say that since truth belongs to the intellect, as stated above (Q. XVI, A. 1), it is appropriated to the Son, without, however, being a property of His. For truth, as we said above (Q. XVI, A. 1), can be considered as existing in the thought or in the thing itself. Hence, as intellect and thing in their essential meaning are referred to the essence, and not to the persons, so the same is to be said of truth. The definition quoted from Augustine belongs to truth as appropriated to the Son. The "book of life" directly means knowledge, but indirectly it means life. For, as above explained (Q. XXIV, A. 1), it is God's knowledge regarding those who are to possess eternal life. Consequently, it is appropriated to the Son, although life is appropriated to the Holy Ghost, as implying a certain kind of interior movement, agreeing in that sense with the property of the Holy Ghost as Love. To be written by another is not of the essence of a book considered as such, but this belongs to it only as a work produced. So this does not imply origin, nor is it personal, but an appropriation to a person. The expression "Who is" is appropriated to the person of the Son not by reason of itself, but by reason of an addition, because, in God's word to Moses, there was prefigured the delivery of the human race accomplished by the Son. Yet, because the word "Who" is taken in a relative sense, it may sometimes relate to the person of the Son, and in that sense it would be taken personally; as, for instance, were we to say, The Son is the begotten "Who is," since God begotten is personal. But taken indefinitely, it is an essential term. And although the pronoun "this" (*iste*) seems grammatically to point to a particular person, nevertheless everything that we can point to can be grammatically treated as a person, although in its own nature it is not a person; as we may say, this stone, and this ass. So, speaking in a grammatical sense, so far as the word God signifies and stands for the divine essence, the latter may be designated by the pronoun this, according to Exod. 15. 2: *This is my God, and I will glorify Him.*

QUESTION XL

OF THE PERSONS AS COMPARED TO THE RELATIONS OR PROPERTIES

(In Four Articles)

WE now consider the persons in connection with the relations, or properties; and there are four points of inquiry: (1) Whether relation is the same as person? (2) Whether the relations distinguish and constitute the persons? (3) Whether the hypostases would remain distinct if the relations were abstracted from the persons by the intellect? (4) Whether the relations, according to our mode of understanding, presuppose the acts of the persons, or contrariwise?

ARTICLE 1. *Whether Relation Is the Same As Person?*

We proceed thus to the First Article: It would seem that in God relation is not the same as person.

Objection 1. For when things are identical, if one is multiplied the others are multiplied. But in one person there are several relations; as in the person of the Father there is paternity and common spiration. Again, one relation exists in two persons, as common spiration in the Father and in the Son. Therefore relation is not the same as person.

Obj. 2. Further, according to the Philosopher[1] "nothing is contained by itself." But relation is in the person; nor can it be said that this occurs because they are identical, for otherwise relation would be also in the essence. Therefore relation, or property, is not the same as person in God.

Obj. 3. Further, when several things are identical, what is predicated of one is predicated of

the others. But all that is predicated of a person is not predicated of his property. For we say that the Father begets, but not that the paternity is begetting. Therefore property is not the same as person in God.

On the contrary, in God "what is" and "whereby it is" are the same, according to Boëthius (*De Hebdom.*).[2] But the Father is Father by paternity. Therefore He is the same as paternity. In the same way, the other properties are the same as the persons.

I answer that, Different opinions have been held on this point. Some have said[3] that the properties are not the persons, nor in the persons; and these have thought thus owing to the mode of signification of the relations, which do not indeed signify existence *in* something, but rather existence *towards* something. Hence, they styled the relations "assistant," as above explained (Q. XXVIII, A. 2). But since relation, considered as really existing in God, is the divine essence Itself, and the essence is the same as person, as appears from what was said above (Q. XXXIX, A. 1), relation must necessarily be the same as person.

Others,[4] therefore, considering this identity, said that the properties were indeed the persons; but not *in* the persons; for, they said, there are no properties in God except in our way of speaking, as stated above (Q. XXXII, A. 2). We must, however, say that there are properties in God, as we have shown (*ibid.*). These are designated by abstract terms, being forms, as it were, of the persons. So, since the nature of a form requires it to be *in* that of which it is the form, we must say that the properties are in the persons, and yet that they are the persons; as we say that the essence is in God, and yet is God.

Reply Obj. 1. Person and property are really the same, but differ logically. Consequently, it does not follow that if one is multiplied, the other must also be multiplied. We must, however, consider that in God, by reason of the divine simplicity, a twofold real identity exists as regards what in creatures are distinct. For, since the divine simplicity excludes the composition of matter and form, it follows that in God the abstract is the same as the concrete, as Godhead and God. And as the divine simplicity excludes the composition of subject and accident, it follows that whatever is attributed

---

[1] *Physics*, IV, 3 (210ᵃ25).

[2] PL 64, 1311.

[3] Gilbert de la Porrée. Cf. St. Thomas, *De Pot.*, VIII, 2. Also, see above, Q. XXVIII, A. 2.

[4] Prepositinus, *Summa* (fol. 67rb).

to God is His essence Itself; and so, wisdom and power are the same in God, because they are both in the divine essence. According to this twofold identity, property in God is the same as person. For personal properties are the same as the persons because the abstract and the concrete are the same in God, since they are the subsisting persons themselves, as paternity is the Father Himself, and filiation is the Son, and procession is the Holy Ghost. But the non-personal properties are the same as the persons according to the other reason of identity, whereby whatever is attributed to God is His own essence. Thus, common spiration is the same as the person of the Father, and the person of the Son; not that it is one self-subsisting person, but that as there is one essence in the two persons, so also there is one property in the two persons, as above explained (Q. XXX, A. 2).

Reply Obj. 2. The properties are said to be in the essence only by mode of identity. But in the persons they exist by mode of identity, not merely in reality, but also in the mode of signification, as the form exists in its suppositum. Thus the properties determine and distinguish the persons, but not the essence.

Reply Obj. 3. Notional participles and verbs signify the notional acts, and acts belong to supposita. Now, properties do not signify supposita, but forms of supposita. And so their mode of signification is against notional participles and verbs being predicated of the properties.

ARTICLE 2. *Whether the Persons Are Distinguished by the Relations?*

We proceed thus to the Second Article: It would seem that the persons are not distinguished by the relations.

Objection 1. For simple things are distinct by themselves. But the persons are supremely simple. Therefore they are distinguished by themselves, and not by the relation.

Obj. 2. Further, a form is distinguished only in relation to its genus. For white is distinguished from black only by quality. But hypostasis signifies an individual in the genus of substance. Therefore the hypostases cannot be distinguished by relations.

Obj. 3. Further, what is absolute comes before what is relative. But the distinction of the divine persons is the primary distinction. Therefore the divine persons are not distinguished by the relations.

Obj. 4. Further, whatever presupposes distinction cannot be the first principle of distinc-

tion. But relation presupposes distinction, which comes into its definition; for a relation is what is towards another. Therefore the first distinctive principle in God cannot be relation.

On the contrary, Boëthius says (*De Trin.*):[1] "Relation alone multiplies the Trinity" of the divine Persons.

I answer that, In whatever multitude of things is found something common to all, it is necessary to seek out the principle of distinction. So, as the three persons agree in the unity of essence, we must seek to know the principle of distinction whereby they are several. Now, there are two principles of difference between the divine persons, and these are origin and relation. Although these do not really differ, yet they differ in the mode of signification; for origin is signified by way of act, as generation; and relation by way of the form, as paternity.

Some,[2] then, considering that relation follows upon act, have said that the divine hypostases are distinguished by origin, so that we may say that the Father is distinguished from the Son, because the former begets and the latter is begotten. Further, that the relations, or the properties, make known the distinctions of the hypostases or persons as resulting therefrom; as also in creatures the properties manifest the distinctions of individuals, which distinctions are caused by the material principles.

This opinion, however, cannot stand—for two reasons. First, because, in order that two things be understood as distinct, their distinction must be understood as resulting from something intrinsic to both; thus in things created it results from their matter or their form. Now origin of a thing does not designate anything intrinsic, but means the way from something, or to something; as generation signifies the way to the thing generated, and as proceeding from the generator. Hence it is not possible that what is generated and the generator should be distinguished by generation alone, but in the generator and in the thing generated we must presuppose whatever makes them to be distinguished from each other. In a divine person there is nothing to presuppose but essence, and relation or property. Hence, since the persons agree in essence, it only remains to be said that the persons are distinguished from each other by the

---

[1] Chap. 6. (PL 64, 1255).

[2] See *De Pot.*, VIII, 3, 13, where Richard of St. Victor is mentioned (*De Trin.*, IV, 15–PL 196, 939); cf. Bonaventure, *In Sent.*, I, dist. XXVI, A. 1, Q. 2, arg. 3 (QR 1, 455); Q. 3, arg. 3 (QR 1, 456).

relations. Secondly, because the distinction of the divine persons is not to be so understood as if what is common to them all is divided, because the common essence remains undivided, but the distinguishing principles themselves must constitute the things which are distinct. Now the relations or the properties distinguish or constitute the hypostases or persons, since they are themselves the subsisting persons; as paternity is the Father, and sonship is the Son, because in God the abstract and the concrete do not differ. But it is against the notion of origin that it should constitute hypostasis or person. For origin taken in an active sense signifies proceeding from a subsisting person, so that it presupposes the latter; while in a passive sense origin, as nativity, signifies the way to a subsisting person, and as not yet constituting the person.

It is therefore better to say that the persons or hypostases are distinguished rather by relations than by origin. For, although in both ways they are distinguished, nevertheless in our mode of understanding they are distinguished chiefly and firstly by relations; hence this name Father signifies not only a property, but also the hypostasis; but this term Begetter or Begetting signifies property only, because this name Father signifies the relation which is distinctive and constitutive of the hypostasis; and this term Begetter or Begotten signifies the origin which is not distinctive and constitutive of the hypostasis.

Reply Obj. 1. The persons are the subsisting relations themselves. Hence it is not against the simplicity of the divine persons for them to be distinguished by the relations.

Reply Obj. 2. The divine persons are not distinguished as regards being, in which they subsist, nor in anything absolute, but only as regards something relative. Hence relation suffices for their distinction.

Reply Obj. 3. The more prior a distinction is, the nearer it approaches to unity, and so it must be the least possible distinction. So the distinction of the persons must be by that which distinguishes the least possible; and this is by relation.

Reply Obj. 4. Relation presupposes the distinction of the supposita when it is an accident; but when the relation is subsistent, it does not presuppose, but brings about distinction. For when it is said that relation is to be towards another, the word "another" signifies the correlative which is not prior but simultaneous in the order of nature.

ARTICLE 3. *Whether the Hypostases Remain If the Relations Are Abstracted by the Intellect from the Persons?*

We proceed thus to the Third Article: It would seem that the hypostases remain if the properties or relations are abstracted by the intellect from the persons.

Objection 1. For that to which something is added, may be understood when the addition is taken away; as for instance man is something added to animal which can be understood if rational be taken away. But person is something added to hypostasis, for person is a hypostasis distinguished by a property of dignity. Therefore, if a personal property be taken away from a person, the hypostasis remains.

Obj. 2. Further, that the Father is Father, and that He is someone, are not due to the same reason. For as He is the Father by paternity, supposing He is some one by paternity it would follow that the Son, in Whom there is not paternity, would not be someone. So when paternity is mentally abstracted from the Father, He still remains someone—that is, a hypostasis. Therefore, if property be removed from person, the hypostasis remains.

Obj. 3. Further, Augustine says (*De Trin.* v, 6):[1] "Unbegotten is not the same as Father; for if the Father had not begotten the Son, nothing would prevent Him being called unbegotten." But if He had not begotten the Son, there would be no paternity in Him. Therefore, if paternity be removed, there still remains the hypostasis of the Father as unbegotten.

On the contrary, Hilary says (*De Trin.* iv):[2] "The Son has nothing else than birth." But He is Son by birth. Therefore, if sonship be removed, the Son's hypostasis no more remains, and the same holds as regards the other persons.

I answer that, Abstraction by the intellect is twofold,—when the universal is abstracted from the particular, as animal abstracted from man; and when the form is abstracted from the matter, as the form of a circle is abstracted by the intellect from all sensible matter.

The difference between these two abstractions consists in the fact that in the abstraction of the universal from the particular that from which the abstraction is made does not remain; for when the difference of rationality is removed from man, man no longer remains in the intellect, but animal alone remains. But in the abstraction of the form from the matter, both the

1 PL 42, 914.
2 PL 10, 103.

form and the matter remain in the intellect; as, for instance, if we abstract the form of a circle from brass, there remains in our intellect separately the understanding both of a circle and of brass.

Now, although there is in reality no universal nor particular in God, nor form and matter, nevertheless, as regards the mode of signification there is a certain likeness of these things in God; and thus Damascene says (*De Fide Orthod.* iii, 6)[1] that "substance is common and hypostasis is particular." So, if we speak of the abstraction of the universal from the particular, the common essence remains in the intellect if the properties are removed; but not the hypostasis of the Father, which is, as it were, a particular.

But, as regards the abstraction of the form from the matter, if the non-personal properties are removed, then the idea of the hypostases and persons remains; as, for instance, if the fact of the Father's being unbegotten or spirating be abstracted by the intellect from the Father, the Father's hypostasis or person remains.

If, however, the personal property be removed by the intellect, the idea of the hypostasis no longer remains. For the personal properties are not to be understood as added to the divine hypostases, as a form is added to a pre-existing subject, but they carry with them their own supposita, since they are themselves subsisting persons; thus paternity is the Father Himself. For hypostasis signifies something distinct in God, since hypostasis means an individual substance. So, as relation distinguishes and constitutes the hypostases, as above explained (A. 2), it follows that if the personal relations are removed by the intellect, the hypostases no longer remain.

Some, however, think, as above noted (A. 2), that the divine hypostases are not distinguished by the relations, but only by origin, so that the Father is a hypostasis because He is not from another, and the Son is a hypostasis because He is from another by generation. But the consequent relations which are to be regarded as properties of dignity, constitute the notion of person, and are thus called personal properties. Hence, if these relations are removed by the intellect, the hypostasis, but not the persons, remain.

But this is impossible, for two reasons: first, because the relations distinguish and constitute the hypostases, as shown above (A. 2); secondly, because every hypostasis of a rational nature is a person, as appears from the definition of

Boëthius (*De Duab. Natur.*)[2] that, person is "the individual substance of a rational nature." Hence, to have hypostasis and not person it would be necessary to abstract the rationality from nature, but not the property from the person.

Reply Obj. 1. Person does not add to hypostasis a distinguishing property absolutely, but a distinguishing property of dignity, all of which must be taken in place of a difference. Now, this distinguishing property is one of dignity because it is understood as subsisting in a rational nature. Hence, if the distinguishing property be removed from the person, the hypostasis no longer remains, while it would remain were the rationality of the nature removed; for both person and hypostasis are individual substances. Consequently, in God the distinguishing relation belongs to the notion of both.

Reply Obj. 2. By paternity the Father is not only Father, but is a person, and is someone, or a hypostasis. It does not follow, however, that the Son is not someone or a hypostasis, just as it does not follow that He is not a person.

Reply Obj. 3. Augustine does not mean to say that the hypostasis of the Father would remain as unbegotten if His paternity were removed, as if innascibility constituted and distinguished the hypostasis of the Father; for this would be impossible, since being unbegotten says nothing positive and is only a negation, as he himself says.[3] But he speaks in a general sense, since not every unbegotten being is the Father. So, if paternity be removed, the hypostasis of the Father does not remain in God, as distinguished from the other persons, but only as distinguished from creatures. And this is the way the Jews understand it.

ARTICLE 4. *Whether the Properties Presuppose the Notional Acts?*

We proceed thus to the Fourth Article: It would seem that the notional acts are understood before the properties.

Objection 1. For the Master of the Sentences says (1 *Sent.* D. xxvii)[4] that, "the Father always is, because He begets the Son." So it seems that generation precedes paternity in the order of understanding.

Obj. 2. Further, in the understanding every relation presupposes that on which it is founded; as equality presupposes quantity. But paternity is a relation founded on the action of genera-

---

[1] PG 94, 1001.

[2] Chap. 3 (PL 64, 1343).
[3] *De Trin.*, v, 6 (PL 42, 915).
[4] Peter Lombard (QR 1, 171).

tion. Therefore paternity presupposes generation.

Obj. 3. Further, active generation is to paternity as nativity is to sonship. But sonship presupposes nativity, for the Son is so called because He is born. Therefore paternity also presupposes generation.

On the contrary, Generation is the operation of the person of the Father. But paternity constitutes the person of the Father. Therefore, in the order of understanding, paternity is prior to generation.

I answer that, According to the opinion that the properties do not distinguish and constitute the hypostases, but only manifest them as already distinct and constituted,[1] we must absolutely say that the relations in our mode of understanding follow upon the notional acts, so that we can say, absolutely, that "because He begets, He is the Father."

A distinction, however, is needed if we suppose that the relations distinguish and constitute the divine hypostases. For origin has in God an active and passive signification—active, as generation is attributed to the Father, and spiration, taken for the notional act, is attributed to the Father and the Son; passive, as nativity is attributed to the Son, and procession to the Holy Ghost. For, in the order of understanding, origin, in the passive sense, precedes absolutely the personal properties of the person proceeding, because origin, as passively understood, signifies the way to a person constituted by the property. Likewise, origin signified actively is prior in the order of understanding to the non-personal relation of the person originating; as the notional act of spiration precedes, in the order of understanding, the unnamed relative property common to the Father and the Son. The personal property of the Father can be considered in a twofold sense: first, as a relation, and thus again in the order of understanding it presupposes the notional act, for relation, as such, is founded upon an act; secondly, according as it constitutes the person, and thus the notional act presupposes the relation, as an action presupposes a person acting.

Reply Obj. 1. When the Master says that "because He begets, He is Father," the term "Father" is taken as meaning relation only, but not as signifying the subsisting person; for then it would be necessary to say conversely that because He is Father He begets.

Reply Obj. 2. This objection avails of pater-

nity as a relation, but not as constituting a person.

Reply Obj. 3. Nativity is the way to the person of the Son; and so, in the order of understanding, it precedes sonship, even as constituting the person of the Son. But active generation signifies a proceeding from the person of the Father. Therefore it presupposes the personal property of the Father.

QUESTION XLI
OF THE PERSONS IN REFERENCE TO THE NOTIONAL ACTS
(*In Six Articles*)

WE now consider the persons in reference to the notional acts, concerning which six points of inquiry arise: (1) Whether the notional acts are to be attributed to the persons? (2) Whether these acts are necessary or voluntary? (3) Whether as with regard to these acts a person proceeds from nothing or from something? (4) Whether in God there exists a power as regards the notional acts? (5) What this power means? (6) Whether several persons can be the term of one notional act?

ARTICLE 1. *Whether the Notional Acts Are To Be Attributed to the Persons?*

We proceed thus to the First Article: It would seem that the notional acts are not to be attributed to the persons.

Objection 1. For Boëthius says (*De Trin.*):[2] "Whatever is predicated of God, of whatever genus it be, becomes the divine substance, except what pertains to the relation." But action is one of the ten genera. Therefore, any action attributed to God belongs to His essence, and not to a notion.

Obj. 2. Further, Augustine says (*De Trin.* v, 4, 5)[3] that everything which is said of God, is said of Him as regards either His substance, or relation. But whatever belongs to the substance is signified by the essential attributes; and whatever belongs to the relations, by the names of the persons, or by the names of the properties. Therefore, beyond these, notional acts are not to be attributed to the persons.

Obj. 3. Further, the property of action is of itself to cause passion. But we do not place passions in God. Therefore neither are notional acts to be placed in God.

On the contrary, Augustine (Fulgentius, *De*

---

[1] Richard of St. Victor, *De Trin.*, IV, 15 (PL 196, 939); see above, A. 2.

[2] Chap. 4 (PL 64, 1252).

[3] PL 42, 913, 914.

Fide ad Petrum ii)[1] says: "It is a property of the Father to beget the Son." But to beget is an act. Therefore notional acts are to be placed in God.

I answer that, In the divine persons distinction is founded on origin. But origin can be properly designated only by certain acts. Therefore, to signify the order of origin in the divine persons, we must attribute notional acts to the persons.

Reply Obj. 1. Every origin is designated by an act. In God there is a twofold order of origin: one, according as the creature proceeds from Him, and this is common to the three persons; and so those actions which are attributed to God to designate the proceeding of creatures from Him, belong to His essence. Another order of origin in God regards the procession of person from person, and so the acts which designate the order of this origin are called notional, because the notions of the persons are the relations of the persons to one another, as is clear from what was above explained (Q. XXXII, A. 3).

Reply Obj. 2. The notional acts differ from the relations of the persons only in their mode of signification, and in reality are entirely the same. Hence the Master says that generation and nativity "in other words are paternity and sonship" (1 *Sent.* D. xxvi).[2] To see this, we must consider that the origin of one thing from another is first known from movement, for that anything be changed from its disposition by movement evidently arises from some cause. Hence action, in its primary sense, means origin of movement; for, as movement derived from another into a mobile object, is called passion, so the origin of movement itself as beginning from another and terminating in what is moved is called action. Hence, if we take away movement action implies nothing more than order of origin, in so far as action proceeds from some cause or principle to what is from that principle. Consequently, since in God no movement exists, the personal action of the one producing a person is only the reference of the principle to the person who is from the principle; which references are the relations, or the notions. Nevertheless we cannot speak of devine and intelligible things except after the manner of sensible things, from which we derive our knowledge, and wherein actions and passions, so far as these imply movement, differ from the relations which result from action and passion, and therefore it was necessary to signify the relations of the

persons separately after the manner of act, and separately after the manner of relations. Thus it is evident that they are really the same, differing only in their mode of signification.

Reply Obj. 3. Action, so far as it means origin of movement, naturally involves passion; but action in that sense is not attributed to God. Hence, passions are attributed to Him only from a grammatical standpoint, and in accordance with our manner of speaking, as we attribute to beget to the Father, and to the Son to be begotten.

ARTICLE 2. *Whether the Notional Acts Are Voluntary?*

We proceed thus to the Second Article: It would seem that the notional acts are voluntary.

Objection 1. For Hilary says (*De Synod.*):[3] "Not by natural necessity was the Father led to beget the Son."

Obj. 2. Further, the Apostle says, *He transferred us to the kingdom of the Son of His love* (Col. 1. 13). But love belongs to the will. Therefore the Son was begotten of the Father by will.

Obj. 3. Further, nothing is more voluntary than love. But the Holy Ghost proceeds as Love from the Father and the Son. Therefore He proceeds voluntarily.

Obj. 4. Further, the Son proceeds by mode of the intellect, as the Word. But every word proceeds by the will from a speaker. Therefore the Son proceeds from the Father by will, and not by nature.

Obj. 5. Further, what is not voluntary is necessary. Therefore if the Father begot the Son not by the will, it seems to follow that He begot Him by necessity; and this is against what Augustine says (*Ad Orosium* qu. vii).[4]

On the contrary, Augustine says, in the same book,[5] that, "the Father begot the Son neither by will, nor by necessity."

I answer that, When anything is said to be, or to be made by the will, this can be understood in two senses. In one sense, the ablative designates only concomitance, as I can say that I am a man by my will—that is, I will to be a man; and in this way it can be said that the Father begot the Son by will, as also He is God by will, because He wills to be God, and wills to beget the Son. In the other sense, the ablative expresses the relation of a principle, as it is said that the workman works by his will, as the will is the

---

[1] PL 65, 675.
[2] Peter Lombard (QR 1, 165).

[3] PL 10, 520.
[4] Among the works of Augustine, *Dial.* 65 *Quaest.*, Q. 7 (PL 40, 736).
[5] *Ibid.*

principle of his work; and thus in that sense it must be said that God the Father did not beget the Son by His will, but that He produced the creature by His will. Hence in the book *De Synod.*, it is said[1]: "If anyone say that the Son was made by the Will of God, as a creature is said to be made, let him be anathema."

The reason of this is that will and nature differ in their manner of causation, in such a way that nature is determined to one, while the will is not determined to one; and this because the effect is assimilated to the form of the agent, whereby the latter acts. Now it is manifest that of one thing there is only one natural form whereby it exists; and hence it will act according to the kind of thing it is. But the form whereby the will acts is not only one, but many, according to the number of notions understood. Hence what the will does is not dependent upon what kind of thing the agent is, but is what the agent wills and understands it to be. So the will is the principle of those things which may be this way or that way, but of those things which can be only in one way, the principle is nature.

What, however, can exist in different ways is far from the divine nature, and belongs to the nature of a created being, because God is of Himself necessary being, whereas a creature is made from nothing. Thus, the Arians,[2] wishing to prove the Son to be a creature, said that the Father begot the Son by will, taking will in the sense of principle. But we, on the contrary, must assert that the Father begot the Son not by will, but by nature. Therefore Hilary says (*De Synod.*)[3]: "The will of God gave to all creatures their substance: but perfect birth gave the Son a nature derived from a substance impassible and unborn. All things created are such as God willed them to be; but the Son, born of God subsists in the perfect likeness of God."

Reply Obj. 1. This saying is directed against those[4] who did not admit even the concomitance of the Father's will in the generation of the Son, for they said that the Father begot the Son in such a manner by nature that the will to beget was wanting, just as we ourselves suffer many things against our will from natural necessity— as, for instance, death, old age, and like ills. This appears from what precedes and from what follows as regards the words quoted, for thus we read: "Not against His will, nor as it were, forced, nor as if He were led by natural necessity did the Father beget the Son."

[1] Hilary (PL 10, 520).
[2] Cf. Hilary, *De Synod.* (PL 10, 520).
[3] *Ibid.*   [4] Cf. Hilary, *Ibid.*

Reply Obj. 2. The Apostle calls Christ the Son of the love of God, since He is superabundantly loved by God; not, however, as if love were the principle of the Son's generation.

Reply Obj. 3. The will, as a kind of nature, wills something naturally, as man's will naturally tends to happiness; and likewise God naturally wills and loves Himself; but in regard to things other than Himself, the will of God is, in a way, undetermined in itself, as above explained (Q. XIX, A. 3). Now, the Holy Ghost proceeds as Love, since God loves Himself, and hence He proceeds naturally, although He proceeds by mode of the will.

Reply Obj. 4. Even as regards intellectual conceptions, a reduction is made to those first principles which are naturally understood. But God naturally understands Himself, and thus the conception of the divine Word is natural.

Reply Obj. 5. A thing is said to be necessary of itself, and by reason of another. Taken in the latter sense, it has a twofold meaning: first, as an efficient and compelling cause, and thus necessary means what is violent; secondly, it means a final cause, when a thing is said to be necessary as the means to an end, so far as without it the end could not be attained, or, at least, so well attained. In neither of these ways is the divine generation necessary, because God is not the means to an end, nor is He subject to compulsion. But a thing is said to be necessary "of itself" which cannot not be; in this sense it is necessary for God to be, and in the same sense it is necessary that the Father beget the Son.

ARTICLE 3. *Whether the Notional Acts Proceed from Something?*

We proceed thus to the Third Article: It would seem that the notional acts do not proceed from anything.

Objection 1. For if the Father begets the Son from something, this will be either from Himself or from something else. If from something else, since that from which a thing is generated exists in what is generated, it follows that something different from the Father exists in the Son, and this contradicts what is laid down by Hilary (*De Trin.* vii)[5] that, "In them nothing diverse or different exists." If the Father begets the Son from Himself, since again that from which a thing is generated, if it remains, receives as predicate the thing generated from it—just as we say, "The man is white," since the man remains, when from not white he is made white—it follows that either the Father does not remain

[5] PL 10. 232.

after the Son is begotten, or that the Father is the Son, which is false. Therefore the Father does not beget the Son from something, but from nothing.

Obj. 2. Further, that from which anything is generated is the principle of what is generated. So if the Father generate the Son from His own essence or nature, it follows that the essence or nature of the Father is the principle of the Son. But it is not a material principle, because in God nothing material exists; and therefore it is, as it were, an active principle, as the begetter is the principle of the one begotten. Thus it follows that the essence generates, which was disproved above (Q. XXXIX, A. 5).

Obj. 3. Further, Augustine says (*De Trin.* vii, 6)[1] that "the three persons are not from the same essence, because the essence is not another thing from person." But the person of the Son is not other than the essence. Therefore the Son is not from the Father's essence.

Obj. 4. Further, every creature is from nothing. But in Scripture the Son is called a creature; for it is said (Ecclus. 24. 5), in the person of the Wisdom begotten, *I came out of the mouth of the Most High, the first-born before all creatures;* and further on (verse 14) it is said as uttered by the same Wisdom, *From the beginning, and before the world was I created.* Therefore the Son was not begotten from something, but from nothing. Likewise we can object concerning the Holy Ghost, by reason of what is said (Zach. 12. 1): *Thus saith the Lord Who stretcheth forth the heavens, and layeth the foundations of the earth, and formeth the spirit of man within him;* and (Amos 4. 13) according to another version (The Septuagint): *I Who form the earth, and create the spirit.*

On the contrary, Augustine (Fulgentius, *De Fide ad Petrum* i, 2)[2] says: "God the Father, of His nature, without beginning, begot the Son equal to Himself."

I answer that, The Son was not begotten from nothing, but from the Father's substance. For it was explained above (Q. XXVII, A. 2; Q. XXXIII, AA. 2, 3) that paternity, sonship and nativity really and truly exist in God. Now, this is the difference between true generation, whereby one proceeds from another as a son, and making, that the maker makes something out of external matter, as a carpenter makes a bench out of wood, whereas a man begets a son from himself. Now, as a created workman makes a thing out of matter, so God makes things out

[1] PL 42, 945.
[2] PL 65, 676.

of nothing, as will be shown later on (Q. XLV, A. 2), not as if this nothing were a part of the substance of the thing made, but because the whole substance of a thing is produced by Him without anything else whatever presupposed. So, were the Son to proceed from the Father as out of nothing, then the Son would be to the Father what the thing made is to the maker, to which, as is evident, the name of sonship would not apply except by a kind of likeness. Thus, if the Son of God proceeds from the Father out of nothing, He could not be properly and truly called the Son, whereas the contrary is stated (I John 5. 20): *That we may be in His true Son Jesus Christ.* Therefore the true Son of God is not from nothing; nor is He made, but begotten.

That certain creatures made by God out of nothing are called sons of God is to be taken in a metaphorical sense, according to a kind of assimilation to Him Who is the true Son. And so, as He is the only true and natural Son of God, He is called the only begotten, according to John 1. 18, *The only begotten Son, Who is in the bosom of the Father, He hath declared Him;* and so far as others are entitled sons of adoption by assimilation to Him, He is called the *first begotten,* according to Rom. 8. 29: *Whom He foreknew He also predestinated to be made conformable to the image of His Son, that He might be the first born of many brethren.*

Therefore the Son of God is begotten of the substance of the Father, but not in the same way as man is born of man, for a part of the human substance in generation passes into the substance of the one begotten, whereas the divine nature cannot be parted. And so it necessarily follows that the Father in begetting the Son does not transmit any part of His nature, but communicates His whole nature to Him, the distinction only of origin remaining, as explained above (Q. XL, A. 2).

Reply Obj. 1. When we say that the Son was born of the Father, the preposition "of" designates a consubstantial generating principle, but not a material principle. For that which is produced from matter is made by a change of form in that from which it is produced. But the divine essence is unchangeable, and is not able to receive another form.

Reply Obj. 2. When we say the Son is begotten of the essence of the Father, as the Master of the Sentences explains (1 *Sent.* D. v),[3] this denotes the relation of a kind of active principle, and as he expounds, the Son is begotten of the

[3] QR 1, 49.

essence of the Father—that is, of the Father Who is essence; and so Augustine says (*De Trin.* xv, 13).[1] "When I say of the Father Who is essence, it is the same as if I said more explicitly, of the essence of the Father."

This, however, is not enough to explain the real meaning of the words. For we can say that the creature is from God Who is essence, but not that it is from the essence of God. So we may explain them otherwise, by observing that the preposition "of" (*de*) always denotes consubstantiality. We do not say that a house is "of" (*de*) the builder, since he is not the consubstantial cause. We can say, however, that something is "of" another if this is its consubstantial principle, no matter in what way it is so, whether it be an active principle, as the son is said to be of the father, or a material principle, as a knife is of iron; or a formal principle, at least in those things in which the forms are subsisting, and not accidental to another, for we can say that an angel is "of" an intellectual nature. In this way, then, we say that the Son is begotten of the essence of the Father, since the essence of the Father, communicated by generation, subsists in the Son.

Reply Obj. 3. When we say that the Son is begotten of the essence of the Father, a term is added which saves the distinction. But when we say that the three persons are of the divine essence, there is nothing expressed to warrant the distinction signified by the preposition, so there is no parity of argument.

Reply Obj. 4. When we say Wisdom was created, this may be understood not of Wisdom which is the Son of God, but of created wisdom given by God to creatures; for it is said, *He created her* (namely, Wisdom) *in the Holy Ghost, and He poured her out over all His works* (Ecclus. 1. 9, 10). Nor is it inconsistent for Scripture in one text to speak of the Wisdom begotten and wisdom created, for wisdom created is a kind of participation of the uncreated Wisdom. The saying may also be referred to the created nature assumed by the Son, so that the sense be, "From the beginning and before the world was I made"—that is, I was foreseen as united to the creature. Or the mention of wisdom as both created and begotten conveys to us the mode of the divine generation; for in generation what is generated receives the nature of the generator, and this pertains to perfection, whereas in creation the Creator is not changed, but the creature does not receive the Creator's nature. Thus the Son is called both created and

begotten, in order that from the idea of creation the immutability of the Father may be understood, and from generation the unity of nature in the Father and the Son. In this way Hilary expounds the sense of this text of Scripture (*De Synod.*).[2] The other passages quoted do not refer to the Holy Ghost, but to the created spirit, sometimes called wind, sometimes air, sometimes the breath of man, sometimes also the soul, or any other invisible substance.

ARTICLE 4. *Whether in God There Is a Power With Regard to the Notional Acts?*

We proceed thus to the Fourth Article: It would seem that in God there is no power with regard to the notional acts.

Objection 1. For every kind of power is either active, or passive, neither of which can be applied here, since there is no passive power in God, as above explained (Q. XXV, A. 1); nor can active power belong to one person with respect to another, since the divine persons were not made, as stated above (A. 3). Therefore in God there is no power with respect to the notional acts.

Obj. 2. Further, the object of power is what is possible. But the divine persons are not regarded as possible, but as necessary. Therefore, as regards the notional acts, whereby the divine persons proceed, there cannot be power in God.

Obj. 3. Further, the Son proceeds as the word, which is the concept of the intellect, and the Holy Ghost proceeds as love, which pertains to the will. But in God power is spoken of in relation to effects, and not in relation to intellect and will, as stated above (Q. XXV, A. 1 ANS. 3, 4). Therefore, in God power does not exist in relation to the notional acts.

On the contrary, Augustine says (*Contra Maxim.* ii, 7):[3] "If God the Father could not beget a co-equal Son, where is the omnipotence of God the Father?" Power therefore exists in God with respect to the notional acts.

I answer that, As the notional acts exist in God, so must there be also a power in God with respect to these acts, since power only means the principle of act. So, as we understand the Father to be principle of generation, and the Father and the Son to be the principle of spiration, we must attribute the power of generating to the Father, and the power of spiration to the Father and the Son; for the power of generation means that whereby the generator generates. Now every generator generates by something.

---

[1] PL 42, 1076.

[2] PL 10, 494.

[3] PL 42, 762.

Therefore in every generator we must suppose the power of generating, and in the spirator the power of spirating.

Reply Obj. 1. As a person, according to the notional acts, does not proceed as if made, so the power in God with respect to the notional acts has no reference to a person as if made, but only with respect to the person as proceeding.

Reply Obj. 2. Possible, as opposed to what is necessary, is a consequence of a passive power, which does not exist in God. Hence, in God there is no such thing as possibility in this sense, but only in the sense of possible as contained in what is necessary; and in this latter sense it can be said that as it is possible for God to be, so also is it possible that the Son should be generated.

Reply Obj. 3. Power signifies a principle, and a principle implies distinction from that of which it is the principle. Now we must observe a twofold distinction in things said of God: one is a real distinction, the other is a distinction of reason only. By a real distinction, God by His essence is distinct from those things of which He is the principle by creation, just as one person is distinct from the other of which He is principle by a notional act. But in God the distinction of action and agent is one of reason only, otherwise action would be an accident in God. And therefore with respect to those actions according to which certain things proceed which are distinct from God, either personally or essentially, we may ascribe power to God in its proper notion of principle. And as we ascribe to God the power of creating, so we may ascribe the power of begetting and of spirating. But to understand and to will are not such actions as to designate the procession of something distinct from God, either essentially or personally. Therefore, with regard to these actions we cannot ascribe power to God in its proper sense, but only after our way of understanding and speaking, since we designate by different terms the intellect and the act of understanding in God, whereas in God the act of understanding is His very essence and has no principle.

ARTICLE 5. *Whether the Power of Begetting Signifies a Relation, and Not the Essence?*

We proceed thus to the Fifth Article: It would seem that the power of begetting, or of spirating, signifies the relation and not the essence.

Objection 1. For power signifies a principle, as appears from its definition; for active power is the principle of action, as we find in the *Meta-*

physics.[1] But in God, principle with respect to Person is said notionally Therefore, in God, power does not signify essence but relation.

Obj. 2. Further, in God, that which is possible (*posse*) and to act are not distinct. But in God, begetting signifies relation. Therefore, the same applies to the power of begetting.

Obj. 3. Further, terms signifying the essence in God, are common to the three persons. But the power of begetting is not common to the three persons, but proper to the Father. Therefore it does not signify the essence.

On the contrary, As God has the power to beget the Son, so also He wills to beget Him. But the will to beget signifies the essence. Therefore, also, the power to beget.

I answer that, Some have said[2] that the power to beget signifies relation in God. But this is not possible. For in every agent that is properly called power by which the agent acts. Now, everything that produces something by its action produces something like itself, as to the form by which it acts; just as man begotten is like his begetter in his human nature, in virtue of which the father has the power to beget a man. In every begetter, therefore, that is the power of begetting in which the begotten is like the begetter. Now the Son of God is like the Father, Who begets Him, in the divine nature. Therefore the divine nature in the Father is in Him the power of begetting. And so Hilary says (*De Trin.* v):[3] "The birth of God cannot but contain that nature from which it proceeded; for He cannot subsist other than God, Who subsists from no other source than God."

We must therefore say that the power of begetting signifies principally the divine essence as the Master says (1 *Sent.* D. vii),[4] and not the relation only. Nor does it signify the essence as identified with the relation, so as to signify both equally. For although paternity is signified as the form of the Father, nevertheless it is a personal property, being in relation to the person of the Father what the individual form is to the individual creature. Now the individual form in things created constitutes the person begetting but is not that by which the begetter begets; otherwise Socrates would beget Socrates. So neither can paternity be understood as that by which the Father begets, but as constituting the person of the Father; otherwise the Father would beget the Father But that by which the

[1] Aristotle, v, 12 (1019ᵃ15).

[2] Cf. Bonaventure, *In Sent.*, 1, dist. VII, A. 1, Q .1. (QR 1, 136), where this opinion is attributed to "the moderns."

[3] PL 10, 155.   [4] QR 1, 56.

Father begets is the divine nature, in which the Son is like to Him. And in this sense Damascene says (*De Fide Orthod.* i, 8)[1] that "generation is the work of nature, not of nature as generating, but as that by which the generator generates." And therefore the power of begetting signifies the divine nature directly, but the relation indirectly.

Reply Obj. 1. Power does not signify the relation itself of a principle, for thus it would be in the genus of relation, but it signifies that which is a principle; not, indeed, in the sense in which we call the agent a principle, but in the sense of being that by which the agent acts. Now the agent is distinct from that which it makes, and the generator from that which it generates; but that by which the generator generates is common to generated and generator, and so much more perfectly as the generation is more perfect. Since, therefore, the divine generation is most perfect, that by which the Begetter begets, is common to Begotten and Begetter and the same in number, and not only in species, as in things created. Therefore, from the fact that we say that the divine essence is the principle by which the Begetter begets, it does not follow that the divine essence is distinct, which would follow if we were to say that the divine essence begets.

Reply Obj. 2. As in God, the power of begetting is the same as the act of begetting, so the divine essence is the same in reality as the act of begetting or paternity, although there is a distinction of reason.

Reply Obj. 3. When I speak of the power of begetting, power is signified directly, begetting indirectly, just as if I were to say, the essence of the Father. Therefore in respect of the essence which is signified, the power of begetting is common to the three persons, but in respect of the notion that is connoted it is proper to the person of the Father.

ARTICLE 6. *Whether Several Persons Can Be the Term of One Notional Act?*

We proceed thus to the Sixth Article: It would seem that a notional act can be directed to several Persons, so that there may be several Persons begotten or spirated in God.

Objection 1. For whoever has the power of begetting can beget. But the Son has the power of begetting. Therefore He can beget. But He can not beget Himself. Therefore He can beget another son. Therefore there can be several Sons in God.

[1] PG 94, 812.

Obj. 2. Further, Augustine says (*Contra Maxim.* ii, 12) :[2] "The Son did not beget a Creator; not that He could not, but that it behoved Him not."

Obj. 3. Further, God the Father has greater power to beget than has a created father. But a man can beget several sons. Therefore God can also: the more so that the power of the Father is not diminished after begetting the Son.

On the contrary, In God *that which is possible,* and *that which is* do not differ. If, therefore, in God it were possible for there to be several Sons, there would be several Sons. And thus there would be more than three Persons in God; which is heretical.

I answer that, As Athanasius says,[3] in God there is only "one Father, one Son, one Holy Ghost." For this four reasons may be given.

The first reason is in regard to the relations by which alone are the Persons distinct. For since the divine Persons are the relations themselves as subsistent, there would not be several Fathers, or several Sons in God, unless there were more than one paternity, or more than one sonship. And this, indeed, would not be possible except owing to a material distinction, since forms of one species are not multiplied except in respect of matter, which is not in God. Therefore there can be but one subsistent sonship in God, just as there could be but one subsistent whiteness.

The second reason is taken from the manner of the processions. For God understands and wills all things by one simple act. Therefore there can be but one person proceeding after the manner of word, which person is the Son; and but one person proceeding after the manner of love, which person is the Holy Ghost.

The third reason is taken from the manner in which the persons proceed. For the persons proceed naturally, as we have said (A. 2), and nature is determined to one.

The fourth reason is taken from the perfection of the divine persons. For this reason is the Son perfect, that the entire divine sonship is contained in Him, and that there is but one Son. The argument is similar in regard to the other persons.

Reply Obj. 1. Although we can grant absolutely that the Son has the same power as the Father, we cannot grant that the Son has the power *generandi* (of begetting) thus taking *generandi* as the gerund of the active verb, so that the sense would be that the Son has the power

[2] PL 42, 768.
[3] Creed, "*Quicumque*" (MA 11, 1354; DZ 39).

to beget. Just as, although Father and Son have the same being, it does not follow that the Son is the Father, by reason of the notional term added. But if the word *generandi* (of being begotten) is taken as the gerundive of the passive verb, the power *generandi* is in the Son—that is, the power of being begotten. The same is to be said if it be taken as the gerundive of an impersonal verb, so that the sense would be *the power* of generation—that is, a power by which it is generated by some person.

Reply Obj. 2. Augustine does not mean to say by those words that the Son could beget a Son, but that if He did not, it was not because He could not, as we shall see later on (Q. XLII, A. 6 ANS. 3).

Reply Obj. 3. Divine perfection and the immateriality in God require that there cannot be several Sons in God, as we have explained. Therefore that there are not several Sons is not due to any lack of power to beget in the Father.

QUESTION XLII
OF EQUALITY AND LIKENESS AMONG
THE DIVINE PERSONS
(*In Six Articles*)

WE now have to consider the persons as compared to one another: first, with regard to equality and likeness; secondly, with regard to mission (Q. XLIII). Concerning the first there are six points of inquiry.

(1) Whether there is equality among the divine persons? (2) Whether the person who proceeds is equal to the one from Whom He proceeds in eternity? (3) Whether there is any order among the divine persons? (4) Whether the divine persons are equal in greatness? (5) Whether the one divine person is in another? (6) Whether they are equal in power?

ARTICLE I. *Whether There Is Equality in God?*

We proceed thus to the First Article: It would seem that equality does not apply to the divine persons.

Objection 1. For equality is in relation to things which are "one in quantity" as the Philosopher says.[1] But in the divine persons there is no quantity, neither continuous intrinsic quantity, which we call size, nor continuous extrinsic quantity, which we call place and time. Nor can there be equality by reason of discrete quantity, because two persons are more than one. Therefore equality does not apply to the divine persons.

[1] *Metaphysics*, v, 15 (1021ᵃ12).

Obj. 2. Further, the divine persons are of one essence, as we have said (Q. XXXIX, A. 2). Now essence is signified by way of form. But agreement in form makes things alike, not equal. Therefore, we may speak of likeness in the divine persons, but not of equality.

Obj. 3. Further, things wherein there is to be found equality are equal to one another, for equality is reciprocal. But the divine persons cannot be said to be equal to one another. For as Augustine says (*De Trin.* vi, 10):[2] "If an image answers perfectly to that whereof it is the image, it may be said to be equal to it; but that which it represents cannot be said to be equal to the image." But the Son is the image of the Father, and so the Father is not equal to the Son. Therefore equality is not to be found among the divine persons.

Obj. 4. Further, equality is a relation. But no relation is common to the three persons, for the persons are distinct by reason of the relations. Therefore equality is not becoming to the divine persons.

On the contrary, Athanasius says[3] that "the three persons are co-eternal and co-equal to one another."

I answer that, We must admit equality among the divine persons. For, according to the Philosopher,[4] equality signifies "the negation of greater or less." Now we cannot admit anything greater or less in the divine persons; for as Boëthius says (*De Trin.* i):[5] "They must admit a difference"—namely, of Godhead—"who speak of either increase or decrease, as the Arians do, who sunder the Trinity by distinguishing degrees as of numbers, thus involving a plurality." Now the reason of this is that unequal things cannot have the same quantity. But quantity, in God, is nothing else than His essence. Therefore it follows, that if there were any inequality in the divine persons, they would not have the same essence; and thus the three persons would not be one God, which is impossible. We must therefore admit equality among the divine persons.

Reply Obj. 1. Quantity is twofold. There is quantity of bulk or dimensive quantity, which is to be found only in corporeal things, and has, therefore, no place in God. There is also quantity of virtue, which is measured according to the perfection of some nature or form; to this sort of quantity we allude when we speak of

[2] PL 42, 931.
[3] Creed "*Quicumque*" (MA II, 1355; DZ 39).
[4] *Metaphysics*, x, 5 (1056ᵃ22).
[5] PL 64, 1249.

something as being more, or less, hot, in so far as it is more, or less, perfect in heat. Now this virtual quantity is measured first by its source —that is, by the perfection of that form or nature, and this is the greatness of spiritual things, just as we speak of great heat on account of its intensity and perfection. And so Augustine says (*De Trin.* vi, 8)[1] that "in things which are great, but not in bulk, to be greater is to be better," for the more perfect a thing is, the better it is. Secondly, virtual quantity is measured by the effects of the form. Now the first effect of form is being, for everything has being by reason of its form. The second effect is operation, for every agent acts through its form. Consequently virtual quantity is measured both in regard to being and in regard to action; in regard to being, in so far as things of a more perfect nature are of longer duration, and in regard to action, in so far as things of a more perfect nature are more powerful to act. And so as Augustine (Fulgentius, *De Fide ad Petrum*, i)[2] says: We understand equality to be in the Father, Son, and Holy Ghost, "inasmuch as no one of them either precedes in eternity, or excels in greatness, or surpasses in power."

Reply Obj. 2. Where we have equality with respect to virtual quantity, equality includes likeness and something besides, because it excludes excess. For whatever things have a common form may be said to be alike, even if they do not participate in that form equally, just as the air may be said to be like fire in heat; but they cannot be said to be equal, if one participates in the form more perfectly than another. And because not only is the same nature in both Father and Son, but also because it is in both in perfect equality, therefore we say not only that the Son is like to the Father, in order to exclude the error of Eunomius,[3] but also that He is equal to the Father to exclude the error of Arius.[4]

Reply Obj. 3. Equality or likeness in God may be designated in two ways—namely, by nouns and by verbs. When designated by nouns, equality in the divine persons is mutual, and so is likeness; for the Son is equal and like to the Father, and conversely. This is because the divine essence is not more the Father's than the Son's. Hence, just as the Son has the greatness of the Father, and is therefore equal to the Father, so the Father has the greatness of the Son, and is therefore equal to the Son. But in reference to creatures, Dionysius says (*Div. Nom.* ix):[5] "Equality and likeness are not mutual." For things caused are said to be like their causes because they have the form of their causes, but not conversely, for the form is principally in the cause, and secondarily in the thing caused.

But verbs signify equality with movement. And although movement is not in God, there is something that receives. Since, therefore, the Son receives from the Father, this, namely, that He is equal to the Father, and not conversely, for this reason we say that the Son is equalled to the Father, but not conversely.

Reply Obj. 4. In the divine persons there is nothing for us to consider but the essence which they have in common and the relations in which they are distinct. Now equality implies both—namely, distinction of persons, for nothing can be said to be equal to itself; and unity of essence, since for this reason are the persons equal to one another, that they are of the same greatness and essence. Now it is clear that the relation of a thing to itself is not a real relation. Nor, again, is one relation referred to another by a further relation; for when we say that paternity is opposed to sonship, opposition is not a relation mediating between paternity and sonship. For in both these cases relation would be multiplied indefinitely. Therefore equality and likeness in the divine persons is not a real relation distinct from the personal relations: but in its meaning it includes both the relations which distinguish the persons and the unity of essence. For this reason the Master says (1 *Sent.* D. xxxi)[6] that in these "it is only the terms that are relative."

ARTICLE 2. *Whether the Person Proceeding Is Co-Eternal With His Principle, As the Son With the Father?*

We proceed thus to the Second Article: It would seem that the person proceeding is not co-eternal with His principle, as the Son with the Father.

Objection 1. For Arius gives twelve modes of generation.[7] The first mode is like the issue of a line from a point, wherein is wanting equality of simplicity. The second is like the emission of rays from the sun, wherein is absent equality of nature. The third is like the mark or impression made by a seal, wherein is wanting consubstantiality and power of making. The fourth is the

---

[1] PL 42, 929.   [2] PL 65, 674.
[3] Cf. Augustine, *De Hæres.*, 54 (PL 42, 40).
[4] *Ibid.*, Sect. 49 (PL 42, 39).

[5] Sect. 6 (PG 3, 913).
[6] QR I, 100.
[7] Cf. Candidus Arianus, *De Gener. Div.*, (PL 8, 1015).

infusion of a good will from God, wherein also consubstantiality is wanting. The fifth is the emanation of an accident from its subject; but the accident has no subsistence. The sixth is the abstraction of a species from matter, as sense receives the species from the sensible thing, wherein is wanting equality of spiritual simplicity. The seventh is the stirring of the will by knowledge, which stimulation is merely temporal. The eighth is transformation, as an image is made of brass; which transformation is material. The ninth is motion from a mover; and here again we have effect and cause. The tenth is the taking of species from genera; but this mode has no place in God, for the Father is not predicated of the Son as the genus of a species. The eleventh is the realization of an idea (*ideatio*), as an external box arises from the one in the mind. The twelfth is birth, as a man is begotten of his father; which implies priority and posteriority of time. Thus it is clear that equality of nature or of time is absent in every mode whereby one thing is from another. So if the Son is from the Father, we must say that He is less than the Father, or later than the Father, or both.

Obj. 2. Further, everything that comes from another has a principle. But nothing eternal has a principle. Therefore the Son is not eternal; nor is the Holy Ghost.

Obj. 3. Further, everything which is corrupted ceases to be. Hence everything generated begins to be; for the end of generation is existence. But the Son is generated by the Father. Therefore He begins to be, and is not co-eternal with the Father.

Obj. 4. Further, if the Son be begotten by the Father, either He is always being begotten, or there is some instant in which He is begotten. If He is always being begotten, since during the process of generation a thing must be imperfect, as appears in successive things which are always in process of becoming, as time and motion, it follows that the Son must be always imperfect, which cannot be admitted. Thus there is an instant to be assigned for the begetting of the Son, and before that moment the Son did not exist.

On the contrary, Athanasius declares[1] that "all the three persons are co-eternal with each other."

I answer that, We must say that the Son is co-eternal with the Father. In proof of this we must consider that for a thing which proceeds from a principle to be posterior to its principle may

be due to two reasons: one on the part of the agent, and the other on the part of the action. On the part of the agent this happens differently as regards free agents and natural agents. In free agents, on account of the choice of time; for as a free agent can choose the form it gives to the effect, as stated above (Q. XLI, A. 2), so it can choose the time in which to produce its effect. In natural agents, however, the same thing happens because the agent does not have its perfection of natural power from the very first, but obtains it after a certain time; as, for instance, a man is not able to generate from the very first. Considered on the part of action, anything derived from a principle cannot exist simultaneously with its principle when the action is successive. So, given that an agent, as soon as it exists, begins to act thus, the effect would not exist in the same instant, but in the instant of the action's termination. Now it is manifest, according to what has been said (Q. XLI, A. 2), that the Father does not beget the Son by will, but by nature; and also that the Father's nature was perfect from eternity; and again that the action whereby the Father produces the Son is not successive, because thus the Son of God would be successively generated, and this generation would be material, and accompanied with movement, which is impossible. Therefore we conclude that the Son existed whenever the Father existed; and thus the Son is co-eternal with the Father, and likewise the Holy Ghost is co-eternal with both.

Reply Obj. 1. As Augustine says (*De Verbis Domini, Serm.* 117),[2] no mode of the procession of any creature perfectly represents the divine generation. Hence we need to gather a likeness of it from many of these modes, so that what is wanting in one may be somewhat supplied from another; and thus it is declared in the council of Ephesus:[3] "Let Splendour tell thee that the co-eternal Son existed always with the Father; let the Word announce the impassibility of His Birth; let the name Son insinuate His consubstantiality." Yet, above them all the procession of the word from the intellect represents it more exactly, since the intellectual word is not posterior to its source except in an intellect passing from potency to act; and this cannot be said of God.

Reply Obj. 2. Eternity excludes the principle of duration, but not the principle of origin.

Reply Obj. 3. Every corruption is a change; and so all that corrupts begins not to be and

---

[1] Cf. Creed *"Quicumque"* (MA II 1355; DZ 39).

[2] Chap. 6 (PL 38, 666); chap. 10 (669).

[3] *Acts,* pt. III, chap. 10 (MA V, 214).

ceases to be. The divine generation, however, is not changed, as stated above (Q. XXVII, A. 2). Hence the Son is ever being begotten, and the Father is always begetting.

Reply Obj. 4. In time there is something indivisible—namely, the instant; and there is something else which endures—namely, time. But in eternity the indivisible now stands always still, as we have said above (Q. X, A. 2, Ans. 1, A. 4, Ans. 2). But the generation of the Son is not in the now of time, or in time, but in eternity. And so to express the presentiality and permanence of eternity, we can say that "He is ever being born," as Origen said (*Hom. in John* 1).[1] But as Gregory[2] and Augustine[3] said, it is better to say "ever born," so that "ever" may denote the permanence of eternity, and "born" the perfection of the only Begotten. Thus, therefore, neither is the Son imperfect, nor was there a time when He was not, as Arius said.[4]

ARTICLE 3. *Whether in the Divine Persons There Exists an Order of Nature?*

We proceed thus to the Third Article: It would seem that among the divine persons there does not exist an order of nature.

Objection 1. For whatever exists in God is the essence, or a person, or a notion. But the order of nature does not signify the essence, nor any of the persons, or notions. Therefore there is no order of nature in God.

Obj. 2. Further, wherever order of nature exists, one comes before another, at least, according to nature and intellect. But in the divine persons "there exists neither priority nor posteriority," as declared by Athanasius.[5] Therefore, in the divine persons there is no order of nature.

Obj. 3. Further, wherever order exists, distinction also exists. But there is no distinction in the divine nature. Therefore it is not subject to order, and order of nature does not exist in it.

Obj. 4. Further, the divine nature is the divine essence. But there is no order of essence in God. Therefore neither is there of nature.

On the contrary, Where plurality exists without order, confusion exists. But in the divine persons there is no confusion, as Athanasius says.[6] Therefore in God order exists.

I answer that, Order always has reference to

some principle. Therefore since there are many kinds of principle—namely, according to site, as a point; according to intellect, as the principle of demonstration; and according to individual causes—so are there many kinds of order. Now principle according to origin, without priority, is asserted in God as we have stated (Q. XXXIII, A. 1); so there must likewise be order according to origin, without priority; and this is called the order of nature, in the words of Augustine (*Contra Maxim.*):[7] "Not whereby one is prior to another, but whereby one is from another."

Reply Obj. 1. The order of nature signifies the notion of origin in general, not a special kind of origin.

Reply Obj. 2. In things created, even when what is derived from a principle is coeval in duration with its principle, the principle still comes first according to nature and reason, if we consider the principle. If, however, we consider the relations of cause and effect, or of the principle and the thing proceeding from it, it is clear that the things so related are simultaneous in nature and reason, since the one enters the definition of the other. But in God the relations themselves are the persons subsisting in one nature. So, neither on the part of the nature, nor on the part of the relations, can one person be prior to another, not even according to nature and reason.

Reply Obj. 3. The order of nature means not the ordering of nature itself, but the existence of order in the divine Persons according to natural origin.

Reply Obj. 4. Nature in a certain way implies the notion of a principle, but essence does not; and so the order of origin is more correctly called the order of nature than the order of essence.

ARTICLE 4. *Whether the Son Is Equal to the Father in Greatness?*

We proceed thus to the Fourth Article: It would seem that the Son is not equal to the Father in greatness.

Objection 1. For He Himself said (John 14. 28): *The Father is greater than I;* and the Apostle says (I Cor. 15. 28): *The Son Himself shall be subject to Him that put all things under Him.*

Obj. 2. Further, Paternity is part of the Father's dignity. But paternity does not belong to the Son. Therefore the Son does not possess all the Father's dignity; and so He is not equal in greatness to the Father.

---

[1] *Hom.*, IX (PG 13, 357).
[2] *Moral.*, XXIX, chap. 1 (PL 76, 477).
[3] 83 *Quaest.*, qu. 37 (PL 40, 27).
[4] Cf. Athanasius, *Contra Arianos*, Orat. 1 (PG 26, 19); Alexander, *Epist. De Ariana Haeres.* (PG 18, 573; MA 2, 796).
[5] Cf. Creed "*Quicumque*" (MA 11, 1354; DZ 39).
[6] *Ibid.*

[7] 11, 14 (PL 42, 775).

Obj. 3. Further, wherever there exist a whole and a part, many parts are more than one only, or than fewer parts; as three men are more than two, or than one. But in God a universal whole exists, and a part; for under relation or notion, several notions are included. Therefore, since in the Father there are three notions, while in the Son there are only two, the Son is evidently not equal to the Father.

On the contrary, It is said (Phil. 2. 6): *He thought it not robbery to be equal with God.*

I answer that, The Son is necessarily equal to the Father in greatness. For the greatness of God is nothing but the perfection of His nature. Now it belongs to the very nature of paternity and sonship that the Son by generation should attain to the possession of the perfection of the nature which is in the Father, in the same way as it is in the Father Himself. But since in men generation is a certain kind of change of one proceeding from potency to act, it follows that a man is not equal at first to the father who begets him, but attains to equality by due growth, unless owing to a defect in the principle of generation it should happen otherwise. From what precedes (Q. XXVII, A. 2; Q. XXXIII, AA. 2, 3), it is evident that in God there exist proper and true paternity and sonship. Nor can we say that the power of generation in the Father was defective, or that the Son of God arrived at perfection in a successive manner and by change. Therefore we must say that the Son was eternally equal to the Father in greatness. Hence, Hilary says (*De Synod.,* Can. 27):[1] "Remove bodily weakness, remove the beginning of conception, remove pain and all human shortcomings, then every son, by reason of his natural nativity, is the father's equal, because he has a like nature."

Reply Obj. 1. These words are to be understood of Christ's human nature, wherein He is less than the Father, and subject to Him; but in His divine nature He is equal to the Father. This is expressed by Athanasius,[2] "Equal to the Father in His Godhead; less than the Father in humanity; and by Hilary (*De Trin.* ix):[3] "By the authority of giving, the Father is greater; but He is not less to Whom the same being is given"; and (*De Synod.*):[4] "The Son subjects Himself by His inborn piety"—that is, by His recognition of paternal authority, whereas "creatures are subject by their created weakness."

Reply Obj. 2. Equality is measured by greatness. In God greatness signifies the perfection of nature, as above explained (A. 1, Ans. 1), and belongs to the essence. Thus equality and likeness in God have reference to the essence; nor can there be inequality or unlikeness arising from the distinction of the relations. For which reason Augustine says (*Contra Maxim.* ii, 18),[5] "The question of origin is, Who is from whom? but the question of equality is, Of what kind, or how great, is he?" Therefore, paternity is the Father's dignity, as also the Father's essence, since dignity is something absolute, and pertains to the essence. As, therefore, the same essence, which in the Father is paternity, in the Son is sonship, so the same dignity which, in the Father is paternity, in the Son is sonship. It is thus true to say that the Son possesses whatever dignity the Father has; but we cannot argue—the Father has paternity, therefore the Son has paternity, for there is a transition from substance to relation. For the Father and the Son have the same essence and dignity, which exist in the Father by the relation of giver and in the Son by the relation of receiver.

Reply Obj. 3. In God relation is not a universal whole, although it is predicated of many relations, because all the relations are one in essence and being, which is irreconcilable with the notion of universal, the parts of which are distinguished in being. Person likewise is not a universal term in God as we have seen above (Q. XXX, A. 4, Ans. 3). Therefore all the relations together are not greater than only one; nor are all the persons something greater than only one, because the whole perfection of the divine nature exists in each person.

ARTICLE 5. *Whether the Son Is in the Father, and Conversely?*

We proceed thus to the Fifth Article: It would seem that the Son is not in the Father and conversely.

Objection 1. For the Philosopher[6] gives eight modes of one thing existing in another, according to none of which is the Son in the Father, or conversely, as is clear to anyone who examines each mode. Therefore the Son and the Father are not in each other.

Obj. 2. Further, nothing that has come out from another is within it. But the Son from eternity came out from the Father, according to Micheas 5. 2: *His going forth is from the beginning, from the days of eternity.* Therefore the Son is not in the Father.

Obj. 3. Further, one of two opposites cannot be in the other. But the Son and the Father are

[1] PL 10, 528.
[2] Cf. Creed *"Quicumque"* (MA II, 1355; DZ 40).
[3] PL 10, 325.   [4] PL 10, 532.
[5] PL 42, 786.   [6] *Physics*, IV, 3 (210ª14).

relatively opposed. Therefore one cannot be in the other.

On the contrary, It is said (John 14. 10): *I am in the Father, and the Father is in Me.*

I answer that, There are three points of consideration as regards the Father and the Son: the essence, the relation, and the origin; and according to each the Son and the Father are in each other. The Father is in the Son by His essence, because the Father is His own essence, and communicates His essence to the Son not by any change on His part. Hence it follows that as the Father's essence is in the Son, the Father Himself is in the Son, likewise, since the Son is His own essence, it follows that He Himself is in the Father in Whom is His essence. This is expressed by Hilary (*De Trin.* v),[1] "The unchangeable God, so to speak, follows His own nature in begetting an unchangeable subsisting God. So we understand the nature of God to subsist in Him, for He is God in God." It is also manifest that as regards the relations, each of two relative opposites is in the understanding of the other. Regarding origin also, it is clear that the procession of the intelligible word is not something external, but remains in the speaker of the word. What also is said by the word is contained in the word. And the same applies to the Holy Ghost.

Reply Obj. 1. What is in creatures does not sufficiently represent what exists in God; so according to none of the modes enumerated by the Philosopher are the Son and the Father in each other. The mode the most nearly approaching to the reality is to be found in that whereby something exists in its originating principle, except that the unity of essence between the principle and that which proceeds from it is wanting in things created.

Reply Obj. 2. The Son's going forth from the Father is according to the mode of the interior procession whereby the word emerges from the heart and remains in it. Hence this going forth in God is only by the distinction of the relations, not by any kind of essential separation.

Reply Obj. 3. The Father and the Son are relatively opposed, but not essentially, while, as above explained, one relative opposite is in the other.

ARTICLE 6. *Whether the Son Is Equal to the Father in Power?*

We proceed thus to the Sixth Article: It would seem that the Son is not equal to the Father in power.

Objection 1. For it is said (John 5. 19): *The Son cannot do anything of Himself but what He seeth the Father doing.* But the Father can act of Himself. Therefore the Father's power is greater than the Son's.

Obj. 2. Further, greater is the power of him who commands and teaches than of him who obeys and hears. But the Father commands the Son according to John 14. 31: *As the Father gave Me commandment, so do I.* The Father also teaches the Son: *The Father loveth the Son, and showeth Him all things that Himself doth* (John 5. 20). Also, the Son hears: *As I hear, so I judge* (John 5. 30). Therefore, the Father has greater power than the Son.

Obj. 3. Further, it belongs to the Father's omnipotence to be able to beget a Son equal to Himself. For Augustine says (*Contra Maxim.* ii, 7),[2] "Were He unable to beget one equal to Himself, where would be the omnipotence of God the Father?" But the Son cannot beget a Son, as proved above (Q. XLI, A. 6, ANS. 1, 2). Therefore the Son cannot do all that belongs to the Father's omnipotence; and hence He is not equal to Him in power.

On the contrary, It is said (John 5. 19): *Whatsoever things the Father doth, these the Son also doth in like manner.*

I answer that, The Son is necessarily equal to the Father in power. Power of action is a consequence of perfection of nature. In creatures, for instance, we see that the more perfect the nature, the greater power is there for action. Now it was shown above (A. 4) that the very notion of the divine paternity and sonship requires that the Son should be the Father's equal in greatness—that is, in perfection of nature. Hence it follows that the Son is equal to the Father in power; and the same applies to the Holy Ghost in relation to both.

Reply Obj. 1. The words, *the Son cannot of Himself do anything,* do not withdraw from the Son any power possessed by the Father, since it is immediately added, *Whatsoever things the Father doth, the Son doth in like manner;* but their meaning is to show that the Son derives His power from the Father, of Whom He receives His nature. Hence, Hilary says (*De Trin.* ix),[3] "The unity of the divine nature implies that the Son so acts of Himself (*per se*), that He does not act by Himself (*a se*)."

Reply Obj. 2. The Father's "showing" and the Son's "hearing" are to be taken in the sense that the Father communicates knowledge to the Son,

[1] PL 10, 155.
[2] PL 42, 762.
[3] PL 10, 319.

just as He communicates His essence. The command of the Father can be explained in the same sense, as giving Him from eternity knowledge and will to act, by begetting Him. Or, preferably, this may be referred to Christ in His human nature.

Reply Obj. 3. As the same essence is paternity in the Father, and sonship in the Son, so by the same power the Father begets, and the Son is begotten. Hence it is clear that the Son can do whatever the Father can do; yet it does not follow that the Son can beget, for to argue thus would imply transition from substance to relation, for generation signifies a divine relation. So the Son has the same power as the Father, but with another relation; the Father possessing power as giving, signified when we say that He is able to beget, while the Son possesses the power as receiving, signified by saying that He can be begotten.

QUESTION XLIII
THE MISSION OF THE DIVINE PERSONS
(In Eight Articles)

WE next consider the mission of the divine persons, concerning which there are eight points of inquiry: (1) Whether it is suitable for a divine person to be sent? (2) Whether mission is eternal, or only temporal? (3) In what sense a divine person is invisibly sent? (4) Whether it is fitting that each person be sent? (5) Whether both the Son and the Holy Ghost are invisibly sent? (6) To whom the invisible mission is directed? (7) Of the visible mission. (8) Whether any person sends Himself visibly or invisibly?

ARTICLE 1. *Whether a Divine Person Can Be Suitably Sent?*

We proceed thus to the First Article: It would seem that a divine person cannot be suitably sent.

Objection 1. For one who is sent is less than the sender. But one divine person is not less than another. Therefore one person is not sent by another.

Obj. 2. Further, what is sent is separated from the sender; hence Jerome says,[1] commenting on Ezechiel 16. 53: "What is joined and tied in one body cannot be sent." But in the divine persons "there is nothing that is separable," as Hilary says (*De Trin.* vii).[2] Therefore one person is not sent by another.

Obj 3. Further, whoever is sent, departs from one place and comes again into another. But

[1] Bk. v (PL 25, 164). [2] PL 10, 233.

this does not apply to a divine person, Who is everywhere. Therefore it is not suitable for a divine person to be sent.

On the contrary, It is said (John 8. 16): *I am not alone, but I and the Father that sent Me.*

I answer that, the notion of mission includes two things: the relation of the one sent to the sender, and that of the one sent to the end to which he is sent. Anyone being sent implies a certain kind of procession of the one sent from the sender: either according to command, as the master sends the servant; or according to counsel, as an adviser may be said to send the king to battle; or according to origin, as a tree sends forth its flower. The relation to the term to which he is sent is also shown, so that in some way he begins to be present there: either because he was in no way present before in the place where he is sent, or because he begins to be there in some way in which he was not there before.

Thus the mission of a divine person is a fitting thing, as meaning in one way the procession of origin from the sender, and as meaning a new way of existing in another; thus the Son is said to be sent by the Father into the world, because He began to exist in the world by taking on flesh; and yet *He was* previously *in the world* (John 1. 1).

Reply Obj. 1. Mission implies inferiority in the one sent when it means procession from the sender as principle, by command or counsel, because the one commanding is the greater, and the counsellor is the wiser. In God, however, it means only procession of origin, which is according to equality, as explained above (Q. XLII, AA. 4, 6).

Reply Obj. 2. What is so sent as to begin to exist where previously it did not exist, is locally moved by being sent; hence it is necessarily separated locally from the sender. This, however, has no place in the mission of a divine person; for the divine person sent neither begins to exist where he did not previously exist, nor ceases to exist where He was. Hence such a mission takes place without a separation, having only distinction of origin.

Reply Obj. 3. This objection rests on the idea of mission according to local motion, which is not in God.

ARTICLE 2. *Whether Mission Is Eternal, or Only Temporal?*

We proceed thus to the Second Article: It would seem that mission can be eternal.

Objection 1. For Gregory says (*Hom.* xxvi, *in*

Ev.),[1] "The Son is sent as He is begotten." But the Son's generation is eternal. Therefore mission is eternal.

Obj. 2. Further, a thing is changed if it becomes something temporally. But a divine person is not changed. Therefore the mission of a divine person is not temporal, but eternal.

Obj. 3. Further, mission implies procession. But the procession of the divine persons is eternal. Therefore mission is also eternal.

On the contrary, It is said (Gal. 4. 4): *When the fulness of the time was come, God sent His Son.*

I answer that, A certain difference is to be observed in all the words that express the origin of the divine persons. For some express only relation to the principle, as procession and going forth. Others express the term of procession together with the relation to the principle. Of these some express the eternal term, as generation and spiration; for generation is the procession of the divine person into the divine nature, and spiration taken passively is the procession of the subsisting love. Others express the temporal term with the relation to the principle, as mission and giving. For a thing is sent that it may be in something else, and is given that it may be possessed. But that a divine person be possessed by any creature, or exist in it in a new mode, is temporal.

Hence mission and giving have only a temporal signification in God, but generation and spiration are exclusively eternal, and procession and giving, in God, have both an eternal and a temporal signification; for the Son may proceed eternally as God, but temporally, by becoming man, according to His visible mission, or likewise by dwelling in man according to his invisible mission.

Reply Obj. 1. Gregory speaks of the temporal generation of the Son, not from the Father, but from His mother. Or it may be taken to mean that He could be sent because eternally begotten.

Reply Obj. 2. That a divine person may newly exist in anyone, or be possessed by anyone in time, does not come from change of the divine person, but from change in the creature; as God Himself is called Lord temporally by change of the creature.

Reply Obj. 3. Mission signifies not only procession from the principle, but also determines the temporal term of the procession. Hence mission is only temporal. Or we may say that it includes the eternal procession with the addition

of a temporal effect. For the relation of a divine person to His principle must be eternal. Hence the procession may be called a twin procession, eternal and temporal, not that there is a double relation to the principle, but a double term, temporal and eternal.

ARTICLE 3. *Whether the Invisible Mission of the Divine Person Is Only According to the Gift of Sanctifying Grace?*

We proceed thus to the Third Article: It would seem that the invisible mission of the divine person is not only according to the gift of sanctifying grace.

Objection 1. For the sending of a divine person means that He is given. Hence if the divine person is sent only according to the gift of sanctifying grace, the divine person Himself will not be given, but only His gifts. And this is the error of those who say that the Holy Ghost is not given, but that His gifts are given.

Obj. 2. Further, this preposition, "according to," denotes the relation of some cause. But the divine person is the cause why the gift of sanctifying grace is possessed, and not conversely, according to Rom. 5. 5, *the charity of God is poured forth in our hearts by the Holy Ghost, Who is given to us.* Therefore it is improperly said that the divine person is sent according to the gift of sanctifying grace.

Obj. 3. Further, Augustine says (*De Trin.* iv, 20)[2] that "the Son, when perceived in time by the mind, is sent." But the Son is known not only by sanctifying grace, but also by gratuitous grace, as by faith and knowledge. Therefore the divine person is not sent only according to the gift of sanctifying grace.

Obj. 4. Further, Rabanus says[3] that the Holy Ghost was given to the apostles for the working of miracles. This, however, is not a gift of sanctifying grace, but a gratuitous grace. Therefore the divine person is not given only according to the gift of sanctifying grace.

On the contrary, Augustine says (*De Trin.*)[4] that "the Holy Ghost proceeds temporally for the creature's sanctification." But mission is a temporal procession. Since then the creature's sanctification is by sanctifying grace, it follows that the mission of the divine person is only by sanctifying grace.

I answer that, The divine person is fittingly sent in the sense that He exists in a new way in

---

[1] Bk. II (PL 76, 1198).

[2] PL 42, 907.

[3] *Ennar. in Epist. Pauli,* Bk. XI, on I Cor. 12.11 (PL 112, 109).

[4] XV, 27 (PL 42, 1095).

anyone, and He is given as possessed by anyone; and neither of these is otherwise than by sanctifying grace. For God is in all things by His essence, power, and presence, according to His one common mode, as the cause existing in the effects which participate in His goodness. Above and beyond this common mode, however, there is one special mode belonging to the rational nature wherein God is said to be present as the thing known is in the knower, and the beloved in the lover. And since the rational creature by its operation of knowledge and love attains to God Himself, according to this special mode God is said not only to exist in the rational creature, but also to dwell in it as in His own temple. So no other effect can be put down as the reason why the divine person is in the rational creature in a new mode, except sanctifying grace. Hence, the divine person is sent, and proceeds temporally only according to sanctifying grace.

Again, we are said to possess only what we can freely use or enjoy, and to have the power of enjoying the divine person can only be according to sanctifying grace. And yet the Holy Ghost is possessed by man, and dwells within him, in the very gift itself of sanctifying grace. Hence the Holy Ghost Himself is given and sent.

Reply Obj. 1. By the gift of sanctifying grace the rational creature is perfected so that it can freely use not only the created gift itself, but enjoy also the divine person Himself; and so the invisible mission takes place according to the gift of sanctifying grace. And yet the divine person Himself is given.

Reply Obj. 2. Sanctifying grace disposes the soul to possess the divine person, and this is signified when it is said that the Holy Ghost is given according to the gift of grace. Nevertheless the gift itself of grace is from the Holy Ghost, which is meant by the words, *the charity of God is poured forth in our hearts by the Holy Ghost.*

Reply Obj. 3. Although the Son can be known by us according to other effects, yet neither does He dwell in us, nor is He possessed by us according to those effects.

Reply Obj. 4. The working of miracles manifests sanctifying grace as also does the gift of prophecy and any other gratuitous graces. Hence gratuitous grace is called the *manifestation of the Spirit* (I Cor. 12. 7). So the Holy Ghost is said to be given to the apostles for the working of miracles, because sanctifying grace was given to them with the outward sign. Were the sign only of sanctifying grace given to them without the grace itself, it would not be simply said that the Holy Ghost was given, except with some qualifying term; just as we read of certain ones receiving the gift of the spirit of prophecy, or of miracles, as having from the Holy Ghost the power of prophesying or of working miracles.

ARTICLE 4. *Whether the Father Can Be Fittingly Sent?*

We proceed thus to the Fourth Article: It would seem that it is fitting also that the Father should be sent.

Objection 1. For being sent means that the divine person is given. But the Father gives Himself since He can only be possessed by His giving Himself. Therefore it can be said that the Father sends Himself.

Obj. 2. Further, the divine person is sent according to the indwelling of grace. But by grace the whole Trinity dwells in us according to John 14. 23: *We will come to him and make Our abode with him.* Therefore each one of the divine persons is sent.

Obj. 3. Further, whatever belongs to one person, belongs to them all, except the notions and persons. But mission does not signify any person, nor even a notion, since there are only five notions, as stated above (Q. XXXII, A. 3). Therefore every divine person can be sent.

On the contrary, Augustine says (*De Trin.* ii, 5),[1] "The Father alone is never described as being sent."

I answer that, The very notion of mission means procession from another, and in God it means procession according to origin, as above expounded (A. 1). Hence, as the Father is not from another, in no way is it fitting for Him to be sent, but this can only belong to the Son and to the Holy Ghost, to Whom it belongs to be from another.

Reply Obj. 1. In the sense of giving as a free bestowal of something, the Father gives Himself, as freely bestowing Himself to be enjoyed by the creature. But as implying the authority of the giver with respect to what is given, to be given only applies in God to the Person Who is from another; and the same as regards being sent.

Reply Obj. 2. Although the effect of grace is also from the Father, Who dwells in us by grace, just as the Son and the Holy Ghost, still He is not described as being sent, for He is not from another. Thus Augustine says (*De Trin.* iv, 20)[2] that "The Father, when known by anyone in

[1] PL 42, 849; *Contra Serm. Arian.*, 4 (PL 42, 686).
[2] PL 42, 908.

time, is not said to be sent; for there is no one whence He is, or from whom He proceeds."

Reply Obj 3. Mission, meaning procession from the sender, includes the signification of a notion, not of a special notion, but in general; thus "to be from another" is common to two of the notions.

ARTICLE 5. *Whether It Is Fitting for the Son To Be Sent Invisibly?*

We proceed thus to the Fifth Article: It would seem that it is not fitting for the Son to be sent invisibly.

Objection 1. For invisible mission of the divine person is according to the gift of grace. But all gifts of grace belong to the Holy Ghost, according to I Cor. 12. 11: *One and the same Spirit worketh all things.* Therefore only the Holy Ghost is sent invisibly.

Obj. 2. Further, the mission of the divine person is according to sanctifying grace. But the gifts belonging to the perfection of the intellect are not gifts of sanctifying grace, since they can be held without the gift of charity, according to I Cor. 13. 2: *If I should have prophecy, and should know all mysteries, and all knowledge, and if I should have all faith so that I could move mountains, and have not charity, I am nothing.* Therefore, since the Son proceeds as the word of the intellect, it seems unfitting for Him to be sent invisibly.

Obj. 3. Further, the mission of the divine person is a procession, as expounded above (AA. 1, 4). But the procession of the Son and of the Holy Ghost differ from each other. Therefore they are distinct missions, if both are sent; and then one of them would be superfluous, since one would suffice for the creature's sanctification.

On the contrary, It is said of divine Wisdom (Wisd. 9. 10): *Send her from heaven to Thy Saints, and from the seat of Thy greatness.*

I answer that, The whole Trinity dwells in the mind by sanctifying grace, according to John 14. 23: *We will come to him, and will make Our abode with him.* But that a divine person be sent to anyone by invisible grace signifies both that this person dwells in a new way within him and that He has His origin from another. Hence, since both to the Son and to the Holy Ghost it belongs to dwell in the soul by grace, and to be from another, it therefore belongs to both of them to be invisibly sent. As to the Father, though He dwells in us by grace, still it does not belong to Him to be from another, and consequently He is not sent.

Reply Obj. 1. Although all the gifts, considered as such, are attributed to the Holy Ghost, because He is by His nature the first Gift, since He is Love, as stated above (Q. XXXVIII, A. 2), some gifts nevertheless, by reason of their proper notions, are appropriated in a certain way to the Son, those, namely, which belong to the intellect, and in respect of which we speak of the mission of the Son. Hence Augustine says (*De Trin.* iv, 20)[1] that "The Son is sent to anyone invisibly, whenever He is known and perceived by anyone."

Reply Obj. 2. The soul is made like God by grace. Hence for a divine person to be sent to anyone by grace there must be a likening of the soul to the divine person Who is sent, by some gift of grace. Because the Holy Ghost is Love, the soul is assimilated to the Holy Ghost by the gift of charity; hence the mission of the Holy Ghost is according to the mode of charity. The Son however is the Word, not any sort of word, but one Who breathes forth Love. Hence Augustine says (*De Trin.* ix, 10):[2] "The Word we speak of is knowledge with love." Thus the Son is sent not in accordance with every and any kind of intellectual perfection, but according to that disposition or instruction which breaks forth into the affection of love, as is said (John 6. 45): *Everyone that hath heard from the Father and hath learned, cometh to Me,* and (Ps. 38. 4): *In my meditation a fire shall flame forth.* Thus Augustine plainly says (*De Trin.* iv, 20):[3] "The Son is sent, whenever He is known and perceived by anyone." Now perception implies a certain experimental knowledge; and this is properly called wisdom (*sapientia*), as it were a sweet knowledge (*sapida scientia*), according to Ecclus. 6. 23: *The wisdom of doctrine is according to her name.*

Reply Obj. 3. Since mission implies the origin of the person Who is sent, and His indwelling by grace, as above explained (AA. 1, 3), if we speak of mission acording to origin, in this sense the Son's mission is distinguished from the mission of the Holy Ghost, as generation is distinguished from procession. If we consider mission as regards the effect of grace, in this sense the two missions are united in the root of grace, but are distinguished in the effects of grace, which consist in the illumination of the intellect and the kindling of the affection. Thus it is manifest that one mission cannot be without the other, because neither takes place without sanctifying grace, nor is one person separated from the other.

[1] PL 42, 907.   [2] PL 42, 969.   [3] PL 42, 907.

ARTICLE 6. *Whether the Invisible Mission Is to All Who Are Sharers of Grace?*

We proceed thus to the Sixth Article: It would seem that the invisible mission is not to all who are sharers of grace.

Objection 1. For the Fathers of the Old Testament had their share of grace. Yet no invisible mission was made to them; for it is said (John 7. 39): *The Spirit was not yet given, because Jesus was not yet glorified.* Therefore the invisible mission is not to all who share in grace.

Obj. 2. Further, progress in virtue is only by grace. But the invisible mission is not according to progress in virtue, because progress in virtue is continuous, since charity ever increases or decreases; and thus the mission would be continuous. Therefore the invisible mission is not to all who share in grace.

Obj. 3. Further, Christ and the blessed have fulness of grace. But mission is not to them, for mission implies distance, whereas Christ, as man, and all the blessed are perfectly united to God. Therefore the invisible mission is not to all sharers in grace.

Obj. 4. Further, the Sacraments of the New Law contain grace, and it is not said that the invisible mission is sent to them. Therefore the invisible mission is not to all that have grace.

On the contrary, According to Augustine (De *Trin.* xv, 27),[1] the invisible mission is "for the creature's sanctification." Now every creature that has grace is sanctified. Therefore the invisible mission is to every such creature.

.I answer that, As above stated (A. 1), mission in its very notion implies that he who is sent either begins to exist where he was not before, as occurs to creatures, or begins to exist where he was before, but in a new way, in which sense mission is ascribed to the divine persons. Thus, mission as regards the one to whom it is sent implies two things, the indwelling of grace, and a certain renewal by grace. Thus the invisible mission is sent to all in whom these two things are to be found.

Reply Obj. 1. The invisible mission was directed to the Old Testament Fathers as appears from what Augustine says (*De Trin.* iv, 20),[2] that the invisible mission of the Son "is in man or with men. This was done in former times with the Fathers and Prophets." Thus the words, "the Spirit was not yet given," are to be applied to that giving accompanied with a visible sign which took place on the day of Pentecost.

[1] PL 42, 1095.
[2] PL 42, 907.

Reply Obj. 2. The invisible mission takes place also as regards progress in virtue or increase of grace. Hence Augustine says (*De Trin.* iv, 20),[3] that "the Son is sent to each one when He is known and perceived by anyone, so far as He can be known and perceived according to the capacity of the soul, whether journeying towards God, or united perfectly to Him." But as regards the increase in grace, the invisible mission takes place especially when anyone advances through some new action or in a new state of grace; as, for example, progress in reference to the gift of miracles or of prophecy, or in the fervour of charity leading a man to expose himself to the danger of martyrdom, or to renounce his possessions, or to undertake any arduous work.

Reply Obj. 3. The invisible mission is directed to the blessed at the very beginning of their Happiness. The invisible mission is made to them subsequently, not by intensity of grace, but by the further revelation of mysteries, which goes on till the day of judgment. Such an increase is by the extension of grace, because it extends to a greater number of things. To Christ the invisible mission was sent at the first moment of His conception, but not afterwards, since from the beginning of His conception He was filled with all wisdom and grace.

Reply Obj. 4. Grace resides instrumentally in the sacraments of the New Law, as the form of a thing designed resides in the instruments of the art designing, according to a process flowing from the agent to the thing acted upon. But mission is only spoken of as directed to its term. Hence the mission of the divine person is not sent to the sacraments, but to those who receive grace through the sacraments.

ARTICLE 7. *Whether It Is Fitting for the Holy Ghost To Be Sent Visibly?*

We proceed thus to the Seventh Article: It would seem that the Holy Ghost is not fittingly sent in a visible manner.

Objection 1. For the Son as visibly sent to the world is said to be less than the Father. But the Holy Ghost is never said to be less than the Father. Therefore the Holy Ghost is not fittingly sent in a visible manner.

Obj. 2. Further, the visible mission takes place by way of union to a visible creature, as the Son's mission according to the flesh. But the Holy Ghost did not assume any visible creature, and hence it cannot be said that He exists otherwise in some creatures than in others, unless

[3] PL 42, 907.

perhaps as in a sign, as He is also present in the sacraments, and in all the figures of the law. Thus the Holy Ghost is either not sent visibly at all, or His visible mission takes place in all these things.

Obj. 3. Further, every visible creature is an effect showing forth the whole Trinity. Therefore the Holy Ghost is not sent by reason of those visible creatures more than any other person.

Obj. 4. Further, the Son was visibly sent according to the noblest of visible creatures—namely, the human nature. Therefore if the Holy Ghost is sent visibly, He ought to be sent according to rational creatures.

Obj. 5. Further, whatever is done visibly by God is dispensed by the ministry of the angels, as Augustine says (*De Trin.* iii, 10, 11).[1] So visible appearances, if there have been any, came by means of the angels. Thus the angels are sent, and not the Holy Ghost.

Obj. 6. Further, if the Holy Ghost is sent in a visible manner it is only for the purpose of manifesting the invisible mission, because invisible things are made known by the visible. So those to whom the invisible mission was not sent, ought not to receive the visible mission; and to all who received the invisible mission, whether in the New or in the Old Testament, the visible mission ought likewise to be sent. And this is clearly false. Therefore the Holy Ghost is not sent visibly.

On the contrary, It is stated (Matt. 3. 16) that, when our Lord was baptized, the Holy Ghost descended upon Him in the shape of a dove.

I answer that, God provides for all things according to the manner of each thing. Now the nature of man requires that he be led to the invisible by visible things, as explained above (Q. XII, A. 12). Therefore the invisible things of God must be made manifest to man by the things that are visible. As God, therefore, in a certain way has demonstrated Himself and His eternal processions to men by visible creatures, according to certain signs, so was it fitting that the invisible missions also of the divine persons should be made manifest by some visible creatures.

This mode of manifestation applies in different ways to the Son and to the Holy Ghost. For it belongs to the Holy Ghost, Who proceeds as Love, to be the gift of sanctification; to the Son as the principle of the Holy Ghost, it belongs to be the author of this sanctification.

[1] PL 42, 879, 882.

Thus the Son has been sent visibly as the author of sanctification, the Holy Ghost as the sign of sanctification.

Reply Obj. 1. The Son assumed the visible creature, wherein He appeared, into the unity of His person, so that whatever can be said of that creature can be said of the Son of God; and so, by reason of the nature assumed, the Son is called less than the Father. But the Holy Ghost did not assume the visible creature, in which He appeared, into the unity of His person, so that what is said of it cannot be predicated of Him. Hence He cannot be called less than the Father by reason of any visible creature.

Reply Obj. 2. The visible mission of the Holy Ghost does not take place according to the imaginary vision which is that of prophecy, because, as Augustine says (*De Trin.* ii, 6):[2] "The prophetic vision is not displayed to corporeal eyes by corporeal shapes, but is shown in the spirit by the spiritual images of bodies. But whoever saw the dove and the fire, saw them by their eyes. Nor, again, has the Holy Ghost the same relation to these images that the Son has to the rock, because it is said, 'The rock was Christ' (I Cor. 1. 4). For that rock was already created, and after the manner of an action was named Christ, Whom it typified, whereas the dove and the fire suddenly appeared to signify only what was happening. They seem, however, to be like to the flame of the burning bush seen by Moses and to the column which the people followed in the desert, and to the lightning and thunder issuing forth when the law was given on the mountain. For the purpose of the bodily appearances of those things was that they might signify, and then pass away." Thus the visible mission neither takes place by prophetic vision, which belongs to the imagination, and not to the body, nor by the sacramental signs of the Old and New Testament, wherein certain pre-existing things are employed to signify something. But the Holy Ghost is said to be sent visibly because He showed Himself in certain creatures as in signs especially made for that purpose.

Reply Obj. 3. Although the whole Trinity makes those creatures, still they are made in order to show forth in some special way this or that person. For as the Father, Son, and Holy Ghost are signified by diverse names, so also can They each one be signified by different things; although neither separation nor diversity exists amongst Them.

Reply Obj. 4. It was necessary for the Son

[2] PL 42, 852.

to be declared as the author of sanctification, as explained above. Thus the visible mission of the Son was necessarily made according to the rational nature to which it belongs to act, and which is capable of sanctification; any other creature however could be the sign of sanctification. Nor was such a visible creature, formed for such a purpose, necessarily assumed by the Holy Ghost into the unity of His person, since it was not assumed or used for the purpose of action, but only for the purpose of a sign; and so likewise it was not required to last beyond what its use required.

Reply Obj. 5. Those visible creatures were formed by the ministry of the angels not to signify the person of an angel, but to signify the Person of the Holy Ghost. Thus, as the Holy Ghost resided in those visible creatures as the one signified in the sign, on that account the Holy Ghost is said to be sent visibly, and not an angel.

Reply Obj. 6. It is not necessary that the invisible mission should always be made manifest by some visible external sign; but, as is said (I Cor. 12. 7)—*the manifestation of the Spirit is given to every man unto profit*—that is, of the Church. This utility consists in the confirmation and propagation of the faith by such visible signs. This has been done chiefly by Christ and by the apostles, according to Heb. 2. 3, *which having begun to be declared by the Lord, was confirmed unto us by them that heard.*

Thus in a special sense, a mission of the Holy Ghost had to be directed to Christ, to the apostles, and to some of the early saints on whom the Church was in a way founded; in such a manner, however, that the visible mission made to Christ should show forth the invisible mission made to Him, not at that particular time, but at the first moment of His conception. The visible mission was directed to Christ at the time of His baptism by the figure of a dove, a fecund animal, to show forth in Christ the authority of the giver of grace by spiritual regeneration; hence the Father's voice spoke, *This is My beloved Son* (Matt. 3. 17), that others might be regenerated to the likeness of the only Begotten. The Transfiguration showed it forth in the appearance of a bright cloud, to show the lavishness of doctrine; and hence it was said, *Hear ye Him* (Matt. 17. 5). To the apostles the mission was directed in the form of breathing to show forth the power of their ministry in the dispensation of the sacraments; and hence it was said, *Whose sins you shall forgive, they are forgiven* (John 20. 23),

and again under the sign of fiery tongues, to show forth the office of teaching; hence it is said that, *they began to speak with divers tongues* (Acts 2. 4). The visible mission of the Holy Ghost was fittingly not sent to the fathers of the Old Testament because the visible mission of the Son was to be accomplished before that of the Holy Ghost, since the Holy Ghost manifests the Son, as the Son manifests the Father. Visible apparitions of the divine persons were, however, given to the Fathers of the Old Testament, which, indeed cannot be called visible missions, because, according to Augustine (*De Trin.* ii, 17),[1] they were not sent to designate the indwelling of the divine person by grace but for the manifestation of something else.

ARTICLE 8. *Whether a Divine Person Is Sent Only by the Person From Whom He Proceeds Eternally?*

We proceed thus to the Eighth Article: It would seem that a divine person is sent only by the one from whom He proceeds eternally.

Objection 1. For as Augustine says (*De Trin.* iv),[2] "The Father is sent by no one because He is from no one." Therefore if a divine person is sent by another, He must be from that other.

Obj. 2. Further, the sender has authority over the one sent. But there can be no authority as regards a divine person except from origin. Therefore the divine person sent must proceed from the one sending.

Obj. 3. Further, if a divine person can be sent by one from whom He does not proceed, then the Holy Ghost may be given by a man, although He does not proceed from him, which is contrary to what Augustine says (*De Trin.* xv).[3] Therefore the divine person is sent only by the one from whom He proceeds.

On the contrary, The Son is sent by the Holy Ghost, according to Isa. 48. 16, *Now the Lord God hath sent Me and His Spirit.* But the Son is not from the Holy Ghost. Therefore a divine person is sent by one from Whom He does not proceed.

I answer that, There are different opinions on this point. Some say[4] that the divine person is sent only by the one from whom He proceeds eternally; and so, when it is said that the Son of God is sent by the Holy Ghost, this is to be

[1] PL 42, 866.
[2] Chap. 20 (PL 42, 908); *Contra Serm. Arian.*, chap. 4 (PL 42, 686).
[3] Chap. 26 (PL 42, 1092); Bk. II, chap. 6 (PL 42, 908).
[4] Augustine, *De Trin.*, II, 5 (PL 42, 849); Peter Lombard, *Sent.*, I, dist. xv, 1 (QR I, 95); Bonaventure, *In Sent.*, I dist. xv, A. 1, Q. 4 (QR I, 265).

explained as regards His human nature, by reason of which He was sent to preach by the Holy Ghost. Augustine, however, says (*De Trin.* ii, 5)[1] that the Son is sent by Himself, and by the Holy Ghost; and the Holy Ghost is sent by Himself, and by the Son;[2] so that to be sent in God does not apply to each person, but only to the person existing from another, whereas to send belongs to each person.

There is some truth in both of these opinions; because when a person is described as being sent, the person Himself existing from another is designated, with the visible or invisible effect because of which the mission of the divine person takes place. Thus if the sender be designated as the principle of the person sent, in this sense not each person sends, but that person only Who is the principle of that person who is sent; and thus the Son is sent only by the Father, and the Holy Ghost by the Father and the Son. If, however, the person sending is understood as the principle of the effect implied in the mission, in that sense the whole Trinity sends the person sent. This reason does not prove that a man can send the Holy Ghost, because man cannot cause the effect of grace.

The *answers to the objections* appear from the above.

[1] PL 42, 849; *Contra Maximin.*, II, 20 (PL 42,789).
[2] *De Trin.*, II, 5 (PL 42, 849); xv, 19 (1084).

TREATISE ON THE CREATION

QUESTION XLIV

The procession of creatures from God, and of the first cause of all beings

(In Four Articles)

AFTER treating of the divine persons, we must consider the procession of creatures from God. This consideration will be threefold: (1) of the production of creatures; (2) of the distinction between them (Q. XLVII); (3) of their preservation and government (Q. CIII). Concerning the first point there are three things to be considered: (1) the first cause of beings; (2) the mode of procession of creatures from the first cause (Q. XLV); (3) the principle of the duration of things (Q. XLVI).

Under the first head there are four points of inquiry: (1) Whether God is the efficient cause of all beings? (2) Whether primary matter is created by God, or is an independent co-ordinate principle with Him? (3) Whether God is the exemplary cause of beings, or whether there are other exemplary causes? (4) Whether He is the final cause of things?

ARTICLE 1. Whether It Is Necessary That Every Being Be Created by God?

We proceed thus to the First Article: It would seem that it is not necessary that every being be created by God.

Objection 1. For there is nothing to prevent a thing from being without that which does not belong to its very notion, as a man can be found without whiteness. But the relation of the thing caused to its cause does not appear to be of the very notion of beings, for some beings can be understood without it; therefore they can exist without it, and therefore it is possible that some beings should not be created by God.

Obj. 2. Further, a thing requires an efficient cause in order to exist. Therefore whatever cannot not be does not require an efficient cause. But no necessary thing can not exist, because whatever necessarily exists cannot not be. Therefore as there are many necessary things in existence, it appears that not all beings are from God.

Obj. 3. Further, whatever things have a cause, can be demonstrated by that cause. But in mathematics demonstration is not made by the efficient cause, as appears from the Philosopher.[1] Therefore not all beings are from God as from their efficient cause.

On the contrary, It is said (Rom. 11. 36): *Of Him, and by Him, and in Him are all things.*

I answer that, It must be said that every being that is in any way is from God. For whatever is found in anything by participation must be caused in it by that to which it belongs essentially, as iron becomes hot by fire. Now it has been shown above (Q. III, A. 4) when treating of the divine simplicity that God is Being itself self-subsisting; and also it was shown (Q. VII, A. 1, ANS. 3; A. 2) that subsisting being must be one; as, if whiteness were self-subsisting, it would be one, since whiteness is multiplied by its receivers. Therefore all beings apart from God are not their own being, but are beings by participation. Therefore it must be that all things which are diversified by the diverse participation of being, so as to be more or less perfect, are caused by one First Being, Who is most perfect.

Hence Plato said[2] that unity must come before multitude; and Aristotle said[3] that "whatever is greatest in being and greatest in truth, is the cause of every being and of every truth," just as "whatever is the greatest in heat is the cause of all heat."

Reply Obj. 1. Though the relation to its cause is not part of the definition of a being caused, still it follows, as a consequence, on what belongs to its notion; because from the fact that a thing is a being by participation, it follows that it is caused by another. Hence such a being cannot be without being caused, just as man cannot be without being capable of laughter. But, since to be caused does not enter into the

---

[1] *Metaphysics*, III, 2 (996ª29).
[2] According to Augustine, *City of God*, VIII, 6 (PL 41 231). cf. Plotinus, v *Ennead*, III, 12 (BU v, 65).
[3] *Metaphysics*, II, 1 (993ᵇ25).

notion of being as such, therefore is it possible for us to find a being uncaused.

Reply Obj. 2. This objection has led some to say that what is necessary has no cause.[1] But this is manifestly false in demonstrative sciences, where necessary principles are the causes of necessary conclusions. And therefore Aristotle says [2] that there are some necessary things which have a cause of their necessity. But the reason why an efficient cause is required is not merely because the effect is able not to be, but because the effect would not be if the cause were not. For this conditional proposition is true whether the antecedent and consequent be possible or impossible.

Reply Obj. 3. Mathematical beings are taken as something abstract according to reason, though they are not abstract in reality. Now it pertains to each thing to have an efficient cause according as it has being. And therefore although mathematical beings have an efficient cause, still their relation to that cause is not the reason why they fall under the consideration of the mathematician. And therefore in the mathematical sciences nothing is demonstrated by means of an efficient cause.

ARTICLE 2. *Whether Primary Matter Is Created by God?*

We proceed thus to the Second Article: It would seem that primary matter is not created by God.

Objection 1. For whatever is made is composed of a subject and of something else.[3] But primary matter has no subject. Therefore primary matter cannot have been made by God.

Obj. 2. Further, action and passion are divided against each other. But as the first active principle is God, so the first passive principle is matter. Therefore God and primary matter are two principles divided against each other, neither of which is from the other.

Obj. 3. Further, every agent produces its like, and thus, since every agent acts in so far as it is in act, it follows that everything made is in some way in act. But primary matter is only in potency, in so far as it is primary matter. Therefore it is against the notion of primary matter to be a thing made.

On the contrary, Augustine says,[4] "Two

things hast Thou made, O Lord; one nigh unto Thyself"—namely, angels—"the other nigh unto nothing"—namely, primary matter.

I answer that, The ancient philosophers gradually, and as it were step by step, advanced to the knowledge of truth.[5] At first being of grosser mind, they failed to realize that any beings existed except sensible bodies.[6] And those among them who admitted movement in them, did not consider it except as regards certain accidents, for instance, in relation to rarefaction and condensation, by union and separation.[7] And supposing as they did that corporeal substance itself was uncreated, they assigned certain causes for these accidental changes, as for instance, affinity, discord, intellect, or something of that kind.[8] But advancing further, they understood that there was a distinction between the substantial form and matter, which latter they imagined to be uncreated,[9] and they perceived transmutation to take place in bodies in regard to essential forms. Such transmutations they attributed to certain universal causes, such "as the oblique circle," according to Aristotle,[10] or ideas, according to Plato.[11]

But we must take into consideration that matter is contracted by form to a determinate species, as a substance belonging to a certain species is contracted by an accident which comes to it to a determinate mode of being; for instance, man by whiteness. Each of these opinions, therefore, considered "being" under some particular aspect, either as this or as such; and so they assigned particular efficient causes to things.

Then others there were who arose to the consideration of being, as being, and who assigned a cause to things, not only as these, or as such, but as beings.[12] Therefore whatever is the cause of things considered as beings, must be the cause of things not only according as they are "such" by accidental forms, nor according as they are "these" by substantial forms, but also

---

[1] Aristotle, *Physics*, VIII, 1 (252ᵃ35).
[2] *Metaphysics*, V, 5 (1015ᵇ9).
[3] Aristotle, *Physics*, I, 7 (190ᵇ1).
[4] *Confessions*, XII, 7 (PL 32, 828).

[5] Cf. Aristotle, *Metaphysics*, I, 3–4 (983ᵇ6–985ᵇ22).
[6] Cf. Aristotle, *Physics*, IV, 6 (213ᵃ29); *Metaphysics*, III, 5 (1002ᵃ8); Augustine, *City of God*, VIII, 2 (PL 41, 225).
[7] Cf. Aristotle, *Generation and Corruption*, II, 9 (335ᵇ 24, 35); *Physics*, I, 4 (187ᵃ15, 30).
[8] Cf. Aristotle, *Physics*, I, 5, 8 (188ᵇ34; 191ᵃ27); VIII, 1 (250ᵇ24); *Metaphysics*, I, 4 (985ᵃ8).
[9] Plato. Cf. above, Q. XV, A. 3, ANS. 3; below, Q. XLVI, A. 1, obj. 3, and ANS. 3. Cf. also St. Thomas, *In Phys.*, I, lect. 15.
[10] *Generation and Corruption*, II, 10 (336ᵃ32).
[11] *Ibid.* Cf. Plato, *Phaedo*, (96).
[12] Cf. Gilson, *L'Esprit de la Phil. Méd.*, I, 240–242; Pegis, *St. Thomas and the Greeks*, pp. 101–104.

according to all that belongs to their being in any way whatsoever. And thus it is necessary to say that also primary matter is created by the universal cause of being.

Reply Obj. 1. The Philosopher[1] is speaking of becoming in particular—that is, from form to form, either accidental or substantial. But here we are speaking of things according to their emanation from the universal principle of being, from which emanation matter itself is not excluded, although it is excluded from the former mode of being made.

Reply Obj. 2. Passion is an effect of action. Hence it is reasonable that the first passive principle should be the effect of the first active principle, since every imperfect thing is caused by one perfect. For the first principle must be most perfect, as Aristotle says.[2]

Reply Obj. 3. The reason advanced does not show that matter is not created, but that it is not created without form; for although everything created is actual, still it is not pure act. Hence it is necessary that even what is potential in it should be created, if all that belongs to its being is created.

ARTICLE 3. *Whether the Exemplary Cause Is Anything Beside God?*

We proceed thus to the Third Article: It would seem that the exemplary cause is something beside God.

Objection 1. For the effect is like its exemplary cause. But creatures are far from being like God. Therefore God is not their exemplary cause.

Obj. 2. Further, whatever is by participation is reduced to something self-existing, as a thing ignited is reduced to fire, as stated above (A. 1). But whatever exists in sensible things exists only by participation of some species. This appears from the fact that in all sensible things is found not only what belongs to the species, but also individuating principles added to the principles of the species. Therefore it is necessary to admit self-existing species, as, for instance, a *per se* man, and a *per se* horse, and the like, which are called the exemplars. Therefore exemplary causes exist beside God.

Obj. 3. Further sciences and definitions are concerned with species themselves, but not as these are in particular things, because there is no science or definition of particular things. Therefore there are some beings, which are beings or species not existing in singular things,

and these are called exemplars. Therefore the same conclusion follows as above.

Obj. 4. Further, this likewise appears from Dionysius, who says (*Div. Nom.* v.)[3] that "self-subsisting being is before self-subsisting life, and before self-subsisting wisdom."

On the contrary, The exemplar is the same as the idea. But ideas, according to Augustine (QQ. LXXXIII, qu. 46),[4] are "the master forms, which are contained in the divine intelligence." Therefore the exemplars of things are not outside God.

I answer that, God is the first exemplary cause of all things. In proof of which we must consider that if for the production of anything an exemplar is necessary, it is in order that the effect may receive a determinate form. For an artificer produces a determinate form in matter by reason of the exemplar before him, whether it is the exemplar beheld externally, or the exemplar interiorly conceived in the mind. Now it is manifest that things made by nature receive determinate forms. This determination of forms must be reduced to the divine wisdom as its first principle, for divine wisdom devised the order of the universe, which order consists in the variety of things. And therefore we must say that in the divine wisdom are the types of all things, which types we have called ideas—that is, exemplary forms existing in the divine mind (Q. XV, A. 1). And these ideas, though multiplied by their relations to things, in reality are not other than the divine essence, according as the likeness to that essence can be shared in different ways by different things. In this manner therefore God Himself is the first exemplar of all things. Moreover, in created things one thing may be called the exemplar of another by the reason of the likeness of one thing to another, either in species, or by the analogy of some kind of imitation.

Reply Obj. 1. Although creatures do not attain to a natural likeness to God according to likeness of species, as a man begotten is like the man begetting, still they do attain to likeness to Him, according as they represent the type known by God, as a material house is like the house in the architect's mind.

Reply Obj. 2. It is of a man's nature to be in matter, and so a man without matter is impossible. Therefore although this man is a man by participation of the species, he cannot be reduced to anything self-existing in the same species, but to a superior species, such as separate

[1] *Physics*, I, 7 (190[b]1).
[2] *Metaphysics*, XII, 7 (1072[b]29).

[3] Sect. 5 (PG 3, 820).
[4] PL 40, 30.

substances. The same applies to other sensible things.

Reply Obj. 3. Although every science and definition is concerned only with beings, still it is not necessary that a thing should have the same mode in intellect as the being has in understanding. For we abstract universal species by the power of the agent intellect from the particular conditions, but it is not necessary that the universals should subsist outside the particulars in order to be their exemplars.

Reply Obj. 4. As Dionysius says (*Div. Nom.* xi, 6),[1] by "self-existing life and self-existing wisdom" sometimes God Himself is named, sometimes the powers given to things themselves; but not any self-subsisting things, as the ancients asserted.

ARTICLE 4. *Whether God Is the Final Cause of All Things?*

We proceed thus to the Fourth Article: It would seem that God is not the final cause of all things.

Objection 1. For to act for an end seems to imply need of the end. But God needs nothing. Therefore it does not become Him to act for an end.

Obj. 2. Further, the end of generation, and the form of the thing generated, and the agent cannot be identical,[2] because the end of generation is the form of the thing generated. But God is the first agent producing all things. Therefore He is not the final cause of all things.

Obj. 3. Further, all things desire their end. But all things do not desire God, for all do not even know Him. Therefore God is not the end of all things.

Obj. 4. Further, the final cause is the first of causes. If, therefore, God is the efficient cause and the final cause, it follows that before and after exist in Him; which is impossible.

On the contrary, It is said (Prov. 16. 4): *The Lord has made all things for Himself.*

I answer that, Every agent acts for an end; otherwise one thing would not follow more than another from the action of the agent, unless it were by chance. Now the end of the agent and of the thing acted upon considered as such is the same, but in a different way with respect to each. For the impression which the agent endeavours to produce, and which the thing acted upon endeavours to receive, are one and the same. Some things, however, are both agent and thing acted upon at the same time; these are

[1] PG 3, 953.
[2] Aristotle, *Physics*, II, 7 (198[a]26).

imperfect agents, and to these it pertains to intend, even while acting, the acquisition of something. But it does not pertain to the First Agent, Who is agent only, to act for the acquisition of some end; He purposes only to communicate His perfection, which is His goodness, while every creature endeavours to acquire its own perfection, which is the likeness of the divine perfection and goodness. Therefore the divine goodness is the end of all things.

Reply Obj. 1. To act from need belongs only to an imperfect agent, which by its nature is both agent and thing acted upon. But this does not belong to God, and therefore He alone is the most perfectly free giver, because He does not act for His own profit, but only for His own goodness.

Reply Obj. 2. The form of the thing generated is not the end of generation, except in so far as it is the likeness of the form of the generator, which endeavours to communicate its own likeness; otherwise the form of the thing generated would be more noble than the generator, since the end is more noble than the means to the end.

Reply Obj. 3. All things desire God as their end when they desire some good thing, whether this desire be intellectual or sensible, or natural, that is, without knowledge; because nothing is good and desirable except according as it participates in the likeness to God.

Reply Obj. 4. Since God is the efficient, the exemplary and the final cause of all things, and since primary matter is from Him, it follows, that the first principle of all things is one in reality. But this does not prevent us from considering many things in Him according to reason, some of which come into our intellect before others.

QUESTION XLV
THE MODE OF EMANATION OF THINGS
FROM THE FIRST PRINCIPLE
(*In Eight Articles*)

THE next question concerns the mode of the emanation of things from the First Principle, and this is called creation, and includes eight points of inquiry: (1) What is creation? (2) Whether God can create anything? (3) Whether creation is a being in nature? (4) To what things it belongs to be created? (5) Whether it belongs to God alone to create? (6) Whether creation is common to the whole Trinity, or proper to any one Person? (7) Whether any trace of the Trinity is to be found in created things? (8) Whether the work of creation is mingled with the works of nature and of the will?

ARTICLE I. *Whether To Create Is To Make Something from Nothing?*

We proceed thus to the First Article: It would seem that to create is not to make anything from nothing.

Objection I. For Augustine says (*Contra Adv. Leg. et Proph.* i):[1] "To make concerns what did not exist at all; but to create is to make something by bringing forth something from what was already."

Obj 2. Further, the nobility of action and of motion is considered from their terms. Action is therefore nobler from good into good, and from being into being, than from nothing to something. But creation appears to be the most noble action, and first among all actions. Therefore it is not from nothing to something, but rather from being into being.

Obj. 3. Further, the preposition from (*ex*) implies relation of some cause, and especially of the material cause; as when we say that a statue is made from brass. But "nothing" cannot be the matter of being, nor in any way its cause. Therefore to create is not to make something from nothing.

On the contrary, On the text of Gen.i., *In the beginning God created,* etc., the gloss has,[2] To create is "to make something from nothing."

I answer that, As said above (Q. XLIV, A. 2), we must consider not only the emanation of a particular being from a particular agent, but also the emanation of all being from the universal cause, which is God; and this emanation we designate by the name of creation. Now what proceeds by particular emanation is not presupposed to that emanation; as when a man is generated, he was not before, but man is made from not-man, and white from not-white. Hence if the emanation of the whole universal being from the first principle be considered, it is impossible that any being should be presupposed to this emanation. For nothing is the same as no being. Therefore as the generation of a man is from the not-being which is not-man, so creation, which is the emanation of all being, is from the not-being which is nothing.

Reply Obj. I. Augustine uses the word crea-

tion in an equivocal sense, according as to be created signifies improvement in things, as when we say that a bishop is created. We do not, however, speak of creation in that way here, but as it is described above.

Reply Obj 2. Changes receive species and dignity not from the term from which, but from the term to which. Therefore a change is more perfect and excellent when the term to which of the change is more noble and excellent, although the term from which, corresponding to the term to which, may be more imperfect; thus generation is absolutely nobler than and prior to alteration, because the substantial form is nobler than the accidental form; and yet the privation of the substantial form, which is the term from which in generation, is more imperfect than the contrary, which is the term from which in alteration. Similarly creation is more perfect than and prior to generation and alteration, because the term to which is the whole substance of the thing, whereas what is understood as the term from which is not-being absolutely.

Reply Obj. 3. When anything is said to be made from nothing, this preposition from (*ex*) does not designate the material cause, but only order; as when we say, "from morning comes midday"—that is, after morning is midday. But we must understand that this preposition from (*ex*) can include the negation conveyed when I say the word nothing, or can be included in it. If taken in the first sense, then we affirm the order by stating the relation between what is now and its previous non-being. But if the negation includes the preposition, then the order is denied, and the sense is, "It is made from nothing"—*i.e.,* "it is not made from anything"—as if we were to say, "He speaks of nothing," because he does not speak of anything. And this is verified in both ways when it is said that anything is made from nothing. But in the first way this preposition from (*ex*) implies order, as has been said in this reply. In the second sense, it implies the material cause, which is denied.

ARTICLE 2. *Whether God Can Create Anything?*

We proceed thus to the Second Article: It would seem that God cannot create anything.

Objection I. Because, according to the Philosopher,[3] the ancient philosophers considered it as a common concept of the mind that "nothing

---

[1] Chap. 23 (PL 42, 633).
[2] *Glossa ordin.,* (I, 23F); cf. Bede, *In Penat.,* on Gen. I.I (PL 91, 191); See Peter Lombard, *Sent.,* II, dist. I, 2 (QR I, 307).
[3] *Physics,* I, 4 (187ª28).

is made from nothing." But the power of God does not extend to the contraries of first principles; as, for instance, that God could make the whole to be less than its part, or that affirmation and negation are both true at the same time. Therefore God cannot make anything from nothing, or create.

Obj. 2. Further, if to create is to make something from nothing, to be created is to be made. But to be made is to be changed. Therefore creation is change. But every change occurs in some subject, as appears by the definition of motion, for motion is the act of what is in potency. Therefore it is impossible for anything to be made out of nothing by God.

Obj. 3. Further, what has been made must have at some time been becoming. But it cannot be said that what is created, at the same time is becoming and has been made, because in permanent things what is becoming, is not, and what has been made, already is; and so it would follow that something would be and not be at the same time. Therefore when anything is made its becoming precedes its having been made. But this is impossible unless there is a subject in which the becoming is sustained. Therefore it is impossible that anything should be made from nothing.

Obj. 4. Further, infinite distance cannot be crossed. But infinite distance exists between being and nothing. Therefore it does not happen that something is made from nothing.

On the contrary, It is said (Gen. 1. 1): *In the beginning God created heaven and earth,* upon which a Gloss says[1] that to create is "to make something out of nothing."

I answer that, Not only is it not impossible that anything should be created by God, but it is necessary to say that all things were created by God, as appears from what has been said (Q. XLIV, A. 1). For when anyone makes one thing from another, this latter thing from which he makes is presupposed to his action, and is not produced by his action; thus the craftsman works from natural things, as wood or brass, which are caused not by the action of art, but by the action of nature. So also nature itself causes natural things as regards their form, but presupposes matter. If therefore God did only act from something presupposed, it would follow that the thing presupposed would not be caused by Him. Now it has been shown above (Q. XLIV, AA. 1, 2), that nothing can be among beings, unless it is from God, Who is the univer-

sal cause of all being. Hence it is necessary to say that God brings things into being from nothing.

Reply Obj. 1. The ancient philosophers, as is said above (Q. XLIV, A. 2), considered only the emanation of particular effects from particular causes, which necessarily presuppose something in their action; from this came their common opinion that nothing is made from nothing. But this has no place in the first emanation from the universal principle of things.

Reply Obj. 2. Creation is not change, except according to a mode of understanding. For change means that the same something should be different now from what it was previously. Sometimes, indeed, the same actual thing is different now from what it was before, as in motion according to quantity, quality and place, but sometimes it is the same being only in potency, as in substantial change, the subject of which is matter. But in creation, by which the whole substance of a thing is produced, the same thing can be taken as different now and before only according to our way of understanding, so that a thing is understood as first not existing at all, and afterwards as existing. But as "action and passion coincide in the substance of motion," and differ only according to different relations,[2] it must follow that when motion is taken away, only different relations remain in the Creator and in the creature. But because the mode of signification follows the mode of understanding as was said above (Q. XIII, A. 1), creation is signified by mode of change; and on this account it is said that to create is to make something from nothing. And yet to make and to be made are more suitable expressions here than to change and to be changed, because to make and to be made imply a relation of cause to the effect, and of effect to the cause, and imply change only as a consequence.

Reply Obj. 3. In things which are made without motion, to become and to be already made are simultaneous, whether such making is the term of motion, as illumination (for a thing is being illuminated and is illuminated at the same time) or whether it is not the term of motion, as the word is being made in the mind and is made at the same time. In these things what is being made, is; but when we speak of its being made, we mean that it is from another, and was not previously. Hence since creation is without motion, a thing is being created and is created at the same time.

---

[1] *Glossa ordin.,* (1, 23F); see note above (A. 1).

[2] Aristotle, *Physics,* III, 3 (202^{b}20).

Reply Obj. 4. This objection proceeds from a false imagination, as if there were an infinite medium between nothing and being, which is plainly false. This false imagination comes from creation being taken to signify a change existing between two terms.

ARTICLE 3. *Whether Creation Is Anything in the Creature?*

We proceed thus to the Third Article: It would seem that creation is not anything in the creature.

Objection 1. For as creation taken in a passive sense is attributed to the creature, so creation taken in an active sense is attributed to the Creator. But creation taken actively is not anything in the Creator, because otherwise it would follow that in God there would be something temporal. Therefore creation taken passively is not anything in the creature.

Obj. 2. Further, there is no medium between the Creator and the creature. But creation is signified as the medium between them both, since it is not the Creator, as it is not eternal; nor is it a creature, because in that case it would be necessary for the same reason to suppose another creation to create it, and so on to infinity. Therefore creation is not anything in the creature.

Obj. 3. Further, if creation is anything beside the created substance, it must be an accident belonging to it. But every accident is in a subject. Therefore a thing created would be the subject of creation, and so the same thing would be the subject and also the term of creation. This is impossible, because the subject is before the accident, and preserves the accident, while the term is after the action and passion whose term it is, and as soon as it exists, action and passion cease. Therefore creation itself is not any thing.

On the contrary, It is greater for a thing to be made according to its entire substance than to be made according to its substantial or accidental form. But generation taken absolutely, or relatively, whereby anything is made according to the substantial or the accidental form, is something in the thing generated. Therefore much more is creation, whereby a thing is made according to its whole substance, something in the thing created.

I answer that, Creation places something in the thing created according to relation only, because what is created, is not made by movement, or by change. For what is made by movement or by change is made from something pre-

existing. And this happens, indeed, in the particular productions of some beings, but cannot happen in the production of all being by the universal cause of all beings, which is God. Hence God by creation produces things without movement. Now when movement is removed from action and passion, only relation remains, as was said above (A. 2, ANS. 2). Hence creation in the creature is only a certain relation to the Creator as to the principle of its being; even as in passion, which implies movement, is implied a relation to the principle of motion.

Reply Obj. 1. Creation signified actively means the divine action, which is God's essence, with a relation to the creature. But in God relation to the creature is not a real relation, but only a relation of reason; but the relation of the creature to God is a real relation, as was said above (Q. XIII, A. 7) in treating of the divine names.

Reply Obj. 2. Because creation is signified as a change, as was said above (A. 2, ANS. 2), and change is a kind of medium between the mover and the thing moved, therefore also creation is signified as a medium between the Creator and the creature. Nevertheless passive creation is in the creature, and is a creature. Nor is there need of a further creation in its creation; because relations, from the fact that they are relations, that is, are said of something else, are not referred by any other relations, but by themselves; as was also shown above (Q. XLII, A. I, ANS. 4), in treating of the equality of the Persons.

Reply Obj. 3. The creature is the term of creation as signifying a change, but is the subject of creation, taken as a real relation, and is prior to it in being, as the subject is to the accident. Nevertheless creation has a certain aspect of priority on the part of the object of which it is said, which is the beginning of the creature. Nor is it necessary to say that as long as the creature is it is being created, because creation implies a relation of the creature to the Creator, with a certain newness or beginning.

ARTICLE 4. *Whether To Be Created Belongs to Composite and Subsisting Things?*

We proceed thus to the Fourth Article: It would seem that to be created does not belong to composite and subsisting things.

Objection 1. For in the book, *De Causis* (prop. IV),[1] it is said, "The first of creatures is being." But the being of a thing created is not

             [1] BA 166.

subsisting. Therefore creation properly speaking does not belong to subsisting and composite things.

Obj. 2. Further, whatever is created is from nothing. But composite things are not from nothing, but are the result of their own component parts. Therefore composite things are not created.

Obj. 3. Further, what is presupposed in the second emanation is properly produced by the first; as natural generation produces the natural thing, which is presupposed in the operation of art. But the thing supposed in natural generation is matter. Therefore matter, and not the composite, is, properly speaking, that which is created.

On the contrary, It is said (Gen. 1. 1): *In the beginning God created heaven and earth*. But heaven and earth are subsisting composite things. Therefore creation is proper to these things.

I answer that, To be created is, in a manner, to be made, as was shown above (A. 2, ANS.2.). Now, to be made is directed to the being of a thing. Hence to be made and to be created properly belong to whatever being belongs; which, indeed, belongs properly to subsisting things, whether they are simple things, as in the case of separate substances, or composite, as in the case of material substances. For being belongs to that which has being—that is, to what subsists in its own being. But forms and accidents and the like are called beings not as if they themselves were, but because something is by them; as whiteness is called a being, because its subject is white by it. Hence, according to the Philosopher[1] accident is more properly said to be of a being than a being. Therefore, as accidents and forms and the like non-subsisting things are to be said to co-exist rather than to exist, so they ought to be called rather concreated than created things; but, properly speaking, created things are subsisting beings.

Reply Obj. 1. In the proposition "the first of created things is being," the word "being" does not refer to the created substance, but to the proper notion of the object of creation. For a created thing is called created because it is a being, not because it is "this" being, since creation is the emanation of all being from the Universal Being, as was said above (A. 1). We use a similar way of speaking when we say that the first visible thing is colour, although, strictly speaking, the thing coloured is what is seen.

[1] *Metaphysics*, VII, 1 (1028ª18).

Reply Obj. 2. Creation does not mean the building up of a composite thing from pre-existing principles, but it means that the composite is created so that it is brought into being at the same time with all its principles.

Reply Obj. 3. This reason does not prove that matter alone is created, but that matter does not exist except by creation; for creation is the production of the whole being, and not only of matter.

ARTICLE 5. *Whether It Pertains to God Alone To Create?*

We proceed thus to the Fifth Article: It would seem that it does not pertain to God alone to create.

Objection 1. Because, according to the Philosopher,[2] what is perfect can make its own likeness. But immaterial creatures are more perfect than material creatures, which nevertheless can make their own likeness, for fire generates fire, and man begets man. Therefore an immaterial substance can make a substance like to itself. But immaterial substance can be made only by creation, since it has no matter from which to be made. Therefore a creature can create.

Obj. 2. Further, the greater the resistance is on the part of the thing made, so much the greater power is required in the maker. But a contrary resists more than nothing. Therefore it requires more power to make (something) from its contrary, which nevertheless a creature can do, than to make a thing from nothing. Much more therefore can a creature do this.

Obj. 3. Further, the power of the maker is considered according to the measure of what is made. But created being is finite, as we proved above when treating of the infinity of God (Q. VII, AA. 2, 3, 4). Therefore only a finite power is needed to produce a creature by creation. But to have a finite power is not contrary to the nature of a creature. Therefore it is not impossible for a creature to create.

On the contrary, Augustine says (*De Trin.* iii, 8)[3] that "neither good nor bad angels can create anything." Much less therefore can any other creatures.

I answer that, It sufficiently appears at the first glance, according to what precedes (A. 1, Q. XLIV, AA. 1, 2), that to create can be the proper action of God alone. For the more universal effects must be reduced to the more universal and prior causes. Now among all effects

[2] *Soul*, II, 4 (415ª26); also *Meteorology*, IV, 3 (380ª14).
[3] PL 42, 876.

the most universal is being itself, and hence it must be the proper effect of the first and most universal cause, and that is God. Hence also it is said (*De Causis*, prop. iii)[1] that neither intelligence nor the soul gives us being, except in so far as it works by divine operation. Now to produce being absolutely, not as this or that being, belongs to the notion of creation. Hence it is manifest that creation is the proper act of God alone.

It happens, however, that something may participate the proper action of another not by its own power, but instrumentally, in so far as it acts by the power of another; as air can heat and ignite by the power of fire. And so some have supposed that although creation is the proper act of the universal cause, still some inferior cause acting by the power of the first cause can create. And thus Avicenna asserted[2] that the first separate substance created by God created another after itself, and the substance of the world and its soul; and that the substance of the world creates the matter of the inferior bodies. And in the same manner the Master says (*Sent.* iv, D. 5)[3] that God can communicate to a creature the power of creating, so that the latter can create ministerially, not by its own power.

But this cannot be, because the secondary instrumental cause does not participate the action of the superior cause, except in so far as by something proper to itself it works to dispose the effect of the principal agent. If therefore it effects nothing according to what is proper to itself, it is used to no purpose, nor would there be any need of certain instruments for certain actions. Thus we see that a saw, in cutting wood, which it does by the property of its own form, produces the form of a bench, which is the proper effect of the principal agent. Now the proper effect of God creating is what is presupposed to all other effects, and that is absolute being. Hence nothing else can act dispositively and instrumentally to this effect, since creation is not from anything presupposed which can be disposed by the action of the instrumental agent. So therefore it is impossible for any creature to create, either by its own power, or instrumentally—that is, ministerially.

And above all it is absurd to suppose that a body can create, for no body acts except by touching or moving; and thus it requires in its action some pre-existing thing which can be touched or moved, which is contrary to the very notion of creation.

Reply Obj. 1. A perfect thing participating any nature, makes a likeness to itself not by absolutely producing that nature, but by applying it to something else. For an individual man cannot be the cause of human nature absolutely, because he would then be the cause of himself; but he is the cause of human nature being in the man begotten, and thus he presupposes in his action a determinate matter whereby he is an individual man. But as this man participates human nature, so every created being participates, so to speak, the nature of being; for God alone is His own being, as we have said above (Q. VII, AA. 1, 2). Therefore no created being can produce a being absolutely, except in so far as it causes *being* in *this,* and so it is necessary to presuppose that whereby a thing is this thing, before the action by which it makes its own likeness. But in an immaterial substance it is not possible to presuppose anything whereby it is this thing, because it is this thing by its form, whereby it has being, since it is a subsisting form. Therefore an immaterial substance cannot produce another immaterial substance like itself as regards its being, but only as regards some added perfection; as we may say that a superior angel illuminates as inferior, as Dionysius says (*Cæl. Hier.* viii, 2).[4] In this way even in heaven there is paternity, as the Apostle says (Eph. 3. 15): *From whom all paternity in heaven and on earth is named.* From which it evidently appears that no created being can cause anything, unless something is presupposed, which is against the notion of creation.

Reply Obj. 2. A thing is made from its contrary accidentally,[5] but per se from the subject which is in potency. And so the contrary resists the agent because it impedes the potency from the act to which the agent intends to reduce the matter, as fire intends to reduce the matter of water to an act like to itself, but is impeded by the form and contrary dispositions, whereby the potency (of the water) is restrained from being reduced to act; and the more the potency is restrained, the more power is required in the agent to reduce the matter to act. Hence a much greater power is required in the agent

---

[1] BA 165.

[2] *Meta.*, tr. IX, chap. 4 (104vb); cf. Algazel, *Meta.*, tr. v (MK 119); Averroes, *Dest. Dest.*, disp. 3 (IX, 52E); cf. also Albert, *Summa de Creat.*, II, Q. 61, A. 2 (BO XXXV, 524).

[3] QR II, 575.

[4] PG 3, 240.

[5] Aristotle, *Physics*, I, 7 (190b27).

when no potency pre-exists. Thus therefore it appears that it is an act of much greater power to make a thing from nothing, than from its contrary.

Reply Obj. 3. The power of the maker is weighed not only from the substance of the thing made, but also from the mode of its being made; for a greater heat heats not only more, but faster. Therefore although to create a finite effect does not show an infinite power, yet to create it from nothing does show an infinite power, which appears from what has been said (Ans. 2). For if a greater power is required in the agent in proportion to the distance of the potency from the act, it follows that the power of that which produces something from no presupposed potency is infinite, because there is no proportion between no potency and the potency presupposed by the power of a natural agent, as there is no proportion between non-being and being. And because no creature has absolutely an infinite power, any more than it has an infinite being, as was proved above (Q. VII, A. 2), it follows that no creature can create.

ARTICLE 6. *Whether To Create Is Proper to Any of the Persons?*

We proceed thus to the Sixth Article: It would seem that to create is proper to some Person.

Objection 1. For what comes first is the cause of what is after, and what is perfect is the cause of what is imperfect. But the procession of the divine Person is prior to the procession of the creature, and is more perfect, because the divine Person proceeds in perfect likeness of its principle; the creature however proceeds in imperfect likeness. Therefore the processions of the divine Persons are the cause of the processions of things, and so to create is proper to a Person.

Obj. 2. Further, the divine Persons are distinguished from each other only by their processions and relations. Therefore whatever difference is attributed to the divine Persons belongs to them according to the processions and relations of the Persons. But the causation of creatures is diversely attributed to the divine Persons; for in the Creed,[1] to the Father is attributed that He is the "Creator of all things visible and invisible," to the Son is attributed that "by Him all things were made," and to the Holy Ghost is attributed that He is "Lord and Life-giver." Therefore the causation of crea-

[1] Nicaean Creed (MA II, 666; DZ 54).

tures belongs to the Persons according to processions and relations.

Obj. 3. Further, if it be said that the causation of the creature flows from some essential attribute appropriated to some one Person, this does not appear to be sufficient, because every divine effect is caused by every essential attribute—namely, by power, goodness, and wisdom—and thus does not pertain to one more than to another. Therefore any determinate mode of causation ought not to be attributed to one Person more than to another, unless they are distinguished in creating according to relations and processions.

On the contrary, Dionysius says (*Div. Nom.* ii)[2] that all things created are the common work of the whole Godhead.

I answer that, To create is, properly speaking, to cause or produce the being of things. And as every agent produces its like, the principle of action can be considered from the effect of the action; for fire generates fire. And therefore to create pertains to God according to His being, that is, His essence, which is common to the three Persons. Hence to create is not proper to any one Person, but is common to the whole Trinity.

Nevertheless the divine Persons, according to the nature of their procession, have a causality respecting the creation of things. For as was said above (Q. XIV, A. 8; Q. XIX, A. 4), when treating of the knowledge and will of God, God is the cause of things by His intellect and will, just as the craftsman is cause of the things made by his craft. Now the craftsman works through the word conceived in his intellect, and through the love of his will regarding some object. Hence also God the Father made the creature through His Word, which is His Son, and through His Love, which is the Holy Ghost. And so the processions of the Persons are the types of the productions of creatures in so far as they include the essential attributes, which are knowledge, and will.

Reply Obj. 1. The processions of the divine Persons are the cause of creation, as above explained.

Reply Obj. 2. As the divine nature, although common to the three Persons, still belongs to them in a kind of order, since the Son receives the divine nature from the Father, and the Holy Ghost from both, so also likewise the power of creation, whilst common to the three Persons, belongs to them in a kind of order. For the Son receives it from the Father, and the

[2] Sect. 3 (PG 3, 637).

Holy Ghost from both. Hence to be the Creator is attributed to the Father as to Him Who does not have the power of creation from another. And of the Son it is said (John 1. 3), *Through Him all things were made,* since He has the same power, but from another; for this preposition "through" usually denotes a mediate cause, or a principle from a principle. But to the Holy Ghost, Who has the same power from both, is attributed that by His rule He governs and quickens what is created by the Father through the Son. Again, the general notion of this appropriation may be taken from the appropriation of the essential attributes. For, as above stated (Q. XXXIX, A. 8), to the Father is appropriated power which is chiefly shown in creation, and therefore it is attributed to Him to be the Creator. To the Son is appropriated wisdom, through which the agent acts through the intellect; and therefore it is said: *Through Whom all things were made.* And to the Holy Ghost is appropriated goodness, to which belong both government, which brings things to their due ends, and the giving of life—for life consists in a certain interior movement, and the first mover is the end and goodness.

Reply Obj. 3. Although every effect of God proceeds from each attribute, each effect is reduced to that attribute to which it is connected through its proper notion; thus the order of things is reduced to wisdom, and the justification of the sinner to mercy and goodness pouring itself out superabundantly. But creation, which is the production of the very substance of a thing, is reduced to power.

ARTICLE 7. *Whether in Creatures Is Necessarily Found a Trace of the Trinity?*

We proceed thus to the Seventh Article: It would seem that in creatures there is not necessarily found a trace of the Trinity.

Objection 1. For anything can be discovered through its traces. But the trinity of persons cannot be discovered from creatures, as was above stated (Q. XXXII, A. 1). Therefore there is no trace of the Trinity in creatures.

Obj. 2. Further, whatever is in creatures is created. Therefore if the trace of the Trinity is found in creatures according to some of their properties, and if everything created has a trace of the Trinity, it follows that we can find a trace of the Trinity in each of these (properties), and so on to infinitude.

Obj. 3. Further, the effect represents only its own cause. But the causality of creatures be-

longs to the common nature and not to the relations whereby the Persons are distinguished and numbered. Therefore in the creature is to be found a trace not of the Trinity but of the unity of essence.

On the contrary, Augustine says (*De Trin.* vi, 10),[1] that "the trace of the Trinity appears in creatures."

I answer that, Every effect in some degree represents its cause, but in different ways. For some effects represent only the causality of the cause, but not its form; as smoke represents fire. Such a representation is called representation by trace; for a trace shows that someone has passed by but not who it is. Other effects represent the cause as regards the likeness of its form, as fire generated represents fire generating, and a statue of Mercury represents Mercury; and this is called the representation of image.

Now the processions of the divine Persons are referred to the acts of intellect and will, as was said above (Q. XXVII). For the Son proceeds as the word of the intellect, and the Holy Ghost proceeds as love of the will. Therefore in rational creatures, possessing intellect and will, there is found the representation of the Trinity by way of image, since there is found in them the word conceived, and the love proceeding.

But in all creatures there is found the trace of the Trinity, since in every creature are found some things which are necessarily reduced to the divine Persons as to their cause. For every creature subsists in its own being, and has a form, whereby it is determined to a species, and has an order to something else. Therefore as it is a created substance, it represents the cause and principle; and so in that manner it shows the Person of the Father, Who is the principle from no principle. According as it has a form and species, it represents the Word as the form of the thing made by art is from the conception of the craftsman. According as it has order, it represents the Holy Ghost, since He is love, because the order of the effect to something else is from the will of the Creator.

And therefore Augustine says (*De Trin.* vi, *loc. cit.*) that the trace of the Trinity is found in every creature according as it is one individual, and according as it is formed by a species, and according as it possesses order. And to these also are reduced those three, *number, weight,* and *measure,* mentioned in the Book of

[1] PL 42, 932.

Wisdom (II. 21). For measure refers to the substance of the thing limited by its principles, number refers to the species, weight refers to the order. And to these three are reduced the other three mentioned by Augustine (*De Nat. Boni,* iii),[1] "mode, species, and order," and also those he again mentions (QQ. LXXXIII, *qu.* 18)[2]: "that which persists; that which is distinguished; that which agrees." For a thing persists by its substance, is distinct by its form, and agrees by its order. Other similar expressions may be easily reduced to the above.

Reply Obj. 1. The representation of the trace is to be referred to the appropriations, in which manner we are able to arrive at a knowledge of the trinity of the divine persons from creatures, as we have said (Q. XXXII, A. 1, Ans. 1).

Reply Obj. 2. A creature is properly a thing self-subsisting, and in such are the three above-mentioned things to be found. Nor is it necessary that these three things should be found in all that exists in the creature, but only to a subsisting being is the trace ascribed in regard to those three things.

Reply Obj. 3. The processions of the persons are also in some way the cause and type of creation, as appears from the above (A. 6).

ARTICLE 8. *Whether Creation Is Mingled with Works of Nature and Art?*

We proceed thus to the Eighth Article: It would seem that creation is mingled in works of nature and art.

Objection 1. For in every operation of nature and art some form is produced. But it is not produced from anything, since matter has no part in it. Therefore it is produced from nothing; and thus in every operation of nature and art there is creation.

Obj. 2. Further, the effect is not more powerful than its cause. But in natural things the only agent is the accidental form, which is an active or a passive form. Therefore the substantial form is not produced by the operation of nature. And therefore it must be produced by creation.

Obj. 3. Further, in nature like begets like. But some things are found generated in nature by a thing unlike to them, as is evident in animals generated through putrefaction. Therefore the form of these is not from nature, but by creation; and the same reason applies to other things.

[1] PL 42, 553.
[2] PL 40, 15.

Obj. 4. Further, what is not created, is not a creature. If therefore in nature's productions there were not creation, it would follow that nature's productions are not creatures; which is heretical.

On the contrary, Augustine[3] distinguishes the work of propagation, which is a work of nature, from the work of creation.

I answer that, The doubt on this subject arises from the forms which, some said,[4] do not begin by the action of nature, but previously exist in matter; for they asserted that forms are latent. This arose from ignorance concerning matter, and from not knowing how to distinguish between potency and act. For because forms pre-exist in matter in potency, they asserted that they pre-existed absolutely. Others, however, said[5] that the forms were given or caused by a separate agent by way of creation, and accordingly, that to each operation of nature is joined creation. But this opinion arose from ignorance concerning form. For they failed to consider that the form of the natural body is not subsisting, but is that by which a thing is. And therefore, since to be made and to be created belong properly to a subsisting thing alone, as shown above (A. 4), it does not belong to forms to be made or to be created, but to be concreated. What, indeed, is properly made by the natural agent is the composite, which is made from matter.

Hence creation does not enter in the works of nature, but it presupposed to the work of nature.

Reply Obj. 1. Forms begin to be in act when the composite things are made, not as though they were made per se, but only accidentally.

Reply Obj. 2. The active qualities in nature act by virtue of substantial forms, and therefore the natural agent not only produces its like according to quality, but according to species.

Reply Obj. 3. For the generation of imperfect animals, a universal agent suffices, and this is to be found in the celestial power to which they are assimilated, not in species, but according to a kind of analogy. Nor is it necessary to say that their forms are created by a separate agent. However for the generation of perfect animals the universal agent does not

[3] *De Gen. ad Lit.,* V, 11, 20 (PL 34, 330, 335).
[4] Anaxagoras, in Aristotle, *Physics,* I, 4 (187ª29); cf. St. Thomas, *De Pot.,* Q. III, A. 8.
[5] Cf. St. Thomas, *De Pot.,* Q. III, A. 8. Averroes ascribed this doctrine to Plato—*In Meta.,* VII, 31 (VIII, 180K).

suffice, but a proper agent is required, in the shape of a univocal generator.

Reply Obj. 4. The operation of nature takes place only on the presupposition of created principles; and thus the products of nature are called creatures.

QUESTION XLVI

OF THE BEGINNING OF THE DURATION

OF CREATURES

(In Three Articles)

NEXT must be considered the beginning of the duration of creatures, about which there are three points for treatment: (1) Whether creatures always existed? (2) Whether that they began to exist is an article of Faith? (3) How God is said to have created heaven and earth in the beginning?

ARTICLE 1. *Whether the Universe of Creatures Always Existed?*

We proceed thus to the First Article: It would seem that the universe of creatures, now called the world, had no beginning, but existed from eternity.

Objection 1. For everything which begins to be is a possible being before it exists; otherwise it would be impossible for it to come into being. If therefore the world began to be, it was a possible being before it began to be. But what is possible to be is matter, which is in potency to being, which results from a form, and to non-being, which results from privation of form. If therefore the world began to be, matter must have existed before the world. But matter cannot exist without form, while the matter of the world with its form is the world. Therefore the world existed before it began to exist; which is impossible.[1]

Obj. 2. Further, nothing which has power to be always, is at times and at times is not, because a thing exists as far as the power of that thing extends. But every incorruptible thing has power to be always, for its power does not extend to any determinate time. Therefore no incorruptible thing is at times, and at times is not. But everything which has a beginning at some time is, and at some time is not. Therefore no incorruptible thing begins to be. But there are many incorruptible things in the world, as the celestial bodies and all intellectual

substances. Therefore the world did not begin to be.[2]

Obj. 3. Further, what is unbegotten has no beginning. But the Philosopher says[3] that "matter is unbegotten," and also[4] that "the heaven is unbegotten." Therefore the universe did not begin to be.[5]

Obj. 4. Further, a vacuum exists where there is not a body, though there could be. But if the world began to exist, there was first no body where the body of the world now is; and yet it could be there, otherwise it would not be there now. Therefore before the world there was a vacuum, which is impossible.[6]

Obj. 5. Further, nothing begins anew to be moved except through the mover or the thing moved being otherwise now than it was before. But what is otherwise now than it was before, is moved. Therefore before every new movement there was a previous movement. Therefore movement always was; and therefore also the thing moved always was, because movement is only in a thing moved.[7]

Obj. 6. Further, every mover is either natural or voluntary. But neither begins to move except by some pre-existing movement. For nature always moves in the same manner; hence unless some change precede either in the nature of the mover, or in the movable thing there cannot arise from the natural mover a movement which was not there before. And the will, without itself being changed, puts off doing what it proposes to do; but this can be only by some imagined change, at least as regards time. Thus he who wills to make a house to-morrow, and not to-day, awaits something which will be to-morrow, but is not to-day, and at least awaits for to-day to pass, and for to-morrow to come; and this cannot be without change, because time is the measure of movement. Therefore it remains that before every new movement, there was another movement. And so the same conclusion follows as before.[8]

Obj. 7. Further, whatever is always in its beginning and always in its end cannot cease and cannot begin, because what begins is not in its end, and what ceases is not in its beginning.

---

[1] This is the position of the Peripatetics, according to Maimonides, *Guide*, PT. II, chap. 14 (FR 174); cf. Averroes, *Destruct., Destruct.*, disp. 1 (IX, 34H); *In Phys.*, VIII, 4 (IV, 340K).

[2] Aristotle, *Heavens*, I, 12 (281ᵇ18); Averroes, *In de Cælo*, I, 119 (IV, 340K).

[3] *Physics*, I, 9 (192ᵃ28).

[4] *Heavens*, I, 3 (270ᵃ13).

[5] Cf. Maimonides, *Guide*, II, 13 (FR 173).

[6] Averroes, *In De Cælo*, III, 29 (V, 199H).

[7] Aristotle's argument, according to Maimonides, *Guide*, II, 14 (FR 174); cf. Averroes, *In Phys.*, VIII, 7 (IV, 342M).

[8] Avicenna, *Meta.*, IX, 1 (102ra); Averroes, *In Phys.*, VIII, 8 (IV, 344E); 15 (V, 349I); *Destruct. Destruct.*, 1 (IX, 16A).

But time always is in its beginning and end, because there is no time except *now* which is the end of the past and the beginning of the future. Therefore time cannot begin or end, and consequently neither can movement, the measure of which is time.[1]

Obj. 8. Further, God is before the world either in the order of nature only, or also by duration. If in the order of nature only, therefore, since God is eternal, the world also is eternal. But if God is prior by duration, since what is prior and posterior in duration constitutes time, it follows that time existed before the world, which is impossible.[2]

Obj. 9. Further, if there is a sufficient cause, there is an effect, for a cause to which there is no effect is an imperfect cause, requiring something else to make the effect follow. But God is the sufficient cause of the world, being the final cause, by reason of His goodness, the exemplary cause by reason of His wisdom, and the efficient cause, by reason of His power as appears from the above (Q. XLIV, AA. 1, 3, 4). Since therefore God is eternal, the world also is eternal.[3]

Obj. 10. Further, where there is an eternal action, there is an eternal effect. But the action of God is His substance, which is eternal. Therefore the world is eternal.

On the contrary, It is said (John 17. 5), *Glorify Me O Father with Thyself with the glory which I had before the world was;* and (Prov. 8. 22), *The Lord possessed Me in the beginning of His ways, before He made anything from the beginning.*

I answer that, Nothing except God can be from eternity. And this statement is not impossible to uphold, for it has been shown above (Q. XIX, A. 4) that the will of God is the cause of things. Therefore things are necessary according as it is necessary for God to will them, since the necessity of the effect depends on the necessity of the cause.[4] Now it was shown above (Q. XIX, A. 3), that, absolutely speaking, it is not necessary that God should will anything except Himself. It is not therefore necessary for God to will that the world should always exist; but the world is eternal to the extent that God wills it to be eternal, since the

being of the world depends on the will of God, as on its cause. It is not therefore necessary for the world to be always. And hence it cannot be proved by demonstration.

Nor are Aristotle's reasons[5] demonstrative absolutely, but relatively that is, as contradicting the reasons of some of the ancients who asserted that the world began to exist in some ways impossible in truth. This appears in three ways.[6] First, because, both in the *Physics*[7] and in the *Heavens*[8] he advances some opinions as those of Anaxagoras, Empedocles and Plato, and brings forward reasons to refute them. Secondly, because wherever he speaks of this subject, he quotes the testimony of the ancients, which is not the way of a demonstrator, but of one persuading of what is probable. Thirdly, because he expressly says[9] that there are dialectical problems, of which we do not have proofs, such as, "whether the world is eternal."

Reply Obj. 1. Before the world existed it was possible for the world to be: not, indeed, according to a passive power which is matter, but according to the active power of God; and also, according as a thing is called absolutely possible not in relation to any power, but from the sole relation of the terms which are not contrary to each other, in which sense possible is opposed to impossible, as appears from the Philosopher.[10]

Reply Obj. 2. Whatever has power always to be, from the fact of having that power cannot sometimes be and sometimes not be; but before it received that power, it did not exist.

Hence this reason, which is given by Aristotle,[11] does not prove absolutely that incorruptible things never began to exist, but that they did not begin by the natural mode whereby things generated and corruptible begin.

Reply Obj. 3. Aristotle proves[12] that "matter is unbegotten" from the fact that "it has not a subject" from which to derive its existence, and he proves[13] that "heaven is ungenerated," because it has no contrary from which to be generated. Hence it appears that no conclusion follows either way, except that matter and heaven did not begin by generation, as some said,[14] es-

---

[1] Aristotle, *Physics*, VIII, 1 (251ᵇ19); cf. Averroes, *In Phys.*, VIII, comm. 11 (IV, 346c).
[2] Avicenna, *Meta.*, IX, 1 (101vab); cf. Averroes, *Dest. Dest.*, disp. 1 (IX, 27C).
[3] Avicenna, *Meta.* IX, 1 (101vb); cf. Alexander of Hales, *Summa Theol.*, I, 64 (QR I, 93); Bonaventure, *In Sent.*, II, d. 1, pt. I, A. 1, Q. 2 (QR II, 20).
[4] Aristotle, *Metaphysics*, V, 5 (1015ᵇ9).

[5] *Physics*, VIII, 1 (250ᵇ24).
[6] Cf. Maimonides, *Guide*, II, 15 (FR 176).
[7] VIII, 1 (250ᵇ24; 251ᵇ17).
[8] I, 10 (279ᵇ4, 280ᵃ30).
[9] *Topics*, I, 9 (104ᵇ16).
[10] *Metaphysics*, V, 12 (1019ᵇ19).
[11] *Heavens*, I, 12 (281ᵇ18).
[12] *Physics*, I, 9 (192ᵃ28).
[13] *Heavens*, I, 3 (270ᵃ13).
[14] Cf. Aristotle, *Heavens*, I, 10 (279ᵇ13).

pecially about heaven. But we say that matter and heaven were produced into being by creation, as appears above (Q. XLIV, A. 2).

Reply Obj. 4. The notion of a vacuum not only implies that in which nothing is, but also requires a space capable of holding a body and in which there is not a body, as appears from Aristotle.[1] We hold however that before the world was there was no place or space.

Reply Obj. 5. The first mover was always in the same state, but the first movable thing was not always so, because it began to be whereas before it was not. This, however, was not through change, but by creation, which is not change, as said above (Q. XLV, A. 2 Ans. 2). Hence it is evident that this reason, which Aristotle gives,[2] is valid against those who admitted the existence of eternal movable things, but not eternal movement, as appears from the opinions of Anaxagoras and Empedocles.[3] But we hold that from the moment movable things began to exist movement also existed.

Reply Obj. 6. The first agent is a voluntary agent. And although He had the eternal will to produce some effect, yet He did not produce an eternal effect. Nor is it necessary for some change to be presupposed, not even on account of imaginary time. For we must take into consideration the difference between a particular agent that presupposes something and produces something else, and the universal agent, who produces the whole. The particular agent produces the form, and presupposes the matter; and hence it is necessary that it introduce the form in due proportion into a suitable matter. And so it is reasonable to say that it introduces the form into such matter, and not into another, on account of the different kinds of matter. But it does not seem reasonable to say so of God Who produces form and matter together, whereas it is considered reasonable to say of Him that He produces matter fitting to the form and to the end. Now, a particular agent presupposes time just as it presupposes matter. Hence it is reasonably considered as acting in time *after* and not in time *before,* according to an imaginary succession of time after time. But the universal agent Who produces the thing and time also, is not considered as acting now, and not before, according to an imaginary succession of time succeeding time, as if time were presupposed to His action; but He must be considered as giving time to His effect as much as and when He willed, and according to what was fitting to demonstrate His power. For the world leads more evidently to the knowledge of the divine creating power if it was not always than if it had always been, since everything which was not always manifestly has a cause, while this is not so manifest of what always was.

Reply Obj. 7. As is stated,[4] "before and after belong to time," according as they are "in movement." Hence beginning and end in time must be taken in the same way as in movement. Now, granted the eternity of movement, it is necessary that any given moment in movement be a beginning and an end of movement, which need not be if movement has a beginning. The same reason applies to the *now* of time. Thus it appears that the notion of the instant *now,* as being always the beginning and end of time, presupposes the eternity of time and movement. Hence Aristotle brings forward this reason[5] against those who asserted the eternity of time, but denied the eternity of movement.

Reply Obj. 8. God is prior to the world by priority of duration. But the word prior signifies priority not of time, but of eternity. Or we may say that it signifies the eternity of imaginary time, and not of time really existing; just as when we say that above heaven there is nothing, the word above signifies only an imaginary place, according as it is possible to imagine other dimensions beyond those of the heavenly body.

Reply Obj. 9. As the effect follows from the cause that acts naturally according to the mode of its form, so likewise it follows from the voluntary agent, according to the form preconceived and determined by the agent, as appears from what was said above (Q. XIX, A. 4; Q. XLI, A. 2). Therefore, although God was from eternity the sufficient cause of the world, we should not say that the world was produced by Him, except as preordained by His will—that is, that it should have being after not being, in order more manifestly to declare its author.

Reply Obj. 10. Given the action, the effect follows according to the requirement of the form, which is the principle of action. But in agents acting by will, what is conceived and preordained is taken as the form, which is the principle of action. Therefore from the eternal action of God an eternal effect does not follow, but such an effect as God willed, an effect, that is, which has being after not being.

[1] *Physics,* IV, 1 (208ᵇ26).
[2] *Ibid.,* VIII, 1 (251ᵃ25).
[3] Cf. Aristotle, *Physics,* VIII, 1 (250ᵇ24).

[4] Aristotle, *Physics,* IV, 11 (219ᵃ17).
[5] *Ibid.,* VIII, 1 (251ᵇ29).

ARTICLE 2. *Whether It Is an Article of Faith That the World Began?*

We proceed thus to the Second Article: It would seem that it is not an article of faith but a demonstrable conclusion that the world began.

Objection 1. For everything that is made has a beginning of its duration. But it can be proved demonstratively that God is the effecting cause of the world; indeed this is asserted by the more credible philosophers.[1] Therefore it can be demonstratively proved that the world began.[2]

Obj. 2. Further, if it is necessary to say that the world was made by God, is must therefore have been made from nothing, or from something. But it was not made from something; otherwise the matter of the world would have preceded the world, against which are the arguments of Aristotle, who held that heaven was ungenerated. Therefore it must be said that the world was made from nothing; and thus it has being after not being. Therefore it must have begun to be.[3]

Obj. 3. Further, everything "which works by intellect, works from some principle,"[4] as appears in all craftsmen. But God acts by intellect; therefore His work has a principle. The world, therefore, which is His effect, did not always exist.[5]

Obj. 4. Further, it appears clearly that certain arts have developed, and certain countries have begun to be inhabited at some fixed time. But this would not be the case if the world had been always. Therefore it is manifest that the world did not always exist.

Obj. 5. Further, it is certain that nothing can be equal to God. But if the world had always been it would be equal to God in duration. Therefore it is certain that the world did not always exist.[6]

Obj. 6. Further, if the world always was, infinite days have preceded this present day. But it is impossible to pass through an infinite medium. Therefore we should never have arrived at this present day; which is manifestly false.[7]

Obj. 7. Further, if the world was eternal, generation also was eternal. Therefore one man was begotten of another in an infinite series. But the father is the efficient cause of the son.[8] Therefore in efficient causes there could be an infinite series, which is disproved in the *Metaphysics*.[9]

Obj. 8. Further, if the world and generation always were, there have been an infinite number of men. But man's soul is immortal. Therefore an infinite number of human souls would actually now exist, which is impossible. Therefore it can be known with certainty that the world began, and is held not only by faith.[10]

On the contrary, The articles of faith cannot be proved demonstratively, because faith is of things *that appear not* (Heb. 11. 1). But that God is the Creator of the world; hence that the world began, is an article of faith, for we say, "I believe in one God," etc.[11] And again, Gregory says (*Hom.* i. *in Ezech.*),[12] that Moses prophesied of the past, saying, *In the beginning God created heaven and earth,* in which words the newness of the world is conveyed. Therefore the newness of the world is known only by revelation; and therefore it cannot be proved demonstratively.

I answer that, We hold by faith alone, and it cannot be proved by demonstration, that the world did not always exist, as was said above of the mystery of the Trinity (Q. XXXII, A. 1). The reason of this is that the newness of the world cannot be demonstrated from the world itself. For the principle of demonstration is the essence of a thing. Now everything according to the notion of its species abstracts from here and now; hence it is said that "universals are everywhere and always."[13] Hence it cannot be demonstrated that man, or heaven, or a stone did not always exist.

Likewise neither can it be demonstrated on the part of the efficient cause, which acts by will. For the will of God cannot be investigated by reason, except as regards those things which God must will of necessity, and what He wills about creatures is not among these, as was said above (Q. XIX, A. 3). But the divine will can

---

[1] See above, Q. XLIV, A. 2.

[2] The position of Alexander of Hales, *Summa Theol.*, I, 64 (QR I, 95); and Bonaventure, *In Sent.*, II, d. 1, A. 1, Q. 2 (QR II, 22); cf. Albert, *In Phys.*, VIII, 1, 13 (BO III, 552); *Summa Theol.*, pt. II, tr. 1, Q. 4 (BO XXXII, 108).

[3] Alexander of Hales, *Summa Theol.*, I, 64 (QR I, 93).

[4] Aristotle, *Physics*, III, 4 (203ª31).

[5] Cf. Albert the Great, *In Phys.*, VIII, 1, 12 (BO III, 548).

[6] Alexander of Hales, *Summa Theol.*, I, 64 (QR I, 93).

[7] Algazel, according to Averroes, *Dest. Dest.*, disp. 1 (IX, 18C); cf. Maimonides, *Guide*, I, 74 (FR 138); Bonaventure, *In Sent.*, II, d. 1, Pt. I, A. 1, Q. 2 (QR II, 21).

[8] Aristotle, *Physics*, II, 3 (194ᵇ30).

[9] Aristotle, II, 2 (994ª5); cf. Averroes, *Dest. Dest.*, disp. I (IX, 20A).

[10] Algazel, according to Averroes, *Dest. Dest.*, disp. 1 (IX, 20A); cf. Maimonides, *Guide*, I, 73 (FR 131); Bonaventure, *In Sent.*, II, d. 1, Pt. I, A. 1, Q. 2 (QR II, 21).

[11] Nicaean Creed (MA II, 666; DZ 54).

[12] PL 76, 786.

[13] Aristotle, *Posterior Analytics*, I, 31 (87ᵇ33).

be manifested to man by revelation, on which faith rests. Hence that the world began to exist is an object of faith, but not of demonstration or science. And it is useful to consider this, lest anyone, presuming to demonstrate what is of faith, should bring forward reasons that are not cogent, so as to give occasion to unbelievers to laugh, thinking that on such reasons we believe things that are of faith.

Reply Obj. 1. As Augustine says[1] the opinion of philosophers who asserted the eternity of the world was twofold. For some said that the substance of the world was not from God, which is an intolerable error; and therefore it is refuted by proofs that are cogent. Some, however, said that the world was eternal, although made by God. "For they hold that the world has a beginning, not of time, but of creation, so that in a certain hardly intelligible way it was always made." "And they try to explain their meaning thus" as Augustine says[2]: "for just as, if the foot were always in the dust from eternity, there would always be a footprint which without doubt was caused by him who trod on it, so also the world always was, because its Maker always existed." To understand this we must consider that the efficient cause, which acts by motion, of necessity precedes its effect in time; because the effect is only in the end of the action, and every agent must be the beginning of action. But if the action is instantaneous and not successive, it is not necessary for the maker to be prior to the thing made in duration, as appears in the case of illumination. Hence they say[3] that it does not follow necessarily if God is the active cause of the world, that He should be prior to the world in duration, because creation, by which He produced the world, is not a successive change, as was said above (Q. XIV, A. 7).

Reply Obj. 2. Those who would say that the world was eternal, would say that the world was made by God from nothing; not that it was made after nothing, according to what we understand by the word creation, but that it was not made from anything; and so also some of them do not reject the word creation, as appears from Avicenna.[4]

Reply Obj. 3. This is the argument of Anaxagoras (as quoted in the *Physics*).[5] But it does not lead to a necessary conclusion, except as to that intellect which deliberates in order to

find out what should be done, which is like movement. Of such a character is the human intellect, but not the divine intellect (Q. XIV, AA. 7, 12).

Reply Obj. 4. Those who hold the eternity of the world hold that some region was changed an infinite number of times, from being uninhabitable to being inhabitable and *vice versa*, and likewise they hold that the arts, by reason of various corruptions and accidents, were subject to an infinite variety of discovery and decay.[6] Hence Aristotle says[7] that it is absurd from such particular changes to accept the opinion of the newness of the whole world.

Reply Obj. 5. Even supposing that the world always was, it would not be equal to God in eternity, as Boëthius says (*De Consol.* v, 6),[8] because the divine Being is all being simultaneously without succession; but with the world it is otherwise.

Reply Obj. 6. Passage is always understood as being from term to term. Whatever by-gone day we choose, from it to the present day there is a finite number of days which can be passed through. The objection is founded on the idea that, given two extremes, there is an infinite number of mean terms.

Reply Obj. 7. In efficient causes it is impossible to proceed to infinity *per se*—thus, there cannot be an infinite number of causes that are *per se* required for a certain effect; for instance, that a stone be moved by a stick, the stick by the hand, and so on to infinity. But it is not impossible to proceed to infinity accidentally as regards efficient causes; for instance, if all the causes thus infinitely multiplied should have the order of only one cause, their multiplication being accidental; as an artificer acts by means of many hammers accidentally, because one after the other is broken. It is accidental, therefore, that one particular hammer acts after the action of another, and likewise it is accidental to this particular man as generator to be generated by another man; for he generates as a man, and not as the son of another man. For all men generating hold one grade in efficient causes—namely, the grade of a particular generator. Hence it is not impossible for a man to be generated by man to infinity; but such a thing would be impossible if the generation of this man depended upon this man, and on an

---

[1] *City of God*, XI, 4 (PL 41, 319).

[2] *Ibid.*, X, 31 (PL 41, 311).

[3] Cf. Averroes, *Dest. Dest.*, I (IX, 27H).

[4] *Meta.*, IX, 4 (104va).

[5] Aristotle, III, 4 (203ª31).

[6] Cf. Augustine, *City of God*, XII, 10 (PL 41, 358); Aristotle, *Meteorology*, I, 14 (351ª19); Averroes, *In Meta.*, XII, 50 (VIII, 334D).

[7] *Meteorology*, I, 14 (352ª26).   [8] PL 63, 859.

elementary body, and on the sun, and so on to infinity.

Reply Obj. 8. Those who hold the eternity of the world evade this reason in many ways. For some do not think it impossible for there to be an actual infinity of souls, as appears from the *Metaphysics* of Algazel, who says[1] that such a thing is an accidental infinity. But this was disproved above (Q. VII, A. 4). Some say that the soul is corrupted with the body.[2] And some say that of all souls only one endures.[3] But others, as Augustine says,[4] asserted on this account a cycle of souls—namely, that souls separated from their bodies return again to bodies after a course of time. A fuller consideration of these matters will be given later (Q. LXXV, A. 6; Q. LXXVI, A. 2; Q. CXVIII, A. 6). But we must consider that this argument concerns only a particular case. Hence one might say that the world was eternal, or at least some creature, as an angel, but not man. But we are considering the question in general, as to whether any creature can exist from eternity.

ARTICLE 3. *Whether the Creation of Things Was in the Beginning of Time?*

We proceed thus to the Third Article: It would seem that the creation of things was not in the beginning of time.

Objection 1. For whatever is not in time, is not in any part of time. But the creation of things was not in time; for by the creation the substance of things was brought into being, and time does not measure the substance of things, and especially of incorporeal things. Therefore, creation was not in the beginning of time.

Obj. 2. Further, the Philosopher proves[5] that "everything which is made, was being made"; and so to be made implies a before and after. But in the beginning of time, since the beginning of time is indivisible, there is no before and after. Therefore, since to be created is a kind of being made, it appears that things were not created in the beginning of time.

Obj. 3. Further, even time itself is created. But time cannot be created in the beginning of time, since time is divisible, and the beginning of time is indivisible. Therefore, the creation of things was not in the beginning of time.

On the contrary, It is said (Gen. 1. 1): *In*

the beginning God created heaven and earth.

I answer that, The words of Genesis, *In the beginning God created heaven and earth,* are expounded in a threefold sense in order to exclude three errors. For some said[6] that the world always was, and that time had no beginning; and to exclude this the words *In the beginning* are expounded—namely, of time. And some said[7] that there are two principles of creation, one of good things and the other of evil things, against which *In the beginning* is expounded—in the Son. For as the efficient principle is appropriated to the Father by reason of power, so the exemplary principle is appropriated to the Son by reason of wisdom, in order that, as it is said (Ps. 103. 24), *Thou hast made all things in wisdom,* it may be understood that God made all things in the beginning—that is, in the Son; according to the word of the Apostle (Col. 1. 16), *In Him*—namely, the Son—*were created all things.* But others said[8] that corporeal things were created by God through the medium of spiritual creatures; and to exclude this it is expounded thus: *In the beginning*—that is, before all things—*God created heaven and earth.* For four things are stated to be created together—namely, the empyrean heaven, corporeal matter, by which is meant the earth, time, and the angelic nature.

Reply Obj. 1. Things are said to be created in the beginning of time not as if the beginning of time were a measure of creation, but because together with time heaven and earth were created.

Reply Obj. 2. This saying of the Philosopher is understood of the *being made* which comes about by motion, or as the term of motion. Because, since in every motion there is before and after, before any one point in a given motion—that is, whilst anything is in the process of being moved and made, there is a before and also an after, because what is in the beginning of motion or in its term is not in being moved. But creation is neither motion nor the term of motion, as was said above (Q. XLV, AA. 2, 3). Hence a thing is created in such a way that it was not being created before.

Reply Obj. 3. Nothing is made except as it exists. But nothing exists of time except *now.* Hence time cannot be made except according to some *now;* not because there is time in the first *now,* but because from it time begins.

---

[1] I, 1, 6 (MK 40). Cf. Averroes, *Dest. Dest.,* 1 (IX, 20A).
[2] The ancient naturalists, such as Democritus. Cf. Aristotle, *Physics,* VIII, 1 (251b16).
[3] Averroes, *Dest. Dest.,* I, (IX, 20K).
[4] *Serm.,* CCXLI, 4 (PL 38, 1135); *City of God,* XII, 13 (PL 41, 367).   [5] *Physics,* VI, 6 (237b10).
[6] See above, A 1, 2, Ans. 2, 4, 8. Cf. Augustine, *City of God,* X, 31; XI, 4; XII, 10 (PL 41, 311, 319, 357).
[7] See below, Q. XLIX, A. 3.
[8] See above, Q. XLV, A. 5; and below, Q. LXV, A. 4.

QUESTION XLVII

OF THE DISTINCTION OF THINGS IN GENERAL

(In Three Articles)

AFTER considering the production of creatures in being we come to the consideration of the distinction of things. This consideration will be threefold—first, of the distinction of things in general; secondly, of the distinction of good and evil (Q. XLVIII); thirdly of the distinction of the spiritual and corporeal creature (Q. L).

Under the first head there are three points of inquiry : (1) The multitude or distinction of things. (2) Their inequality. (3) The unity of the world.

ARTICLE 1. *Whether the Multitude and Distinction of Things Come from God?*

We proceed thus to the First Article: It would seem that the multitude and distinction of things does not come from God.

Objection 1. For one naturally always makes one. But God is supremely one, as appears from what precedes (Q. XI, A. 4). Therefore He produces but one effect.

Obj. 2. Further, the representation is assimilated to its exemplar. But God is the exemplary cause of His effect, as was said above (Q. XLIV, A. 3). Therefore, as God is one, His effect is one only, and not diverse.

Obj. 3. Further, the means are proportioned to the end. But the end of the creature is one—namely, the divine goodness, as was shown above (Q. XLIV, A. 4). Therefore the effect of God is but one.

On the contrary, It is said (Gen. 1. 4, 7) that God *divided the light from the darkness,* and *divided waters from waters.* Therefore the distinction and multitude of things is from God.

I answer that, The distinction of things has been ascribed to many causes. For some attributed the distinction to matter, either by itself or with the agent. Democritus, for instance, and all the ancient natural philosophers,[1] who admitted no cause but matter, attributed it to matter alone; and in their opinion the distinction of things comes from chance according to the movement of matter. Anaxagoras, however, attributed the distinction and multitude of things to matter and to the agent together;[2] and he said that the intellect distinguishes things by drawing out what is mixed up in matter.

But this cannot stand, for two reasons. First, because, as was shown above (Q. XLIV, A. 2), even matter itself was created by God. Hence we must reduce whatever distinction comes from matter to a higher cause. Secondly, because matter is for the sake of the form, and not the form for the matter, and the distinction of things comes from their proper forms. Therefore the distinction of things is not on account of the matter, but rather, on the contrary, created matter is formless in order that it may be accommodated to different forms.

Others have attributed the distinction of things to secondary agents, as did Avicenna,[3] who said that God by understanding Himself, produced the first intelligence, in which, since it was not its own being, there is necessarily composition of potency and act, as will appear later (Q. L, A. 2, Ans. 3). And so the first intelligence, in so far as it understood the first cause, produced the second intelligence; and in so far as it understood itself as in potency it produced the body of the heavens, which causes movement, and in so far as it understood itself as having actuality it produced the soul of the heavens.

But this opinion cannot stand, for two reasons. First, because it was shown above (Q. XLV, A. 5) that to create pertains to God alone, and hence what can be caused only by creation is produced by God alone—namely, all those things which are not subject to generation and corruption. Secondly, because, according to this opinion the universality of things would not proceed from the intention of the first agent, but from the concurrence of many active causes; and such an effect we can describe only as being produced by chance. Therefore, the perfection of the universe, which consists of the diversity of things, would thus be a thing of chance, which is impossible.

Hence we must say that the distinction and multitude of things come from the intention of the first agent, who is God. For He brought things into being in order that His goodness might be communicated to creatures, and be represented by them; and because His goodness could not be adequately represented by one creature alone, He produced many and diverse creatures, that what was wanting to one in the representation of the divine goodness might be supplied by another. For goodness, which in God is simple and uniform, in creatures is manifold and divided; and hence the whole universe together participates the divine

---

[1] Cf. Aristotle, *Physics,* II, 2 (194ᵃ20); II, 4 (196ᵃ24); III, 4 (203ᵃ34).　　　[2] Cf. *Ibid.,* III, 4 (203ᵃ23).

[3] *Meta.* IX, 4 (104va); cf. I, 7 (73rb).

goodness more perfectly, and represents it better than any single creature whatever.

And because the divine wisdom is the cause of the distinction of things, therefore Moses said that things are made distinct by the word of God, which is the conception of His wisdom; and this is what we read in Genesis (1. 3, 4): *God said: Be light made. . . . And He divided the light from the darkness.*

Reply Obj. 1. The natural agent acts by the form which makes it what it is, and which is only one in one thing; and therefore its effect is one only. But the voluntary agent, such as God is, as was shown above (Q. XIX, A. 4), acts by an intellectual form. Since, therefore, it is not against God's unity and simplicity to understand many things, as was shown above (Q. XV, A. 2), it follows that, although He is one, He can make many things.

Reply Obj. 2. This reason would apply to the representation which reflects the exemplar perfectly, and which is multiplied by reason of matter only; hence the uncreated image, which is perfect, is only one. But no creature perfectly represents the first exemplar, which is the divine essence; and, therefore, it can be represented by many things. Still, according as ideas are called exemplars, the plurality of ideas corresponds in the divine mind to the plurality of things.

Reply Obj. 3. In speculative things the means of demonstration, which demonstrates the conclusion perfectly, is one only whereas probable means of proof are many. Likewise when operation is concerned, if the means be equal, so to speak, to the end, one only is sufficient. But the creature is not such a means to its end, which is God. And hence the multiplication of creatures is necessary.

ARTICLE 2. *Whether the Inequality of Things Is from God?*

We proceed thus to the Second Article: It would seem that the inequality of things is not from God.

Objection 1. For it belongs to the best to produce the best. But among things that are best, one is not greater than another. Therefore, it belongs to God, Who is the Best, to make all things equal.

Obj. 2. Further, equality is the effect of unity[1]. But God is one. Therefore, He has made all things equal.

Obj. 3. Further, it is the part of justice to give unequal to unequal things. But God is just in all His works. Since, therefore, no inequality of

things is presupposed to the operation whereby He gives being to things, it seems that He has made all things equal.

On the contrary, It is said (Ecclus. 33. 7): *Why does one day excel another, and one light another, and one year another year, one sun another sun?* (Vulg.—*when all come of the sun*). *By the knowledge of the Lord they were distinguished.*

I answer that, When Origen wished to refute those who said that the distinction of things arose from the contrary principles of good and evil, he said[2] that in the beginning all things were created equal by God. For he asserted that God first created only the rational creatures, and all equal, and that inequality arose in them from free choice, some being turned to God more and some less, and others turned more and others less away from God. And so those rational creatures which were turned to God by free choice, were advanced to the different orders of angels according to the diversity of merits. And those who were turned away from God were bound down to various bodies according to the diversity of their sin; and he said this was the cause of the creation and diversity of bodies.

But according to this opinion, it would follow that the universe of bodily creatures would not be the effect of the goodness of God as communicated to creatures, but it would be for the sake of the punishment of sin, which is contrary to what is said: *God saw all the things that He had made, and they were very good* (Gen. 1. 31). And, as Augustine says:[3] "What can be more foolish than to say that the divine Architect provided this one sun for the one world not to be an ornament to its beauty, nor for the benefit of corporeal things, but that it happened through the sin of one soul, so that, if a hundred souls had sinned, there would be a hundred suns in the world?"

Therefore it must be said that as the wisdom of God is the cause of the distinction of things, so the same wisdom is the cause of their inequality. This may be explained as follows. A twofold distinction is found in things: one is a formal distinction as regards things differing specifically; the other is a material distinction as regards things differing numerically only. And as the matter is on account of the form, material distinction exists for the sake of the formal distinction. Hence we see that in incorruptible things there is only one individual of each species, since the species is sufficiently pre-

---

[1] Aristotle, *Metaphysics*, v, 15 (1021ᵃ12).

[2] *Peri Archon*, I, 6 (PG 11, 166); 8 (178); II, 9 (229).

[3] *City of God*, XI, 23 (PL 41, 337).

served in the one, but in things generated and corruptible there are many individuals of one species for the preservation of the species. From this it appears that formal distinction is of greater consequence than material. Now, formal distinction always requires inequality, because, as the Philosopher says,[1] "the forms of things are like numbers in which species vary by addition or subtraction of unity." Hence in natural things species seem to be arranged in degrees; as the mixed things are more perfect than the elements, and plants than minerals, and animals than plants, and men than other animals; and in each of these one species is more perfect than others. Therefore, as the divine wisdom is the cause of the distinction of things for the sake of the perfection of the universe, so is it the cause of inequality. For the universe would not be perfect if only one grade of goodness were found in things.

Reply Obj. 1. It pertains to the best agent to produce an effect which is best in its entirety, but this does not mean that He makes every part of the whole the best absolutely, but in proportion to the whole; in the case of an animal, for instance, its goodness would be taken away if every part of it had the dignity of an eye. Thus, therefore, God also made the universe to be best as a whole, according to the mode of a creature, not making each single creature best, but one better than another. And therefore we find it said of each creature, *God saw the light that it was good* (Gen. 1. 4); and in like manner of each one of the rest. But of all together it is said, *God saw all the things that He had made, and they were very good* (Gen. 1. 31).

Reply Obj. 2. The first effect of unity is equality, and then comes multiplicity. And therefore from the Father, to Whom, according to Augustine,[2] is appropriated unity, the Son proceeds, to Whom is appropriated equality, and then from Him the creature proceeds, to which belongs inequality; but nevertheless even creatures share in a certain equality—namely, of proportion.

Reply Obj. 3. This is the argument that persuaded Origen, but it holds only as regards the distribution of rewards, the inequality of which is due to unequal merits. But in the constitution of things there is no inequality of parts through any preceding inequality, either of merits or of the disposition of the matter; but inequality comes from the perfection of the whole. This appears also in works done by art; for the roof

of a house differs from the foundations not because it is made of other material, but in order that the house may be made perfect of different parts, the artificer seeks different material; indeed, he would make such material if he could.

ARTICLE 3. *Whether There Is Only One World?*

We proceed thus to the Third Article: It would seem that there is not only one world, but many.

Objection 1. Because, as Augustine says (QQ. LXXXIII, *qu.* 46),[3] it is unfitting to say that God has created things without a reason. But for the same reason that He created one, He could create many, since His power is not limited to the creation of one world, but rather it is infinite, as was shown above (Q. XXV, A. 2), Therefore God has produced many worlds.

Obj. 2. Further, nature does what is best, and much more does God. But it is better for there to be many worlds than one, because many good things are better than a few. Therefore many worlds have been made by God.

Obj. 3. Further, everything which has a form in matter can be multiplied in number, the species remaining the same, because multiplication in number comes from matter. But the world has a form in matter. Thus as when I say man I mean the form, and when I say this man, I mean the form in matter; so when we say world, the form is signified, and when we say this world, the form in matter is signified. Therefore there is nothing to prevent the existence of many worlds.

On the contrary, It is said (John 1. 10): *The World was made by Him,* where the world is named as one, as if only one existed.

I answer that, The very order of things created by God shows the unity of the world. For this world is called one by the unity of order, whereby some things are ordered to others. But whatever things come from God have relation of order to each other and to God Himself, as shown above (Q. XI, A. 3; Q. XXI, A. 1 ANS. 3). Hence it is necessary that all things should belong to one world. Therefore those only can assert that many worlds exist who do not acknowledge any ordering wisdom, but rather believe in chance, as Democritus,[4] who said that this world, besides an infinite number of other worlds, was made from a clashing together of atoms.

---

[1] *Metaphysics,* VIII, 3 (1043ᵇ34).
[2] *Christian Doctrine,* I, 5 (PL 34, 21).
[3] PL 40, 30.
[4] See Aristotle, *Heavens,* III, 4 (303ᵃ4); Cicero, *De Nat. Deor.,* I, 26 (DD IV, 96); Ambrose, *In Hexaëm.,* I, 1 (PL 14, 135).

Reply Obj. 1. This reason proves that the world is one because all things must be arranged in one order, and to one end. Therefore from the unity of order in things Aristotle infers[1] the unity of God governing all; and Plato,[2] from the unity of the exemplar, proves the unity of the world, as the thing designed.

Reply Obj. 2. No agent intends material plurality as the end, since material multitude has no certain limit, but of itself tends to infinity, and the infinite is opposed to the notion of end. Now when it is said that many worlds are better than one, this has reference to material multitude. But the best in this sense is not the intention of the divine agent because for the same reason it might be said that if He had made two worlds, it would be better if He had made three, and so on to infinity.

Reply Obj. 3. The world is composed of the whole of its matter. For it is not possible for there to be another earth than this one, since every earth would naturally be carried to this central one, wherever it was. The same applies to the other bodies which are parts of the world.

QUESTION XLVIII
The distinction of things in particular
(*In Six Articles*)

We must now consider the distinction of things in particular; and first the distinction of good and evil; and then the distinction of the spiritual and corporeal creatures. (Q. L.)

Concerning the first, we inquire into evil and its cause (Q. XLIX).

Concerning evil, six points are to be considered: (1) Whether evil is a nature? (2) Whether evil is found in things? (3) Whether good is the subject of evil? (4) Whether evil totally corrupts good? (5) The division of evil into pain and fault. (6) Whether pain, or fault, has more the character of evil?

ARTICLE 1. *Whether Evil Is a Nature?*

We proceed thus to the First Article: It would seem that evil is a nature.

Objection 1. For every genus is a nature. But evil is a genus; for the Philosopher says[3] that "good and evil are not in a genus, but are genera of other things." Therefore evil is a nature.

Obj. 2. Further, every difference which con-stitutes a species is a nature. But evil is a difference constituting a species in morals; for a bad habit differs in species from a good habit, as liberality from illiberality. Therefore evil signifies a nature.

Obj. 3. Further, each extreme of two contraries is a nature. But evil and good are not opposed as privation and habit, but as contraries, as the Philosopher shows[4] by the fact that between good and evil there is a medium, and from evil there can be a return to good. Therefore evil signifies a nature.

Obj. 4. Further, what is not, acts not. But evil acts, for it corrupts good. Therefore evil is a being and a nature.

Obj. 5. Further, nothing belongs to the perfection of the universe except what is a being and a nature. But evil pertains to the perfection of the universe of things, for Augustine says (*Enchir.* 10)[5] that "the admirable beauty of the universe is made up of all things. In which even what is called evil, well ordered and in its place, eminently sets off the good." Therefore evil is a nature.

On the contrary, Dionysius says (*Div. Nom.* iv),[6] "Evil is neither a being nor a good."

I answer that, One opposite is known through the other, as darkness is known through light. Hence also what evil is must be known from the notion of good. Now, we have said above that good is everything desirable; and thus, since every nature desires its own being and its own perfection, it must be said also that the being and the perfection of any nature has the character of goodness. Hence it cannot be that evil signifies being, or any form or nature. Therefore it must be that by the name of evil is signified a certain absence of good. And this is what is meant by saying that "evil is neither a being nor a good." For since being, as such, is good, the taking away of the one implies the taking away of the other.

Reply Obj. 1. Aristotle speaks there according to the opinion of the Pythagoreans, who thought that evil was a kind of nature; and therefore they held that good and evil are genera.[7] For Aristotle, especially in his logical works, brings foward examples that in his time were probable in the opinion of some philosophers. Or, it may be said that, as the Philosopher says,[8] "the first kind of contrariety is habit and privation," as being verified in all con-

---

[1] *Metaphysics,* XII, 10 (1076ᵃ4).
[2] Cf. *Timaeus* (31); cf. also St. Thomas, *In de Cælo,* I, 19; Averroes, *In de Cælo,* I, 92 (v, 61, L).
[3] *Categories,* 10 (14ᵃ23).
[4] *Ibid.* (12ᵃ22; ᵇ26).   [5] PL 40, 236.
[6] Sect. 20 (PG 3, 717).
[7] Cf. Aristotle, *Metaphysics,* I, 5 (986ᵃ33).
[8] *Metaphysics,* X, 4 (1055ᵃ33).

traries; since one contrary is always imperfect in relation to another, as black in relation to white, and bitter in relation to sweet. And in this way good and evil are said to be genera not simply, but in regard to contraries; because, as every form has the character of good, so every privation, as such, has the character of evil.

Reply Obj. 2. Good and evil are not constitutive differences except in morals, which receive their species from the end, which is the object of the will, the source of all morality. And because good has the nature of an end, therefore good and evil are specific differences in moral things; good in itself, but evil as the absence of the due end. Yet neither does the absence of the due end by itself constitute a moral species, except as it is joined to an improper end; just as we do not find the privation of the substantial form in natural things unless it is joined to another form. Thus, therefore, the evil which is a constitutive difference in morals is a certain good joined to the privation of another good, just as the end proposed by the intemperate man is not the privation of the good of reason, but the delight of sense without the order of reason. Hence evil is not a constitutive difference as such, but by reason of the good that is joined to it.

Reply Obj. 3. This answer appears from the above. For the Philosopher speaks there of good and evil in morality. Because in that respect, between good and evil there is a medium, as good is considered as something ordered, and evil as a thing not only out of order, but also as injurious to another. Hence the Philosopher says[1] that a prodigal man is "foolish," but not evil. And from this evil in morality, there may be a return to good, but not from any sort of evil; for from blindness there is no return to sight, although blindness is an evil.

Reply Obj. 4. A thing is said to act in a threefold sense. In one way, formally, as when we say that whiteness makes white; and in that sense evil considered even as a privation is said to corrupt good, since it is itself a corruption or privation of good. In another sense a thing is said to act effectively, as when a painter makes a wall white. Thirdly, it is said in the sense of the final cause, as the end is said to effect by moving the efficient cause. But in these two ways evil does not effect anything of itself, that is, as a privation, but by virtue of the good joined to it. For every action comes from some form, and everything which is desired as an end is a perfection. And therefore, as Dionysius

[1] *Ethics*, IV, I (1121ᵃ25).

says (*Div. Nom.* iv),[2] evil does not act, nor is it desired, except by virtue of some good joined to it, while of itself it is nothing definite, and beside the scope of our will and intention.

Reply Obj. 5. As was said above, (Q. II, A. 3; Q. XIX, A. 5, Ans. 2; Q. XXI, A. I, Ans. 3; Q. XLIV, A. 3) the parts of the universe are ordered to each other according as one acts on the other, and according as one is the end and exemplar of the other. But, as was said above, this can only happen to evil as joined to some good. Hence evil neither belongs to the perfection of the universe, nor does it come under the order of the same, except accidentally, that is, by reason of some good joined to it.

ARTICLE 2. *Whether Evil Is Found in Things?*

We proceed thus to the Second Article: It would seem that evil is not found in things.

Objection 1. For whatever is found in things, is either something, or a privation of something, which is a non-being. But Dionysius says (*Div. Nom.* iv)[3] that evil is distant from existence, and even more distant from non-existence. Therefore evil is not at all found in things.

Obj. 2. Further, being and thing are convertible. If, therefore, evil is a being in things, it follows that evil is a thing, which is contrary to what has been (A. I).

Obj. 3. Further, "the white unmixed with black is the most white," as the Philosopher says.[4] Therefore also the good unmixed with evil is the greater good. But God makes always what is best, much more than nature does. Therefore in things made by God there is no evil.

On the contrary, According to this, all prohibitions and penalties would be removed, for they exist only for evils.

I answer that, As was said above (Q. XLVII, A. 2), the perfection of the universe requires that there should be inequality in things, so that every grade of goodness may be realized. Now, one grade of goodness is that of the good which cannot fail. Another grade of goodness is that of the good which can fail in goodness. And these grades are to be found in being itself; for some things there are which cannot lose their being as incorruptible things, while some there are which can lose it, as things corruptible.

As, therefore, the perfection of the universe requires that there should be not only beings incorruptible, but also corruptible beings, so the perfection of the universe requires that there should be some which can fail in goodness, and

[2] Sect. 20 (PG 3, 720); 32 (733).
[3] Sect. 19 (PG 3, 716).   [4] *Topics*, III, 5 (119ᵃ27).

thence it follows that sometimes they do fail. Now it is in this that evil consists, namely, in the fact that a thing fails in goodness. Hence it is clear that evil is found in things, as corruption also is found; for corruption is itself an evil.

Reply Obj. 1. Evil is distant both from absolute being and from absolute non-being, because it is neither a habit nor a pure negation, but a privation.

Reply Obj. 2. As the Philosopher says,[1] being is twofold. In one way it is considered as signifying the entity of a thing, according as it is divided by the ten predicaments; and in that sense it is convertible with thing, and in this way no privation is a being. and neither therefore is evil a being. In another sense being signifies the truth of a proposition which consists in composition whose mark is this word *is;* and in this sense being is what answers to the question, Does it exist? and thus we speak of blindness as being in the eye, or of any other privation. In this way even evil can be called a being. Through ignorance of this distinction some,[2] considering that things are called evil, or that evil is said to be in things, believed that evil was a kind of thing.

Reply Obj. 3. God and nature and any other agent make what is best in the whole, but not what is best in every single part, except in order to the whole, as was said above (Q. XLVII, A. 2 ANS. 1). And the whole itself, which is the universe of creatures, is better and more perfect if some things in it can fail in goodness. and do sometimes fail, God not preventing this. This happens, first, because "it belongs to Providence not to destroy, but to save nature," as Dionysius says (*Div. Nom.* iv)[3]; it belongs to nature however that what may fail should sometimes fail; secondly. because, as Augustine says (*Enchir.* 11),[4] "God is so powerful that He can even make good out of evil." Hence many good things would be taken away if God permitted no evil to exist; for fire would not be generated if air was not corrupted, nor would the life of a lion be preserved unless the ass were killed. Neither would avenging justice nor the patience of a sufferer be praised if there were no injustice.

ARTICLE 3. *Whether Evil Is in Good As in a Subject?*

We proceed thus to the Third Article: It would seem that evil is not in good as in a subject.

Objection 1. For good is something that exists. But Dionysius says (*Div. Nom.* iv, 4)[5] that "evil does not exist, nor is it in that which exists." Therefore, evil is not in good as in a subject.

Obj. 2. Further, evil is not a being, whereas good is a being. But non-being does not require being as its subject. Therefore, neither does evil require good as its subject.

Obj. 3. Further, one contrary is not the subject of another. But good and evil are contraries. Therefore, evil is not in good as in its subject.

Obj. 4. Further, the subject of whiteness is called white. Therefore, also, the subject of evil is evil. If, therefore, evil is in good as in its subject, it follows that good is evil, against what is said (Isa. 5. 20): *Woe to you who call evil good, and good evil!*

On the contrary, Augustine says (*Enchir.* 14)[6] that evil exists only in good.

I answer that, As was said above (A. 1), evil implies the absence of good. But not every absence of good is evil. For absence of good can be taken in a privative and in a negative sense. Absence of good, taken negatively is not evil; otherwise, it would follow that what does not exist is evil, and also that everything would be evil, through not having the good belonging to something else; for instance, a man would be evil who had not the swiftness of the roe, or the strength of a lion. But the absence of good, taken in a privative sense, is an evil; as, for instance, the privation of sight is called blindness.

Now, the subject of privation and of form is one and the same—namely, being in potency, whether it be being in potency absolutely, as primary matter, which is the subject of the substantial form, and of privation of the opposite form; or whether it be being in potency relatively and in act absolutely, as in the case of a transparent body, which is the subject both of darkness and light. It is, however. manifest that the form which makes a thing actual is a perfection and a good, and thus every actual being is a good; and likewise every potential being, as such, is a good, as having a relation to good. For as it has being in potency, so has it good in potency. Therefore, the subject of evil is good.

Reply Obj. 1. Dionysius means that evil is not in existing things as a part, or as a natural property of any existing thing.

Reply Obj. 2. Non-being, understood negatively, does not require a subject; but privation is negation in a subject, as the Philosopher says,[7] and such non-being is an evil.

---

[1] *Metaphysics*, v, 7 (1017ª22).
[2] Cf. above, A. 1, Ans. 1; below, Q. XLIX, A. 3.
[3] Sect. 33 (PG 3, 733).   [4] PL 40, 236.
[5] Sect. 33 (PG 3, 733).   [6] PL 40, 238.
[7] *Metaphysics*, IV, 2 (1004ª15).

Reply Obj. 3. Evil is not in the good opposed to it as in its subject, but in some other good, for the subject of blindness is not sight, but animal. Yet, it appears, as Augustine says (*Enchir.* 14), [1] that "the rule of dialectics here fails, where it is laid down that contraries cannot exist together." But this is to be taken as referring to good and evil in general, but not in reference to any particular good and evil. For white and black, sweet and bitter, and the like contraries, are only considered as contraries in a special sense, because they exist in some determinate genera, whereas good enters into every genus. Hence one good can coexist with the privation of another good.

Reply Obj. 4. The prophet invokes woe to those who say that good as such is evil. But this does not follow from what is said above, as is clear from the explanation given.

ARTICLE 4. *Whether Evil Corrupts the Whole Good?*

We proceed thus to the Fourth Article: It would seem that evil corrupts the whole good.

Objection 1. For one contrary is wholly corrupted by another. But good and evil are contraries. Therefore evil can corrupt the whole good.

Obj. 2. Further, Augustine says (*Enchir.* 12)[2] that "evil hurts in so far as it takes away good." But good is all of a piece and uniform. Therefore it is wholly taken away by evil.

Obj. 3. Further, evil, as long as it lasts, hurts, and takes away good. But that from which something is always being removed, is at some time consumed, unless it is infinite, which cannot be said of any created good. Therefore evil wholly consumes good.

On the contrary, Augustine says (*Enchir., loc. cit.*) that evil cannot wholly consume good.

I answer that, Evil cannot wholly consume good. To prove this we must consider that good is threefold. One kind of good is wholly destroyed by evil, and this is the good opposed to the evil, as light is wholly destroyed by darkness, and sight by blindness. Another kind of good is neither wholly destroyed nor diminished by evil, and that is the good which is the subject of evil; for by darkness the substance of the air is not injured. And there is also a kind of good which is diminshed by evil, but is not wholly taken away; and this good is the aptitude of a subject to actuality.

The diminution, however, of this kind of good is not to be considered by way of subtraction, as diminution in quantity, but rather by way of abatement, as diminution in qualities and forms. The lessening likewise of this aptitude is to be taken as contrary to its intensity. For this kind of aptitude receives its intensity by the dispositions whereby the matter is prepared for act, which, the more they are multiplied in the subject, the more is it fitted to receive its perfection and form; and, on the contrary, it receives its lessening by contrary dispositions, which, the more they are multiplied in the matter, and the more they are intensified, the more is the potency lessened as regards the act.

Therefore, if contrary dispositions cannot be multiplied and intensified to infinity, but only to a certain limit, neither is the aforesaid aptitude diminished or lessened infinitely, as appears in the active and passive qualities of the elements; for coldness and humidity, whereby the aptitude of matter to the form of fire is diminished or lessened, cannot be infinitely multiplied. But if the contrary dispositions can be infinitely multiplied, the aforesaid aptitude is also infinitely diminished or lessened; yet, nevertheless, it is not wholly taken away, because its root always remains, which is the substance of the subject. Thus, if opaque bodies were interposed to infinity between the sun and the air, the aptitude of the air to light would be infinitely diminished, but still it would never be wholly removed while the air remained, which in its very nature is transparent. Likewise, addition in sin can be made to infinity, whereby the aptitude of the soul to grace is more and more lessened; and these sins, indeed, are like obstacles interposed between us and God, according to Isa. 59. 2: *Our sins have divided between us and God.* Yet the aforesaid aptitude of the soul is not wholly taken away, for it belongs to its very nature.

Reply Obj. 1. The good which is opposed to evil is wholly taken away, but other goods are not wholly removed, as said above.

Reply Obj. 2. The aforesaid aptitude is a medium between subject and act. Hence, where it touches act, it is diminished by evil, but where it touches the subject, it remains as it was. Therefore, although good is like to itself, yet, on account of its relation to different things, it is not wholly, but only partially taken away.

Reply Obj. 3. Some,[3] imagining that the diminution of this kind of good is like the diminu-

---

[1] PL 40, 238.
[2] PL 40, 237; cf. also, *De Mor. Eccl.,* II, 3 (PL 32, 1347).

[3] Cf. Wm. of Auxerre, *Summa Aurea,* II, 26, 5 (fol. 87a)

tion of quantity, said that just as the continuous is infinitely divisible, if the division be made in an ever same proportion (for instance, half of half, or a third of a third), so is it in the present case. But this explanation does not avail here. For when in a division we keep the same proportion, we continue to subtract less and less; for half of half is less than half the whole. But a second sin does not necessarily diminish the above mentioned aptitude less than a preceding sin, but perhaps either equally or more.

Therefore it must be said that, although this aptitude is a finite thing, still it may be so diminished infinitely, not *per se*, but accidentally according as the contrary dispositions are also increased infinitely, as explained above.

ARTICLE 5. *Whether Evil Is Adequately Divided into Pain* (Poena) *and Fault* (Culpa)?

We proceed thus to the Fifth Article: It would seem that evil is not adequately divided into pain and fault.

Objection 1. For every defect is a kind of evil. But in all creatures there is the defect of not being able to keep themselves in being, which nevertheless is neither a pain nor a fault. Therefore evil is inadequately divided into pain and fault.

Obj. 2. Further, in irrational things there is neither fault nor pain; but, nevertheless, they have corruption and defect, which are evils. Therefore not every evil is a pain or a fault.

Obj. 3. Further, temptation is an evil, but it is not a fault; for "temptation which involves no consent, is not a sin, but an occasion for the exercise of virtue," as is said in a gloss on 2 Cor. 12;[1] nor is it a pain, because temptation precedes the fault, and the pain follows afterwards. Therefore, evil is not sufficiently divided into pain and fault.

Obj. 4. *On the contrary*, It would seem that this division is superfluous; for, as Augustine says (*Enchir.* 12),[2] a thing is evil because it hurts. But whatever hurts is penal. Therefore every evil comes under pain.

I answer that, Evil, as was said above (A. 3) is the privation of good, which chiefly and of itself consists in perfection and act. Act, however, is twofold: first, and second. The first act is the form and integrity of a thing, the second act is its operation. Therefore evil also is two-

fold. In one way it occurs by the taking away of the form, or of any part required for the integrity of the thing, as blindness is an evil, as also it is an evil to be wanting in any member of the body. In another way evil exists by the withdrawal of the due operation, either because it does not exist, or because it has not its due mode and order.

But because good in itself is the object of the will, evil, which is the privation of good, is found in a special way in rational creatures which have a will. Therefore the evil which comes from the withdrawal of the form and integrity of the thing has the nature of a pain, and especially so on the supposition that all things are subject to divine providence and justice, as was shown above (Q. XXII, A. 2), for it is of the very nature of a pain to be against the will. But the evil which consists in the taking away of the due operation in voluntary things has the nature of a fault; for this is imputed to anyone as a fault to fall as regards perfect action, of which he is master by the will. Therefore every evil in voluntary things is to be looked upon as a pain or a fault.

Reply Obj. 1. Because evil is the privation of good, and not pure negation, as was said above (A. 3), therefore not every defect of good is an evil, but the defect of the good which is naturally due. For the want of sight is not an evil in a stone, but it is an evil in an animal, since it is against the nature of a stone to see. So, likewise, it is against the nature of a creature to be preserved in being by itself, because being and conservation come from one and the same source. Hence this kind of defect is not an evil as regards a creature.

Reply Obj. 2. Pain and fault do not divide evil absolutely considered, but evil that is found in voluntary things.

Reply Obj. 3. Temptation, as implying provocation to evil, is always an evil of fault in the tempter; but in the one tempted it is not, properly speaking, a fault, unless through the temptation some change is wrought in the one who is tempted; for thus the action of the agent is in the one acted upon. And if the tempted is changed to evil by the tempter he falls into fault.

Reply Obj. 4. It must be said that the very notion of pain includes the idea of injury to the agent in himself, whereas the notion of fault includes the idea of injury to the agent in his operation; and thus both are contained under the notion of evil, as including the notion of injury.

---

[1] *Glossa ordin.*, (VI, 76E); *Glossa* Lombardi (PL 192, 84).
[2] PL 40, 237; *De Mor. Eccl.*, II, 3 (PL 32, 1347).

ARTICLE 6. *Whether Pain Has the Nature of Evil More Than Fault Has?*

We proceed thus to the Sixth Article: It would seem that pain has more of evil than fault.

Objection 1. For fault is to pain what merit is to reward. But reward has more of good than merit, as its end. Therefore pain has more evil in it than fault has.

Obj. 2. Further, that is the greater evil which is opposed to the greater good. But pain, as was said above (A. 5), is opposed to the good of the agent, while fault is opposed to the good of the action. Therefore, since the agent is better than the action, it seems that pain is worse than fault.

Obj. 3. Further, the privation of the end is a pain consisting in forfeiting the vision of God, whereas the evil of fault is privation of the order to the end. Therefore pain is a greater evil than fault.

On the contrary, A wise workman chooses a less evil in order to prevent a greater, as the surgeon cuts off a limb to save the whole body. But divine wisdom inflicts pain to prevent fault. Therefore fault is a greater evil than pain.

I answer that, Fault has more of the notion of evil than pain has; not only more than pain of sense, consisting in the privation of corporeal goods, which is the kind of pain most men understand, but also more than any kind of pain, taking pain in its most general meaning, so as to include privation of grace or glory.

There is a twofold reason for this. The first is that one becomes evil by the evil of fault, but not by the evil of pain, as Dionysius says (*Div. Nom.* iv):[1] "To be punished is not an evil; but it is an evil to be made worthy of punishment." And this is because, since good absolutely considered consists in act, and not in potency, and the ultimate act is operation, or the use of something possessed, it follows that the absolute good of man consists in good operation, or the good use of something possessed. Now we use all things by the will, by which a man uses well what he has, man is called good, and from a bad will he is called bad. For a man who has a bad will can use ill even the good he has, as when a grammarian of his own will speaks incorrectly. Therefore, because the fault itself consists in the disordered act of the will, and the pain consists in the privation of something used by the will, fault has more of evil in it than pain has.

The second reason can be taken from the fact

[1] Sect. 22 (PG 3, 724).

that God is the author of the evil of pain, but not of the evil of fault. And this is because the evil of pain takes away the creature's good, which may be either something created, as sight, destroyed by blindness, or something uncreated, as by being deprived of the vision of God, the creature forfeits its uncreated good. But the evil of fault is properly opposed to uncreated good, for it is opposed to the fulfilment of the divine will, and to divine love, whereby the divine good is loved for itself, and not only as shared by the creature. Therefore it is plain that fault has more evil in it than pain has.

Reply Obj. 1. Although fault ends in pain, as merit in reward, yet fault is not intended on account of the pain, as merit is for the reward; but rather, on the contrary, pain is brought about so that the fault may be avoided, and thus fault is worse than pain.

Reply Obj. 2. The order of action which is destroyed by fault is the more perfect good of the agent, since it is the second perfection, than the good taken away by pain, which is the first perfection.

Reply Obj. 3. Pain and fault are not to be compared as end and order to the end, because one may be deprived of both of these in some way, both by fault and by pain; by pain, accordingly as a man is removed from the end and from the order to the end; by fault, according as this privation belongs to the action which is not ordered to its due end.

QUESTION XLIX

THE CAUSE OF EVIL

(In Three Articles)

WE next inquire into the cause of evil. Concerning this there are three points of inquiry: (1) Whether good can be the cause of evil? (2) Whether the supreme good, God, is the cause of evil? (3) Whether there be any supreme evil, which is the first cause of all evils?

ARTICLE 1. *Whether Good Can Be the Cause of Evil?*

We proceed thus to the First Article: It would seem that good cannot be the cause of evil.

Objection 1. For it is said (Matt. 7. 18): *A good tree cannot bring forth evil fruit.*

Obj. 2. Further, one contrary cannot be the cause of another. But evil is the contrary to good. Therefore good cannot be the cause of evil.

Obj. 3. Further, a deficient effect can proceed only from a deficient cause. But evil is a deficient effect. Therefore its cause, if it has one, is deficient. But everything deficient is an evil. Therefore the cause of evil can only be evil.

Obj. 4. Further, Dionysius says (*Div. Nom.* iv)[1] that evil has no cause. Therefore good is not the cause of evil.

On the contrary, Augustine says (*Contra Julian.* i 9):[2] "There is no possible source of evil except good."

I answer that, It must be said that every evil in some way has a cause. For evil is the absence of the good which is natural and due to a thing. But that anything fail from its natural and due disposition can come only from some cause drawing it out of its proper disposition. For a heavy thing is not moved upwards except by some impelling force, nor does an agent fail in its action except from some impediment. But only good can be a cause, because nothing can be a cause except in so far as it is a being, and every being, as such, is good. And if we consider the special kinds of causes, we see that the agent, the form, and the end, imply some kind of perfection which belongs to the notion of good. Even matter, as a potency to good, has the nature of good.

Now that good is the cause of evil by way of the material cause was shown above (Q. XLVIII, A. 3). For it was shown that good is the subject of evil. But evil has no formal cause, rather is it a privation of form; likewise, neither has it a final cause, but rather is it a privation of order to the proper end, since not only the end has the nature of good, but also the useful, which is ordered to the end. Evil, however, has a cause by way of an agent, not per se, but accidentally.

In proof of this, we must know that evil is caused in the action otherwise than in the effect. In the action evil is caused by reason of the defect of some principle of action, either of the principal or the instrumental agent; thus the defect in the movement of an animal may happen by reason of the weakness of the motive power, as in the case of children, or by reason only of the ineptitude of the instrument. as in the lame. On the other hand, evil is caused in a thing, but not in the proper effect of the agent, sometimes by the power of the agent, sometimes by reason of a defect, either of the agent or of the matter. It is caused by reason of the power or perfection of the agent when there necessarily follows on the form intended by the agent the privation of another form; as. for instance, when on the form of fire there follows the privation of the form of air or of water. Therefore, as the more

perfect the fire is in strength, so much the more perfectly does it impress its own form, so also the more perfectly does it corrupt the contrary. Hence that evil and corruption befall air and water comes from the perfection of the fire; but this is accidental, because fire does not aim at the privation of the form of water, but at the bringing in of its own form, though by doing this it also accidentally causes the other. But if there is a defect in the proper effect of the fire —as, for instance, that it fails to heat—this comes either by defect of the action, which implies the defect of some principle, as was said above, or by the indisposition of the matter, which does not receive the action of fire acting on it. But this very fact that it is a deficient being is accidental to good to which of itself it pertains to act. Hence it is true that evil in no way has any but an accidental cause; and thus is good the cause of evil.

Reply Obj. 1. As Augustine says (*Contra Julian.* i):[3] "The Lord calls an evil will the evil tree, and a good will a good tree." Now, a good will does not produce a morally bad act, since it is from the good will itself that a moral act is judged to be good. Nevertheless the movement itself of an evil will is caused by the rational creature, which is good. And thus good is the cause of evil.

Reply Obj. 2. Good does not cause that evil which is contrary to itself, but some other evil; thus the goodness of the fire causes evil to the water, and man, good as to his nature, causes an act morally evil. And, as explained above (Q. XIX, A. 9), this is by accident. Moreover, it does happen sometimes that one contrary causes another by accident, for instance, the exterior surrounding cold heats by causing the withdrawing inwards of heat.

Reply Obj. 3. Evil has a deficient cause in voluntary things otherwise than in natural things. For the natural agent produces the same kind of effect as it is itself, unless it is impeded by some exterior thing; and this indeed is a defect in it. Hence evil never follows in the effect unless some other evil pre-exists in the agent or in the matter, as was said above. But in voluntary things the defect of the action comes from the will actually deficient in so far as it does not actually subject itself to its proper rule. This defect, however, is not a fault, but fault follows upon it from the fact that the will acts with this defect.

Reply Obj. 4. Evil has no direct cause, but only an accidental cause, as was said above.

ARTICLE 2. *Whether the Supreme Good, God, Is the Cause of Evil?*

We proceed thus to the Second Article: It would seem that the supreme good, God, is the cause of evil.

Objection 1. For it is said (Isa. 45. 5, 7): *I am the Lord, and there is no other God, forming the light and creating darkness, making peace, and creating evil.* And (Amos 3. 6), *Shall there be evil in a city, which the Lord hath not done?*

Obj. 2. Further, the effect of the secondary cause is reduced to the first cause. But good is the cause of evil, as was said above (A. 1). Therefore, since God is the cause of every good, as was shown above (Q. II, A. 3; Q. VI, AA. 1, 4), it follows that also every evil is from God.

Obj. 3. Further, as is said by the Philosopher,[1] the cause of both safety and danger of the ship is the same. But God is the cause of the safety of all things. Therefore He is the cause of all perdition and of all evil.

On the contrary, Augustine says (QQ. LXXXIII, qu. 21)[2] that, "God is not the author of evil, because He is not the cause of tending to non-being."

I answer that, As appears from what was said (A. 1), the evil which consists in the defect of action is always caused by the defect of the agent. But in God there is no defect, but the highest perfection, as was shown above (Q. IV, A. 1). Hence, the evil which consists in defect of action, or which is caused by defect of the agent, is not reduced to God as to its cause.

But the evil which consists in the corruption of some things is reduced to God as the cause. And this appears as regards both natural things and voluntary things. For it was said (A. 1) that some agent, in so far as it produces by its power a form to which follows corruption and defect, causes by its power that corruption and defect. But it is manifest that the form which God chiefly intends in things created is the good of the order of the universe. Now, the order of the universe requires, as was said above (Q. XXII, A. 2 ANS. 2; Q. XLVIII, A. 2), that there should be some things that can, and do sometimes, fail. And thus God, by causing in things the good of the order of the universe, consequently and as it were by accident, causes the corruptions of things, according to I Kings 2. 6: *The Lord killeth and maketh alive.* But when we read that *God hath not made death* (Wis. 1. 13), the sense is that God does not will death for its own sake. Nevertheless the order of justice belongs

to the order of the universe, and this requires that penalty should be dealt out to sinners. And so God is the author of the evil which is penalty, but not of the evil which is fault, by reason of what is said above.

Reply Obj. 1. These passages refer to the evil of penalty, and not to the evil of fault.

Reply Obj. 2. The effect of the deficient secondary cause is reduced to the first non-deficient cause as regards what it has of being and perfection, but not as regards what it has of defect; just as whatever there is of motion in the act of limping is caused by the moving power, whereas what is awry in it does not come from the moving power, but from the curvature of the leg. And, likewise, whatever there is of being and action in a bad action is reduced to God as the cause, whereas whatever defect is in it is not caused by God, but by the deficient secondary cause.

Reply Obj. 3. The sinking of a ship is attributed to the sailor as the cause from the fact that he does not fulfil what the safety of the ship requires; but God does not fail in doing what is necessary for the safety of all. Hence there is no parity.

ARTICLE 3. *Whether There Be One Supreme Evil Which Is the Cause of Every Evil?*

We proceed thus to the Third Article: It would seem that there is one supreme evil which is the cause of every evil.

Objection 1. For contrary effects have contrary causes. But contrariety is found in things, according to Ecclus. 33. 15: *Good is set against evil, and life against death; so also is the sinner against a just man.* Therefore there are contrary principles, one of good, the other of evil.

Obj. 2. Further, if one contrary is in nature, so is the other.[3] But the supreme good is in nature, and is the cause of every good, as was shown above (Q. II, A. 3; Q. VI, AA. 2, 4). Therefore, also, there is a supreme evil opposed to it as the cause of every evil.

Obj. 3. Further, as we find good and better things, so we find evil and worse. But good and better are so considered in relation to what is best. Therefore evil and worse are so considered in relation to some supreme evil.

Obj. 4. Further, everything participated is reduced to what is essential. But things which are evil among us are evil not essentially, but by participation. Therefore we must seek for some supreme evil, which is the cause of every evil.

Obj. 5. Further, whatever is accidental is re-

---

[1] *Physics,* II, 3 (195ᵃ3).　　[2] PL 40, 16.

[3] Aristotle, *Heavens,* II, 3 (286ᵃ23).

duced to that which is *per se*. But good is the accidental cause of evil. Therefore, we must suppose some supreme evil which is the *per se* cause of evils. Nor can it be said that evil has no *per se* cause, but only an accidental cause; for it would then follow that evil would not exist in the many, but only in the few.

Obj. 6. Further, the evil of the effect is reduced to the evil of the cause, because the deficient effect comes from the deficient cause, as was said above (AA. 1, 2). But we cannot proceed to infinity in this matter. Therefore, we must suppose one first evil as the cause of every evil.

On the contrary, The supreme good is the cause of every being, as was shown above (Q. II, A. 3; Q. VI, A. 4). Therefore there cannot be any principle opposed to it as the cause of evils.

I answer that, It appears from what precedes that there is no one first principle of evil, as there is one first principle of good.

First, indeed, because the first principle of good is essentially good, as was shown above (Q. VI, AA. 3, 4). But nothing can be essentially bad. For it was shown above that every being, as such, is good (Q. V, A. 3), and that evil can exist only in good as in its subject (Q. XLVIII, A. 3).

Secondly, because the first principle of good is the highest and perfect good which contains beforehand in itself all goodness, as shown above (Q. VI, A. 2). But there cannot be a supreme evil, because, as was shown above (Q. XLVIII, A. 4), although evil always lessens good, yet it never wholly consumes it; and thus, since good always remains, nothing can be wholly and perfectly bad. Therefore, the Philosopher says[1] that "if the wholly evil could be, it would destroy itself," because all good being destroyed (which it need be for something to be wholly evil), evil itself would be taken away, since its subject is good.

Thirdly, because the very notion of evil is against the notion of a first principle; both because evil is caused by good, as was shown above (A. 1), and because evil can be only an accidental cause, and thus it cannot be the first cause, for "the accidental cause is subsequent to the *per se* cause," as appears in the *Physics*.[2]

Those, however, who upheld two first principles, one good and the other evil,[3] fell into this error from the same source, from which also arose other strange notions of the ancients,

namely, because they failed to consider the universal cause of all being, and considered only the particular causes of particular effects. For on that account, if they found a thing hurtful to something by the power of its own nature, they thought that the nature of that thing was evil; as, for instance, if one should say that the nature of fire was evil because it burnt the house of a poor man. The judgment, however, of the goodness of anything does not depend upon its order to any particular thing, but rather upon what it is in itself, and on its order to the whole universe, wherein every thing has its own perfectly ordered place, as was said above (Q. XLVII, A. 2 Ans. 1).

Likewise, those who found two contrary particular causes of two contrary particular effects did not know how to reduce these contrary particular causes to the universal common cause, and therefore they extended the contrariety of causes even to the first principles. But since all contraries agree in something common, it is necessary to search for one common cause for them above their own contrary proper causes; just as above the contrary qualities of the elements exists the power of a heavenly body, and likewise above all things that exist, in anyway whatsoever there exists one first principle of being, as was shown above (Q. II, A. 3).

Reply Obj. 1. Contraries agree in one genus, and they also agree in the aspect of being; and therefore, although they have contrary particular causes, nevertheless we must come at last to one first common cause.

Reply Obj. 2. Privation and habit belong naturally to the same subject. Now the subject of privation is a being in potency, as was said above (Q. XLVIII, A. 3). Hence, since evil is privation of good, as appears from what was said above (*ibid.*, AA. 1, 2, 3), it is opposed to that good which has some potency, but not to the supreme good, who is pure act.

Reply Obj. 3. Increase in intensity is in proportion to the nature of a thing. And as the form is a perfection, so privation removes a perfection. Hence every form, perfection, and good is intensified by approach to the perfect term, but privation and evil by receding from that term. Hence a thing is not said to be evil and worse by reason of approach to the supreme evil, as, for instance, it is said to be good and better by reason of approach to the supreme good.

Reply Obj. 4. No being is called evil by participation, but by privation of participation. Hence it is not necessary to reduce it to any essential evil.

---

[1] *Ethics*, IV, 5 (1126ᵃ12).   [2] Aristotle, II, 6 (198ᵃ8).
[3] Cf. *Contra Gent.*, II, 41; cf. also Augustine, *De Haeres*, XXI, XLVI (PL 42, 29, 37); cf. also Aristotle, *Metaphysics*, I, 4 (985ᵃ3).

Reply Obj. 5. Evil can only have an accidental cause, as was shown above (A. 1). Hence reduction to any *per se* cause of evil is impossible. And to say that evil is in the greater number is simply false. For things which are generated and corrupted, in which alone can there be natural evil, are the smaller part of the whole universe. And again, in every species the defect of nature is in the smaller number. In man alone

does evil appear as in the greater number, because the good of man as regards the senses is not the good of man as man—that is, in regard to reason, and more men follow the senses than the reason.

Reply Obj. 6. In the causes of evil we do not proceed to infinity but reduce all evils to some good cause, from which evil follows accidentally.

TREATISE ON THE ANGELS

QUESTION L

OF THE SUBSTANCE OF THE ANGELS ABSOLUTELY CONSIDERED

(In Five Articles)

NEXT we consider the distinction of corporeal and spiritual creatures: first, the purely spiritual creature which in Holy Scripture is called angel; secondly, the creature purely corporeal (Q. LXV); thirdly, the composite creature, corporeal and spiritual, which is man (Q. LXXV).

Concerning the angels, we consider first what belongs to their substance; secondly, what belongs to their intellect (Q. LIV); thirdly, what belongs to their will (Q. LIX); fourthly, what belongs to their creation (Q. XLI).

Their substance we consider absolutely, and in relation to corporeal things (Q. LI).

Concerning their substance absolutely considered, there are five points of inquiry: (1) Whether there is any entirely spiritual creature, altogether incorporeal? (2) Supposing that an angel is such, we ask whether it is composed of matter and form? (3) We ask concerning their number. (4) Of their difference from each other. (5) Of their immortality or incorruptibility.

ARTICLE 1. *Whether an Angel Is Entirely Incorporeal?*

We proceed thus to the First Article: It would seem that an angel is not entirely incorporeal.

Objection 1. For what is incorporeal only as regards ourselves, and not in relation to God, is not absolutely incorporeal. But Damascene says (*De Fid. Orth.* ii)[1] that "an angel is said to be incorporeal and immaterial as regards us; but compared to God it is corporeal and material." Therefore it is not incorporeal absolutely.

Obj. 2. Further, nothing is moved except a body, as the Philosopher says.[2] But Damascene says (*De Fid. Orth.* ii)[3] that an angel is "an ever movable intellectual substance." Therefore an angel is a corporeal substance.

Obj. 3. Further, Ambrose says (*De Spir. Sanct.* i, 7):[4] "Every creature is limited within its own nature." But to be limited is proper to bodies. Therefore, every creature is corporeal. Now angels are God's creatures, as appears from Ps. 148. 2: *Praise ye* the Lord, *all His angels;* and, farther on (*verse* 4), *For He spoke, and they were made; He commanded, and they were created.* Therefore angels are corporeal.

On the contrary, It is said (Ps. 103. 4): *Who makes His angels spirits.*

I answer that, We must admit some incorporeal creatures. For what is principally intended by God in creatures is good, and this consists in assimilation to God Himself. And the perfect assimilation of an effect to a cause is accomplished when the effect imitates the cause according to that whereby the cause produces the effect; as for instance, heat makes heat. Now, God produces the creature by His intellect and will (Q. XIV, A. 8; Q. XIX, A. 4). Hence the perfection of the universe requires that there should be intellectual creatures. Now intelligence cannot be the action of a body, nor of any corporeal power, for every body is limited to here and now. Hence the perfection of the universe requires the existence of an incorporeal creature.

The ancients, however, not properly realizing the force of intelligence, and failing to distinguish between sense and intellect, thought that nothing existed in the world but what could be apprehended by sense and imagination.[5] And because bodies alone fall under imagination, "they supposed that no being existed except bodies," as the Philosopher observes.[6] The error of the Sadducees, who said there was no spirit (Acts 23. 8), also arose from this source.

But the very fact that intellect is above sense shows reasonably that there are some incorporeal things comprehensible by the intellect alone.

Reply Obj. 1. Incorporeal substances rank between God and corporeal creatures. Now the medium compared to one extreme appears to

[1] Chap. 3 (PG 94, 886).
[2] *Physics*, VI, 4 (234b10).
[3] Chap. 3 (PG 94, 886).

[4] PL 16, 753.
[5] Cf. Aristotle, *Soul*, III, 3 (427a21).
[6] *Physics*, IV, 6 (213a29).

be the other extreme, as what is tepid compared to heat seems to be cold; and thus it is said that the angels, compared to God, are material and corporeal, not, however, as if anything corporeal existed in them.

Reply Obj. 2. Movement is there taken in the sense in which it is applied to intelligence and will. Therefore an angel is called an ever moving substance because he is always actually intelligent, and not as if he were sometimes actually and sometimes potentially, as we are. Hence it is clear that the objection rests on an equivocation.

Reply Obj. 3. To be circumscribed by local limits is proper to bodies only; but to be circumscribed by essential limits belongs to all creatures, both corporeal and spiritual. Hence Ambrose says (*ibid.*) that "although some things are not contained in corporeal place, still they are none the less circumscribed by their substance."

ARTICLE 2. *Whether an Angel Is Composed of Matter and Form?*

We proceed thus to the Second Article: It would seem that an angel is composed of matter and form.

Objection 1. For everything which is contained under any genus is composed of the genus and of the difference which added to the genus makes the species. But the genus comes from the matter, and the difference from the form.[1] Therefore everything which is in a genus is composed of matter and form. But an angel is in the genus of substance. Therefore he is composed of matter and form.[2]

Obj. 2. Further, wherever the properties of matter exist, there is matter.[3] Now the properties of matter are to receive and to substand;[4] hence Boëthius says (*De Trin.*)[5] that "a simple form cannot be a subject"; but the above properties are found in the angel. Therefore an angel is composed of matter and form.[6]

Obj. 3. Further, form is act. So what is form

only is pure act. But an angel is not pure act, for this belongs to God alone. Therefore an angel is not form only, but has a form in matter.[7]

Obj. 4. Further, form is properly limited and bounded by matter So the form which is not in matter is an infinitam form. But the form of an angel is not infinite, for every creature is finite Therefore the form of an angel is in matter.[8]

On the contrary, Dionysius says (*Div. Nom* iv)[9]: "Just as first creatures are understood to be as immaterial so they are understood to be incorporeal"

I answer that, Some assert[10] that the angels are composed of matter and form, which opinion Avicebron endeavoured to establish in his book of the *Fount of Life.* For he supposes that whatever things are distinguished by the intellect are really distinct.[11] Now as regards incorporeal substance, the intellect apprehends something by which it is distinguished from corporeal substance, and something by which it agrees with it. Hence he concludes that what distinguishes incorporeal from corporeal substance is a kind of form to it, and whatever is subject to this distinguishing form, as it were something common, is its matter.[12] Therefore he asserts, the universal matter of spiritual and corporeal things is the same,[13] so that it must be understood that the form of incorporeal substance is impressed in the matter of spiritual things in the same way as the form of quantity is impressed in the matter of corporeal things.[14]

But one glance is enough to show that there cannot be one matter of spiritual and of corporeal things. For it is not possible that a spiritual and a corporeal form should be received into the same part of matter, otherwise a thing one and the same numerically, would be corporeal and spiritual. Hence it would follow that one part of matter receives the corporeal

---

[1] Aristotle, *Metaphysics*, VIII, 2(1043ᵃ19); cf. Boëthius *De Div.* (PL 64, 879).

[2] This is the argument of Alexander of Hales, *Summa Theol.*, I-II, n. 106 (QR II, 135), and of Bonaventure, *In Sent.*, II, d. 3, A. I, Q. I (QR II, 90); cf. Avicebron, *Fons Vitae*, III, 18 (BK 118).

[3] Cf. Avicebron, *Fons Vitae*, IV, I (BK 211. 10).

[4] *Op. cit.*, IV, 10 (BK 231. 21); II, 8 (BK 38. 4); cf. Albert the Great, *In Sent.*, II, d. 1, A. 4 (BO XXVII, 13).

[5] Chap. 2 (PL 64, 1250).

[6] Boëthius, *Ibid.*, cf. Albert the Great, *In Sent.*, II, d. 3, A. 4 (BO XXVII, 66); Bonaventure, *In Sent.*, II, d. 3, A. I, Q. I (QR II, 90); Alexander of Hales, *Summa Theol.*, I-II, 106 (QR II, 136).

[7] Cf. Bonaventure, *In Sent.*, II, d. 3, A. I, Q. ? (QR II, 91).

[8] Cf. Bonaventure, *Ibid.;* cf. Albert, *Summa de Creatur.* II, Q. 7, A. 3, arg. 7 (BO XXXV, 101); Gundissalinus *De An.*, VII (MK 56); Avicebron, *Fons Vitae*, IV, ((BK 223,1).

[9] Sect. 1 (PG 3, 693).

[10] Alexander of Hales and Bonaventure, and the Fran ciscan teachers in general, with the exception of John o Rochelle. Cf. Kleineidam, *Das Problem*, (pp. 23–46) Lottin, RNP (1932), pp. 21–41.

[11] *Fons Vitae*, II, 16 (BK 51); III, 46 (BK 182).

[12] *Ibid.*, IV, 2 (BK 213. 23); cf. I, 12 (BK 15); cf. St Thomas, *De Subst. Separatis*, chap. 4.

[13] *Ibid.*, IV (BK 211–256; especially pp. 226, 233). Cf Gundissalinus, *De An.*, 7 (MK 53); Albert, *Summa d Creatur.*, II, Q. 7, A. 3 (BO XXXV, 100).

[14] Cf. *Fons Vitae*, II, 12 (BK 44).

form, and another receives the spiritual form. Matter, however, is not divisible into parts except as regarded under quantity; and without quantity substance is indivisible, as Aristotle says.[1] Therefore it would follow that the matter of spiritual things is subject to quantity, which cannot be. Therefore it is impossible that corporeal and spiritual things should have the same matter.

It is, further, impossible for an intellectual substance to have any kind of matter. For the operation belonging to anything is according to the mode of its substance Now to understand is an altogether immaterial operation, as appears from its object, from which any act receives its species and nature. For a thing is understood in so far as it is abstracted from matter, because forms in matter are individual forms which the intellect cannot apprehend as such. Hence it must be that every intellectual substance is altogether immaterial.

But things distinguished by the intellect are not necessarily distinguished in reality, because the intellect does not apprehend things according to their mode, but according to its own mode. Hence material things which are below our intellect exist in our intellect in a simpler mode than they exist in themselves. Angelic substances, on the other hand, are above our intellect, and hence our intellect cannot attain to apprehend them as they are in themselves, but by its own mode, according as it apprehends composite things; and in this way also it apprehends God (Q. III, A. 3, Ans. I).

Reply Obj. 1. Difference is what constitutes the species. Now everything is constituted in a species according as it is determined to some special grade of being because the species of things are "like numbers, which differ by the addition and subtraction of unity," as the Philosopher says.[2] But in material things there is one thing which determines to a special grade, and that is the form, and another thing which is determined, and this is the matter; and hence from the latter the genus is derived, and from the former the difference. But in immaterial things there is no separate thing determining and thing determined; each thing by its own self holds a determinate grade in being, and therefore in them genus and difference are not derived from different things, but from one and the same. Nevertheless, they differ in our mode of consideration; for, in so far as our intellect considers it as indeterminate, it derives the no-

tion of genus; and in so far as it considers it determinately, it derives the notion of difference.

Reply Obj. 2. This reason is given in the book on the *Fount of Life,* and it would be necessary if the mode of receiving of the intellect and of matter were the same. But this is clearly false. For matter receives the form, that thereby it may be constituted in some species, either of air, or of fire, or of something else. But the intellect does not receive the form in the same way; otherwise the opinion of Empedocles[3] would be true, to the effect that "we know earth by earth, and fire by fire." But the intelligible form is in the intellect according to the very nature of a form, for as such is it known by the intellect. Hence such a way of receiving is not that of matter, but of an immaterial substance.

Reply Obj. 3. Although there is no composition of matter and form in an angel, yet there is act and potency. And this can be made evident if we consider material things, which contain a twofold composition. The first is that of form and matter, whereby the nature is constituted. Such a composite nature is not its own being, but being is its act. Hence the nature itself is related to its own being as potency to act. Therefore if there be no matter, and supposing that the form itself subsists without matter, there nevertheless still remains the relation of the form to its own being, as of potency to act. And such a kind of composition is to be understood in the angels; and this is what some say,[4] that an angel is composed of, that by which *he is* and *what is,* or *being,* and *what is,* as Boëthius says.[5] For *what is,* is the form itself subsisting, and the being itself is that by which the substance is; just as the running is that by which the runner runs. But in God *being* and *what is* are not different, as was explained above (Q. III, A. 4). Hence God alone is pure act.

Reply Obj. 4. Every creature is finite absolutely, since its being is not absolutely subsisting but is limited to some nature to which it belongs. But there is nothing against a creature being considered relatively infinite. Material creatures are infinite on the part of matter but finite in their form, which is limited by the matter which receives it. But immaterial created substances are finite in their being, whereas they are infinite in the sense that their forms are not received in anything else; as if we were to say, for example, that whiteness existing

---

[1] *Physics,* III, 5 (204 ᵃ9).
[2] *Metaphysics,* VIII, 3 (1043ᵇ34).
[3] Aristotle, *Soul,* 1, 2 (404ᵇ13).
[4] Hugh of St. Cher in Lottin, RNP (1932), p. 25. Also Philip the Chancellor, *ibid.*, p. 28.
[5] *De Hebdom.* (PL 64, 1311).

separate is infinite as regards the nature of whiteness, because it is not contracted to any one subject, while its being is finite as determined to some one special nature.

Hence it is said[1] that "intelligence is finite from above, as receiving its being from above itself, and is infinite from below, as not received in any matter."

ARTICLE 3. *Whether the Angels Exist in Any Great Number?*

We proceed thus to the Third Article: It would seem that the angels are not in great numbers.

Objection 1. For number is a species of quantity, and follows the division of a continuous body. But this cannot be in the angels, since they are incorporeal, as was shown above (A. 1). Therefore the angels cannot exist in any great number.

Obj. 2. Further, the more a thing approaches to unity, so much the less is it multiplied, as is evident in numbers. But among other created natures the angelic nature approaches nearest to God. Therefore since God is supremely one, it seems that there is the least possible number in the angelic nature.

Obj. 3. Further, the proper effect of the separate substances seems to be the movements of the heavenly bodies. But the movements of the heavenly bodies fall within some small determined number, which we can apprehend. Therefore the angels are not in greater number than the movements of the heavenly bodies.

Obj. 4. Dionysius says (*Div. Nom.* iv)[2] that "all intelligible and intellectual substances subsist because of the rays of the divine goodness." But a ray is only multiplied according to the different things that receive it. Now it cannot be said that their matter is receptive of an intelligible ray, since intellectual substances are immaterial, as was shown above (A. 2). Therefore it seems that the multiplication of intellectual substances can only be according to the requirements of the first bodies—that is, of the heavenly bodies, so that in some way the outpouring of the aforesaid rays may be terminated in them. And hence, the same conclusion is to be drawn as before.

On the contrary, It is said (Dan. 7. 10): *Thousands of thousands ministered to Him, and ten thousand times a hundred thousand stood before Him.*

I answer that, There have been various opinions with regard to the number of the separate substances. Plato contended[3] that the separate substances are the species of sensible things, as if we were to maintain that human nature is a separate substance of itself. And according to this view it would have to be maintained that the number of the separate substances is the number of the species of sensible things.[4] Aristotle, however, rejects this view[5] because matter is of the very nature of the species of sensible things. Consequently the separate substances cannot be the exemplary species of these sensible things, but have their own natures, which are higher than the natures of sensible things. Nevertheless Aristotle held[6] that those more perfect natures bear relation to these sensible things, as movers and ends; and therefore he strove to find out the number of the separate substances according to the number of the first movements.

But since this appears to militate against the teachings of Sacred Scripture, Rabbi Moses the Jew, wishing to bring both into harmony, held[7] that the angels, in so far as they are styled immaterial substances, are multiplied according to the number of heavenly movements or bodies, as Aristotle held (*loc. cit.*); while he contended that in the Scriptures even men bearing a divine message are styled angels;[8] and again, even "the powers of natural things,"[9] which manifest God's almighty power. It is, however, quite foreign to the custom of the Scriptures for the powers of irrational things to be designated as angels.

Hence it must be said that the angels, even according as they are immaterial substances, exist in exceeding great number, far beyond all material multitude. This is what Dionysius says (*Cæl. Hier.* xiv):[10] "There are many blessed armies of the heavenly minds, surpassing the weak and limited reckoning of our material numbers." The reason for this is that because, since it is the perfection of the universe that God chiefly intends in the creation of things, the more perfect some things are, in so much greater profusion are they created by God. Now, as in bodies such profusion is observed in regard to their magnitude, so in things incorporeal is it observed in regard to their mul-

---

[1] *Lib. de Causis,* 15 (BA 178).
[2] Sect. 1 (PG 3, 693).
[3] Cf. Aristotle, *Metaphysics,* I, 6 (987[b]7).
[4] *Ibid.,* I, 9 (990[b]6).
[5] *Ibid.,* VIII, 1 (1042[a]25).
[6] *Metaphysics,* XII, 8 (1073[a]33, 1074[a]20).
[7] *Guide,* II, 4 (FR 157).
[8] *Ibid.,* II, 6 (FR 160).
[9] *Ibid.,* II, 6 (FR 161).
[10] Sect. 1 (PG 3, 321).

titude. We see, in fact, that incorruptible bodies, which are the most perfect of bodies, exceed corruptible bodies almost incomparably in magnitude; for the entire sphere of things active and passive is something very small in comparison with the heavenly bodies. Hence it is reasonable to conclude that the immaterial substances as it were incomparably exceed material substances as to multitude.

Reply Obj. 1. In the angels number is not that of discrete quantity, brought about by division of what is continuous, but that which is caused by distinction of forms, according as multitude is reckoned among the transcendentals, as was said above (Q. XXX, A. 3).

Reply Obj. 2. From the fact that angelic nature is nearest to God, it must have least of multitude in its composition, but not so as to be found in few subjects.

Reply Obj. 3. This is Aristotle's argument,[1] and it would conclude necessarily if the separate substances were made for corporeal substances. For thus the immaterial substances would exist to no purpose, unless some movement from them were to appear in corporeal things. But it is not true that the immaterial substances exist on account of the corporeal, because the end is nobler than the means to the end. Hence Aristotle says also (*loc. cit.*) that this is not a necessary argument, but a probable one. He was forced to make use of this argument since only through sensible things can we come to know intelligible ones.

Reply Obj. 4. This argument comes from the opinion of such as hold that matter is the cause of the distinction of things; but this was refuted above (Q. XLVII, A. 1). Accordingly, the multiplication of the angels is not to be taken according to matter, nor according to bodies, but according to the divine wisdom devising the various orders of immaterial substances.

ARTICLE 4. *Whether the Angels Differ in Species?*

We proceed thus to the Fourth Article: It would seem that the angels do not differ in species.

Objection 1. For since the difference is nobler than the genus, all things which agree in what is noblest in them, agree likewise in their ultimate constitutive difference; and so they are the same according to species. But all the angels agree in what is noblest in them—that is to say, in intellectuality. Therefore all the angels are of one species.

Obj. 2. Further, more and less do not change a species. But the angels seem to differ only from one another according to more and less—namely, as one is simpler than another, and of keener intellect. Therefore the angels do not differ specifically.

Obj. 3. Further, soul and angel are divided against each other. But all souls are of the one species. So therefore are the angels.

Obj. 4. Further, the more perfect a thing is in nature, the more ought it to be multiplied. But this would not be so if there were but one individual under one species. Therefore there are many angels of one species.

On the contrary, In things of one species there is no such thing as first and second (prius et posterius), as the Philosopher says.[2] But in the angels even of the one order there are first, middle, and last, as Dionysius says.[3] Therefore the angels are not of the same species.

I answer that, Some have said[4] that all spiritual substances, even souls, are of the one species. Others again,[5] that all the angels are of the one species, but not souls; while others[6] allege that all the angels of one hierarchy, or even of one order, are of the one species.

But this is impossible. For such things as agree in species but differ in number, agree in form, but are distinguished materially. If, therefore, the angels are not composed of matter and form, as was said above (A. 2), it follows that it is impossible for two angels to be of one species, just as it would be impossible for there to be several whitenesses apart, or several humanities, since whitenesses are not several, except in so far as they are in several substances. And if the angels had matter, not even then could there be several angels of one species. For it would be necessary for matter to be the principle of distinction of one from the other, not, indeed, according to the division of quantity, since they are incorporeal, but according to the diversity of their powers; and such diversity of matter causes diversity not only of species, but of genus.

Reply Obj. 1. Difference is nobler than genus

---

[2] *Metaphysics*, III, 3 (999ᵇ6).

[3] *Cæl. Hier.*, 2 (PG 3, 273).

[4] Cf. *Contra Gent.*, II, 95, where Origen is named (*Peri Archon*, I, 8; II, 9; PG 11, 176, 229).

[5] Bonaventure, *In Sent.*, II, d. 3, Pt. I, A. 2, Q. 1 (Q. II, 103); d. 9, A. 1, Q. 1 (QR II, 242); cf. Albert, *In Sent.*, II, d. 9, A. 7 (BO XXVII, 204); d. 25, A.5 (BO XXVII, 430); *S.T*, Pt. II, tr. 2, Q. 8 (BO XXXII, 137). Cf. Denifle, *Chartularium*; condemned propositions 81, 96 (1277), n. 473 (I, 548).

[6] Alexander of Hales, *Summa Theol.*, I–II, n. 113 (QR II, 153); n. 114 (QR II, 155).

[1] *Metaphysics*, XII, 8 (1073ᵃ37).

as the determined is more noble than the undetermined, and the proper than the common,
but not as one nature is nobler than another;
otherwise it would be necessary that all irrational animals be of the same species, or that
there should be in them some form which is
higher than the sensible soul. Therefore irrational animals differ in species according to the
various determined degrees of sensitive nature;
and in like manner all the angels differ in species according to the diverse degrees of intellectual nature.

Reply Obj. 2. More and less change the
species not according as they are caused by
the intensity or lessening of one form, but according as they are caused by forms of different degrees; for instance, if we say that fire
is more perfect than air. And in this way the
angels are diversified according to more and
less.

Reply Obj. 3. The good of the species preponderates over the good of the individual.
Hence it is much better for the species to be
multiplied in the angels than for individuals to
be multiplied in the one species.

Reply Obj. 4. Numerical multiplication, since
it can be drawn out infinitely, is not intended by
the agent, but only specific multiplication, as
was said above (Q. XLVII, A. 3, ANS. 2). Hence
the perfection of the angelic nature calls for the
multiplying of species, but not for the multiplying of individuals in one species.

ARTICLE 5. *Whether the Angels Are
Incorruptible?*

We proceed thus to the Fifth Article: It
would seem that the angels are not incorruptible.

Objection 1. For Damascene, speaking of the
angel, says (*De Fide Orth.* ii, 3)[1] that he is "an
intellectual substance, partaking of immortality
by favour, and not by nature."

Obj. 2. Further, Plato says in the *Timæus:*[2]
"O gods of gods, whose maker and father am I:
You are indeed my works, dissoluble by nature,
yet indissoluble because I so will it." But gods
such as these can only be understood to be the
angels. Therefore the angels are corruptible by
their nature.

Obj. 3. Further, according to Gregory (*Moral.*
xvi),[3] "all things would tend towards nothing,
unless the hand of the Almighty preserved

them." But what can be brought to nothing is
corruptible. Therefore, since the angels were
made by God, it would appear that they are
corruptible of their own nature.

On the contrary, Dionysius says (*Div. Nom.*
iv)[4] that "the intellectual substances have unfailing life, being free from all corruption,
death, matter, and generation."

I answer that, It must necessarily be maintained that the angels are incorruptible of their
own nature. The reason for this is that nothing
is corrupted except by its form being separated
from the matter. Hence, since an angel is a subsisting form, as is clear from what was said
above (A. 2), it is impossible for its substance
to be corruptible. For what belongs to anything
considered in itself can never be separated from
it; but what belongs to a thing considered in relation to something else can be separated, when
that something else, in view of which it belonged to it, is taken away. Roundness can never
be taken from the circle because it belongs to
it of itself, but a bronze circle can lose roundness if the bronze be deprived of its circular
shape. Now to be belongs to a form considered
in itself, for everything is a being in act according as it has form, but matter is a being in
act by the form. Consequently a subject composed of matter and form ceases to be in act
through the form being separated from the matter. But if the form subsists in its own being,
as happens in the angels, as was said above (A.
2), it cannot lose its being. Therefore, the angel's immateriality is the reason why it is incorruptible by its own nature.

A sign of this incorruptibility can be gathered from its intellectual operation; for since
everything acts according as it is in act, the operation of a thing indicates its mode of being.
Now the species and nature of the operation is
understood from the object. But an intelligible
object, being above time, is everlasting. Hence
every intellectual substance is incorruptible of
its own nature.

Reply Obj. 1. Damascene is dealing with perfect immortality, which includes complete immutability, since *"every change is a kind of
death,"* as Augustine says (*Contra Maxim.*).[5]
The angels obtain perfect immutability only by
grace, as will appear later (Q. LXII, AA. 2, 8).

Reply Obj. 2. By the expression "gods" Plato
understands the heavenly bodies, which he supposed to be made up of elements which are
composite, and therefore dissoluble of their

---

[1] PG 94, 868.
[2] Translation of Chalcidius, Sect. 16 (DD-169)-*Timæus*
(41).
[3] Chap. 37 (PL 75, 1143).

[4] Sect. 1 (PG 3, 693).
[5] Bk II, Chap. 12 (PL 42, 768).

own nature; yet they are for ever preserved in being by the Divine will.

Reply Obj. 3. As was observed above (Q. XLIV, A. I, Ans. 2) there is a kind of necessary thing which has a cause of its necessity. Hence it is not contradictory for a necessary or incorruptible being to depend for its being on another as its cause. Therefore, when it is said that all things, even the angels, would lapse into nothing unless preserved by God, it is not to be gathered therefrom that there is any principle of corruption in the angels, but that the being of the angels is dependent upon God as its cause. For a thing is said to be corruptible not merely because God can reduce it to non-being, by withdrawing His act of preservation, but because it has some principle of corruption within itself, or some contrariety, or at least the potency of matter.

QUESTION LI
OF THE ANGELS IN COMPARISON WITH BODIES
(In Three Articles)

WE next inquire about the angels in comparison with corporeal things; and in the first place about their comparison with bodies; secondly, of the angels in comparison with corporeal places (Q. LII); and, thirdly, of their comparison with local movement (Q. LIII).

Under the first heading there are three points of inquiry: (1) Whether angels have bodies naturally united to them? (2) Whether they assume bodies? (3) Whether they exercise functions of life in the bodies assumed?

ARTICLE 1. *Whether the Angels Have Bodies Naturally United To Them?*

We proceed thus to the First Article: It would seem that angels have bodies naturally united to them.

Objection 1. For Origen says (*Peri Archon* i):[1] "It is God's attribute alone—that is, it belongs to the Father, the Son, and the Holy Ghost, as a property of nature, that He is understood to exist without any material substance and without any companionship of corporeal addition." Bernard likewise says (*Hom. vi. super Cant.*):[2] "Let us assign incorporeity to God alone even as we do immortality, whose nature alone, neither for its own sake nor on account of anything else, needs the help of any corporeal organ. But it is clear that every cre-

ated spirit needs corporeal assistance." Augustine also says (*Gen. ad lit.* iii):[3] "The demons are called animals of the air because their nature is akin to that of aerial bodies." But the nature of demons and angels is the same. Therefore angels have bodies naturally united to them.

Obj. 2. Further, Gregory (*Hom.* x. *in Ev.*)[4] calls an angel "a rational animal." But every animal is composed of body and soul. Therefore angels have bodies naturally united to them.

Obj. 3. Further, life is more perfect in the angels than in souls. But the soul not only lives, but gives life to the body. Therefore the angels animate bodies which are naturally united to them.

On the contrary, Dionysius says (*Div. Nom.* iv)[5] that the angels "are understood to be incorporeal."

I answer that, The angels have not bodies naturally united to them. For whatever belongs to any nature as an accident is not found universally in that nature; thus, for instance, to have wings, because it is not of the essence of an animal, does not belong to every animal. Now since to understand is not the act of a body, nor of any corporeal energy, as will be shown later (Q. LXXV, A. 2), it follows that to have a body united to it is not of the nature of an intellectual substance, as such, but it comes to some intellectual substance on account of something else, just as it belongs to the human soul to be united to a body, because it is imperfect and exists potentially in the genus of intellectual substances, not having the fulness of knowledge in its own nature, but acquiring it from sensible things through the bodily senses, as will be explained later on (Q. LXXXIV, A. 6; Q. LXXXIX, A. 1). Now whenever we find something imperfect in any genus we must presuppose something perfect in that genus. Therefore in the intellectual nature there are some perfectly intellectual substances, which do not need to acquire knowledge from sensible things. Consequently not all intellectual substances are united to bodies, but some are quite separated from bodies, and these we call angels.

Reply Obj. 1. As was said above (Q. L, A. 1), it was the opinion of some that every being is a body, and consequently some seem to have thought[6] that there were no incorporeal sub-

---

[1] Chap. 6 (PG 11, 170).
[2] *Serm.*, VI (PL 183, 803).
[3] Chap. 10 (PL 34, 284).
[4] PL 76, 1110.
[5] Sect. 1 (PG 3, 693).
[6] Origen, *op. cit.;* Alcher of Clairvaux, *De Spir. et An.,* XVIII (PL 40, 793); Gennadius, *De Eccl. Dog.,* XI (PL 58, 984); cf. below, Q. LIV, A. 5.

stances except as united to bodies; so much so that some even held that "God is the soul of the world," as Augustine tells us.[1] As this is contrary to Catholic Faith, which asserts that God is exalted above all things, according to Psalm 8. 2: *Thy magnificence is exalted beyond the heavens,* Origen,[2] while refusing to say such a thing of God, followed the above opinion of others regarding the other substances, being deceived here as he was also in many other points by following the opinions of the ancient philosophers. Bernard's expression can be explained that the created spirit needs some bodily instrument, which is not naturally united to it, but assumed for some purpose, as will be explained (A. 2). Augustine speaks,[3] not as asserting the fact, but merely using the opinion of the Platonists, who maintained that there are some aerial animals, which they termed demons.

Reply Obj. 2. Gregory calls the angel a rational animal metaphorically, on account of the likeness of the reason.

Reply Obj. 3. To give life effectively is a perfection absolutely speaking; hence it belongs to God, as is said (I Kings 2. 6): *The Lord killeth, and maketh alive.* But to give life formally belongs to a substance which is part of some nature, and which has not within itself the full nature of the species. Hence an intellectual substance which is not united to a body is more perfect than one which is united to a body.

ARTICLE 2. *Whether Angels Assume Bodies?*

We proceed thus to the Second Article: It would seem that angels do not assume bodies.

Objection 1. For there is nothing superfluous in the work of an angel, as there is nothing of the kind in the work of nature. But it would be superfluous for the angels to assume bodies, because an angel has no need for a body, since his own power exceeds all bodily power. Therefore an angel does not assume a body.

Obj. 2. Further, every assumption is terminated in some union, because to assume implies a taking to oneself (*ad se sumere*). But a body is not united to an angel as to a form, as stated (A. 1), while in so far as it is united to the angel as to a mover, it is not said to be assumed, otherwise it would follow that all bodies moved by the angels are assumed by them. Therefore the angels do not assume bodies.

Obj. 3. Further, angels do not assume bodies from the earth or water, or they could not suddenly disappear; nor again from fire, otherwise they would burn whatever things they touched; nor again from air, because air is without shape or colour. Therefore the angels do not assume bodies.

On the contrary, Augustine says[4] that angels appeared to Abraham under assumed bodies.

I answer that, Some have maintained[5] that the angels never assume bodies, but that all that we read in Scripture of apparitions of angels happened in prophetic vision—that is, according to imagination. But this is contrary to the intent of Scripture; for whatever is seen in imaginary vision is only in the beholder's imagination, and consequently is not seen indifferently by everybody. Yet Divine Scripture from time to time introduces angels so apparent as to be seen commonly by all; just as the angels who appeared to Abraham were seen by him and by his whole family, by Lot, and by the citizens of Sodom; in like manner the angel who appeared to Tobias was seen by all present. From all this it is clearly shown that such apparitions were seen by bodily vision, whereby the object seen exists outside the person beholding it, and can accordingly be seen by all. Now by such vision only a body can be seen. Consequently, since the angels are not bodies, nor have they bodies naturally united with them, as is clear from what has been said (A. 1; Q. L, A. 1), it follows that they sometimes assume bodies.

Reply Obj. 1. Angels need an assumed body, not for themselves, but on our account, that by conversing familiarly with men they may give evidence of that intellectual companionship which men expect to have with them in the life to come. Moreover that angels assumed bodies under the Old Law was a figurative indication that the Word of God would take a human body, because all the apparitions in the Old Testament were ordered to that one whereby the Son of God appeared in the flesh.

Reply Obj. 2. The body assumed is united to the angel not as its form, nor merely as its mover, but as its mover represented by the assumed movable body. For as in the Sacred Scripture the properties of intelligible things are set forth by the likenesses of things sensible, in the same way by Divine power sensible bodies are so fashioned by angels as fittingly to represent the intelligible properties of an angel. And this is what we mean by an angel assuming a body.

---

[1] *City of God*, VII, 6 (PL 41, 199); cf. Varro, *De Lingua Lat.*, v, 59 (DD 486).
[2] *Peri Archon*, I, 6 (PG 11, 170).
[3] *City of God*, VIII, 16; IX, 8 (PL 41, 241, 263). Cf. Apuleius. *Lib. de Deo Socratis* (DD 135).

[4] *City of God*, XVI, 29 (PL 41, 508).
[5] Maimonides, *Guide for the Perplexed*, II, 6 (FR 162).

Reply Obj. 3. Although air as long as it is in a state of rarefaction has neither shape nor colour, yet when condensed it can both be shaped and coloured as appears in the clouds. Even so the angels assume bodies of air, condensing it by Divine power in so far as is needful for forming the assumed body.

ARTICLE 3. *Whether the Angels Exercise Functions of Life in the Bodies Assumed?*

We proceed thus to the Third Article: It would seem that the angels exercise functions of life in assumed bodies.

Objection 1. For pretence of truth is unbecoming in angels. But it would be pretence if the body assumed by them, which seems to live and to exercise vital functions, did not possess these functions. Therefore the angels exercise functions of life in the assumed body.

Obj. 2. Further, in the works of the angels there is nothing without a purpose. But eyes, nostrils, and the other instruments of the senses would be fashioned without a purpose in the body assumed by the angel if he perceived nothing by their means. Consequently, the angel perceives by the assumed body; and this is the most special function of life.

Obj. 3. Further, to move by the movement of progression is one of the functions of life, as the Philosopher says.[1] But the angels are manifestly seen to move in their assumed bodies. For it is said (Gen. 18. 16) that *Abraham walked with* the angels, who had appeared to him, *bringing them on the way;* and when Tobias said to the angel (Tob. 5. 7, 8: *Knowest thou the way that leadeth to the city of the Medes?* he answered: *I know it; and I have often walked through all the ways thereof.* Therefore the angels often exercise functions of life in assumed bodies.

Obj. 4. Further, speech is the function of a living subject, for it is produced by the voice, while the voice itself is a sound conveyed from the mouth of an animal, as it is said in the book on the *Soul*.[2] But it is evident from many passages of Sacred Scripture that angels spoke in assumed bodies. Therefore in their assumed bodies they exercise functions of life.

Obj. 5. Further, eating is a purely animal function. Hence the Lord after His Resurrection ate with His disciples in proof of having resumed life (Luke 24). Now when angels appeared in their assumed bodies they ate, and Abraham offered them food after having pre-

[1] *Soul*, II, 2 (413ª23).
[2] Aristotle, II, 8 (420ᵇ5).

viously adored them as God (Gen. 18). Therefore the angels exercise functions of life in assumed bodies.

Obj. 6. Further, to beget offspring is a vital act. But this has taken place with the angels in their assumed bodies; for it is related: *After the sons of God went in to the daughters of men, and they brought forth children, these are the mighty men of old, men of renown* (Gen. 6, 4). Consequently the angels exercised vital functions in their assumed bodies.

On the contrary, The bodies assumed by angels have no life, as was stated in the previous article (ANS. 3). Therefore they cannot exercise functions of life through assumed bodies.

I answer that, Some functions of living subjects have something in common with other operations, just as speech, which is the function of a living creature, agrees with other sounds of inanimate things, in so far as it is sound, and moving from here to there agrees with other movements, in so far as it is movement. Consequently vital functions can be performed in assumed bodies by the angels as to that which is common in such operations, but not as to that which is proper to living subjects; because, according to the Philosopher,[3] "that which has the power has the action." Hence nothing can have a function of life except what has life, which is the potential principle of such action.

Reply Obj. 1. As it is in no way contrary to truth for intelligible things to be set forth in Scripture under sensible figures, since it is not said for the purpose of maintaining that intelligible things are sensible but in order that properties of intelligible things may be understood according to likeness through sensible figures, so it is not contrary to the truth of the holy angels that through their assumed bodies they appear to be living men, although they really are not. For the bodies are assumed merely for this purpose, that the spiritual properties and works of the angels may be manifested by the properties of man and of his works. This could not so fittingly be done if they were to assume true men because the properties of such men would lead us to men, and not to angels.

Reply Obj. 2. Sensation is entirely a vital function. Consequently it can in no way be said that the angels perceive through the organs of their assumed bodies. Yet such bodies are not fashioned in vain, for they are not fashioned for the purpose of sensation through them, but to this end, that by such bodily organs the spiritual powers of the angels may be made manifest;

[3] *Sleep*, I (454ª8).

just as by the eye the power of the angel's knowledge is pointed out, and other powers by the other members, as Dionysius teaches (*Cœl. Hier.*).[1]

Reply Obj. 3. Motion which is from a conjoined mover is a proper function of life; but the bodies assumed by the angels are not thus moved, since the angels are not their forms. Yet the angels are moved accidentally when such bodies are moved, since they are in them as movers are in the moved; and they are here in such a way as not to be elsewhere, which cannot be said of God. Accordingly, although God is not moved when the things are moved in which He exists, since He is everywhere, yet the angels are moved accidentally according to the movement of the bodies assumed. But they are not moved according to the motion of the heavenly bodies, even though they be in them as the movers in the things moved, because the heavenly bodies do not change place in their entirety; nor for the spirit which moves the world is there any fixed locality according to any restricted part of the world's substance, which now is in the east, and now in the west, but according to a fixed quarter; because the moving energy is always in the east, as stated in the eighth book of the *Physics*.[2]

Reply Obj. 4. Properly speaking, the angels do not talk through their assumed bodies, yet there is a semblance of speech, in so far as they fashion sounds in the air like to human voices.

Reply Obj. 5. Properly speaking, the angels cannot be said to eat, because eating involves the taking of food convertible into the substance of the eater. Although after the Resurrection food was not converted into the substance of Christ's body, but resolved into adjoining (praejacens) matter, nevertheless Christ had a body of such a true nature that food could be changed into it; hence it was a true eating. But the food taken by angels was neither changed into the assumed body, nor was the body of such a nature that food could be changed into it. Consequently, it was not a true eating, but figurative of spiritual eating. This is what the angel said to Tobias: *When I was with you, I seemed indeed to eat and to drink; but I use an invisible meat and drink* (Tob. 12. 19). Abraham offered them food, deeming them to be men, in whom, nevertheless, he venerated God, "as God is wont to be in the prophets," as Augustine says.[3]

Reply Obj. 6. As Augustine says:[4] "Many persons affirm that they have had the experience, or have heard from such as have experienced it, that the Satyrs and Fauns, whom the common folk call incubi, have often presented themselves before women, and have sought and procured intercourse with them. Hence it seems folly to deny it. But God's holy angels could not fall in such fashion before the deluge. Hence by the sons of God are to be understood the sons of Seth, who were good; while by the daughters of men the Scripture designates those who sprang from the race of Cain. Nor is it to be wondered at that giants should be born of them; for they were not all giants, albeit there were many more before than after the deluge." Still if some are occasionally begotten from demons, it is not from the seed of such demons, nor from their assumed bodies, but from the seed of men taken for the purpose, as when the demon assumes first the form of a woman, and afterwards of a man; just as they take the seed of other things for other generating purposes, as Augustine says (*De Trin.* iii)[5], so that the person born is not the child of a demon, but of the man from whom the seed is taken.

QUESTION LII

OF THE ANGELS IN RELATION TO PLACE
(*In Three Articles*)

WE now inquire into the place of the angels. Touching this there are three subjects of inquiry: (1) Is the angel in a place? (2) Can he be in several places at once? (3) Can several angels be in the same place?

ARTICLE 1. *Whether an Angel Is In a Place?*

We proceed thus to the First Article: It would seem that an angel is not in a place.

Objection 1. For Boëthius says (*De Hebd.*):[6] "The common opinion of the learned is that things incorporeal are not in a place." And again, Aristotle observes[7] that "it is not everything existing which is in a place, but only a movable body." But an angel is not a body, as was shown above (Q. L.). Therefore an angel is not in a place.

Obj. 2. Further, place is a quantity having position. But everything which is in a place has some position. Now to have a position cannot befit an angel, since his substance is devoid of

---

[1] Chap. 15, sect. 3 (PG 3, 328).
[2] Cf. Aristotle, *Heavens*, II, 2 (285[b]18).
[3] *City of God*, XVI, 29 (PL 41, 509).
[4] *City of God*, XV, 23 (PL 41, 468).
[5] Chaps. 8, 9 (PL 42, 876, 878).
[6] PL 64, 1311.
[7] *Physics*, IV, 5 (212[b]28).

quantity, the proper difference of which is to have a position. Therefore an angel is not in a place.

Obj. 3. Further, to be in a place is to be measured and to be contained by such place, as is evident from the Philosopher.[1] But an angel can neither be measured nor contained by a place, because the container is more formal than the contained; as for example, air with regard to water.[2] Therefore an angel is not in a place.

On the contrary, It is said in the Collect:[3] "Let Thy holy angels who dwell herein, keep us in peace."

I answer that, It is befitting an angel to be in a place; yet an angel and a body are said to be in a place in an equivocal sense. A body is said to be in a place in such a way that it is applied to such place according to the contact of dimensive quantity; but there is no such quantity in the angels, for theirs is a virtual one. Consequently an angel is said to be in a corporeal place by application of the angelic power in any manner whatever to any place.

Accordingly there is no need for saying that an angel can be deemed commensurate with a place, or that he occupies a space in the continuous, for this is proper to a body in a place according as it is endowed with dimensive quantity. In similar fashion it is not necessary on this account for the angel to be contained by a place, because an incorporeal substance virtually contains the thing with which it comes into contact, and is not contained by it; for the soul is in the body as containing it, not as contained by it. In the same way an angel is said to be in a place which is corporeal, not as the thing contained, but as somehow containing it.

And from this the answers to the objections appear.

ARTICLE 2. *Whether an Angel Can Be In Several Places At Once?*

We proceed thus to the Second Article: It would seem that an angel can be in several places at once.

Objection 1. For an angel is not less endowed with power than the soul. But the soul is in several places at once, for it is "entirely in every part of the body," as Augustine says (*De Trin.* vi).[4] Therefore an angel can be in several places at once.

Obj. 2. Further, an angel is in the body which he assumes; and, since the body which he assumes is continuous, it would appear that he is in every part of it. But according to its various parts there are various places. Therefore the angel is at one time in various places.

Obj. 3. Further, Damascene says (*De Fid. Orth.*)[5] that "where the angel operates, there he is." But occasionally he operates in several places at one time, as is evident from the angel destroying Sodom (Gen. 19. 25). Therefore an angel can be in several places at the one time.

On the contrary, Damascene says (*ibid.*)[6] that "while the angels are in heaven, they are not on earth."

I answer that, An angel's power and nature are finite, whereas the Divine power and essence, which is the universal cause of all things, is infinite. Consequently God through His power touches all things, and is not merely present in some places, but is everywhere. Now since the angel's power is finite, it does not extend to all things, but to one determined thing. For whatever is related to one power must be related to it as one determined thing. Consequently since all being is related as one thing to God's universal power, so is one particular being related as one with the angelic power. Hence, since the angel is in a place by the application of his power to the place, it follows that he is not everywhere, nor in several places, but in only one place.

Some, however, have been deceived in this matter. For some[7] who were unable to go beyond the reach of their imaginations supposed the indivisibility of the angel to be like that of a point; consequently they thought that an angel could be only in a place which is a point. But they were manifestly deceived, because a point is something indivisible having position, while the angel is indivisible, and beyond the genus of quantity and situation. Consequently there is no occasion for determining in his regard one indivisible place as to situation; any place which is either divisible or indivisible, great or small suffices, according as he voluntarily applies his power to a great or to a small body. So the entire body to which he is applied by his power, corresponds as one place to him.

Neither, if any angel moves the heavens, is it necessary for him to be everywhere. First of all, because his power is applied only to what is

---

[1] *Ibid.*, 12 (221ª18).
[2] *Ibid.*, 5 (213ª2).
[3] Prayer at Compline, Dominican Breviary.
[4] Chap. 6 (PL 42, 929).

[5] Bk I, Chap. 13 (PG 94, 853).
[6] Bk II, Chap. 3 (PG 94, 869).
[7] Cf. Bonaventure, *In Sent.*, II, d. II, pt. 2, A. 2, Q. 3 (QR II, 81); cf. below, Q. LIII, A. 3, obj. I.

first moved by him. Now there is one part of the heavens in which there is movement first of all, namely, the part to the east; hence the Philosopher[1] attributes the power of the heavenly mover to the part which is in the east. Secondly, because philosophers[2] do not hold that one separate substance moves all the spheres immediately. Hence it need not be everywhere.

So, then, it is evident that to be in a place appertains quite differently to a body, to an angel, and to God. For a body is in a place in a circumscribed fashion, since it is measured by the place. An angel, however, is not there in a circumscribed fashion, since he is not measured by the place, but definitively, because he is in one place in such a manner that he is not in another. But God is neither circumscriptively nor definitely there, because He is everywhere.

From this we can easily gather an answer to the objections, because the entire subject to which the angelic power is immediately applied is considered as one place, even though it be continuous.

ARTICLE 3. *Whether Several Angels Can Be at the Same Time in the Same Place?*

We proceed thus to the Third Article: It would seem that several angels can be at the same time in the same place.

Objection 1. For several bodies cannot be at the same time in the same place, because they fill the place. But angels do not fill a place, because only a body fills a place, so that it be not a vacuum, as appears from the Philosopher.[3] Therefore several angels can be in the one place.

Obj. 2. Further, there is a greater difference between an angel and a body than there is between two angels. But an angel and a body are at the one time in the one place, because there is no place which is not filled with a sensible body, as we find proved in the *Physics*.[4] Much more, then, can two angels be in the same place.

Obj. 3. Further, "the soul is in every part of the body," according to Augustine (*De Trin.* vi).[5] But demons, although they do not possess minds, do possess bodies occasionally, and thus the soul and the demon are at the one time in

the same place; and consequently for the same reason all other spiritual substances.

On the contrary, There are not two souls in the same body. Therefore for a like reason there are not two angels in the same place.

I answer that, There are not two angels in the same place. The reason of this is because it is impossible for two complete causes to be the causes immediately of one and the same thing. This is evident in every genus of causes; for there is one proximate form of one thing, and there is one proximate mover, although there may be several remote movers. Nor can it be objected that several individuals may row a boat, since no one of them is a perfect mover, because no one man's strength is sufficient for moving the boat, while all together are as one mover, in so far as their united strengths all combine in producing the one movement. Hence, since the angel is said to be in one place by the fact that his power touches the place immediately by way of a perfect container, as was said (A. 1), there can be but one angel in one place.

Reply Obj. 1. Several angels are not hindered from being in the same place because of their filling the place, but for another reason, as has been said.

Reply Obj. 2. An angel and a body are not in a place in the same way. Hence the conclusion does not follow.

Reply Obj. 3. Not even a demon and a soul are compared to a body according to the same relation of cause, since the soul is its form, while the demon is not. Hence the inference does not follow.

QUESTION LIII
OF THE LOCAL MOVEMENT OF THE ANGELS
(*In Three Articles*)

WE must next consider the local movement of the angels, under which heading there are three points of inquiry: (1) Whether an angel can be moved locally? (2) Whether in passing from place to place he passes through intervening space? (3) Whether the angel's movement is in time or instantaneous?

ARTICLE 1. *Whether an Angel Can Be Moved Locally?*

We proceed thus to the First Article: It seems that an angel cannot be moved locally.

Objection 1. For, as the Philosopher proves,[6]

---

[1] Cf. *Heavens*, II, 2 (285ᵇ18)

[2] Cf. Avicenna, *Meta.*, IX, 2 (103vb); Averroes, *In Meta.*, XII, 43 (VIII, 326l); Aristotle, *Metaphysics*, XII, 8 (1073ª32).

[3] *Physics*, IV, 7 (213ᵇ33).

[4] Aristotle, IV, 8, 9 (214ᵇ12; 216ᵇ23).

[5] Chap. 6 (PL 42, 929); *De Immort. An.*, 16 (PL 32, 1034); *Contra Epist. Manich.*, 16 (PL 42, 185).

[6] *Physics*, VI, 4 (234ᵇ10); cf. VI, 10 (240ᵇ8).

"nothing which is devoid of parts is moved"; because, while it is in the term from which, it is not moved; nor while it is in the term to which, for it is then already moved. Consequently it remains that everything which is moved, while it is being moved, is partly in the term from which and partly in the term to which. But an angel is without parts. Therefore an angel cannot be moved locally.

Obj. 2. Further, "motion is the act of an imperfect being," as the Philosopher says.[1] But a beatified angel is not imperfect. Consequently a beatified angel is not moved locally.

Obj. 3. Further, movement is only because of want. But the holy angels have no want. Therefore the holy angels are not moved locally.

On the contrary, It is the same thing for a beatified angel to be moved as for a beatified soul to be moved. But it must necessarily be said that a blessed soul is moved locally, because it is an article of faith that Christ's soul descended into Hell. Therefore a beatified angel is moved locally.

I answer that, A beatified angel can be moved locally. As, however, to be in a place belongs equivocally to a body and to an angel, so likewise does local motion. For a body is in a place in so far as it is contained under the place, and is commensurate with the place. Hence it is necessary for local movement of a body to be commensurate with the place, and according to its demands. Hence it is that "the continuity of motion is according to the continuity of magnitude; and according to priority and posteriority in magnitude is the priority and posteriority of the local motion of bodies," as the Philosopher says.[2] But an angel is not in a place as commensurate and contained, but rather as containing it. Hence it is not necessary for the local motion of an angel to be commensurate with the place, nor for it to be according to the exigency of the place, so as to have continuity therefrom, but it is a non-continuous motion. For since the angel is in a place only by virtual contact, as was said above (Q. LII, A. 1), it follows necessarily that the motion of an angel in a place is nothing else than the various contacts of various places successively, and not at once, because an angel cannot be in several places at one time, as was said above (Q. LII, A. 2). Nor is it necessary for these contacts to be continuous. Nevertheless a certain kind of continuity can be found in such contacts. Because, as was said above (*ibid.*, A. 2), there is nothing to hinder us from assigning a divisible

place to an angel according to virtual contact, just as a divisible place is assigned to a body by contact of magnitude. Hence as a body successively, and not all at once, quits the place in which it was before, and from this arises continuity in its local motion, so likewise an angel can successively quit the divisible place in which he was before, and so his motion will be continuous. And he can all at once quit the whole place, and in the same instant apply himself to the whole of another place, and thus his motion will not be continuous.

Reply Obj. 1. This argument fails of its purpose for a twofold reason. First of all, because Aristotle's demonstration proceeds from what is indivisible according to quantity, to which corresponds a place necessarily indivisible. And this cannot be said of an angel.

Secondly, because Aristotle's demonstration deals with motion which is continuous. For if the motion were not continuous, it might be said that a thing is moved while it is in the term from which, and while it is in the term to which, because the very succession of *wheres* regarding the same thing, would be called motion; hence, in whichever of those *wheres* the thing might be, it could be said to be moved. But the continuity of motion prevents this, because nothing which is continuous is in its term, as is clear, because the line is not in the point. Therefore it is necessary for the thing moved to be not totally in either of the terms while it is being moved, but partly in the one, and partly in the other. Therefore, according as the angel's motion is not continuous, Aristotle's demonstration does not hold good. But according as the angel's motion is held to be continuous, it can be so granted, that, while an angel is in motion, he is partly in the term from which, and partly in the term to which (yet so that such "partlyness" be not referred to the angel's substance, but to the place); because at the outset of his continuous motion the angel is in the whole divisible place from which he begins to be moved, but while he is actually in motion, he is in part of the first place which he quits, and in part of the second place which he occupies. This very fact that he can occupy the parts of two places appertains to the angel from this, that he can occupy a divisible place by applying his power, as a body does by application of magnitude. Hence it follows regarding a body which is movable according to place that it is divisible according to magnitude, but regarding an angel, that his power can be applied to something which is divisible.

[1] *Physics*, III, 2 (201ᵇ31).   [2] *Ibid.*, IV, 11 (219ᵃ12).

Reply Obj. 2. The motion of that which is in potency is the act of that which is imperfect. But the motion which is by application of power is the act of one in act: because the power of a thing is according as it is in act.

Reply Obj. 3. The motion of that which is in potency is on account of its own need, but the motion of what is in act is not for any need of its own, but for another's need. In this way, because of our need, the angel is moved locally, according to Heb. 1. 14: *They are all* [Vulg., *Are they not all . . . ?*] *ministering spirits, sent to minister for them who receive the inheritance of salvation.*

ARTICLE 2. *Whether an Angel Passes Through Intermediate Space?*

We proceed thus to the Second Article: It would seem that an angel does not pass through intermediate space.

Objection 1. For everything that passes through a middle space first travels along a place of its own dimensions, before passing through a greater. But the place responding to an angel, who is indivisible, is confined to a point. Therefore if the angel passes through middle space, he must number infinite points in his movement, which is not possible.

Obj. 2. Further, an angel is of simpler substance than the soul. But our soul by taking thought can pass from one extreme to another without going through the middle; for I can think of France and afterwards of Syria, without ever thinking of Italy, which stands between them. Therefore much more can an angel pass from one extreme to another without going through the middle.

On the contrary, If the angel be moved from one place to another, then, when he is in the term to which, he is not moved, but is changed. But a process of changing precedes every actual change. Consequently he was being moved while existing in some place. But he was not moved so long as he was in the term from which. Therefore, he was moved while he was in mid-space, and so it was necessary for him to pass through intervening space.

I answer that, As was observed above in the preceding article, the local motion of an angel can be continuous, and non-continuous. If it be continuous, the angel cannot pass from one extreme to another without passing through the mid-space, because, as is said by the Philosopher,[1] "The middle is that into which a thing which is continually changed comes, before arriving at the last into which it is changed"; for the order of first and last in continuous movement is according to the order of first and last in magnitude, as he says.[2]

But if an angel's motion be not continuous, it is possible for him to pass from one extreme to another without going through the middle, which is evident thus. Between the two extreme limits there are infinite intermediate places, whether the places be taken as divisible or as indivisible. This is clearly evident with regard to places which are indivisible, because between every two points there are infinite intermediate points, since "no two points follow one another without a middle," as is proved in the *Physics*.[3] And the same must of necessity be said of divisible places, and this is shown from the continuous motion of a body. For a body is not moved from place to place except in time. But in the whole time which measures the motion of a body, there are not two *nows* in which the body moved is not in one place and in another; for if it were in one and the same place in two *nows*, it would follow that it would be at rest there, since to be at rest is nothing else than to be in the same place now and previously. Therefore, since there are infinite *nows* between the first and the last *now* of the time which measures the motion, there must be infinite places between the first from which the motion begins, and the last where the motion ceases. This again is made evident from sensible experience. Let there be a body of a palm's length, and let there be a plane measuring two palms, along which it travels; it is evident that the first place from which the motion starts is that of the one palm, and the place wherein the motion ends is that of the other palm. Now it is clear that when it begins to move, it gradually quits the first palm and enters the second. According, then, as the magnitude of the palm is divided, even so are the intermediate places multiplied, because every distinct point in the magnitude of the first palm is the beginning of a place, and a distinct point in the magnitude of the other palm is the limit of the same. Accordingly, since magnitude is infinitely divisible, and the points in every magnitude are likewise infinite in potency, it follows that between every two places there are infinite intermediate places.

Now a movable body only exhausts the infinity of the intermediate places by the continuity of its motion, because as the intermedi-

---

[1] *Physics*, V, 3 (226ᵇ23).

[2] *Ibid.*, IV, 11 (219ᵃ16).

[3] VI, 1 (231ᵇ9).

ate places are infinite in potency, so likewise must there be reckoned some infinitudes in motion which is continuous. Consequently, if the motion be not continuous, then all the parts of the motion will be actually numbered. If, therefore, any movable body be moved, but not by continuous motion, it follows, either that it does not pass through all the intermediate places, or else that it actually numbers infinite places, which is not possible. Accordingly, then, as the angel's motion is not continuous, he does not pass through all intermediate places.

Now, the actual passing from one extreme to the other, without going through the mid-space, is quite in keeping with an angel's nature, but not with that of a body, because a body is measured by and contained under a place; hence it is bound to follow the laws of place in its movement. But an angel's substance is not subject to place as contained thereby, but is above it as containing it. Hence it is under his control to apply himself to a place just as he wills, either through or without the intervening place.

Reply Obj. 1. The place of an angel is not taken as equal to him according to magnitude, but according to contact of power, and so the angel's place can be divisible, and is not always a mere point. Yet even the intermediate divisible places are infinite, as was said above, but they are consumed by the continuity of the motion, as is evident from the foregoing.

Reply Obj. 2. While an angel is moved locally, his essence is applied to various places; but the soul's essence is not applied to the things thought of, but rather the things thought of are in it. So there is no comparison.

Reply Obj. 3. In continuous motion the actual change is not a part of the motion, but its term; hence motion must precede change. Accordingly such motion is through the mid-space. But in motion which is not continuous, the change is a part, as a unit is a part of number; hence the succession of the various places, even without the mid-space, constitutes such motion.

ARTICLE 3. *Whether the Movement of an Angel Is Instantaneous?*

We proceed thus to the Third Article: It would seem that an angel's movement is instantaneous.

Objection 1. For the greater the power of the mover, and the less the moved resist the mover, the more rapid is the movement. But the power of an angel moving himself exceeds beyond all proportion the power which moves a body. Now the proportion of velocities is reckoned according to the lessening of the time. But between one length of time and any other length of time there is proportion. If therefore a body be moved in time, an angel is moved in an instant.

Obj. 2. Further, the angel's movement is simpler than any bodily change. But some bodily change is effected in an instant, such as illumination; both because the subject is not illuminated successively, as it gets hot successively, and because a ray does not reach sooner what is near than what is remote. Much more therefore is the angel's movement instantaneous.

Obj. 3. Further, if an angel be moved from place to place in time, it is manifest that in the last instant of such time he is in the term to which; but in the whole of the preceding time, he is either in the place immediately preceding, which is taken as the term from which; or else he is partly in the one, and partly in the other. But if he be partly in the one and partly in the other, it follows that he is divisible; which is impossible. Therefore during the whole of the preceding time he is in the term from which. Therefore he rests there, since to be at rest is to be in the same place now and previously, as was said (A. 2). Therefore it follows that he is not moved except in the last instant of time.

On the contrary, In every change there is a before and after. Now the before and after of movement is reckoned by time. Consequently every movement, even of an angel, is in time, since there is a before and after in it.

I answer that, Some have maintained[1] that the local motion of an angel is instantaneous. They said that when an angel is moved from place to place, during the whole of the preceding time he is in the term from which, but in the last instant of such time he is in the term to which. Nor is there any need for a medium between the terms, just as there is no medium between time and the limit of time. But there is a mid-time between two *nows* of time; hence they say that a last *now* cannot be assigned in which it was in the term from which, just as in illumination, and in the substantial generation of fire, there is no last instant to be assigned in which the air was dark, or in which the matter

[1] Albert, *In Sent.*, I, d. 37, A. 23 (BO XXVI, 260); A. 24 (BO XXVI, 262); *Summa de Creatur.*, I, 4, 59 (BO XXXIV, 627).

was under the privation of the form of fire, but a last time can be assigned, so that in the last instant of such time there is light in the air, or the form of fire in the matter. And so illumination and substantial generation are called instantaneous movements.[1]

But this does not hold good in the present case; and it is shown thus. It is of the nature of rest that the subject in repose be not otherwise disposed now than it was before, and therefore in every *now* of time which measures rest, the subject reposing is in the same *where* in the first, in the middle, and in the last *now*. On the other hand, it is of the very nature of movement for the subject moved to be otherwise now than it was before, and therefore in every *now* of time which measures movement, the movable subject is in various dispositions; hence in the last *now* it must have a different form from what it had before. So it is evident that to rest during the whole time in some (disposition), for instance, in whiteness, is to be in it in every instant of such time. Hence it is not possible for anything to rest in one term during the whole of the preceding time, and afterwards in the last instant of that time to be in the other term. But this is possible in movement, because to be moved in any whole time is not to be in the same disposition in every instant of that time. Therefore all instantaneous changes of the kind are terms of a continuous movement; just as generation is the term of the alteration of matter, and illumination is the term of the local motion of the illuminating body. Now the local motion of an angel is not the term of any other continuous movement, but is of itself, depending upon no other movement. Consequently it is impossible to say that he is in any place during the whole time, and that in the last *now* he is in another place, but some *now* must be assigned in which he was last in the preceding place. But where there are many *nows* succeeding one another, there is necessarily time, since time is nothing else than the numbering of before and after in movement. It remains, then, that the movement of an angel is in time. It is in continuous time if his movement be continuous, and in non-continuous time if his movement be non-continuous; for, as was said (A. 1), his movement can be of either kind, since the continuity of time comes of the continuity of movement, as the Philosopher says.[2]

But that time, whether it be continuous or not, is not the same as the time which meas-

ures the motion of the heavens, and whereby all corporeal things are measured, which have changeableness from the motion of the heavens; because the angel's motion does not depend upon the motion of the heavens.

Reply Obj. 1. If the time of the angel's movement be not continuous, but a kind of succession of *nows*, it will have no proportion to the time which measures the motion of corporeal things, which is continuous; since it is not of the same nature. If, however, it be continuous, it is indeed proportionable, not because of the proportion of the mover and the movable, but on account of the proportion of the magnitudes in which the movement exists. On that account, the swiftness of the angel's movement is not measured by the quantity of his power, but according to the determination of his will.

Reply Obj. 2. Illumination is the term of a movement, and is an alteration, not a local motion, as though the light were understood to be moved to what is near, before being moved to what is remote. But the angel's movement is local, and, besides, it is not the term of movement; hence there is no comparison.

Reply Obj. 3. This objection is based on continuous time. But the time of an angel's movement can be non-continuous. So an angel can be in one place in one instant, and in another place in the next instant, without any time intervening. If the time of the angel's movement be continuous, he is changed through infinite places throughout the whole time which precedes the last *now*, as was already shown (A. 2). Nevertheless he is partly in one of the continuous places, and partly in another, not because his substance is susceptible of parts, but because his power is applied to a part of the first place and to a part of the second, as was said above (A. 1).

QUESTION LIV

Of the Knowledge of the Angels

(In Five Articles)

After considering what belongs to the angel's substance, we now proceed to his knowledge. This investigation will be fourfold. In the first place inquiry must be made into his power of knowledge; secondly, into his medium of knowledge (Q. LV); thirdly, into the things known by him (Q. LVI); and fourthly, into the manner whereby he knows them. (Q. LVIII).

Under the first heading there are five points of inquiry: (1) Is the angel's act of understand-

---

[1] Cf. Averroes, *In Phys.*, VI, 59 (IV, 284 I).
[2] *Physics*, IV, 11 (219ᵃ13).

ing his substance? (2) Is his being his act of understanding? (3) Is his substance his power of understanding? (4) Is there in the angels an agent and a possible intellect? (5) Is there in them any other knowing power besides the intellect?

ARTICLE 1. *Whether an Angel's Act of Understanding Is His Substance?*

We proceed thus to the First Article: It would seem that the angel's act of understanding is his substance.

Objection 1. For the angel is both higher and simpler than the agent intellect of a soul. But the substance of the agent intellect is its own action, as is evident from Aristotle[1] and from his Commentator.[2] Therefore much more is the angel's substance his action,—that is his act of understanding.

Obj. 2. Further, the Philosopher says[3] that "the action of the intellect is life." But since "in living things to live is to be," as he says,[4] it seems that life is essence. Therefore the action of the intellect is the essence of an angel who understands.

Obj. 3. Further, if the extremes be one, then the middle does not differ from them, because extreme is farther from extreme than the middle is. But in an angel the intellect and the thing understood are the same, at least in so far as he understands his own essence. Therefore the act of understanding, which is between the intellect and the thing understood, is one with the substance of the angel who understands.

On the contrary, The action of a thing differs more from its substance than does its being. But no creature's being is its substance, for this belongs to God only, as is evident from what was said above (Q. III, A. 4; Q. VII, A. 1, Ans. 3; Q. XLIV, A. 1). Therefore neither the action of an angel, nor of any other creature, is its substance.

I answer that, It is impossible for the action of an angel, or of any other creature, to be its own substance. For an action is properly the actuality of a power, just as being is the actuality of a substance, or of an essence. Now it is impossible for anything which is not a pure act, but which has some admixture of potency, to be its own actuality, because actuality is opposed to potentiality. But God alone is pure act. Hence only in God is His substance the same as His being and His action.

[1] *Soul,* III, 5 (430ᵃ18).
[2] *Comm.* 19 (VI, 162c).
[3] *Metaphysics,* XII, 7 (1072ᵇ27).
[4] *Soul,* II, 4 (415ᵇ13).

Besides, if an angel's act of understanding were his substance, it would be necessary for it to be subsisting. Now a subsisting act of intelligence can be but one, just as an abstract thing that subsists can be but one. Consequently the substance of one angel would neither be distinguished from God's substance, which is His very act of understanding subsisting, nor from the substance of another angel.

Also, if the angel were his own act of understanding, there could then be no degrees of understanding more or less perfectly; for this comes about through the diverse participation of the act of understanding.

Reply Obj. 1. When the agent intellect is said to be its own action, such predication is not essential, but concomitant, because, since its very nature consists in act, instantly, so far as lies in itself, action accompanies it, which cannot be said of the possible intellect, for this has no actions until after it has been reduced to act.

Reply Obj. 2. The relation between *life* and *to live* is not the same as that between *essence* and *to be,* but rather as that between *a race* and *to run,* one of which signifies the act in the abstract, and the other in the concrete. Hence it does not follow, if *to live* is *to be,* that *life* is *essence.* Although life is sometimes put for the essence, as Augustine says (*De Trin.* x),[5] "Memory and understanding and will are one essence, one life," yet it is not taken in this sense by the Philosopher when he says that "the act of the intellect is life."

Reply Obj. 3. The action which passes to something extrinsic, is really a medium between the agent and the subject receiving the action. The action which remains within the agent is not really a medium between the agent and the object, but only according to the manner of expression; for it really follows the union of the object with the agent. For the act of understanding is brought about by the union of the thing understood with the one who understands it, as an effect which differs from both.

ARTICLE 2. *Whether in the Angel's Act of Understanding Is His Being?*

We proceed thus to the Second Article: It would seem that in the angel's act of understanding is his being. For "in living things to live is to be," as the Philosopher says[6]. But to understand is in a sense to live.[7] Therefore in the angel to understand is to be.

[5] Chap. 11 (PL 42, 983).
[6] *Soul,* II, 4 (415ᵇ13).
[7] *Ibid.,* II, 2 (413ᵃ23).

Obj. 2. Further, cause bears the same relation to cause, as effect to effect. But the form whereby the angel exists is the same as the form by which he understands at least himself. Therefore in the angel to understand is to be.

On the contrary, The angel's act of understanding is his motion, as is clear from Dionysius (*Div. Nom.* iv).[1] But to be is not motion. Therefore in the angel to be is not to understand.

I answer that, The action of the angel, as also the action of any creature, is not his being. For as it is said[2] there is a twofold class of action: one which passes out to something beyond, and causes passion in it, as burning and cutting; and another which does not pass to a thing outside, but which remains within the agent, as to feel, to understand, to will. By such actions nothing outside is changed, but the whole action takes place within the agent. It is quite clear regarding the first kind of action that it cannot be the agent's very being, because the agent's being is signified as within him, while such an action denotes something as issuing from the agent into the thing done. But the second action of its own nature has infinity, either absolutely or relatively. As an example of infinity absolutely, we have the act to understand, of which the object is the true, and the act to will, of which the object is the good, each of which is convertible with being; and so, to understand and to will, of themselves, bear relation to all things, and each receives its species from its object. But the act of sensation is relatively infinite, for it bears relation to all sensible things; as sight does to all things visible. Now the being of every creature is restricted to one in genus and species; God's being alone is infinite absolutely, comprehending all things in itself, as Dionysius says (*Div. Nom.* v).[3] Hence the Divine nature alone is its own act of understanding and its own act of will.

Reply Obj. 1. Life is sometimes taken for the being itself of the living thing, sometimes also for a vital operation, that is, for one whereby something is shown to be living. In this way the Philosopher says that to understand is, in a sense, to live; for there he distinguishes the various grades of living things according to the various functions of life.

Reply Obj. 2. The essence itself of an angel is the reason of his entire being, but not the reason of his whole act of understanding, since he

cannot understand everything by his essence. Consequently according to its proper notion as such an essence, it is compared to the being itself of the angel, whereas to his act of understanding it is compared as included in the notion of a more universal object, namely, truth or being. Thus it is evident, that, although the form it the same, yet it is not the principle of being and of understanding according to the same notion. On this account it does not follow that in the angel to be is the same as to understand.

ARTICLE 3. *Whether an Angel's Knowing Power Is His Essence?*

We proceed thus to the Third Article: It would seem that in an angel the power or faculty of understanding is not different from his essence.

Objection 1. For, mind and intellect express the power of understanding. But in many passages of his writings, Dionysius[4] styles angels "intellects and minds." Therefore the angel is his own power of understanding.

Obj. 2. Further, if the angel's power of understanding be anything other than his essence, then it must be an accident; for that which is other than the essence of anything, we call its accident. But "a simple form cannot be a subject," as Boëthius states (*De Trin.*).[5] Thus an angel would not be a simple form, which is contrary to what has been previously said (Q. L, A. 2).

Obj. 3. Further, Augustine says,[6] that God made the angelic nature "nigh unto Himself," while He made primary matter "nigh unto nothing"; from this it would seem that the angel is of a simpler nature than primary matter, as being closer to God. But primary matter is its own power. Therefore much more is an angel his own power of understanding.

On the contrary, Dionysius says (*Cæl. Hier.* xi)[7] that "the angels are divided into substance, power, and operation." Therefore, substance, power, and operation, are all distinct in them.

I answer that, Neither in an angel nor in any creature is the power or operative faculty the same as its essence. Which is made evident thus. Since every power is ordered to an act, then according to the diversity of acts must be the di-

---

[1] Sect. 8 (PG 3, 704).
[2] *Metaphysics,* IX, 8 (1050ᵃ23).
[3] Sect. 4 (PG 3, 817).

[4] *De Cæl. Hier.,* II, 1 (PG 3, 137); VI, 1 (200); XII, 2 (292); *De Div. Nom.,* VII, 2 (PG 3, 868).
[5] Chap. 2. (PL 64, 1250).
[6] *Confessions,* XII, 7 (PL 32, 828).
[7] Sect. 2 (PG 3, 284).

versity of powers; and on this account it is said that each proper act responds to its proper power. But in every creature the essence differs from the being, and is related to it as potency is to act, as is evident from what has been already said (Q. XLIV, A. 1). Now the act to which the operative power is related is operation. But in the angel to understand is not the same as to be, nor is any other operation either in him, or in any other created thing. Hence the angel's essence is not his power of understanding, nor is the essence of any creature its power of operation.

Reply Obj. 1. An angel is called "intellect and mind" because all his knowledge is intellectual, whereas the knowledge of a soul is partly intellectual and partly sensitive.

Reply Obj. 2. A simple form which is pure act cannot be the subject of accident, because subject is related to accident as potency is to act. God alone is such a form, and of such is Boëthius speaking there. But a simple form which is not its own being, but is related to it as potency is to act, can be the subject of accident; and especially of such accident as follows the species; but such accident belongs to the form, whereas an accident which belongs to the individual, and which does not belong to the whole species, results from the matter, which is the principle of individuation. And such a simple form is an angel.

Reply Obj. 3. The power of matter is a potentiality in regard to substantial being itself, while the power of operation regards accidental being. Hence there is no comparison.

ARTICLE 4. *Whether There Is An Agent and a Possible Intellect in an Angel?*

We proceed thus to the Fourth Article: It would seem that there is both an agent and a possible intellect in an angel.

Objection 1. The Philosopher says[1] that, "in the soul, just as in every nature, there is something whereby it can become all things, and there is something whereby it can make all things." But an angel is a kind of nature. Therefore there is an agent and a possible intellect in an angel.

Obj. 2. Further, the proper function of the possible intellect is to receive, whereas to enlighten is the proper function of the agent intellect, as is made clear in the book on the *Soul*.[2] But an angel receives enlightenment from a higher angel, and enlightens a lower one. There-

fore there is in him an agent and a possible intellect.

On the contrary, The dictinction of agent and possible intellect in us is in relation to the phantasms, which are related to the possible intellect as colours to the sight are related, but to the agent intellect as colours to the light, as is clear from the book on the *Soul*.[3] But this is not so in the angel. Therefore there is no agent and possible intellect in the angel.

I answer that, The necessity for admitting a possible intellect in us is derived from the fact that we understand sometimes only in potency, and not in act. Hence there must be some power, which, previous to the act of understanding, is in potency to intelligible things, but which is brought into act in their regard when it knows them, and still more when it considers them. This is the power which is called the possible intellect. The necessity for admitting an agent intellect is due to this, that the natures of the material things which we understand do not exist outside the soul as immaterial and actually intelligible, but are only intelligible in potency so long as they are outside the soul. Consequently it is necessary that there should be some power capable of rendering such natures actually intelligible, and this power in us is called the agent intellect.

But each of these necessities is absent from the angels. They are neither sometimes understanding only in potency with regard to such things as they naturally understand, nor, again, are their intelligibles intelligible in potency, but they are actually such; for they first and principally understand immaterial things, as will appear later (QQ. LXXXIV, A. 7. and LXXXV, A. 1). Therefore there cannot be an agent and a possible intellect in them, except equivocally.

Reply Obj. 1. As the words themselves show, the Philosopher understands those two things to be in every nature in which there happens to be generation or becoming. Knowledge, however, is not generated in the angels, but is present naturally. Hence there is no need for admitting an agent and a possible intellect in them.

Reply Obj. 2. It is the function of the agent intellect to enlighten not another intellect, but things which are intelligible in potency, in so far as by abstraction it makes them to be actually intelligible. It pertains to the possible intellect to be in potency with regard to things which are naturally capable of being known, and sometimes to be put in act concerning them. Hence for one angel to enlighten another does not be-

---

[1] *Soul*, III, 5 (430ª14).
[2] Aristotle, III, 4, 5 (429ª15; 430ª14).
[3] Aristotle, III, 5, 7 (430ª15; 431ª14).

long to the notion of an agent intellect; neither does it belong to the notion of the possible intellect for the angel to be enlightened with regard to supernatural mysteries, to the knowledge of which he is sometimes in potency. But if anyone wishes to call these by the names of agent and possible intellect, he will then be speaking equivocally; and we need not trouble about names.

ARTICLE 5. *Whether There Is Only Intellectual Knowledge in the Angels?*

We proceed thus to the Fifth Article: It would seem that the knowledge of the angels is not exclusively intellectual.

Objection 1. For Augustine says[1] that in "the angels there is life which understands and feels." Therefore there is a sensitive power in them as well.

Obj. 2. Further, Isidore says[2] that the angels have known many things by experience. But "experience comes of many remembrances," as stated in the *Metaphysics*.[3] Consequently they have likewise a power of memory.

Obj. 3. Further, Dionysius says (*Div. Nom.* iv)[4] that there is a "perverted phantasy" in the demons. But phantasy belongs to the imaginative faculty. Therefore the power of the imagination is in the demons; and for the same reason it is in the angels, since they are of the same nature.

On the contrary, Gregory says (Hom. 29 *in Ev.*),[5] that "man senses in common with the brutes, and understands with the angels."

I answer that, In our soul there are certain powers whose operations are exercised by corporeal organs; such powers are acts of sundry parts of the body, as sight of the eye, and hearing of the ear. There are some other powers of the soul whose operations are not performed through bodily organs, as intellect and will, and these are not acts of any parts of the body. Now the angels have no bodies naturally joined to them, as is manifest from what has been said already (Q. LI, A. 1). Hence of the soul's powers only intellect and will can belong to them.

The Commentator (*Metaph.* xii)[6] says the same thing, namely that the separated substances are divided into intellect and will. And it is in keeping with the order of the universe for the highest intellectual creature to be en-

tirely intelligent, and not in part, as is our soul. For this reason the angels are called "intellects and minds," as was said above (A. 3, ANS. 1).

A twofold answer can be returned to the *contrary objections*. First, it may be replied that those authorities are speaking according to the opinion of such men[7] as contended that angels and demons have bodies naturally united to them. Augustine often makes use of this opinion in his books[8] although he does not mean to assert it; hence he says[9] that "such an inquiry does not call for much labour."

Secondly, it may be said that such authorities and the like are to be understood as by way of likeness. Because, since sense has a sure apprehension of its proper sensible, it is a common usage of speech, when we understand something for certain, to say that we sense it. And hence it is that we use the word *sententia* (opinion, sentiment). Experience can be attributed to the angels according to the likeness of the things known, although not by likeness of the knowing power. We have experience when we know single objects through the senses; the angels likewise know single objects, as we shall show (Q. LVII, A. 2), yet not through the senses. But memory can be allowed in the angels, according as Augustine (*De Trin.* x)[10] puts it in the mind, although it cannot belong to them in so far as it is a part of the sensitive soul. In like fashion "a perverted phantasy" is attributed to demons since they have a false practical estimate of what is the true good, while deception in us comes properly from the phantasy, whereby we sometimes hold fast to images of things as to the things themselves, as is manifest in sleepers and lunatics.

QUESTION LV

OF THE MEDIUM OF THE ANGELIC KNOWLEDGE

(*In Three Articles*)

NEXT in order, the question arises as to the medium of the angelic knowledge. Under this heading there are three points of inquiry: (1) Do the angels know everything by their substance, or by some species? (2) If by species, is it by connatural species, or is it by species derived from things? (3) Do the higher angels know by more universal species than the lower angels?

---

[1] *City of God*, VIII, 6 (PL 41, 231).
[2] *Sent.*, I, 10 (PL 83, 556).　　　[3] I, 1 (980ᵇ29).
[4] Sect. 23 (PG 3, 725).　　　[5] PL 76, 1214.
[6] Comm. 36 (VIII, 318 H).

[7] See above, Q. LI, A 1, ANS. 1.
[8] Cf. *De Gen. ad Litt.*, II, 17 (PL 34, 278); III, 10 (284),
[9] *City of God*, XXI, 10 (PL 41, 724).
[10] Chap. 11 (PL 42, 983).

ARTICLE 1. *Whether the Angels Know All Things by Their Substance?*

We proceed thus to the First Article: It would seem that the angels know all things by their substance.

Objection 1. For Dionysius says (*Div. Nom.* vii)[1] that "the angels, according to the proper nature of a mind, know the things which are happening upon earth." But the angel's nature is his essence. Therefore the angel knows things by his essence.

Obj. 2. Further, according to the Philosopher,[2] "in things which are without matter, the intellect is the same as what is understood." But what is understood is the same as the one who understands it, by reason of that whereby it is understood. Therefore in things without matter, such as the angels, that whereby something is understood is the very substance of the one understanding it.

Obj. 3. Further, everything which is in another is there according to the mode of what it is in. But an angel has an intellectual nature. Therefore whatever is in him is there in an intelligible mode. But all things are in him, because the lower orders of beings are essentially in the higher, while the higher are in the lower participatively. And therefore Dionysius says (*Div. Nom.* iv)[3] that God "enfolds the whole in the whole," that is all in all. Therefore the angel knows all things in his substance.

On the contrary, Dionysius says (*ibid.*)[4] that "the angels are enlightened by the ideas of things." Therefore they know by the ideas of things, and not by their own substance.

I answer that, The medium through which the intellect understands is related to the intellect understanding it as its form, because it is by the form that the agent acts. Now in order that the power may be perfectly completed by the form, it is necessary for all things to which the power extends to be contained under the form. Hence it is that in things which are corruptible the form does not perfectly complete the potency of the matter, because the potency of the matter extends to more things than are contained under this or that form. But the intellectual power of the angel extends to understanding all things, because the object of the intellect is universal being or universal truth. The angel's essence, however, does not comprise all things in

itself, since it is an essence restricted to a genus and species. This is proper to the Divine essence, which is infinite, to comprise absolutely all things in Itself in a perfect manner. Therefore God alone knows all things by His essence. But an angel cannot know all things by his essence, and his intellect must be perfected by some species in order to know things.

Reply Obj. 1. When it is said that the angel knows things according to his own nature, the words "according to" do not determine the medium of such knowledge, since the medium is the likeness of the thing known; but they denote the knowing power, which belongs to the angel according to his own nature.

Reply Obj. 2. As the sense in act is the sensible in act, as stated in the book on the *Soul*,[5] not in such a way that the sensitive power is the likeness itself of the sensible thing contained in the sense, but because one thing is made from both as from act and potency, so likewise the intellect in act is said to be the thing understood in act, not that the substance of the intellect is itself the likeness by which it understands, but because that likeness is its form. Now, it is precisely the same thing to say "in things which are without matter, the intellect is the same thing as the thing understood, as to say that the intellect in act is the thing understood in act"[6]; for a thing is actually understood because it is immaterial.

Reply Obj. 3. The things which are beneath the angel and those which are above him are in a certain way in his substance, not indeed perfectly, nor according to their proper notion—because the angel's essence, as being finite, is distinguished by its own notion from other things—but according to some common notion. Yet all things are perfectly and according to their own notion in God's essence, as in the first and universal operative power, from which proceeds whatever is proper or common to anything. Therefore God has a proper knowledge of all things by His own essence, and this the angel has not, but only a common knowledge.

ARTICLE 2. *Whether the Angels Understand by Species Drawn from Things?*

We proceed thus to the Second Article: It would seem that the angels understand by species drawn from things.

Objection 1. For everything understood is apprehended by some likeness within him who understands it. But the likeness of the thing ex-

1 Sect. 2 (PG 3, 869).
2 *Metaphysics*, XII, 9 (1075ª3); *Soul*, III, 4 (430ª3).
3 Sect. 7 (PG 3, 701).
4 Chap. IV, 1 (PG 3, 692)
5 Aristotle, III, 2 (426ª10).
6 Aristotle, *Soul*, III, 4 (430ª3).

isting in another is there either by way of an exemplar, so that the likeness is the cause of the thing, or else by way of an image, so that it is caused by the thing. All knowledge, then, of the person understanding must either be the cause of the thing understood, or else caused by it. Now the angel's knowledge is not the cause of existing things. That belongs to the Divine knowledge alone. Therefore it is necessary for the species by which the angelic mind understands to be derived from things.

Obj. 2. Further, the angelic light is stronger than the light of the agent intellect of the soul. But the light of the agent intellect abstracts intelligible species from phantasms. Therefore the light of the angelic intellect can also abstract species from sensible things. So there is nothing to hinder us from saying that the angel understands through species drawn from things.

Obj. 3. Further, the species in the intellect are indifferent to what is present or distant, except in so far as they are taken from sensible things. Therefore, if the angel does not understand by species drawn from things, his knowledge would be indifferent as to things present and distant; and so he would be moved locally to no purpose.

On the contrary, Dionysius says (*Div. Nom.* vii)[1] that "the angels do not gather their Divine knowledge from things divisible or sensible."

I answer that, The species whereby the angels understand are not drawn from things, but are connatural to them. For we must observe that there is a similarity between the distinction and order of spiritual substances and the distinction and order of corporeal substances. The highest bodies have in their nature a potency which is fully perfected by the form, whereas in the lower bodies the potency of matter is not entirely perfected by the form, but receives from some agent, now one form, now another. In like fashion also the lower intellectual substances—that is to say, human souls—have a power of understanding which is not naturally complete, but is successively completed in them by their drawing intelligible species from things. But in the higher spiritual substances—that is, the angels—the power of understanding is naturally complete by connatural intelligible species, in so far as they have such species connatural to them, so as to understand all things which they can know naturally.

The same is evident from the manner of being of such substances. The lower spiritual sub-

stances—that is, souls—have a being akin to a body, in so far as they are the forms of bodies; and consequently from their very mode of being it is appropriate to them to seek their intelligible perfection from bodies, and through bodies; otherwise they would be united with bodies to no purpose. On the other hand, the higher substances—that is, the angels—are utterly free from bodies, and subsist immaterially and in their own intelligible being; consequently they attain their intelligible perfection through an intelligible outpouring, whereby they received from God the species of things known, at the same time as their intellectual nature. Hence Augustine says (*Gen. ad lit.* ii, 8): "The other things which are lower than the angels are so created that they first receive existence in the knowledge of the rational creature, and then in their own nature."[2]

Reply Obj. 1. There are likenesses of creatures in the angel's mind, not, indeed, derived from creatures, but from God, Who is the cause of creatures, and in Whom the likenesses of creatures first exist. Hence Augustine says (*ibid.*) that, "As the type according to which the creature is fashioned is in the Word of God before the creature which is fashioned, so the knowledge of the same type exists first in the intellectual creature, and is afterwards the very fashioning of the creature."

Reply Obj. 2. To go from one extreme to the other it is necessary to pass through the middle. Now the being of a form in the imagination, which form is without matter but not without material conditions, stands midway between the being of a form which is in matter, and the being of a form which is in the intellect by abstraction from matter and from material conditions. Consequently, however powerful the angelic intellect might be, it could not reduce material forms to intelligible being, except it were first to reduce them to the being of imagined forms, which is impossible, since the angel has no imagination, as was said above (Q. LIV, A. 5). Even granted that he could abstract intelligible species from material things, yet he would not do so, because he would not need them, for he has connatural intelligible species.

Reply Obj. 3. The angel's knowledge is indifferent as to what is near or distant according to place. Nevertheless his local movement is not purposeless on that account, for he is not moved to a place for the purpose of acquiring knowledge, but for the purpose of operation.

---

[1] Sect. 2 (PG 3, 868).

[2] PL 34, 269.

ARTICLE 3. *Whether the Higher Angels Understand by More Universal Species Than the Lower Angels?*

We proceed thus to the Third Article: It would seem that the higher angels do not understand by more universal species than the lower angels.

Objection 1. For the universal, it seems, is what is abstracted from particulars. But angels do not understand by species abstracted from things. Therefore it cannot be said that the species of the angelic intellect are more or less universal.

Obj. 2. Further, whatever is known in particular is more perfectly known than what is known universally because to know anything universally is, in a fashion, midway between potency and act. If, therefore, the higher angels know by more universal forms than the lower, it follows that the higher have a more imperfect knowledge than the lower, which is not befitting.

Obj. 3. Further, the same cannot be the proper type of many. But if the higher angel knows various things by one universal form, which the lower angel knows by several special forms, it follows that the higher angel uses one universal form for knowing various things. Therefore he will not be able to have a proper knowledge of each, which seems unbecoming.

On the contrary, Dionysius says (*Cæl. Hier.* xii)[1] that the higher angels have a more universal knowledge than the lower. And in *De Causis*[2] it is said that "the higher angels have more universal forms."

I answer that, Some things are of a more exalted nature because they are nearer to and more like to the first, which is God. Now in God the whole fulness of intellectual knowledge is contained in one thing, that is to say, in the Divine essence, by which God knows all things. This plenitude of knowledge is found in created intellects in a lower manner, and less simply. Consequently it is necessary for the lower intelligences to know by many forms what God knows by one, and by so many the more according as the intellect is lower.

Thus the higher the angel is, by so much the fewer species will he be able to apprehend the whole universe of intelligible things. Therefore his forms must be more universal, each one of them, as it were, extending to more things. An example of this can in some measure be observed in ourselves. For some people there are

---

who cannot grasp an intelligible truth unless it be explained to them in every part and detail; this comes of their weakness of intellect, while there are others of stronger intellect, who can grasp many things from few.

Reply Obj. 1. It happens to the universal to be abstracted from particulars in so far as the intellect knowing it derives its knowledge from things. But if there be an intellect which does not derive its knowledge from things, the universal which it knows will not be abstracted from things, but will be in a certain way existing before them; either according to the order of causes, as the universal ideas of things are in the Word of God, or at least in the order of nature, as the universal ideas of things are in the angelic intellect.

Reply Obj. 2. To know anything universally can be taken in two senses. In one way, on the part of the thing known, namely, that only the universal nature of the thing is known. To know a thing thus is something less perfect, for he would have but an imperfect knowledge of a man who only knew him to be an animal. In another way, on the part of the medium of knowing. In this way it is more perfect to know a thing in the universal; for the intellect which by one universal medium can know the singulars which are properly contained in it is more perfect than one which cannot.

Reply Obj. 3. The same cannot be the proper and adequate type of several things. But if it be superior, then it can be taken as the proper type and likeness of many. Just as in man, there is a universal prudence with respect to all the acts of the virtues, which can be taken as the proper type and likeness of the particular prudence which in the lion leads to acts of magnanimity, and in the fox to acts of wariness, and so on of the rest. The Divine essence, on account of Its eminence, is in like fashion taken as the proper type of the singulars contained therein; hence each singular is likened to It according to its proper type. The same applies to the universal idea which is in the mind of the angel, so that, on account of its excellence, many things can be known through it with a proper knowledge.

QUESTION LVI
Of the angels' knowledge of immaterial things
(In Three Articles)

We now inquire into the knowledge of the angels with regard to the things known by them.

---

[1] Sect. 2 (PG 3, 292).   [2] Sect. 9 (BA 173).

We shall treat of their knowledge: first, of immaterial things, secondly of things material (Q. LVII). Under the first heading there are three points of inquiry: (1) Does an angel know himself? (2) Does one angel know another? (3) Does the angel know God by his own natural powers?

ARTICLE 1. *Whether an Angel Knows Himself?*

We proceed thus to the First Article: It would seem that an angel does not know himself.

Objection 1. For Dionysius says that "the angels do not know their own powers." (*Cœl. Hier.* vi).[1] But, when the substance is known, the power is known. Therefore an angel does not know his own essence.

Obj. 2. Further, an angel is a singular substance; otherwise he would not act, since acts belong to singular subsistences. But no singular is intelligible. Therefore it cannot be understood. Therefore, since the angel possesses only knowledge which is intellectual, no angel can know himself.

Obj. 3. Further, the intellect is moved by the intelligible thing, because, as stated in the book on the *Soul*,[2] "to understand is in some way to be acted upon." But nothing is moved by or is acted upon by itself, as appears in corporeal things. Therefore the angel cannot understand himself.

On the contrary, Augustine says (*Gen. ad lit.* ii)[3] that "the angel knew himself when he was confirmed, that is, enlightened by truth."

I answer that, As is evident from what has been previously said (QQ. XIV, A. 2; LIV, A. 2), the object is otherwise in an immanent, and in a transient, action. In a transient action the object or matter into which the action passes is something separate from the agent, as the thing heated is from what gave it heat, and the building from the builder; but in an immanent action, for the action to proceed the object must be united with the agent, just as the sensible object must be in contact with sense in order that sense may actually perceive. And the object which is united to a power bears the same relation to actions of this kind as does the form which is the principle of action in other agents; for, as heat is the formal principle of heating in the fire, so is the species of the thing seen the formal principle of vision to the eye. It must, however, be borne in mind that this

species of the object exists sometimes only in potency in the knowing power, and then there is only knowledge in potency; and in order that there may be actual knowledge, it is required that the knowing power be reduced to act by the species. But if it always actually possesses the species, it can thereby have actual knowledge without any preceding change or reception. From this it is evident that it is not of the nature of knower, as knowing, to be moved by the object, but as knowing in potency. Now, for the form to be the principle of the action, it makes no difference whether it be inherent in something else, or whether it be self-subsisting; because heat would give forth heat none the less if it were self-subsisting than it does by inhering in something else. So therefore, if in the genus of intelligible beings there be any subsisting intelligible form, it will understand itself. And since an angel is immaterial, he is a subsisting form; and, consequently, he is actually intelligible. Hence it follows that he understands himself by his form, which is his substance.

Reply Obj. 1. That is the text of the old translation, which is amended in the new one, and runs thus: "furthermore they," that is to say the angels, "knew their own powers," instead of which the old translation read—" and furthermore they do not know their own powers." Although even the letter of the old translation might be kept in this respect, that the angels do not know their own power perfectly, according as it proceeds from the order of the Divine Wisdom, Which to the angels is incomprehensible.

Reply Obj. 2. We have no knowledge of singulars corporeal not because of their singularity, but on account of the matter, which is their principle of individuation. Accordingly, if there be any singulars subsisting without matter, as the angels are, there is nothing to prevent them from being actually intelligible.

Reply Obj. 3. It belongs to the intellect, in so far as it is in potency, to be moved and to be acted upon. Hence this does not happen in the angelic intellect, especially as regards the fact that he understands himself. Besides the action of the intellect is not of the same nature as the action found in corporeal things, which passes out into some other matter.

ARTICLE 2. *Whether One Angel Knows Another?*

We proceed thus to the Second Article: It would seem that one angel does not know another.

---

[1] Sect. 1 (PG 3, 200).
[2] Aristotle, III, 4 (429ᵃ14).
[3] Chap. 8 (PL 34, 269).

Objection 1. For the Philosopher says[1] that if the human intellect were to have in itself any one of the natures of sensible things, then such a nature existing within it would prevent it from apprehending external things, as likewise, if the pupil of the eye were coloured with some particular colour, it could not see every colour. But as the human intellect is disposed for understanding corporeal things, so is the angelic mind for understanding immaterial things. Therefore, since the angelic intellect has within itself some one determinate nature from the number of such natures, it would seem that it cannot understand other natures.

Obj. 2. Further, it is stated in *De Causis*[2] that every intelligence knows what is above it, in so far as it is caused by it; and what is beneath it, in so far as it is its cause. But one angel is not the cause of another. Therefore one angel does not know another.

Obj. 3. Further, one angel cannot be known to another angel by the essence of the one knowing, because all knowledge is effected by way of a likeness. But the essence of the angel knowing is not like the essence of the angel known, except generically, as is clear from what has been said before (QQ. L, A. 4; LV, A. 1 Ans. 3). Hence, it follows that one angel would not have a proper knowledge of another, but only a general knowledge. In like manner it cannot be said that one angel knows another by the essence of the angel known, because that whereby the intellect understands is something within the intellect, while the Trinity alone can penetrate the mind. Again, it cannot be said that one angel knows the other by a species, because that species does not differ from the angel understood, since each is immaterial. Therefore in no way does it appear that one angel can understand another.

Obj. 4. Further, if one angel did understand another, this would be either by an innate species; and so it would follow that, if God were now to create another angel, such an angel could not be known by the existing angels; or else he would have to be known by a species drawn from things, and so it would follow that the higher angels could not know the lower, from whom they receive nothing. Therefore in no way does it seem that one angel knows another.

On the contrary, We read in *De Causis*[3] that "every intelligence knows the things which are not corrupted."

I answer that, As Augustine says (*Gen. ad lit.* ii),[4] such things as pre-existed from eternity in the Word of God, came forth from Him in two ways: first, into the angelic intellect; and secondly, so as to subsist in their own natures. They proceeded into the angelic intellect because God impressed upon the angelic mind the images of the things which He produced in their own natural being. Now in the Word of God from eternity there existed not only the ideas of corporeal things, but likewise the ideas of all spiritual creatures. So in every one of these spiritual creatures, the ideas of all things, both corporeal and spiritual, were impressed by the Word of God; yet so that in every angel there was impressed the idea of his own species according to both its natural and its intelligible being, so that he should subsist in the nature of his species, and understand himself by it, while the forms of other spiritual and corporeal natures were impressed in him only according to their intelligible being, so that by such impressed species he might know corporeal and spiritual creatures.

Reply Obj. 1. The spiritual natures of the angels are distinguished from one another in a certain order, as was already observed (Q. L, A. 4, Ans. 1, 2; Q. X, A. 6; Q. XLVII, A. 2). So the nature of an angel does not hinder him from knowing the other angelic natures, since both the higher and lower bear affinity to his nature, the only difference being according to their various degrees of perfection.

Reply Obj. 2. The nature of cause and effect does not lead one angel to know another, unless by reason of likeness, so far as cause and the thing caused are alike. Therefore if likeness without causality be admitted in the angels, this will suffice for one to know another.

Reply Obj. 3. One angel knows another by the species of such angel existing in his intellect, which differs from the angel whose likeness it is not according to material and immaterial being, but according to natural and intentional being. The angel is himself a subsisting form in his natural being, but his species in the intellect of another angel is not so, for there it possesses only an intelligible being. As the form of colour on the wall has a natural being, but, in the medium which carries it, it has only intentional being.

Reply Obj. 4. God made every creature proportionate to the universe which He determined to make. Therefore had God resolved to make more angels or more natures of things,

[1] *Soul,* III, 4 (429ᵃ20).   [2] Sect. 7 (BA 170).
[3] Sect. 10 (BA 174).   [4] Chap. 8 (PL 34, 269).

He would have impressed more intelligible species in the angelic minds; just as a builder who, if he had intended to build a larger house, would have made larger foundations. Hence, for God to add a new creature to the universe means that He would likewise add a new intelligible species to an angel.

ARTICLE 3. *Whether an Angel Knows God by His Own Natural Powers?*

We proceed thus to the Third Article: It would seem that the angels cannot know God by their natural powers.

Objection. 1. For Dionysius says (*Div. Nom.* i)[1] that God "by His incomprehensible might is placed above all heavenly minds." Afterwards he adds that, "since He is above all substances, He is remote from all knowledge."

Obj. 2. Further, God is infinitely beyond the intellect of an angel. But what is infinitely beyond cannot be reached. Therefore it appears that an angel cannot know God by his natural powers.

Obj. 3. Further, it is written (I Cor. 13. 12): *We see now through a glass in a dark manner; but then face to face.* From this it appears that there is a twofold knowledge of God: the one, whereby He is seen in His essence, according to which He is said to be seen face to face; the other whereby He is seen in the mirror of creatures. As was already shown (Q. XII, A. 4), an angel cannot have the former knowledge by his natural powers. Nor does vision through a mirror belong to the angels, since they do not derive their knowledge of God from sensible things, as Dionysius observes (*Div. Nom.* vii).[2] Therefore the angels cannot know God by their natural powers.

On the contrary, The angels are mightier in knowledge than men. Yet men can know God through their natural powers, according to Rom. 1. 19: *what is known of God is manifest in them.* Therefore much more so can the angels.

I answer that, The angels can have some knowledge of God by their own natural powers. In evidence of this it must be borne in mind that a thing is known in three ways: first, by the presence of its essence in the knower, as light can be seen in the eye; and so we have said that an angel knows himself (A. 1.);— secondly, by the presence of its likeness in the power which knows it, as a stone is seen by the eye from its likeness being in the eye;—thirdly, when the likeness of the object known is not

drawn immediately from the thing known itself, but from something else in which it is made to appear, as when we behold a man in a mirror.

To the first-named class is likened that knowledge of God by which He is seen through His essence; and knowledge such as this cannot accrue to any creature from its natural powers, as was said above (Q. XII, A. 4). The third class comprises the knowledge whereby we know God while we are on earth, by His likeness reflected in creatures, according to Rom. 1. 20: *The invisible things of God are clearly seen, being understood by the things that are made.* Hence, too, we are said to see God in a mirror. But the knowledge by which according to his natural powers the angel knows God, stands midway between these two, and is likened to that knowledge by which a thing is seen through the species received from it. For since God's image is impressed on the very nature of the angel by His essence, the angel knows God in sofar as he is the likeness of God. Yet he does not see God's essence, because no created likeness is sufficient to represent the Divine essence. Such knowledge then approaches rather to the knowledge of reflection, because the angelic nature is itself a kind of mirror representing the Divine likeness.

Reply Obj. 1. Dionysius is speaking of the knowledge of comprehension, as his words expressly state. In this way God is not known by any created intellect.

Reply Obj. 2. Since an angel's intellect and essence are infinitely remote from God, it follows that he cannot comprehend Him; nor can he see God's essence through his own nature. Yet it does not follow on that account that he can have no knowledge of Him at all, because, as God is infinitely remote from the angel, so the knowledge which God has of Himself is infinitely above the knowledge which an angel has of Him.

Reply Obj. 3. The knowledge which an angel naturally has of God is midway between these two kinds of knowledge; nevertheless it approaches more to one of them, as was said above.

QUESTION LVII

OF THE ANGELS' KNOWLEDGE OF
MATERIAL THINGS
(*In Five Articles*)

WE next investigate the material things which are known by the angels. Under this heading there are five points of inquiry: (1) Whether

---

[1] Sect. 4 (PG 3, 593).
[2] Sect. 2 (PG 3, 868).

the angels know the natures of material things? (2) Whether they know singular things? (3) Whether they know the future? (4) Whether they know secret thoughts? (5) Whether they know all mysteries of grace?

ARTICLE 1. *Whether the Angels Know Material Things?*

We proceed thus to the First Article: It would seem that the angels do not know material things.

Objection 1. For the thing understood is the perfection of him who understands it. But material things cannot be the perfections of angels, since they are beneath them. Therefore the angels do not know material things.

Obj. 2. Further, intellectual vision is only of such things as exist within the soul by their essence, as is said in a gloss.[1] But material things cannot enter by their essence into man's soul, nor into the angel's mind. Therefore they cannot be known by intellectual vision, but only by imaginary vision, whereby the likenesses of bodies are apprehended, and by sensible vision, which regards bodies in themselves. Now there is neither imaginary nor sensible vision in the angels, but only intellectual. Therefore the angels cannot know material things.

Obj. 3. Further, material things are not actually intelligible, but are knowable by apprehension of sense and of imagination, which does not exist in angels. Therefore angels do not know material things.

On the contrary, Whatever the lower power can do, the higher can do likewise. But man's intellect, which in the order of nature is inferior to the angel's, can know material things. Therefore much more can the mind of an angel.

I answer that, The established order of things is for higher beings to be more perfect than lower, and for whatever is contained deficiently, partially, and in manifold manner in the lower beings, to be contained in the higher eminently, and in a certain degree of fulness and simplicity. Therefore, in God, as in the highest source of things, all things pre-exist supersubstantially in respect of His simple Being itself, as Dionysius says (*Div. Nom.* i).[2] But among other creatures the angels are nearest to God, and resemble Him most; hence they share more fully and more perfectly in the Divine goodness, as Dionysius says (*Cæl. Hier.* iv).[3] Consequently,

all material things pre-exist in the angels more simply and less materially even than in themselves, yet in a more manifold manner and less perfectly than in God.

Now whatever exists in any thing, is contained in it after the manner of that thing. But the angels are intellectual beings of their own nature. Therefore, as God knows material things by His essence, so do the angels know them, through the fact that they are in the angels by their intelligible species.

Reply Obj. 1. The thing understood is the perfection of the one who understands by reason of the intelligible species which he has in his intellect. And thus the intelligible species which are in the intellect of an angel are perfections and acts in regard to that intellect.

Reply Obj. 2. Sense does not apprehend the essences of things, but only their outward accidents. In like manner neither does the imagination, for it apprehends only the likenesses of bodies. The intellect alone apprehends the essence of things. Hence it is said[4] that "the object of the intellect is *what a thing is,*" regarding which it does not err, as neither does sense regarding its proper sensible object. So therefore the essences of material things are in the intellect of man and angels as the thing understood is in him who understands, and not according to their real being. But some things are in an intellect or in the soul according to both ways of being; and in either case there is intellectual vision.

Reply Obj. 3. If an angel were to draw his knowledge of material things from the material things themselves, he would have to make them intelligible in act by abstracting them. But he does not derive his knowledge of them from the material things themselves. He has knowledge of material things by actually intelligible species of things, which species are connatural to him; just as our intellect has, by species which it makes intelligible by abstraction.

ARTICLE 2. *Whether an Angel Knows Singulars?*

We proceed thus to the Second Article: It would seem that angels do not know singulars.

Objection 1. For the Philosopher says[5]: "The sense has for its object singulars, but reason, or the intellect, universals." Now, in the angels there is no power of knowing except the intellectual power, as is evident from what was said above (Q. LIV, A. 5). Consequently they do not know singulars.

---

[1] *Glossa ordin.,* on II Cor. 12.2 (VI, 76A); *Glossa* Lombardi, on II Cor. 12.2 (PL 192, 80); cf. Aug., *De Gen. ad Lit.,* XII, 28 (PL 34, 478).
[2] Sect. 5 (PG 3, 592); V, 9 (825)
[3] Sect. 2 (PG 3, 180).

[4] Aristotle, *Soul,* III, 6 (430^b28).
[5] *Posterior Analytics,* I, 18, 24 (81^b6; 86^a29).

Obj. 2. Further, all knowledge comes about by some assimilation of the knower to the thing known. But it is not possible for any assimilation to exist between an angel and a singular thing, in so far as it is singular, because, as was observed above (Q. L, A. 2), an angel is immaterial, while matter is the principle of singularity. Therefore the angel cannot know singulars.

Obj. 3. Further, if an angel does know singulars, it is either by singular or by universal species. It is not by singular species, because in this way he would require to have an infinite number of species. Nor is it by universal species, since the universal is not the sufficient principle for knowing the singular as such, because singular things are not known in the universal except in potency. Therefore the angel does not know singulars.

On the contrary, No one can guard what he does not know. But angels guard individual men, according to Ps. 90. 11: *He hath given His angels charge over Thee.* Consequently the angels know singulars.

I answer that, Some have denied to the angels all knowledge of singulars.[1] In the first place this detracts from the Catholic faith, which asserts that these lower things are administered by angels, according to Heb. 1. 14: *They are all ministering spirits.* Now, if they had no knowledge of singulars, they could exercise no provision over what is going on in this world, since acts belong to individuals; and this is against the text of Eccles. 5. 5 : *Say not before the angel: There is no providence.* Secondly, it is also contrary to the teachings of philosophy,[2] according to which the angels are stated to be the movers of the heavenly spheres, and to move them according to intellect and will.

Consequently others have said[3] that the angel possesses knowledge of singulars, but in their universal causes, to which all particular effects are reduced; as if the astronomer were to foretell a coming eclipse from the dispositions of the movements of the heavens. This opinion does not escape the previously mentioned difficulties because to know a singular merely in its universal causes is not to know it as singular, that is, as it exists here and now. The astronomer,

---

[1] Albert the Great, *In Sent.,* II, d. III, A. 16 (BO XXVII, 94) attributes this doctrine to the Jewish philosophers; cf. Maimonides, *Guide,* Pt. II, chap. 11 (FR 167); Isaac, *Lib. de Def.* (Muckle, AHDLM, 1937, pp. 312, 315); cf. St. Thomas, *De Subst. Separatis,* XI.

[2] Cf. Maimonides, *Guide,* II, 4 (FR 156); cf. also above, Q. LII, A. 2.

[3] Avicenna, *Meta.,* IX, 6 (105vb); cf. above, Q. XIV, A. 11.

knowing from computation of the heavenly movements that an eclipse is about to happen, knows it in the universal; yet he does not know it as taking place now, unless he apprehends it by the senses. But administration, providence and motion are of singulars as they are here and now existing.

Therefore it must be said differently, that, as man by his various powers of knowledge knows all classes of things, apprehending universals and immaterial things by his intellect, and things singular and corporeal by the senses, so an angel knows both by his one intellectual power. For the order of things runs in this way, that the higher a thing is, so much the more is its power unified and far-reaching; thus in man himself it is manifest that the common sense which is higher than the proper sense, although it is but a single power, knows everything known by the five outward senses, and some other things which no outer sense knows; for example, the difference between white and sweet. The same is to be observed in other cases. Accordingly, since an angel is above man in the order of nature, it is unfitting to say that a man knows by any one of his powers something which an angel by his one power of knowledge, namely, the intellect, does not know. Hence Aristotle pronounces it ridiculous to say that a discord, which is known to us, should be unknown to God.[4]

The manner in which an angel knows singular things can be considered from this, that, as things proceed from God in order that they may subsist in their own natures, so likewise they proceed in order that they may exist in the angelic mind. Now it is clear that there comes forth from God into things not only whatever belongs to their universal nature, but likewise all that goes to make up their principles of individuation, since He is the cause of the entire substance of the thing, as to both its matter and its form. And according as He causes, so does He know, for His knowledge is the cause of a thing, as was shown above (Q. XIV, A. 8). Therefore as by His essence, by which He causes all things, God is the likeness of all things, and knows all things, not only as to their universal natures, but also as to their singularity, so through the species implanted in them do the angels know things, not only as to their universal nature, but likewise in their singularity, in so far as they are the manifold representations of that one simple essence.

Reply Obj. 1. The Philosopher is speaking of

---

[4] *Soul,* I, 5 (410ᵇ4); *Metaphysics,* III, 4 (1000ᵇ5).

our intellect, which apprehends things only by a process of abstraction; and by such abstraction from material conditions the thing abstracted becomes a universal. Such a manner of understanding is not in keeping with the nature of the angels, as was said above (Q. LV, A. 2, A. 3 ANS. 1), and consequently there is no comparison.

Reply Obj. 2. It is not according to their nature that the angels are likened to material things, as one thing resembles another by agreement in genus, species, or accident, but as the higher bears resemblance to the lower, as the sun does to fire. Even in this way there is in God a resemblance of all things, as to both matter and form, in so far as there pre-exists in Him as in its cause whatever is to be found in things. For the same reason, the species in the angel's intellect, which are likenesses drawn from the Divine essence, are the likenesses of things not only as to their form, but also as to their matter.

Reply Obj. 3. Angels know singulars by universal forms, which nevertheless are the likenesses of things both as to their universal principles, and as to their individuating principles. The way in which many things can be known by the same species has been already stated above (Q. LV, A. 3 Ans. 3).

ARTICLE 3. *Whether Angels Know the Future?*

We proceed thus to the Third Article: It would seem that the angels know future events.

Objection 1. For angels are mightier in knowledge than men. But some men know many future events. Therefore much more do the angels.

Obj. 2. Further, the present and the future are differences of time. But the angel's intellect is above time because, as is said in *De Causis*,[1] an intelligence is equated with eternity, that is, with timeless duration (aevus). Therefore, to the angel's intellect, past and future are not different, but he knows each indifferently.

Obj. 3. Further, the angel does not know by species derived from things, but by innate universal species. But universal species refer equally to the past and the future. Therefore it appears that the angels know indifferently things past, present, and future.

Obj. 4. Further, as a thing is spoken of as distant by reason of time, so is it by reason of place. But angels know things which are distant according to place. Therefore they likewise know things distant according to future time.

On the contrary, Whatever is the proper sign of the Divinity does not belong to the angels.

But to know future events is the exclusive sign of the Divinity, according to Isa. 41. 23: *Show the things that are to come hereafter, and we shall know that ye are gods.* Therefore the angels do not know future events.

I answer that, The future can be known in two ways. First, it can be known in its cause. And thus, future events which proceed necessarily from their causes are known with sure knowledge, as that the sun will rise to-morrow. But events which proceed from their causes in the majority of cases, are not known for certain, but conjecturally; thus the doctor knows beforehand the health of the patient. This manner of knowing future events exists in the angels, and by so much the more than it does in us, as they understand the causes of things both more universally and more perfectly; thus doctors who penetrate more deeply into the causes of an ailment can pronounce a surer verdict on the future issue thereof. But events which proceed from their causes in the minority of cases are quite unknown, such as casual and chance events.

In another way future events are known in themselves. To know the future in this way belongs to God alone; and not merely to know those events which happen of necessity, or in the majority of cases, but even casual and chance events, for God sees all things in His eternity, which, being simple, is present to all time, and embraces all time. And therefore God's one glance is cast over all things which happen in all time as present before Him, and He beholds all things as they are in themselves, as was said before when dealing with God's knowledge (Q. XIV, A. 13). But the intellect of an angel, and every created intellect, fall far short of God's eternity; hence the future as it is in itself cannot be known by any created intellect.

Reply Obj. 1. Men cannot know future things except in their causes, or by God's revelation. The angels know the future in the same way, but much more acutely.

Reply Obj. 2. Although the angel's intellect is above that time according to which corporeal movements are reckoned, yet there is a time in his intellect according to the succession of intelligible concepts; of which Augustine says (*Gen. ad lit.* viii)[2] that "God moves the spiritual creature according to time." And thus, since there is succession in the angel's intellect, not all things that happen through all time are present to the angelic intellect.

---

[1] Sect. 2 (BA 165).

[2] Chap. 22 (PL 34, 389); cf. chap. 20 (388).

Reply Obj. 3. Although the species in the intellect of an angel, in so far as they are species, refer equally to things present, past, and future, nevertheless the present, past, and future do not bear the same relations to the species. Present things have a nature according to which they resemble the species in the mind of an angel, and so they can be known thereby. Things which are yet to come have not yet a nature whereby they are likened to such species; consequently, they cannot be known by those species.

Reply Obj. 4. Things distant according to place are already existing in nature, and share in some species, whose likeness is in the angel; but this is not true of future things, as has been stated. Consequently there is no comparison.

ARTICLE 4. *Whether Angels Know Secret Thoughts?*

We proceed thus to the Fourth Article: It would seem that the angels know secret thoughts.

Objection 1. For Gregory (*Moral.* xviii),[1] explaining Job 28. 17: *Gold or crystal cannot equal it,* says that "then, namely in the bliss of those rising from the dead, one shall be as evident to another as he is to himself, and when once the mind of each is seen, his conscience will at the same time be penetrated." But those who rise shall be like the angels, as is stated (Matt. 22. 30). Therefore an angel can see what is in another's conscience.

Obj. 2. Further, intelligible species bear the same relation to the intellect as shapes do to bodies. But when the body is seen its shape is seen. Therefore, when an intellectual substance is seen, the intelligible species within it is also seen. Consequently, when one angel beholds another, or even a soul, it seems that he can see the thoughts of both.

Obj. 3. Further, the ideas in our intellect resemble the angel more than do the images in our imagination, because the former are actually understood, while the latter are understood only potentially. But the images in our imagination can be known by an angel as corporeal things are known, because the imagination is a corporeal power. Therefore it seems that an angel can know the thoughts of the intellect.

On the contrary, What is proper to God does not belong to angels. But it is proper to God to read the secrets of hearts, according to Jer. 17. 9: *The heart is perverse above all things, and unsearchable; who can know it? I am the Lord,*

[1] Chap. 48 (PL 76, 84).

Who search the heart. Therefore angels do not know the secrets of hearts.

I answer that, A secret thought can be known in two ways: first, in its effect. In this way it can be known not only by an angel, but also by man; and with so much the greater subtlety according as the effect is the more hidden. For thought is sometimes discovered not merely by outward act, but also by change of countenance; and doctors can tell some affections of the soul by the mere pulse. Much more then can angels, or even demons, the more deeply they penetrate these hidden bodily modifications. Hence Augustine says (*De divin. dæmon.*)[2] that demons "sometimes with the greatest facility learn man's dispositions, not only when expressed by speech, but even when conceived in thought, when the soul expresses them by certain signs in the body"; although (*Retract.* ii, 30)[3] he says it cannot be asserted how this is done.

In another way thoughts can be known as they are in the mind, and affections as they are in the will, and in this way God alone can know the thoughts of hearts and affections of wills. The reason of this is that the will of the rational creature is subject to God only, and He alone can work in it Who is its principal object and last end; this will be developed later (Q. CV, A. 5; Q. CVI, A. 2; I-II, Q. IX, A. 6). Consequently all that is in the will, and all things that depend only on the will, are known to God alone. Now it is evident that it depends entirely on the will for anyone actually to consider anything, because a man who has a habit of knowledge, or who has intelligible species within him, uses them at will. Hence the Apostle says (I Cor. 2. 11): *For what man knoweth the things of a man, but the spirit of a man that is in him?*

Reply Obj. 1. In the present life one man's thought is not known by another owing to a twofold hindrance; namely, on account of the weight of the body, and because the will shuts up its secrets. The first obstacle will be removed at the Resurrection, and does not exist at all in the angels, while the second will remain, and is in the angels now. Nevertheless the brightness of the body will show forth the quality of the mind, as to its amount of grace and of glory. In this way one will be able to see the mind of another.

Reply Obj. 2. Although one angel sees the intelligible species of another by the fact that the species are proportioned to the rank of

[2] Chap. 5 (PL 40, 586).
[3] PL 32, 643.

these substances according to greater or lesser universality, yet it does not follow that one knows how far another makes use of them by actual consideration.

Reply Obj. 3. The appetite of the brute does not control its act, but follows the impression of some other corporeal or spiritual cause. Since, therefore, the angels know corporeal things and their dispositions, they can thereby know what is passing in the appetite or in the imaginative apprehension of the brute beasts, and even of man, in so far as the sensitive appetite sometimes acts following some bodily impression, as always happens in brutes. Yet the angels do not necessarily know the movements of the sensitive appetite and the imaginative apprehension of man in so far as these are moved by the will and reason, because even "the lower part of the soul has some share of reason, as obeying its ruler," as is said in the *Ethics*.[1] But it does not follow that if the angel knows what is passing through man's sensitive appetite or imagination, he knows what is in the thought or will, because the intellect or will is not subject to the sensitive appetite or the imagination, but can make various uses of them.

ARTICLE 5. *Whether the Angels Know the Mysteries of Grace?*

We proceed thus to the Fifth Article: It would seem that the angels know mysteries of grace.

Objection 1. For, the mystery of the Incarnation is the most excellent of all mysteries. But the angels knew of it from the beginning; for Augustine (*Gen. ad lit.* v, 19)[2] says: "This mystery was hidden in God through the ages, yet so that it was known to the princes and powers in heavenly places." And the Apostle says (I Tim. 3. 16): *That great mystery of godliness appeared unto angels.* (Vulg., *Great is the mystery of godliness, which . . . appeared unto angels.*) Therefore the angels know the mysteries of grace.

Obj. 2. Further, the reasons of all mysteries of grace are contained in the Divine wisdom. But the angels behold God's wisdom, which is His essence. Therefore they know the mysteries of grace.

Obj. 3. Further, the prophets are enlightened by the angels, as is clear from Dionysius (*Cœl. Hier.* iv).[3] But the prophets knew mysteries of

grace; for it is said (Amos 3. 7): *For the Lord God doth nothing without revealing His secret to His servants the prophets.* Therefore angels know the mysteries of grace.

On the contrary, No one learns what he knows already. Yet even the highest angels seek out and learn mysteries of grace. For it is stated (*Cœl. Hier.* vii)[4] that Sacred Scripture describes "some heavenly essences as questioning Jesus, and learning from Him the knowledge of His Divine work for us; and Jesus as teaching them directly," as is evident in Isa. 63. 1, where, on the angels asking, *Who is he who cometh up from Edom?* Jesus answered, *It is I, Who speak justice.* Therefore the angels do not know mysteries of grace.

I answer that, There is a twofold knowledge in the angel. The first is his natural knowledge, according to which he knows things both by his essence, and by innate species. By such knowledge the angels cannot know mysteries of grace. For these mysteries depend upon the pure will of God; but if an angel cannot learn the thoughts of another angel, which depend upon the will of such angel, much less can he ascertain what depends entirely upon God's will. The Apostle reasons in this fashion (I Cor. 2. 11): *No one knoweth the things of a man,*[5] *but the spirit of a man that is in him. So, the things also that are of God no man knoweth but the Spirit of God.*

There is another knowledge of the angels, which renders them happy; it is the knowledge whereby they see the Word, and things in the Word. By such vision they know mysteries of grace, but not all mysteries; nor do they all know them equally, but just as God wills them to learn by revelation, as the Apostle says (I Cor. 2. 10): *But to us God hath revealed them through His Spirit;* yet so that the higher angels beholding the Divine wisdom more clearly, learn more and deeper mysteries in the vision of God, which mysteries they communicate to the lower angels by enlightening them. Some of these mysteries they knew from the very beginning of their creation; others they are taught afterwards, as befits their ministrations.

Reply Obj. 1. One can speak in two ways of the mystery of the Incarnation. First of all, in general; and in this way it was revealed to all from the commencement of their happiness. The reason of this is, that this is a kind of general principle to which all their duties are ordered. For *all are* (Vulg., *Are they not all*)

---

[1] Aristotle, I, 13 (1102[b]31).
[2] PL 34, 334.
[3] Sect. 2 (PG 3, 180).

[4] Sect. 3 (PG 3, 209).
[5] Vulg., *What man knoweth the things of a man, but . . .?*

ministering spirits, sent to minister for them who shall receive the inheritance of salvation (Heb. 1. 14); and this is brought about by the mystery of the Incarnation. Hence it was necessary for all of them to be instructed in this mystery from the very beginning. We can speak of the mystery of the Incarnation in another way, as to its special conditions. Thus not all the angels were instructed on all points from the beginning; even the higher angels learned these afterwards, as appears from the passage of Dionysius already quoted.

Reply Obj. 2. Although the angels in bliss behold the Divine wisdom, yet they do not comprehend it. So it is not necessary for them to know everything hidden in it.

Reply Obj. 3. Whatever the prophets knew by revelation of the mysteries of grace was revealed in a more excellent way to the angels. And although God revealed in general to the prophets what He was one day to do regarding the salvation of the human race, still the apostles knew some particulars of the same, which the prophets did not know. Thus we read (Eph. 3. 4, 5): *As you reading, may understand my knowledge in the mystery of Christ, which in other generations was not known to the sons of men, as it is now revealed to His holy apostles.* Among the prophets also, the later ones knew what the former did not know; according to Ps. 118. 100: *I have had understanding above ancients,* and Gregory says: "The knowledge of Divine things increased as time went on" (*Homil.* iv, *in Ezech.*).[1]

QUESTION LVIII
OF THE MODE OF THE ANGELIC KNOWLEDGE
(*In Seven Articles*)

AFTER the foregoing we have now to treat of the mode of the angelic knowledge, concerning which there are seven points of inquiry: (1) Whether the angel's intellect be sometimes in potency, and sometimes in act? (2) Whether the angel can understand many things at the same time? (3) Whether the angel's knowledge is discursive? (4) Whether he understands by composing and dividing? (5) Whether there can be falsity in the angel's intellect? (6) Whether his knowledge can be styled as morning and evening? (7) Whether the morning and evening knowledge are the same, or do they differ?

[1] PL 76, 980.

ARTICLE 1. *Whether the Angel's Intellect Is Sometimes in Potency, and Sometimes in Act?*

We proceed thus to the First Article: It would seem that the angel's intellect is sometimes in potency and sometimes in act.

Objection 1. "For motion is the act of what is in potency," as stated in the *Physics*.[2] But the angels' minds are moved by understanding, as Dionysius says (*Div. Nom.* iv).[3] Therefore the angelic minds are sometimes in potency.

Obj. 2. Further, since desire is of a thing not possessed but possible to have, whoever desires to know anything is in potency to it. But it is said (I Pet. 1. 12): *On Whom the angels desire to look.* Therefore the angel's intellect is sometimes in potency.

Obj. 3. Further, in the book *De Causis*[4] it is stated that "an intelligence understands according to the mode of its substance." But the angel's intelligence has some admixture of potency. Therefore it sometimes understands in potency.

On the contrary, Augustine says (*Gen. ad lit.* ii):[5] "Since the angels were created in the eternity of the Word, they enjoy holy and devout contemplation." Now a contemplating intellect is not in potency, but in act. Therefore the intellect of an angel is not in potency.

I answer that, As the Philosopher states,[6] the intellect is in potency in two ways: First, "as before learning or discovering," that is, before it has the habit of knowledge; secondly, as "when it possesses the habit of knowledge, but does not actually consider." In the first way an angel's intellect is never in potency with regard to the things to which his natural knowledge extends. For, as the higher, namely, the heavenly, bodies have no potency to being which is not fully actualized, in the same way the heavenly intellects, the angels, have no intelligible potency which is not fully completed by connatural intelligible species. But with regard to things divinely revealed to them, there is nothing to hinder them from being in potency, because even the heavenly bodies are at times in potency to being enlightened by the sun.

In the second way an angel's intellect can be in potency with regard to things learnt by natural knowledge, for he is not always actually considering everything that he knows by nat-

[2] III, 1 (201ᵃ10).
[3] Sect. 8 (PG 3, 704).
[4] Sect. 7 (BA 171).
[5] Chap. 8 (PL 34, 270).
[6] *Soul,* III, 4 (429ᵇ8); *Physics,* VIII, 4 (255ᵃ33).

ural knowledge. But as to the knowledge of the Word, and of the things he sees in the Word, he is never in this way in potency, because he is always actually beholding the Word, and the things he sees in the Word. For the bliss of the angels consists in such vision, and "beatitude does not consist in habit, but in act," as the Philosopher says.[1]

Reply Obj. 1. Motion is taken there not as the act of something imperfect, that is, of something existing in potency, but as the act of something perfect, that is, of one actually existing. In this way understanding and feeling are termed motion, as stated in the book on the *Soul*.[2]

Reply Obj. 2. Such desire on the part of the angels does not exclude the thing desired, but weariness of it. Or they are said to desire the vision of God with regard to fresh revelations, which they receive from God to fit them for the tasks which they have to perform.

Reply Obj. 3. In the angel's substance there is no potency divested of act. In the same way, the angel's intellect is never so in potency as to be without act.

ARTICLE 2. *Whether an Angel Can Understand Many Things at the Same Time?*

We proceed thus to the Second Article: It would seem that an angel cannot understand many things at the same time.

Objection 1. For the Philosopher says[3] that "it may happen that we know many things, but understand only one."

Obj. 2. Further, nothing is understood unless the intellect be informed by an intelligible species, just as the body is formed by shape. But one body cannot be formed by many shapes. Therefore neither can one intellect simultaneously understand various intelligible things.

Obj. 3. Further, to understand is a kind of movement. But no movement terminates in various terms. Therefore many things cannot be understood at the same time.

On the contrary, Augustine says (*Gen. ad lit.* iv, 32):[4] "The spiritual power of the angelic mind comprehends most easily at the same time all things that it wills."

I answer that, As unity of term is requisite for unity of movement, so is unity of object required for unity of operation. Now it happens that several things may be taken as several or as one, like the parts of a continuous whole.

For if each of the parts be considered in itself, they are many; consequently neither by sense nor by intellect are they grasped by one operation, nor all at once. In another way they are taken according as they are one in the whole; and so they are known both by sense and intellect all at once and by one operation, as long as the entire continuous whole is considered, as is stated in the book on the *Soul*.[5] In this way our intellect understands at the same time both the subject and the predicate, as forming parts of one proposition; and also two things compared together, according as they agree in one point of comparison. From this it is evident that many things, in so far as they are distinct, cannot be understood at the same time; but in so far as they are joined under one intelligible aspect, they can be understood together. Now everything is actually intelligible according as its likeness is in the intellect. All things, then, which can be known by one intelligible species, are known as one intelligible thing, and therefore are understood simultaneously. But things known by various intelligible species are apprehended as different intelligible things.

Consequently, by such knowledge as the angels have of things through the Word, they know all things under one intelligible species, which is the Divine essence. Therefore, as regards such knowledge, they know all things at once; just as in heaven "our thoughts will not be fleeting, going and returning from one thing to another, but we shall survey all our knowledge at the same time by one glance," as Augustine says (*De Trin.* xv, 16).[6] But by that knowledge with which the angels know things by innate species they can at the one time know all things which are known under one species, but not such as are under various species.

Reply Obj. 1. To understand many things as one, is, so to speak, to understand one thing.

Reply Obj. 2. The intellect is informed by the intelligible species which it has within it. So it can behold at the same time many intelligible things under one species; as one body can by one shape be likened to many bodies.

To the third objection the answer is the same as to the first.

ARTICLE 3. *Whether an Angel's Knowledge Is Discursive?*

We proceed thus to the Third Article: It would seem that the knowledge of an angel is discursive.

---

[1] *Ethics*, I, 8 (1098^{b}33).   [2] Aristotle, III, 7 (431^{a}4).
[3] *Topics*, II, 10 (114^{b}34).   [4] PL 34, 316.
[5] Aristotle, III, 6 (430^{b}7).   [6] PL 42, 1079.

Objection 1. For the discursive movement of the mind comes from one thing being known through another. But the angels know one thing through another, for they know creatures through the Word. Therefore the intellect of an angel knows by discursive method.

Obj. 2. Further, whatever a lower power can do, the higher can do. But the human intellect can syllogize, and know causes in effects, all of which is discursive. Therefore the intellect of the angel, which is higher in the order of nature, can with greater reason do this.

Obj. 3. Further, Isidore says[1] that demons learn many things by experience. But experimental knowledge is discursive, for, "one experience comes of many remembrances, and one universal from many experiences," as Aristotle observes.[2] Therefore an angel's knowledge is discursive.

On the contrary, Dionysius says (*Div. Nom.* vii)[3] that the "angels do not acquire Divine knowledge from separate discourses, nor are they led to something particular from something common."

I answer that, As has often been stated (A. 1; Q. L, A. 3; Q. LV, A. 2), the angels hold that grade among spiritual substances which the heavenly bodies hold among corporeal substances, for Dionysius calls them "heavenly minds" (*loc. cit.*).[4] Now, the difference between heavenly and earthly bodies is this, that earthly bodies obtain their ultimate perfection by change and motion, while the heavenly bodies have their ultimate perfection at once from their very nature. So, likewise, the lower, namely, the human, intellects obtain their perfection in the knowledge of truth by a kind of movement and discursive intellectual operation; that is to say, as they advance from one known thing to another. But, if from the knowledge of a known principle they were straightway to perceive as known all its consequent conclusions, then discourse would have no place in them. Such is the condition of the angels, because in those things which they first know naturally, they at once behold all things whatsoever that can be known in them.

Therefore they are called intellectual beings, because even with ourselves the things which are instantly naturally apprehended are said to be understood (*intelligi*); hence intellect is defined as the habit of first principles. But human souls which acquire knowledge of truth by the discursive method are called rational; and this comes of the feebleness of their intellectual light. For if they possessed the fulness of intellectual light, like the angels, then in the first aspect of principles they would at once comprehend their whole range, by perceiving whatever could be reasoned out from them.

Reply Obj. 1. Discursion expresses movement of a kind. Now all movement is from something before to something after. Hence discursive knowledge comes about according as from something previously known one attains to the knowledge of what is afterwards known, and which was previously unknown. But if in the thing perceived something else be seen at the same time, as a thing and its image are seen simultaneously in a mirror, it is not discursive knowledge. And in this way the angels know things in the Word.

Reply Obj. 2. The angels can syllogize, in the sense of knowing a syllogism, and they see effects in causes, and causes in effects; yet they do not acquire knowledge of an unknown truth in this way, by syllogizing from causes to effect, or from effect to cause.

Reply Obj. 3. Experience is affirmed of angels and demons simply by way of likeness, since they know sensible things which are present, yet without any discursion.

Article 4. *Whether the Angels Understand by Composing and Dividing?*

We proceed thus to the Fourth Article: It would seem that the angels understand by composing and dividing.

Objection 1. For where there is multiplicity of things understood, there is composition of the same as is said in the book on the *Soul*.[5] But there is a multitude of things understood in the angelic intellect, because angels apprehend different things by various species, and not all at one time. Therefore there is composition and division in the angel's intellect.

Obj. 2. Further, negation is more distant from affirmation than any two opposite natures are, because the first of distinctions is that of affirmation and negation. But the angel knows certain distant natures not by one, but by diverse species, as is evident from what was said (A. 2). Therefore he must know affirmation and nega-

[1] *Sent.,* I, 10 (PL 83, 556).
[2] *Posterior Analytics,* II, 19 (100ᵇ4); *Metaphysics,* I, 1 (980ᵇ28).
[3] Sect. 2 (PG 3, 868).
[4] I, 4 (PG 3, 593); cf. also *Cæl. Hier.,* II, 1 (PG 3, 137).
[5] Aristotle, III, 6 (430ᵃ27).

tion by diverse species. And so it seems that he understands by composing and dividing.

Obj. 3. Further, speech is a sign of the intellect. But in speaking to men, angels use affirmative and negative expressions, which are signs of composition and of division in the intellect, as is manifest from many passages of Sacred Scripture. Therefore it seems that the angel understands by composing and dividing.

On the contrary, Dionysius says (*Div. Nom.* vii)[1] that "the intellectual power of the angel shines forth with the clear simplicity of divine concepts." But a simple intelligence is without composition and division as it is stated in the book on the *Soul*.[2] Therefore the angel understands without composition or division.

I answer that, As in the intellect, when reasoning, the conclusion is compared with the principle, so in the intellect composing and dividing, the predicate is compared with the subject. For if our intellect were to see at once the force of the conclusion in the principle, it would never understand by discursion and reasoning. In like manner, if the intellect in apprehending the quiddity of the subject were at once to have knowledge of all that can be attributed to, or removed from, the subject, it would never understand by composing and dividing, but only by understanding the essence. Thus it is evident that for the self-same reason our intellect understands by discursion, and by composing and dividing, namely, that in the first apprehension of anything newly apprehended it does not at once grasp all that is virtually contained in it. And this comes from the weakness of the intellectual light within us, as has been said (A. 3). Hence, since the intellectual light is perfect in the angel, for he is "a pure and most clear mirror," as Dionysius says (*Div. Nom.* iv),[3] it follows that as the angel does not understand by reasoning, so neither does he by composing and dividing.

Nevertheless, he understands the composition and the division of enunciations, just as he apprehends the reasoning of syllogisms, for he understands simply such things as are composite, things movable immovably, and material things immaterially.

Reply Obj. 1. Not every multitude of things understood causes composition, but a multitude of such things understood that one of them is attributed to, or denied of, another. When an angel apprehends the quiddity of anything, he at the same time understands whatever can be either attributed to it, or denied of it. Hence, in apprehending an essence, he by one simple perception grasps all that we can learn by composing and dividing.

Reply Obj. 2. The various quiddities of things differ less as to their mode of existing than do affirmation and negation. Yet, as to the way in which they are known, affirmation and negation have something more in common, because directly the truth of an affirmation is known, the falsehood of the opposite negation is known also.

Reply Obj. 3. The fact that angels use affirmative and negative forms of speech shows that they know both composition and division, yet not that they know by composing and dividing, but by knowing absolutely the essence of a thing.

ARTICLE 5. *Whether There Can Be Falsity in the Intellect of an Angel?*

We proceed thus to the Fifth Article: It would seem that there can be falsity in the angel's intellect.

Objection 1. For perversity appertains to falsehood. But, as Dionysius says (*Div. Nom.* iv),[4] there is "a perverted fancy" in the demons. Therefore it seems that there can be falsity in the intellect of the angels.

Obj. 2. Further, nescience is the cause of estimating falsely. But, as Dionysius says (*Eccl. Hier.* vi),[5] there can be nescience in the angels. Therefore it seems there can be falsehood in them.

Obj. 3. Further, everything which falls short of the truth of wisdom, and which has a depraved reason, has falsity or error in its intellect. But Dionysius (*Div. Nom.* vii)[6] affirms this of the demons. Therefore it seems that there can be error in the intellect of the angels.

On the contrary, The Philosopher says[7] that "the intellect is always true." Augustine likewise says (QQ. LXXXIII, qu 32)[8] that "nothing is understood except truth." But angels do not know anything except by understanding. Therefore there can be neither deception nor falsity in the angel's knowledge.

I answer that, The truth of this question depends partly upon what has gone before. For it

---

[1] Sect. 2 (PG 3, 868).
[2] Aristotle, III, 6 (430ª26).
[3] Sect. 22 (PG 3, 724).

[4] Sect. 23 (PG 3, 725).
[5] Sect. 1 (PG 3, 200).
[6] Sect. 3 (PG 3, 868).
[7] *Soul*, III, 6, 10 (430ᵇ27; 433ª26).
[8] PL 40, 22; cf. Q. 44 (PL 40, 38).

has been said (A. 4) that an angel understands not by composing and dividing, but by understanding essence. "Now the intellect is always true as regards essence," just as the sense regarding its proper object, as is said in the book on the *Soul*.[1] But in us deception and falsehood creep in by accident when we understand the essence of a thing by some kind of composition, and this happens either when we take the definition of one thing for another, or when the parts of a definition do not hang together, as if we were to accept as the definition of some creature, "a four-footed flying beast," for there is no such animal. And this comes about in things composite, the definition of which is drawn from diverse elements, one of which is as matter to the other. But "there is no falsity in the understanding of simple quiddities," as is stated in the *Metaphysics*;[2] for either they are not grasped at all, and so we understand nothing respecting them, or else they are known as they are.

So therefore, no falsity, error, or deception can exist per se in the mind of any angel; yet it does so happen accidentally, but differently from the way it befalls us. For we sometimes get at the quiddity of a thing by a composing and dividing process, as when, by division and demonstration, we seek out the truth of a definition. Such is not what takes place in the angels, but through the essence of a thing they know everything that can be said regarding it. Now it is quite evident that the quiddity of a thing can be a principle of knowledge with regard to everything belonging to such thing, or excluded from it, but not of what may be dependent on God's supernatural ordinance. Consequently, owing to their upright will, from their knowledge of the quiddity of the thing the good angels form no judgments of those things which pertain to the thing supernaturally save under the Divine ordinance; hence there can be no error or falsity in them. But since the intellects of demons are led away from the Divine wisdom by a perverse will, they at times judge of things simply according to the natural conditions of the same. Nor are they ever deceived as to what pertains naturally to a thing, but they can be misled with regard to supernatural matters; for example, on seeing a dead man, they may suppose that he will not rise again, or, on seeing the man Christ, they may judge Him not to be God.

From all this the answers to *the objections on both sides* of the question are evident. For the perversity of the demons comes of their not being subject to the Divine wisdom; while nescience is not in the angels as regards things naturally knowable, but supernaturally knowable. It is, furthermore, evident that their understanding of essence is always true, save accidentally, according as it is, in an undue manner, referred to some composition or division.

ARTICLE 6. *Whether There Is a "Morning" and an "Evening" Knowledge in the Angels?*

We proceed thus to the Sixth Article: It would seem that there is neither an evening nor a morning knowledge in the angels.

Objection 1. For evening and morning have an admixture of darkness. But there is no darkness in the knowledge of an angel, since there is no error nor falsity. Therefore the angelic knowledge ought not to be termed the morning and evening knowledge.

Obj. 2. Further, between evening and morning the night intervenes, while noonday falls between morning and evening. Consequently, if there be a morning and an evening knowledge in the angels, for the same reason it appears that there ought to be a noonday and a night knowledge.

Obj. 3. Further, knowledge is diversified according to the difference of the things known; hence the Philosopher says,[3] "The sciences are divided just as things are." But there is a three-fold being of things: namely, in the Word; in their own natures; and in the angelic knowledge, as Augustine observes (*Gen. ad lit.* ii, 8).[4] If, therefore, a morning and an evening knowledge be admitted in the angels because of the being of things in the Word, and in their own nature, then there ought to be admitted a third class of knowledge, on account of the being of things in the angelic mind.

On the contrary, Augustine[5] divides the knowledge of the angels into morning and evening knowledge.

I answer that, The expression "morning" and "evening" knowledge was devised by Augustine, who interprets the six days wherein God made all things[6] not as ordinary days measured by the solar circuit, since the sun was only made on the fourth day, but as one day, namely, the day of angelic knowledge as directed to six classes of things. As in the ordinary day, morning is the

---

[1] Aristotle, III, 6 (430[b]27).
[2] Aristotle, IX, 10 (1051[b]26).

[3] *Soul*, III, 8 (431[b]24).
[4] PL 34, 269.
[5] *Gen. ad lit.*, IV, 22 (PL 34, 312); *City of God*, XI, 7 (PL 41, 322).
[6] *Gen. ad. lit.*, IV, 22, 26 (PL 34, 312, 314).

beginning, and evening the close of day, so, their knowledge of the primordial being of things is called morning knowledge; and this is according as things are in the Word. But their knowledge of the very being of the thing created, as it stands in its own nature, is termed evening knowledge, because the being of things flows from the Word, as from a kind of primordial principle, and this flow is terminated in the being which they have in their own nature.

Reply Obj. 1. Evening and morning in the angelic knowledge are not taken as compared to the admixture of darkness, but as compared to beginning and end. Or else it can be said, as Augustine puts it (*Gen. ad lit.* iv, 23),[1] that there is nothing to prevent us from calling something light in comparison with one thing and darkness with respect to another. In the same way the life of the faithful and the just is called light in comparison with the wicked, according to Eph. 5. 8: *You were heretofore darkness; but now, light in the Lord;* yet this very life of the faithful, when set in contrast to the life of glory, is termed darkness, according to II Pet. 1. 19: *You have the firm prophetic word, whereunto you do well to attend, as to a light that shineth in a dark place.* So the angel's knowledge by which he knows things in their own nature is day in comparison with ignorance or error; yet it is dark in comparison with the vision of the Word.

Reply Obj. 2. The morning and evening knowledge belong to the day, that is, to the enlightened angels, who are set apart from the darkness, that is, from the evil spirits. The good angels, while knowing the creature, do not adhere to it, for that would be to turn to darkness and to night, but they refer this back to the praise of God, in Whom, as in their principle, they know all things. Consequently after evening there is no night, but morning, so that morning is the end of the preceding day, and the beginning of the following, in so far as the angels refer to God's praise their knowledge of the preceding work. Noonday is comprised under the name of day as the middle between the two extremes. Or else the noon can be referred to their knowledge of God Himself, Who has neither beginning nor end.

Reply Obj. 3. The angels themselves are also creatures. Accordingly the being of things in the angelic knowledge is comprised under evening knowledge, as also the being of things in their own nature.

[1] PL 34, 312.

ARTICLE 7. *Whether the Morning and Evening Knowledge Are One?*

We proceed thus to the Seventh Article: It would seem that the morning and the evening knowledge are one.

Objection 1. For it is said (Gen. 1. 5): *There was evening and morning, one day.* But by the expression day the knowledge of the angels is to be understood, as Augustine says.[2] Therefore the morning and the evening knowledge of the angels are one and the same.

Obj. 2. Further, it is impossible for one power to have two operations at the same time. But the angels are always actually knowing by their morning knowledge, because they are always beholding God and things in God, according to Matt. 18. 10. Therefore, if the evening knowledge were different from the morning, the angel could never exercise his evening knowledge.

Obj. 3. Further, the Apostle says (I Cor. 13. 10): *When that which is perfect is come, then that which is in part shall be done away.* But, if the evening knowledge be different from the morning, it is compared to it as the less perfect to the perfect. Therefore the evening knowledge cannot exist together with the morning knowledge.

On the contrary, Augustine says (*Gen. ad lit.* iv, 23):[3] "There is a vast difference between knowing anything as it is in the Word of God, and as it is in its own nature; so that the former belongs to the day, and the latter to the evening."

I answer that, As was observed (A. 6), the evening knowledge is that by which the angels know things in their proper nature. This cannot be understood as if they drew their knowledge from the proper nature of things, so that the preposition "in" denotes the relation to a principle; because, as has been already stated (Q. LV, A. 2), the angels do not draw their knowledge from things. It follows, then, that when we say "in their proper nature" we refer to the aspect of the thing known in so far as it falls under knowledge; that is to say, that the evening knowledge is in the angels in so far as they know the being of things which those things have in their own nature.

Now they know this through a twofold medium, namely, by innate species, and by the ideas of things existing in the Word. For by seeing the Word, they know not merely the being which things have in the Word, but the being as

[2] *De Gen. ad lit.,* IV, 22 (PL 34, 312); *City of God,* XI, 7 (PL 41, 322).   [3] PL 34, 312.

possessed by the things in their own nature; as God by contemplating Himself sees that being which things have in their own nature. If, therefore, it be called evening knowledge in so far as when the angels behold the Word they know the being which things have in their proper nature, then the morning and the evening knowledge are essentially one and the same, and only differ as to the things known. If it be called evening knowledge in so far as through innate forms they know the being which things have in their own natures, then the morning and the evening knowledge differ. Thus Augustine seems to understand it when he assigns one as inferior to the other (*loc. cit.*).

Reply Obj. 1. The six days, as Augustine understands them, are taken as the six classes of things known by the angels, so that the day's unity is taken according to the unity of the thing understood; which, nevertheless, can be apprehended by various ways of knowing it.

Reply Obj. 2. There can be two operations of the same power at the one time, one of which is referred to the other; as is evident when the will at the same time wills the end and the means to the end, and the intellect at the same instant understands principles and conclusions through those principles, when it has already acquired knowledge. As Augustine says, (*loc. cit.*) the evening knowledge is referred to the morning knowledge in the angels. Hence there is nothing to hinder both from being at the same time in the angels.

Reply Obj. 3. On the coming of what is perfect, the opposite imperfect is done away; just as faith, which is of the things that are not seen, is made void when vision succeeds. But the imperfection of the evening knowledge is not opposed to the perfection of the morning knowledge. For that a thing be known in itself is not opposite to its being known in its cause. Nor, again, is there anything contrary in knowing a thing through two mediums, one of which is more perfect and the other less perfect, just as we can have a demonstrative and a probable medium for reaching the same conclusion. In like manner the same thing can be known by the angel through the uncreated Word and through an innate species.

QUESTION LIX
The will of the angels
(*In Four Articles*)

In the next place we must treat of things concerning the will of the angels. In the first place

we shall treat of the will itself; secondly, of its movement, which is love (q. LX). Under the first heading there are four points of inquiry: (1) Whether there is will in the angels? (2) Whether the will of the angel is his nature, or his intellect? (3) Is there free choice in the angels (4) Is there an irascible and a concupiscible appetite in them?

ARTICLE 1. *Whether There Is Will in the Angels?*

We proceed thus to the First Article: It would seem that there is no will in the angels.

Objection 1. For as the Philosopher says,[1] "The will is in the reason." But there is no reason in the angels, but something higher than reason. Therefore there is no will in the angels, but something higher than the will.

Obj. 2. Further, the will is comprised under the appetite, as is evident from the Philosopher.[2] But, appetite argues something imperfect, because it is a desire of something not as yet possessed. Therefore, since there is no imperfection in the angels, especially in the blessed ones, it seems that there is no will in them.

Obj. 3. Further, the Philosopher says[3] that the will is a mover which is moved, for it is moved by the desirable thing understood. Now the angels are immovable, since they are incorporeal. Therefore there is no will in the angels.

On the contrary, Augustine says (*De Trin.* x, 12)[4] that the image of the Trinity is found in the mind according to memory, understanding, and will. But God's image is found not only in the mind of man, but also in the angelic mind, since it also is capable of knowing God. Therefore there is will in the angels.

I answer that, We must necessarily place a will in the angels. In evidence of this it must be borne in mind that since all things flow from the Divine will, all things in their own way are inclined by appetite towards good, but in different ways. Some are inclined to good by their natural inclination, without knowledge, as plants and inanimate bodies. Such inclination towards good is called a natural appetite. Others, again, are inclined towards good, but with some knowledge; not that they know the aspect of goodness, but that they know some particular good; as the sense, which knows the sweet,

---

[1] *Soul*, III, 9 (432^{b}5).　　　[2] *Ibid.*, 9, 10 (432^{b}5; 433^{a}23).
[3] *Ibid.*, 10 (433^{b}16).
[4] PL 42, 984.

the white, and so on. The inclination which follows this knowledge is called a sensitive appetite. Other things, again, have an inclination towards good, but with a knowledge whereby they know the aspect of good itself; this is proper to the intellect. This is most perfectly inclined towards good; not, indeed, as if it were merely guided by another towards good, like things devoid of knowledge, nor towards some particular good only, as things which have only sensitive knowledge, but as inclined towards good universal in itself. Such inclination is termed will. Accordingly, since the angels by their intellect know the universal aspect of good itself, it is manifest that there is a will in them.

Reply Obj. 1. Reason transcends sense in a different way from that in which intellect surpasses reason. Reason surpasses sense according to the diversity of the things known, for sense is of particulars, while reason is of universals. Therefore there must be one appetite tending towards the universal good, which appetite belongs to reason, and another with a tendency towards particular good, which appetite belongs to sense. But intellect and reason differ as to their manner of knowing, because the intellect knows by simple intuition, while reason knows by a process of discursion from one thing to another. Nevertheless by such discursion reason comes to know what intellect learns without it, namely, the universal. Consequently the object presented to the appetitive power on the part of reason and on the part of intellect is the same. Therefore in the angels, who are only intellectual, there is no appetite higher than the will.

Reply Obj. 2. Although the name of the appetitive part is derived from seeking things not yet possessed, yet the appetitive part reaches out not to these things only, but also to many other things; thus the name of a stone (*lapis*) is derived from injuring the foot (*læsione pedis*), though not this alone belongs to a stone. In the same way the irascible power is so denominated from anger (*ira*), though at the same time there are several other passions in it, as hope, daring, and the rest.

Reply Obj. 3. The will is called a mover which is moved according as to will and to understand are termed movements of a kind; and there is nothing to prevent movement of this kind from existing in the angels, since such movement is "the act of a perfect agent," as stated in the book on the *Soul*.[1]

[1] Aristotle, III, 7 (431ᵇ6).

ARTICLE 2. *Whether in the Angels the Will Differs from the Intellect?*

We proceed thus to the Second Article: It would seem that in the angels the will does not differ from the intellect and from the nature.

Objection 1. For an angel is more simple than a natural body. But a natural body is inclined through its form towards its end, which is its good. Therefore much more so is the angel. Now the angel's form is either the nature itself in which he subsists, or else it is the species within his intellect. Therefore the angel inclines towards the good through his own nature, and through an intelligible species. But such inclination towards the good belongs to the will. Therefore the will of the angel does not differ from his nature or his intellect.

Obj. 2. Further, the object of the intellect is the true, while the object of the will is the good. Now the good and the true differ not really but only logically (Q. XVI, A. 4). Therefore will and intellect are not really different.

Obj. 3. Further, the distinction of common and proper does not differentiate the powers, for the same power of sight perceives colour and whiteness. But the good and the true seem to be related to one another as common to particular; for the true is a particular good, namely, of the intellect. Therefore the will, whose object is the good, does not differ from the intellect, whose object is the true.

On the contrary, The will in the angels regards good things only, while their intellect regards both good and evil things, for they know both. Therefore the will of the angels is distinct from their intellect.

I answer that, In the angels the will is a special force or power, which is neither their nature nor their intellect. That it is not their nature is manifest from this, that the nature or essence of a thing is completely comprised within it; whatever, then, extends to anything beyond it, is not its essence. Hence we see in natural bodies that the inclination to being does not come from anything superadded to the essence, but from the matter which desires being before possessing it, and from the form which keeps it in such being when once it exists. But the inclination towards something extrinsic comes from something superadded to the essence; as tendency to a place comes from heaviness or lightness, while the inclination to make something like itself comes from the active qualities.

Now the will has a natural tendency towards

good. Consequently there alone are essence and will the same where all good is contained within the essence of him who wills, that is to say, in God, Who wills nothing beyond Himself except on account of His goodness. This cannot be said of any creature, because infinite goodness is outside of the essence of any caused thing. Accordingly, neither the will of the angel, nor that of any creature, can be the same thing as its essence.

In like manner neither can the will be the same thing as the intellect of angel or man. For knowledge comes about in so far as the thing known is within the knower. Consequently the intellect extends itself to what is outside it, according as what in its essence is outside it is disposed to be somehow within it. On the other hand, the will goes out to what is beyond it, according as by a kind of inclination it tends, in some manner, to what is outside it. But the power that has within itself what exists outside it, is not the same as the power that tends to the thing outside. Consequently intellect and will must necessarily be different powers in every creature. It is not so with God, for He has within Himself both universal being and the universal good. Therefore both intellect and will are His essence.

Reply Obj. 1. A natural body is moved to its own being by its substantial form, while it is inclined to something outside by something additional, as has been said.

Reply Obj. 2. Powers are not differentiated by any material difference of their objects, but according to their formal distinction, which is taken from the nature of the object. Consequently the diversity derived from the notion of good and true suffices for the difference of intellect and will.

Reply Obj. 3. Because the good and the true are really convertible, it follows that the good is understood by the intellect under the aspect of the true, while the true is desired by the will under the aspect of the good. Nevertheless the diversity of their aspects is sufficient for diversifying the powers, as was said above (*ad* 2).

ARTICLE 3. *Whether There Is Free Choice in the Angels?*

We proceed thus to the Third Article: It would seem that there is no free choice in the angels.

Objection 1. For the act of free choice is to choose. But there can be no choice with the angels, because "choice is the desire of something after taking counsel, while counsel is a kind of inquiry," as stated in the *Ethics*.[1] But the angels' knowledge is not the result of inquiring, for this pertains to the discursiveness of reason. Therefore it appears that there is no free choice in the angels.

Obj. 2. Further, free choice implies indifference to alternatives. But in the angels on the part of their intellect there is no such indifference, because, as was observed already (Q. LVIII, A. 5), their intellect is not deceived as to things which are naturally intelligible to them. Therefore neither on the part of their appetite can there be free choice.

Obj. 3. Further, the natural endowments of the angels belong to them according to degrees of more or less, because in the higher angels the intellectual nature is more perfect than in the lower. But free choice does not admit of degrees. Therefore there is no free choice in them.

On the contrary, Free choice is part of man's dignity. But the angels' dignity surpasses that of men. Therefore, since free choice is in men, with much more reason is it in the angels.

I answer that, There are some things which act not from any choice, but, as it were, moved and made to act by others; just as the arrow is directed to the target by the archer. Others act from some kind of choice, but not from free choice, such as irrational animals, for the sheep flies from the wolf by a kind of judgment whereby it considers it to be hurtful to itself; such a judgment is not a free one, but implanted by nature. Only an agent endowed with an intellect can act with a judgment which is free in so far as it apprehends the common notion of good, from which it can judge this or the other thing to be good. Consequently, wherever there is intellect, there is free choice. It is therefore manifest that just as there is intellect, so is there free choice in the angels, and in a higher degree of perfection than in man.

Reply Obj. 1. The Philosopher is speaking of choice as it is in man. As a man's estimation in speculative matters differs from an angel's in this, that the one needs not to inquire, while the other does so need, so is it in practical matters. Hence there is choice in the angels, yet not with the inquisitive deliberation of counsel, but by the immediate acceptance of truth.

Reply Obj. 2. As was observed already (A. 2, Q. XII, A. 4), knowledge is effected by the presence of the known within the knower. Now it is a mark of imperfection in anything not to have within it what it should naturally have. Consequently an angel would not be perfect in

[1] Aristotle, III, 2, 3 ($1112^{a}15$; $1112^{b}23$).

his nature if his intellect were not determined to every truth which he can know naturally. But the act of the appetitive power comes from the fact that the affection is directed to something outside. Yet the perfection of a thing does not depend on everything to which it is inclined, but only from something which is higher than it. Therefore it does not argue imperfection in an angel if his will be not determined with regard to things beneath him; but it would argue imperfection in him, were he to be indeterminate to what is above him.

Reply Obj. 3. Free choice exists in a nobler manner in the higher angels than it does in the lower, as also does the judgment of the intellect. Yet it is true that liberty, in so far as the removal of compulsion is considered, is not susceptible of greater and less degree; because privations and negations are not lessened nor increased of themselves, but only by their cause, or through the addition of some qualification.

ARTICLE 4. *Whether There Is an Irascible and a Concupiscible Appetite in the Angels?*

We proceed thus to the Fourth Article: It would seem that there is an irascible and a concupiscible appetite in the angels.

Objection 1. For Dionysius says (*Div. Nom.* iv)[1] that in the demons there is "unreasonable fury and wild concupiscence." But demons are of the same nature as angels, for sin has not altered their nature. Therefore there is an irascible and a concupiscible appetite in the angels.

Obj. 2. Further, love and joy are in the concupiscible, while anger, hope, and fear, are in the irascible appetite. But in the Sacred Scriptures these things are attributed both to the good and to the wicked angels. Therefore there is an irascible and a concupiscible appetite in the angels.

Obj. 3. Further, some virtues are said to reside in the irascible appetite and some in the concupiscible; thus charity and temperance appear to be in the concupiscible, while hope and fortitude are in the irascible. But these virtues are in the angels. Therefore there is both a concupiscible and an irascible appetite in the angels.

On the contrary, The Philosopher says[2] that the irascible and concupiscible are in the sensitive part, which does not exist in angels. Consequently there is no irascible or concupiscible appetite in the angels.

I answer that, The intellectual appetite is not divided into irascible and concupiscible; only the sensitive appetite is so divided. The reason of this is because, since the powers are distinguished from one another not according to the material distinction of objects but only by the formal aspect of objects, if to any power there corresponds an object according to some common notion, there will be no distinction of powers according to the diversity of the proper objects contained under that common notion. Just as, if the proper object of the power of sight be colour as such, then there are not several powers of sight distinguished according to the difference of black and white; but if the proper object of any power were white, as white, then the power of seeing white would be distinguished from the power of seeing black.

Now it is quite evident from what has been said (A. 1; Q. XVI, A. 1), that the object of the intellectual appetite, which is called the will, is good according to the common notion of goodness; nor can there be any appetite except of what is good. Hence, in the intellectual part, the appetite is not divided according to the distinction of some particular goods, as the sensitive appetite is divided, which does not consider the good according to its common notion, but some particular good. Accordingly, since there exists in the angels only an intellectual appetite, their appetite is not distinguished into irascible and concupiscible, but remains undivided. And it is called the will.

Reply Obj. 1. Fury and concupiscence are metaphorically said to be in the demons, as anger is sometimes attributed to God, on account of the resemblance in the effect.

Reply Obj. 2. Love and joy, in so far as they are passions, are in the concupiscible appetite, but in so far as they express a simple act of the will, they are in the intellectual part; in this sense to love is to wish well to anyone, and to rejoice is for the will to repose in some good possessed. Universally speaking, none of these things is said of the angels, as by way of passions, as Augustine says.[3]

Reply Obj. 3. Charity, as a virtue, is not in the concupiscible appetite, but in the will, because the object of the concupiscible appetite is the good as delightful to the senses. But the Divine goodness, which is the object of charity, is not of any such kind. For the same reason it must be said that hope does not exist in the irascible appetite, because the object of the irascible appetite is something arduous belonging to the sensible order, which the virtue of hope

[1] Sect. 23 (PG 3, 725).   [2] *Soul*, III, 9 (432^{b}6).   [3] *City of God*, IX, 5 (PL 41, 261).

does not regard, since the object of hope is something arduous and divine. Temperance, however, considered as a human virtue, deals with the desires of sensible pleasures, which belong to the concupiscible power. Similarly, fortitude has to do with daring and fear, which reside in the irascible part. Consequently temperance, in so far as it is a human virtue, resides in the concupiscible part, and fortitude in the irascible. But they do not exist in the angels in this manner. For in them there are no passions of concupiscence, nor of fear and daring, which have to be regulated by temperance and fortitude. But temperance is said of them according as in moderation they display their will in conformity with the Divine will. Fortitude is likewise attributed to them, in so far as they firmly carry out the Divine will. All of this is done by their will, and not by the irascible or concupiscible appetite.

QUESTION LX

OF THE LOVE OR DILECTION OF THE ANGELS

(In Five Articles)

THE next subject for our consideration is that act of the will which is love or dilection; because every act of the appetitive power comes of love.

Under this heading there are five points of inquiry: (1) Whether there is natural love in the angels? (2) Whether there is in them love of choice? (3) Whether the angel loves himself with natural love or with love of choice? (4) Whether one angel loves another with natural love as he loves himself? (5) Whether the angel loves God more than self with natural love?

ARTICLE 1. *Whether There Is Natural Love or Dilection in an Angel?*

We proceed thus to the First Article: It would seem that there is no natural love or dilection in the angels.

Objection 1. For, natural love is divided against intellectual love, as stated by Dionysius (*Div. Nom.* iv).[1] But an angel's love is intellectual. Therefore it is not natural.

Obj. 2. Further, those who love with natural love are more acted upon than active in themselves, for nothing has control over its own nature. Now the angels are not acted upon, but act of themselves, because they possess free choice, as was shown above (Q. LIX, A. 3). Consequently there is no natural love in them.

[1] Sect. 15 (PG 3, 713).

Obj. 3. Further, every love is either lawful or unlawful. Now lawful love pertains to charity, while unlawful love pertains to wickedness. But neither of these pertains to nature, because charity is above nature, while wickedness is against nature. Therefore there is no natural love in the angels.

On the contrary, Love results from knowledge, for nothing is loved unless it is known, as Augustine says (*De Trin.* x, 1, 2).[2] But there is natural knowledge in the angels. Therefore there is also natural love.

I answer that, We must necessarily place natural love in the angels. In evidence of this we must bear in mind that what comes first is always kept in what comes after it. Now nature comes before intellect, because the nature of any thing is its essence. Consequently whatever belongs to nature must be preserved likewise in such subjects as have intellect. But it is common to every nature to have some inclination, and this is its natural appetite or love. This inclination is found to exist differently in different natures, but in each according to its mode. Consequently, in the intellectual nature there is to be found a natural inclination coming from the will; in the sensitive nature, according to the sensitive appetite; but in a nature devoid of knowledge, only according to the tendency of the nature to something. Therefore, since an angel is an intellectual nature, there must be a natural love in his will.

Reply Obj. 1. Intellectual love is divided against the natural love which is merely natural, in so far as it belongs to a nature which has not likewise the perfection of either sense or intellect.

Reply Obj. 2. All things in the world are moved to act by something else except the First Agent, Who acts in such a manner that He is in no way moved to act by another, and in Whom, nature and will are the same. So there is nothing unfitting in an angel being moved to act in so far as such natural inclination is implanted in him by the Author of his nature. Yet he is not so moved to act that he does not act himself, because he has a free will.

Reply Obj. 3. As natural knowledge is always true, so is natural love always well regulated, because natural love is nothing else than the inclination implanted in nature by its Author. To say that a natural inclination is not well regulated is to detract from the Author of nature. Yet the rectitude of natural love is different from the rectitude of charity and virtue, be-

[2] PL 42, 973, 975; cf. also VIII, 4 (951).

cause the one rectitude perfects the other; even so the truth of natural knowledge is of one kind, and the truth of infused or acquired knowledge is of another.

ARTICLE 2. *Whether There Is Love of Choice in the Angels?*

We proceed thus to the Second Article: It would seem that there is no love of choice in the angels.

Objection 1. For love of choice appears to be rational love, since choice follows counsel, which lies in inquiry, as stated in the *Ethics*.[1] Now rational love is contrasted with intellectual, which is proper to angels, as is said (*Div. Nom.* iv).[2] Therefore there is no love of choice in the angels.

Obj. 2. Further, the angels have only natural knowledge besides such as is infused, since they do not proceed by discourse from principles to acquire conclusions. Hence they are disposed to everything they can naturally know, as our intellect is disposed towards first principles, which it can know naturally. Now love follows knowledge, as has been already stated (A. 1; Q. XVI, A. 1). Consequently, besides their love from grace, there is only natural love in the angels. Therefore there is no love of choice in them.

On the contrary, We neither merit nor demerit by our natural acts. But by their love the angels merit or demerit. Therefore there is love of choice in them.

I answer that, There exists in the angels a natural love, and a love of choice. Their natural love is the principle of their love of choice, because, what pertains to that which precedes, has always the nature of a principle. Therefore, since nature is first in everything, what belongs to nature must be a principle in everything.

This appears in man, with respect to both his intellect and his will. For the intellect knows principles naturally; and this knowledge in man causes the knowledge of conclusions, which are known by him not naturally, but by discovery, or by teaching. In like manner, the end is to the will as the principle to the intellect, as is laid down in the *Physics*.[3] Consequently the will tends naturally to its last end; for every man naturally wills happiness, and all other wills are caused by this natural will, since whatever a man wills he wills on account of the end. Therefore the love of that good, which a man naturally wills as an end, is his natural love; but the love which comes of this, which is of a good

[1] Aristotle, III, 2 (1112ª15).   [2] Sect. 16 (PG 3, 713).
[3] Aristotle, II, 9 (200ª22).

loved for the sake of the end, is the love of choice.

There is however a difference on the part of the intellect and on the part of the will. Because, as was stated already (Q. LIX, A. 2), the intellect's knowledge is brought about by the presence of the thing known within the knower. It comes of the imperfection of man's intellectual nature that his mind does not simultaneously possess all things capable of being understood, but only a few things from which he is moved in a measure to grasp other things. The act of the appetitive power, on the contrary, follows the inclination of man towards things; some of which are good in themselves, and consequently are desirable in themselves, while others have the aspect of good only in relation to something else, and are desirable on account of something else. Consequently it does not argue imperfection in the person desiring for him to seek one thing naturally as his end, and something else from choice as ordered to such end. Therefore, since the intellectual nature of the angels is perfect, only natural and not discursive knowledge is to be found in them, but there is to be found in them both natural love and love of choice. In saying all this, we are passing over all that regards those things which are above nature, since nature is not the sufficient principle of these things. But we shall speak of them later on (Q. LXII).

Reply Obj. 1. Not all love of choice is rational love, according as rational is contrasted to intellectual love. For that is called rational love which follows discursive knowledge, but, as was said above (Q. LIX, A. 3, Ans. 1), when treating of free choice, every choice does not follow a discursive act of the reason, but only human choice. Consequently the conclusion does not follow.

The reply to the second objection follows from what has been said.

ARTICLE 3. *Whether the Angel Loves Himself with Both Natural Love, and Love of Choice?*

We proceed thus to the Third Article: It would seem that the angel does not love himself both with a natural love and a love of choice.

Objection 1. For, as was said (A. 2), natural love regards the end itself, while love of choice regards the means to the end. But the same thing, in the same respect, cannot be both the end and a means to the end. Therefore natural love and the love of choice cannot have the same object.

Obj. 2. Further, as Dionysius observes (*Div*

Nom. iv):[1] "Love is a uniting and a binding power." But uniting and binding imply various things brought together into one. Therefore the angel cannot love himself.

Obj. 3. Further, love is a kind of movement. But every movement tends towards something else. Therefore it seems that an angel cannot love himself with either natural or elective love.

On the contrary, The Philosopher says:[2] "Love for others comes of love for oneself."

I answer that, Since the object of love is good, and good is to be found both in substance and in accident, as is clear from the *Ethics,*[3] a thing may be loved in two ways: first of all as a subsisting good; and secondly as an accidental or inherent good. That is loved as a subsisting good which is so loved that we wish well to it. But that which we wish for another is loved as an accidental or inherent good; thus knowledge is loved not that any good may come to it but that it may be possessed. This kind of love has been called by the name of concupiscence, while the first is called friendship.

Now it is manifest that in things devoid of knowledge everything naturally seeks to procure what is good for itself; as fire seeks to mount upwards. Consequently both angel and man naturally seek their own good and perfection. This is to love self. Hence angel and man naturally love self, in so far as by natural appetite each desires what is good for self. On the other hand, each loves self with the love of choice, in so far as from choice he wishes for something which will benefit himself.

Reply Obj. 1. It is not under the same but under quite different aspects that an angel or a man loves self with natural and with elective love, as was observed above.

Reply Obj. 2. As to be one is more than to be united, so there is more oneness in love which is directed to self than in love which unites one to others. Dionysius used the terms uniting and binding in order to show the derivation of love from self to things outside self; just as uniting is derived from unity.

Reply Obj. 3. As love is an action which remains within the agent, so also is it a movement which remains within the lover, but does not of necessity tend towards something else; yet it can be reflected back upon the lover so that he loves himself, just as knowledge is reflected back upon the knower in such a way that he knows himself.

[1] Sect. 15 (PG 3, 713).
[2] *Ethics,* IX, 4 (1166ª1).
[3] Aristotle, I, 6 (1096ª19).

ARTICLE 4. *Whether an Angel Loves Another with Natural Love as He Loves Himself?*

We proceed thus to the Fourth Article: It would seem that an angel does not love another with natural love as he loves himself.

Objection 1. For love follows knowledge. But an angel does not know another as he knows himself, because he knows himself by his essence, while he knows another by his likeness, as was said above (Q. LVI, AA. 1, 2). Therefore it seems that one angel does not love another with natural love as he loves himself.

Obj. 2. Further, the cause is more powerful than the effect; and the principle than what is derived from it. But love for another comes of love for self, as the Philosopher says.[4] Therefore one angel does not love another as himself, but loves himself more.

Obj. 3. Further, natural love is of something as an end, and cannot be taken away. But one angel is not the end of another; and again, such love can be taken away from him, as is the case with the demons, who have no love for the good angels. Therefore an angel does not love another with natural love as he loves himself.

On the contrary, That seems to be natural which is found in all things, even those lacking reason. But, *every beast loves its like,* as is said Ecclus. 13. 19. Therefore an angel naturally loves another as he loves himself.

I answer that, As was observed (A. 3), both angel and man naturally loves self. Now what is one with a thing is that thing itself. Consequently every thing loves what is one with itself. So, if this be one with it by natural union, it loves it with natural love; but if it be one with it by union, which is not natural, then it loves it with love which is not natural. Thus a man loves his fellow citizen with the love of political virtue, while he loves a blood relation with natural affection, in so far as he is one with him in the principle of natural generation.

Now it is evident that what is generically or specifically one with another is one according to nature. And so everything loves another which is one with it in species with a natural affection, in so far as it loves its own species. This is manifest even in things devoid of knowledge; for fire has a natural inclination to communicate its form to another thing, in which consists this other thing's good, as it is naturally inclined to seek its own good, namely, to be borne upwards.

So then, it must be said that one angel loves

[4] *Ethics,* IX, 4 (1166ª1).

another with natural affection in so far as he is one with him in nature. But so far as an angel has something else in common with another angel, or differs from him in other respects, he does not love him with natural love.

Reply Obj. 1. The expression "as himself" in one way can qualify the knowledge and the love on the part of the one known and loved, and thus one angel knows another as himself, because he knows the other to be even as he knows himself to be. In another way the expression can qualify the knowledge and the love on the part of the knower and lover. And thus one angel does not know another as himself, because he knows himself by his essence, and the other not by the other's essence. In like manner he does not love another as he loves himself, because he loves himself by his own will, but he does not love another by the other's will.

Reply Obj. 2. The expression "as" does not denote equality, but likeness. For since natural affection rests upon natural unity, the angel naturally loves less what is less one with him. Consequently he loves more what is numerically one with himself than what is one only generically or specifically. But it is natural for him to have a like love for another as for himself, in this respect, that as he loves self in wishing well to self, so he loves another in wishing well to him.

Reply Obj. 3. Natural love is said to be of the end itself, not as of that end to which good is willed, but rather as of that good which one wills for oneself, and in consequence for another, as united to oneself. Nor can such natural love be stripped from the wicked angels without their still retaining a natural affection towards the good angels, in so far as they share the same nature with them. But they hate them in so far as they are unlike them according to uprightness and improbity.

ARTICLE 5. *Whether an Angel by Natural Love Loves God More Than He Loves Himself?*

We proceed thus to the Fifth Article: It would seem that the angel does not love God by natural love more than he loves himself.

Objection 1. For, as was stated (A. 4), natural love rests upon natural union. Now the Divine nature is far above the angelic nature. Therefore according to natural love the angel loves God less than self, or even than another angel.

Obj. 2. Further, That on account of which a thing is such, is still more so. But every one loves another with natural love for his own sake, because one thing loves another as good for it-

self. Therefore the angel does not love God more than self with natural love.

Obj. 3. Further, nature is self-centred in its operation, for we behold every agent acting naturally for its own preservation. But nature's operation would not be self-centred were it to tend towards anything else more than to nature itself. Therefore the angel does not love God more than himself from natural love.

Obj. 4. Further, it is proper to charity to love God more than self. But to love from charity is not natural to the angels, for "it is poured out upon their hearts by the Holy Spirit Who is given to them," as Augustine says.[1] Therefore the angels do not love God more than themselves by natural love.

Obj. 5. Further, natural love lasts as long as nature endures. But the love of God more than self does not remain in the angel or man who sins; for, as Augustine says,[2] "Two loves have made two cities; namely, love of self unto the contempt of God has made the earthly city, while love of God unto the contempt of self has made the heavenly city." Therefore it is not natural to love God more than self.

On the contrary, All the moral precepts of the law come of the law of nature. But the precept of loving God more than self is a moral precept of the law. Therefore, it is of the law of nature. Consequently from natural love the angel loves God more than himself.

I answer that, There have been some who maintained[3] that an angel loves God more than himself with natural love, both as to the love of concupiscence, through his seeking the Divine good for himself rather than his own good, and in a fashion, as to the love of friendship, in so far as he naturally desires a greater good to God than to himself, because he naturally wishes God to be God, while as for himself, he wills to have his own nature. But absolutely speaking, out of natural love he loves himself more than he does God, because he naturally loves himself before God, and with greater intensity.

The falsity of such an opinion stands in evidence, if we consider where natural movement tends in the natural order of things, because the natural tendency of things devoid of reason shows the nature of the natural inclination residing in the will of an intellectual nature. Now, in natural things, everything which, as such, nat-

---

[1] *City of God,* XII, 9 (PL 41, 357).
[2] *Ibid.,* XIV, 28 (PL 41, 436).
[3] Wm. of Auxerre, *Summa Aurea,* II, 1, 4 (fol. 36rb). Cf. Albertus Magnus, *In Sent.,* II, dist. III, a18 (BO XXVII, 98).

urally belongs to another, is principally and more strongly inclined to that other to which it belongs than towards itself. Such a natural tendency is evidenced from things which are moved according to nature, because "according as a thing is moved naturally, it has an inborn aptitude to be thus moved," as stated in the *Physics*.[1] For we observe that the part naturally exposes itself in order to safeguard the whole; as, for instance, the hand is without deliberation exposed to the blow for the whole body's safety. And since reason copies nature, we find the same imitation among the political virtues; for it pertains to the virtuous citizen to expose himself to the danger of death for the conservation of the whole commonwealth; and if man were a natural part of this state, then such inclination would be natural to him.

Consequently, since God is the universal good, and under this good both man and angel and all creatures are comprised, because every creature according to its being naturally belongs to God, it follows that from natural love angel and man alike love God before themselves and with a greater love. Otherwise, if either of them loved self more than God, it would follow that natural love would be perverse, and that it would not be perfected but destroyed by charity.

Reply Obj. 1. Such reasoning holds good of things divided on a basis of equality, of which one is not the reason of the existence and goodness of the other; for in such natures each loves itself naturally more than it does the other, since it is more one with itself than it is with the other. But where one is the whole reason of the existence and goodness of the other, that one is naturally more loved than self; because, as we said above, each part naturally loves the whole more than itself, and each individual naturally loves the good of the species more than its own particular good. Now God is not only the good of one species, but is absolutely the universal good; hence everything in its own way naturally loves God more than itself.

Reply Obj. 2. When it is said that God is loved by an angel "in so far" as He is good to the angel, if the expression "in so far" denotes an end, then it is false; for he does not naturally love God for his own good, but for God's sake. If it denotes the nature of love on the lover's part, then it is true, for it would not be in the nature of anyone to love God, except from this —that everything is dependent on that good which is God.

Reply Obj. 3. Nature's operation is self-

[1] Aristotle, II, 8 (199ª9).

centred not merely as to what is particular in it but much more as to what is common; for everything is inclined to preserve not merely its individuality, but likewise its species. And much more has everything a natural inclination towards what is the absolutely universal good.

Reply Obj. 4. God, in so far as He is the universal good, from Whom every natural good depends, is loved by everything with natural love. So far as He is the good which naturally makes all happy with supernatural Happiness, He is loved with the love of charity.

Reply Obj. 5. Since God's substance and universal goodness are one and the same, all who behold God's essence are by the same movement of love moved towards the Divine essence as it is distinct from other things, and according as it is the universal good. And because He is naturally loved by all so far as He is the universal good, it is impossible that whoever sees Him in His essence should not love Him. But such as do not behold His essence know him by some particular effects, which are sometimes opposed to their will. So in this way they are said to hate God; yet nevertheless, so far as He is the universal good of all, everything naturally loves God more than itself.

QUESTION LXI

OF THE PRODUCTION OF THE ANGELS IN THE ORDER OF NATURAL BEING

(*In Four Articles*)

AFTER dealing with the nature of the angels, their knowledge and will, it now remains for us to treat of their creation, or, speaking in a general way, of their origin. Such consideration is threefold. In the first place we must see how they were brought into natural being; secondly, how they were made perfect in grace or glory (Q. LXII); and thirdly, how some of them became wicked (Q. LXIII).

Under the first heading there are four points of inquiry: (1) Whether the angel has a cause of his being? (2) Whether he has existed from eternity? (3) Whether he was created before corporeal creatures? (4) Whether the angels were created in the empyrean heaven?

ARTICLE 1. *Whether the Angels Have a Cause of Their Being?*

We proceed thus to the First Article: It would seem that the angels have no cause of their being.

Objection 1. For the first chapter of Genesis treats of things created by God. But there is no mention of angels. Therefore the angels were not created by God.

Obj. 2. Further, the Philosopher says[1] that if any substance be a form "without matter, straightway it is being and unity of itself, and has no cause of its being and unity." But the angels are immaterial forms, as was shown above (Q. L, A. 2). Therefore they have no cause of their being.

Obj. 3. Further, whatever is produced by any agent, from the very fact of its being produced, receives form from it. But since the angels are forms, they do not derive their form from any agent. Therefore the angels have no active cause.

On the contrary, It is said (Ps. 148. 2): *Praise ye Him all His angels;* and further on, *verse* 5: *For He spoke and they were made.*

I answer that, It must be affirmed that angels and everything that is, except God, were made by God. God alone is His own being, while in everything else the essence differs from the being, as was shown above (Q. III, A. 4; Q. VII, A. I, ANS. 3; Q. XLIV, A. I). From this it is clear that God alone is being through His own essence, while all other things are beings by participation. Now whatever is by participation is caused by what is essentially; as everything ignited is caused by fire. Consequently the angels, of necessity, were made by God.

Reply Obj. 1. Augustine says[2] that "the angels were not passed over in that account of the first creation of things, but are designated by the name of heavens, or of light." And they were either passed over, or else designated by the names of corporeal things, because Moses was addressing an undeveloped people, as yet incapable of understanding an incorporeal nature; and if it had been divulged that there were creatures existing beyond corporeal nature, it would have proved to them an occasion of idolatry, to which they were inclined, and from which Moses especially meant to restrain them.

Reply Obj. 2. Substances that are subsisting forms have no formal cause of their being and unity, nor an agent cause for changing matter from a state of potency to act; but they have a cause productive of their entire substance.

From this the solution of the third difficulty is manifest.

ARTICLE 2. *Whether the Angel Was Produced by God from Eternity?*

We proceed thus to the Second Article: It would seem that the angel was produced by God from eternity.

Objection 1. For God is the cause of the angel by His being, for He does not act through something added to His essence. But His being is eternal. Therefore He produced the angels from eternity.

Obj. 2. Further, everything which exists at one period and not at another is subject to time. But the angel is above time, as is laid down in the Book *De Causis.*[3] Therefore the angel is not at one time existing and at another non-existing, but exists always.

Obj. 3. Further, Augustine proves[4] the soul's incorruptibility by the fact that the mind is capable of truth. But as truth is incorruptible, so is it eternal. Therefore the intellectual nature of the soul and of the angel is not only incorruptible, but likewise eternal.

On the contrary, It is said (Proverbs 8. 22), in the person of begotten Wisdom: *The Lord possessed me in the beginning of His ways, before He made anything from the beginning.* But, as was shown above (A. 1), the angels were made by God. Therefore at one time the angels were not.

I answer that, God alone, Father, Son, and Holy Ghost, is from eternity. Catholic Faith holds this without doubt, and everything to the contrary must be rejected as heretical. For God so produced creatures that He made them from nothing, that is, after there had been nothing.

Reply Obj. 1. God's being is His will. So the fact that God produced the angels and other creatures by His being does not exclude that He made them also by His will. But, as was shown above (Q. XIX, A. 3; Q. XLVI, A. I), God's will does not act by necessity in producing creatures. Therefore He produced such as He willed, and when He willed.

Reply Obj. 2. An angel is above that time which is the measure of the movement of the heavens, because he is above every movement of a corporeal nature. Nevertheless he is not above the time which is the measure of the succession of his being after his non-being, and which is also the measure of the succession which is in his operations. Hence Augustine says (*Gen. ad lit.* viii, 20, 22)[5] that "God

---

[1] *Metaphysics,* VIII, 6 (1045ª36).
[2] *City of God,* XI, 9, 33 (PL 41, 323, 347).

[3] Sect. 2 (BA 165); this is said of the soul rather than of angels. Cf. above, Q. LVII, A. 3, obj. 3.
[4] *Solil.,* II, 19 (PL 32, 901).   [5] PL 34, 388, 389.

moves the spiritual creature according to time."

Reply Obj. 3. Angels and intellectual souls are incorruptible by the very fact of their having a nature whereby they are capable of truth. But they did not possess this nature from eternity. It was bestowed upon them when God Himself willed it. Consequently it does not follow that the angels existed from eternity.

ARTICLE 3. *Whether the Angels Were Created Before the Corporeal World?*

We proceed thus to the Third Article: It would seem that the angels were created before the corporeal world.

Objection 1. For Jerome says (*In Ep. ad Tit.* i, 2)[1]: "Six thousand years of our time have not yet elapsed; yet how shall we measure the time, how shall we count the ages, in which the Angels, Thrones, Dominations, and the other orders served God?" Damascene also says (*De Fid. Orth.* ii)[2]: "Some say that the angels were begotten before all creation; as Gregory the Theologian declares,[3] He first of all devised the angelic and heavenly powers, and the devising was the making thereof."

Obj. 2. Further, the angelic nature stands midway between the Divine and the corporeal natures. But the Divine nature is from eternity, while corporeal nature is from time. Therefore the angelic nature was produced before the creation of time, and after eternity.

Obj. 3. Further, the angelic nature is more remote from the corporeal nature than one corporeal nature is from another. But one corporeal nature was made before another. Hence the six days of the production of things are set forth in the opening of Genesis. Much more, therefore, was the angelic nature made before every corporeal nature.

On the contrary, It is said (Gen. 1. 1): *In the beginning God created heaven and earth.* Now, this would not be true if anything had been created previously. Consequently the angels were not created before corporeal nature.

I answer that, There is a twofold opinion on this point to be found in the writings of the Fathers. The more probable one holds that the angels were created at the same time as corporeal creatures. For the angels are part of the universe; they do not constitute one universe of themselves, but both they and corporeal natures unite in constituting one universe. This appears from the relationship of creature to creature, because the order of things to each other makes up the good of the universe. But no part is perfect if separate from its whole. Consequently it is improbable that God, Whose *works are perfect,* as it is said Deut. 32. 4, should have created the angelic creature before other creatures. At the same time the contrary is not to be deemed erroneous; especially on account of the opinion of Gregory Nazianzen,[4] whose authority in Christian doctrine is of such weight that no one has ever raised objection to his teaching, as is also the case with the doctrine of Athanasius, as Jerome says.[5]

Reply Obj. 1. Jerome is speaking according to the teaching of the Greek Fathers, all of whom hold the creation of the angels to have taken place previously to that of the corporeal world.

Reply Obj. 2. God is not a part of, but is above the whole universe, possessing within Himself the entire perfection of the universe in a more eminent way. But an angel is a part of the universe. Hence the comparison does not hold.

Reply Obj. 3. All corporeal creatures are one in matter, while the angels do not agree with them in matter. Consequently the creation of the matter of the corporeal creature involves in a manner the creation of all things; but the creation of the angels does not involve creation of the universe.

If *the contrary* view be held, then in the text of Genesis 1., *In the beginning God created heaven and earth,* the words, *In the beginning,* must be interpreted, "In the Son," or "In the beginning of time"; but not, "In the beginning, before which there was nothing," unless we say, "Before which there was nothing of the nature of corporeal creatures."

ARTICLE 4. *Whether the Angels Were Created in the Empyrean Heaven?*

We proceed thus to the Fourth Article: It would seem that the angels were not created in the empyrean heaven.

Objection 1. For the angels are incorporeal substances. Now a substance which is incorporeal is not dependent upon a body for its existence, and as a consequence, neither is it for its being made. Therefore the angels were not created in any corporeal place.

Obj. 2. Further, Augustine remarks (*Gen. ad lit.* iii, 10),[6] that the angels were created in the

---

[1] PL 26, 594. [2] Chap. 3 (PG 94, 873).
[3] Orat. xxxviii, *In Theoph.*, (PG 36, 320).

[4] Orat. xxxviii, *In Theoph.*, (PG 36, 320).
[5] Cf. Rufinus, *Prol. in Orat. Greg. Naz.* (CV XLVI, 5.3; cf. PG 35, 305).
[6] PL 34, 284; also, VIII, 20 (388).

upper atmosphere: therefore not in the empyrean heaven.

Obj. 3. Further, the empyrean heaven is said to be the highest heaven. If therefore the angels were created in the empyrean heaven, it would not be fitting for them to mount up to a still higher heaven. And this is contrary to what is said in Isaias, speaking in the person of the sinning angel: *I will ascend into heaven* (Isa. 14. 13).

On the contrary, Strabus,[1] commenting on the text *In the beginning God created heaven and earth*, says that by heaven he does not mean the visible firmament, but the empyrean, that is, the fiery or intellectual firmament, which is not so styled from its heat, but from its splendour, and which was filled with angels directly it was made.

I answer that, As was observed (A. 3), the one universe is made up of corporeal and spiritual creatures. Consequently spiritual creatures were so created as to bear some relationship to the corporeal creature, and to rule over every corporeal creature. Hence it was fitting for the angels to be created in the highest corporeal place, as presiding over all corporeal nature, whether it be styled the empyrean heaven, or whatever else it be called. So Isidore says[2] that the highest heaven is the heaven of the angels, explaining the passage of Deuteronomy 10. 14: *Behold heaven is the Lord's thy God, and the heaven of heaven.*

Reply Obj. 1. The angels were not created in a corporeal place as if depending upon a body either as to their being or as to their being made, because God could have created them before all corporeal creation, as many holy Doctors hold. They were made in a corporeal place in order to show their relationship to corporeal nature, and that they are by their power in touch with bodies.

Reply Obj. 2. By the uppermost atmosphere Augustine possibly means the highest part of heaven, to which the atmosphere has a kind of proportion owing to its subtlety and transparency. Or else he is not speaking of all the angels, but only of such as sinned, who, in the opinion of some, belonged to the inferior orders. But there is nothing to hinder us from saying that the higher angels, as having an exalted and universal power over all corporeal things, were created in the highest place of the corporeal creature; while the other angels, as having

more restricted powers, were created among the inferior bodies.

Reply Obj. 3. Isaias is not speaking there of any corporeal heaven, but of the heaven of the Blessed Trinity, to which the sinning angel wished to ascend when he desired to be equal in some manner to God, as will appear later on (Q. LXIII, A. 3).

QUESTION LXII

OF THE PERFECTION OF THE ANGELS
IN THE ORDER OF GRACE AND OF GLORY
(*In Nine Articles*)

IN due sequence we have to inquire how the angels were made in the order of grace and of glory; under which heading there are nine points of inquiry: (1) Were the angels created in Happiness? (2) Did they need grace in order to turn to God? (3) Were they created in grace? (4) Did they merit their Happiness? (5) Did they at once enter into Happiness after merit? (6) Did they receive grace and glory according to their natural capacities? (7) After entering into glory, did their natural love and knowledge remain? (8) Could they have sinned afterwards? (9) After entering into glory, could they advance farther?

ARTICLE 1. *Whether the Angels Were Created in Happiness?*

We proceed thus to the First Article: It would seem that the angels were created in Happiness.

Objection 1. For it is stated (*De Eccl. Dogm.* xxix)[3] that "the angels who continue in the beatitude wherein they were created, do not of their nature possess the good they have." Therefore the angels were created in Happiness.

Obj. 2. Further, the angelic nature is nobler than the corporeal creature. But the corporeal creature at once in the beginning of its creation was made perfect and complete; nor did its lack of form precede in time its formation, but only in nature, as Augustine says (*Gen. ad lit.* i, 15).[4] Therefore neither did God create the angelic nature imperfect and incomplete. But its formation and perfection are derived from its Happiness, whereby it enjoys God. Therefore it was created blessed.

Obj. 3. Further, according to Augustine (*Gen. ad lit.* iv, 34; v, 5),[5] the things which we read of as being made in the works of the six days were all made together at one time, and so all

1 Cf. *Glossa ordin.*, on Gen. 1.1 (1, 23, F).
2 Cf. *Glossa ordin.*, on Deut. 10.14 (1, 343A). See also Isadore, *De Ord. Creatur.*, chap. 6 (PL 83, 927).

3 Gennadius, 59 (PL 58, 995).
4 PL 34, 257; also, v, 5 (326).   5 PL 34, 319, 326.

the six days must have existed instantly from the beginning of creation. But, according to his exposition,[1] in those six days, "the morning" was the angelic knowledge, according to which they knew the Word and things in the Word. Therefore straightway from their creation they knew the Word, and things in the Word. But the Happiness of the angels comes of seeing the Word. Consequently the angels were happy at once from the very beginning of their creation.

On the contrary, To be established or confirmed in good is of the nature of Happiness. But the angels were not confirmed in good as soon as they were created; the fall of some of them shows this. Therefore the angels were not happy from their creation.

I answer that, By the name of Happiness (beatitude) is understood the ultimate perfection of rational or of intellectual nature; and hence it is that it is naturally desired, since everything naturally desires its ultimate perfection. Now there is a twofold ultimate perfection of rational or of intellectual nature. The first is one which it can procure of its own natural power, and this is in a measure called beatitude or happiness. Hence Aristotle says[2] that man's ultimate happiness consists in the most perfect contemplation, by which in this life he can contemplate the highest intelligible object; and that is God. Above this happiness there is still another, which we look forward to in the future, whereby *we shall see God as He is* (I John, 3. 2). This is beyond the nature of every created intellect, as was shown above (Q. XII, A. 4).

So, then, it remains to be said, that, as regards this first happiness, which the angel could procure by his natural power, he was created already happy. Because the angel does not acquire such happiness by any discursive motion, as man does, but, as was observed above (Q. LVIII, A. 4), is straightway in possession of it, owing to his natural dignity. But the angels did not have from the beginning of their creation that ultimate Happiness which is beyond the power of nature, because such Happiness is no part of their nature, but its end; and consequently they ought not to have it immediately from the beginning.

Reply Obj. 1. Happiness is there taken for that natural perfection which the angel had in the state of innocence.

Reply Obj. 2. The corporeal creature instantly in the beginning of its creation could not have the perfection to which it is brought by its oper-

ation. Consequently, according to Augustine (*Gen. ad lit.* v, 4, 5),[3] the growing of plants from the earth did not take place at once among the first works, in which only the germinating power of the plants was bestowed upon the earth. In the same way, the angelic creature in the beginning of its creation had the perfection of its nature, but it did not have the perfection to which it had to come by its operation.

Reply Obj. 3. The angel has a twofold knowledge of the Word: the one which is natural, and the other according to glory. He has a natural knowledge whereby he knows the Word through a likeness of it shining in his nature, and he has a knowledge of glory whereby he knows the Word through His essence. By both kinds of knowledge the angel knows things in the Word, imperfectly by his natural knowledge, and perfectly by his knowledge of glory. Therefore the first knowledge of things in the Word was present to the angel from the outset of his creation, while the second was not, but only when the angels became blessed by turning to the good. And this is properly termed their morning knowledge.

ARTICLE 2. *Whether an Angel Needs Grace in Order To Turn to God?*

We proceed thus to the Second Article: It would seem that the angel had no need of grace in order to turn to God.

Objection 1. For, we have no need of grace for what we can accomplish naturally. But the angel naturally turns to God, because he loves God naturally, as is clear from what has been said (Q. LX, A. 5). Therefore an angel did not need grace in order to turn to God.

Obj. 2. Further, it seems that we need help only for difficult tasks. Now it was not a difficult task for the angel to turn to God, because there was no obstacle in him to such turning. Therefore the angel had no need of grace in order to turn to God.

Obj. 3. Further, to turn oneself to God is to dispose oneself for grace; hence it is said (Zach. 1. 3): *Turn ye to Me, and I will turn to you.* But we do not stand in need of grace in order to prepare ourselves for grace, for thus we should go on to infinity. Therefore the angel did not need grace to turn to God.

On the contrary, It was by turning to God that the angel reached to Happiness. If, then, he had needed no grace in order to turn to God, it would follow that he did not require grace in order to possess everlasting life. But this is con-

---

[1] Bk. IV, 22 (PL 34, 312).
[2] *Ethics,* X, 7, 8 (1177ᵃ12; 1178ᵇ23).
[3] PL 34, 324, 338.

trary to the saying of the Apostle (Rom. 6. 23): *The grace of God is life everlasting.*

I answer that, The angels stood in need of grace in order to turn to God, as the object of Happiness. For, as was observed above (Q. LX, A. 2), the natural movement of the will is the principle of all things that we will. But the will's natural inclination is directed towards what is in keeping with its nature. Therefore, if there is anything which is above nature, the will cannot be inclined towards it, unless helped by some other supernatural principle. Thus it is clear that fire has a natural tendency to give forth heat, and to generate fire; but to generate flesh is beyond the natural power of fire, and consequently, fire has no tendency to this, except in so far as it is moved instrumentally by the nutritive soul.

Now it was shown above (Q. XII, A. 4), when we were treating of God's knowledge, that to see God in His essence, in which the ultimate Happiness of the rational creature consists, is beyond the nature of every created intellect. Consequently no rational creature can have the movement of the will directed towards such Happiness unless it is moved through a supernatural agent. This is what we call the help of grace. Therefore it must be said that an angel could not of his own will be turned to such Happiness, except by the help of grace.

Reply Obj. 1. The angel loves God naturally, so far as God is the author of his natural being. But here we are speaking of turning to God, so far as God bestows Happiness by the vision of His essence.

Reply Obj. 2. A thing is difficult which is beyond a power; and this happens in two ways. First of all, because it is beyond the natural capacity of the power. And then, if it can be attained by some help, it is said to be difficult, but if it can in no way be attained, then it is impossible; thus it is impossible for a man to fly. In another way a thing may be beyond the power, not according to the natural order of such power, but owing to some added hindrance; as to mount upwards is not contrary to the natural order of the moving power of the soul, because the soul, considered in itself, can be moved in any direction, but is hindered from so doing by the weight of the body; consequently it is difficult for a man to mount upwards. To be turned to his ultimate Happiness is difficult for man both because it is beyond his nature, and because he has a hindrance from the corruption of the body and the infection of sin. But it is difficult for an angel only because it is supernatural.

Reply Obj. 3. Every movement of the will towards God can be termed a conversion to God. And so there is a threefold turning to God. The first is by the perfect love of God; this belongs to the creature enjoying the possession of God, and for such conversion, perfecting grace is required. The next turning to God is that which merits Happiness; and for this there is required habitual grace, which is the principle of merit. The third turning to God is that whereby a man disposes himself so that he may have grace; for this no habitual grace is required, but the operation of God, Who draws the soul towards Himself, according to Lament. 5. 21: *Convert us, O Lord, to Thee, and we shall be converted.* Hence it is clear that there is no need to go on to infinity.

ARTICLE 3. *Whether the Angels Were Created in Grace?*

We proceed thus to the Third Article: It would seem that the angels were not created in grace.

Objection 1. For Augustine says (*Gen. ad lit.* ii. 8)[1] that the angelic nature was first made without form, and was called heaven; but afterwards it received its form, and was then called light. But such formation comes from grace. Therefore they were not created in grace.

Obj. 2. Further, grace turns the rational creature towards God. If, therefore, the angel had been created in grace, no angel would ever have turned away from God.

Obj. 3. Further, grace comes midway between nature and glory. But the angels were not made blessed in their creation. Therefore it seems that they were not created in grace, but that they were first created in nature only, and then received grace, and that last of all they were made blessed.

On the contrary, Augustine says,[2] "Who wrought the good will of the angels? Who, save Him Who created them with His will, that is, with the pure love wherewith they cling to Him, at the same time building up their nature and bestowing grace on them?"

I answer that, Although there are conflicting opinions on this point, some holding that the angels were created only in a natural state,[3]

---

[1] PL 34, 269; also, I, 3, 9 (247, 248); III, 201 (292).

[2] *City of God*, XII, 9 (PL 41, 357).

[3] William of Auxerre, *Summa Aurea*, II, I, I (fol. 35rb); Alexander of Hales, *Summa Theol.*, I-II, n 100 (QR II, 126); Bonaventure, *In Sent.*, II, d. IV, A. I, Q. II (QR II, 134). See also Hugh of St. Victor, *De Sacram.*, I, pt. v, chap. 19 (PL 176, 254); Lombard, *Sent.*, II, d. III, chap. 4 (QR I, 320); d. IV, chap. I (QR I, 324).

while others maintain that they were created in grace;[1] yet it seems more probable, and more in keeping with the sayings of holy men, that they were created in sanctifying grace. For we see that all things which, in the process of time, created by the work of Divine Providence, were produced by the operation of God, were created in the first fashioning of things according to seedlike forms (*seminales rationes*), as Augustine says (*Gen. ad lit*. viii, 3),[2] such as trees, animals, and the rest. Now it is evident that sanctifying grace bears the same relation to Happiness as the seedlike form in nature does to the natural effect; hence (I John 3. 9) grace is called the *seed of God*. As, then, in Augustine's opinion it is contended that the seedlike forms of all natural effects were implanted in the creature when corporeally created, so, straightway from the beginning the angels were created in grace.

Reply Obj. 1. Such absence of form in the angels can be understood either in relation to their formation in glory, and so the absence of formation preceded formation by priority of time. Or else it can be understood of the formation according to grace, and so it did not precede in the order of time, but in the order of nature; as Augustine holds with regard to the formation of corporeal things (*Gen. ad lit*. i, 15).[3]

Reply Obj. 2. Every form inclines the subject after the mode of the subject's nature. Now it is the mode of an intellect nature to be inclined freely towards the objects it desires. Consequently the inclination of grace does not impose necessity; but he who has grace can fail to make use of it, and can sin.

Reply Obj. 3. Although in the order of nature grace comes midway between nature and glory, nevertheless, in the order of time, in created nature, glory is not simultaneous with nature, because glory is the end of the operation of nature helped by grace. But grace does not stand as the end of operation, because it is not of works, but as the principle of right operation. Therefore it was fitting for grace to be given straightway with nature.

ARTICLE 4. *Whether a Blessed Angel Merits His Happiness?*

We proceed thus to the Fourth Article: It would seem that the blessed angel did not merit his Happiness.

[1] Praepositinus, *Summa* (cf. note to *S.T.* of Alexander of Hales—QR ii, 125, n. 2); Albert the Great, *In Sent.*, ii, d. 3, A. 12 (BO XXVII, 85); See below, Q. XCV, A. 1.
[2] PL 34, 374; V, 4, 23 (324, 338).
[3] PL 34, 257; V, 5 (326).

Objection 1. For merit arises from the difficulty of the meritorious act. But the angel experienced no difficulty in acting well. Therefore a good action was not meritorious for him.

Obj. 2. Further, we do not merit by merely natural operations. But it was quite natural for the angel to turn to God. Therefore he did not thereby merit Happiness.

Obj. 3. Further, if a blessed angel merited his Happiness, he did so either before he had it, or else afterwards. But it was not before, because, in the opinion of many, he had no grace before by which to merit it. Nor did he merit it afterwards, because thus he would be meriting it now, which is clearly false, because in that case a lower angel could by meriting rise up to the rank of a higher, and the distinct degrees of grace would not be permanent, which is not admissible. Consequently the angel did not merit his Happiness.

On the contrary, It is stated (Apoc. 21. 17) that the *measure of the angel* in that heavenly Jerusalem is *the measure of a man*. But man can only reach Happiness by merit. Therefore the same is the case with the angel.

I answer that, Perfect Happiness is natural only to God, because being and Happiness are one and the same thing in Him. Happiness, however, is not of the nature of the creature, but is its end. Now everything attains its last end by its operation. Such operation leading to the end is either productive of the end, when such end is not beyond the power of the agent working for the end, as the healing art is productive of health; or else it is deserving of the end, when such end is beyond the capacity of the agent striving to attain it, and therefore it is looked for from another's bestowing. Now it is evident from what has gone before (A. 1; Q. XII, A. 4), ultimate Happiness exceeds both the angelic and the human nature. It remains, then, that both man and angel merited their Happiness.

And if the angel was created in grace, without which there is no merit, there would be no difficulty in saying that he merited Happiness; as also, if one were to say that he had grace in any way before he had glory. But if he had no grace before entering upon Happiness, it would then have to be said that he had Happiness without merit, even as we have grace. This, however, is against the idea of Happiness, "which has the notion of an end, and is the reward of virtue," as even the Philosopher says.[4] Or else it will have to be said, as some others have main-

[4] *Ethics*, I, 7, 9 (1097[a]34; 1099[b]16).

tained,[1] that the angels merit Happiness by their divine ministrations while they already enjoy that Happiness. This is quite contrary, again, to the notion of merit, since merit conveys the idea of a means to an end, while what is already in its end cannot, properly speaking, be moved towards that end; and so no one merits what he already enjoys. Or else it will have to be said that one and the same act of turning to God, so far as it comes of free choice, is meritorious, and so far as it attains the end, is the enjoyment of Happiness. Even this view will not stand, because free choice is not the sufficient cause of merit, and, consequently, an act cannot be meritorious as coming from free choice, except in so far as it is informed by grace; but it cannot at the same time be informed by imperfect grace, which is the principle of meriting, and by perfect grace, which is the principle of enjoying. Hence it does not appear to be possible for anyone to enjoy Happiness and at the same time to merit it. Consequently it is better to say that the angel had grace before he was admitted to Happiness, and that by such grace he merited Happiness.

Reply Obj. 1. The angel's difficulty of doing well does not come from any contrariety or hindrance of natural powers, but from the fact that the good work is beyond his natural capacity.

Reply Obj. 2. An angel did not merit Happiness by natural turning towards God, but by the turning towards God of charity, which comes of grace.

The answer to the third objection is evident from what we have said.

ARTICLE 5. *Whether the Angel Obtained Happiness Immediately After One Act of Merit?*

We proceed thus to the Fifth Article: It would seem that the angel did not possess Happiness instantly after one act of merit.

Objection 1. For it is more difficult for a man to do well than for an angel. But man is not rewarded at once after one act of merit. Therefore neither was the angel.

Obj. 2. Further, an angel could act at once, and in an instant, from the very outset of his creation, for even natural bodies begin to be moved in the very instant of their creation; and if the movement of a body could be instantaneous, like operations of mind and will, it would have movement in the first instant of its generation. Consequently, if the angel merited Hap-

[1] Cf. Peter Lombard, *Sent.*, II, v, 6 (QR I, 329); also, Albertus Magnus, *In Sent.*, II, v, 7 (BO XXVII, 124).

piness by one act of his will, he merited it in the first instant of his creation; and so, if their Happiness was not kept back, then the angels were in Happiness in the first instant.

Obj. 3. Further, there must be many intervals between things which are far apart. But the Happiness state of the angels is very far from their natural condition, while merit comes midway between. Therefore the angel would have to pass through many stages of merit in order to reach Happiness.

On the contrary, Man's soul and an angel are ordered alike for Happiness; consequently equality with angels is promised to the saints (Luke, 20. 36). Now the soul separated from the body, if it has merit deserving Happiness, enters at once into Happiness, unless there be some obstacle. Therefore so does an angel. Now an angel instantly, in his first act of charity, had the merit of Happiness. Therefore, since there was no obstacle within him, he passed at once into Happiness by only one meritorious act.

I answer that, The angel was made blessed instantly after the first act of charity, whereby he merited Happiness. The reason for this is that grace perfects nature according to the manner of the nature; just as every perfection is received in the subject capable of perfection, according to its mode. Now it is proper to the angelic nature to receive its natural perfection not by passing from one stage to another, but to have it at once naturally, as was shown above (Q. LVIII, A. 3). But as the angel is of his nature ordered to natural perfection, so is he by merit ordered to glory. Hence instantly after merit the angel secured Happiness. Now the merit of Happiness in angel and man alike can be from merely one act, because man merits Happiness by every act informed by charity. Hence it remains that an angel was made blessed straightway after one act informed by charity.

Reply Obj. 1. Man was not intended naturally to secure his ultimate perfection at once, like the angel. Hence a longer way was assigned to man than to the angel for meriting Happiness.

Reply Obj. 2. The angel is above the time of corporeal things; hence the various instants regarding the angels are not to be taken except as reckoning the succession of their acts. Now their act which merited Happiness could not be in them simultaneously with the act of Happiness, which is enjoyment, since the one belongs to imperfect grace and the other to perfected grace. Consequently, we must admit different instants, in one of which the angel merited Happiness, and in another was made happy.

Reply Obj. 3. It is of the nature of an angel instantly to attain the perfection to which he is ordained. Consequently, only one meritorious act is required; hence this act can be called an interval because through it the angel is brought to Happiness.

ARTICLE 6. *Whether the Angels Received Grace and Glory According to the Degree of Their Natural Gifts?*

We proceed thus to the Sixth Article: It would seem that the angels did not receive grace and glory according to the degree of their natural gifts.

Objection 1. For grace is bestowed of God's will alone. Therefore the degree of grace depends on God's will, and not on the degree of their natural gifts.

Obj. 2. Further, a human act seems to be more closely allied with grace than nature is, because a human act is preparatory to grace. But grace does not come of *works,* as is said Rom. 11. 6. Therefore much less does the degree of grace depend upon the degree of their natural gifts.

Obj. 3. Further, man and angel are alike ordained for happiness or grace. But man does not receive more grace according to the degree of his natural gifts. Therefore neither does the angel.

On the contrary, Is the saying of the Master of the Sentences (*Sent.* ii, d. 3),[1] that "those angels who were created with more subtle natures and of keener intelligence in wisdom, were likewise endowed with greater gifts of grace."

I answer that, It is reasonable to suppose that gifts of graces and perfection of Happiness were bestowed on the angels according to the degree of their natural gifts. The reason for this can be drawn from two sources.

First of all, on the part of God, Who, in the order of His wisdom, established various degrees in the angelic nature. Now as the angelic nature was made by God for attaining grace and Happiness, so likewise the grades of the angelic nature seem to be ordained for the various degrees of grace and glory; just as when, for example, the builder chisels the stones for building a house, from the fact that he prepares some more artistically and more fittingly than others, it is clear that he is setting them apart for the more ornate part of the house. So it seems that

[1] Chap. 2 (QR I, 318).

God destined those angels for greater gifts of grace and fuller Happiness, whom He made of a higher nature.

Secondly, the same is evident on the part of the angel. The angel is not a compound of different natures, so that the inclination of the one hinders or retards the tendency of the other; as happens in man, in whom the movement of his intellectual part is either retarded or hindered by the inclination of his sensitive part. But when there is nothing to retard or hinder it, nature is moved with its whole energy. So it is reasonable to suppose that the angels who had a higher nature were turned to God more forcefully and efficaciously. The same thing happens in men, since greater grace and glory are bestowed according to the greater intensity of their turning to God. Hence it appears that the angels who had the greater natural powers, had the more grace and glory.

Reply Obj. 1. As grace comes of God's will alone, so likewise does the nature of the angel; and as God's will ordered nature for grace, so did it order the various degrees of nature to the various degrees of grace.

Reply Obj. 2. The acts of the rational creature are from the creature itself, whereas nature is immediately from God. Accordingly it seems rather that grace is bestowed according to degree of nature than according to works.

Reply Obj. 3. Diversity of natural gifts is in one way in the angels, who differ according to species, and in quite another way in men, who differ only numerically. For specific difference is on account of the end, while numerical difference is because of the matter. Furthermore, there is something in man which can impede or retard the movement of his intellectual nature, but not in the angels. Consequently the argument is not the same for both.

ARTICLE 7. *Whether Natural Knowledge and Love Remain in the Beatified Angels?*

We proceed thus to the Seventh Article: It would seem that natural knowledge and love do not remain in the beatified angels.

Objection 1. For it is said (I Cor. 13. 10): *When that which is perfect is come, then that which is in part shall be done away.* But natural love and knowledge are imperfect in comparison with knowledge and love that is blessed. Therefore, in Happiness, natural knowledge and love cease.

Obj. 2. Further, where one suffices, another is superfluous. But the knowledge and love of glory suffice for the blessed angels. Therefore it

would be superfluous for their natural knowledge and love to remain.

Obj. 3. Further, the same power has not two simultaneous acts, as the same line cannot, at the same end, be terminated in two points. But the blessed angels are always exercising their beatified knowledge and love; for, as is said in the *Ethics*,[1] "happiness consists not in habit, but in act." Therefore there can never be natural knowledge and love in the angels.

On the contrary, So long as a nature endures, its operation remains. But Happiness does not destroy nature, since it is its perfection. Therefore it does not take away natural knowledge and love.

I answer that, Natural knowledge and love remain in the angels. For as principles of operations are mutually related, so are the operations themselves. Now it is manifest that nature is related to Happiness as first to second, because Happiness always is added to nature. But the first must always be preserved in the second. Consequently nature must be preserved in Happiness, and in like manner the act of nature must be preserved in the act of Happiness.

Reply Obj. 1. The advent of a perfection removes the opposite imperfection. Now the imperfection of nature is not opposed to the perfection of Happiness, but underlies it; just as the imperfection of the power underlies the perfection of the form, and the power is not taken away by the form, but the privation which is opposed to the form. In the same way, the imperfection of natural knowledge is not opposed to the perfection of the knowledge in glory, for nothing hinders us from knowing a thing at the same time through various mediums, as a thing may be known at the one time through a probable medium and through a demonstrative one. In like manner, an angel can know God by His essence, and this appertains to his knowledge of glory; and at the same time he can know God by his own essence, which belongs to his natural knowledge.

Reply Obj. 2. All things which make up Happiness are sufficient of themselves. But in order for them to exist, they presuppose the natural gifts, because no Happiness is self-subsisting except the uncreated Happiness.

Reply Obj. 3. There cannot be two operations of the one power at the one time, unless one is ordered to the other. But natural knowledge and love are ordered to the knowledge and love of glory. Accordingly there is nothing to hinder natural knowledge and love from existing in the angel together with those of glory.

[1] Aristotle, I, 8 (1098[b]33).

ARTICLE 8. *Whether a Blessed Angel Can Sin?*

We proceed thus to the Eighth Article: It would seem that a blessed angel can sin.

Objection 1. For, as was said above (A. 7), Happiness does not do away with nature. But it is of the very notion of created nature that it can fail. Therefore a blessed angel can sin.

Obj. 2. Further, "the rational powers are related to opposites," as the Philosopher observes.[2] But the will of the angel in Happiness does not cease to be rational. Therefore it is inclined towards good and evil.

Obj. 3. Further, it pertains to the liberty of choice that man be able to choose good or evil. But the freedom of choice is not lessened in the blessed angels. Therefore they can sin.

On the contrary, Augustine says (*Gen. ad lit.* xi)[3] that there is "in the holy angels" that nature which is not able to sin. Therefore the holy angels cannot sin.

I answer that, The blessed angels are not able to sin. The reason for this is because their Happiness consists in seeing God through His essence. Now, God's essence is the very essence of goodness. Consequently the angel seeing God is in the same way towards God as anyone else not seeing God is to the common notion of goodness. Now it is impossible for any man either to will or to do anything except aiming at what is good, or for him to wish to turn away from good as such. Therefore the blessed angel can neither will nor act, except as aiming towards God. Now whoever wills or acts in this manner is not able to sin. Consequently the blessed angel cannot sin.

Reply Obj. 1. Created good, considered in itself, can fail. But from its perfect union with the uncreated good, such as is the union of Happiness, it is rendered unable to sin, for the reason already given.

Reply Obj. 2. The rational powers are related to opposites in the things to which they are not ordered naturally; but as to the things to which they are naturally ordered, they are not related to opposites. For the intellect cannot not assent to naturally known principles; in the same way, the will cannot not adhere to good, as good, because the will is naturally ordered to good as to its proper object. Consequently the will of the angels is related to opposites, as to doing many things, or not doing them. But they have no relation to opposites with regard to God Himself, Whom they see to be the essence itself of good-

[2] *Metaphysics*, IX, 2 (1046[b]5).
[3] Chap. 7 (PL 34, 433).

ness, but in all things their aim is towards God, whichever alternative they choose. And this is without sin.

Reply Obj. 3. Free choice in its choice of means to an end is disposed just as the intellect is to conclusions. Now it is evident that it pertains to the power of the intellect to be able to proceed to different conclusions, according to given principles, but for it to proceed to some conclusion by neglecting the order of the principles comes of its own defect. Hence it pertains to the perfection of its liberty for free choice to be able to choose between opposite things, keeping the order of the end in view. But it pertains to the defect of liberty for it to choose anything by turning away from the order of the end. And this is to sin. Hence there is greater liberty of choice in the angels, who are not able to sin, than there is in ourselves, who are able to sin.

ARTICLE 9. *Whether the Blessed Angels Advance in Happiness?*

We proceed thus to the Ninth Article: It would seem that the blessed angels can advance in Happiness.

Objection 1. For charity is the principle of merit. But there is perfect charity in the angels. Therefore the blessed angels can merit. Now, as merit increases, the reward of Happiness increases. Therefore the blessed angels can progress in Happiness.

Obj. 2. Further, Augustine says[1] that God "makes use of us for our own gain, and for His own goodness." The same thing happens to the angels, whom He uses for spiritual ministrations, since *they are all* (Vulg., *Are they not all . . . ?*) *ministering spirits, sent to minister for them who shall receive the inheritance of salvation* (Heb. 1. 14). This would not be for their gain were they not to merit thereby, nor to advance in Happiness. It remains, then, that the blessed angels can merit, and can advance in Happiness.

Obj. 3. Further, it argues imperfection for anyone not occupying the foremost place not to be able to advance. But the angels are not in the highest degree of Happiness. Therefore, if unable to ascend higher, it would appear that there is imperfection and defect in them, which is not admissible.

On the contrary, Merit and progress belong to this present condition of life. But angels are not wayfarers travelling towards beatitude, they are already in possession of Happiness.

[1] *Christian Doctrine,* 1, 32 (PL 34, 32).

Consequently the blessed angels can neither merit nor advance in Happiness.

I answer that, In every movement the mover's intention is centred upon one determined end, to which he intends to lead the movable subject, because intention looks to the end, which the notion of infinity opposes. Now it is evident, since the rational creature cannot of its own power attain to its Happiness, which consists in the vision of God, as is clear from what has gone before (A. 1, Q. XII, A. 4), that it needs to be moved by God towards its Happiness. Therefore there must be some one determined thing to which every rational creature is directed as to its last end.

Now this one determinate thing cannot, in the vision of God, consist precisely in that which is seen, for the Supreme Truth is seen by all the blessed in various degrees. But it pertains to the mode of vision, that diverse terms are fixed beforehand by the intention of Him Who directs towards the end. For it is impossible that as the rational creature is led on to the vision of the Supreme Essence, it should be led on in the same way to the supreme mode of vision, which is comprehension, for this belongs to God only; as is evident from what was said above (Q. XII, A. 7; Q. XIV, A. 3). But since infinite efficacy is required for comprehending God, while the creature's efficacy in beholding is only finite, and since every finite thing is in infinite degrees removed from the infinite, it comes to pass that the rational creature understands God more or less clearly according to many degrees. And as Happiness consists in the vision itself, so the degree of vision lies in a certain mode of the vision.

Therefore every rational creature is so led by God to the end of its Happiness that from God's predestination it is brought even to a determinate degree of Happiness. Consequently when that degree is once secured it cannot pass to a higher degree.

Reply Obj. 1. Merit belongs to him who is moved to an end. Now the rational creature is moved towards its end, not only by being acted upon, but also by working actively. If the end is within the power of the rational creature, then its action is said to procure the end, just as man acquires knowledge by reflection; but if the end be beyond its power, and is looked for from another, then the action will be meritorious of the end. But what is already in the ultimate term is not said to be moved, but to have been moved. Consequently, to merit belongs to the imperfect charity of this life, while perfect charity does not merit but rather enjoys the reward. Even as in acquired habits, the operation preceding the habit is productive of the habit, but the operation from an acquired habit is both perfect and enjoyable. In the same way the act of perfect charity has no aspect of merit, but belongs rather to the perfection of the reward.

Reply Obj. 2. A thing can be termed useful in two ways. First of all, as being on the way to an end; and so the merit of Happiness is useful. Secondly, as the part is useful for the whole; as for instance the wall for a house. In this way the angelic ministerings are useful for the blessed angels since they are a part of their Happiness; for to pour out acquired perfection upon others is of the nature of what is perfect, considered as perfect.

Reply Obj. 3. Although a blessed angel is not absolutely in the highest degree of Happiness, yet, as to himself he is in the highest degree, according to Divine predestination. Nevertheless the joy of the angels can be increased with regard to the salvation of such as are saved by their ministrations, according to Luke 15. 10: *There is* (Vulg., *shall be*) *joy before the angels of God upon one sinner doing penance.* Such joy belongs to their accidental reward, which can be increased up to the judgment day. Hence some writers say[1] that they can merit as to their accidental reward. But it is better to say that the Blessed can in no way merit, without being at the same time a wayfarer and one comprehending, like Christ, Who alone was such. For the Blessed acquire such joy by virtue of their Happiness, rather than by merit.

QUESTION LXIII
The Malice of the Angels with
regard to Sin
(In Nine Articles)

In the next place we must consider how angels became evil: first of all with regard to the evil of fault; and secondly, as to the evil of punishment (Q. LXIV). Under the first heading there are nine points for consideration: (1) Can there be evil of faults in the angels? (2) What kind of sins can be in them? (3) What did the angel seek in sinning? (4) Supposing that some became evil by a sin of their own choosing, are any of them naturally evil? (5) Supposing that it is not so, could any one of them become

evil in the first instant of his creation by an act of his own will? (6) Supposing that he did not, was there any interval between his creation and fall? (7) Was the highest of them who fell, absolutely the highest among the angels? (8) Was the sin of the foremost angel the cause of the others sinning? (9) Did as many sin as remained steadfast?

ARTICLE 1. *Whether the Evil of Fault Can Be in the Angels?*

We proceed thus to the First Article: It would seem that there can be no evil of fault in the angels.

Objection 1. For there can be no evil, except in things which are in potency, as is said by the Philosopher,[2] because the subject of privation is a being in potency. But the angels have not being in potency, since they are subsisting forms. Therefore there can be no evil of fault, in them.

Obj. 2. Further, the angels are higher than the heavenly bodies. But philosophers say[3] that there cannot be evil in the heavenly bodies. Therefore neither can there be in the angels.

Obj. 3. Further, what is natural to a thing is always in it. But it is natural for the angels to be moved by the movement of love towards God. Therefore such love cannot be withdrawn from them. But in loving God they do not sin. Consequently the angels cannot sin.

Obj. 4. Further, desire is only of what is good or apparently good. Now for the angels there can be no apparent good which is not a true good, because in them either there can be no error at all, or at least not before guilt. Therefore the angels can desire only what is truly good. But no one sins by desiring what is truly good. Consequently the angel does not sin by desire.

On the contrary, It is said (Job. 4. 18): *In His angels He found wickedness.*

I answer that, An angel or any other rational creature considered in his own nature, is able to sin; and to whatever creature it belongs not to be able to sin, such creature has it as a gift of grace, and not from the condition of nature. The reason of this is because sinning is nothing else than a deviation from that rightness which an act ought to have, whether we speak of sin in nature, in things made or in morals. That act alone, the rule of which is the very power of

---

[1] Wm. of Paris, *De Univ.*, III–II, chap. 156 (II, 948); cf. *Glossa ordin.*, on Num. 25.5 (I, 311C); Origen, *In Num.*, hom. XX (PG 12, 735); *In Luc.*, hom. XIII (PG 13, 1832).

[2] *Metaphysics*, IX, 9 (1051ᵃ18).

[3] Aristotle, *Metaphysics*, IX, 9 (1051ᵃ19); Avicenna, *Meta.*, IX, 6 (106ra); cf. *De Error. Philosoph.*, VI, 12 (MD 13); Averroes, *In Meta.*, IX, 19 (VIII, 245F).

the agent, can never fall short of rectitude. Were the craftsman's hand the rule itself engraving, he could not engrave the wood otherwise than rightly; but if the rightness of engraving be judged by another rule, then the engraving may be right or faulty. Now the Divine will is the sole rule of God's act, because it is not ordered to any higher end. But every created will has rectitude of act so far only as it is regulated according to the Divine will, to which the last end is to be referred, just as every will of a subordinate ought to be regulated by the will of his superior; for instance, the soldier's will, according to the will of his commanding officer. Thus only in the Divine will is there not able to be sin, whereas there can be sin in the will of every creature, considering the condition of its nature.

Reply Obj. 1. In the angels there is no potency to natural being. Yet there is potency in their intellectual part, according as it is inclined to this or that thing. In the respect there can be evil in them.

Reply Obj. 2. The heavenly bodies have none but a natural operation. Therefore as there can be no evil of corruption in their nature, so neither can there be evil of disorder in their natural action. But besides their natural action there is the action of free choice in the angels, by reason of which evil may be in them.

Reply Obj. 3. It is natural for the angel to turn to God by the movement of love, according as God is the principle of his natural being. But for him to turn to God as the object of supernatural Happiness, comes of freely given love, from which he could be turned away by sinning.

Reply Obj. 4. Mortal sin occurs in two ways in the act of free choice. First, when something evil is chosen; as man sins by choosing adultery, which is evil of itself. Such sin always comes of ignorance or error. Otherwise what is evil would never be chosen as good. The adulterer errs in the particular, choosing this delight of a disordered act as something good to be performed now, from the inclination of passion or of habit, even though he does not err in his universal judgment, but retains a right opinion in this respect. In this way there can be no sin in the angel, because there are no passions in the angels to fetter reason or intellect, as is manifest from what has been said above (Q. LIX, A. 4); nor, again, could any habit inclining to sin precede their first sin. In another way sin comes of free choice by choosing something good in itself, but not according to the order of due measure or rule, so that the defect which induces

sin is only on the part of the choice which does not have its due order (except on the part of the thing chosen); as if one were to pray without heeding the order established by the Church. Such a sin does not presuppose ignorance, but merely absence of consideration of the things which ought to be considered. In this way the angel sinned, by seeking his own good, from his own free choice, without being ordered to the rule of the Divine will.

ARTICLE 2. *Whether Only the Sin of Pride and Envy Can Exist in an Angel?*

We proceed thus to the Second Article: It would seem that there can be other sins in the angels besides those of pride and envy.

Objection 1. Because whosoever can delight in any kind of sin can fall into the sin itself. But the demons delight even in the obscenities of carnal sins, as Augustine says.[1] Therefore there can also be carnal sins in the demons.

Obj. 2. Further, as pride and envy are spiritual sins, so are acedia, avarice, and anger. But spiritual sins are concerned with the spirit, just as carnal sins are with the flesh. Therefore not only can there be pride and envy in the angels, but likewise acedia and avarice.

Obj. 3. Further, according to Gregory (*Moral.* xxxi),[2] "many vices spring from pride; and in like manner from envy." But, if the cause is granted, the effect follows. If, therefore, there can be pride and envy in the angels, for the same reason there can likewise be other vices in them.

On the contrary, Augustine says[3] that "the devil is not a fornicator nor a drunkard, nor anything of the like sort; yet he is proud and envious."

I answer that, Sin can be in a subject in two ways: first of all by actual guilt, and secondly by affection. As to guilt, all sins are in the demons, since by leading men to sin they incur the guilt of all sins. But as to affection, only those sins can be in the demons which can belong to a spiritual nature. Now a spiritual nature cannot be affected by such goods as are proper to bodies, but only by such as are in keeping with spiritual things, because nothing is affected except with regard to something which is in some way suited to its nature. But there can be no sin when anyone is incited to good of the spiritual order, unless in such affection the rule of the superior be not kept. And this is the sin

[1] *City of God*, II, 4, 26 (PL 41, 50, 74).
[2] Chap. 45 (PL 76, 620).
[3] *City of God*, XIV, 3 (PL 41, 406).

of pride,—not to be subject to a superior where subjection is due. Consequently the first sin of the angel can be none other than pride.

Yet, as a consequence, it was possible for envy also to be in them, since for the affection to tend to the desire of something involves on its part resistance to anything contrary. Now the envious man sorrows over the good possessed by another, because he considers his neighbour's good to be a hindrance to his own. But another's good could not be considered a hindrance to the good coveted by the wicked angel except in so far as he coveted a singular excellence, which would cease to be singular because of the excellence of some other. So, after the sin of pride, there followed the evil of envy in the sinning angel whereby he grieved over man's good, and also over the Divine excellence, according as against the devil's will God makes use of man for the Divine glory.

Reply Obj. 1. The demons do not delight in the obscenities of the sins of the flesh as if they themselves were disposed to carnal pleasures; it is wholly through envy that they take pleasure in all sorts of human sins, so far as these are hindrances to a man's good.

Reply Obj. 2. Avarice, considered as a special kind of sin, is the immoderate desire of temporal things which serve the use of human life, and which can be estimated in value by money; to these things demons are not inclined, any more than they are to carnal pleasures. Consequently avarice properly so called cannot be in them. But if every immoderate greed of possessing any created good be termed avarice, in this way avarice is contained under the pride which is in the demons. But anger implies passion, and so does concupiscence. Consequently they can only exist metaphorically in the demons. Acedia is a kind of sadness, whereby a man becomes sluggish in spiritual exercises because they weary the body, which does not apply to the demons. So it is evident that pride and envy are the only spiritual sins which can be found in demons, yet so that envy is not to be taken for a passion, but for a will resisting the good of another.

Reply Obj. 3. Under envy and pride, as found in the demons. are comprised all other sins derived from them.

ARTICLE 3. *Whether the Devil Desired To Be As God?*

We proceed thus to the Third Article: It would seem that the devil did not desire to be as God.

Objection 1. For what does not fall under apprehension, does not fall under desire, because the good which is apprehended moves the appetite, whether sensible, rational, or intellectual, and sin consists only in such desire. But for any creature to be God's equal does not fall under apprehension, because it implies a contradiction, for if the finite equals the infinite, then it would itself be infinite. Therefore an angel could not desire to be as God.

Obj. 2. Further, the natural end can always be desired without sin. But to be likened to God is the end to which every creature naturally tends. If, therefore, the angel desired to be as God, not by equality, but by likeness, it would seem that he did not thereby sin.

Obj. 3. Further, the angel was created with greater fulness of wisdom than man. But no man, save a fool, ever makes choice of being the equal of an angel, still less of God, because choice regards only things which are possible, regarding which one takes deliberation. Therefore much less did the angel sin by desiring to be as God.

On the contrary, It is said, in the person of the devil (Isa. 14. 13, 14), *I will ascend into heaven. . . . I will be like the Most High.* And Augustine (*De Qu. Vet. Test.,* cxiii)[1] says that being inflated with pride, "he wished to be called God."

I answer that, Without doubt the angel sinned by seeking to be as God. But this can be understood in two ways: first, by equality; secondly, by likeness. He could not seek to be as God in the first way, because by natural knowledge he knew that this was impossible, and there was no habit preceding his first sinful act, nor any passion fettering his knowing power, so as to lead him to choose what was impossible by failing with regard to some particular, as sometimes happens in ourselves. And even supposing it were possible, it would be against the natural desire, because there exists in everything the natural desire of preserving its own being, which would not be preserved were it to be changed into another nature. Consequently, no thing of a lower order can ever desire the grade of a higher nature, just as an ass does not desire to be a horse; for were it to be so upraised, it would cease to be itself. But here the imagination plays us false; for one is liable to think that because a man seeks to occupy a higher grade as to accidentals, which can increase without the destruction of the subject, he can also seek a higher grade of nature, to

[1] Ambrosiaster (PL 35, 2341).

which he could not attain without ceasing to be. Now it is quite evident that God surpasses the angels not merely in accidentals, but also in degree of nature; and one angel, another. Consequently it is impossible for one angel of lower degree to desire equality with a higher, and still more to covet equality with God.

To desire to be as God according to likeness can happen in two ways. In one way, as to that likeness whereby everything is made to be likened to God. And so, if anyone desire in this way to be Godlike, he commits no sin, provided that he desires such likeness in proper order, that is to say, that he may obtain it of God. But he would sin were he to desire to be like God even in the right way, as of his own, and not of God's power. In another way one may desire to be like God in some respect which is not natural to one, as if one were to desire to create heaven and earth, which is proper to God, in which desire there would be sin. It was in this way that the devil desired to be as God. Not that he desired to resemble God by being subject to no one else absolutely, for so he would be desiring his own non-being, since no creature can be except by participating being under God. But he desired to be like God in this respect,—by desiring, as his last end of Happiness that which he could attain by the power of his own nature, turning his desire away from supernatural Happiness, which is attained by God's grace. Or, if desiring as his last end that likeness of God which is bestowed by grace, he sought to have it by the power of his own nature, and not from Divine assistance according to God's ordering. This harmonizes with Anselm's opinion, who says[1] that he sought that to which he would have come had he stood fast. These two views in a manner coincide; because according to both, he sought to have final happiness of his own power, whereas this is proper to God alone.

Since, then, what exists of itself is the principle and cause of what exists of another, it follows also from this that he sought to have dominion over others, wherein he also perversely wished to be like God.

From this we have *the answer to all the objections.*

ARTICLE 4. *Whether Any of the Demons Are Naturally Wicked?*

We proceed thus to the Fourth Article: It would seem that some demons are naturally wicked.

[1] *De casu diaboli,* chap. 6 (PL 158, 337).

Objection 1. For Porphyry says, as quoted by Augustine[2]: "There is a class of demons of crafty nature, pretending that they are gods and the souls of the dead." But to be deceitful is to be evil. Therefore some demons are naturally wicked.

Obj. 2. Further, as the angels are created by God, so are men. But some men are naturally wicked, of whom it is said (Wisd. 12. 10): *Their malice* was *natural.* Therefore some angels may be naturally wicked.

Obj. 3. Further, some irrational animals have wicked dispositions by nature; thus the fox is naturally sly, and the wolf naturally rapacious, yet they are God's creatures. Therefore, although the demons are God's creatures, they may be naturally wicked.

On the contrary, Dionysius says (*Div. Nom.* iv)[3] that "the demons are not naturally wicked."

I answer that, Everything which is, so far as it is and has some nature, tends naturally towards some good, since it comes from a good principle; because the effect always reverts to its principle. Now a particular good may happen to have some evil connected with it; thus fire has this evil connected with it that it consumes other things. But with the universal good no evil can be connected. If, then, there be anything whose nature is ordered towards some particular good, it can tend naturally to some evil; not as evil, but accidentally, as joined to some good. But if anything of its nature be ordered to good in general, then of its own nature it cannot be inclined to evil. Now it is manifest that every intellectual nature is ordered to the universal good, which it can apprehend and which is the object of the will. Hence, since the demons are intellectual substances, they can in no way have a natural inclination towards any evil whatsoever. Consequently they cannot be naturally evil.

Reply Obj. 1. Augustine in the same place rebukes Porphyry for saying that the demons are naturally deceitful saying that they are not naturally so, but of their own will. Now the reason why Porphyry held that they are naturally deceitful was that, as he contended, demons are animals with a sensitive nature. Now the sensitive nature is inclined towards some particular good, to which evil may be joined. In this way, then, it can have a natural inclination to evil; yet only accidentally, in so far as evil is joined to good.

[2] *City of God,* x, 11 (PL 41, 289).
[3] Sect. 23 (PG 3, 724).

Reply Obj. 2. The malice of some men can be called natural either because of custom which is a second nature, or on account of the natural proclivity on the part of the sensitive nature to some inordinate passion, as some people are said to be naturally wrathful or lustful; but not on the part of the intellectual nature.

Reply Obj. 3. Brute beasts have a natural inclination in their sensitive nature towards certain particular goods, to which certain evils are joined; thus the fox in seeking its food has a natural inclination to do so with a certain skill coupled with deceit. Therefore it is not evil in the fox to be sly, since it is natural to him, as it is not evil in the dog to be fierce, as Dionysius observes (*De Div. Nom.* iv).[1]

ARTICLE 5. *Whether the Devil Was Wicked by the Fault of His Own Will in the First Instant of his Creation?*

We proceed thus to the Fifth Article: It would seem that the devil was wicked by the fault of his own will in the first instant of his creation.

Objection 1. For it is said of the devil (John 8 44): *He was a murderer from the beginning.*

Obj. 2. Further, according to Augustine (*Gen. ad lit.* i, 15),[2] "the lack of form in the creature did not precede its formation in order of time, but merely in order of nature." Now according to him (*ibid.* ii, 8),[3] the heaven, which is said to have been created in the beginning, signifies the angelic nature while as yet not fully formed; and when it is said that God said: *Be light made: and light was made,* we are to understand the full formation of the angel by turning to the Word. Consequently, the nature of the angel was created, and light was made, in the one instant. But at the same moment that light was made, it was made distinct from darkness, whereby the angels who sinned are denoted. Therefore in the first instant of their creation some of the angels were made blessed, and some sinned.

Obj. 3. Further, sin is opposed to merit. But some intellectual nature can merit in the first instant of its creation, as the soul of Christ, or also the good angels. Therefore the demons likewise could sin in the first instant of their creation.

Obj. 4. Further, the angelic nature is more

powerful than the corporeal nature. But a corporeal thing begins to have its operation in the first instant of its creation; as fire begins to move upwards in the first instant it is produced. Therefore the angel could also have his operation in the first instant of his creation. Now this operation was either ordered or inordinate. If ordered, then, since he had grace, he thereby merited Happiness. But with the angels the reward follows immediately upon merit, as was said above (Q. LXII, A. 5). Consequently they would have become blessed at once, and so would never have sinned, which is false. It remains, then, that they sinned by inordinate action in their first instant.

On the contrary, It is written (Gen. 1. 31): *God saw all the things that He had made, and they were very good.* But among them were also the demons. Therefore the demons were at some time good.

I answer that, Some have maintained[4] that the demons were wicked immediately in the first instant of their creation, not by their nature, but by the sin of their own will, because, "as soon as he was made, the devil refused justice." To this opinion, as Augustine says,[5] "if anyone subscribes, he does not agree with those Manichean heretics who say that the devil's nature is evil of itself." Since this opinion, however, is in contradiction with the authority of Scripture,—for it is said of the devil under the figure of the prince of Babylon (Isa. 14. 12): *How art thou fallen . . . O Lucifer, who didst rise in the morning!* and it is said to the devil in the person of the King of Tyre (Ezech. 28. 13): *Thou wast in the pleasures of the paradise of God,*—consequently, this opinion was reasonably rejected by the masters[6] as erroneous.

Hence others have said[7] that the angels, in the first instant of their creation, could have sinned, but did not. Yet this view also is rejected by some,[8] because, when two operations follow one upon the other, it seems impossible for each operation to terminate in the same "now." But it is clear that the angel's sin was an act subsequent to his creation. But the term

---

[1] Sect. 25 (PG 3, 728).
[2] PL 34, 257; also, v, 5 (PL 34, 269).
[3] PL 34, 269; cf. I, 3, 4, 9 (218, 219, 259); III, 20 (292).

[4] Certain unnamed theologians. Cf. Peter Lombard, *Sent.*, II, d. III, chap. 4 (QR 1, 319); Denifle, *Chartularium*, n. 130 (I, 173); n. 278 (I, 316).
[5] *City of God*, XI, 13 (PL 41, 329).
[6] At Paris. Cf. Denifle, *Chartularium*, n. 128 (I, 171).
[7] Albertus Magnus discusses this opinion. *In Sent.*, II, d. III, A. 14 (BO XXVII, 86); cf. Bonaventure, *In Sent.*, II, d. III, pt. 2, A. 1, Q. 2 (QR II, 117).
[8] Albertus Magnus, *In Sent.*, II, d. III, A. 14 (BO XXVII 87).

of the creative act is the angel's very being, while the term of the sinful act is that they are being wicked. It seems, then, an impossibility for the angel to have been wicked in the first instant in which he began to be.

This reason, however, does not seem sufficient. For it holds good only in temporal motions which take place successively; thus, if local motion follows a change, then the change and the local motion cannot be terminated in the same instant. But if the changes are instantaneous, then all at once and in the same instant there can be a term to the first and the second change; thus in the same instant in which the moon is lit up by the sun, the atmosphere is lit up by the moon. Now, it is manifest that creation is instantaneous; so also is the movement of free choice in the angels, for, as has been already stated, they have no occasion for comparison or discursive reasoning (Q. LVIII, A. 3). Consequently, there is nothing to hinder the term of creation and of free choice from being in the same instant.

We must therefore reply otherwise that it was impossible for the angel to sin in the first instant by an inordinate act of free choice. For although a thing can begin to act in the first instant in which it begins to be, nevertheless, that operation which begins immediately with the being of a thing is in it from the agent from which it has its being; just as upward movement in fire comes of its generator. Therefore, if there be anything which derives being from a deficient agent, which can be the cause of a defective action, it can in the first instant in which it begins to be have a defective operation; just as the leg which is defective from birth through a defect in the principle of generation, begins at once to limp. But the agent which brought the angels into being, namely, God, cannot be the cause of sin. Consequently it cannot be said that the devil was wicked in the first instant of his creation.

Reply Obj. 1. As Augustine says,[1] when it is stated that "the devil sins from the beginning," "he is not to be thought of as sinning from the beginning wherein he was created, but from the beginning of sin"; that is to say, because he never drew back from his sin.

Reply Obj. 2. That distinction of light and darkness, whereby the sins of the demons are understood by the term darkness, must be taken as according to God's foreknowledge. Hence Augustine says,[2] that "He alone could discern

light and darkness, Who also could foreknow, before they fell, those who would fall."

Reply Obj. 3. All that is in merit is from God, and consequently an angel could merit in the first instant of his creation. The same reason does not hold good of sin, as has been said.

Reply Obj. 4. God did not distinguish between the angels before the turning away of some of them and the turning of others to Himself, as Augustine says.[3] Therefore, as all were created in grace, all merited in their first instant. But some of them at once placed an impediment to their happiness, thereby destroying their preceding merit; and consequently they were deprived of the happiness which they had merited.

ARTICLE 6. *Whether There Was Any Interval Between the Creation and the Fall of the Angel?*

We proceed thus to the Sixth Article: It would seem that there was some interval between the angel's creation and his fall.

Objection 1. For, it is said (Ezech. 28. 15): *Thou didst walk perfect* (Vulg., *Thou hast walked in the midst of the stones of fire; thou wast perfect....*) *in thy ways from the day of thy creation, until iniquity was found in thee.* But since walking is continuous movement, it requires an interval. Therefore there was some interval between the devil's creation and his fall.

Obj. 2. Further, Origen says (*Hom.* i *in Ezech.*)[4] that the serpent of old "did not from the first walk upon his breast and belly"; which refers to his sin. Therefore the devil could not sin at once in the first instant of his creation.

Obj. 3. Further, to be able to sin is common alike to man and angel. But there was some delay between man's formation and his sin. Therefore, for the like reason there was some interval between the devil's formation and his sin.

Obj. 4. Further, the instant wherein the devil sinned was distinct from the instant wherein he was created. But there is a middle time between every two instants. Therefore there was an interval between his creation and his fall.

On the contrary, It is said of the devil (John 8. 44): *He stood not in the truth;* and, as Augustine says,[5] "we must understand this in the sense that he was in the truth, but did not remain in it."

[1] *City of God,* XI, 15 (PL 41, 330).
[2] *Ibid.,* XI, 19 (PL 41, 333).
[3] *Ibid.,* XI, 11 (PL 41, 327).
[4] PG 13, 670.
[5] *City of God,* XI, 15 (PL 41, 330).

I answer that, There is a twofold opinion on this point.[1] But the more probable one, which is also more in harmony with the teachings of the Saints, is that the devil sinned at once after the first instant of his creation. This must be maintained if it be held that he elicited an act of free choice in the first instant of his creation, and that he was created in grace, as we have said (A. 5, Q. LXII, A. 3). For since the angels attain Happiness by one meritorious act, as was said above (Q. LXII, A. 5), if the devil, created in grace, merited in the first instant, he would at once have received Happiness after that first instant, if he had not placed an impediment by sinning.

If, however, it be contended that the angel was not created in grace, or that he could not have an act of free choice in the first instant, then there is nothing to prevent some interval being interposed between his creation and fall.

Reply Obj. 1. Sometimes in Holy Scripture spiritual instantaneous movements are metaphorically represented by corporeal movements which are measured by time. In this way by "walking" we are to understand the movement of free choice tending towards good.

Reply Obj. 2. Origen says, "The serpent of old did not from the first walk upon his breast and belly," because of the first instant in which he was not wicked.

Reply Obj. 3. An angel has inflexible free choice after choosing; consequently, if after the first instant, in which he had a natural movement to good, he had not at once placed a barrier to Happiness, he would have been confirmed in good. It is not so with man, and therefore the argument does not hold good.

Reply Obj. 4. It is true to say that "there is a middle time between every two instants," so far as "time is continuous," as it is proved in the *Physics*.[2] But in the angels, who are not subject to the heavenly movement, which is primarily measured by continuous time, time is taken to mean the succession of their intellectual acts, or of their affections. So the first instant in the angels is understood to correspond to the operation of the angelic mind, by which it turns to itself by its evening knowledge, because on the first day evening is mentioned, but not morning. This operation was good in them all. From such operation some of them were turned to the praise of the Word by their morning knowledge, while others, remaining within themselves, became night, "swelling

up with pride," as Augustine says (*Gen. ad lit.* iv. 24).[3] Hence the first operation was common to them all, but in their second they were separated. Consequently they were all of them good in the first instant, but in the second the good were set apart from the wicked.

ARTICLE 7. *Whether the Highest Angel Among Those Who Sinned Was the Highest of All?*

We proceed thus to the Seventh Article: It would seem that the highest among the angels who sinned was not the highest of all.

Objection 1. For it is stated (Ezech. 28. 14): *Thou wast a cherub stretched out, and protecting, and I set thee in the holy mountain of God.* Now the order of the Cherubim is under the order of the Seraphim, as Dionysius says (*Cæl. Hier.* vii).[4] Therefore, the highest angel among those who sinned was not the highest of all.

Obj. 2. Further, God made intellectual nature in order that it might attain to Happiness. If therefore the highest of the angels sinned, it follows that the Divine ordinance was frustrated in the noblest creature; which is unfitting.

Obj. 3. Further, the more a subject is inclined towards anything, so much the less can it fall away from it. But the higher an angel is, so much the more is he inclined towards God. Therefore so much the less can he turn away from God by sinning. And so it seems that the angel who sinned was not the highest of all, but one of the lower angels.

On the contrary, Gregory (*Hom.* xxxiv *in Ev.*)[5] says that "the chief angel who sinned, being set over all the hosts of angels," surpassed them in brightness, "and was by comparison the most illustrious among them."

I answer that, Two things have to be considered in sin, namely, the proneness to sin, and the motive for sinning. If, then, in the angels we consider the proneness to sin, it seems that the higher angels were less likely to sin than the lower. On this account Damascene says (*De Fid. Orth.* ii),[6] that the highest of those who sinned "was set over the terrestrial order." This opinion seems to agree with the view of the Platonists, which Augustine quotes.[7] For they said that all the gods were good, whereas some of the demons were good, and some bad; naming as gods the intellectual sub-

---

[1] See above, Q. LXII, A. 3.
[2] Aristotle, VI, 1 (231^{b}9); cf. IV, 11 (219^{a}13).
[3] PL 34, 313.
[4] Sect. 1 (PG 3, 205).
[5] PL 76, 1250.
[6] Chap. 4 (PG 94, 873).
[7] *City of God,* VIII, 13, 14 (PL 41, 237, 238); X, 11 (PL 41, 289).

stances which are above the lunar sphere, and calling by the name of demons the intellectual substances which are beneath it, yet higher than men in the order of nature. But this opinion is to be rejected as contrary to faith, because the whole corporeal creation is governed by God through the angels, as Augustine says (De Trin. iii. 4).[1] Consequently there is nothing to prevent us from saying that the lower angels were divinely set aside for presiding over the lower bodies, the higher over the higher bodies, and the highest to stand before God. And in this sense Damascene says (loc. cit.) that they who fell were of the lower grade of angels; yet in that order some of them remained good.

But if the motive for sinning be considered, we find that it existed in the higher angels more than in the lower. For, as has been said (A. 2), the demons' sin was pride; and the motive of pride is excellence, which was greater in the higher spirits. Hence Gregory says (loc. cit.) that he who sinned was the very highest of all.

This seems to be the more probable view, because the angels' sin did not come of any proneness, but of free choice alone. Consequently that argument seems to have the more weight which is drawn from the motive in sinning. Yet the other view is not to be dismissed, because there might be some motive for sinning in him also who was the chief of the lower angels.

Reply Obj. 1. Cherubim is interpreted "fulness of knowledge," while Seraphim means "those who are on fire," or "who set on fire." Consequently Cherubim is derived from knowledge, which is compatible with mortal sin; but Seraphim is derived from the heat of charity, which is incompatible with mortal sin. Therefore the first angel who sinned is called not a Seraph, but a Cherub.

Reply Obj. 2. The Divine intention is not frustrated in those who sin, or in those who are saved; for God knows beforehand the end of both, and He procures glory from both, saving these of His goodness, and punishing those of His justice. But the intellectual creature, when it sins, falls away from its due end. Nor is this unfitting in any exalted creature, because the intellectual creature was so made by God that it lies within its own choice to act for its end.

Reply Obj. 3. However great was the inclination towards good in the highest angel, there was no necessity imposed upon him. Consequently he was able through free choice not to follow it.

[1] PL 42, 873.

ARTICLE 8. Whether the Sin of the Highest Angel Was the Cause of the Others Sinning?

We proceed thus to the Eighth Article: It would seem that the sin of the highest angel was not the cause of the others sinning.

Objection 1. For the cause precedes the effect. But, as Damascene observes (De Fid. Orth. ii),[2] they all sinned at the one time. Therefore the sin of one was not the cause of the others sinning.

Obj. 2. Further, an angel's first sin can only be pride, as was shown above (A. 2). But pride seeks excellence. Now it is more contrary to excellence for anyone to be subject to an inferior than to a superior, and so it does not appear that the angels sinned by desiring to be subject to a higher angel rather than to God. Yet the sin of one angel would have been the cause of the others sinning if he had induced them to be his subjects. Therefore it does not appear that the sin of the highest angel was the cause of the others sinning.

Obj. 3. Further, it is a greater sin to wish to be subject to another against God than to wish to be over another against God, because there is less motive for sinning. If, therefore, the sin of the foremost angel was the cause of the others sinning, in that he induced them to subject themselves to him, then the lower angels would have sinned more deeply than the highest one, which is contrary to a gloss on Ps. 103. 26: This dragon which Thou hast formed: "He who was the more excellent than the rest became the greater in malice."[3] Therefore the sin of the highest angel was not the cause of the others sinning.

On the contrary, It is said (Apoc. 12. 4) that the dragon drew with him the third part of the stars of heaven.

I answer that, The sin of the highest angel was the cause of the others sinning, not as compelling them, but as inducing them by a kind of exhortation. A token thereof appears in this, that all the demons are subjects of that highest one, as is evident from our Lord's words: Go (Vulg., Depart from Me), you cursed, into everlasting fire, which was prepared for the devil and his angels (Matt. 25. 41). For the order of Divine justice exacts that whosoever consents to another's evil suggestion shall be subjected to him in his punishment according to (II Pet. 2. 19): By whom a man is overcome, of the same also he is the slave.

[2] Chap. 4 (PG 94, 876).

[3] Glossa ordin., (III, 241A); Glossa Lombardi (PL 191, 941). Cf. Aug., Enarr. in Ps., CIII, 4 (PL 37, 1381).

Reply Obj. 1. Although the demons all sinned in the one instant, yet the sin of one could be the cause of the rest sinning. For the angel needs no delay of time for choice, exhortation, or consent, as man, who requires deliberation in order to choose and consent, and vocal speech in order to exhort, both of which are the work of time. And it is evident that even man begins to speak in the very instant when he takes thought; and in the last instant of speech, another who catches his meaning can assent to what is said, as is especially evident with regard to primary concepts, which everyone accepts directly they are heard. Taking away, then, the time for speech and deliberation which is required in us, in the same instant in which the highest angel expressed his affection by intelligible speech, it was possible for the others to consent to it.

Reply Obj. 2. Other things being equal, the proud would rather be subject to a superior than to an inferior. Yet he chooses rather to be subject to an inferior than to a superior if he can procure an advantage under an inferior which he cannot under a superior. Consequently it was not against the demons' pride for them to wish to serve an inferior by yielding to his rule; for they wanted to have him as their prince and leader so that they might attain their ultimate happiness of their own natural powers, especially because in the order of nature they were even then subject to the highest angel.

Reply Obj. 3. As was observed above (Q. LXII, A. 6), an angel has nothing in him to retard his action, and with his whole might he is moved to whatsoever he is moved, be it good or bad. Consequently since the highest angel had greater natural power than the lower angels, he fell into sin with a more intense movement, and therefore he became the greater in malice.

ARTICLE 9. *Whether Those Who Sinned Were as Many as Those Who Remained Firm?*

We proceed thus to the Ninth Article: It would seem that more angels sinned than stood firm.

Objection 1. For, as the Philosopher says:[1] "Evil is in many, but good is in few."

Obj. 2. Further, justice and sin are to be found in the same way in men and in angels. But there are more wicked men to be found than good, according to Eccles. 1. 15: *The number of fools is infinite.* Therefore for the same reason it is so with the angels.

Obj. 3. Further, the angels are distinguished according to persons and orders. Therefore if

[1] *Topics,* ii, 6 (112ᵇ11).

more angelic persons stood firm, it would appear that those who sinned were not from all the orders.

On the contrary, It is said (IV Kings 6. 16): *There are more with us than with them,* which is expounded of the good angels who are with us to aid us, and the wicked spirits who are our foes.

I answer that, More angels stood firm than sinned. Because sin is contrary to the natural inclination, while that which is against the natural order happens with less frequency; for nature procures its effect either always, or more often than not.

Reply Obj. 1. The Philosopher is speaking with regard to men, in whom evil comes to pass from seeking after sensible pleasures, which are known to most men, and from forsaking the good dictated by reason, which good is known to the few. In the angels there is only an intellectual nature. Hence the argument does not hold.

And from this we have the *answer to the second difficulty.*

Reply Obj. 3. According to those who hold that the chief devil belonged to the lower order[2] of the angels, who are set over earthly affairs, it is evident that some of every order did not fall, but only those of the lowest order. According to those who maintain that the chief devil was of the highest order,[3] it is probable that some fell of every order; just as men are taken up into every order to supply for the angelic ruin. In this view the liberty of free choice is more established, which in every degree of creature can be turned to evil. In the Sacred Scripture, however, the names of some orders, as of Seraphim and Thrones, are not attributed to demons, since they are derived from the ardour of love and from God's indwelling, which are not consistent with mortal sin. Yet the names of Cherubim, Powers, and Principalities are attributed to them, because these names are derived from knowledge and from power, which can be common to both good and bad.

QUESTION LXIV

THE PUNISHMENT OF THE DEMONS

(In Four Articles)

IT now remains to deal with the punishment of the demons, under which heading there are four points of inquiry: (1) Of their darkness of intellect. (2) Of their obstinacy of will. (3) Of their grief. (4) Of their place of punishment.

[2] Damascene, *De Fide Orth.,* ii, 4 (PG 94, 873).
[3] Gregory, *In Evang.,* Bk. ii, hom. xxxiv (PL 76, 1250).
Cf. Wm. of Paris, *De Univ.,* ii–ii, chap. 11 (ii, 805).

ARTICLE 1. *Whether the Demons' Intellect Is Darkened by Privation of the Knowledge of All Truth?*

We proceed thus to the First Article: It would seem that the demons' intellect is darkened by being deprived of the knowledge of all truth.

Objection 1. For if they knew any truth at all, they would most of all know themselves, which is to know separated substances. But this is not in keeping with their unhappiness, for this seems to belong to great happiness, so much so that some writers have assigned as man's last happiness the knowledge of the separated substances.[1] Therefore the demons are deprived of all knowledge of truth.

Obj. 2. Further, what is most manifest in its nature seems to be specially manifest to the angels, whether good or bad. That the same is not most manifest with regard to ourselves comes from the weakness of our intellect which draws its knowledge from phantasms; as it comes from the weakness of its eye that the owl cannot behold the light of the sun. But the demons cannot know God, Who is most manifest of Himself, because He is the sovereign truth; and this is because they are not clean of heart, whereby alone can God be seen. Therefore neither can they know other things.

Obj. 3. Further, according to Augustine (*Gen. ad lit.* iv, 22),[2] the proper knowledge of the angels is twofold; namely, morning and evening. But the demons have no morning knowledge, because they do not see things in the Word; nor have they the evening knowledge, because this evening knowledge refers the things known to the Creator's praise; hence, after evening comes morning, as it says in the first book of Gen. Therefore the demons can have no knowledge of things.

Obj. 4. Further, the angels at their creation knew the mystery of the kingdom of God, as Augustine says (*Gen. ad lit.* v, 19).[3] But the demons are deprived of such knowledge; *for if they had known it, they would never have crucified the Lord of glory,* as is said I Cor. 2. 8. Therefore, for the same reason, they are deprived of all other knowledge of truth.

Obj. 5. Further, whatever truth anyone knows is known either naturally, as we know first principles, or by deriving it from someone else, as we know by learning, or by long experience, as the things we learn by discovery. Now, the demons

cannot know the truth by their own nature, because, as Augustine says,[4] the good angels are separated from them as light is from darkness, and every manifestation is made through light, as is said Eph. 5. 13. In like manner they cannot learn by revelation, nor by learning from the good angels, because *there is no fellowship of light with darkness* (Vulg., *What fellowship hath . . . ?*) (II Cor. 6. 14). Nor can they learn by long experience because experience comes of the senses. Consequently there is no knowledge of truth in them.

On the contrary, Dionysius says (*Div. Nom.* iv)[5] that, "certain gifts were bestowed upon the demons which, we say, have not been changed at all, but remain entire and most brilliant." Now, the knowledge of truth stands among those natural gifts. Consequently there is some knowledge of truth in them.

I answer that, The knowledge of truth is twofold: one which comes of nature, and one which comes of grace. The knowledge which comes of grace is likewise twofold: the first is purely speculative, as when Divine secrets are imparted to an individual; the other is affective, and produces love for God; which knowledge properly belongs to the gift of Wisdom.

Of these three kinds of knowledge the first was neither taken away nor lessened in the demons. For it follows from the very nature of the angel, who, according to his nature, is an intellect or mind. For on account of the simplicity of his substance, nothing can be withdrawn from his nature, so as to punish him by subtracting from his natural powers, as a man is punished by being deprived of a hand or foot or of something else. Therefore Dionysius says (*loc. cit.*) that the natural gifts remain entire in them. Consequently their natural knowledge was not diminished. The second kind of knowledge, however, which comes of grace, and consists in speculation, has not been utterly taken away from them, but lessened; because, of these Divine secrets only so much is revealed to them as is necessary, and that is done either by means of the angels, or "through some temporal workings of Divine power," as Augustine says;[6] but not in the same degree as to the holy angels, to whom many more things are revealed, and more clearly, in the Word Himself. But of the third knowledge, as likewise of charity, they are utterly deprived.

Reply Obj. 1. Happiness consists in drawing near to something higher. The separated sub-

---

[1] See below, Q. LXXXVIII, A. 1.
[2] PL 34, 317; cf. also *City of God*, XI, 7 (PL 41, 322).
[3] PL 34, 334.

[4] *City of God*, XI, 19, 33 (PL 41, 333, 346).
[5] Sect. 23 (PG 3, 725).   [6] *City of God*, IX, 21 (PL 41, 274).

stances are above us in the order of nature; hence man can have happiness of a kind by knowing the separated substances, although his perfect happiness consists in knowing the first substance, namely, God. But it is natural for one separate substance to know another, as it is natural for us to know sensible natures. Hence, as man's happiness does not consist in knowing sensible natures, so neither does the angel's happiness consist in knowing separated substances.

Reply Obj. 2. What is most manifest in its nature is hidden from us because it exceeds the proportion of our intellect, and not merely because our intellect draws knowledge from phantasms. Now the Divine substance surpasses the proportion not only of the human intellect, but even of the angelic. Consequently, not even an angel can of his own nature know God's substance. Yet on account of the perfection of his intellect he can of his nature have a higher knowledge of God than man can have. Such knowledge of God remains also in the demons. Although they do not possess the purity which comes with grace, nevertheless they have purity of nature; and this suffices for the knowledge of God which belongs to them from their nature.

Reply Obj. 3. The creature is darkness in comparison with the excellence of the Divine light, and therefore the creature's knowledge in its own nature is called evening knowledge. For the evening is akin to darkness, yet it possesses some light; but when the light fails utterly, then it is night. So then the knowledge of things in their own nature, when referred to the praise of the Creator, as it is in the good angels, has something of the Divine light, and can be called evening knowledge; but if it be not referred to God, as is the case with the demons, it is not called evening, but "nocturnal" knowledge. Accordingly we read in Genesis (1. 5) that the darkness, which God separated from the light, *He called night.*

Reply Obj. 4. All the angels had some knowledge from the very beginning respecting the mystery of God's kingdom, which found its completion in Christ; and most of all from the moment when they were blessed by the vision of the Word, which the demons never had. Yet all the angels did not perfectly nor equally apprehend it; hence the demons much less fully understood the mystery of the Incarnation when Christ was in the world. For, as Augustine observes,[1] "It was not manifested to them as it was to the holy angels, who enjoy a participated eternity of the Word; but it was made known by

[1] *City of God,* IX, 21 (PL 41, 274).

some temporal effects, so as to strike terror into them." For had they perfectly and certainly known that he was the Son of God and the effect of His passion, they would never have procured the crucifixion of the Lord of glory.

Reply Obj. 5. The demons know a truth in three ways: first of all by the subtlety of their nature; for although they are darkened by privation of the light of grace, yet they are enlightened by the light of their intellectual nature. Secondly, by revelation from the holy angels; for while not agreeing with them in conformity of will, they do agree, nevertheless, by their likeness of intellectual nature, according to which they can accept what is manifested by others. Thirdly, they know by long experience; not as deriving it from the senses, but when the likeness of their innate intelligible species is completed in individual things, they know some things as present, which they previously did not know would come to pass, as we said when dealing with the knowledge of the angels (Q. LVII, A. 3 ANS. 3).

ARTICLE 2. *Whether the Will of the Demons Is Obstinate in Evil?*

We proceed thus to the Second Article: It would seem that the will of the demons is not obstinate in evil.

Objection 1. For liberty of choice belongs to the nature of an intellectual being, which nature remains in the demons, as we said above (A. 1). But liberty of choice is per se and first ordered to good rather than to evil. Therefore the demons' will is not so obstinate in evil as not to be able to return to what is good.

Obj. 2. Further, since God's mercy is infinite, it is greater than the demons' malice, which is finite. But no one returns from the malice of sin to the goodness of justice save through God's mercy. Therefore the demons can likewise return from their state of malice to the state of justice.

Obj. 3. Further, if the demons have a will obstinate in evil, then their will would be especially obstinate in the sin whereby they fell. But that sin, namely, pride, is in them no longer, because the motive for the sin no longer endures, namely, excellence. Therefore the demon is not obstinate in malice.

Obj. 4. Further, Gregory says (*Moral.* iv)[2] that "man can be reinstated by another, since he fell through another." But, as was observed already (Q. LXIII, A. 8), the lower demons fell through the highest one. Therefore their fall can

[2] Chap. 3 (PL 75, 642).

be repaired by another. Consequently they are not obstinate in malice.

Obj. 5. Further, whoever is obstinate in malice never performs any good work. But the demon performs some good works, for he confesses the truth, saying to Christ: *I know Who Thou art, the holy one of God* (Mark 1. 24). *The demons* also *believe and tremble* (Jas. 2. 19). And Dionysius observes (*Div. Nom.* iv),[1] that "they desire what is good and best, which is, to be, to live, to understand." Therefore they are not obstinate in malice.

On the contrary, It is said (Ps. 73. 23): *The pride of them that hate Thee, ascendeth continually,* and this is understood of the demons. Therefore they remain ever obstinate in their malice.

I answer that, It was Origen's opinion[2] that every will of the creature can by reason of free choice be inclined to good and evil, with the exception of the soul of Christ on account of the union of the Word. Such a statement deprives angels and men of true happiness, because everlasting stability is of the very nature of true happiness (hence it is termed "life everlasting"). It is also contrary to the authority of Sacred Scripture, which declares that demons and wicked men shall be sent into everlasting punishment, and the good brought into everlasting life. Consequently such an opinion must be considered erroneous; and according to Catholic Faith, it must be held firmly both that the will of the good angels is confirmed in good, and that the will of the demons is obstinate in evil.

We must seek for the cause of this obstinacy not in the gravity of the sin, but in the condition of their nature or state. For as Damascene says (*De Fid. Orth.* ii),[3] "death is to men what the fall is to the angels." Now it is clear that all the mortal sins of men, grave or less grave, are pardonable before death; but after death they are without remission, and endure for ever.

To find the cause, then, of this obstinacy, it must be borne in mind that the power of desire is in all things proportioned to the power of apprehending whereby it is moved, as the movable by its mover. For the sensitive appetite seeks a particular good, while the will seeks the universal good, as was said above (Q. LIX, A. 1); as also the sense apprehends particular objects, while the intellect considers universals. Now the angel's apprehension differs from man's in this respect, that the angel by his intellect apprehends immovably, as we apprehend immovably first principles which are the object of the intellect. But man by his reason apprehends movably, passing from one consideration to another, and having the way open by which he may proceed to either of two opposites. Consequently man's will adheres to a thing movably, and with the power of forsaking it and of clinging to the opposite, but the angel's will adheres fixedly and immovably.

Therefore, if his will be considered before its adhering, it can freely adhere either to this or to its opposite, in such things namely, as he does not will naturally; but after he has once adhered, he clings immovably. So it is customary to say that man's free choice is flexible to the opposite both before and after choice; but the angel's free choice is flexible to either opposite before the choice, but not after. Therefore the good angels, always adhering to justice, are confirmed therein; but the wicked ones, sinning, are obstinate in sin. Later on we shall treat of the obstinacy of men who are damned. (*Suppl.,* Q. XCVIII, AA. 1, 3.)

Reply Obj. 1. The good and wicked angels have free choice, but according to the manner and condition of their nature, as has been said.

Reply Obj. 2. God's mercy frees from sin those who repent. But those who are not capable of repenting, cling immovably to sin, and are not freed by the Divine mercy.

Reply Obj. 3. The devil's first sin still remains in him according to desire, although not as to his believing that he can obtain what he desired. Even so, if a man were to believe that he can commit murder, and wills to commit it, and afterwards the power is taken from him, nevertheless the will to murder can stay with him, so that he would he had done it, or still would do it if he could.

Reply Obj. 4. The fact that man sinned from another's suggestion is not the whole cause for man's sin being pardonable. Consequently the argument does not hold good.

Reply Obj. 5. A demon's act is twofold. One comes of deliberate will, and this is properly called his own act. Such an act on the demon's part is always wicked, because, although at times he does something good, yet he does not do it well; as when he tells the truth in order to deceive, and when he believes and confesses, yet not willingly, but compelled by the evidence of things. Another kind of act is natural to the demon; this can be good, and bears witness to the goodness of nature. Yet he abuses even such good acts to evil purpose.

[1] Sect. 23 (PG 3, 725).
[2] *Peri Archon,* 1, 6. (PG 11, 168); chap. 8 (178).
[3] Chap. 4 (PG 94, 877).

ARTICLE 3. *Whether There Is Sorrow in the Demons?*

We proceed thus to the Third Article: It would seem that there is no sorrow in the demons.

Objection 1. For since sorrow and joy are opposites, they cannot be together in the same subject. But there is joy in the demons; for Augustine writing against the Manichees (*De Gen. contra Manich.* ii, 17)[1] says: "The devil has power over them who despise God's commandments, and he rejoices over this sinister power." Therefore there is no sorrow in the demons.

Obj. 2. Further, sorrow is the cause of fear; for those things cause fear while they are future which cause sorrow when they are present. But there is no fear in the demons, according to Job. 41. 24, *Who was made to fear no one.* Therefore there is no grief in the demons.

Obj. 3. Further, it is a good thing to be sorry for evil. But the demons can do no good action. Therefore they cannot be sorry, at least for the evil of sin; which applies to the worm of conscience.

On the contrary, The demon's sin is greater than man's sin. But man is punished with sorrow on account of the pleasure taken in sin, according to Apoc. 18. 7, *As much as she hath glorified herself, and lived in delicacies, so much torment and sorrow give ye to her.* Consequently much more is the devil punished with the grief of sorrow, because he especially glorified himself.

I answer that, Fear, sorrow, joy, and the like, so far as they are passions, cannot be in the demons; for thus they are proper to the sensitive appetite, which is a power in a corporeal organ. According, however, as they denote simple acts of the will, they can be in the demons. And it must be said that there is sorrow in them, because sorrow, as denoting a simple act of the will, is nothing else than the resistance of the will to what is, or to what is not. Now it is evident that the demons would wish many things not to be which are, and others to be which are not; for, out of envy, they would wish others to be damned, who are saved. Consequently, sorrow must be said to exist in them, and especially because it is of the very notion of punishment for it to be distasteful to the will. Moreover, they are deprived of happiness, which they desire naturally; and their wicked will is curbed in many respects.

Reply Obj. 1. Joy and sorrow about the same

[1] PL 34, 209.

thing are opposites, but not about different things. Hence there is nothing to hinder a man from being sorry for one thing, and joyful for another, especially so far as sorrow and joy imply simple acts of the will; because, not merely in different things, but even in one and the same thing, there can be something that we will, and something that we will not.

Reply Obj. 2. As there is sorrow in the demons over present evil, so also there is fear of future evil. Now when it is said, *He was made to fear no one,* this is to be understood of the fear of God which restrains from sin. For it is written elsewhere that *the devils believe and tremble* (Jas. 2. 19).

Reply Obj. 3. To be sorry for the evil of sin on account of the sin bears witness to the goodness of the will, to which the evil of sin is opposed. But to be sorry for the evil of punishment, or for the evil of sin on account of the punishment, bears witness to the goodness of nature, to which the evil of punishment is opposed. Hence Augustine says[2] that "sorrow for good lost by punishment is the witness to a good nature." Consequently, since the demon has a perverse and obstinate will, he is not sorry for the evil of sin.

ARTICLE 4. *Whether Our Atmosphere Is the Demon's Place of Punishment?*

We proceed thus to the Fourth Article: It would seem that this atmosphere is not the demons' place of punishment.

Objection 1. For a demon is a spiritual nature. But a spiritual nature is not affected by place. Therefore there is no place of punishment for demons.

Obj. 2. Further, man's sin is not graver than the demons'. But man's place of punishment is hell. Much more, therefore, is it the demon's place of punishment, and consequently not the darksome atmosphere.

Obj. 3. Further, the demons are punished with the pain of fire. But there is no fire in the misty atmosphere. Therefore the dark atmosphere is not the place of punishment for the demons.

On the contrary, Augustine says (*Gen. ad lit.* iii, 10)[3] that "the darksome atmosphere is as a prison to the demons until the judgment day."

I answer that, The angels in their own nature stand midway between God and men. Now the order of Divine providence so disposes that it procures the welfare of the inferior orders

[2] *City of God,* XIX, 13 (PL 41, 641).

[3] PL 34, 285.

through the superior. But man's welfare is disposed by Divine providence in two ways: first of all, directly, when a man is brought to good and withheld from evil; and this is fittingly done through the good angels. In another way, indirectly, as when anyone assailed is exercised by fighting against opposition. It was fitting for this procuring of man's welfare to be brought about through the wicked spirits, lest they should cease to be of service in the natural order. Consequently a twofold place of punishment is due to the demons: one, by reason of their sin, and this is hell; and another in order that they may tempt men, and thus the dark atmosphere is their due place of punishment.

Now the procuring of men's salvation is prolonged even to the judgment day; consequently, the ministry of the angels and wrestling with demons endure until then. Hence until then the good angels are sent to us here, and the demons are in this dark atmosphere for our trial, although some of them are even now in hell, to torment those whom they have led astray; just as some of the good angels are with the holy souls in heaven. But after the judgment day all the wicked, both men and angels, will be in hell, and the good in heaven.

Reply Obj. 1. A place is not penal to angel or soul as if affecting the nature by changing it, but as affecting the will by saddening it, as long as the angel or the soul apprehends that it is in a place not agreeable to its will.

Reply Obj. 2. One soul is not set over another in the order of nature, as the demons are over men in the order of nature. Consequently there is no parallel.

Reply Obj. 3. Some have maintained that the pain of sense for demons and souls is postponed until the judgment day,[1] and that the happiness of the saints is likewise postponed until the judgment day. But this is erroneous, and contrary to the teaching of the Apostle (II Cor. 5. 1): *If our earthly house of this habitation be dissolved, we have a house in heaven.* Others, again,[2] while not admitting the same of souls, admit it as to demons. But it is better to say that the same judgment is passed upon wicked souls and wicked angels, even as on good souls and good angels.

Consequently, it must be said that although a heavenly place belongs to the glory of the angels, yet their glory is not lessened by their coming to us; for they consider that place to be their own; in the same way as we say that the bishop's honour is not lessened while he is not actually sitting on his throne. In like manner it must be said, that although the demons are not actually bound within the fire of hell while they are in this dark atmosphere, nevertheless their punishment is none the less, because they know that such confinement is their due. Hence it is said in a gloss upon Jas. 3. 6[3] that they carry the fire of hell with them wherever they go. Nor is this contrary to what is said (Luke 8. 31), *They besought the Lord not to cast them into the abyss;* for they asked for this, deeming it to be a punishment for them to be cast out of a place where they could injure men. Hence it is stated, *They* (Vulg., *He*) *besought Him that He would not expel them* (Vulg., *him*) *out of the country* (Mark 5. 10).

[1] Cf. St. Thomas, *Contra Gent.* IV, 91; cf. also Hilary, *Tract. in Ps.*, Ps. 2 (PL 9, 290); Gregory the Great, *Dial.*, IV, 28 (PL 77, 365).

[2] William of Paris, *De Univ.*, II–II, chap. 70 (II, 871); cf. Peter of Poitiers, *Sent.*, II, 4 (PL 211, 951).

[3] *Glossa ordin.*, (VI, 213F).

TREATISE ON THE WORK OF
THE SIX DAYS

QUESTION LXV

The work of creation of corporeal creatures

(In Four Articles)

From the consideration of spiritual creatures we proceed to that of corporeal creatures, in the production of which, as Holy Scripture makes mention, three works are found, namely, the work of creation, as given in the words, *In the beginning God created heaven and earth* (Gen. i. i); the work of distinction as given in the words, *He divided the light from the darkness, and the waters that are above the firmament from the waters that are under the firmament* (Gen. i. 4, 7); and the work of adornment, expressed thus, *Let there be lights in the firmament* (Gen. i. 14).

First, then, we must consider the work of creation; secondly, the work of distinction (Q. LXVI); and thirdly, the work of adornment (Q. LXX). Under the first head there are four points of inquiry: (1) Whether corporeal creatures are from God? (2) Whether they were created on account of God's goodness? (3) Whether they were created by God through the medium of the angels? (4) Whether the forms of bodies are from the angels or immediately from God.

Article i. *Whether Corporeal Creatures Are From God?*

We proceed thus to the First Article: It would seem that corporeal creatures are not from God.

Objection 1. For it is said (Eccles. 3. 14): *I have learned that all the works which God hath made, continue for ever.* But visible bodies do not continue for ever, for it is said (II Cor. 4. 18): *The things which are seen are temporal, but the things which are not seen are eternal.* Therefore God did not make visible bodies.

Obj. 2. Further, it is said (Gen. i. 31): *God saw all the things that He had made, and they were very good.* But corporeal creatures are evil, since we find them harmful in many ways, as may be seen in serpents, in the sun's heat, and other like things. Now a thing is called evil in so far as it is harmful. Corporeal creatures, therefore, are not from God.

Obj. 3. Further, what is from God does not withdraw us from God, but leads us to Him. But corporeal creatures withdraw us from God. Hence the Apostle says (II Cor. 4. 18): *While we look not at the things which are seen.* Corporeal creatures, therefore, are not from God.

On the contrary, It is said (Ps. 145. 6): *Who made heaven and earth, the sea, and all things that are in them.*

I answer that, Certain heretics maintain[1] that visible things are not created by the good God, but by an evil principle, and allege in proof of their error the words of the Apostle (II Cor. 4. 4), *The god of this world hath blinded the minds of unbelievers.* But this position is altogether untenable. For, if things that differ agree in some point, there must be some cause for that agreement, since things diverse in nature cannot be united of themselves. Hence whenever in different things some one thing common to all is found, it must be that these different things receive that one thing from some one cause, as different bodies that are hot receive their heat from fire. But being is found to be common to all things, however different otherwise. There must, therefore, be one principle of being from which all things in whatever way existing have their being, whether they are invisible and spiritual, or visible and corporeal. But the devil is called the god of this world not as having created it, but because worldlings serve him, of whom also the Apostle says, speaking in the same sense, *Whose god is their belly* (Phil. 3. 19).

Reply Obj. 1. All the creatures of God in some respects continue for ever, at least as to matter, since what is created will never be annihilated, even though it be corruptible. And the nearer a creature approaches God, Who is immovable, the more it also is immovable. For corruptible creatures endure for ever as regards their matter, though they change as regards

---

[1] The Manichees. See above, Q. XLIX, A. 3.

their substantial form. But incorruptible creatures endure wtih respect to their substance, though they are changeable in other respects, such as place; for instance, the heavenly bodies; or the affections, as spiritual creatures. But the Apostle's words, *The things which are seen are temporal,* though true even as regards such things considered in themselves (in so far as every visible creature is subject to time, either as to being or as to movement), are intended to apply to visible things in so far as they are offered to man as rewards. For such rewards consisting in these visible things are temporal, while those that are invisible endure for ever. Hence he said before (*ibid.* 17): It *worketh for us . . . an eternal weight of glory.*

Reply Obj. 2. Corporeal creatures according to their nature are good, though this good is not universal, but particular and limited, the consequence of which is a certain opposition of contrary qualities, though each quality is good in itself. To those, however, who estimate things, not by their nature, but by the good they themselves can derive from them, everything which is harmful to themselves seems evil absolutely. For they do not consider that what is in some way injurious to one person to another is beneficial, and that even to themselves the same thing may be evil in some respects, but good in others. And this could not be if bodies were essentially evil and harmful.

Reply Obj. 3. Creatures of themselves do not withdraw us from God, but lead us to Him; for *the invisible things of God are clearly seen, being understood by the things that are made* (Rom. 1. 20). If, then, they withdraw men from God, it is the fault of those who use them foolishly. Thus it is said (Wisd. 14. 11): *Creatures are turned into a snare to the feet of the unwise.* And the very fact that they can thus withdraw us from God proves that they came from Him, for they cannot lead the foolish away from God except by the allurements of some good that they have from Him.

ARTICLE 2. *Whether Corporeal Things Were Made On Account Of God's Goodness?*

We proceed thus to the Second Article: It would seem that corporeal creatures were not made on account of God's goodness.

Objection 1. For it is said (Wisd. 1. 14) that *God created all things that they might be.* Therefore all things were created for their own being's sake, and not on account of God's goodness.

Obj. 2. Further, good has the nature of an end. Therefore the greater good in things is the end of the lesser good. But spiritual creatures are related to corporeal creatures as the greater good to the lesser. Corporeal creatures, therefore, are created for the sake of spiritual creatures, and not on account of God's goodness.

Obj. 3. Further, justice does not give unequal things except to the unequal. Now God is just. Therefore inequality not created by God must precede all inequality created by Him. But an inequality not created by God can only arise from free choice, and consequently all inequality results from the different movements of free choice. Now, corporeal creatures are unequal to spiritual creatures. Therefore the former were made on account of movements of free choice, and not on account of God's goodness.

On the contrary, Is is said (Prov. 16. 4): *The Lord hath made all things for Himself.*

I answer that, Origen laid down[1] that corporeal creatures were not made according to God's original purpose, but in punishment of the sin of spiritual creatures. For he maintained that God in the beginning made spiritual creatures only, and all of equal nature[2]; but that of these by the use of free choice some turned to God, and, according to the measure of their conversion, were given a higher or a lower rank, retaining their simplicity, while others turned from God, and became bound to different kinds of bodies according to the degree of their turning away.

But this position is erroneous. In the first place, because it is contrary to Scripture, which, after narrating the production of each kind of corporeal creatures, adds, *God saw that it was good* (Gen. 1.), as if to say that everything was brought into being for the reason that it was good for it to be. But according to Origen's opinion, the corporeal creature was made not because it was good that it should be, but that the evil in another might be punished. Secondly, because it would follow that the arrangement which now exists of the corporeal world would arise from chance. For if the sun's body was made what it is that it might serve for a punishment suitable to some sin of a spiritual creature, it would follow that if other spiritual creatures had sinned in the same way as the one to punish whom the sun had been created, many suns would exist in the world; and so of other things. But such a consequence is altogether inadmissible.

Hence setting aside this theory as false, we must consider that the entire universe is con-

[1] *Peri Archon,* III, 5 (PG 11, 329).
[2] *Ibid.,* I, 6, 8; II, 9; III, 5 (PG 11. 166, 178, 229, 329).

stituted by all creatures, as a whole consists of its parts. Now if we wish to assign an end to any whole, and to the parts of that whole, we shall find, first, that each of the parts exists for the sake of its proper act, as the eye for the act of seeing; secondly, that less admirable parts exist for the more admirable, as the senses for the intellect, the lungs for the heart; and, thirdly, that all parts are for the perfection of the whole, as the matter for the form, since the parts are, as it were, the matter of the whole. Furthermore, the whole man is on account of an extrinsic end, that end being the enjoyment of God. So, therefore, in the parts of the universe also every creature exists for its own proper act and perfection, and the less noble for the nobler, as those creatures that are less noble than man exist for the sake of man, whilst individual creatures exist for the perfection of the entire universe. Furthermore, the entire universe, with each of its parts, is ordered towards God as its end, in so far as it imitates, as it were, and shows forth the Divine goodness, to the glory of God. Reasonable creatures, however, in some special and higher manner have God as their end, since they can attain to Him by their own operations, by knowing and loving Him. Thus it is plain that the Divine goodness is the end of all corporeal things.

Reply Obj. 1. In the very fact of any creature possessing being it represents the Divine Being and Its goodness. And, therefore the fact that God created all things that they might have being does not exclude that He created them for His own goodness.

Reply Obj. 2. The proximate end does not exclude the ultimate end. Therefore that corporeal creatures were, in a manner, made for the sake of the spiritual, does not prevent their being made on account of God's goodness.

Reply Obj. 3. Equality of justice has its place in retribution, since equal rewards or punishments are due to equal merit or demerit. But this does not apply to things as at first instituted. For just as an architect, without injustice, places stones of the same kind in different parts of a building not on account of any antecedent difference in the stones, but with a view to securing that perfection of the entire building, which could not be obtained except by the different positions of the stones, even so, God from the beginning, to secure perfection in the universe, has set therein creatures of various and unequal natures, according to His wisdom, and without injustice, since no diversity of merit is presupposed.

ARTICLE 3. *Whether Corporeal Creatures Were Produced by God Through the Medium of the Angels?*

We proceed thus to the Third Article: It would seem that corporeal creatures were produced by God through the medium of the angels.

Objection 1. For, as all things are governed by the Divine wisdom, so by it were all things made, according to Ps. 103. 24: *Thou hast made all things in wisdom.* But "it pertains to wisdom to order," as stated in the beginning of the *Metaphysics.*[1] Hence in the government of things "the lower is ruled by the higher in a certain fitting order," as Augustine says (*De Trin.* iii, 4).[2] Therefore in the production of things it was ordained that the corporeal should be produced by the spiritual, as the lower by the higher.

Obj. 2. Further, diversity of effects shows diversity of causes, since like always produces like. If then all creatures, both spiritual and corporeal, were produced immediately by God, there would be no diversity in creatures, for one would not be farther removed from God than another. But this is clearly false; for the Philosopher says that some things are corruptible because they are far removed from God.[3]

Obj. 3. Further, infinite power is not required to produce a finite effect. But every corporeal thing is finite. Therefore, it could be, and was, produced by the finite power of spiritual creatures; for in such beings there is no distinction between to be and to be able, especially as no dignity befitting a nature is denied to that nature, unless it be from some fault of that nature.

On the contrary, It is said (Gen. 1. 1): *In the beginning God created heaven and earth,* by which are understood corporeal creatures. These, therefore, were produced immediately by God.

I answer that, Some have maintained that creatures proceeded from God by degrees,[4] in such a way that the first creature proceeded from Him immediately, and in its turn produced another, and so on until the production of corporeal creatures. But this position is untenable, since the first production of corporeal creatures is by creation, by which matter itself is produced; for in the act of coming into being the

---

[1] Aristotle, I, 2 (982ᵃ18).
[2] PL 42, 873.
[3] *Generation and Corruption*, II, 10 (336ᵇ30).
[4] Avicenna. See above, Q. XLV, A. 5; see also Avicebron, *Fons Vitae*, II, 34; (BK. 71.3); III, 2 (BK. 76.26); III, 6 (BK. 90.15); also see below, Q. LXXIV, A. 3, Ans. 5.

imperfect must be made before the perfect, and it is impossible that anything should be created, save by God alone.

In proof of this it must be borne in mind that the higher the cause, the more numerous the objects to which its causation extends. Now the underlying principle in things is always more universal than that which informs and restricts it; thus, being is more universal than living, living than understanding, matter than form. The more widely, then, one thing underlies others, the more directly does that thing proceed from a higher cause. Thus the thing that underlies primarily all things belongs properly to the causality of the supreme cause. Therefore no secondary cause can produce anything, unless there is presupposed in the thing produced something that is caused by a higher cause. But creation is the production of a thing in its entire substance, nothing being presupposed, either uncreated or created. Hence it remains that nothing can create except God alone, Who is the first cause. Therefore, in order to show that all bodies were created immediately by God, Moses said: *In the beginning God created heaven and earth.*

Reply Obj. 1. In the production of things an order exists, but not such that one creature is created by another, for that is impossible, but rather such that by the Divine wisdom diverse grades are constituted in creatures.

Reply Obj. 2. God Himself, though one, has knowledge of many and different things without detriment to the simplicity of His nature, as has been shown above (Q. XV, A. 2), so that by His wisdom He is the cause of diverse things, produced according to the diversity of things as known by Him, even as an artificer, by apprehending diverse forms, produces diverse works of art.

Reply Obj. 3. The amount of the power of an agent is measured not only by the thing made, but also by the manner of making it; for one and the same thing is made in one way by a higher power, in another by a lower. But the production of finite things, where nothing is presupposed as existing, is the work of infinite power, and, as such, can belong to no creature.

ARTICLE 4. *Whether the Forms of Bodies Are From the Angels?*

We proceed thus to the Fourth Article: It would seem that the forms of bodies are from the angels.

Objection 1. For Boëthius says (*De Trin.*)[1]

[1] Chap. 2 (PL 64, 1250).

"From forms that are without matter come the forms that are in matter." But forms that are without matter are spiritual substances, and forms that are in matter are the forms of bodies. Therefore, the forms of bodies are from spiritual substances.

Obj. 2. Further, all that is by participation is reduced to that which is by essence. But spiritual substances are forms by their essence, whereas corporeal creatures have forms by participation. Therefore the forms of corporeal things are derived from spiritual substances.

Obj. 3. Further, spiritual substances have more power of causing than the heavenly bodies. But the heavenly bodies give form to things here below, for which reason they are said to cause generation and corruption. Much more, therefore, are material forms derived from spiritual substances.

On the contrary, Augustine says (*De Trin.* iii, 8):[2] "We must not suppose that this corporeal matter serves the angels at their nod, but rather that it obeys God thus." But corporeal matter may be said thus to serve that from which it receives its form. Corporeal forms, then, are not from the angels, but from God.

I answer that, It was the opinion of some that all corporeal forms are derived from spiritual substances, which we call the angels. And there are two ways in which this has been stated.

For Plato held that the forms of corporeal matter are derived from, and formed by, forms immaterially subsisting,[3] by a kind of participation.[4] Thus he held[5] that there exists an immaterial man, and an immaterial horse, and so forth, and that from such the singular sensible things that we see are constituted, in so far as in corporeal matter there endures the impression received from these separate forms, by a kind of assimilation, or as he calls it, participation. And, according to the Platonists, the order of forms corresponds to the order of those separate substances;[6] for example, that there is a single separate substance, which is a horse and the cause of all horses, whilst above this is separate life, or *per se* life, as they term it, which is the cause of all life, and that above this again is that which they call being itself, which is the cause of all being.

[2] PL 42, 875.
[3] Aristotle, *Metaphysics*, I, 9 (991^{b}3); *Phaedo* (100).
[4] Aristotle, *op. cit.*, I, 6 (987^{b}9).
[5] Aristotle, *Ibid.*, III, 2 (997^{b}8).
[6] *Lib. de Causis*, I (BA 163.14). Cf. Proclus, *Inst. Theol.*, prop. CI (DD LXXXIV). See also Dionysius, *De Div. Nom.*, v, 1 (PG 3, 816).

Avicenna,[1] however, and certain others,[2] have maintained that the forms of corporeal things do not subsist *per se* in matter, but in the intellect only. Thus they say that from forms existing in the intellect of spiritual creatures (called intelligences by them, but angels by us) proceed all the forms in corporeal matter, as the form of his handiwork proceeds from the forms in the mind of the craftsman.[3] This theory seems to be the same as that of certain heretics of modern times,[4] who say that God indeed created all things, but that the devil formed corporeal matter, and differentiated it into species.

But all these opinions seem to have a common root. They all, in fact, sought for a cause of forms as though the form were of itself brought into being. Whereas, as Aristotle[5] proves, what is, properly speaking, made, is the composite. Now, such are the forms of corruptible things that at one time they exist and at another they do not exist, without being themselves generated or corrupted, but by reason of the generation or corruption of the composite, since even forms have not being, but composites have being through forms; for, according to a thing's mode of being, is the mode in which it is brought into being. Since, then, like is produced from like, we must not look for the cause of corporeal forms in any immaterial form, but in something that is composite, as this fire is generated by that fire. Corporeal forms, therefore, are caused not as emanations from some immaterial form, but by matter being brought from potency into act by some composite agent. But since the composite agent, which is a body, is moved by a created spiritual substance, as Augustine says (*De Trin.* iii, 4),[6] it follows further that even corporeal forms are derived from spiritual substances, not as emanating from them, but as the term of their movement. And, further still, the species of the angelic intellect, which are, as it were, the seminal types of corporeal forms, must be referred to God as the first cause.

But in the first production of corporeal creatures no transmutation from potency to act can have taken place, and accordingly, the corporeal forms that bodies had when first produced came immediately from God, whose bidding alone matter obeys, as its proper cause. To signify this, Moses prefaces each work with the words, *God said, Let this thing be,* or *that,* to denote

the formation of all things by the Word of God, from Whom, according to Augustine,[7] is "all form and fitness and concord of parts."

Reply Obj. 1. By forms without matter Boëthius understands the types of things in the mind of God. Thus the Apostle says (Heb. 11. 3): *By faith we understand that the world was framed by the Word of God; that from invisible things visible things might be made.* But if by immaterial forms he understands the angels, we say that from them come material forms, not by emanation, but by motion.

Reply Obj. 2. Participated forms in matter are reduced, not to self-subsisting forms of the same nature, as the Platonists held, but either to intelligible forms or the angelic intellect, from which they proceed by movement, or, still higher, to the types in the Divine intellect, by which the seeds of forms are implanted in created things, that they may be able to be brought by movement into act.

Reply Obj. 3. The heavenly bodies inform earthly ones by movement, not by emanation.

QUESTION LXVI

Of the order of creation with regard to distinction

(In Four Articles)

We must next consider the work of distinction; first, the ordering of creation with regard to distinction; secondly, the distinction itself. Under the first head there are four points of inquiry: (1) Whether formlessness of created matter preceded in time its distinction? (2) Whether the matter of all corporeal things is the same? (3) Whether the empyrean heaven was created contemporaneously with formless matter? (4) Whether time was created simultaneously with it?

ARTICLE 1. *Whether Formlessness of Created Matter Preceded in Time Its Formation?*

We proceed thus to the First Article: It would seem that formlessness of matter preceded in time its formation.

Objection 1. For it is said (Gen. 1. 2): *The earth was void and empty,* or *invisible and shapeless,* according to another version,[8] by which is understood "the formlessness of matter," as Augustine says.[9] Therefore matter was formless until it received its form.

---

[1] *Meta.,* vii, 2 (96rb).

[2] Avicebron, *Fons Vitae,* iii, 23 (132.24).

[3] Avicenna, *Meta.,* ix, 3 (103vb); *De An.,* iv, 4 (20vb).

[4] The Albigensians; see the Lateran Council, iv (1215) (MA xxii, 962; DZ 428).

[5] *Metaphysics,* vii, 8, 9 (1033[b]17, 1034[b]10). [6] PL 42, 873.

[7] *In Joan.,* tract. 1, on 1.3 (PL 35, 1386).

[8] The Septuagint.

[9] *Confessions,* xii, 15 (PL 32, 831); cf. also *Gen. ad lit.,* ii, 11 (PL 34, 272).

Obj. 2. Further, nature in its working imitates the working of God, as a secondary cause imitates a first cause. But in the working of nature formlessness precedes form in time. It does so, therefore, in the Divine working.

Obj. 3. Further, matter is higher than accident, for matter is part of substance. But God can effect that accident exist without substance, as in the Sacrament of the Altar. He could, therefore, cause matter to be without form.

On the contrary, An imperfect effect proves imperfection in the agent. But God is an agent absolutely perfect; therefore it is said of Him (Deut. 32. 4): *The works of God are perfect.* Therefore the work of His creation was at no time formless.

Further, the formation of corporeal creatures was effected by the work of distinction. But confusion is opposed to distinction, as formlessness to form. If, therefore, formlessness preceded in time the formation of matter, it follows that at the beginning confusion, called by the ancients chaos,[1] existed in the corporeal creation.

I answer that, On this point holy men differ in opinion. Augustine, for instance (*Gen. ad lit.* i, 15),[2] believes that the formlessness of corporeal matter was not prior in time to its formation, but only in origin or the order of nature, whereas others, as Basil (*Hom.* ii *in Hexaëm.*),[3] Ambrose (*in Hexaëm.* 7),[4] and Chrysostom (*Hom.* ii *in Gen.*),[5] hold that formlessness of matter preceded in time its formation. And although these opinions seem contradictory, in reality they differ but little; for Augustine takes the formlessness of matter in a different sense from the others.

In the sense of Augustine it means the lack of all form, and if we understand it in this way we cannot say that the formlessness of matter was prior in time either to its formation or to its distinction. As to formation, the argument is clear. For if formless matter preceded in duration, it was already in act; for this is implied by duration, since the end of creation is being in act, and what is act is itself a form. To say, then, that matter preceded, but without form, is to say being in act without act, which is a contradiction in terms. Nor can it be said that it possessed some common form, on which afterwards follow the different forms, that distinguish it.

For this would be to hold the opinion of the ancient natural philosophers, who maintained that primary matter was some body in act, as fire, air, water, or some intermediate substance. Hence, it followed that "to be made means only to be changed";[6] for since that preceding form bestowed actual substantial being, and made some particular thing to be, it would result that the supervening form would not simply make an actual being, but *this* actual being; which is proper to the accidental form. Thus the consequent forms would be merely accidents, implying not generation, but alteration. Hence we must assert that primary matter was not created altogether formless, nor under any one common form, but under distinct forms. And so, if the formlessness of matter be taken as referring to the condition of primary matter, which in itself is formless, this formlessness did not precede in time its formation or distinction, but only in origin and nature, as Augustine says; in the same way as potency is prior to act, and the part to the whole. But the other holy writers understand by formlessness not the exclusion of all form, but the absence of that beauty and comeliness which are now apparent in the corporeal creation. Accordingly they say that the formlessness of corporeal matter preceded its form in duration. And so, when this is considered, it appears that Augustine agrees with them in some respects, and in others disagrees, as will be shown later (Q. LXIX, A. 1; and Q. LXXIV, A. 2).

As far as may be gathered from the text of Genesis a threefold beauty was wanting to corporeal creatures, for which reason they are said to be without form. For the beauty of light was wanting to all that transparent body which we call the heavens, and so it is said that *darkness was upon the face of the deep.* And the earth lacked beauty in two ways: first, that beauty which it acquired when its watery veil was withdrawn, and so we read that *the earth was void,* or *invisible,* since the waters covered and concealed it from view; secondly, that which it derives from being adorned by herbs and plants, for which reason it is called *empty,* or, according to another reading,[7] *shapeless*—that is, unadorned. Thus after mention of two created natures, the heaven and the earth, the formlessness of the heaven is indicated by the words, *darkness was upon the face of the deep,* since the air is included under heaven; and the formlessness of the earth by the words, *the earth was void and empty.*

---

[1] Cf. Aristotle, *Physics,* I, 4 (187ᵃ23); *Metaphysics,* XII, 2 (1069ᵇ22).

[2] PL 34, 257; cf. also *Confessions,* XII, 40 (PL 32, 843).

[3] PG 29, 29.

[4] PL 14, 148.

[5] PG 53, 30. See also Peter Lombard, *Sent.,* II, XII, 2 (QR I, 359).

[6] Aristotle, *Physics,* I, 4 (187ᵃ12).

[7] The Septuagint.

Reply Obj. 1. The word earth is taken differently in this passage by Augustine, and by other writers. Augustine holds that by the words "earth" and "water," in this passage, primary matter itself is signified, on account of its being impossible for Moses to make the idea of such matter intelligible to an undeveloped people, except under the likeness of well-known objects. Hence he uses a variety of figures in speaking of it, calling it not water only, nor earth only, lest they should think it to be in very truth water or earth. At the same time it has so far a likeness to earth in that it is susceptible of form, and to water in its adaptability to a variety of forms. In this respect, then, the earth is said to be *void and empty*, or *invisible and shapeless*, that matter is known by means of form. Hence, considered in itself, it is called *invisible* or *void*, and its potency is completed by form; thus Plato says that matter is "place."[1] But other holy writers understand by earth the element of earth, and we have said how, in this sense, the earth was, according to them, without form.

Reply Obj. 2. Nature produces effect in act from being in potency; and consequently in the operations of nature potency must precede act in time and formlessness precede form. But God produces being in act out of nothing, and can, therefore, produce a perfect thing in an instant, according to the greatness of His power.

Reply Obj. 3. Accident, in so far as it is a form, is a kind of act, but matter is essentially being in potency. Hence it is more inconsonant that matter should be in act without form than for accident to be without subject.

In *reply to the first argument in the contrary sense*, we say that if, according to some holy writers, formlessness was prior in time to the informing of matter, this arose not from want of power on God's part, but from His wisdom, and from the design of preserving due order in the disposition of creatures by developing perfection from imperfection.

In *reply to the second argument*, we say that certain of the ancient natural philosophers maintained "confusion" devoid of all distinction, except Anaxagoras, who taught that the intellect alone was distinct and without admixture. But previous to the work of distinction Holy Scripture enumerates several kinds of differentiation, the first being that of the heaven from the earth, in which even a material distinction is expressed, as will be shown later (A. 3; Q. LXVIII, A. 1). This is signified by the words, *In the beginning*

---

[1] Cf. Aristotle, *Physics*, IV, 2 (209ᵇ11); *Timaeus* (52); and translation of Chalcidius, Sect. 26 (DD 179).

God created heaven and earth. The second distinction mentioned is that of the elements according to their forms, since both earth and water are named. That air and fire are not mentioned by name is due to the fact that the corporeal nature of these would not be so evident as that of earth and water to the primitive people to whom Moses spoke. Plato,[2] nevertheless, understood air to be signified by the words, *Spirit of God,* since spirit is another name for air, and considered that by the word heaven is meant fire, for he held heaven to be composed of fire, as Augustine relates.[3] But Rabbi Moses,[4] though otherwise agreeing with Plato, says that fire is signified by the word darkness, since, said he, fire does not shine in its own sphere. However, it seems more reasonable to hold to what we stated above; because by the words *Spirit of God* Scripture usually means the Holy Ghost, Who is said to "move over the waters," not, indeed, in bodily shape, but as the craftsman's will may be said to move over the material to which he intends to give a form. The third distinction is that of place, since the earth is said to be under the waters that rendered it invisible, whilst the air, the subject of darkness, is described as being above the waters, in the words: *Darkness was upon the face of the deep.* The remaining distinctions will appear from what follows (Q. LXIX).

ARTICLE 2. *Whether the Formless Matter of All Corporeal Things Is One?*

We proceed thus to the Second Article: It would seem that the formless matter of all corporeal things is one.

Objection 1. For Augustine says:[5] "I find two things Thou hast made, one formed, the other formless," and he says that the latter was "the earth invisible and shapeless," whereby, he says, the matter of all corporeal things is designated. Therefore the matter of all corporeal things is the same.

Obj. 2. Further, the Philosopher says:[6] "Things that are one in genus are one in matter." But all corporeal things are in the same genus of body. Therefore the matter of all bodies is the same.

Obj. 3. Further, different acts are realized in different potencies, and the same act in the same potency. But all bodies have the same form, cor-

---

[2] Aristotle, *Physics*, VIII, 5 (256ᵇ25); *Metaphysics*, I, 8 (989ᵇ15).

[3] *City of God*, VIII, 11 (PL 41, 236); *Timaeus* (31; 32).

[4] *Guide*, II, 30 (FR 213).

[5] *Confessions*, XII, 15 (PL 32, 831).

[6] *Metaphysics*, V, 6 (1016ᵃ24).

poreity. Therefore all bodies have the same matter.

Obj. 4. Further, matter considered in itself is only in potency. But distinction is due to form. Therefore matter considered in itself is the same in all corporeal things.

On the contrary, Things of which the matter is the same are mutually interchangeable, and mutually active or passive, as is said.[1] But heavenly and earthly bodies do not act upon each other mutually. Therefore their matter is not the same.

I answer that, On this question the opinions of philosophers have differed. Plato and all who preceded Aristotle held that all bodies are of the nature of the four elements.[2] Hence, because the four elements have one common matter, as their mutual generation and corruption prove, it followed that the matter of all bodies is the same. But the fact of the incorruptibility of some bodies was ascribed by Plato[3] not to the condition of matter, but to the will of the artificer, God, Whom he represents as saying to the heavenly bodies: "By your own nature you are subject to dissolution, but by My will you are indissoluble, for My will is more powerful than the link that binds you together." But this theory Aristotle disproves[4] by the natural movements of bodies. For since, he says, the heavenly bodies have a natural movement different from that of the elements, it follows that they have a different nature from them. For movement in a circle, which is proper to the heavenly bodies, is not by contraries, whereas the movements of the elements are mutually contrary, one tending upwards, another downwards; so, therefore, the heavenly body is without contrariety, whereas the elemental bodies have contrariety in their nature. And as generation and corruption are from contraries it follows that, whereas the elements are corruptible, the heavenly bodies are incorruptible.

But in spite of this difference of natural corruption and incorruption, Avicebron taught[5] unity of matter in all bodies, arguing from their unity of form. And, indeed, if corporeity were one form in itself, on which the other forms that distinguish bodies from each other supervene,

this argument would necessarily be true; for this form of corporeity would inhere in matter immutably, and so far all bodies would be incorruptible. But corruption would then be merely accidental through the disappearance of the forms that follow—that is to say, it would not be absolute corruption, but relative, since a being in act would subsist under the privation. Thus the ancient natural philosophers taught[6] that the substratum of bodies was some actual being, such as air or fire.

But supposing that there is no form in corruptible bodies which remains as a substratum beneath generation and corruption, it follows necessarily that the matter of corruptible and incorruptible bodies is not the same. For matter, as it is in itself, is in potency to form.

Considered in itself, then, matter must be in potency in respect to all those forms to which it is common, and in receiving any one form it is in act only as regards that form. Hence it remains in potency to all other forms. And this is the case even where some forms are more perfect than others, and contain these others virtually in themselves. For potency in itself is indifferent with respect to perfection and imperfection, so that under an imperfect form it is in potency to a perfect form, and *vice versa*. Matter, therefore, while existing under the form of an incorruptible body, would be in potency to the form of a corruptible body; and as it does not actually possess the latter, it has both form and the privation of form; for want of a form in that which is in potency thereto is privation. But this is the disposition of a corruptible body. It is therefore impossible that bodies by nature corruptible, and those by nature incorruptible, should possess the same matter.

Neither can we say, as Averroes[7] imagines, that the heavenly body itself is the matter of the heaven—being in potency with regard to place, though not to being, and that its form is a separate substance united to it as its moving force. For it is impossible to suppose any being in act unless in its totality it be act and form, or be something which has act or form. Setting aside, then, in thought, the separate substance stated to be a mover, if the heavenly body is not something having form—that is, something composed of a form and the subject of that form—it follows that in its totality it is form and act. But every such thing is something intelligible in act, which the heavenly bodies are not, being sensible. It follows, then, that the matter of the

[1] Aristotle, *Generation and Corruption,* I, 6 (322^{b}18).

[2] Cf. Aristotle, *Physics,* I, 4 (187^{a}12); *Timaeus* (31); see Macrobius, *In Somn. Scip.,* I, 6 (DD 24B); Augustine, *City of God,* VIII, 15 (PL 41, 240); see below, Q. LXVIII, A. I.

[3] *Timaeus* (41); trans. of Chalcidius, 16 (DD 169); cf. Augustine, *City of God,* XIII, 16 (PL 41, 388).

[4] *Heavens,* I, 2, 3 (269^{a}30; 270^{a}12).

[5] *Fons Vitae,* I, 17 (BK 21.20; 22.10).

[6] See above, A. I.

[7] *De Subst. Orbis,* chap. 3 (IX, 9A).

heavenly bodies, considered in itself, is in potency to that form alone which it actually possesses. Nor does it concern the point at issue to inquire whether this is a soul or any other thing.[1] Hence this form perfects this matter in such a way that there remains in it no potency with respect to being, but only to place, as Aristotle says.[2] So, then, the matter of the heavenly bodies and of the elements is not the same, except by analogy, in so far as they agree in the character of potency.

Reply Obj. 1. Augustine follows in this the opinion of Plato,[3] who does not admit a fifth essence. Or we may say that formless matter is one with the unity of order, as all bodies are one in the order of corporeal creatures.

Reply Obj. 2. If genus is taken in a physical sense, "corruptible and incorruptible things are not in the same genus" on account of their different modes of potency, as is said in the *Metaphysics*.[4] Logically considered, however, there is but one genus of all bodies, since they are all included in the one notion of corporeity.

Reply Obj. 3. The form of corporeity is not one in all bodies, since it is no other than the various forms by which bodies are distinguished, as stated above.

Reply Obj. 4. As potency is referred to act, potential beings are differentiated by their different acts, as sight is by colour, hearing by sound. Therefore the matter of the celestial bodies is different from that of the elemental body because the matter of the celestial body is not in potentiality to an elemental form.

ARTICLE 3. *Whether the Empyrean Heaven Was Created At the Same Time As Formless Matter?*

We proceed thus to the Third Article: It would seem that the empyrean heaven was not created at the same time as formless matter.

Objection 1. For the empyrean, if it is anything at all, must be a sensible body. But all sensible bodies are movable, and the empyrean heaven is not movable. For if it were so, its movement would be ascertained by the movement of some visible body, which is not the case. The empyrean heaven, then, was not created at the same time as formless matter.

Obj. 2. Further, Augustine says (*De Trin.* iii, 4)[5] that "the lower bodies are governed by the higher in a certain order." If, therefore, the em-

pyrean heaven is the highest of bodies, it must necessarily exercise some influence on bodies below it. But this does not seem to be the case, especially as it is presumed to be without motion; for one body cannot move another unless it be moved itself also. Therefore the empyrean heaven was not created together with formless matter.

Obj. 3. Further, if it is held[6] that the empyrean heaven is the place of contemplation, and not ordained to natural effects, Augustine says on the contrary (*De Trin.* iv, 20):[7] "In so far as we mentally apprehend eternal things, so far are we not of this world," from which it is clear that contemplation lifts the mind above corporeal things. Corporeal place, therefore, cannot be the seat of contemplation.

Obj. 4. Further, among the heavenly bodies there is a body partly transparent and partly luminous, which we call the sidereal heaven. There exists also a heaven wholly transparent, called by some[8] the aqueous or crystalline heaven. If, then, there exists a still higher heaven, it must be wholly luminous. But this cannot be, for then the air would be constantly illuminated, and there would be no night. Therefore the empyrean heaven was not created together with formless matter.

On the contrary, Strabus says[9] that in the passage, *In the beginning God created heaven and earth,* "heaven denotes not the visible firmament, but the empyrean or fiery heaven."

I answer that, The empyrean heaven rests only on the authority of Strabus and Bede, and also of Basil, all of whom agree in one respect, namely, in holding it to be the place of the blessed. Strabus[10] and Bede[11] say that as soon "as created it was filled with the angels"; and Basil[12] says: "Just as the lost are driven into the lowest darkness, so the reward for worthy deeds is laid up in the light beyond this world, where the just shall obtain the abode of rest." But they differ in the reasons on which they base their statement. Strabus and Bede teach that there is an empyrean heaven, because the firmament, which they take to mean the sidereal heaven, is said to have been made not in the beginning, but on the second day; but the reason given by Basil[13] is that otherwise God would seem to have made darkness His first work, as the Manicheans

---

[1] See below, Q. LXX.

[2] *Metaphysics*, XII, 2 (1069ᵇ26).

[3] Cf. Nemesius, *De Nat. Hom.*, v (PG 40, 625); also St. Thomas, *In de Cœlo*, I, 4.

[4] Aristotle, X, 10 (1058ᵇ28).

[5] PL 42, 873.

[6] Cf. Albert, *In Sent.*, II, dist. II, A. 5 (BO XXVII, 54).

[7] PL 42, 907.

[8] Cf. below, Q. LXVIII, AA. 2, 4.

[9] Cf. *Glossa ordin.*, *super Gen.*, I, 1 (I, 23F).   [10] *Ibid.*

[11] *Hexaëm.*, I (PL 91, 18); *In Pentat.*, I (PL 91, 191).

[12] *In Hexaëm.*, II (PG 29, 41).

[13] *Ibid.*, II (PG 29, 37).

falsely assert, when they call the God of the Old Testament the God of darkness.

These reasons, however, are not very compelling. For the question of the firmament, said to have been made on the second day, is solved in one way by Augustine[1] and in another by other holy writers.[2] But the question of the darkness is explained according to Augustine[3] by supposing that formlessness, signified by darkness, preceded form not by duration but by origin. According to others,[4] however, since darkness is no creature, but a privation of light, it is a proof of Divine wisdom that the things it created from nothing it produced first of all in an imperfect state, and afterwards brought them to perfection.

But a better reason can be drawn from the state of glory itself. For in the reward to come a twofold glory is looked for, spiritual and corporeal, not only in the human body to be glorified, but in the whole world which is to be made new. Now the spiritual glory began with the beginning of the world, in the blessedness of the angels, equality with whom is promised to the saints. It was fitting, then, that even from the first there should be made some beginning of bodily glory in something corporeal, free at the very outset from the servitude of corruption and change, and wholly luminous, even as the whole bodily creation, after the Resurrection, is expected to be. So, then, that heaven is called the empyrean, that is, fiery, not from its heat, but from its brightness.[5] It is to be noticed, however, that Augustine[6] says that Porphyry "sets the demons apart from the angels by supposing that the former inhabit the air, the latter the ether, or empyrean." But Porphyry, as a Platonist, held the heaven known as sidereal to be fiery,[7] and therefore called it empyrean or ethereal, taking ethereal to denote the burning of flame, and not as Aristotle understands it, swiftness of movement.[8] This much has been said to prevent anyone from supposing that Augustine maintained an empyrean heaven in the sense understood by modern writers.[9]

Reply Obj. 1. Sensible corporeal things are movable in the present state of the world, for by the movement of corporeal creatures is secured the multiplication of the elements. But when glory is finally consummated, the movement of bodies will cease. And such must have been from the beginning the condition of the empyrean heaven.

Reply Obj. 2. It is sufficiently probable, as some assert,[10] that the empyrean heaven, having the state of glory for its ordained end, does not influence inferior bodies of another order—those, namely, that are directed only to natural ends. Yet it seems still more probable that it does influence bodies that are moved, even though it is itself not moved, just as angels of the highest rank, who stand by the throne of God, influence those of lower degree who act as messengers, though they themselves are not sent, as Dionysius teaches (*Cæl. Hier.* xiii).[11] For this reason it may be said that the influence of the empyrean upon that which is called the first heaven, and is moved, produces therein not something that comes and goes as a result of movement, but something of a fixed and stable nature, as the power of conservation or causation, or something of that kind pertaining to dignity.

Reply Obj. 3. Corporeal place is assigned to contemplation not as necessary, but as fitting, that the splendour without may correspond to that which is within. Hence Basil (*Hom.* ii *in Hexaëm.*)[12] says: "The ministering spirit could not live in darkness, but made his habitual dwelling in light and joy."

Reply Obj. 4. As Basil says (*ibid.*): "It is certain that the heaven was created spherical in shape, of dense body, and sufficiently strong to separate what is outside it from what it encloses. On this account it darkens the region external to it, the light by which itself is lit up being shut out from that region." But since the body of the firmament, though solid, is transparent, since it does not exclude light (and this is clear from the fact that we can see the stars through the intervening heavens), we may also say that the empyrean heaven has light, not condensed so as to emit rays, as the sun does, but of a more subtle nature. Or it may have the brightness of glory which differs from natural brightness.

ARTICLE 4. *Whether Time Was Created Simultaneously With Formless Matter?*

We proceed thus to the Fourth Article: It would seem that time was not created simultaneously with formless matter.

---

[1] *Gen. ad lit.*, 1, 9 (PL 34, 252); cf. also 11, 4 (265).
[2] Bede, *Hexaëm.*, 1 (PL 91, 13); cf. *Glossa ordin.*, on Gen. 1.1 (1, 23F); on Gen. 1.6 (1, 24G); also, *Glossa interl.*, on Gen. 1.6 (1, 25r).
[3] *Contra Adv. Legis et Proph.*, 1, 8, 9 (PL 42, 608, 609).
[4] Bede, *Hexaëm.*, 1, on Gen. 1.2 (PL 91, 15).
[5] Cf. *Glossa ordin.*, on Gen. 1.1 (1, 23F).
[6] *City of God*, x, 9 (PL 41, 287).
[7] See below, Q. LXVIII, A. 1.
[8] *Heavens*, 1, 3 (270[b]20); *Meteorology*, 1, 3 (339[b]21).
[9] Following the authority of Bede and Strabus. See below, Q. LXVIII, A. 4.

[10] Albert, *In Sent.*, 11, dist. 11, A. 5 (BO XXVII, 54).
[11] Sect. 3 (PG 3, 301).　　　　[12] PG 29, 41.

Objection 1. For Augustine says:[1] "I find two things that Thou didst create before time was," namely the first corporeal matter, and the angelic nature. Therefore time was not created with formless matter.

Obj. 2. Further, time is divided by day and night. But in the beginning there was neither day nor night, for these began when *God divided the light from the darkness.* Therefore in the beginning time was not.

Obj. 3. Further, time is the measure of the firmament's movement; and the firmament is said to have been made on the second day. Therefore in the beginning time was not.

Obj. 4. Further, movement precedes time, and therefore should be reckoned among the first things created, rather than time.

Obj. 5. Further, as time is the extrinsic measure of things, so is place. Place, then, as truly as time, must be reckoned among the things first created.

On the contrary, Augustine says (*Gen. ad lit.* i, 1):[2] Both spiritual and corporeal creatures were created "at the beginning of time."

I answer that, It is commonly said that the first things created were these four—the angelic nature, the empyrean heaven, formless corporeal matter, and time.[3] It must be observed, however, that this is not the opinion of Augustine. For he specifies[4] only two things as first created—the angelic nature and corporeal matter—making no mention of the empyrean heaven. But these two, namely, the angelic nature and formless matter, precede the formation by nature only, and not by duration; and therefore, as they precede formation, so do they precede movement and time. Time, therefore, cannot be included among them. But the enumeration above given is that of other holy writers,[5] who hold that the formlessness of matter preceded by duration its form, and this view postulates the existence of time as the measure of duration; for otherwise there would be no such measure.

Reply Obj. 1. The teaching of Augustine rests on the opinion that the angelic nature and formless matter precede time by origin or nature.

Reply Obj. 2. As in the opinion of some holy writers[6] matter was in some measure formless before it received its full form, so time was in a manner formless before it was fully formed and distinguished into day and night.

Reply Obj. 3. If the movement of the firmament did not begin immediately from the beginning, then the time that preceded was the measure, not of the firmament's movement, but of the first movement of whatsoever kind. For it is accidental to time to be the measure of the firmament's movement, in so far as this is the first movement. But if the first movement was another than this, time would have been its measure, for everything is measured by the first of its kind. And it must be granted that at once from the beginning, there was movement of some kind, at least in the succession of concepts and affections in the angelic mind. But movement without time cannot be conceived, since time is nothing else than the measure of priority and succession in movement.

Reply Obj. 4. Among the first created things are to be reckoned those which have a general relationship to things. And, therefore, among these time must be included, as having the nature of a common measure; but not movement, which is related only to the movable subject.

Reply Obj. 5. Place is understood as existing in the empyrean heaven, which is the boundary of the universe. And since place has reference to things permanent, it was created at once in its totality. But time, as not being permanent, was created in its beginning; even as in the same way we cannot lay hold of any part of time save the *now.*

QUESTION LXVII
OF THE WORK OF DISTINCTION IN ITSELF
(*In Four Articles*)

WE must consider next the work of distinction in itself. First, the work of the first day; secondly, the work of the second day (Q. LXVIII); thirdly, the work of the third day (Q. LXIX).

Under the first head there are four points of inquiry: (1) Whether the word light is used in its proper sense in speaking of spiritual things? (2) Whether light, in corporeal things, is itself corporeal? (3) Whether light is a quality? (4) Whether light was fittingly made on the first day?

ARTICLE 1. *Whether the Word Light Is Used in Its Proper Sense in Speaking of Spiritual Things?*

We proceed thus to the First Article: It would seem that light is used in its proper sense in spiritual things.

Objection 1. For Augustine says (*Gen. ad lit.*

[1] *Confessions,* XII, 15 (PL 32, 831).   [2] PL 34, 247.
[3] Albert, *Summa de Creat.,* I (BO XXXIX, 307).
[4] *Confessions,* XII, 15 (PL 32, 831).
[5] See above, A. 1.   [6] See above, A. 1.

iv, 28)[1] that in spiritual things "light is better and surer; and that Christ is not called Light in the same sense as He is called the Stone; the former is to be taken literally, and the latter figuratively."

Obj. 2. Further, Dionysius (*Div. Nom.* iv)[2] includes Light among the intelligible names of God. But such names are used in their proper sense in spiritual things. Therefore light is used in its proper sense in spiritual matters.

Obj. 3. Further, the Apostle says (Eph. 5. 13): *All that is made manifest is light.* But to be made manifest belongs more properly to spiritual things than to corporeal. Therefore also does light.

On the contrary, Ambrose says (*De Fid.* ii)[3] that Splendour is among those things which are said of God metaphorically.

I answer that, Any word may be used in two ways—that is to say, either in its original application or according to custom. This is clearly shown in the word "sight," originally applied to the act of the sense, and then, as sight is the noblest and most trustworthy of the senses, extended in common speech to all knowledge obtained through the other senses. Thus we say, "See how it tastes," or smells, or is hot. Further, sight is applied to knowledge obtained through the intellect, as in those words: *Blessed are the clean of heart, for they shall see God* (Matt. 5. 8). And thus it is with the word light. In its primary meaning it signifies that which makes manifest to the sense of sight; afterwards it was extended to that which makes manifest to knowledge of any kind. If, then, the word is taken in its strict and primary meaning, it is to be understood metaphorically when applied to spiritual things, as Ambrose says (*loc. cit.*). But if taken according to the usage of speech, as applied to manifestation of every kind, it may properly be applied to spiritual things.

The answer to the objections will sufficiently appear from what has been said.

ARTICLE 2. *Whether Light is a Body?*

We proceed thus to the Second Article: It would seem that light is a body.

Objection 1. For Augustine says (*De Lib. Arb.* iii, 5)[4] that "light takes the first place among bodies." Therefore light is a body.

Obj. 2. Further, the Philosopher says[5] that light is a species of fire. But fire is a body, and therefore so is light.

Obj. 3. Further, to be borne, to be divided, to be reflected, is proper to bodies; and all these are attributed to light and its rays. Moreover, different rays of light, as Dionysius says (*Div. Nom.*),[6] are united and separated, which seems impossible unless they are bodies. Therefore light is a body.

On the contrary, Two bodies cannot occupy the same place simultaneously. But this is the case with light and air. Therefore light is not a body.

I answer that, Light cannot be a body, which appears in three ways. First, on the part of place. For the place of any one body is different from that of any other, nor is it possible, naturally speaking, for any two bodies, of whatever nature, to exist simultaneously in the same place, since contiguity requires distinction of place.

The second reason is from the nature of movement. For if light were a body, illumination would be the local motion of a body. Now no local motion of a body can be instantaneous, as everything that moves from one place to another must pass through the intervening space before reaching the end, whereas illumination is instantaneous. Nor can it be argued that the time required is too short to be perceived; for though this may be the case in short distances, it cannot be so in distances so great as that which separates the East from the West. Yet as soon as the sun is at the horizon, the whole hemisphere is illuminated from end to end. It must also be borne in mind on the part of movement that whereas all bodies have their natural determinate movement, that of light is indifferent as regards direction, working equally in a circle as in a straight line. Hence it appears that the diffusion of light is not the local motion of a body.

The third reason is from generation and corruption. For if light were a body, it would follow that whenever the air is darkened by the absence of the luminary, the body of light would be corrupted, and its matter would receive a new form. But unless we are to say that darkness is a body, this does not appear to be the case. Neither does it appear from what matter a body can be daily generated large enough to fill the intervening hemisphere. Also it would be absurd to say that a body of so great bulk is corrupted by the mere absence of the luminary. And should anyone reply that it is not corrupted, but approaches and moves round with the sun, we may ask why it is that

---

[1] PL 34, 315.   [2] Sect. 5 (PG 3, 700).
[3] Prol. (PL 16, 584).   [4] PL 32, 1279.
[5] *Topics*, v, 5 (134[b]29).   [6] II, 4 (PG 3, 641).

when a lighted candle is obscured by the intervening object the whole room is darkened? It is not that the light is condensed round the candle when this is done, since it burns no more brightly then than it burned before.

Since, therefore, these things go against not only reason, but also the sense, we must conclude that light cannot be a body.

Reply Obj. 1. Augustine takes light to be a luminous body in act—in other words, to be fire, the noblest of the four elements.

Reply Obj. 2. Aristotle refers to light as fire existing in its proper matter; just as fire in aerial matter is called flame, or in earthly matter is called *coal.* Nor must too much attention be paid to the instances brought in by Aristotle in his works on logic, as he mentions them as probable opinions of other writers.

Reply Obj. 3. All these properties are assigned to light metaphorically, and might in the same way be attributed to heat. For because "motion from place to place is naturally the first of movements," as is proved in the *Physics*,[1] we use terms belonging to local motion in speaking of alteration and movement of all kinds. For even the word distance is extended from the idea of place, to that of all contraries, as is said in the *Metaphysics*.[2]

ARTICLE 3. *Whether Light Is a Quality?*

We proceed thus to the Third Article: It would seem that light is not a quality.

Objection 1. For every quality remains in its subject, even though the active cause of the quality be removed, as heat remains in water removed from the fire. But light does not remain in the air when the source of light is withdrawn. Therefore light is not a quality.

Obj. 2. Further, every sensible quality has its contrary, as cold is contrasted to heat, blackness to whiteness. But this is not the case with light since darkness is merely a privation of light. Light therefore is not a sensible quality.

Obj. 3. Further, a cause is more powerful than its effect. But the light of the heavenly bodies is a cause of substantial forms of lower bodies,[3] and also gives spiritual being to colours, by making them actually visible. Light, then, is not a sensible quality, but rather a substantial or spiritual form.

On the contrary, Damascene (*De Fid. Orth.* i)[4] says that light is a species of quality.

[1] Aristotle, VIII, 7 (260ᵃ28).   [2] Aristotle, x, 4 (1055ᵃ9).
[3] On the Neoplatonic doctrine of light cf. Albert, *De Caus. et Proc. Univ.*, I, 21 (BO X, 469). Cf. also Avicenna, *Meta.*, IX, 2 (102rb); also, Baeumker, *Witelo* (p. 389).
[4] Chap. 8 (PG 94, 816).

I answer that, Some writers have said[5] that the light in the air has not a natural being such as the colour on a wall has, but only an intentional being, as the likeness of colour in the air. But this cannot be the case for two reasons. First, because light gives a name to the air, since by it the air becomes actually luminous. But colour does not do this, for we do not speak of the air as coloured. Secondly, because light produces natural effects, for by the rays of the sun bodies are warmed and natural changes cannot be brought about by intentions.

Others have said[6] that light is the sun's substantial form, but this also seems impossible for two reasons. First, because substantial forms are not of themselves sensible; for "what a thing is, is the object of the intellect," as is said in the book on the *Soul*,[7] whereas light is visible of itself. In the second place, because it is impossible that what is the substantial form of one thing should be the accidental form of another, since substantial forms of themselves constitute species; hence the substantial form always and everywhere accompanies the species. But light is not the substantial form of air, for if it were, the air would be destroyed when light is withdrawn. Hence it cannot be the substantial form of the sun.

We must say, then, that as heat is an active quality consequent on the substantial form of fire, so light is an active quality consequent on the substantial form of the sun, or of another body that is of itself luminous, if there is any such body. A proof of this is that the rays of different stars produce different effects according to the diverse natures of bodies.

Reply Obj. 1. Since quality follows upon substantial form, the mode in which the subject receives a quality differs as the mode differs in which a subject receives a substantial form. For when matter receives form perfectly, the qualities consequent upon the form are firm and enduring; as when, for instance, water is changed into fire. When, however, substantial form is received imperfectly, according, as it were, to a kind of beginning, the consequent quality lasts for a time but is not permanent; as may be seen when water which has been heated returns in time to its natural state. But illumina-

[5] Bonaventure, *In Sent.*, II, d. XIII, A. 3, Q. 2 (QR II, 328); cf. Averroes, *In De An.*, II, 70 (VI, 87E); Albert, *In De An.*, II, 3, chap. 12 (BO V, 255).
[6] Bonaventure, *In Sent.*, II, d. XIII, A. 2, Q. 2 (QR II, 320): cf. St. Thomas, *In De An.*, II, 14; also Avicebron, *Fons Vitae*, IX, 14 (BK 243); Robert Grosseteste, *De Luce* (BR 52.15). Baeumker, *Witelo* (p. 357; p. 397).
[7] Aristotle, III, 6 (430ᵇ28).

tion is not produced by the transmutation of matter, as though matter received a substantial form and illumination were a certain inception of substantial form. For this reason light disappears on the disappearance of its active cause.

Reply Obj. 2. It is accidental to light not to have a contrary, since it is the natural quality of the first corporeal cause of change, which is itself removed from contrariety.

Reply Obj. 3. As heat acts towards the form of fire as an instrumental cause, by virtue of the substantial form, so does light act instrumentally, by virtue of the heavenly bodies, towards producing substantial forms; and towards rendering colours actually visible, since it is a quality of the first sensible body.

ARTICLE 4. *Whether the Production of Light Is Fittingly Assigned to the First Day?*

We proceed thus to the Fourth Article: It would seem that the production of light is not fittingly assigned to the first day.

Objection 1. For light, as stated above (A. 3), is a quality. But qualities are accidents, and do not possess the character of first, but rather the character of last. The production of light, then, ought not to be assigned to the first day.

Obj. 2. Further, it is light that distinguishes night from day, and this is effected by the sun, which is recorded as having been made on the fourth day. Therefore the production of light could not have been on the first day.

Obj. 3. Further, night and day are brought about by the circular movement of a luminous body. But movement of this kind is proper to the firmament, and we read that the firmament was made on the second day. Therefore the production of light, dividing night from day, ought not to be assigned to the first day.

Obj. 4. Further, if it be said that spiritual light is here spoken of, it may be replied that the light made on the first day is distinguished from darkness. But in the beginning spiritual darkness was not, for even the demons were in the beginning good, as has been shown (Q. LXIII, A. 5). Therefore the production of light ought not to be assigned to the first day.

On the contrary, That without which there could not be day, must have been made on the first day. But there can be no day without light. Therefore light must have been made on the first day.

I answer that, There are two opinions as to the production of light. Augustine seems to say[1] that Moses could not have fittingly passed over

the production of the spiritual creature, and therefore when we read, *In the beginning God created heaven and earth,* a spiritual nature as yet formless is to be understood by the word *heaven,* and formless matter of the corporeal creature by the word *earth.* And spiritual nature was formed first, as being of higher dignity than corporeal. The forming, therefore, of this spiritual nature is signified by the production of light, that is to say, of spiritual light. For a spiritual nature receives its form by the enlightenment whereby it is led to adhere to the Word of God.

Other writers think that the production of spiritual creatures was purposely omitted by Moses, and give various reasons. Basil says[2] that Moses begins his narrative from the beginning of time which belongs to sensible things, but that the spiritual or angelic creation is passed over, as created beforehand.

Chrysostom gives as a reason[3] for the omission that Moses was addressing a primitive people, to whom material things alone appealed, and whom he was endeavouring to withdraw from the service of idols. It would have been to them a pretext for idolatry if he had spoken to them of natures spiritual in substance and nobler than all corporeal creatures; for they would have paid them Divine worship, since they were prone to worship as gods even the sun, moon, and stars, which was forbidden them (Deut. 4.).

But mention is made of several kinds of formlessness, in regard to the corporeal creature (Gen. 1. 2). One is where we read that *the earth was void and empty,* and another where it is said that *darkness was upon the face of the deep.* Now it was required, for two reasons, that the formlessness of darkness should be removed first of all by the production of light. In the first place because light is a quality of the first body, as was stated (A. 3), and thus it was fitting that the world should first receive its form by means of light. The second reason is because light is a common quality. For light is common to lower and higher bodies. But as in knowledge we proceed from the more common, so also in operation, for the living thing is generated before the animal, and the animal before man, as is shown in the book on the *Generation of Animals.*[4] It was fitting, then, as an evidence of the Divine wisdom, that among the works of distinction the production of light

[1] *Gen. ad lit.*, I, 1, 3, 4, 9. (PL 34, 247–8–9, 252).
[2] *Hom.* I, *in Hexaëm.*, (PG 29, 4).
[3] *Hom.* V, *in Gen.* (PG 53, 52).
[4] Aristotle, II, 3 (736^{b}2).

should take first place, since light is a form of the primary body, and because it is more common quality.

Basil, indeed, adds a third reason:[1] that all other things are made manifest by light. And there is yet a fourth, already touched upon in the objections: that day cannot be unless light exists, which was made therefore on the first day.

Reply Obj. 1. According to the opinion of those who hold that the formlessness of matter preceded its formation in duration,[2] matter must be held to have been created at the beginning with substantial forms, afterwards receiving those that are accidental, among which light holds the first place.

Reply Obj. 2. In the opinion of some[3] the light here spoken of was a kind of luminous cloud, and that on the making of the sun this returned to the matter of which it had been formed (*materia praejacens*). But this cannot well be maintained, as in the beginning of Genesis Holy Scripture records the institution of that order of nature which henceforth is to endure. We cannot, then, say that what was made at that time afterwards ceased to exist.

Others, therefore, held[4] that this luminous cloud continues in existence, but so closely attached to the sun as to be indistinguishable. But this is as much as to say that it is superfluous, whereas none of God's works have been made in vain. On this account it is held by some[5] that the sun's body was made out of this cloud. This, too, is impossible if it is held that the body of the sun is different in its nature from the four elements, and naturally incorruptible. For in that case its matter cannot take on another form.

I answer, then, with Dionysius (*Div. Nom.* iv),[6] that the light was the sun's light, formless as yet, being already the solar substance, and possessing illuminative power in a general way, to which was afterwards added the special and determinative power required to produce determinate effects. Thus, then, in the production of this light a triple distinction was made between light and darkness. First, as to the cause, according as in the substance of the sun

we have the cause of light, and in the opaque nature of the earth the cause of darkness. Secondly, as to place, for in one hemisphere there was light, in the other darkness. Thirdly, as to time, because there was light for one and darkness for another in the same hemisphere; and this is signified by the words *He called the light day, and the darkness night.*

Reply Obj. 3. Basil says (*Homil.* ii *in Hexaëm.*)[7] that day and night were then caused by sending out and contraction of light, rather than by movement. But Augustine objects to this (*Gen. ad lit.* i)[8] that there was no reason for this alternation of emission and contraction since there were neither men nor animals on the earth at that time, for whose service this was required. Nor does the nature of a luminous body seem to admit of the withdrawal of light, so long as the body is actually present; though this might be effected by miracle. As to this, however, Augustine remarks[9] that in the first founding of the order of nature we must not look for miracles, but for what is in accordance with nature.

We hold, then, that the movement of the heavens is twofold. Of these movements, one is common to the entire heaven, and is the cause of day and night. This, as it seems, had its beginning on the first day. The other varies in proportion as it affects various bodies, and by its variations is the cause of the succession of days, months, and years. Thus it is that in the account of the first day the distinction between day and night alone is mentioned, this distinction being brought about by the common movement of the heavens. The further distinction into successive days, seasons, and years recorded as begun on the fourth day, in the words, *let them be for seasons, and for days, and years* is due to proper movements.

Reply Obj. 4. As Augustine teaches,[10] formlessness did not precede forms in duration; and so we must understand the production of light to signify the formation of spiritual creatures, not, indeed, with the perfection of glory, in which they were not created, but with the perfection of grace, which they possessed from their creation as said above (Q. LXII, A. 3). Thus the division of light from darkness will denote the distinction of the spiritual creature from other created things as yet without form. But if all created things received their form at the

---

[1] *Hom.* II *in Hexaëm.*, (PG 29, 44).

[2] Cf. above, Q. LXVI, A. I.

[3] Cf. Alexander of Hales, *Summa Theol.*, I–II, n. 263 (QR II, 323); also Bonaventure, *In Sent.*, II, d. XIII, dub. 2 (QR II, 331); and, Peter Lombard, *Sent.*, II, d. XIII, A. 2 (QR I, 364).

[4] Cf. Peter Lombard, *Sent.*, II, dist. XIII, A. 5 (QR I, 366).

[5] See above (in the body of the article).

[6] Sect. 4 (PG 3, 700).

[7] PG 29, 48.   [8] Chap. 16 (PL 34, 258).

[9] *Ibid.*, II, 1 (PL 34, 263).

[10] *Confessions*, XII, 40 (PL 32, 843); *Gen. ad lit.*, I, 15 (PL 34, 257).

same time, the darkness must be held to mean the spiritual darkness, not as existing from the beginning, because the devil was not created wicked, but such as God foresaw would exist.

QUESTION LXVIII
OF THE WORK OF THE SECOND DAY
(*In Four Articles*)

WE must next consider the work of the second day. Under this head there are four points of inquiry: (1) Whether the firmament was made on the second day? (2) Whether there are waters above the firmament? (3) Whether the firmament divides waters from waters? (4) Whether there is more than one heaven?

ARTICLE 1. *Whether the Firmament Was Made on the Second Day?*

We proceed thus to the First Article: It would seem that the firmament was not made on the second day.

Objection 1. For it is said (Gen. 1. 8): *God called the firmament heaven.* But the heaven existed before any day, as is clear from the words, *In the beginning God created heaven and earth.* Therefore the firmament was not made on the second day.

Obj. 2. Further, the work of the six days is ordered conformably to the order of Divine wisdom. Now it would not become the Divine wisdom to make afterwards that which is naturally first. But though the firmament naturally precedes the earth and the waters, these are mentioned before the formation of light, which was on the first day. Therefore the firmament was not made on the second day.

Obj. 3. Further, all that was made in the six days was formed out of matter created before days began. But the firmament cannot have been formed out of pre-existing matter, for if so it would be liable to generation and corruption. Therefore the firmament was not made on the second day.

On the contrary, It is written (Gen. 1. 6): *God said: let there be a firmament,* and further on (*verse* 8): *And the evening and morning were the second day.*

I answer that, In discussing questions of this kind two rules are to be observed, as Augustine teaches (*Gen. ad lit.* i. 18).[1] The first is, to hold the truth of Scripture without wavering. The second is that since Holy Scripture can be explained in a multiplicity of senses, one should adhere to a particular explanation only in such

measure as to be ready to abandon it if it be proved with certainty to be false, lest Holy Scripture be exposed to the ridicule of unbelievers, and obstacles be placed to their believing.

We say, therefore, that the words which speak of the firmament as made on the second day can be understood in two senses. They may be understood, first, of the starry firmament, on which point it is necessary to set forth the different opinions of men.[2] Some of these believed it to be composed of the elements; and this was the opinion of Empedocles,[3] who, however, held further that the body of the firmament was not susceptible of dissolution, because in its composition there is no strife, but only harmony. Others held the firmament to be of the nature of the four elements, not, indeed, compounded of them, but being as it were a simple element. Such was the opinion of Plato,[4] who held that element to be fire. Others, again, have held that the heaven is not of the nature of the four elements, but is itself a fifth body, existing over and above these. This is the opinion of Aristotle.[5]

According to the first opinion, it can be granted absolutely that the firmament was made, even as to substance, on the second day. For it is part of the work of creation to produce the substance of the elements, while it belongs to the work of distinction and adornment to give forms to the elements that pre-exist.

But the belief that the firmament was made, as to its substance, on the second day is incompatible with the opinion of Plato, according to whom the making of the firmament implies the production of the element of fire. This production, however, belongs to the work of creation, at least according to those who hold that formlessness of matter preceded in time its formation, since the first forms received by matter are those of the elements.

Still less compatible with the belief that the substance of the firmament was produced on the second day is the opinion of Aristotle,[6] seeing that the mention of days denotes succession of time, whereas the firmament, being naturally incorruptible, is of a matter not susceptible of

---

[1] PL 34, 260; also Chaps. 18, 19, 21 (PL 34. 260–262).

[2] Cf. Basil, *In Hexaëm.*, I, (PG 29, 26); Damascene, *De Fide Orth.*, II, 6 (PG 94, 879).

[3] Cf. Aristotle, *Generation and Corruption*, I, 2 (315ᵃ3); Ambrose, *In Hexaëm.*, I, 6 (PL 14, 146); Hugh of St. Victor, *De Sacram.*, I, I, 6 (PL 176, 190).

[4] *Timaeus*, §15, translation of Chalcidius (DD 168). Cf. Augustine, *City of God*, VIII, 15 (PL 41, 240); *Gen. ad lit.*, II, 3 (PL 34, 265); cf. Lombard, *Sent.*, II, d. XIV, 4 (QR I, 370).

[5] *Heavens*, I, 2 (269ᵇ13).   [6] *Ibid.*, I, 3 (270ᵃ12).

change of form; hence it could not be made out of matter existing antecedently in time.

Therefore to produce the substance of the firmament belongs to the work of creation. But its formation, in some degree, belongs to the second day, according to both opinions; for as Dionysius says (*Div. Nom.* iv),[1] the light of the sun was without form during the first three days, and afterwards, on the fourth day, received its form.

If, however, we take these days to denote merely sequence in the natural order, as Augustine holds (*Gen. ad lit.* iv, 34),[2] and not succession in time, there is then nothing to prevent our saying, whilst holding any one of the opinions given above, that the substantial formation of the firmament belongs to the second day.

Another possible explanation is to understand by the firmament that was made on the second day, not that in which the stars are set, but the part of the atmosphere where the clouds are condensed, and which has received the name of firmament from the firmness and density of the air. "For a body is called firm," that is dense and solid, "thereby differing from a mathematical body" as is remarked by Basil (*Hom.* iii *in Hexaëm.*).[3] If, then, this explanation is adopted none of these opinions will be found contrary to reason. Augustine, in fact (*Gen. ad lit.* ii, 4),[4] recommends it thus: "I consider this view of the question worthy of all commendation, as neither contrary to faith nor difficult to be proved and believed."

Reply Obj. 1. According to Chrysostom (*Hom.* ii *in Genes.*),[5] Moses prefaces his record by speaking of the works of God collectively, in the words, *In the beginning God created heaven and earth,* and then proceeds to explain them part by part; in somewhat the same way as one might say: "This house was constructed by that builder," and then add: "First he laid the foundations, then built the walls, and thirdly, put on the roof." In accepting this explanation we are, therefore, not bound to hold that a different heaven is spoken of in the words: *In the beginning God created heaven and earth,* and when we read that the firmament was made on the second day.

We may also say that the heaven recorded as created in the beginning is not the same as that made on the second day; and there are several senses in which this may be understood. Augustine says (*Gen. ad lit.* i, 9)[6] that the heaven recorded as made on the first day is the formless spiritual nature, and that the heaven of the second day is the corporeal heaven. According to Bede (*Hexaëm.* i)[7] and Strabus,[8] the heaven made on the first day is the empyrean, and the firmament made on the second day, the starry heaven. According to Damascene (*De Fid. Orth.* ii),[9] that of the first day was "spherical in form and without stars," the same, in fact, that the philosophers speak of,[10] calling it the ninth sphere, and the primary movable body, which moves with a diurnal movement, while by the firmament made on the second day he understands the starry heaven.

According to another theory, touched upon by Augustine,[11] the heaven made on the first day was the starry heaven, and the firmament made on the second day was that region of the air where the clouds are condensed, which is also called heaven, but equivocally. And to show that the word is here used in an equivocal sense, it is expressly said that *God called the firmament heaven,* just as in a preceding verse it is said that *God called the light day* (since the word *day* is also used to denote a space of twenty-four hours). Other instances of a similar use occur, as pointed out by Rabbi Moses.[12]

The *second and third objections* are sufficiently answered by what has been already said.

ARTICLE 2. *Whether There Are Waters Above the Firmament?*

We proceed thus to the Second Article: It would seem that there are not waters above the firmament.

Objection 1. For water is heavy by nature, and heavy things tend naturally downwards, not upwards. Therefore there are not waters above the firmament.

Obj. 2. Further, water is fluid by nature, and fluids cannot rest on a sphere, as experience shows. Therefore, since the firmament is a sphere, there cannot be water above it.

Obj. 3. Further, water is an element, and appointed to the generation of composite bodies, according to the relation in which imperfect things stand towards perfect. But bodies of composite nature have their place upon the

---

[1] Sect. 4 (PG 3, 700).   [2] PL 34, 319; also, v, 5 (325).
[3] PG 29, 64.   [4] PL 34, 266.   [5] PG 53, 30.
[6] PL 34, 252.

[7] PL 91, 13.
[8] Cf. *Glossa ordin.*, on Gen. 1, 1 (1, 23 F); on Gen. 1.6 (1, 24G); cf. also *Glossa interl.*, on Gen. 1.6 (1, 25r). See above, Q. LXVI, A. 3.
[9] Chap. 6 (PG 94, 880).
[10] Especially Michael the Scot. See below, A. 2, Ans. 3; A. 3.
[11] *Gen. ad lit.*, II, 1, 4 (PL 34, 263, 265).
[12] *Guide.* II, 30 (FR 213); cf. below, Q. LXIX, A. 1 Ans. 5.

earth, and not above the firmament, so that water would be useless there. But none of God's works are useless. Therefore there are not waters above the firmament.

On the contrary, It is written (Gen. 1. 7): (*God*) *divided the waters that were under the firmament, from those that were above the firmament.*

I answer with Augustine (*Gen. ad lit.* ii, 5)[1] that, "These words of Scripture have more authority than the most exalted human intellect. Hence, whatever these waters are, and whatever their mode of existence, we cannot for a moment doubt that they are there." As to the nature of these waters, all are not agreed. Origen says[2] that the waters that are above the firmament are spiritual substances. Hence it is written (Ps. 148. 4): *Let the waters that are above the heavens praise the name of the Lord,* and (Dan. 3. 60): *Ye waters that are above the heavens, bless the Lord.* To this Basil answers (*Hom.* iii *in Hexaëm.*)[3] that these words do not mean that these waters are rational creatures, but that the thoughtful contemplation of them by those who understand fulfils the glory of the Creator. Hence in the same context, fire, hail, and other like creatures, are invoked in the same way, though no one would attribute reason to these.

We must hold, then, these waters to be material, but their exact nature will be differently defined according as opinions on the firmament differ. For if by the firmament we understand the starry heaven, and as being of the nature of the four elements, for the same reason it may be believed that the waters above the heaven are of the same nature as the elemental waters.

But if by firmament we understand the starry heaven, not, however, as being of the nature of the four elements, then the waters above the firmament will not be of the same nature as the elemental waters, but just as, according to Strabus,[4] one heaven is called empyrean, that is, fiery, on account of the splendour of the sun, so this other heaven will be called aqueous[5] solely on account of its transparence; and this heaven is above the starry heaven. Again, if the firmament is held to be of other nature than the elements, it may still be said to divide the waters,[6] if we understand by water not the ele-

ment but formless matter. Augustine, in fact, says (*Super Gen. cont. Manich.* i, 7)[7] that whatever divides bodies from bodies can be said to divide waters from waters.

If, however, we understand by the firmament that part of the air in which the clouds are condensed,[8] then the waters above the firmament must rather be the vapours resolved from the waters which are raised above a part of the atmosphere, and from which the rain falls. But to say, as some writers alluded to by Augustine (*Gen. ad lit.* ii, 4),[9] that waters resolved into vapour may be lifted above the starry heaven, is impossible. The solid nature of the firmament, the intervening region of fire, wherein all vapour must be consumed, the tendency in light and rarefied bodies to drift to one spot beneath the vault of the moon, as well as the fact that vapours are perceived not to rise even to the tops of the higher mountains, all go to show the impossibility of this. Nor is it less absurd to say, in support of this opinion, that bodies may be rarefied infinitely, since natural bodies cannot be infinitely rarefied or divided, but up to a certain point only.

Reply Obj. 1. Some have attempted to solve this difficulty by supposing that in spite of the natural heaviness of water, it is kept in its place above the firmament by the Divine power. Augustine (*Gen. ad lit.* ii, 1),[10] however, will not admit this solution, but says, "It is our business here to inquire how God has constituted the natures of His creatures, not how far it may have pleased Him to work on them by way of miracle."

We leave this view, then, and answer that according to the last two opinions on the firmament and the waters the solution appears from what has been said. According to the first opinion, an order of the elements must be supposed different from that given by Aristotle,[11] that is to say, that the waters surrounding the earth are of a dense consistency, and those around the firmament of a rarer consistency, in proportion to the respective density of the earth and of the heaven.

Or by the water we may understand the matter of bodies to be signified, as we have said.

Reply Obj. 2. The solution is clear from what has been said, according to the last two opinions. But according to the first opinion, Basil gives two replies (*Hom.* iii *in Hexaëm.*).[12] He answers first, that a body seen as concave from

[1] PL 34, 267.
[2] Cf. Epiphanius, *Epist. Ad Joann,* trans. by St. Jerome, *Epist.* LI (PL 22, 523).
[3] PG 29, 76.   [4] See above, A. 1 Ans. I.
[5] Cf. Albert, *In Sent.,* II, dist. XIV, A. 2 (BO XXVII, 260).
[6] *Ibid.,* A. 1 (258).
[7] PL 34, 179.   [8] See above, A. 1, Ans. I.
[9] PL 34, 265.   [10] PL 34, 263.
[11] *Heavens,* II, 4 (287ª32).   [12] PG 29, 60.

beneath need not necessarily be rounded or convex above. Secondly, that the waters above the firmament are not fluid, but exist outside it in a solid state, as a mass of ice, and that this is the crystalline heaven of some writers.[1]

Reply Obj. 3. According to the third opinion given, the waters above the firmament have been raised in the form of vapours and serve to give rain to the earth. But according to the second opinion, they are above the heaven that is wholly transparent and starless. This, according to some,[2] is the first movable body, the cause of the daily revolution of the entire heaven, whereby the continuance of generation is secured. In the same way the starry heaven, by the zodiacal movement, is the cause whereby different bodies are generated or corrupted,[3] through the rising and setting of the stars, and their various influences.[4] But according to the first opinion these waters are set there to temper the heat of the celestial bodies, as Basil supposes (*loc. cit.*). And Augustine says (*Gen. ad lit.* ii, 5)[5] that some have considered this to be proved by the extreme cold of Saturn owing to its nearness to the waters that are above the firmament.

ARTICLE 3. *Whether the Firmament Divides Waters from Waters?*

We proceed thus to the Third Article: It would seem that the firmament does not divide waters from waters.

Objection 1. For bodies that are of one and the same species have naturally one and the same place. But the Philosopher says:[6] "All water is the same in species." Water therefore cannot be distinct from water by place.

Obj. 2. Further, should it be said that the waters above the firmament differ in species from those under the firmament, it may be argued, on the contrary, that things distinct in species need nothing else to distinguish them. If, then, these waters differ in species, it is not the firmament that distinguishes them.

Obj. 3. Further, it would appear that what distinguishes waters from waters must be something which touches them on either side, as a wall standing in the midst of a river. But it is evident that the waters below do not reach up to the firmament. Therefore the firmament does not divide the waters from the waters.

On the contrary, It is written (Gen. 1. 6): *Let there be a firmament made amidst the waters; and let it divide the waters from the waters.*

I answer that, The text of Genesis, considered superficially, might lead to the adoption of a theory similar to that held by certain philosophers of antiquity, who taught that water was a body infinite in dimension, and the primary element of all bodies.[7] Thus in the words, *Darkness was upon the face of the deep,* the word *deep* might be taken to mean the infinite mass of water, understood as the principle of all other bodies. These philosophers also taught[8] that not all corporeal things are confined beneath the heaven perceived by our senses, but that a body of water, infinite in extent, exists above that heaven. On this view the firmament of heaven might be said to divide the waters without from those within—that is to say, from all bodies under the heaven, since they took water to be the principle of them all.

As, however, this theory can be shown to be false by true reasons, it cannot be held to be the sense of Holy Scripture. It should rather be considered that Moses was speaking to a primitive people, and that out of condescension to their weakness he put before them only such things as are apparent to sense. Now even the most uneducated can perceive by their senses that earth and water are corporeal, whereas it is not evident to all that air also is corporeal, for there have even been philosophers who said that air is nothing, and called a space filled with air a vacuum.[9]

Moses, then, while he expressly mentions water and earth, makes no express mention of air, to avoid setting before ignorant persons something beyond their knowledge. In order, however, to express the truth to those capable of understanding it, he implies in the words, *Darkness was upon the face of the deep,* the existence of air as attendant, so to say, upon the water. For it may be understood from these words that over the face of the water a transparent body was extended, the subject of light and darkness, which, in fact, is the air.

---

[1] See below, A. 4.

[2] Cf. above. (Albert the Great, *In Sent.*, 11). See also Duhem, *Le Système du Monde* (III, 336; 352).

[3] Cf. Alpetragius (Duhem, *op. cit.*, 11, 149); Messahalam, (Duhem, 11, 205); Michael the Scot (*Ibid.*, 111, 247).

[4] Cf. Thabit Ben Kourrah (*Ibid.*, 11, 242).

[5] PL 34, 266.

[6] *Topics*, 1, 5 (103ᵃ19).

[7] Thales; cf. Aristotle, *Metaphysics*, 1, 3 (983ᵇ20). See also Augustine, *City of God*, VIII, 2 (PL 41, 225).

[8] Cf. Albert the Great, *In Sent.*, 11, d. XIV, A. 2 (BO XXVII, 260); also Damascene, *De Fide Orth.*, 11, 6 (PG 94, 879); Avicenna, *Meta.*, IX, 2 (103va); St. Thomas, *In De Cœlo*, 11, 19.

[9] Cf. Aristotle, *Physics*, IV, 6 (213ᵃ27); also Alexander of Hales, *Summa Theol.*, 1-11, 284 (QR 11, 345).

Whether, then, we understand by the firmament the starry heaven, or the cloudy region of the air, it is proper to say that it divides the waters from the waters, according as we take water to denote formless matter, or any kind of transparent body as fittingly designated under the name of waters. For the starry heaven divides the lower transparent bodies from the higher, and the cloudy region divides that higher part of the air where the rain and similar things are generated from the lower part, which is connected with the water and included under that name.

Reply Obj. 1. If by the firmament is understood the starry heaven, the waters above are not of the same species as those beneath. But if by the firmament is understood the cloudy region of the air, both these waters are of the same species, and two places are assigned to them, though not for the same purpose, the higher being the place of their generation, the lower, the place of their repose.

Reply Obj. 2. If the waters are held to differ in species, the firmament cannot be said to divide the waters as the cause of their distinction, but only as the boundary of each.

Reply Obj. 3. On account of the air and other similar bodies being invisible, Moses includes all such bodies under the name of water, and thus it is evident that waters are found on each side of the firmament, whatever be the sense in which the word is used.

ARTICLE 4. *Whether There Is Only One Heaven?*

We proceed thus to the Fourth Article: It would seem that there is only one heaven.

Objection 1. For the heaven is contrasted with the earth, in the words, *In the beginning God created heaven and earth.* But there is only one earth. Therefore there is only one heaven.

Obj. 2. Further, that which consists of the entire sum of its own matter, must be one; and such is the heaven, as the Philosopher proves.[1] Therefore there is but one heaven.

Obj. 3. Further, whatever is predicated of many things univocally is predicated of them according to some common notion. But if there are more heavens than one, they are so called univocally, for if equivocally only, they could not properly be called many. If, then, they are many, there must be some common notion by reason of which each is called heaven, but this common notion cannot be assigned. Therefore there cannot be more than one heaven.

[1] *Heavens*, I, 9 (279ª7).

On the contrary, It is said (Ps. 148. 4): *Praise Him, ye heavens of heavens.*

I answer that, On this point there seems to be a diversity of opinion between Basil and Chrysostom. The latter says that there is only one heaven (*Hom.* iv *in Gen.*),[2] and that the words *heavens of heavens* are merely the translation of the Hebrew idiom according to which the word is always used in the plural, just as in Latin there are many nouns that are wanting in the singular. On the other hand, Basil (*Hom.* iii *in Hexaëm.*),[3] whom Damascene follows (*De Fid. Orth.* ii),[4] says that there are many heavens. The difference, however, is more nominal than real. For Chrysostom means by the one heaven the whole body that is above the earth and the water, for which reason the birds that fly in the air are called birds of heaven. But since in this body there are many distinct parts, Basil said that there are more heavens than one.

In order, then, to understand the distinction of heavens, it must be borne in mind that Scripture speaks of heaven in a threefold sense. Sometimes it uses the word in its proper and natural meaning, when it denotes that body on high which is luminous actually or potentially, and incorruptible by nature. In this body there are three heavens; the first is the empyrean, which is wholly luminous[5]; the second is the aqueous or crystalline, wholly transparent; and the third is called the starry heaven, in part transparent, and in part actually luminous, and divided into eight spheres. One of these is the sphere of the fixed stars; the other seven, which may be called the eight heavens, are the spheres of the planets.

In the second place, the name heaven is applied to a body that participates in any property of the heavenly body, as sublimity and luminosity, actual or potential. Thus Damascene (*ibid.*) holds as one heaven all the space between the waters and the moon's orb, calling it the aerial. According to him, then, there are three heavens, the aerial, the starry, and one higher than both these, of which the Apostle is understood to speak when he says of himself that he was *rapt to the third heaven* (2 Cor. 12. 2).

[2] PG 53, 41.   [3] PG 29, 56.
[4] Chap. 6 (PG 94, 880, 884).
[5] This and the following names are found in *Glossa ordin.*, on Gen. 1.1 (1, 23F); Bede, *In Pentat.*, Bk. 1, on Gen. 1.1 (PL 91, 192); on the names, disposition and number of the heavens, see Alexander of Hales, *Summa Theol.*, I–II, n. 266 (QR II, 327); Albert, *In Sent.*, II, d. xv, A. 3 (BO XXVII, 275); *Summa de Creatur.*, Pt. I, tr. 3, Q. 10 (BO XXXIV, 415); Bonaventure, *In Sent.*, II, d. ii, dub. 2 (QR II, 85). Cf. Denifle. *Chartularium.* n. 128 (I. 171).

But since this space contains two elements, namely, fire and air, and in each of these there is what is called a higher and a lower region, Rabanus subdivides this space into four distinct heavens.[1] The higher region of fire he calls "the fiery heaven"; the lower, "the Olympian heaven" from a lofty mountain of that name; the higher region of air he calls, from its brightness, "the ethereal heaven," the lower, the "aerial." When, therefore, these four heavens are added to the three enumerated above, there are seven corporeal heavens in all, in the opinion of Rabanus.

Thirdly, there are metaphorical uses of the word heaven, as when this name is applied to the Blessed Trinity, Who is the Light and the Most High Spirit. It is explained by some, as thus applied, in the words, *I will ascend into heaven*, whereby the evil spirit is represented as seeking to make himself equal with God. Sometimes also spiritual goods, the recompense of the Saints, from being the highest of all good gifts, are signified by the word heaven, and, in fact, are so signified, according to Augustine (*De Serm. Dom. in Monte*),[2] in the words, *Your reward is very great in heaven* (Matt. 5. 12).

Again, three kinds of supernatural visions, bodily, imaginative, and intellectual, are called sometimes so many heavens, in reference to which Augustine (*De Gen. ad lit.* xii)[3] expounds Paul's rapture *to the third heaven*.

Reply Obj. 1. The earth stands in relation to the heaven as the centre of a circle to its circumference. But as one centre may have many circumferences, so, though there is but one earth, there may be many heavens.

Reply Obj. 2. The argument holds good as to the heaven, in so far as it denotes the entire sum of corporeal creation, for in that sense it is one.

Reply Obj. 3. All the heavens have in common sublimity and some degree of luminosity, as appears from what has been said.

QUESTION LXIX

OF THE WORK OF THE THIRD DAY

(*In Two Articles*)

WE next consider the work of the third day. Under this head there are two points of inquiry: (1) About the gathering together of the waters. (2) About the production of plants.

[1] Bede, *In Pentat.*, on Gen. 1.1 (PL 91, 192).
[2] 1, 5 (PL 34, 1237).
[3] Chap. 28, 29, 34 (PL 34, 478, 479, 482).

ARTICLE 1. *Whether It Was Fitting That the Gathering Together of the Waters Should Take Place, As Recorded, on the Third Day?*

We proceed thus to the First Article: It would seem that it was not fitting that the gathering together of the waters should take place on the third day.

Objection 1. For what was made on the first and second days is expressly said to have been *made* in the words, *God said: Be light made, and Let there be a firmament made*. But the third day is divided against the first and second days. Therefore the work of the third day should have been described as a making, not as a gathering together.

Obj. 2. Further, the earth hitherto had been completely covered by the waters, and so it was described as invisible. There was then no place on the earth to which the waters could be gathered together.

Obj. 3. Further, things which are not continuous to one another cannot occupy one place. But not all the waters are continuous to one another, and therefore all were not gathered together into one place.

Obj. 4. Further, a gathering together pertains to local movement. But the waters flow naturally, and take their course towards the sea. In their case, therefore, a Divine precept of this kind was unnecessary.

Obj. 5. Further, the earth is given its name at its first creation by the words, *In the beginning God created heaven and earth*. Therefore the imposition of its name on the third day seems to be recorded without necessity.

On the contrary, The authority of Scripture suffices.

I answer that, It is necessary to reply differently to this question according to the different interpretations given by Augustine and other holy writers.[4] In all these works, according to Augustine (*Gen. ad lit.* i, 15; iv, 34; *De Gen. contr. Manich.* i, 7),[5] there is no order of duration, but only of origin and nature. He says that the formless spiritual and formless corporeal natures were created first of all, and that the latter are at first indicated by the words earth and water. Not that this formlessness preceded formation, in time, but only in origin; nor yet that one formation preceded another in duration, but merely in the order of nature. Agreeably, then, to this order, the formation of the highest or

[4] See above, Q. XLVI, A. 1.
[5] PL 34, 257, 319; PL 34, 178; cf. also *Gen. ad lit.*, I, 1, 3, 4, 9 (PL 34, 247–9, 252).

spiritual nature is recorded in the first place, where it is said that light was made on the first day. For as the spiritual nature is higher than the corporeal, so the higher bodies are nobler than the lower. Hence the formation of the higher bodies is indicated in the second place, by the words, *Let there be made a firmament,* by which is to be understood the impression of celestial forms on formless matter that preceded with priority not of time, but of origin only. But in the third place the impression of elemental forms on formless matter is recorded, also with a priority of origin only. Therefore the words, *Let the waters be gathered together, and the dry land appear,* mean that corporeal matter was impressed with the substantial form of water, so as to have such movement, and with the substantial form of earth, so as to have such an appearance.[1]

According, however, to other holy writers[2] an order of duration in the works is to be understood, by which is meant that the formlessness of matter precedes its formation, and one form another, in order of time. Nevertheless, they do not hold that the formlessness of matter implies the total absence of form, since heaven, earth, and water already existed, for these three are named as already clearly perceptible to the senses; rather they understand by formlessness the want of due distinction and of perfect beauty, and in respect of these three Scripture mentions three kinds of formlessness. Heaven, the highest of them, was without form so long as darkness filled it, because it was the source of light. The formlessness of water, which holds the middle place, is called the deep, because, as Augustine says (*Contr. Faust.* xxii, 11),[3] this word signifies the mass of waters without order. Thirdly, the formless state of the earth is touched upon when the earth is said to be void or invisible, because it was covered by the waters.

Thus, then, the formation of the highest body took place on the first day. And since time results from the movement of the heaven, and is the numerical measure of the movement of the highest body, from this formation resulted the distinction of time, namely, that of night and day. On the second day the intermediate body, water, was formed, receiving from the firmament a sort of distinction and order (so that water be understood as including certain other things, as explained above, Q. LXVIII, A. 3). On the third day the earth, the lowest body, re-

ceived its form by the withdrawal of the waters, and there resulted the distinction in the lowest body, namely, of land and sea. Hence Scripture, having clearly expressed the formless state of the earth, by saying that it was invisible or void, expresses the manner in which it received its form by the equally suitable words, *Let the dry land appear.*

Reply Obj. 1. According to Augustine,[4] Scripture does not say of the work of the third day, that it was made, as it says of those that precede, in order to show that higher and spiritual forms, such as the angels and the heavenly bodies, are perfect and stable in being, whereas inferior forms are imperfect and mutable. Hence the impression of such forms is signified by the gathering of the waters and the appearing of the land. "For water," to use Augustine's words, "glides and flows away, the earth abides."[5] Others, again, hold[6] that the work of the third day was perfected on that day only as regards movement from place to place, and that for this reason Scripture had no reason to speak of it as made.

Reply Obj. 2. This argument is easily solved, according to Augustine's opinion (*De Gen. contr. Manich.* i),[7] because we need not suppose that the earth was first covered by the waters and that these were afterwards gathered together, but that they were produced in this very gathering together.

But according to other writers there are three solutions, which Augustine gives (*Gen. ad lit.* i, 12).[8] The first supposes that the waters were heaped up to a greater height at the place where they were gathered together, for it has been proved in regard to the Red Sea that the sea is higher than the land, as Basil remarks (*Hom.* iv *in Hexaëm.*).[9] The second explains the water that covered the earth as being rarefied or nebulous, which was afterwards condensed when the waters were gathered together. The third suggests the existence of hollows in the earth to receive the confluence of waters. Of the above the first seems the most probable.

Reply Obj. 3. All the waters have the sea as their goal, into which they flow by channels hidden or apparent, and this may be the reason why they are said to be gathered together into one place. Or, "one place" is to be understood not absolutely, but as contrasted with the place of the dry land, so that the sense would be, "Let

---

[1] *De Gen. ad lit.,* II, 11 (PL 34, 272).
[2] See above, Q. XLVI, A. 1. [3] PL 42, 405.
[4] *De Gen. ad lit.,* II, 11 (PL 34, 273). [5] *Ibid.*
[6] Cf. Peter Lombard, *Sent.,* II, d. XIV, 8 (QR I, 372); *Glossa ordin.,* on Gen. 1.8 (I, 25E); Bede, *Hexaëm.,* I (PL 91, 20). [7] PL 34, 181; *Gen. ad lit.,* II, 11 (PL 34, 272).
[8] PL 34, 255. [9] PG 29, 84.

the waters be gathered together in one place,"
that is, apart from the dry land. That the waters
occupied more places than one seems to be implied by the words that follow, *The gathering
together of the waters He called seas.*

Reply Obj. 4. The Divine command gives
bodies their natural movement, and by these
natural movements they are said to *fulfil His
word.* Or we may say that it was according to
the nature of water completely to cover the
earth, just as the air completely surrounds both
water and earth; but as a necessary means towards an end, namely, that plants and animals
might be on the earth, it was necessary for the
waters to be withdrawn from a portion of the
earth. Some philosophers[1] attribute this uncov-
ering of the earth's surface to the action of the
sun lifting up the vapours and thus drying the
land. Scripture, however, attributes it to the
Divine power, not only in the Book of Genesis,
but also Job 38. 10, where in the person of the
Lord it is said, *I set My bounds around the sea,*
and Jer. 5. 22, where it is written: *Will you not
then fear Me, saith the Lord, who have set the
sand a bound for the sea?*

Reply Obj. 5. According to Augustine (*De
Gen. contr. Manich.* i),[2] primary matter is
meant by the word earth, where it is first mentioned, but in the present passage it is to be
taken for the element itself. Again it may be
said with Basil (*Hom.* iv *in Hexaëm.*)[3] that the
earth is mentioned in the first passage in respect
of its nature, but here in respect of its principal
property, namely, dryness. Hence it is written:
He called the dry land, Earth. It may also be
said with Rabbi Moses,[4] that the expression, *He
called,* denotes throughout an equivocal use of
the name imposed. Thus we find it said at first
that *He called the light day,* for the reason that
later on a period of twenty-four hours is also
called day, where it is said that *there was evening and morning, one day.* In like manner it is
said that *the firmament,* that is, the air, *He
called heaven,* for that which was first created
was also called *heaven.* And here, again, it is
said that *the dry land,* that is, the part from
which the waters had withdrawn, *He called,
Earth,* as distinct from the sea; although the
name earth is equally applied to that which is
covered with waters or not. So by the expression
He called we are to understand throughout
that the nature or property He bestowed corre-
sponded to the name He gave.

ARTICLE 2. *Whether It Was Fitting That the
Production of Plants Should Take Place on the
Third Day?*

We proceed thus to the Second Article: It
would seem that it was not fitting that the production of plants should take place on the third
day.

Objection 1. For plants have life, as animals
have. But the production of animals belongs to
the work, not of distinction, but of adornment.
Therefore the production of plants, as also belonging to the work of adornment, ought not to
be recorded as taking place on the third day,
which is devoted to the work of distinction.

Obj. 2. Further, a work by which the earth is
accursed should have been recorded apart from
the work by which it receives its form. But the
words of Gen. 3. 17, *Cursed is the earth in thy
work, thorns and thistles shall it bring forth to
thee,* show that by the production of certain
plants the earth was accursed. Therefore the
production of plants in general should not have
been recorded on the third day, which is concerned with the work of formation.

Obj. 3. Further, as plants are firmly fixed to
the earth, so are stones and metals, which are,
nevertheless, not mentioned in the work of formation. Plants, therefore, ought not to have
been made on the third day.

On the contrary, It is said (Gen. 1. 12): *The
earth brought forth the green herb,* after which
there follows, *The evening and the morning
were the third day.*

I answer that, On the third day, as said (A. 1),
the formless state of the earth comes to an end.
But this state is described as twofold. On the
other hand, the earth was *invisible* or *void,* being covered by the waters; on the other hand,
it was *shapeless* or *empty,* that is, without that
comeliness which it owes to the plants that
clothe it, as it were, with a garment. Thus, therefore, in either respect this formless state ends
on the third day: first, when *the waters were
gathered together into one place and the dry
land appeared;* secondly, when the *earth brought
forth the green herb.*

But concerning the production of plants, Augustine's opinion differs from that of others. For
other commentators,[5] in accordance with the
surface meaning of the text, consider that the
plants were produced in act in their various species, on this third day; Augustine (*Gen. ad lit.*

[1] Aristotle, *Meteorology,* II, 1 (353[b]5).
[2] Chaps. 7, 12 (PL 34, 178, 182).
[3] PG 29, 89.　　[4] *Guide,* II, 30 (FR 213).

[5] *Glossa ordin.,* on Gen. 1.11 (I, 25F); Bede, *Hexaëm.,,* I
(PL 91, 21); cf. Basil, *In Hexaëm.,* V (PG 29, 99); Ambrose, *In Hexaëm.,* III, 6 (PL 14 178).

v, 4; viii, 3)[1] however says that "the earth is said to have then produced plants and trees in their causes, that is, it received then the power to produce them." He supports this view by the authority of Scripture, for it is said (Gen. 2. 4, 5): *These are the generations of the heaven and the earth, when they were created, in the day that ... God made the heaven and the earth, and every plant of the field before it sprung up in the earth, and every herb of the ground before it grew.* Therefore, the production of plants in their causes, within the earth, took place before they sprang up from the earth's surface. And this is confirmed by reason, as follows. In these first days God created all things in their origin or causes, and from this work He subsequently rested. Yet afterwards, by governing His creatures, in the work of propagation, *He worketh until now.* Now the production of plants from out the earth is a work of propagation, and therefore they were not produced in act on the third day, but in their causes only. However, in accordance with other writers,[2] it may be said that the first constitution of species belongs to the work of the six days, but the reproduction among them of like from like, to the government of the universe. And Scripture indicates this in the words, *before it sprung up in the earth,* and *before it grew,* that is, before like was produced from like, just as now happens in the natural course by the production of seed. Therefore Scripture says pointedly (Gen. 1. 11): *Let the earth bring forth the green herb, and such as may seed,* as indicating the production of perfect species, from which the seed of others should arise. Nor does the question where the seminal power may reside, whether in root, stem, or fruit, affect the argument.

Reply Obj. 1. Life in plants is hidden, since they lack sense and local motion, by which the animate and the inanimate are chiefly discernible. And therefore, since they are firmly fixed in the earth, their production is treated as a part of the earth's formation.

Reply Obj. 2. Even before the earth was accursed, thorns and thistles had been produced, either virtually or actually. But they were not produced in punishment of man, as though the earth, which he tilled to gain his food, produced unfruitful and noxious plants. Hence it was said: "Shall it bring forth *to thee.*"

Reply Obj. 3. Moses put before the people such things only as were manifest to their senses, as we have said (QQ. LXVII, A. 4; LXVIII,

A. 3). But minerals are generated in hidden ways within the bowels of the earth. Moreover, they seem hardly distinct from earth, and would seem to be species of the earth. For this reason, therefore, he makes no mention of them.

QUESTION LXX

OF THE WORK OF ADORNMENT, AS REGARDS THE FOURTH DAY

(In Three Articles)

WE must next consider the work of adornment, first as to each day by itself, secondly as to all seven days in general (Q. LXXIV).

In the first place, then, we consider the work of the fourth day, secondly that of the fifth day (Q. LXXI), thirdly that of the sixth day (Q. LXXII), and fourthly, such matters as belong to the seventh day (Q. LXXIII).

Under the first head there are three points of inquiry: (1) As to the production of the lights? (2) As to the end of their production? (3) Whether they are living things?

ARTICLE 1. *Whether the Lights Ought to Have Been Produced on the Fourth Day?*

We proceed thus to the First Article: It would seem that the lights ought not to have been produced on the fourth day.

Objection 1. For the heavenly luminaries are by nature incorruptible bodies. Therefore their matter cannot exist without their form. But as their matter was produced in the work of creation before there was any day, so therefore were their forms. It follows, then, that the lights were not produced on the fourth day.

Obj. 2. Further, the luminaries are, as it were, vessels of light. But light was made on the first day. The luminaries, therefore, should have been made on the first day, not on the fourth.

Obj. 3. Further, the lights are fixed in the firmament, as plants are fixed in the earth. For the Scripture says: *He set them in the firmament.* But plants are described as produced when the earth, to which they are attached, received its form. The lights, therefore, should have been produced at the same time as the firmament, that is to say, on the second day.

Obj. 4. Further, plants are an effect of the sun, moon, and other heavenly bodies. Now, cause precedes effect in the order of nature. The lights, therefore, ought not to have been produced on the fourth day, but on the third or before.

Obj. 5. Further, as astronomers say, there are many stars larger than the moon. Therefore

---

[1] PL 34, 325, 374.
[2] See above, in the body of the article.

the sun and the moon alone are not correctly described as the *two great lights*.

On the contrary, the authority of Scripture suffices.

I answer that, In recapitulating the Divine works, Scripture says (Gen. 2. 1): *So the heavens and the earth were finished and all the furniture of them,* thereby indicating that the work was threefold. In the first work, that of creation, the heaven and the earth were produced, but as yet without form. In the second, or work of distinction, the heaven and the earth were perfected, either by adding substantial form to formless matter, as Augustine holds (*Gen. ad lit.* ii, 11),[1] or by giving them the order and beauty due to them, as other holy writers suppose.[2] To these two works is added the work of adornment, which is distinct from perfection. For the perfection of the heaven and the earth seems to regard those things that belong to them intrinsically, but the adornment those that are extrinsic, just as the perfection of a man lies in his proper parts and forms, and his adornment in clothing or the like. Now just as distinction of certain things is made most evident by their local motion, as separating one from another, so the work of adornment is set forth by the production of things having movement in the heavens, and upon the earth. But it has been stated above (Q. LXIX, A. 1), that three things are recorded as created, namely, the heaven, the water, and the earth; and these three received their form from the three days' work of distinction, so that heaven was formed on the first day, on the second day the waters were separated, and on the third, the earth was divided into sea and dry land. So also is it in the work of adornment: on the first day of this work, which is the fourth of creation, are produced the lights, to adorn the heaven by their movements; on the second day, which is the fifth, birds and fishes are called into being, to make beautiful the intermediate element, for they move in air and water, which are here taken as one; while on the third day, which is the sixth, animals are brought forth, to move upon the earth and adorn it. It must also here be noted that Augustine's opinion (*Gen. ad lit.* v, 5)[3] on the production of the lights is not at variance with that of other holy writers,[4] since he says that they were made actually, and not merely virtually, for the firmament has not the power of producing lights, as

the earth has of producing plants. Therefore Scripture does not say: *Let the firmament produce lights,* though it says: *Let the earth bring forth the green herb.*

Reply Obj. 1. In Augustine's opinion[5] there is no difficulty here, for he does not hold a succession of time in these works, and so there was no need for the matter of the lights to exist under another form. Nor is there any difficulty in the opinion of those who hold the heavenly bodies to be of the nature of the four elements,[6] for it may be said that they were formed out of matter already existing, as animals and plants were formed. For those, however, who hold the heavenly bodies to be of another nature from the elements, and naturally incorruptible,[7] the answer must be that the substance of the lights was created at the beginning, but that their substance, at first formless, is formed on this day, by receiving not its substantial form, but a determination of power. As to the fact that the lights are not mentioned as existing from the beginning, but only as made on the fourth day, Chrysostom (*Hom.* vi *in Gen.*)[8] explains this by the need of guarding the people from the danger of idolatry, since the lights are proved not to be gods by the fact that they were not from the beginning.

Reply Obj. 2. No difficulty exists if we follow Augustine in holding the light made on the first day to be spiritual, and that made on this day to be corporeal.[9] If, however, the light made on the first day is understood to be itself corporeal,[10] then it must be held to have been produced on that day merely as light in general, and that on the fourth day the lights received a definite power to produce determinate effects. Thus we observe that the rays of the sun have one effect, those of the moon another, and so forth. Hence, speaking of such a determination of power, Dionysius (*De Div. Nom.* iv)[11] says that the sun's light which previously was without form, was formed on the fourth day.

Reply Obj. 3. According to Ptolemy[12] the luminaries are not fixed in the spheres, but have their own motion distinct from the motion of the spheres. Hence Chrysostom says (*ibid.*) that He is said to have set them in the firmament not because He fixed them there immovably, but because He bade them be there, even as He

---

[1] PL 34, 272.
[2] See above, Q. LXVI, A. 1; Q. LXIX, A. 1.
[3] PL 34, 326.
[4] Cf. *Glossa ordin.*, on Gen. 1.14 (I, 26b); Bede, *Hexaëm.*, I (PL 91, 21).
[5] *Gen. ad lit.*, IV, 34; V, 5 (PL 34, 319, 325).
[6] See above, Q. LXVIII, A. 1.   [7] *Ibid.*
[8] PG 53, 58.   [9] *Gen. ad lit.*, I, 12 (PL 34, 255).
[10] Cf. above, Q. LXVII, A. 4, Ans. 2.
[11] Sect. 4 (PG 3, 700).
[12] *Syntaxis Mathematica,* (*Almagest*), I, 20 (HB I, 26.23); III, 3 (HB I, 216.24).

placed man in Paradise, to be there. In the opinion of Aristotle, however, the stars are fixed in their orbits, and in reality have no other movement but that of the spheres; and yet our senses perceive the movement of the luminaries and not that of the spheres.[1] But Moses describes what is obvious to sense, out of condescension to the ignorance of the people, as we have already said (QQ. LXVII, A. 4; LXVIII, A. 3). The objection, however, falls to the ground if we regard the firmament made on the second day as having a natural distinction from that in which the stars are placed, even though the distinction is not apparent to the senses, the testimony of which Moses follows, as stated above (*ibid.*). For although to the senses there appears but one firmament, if we admit a higher and a lower firmament, the lower will be that which was made on the second day, and on the fourth the stars were fixed in the higher firmament.

Reply Obj. 4. In the words of Basil (*Hom.* v. *in Hexaëm.*),[2] plants were recorded as produced before the sun and moon, to prevent idolatry, since those who believe the heavenly bodies to be gods hold that plants originate primarily from these bodies. Although as Chrysostom remarks (*Hom.* vi *in Gen.*),[3] the sun, moon, and stars co-operate in the work of production by their movements, as the husbandman co-operates by his labour.

Reply Obj. 5. As Chrysostom says,[4] the two lights are called great, not so much with regard to their dimensions as to their efficacy and power. For though the stars be of greater bulk than the moon, yet the influence of the moon is more perceptible to the senses in this lower world. Moreover, as far as the senses are concerned, its apparent size is greater.

ARTICLE 2. *Whether the Cause Assigned for the Production of the Lights Is Fitting?*

We proceed thus to the Second Article: It would seem that the cause assigned for the production of the lights is not fitting.

Objection 1. For it is said (Jer. 10. 2): *Be not afraid of the signs of heaven, which the heathens fear.* Therefore the heavenly lights were not made to be signs.

Obj. 2. Further, sign is divided against cause. But the lights are the cause of what takes place upon the earth. Therefore they are not signs.

Obj. 3. Further, the distinction of seasons and days began from the first day. Therefore the

---

[1] *Heavens*, II, 8 (289ᵇ32).
[2] PG 29, 96.   [3] PG 53, 58.
[4] Cf. Basil, *In Hexaëm.*, VI (PG 29, 137).

lights were not made *for seasons, and days, and years,* that is, in order to distinguish them.

Obj. 4. Further, nothing is made for the sake of that which is inferior to itself, since the end is better than the means. But the lights are nobler than the earth. Therefore they were not made *to enlighten it.*

Obj. 5. Further, the new moon cannot be said *to rule the night.* But the moon when first made was probably at the full; for men begin to count from the full moon. The moon, therefore, was not made to *rule the night.*

On the contrary, The authority of Scripture suffices.

I answer that, As we have said above (Q. LXV, A. 2), a corporeal creature can be considered as made either for the sake of its proper act, or for other creatures, or for the whole universe, or for the glory of God. Of these reasons only that which points out the usefulness of these things to man is touched upon by Moses, in order to withdraw his people from idolatry. Hence it is written (Deut. 4. 19): *Lest perhaps lifting up thy eyes to heaven, thou see the sun and the moon and all the stars of heaven, and being deceived by error thou adore and serve them, which the Lord thy God created for the service of all nations.* Now, he explains this service at the beginning of Genesis as threefold. First, the lights are of service to man in regard to sight, which directs him in his works, and is most useful for knowing things. In reference to this he says: *Let them shine in the firmament and give life to the earth.* Secondly, as regards the changes of the seasons, which prevent weariness, preserve health, and provide for the necessities of food, all of which things could not be secured if it were always summer or winter. In reference to this he says: *Let them be for seasons, and for days, and years.* Thirdly, as regards the convenience of business and work, in so far as the lights are set in the heavens to indicate fair or foul weather, as favourable to various occupations. And in this respect he says: *Let them be for signs.*

Reply Obj. 1. The lights in the heaven are set for signs of changes effected in corporeal creatures, but not of those changes which depend upon free choice.

Reply Obj. 2. We are sometimes brought to the knowledge of hidden effects through their sensible causes, and conversely. Hence nothing prevents a sensible cause from being a sign. But he says signs, rather than causes, to guard against idolatry.

Reply Obj. 3. The general division of time

into day and night took place on the first day as regards the diurnal movement, which is common to the whole heaven and may be understood to have begun on that first day. But the particular distinctions of days and seasons and years, according as one day is hotter than another, one season than another, and one year than another, are due to certain particular movements of the stars which movements may have had their beginning on the fourth day.

Reply Obj. 4. Light was given to the earth for the service of man, who, by reason of his soul, is above the heavenly bodies. Nor is it untrue to say that a higher creature may be made for the sake of a lower, considered not in itself, but as ordered to the good of the universe.

Reply Obj. 5. When the moon is at its perfection it rises in the evening and sets in the morning, and thus it rules the night, and it was probably made in its full perfection as were plants yielding seed, as also were animals and man himself. For although the perfect is developed from the imperfect by natural processes, yet the perfect must exist absolutely before the imperfect. Augustine, however (*Gen. ad lit.* ii),[1] does not say this, for he says that it is not unfitting that God made things imperfect, which He afterwards perfected.

ARTICLE 3. *Whether the Lights of Heaven Are Living Beings?*

We proceed thus to the Third Article: It would seem that the lights of heaven are living beings.

Objection 1. For the nobler a body is, the more nobly it should be adorned. But a body less noble than the heaven is adorned with living beings, with fish, birds, and the beasts of the field. Therefore the lights of heaven, as pertaining to its adornment, should be living beings also.

Obj. 2. Further, the nobler a body is, the nobler must be its form. But the sun, moon, and stars are nobler bodies than plants or animals, and must therefore have nobler forms. Now the noblest of all forms is the soul, as being the first principle of life. Hence Augustine (*De Vera Relig.* xxix)[2] says: "Every living substance stands higher in the order of nature than one that has not life." The lights of heaven, therefore, are living beings.

Obj. 3. Further, a cause is nobler than its effect. But the sun, moon, and the other lights are a cause of life, as is especially evidenced in the case of animals generated from putrefaction, which receive life from the power of the sun and

stars. Much more, therefore, have the heavenly bodies a living soul.

Obj. 4. Further, the movements of the heaven and the heavenly bodies are natural,[3] and natural movement is from an intrinsic principle. Now the principle of movement in the heavenly bodies is a substance capable of apprehension, and is moved as the desirer is moved by the object desired.[4] Therefore, it seems, the apprehending principle is intrinsic to the heavenly bodies, and consequently they are living beings.

Obj. 5. Further, the first of movables is the heaven. Now, of all things that are endowed with movement the first moves itself, as is proved in the *Physics*,[5] because what is such of itself precedes that which is by another. But only beings that are living move themselves, as is shown in the same book.[6] Therefore the heavenly bodies are living beings.

On the contrary, Damascene says (*De Fid. Orth.* ii, 6),[7] "Let no one esteem the heavens or the heavenly bodies to be living beings, for they have neither life nor sense."

I answer that, Philosophers have differed on this question. Anaxagoras, for instance, as Augustine mentions,[8] "was condemned by the Athenians for teaching that the sun was a fiery mass of stone, and neither a god nor even a living being." On the other hand, the Platonists held that the heavenly bodies have life.[9] Nor was there less diversity of opinion among the Doctors of the Church. It was the belief of Origen (*Peri Archon* i)[10] and Jerome[11] that these bodies were alive, and the latter seems to explain in that sense the words (Eccles. 1. 6), *The spirit goeth forward, surveying all places round about.* But Basil (*Hom.* iii, *in Hexaëm.*)[12] and Damascene (*loc. cit.*) maintain that the heavenly bodies are inanimate. Augustine leaves the matter in doubt, without committing himself to either theory, though he goes so far as to say that if the heavenly bodies are really living beings, their souls must be akin to the angelic nature (*Gen. ad lit.* ii, 18 and *Enchiridion* lviii).[13]

In examining the truth of this question, where

---

[1] Chap. 15 (PL 34, 276).   [2] PL 34, 145.

[3] Aristotle, *Heavens*, i, 2 (269ᵃ30).
[4] Aristotle, *Metaphysics*, xii, 7 (1072ᵃ26).
[5] Aristotle, viii, 5 (256ᵃ21).   [6] viii, 4 (255ᵃ6).
[7] PG 94, 885.   [8] *City of God*, xviii, 41 (PL 41, 601).
[9] Cf. Macrobius, *In Somn. Scip.*, i, 14 (DD 45B). Augustine, in the *City of God*, xiii, 16 (PL 41, 388), attributes this doctrine to the Platonists. Cf. also Boëthius, *In Porphyrium*, iii (PL 64, 123); cf. *Timaeus* (41); cf. also Avicenna, *Meta.*, ix, 2 (102vb); Averroes, *In Meta.*, xii 36 (viii, 318G).
[10] Chap. 7 (PG 11, 173).
[11] *In Eccle.* i, 6 (PL 23, 1068).
[12] PG 29, 76.   [13] PL 34, 279; PL 40, 260.

such diversity of opinion exists, we shall do well to bear in mind that the union of soul and body exists for the sake of the soul and not of the body; for the form does not exist for the matter, but the matter for the form. Now the nature and power of the soul are apprehended through its operation, which is to a certain extent its end. Yet for some of these operations, as sensation and nutrition, our body is a necessary instrument. Hence it is clear that the sensitive and nutritive souls must be united to a body in order to exercise their functions. There are, however, operations of the soul which are not exercised through the medium of the body, though the body ministers, as it were, to their production. The intellect, for example, makes use of the phantasms derived from the bodily senses, and thus far is dependent on the body, although capable of being separated from it.

It is not, however, possible that the functions of nutrition, growth, and generation, through which the nutritive soul operates, can be exercised by the heavenly bodies, for such operations are incompatible with a body naturally incorruptible. Equally impossible is it that the functions of the sensitive soul can appertain to the heavenly body, since all the senses depend on the sense of touch, which perceives elemental qualities, and all the organs of the senses require a certain proportion in the admixture of elements, whereas the nature of the heavenly bodies is not elemental. It follows, then, that of the operations of the soul the only ones left to be attributed to the heavenly bodies are those of understanding and moving; for desire follows both sensitive and intellectual perception, and is ordered to both. But the operations of the intellect, which does not act through the body, do not need a body as their instrument, except to supply phantasms through the senses. Moreover, the operations of the sensitive soul, as we have seen, cannot be attributed to the heavenly bodies. Accordingly, the union of a soul to a heavenly body cannot be for the purpose of the operations of the intellect.

It remains, then, only to consider whether the movement of the heavenly bodies demands a soul as the moving power, not that the soul, in order to move the heavenly body, need be united to the latter as its form, but by contact of power, as a mover is united to that which he moves. Therefore Aristotle,[1] after showing that the first mover is made up of two parts, the moving and the moved, goes on to show the nature of the union between these two parts. This, he says, is

effected by contact which is mutual if both are bodies; on the part of one only, if one is a body and the other not. The Platonists explain the union of soul and body in the same way, as a contact of "a moving power with the thing moved,"[2] and since Plato holds the heavenly bodies to be living beings, this means nothing else but that substances of spiritual nature are united to them, and act as their moving power. A proof that the heavenly bodies are moved by the direct influence and contact of some apprehending substance, and not, like heavy and light bodies, by nature, lies in the fact that whereas nature moves to one fixed end in whose attainment it rests, this does not appear in the motion of heavenly bodies. Hence it follows that they are moved by some apprehending substances. Augustine appears to be of the same opinion when he expresses his belief that "all corporeal things" are ruled by God "through the spirit of life" (*De Trin.* iii, 4).[3]

From what has been said, then, it is clear that the heavenly bodies are not living beings in the same sense as plants and animals, and that if they are called so, it can only be equivocally. It will also be seen that the difference of opinion between those who affirm and those who deny that these bodies have life, is not a difference of things but of words.

Reply Obj. 1. Certain things belong to the adornment of the universe by reason of their proper movement; and in this way the heavenly luminaries agree with others that conduce to that adornment, for they are moved by a living substance.

Reply Obj. 2. One being may be nobler than another absolutely, but not in a particular respect. While, then, it is not conceded that the forms of heavenly bodies are nobler than the souls of animals absolutely, it must be conceded that they are superior to them with regard to the character of form, since their form perfects their matter entirely, so that it is not in potency to other forms, whereas a soul does not do this. Also as regards movement, the power that moves the heavenly bodies is of a nobler kind.

Reply Obj. 3. Since the heavenly body is a mover moved, it is of the nature of an instrument, which acts by the power of the principle agent; and therefore since this agent is a living substance the heavenly body can impart life in virtue of that agent.

Reply Obj. 4. The movement of the heavenly bodies are natural not on account of their active principle, but on account of their passive prin-

---

[1] *Physics*, VIII, 5 (257ª33).

[2] See Q. LXXVI, A. I.   [3] PL 42, 873.

ciple; that is to say, from a certain natural aptitude for being moved by an intelligent power.

Reply Obj. 5. The heaven is said to move itself in as far as it is compounded of mover and moved; not by the union of the mover, as the form, with the moved, as the matter, but by contact with the moving power, as we have said. So far, then, the principle that moves it may be called intrinsic, and consequently its movement natural with respect to that active principle; just as we say that voluntary movement is natural to the animal as animal.[1]

QUESTION LXXI
OF THE WORK OF THE FIFTH DAY
(*In One Article*)

WE must next consider the work of the fifth day. It would seem that this work is not fittingly described.

Objection 1. For the waters produce that which the power of water is adequate to produce. But the power of water does not suffice for the production of every kind of fishes and birds since we find that many of them are generated from seed. Therefore the words, *Let the waters bring forth the creeping creature having life, and the fowl that may fly over the earth,* do not fittingly describe this work.

Obj. 2. Further, fishes and birds are not produced from water only, but earth seems to predominate over water in their composition, as is shown by the fact that their bodies tend naturally to the earth and rest upon it. It is not, then, fittingly said that fishes and birds are produced from water.

Obj. 3. Further, fishes move in the waters, and birds in the air. If, then, fishes are produced from the waters, birds ought to be produced from the air, and not from the waters.

Obj. 4. Further, not all fishes creep through the waters, for some, as seals, have feet and walk on land. Therefore the production of fishes is not sufficiently described by the words, *Let the waters bring forth the creeping creature having life.*

Obj. 5. Further, land animals are more perfect than birds and fishes, which appears from the fact that they have more distinct limbs, and generation of a higher order. For they bring forth animals, whereas birds and fishes bring forth eggs. But the more perfect has precedence in the order of nature. Therefore fishes and birds ought not to have been produced on the fifth day, before the land animals.

[1] Aristotle, *Physics,* VIII, 4 (254ᵇ14).

On the contrary, The authority of Scripture suffices.

I answer that, As said above (Q. LXX, A. 1), the order of the work of adornment corresponds to the order of the work of distinction. Hence, as among the three days assigned to the work of distinction, the middle, or second, day is devoted to the work of the distinction of water, which is the intermediate body, so in the three days of the work of adornment, the middle day, which is the fifth, is assigned to the adornment of the intermediate body, by the production of birds and fishes. As, then, Moses makes mention of the lights and the light on the fourth day, to show that the fourth day corresponds to the first day on which he had said that the light was made, so on this fifth day he mentions the waters and the firmament of heaven to show that the fifth day corresponds to the second. It must, however, be observed that Augustine differs from other writers in his opinion about the production of fishes and birds, as he differs about the production of plants. For while others say that fishes and birds were produced on the fifth day actually,[2] he holds that the nature of the waters produced them on that day potentially.[3]

Reply Obj. 1. It was laid down by Avicenna[4] that animals of all kinds can be generated by various minglings of the elements, and naturally, without any kind of seed. This, however, seems wrong, since nature produces its effects by determinate means, and, consequently, those things that are naturally generated from seed cannot be generated naturally in any other way. It ought, then, rather to be said that in the natural generation of all animals that are generated from seed, the active principle lies in the formative power of the seed, but that in the case of animals generated from putrefaction, the formative power is the influence of the heavenly bodies. The material principle, however, in the generation of either kind of animals is either some element, or something compounded of the elements. But at the first beginning of things the active principle was the Word of God, which produced animals from material elements, either in act, as some holy writers say,[5] or virtually, as Augustine teaches.[6] Not as though the power possessed by water or earth of producing all animals resides in the earth and water themselves,

[2] Cf. Basil, *In Hexaëm.,* VII (PG 29, 148); Ambrose, *In Hexaëm.* v, 1 (PL 14, 219); Bede, *In Hexaëm.,* 1 (PL 91, 25).   [3] *Gen. ad lit.,* v, 5 (PL 34, 326).

[4] *De Anima,* XV, 1 (59va).

[5] Cf. Basil, *In Hexaëm.* VIII (PG 29, 163); Ambrose, *In Hexaëm.,* VI, 2 (PL 14, 258); Bede, *In Hexaëm.,* 1 (PL 91, 27).   [6] *Gen. ad lit.,* v, 5 (PL 34, 326).

as Avicenna held,[1] but in the power originally given to the elements of producing them from elemental matter by the power of seed or the influence of the stars.

Reply Obj. 2. The bodies of birds and fishes may be considered from two points of view. If considered in themselves, it will be evident that the earthly element must predominate, since the element that is least active, namely, the earth, must be the most abundant in quantity in order that the mingling may be duly tempered in the body of the animal. But if considered as by nature constituted to move with certain specific motions, thus they have some special affinity with the bodies in which they move; and hence the words in which their generation is described.

Reply Obj. 3. The air, as not being so apparent to the senses, is not enumerated by itself, but with other things: partly with the water, because the lower region of the air is thickened by watery exhalations; partly with the heaven as to the higher region. But birds move in the lower part of the air, and so are said to fly *beneath the firmament,* even if the firmament be taken to mean the region of clouds. Hence the production of birds is ascribed to the water.

Reply Obj. 4. Nature passes from one extreme to another through the medium. And therefore there are creatures of intermediate type between the animals of the air and those of the water, having something in common with both. And they are reckoned as belonging to that class to which they are most allied, through the characters possessed in common with that class, rather than with the other. But in order to include among fishes all such intermediate forms as have special characters like theirs, the words, *Let the waters bring forth the creeping creature having life,* are followed by these: *God created great whales,* etc.

Reply Obj. 5. The order in which the production of these animals is given has reference to the order of those bodies which they are set to adorn, rather than to the superiority of the animals themselves. Moreover, in generation also the more perfect is reached through the less perfect.

QUESTION LXXII
OF THE WORK OF THE SIXTH DAY
(*In One Article*)

WE must now consider the work of the sixth day.

It would seem that this work is not fittingly described.

[1] *De Anim.,* XV, I (59va).

Objection 1. For as birds and fishes have a living soul, so also have land animals. But these animals are not themselves living souls. Therefore the words, *Let the earth bring forth the living creature,* should rather have been, *Let the earth bring forth the living fourfooted creatures.*

Obj. 2. Further, a genus ought not to be divided against its species. But beasts and cattle are quadrupeds. Therefore quadrupeds ought not to be enumerated as a class with beasts and cattle.

Obj. 3. Further, as other animals belong to a determinate genus and species, so also does man. But in the making of man nothing is said of his genus nor species, and therefore nothing ought to have been said about them in the production of other animals, whereas it is said "according to its genus" or "in its species."

Obj. 4. Further, land animals are more like man, whom God is recorded to have blessed, than are birds and fishes. But as birds and fishes are said to be blessed, this should have been said, with much more reason, of the other animals as well.

Obj. 5. Further, certain animals are generated from putrefaction, which is a kind of corruption. But corruption is not appropriate to the first founding of the world. Therefore such animals should not have been produced at that time.

Obj. 6. Further, certain animals are poisonous, and injurious to man. But there ought to have been nothing injurious to man before man sinned. Therefore such animals ought not to have been made by God at all, since He is the Author of good, or at least not until man had sinned.

On the contrary, The authority of Scripture suffices.

I answer that, As on the fifth day the intermediate body, namely the water, is adorned, and thus that day corresponds to the second day; so the sixth day, on which the lowest body, or the earth, is adorned by the production of land animals, corresponds to the third day. Hence the earth is mentioned in both places. And here again Augustine says (*Gen. ad lit.,* v)[2] that the production was potential, and other holy writers that it was actual.[3]

Reply Obj. 1. The different grades of life which are found in different living creatures can be discovered from the various ways in which the Scripture speaks of them, as Basil

[2] Chap. 5 (PL 34, 326).
[3] See note above, Q. LXXI, ANS. I.

says (*Hom. viii in Hexaëm.*).[1] The life of plants, for instance, is very imperfect and difficult to discern, and hence, in speaking of their production, nothing is said of their life, but only their generation is mentioned, since only in generation is a vital act observed in them. For the powers of nutrition and growth are subordinate to the generative life, as will be shown later on (Q. LXXVIII, A. 2). But amongst animals, those that live on land are, generally speaking, more perfect than birds and fishes, not because the fish is devoid of memory, as Basil upholds (*ibid.*) and Augustine rejects (*Gen. ad lit.* iii),[2] but because their limbs are more distinct and their generation of a higher order, (yet some imperfect animals, such as bees and ants, are more acute in certain ways). Scripture, therefore, does not call fishes *living creatures,* but *creeping creatures having life;* but it does call land animals *living creatures* on account of their more perfect life, and seems to imply that fishes are merely bodies having in them something of a soul, whilst land animals, from the higher perfection of their life, are, as it were, living souls with bodies subject to them. But the life of man, as being the most perfect grade, is not said to be produced, like the life of other animals, by the earth or water, but immediately by God.

Reply Obj. 2. By *cattle,* domestic animals are signified, which in any way are of service to man, but by *beasts,* wild animals such as bears and lions are designated. By *creeping things* those animals are meant which either have no feet and cannot rise from the earth, as serpents, or those whose feet are too short to lift them far from the ground, as the lizard and tortoise. But since certain animals, as deer and goats, seem to fall under none of these classes, the word *quadrupeds* is added. Or perhaps the word *quadruped* is used first as being the genus, to which animals are added as species, for even some reptiles, such as lizards and tortoises, are four-footed.

Reply Obj. 3. In other animals, and in plants, mention is made of genus and species to denote the generation of like from like. But it was unnecessary to do so in the case of man, as what had already been said of other creatures might be understood of him. Again, animals and plants may be said to be produced according to their kinds to signify their remoteness from the Divine likeness, whereas man is said to be made *to the image and likeness of God.*

Reply Obj. 4. The blessing of God gives power to multiply by generation, and, having been mentioned in the preceding account of the making of birds and fishes, could be understood of the beasts of the earth without requiring to be repeated. The blessing, however, is repeated in the case of man, since in him generation of children has a special relation to the filling up of the number of the elect, and "to prevent anyone from saying that there was any sin whatever in the act of begetting children." As to plants, "since they experience neither desire of propagation, nor sensation in generating, they are deemed unworthy of the words of the blessing."[3]

Reply Obj. 5. Since the generation of one thing is the corruption of another, it was not incompatible with the first formation of things that from the corruption of the less perfect the more perfect should be generated. Hence animals generated from the corruption of inanimate things, or of plants, may have been generated then. But those generated from corruption of animals could not have been produced then otherwise than potentially.

Reply Obj. 6. In the words of Augustine (*Super. Gen. contr. Manich.* i):[4] "If an unskilled person enters the workshop of an artificer he sees in it many appliances of which he does not understand the use, and which, if he is a foolish fellow, he considers unnecessary. Moreover, should he carelessly fall into the fire, or wound himself with a sharp-edged tool, he is under the impression that many of the things there are hurtful; the craftsman, however, knowing their use, laughs at his folly. And thus some people presume to find fault with many things in this world, through not seeing the reasons for their existence. For though not required for the furnishing of our house, these things are necessary for the perfection of the universe." And, since man before he sinned would have used the things of this world conformably to the order designed, poisonous animals would not have injured him.

QUESTION LXXIII
OF THE THINGS THAT BELONG TO THE SEVENTH DAY
(*In Three Articles*)

WE must next consider the things that belong to the seventh day. Under this head there are three points of inquiry: (1) About the comple-

---

[1] PG 29, 165.
[2] Chap. 8 (PL 34, 283).
[3] Augustine, *Gen. ad lit.,* III, 13 (PL 34, 288).
[4] Chap. 16 (PL 34, 185).

tion of the works. (2) About the resting of God. (3) About the blessing and sanctifying of this day.

ARTICLE 1. *Whether the Completion of the Divine Works Ought To Be Ascribed to the Seventh Day?*

We proceed thus to the First Article: It would seem that the completion of the Divine works ought not to be ascribed to the seventh day.

Objection 1. For all things that are done in this world belong to the Divine works. But the consummation of the world will be at the end of the world (Matt. 13. 39, 40). Moreover, the time of Christ's Incarnation is a time of completion, and therefore it is called *the time of fulness* (Vulg., *the fulness of time*) (Gal. 4. 4). And Christ Himself, at the moment of His death, cried out, *It is consummated* (John 19. 30). Hence the completion of the Divine works does not belong to the seventh day.

Obj. 2. Further, the completion of a work is an act in itself. But we do not read that God acted at all on the seventh day, but rather that He rested from all His work. Therefore the completion of the works does not belong to the seventh day.

Obj. 3. Further, nothing is said to be complete to which many things are added, unless they are superfluous, for a thing is called perfect to which nothing is wanting that it ought to possess. But many things were made after the seventh day, as the production of many individual beings, and even of certain new species that are frequently appearing, especially in the case of animals generated from putrefaction. Also, God creates daily new souls. Again, the work of the Incarnation was a new work, of which it is said (Jer. 31. 22): *The Lord hath created a new thing upon the earth.* Miracles also are new works, of which it is said (Eccles. 36. 6): *Renew thy signs, and work new miracles.* Moreover, all things will be made new when the Saints are glorified, according to Apoc. 21. 5: *And He that sat on the throne said: Behold I make all things new.* Therefore the completion of the Divine works ought not to be attributed to the seventh day.

On the contrary, It is said (Gen. 2. 2): *On the seventh day God ended His work which he had made.*

I answer that, The perfection of a thing is twofold, the first perfection and the second perfection. The first perfection is that according to which a thing is substantially perfect, and this perfection is the form of the whole, which form results from the whole having its parts complete. But the second perfection is the end, which is either an operation, as the end of the harpist is to play the harp, or something that is attained by an operation, as the end of the builder is the house that he makes by building. But the first perfection is the cause of the second, because the form is the principle of operation. Now the final perfection, which is the end of the whole universe, is the perfect happiness of the Saints at the consummation of the world; and the first perfection is the completeness of the universe at its first founding, and this is what is ascribed to the seventh day.

Reply Obj. 1. The first perfection is the cause of the second, as above said. Now, for the attaining of happiness two things are required, nature and grace. Therefore, as said above, the perfection of happiness will be at the end of the world. But this consummation existed previously in its causes, as to nature, at the first founding of the world, as to grace, in the Incarnation of Christ. For, *Grace and truth came by Jesus Christ* (John 1. 17). So, then, on the seventh day was the consummation of nature, in Christ's Incarnation the consummation of grace, and at the end of the world will be the consummation of glory.

Reply Obj. 2. God acted on the seventh day, not by creating new creatures, but by directing and moving His creatures to the work proper to them, and thus He made some beginning of the second perfection. So that, according to our version of the Scripture, the completion of the works is attributed to the seventh day, though according to another[1] it is assigned to the sixth. Either version, however, may stand, since the completion of the universe as to the completeness of its parts belongs to the sixth day, but its completion as regards their operation, to the seventh. It may also be added that in continuous movement, so long as any movement further is possible, movement cannot be called completed till it comes to rest, for rest denotes consummation of movement. Now God might have made many other creatures besides those which He made in the six days, and hence, by the fact that He ceased making them on the seventh day, He is said on that day to have consummated His work.

Reply Obj. 3. Nothing entirely new was afterwards made by God, but all things subsequently made had in a sense been made before in the work of the six days. Some things, indeed, had

---

[1] The Septuagint.

a previous existence materially, as the rib from the side of Adam out of which God formed Eve; whilst others existed not only in matter but also in their causes, as those individual creatures that are now generated existed in the first of their kind. Species, also, that are new, if any such appear, existed beforehand in various active powers, so that animals, and perhaps even new species of animals, are produced by putrefaction by the power which the stars and elements received at the beginning. Again, animals of new kinds arise occasionally from the intercourse of individuals belonging to different species, as the mule is the offspring of an ass and a mare; but even these existed previously in their causes, in the works of the six days. Some also existed beforehand by way of likeness, as the souls now created. And the work of the Incarnation itself was thus foreshadowed, for as we read (Philip. 2. 7), The Son of God *was made in the likeness of men.* And again, the glory that is spiritual was anticipated in the angels by way of likeness; and that of the body in the heaven, especially the empyrean. Hence it is written (Eccles. 1. 10), *Nothing under the sun is new, for it hath already gone before, in the ages that were before us.*

ARTICLE 2. *Whether God Rested on the Seventh Day from All His Work?*

We proceed thus to the Second Article: It would seem that God did not rest on the seventh day from all His work.

Objection 1. For it is said (John 5. 17), *My Father worketh until now, and I work.* God, then, did not rest on the seventh day from all His works.

Obj. 2. Further, rest is opposed to movement, or to labour, which movement causes. But, as God produced His work without movement and without labour, He cannot be said to have rested on the seventh day from His work.

Obj. 3. Further, should it be said that God rested on the seventh day by causing man to rest, against this it may be argued that rest is set down against His work; now the words "God created" or "made" this thing or the other cannot be explained to mean that He made man create or make these things. Therefore the resting of God cannot be explained as His making man to rest.

On the contrary, It is said (Gen. 2. 2): *God rested on the seventh day from all the work which He had done.*

I answer that, Rest is, properly speaking, opposed to movement, and consequently to the labour that arises from movement. But although movement, strictly speaking, is a quality of bodies, yet the word is applied also to spiritual things, and in a twofold sense. On the one hand, every operation may be called a movement, and thus the Divine goodness is said to move and go forth to the thing in communicating itself to that thing, as Dionysius says (*De Div. Nom.* ii).[1] On the other hand, the desire that tends to another, is said to move towards it. Hence rest is taken in two senses, in one sense meaning a cessation from work, in the other, the fulfilling of desire. Now, in either sense God is said to have rested on the seventh day. First, because He ceased from creating new creatures on that day, for, as said above (A. 1, Ans. 3), He made nothing afterwards that had not existed previously, in some degree, in the first works; secondly, because He Himself had no need of the things that He had made, but was happy in the enjoyment of Himself. Hence, when all things were made He is not said to have rested *in* His works, as though needing them for His own happiness, but to have rested *from* them, as in fact resting in Himself, as He suffices for Himself and fulfils His own desire. And even though from all eternity He rested in Himself, yet the rest in Himself which He took after He had finished His works is that rest which belongs to the seventh day. And this, says Augustine, is the meaning of God's "resting from His works" on that day (*Gen. ad lit.* iv).[2]

Reply Obj. 1. God indeed *worketh until now* by preserving and providing for the creatures He has made, but not by the making of new ones.

Reply Obj. 2. Rest is here not opposed to labour or to movement, but to the production of new creatures and to the desire tending to another.

Reply Obj. 3. Even as God rests in Himself alone and is happy in the enjoyment of Himself, so our own sole happiness lies in the enjoyment of God. Thus, also, He makes us find rest in Himself both from His works and our own. It is not, then, unreasonable to say that God rested in giving rest to us. Still, this explanation must not be set down as the only one, and the other is the first and principal explanation.

ARTICLE 3. *Whether Blessing and Sanctifying Are Due to the Seventh Day?*

We proceed thus to the Third Article: It would seem that blessing and sanctifying are not due to the seventh day.

[1] Sect. 4 (PG 3, 640).   [2] Chap. 15 (PL 34, 306).

Objection 1. For it is usual to call a time blessed or holy for that some good thing has happened in it, or some evil been avoided. But whether God works or ceases from work nothing accrues to Him or is lost to Him. Therefore no special blessing nor sanctifying are due to the seventh day.

Obj. 2. Further, the word *benedictio* (blessing) is derived from *bonitas* (goodness). But it is the nature of good to spread and communicate itself, as Dionysius says (*De Div. Nom.* iv).[1] The days, therefore, in which God produced creatures deserved a blessing rather than the day on which He ceased producing them.

Obj. 3. Further, over each creature a blessing was pronounced, as upon each work it was said, *God saw that it was good.* Therefore it was not necessary that after all had been produced, the seventh day should be blessed.

On the contrary, It is written (Gen. 2. 3), *God blessed the seventh day and sanctified it, because in it He had rested from all His work.*

I answer that, As said above (A. 2), God's rest on the seventh day is understood in two ways. First, in that He ceased from producing new works, though He still preserves and provides for the creatures He has made. Secondly, in that after all His works He rested in Himself. According to the first meaning, then, a blessing befits the seventh day, since, as we explained (Q. LXXII, Ans. 4), the blessing referred to the increase by multiplication, for which reason God said to the creatures which He blessed: *Increase and multiply.* Now, this increase is effected through God's Providence over His creatures, securing the generation of like from like. And according to the second meaning, it is right that the seventh day should have been sanctified, since the special sanctification of every creature consists in resting in God. For this reason things dedicated to God are said to be sanctified.

Reply Obj. 1. The seventh day is said to be sanctified not because anything can accrue to God or be taken from Him, but because something is added to creatures by their multiplying and by their resting in God.

Reply Obj. 2. In the first six days creatures were produced in their first causes, but after being thus produced, they are multiplied and preserved, and this work also belongs to the Divine goodness. And the perfection of this goodness is made most clear by the knowledge that in it alone God finds His own rest, and we may find ours in its enjoyment.

[1] Sect. 20 (PG 3, 720). Cf. Sect. 1, 4 (693, 697).

Reply Obj. 3. The good mentioned in the works of each day belongs to the first institution of nature, but the blessing attached to the seventh day to its propagation.

QUESTION LXXIV
OF ALL THE SEVEN DAYS IN COMMON
(*In Three Articles*)

WE next consider all the seven days in common: and there are three points of inquiry: (1) As to the sufficiency of these days. (2) Whether they are all one day, or more than one? (3) As to certain modes of speaking which Scripture uses in narrating the works of the six days.

ARTICLE 1. *Whether These Days Are Sufficiently Enumerated?*

We proceed thus to the First Article: It would seem that these days are not sufficiently enumerated.

Objection 1. For the work of creation is no less distinct from the works of distinction and adornment than these two works are from one another. But separate days are assigned to distinction and to adornment, and therefore separate days should be assigned to creation.

Obj. 2. Further, air and fire are nobler elements than earth and water. But one day is assigned to the distinction of water and another to the distinction of the land. Therefore, other days ought to be devoted to the distinction of fire and air.

Obj. 3. Further, fish differ from birds as much as birds differ from the beasts of the earth, whereas man differs more from other animals than all animals whatsoever differ from each other. But one day is devoted to the production of fishes, and another to that of the beasts of the earth. Another day, then, ought to be assigned to the production of birds, and another to that of man.

Obj. 4. Further, it would seem, on the other hand, that some of the days are superfluous. Light, for instance, stands to the luminaries in the relation of accident to subject. But the subject is produced at the same time as the accident proper to it. The light and the luminaries, therefore, ought not to have been produced on different days.

Obj. 5. Further, these days are devoted to the first instituting of the world. But as on the seventh day nothing was instituted, that day ought not to be enumerated with the others.

I answer that, The reason of the distinction

of these days is made clear by what has been said above (Q. LXX, A. 1), namely, that the parts of the world had first to be distinguished, and then each part adorned and filled, as it were, by the beings that inhabit it. Now the parts into which the corporeal creation is divided are three, according to some holy writers,[1] these parts being the heaven, or highest part, the water, or middle part, and the earth, or lowest part. Thus the Pythagoreans teach that "perfection consists in three things, the beginning, the middle, and the end," as it is stated in the book on the *Heavens*.[2] The first part, then, is distinguished on the first day, and adorned on the fourth, the middle part distinguished on the middle day, and adorned on the fifth and the third part distinguished on the third day and adorned on the sixth. But Augustine, while agreeing with the above writers as to the last three days, differs as to the first three,[3] for, according to him, spiritual creatures are formed on the first day and corporeal on the two others, the higher bodies being formed on the first of these two days, and the lower on the second. Thus, then, the perfection of the Divine works corresponds to the perfection of the number six, which is the sum of its integral factors, one, two, three; for one day is assigned to the forming of spiritual creatures, two to that of corporeal creatures, and three to the work of adornment.

Reply Obj. 1. According to Augustine,[4] the work of creation belongs to the production of formless matter and of the formless spiritual nature, both of which are outside of time, as he himself says.[5] Thus, then, the creation of either is set down before there was any day. But it may also be said, following other holy writers,[6] that the works of distinction and adornment imply certain changes in the creature which are measurable by time, whereas the work of creation lies only in the Divine act producing the substance of beings instantaneously. For this reason, therefore, every work of distinction and adornment is said to take place *in a day*, but creation *in the beginning* which denotes something indivisible.

Reply Obj. 2. Fire and air, as not distinctly known by the unlettered, are not expressly named by Moses among the parts of the world, but reckoned with the intermediate part, or

water, especially as regards the lowest part of the air; or with the heaven, to which the higher region of air approaches, as Augustine says (*Gen. ad lit.* ii, 13).[7]

Reply Obj. 3. The production of animals is recorded with reference to their adorning the various parts of the world, and therefore the days of their production are separated or united according as the animals adorn the same parts of the world, or different parts.

Reply Obj. 4. The nature of light, as existing in a subject, was made on the first day; and the making of the luminaries on the fourth day does not mean that their substance was produced anew, but that they then received a form that they had not before, as said above (Q. LXX, A. 1, Ans. 2).

Reply Obj. 5. According to Augustine (*Gen. ad lit.* iv, 15),[8] after all that has been recorded that is assigned to the six days, something distinct is attributed to the seventh,—namely, that on it God rested in Himself from His works; and for this reason it was right that the seventh day should be mentioned after the six. It may also be said, with the other writers,[9] that the world entered on the seventh day upon a new state, in that nothing new was to be added to it, and that therefore the seventh day is mentioned after the six from its being devoted to cessation from work.

ARTICLE 2. *Whether All These Days Are One Day?*

We proceed thus to the Second Article: It would seem that all these days are one day.

Objection 1. For it is written (Gen. 2. 4, 5): *These are the generations of the heaven and the earth, when they were created, in the day that the Lord . . . made the heaven and the earth, and every plant of the field, before it sprung up in the earth.* Therefore the day in which God made *the heaven and the earth, and every plant of the field,* is one and the same day. But He made the heaven and the earth on the first day, or rather before there was any day, but the plant of the field He made on the third day. Therefore the first and third days are but one day, and for a like reason all the rest.

Obj. 2. Further, it is said (Ecclus. 18. 1): *He that liveth for ever, created all things together.* But this would not be the case if the days of these works were more than one. Therefore they are not many but one only.

---

[1] Cf. Basil, *In Hexaëm.*, 1 (PG 29, 19).
[2] Aristotle, I, 1 (268ª10).
[3] See Q. LXX, A. 1; Q. LXXI; Q. LXXII.
[4] See Q. LXX, A. 1.
[5] *Confessions*, XII, 15 (PL 32, 831).
[6] See Q. LXVI, A. 1.

[7] PL 34, 265.   [8] PL 34, 306.
[9] See Q. LXVI, A. 1; Q. LXIX, A. 2.

Obj. 3. Further, on the seventh day God ceased from all new works. If, then, the seventh day is distinct from the other days, it follows that He did not make that day; which is not admissible.

Obj. 4. Further, the entire work ascribed to one day God perfected in an instant, for with each work are the words (*God*) *said, . . . and it was . . . done.* If then, He had kept back His next work to another day, it would follow that for the remainder of that day He would have ceased from working, which would be needless. The day therefore, of the preceding work is one with the day of the work that follows.

On the contrary, It is written (Gen. 1.), *The evening and the morning were the second day . . . the third day,* and so on. But where there is second and third there are more than one. There was not, therefore, only one day.

I answer that, On this question Augustine differs from other expositors. His opinion is that all the days that are called seven, are one day represented in a sevenfold aspect,[1] while others[2] consider there were seven distinct days, and not one only.

Now these two opinions, taken as explaining the literal text of Genesis, are certainly widely different. For Augustine understands by the word day the knowledge in the mind of the angels, and hence, according to him, the first day denotes their knowledge of the first of the Divine works, the second day their knowledge of the second work, and similarly with the rest. Thus, then, each work is said to have been wrought in some one of these days, since God wrought nothing in the universe without impressing the knowledge of it on the angelic mind, which can know many things at the same time, especially in the Word, in Whom all angelic knowledge is perfected and terminated. So the distinction of days denotes the natural order of the things known, and not a succession in knowledge, or in the things produced. Moreover, angelic knowledge is appropriately called day, since light, the cause of day, is to be found in spiritual things, as Augustine observes (*Gen. ad lit.* iv. 28).[3] In the opinion of the others, however, the days signify a succession both in time and in the things produced.

If, however, these two explanations are looked at as referring to the mode of production, they will be found not greatly to differ, if the diversity of opinion existing on two points, as already shown (QQ. LXVII, A. 1; LXIX, A. 1), between Augustine and other writers is taken into account. First, because Augustine takes the earth and the water, as first created, to signify matter totally without form; but the making of the firmament, the gathering of the waters, and the appearing of dry land, to denote the impression of forms upon corporeal matter. But other holy writers take the earth and the water, as first created, to signify the elements of the universe themselves existing under their proper forms, and the works that follow to mean some sort of distinction in bodies previously existing, as also has been shown (QQ. LXVII, AA. 1, 4; LXIX, A. 1). Secondly, some writers hold that plants and animals were produced actually in the work of the six days;[4] Augustine, that they were produced potentially.[5] Now the opinion of Augustine, that the works of the six days were simultaneous, is consistent with either view of the mode of production. For the other writers agree with him that in the first production of things matter existed under the substantial form of the elements, and agree with him also that in the first instituting of the world animals and plants did not exist actually. There remains, however, a difference as to four points, since, according to the latter, there was a time, after the production of creatures, in which light did not exist, the firmament had not been formed, and the earth was still covered by the waters, nor had the heavenly bodies been formed, which is the fourth difference; and these are not consistent with Augustine's explanation. In order, therefore, to be impartial, we must meet the arguments of either side.

Reply Obj. 1. On the day on which God created the heaven and the earth, He created also every plant of the field, not, indeed, actually, but *before it sprung up in the earth,* that is, potentially. And this work Augustine ascribes to the third day,[6] but other writers to the first instituting of the world.[7]

Reply Obj. 2. God created all things together so far as regards their substance considered in some way formless. But He did not create all things together so far as regards that

---

[1] *Gen. ad lit.,* IV, 26, 33 (PL 34, 314, 318); V, 3, 23 (PL 34, 323, 338); *City of God,* XI, 9 (PL 41, 324); *Ad Orosium* XXVI (Contained among the works of Augustine, *Dial. Sexag. quinq.,* Q. XXVI—PL 40, 741).

[2] Basil, *In Hexaëm.,* II (PG 29, 49); Ambrose, *In Hexaëm.,* I, 10 (PL 41, 155); cf. Gregory, *Moral.,* XXXII, 12 (PL 76, 644).

[3] PL 34, 315.

[4] Q. LXIX, A. 2; Q. LXXI.

[5] Q. LXIX, A. 2; Q. LXXI; Q. LXXII.

[6] *De Gen. ad lit.,* V, 5 (PL 34, 326); VIII, 3 (PL 34, 374).

[7] See Q. LXIX, A. 2.

formation of things which lies in distinction and adornment. Hence the word *creation* is significant.

Reply Obj. 3. On the seventh day God ceased from making new beings, but not from providing for their increase, and it pertains to this latter work that the first day is succeeded by other days.

Reply Obj. 4. All things were not distinguished and adorned together, not from a want of power on God's part, as requiring time in which to work, but that due order might be observed in the instituting of the world. Hence it was fitting that different days should be assigned to the different states of the world as each succeeding work added to the world a fresh state of perfection.

Reply Obj. 5. According to Augustine,[1] the order of days refers to the natural order of the works attributed to the days.

ARTICLE 3. *Whether Scripture Uses Suitable Words to Express the Work of the Six Days?*

We proceed thus to the Third Article: It would seem that Scripture does not use suitable words to express the works of the six days.

Objection 1. For as light, the firmament, and other similar works were made by the Word of God, so were the heaven and the earth. For *all things were made by Him* (John 1. 3). Therefore in the creation of heaven and earth, as in the other works, mention should have been made of the Word of God.

Obj. 2. Further, the water was created by God, yet its creation is not mentioned. Therefore the creation of the world is not sufficiently described.

Obj. 3. Further, it is said (Gen. 1. 31): *God saw all the things that He had made, and they were very good.* It ought, then, to have been said of each work, *God saw that it was good.* The omission, therefore, of these words in the work of creation and in that of the second day, is not fitting.

Obj. 4. Further, the Spirit of God is God Himself. But it does not befit God to move and to occupy place. Therefore the words, *The Spirit of God moved over the waters,* are unsuitable.

Obj. 5. Further, what is already made is not made over again. Therefore to the words, *God said: Let the firmament be made . . . and it was so,* it is superfluous to add, *God made the firmament.* And the like is to be said of other works.

[1] *Gen. ad lit.,* IV, 34, 35; V, 5 (PL 34, 319, 320, 326).

Obj. 6. Further, evening and morning do not sufficiently divide the day, since the day has many parts. Therefore the words, *The evening and morning were the second day* or, *the third day,* are not suitable.

Obj. 7. Further, *first,* not *one,* corresponds to *second* and *third.* It should therefore have been said that, *The evening and the morning were the first day,* rather than *one day.*

Reply Obj. 1. According to Augustine (*Gen. ad lit.* i, 4),[2] the person of the Son is mentioned both in the first creation of the world, and in its distinction and adornment, but differently in either place. For distinction and adornment belong to the work by which the world receives its form. But as the giving form to a work of art is by means of the form of the art in the mind of the artist, which may be called his intelligible word, so the giving form to every creature is by the word of God; and for this reason in the works of distinction and adornment the Word is mentioned. But in creation the Son is mentioned as the beginning, by the words, *In the beginning God created,* since by creation is understood the production of formless matter. But according to those who hold that the elements were created from the first under their proper forms, another explanation must be given; and therefore Basil says (*Hom.* ii *and* iii *in Hexaëm.*)[3] that the words, *God said,* signify a Divine command. Such a command, however, could not have been given before creatures had been produced that could obey it.

Reply Obj. 2. According to Augustine,[4] by the heaven is understood the formless spiritual nature, and by the earth, the formless matter of all bodies, and thus no creature is omitted. But, according to Basil (*Hom.* i *in Hexaëm.*),[5] the heaven and the earth, as "the two extremes," are alone mentioned, the intervening things being left to be understood, since all these move heavenwards, if light, or earthwards, if heavy, And others say[6] that under the word, *earth,* Scripture is accustomed to include all the four elements, as (Ps. 148. 7, 8) after the words, *Praise the Lord from the earth,* is added, *fire, hail, snow,* and *ice.*

Reply Obj. 3. In the account of the creation there is found something to correspond to the words, *God saw that it was good,* used in the work of distinction and adornment, and this appears from the consideration that the Holy

[2] PL 34, 249.   [3] PG 29, 45, 53.
[4] *Gen. ad lit.,* I, I (PL 34, 247), chaps. 4, 9 (249, 252).
[5] PG 29, 17.
[6] Peter Lombard, *Sent.,* II, d. XII, chap. I (QR I, 358); Maimonides, *Guide,* II, 30 (FR 213).

Spirit is Love. Now, there are two things, says Augustine (*Gen. ad lit.* i, 8)[1] on account of which God loves His creatures, their existence and their permanence. That they might then exist, and exist permanently, *the Spirit of God,* it is said, *moved over the waters*—that is to say, over that formless matter, signified by water, even as the love of the artist moves over the materials of his art, that out of them he may form his work. And the words, *God saw that it was good,* signify that the things that He had made were to endure, since they express a certain satisfaction taken by God in His works, as of an artist in his art : not as though He knew the creature otherwise, or that the creature was pleasing to Him otherwise than before He made it. Thus in either work, of creation and of formation, the Trinity of Persons is implied. In creation the Person of the Father is indicated by God the Creator, the Person of the Son by the beginning, in which He created, and the Person of the Holy Ghost by the Spirit that moved over the waters. But in the formation, the Person of the Father is indicated by God that speaks, the Person of the Son by the Word in Which He speaks, and the Person of the Holy Spirit by the satisfaction with which God saw that what was made was good.

And if the words, *God saw that it was good,* are not said of the work of the second day, this is because the work of distinguishing the waters was only begun on that day, but perfected on the third. Hence these words that are said of the third day refer also to the second. Or it may be that Scripture does not use these words of approval of the second day's work, because this is concerned with the distinction of things not evident to mankind. Or, again, because by the firmament is understood absolutely the cloudy region of the air, which is not one of the permanent parts of the universe, nor of the principal parts of the world. The above three reasons are given by Rabbi Moses,[2] others give a mystical reason derived from numbers, and according to these[3] the work of the second day is not marked with approval because the second number recedes from unity.

Reply Obj. 4. Rabbi Moses (*ibid.*) understands by the *Spirit of the Lord,* the air or the wind, as Plato also did,[4] and says that it is so called according to the custom of Scripture, in which these things are throughout attributed to God. But according to the holy writers, the Spirit of the Lord signifies the Holy Ghost, Who is said to *move over the water*—that is to say, over what Augustine holds[5] to mean "formless matter," lest it should be supposed that God loved of necessity the works He was to produce, as though He stood in need of them. For love of that kind is subject to, not superior to, the object of love. Moreover, it is fittingly implied that the Spirit moved over that which was incomplete and unfinished, since that movement is not one of place, but of pre-eminent power, as Augustine says (*Gen. ad lit.* i, 7).[6] It is the opinion, however, of Basil (*Hom.* ii *in Hexaëm.*)[7] that the Spirit moved over the element of water, "fostering and quickening its nature and impressing vital power, as the hen broods over her chickens." For water has especially a life-giving power, since many animals are generated in water, and the seed of all animals is liquid. Also the life of the soul is given by the water of baptism, according to John 3. 5 : *Unless a man be born again of water and the Holy Ghost, he cannot enter into the kingdom of God.*

Reply Obj. 5. According to Augustine (*Gen. ad lit.* ii, 8),[8] these three phrases denote the threefold being of creatures; first, their being in the Word, denoted by the command *Let . . . be made;* secondly, their being in the angelic mind, signified by the words, *It was . . . done;* thirdly, their being in their proper nature, by the words *He made.* And because the formation of the angels is recorded on the first day, it was not necessary there to add, *He made.* It may also be said, following other writers,[9] that the words, *He said,* and, *Let . . . be made,* denote God's command, and the words, *It was done,* the fulfilment of that command. But as it was necessary, for the sake of those especially who have asserted that all visible things were made by the angels,[10] to mention how things were made, it is added, in order to remove that error, that God Himself made them. Hence, in each work, after the words, *It was done,* some act of God is expressed by some such words as, *He made,* or, *He divided,* or, *He called.*

Reply Obj. 6. According to Augustine (*Gen. ad lit.* iv, 22),[11] by the *evening* and the *morning* are understood the evening and the morn-

---

[1] PL 34, 251.   [2] *Guide*, II. 30 (FR 213).
[3] *Glossa ordin.*, super Gen. I, 6 (I, 25B); Jerome, *Adver. Jovin.*, I, 16 (PL 23, 246).
[4] See Q. LXVI, A. 1, Ans. 5.

[5] *De Gen. contra Manich.*, I, 7 (PL 34, 179).
[6] PL 34, 251.   [7] PG 29, 44.   [8] PL 34, 269.
[9] Basil, Chrysostom, Ambrose, Bede.
[10] St. Thomas names Menandrianus in *Expos. in* I, *Decretal,* Op. XXIII (MD IV, 333); cf. Aug., *De Haeres,* 2 (PL 42, 26).
[11] PL 34, 312.

ing knowledge of the angels, which has been explained (Q. LVIII, A. 6, 7). But, according to Basil (*Hom.* ii *in Hexaëm.*),[1] the entire period takes its name, as is customary, from its more important part, the day. An instance of this is found in the words of Jacob, *The days of my pilgrimage,* where night is not mentioned at all. But the evening and the morning are mentioned as being the ends of the day, since day begins with morning and ends with evening, or because evening denotes the beginning of night; and morning the beginning of day. It seems fitting, also, that where the first distinction of creatures is described, divisions of time should be denoted only by what marks their beginning. And the reason for mentioning the evening first is that as the evening ends the day, which begins with the light, the termination of the light

at evening precedes the termination of the darkness, which ends with the morning. But Chrysostom's explanation is that thereby it is intended to show that the natural day does not end with the evening, but with the morning (*Hom.* v *in Gen.*).[2]

Reply Obj. 7. The words *one day* are used when day is first instituted, to denote that one day is made up of twenty-four hours. Hence, by mentioning "one," the measure of a natural day is fixed. Another reason may be to signify that a day is completed by the return of the sun to the point from which it commenced its course. And yet another, because at the completion of a week of seven days, the first day returns, which is one with the eighth day. The three reasons assigned above are those given by Basil (*Hom.* ii *in Hexaëm.*).[3]

[1] PG 29, 49   [2] PG 53, 52.   [3] PG 29, 49.

TREATISE ON MAN

QUESTION LXXV

OF MAN, WHO IS COMPOSED OF A SPIRITUAL AND A CORPOREAL SUBSTANCE; AND FIRST, WHAT PERTAINS TO THE ESSENCE OF THE SOUL

(*In Seven Articles*)

HAVING treated of the spiritual and of the corporeal creature, we now proceed to treat of man, who is composed of a spiritual and of a corporeal substance. We shall treat first of the nature of man, and secondly of his origin. (Q. XC). Now the theologian considers the nature of man in relation to the soul, but not in relation to the body, except in so far as the body has relation to the soul. Hence the first object of our consideration will be the soul. And since Dionysius (*Ang. Hier.* xi)[1] says that three things are to be found in spiritual substances—essence, power, and operation—we shall treat first of what belongs to the essence of the soul; secondly, of what belongs to its power (Q. LXXVII); thirdly, of what belongs to its operation (Q. LXXXIV).

Concerning the first, two points have to be considered: the first is the nature of the soul considered in itself; the second is the union of the soul with the body. (Q. LXXVI). Under the first head there are seven points of inquiry.

(1) Whether the soul is a body? (2) Whether the human soul is something subsistent? (3) Whether the souls of brute animals are subsistent? (4) Whether the soul is man, or whether man is composed of soul and body? (5) Whether the soul is composed of matter and form? (6) Whether the soul is incorruptible? (7) Whether the soul is of the same species as an angel?

ARTICLE 1. *Whether the Soul Is a Body?*

We proceed thus to the First Article: It would seem that the soul is a body.

Objection 1. For the soul is the mover of the body. Nor does it move unless moved. First, because it seems that nothing can move unless it is itself moved, since nothing gives what it has not; for instance, what is not hot does not give heat. Secondly, because if there is anything that moves and is not moved, "it is the

[1] Sect. 2 (PG 3, 284).

cause of eternal, unvarying movement," as we find proved in the *Physics;*[2] and this does not appear to be the case in the movement of an animal, which is caused by the soul. Therefore the soul is a mover moved. But every mover moved is a body. Therefore the soul is a body.

Obj. 2. Further, all knowledge is caused by means of some likeness. But there can be no likeness of a body to an incorporeal thing. If, therefore, the soul were not a body, it could not have knowledge of corporeal things.

Obj. 3. Further, between the mover and the moved there must be contact. But contact is only between bodies. Since, therefore, the soul moves the body, it seems that the soul must be a body.

On the contrary, Augustine says (*De Trin.* vi, 6)[3] that the soul "is simple in comparison with the body, because it does not occupy space by its bulk."

I answer that, To seek the nature of the soul, we must lay down first that the soul is defined as the first principle of life in those things which in our judgment live; for we call living things "animate," and those things which have no life, "inanimate." Now life is shown principally by two actions, knowledge and movement. The philosophers of old,[4] not being able to rise above their imagination, supposed that the principle of these actions was something corporeal; for they asserted that only bodies were real things and that what is not a body is nothing.[5] Hence they maintained that the soul is a kind of body.[6] Although this opinion can be proved to be false in many ways, we shall make use of only one proof, which shows clearly in a general and certain way that the soul is not a body.

It is manifest that not every principle of vital action is a soul, for then the eye would be a soul, as it is a principle of vision, and the same

[2] Aristotle, VIII, 10 (267ᵇ3).
[3] PL 42, 929.
[4] Democritus and Empedocles, in Aristotle, *Soul*, I, 2 (404ᵃ1).
[5] Cf. Q. L, A. 1.
[6] Cf. Macrobius, *In Somn. Scip.*, I, 14 (DD 47b); Nemesius, *De Nat. Hom.*, 2 (PG 40, 536); Augustine, *City of God*, VIII, 5 (PL 41, 230).

might be applied to the other instruments of the soul; but it is the *first* principle of life which we call the soul. Now, though a body may be a principle of life, as the heart is a principle of life in an animal, yet no body can be the first principle of life. For it is clear that to be a principle of life, or to be a living thing, does not pertain to a body as such; since, if that were the case, every body would be a living thing, or a principle of life. Therefore a body is suited to be a living thing or even a principle of life, from the fact that it is this kind of body. Now that it is actually such a kind of body it owes to some principle which is called its act. Therefore the soul, which is the first principle of life, is not a body, but the act of a body; thus heat, which is the principle of making hot, is not a body, but an act of a body.

Reply Obj. 1. As everything which is in motion must be moved by something else, a process which cannot proceed to infinity, we must allow that not every mover is moved. For, since to be moved is to pass from potency to act, the mover gives what it has to the thing moved, in so far as it causes it to be in act. But, as is shown in the *Physics*,[1] "there is a mover which is altogether immovable, and not moved either per se, or accidentally; and such a mover can cause an invariable movement." There is, however, another kind of mover, which, though not moved *per se*, is moved accidentally, and for this reason it does not cause an invariable movement; such a mover is the soul. There is, again, another mover, which is moved per se—namely, the body. And because the philosophers of old believed that nothing existed but bodies,[2] they maintained that every mover is moved, and that the soul is moved per se, and is a body.

Reply Obj. 2. The likeness of the thing known is not of necessity actually in the nature of the knower; but given a thing which knows in potency, and afterwards knows in act, the likeness of the thing known must be in the nature of the knower not actually, but only in potency; thus colour is not actually in the pupil of the eye, but only in potency. Hence it is necessary not that the likeness of corporeal things should be actually in the nature of the soul, but that it be in potency to such a likeness. But the ancient naturalists[3] did not know how to distinguish between act and potency; and so they held that the soul must be a body, and that it must be

composed of the principles of which all bodies are formed in order to know all bodies.

Reply Obj. 3. There are two kinds of contact: of quantity, and of power. By the former a body can be touched only by a body; by the latter a body can be touched by an incorporeal thing, which moves that body.

ARTICLE 2. *Whether the Human Soul Is Something Subsistent?*

We proceed thus to the Second Article: It would seem that the human soul is not something subsistent.

Objection 1. For that which subsists is said to be "this particular thing." Now "this particular thing" is said not of the soul, but of that which is composed of soul and body. Therefore the soul is not something subsistent.

Obj. 2. Further, everything subsistent operates. But the soul does not operate; for, as the Philosopher says,[4] "to say that the soul feels or understands is like saying that the soul weaves or builds." Therefore the soul is not subsistent.

Obj. 3. Further, if the soul were subsistent, it would have some operation apart from the body. But it has no operation apart from the body, not even that of understanding, for the act of understanding does not take place without a phantasm, which cannot exist apart from the body. Therefore the human soul is not something subsistent.

On the contrary, Augustine says (*De Trin.* x, 7):[5] "Whoever understands that the nature of the soul is that of a substance and not that of a body, will see that those who maintain the corporeal nature of the soul are led astray through associating with the soul those things without which they are unable to think of any nature" that is, imaginary pictures of corporeal things. Therefore the nature of the human intellect is not only incorporeal, but it is also a substance, that is, something subsistent.

I answer that, It must necessarily be allowed that the principle of intellectual operation which we call the soul is a principle both incorporeal and subsistent. For it is clear that by means of the intellect man can know the natures of all corporeal things. Now whatever knows certain things cannot have any of them in its own nature because that which is in it naturally would impede the knowledge of anything else. Thus we observe that a sick man's tongue being vitiated by a feverish and bitter humour, cannot perceive anything sweet, and everything seems

---

[1] Aristotle, VIII, 5, 6, 10 (258^{b}4, 15, 267^{b}3).
[2] Cf. Aristotle, *Soul*, I, 2 (403^{b}29).
[3] Cf. Aristotle, *Generation and Corruption*, I, 10 (327^{b}23).
[4] *Soul*, I, 4 (408^{b}11).   [5] PL 42, 979.

bitter to it. Therefore, if the intellectual principle contained the nature of any body it would be unable to know all bodies. Now every body has some determinate nature. Therefore it is impossible for the intellectual principle to be a body. It is likewise impossible for it to understand by means of a bodily organ, since the determinate nature of that bodily organ would prevent the knowledge of all bodies; as when a certain determinate colour is not only in the pupil of the eye, but also in a glass vase, the liquid in the vase seems to be of that same colour.

Therefore the intellectual principle which we call the mind or the intellect has an operation *per se* apart from the body. Now only that which subsists can have an operation *per se*. For nothing can operate except a being in act; hence a thing operates according as it is. For this reason we do not say that heat imparts heat, but that what is hot gives heat. We must conclude, therefore, that the human soul, which is called the intellect or the mind, is something incorporeal and subsistent.

Reply Obj. 1. "This particular thing" can be taken in two senses. Firstly, for anything subsistent; secondly, for that which subsists, and is complete in a specific nature. The former sense excludes the inherence of an accident or of a material form; the latter excludes also the imperfection of the part, so that a hand can be called "this particular thing" in the first sense, but not in the second. Therefore, as the human soul is a part of the human species, it can be called "this particular thing" in the first sense, as being something subsistent; but not in the second, for in this sense what is composed of body and soul is said to be "this particular thing."

Reply Obj. 2. Aristotle wrote those words as expressing not his own opinion, but the opinion of those who said that to understand is to be moved, as is clear from the context.

Or we may reply that to act *per se* belongs to what exists *per se*. But for a thing to exist *per se*, it suffices sometimes that it be not inherent, as an accident or a material form, even though it be part of something. Nevertheless, that is rightly said to subsist *per se* which is neither inherent in the above sense nor part of anything else. In this sense, the eye or the hand cannot be said to subsist *per se;* nor can it for that reason be said to operate *per se*. Hence the operation of the parts is through each part attributed to the whole. For we say that man sees with the eye, and feels with the hand, and not in the same

sense as when we say that what is hot gives heat by its heat; for heat, strictly speaking, does not give heat. We may therefore say that the soul understands, as the eye sees; but it is more correct to say that man understands through the soul.

Reply Obj. 3. The body is necessary for the action of the intellect not as its organ of action, but by reason of the object; for the phantasm is to the intellect what colour is to the sight. Neither does such a dependence on the body prove the intellect to be non-subsistent; otherwise it would follow that an animal is non-subsistent, since it requires external senible things in order to sense.

ARTICLE 3. *Whether the Souls of Brute Animals Are Subsistent?*

We proceed thus to the Third Article: It would seem that the souls of brute animals are subsistent.

Objection 1. For man is of the same genus as other animals; but, as we have just shown (A. 2), the soul of man is subsistent. Therefore the souls of other animals are subsistent.

Obj. 2. Further, the relation of the sensitive power to sensible things is like the relation of the intellectual power to intelligible things. But the intellect, without the body, understands intelligible things. Therefore the sense perceives sensible things without the body. Therefore, since the souls of brute animals are sensitive, it follows that they are subsistent, just as the human intellectual soul is subsistent.

Obj. 3. Further, the soul of brute animals moves the body. But the body is not a mover, but is moved. Therefore the soul of brute animals has an operation without the body.

On the contrary, Is what is written in the Book *De Eccl. Dogm.* (xvi, xvii):[1] "Man alone we believe to have a subsistent soul; but the souls of animals are not subsistent."

I answer that, The ancient philosophers made no distinction between sense and intellect,[2] and referred both to a corporeal principle, as has been said (A. 1; Q. L, A. 1). Plato, however, drew a distinction between intellect and sense; yet he referred both to an incorporeal principle, maintaining that sensing, just as understanding, belongs to the soul as such.[3] From this it follows that even the souls of brute animals are sub-

[1] Gennadius, (PL 58. 984).

[2] Empedocles; cf. Aristotle, *Soul*, III, 3 (427ª21).

[3] Cf. Nemesius, *De Nat. Hom.*, chap. 6 (PG 40, 637); Augustine, *De Musica*, VI, 5 (PL 32, 1168); Robert Grosseteste, *De Intelligentiis* (BR 119); Pseudo-Augustine (Alcher of Clairvaux), *De Spir. et An.*, chap. 13 (PL 40, 788).

sistent.[1] But Aristotle held[2] that of the works of the soul, understanding alone is performed without a corporeal organ. On the other hand, sensation and the consequent operations of the sensitive soul are evidently accompanied with change in the body; thus in the act of vision, the pupil of the eye is changed by the species of colour; and so with the other senses. Hence it is clear that the sensitive soul has no *per se* operation of its own, and that every operation of the sensitive soul belongs to the composite. Therefore we conclude that as the souls of brute animals have no *per se* operations they are not subsistent. For the operation of anything follows the mode of its being.

Reply Obj. 1. Although man is of the same genus as other animals, he is of a different species. Specific difference is derived from the difference of form; nor does every difference of form necessarily imply a diversity of genus.

Reply Obj. 2. The relation of the sensitive power to the sensible is in one way the same as that of the intellectual power to the intelligible, in so far as each is in potency to its object. But in another way their relations differ, in so far as the impression of the thing sensed on the sense is accompanied with change in the body, so that excessive strength of the sensible corrupts sense, a thing that never occurs in the case of the intellect. For an intellect that understands the highest of intelligible things is more able afterwards to understand those that are lower.—If, however, in the process of understanding the body is weary, this result is accidental, in so far as the intellect requires the operation of the sensitive powers in the production of the phantasms.

Reply Obj. 3. A moving power is of two kinds. One, the appetitive power, commands motion. The operation of this power in the sensitive soul is not without the body; for anger, joy, and passions of a like nature are accompanied by a change in the body. The other moving power is that which executes motion in adapting the members for obeying the appetite; and the act of this power does not consist in moving, but in being moved. And so it is clear that to move is not an act of the sensitive soul without the body.

ARTICLE 4. *Whether the Soul Is Man?*

We proceed thus to the Fourth Article: It would seem that the soul is man.

Objection 1. For it is written (II Cor. 4. 16): *Though our outward man is corrupted, yet the inward man is renewed day by day.* But that which is within man is the soul. Therefore the soul is the inward man.

Obj. 2. Further, the human soul is a substance. But it is not a universal substance. Therefore it is a particular substance. Therefore it is a hypostasis or a person, and it can only be a human person. Therefore the soul is man, for a human person is a man.

On the contrary, Augustine[3] commends Varro as holding that "man is not a mere soul, nor a mere body, but both soul and body."

I answer that, The assertion, "the soul is man," can be taken in two senses. First, that man is a soul, though this particular man, Socrates, for instance, is not a soul, but composed of soul and body. I say this because some held[4] that the form alone belongs to the species, while matter is part of the individual, and not of the species. This cannot be true; for to the nature of the species belongs what the definition signifies, and in natural things the definition does not signify the form only, but the form and the matter. Hence in natural things the matter is part of the species; not, indeed, signate matter, which is the principle of individuality, but the common matter. For as it belongs to the notion of this particular man to be composed of this soul, of this flesh, and of these bones, so it belongs to the notion of man to be composed of soul, flesh, and bones; for whatever belongs in common to the substance of all the individuals contained under a given species must belong also to the substance of the species.

It may also be understood in this sense, that this soul is this man; and this could be held if it were supposed that the operation of the sensitive soul were proper to it without the body, because in that case all the operations which are attributed to man would belong to the soul only; and whatever performs the operations proper to a thing is that thing; therefore that which performs the operations of a man is man. But it has been shown above (A. 3) that sensation is not the operation of the soul only. Since, then, sensation is an operation of man, though not proper to him, it is clear that man is not a soul only, but something composed of soul and body. Plato, through supposing that sensation was proper to the soul, could maintain man to be "a soul making use of the body."[5]

---

[1] The doctrine of Plato and the Platonists according to Nemesius, *De Nat. Hom.,* 2 (PG 40, 582).
[2] *Soul,* III, 4 (429ᵃ24).

[3] *City of God,* XIX, 3 (PL 41, 626).
[4] Averroes, *In Meta.,* VII, 21 (VIII, 171 I); 34 (VIII, 184 D). Cf. St. Thomas, *In Meta,* VII, 9.
[5] According to Nemesius, *De Nat. Hom.,* 1 (PG 40, 505). Cf. Plato, *Alcibiades* (130). See below, Q. LXXVI. A. I.

Reply Obj. 1. According to the Philosopher[1] "a thing seems to be chiefly what is principal in it; thus what the governor of a state does, the state is said to do. In this way sometimes what is principal in man is said to be man"; sometimes, indeed, the intellectual part which, in accordance with truth, is called the inward man, and sometimes the sensitive part with the body is called man in the opinion of those whose observation does not go beyond sensible things. And this is called the outward man.

Reply Obj. 2. Not every particular substance is a hypostasis or a person, but that which has the complete nature of its species. Hence a hand, or a foot, is not called a hypostasis, or a person; nor, likewise, is the soul so called, since it is a part of the human species.

ARTICLE 5. *Whether the Soul Is Composed of Matter and Form?*

We proceed thus to the Fifth Article: It would seem that the soul is composed of matter and form.

Objection 1. For potency is opposed to act. Now, whatsoever things are in act participate of the First Act, which is God, by participation of Whom, all things are good, are beings, and are living things, as is clear from the teaching of Dionysius (*Div. Nom.* v).[2] Therefore whatsoever things are in potency participate of the first potency. But the first potency is primary matter. Therefore, since the human soul is, after a manner, in potency, which appears from the fact that sometimes a man is potentially understanding, it seems that the human soul must participate of primary matter as a part of itself.

Obj. 2. Further, wherever the properties of matter are found, there matter is. But the properties of matter are found in the soul—namely, to be a subject, and to be changed; for it is subject to science, and virtue, and it changes from ignorance to knowledge and from vice to virtue. Therefore matter is in the soul.[3]

Obj. 3. Further, things which have no matter have no cause of their being, as the Philosopher says.[4] But the soul has a cause of its being, since it is created by God. Therefore the soul has matter.

Obj. 4. Further, what has no matter and is a form only, is a pure act and is infinite. But this belongs to God alone. Therefore the soul has matter.[5]

On the contrary, Augustine (*Gen. ad lit.* vii, 7, 8, 9)[6] proves that the soul was made neither of corporeal matter nor of spiritual matter.

I answer that, The soul has no matter. We may consider this question in two ways. First, from the notion of a soul in general; for it belongs to the notion of a soul to be the form of a body. Now, either it is a form of virtue of itself in its entirety, or by virtue of some part of itself. If by virtue of itself in its entirety, then it is impossible that any part of it should be matter, if by matter we understand some being only in potency, for a form, as such, is an act; and that which is only in potency cannot be part of an act, since potency is contrary to act as being its opposite. If, however, it be a form by virtue of a part of itself, then we call that part the soul; and that matter, which it actualizes first, we call the first thing animated.

Secondly, we may proceed from the notion of the human soul in particular, in so far as it is intellectual. For it is clear that whatever is received into something is received according to the condition of the recipient. Now a thing is known in as far as its form is in the knower. But the intellectual soul knows a thing in its nature absolutely; for instance, it knows a stone absolutely as a stone, and therefore the form of a stone absolutely, as to its own formal notion, is in the intellectual soul. Therefore the intellectual soul itself is an absolute form, and not something composed of matter and form. For if the intellectual soul were composed of matter and form, the forms of things would be received into it as individuals, and so it would only know the individual; just as it happens with the sensitive powers which receive forms in a corporeal organ, since matter is the principle by which forms are individualized. It follows, therefore, that the intellectual soul, and every intellectual substance which has knowledge of forms absolutely, is without composition of matter and form.

Reply Obj. 1. The First Act is the universal principle of all acts, because It is infinite, virtually "precontaining all things," as Dionysius says (*Div. Nom.* v).[7] Therefore things participate of It not as a part of themselves, but by diffusion of Its processions. Now as potency is receptive of act, it must be proportionate to

---

[1] *Ethics,* IX, 8 (1168[b]31).

[2] Sect. 5 (PG 3, 820).

[3] Cf. Bonaventure, *In Sent.,* II, d. III, pt. I, A. I, Q. I, arg. I, 2 (QR II, 89).

[4] *Metaphysics,* VIII, 6 (1054[b]4).

[5] Cf. Q. L, A. 2, obj. 3; Bonaventure, *In Sent.,* I, d. 8, pt. II, A. I, Q. 2, arg. I (QR I, 167).

[6] PL 34, 359, 360.

[7] Sect. 9 (PG 3, 825).

act. But the acts received which proceed from the First Infinite Act, and are participations of it, are diverse, so that there cannot be one potency which receives all acts, as there is one act from which all participated acts are derived; for then the receptive potency would equal the active potency of the First Act. Now the receptive potency in the intellectual soul is other than the receptive potency of first matter, as appears from the diversity of the things received by each. For primary matter receives individual forms, whereas the intellect receives absolute forms. Hence the existence of such a potency in the intellectual soul does not prove that the soul is composed of matter and form.

Reply Obj. 2. To be a subject and to be changed belong to matter by reason of its being in potency. As, therefore, the potency of the intellect is one thing and the potency of primary matter another, so in each is there a different reason of subjection and change. For the intellect is subject to knowledge, and is changed from ignorance to knowledge by reason of its being in potency with regard to the intelligible species.

Reply Obj. 3. The form causes matter to be, and so does the agent; therefore the agent causes matter to be, by changing it to the act of a form. A subsistent form, however, does not owe its being to some formal principle, nor has it a cause changing it from potency to act. So after the words quoted above, the Philosopher concludes,[1] that in things composed of matter and form "there is no other cause but that which moves from potentiality to act; but whatsoever things have no matter are without qualification true beings."

Reply Obj. 4. Everything participated is compared to the thing participating as its act. But whatever created form be supposed to subsist *per se* must participate being; for even life, or anything of that sort, "is a participator of being," as Dionysius says (*Div. Nom.* v).[2] Now participated being is limited by the capacity of the participator; so that God alone, Who is His own being, is pure act and infinite. But in intellectual substances, there is composition of act and potency, not, indeed, of matter and form, but of form and participated being. Therefore some say that[3] they are composed of that by which they are and that which they are; for being itself is that by which a thing is.

[1] *Metaphysics*, VIII, 6 (1045[b]21).
[2] *Sect.* 5 (PG 3, 820).
[3] See Q. L, A. 2, Ans. 2.

ARTICLE 6. *Whether the Human Soul Is Incorruptible?*

We proceed thus to the Sixth Article: It would seem that the human soul is corruptible.

Objection 1. For those things that have a like beginning and process seem to have a like end. But the beginning, by generation, of men is like that of animals, for they are made from the earth. And the process of life is alike in both; because *all things breathe alike, and man hath nothing more than the beast,* as it is written (Eccles. 3. 19). Therefore, as the same text concludes, *the death of man and beast is one, and the condition of both is equal.* But the souls of brute animals are corruptible. Therefore, also, the human soul is corruptible.

Obj. 2. Further, whatever is out of nothing can return to nothingness, because the end should correspond to the beginning. But as it is written (Wisd. 2. 2), *We are born of nothing;* which is true not only of the body, but also of the soul. Therefore, as is concluded in the same passage, *After this we shall be as if we had not been,* even as to our soul.

Obj. 3. Further, nothing is without its proper operation. But the operation proper to the soul, which is to understand through a phantasm, cannot be without the body. For the soul understands nothing without a phantasm, and "there is no phantasm without the body" as the Philosopher says.[4] Therefore the soul cannot survive the dissolution of the body.

On the contrary, Dionysius says (*Div. Nom.* iv)[5] that human souls owe to Divine goodness that they are "intellectual, and that they have an incorruptible substantial life."

I answer that, We must assert that the human soul which we call the intellectual principle is incorruptible. For a thing may be corrupted in two ways—*per se,* and accidentally. Now it is impossible for anything subsistent to be generated or corrupted accidentally, that is, by the generation or corruption of something else. For generation and corruption belong to a thing, just as being belongs to it, which is acquired by generation and lost by corruption. Therefore, whatever has being *per se* cannot be generated or corrupted except *per se;* while things which do not subsist, such as accidents and material forms, acquire being or lose it through the generation or corruption of composite things. Now it was shown above (AA. 2, 3) that the souls of brutes are not self-subsistent, whereas the hu-

[4] *Soul,* I, I (403[a]9).
[5] Sect. 2 (PG 3, 696).

man soul is; so that the souls of brutes are corrupted when their bodies are corrupted, while the human soul could not be corrupted unless it were corrupted *per se*. This, indeed, is impossible, not only as regards the human soul, but also as regards any subsistent thing that is a form alone. For it is clear that what belongs to a thing by virtue of itself is inseparable from it; but to be belongs to a form, which is an act, by virtue of itself. Therefore matter acquires actual being as it acquires the form, while it is corrupted so far as the form is separated from it. But it is impossible for a form to be separated from itself, and therefore it is impossible for a subsistent form to cease to exist.

Granted even that the soul is composed of matter and form, as some pretend,[1] we should nevertheless have to maintain that it is incorruptible. For corruption is found only where there is contrariety; for generation and corruption are from contraries and into contraries. Therefore the heavenly bodies, since they have no matter subject to contrariety, are incorruptible. Now there can be no contrariety in the intellectual soul, for it receives according to the manner of its being, and those things which it receives are without contrariety; for the notions even of contraries are not themselves contrary, since contraries belong to the same knowledge. Therefore it is impossible for the intellectual soul to be corruptible.

Moreover we may take a sign of this from the fact that everything naturally desires being after its own manner. Now, in things that have knowledge, desire ensues upon knowledge. The senses indeed do not know being, except under the conditions of *here* and *now*, whereas the intellect apprehends being absolutely, and for all time, so that everything that has an intellect naturally desires always to be. But a natural desire cannot be in vain. Therefore every intellectual substance is incorruptible.

Reply Obj. 1. Solomon reasons thus in the person of the foolish, as expressed in the words of Wisd. 2. Therefore the saying that man and animals have a like beginning in generation is true of the body, for all animals alike are made of earth. But it is not true of the soul. For the souls of brutes are produced by some power of the body, whereas the human soul is produced by God. To signify this, it is written as to other animals: *Let the earth bring forth the living soul* (Gen. 1. 24) while of man it is written (*ibid.* 2. 7) that *He breathed into his face the breath of life*. And so in the last chapter of Ecclesiastes

[1] See above, A. 5; also, Q. L, A. 2.

(12. 7) it is concluded: (*Before*) *the dust return into its earth from whence it was; and the spirit return to God Who gave it*. Again the process of life is alike as to the body, concerning which it is written (Eccles. 3. 19): *All things breathe alike*, and (Wis. 2. 2), *The breath in our nostrils is smoke*. But the process is not alike of the soul; for man is intelligent, whereas animals are not. Hence it is false to say: *Man has nothing more than beasts*. Thus death comes to both alike as to the body, but not as to the soul.

Reply Obj. 2. As a thing can be created not by reason of a passive potency, but only by reason of the active power of the Creator, Who can produce something out of nothing, so that when we say that a thing can be reduced to nothing, we do not imply in the creature a potency to non-being, but in the Creator the power of ceasing to sustain being. But a thing is said to be corruptible because there is in it a potency to non-being.

Reply Obj. 3. To understand through a phantasm is the proper operation of the soul by virtue of its union with the body. After separation from the body it will have another mode of understanding, similar to other substances separated from bodies, as will appear later on (Q. LXXXIX, A. 1).

ARTICLE 7. *Whether the Soul Is of the Same Species as an Angel?*

We proceed thus to the Seventh Article: It would seem that the soul is of the same species as an angel.

Objection 1. For each thing is ordered to its proper end by the nature of its species, from which is derived its inclination for that end. But the end of the soul is the same as that of an angel—namely, eternal happiness. Therefore they are of the same species.

Obj. 2. Further, the ultimate specific difference is the noblest, because it completes the nature of the species. But there is nothing nobler either in an angel or in the soul than to be intellectual. Therefore the soul and the angel agree in the ultimate specific difference. Therefore they belong to the same species.

Obj. 3. Further, it seems that the soul does not differ from an angel except in its union with the body. But as the body is outside the essence of the soul, it seems that it does not belong to its species. Therefore the soul and an angel are of the same species.

On the contrary, Things which have different natural operations are of different species. But

the natural operations of the soul and of an angel are different, since, as Dionysius says (*Div. Nom.* vii),[1] "Angelic minds have simple and blessed intelligence, not gathering their knowledge of Divine things from visible things." Subsequently he says the contrary to this of the soul. Therefore the soul and an angel are not of the same species.

I answer that, Origen (*Peri Archon* iii, 5)[2] held that human souls and angels are all of the same species, and this because he supposed that in these substances the difference of degree was accidental, as resulting from their free choice,[3] as we have seen above (Q. XLVII, A. 2). But this cannot be. For in incorporeal substances there cannot be diversity of number without diversity of species and inequality of nature; because, as they are not composed of matter and form, but are subsistent forms, it is clear that there is necessarily among them a diversity in species. For a separate form cannot be understood otherwise than as one of a single species; thus, supposing a separate whiteness to exist, it could only be one, because one whiteness does not differ from another except as in this or that subject. But diversity of species is always accompanied with a diversity of nature; thus in species of colours one is more perfect than another. And the same applies to other species, because differences which divide a genus are contrary to one another. Contraries, however, are related to one another as the perfect to the imperfect, since the "principle of contrariety is habit and privation," as is written in the *Metaphysics*.[4]

The same would follow if the aforesaid substances were composed of matter and form. For if the matter of one be distinct from the matter of another, it follows that either the form is the principle of the distinction of matter—that is to say, that the matter is distinct on account of its relation to divers forms (and even then there would result a difference of species and inequality of nature), or else the matter is the principle of the distinction of forms. But one matter cannot be distinct from another except by a distinction of quantity, which has no place in these incorporeal substances, such as an angel and the soul. And so it is not possible for the angel and the soul to be of the same species. How it is that there can be many souls of one species will be explained later (Q. LXXVI, A. 2, Ans. 1).

[1] Sect. 2 (PG 3, 868).
[2] PG 11, 329.
[3] *Op. cit.*, I, 6, 8; II, 9; III, 5 (PG 11, 166, 178, 229, 329).
[4] Aristotle, x, 4 (1055ᵃ33).

Reply Obj. 1. This argument proceeds from the proximate and natural end. Eternal happiness is the ultimate and supernatural end.

Reply Obj. 2. The ultimate specific difference is the noblest because it is the most determinate, in the same way as act is nobler than potency. Thus, however, the intellectual power is not the noblest, because it is indeterminate and common to many degrees of intellectuality; just as the sensible power is common to many degrees in the sensible nature. Hence, as all sensible things are not of one species, so neither are all intellectual things of one species.

Reply Obj. 3. The body is not of the essence of the soul, but the soul by the nature of its essence can be united to the body, so that, properly speaking, not the soul alone, but the composite, is the species. And the very fact that the soul in a certain way requires the body for its operation shows that the soul is endowed with a grade of intellectuality inferior to that of an angel, who is not united to a body.

QUESTION LXXVI

OF THE UNION OF BODY AND SOUL
(*In Eight Articles*)

WE now consider the union of the soul with the body; and concerning this there are eight points for inquiry: (1) Whether the intellectual principle is united to the body as its form? (2) Whether the intellectual principle is multiplied numerically according to the number of bodies, or is there one intellect for all men? (3) Whether in the body the form of which is an intellectual principle, there is some other soul? (4) Whether in the body there is any other substantial form? (5) Of the qualities required in the body of which the intellectual principle is the form? (6) Whether it be united to such a body by means of another body? (7) Whether by means of an accident? (8) Whether the soul is wholly in each part of the body?

ARTICLE 1. *Whether the Intellectual Principle Is United to the Body As Its Form?*

We proceed thus to the First Article: It seems that the intellectual principle is not united to the body as its form.

Objection 1. For the Philosopher says[5] that "the intellect is separate," and that it is not the act of any body. Therefore it is not united to the body as its form.

Obj. 2. Further, every form is determined according to the nature of the matter of which it is

[5] *Soul,* III, 4 (429ᵇ5).

the form; otherwise no proportion would be required between matter and form. Therefore if the intellect were united to the body as its form, since every body has a determinate nature it would follow that the intellect has a determinate nature; and thus, it would not be capable of knowing all things, as is clear from what has been said (Q. LXXV, A. 2), which is contrary to the notion of intellect. Therefore the intellect is not united to the body as its form.

Obj. 3. Further, whatever receptive power is an act of a body receives a form materially and individually; for what is received must be received according to the mode of the receiver. But the form of the thing understood is not received into the intellect materially and individually, but rather immaterially and universally; otherwise the intellect would not be capable of the knowledge of immaterial and universal objects, but only of individuals, like the senses. Therefore the intellect is not united to the body as its form.

Obj. 4. Further, power and action have the same subject; for the same subject is what can, and does, act. But the intellectual action is not the action of a body, as appears from above (Q. LXXV, A. 2). Therefore neither is the intellectual power a power of the body. But virtue or power cannot be more abstract or more simple than the essence from which the virtue or power is derived. Therefore neither is the substance of the intellect the form of a body.

Obj. 5. Further, whatever has *per se* being is not united to the body as its form, because a form is that by which a thing is, so that the very being of a form does not belong to the form by itself. But the intellectual principle has *per se* being and is subsistent, as was said above (Q. LXXV, A. 2). Therefore it is not united to the body as its form.

Obj. 6. Further, whatever exists in a thing by reason of its nature exists in it always. But to be united to matter belongs to the form by reason of its nature. For form is the act of matter not by any accidental quality, but by its own essence; otherwise matter and form would not make a thing substantially one, but only accidentally one. Therefore a form cannot be without its own proper matter. But the intellectual principle, since it is incorruptible, as was shown above (Q. LXXV, A. 6), remains separate from the body after the dissolution of the body. Therefore the intellectual principle is not united to the body as its form.

On the contrary, According to the Philosopher,[1] difference is derived from the form. But

the difference which constitutes man is *rational*, which is applied to man on account of his intellectual principle. Therefore the intellectual principle is the form of man.

I answer that, We must assert that the intellect which is the principle of intellectual operation is the form of the human body. For that whereby primarily anything acts is a form of the thing to which the act is to be attributed; for instance, that whereby a body is primarily healed is health, and that whereby the soul knows primarily is knowledge; hence health is a form of the body, and knowledge is a form of the soul. The reason is because nothing acts except so far as it is in act; hence a thing acts by that whereby it is in act. Now it is clear that the first thing by which the body lives is the soul. And as life appears through various operations in different degrees of living things, that whereby we primarily perform each of all these vital actions is the soul. For the soul is the primary principle of our nourishment, sensation, and local movement; and likewise of our understanding. Therefore this principle by which we primarily understand, whether it be called the intellect or the intellectual soul, is the form of the body. This is the demonstration used by Aristotle.[2]

But if anyone say that the intellectual soul is not the form of the body[3] he must first explain how it is that this action of understanding is the action of this particular man; for each one is conscious that it is himself who understands. Now an action may be attributed to anyone in three ways, as is clear from the Philosopher.[4] "For a thing is said to move or act either by virtue of its whole self, for instance, as a physician heals; or by virtue of a part, as a man sees by his eye; or through an accidental quality, as when we say that something that is white builds, because it is accidental to the builder to be white." So when we say that Socrates or Plato understands, it is clear that this is not attributed to him accidentally, since it is ascribed to him as man, which is predicated of him essentially. We must therefore say either that Socrates understands by virtue of his whole self, as Plato maintained,[5] holding that man is an intellectual soul, or that the intellect is a part of Socrates. The first cannot stand, as was shown above (Q.

---

[1] *Metaphysics,* VIII, 2 (1043ᵃ19).

[2] *Soul,* II, 2 (414ᵃ12).

[3] Cf. Albert the Great, *Summa de Creat.,* II, 4, 1 (BO XXXV, 34). Also Avicenna, *De An.,* I, 1 (1rb); V, 4 (24va).

[4] *Physics,* V, 1 (224ᵃ31).

[5] See Q LXXV, A. 4; cf. also Albert, *De Intell. et Intelligib.,* II, 8 (BO IX, 515).

LXXV, A. 4), for this reason, that it is one and the same man who is conscious both that he understands, and that he senses. But one cannot sense without a body; therefore the body must be some part of man. It remains therefore that the intellect by which Socrates understands is a part of Socrates, so that in some way it is united to the body of Socrates.

The Commentator held[1] that this union is through the intelligible species, as having a double subject: in the possible intellect, and in the phantasms which are in the corporeal organs. Thus through the intelligible species the possible intellect is linked to the body of this or that particular man. But this link or union does not sufficiently explain the fact that the act of the intellect is the act of Socrates. This can be clearly seen from comparison with the sensitive power, from which Aristotle proceeds to consider things relating to the intellect. For the relation of phantasms to the intellect is like the relation of colours to the sense of sight, as he says in the book on the *Soul*.[2] Therefore, as the species of colours are in the sight, so are the species of phantasms in the possible intellect. Now it is clear that because the colours, the likenesses of which are in the sight, are on a wall, the action of seeing is not attributed to the wall; for we do not say that the wall sees, but rather that it is seen. Therefore, from the fact that the species of phantasms are in the possible intellect it does not follow that Socrates, in whom are the phantasms, understands, but that he or his phantasms are understood.

Some, however, tried to maintain that the intellect is united to the body as its mover,[3] and hence that the intellect and body form one thing so that the act of the intellect could be attributed to the whole. This is groundless however, for many reasons. First, because the intellect does not move the body except through desire, the movement of which presupposes the operation of the intellect. The reason therefore why Socrates understands is not because he is moved by his intellect, but rather, contrariwise, he is moved by his intellect because he understands. Secondly, because, since Socrates is an individual in a nature of one essence composed of matter and form, if the intellect be not the form, it follows that it must be outside the essence, and then the intellect is to the whole Socrates as a mover to the thing moved. The act of intellect however remains in the agent, and does not pass into something else, as does the action of heating. Therefore the act of understanding cannot be attributed to Socrates for the reason that he is moved by his intellect. Thirdly, because the action of a mover is never attributed to the thing moved, except as to an instrument; as the action of a carpenter to a saw. Therefore if understanding is attributed to Socrates, as the action of what moves him, it follows that it is attributed to him as to an instrument. This is contrary to the teaching of the Philosopher, who holds that understanding is not possible through a corporeal instrument.[4] Fourthly, because, although the action of a part be attributed to the whole, as the action of the eye is attributed to a man, yet it is never attributed to another part, except perhaps accidentally; for we do not say that the hand sees because the eye sees. Therefore if the intellect and Socrates are united in the above manner, the action of the intellect cannot be attributed to Socrates. If, however, Socrates be a whole composed of a union of the intellect with whatever else belongs to Socrates, while nevertheless the intellect is united to those other things only as a mover, it follows that Socrates is not one absolutely, and consequently neither a being absolutely, for a thing is a being according as it is one.

There remains, therefore, no other explanation than that given by Aristotle[5]—namely, that this particular man understands because the intellectual principle is his form. Thus from the very operation of the intellect it is made clear that the intellectual principle is united to the body as its form.

The same can be clearly shown from the nature of the human species. For the nature of each thing is shown by its operation. Now the proper operation of man as man is to understand, because he thereby surpasses all other animals. From this, too, Aristotle concludes[6] that the ultimate happiness of man must consist in this operation as properly belonging to him. Man must therefore derive his species from that which is the principle of this operation. But the species of anything is derived from its form. It follows therefore that the intellectual principle is the proper form of man.

But we must observe that the nobler a form is, the more it rises above corporeal matter, the less it is merged in matter, and the more it excels matter by its power and its operation;

[1] *De An.*, III, Comm. v (VI, 2–148c).
[2] III, 7 (431ᵃ14).
[3] Cf. William of Paris, *De An.*, I, pt. VII (II, 72); 6, XXXV (II, 194).
[4] *Soul*, III, 4 (429ᵃ26).
[5] *Ibid.*, II, 2 (414ᵃ12). See *Contra Gent.*, II, 59.
[6] *Ethics*, X, 7 (1177ᵃ17).

hence we find that the form of a mixed body has another operation not caused by its elemental qualities. And the higher we advance in the nobility of forms, the more we find that the power of the form excels the elementary matter; as the vegetative soul excels the form of the metal, and the sensitive soul excels the vegetative soul. Now the human soul is the highest and noblest of forms. Therefore it excels corporeal matter in its power by the fact that it has an operation and a power in which corporeal matter has no share whatever. This power is called the intellect.

It is well to remark that if anyone holds that the soul is composed of matter and form,[1] it would follow that in no way could the soul be the form of the body. For since the form is an act, and matter is only a being in potency, that which is composed of matter and form cannot be the form of another by virtue of itself as a whole. But if it is a form by virtue of some part of itself, then that part which is the form we call the soul, and that of which it is the form we call the first thing animated, as was said above (Q. LXXV, A. 5).

Reply Obj. 1. As the Philosopher says,[2] the ultimate natural form to which the consideration of the natural philosopher is directed, namely, the human soul, is indeed separate; yet it exists in matter. He proves this from the fact that "man and the sun generate man from matter." It is separate indeed according to its intellectual power, because the intellectual power does not belong to a corporeal organ, as the power of seeing is the act of the eye; for understanding is an act which cannot be performed by a corporeal organ, like the act of seeing. But it exists in matter so far as the soul itself, to which this power belongs, is the form of the body, and the term of human generation. And so the Philosopher says[3] that "the intellect is separate" because it is not the power of a corporeal organ.

From this it is clear how to answer the *Second and Third objections.* For, in order that man may be be able to understand all things by means of his intellect, and that his intellect may understand all things immaterial and universal, it is sufficient that the intellectual power be not the act of the body.

Reply Obj. 4. The human soul, by reason of its perfection, is not a form merged in matter, or entirely embraced by matter. Therefore there

is nothing to prevent one of its powers not being the act of the body, although the soul is essentially the form of the body.

Reply Obj. 5. The soul communicates that being in which it subsists to the corporeal matter, out of which, combined with the intellectual soul, there results unity of being so that the being of the whole composite is also the being of the soul. This is not the case with other non-subsistent forms. For this reason the human soul retains its own being after the dissolution of the body, though this is not so with other forms.

Reply Obj. 6. To be united to the body pertains to the soul by reason of itself, as it pertains to a light body by reason of itself to be raised up. And as a light body remains light when removed from its proper place, retaining meanwhile an aptitude and an inclination for its proper place, so the human soul retains its proper being when separated from the body, having an aptitude and a natural inclination to be united to the body.

ARTICLE 2. *Whether the Intellectual Principle Is Multiplied According to the Number of Bodies?*

We proceed thus to the Second Article: It would seem that the intellectual principle is not multiplied according to the number of bodies, but that there is one intellect in all men.

Objection 1. For an immaterial substance is not multiplied in number within one species. But the human soul is an immaterial substance, since it is not composed of matter and form, as was shown above (Q. LXXV, A. 5). Therefore there are not many human souls in one species. But all men are of one species. Therefore there is but one intellect in all men.

Obj. 2. Further, when the cause is removed, the effect is also removed. Therefore, if human souls were multiplied according to the number of bodies, it follows that the bodies being removed, the number of souls would not remain, but from all the souls there would be but a single one remaining. This is heretical, for it would do away with the distinction of rewards and punishments.

Obj. 3. Further, if my intellect is distinct from your intellect, my intellect is an individual, and so is yours; for individuals are things which differ in number but agree in one species.[4] Now whatever is received into anything must be received according to the mode of the receiver. Therefore the species of things would be received individually into my intellect, and also

---

[1] See Q. LXXV, A. 5; Q. L, A. 2.
[2] *Physics*, II, 2 (194[b]12).
[3] *Soul*, III, 4 (429[b]5).
[4] Cf. Averroes, *In De An.*, III, 5 (VI, 2-152D).

into yours, which is contrary to the nature of the intellect which knows universals.

Obj. 4. Further, the thing understood is in the intellect which understands. If, therefore, my intellect is distinct from yours, what is understood by me must be distinct from what is understood by you; and consequently it will be "reckoned as something individual," and be only "potentially something understood,"[1] so that the common intention will have to be abstracted from both, because from things diverse something intelligible common to them may be abstracted. But this is contrary to the nature of the intellect, for then the intellect would seem not to be distinct from the imagination. It seems, therefore, to follow that there is one intellect in all men.

Obj. 5. Further, when the disciple receives knowledge from the master, it cannot be said that the master's knowledge begets knowledge in the disciple, because then also knowledge would be an active form, such as heat is, which is clearly false. It seems, therefore, that the same individual knowledge which is in the master is communicated to the disciple, which cannot be, unless there is one intellect in both.[2] It seems, therefore, that the intellect of the disciple and master is but one; and, consequently, the same applies to all men.

Obj. 6. Further, Augustine (*De Quant. Animæ* xxxii)[3] says: "If I were to say that there are many human souls, I should laugh at myself." But the soul seems to be one chiefly on account of the intellect. Therefore there is one intellect of all men.

On the contrary, The Philosopher says[4] that the relation of universal causes to universals is like the relation of particular causes to individuals. But it is impossible that a soul, one in species, should belong to animals of different species. Therefore it is impossible that one individual intellectual soul should belong to several individuals.

I answer that, It is absolutely impossible for one intellect to belong to all men. This is clear if, as Plato maintained,[5] man is the intellect itself. For it would follow that Socrates and Plato are one man, and that they are not distinct from each other except by something outside the essence of each. The distinction between Socrates and Plato would be no other than that of one man with a tunic and another with a cloak; which is altogether absurd.

It is likewise clear that this is impossible if, according to the opinion of Aristotle,[6] it is supposed that the intellect is a part or a power of the soul which is the form of man. For it is impossible for many distinct individuals to have one form, as it is impossible for them to have one being, for the form is the principle of being.

Again, this is clearly impossible whatever one may hold as to the manner of the union of the intellect to this or that man. For it is manifest that, supposing there is one principal agent and two instruments, we can say that there is one agent absolutely, but several actions; as when one man touches several things with his two hands, there will be one who touches, but two contacts. If, on the contrary, we suppose one instrument and several principal agents, we might say that there are several agents, but one act; for example, if there be many drawing a ship by means of a rope, there will be many drawing, and one pull. If, however, there is one principal agent, and one instrument, we say that there is one agent and one action, as when the smith strikes with one hammer, there is one striker and one stroke. Now it is clear that no matter how the intellect is united or coupled to this or that man, the intellect has the precedence of all the other things which appertain to man; for the sensitive powers obey the intellect, and are at its service. Therefore, if we suppose two men to have several intellects and one sense,—for instance, if two men had one eye,—there would be several seers, but one sight. But if there is one intellect, no matter how diverse may be all those things of which the intellect makes use as instruments, in no way is it possible to say that Socrates and Plato are otherwise than one understanding man. And if to this we add that to understand, which is the act of the intellect, is not effected by any organ other than the intellect itself, it will further follow that there is but one agent and one action; that is to say that all men are but one "understander," and have but one act of understanding, in regard, that is, of one intelligible object.

However, it would be possible to distinguish my intellectual action from yours by the distinction of the phantasms—that is to say, were there one phantasm of a stone in me, and another in you—if the phantasm itself, as it is one thing in me and another in you, were a form of the possible intellect; because the same agent according to divers forms produces divers actions, just as according to divers forms of things with regard to

[1] *Ibid.* (VI, 2,–147A).
[2] *Ibid.* (VI, 2–152D).   [3] PL 32, 1073.
[4] *Physics*, II, 3 (195ᵇ26).   [5] See Q. LXXV, A. 4.
[6] *Soul*, II, 2 (414ᵃ13).

the same eye there are divers visions. But the phantasm itself is not a form of the possible intellect, but rather the intelligible species abstracted from the phantasms. Now in one intellect, from different phantasms of the same species only one intelligible species is abstracted, as appears in one man, in whom there may be different phantasms of a stone; yet from all of them only one intelligible species of a stone is abstracted, by which the intellect of that one man, by one operation, understands the nature of a stone, notwithstanding the diversity of phantasms. Therefore, if there were one intellect for all men, the diversity of phantasms which are in this one and that one would not cause a diversity of intellectual operation in this man and that man as the Commentator teaches.[1] It remains, therefore, that it is altogether impossible and unreasonable to maintain that there exists one intellect for all men.

Reply Obj. 1. Although the intellectual soul, like an angel, has no matter from which it is produced, yet it is the form of a certain matter; in which it is unlike an angel. Therefore, according to the division of matter, there are many souls of one species, while it is quite impossible for many angels to be of one species.

Reply Obj. 2. Everything has unity in the same way that it has being. Consequently we must judge of the multiplicity of a thing as we judge of its being. Now it is clear that the intellectual soul, by virtue of its very being, is united to the body as its form; yet, after the dissolution of the body, the intellectual soul retains its own being. In like manner the multiplicity of souls is in proportion to the multiplicity of bodies; yet, after the dissolution of the bodies, the souls remain multiplied in their being.

Reply Obj. 3. Individuality of the intelligent being, or of the species whereby it understands, does not exclude the understanding of universals; otherwise, since separate intellects are subsistent substances, and consequently individual, they could not understand universals. But the materiality of the knower and of the species whereby it knows, impedes the knowledge of the universal. For as every action is according to the mode of the form by which the agent acts, as heating is according to the mode of the heat, so knowledge is according to the mode of the species by which the knower knows. Now it is clear that common nature becomes distinct and multiplied by reason of the individuating principles which come from the matter. Therefore if

the form, which is the means of knowledge, is material—that is, not abstracted from material conditions—its likeness to the nature of a species or genus will be according to the distinction and multiplication of that nature by means of individuating principles; so that knowledge of the nature of a thing in general will be impossible. But if the species be abstracted from the conditions of individual matter, there will be a likeness of the nature without those things which make it distinct and multiplied; thus there will be knowledge of the universal. Nor does it matter, as to this particular point, whether there be one intellect or many; because, even if there were but one, it would necessarily be an individual intellect, and the species whereby it understands, an individual species.

Reply Obj. 4. Whether the intellect be one or many, what is understood is one; for what is understood is in the intellect not according to itself, but according to its likeness; for "the stone is not in the soul, but its likeness is," as is said in the book on the *Soul*.[2] Yet it is the stone which is understood, not the likeness of the stone, (except by a reflection of the intellect on itself); otherwise, the objects of sciences would not be things, but only intelligible species. Now it happens that different things according to different forms are likened to the same thing. And since knowledge is begotten according to the assimilation of the knower to the thing known, it follows that the same thing may happen to be known by several knowers, as is apparent in regard to the senses; for several see the same colour, according to different likenesses. In the same way several intellects understand one thing understood. But there is this difference, according to the opinion of Aristotle,[3] between the sense and the intelligence—that a thing is perceived by the sense according to the disposition which it has outside the soul—that is, in its individuality, but the nature of the thing understood is indeed outside the soul, but it does not have that mode of being outside the soul which it has according as it is understood. For the common nature is understood as apart from the individuating principles, but it does not have this mode of being outside the soul. But, according to the opinion of Plato,[4] the thing understood exists outside the soul in the same mode as that in which it is understood; for he supposed that the natures of things exist separate from matter.

---

[1] *In De An.*, III, comm. 5 (VI, 2-152E).

[2] Aristotle, III, 8 (431[b]29).
[3] *Ibid.* (432[a]2).
[4] See Q. VI, A. 4.

Reply Obj. 5. One knowledge exists in the disciple and another in the master. How it is caused will be shown later on (Q. CXVII, A. 1).

Reply Obj. 6. Augustine denies a plurality of souls that would involve a plurality of species.

ARTICLE 3. *Whether Besides the Intellectual Soul There Are in Man Other Souls Essentially Different From One Another?*

We proceed thus to the Third Article: It would seem that besides the intellectual soul there are in man other souls essentially different from one another, such as the sensitive soul and the nutritive soul.

Objection 1. For corruptible and incorruptible are not of the same substance. But the intellectual soul is incorruptible, whereas the other souls, as the sensitive and the nutritive, are corruptible, as was shown above (Q. LXXV, A. 6). Therefore in man the essence of the intellectual soul, the sensitive soul, and the nutritive soul, cannot be the same.

Obj. 2. Further, if it be said that the sensitive soul in man is incorruptible, on the contrary, "corruptible and incorruptible differ generically," says the Philosopher.[1] But the sensitive soul in the horse, the lion, and other brute animals, is corruptible. If, therefore, in man it be incorruptible, the sensitive soul in man and brute animals will not be of the same genus. Now, an animal is so called from its having a sensitive soul, and, therefore, animal will not be one genus common to man and other animals, which is incongruous.

Obj. 3. Further, the Philosopher says[2] that the embryo is an animal before it is a man. But this would be impossible if the essence of the sensitive soul were the same as that of the intellectual soul; for an animal is such by its sensitive soul, while a man is a man by the intellectual soul. Therefore in man the essence of the sensitive soul is not the same as the essence of the intellectual soul.

Obj 4. Further, the Philosopher says[3] that the genus is taken from the matter, and difference from the form. But rational, which is the difference constituting man, is taken from the intellectual soul, while he is called animal by reason of his having a body animated by a sensitive soul. Therefore the intellectual soul is related to the body animated by a sensitive soul as form to matter. Therefore in man the intellectual soul is not essentially the same as the sensi-

tive soul, but presupposes it as a material suppositum.

On the contrary, It is said in the Book *De Ecclesiasticis Dogmatibus* XV:[4] "Nor do we say that there are two souls in one man, as James and other Syrians write: one, animal, by which the body is animated, and which is mingled with the blood, the other, spiritual, which obeys the reason; but we say that it is one and the same soul in man, that both gives life to the body by being united to it, and orders itself by its own reasoning."

I answer that, Plato held[5] that there were several souls in one body, distinct even as to organs, to which souls he referred the different vital actions, saying that "the nutritive power is in the liver, the concupiscible in the heart, and the power of knowledge in the brain." Which opinion is rejected by Aristotle[6] with regard to those parts of the soul which use corporeal organs, because in those animals which continue to live when they have been divided, in each part are observed the operations of the soul, as sense and appetite. Now this would not be the case if the various principles of the soul's operations were essentially different, and distributed in the various parts of the body. But with regard to the intellectual part, he seems to leave it in doubt whether it be only logically distinct from the other parts of the soul, or also locally.

The opinion of Plato might be maintained if, as he held,[7] the soul were supposed to be united to the body, not as its form, but as its mover. For it involves nothing unreasonable that the same movable thing be moved by several movers; and still less if it be moved according to its various parts. If we suppose, however, that the soul is united to the body as its form, it is quite impossible for several essentially different souls to be in one body. This can be made clear by three reasons.

In the first place, an animal would not be absolutely one, in which there were several souls. For nothing is absolutely one except by one form, by which a thing has being, because a thing has from the same source both being and unity; and therefore things which are denominated by various forms are not absolutely one,

---

[1] *Metaphysics*, X, 10 (1059ᵃ10).

[2] *Generation of Animals*, II, 3 (736ᵃ35).

[3] *Metaphysics*, VIII, 2 (1043ᵃ5). Cf. VII, 12 (1038ᵃ6).

[4] Gennadius (PL 58, 984); cf. Pseudo-Augustine (Alcher of Clairvaux), *De Spir. et An.*, 48 (PL 40, 814).

[5] Cf. Averroes, *In De An.*, I, 90 (VI, 2–45F); *Timaeus* (69). On the controversy of the Schools concerning the plurality of forms, cf. Denifle, *Chartularium*, 474 (I 559); 517 (I, 625); 518 (I, 627); 523 (I, 634); also Lottin, RNP (1932) pp. 449–467.

[6] *Soul*, II, 2 (413ᵇ13).

[7] See above, A. 1.

as, for instance, *a white man*. If, therefore, man were *living* by one form, the vegetative soul, and *animal* by another form, the sensitive soul, and *man* by another form, the intellectual soul, it would follow that man is not absolutely one. Thus Aristotle argues[1] against Plato that if the idea of an animal is distinct from the idea of a biped, then a biped animal is not absolutely one. For this reason, against those who hold that there are several souls in the body, he asks,[2] what contains them?—that is, what makes them one? It cannot be said that they are united by the one body, because rather does the soul contain the body and make it one, than the reverse.

Secondly, this is proved to be impossible by the mode of predication. Those things which are derived from various forms are predicated of one another either accidentally, (if the forms are not ordered one to another, as when we say that something white is sweet), or essentially, in the second mode of essential predication, (if the forms are ordered one to another, the subject belonging to the definition of the predicate; as a surface is presupposed to colour, so that if we say that a body with a surface is coloured, we have the second manner of essential predication). Therefore, if we have one form by which a thing is an animal, and another form by which it is a man, it follows either that one of these two things could not be predicated of the other, except accidentally, supposing these two forms not to be ordered to one another,—or that one would be predicated of the other according to the second mode of essential predication, if one soul be presupposed to the other. But both of these consequences are clearly false, because animal is predicated of man essentially and not accidentally, and man is not part of the definition of an animal, but the other way about. Therefore of necessity by the same form a thing is animal and man; otherwise man would not really be the thing which is an animal, so that animal can be essentially predicated of man.

Thirdly, this is shown to be impossible by the fact that when one operation of the soul is intense it impedes another, which could never be the case unless the principle of action were essentially one.

We must therefore conclude that in man the sensitive soul, the intellectual soul, and the nutritive soul are numerically one soul. This can easily be explained, if we consider the differences of species and forms. For we observe that the species and forms of things differ from one

another as the perfect and the imperfect; as in the order of things, the animate are more perfect than the inanimate, and animals more perfect than plants, and man than brute animals, and in each of these genera there are various degrees. For this reason Aristotle compares[3] the species of things to numbers, which differ in species by the addition or subtraction of unity. And he compares[4] the various souls to the species of figures, one of which contains another; as a pentagon contains and exceeds a tetragon. Thus the intellectual soul contains virtually whatever belongs to the sensitive soul of brute animals and to the nutritive soul of plants. Therefore, as a surface which is of a pentagonal shape is not tetragonal by one shape and pentagonal by another—since a tetragonal shape would be superfluous as contained in the pentagonal—so neither is Socrates a man by one soul and an animal by another, but by one and the same soul he is both animal and man.

Reply Obj. 1. The sensitive soul is incorruptible not by reason of its being sensitive, but by reason of its being intellectual. When, therefore, a soul is sensitive only, it is corruptible; but when with sensibility it has also intellectuality, it is incorruptible. For although sensibility does not give incorruptibility, yet it cannot deprive intellectuality of its incorruptibility.

Reply Obj. 2. Not forms, but composites, are classified either generically or specifically. Now man is corruptible like other animals. And so the difference of corruptible and incorruptible which is on the part of the forms does not involve a generic difference between man and the other animals.

Reply Obj. 3. The embryo has first of all a soul which is merely sensitive, and when this is removed, it is supplanted by a more perfect soul, which is both sensitive and intellectual; as will be shown farther on (Q. CXVIII, A. 2, ANS. 2).

Reply Obj 4. We must not consider the diversity of natural things as proceeding from the various logical notions or intentions which flow from our manner of understanding, because reason can apprehend one and the same thing in various ways. Therefore since, as we have said, the intellectual soul contains virtually what belongs to the sensitive soul, and something more, reason can consider separately what belongs to the power of the sensitive soul, as something imperfect and material. And because it observes that this is something common to man and to other animals, it forms from this the notion of the genus, while that in which the intellectual

[1] *Metaphysics*, VIII, 6 (1045ª14).
[2] *Soul*, I, 5 (411ᵇ6).

[3] *Metaphysics*, VIII, 3 (1043ᵇ34).   [4] *Soul*, II, 3 (414ᵇ28).

soul exceeds the sensitive soul it takes as formal and perfecting; and from this it gathers the difference of man.

ARTICLE 4. *Whether in Man There Is Another Form Besides the Intellectual Soul?*

We proceed thus to the Fourth Article: It would seem that in man there is another form besides the intellectual soul.

Objection 1. For the Philosopher says[1] that "the soul is the act of a physical body which has life potentially." Therefore the soul is to the body as a form to matter. But the body has a substantial form by which it is a body. Therefore some other substantial form in the body precedes the soul.

Obj. 2. Further, man moves himself as every animal does. "Now everything that moves itself is divided into two parts, of which one moves and the other is moved," as the Philosopher proves.[2] But the part which moves is the soul. Therefore the other part must be such that it can be moved. But primary matter cannot be moved,[3] since it is a being only potentially; indeed, everything that is moved is a body. Therefore in man and in every animal there must be another substantial form, by which the body is constituted.

Obj. 3. Further, the order of forms depends on their relation to primary matter; for *before* and *after* apply by comparison to some beginning. Therefore if there were not in man some other substantial form besides the rational soul, and if this were to inhere immediately in primary matter, it would follow that it ranks among the most imperfect forms which inhere in matter immediately.

Obj. 4. Further, the human body is a mixed body. Now mingling does not result from matter alone, for then we should have mere corruption. Therefore the forms of the elements must remain in a mixed body, and these are substantial forms. Therefore in the human body there are other substantial forms besides the intellectual soul.

On the contrary, Of one thing there is but one substantial being. But the substantial form gives substantial being. Therefore of one thing there is but one substantial form. But the soul is the substantial form of man. Therefore it is impossible for there to be in man another substantial form besides the intellectual soul.

I answer that, If we suppose that the intellectual soul is not united to the body as its form,

but only as its mover as the Platonists maintain,[4] it would necessarily follow that in man there is another substantial form, by which the body is established in its being as movable by the soul. If, however, the intellectual soul be united to the body as its substantial form, as we have said above (A. 1), it is impossible for another substantial form besides the intellectual soul to be found in man.

In order to make this evident, we must consider that the substantial form differs from the accidental form in this, that the accidental form does not make a thing to be absolutely, but to be *such,* as heat does not make a thing to be absolutely, but only to be hot. And by the coming of the accidental form a thing is not said to be made or generated absolutely, but to be made such, or to be in some particular condition; and in like manner, when an accidental form is removed a thing is said to be corrupted, not absolutely, but relatively. Now the substantial form gives being absolutely; therefore by its coming a thing is said to be generated absolutely, and by its removal to be corrupted absolutely. For this reason, the old natural philosophers, who held that primary matter was some actual being— for instance, fire or air, or something of that sort—maintained that nothing is generated absolutely, or corrupted absolutely, and stated that "every becoming is nothing but an alteration," as we read in the *Physics.*[5] Therefore, if besides the intellectual soul there pre-existed in matter another substantial form by which the subject of the soul were made an actual being, it would follow that the soul does not give being absolutely, and consequently that it is not the substantial form; and so at the advent of the soul there would not be absolute but only relative generation, nor at its removal absolute corruption, all of which is clearly false.

And so we must conclude that there is no other substantial form in man besides the intellectual soul, and that the soul, as it virtually contains the sensitive and nutritive souls, so does it virtually contain all inferior forms, and itself alone does whatever the imperfect forms do in other things. The same is to be said of the sensitive soul in brute animals, and of the nutritive soul in plants, and universally of all more perfect forms with regard to the imperfect.

Reply Obj. 1. Aristotle does not say that the

[1] *Soul,* II, 1 (412[a]27).
[2] *Physics,* VIII, 5 (257[b]12).   [3] *Ibid.,* V, 1 (225[a]25).

[4] See above, A. 1. Cf. Alexander of Hales, *Summa Theol.,* I–II, n. 344 (Q II, 419); John of Rochelle, *Summa de An.,* 1, 37, 38, in Manser, JPST (1912) p. 297; Bonaventure, in Gilson, *La Philosophie* (p. 310); cf. also Pegis, *St. Thomas and the Problem of the Soul* (p. 42).
[5] I, 4 (187[a]30).

soul is the act of a body only, but "the act of a physical organic body which has life potentially"; and that this potency "does not reject the soul."[1] And so it is clear that when the soul is called the act, the soul itself is included, as when we say that heat is the act of what is hot, and light of what is lucid; not as though lucid and light were two separate things, but because a thing is made lucid by the light. In like manner, the soul is said to be "the act of a body," etc., because by the soul it is a body, and is organic, and has life potentially. Yet the first act is said to be in potency to the second act, which is operation; for such a potency "does not reject" —that is, does not exclude—the soul.

Reply Obj. 2. The soul does not move the body by its being, as the form of the body, but by the moving power, the act of which presupposes the body to be already actualized by the soul, so that the soul by its moving power is the part which moves, and the animate body is the part moved.

Reply Obj. 3. We observe in matter various degrees of perfection, as being, living, sensing, and understanding. Now what is added is always more perfect. Therefore that form which gives matter only the first degree of perfection is the most imperfect, while that form which gives the first, second, and third degree, and so on, is the most perfect; and yet it inheres in matter immediately.

Reply Obj. 4. Avicenna held[2] that the substantial forms of the elements remain entire in the mixed body and that the mixture is made by the contrary qualities of the elements being reduced to a neutral state. But this is impossible, because the various forms of the elements must necessarily be in various parts of matter, for the distinction of which we must suppose dimensions, without which matter cannot be divisible. Now matter subject to dimension is not to be found except in a body. But various bodies cannot be in the same place. And so it follows that elements in the mixed body would be distinct as to situation. And then there would not be a real mixture which is in respect of the whole, but only a mixture apparent to sense, by the juxtaposition of particles.

Averroes maintained[3] that the forms of elements, by reason of their imperfection, are midway between accidental and substantial forms, and so can be *more* or *less;* and therefore in the mixture they are modified and reduced to a neu-

tral state, so that one form emerges from them. But this is even still more impossible. For the substantial being of each thing consists in something indivisible, and every addition and subtraction varies the species, as in numbers, as stated in the *Metaphysics*.[4] And consequently it is impossible for any substantial form to receive *more* or *less.* Nor is it less impossible for anything to be midway between substance and accident.

Therefore we must say, in accordance with the Philosopher,[5] that the forms of the elements remain in the mixed body not actually but virtually. For the proper qualities of the elements remain, though modified, and in them is the power of the elementary forms. This quality of the mixture is the proper disposition for the substantial form of the mixed body; for instance, the form of a stone, or of any sort of soul.

ARTICLE 5. *Whether the Intellectual Soul Is Properly United to Such a Body?*

We proceed thus to the Fifth Article: It would seem that the intellectual soul is improperly united to such a body.

Objection 1. For matter must be proportionate to the form. But the intellectual soul is incorruptible. Therefore it is not properly united to a corruptible body.

Obj. 2. Further, the intellectual soul is a perfectly immaterial form, in proof of which is its operation, in which corporeal matter does not share. But the more subtle the body, the less it has of matter. Therefore the soul should be united to a most subtle body, to fire, for instance, and not to a mixed body, still less to a terrestrial body.

Obj. 3. Further, since the form is the principle of the species, one form cannot produce a variety of species. But the intellectual soul is one form. Therefore, it should not be united to a body which is composed of parts belonging to various species.

Obj. 4. Further, what is susceptible of a more perfect form should itself be more perfect. But the intellectual soul is the most perfect of souls. Therefore since the bodies of other animals are naturally provided with a covering, for instance, with hair instead of clothes, and hoofs instead of shoes, and are, moreover, naturally provided with arms as claws, teeth, and horns, it seems that the intellectual soul should not have been united to a body which is imperfect as being deprived of such means of protection.

---

[1] *Soul*, II, 2 (412ᵃ27; ᵇ25).
[2] According to Averroes, *In de Gener.*, I, 90 (V, 370K).
[3] *De Cælo* III, 67 (V,227C).

[4] Aristotle, VIII, 3 (1044ᵃ9).
[5] *Generation and Corruption*, I, 10 (327ᵇ22).

On the contrary The Philosopher says[1] that "the soul is the act of a physical organic body having life potentially."

I answer that, Since the form is not for the sake of the matter, but rather the matter for the form, we must gather from the form the reason why the matter is such as it is; and not conversely. Now the intellectual soul, as we have seen above (Q. LV, A. 2) in the order of nature, holds the lowest place among intellectual substances; for it is not naturally gifted with the knowledge of truth, as the angels are, but has to gather knowledge from individual things by way of the senses, as Dionysius says (*Div. Nom.* vii).[2] But nature never fails in necessary things; therefore the intellectual soul had to be endowed not only with the power of understanding, but also with the power of feeling. Now the action of the senses is not performed without a corporeal instrument. Therefore the intellectual soul had to be united to a body which could be an adequate organ of sense.

Now all the other senses are based on the sense of touch. But the organ of touch has to be a medium between contraries, such as hot and cold, wet and dry, and the like, of which the sense of touch has the perception; thus it is in potency with regard to contraries, and is able to perceive them. Therefore the more the organ of touch is reduced to an even temperament, the more sensitive will be the touch. But the intellectual soul has the power of sense in all its completeness, because what belongs to the inferior nature pre-exists more perfectly in the superior, as Dionysius says (*Div. Nom.* v).[3] Therefore the body to which the intellectual soul is united should be a mixed body, above all others reduced to the most even temperament. For this reason among animals man has the best sense of touch. And among men, those who have the best sense of touch have the best intellect. A sign of this is that we observe *those who are refined in body are well endowed in mind,* as stated in the book on the *Soul.*[4]

Reply Obj. 1. Perhaps someone might attempt to answer this by saying that before sin the human body was incorruptible. This answer does not seem sufficient, because before sin the human body was immortal not by nature but by a gift of Divine grace; otherwise its immortality would not be forfeited through sin, as neither was the immortality of the devil.

Therefore we answer otherwise by observing that in matter two conditions are to be found:

one which is chosen in order that the matter be suitable to the form, the other which follows of necessity from the prior disposition. The artisan, for instance, for the form of the saw chooses the matter, iron adapted for cutting through hard material; but that the teeth of the saw may become blunt and rusted follows by necessity of the matter. So the intellectual soul requires a body of an even temperament, which, however, is corruptible by necessity of its matter. If, however, it be said that God could avoid this, we answer that in the formation of natural things we do not consider what God might do, but what is suitable to the nature of things as Augustine says (*Gen. ad lit.* ii, 1).[5] God, however, provided in this case by applying a remedy against death in the gift of grace.

Reply Obj. 2. A body is not necessary to the intellectual soul by reason of its intellectual operation considered as such, but on account of the sensitive power, which requires an organ of an even temperament. Therefore the intellectual soul had to be united to such a body, and not to a simple element, or to a mixed body, in which fire was in excess, because otherwise there could not be an evenness of combination, on account of the excessive active force of fire. And this evenly combined body has a dignity of its own by reason of its being remote from contraries, thereby resembling in a way a heavenly body.

Reply Obj. 3. The parts of an animal, for instance, the eye, hand, flesh, and bones, and so forth, do not make the species, but the whole does; and therefore, properly speaking, we cannot say that these are of different species, but that they are of various dispositions. This is suitable to the intellectual soul, which, although it be one in its essence, yet on account of its perfection is manifold in power; and therefore, for its various operations it requires various dispositions in the parts of the body to which it is united. For this reason we observe that there is a greater variety of parts in perfect than in imperfect animals; and in these a greater variety than in plants.

Reply Obj. 4. The intellectual soul, because it can comprehend universals, has a power extending to the infinite; therefore it cannot be limited by nature either to certain fixed natural judgments, or to certain fixed means whether of defence or of clothing, as is the case with other animals, the souls of which have knowledge and power in regard to fixed particular things. Instead of all these, man has by nature his reason and his hands, which are the organs of organs,

---

[1] *Soul,* II, 1 (412ª27).   [2] Sect. 2 (PG 3, 868).
[3] Sect. 3 (PG 3, 817).   [4] Aristotle, II, 9 (421ª26).   [5] PL 34, 263.

since by their means man can make for himself instruments of an infinite variety, and for any number of purposes.

ARTICLE 6. *Whether the Intellectual Soul Is United to the Body Through the Medium of Accidental Dispositions?*

We proceed thus to the Sixth Article: It would seem that the intellectual soul is united to the body through the medium of accidental dispositions.

Objection 1. For every form exists in its proper, disposed matter. But dispositions to a form are accidents. Therefore we must presuppose accidents to be in matter before the substantial form; and therefore before the soul, since the soul is a substantial form.

Obj. 2. Further, various forms of one species require various parts of matter. But various parts of matter are unintelligible without division in measurable quantities. Therefore we must suppose dimensions in matter before the substantial forms, which are many belonging to one species.

Obj. 3. Further, what is spiritual is connected with what is corporeal by virtual contact. But the virtue of the soul is its power. Therefore it seems that the soul is united to the body by means of a power, which is an accident.

On the contrary, "Accident is posterior to substance, both in the order of time and in the order of reason," as the Philosopher says,[1] Therefore it is unintelligible that any accidental form exist in matter before the soul, which is the substantial form.

I answer that, If the soul were united to the body merely as a mover, there would be nothing to prevent the existence of certain dispositions mediating between the soul and the body; on the contrary, they would be necessary, for on the part of the soul would be required the power to move the body, and on the part of the body, a certain aptitude to be moved by the soul.

If, however, the intellectual soul is united to the body as the substantial form, as we have already said above (A. 1), it is impossible for any accidental disposition to come between the body and the soul, or between any substantial form whatever and its matter. The reason is because since matter is in potentiality to all acts in a certain order, what is absolutely first among the acts must be understood as being first in matter. Now the first among all acts is being. Therefore, it is impossible for matter to be apprehended as hot, or as having quantity, before it is actual.

But matter has actual being by the substantial form, which makes it to exist absolutely, as we have said above (A. 4). Therefore it is impossible for any accidental dispositions to pre-exist in matter before the substantial form, and consequently before the soul.

Reply Obj. 1. As appears from what has been already said (A. 4), the more perfect form virtually contains whatever belongs to the inferior forms; therefore while remaining one and the same, it perfects matter according to the various degrees of perfection. For the same essential form makes man an actual being, a body, a living being, an animal, and a man. Now it is clear that to every genus follow its proper accidents. Therefore as matter is first understood as perfected in its being before it is understood as corporeal, and so on, so those accidents which are proper to being are understood before corporeity; and thus dispositions are understood in matter before the form, not as regards all its effects, but as regards the subsequent effect.

Reply Obj. 2. Dimensions of quantity are accidents following on corporeity, which pertains to the whole of matter. Therefore matter, once understood as corporeal and measurable, can be understood as distinct in its various parts, and as receptive of different forms according to the further degrees of perfection. For although it is essentially the same form which gives matter the various degrees of perfection, as we have said (ANS. 1), yet it differs according to the consideration of reason.

Reply Obj. 3. A spiritual substance which is united to a body as its mover only is united to it by power or virtue. But the intellectual soul is united by its very being to the body as a form; and yet it guides and moves the body by its power and virtue.

ARTICLE 7. *Whether the Soul Is United to the Animal Body By Means of a Body?*

We proceed thus to the Seventh Article: It seems that the soul is united to the animal body by means of a body.

Objection 1. For Augustine says (*Gen. ad lit.* vii, 19),[2] that "the soul administers the body by light," that is, by fire, "and by air, which are most akin to a spirit." But fire and air are bodies. Therefore the soul is united to the human body by means of a body.

Obj. 2. Further a link between two things seems to be that thing the removal of which destroys their union. But when breathing ceases, the soul is separated from the body. Therefore

---

[1] *Metaphysics,* VII, I (1028ᵃ32).

[2] PL 34, 364.

the breath, which is a subtle body, is the means of union between soul and body.

Obj. 3. Further, things which are very distant from one another are not united except by something between them. But the intellectual soul is distant from the body, both because it is incorporeal, and because it is incorruptible. Therefore it seems to be united to the body by means of an incorruptible body, and such would be some heavenly light, which would harmonize the elements, and unite them together.

On the contrary, The Philosopher says:[1] "We need not ask if the soul and body are one, as neither do we ask if wax and its shape are one." But the shape is united to the wax without a body intervening. Therefore also the soul is thus united to the body.

I answer that, If the soul, according to the Platonists,[2] were united to the body, merely as a mover, it would be right to say that some other bodies must intervene between the soul and body of man, or any animal whatever; for a mover appropriately moves what is distant from it by means of something nearer.

If, however, the soul is united to the body as its form, as we have said above (A. 1), it is impossible for it to be united by means of another body. The reason of this is that a thing is one according as it is a being. Now the form, through itself, makes a thing to be actual since it is itself essentially an act; nor does it give being by means of something else. Therefore the unity of a thing composed of matter and form, is through the form itself, which by reason of its very nature is united to matter as its act. Nor is there any other cause of union except the agent, which causes matter to be in act, as the Philosopher says.[3]

From this it is clear how false are the opinions of those who maintained the existence of some mediate bodies between the soul and body of man. Of these certain Platonists said[4] that the intellectual soul has an incorruptible body naturally united to it, from which it is never separated, and by means of which it is united to the corruptible body of man. Others said that the soul is united to the body by means of a corporeal spirit.[5] Others said it is united to the body

by means of light,[6] which, they say, is a body and of the nature of the fifth essence;[7] so that the vegetative soul would be united to the body by means of the light of the sidereal heaven, the sensible soul by means of the light of the crystal heaven, and the intellectual soul by means of the light of the empyrean heaven. Now all this is fictitious and ridiculous, because light is not a body and because the fifth essence does not enter materially into the composition of a mixed body (since it is unchangeable), but only virtually, and lastly, because the soul is immediately united to the body as the form to matter.

Reply Obj. 1. Augustine speaks there of the soul as it moves the body; hence he uses the word "administration." It is true that it moves the grosser parts of the body by the more subtle parts. And the first instrument of the moving power is the breath, as the Philosopher says.[8]

Reply Obj. 2. The union of soul and body ceases at the cessation of breath, not because this is the means of union, but because of the removal of that disposition by which the body is disposed for such a union. Nevertheless the breath is a means of moving, as the first instrument of motion.

Reply Obj. 3. The soul is indeed very distant from the body if we consider the condition of each separately, so that if each had a separate existence, many media would have to intervene. But since the soul is the form of the body, it has not a being apart from being the being of the body, but by its own being is united to the body immediately. This is the case with every form which, if considered as an act, is very distant from matter, which is a being only in potency.

ARTICLE 8. *Whether the Whole Soul Is in Each Part of the Body?*

We proceed thus to the Eighth Article: It would seem that the whole soul is not in each part of the body.

Objection 1. For the Philosopher says in the *Motion of Animals*:[9] "It is not necessary for the soul to be in each part of the body; it suffices that it be in some principle of the body causing the other parts to live, for each part has a natural movement of its own."

---

[1] *Soul,* II, 1 (412ᵇ6).   [2] See above, A. 1.
[3] *Metaphysics,* VIII, 6 (1045ᵇ21).
[4] See Q. LI, A. 1, Ans. 1. Cf. Baeumker, *Witelo* (p. 452).
[5] Ps.-Augustine (Alcher of Clairvaux), *De Spir. et An.,* XIV (PL 40, 789); Costa-Ben-Luca, *De Differ. Spir. et An.,* chap. 4 (BH 138); cf. Avicebron, *Fons Vitae,* III, 2 (BK 75,24), V, 15 (BK 284,24); Dominic Gundissalinus, *De An.,* X (MK 97,35); Hugh of St. Victor, *De Unione Corp. et Spir.* (PL 177, 288); Bonaventure, *In Sent.,* II, d. 1, Pt. II, A. 1, Q. 2 (QR II, 42).

[6] Bonaventure, *In Sent.,* II, d. XIII (QR II, 310); d. XIII, A. 2, Q. 2, ad 5 (QR II, 321); d. XVII, A. 2, Q. 2 (QR II, 421). Cf. also Augustine, *Gen. ad li t.,* VII, 19 (PL 34, 364); Avicenna, *De An.,* IV, 5 (21ra).
[7] Anonymous writers quoted by Alexander of Hales, *Summa Theol.,* I–II, n. 266 (QR II, 327); cf. Bonaventure, *In Sent.* II, d. XVII, A. 2, Q. 2 (QR II, 422); Baeumker, *Witelo* (p. 455).
[8] *Motion of Animals,* 10 (703ᵃ9).
[9] *Ibid.* (703ᵃ34).

Obj. 2. Further, the soul is in the body of which it is the act. But it is the act of an organic body. Therefore it exists only in an organic body. But each part of the human body is not an organic body. Therefore the whole soul is not in each part.

Obj. 3. Further, the Philosopher says[1] that the relation of a part of the soul to a part of the body, such as the sight to the pupil of the eye, is the same as the relation of the soul to the whole body of an animal. If, therefore, the whole soul is in each part of the body, it follows that each part of the body is an animal.

Obj. 4. Further, all the powers of the soul are rooted in the essence of the soul. If, therefore, the whole soul be in each part of the body, it follows that all the powers of the soul are in each part of the body; thus the sight will be in the ear, and hearing in the eye, and this is absurd.

Obj. 5. Further, if the whole soul is in each part of the body, each part of the body is immediately dependent on the soul. Thus one part would not depend on another, nor would one part be nobler than another, which is clearly untrue. Therefore the soul is not in each part of the body.

On the contrary, Augustine says (*De Trin.* vi, 6),[2] that "in each body the whole soul is in the whole body, and in each part is entire."

I answer that, As we have said, (AA. 6, 7) if the soul were united to the body merely as its mover, we might say that it is not in each part of the body, but only in one part through which it would move the others. But since the soul is united to the body as its form, it must necessarily be in the whole body, and in each of its parts. For it is not an accidental form, but the substantial form of the body. Now the substantial form perfects not only the whole, but each part of the whole. For since a whole consists of parts, a form of the whole which does not give being to each of the parts of the body is a form consisting in composition and order, such as the form of a house; and such a form is accidental. But the soul is a substantial form, and therefore it must be the form and the act not only of the whole, but also of each part. Therefore, on the withdrawal of the soul, just as we do not speak of an animal or a man unless equivocally (as we speak of a painted animal or a stone animal), so is it with the hand, the eye, the flesh and bones, as the Philosopher says.[3] A proof of this is that on the withdrawal of the

soul no part of the body retains its proper action, although that which retains its species, retains the action of the species. But act is in that of which it is the act; therefore the soul must be in the whole body, and in each of its parts.

That it is entire in each of its parts may be concluded from this, that since a whole is that which is divided into parts, there are three kinds of totality, corresponding to three kinds of division. There is a whole which is divided into parts of quantity, as a whole line, or a whole body. There is also a whole which is divided into logical and essential parts, as a thing defined is divided into the parts of a definition, and a composite into matter and form. There is, further, a third kind of whole which is of power divided into virtual parts.

The first kind of totality does not apply to forms, except perhaps accidentally, and then only to those forms which have an indifferent relationship to a quantitative whole, and its parts; as whiteness, as far as its essence is concerned, is equally disposed to be in the whole surface, and in each part of the surface, and, therefore, the surface being divided, the whiteness is accidentally divided. But a form which requires diversity in the parts, such as a soul, and specially the soul of perfect animals, is not equally related to the whole and the parts; hence it is not divided accidentally when the whole is divided. So therefore quantitative totality cannot be attributed to the soul, either essentially or accidentally. But the second kind of totality, which depends on logical and essential perfection, properly and essentially belongs to forms; and likewise the totality of power, because a form is the principle of operation.

Therefore if it be asked whether the whole whiteness is in the whole surface and in each of its parts, it is necessary to distinguish. If we mean quantitative totality which whiteness has accidentally, then the whole whiteness is not in each part of the surface. The same is to be said of totality of power, since the whiteness which is in the whole surface moves the sight more than the whiteness which is in a small part thereof. But if we mean totality of species and essence, then the whole whiteness is in each part of a surface.

Since, however, the soul has not quantitative totality, neither essentially, nor accidentally, as we have seen, it is enough to say that the whole soul is in each part of the body, by totality of perfection and of essence, but not by totality of power. For it is not in each part of the body,

[1] *Soul,* II, 1 (412[b]17).   [2] PL 42, 929.
[3] *Soul,* II, 1 (412[b]10); also, *Meteorology,* IV, 12 (389[b]31).

with regard to each of its powers; but with regard to sight, it is in the eye, and with regard to hearing, it is in the ear, and so forth. We must observe, however, that since the soul requires diversity of parts, its relation to the whole is not the same as its relation to the parts; for to the whole it is compared primarily and essentially, as to its proper and proportionate perfectible, but to the parts, secondarily, in so far as they are ordered to the whole.

Reply Obj. 1. The Philosopher is speaking there of the moving power of the soul.

Reply Obj. 2. The soul is the act of an organic body, as of its primary and proportionate perfectible.

Reply Obj. 3. An animal is that which is composed of a soul and a whole body, which is the soul's primary and proportionate perfectible. Thus the soul is not in a part. Hence it does not follow that a part of an animal is an animal.

Reply Obj. 4. Some of the powers of the soul are in it according as it exceeds the entire capacity of the body, namely, the intellect and the will; and so these powers are not said to be in any part of the body. Other powers are common to the soul and body. Therefore each of these powers need not be wherever the soul is, but only in that part of the body which is proportioned to the operation of such a power.

Reply Obj. 5. One part of the body is said to be nobler than another on account of the various powers, of which the parts of the body are the organs. For that part which is the organ of a nobler power is a nobler part of the body, as also is that part which serves the same power in a nobler manner.

QUESTION LXXVII

OF THE THINGS WHICH BELONG TO THE POWERS OF THE SOUL IN GENERAL

(*In Eight Articles*)

WE proceed to consider those things which belong to the powers of the soul; first, in general, secondly, in particular (Q. LXXVIII). Under the first head there are eight points of inquiry: (1) Whether the essence of the soul is its power? (2) Whether there is one power of the soul, or several? (3) How the powers of the soul are distinguished from one another? (4) Of the order of the powers, one to another. (5) Whether the powers of the soul are in it as in their subject? (6) Whether the powers flow from the essence of the soul? (7) Whether one power rises from another? (8) Whether all the powers of the soul remain in the soul after death?

ARTICLE 1. *Whether the Essence of the Soul Is Its Power?*

We proceed thus to the First Article: It would seem that the essence of the soul is its power.

Objection 1. For Augustine says (*De Trin.* ix, 4),[1] that "mind, knowledge, and love are in the soul substantially, or, which is the same thing, essentially"; and (*ibid.* x, 11),[2] that "memory, understanding, and will are one life, one mind, one essence."

Obj. 2. Further, the soul is nobler than primary matter. But primary matter is its own potency. Much more therefore is the soul its own power.

Obj. 3. Further, the substantial form is simpler than the accidental form, a sign of which is that the substantial form is not intensified or relaxed, but is indivisible. But the accidental form is its own power. Much more therefore is that substantial form which is the soul.

Obj. 4. Further, we sense by the sensitive power and we understand by the intellectual power. But "that by which we first sense and understand is the soul," according to the Philosopher.[3] Therefore the soul is its own power.

Obj. 5. Further, whatever does not belong to the essence is an accident. Therefore if the power of the soul is something else beside its essence, it is an accident, which is contrary to Augustine, who says that the foregoing (*see* obj. 1) "are not in the soul as in a subject, as colour or shape, or any other quality, or quantity, are in a body; for whatever is so, does not exceed the subject in which it is, whereas the mind can love and know other things" (*De Trin.* ix, 4).[4]

Obj. 6. Further, a simple form cannot be a subject.[5] But the soul is a simple form, since it is not composed of matter and form, as we have said above (Q. LXXV, A. 5). Therefore the power of the soul cannot be in it as in a subject.

Obj. 7. Further, an accident is not the principle of a substantial difference. But sensitive and rational are substantial differences, and they are taken from sense and reason, which are powers of the soul. Therefore the powers of the soul are not accidents. And so it would seem that the power of the soul is its own essence.

On the contrary, Dionysius (*Cæl. Hier.* xi)[6] says that "heavenly spirits are divided into es-

---

[1] PL 42, 963.   [2] PL 42, 984.
[3] *Soul*, II, 2 (414ᵃ12).   [4] PL 42, 963.
[5] Boëthius, *De Trin.*, chap. 2 (PL 64, 1250).
[6] Sect. 2 (PG 3, 284).

sence, power, and operation." Much more, then, in the soul is the essence distinct from the virtue or power.

I answer that, It is impossible to admit that the power of the soul is its essence, although some have maintained it.[1] For the present purpose this may be proved in two ways. First, because, since power and act divide being and every kind of being, we must refer a power and its act to the same genus. Therefore, if the act be not in the genus of substance, the power directed to that act cannot be in the genus of substance. Now the operation of the soul is not in the genus of substance; for this belongs to God alone, whose operation is His own substance. Therefore the Divine power which is the principle of His operation is the Divine Essence itself. This cannot be true either of the soul, or of any creature, as we have said above when speaking of the angels (Q. LIV, A. 3). Secondly, this may be also shown to be impossible in the soul. For the soul by its very essence is an act. Therefore if the very essence of the soul were the immediate principle of operation, whatever has a soul would always have actual vital actions, as that which has a soul is always an actually living thing. For as a form the soul is not an act ordered to a further act, but the ultimate term of generation. Hence, for it to be in potency to another act does not belong to it according to its essence, as a form, but according to its power. So the soul itself, as the subject of its power, is called the first act, with a further relation to the second act.[2] Now we observe that what has a soul is not always actual with respect to its vital operations; hence also it is said in the definition of the soul that it is "the act of a body having life potentially; which potency, however, does not exclude the soul."[3] Therefore it follows that the essence of the soul is not its power. For nothing is in potency by reason of an act, as act.

Reply Obj. 1. Augustine is speaking of the mind as it knows and loves itself. Thus knowledge and love as referred to the soul as known and loved are substantially or essentially in the soul, for the very substance or essence of the soul is known and loved. In the same way are we to understand what he says in the other passage, that those things are "one life, one mind, one essence." Or, as some say,[4] this passage is true in the sense in which the whole of power is predicated of its parts, being midway between the universal whole and the integral whole. For the universal whole is in each part according to its entire essence and power, as animal in a man and in a horse, and therefore it is properly predicated of each part. But the integral whole is not in each part, neither according to its whole essence, nor according to its whole power. Therefore in no way can it be predicated of each part; yet in a way it is predicated, though improperly, of all the parts together, as if we were to say that the wall, roof, and foundations are a house. But the whole of power is in each part according to its whole essence, not, however, according to its whole power. Therefore in a way it can be predicated of each part, but not so properly as the universal whole. In this sense Augustine says that the memory, understanding, and will are the one essence of the soul.

Reply Obj. 2. The act to which primary matter is in potency is the substantial form. Therefore the potency of matter is nothing else but its essence.

Reply Obj. 3. Action belongs to the composite, as does being; for to act belongs to what exists. Now the composite has substantial being through the substantial form, and it operates by the power which results from the substantial form. Hence an active accidental form is to the substantial form of the agent (for instance, heat compared to the form of fire) as the power of the soul is to the soul.

Reply Obj. 4. That the accidental form is a principle of action is due to the substantial form. Therefore the substantial form is the first principle of action, but not the proximate principle. In this sense the Philosopher says that "the soul is that whereby we understand and sense."

Reply Obj. 5. If we take accident as meaning what is divided against substance, then there can be no medium between substance and accident; because they are divided by affirmation and negation, that is, according to being in a subject, and non-being in a subject. In this sense, as the power of the soul is not its essence, it must be an accident; and it belongs to the second species of accident, that of quality. But if we take accident as one of the five universals, in this sense there is a medium between substance and accident. For to substance pertains all that belongs to the essence of a thing; but whatever is beyond the essence of a thing can-

[1] Wm. of Paris, *De An.*, chap. 3, pt. IV (II, 89) (cf. Gilson, AHDLM, 1926, p. 53). Cf. Peter Lombard, *Sent.*, I, d. III, chap. 2 (QR I, 35). Cf. Lottin, *Mél. de Wulf* (pp. 191–210).

[2] Aristotle, *Soul*, II, 1 (412ª27).

[3] *Ibid.*, II, 1 (412ᵇ25).

[4] Albert the Great, *In Sent.*, I, d. III, A. 34 (BO xxv, 140).

not be called accident in this sense, but only what is not caused by the essential principle of the species. For a property does not belong to the essence of a thing, but is caused by the essential principles of the species; hence it is a medium between the essence and accident as we have said. In this sense the powers of the soul may be said to be a medium between substance and accident, as being natural properties of the soul. When Augustine says that knowledge and love are not in the soul as accidents in a subject, this must be understood in the sense given above (Ans. 1), in so far as they are compared to the soul not as loving and knowing, but as loved and known. His argument applies in this sense; for if love were in the soul loved as in a subject, it would follow that an accident transcends its subject, since even other things are loved through the soul.

Reply Obj. 6. Although the soul is not composed of matter and form, yet it has an admixture of potentiality, as we have said above (Q. LXXV, A. 5, Ans. 4), and for this reason it can be the subject of an accident. The statement quoted is verified in God, Who is the Pure Act, in treating of which subject Boëthius employs that phrase.

Reply Obj. 7. Rational and sensitive, as differences, are not taken from the powers of sense and reason, but from the sensitive and rational soul itself. But because substantial forms, which in themselves are unknown to us, are known by their accidents, nothing prevents us from sometimes substituting accidents for substantial differences.

ARTICLE 2. *Whether There Are Several Powers of the Soul?*

We proceed thus to the Second Article: It would seem that there are not several powers of the soul.

Objection 1. For the intellectual soul approaches nearest to the likeness of God. But in God there is one simple power; and therefore also in the intellectual soul.

Obj. 2. Further, the higher a power is, the more unified it is. But the intellectual soul excels all other forms in power. Therefore above all others it has one virtue or power.

Obj. 3. Further, to operate belongs to what is in act. But by the one essence of the soul, man has being in the different degrees of perfection, as we have seen above (Q. LXXVI, AA. 3, 4). Therefore by the one power of the soul he performs different operations of various degrees.

On the contrary, The Philosopher places several powers in the soul.[1]

I answer that, Of necessity we must place several powers in the soul. To make this evident, we observe that, as the Philosopher says,[2] the lowest order of things cannot acquire perfect goodness, but they acquire a certain imperfect goodness by a few movements. And those which belong to a higher order acquire perfect goodness by many movements. Those yet higher acquire perfect goodness by few movements, and the highest perfection is found in those things which acquire perfect goodness without any movement whatever. Thus he is least of all disposed to health who can only acquire imperfect health by means of a few remedies. Better disposed is he who can acquire perfect health by means of many remedies, and better still, he who can by few remedies. Best of all is he who has perfect health without any remedies. We conclude, therefore, that things which are below man acquire a certain limited goodness, and so they have a few determinate operations and powers. But man can acquire universal and perfect goodness because he can acquire Happiness. Yet he is in the last degree, according to his nature, of those to whom Happiness is possible. Therefore the human soul requires many and various operations and powers. But to angels a smaller variety of powers is sufficient. In God there is no power or action beyond His own Essence.

There is yet another reason why the human soul abounds in a variety of powers: because it is on the confines of spiritual and corporeal creatures, and therefore the powers of both meet together in the soul.

Reply Obj. 1. The intellectual soul approaches to the Divine likeness more than inferior creatures in being able to acquire perfect goodness, although by many and various means; and in this it falls short of more perfect creatures.

Reply Obj. 2. A unified power is superior if it extends to equal things, but a multiform power is superior to it, if it is over many things.

Reply Obj. 3. One thing has one substantial being but may have several operations. So there is one essence of the soul, with several powers.

ARTICLE 3. *Whether the Powers Are Distinguished by Their Acts and Objects?*

We proceed thus to the Third Article: It would seem that the powers of the soul are not distinguished by acts and objects.

[1] *Soul,* II, 3 (414ª31).
[2] *Heavens,* II, 12 (292ª22).

Objection 1. For nothing is determined to its species by what is subsequent and extrinsic to it. But the act is subsequent to the power, and the object is extrinsic to it. Therefore the soul's powers are not specifically distinct by acts and objects.

Obj. 2. Further, contraries are what differ most from each other. Therefore if the powers are distinguished by their objects, it follows that the same power could not have contrary objects. This is clearly false in almost all the powers; for the power of vision extends to white and black, and the power of taste to sweet and bitter.

Obj. 3. Further, if the cause be removed, the effect is removed. Hence if the difference of powers came from the difference of objects, the same object would not come under different powers. This is clearly false, for the same thing is known by the knowing power, and desired by the appetitive power.

Obj. 4. Further, that which of itself is the cause of anything, is its cause in every case. But various objects which belong to various powers belong also to some one power; as sound and colour belong to sight and hearing, which are different powers, yet come under the one power of common sense. Therefore the powers are not distinguished according to the difference of their objects.

On the contrary, Things that are subsequent are distinguished by what precedes. But the Philosopher says[1] that "acts and operations precede the powers according to the reason; and these again are preceded by their opposites," that is their objects. Therefore the powers are distinguished according to their acts and objects.

I answer that, A power as such is ordered to an act. Therefore we seek to know the nature of a power from the act to which it is ordered, and consequently the nature of a power is diversified, as the nature of the act is diversified. Now the nature of an act is diversified according to the various natures of the objects. For every act is either of an active power or of a passive power. Now, the object is to the act of a passive power as the principle and moving cause; for colour is the principle of vision, in so far as it moves the sight. On the other hand, to the act of an active power the object is a term and end; as the object of the power of growth is perfect quantity, which is the end of growth. Now, from these two things an act receives its species, namely, from its principle, or

[1] *Soul*, II, 4 (415ᵃ18).

from its end or term; for the act of heating differs from the act of cooling in this, that the former proceeds from something hot, which is the active principle, to heat; the latter from something cold, which is the active principle, to cold. Therefore the powers are of necessity distinguished by their acts and objects.

Nevertheless, we must observe that things which are accidental do not change the species. For since to be coloured is accidental to an animal, its species is not changed by a difference of colour, but by a difference in that which belongs to the nature of an animal, that is to say, by a difference in the sensitive soul, which is sometimes rational, and sometimes otherwise. Hence rational and irrational are differences dividing animal, constituting its various species. In like manner, therefore, not any variety of objects diversifies the powers of the soul, but a difference in that to which the power of its very nature is directed. Thus the senses of their very nature are directed to the passive quality which of itself is divided into colour, sound, and the like, and therefore there is one sensitive power with regard to colour, namely, sight, and another with regard to sound, namely, hearing. But it is accidental to a passive quality, for instance, to something coloured, to be a musician or a grammarian, great or small, a man or a stone. Therefore by reason of such differences the powers of the soul are not distinguished.

Reply Obj. 1. Act, though subsequent in being to power, is, nevertheless, prior to it in intention and logically; as the end is with regard to the agent. And the object, although extrinsic, is, nevertheless, the principle or end of the action; and those things which are intrinsic to a thing are proportionate to its principle and end.

Reply Obj. 2. If any power were to have one of two contraries as such for its object, the other contrary would belong to another power. But the power of the soul does not regard the nature of the contrary as such, but rather the common aspect of both contraries; as sight does not regard the aspect of white, but of colour. This is because one of two contraries in a manner includes the notion of the other, since they are to one another as perfect and imperfect.

Reply Obj. 3. Nothing prevents things which are the same in subject from being considered under different aspects; therefore they can pertain to various powers of the soul.

Reply Obj. 4. The higher power of itself regards a more universal aspect of the object than the lower power, because the higher a power is, to a greater number of things does it extend. Therefore many things are combined in the one aspect of the object, which the higher power considers of itself, while they differ in the aspects regarded by the lower powers of themselves. Thus it is that various objects pertain to various lower powers, which objects, however, are subject to one higher power.

ARTICLE 4. *Whether Among the Powers of the Soul There Is Order?*

We proceed thus to the Fourth Article: It would seem that there is no order among the powers of the soul.

Objection 1. For in those things which come under one division there is no before and after, but all are naturally simultaneous. But the powers of the soul are contradistinguished from one another. Therefore there is no order among them.

Obj. 2. Further, the powers of the soul are referred to their objects and to the soul itself. On the part of the soul, there is not order among them, because the soul is one. In like manner the objects are various and dissimilar, as colour and sound. Therefore there is no order among the powers of the soul.

Obj. 3. Further, where there is order among powers, we find that the operation of one depends on the operation of another. But the act of one power of the soul does not depend on that of another; for sight can act independently of hearing, and conversely. Therefore there is no order among the powers of the soul.

On the contrary, The Philosopher[1] compares the parts or powers of the soul to figures. But figures have an order among themselves. Therefore also the powers of the soul have order.

I answer that, Since the soul is one, and the powers are many, and since a number of things that proceed from one must proceed in a certain order, there must be some order among the powers of the soul.

Accordingly we may observe a threefold order among them, two of which correspond to the dependence of one power on another, while the third is taken from the order of the objects. Now the dependence of one power on another can be taken in two ways: according to the order of nature, since perfect things are by their nature prior to imperfect things; and according to the order of generation and time, according as from being imperfect, a thing comes to be perfect. Thus, according to the first

kind of order among the powers, the intellectual powers are prior to the sensitive powers; hence they direct them and command them. Likewise the sensitive powers are prior in this order to the powers of the nutritive soul.

In the second kind of order, it is the other way about. For the powers of the nutritive soul are prior by way of generation to the powers of the sensitive soul, for which, therefore, they prepare the body. The same is to be said of the sensitive powers with regard to the intellectual. But in the third kind of order, certain sensitive powers are ordered among themselves, namely, sight, hearing, and smelling. For the visible naturally comes first, since it is common to higher and lower bodies. But sound is audible in the air, which is naturally prior to the mingling of elements, of which smell is the result.

Reply Obj. 1. The species of a given genus are to one another as before and after, like numbers and figures, if considered in their being; although they may be said to be simultaneous according as they receive the predication of the common genus.

Reply Obj. 2. This order among the powers of the soul is both on the part of the soul (which, though it be one according to its essence, has a certain relation to various acts in a certain order) and on the part of the objects, and furthermore on the part of the acts, as we have said above.

Reply Obj. 3. This argument is verified as regards those powers among which order of the third kind exists. Those powers among which the two other kinds of order exist are such that the action of one depends on another.

ARTICLE 5. *Whether All the Powers of the Soul Are in the Soul As Their Subject?*

We proceed thus to the Fifth Article: It would seem that all the powers of the soul are in the soul as their subject.

Objection 1. For as the powers of the body, are to the body, so are the powers of the soul to the soul. But the body is the subject of the corporeal powers. Therefore the soul is the subject of the powers of the soul.

Obj. 2. Further, the operations of the powers of the soul are attributed to the body by reason of the soul, because, as the Philosopher says,[2] "The soul is that by which we sense and understand primarily." But the first principles of the operations of the soul are the powers. Therefore the powers are primarily in the soul.

[1] *Ibid.,* II, 3 (414[b]20).

[2] *Ibid.,* II, 2 (414[a]12).

Obj. 3. Further, Augustine says (*Gen. ad lit.* xii, 7, 24)[1] that the soul senses certain things, not through the body,—in fact, without the body, as fear and the like, and some things through the body. But if the sensitive powers were not in the soul alone as in their subject, the soul could not sense anything without the body. Therefore the soul is the subject of the sensitive powers; and for a similar reason, of all the other powers.

On the contrary, The Philosopher says[2] that "to sense belongs neither to the soul, nor to the body, but to the composite." Therefore the sensitive power is in the composite as its subject. Therefore the soul alone is not the subject of all the powers.

I answer that, The subject of operative power is that which is able to operate, for every accident denominates its proper subject. Now that which is able to operate, and that which does operate is the same. Therefore the subject of power is of necessity the subject of operation, as again the Philosopher says in the beginning of the treatise on *Sleep.* Now, it is clear from what we have said above (Q. LXXV, AA. 2, 3; Q. LXXVI, A. 1, Ans. 1), that some operations of the soul are performed without a corporeal organ, as to understand and to will. Hence the powers of these operations are in the soul as their subject. But some operations of the soul are performed by means of corporeal organs; as sight by the eye, and hearing by the ear. And so it is with all the other operations of the nutritive and sensitive parts. Therefore the powers which are the principles of these operations have their subject in the composite, and not in the soul alone.

Reply Obj. 1. All the powers are said to belong to the soul, not as their subject, but as their principle, because it is by the soul that the composite has the power to perform such operations.

Reply Obj. 2. All such powers are primarily in the soul, as compared to the composite; not as in their subject, but as in their principle.

Reply Obj. 3. Plato's opinion[3] was that sensation is an operation proper to the soul, just as understanding is. Now in many things relating to philosophy Augustine makes use of the opinions of Plato, not asserting them as true, but relating them. However, as far as the present question is concerned, when it is said that the soul senses some things with the body and some

without the body, this can be taken in two ways. Firstly, the words "with the body or without the body" may determine the act of sensing according as it proceeds from the one sensing. Thus the soul senses nothing without the body, because the act of sensing cannot proceed from the soul except by a corporeal organ. Secondly, they may be understood as determining the act of sensing on the part of the object sensed. Thus the soul senses some things with the body, that is, things existing in the body, as when it feels a wound or something of that sort; while it senses some things without the body, that is, which do not exist in the body, but only in the apprehension of the soul, as when it feels sad or joyful on hearing something.

ARTICLE 6. *Whether the Powers of the Soul Flow from Its Essence?*

We proceed thus to the Sixth Article: It would seem that the powers of the soul do not flow from its essence.

Objection 1. For different things do not proceed from one simple thing. But the essence of the soul is one and simple. Since, therefore, the powers of the soul are many and various, they cannot proceed from its essence.

Obj. 2. Further, that from which a thing proceeds is its cause. But the essence of the soul cannot be said to be the cause of the powers, as is clear if one considers the different kinds of causes. Therefore the powers of the soul do not flow from its essence.

Obj. 3. Further, emanation involves some sort of movement. But nothing is moved by itself, as the Philosopher proves;[4] except, perhaps, by reason of a part of itself, as an animal is said to be moved by itself because one of its parts moves and another is moved. Neither is the soul moved, as the Philosopher proves.[5] Therefore the soul does not produce its powers within itself.

On the contrary, The powers of the soul are its natural properties. But the subject is the cause of its proper accidents; hence also "it is included in the definition of accident," as is clear from the *Metaphysics.*[6] Therefore the powers of the soul proceed from its essence as their cause.

I answer that, The substantial and the accidental form partly agree and partly differ. They agree in this, that each is an act, and that by each of them something is in some way in act. They differ, however, in two respects. First,

---

[1] PL 34, 459, 474.
[2] *Sleep,* 1 (454[a]7).
[3] See Q. LXXV, A. 3.

[4] *Physics,* VII, 1 (241[b]24).
[5] *Soul,* I, 4 (408[a]34).
[6] Aristotle, VII, 4 (1029[b]20).

because the substantial form makes a thing to be absolutely, and its subject is a being in potency only. But the accidental form does not make a thing to be absolutely, but to be such, or so great, or in some particular condition; for its subject is a being in act. Hence it is clear that actuality is found in the substantial form prior to its being found in the subject; and since that which is first in a genus is the cause in that genus, the substantial form causes being in act in its subject. On the other hand, actuality is found in the subject of the accidental form prior to its being found in the accidental form; hence the actuality of the accidental form is caused by the actuality of the subject. So the subject, according as it is in potency, is receptive of the accidental form, but according as it is in act, it produces it. This I say of the proper and *per se* accident; for with regard to the extraneous accident, the subject is receptive only, the accident being caused by an extrinsic agent. Secondly, substantial and accidental forms differ because, since that which is the less principal is for the sake of that which is the more principal, matter therefore is on account of the substantial form; while on the contrary, the accidental form exists on account of the completeness of the subject.

Now it is clear, from what has been said (A. 5), that either the subject of the soul's powers is the soul itself alone, which can be the subject of an accident, according as it has something of potentiality, as we have said above (A. 1, Ans. 6; Q. LXXV, A. 5, Ans. 4), or else this subject is the composite. Now the composite is in act through the soul. Hence it is clear that all the powers of the soul, whether their subject be the soul alone, or the composite, flow from the essence of the soul, as from their principle; because it has already been said that the accident is caused by the subject according as it is in act, and is received into it according as it is in potency.

Reply Obj. 1. From one simple thing many things may proceed naturally in a certain order; or again if there be diversity of recipients. Thus, from the one essence of the soul many and various powers proceed, both because order exists among these powers, and also by reason of the diversity of the corporeal organs.

Reply Obj. 2. The subject is both the final cause, and in a way the active cause, of its proper accident. It is also as it were the material cause, in so far as it is receptive of the accident. From this we may gather that the essence of the soul is the cause of all its powers, as their end,

and as their active principle; and of some as receptive of them.

Reply Obj. 3. The emanation of proper accidents from their subject is not by way of change, but by a certain natural consequence; thus one thing results naturally from another, as colour from light.

ARTICLE 7. *Whether One Power of the Soul Arises From Another?*

We proceed thus to the Seventh Article: It would seem that one power of the soul does not arise from another.

Objection 1. For if several things begin to be together, one of them does not arise from another. But all the powers of the soul are created at the same time with the soul. Therefore one of them does not arise from another.

Obj. 2. Further, the power of the soul arises from the soul as an accident from the subject. But one power of the soul cannot be the subject of another, because nothing is the accident of an accident. Therefore one power does not arise from another.

Obj. 3. Further, one opposite does not arise from the other opposite, but everything arises from that which is like it in species. Now the powers of the soul are oppositely divided, as various species. Therefore one of them does not proceed from another.

On the contrary, Powers are known by their actions. But the action of one power is caused by the action of another power, as the action of the imagination by the action of the senses. Therefore one power of the soul is caused by another.

I answer that, In those things which proceed from one according to a natural order, just as the first is the cause of all, so that which is nearer to the first is, in a way, cause of those which are more remote. Now it has been shown above (A. 4) that among the powers of the soul there are several kinds of order. Therefore one power of the soul proceeds from the essence of the soul through the medium of another. But since the essence of the soul is related to the powers both as a principle active and final, and as a receptive principle, either separately by itself, or together with the body, and since the agent and the end are more perfect, while the receptive principle, as such, is less perfect, it follows that those powers of the soul which precede the others, in the order of perfection and nature, are the principles of the others, after the manner of the end and active principle. For we see that the senses are for the sake of the intellect, and not the other way about. The sense, moreover, is a certain deficient participation of the intellect; hence, according to its natural origin, it proceeds from the intellect as the imperfect from the perfect. But considered as receptive principles, the more imperfect powers are principles with regard to the others; thus the soul, according as it has the sensitive power, is considered as the subject, and as something material with regard to the intellect. On this account, the more imperfect powers precede the others in the order of generation, for the animal is generated before the man.

Reply Obj. 1. As the power of the soul flows from the essence, not by a change, but by a certain natural consequence, and is simultaneous with the soul, so is it the case with one power as regards another.

Reply Obj. 2. An accident cannot of itself be the subject of an accident, but one accident is received prior to another into substance, as quantity before quality. In this sense one accident is said to be the subject of another; as surface is of colour, in so far as substance receives one accident through the means of another. The same thing may be said of the powers of the soul.

Reply Obj. 3. The powers of the soul are opposed to one another as perfect and imperfect, as also are the species of numbers and figures. But this opposition does not prevent the origin of one from another, because imperfect things naturally proceed from perfect things.

ARTICLE 8. *Whether All the Powers Remain in the Soul When Separated From the Body?*

We proceed thus to the Eighth Article: It would seem that all the powers of the soul remain in the soul separated from the body.

Objection 1. For we read in the book *De Spiritu et Anima*[1] that "the soul withdraws from the body, taking with itself sense and imagination, reason and intellect and understanding, concupiscibility and irascibility."

Obj. 2. Further, the powers of the soul are its natural properties. But properties are always in that to which they belong, and are never separated from it. Therefore the powers of the soul are in it even after death.

Obj. 3. Further, the powers even of the sensitive soul are not weakened when the body becomes weak; because, as the Philosopher says,[2] "If an old man were given the eye of a young man, he would see even as well as a young man." But weakness is the road to corruption. There-

fore the powers of the soul are not corrupted when the body is corrupted, but remain in the separated soul.

Obj. 4. Further, memory is a power of the sensitive soul, as the Philosopher proves.[3] But memory remains in the separated soul; for it was said to the rich glutton whose soul was in hell: *Remember that thou didst receive good things during thy lifetime* (Luke 16. 25). Therefore memory remains in the separated soul, and consequently the other powers of the sensitive part.

Obj. 5. Further, joy and sorrow are in the concupiscible part, which is a power of the sensitive soul. But it is clear that separate souls grieve or rejoice at the pains or rewards which they receive. Therefore the concupiscible power remains in the separated soul.

Obj. 6. Further, Augustine says (*Gen. ad lit.* xii, 32)[4] that, as the soul, when the body lies senseless, yet not quite dead, sees some things by imaginary vision, so also when by death the soul is quite separate from the body. But the imagination is a power of the sensitive part. Therefore the power of the sensitive part remains in the separated soul; and consequently all the other powers.

On the contrary, It is said (*De Eccl. Dogm.*)[5] that "of two substances only does man consist: the soul with its reason, and the body with its senses." Therefore the body being dead, the sensitive powers do not remain.

I answer that, As we have said already (AA. 5, 6, 7), all the powers of the soul belong to the soul alone as their principle. But some powers belong to the soul alone as their subject; as the intellect and the will. These powers must remain in the soul after the destruction of the body. But other powers are in the composite as their subject, as all the powers of the sensitive and nutritive parts. Now accidents cannot remain after the destruction of the subject. Therefore, when the composite is destroyed, such powers do not remain actually; but they remain virtually in the soul, as in their principle or root.

So it is false that, as some say,[6] these powers remain in the soul even after the corruption of the body. It is much more false that, as they say also, the acts of these powers remain in the separated soul,[7] because these powers have no act apart from the corporeal organ.

---

[1] Pseudo-Augustine (Alcher of Clairvaux), chap. 15 (PL 40, 791).　　[2] *Soul*, I, 4 (408[b]21).

[3] *Memory and Reminiscence*, 1 (450[a]12).

[4] PL 34, 480.

[5] Gennadius. Chap. 29 (PL 58, 985).

[6] Pseudo-Augustine, *loc. cit.*

[7] *Ibid.*, chap. 30 (PL 40, 800).

Reply Obj. 1. That book has no authority, and so what is there written can be despised with the same facility as it was said; although we may say that the soul takes with itself these powers not actually but virtually.

Reply Obj. 2. These powers which we say do not actually remain in the separate soul, are not the properties of the soul alone, but of the composite.

Reply Obj. 3. These powers are said not to be weakened when the body becomes weak because the soul remains unchangeable, and is the virtual principle of these powers.

Reply Obj. 4. The recollection spoken of there is to be taken in the same way as Augustine (*De Trin.* x, 11; xiv, 7)[1] places memory in the mind, not as a part of the sensitive soul.

Reply Obj. 5. In the separate soul, sorrow and joy are not in the sensitive, but in the intellectual appetite, as in the angels.

Reply Obj. 6. Augustine in that passage is speaking as inquiring, not as asserting. Therefore he retracted some things which he had said there (*Retract.* ii, 24).[2]

QUESTION LXXVIII

OF THE POWERS OF THE SOUL IN PARTICULAR

(*In Four Articles*)

WE next treat of the powers of the soul in particular. The theologian, however, has only to inquire in particular of the intellectual and appetitive powers, in which the virtues reside. And since the knowledge of these powers depends to a certain extent on the other powers, our consideration of the powers of the soul taken in particular will be divided into three parts: first, we shall consider those powers which are preliminary to the intellect; secondly, the intellectual powers (Q. LXXIX); thirdly, the appetitive powers (Q. LXXX).

Under the first head there are four points of inquiry: (1) The powers of the soul considered generally. (2) The various species of the vegetative part. (3) The exterior senses. (4) The interior senses.

ARTICLE 1. *Whether There Are To Be Distinguished Five Genera of Powers in the Soul?*

We proceed thus to the First Article: It would seem that there are not to be distinguished five genera of powers in the soul—

namely, vegetative, sensitive, appetitive, locomotive, and intellectual.

Objection 1. For the powers of the soul are called its parts. But only three parts of the soul are commonly assigned by everybody—namely, the vegetative soul, the sensitive soul, and the rational soul. Therefore there are only three genera of powers in the soul, and not five.

Obj. 2. Further, the powers of the soul are the principles of its vital operations. Now, in four ways is a thing said to live. For the Philosopher says,[3] "In several ways a thing is said to live, and even if only one of these is present, the thing is said to live; as intellect and sense, local movement and rest, and lastly, movement of decrease and increase due to nourishment." Therefore there are only four genera of powers of soul, as the appetitive is excluded.

Obj. 3. Further, a special kind of soul ought not to be assigned as regards what is common to all the powers. Now desire is common to each power of the soul. For sight desires an appropriate visible object; hence we read (Ecclus. 40. 22): *The eye desireth favour and beauty, but more than these green sown fields.* In the same way every other power desires its appropriate object. Therefore the appetitive power should not be made a special genus of the powers of the soul.

Obj. 4. Further, the moving principle in animals is sense, intellect, or appetite, as the Philosopher says.[4] Therefore the motive power should not be added to the above as a special genus of soul.

On the contrary, The Philosopher says,[5] "The powers are the vegetative, the sensitive, the appetitive, movement according to place, and the intellectual."

I answer that, There are five genera of powers of the soul, as above numbered. Of these, three are called souls and four are called modes of living.

The reason of this diversity lies in the various souls being distinguished accordingly as the operation of the soul surpasses the operation of the corporeal nature in various ways; for the whole corporeal nature is subject to the soul, and is related to it as its matter and instrument. There exists, therefore, an operation of the soul which so far exceeds the corporeal nature that it is not even performed by any corporeal organ; and such is the operation of the rational soul. Below this, there is another operation of the

---

[1] PL 42, 983, 1043.
[2] PL 32, 640.

[3] *Soul,* II, 2 (413ª22).
[4] *Ibid.,* III, 10 (433ª9).
[5] *Ibid.,* II, 3 (414ª31).

soul, which is indeed performed through a corporeal organ, but not through a corporeal quality, and this is the operation of the sensitive soul; for though hot and cold, wet and dry, and other such corporeal qualities are required for the work of the senses, yet they are not required in such a way that the operation of the senses takes place by virtue of such qualities, but only for the proper disposition of the organ. The lowest of the operations of the soul is that which is performed by a corporeal organ, and by virtue of a corporeal quality. Yet this surpasses the operation of the corporeal nature, because the movements of bodies are caused by an extrinsic principle, while these operations are from an intrinsic principle; for this is common to all the operations of the soul, since every animate thing, in some way, moves itself. Such is the operation of the vegetative soul; for digestion, and what follows, is caused instrumentally by the action of heat, as the Philosopher says.[1]

Now the powers of the soul are distinguished generically by their objects. For the higher a power is, the more universal is the object to which it extends, as we have said above (Q. LXXVII, A. 3, Ans. 4). But the object of the soul's operation may be considered in a threefold order. For in the soul there is a power the object of which is only the body that is united to that soul. The powers of this genus are called vegetative, for the vegetative power acts only on the body to which the soul is united. There is another genus in the powers of the soul, which genus regards a more universal object—namely, every sensible body, not only the body to which the soul is united. And there is yet another genus in the powers of the soul, which genus regards a still more universal object—namely, not only the sensible body, but all being in general. From this it is evident that the latter two genera of the soul's powers have an operation in regard not only to that which is united to them, but also to something extrinsic. Now, since whatever operates must in some way be united to the object about which it operates, it follows of necessity that this something extrinsic, which is the object of the soul's operation, must be related to the soul in a twofold manner. First, in so far as this something extrinsic has a natural aptitude to be united to the soul, and to be by its likeness in the soul. In this way there are two kinds of powers—namely, the sensitive in regard to the less common object—the sensible body, and the intellectual, in regard to the most common object—universal being. Secondly, according as

the soul itself has an inclination and tendency to the something extrinsic. And in this way there are again two kinds of powers in the soul: one—the appetitive—in respect of which the soul is related to something extrinsic as to an end, which is first in the intention; the other—the power of local movement—in respect of which the soul is related to something extrinsic as to the term of its operation and movement; for every animal is moved for the purpose of realizing its desires and intentions.

The modes of living are distinguished according to the degrees of living things. There are some living things in which there exists only vegetative power, as the plants. There are others in which with the vegetative there exists also the sensitive, but not the power of local movement; such are immovable animals, as shellfish. There are others which besides this have powers of local movement, as perfect animals, which require many things for their life, and consequently movement to seek necessaries of life from a distance. And there are some living things which with these have intellectual power—namely, men. But the appetitive power does not constitute a degree of living things; because "wherever there is sense there is also appetite."[2]

Thus the *first two objections* are hereby solved.

Reply Obj. 3. The natural appetite is that inclination which each thing has, of its own nature, for something; hence by its natural appetite each power desires something suitable to itself. But the animal appetite results from the form apprehended; this sort of appetite requires a special power of the soul—apprehension alone does not suffice. For a thing is desired as it exists in its own nature, whereas in the apprehensive power it does not exist according to its own nature, but according to its likeness. Hence it is clear that sight desires naturally a visible object for the purpose of its act only—namely, for the purpose of seeing; but the animal by the appetitive power desires the thing seen not merely for the purpose of seeing it, but also for other purposes. But if the soul did not require things perceived by the senses, except on account of the actions of the senses, that is, for the purpose of sensing them, there would be no need for a special genus of appetitive powers, since the natural appetite of the powers would suffice.

Reply Obj. 4. Although sense and appetite are principles of movement in perfect animals, yet sense and appetite, as such, are not sufficient to

---

[1] *Soul*, II, 4 (416^{b}25).   [2] *Ibid.*, II, 3 (414^{b}1).

cause movement unless another power be added to them; for immovable animals have sense and appetite, and yet they have not the power of motion. Now this moving power is not only in the appetite and sense as commanding the movement, but also in the parts of the body, to make them obey the appetite of the soul which moves them. Of this we have a sign in the fact that when the members are deprived of their natural disposition, they do not move in obedience to the appetite.

ARTICLE 2. *Whether the Parts of the Vegetative Soul Are Fittingly Described as the Nutritive, Augmentative, and Generative?*

We proceed thus to the Second Article: It would seem that the parts of the vegetative soul are not fittingly described—namely, the nutritive, augmentative, and generative.

Objection 1. For these are called natural forces. But the powers of the soul are above the natural forces. Therefore we should not class the above forces as powers of the soul.

Obj. 2. Further, we should not assign a particular power of the soul to that which is common to living and non-living things. But generation is common to all things that can be generated and corrupted, whether living or not living. Therefore the generative force should not be classed as a power of the soul.

Obj. 3. Further, the soul is more powerful than the body. But the body by the same power gives species and quantity; much more, therefore, does the soul. Therefore the power of growth of the soul is not distinct from the generative power.

Obj. 4. Further, everything is preserved in being by that whereby it has being. But the generative power is that whereby a living thing acquires being. Therefore by the same power the living thing is preserved. Now the nutritive force is directed to the preservation of the living thing,[1] being "a power which is capable of preserving whatever receives it." Therefore we should not distinguish the nutritive power from the generative.

On the contrary, The Philosopher says[2] that the operations of this soul are "generation, the use of food, and growth."

I answer that, The vegetative part has three powers. For the vegetative part, as we have said (A. 1), has for its object the body itself, living by the soul, for which body a threefold operation of the soul is required. One is that whereby it acquires being, and to this is directed the generative power. Another is that whereby the living body acquires its due quantity; to this is directed the power of growth. Another is that whereby the body of a living thing is preserved in its being and in its due quantity; to this is directed the nutritive power.

We must, however, observe a difference among these powers. The nutritive power and the power of growth have their effect where they exist, since the body itself united to the soul grows and is preserved by the growth and nutritive powers which exist in one and the same soul. But the generative power has its effect not in one and the same body but in another; for a thing cannot generate itself. Therefore the generative power, in a way, approaches to the dignity of the sensitive soul, which has an operation extending to extrinsic things, although in a more excellent and more universal manner; for that which is highest in an inferior nature approaches to that which is lowest in the higher nature, as is made clear by Dionysius (*Div. Nom.* vii).[3] Therefore, of these three powers, the generative has the greater finality, nobility, and perfection, as the Philosopher says,[4] for "it belongs to a thing which is already perfect to produce another like to itself." And the generative power is served by the growth and nutritive powers; and the power of growth by the nutritive.

Reply Obj. 1. Such forces are called natural both because they produce an effect like that of nature, which also gives being, quantity, and preservation (although the above forces accomplish these things in a more perfect way), and because those forces perform their actions instrumentally, through the active and passive qualities, which are the principles of natural actions.

Reply Obj. 2. Generation of inanimate things is entirely from an extrinsic source, but the generation of living things is in a higher way, through something in the living thing itself, which is the seed containing the forming principle of the body. Therefore there must be in the living thing a power that prepares this seed. And this is the generative power.

Reply Obj. 3. Since the generation of living things is from a seed, it is necessary that in the beginning an animal be generated small in size. For this reason it must have a power in the soul whereby it is brought to its appropriate size. But the inanimate body is generated from determinate matter by an extrinsic agent. Therefore it

---

[1] *Ibid.,* II, 4 (416^{b}14).
[2] *Ibid.,* II, 4 (415^{a}25; ^{b}23).

[3] Sect. 3 (PG 3, 872).
[4] *Soul,* II, 4 (416^{b}24).

receives at once its nature and its quantity, according to the condition of the matter.

Reply Obj. 4. As we have said above (A. I), the operation of the vegetative principle is performed by means of heat, the property of which is to consume humidity. Therefore, in order to restore the humidity thus lost, the nutritive power is required, whereby the food is changed into the substance of the body. This is also necessary for the action of the growth and generative powers.

ARTICLE 3. *Whether the Five Exterior Senses Are Properly Distinguished?*

We proceed thus to the Third Article: It would seem inaccurate to distinguish five exterior senses.

Objection 1. For sense can know accidents. But there are many kinds of accidents. Therefore, as powers are distinguished by their objects, it seems that the senses are multiplied according to the number of the kinds of accidents.

Obj. 2. Further, magnitude and shape, and other things which are called common sensibles, are not sensibles by accident, but are contradistinguished from them by the Philosopher.[1] Now the diversity of objects, as such, diversifies the powers. Since, therefore, magnitude and shape are further from colour than sound is, it seems that there is much more need for another sensitive power that can grasp magnitude or shape than for that which grasps colour or sound.

Obj. 3. Further, one sense is related to one contrariety; as sight regards white and black. But the sense of touch grasps several contrarieties, such as hot or cold, damp or dry, and the like. Therefore it is not a single sense but several. Therefore there are more than five senses.

Obj. 4. Further, a species is not divided against its genus. But taste is a kind of touch. Therefore it should not be classed as a distinct sense from touch.

On the contrary, The Philosopher says,[2] "There is no other besides the five senses."

I answer that, The reason of the distinction and number of the senses has been assigned by some to the organs in which one or other of the elements preponderate, as water, air, or the like.[3] By others it has been assigned to the medium, which is either in conjunction or extrinsic, and

is either water or air, or the like.[4] Others have ascribed it to the various natures of the sensible qualities, according as such quality belongs to a simple body or results from complexity.[5]

But none of these explanations is fitting. For the powers are not for the organs, but the organs for the powers. Therefore there are not various powers for the reason that there are various organs, but nature has provided a variety of organs so that they might be adapted to various powers. In the same way nature provided various mediums for the various senses, according to their fitness for the acts of the powers. And to know the natures of sensible qualities does not pertain to the senses but to the intellect.

The reason of the number and distinction of the exterior senses must therefore be ascribed to that which belongs to the senses properly and *per se.* Now, sense is a passive power, and is naturally changed by the exterior sensible. Therefore the exterior cause of such change is what is *per se* perceived by the sense, and according to the diversity of that exterior cause the sensitive powers are diversified.

Now, change is of two kinds, one natural, the other spiritual. Natural change takes place by the form of the thing which causes the change being received, according to its natural being, into the thing changed, as heat is received into the thing heated. But spiritual change takes place by the form of the thing which causes the change being received according to a spiritual mode of being into the thing changed, as the form of colour is received into the pupil which does not thereby become coloured. Now, for the operation of the senses, a spiritual change is required, whereby an intention of the sensible form is effected in the sensile organ. Otherwise, if a natural change alone sufficed for the sense's action, all natural bodies would feel when they undergo alteration.

But in some senses we find spiritual change only, as in sight, while in others we find not only a spiritual but also a natural change, either on the part of the object only, or likewise on the part of the organ. On the part of the object we find natural change as to place in sound, which is the object of hearing; for sound is caused by percussion and commotion of the air. And we find natural change by alteration, in odour which is the object of smelling; for in order to exhale an odour a body must be in a measure altered by heat. On the part of the organ, natural change

---

[1] *Soul*, II, 6 (418ᵃ8).

[2] *Ibid.*, III, 1 (424ᵇ22).

[3] Cf. Albert the Great, *Summa de Creatur.*, III, Q. XXXIV, A. 4 (BO XXXV, 304). Cf. also Alexander of Hales, *Summa Theol.*, I–II, 356 (QR II, 432).

[4] See preceding note.

[5] Cf. Bonaventure, *Itinerarium Mentis in Deum*, chap. 2 (QR V, 300).

takes place in touch and taste; for the hand that touches something hot becomes hot, while the tongue is moistened by the humidity of the flavoured morsel. But the organs of smelling and hearing are not changed in their respective operations by any natural change unless accidentally.

Now, the sight, which is without natural change either in its organ or in its object, is the most spiritual, the most perfect, and the most universal of all the senses. After this comes the hearing and then the smell, which require a natural change on the part of the object; but local motion is more perfect than, and naturally prior to, the motion of alteration, as the Philosopher proves.[1] Touch and taste are the most material of all, of the distinction of which we shall speak later on (Ans. 3, 4). Hence it is that the three other senses are not exercised through a medium united to them, to obviate any natural change in their organ, as happens as regards these two senses.

Reply Obj. 1. Not every accident has in itself a power of change, but only qualities of the third species, according to which alteration takes place. Therefore only qualities of this kind are the objects of the senses; because "the senses are affected by the same things whereby inanimate bodies are affected," as stated in the *Physics*.[2]

Reply Obj. 2. Size, shape, and the like, which are called common sensibles, are midway between accidental sensibles and proper sensibles, which are the objects of the senses. For the proper sensibles first, and of their very nature, change the senses, since they are qualities that cause alteration. But the common sensibles are all reducible to quantity. As to size and number, it is clear that they are species of quantity. Shape is a quality about quantity, since the notion of shape consists in fixing the bounds of magnitude. Movement and rest are sensed according as the subject is affected in one or more ways in the magnitude of the subject or of its local distance, as in the movement of growth or of local motion, or again, according as it is affected in some sensible qualities, as in the movement of alteration; and thus to sense movement and rest is, in a way, to sense one thing and many. Now quantity is the proximate subject of the qualities that cause alteration, as surface is of colour. Therefore the common sensibles do not move the senses first and of their own nature, but by reason of the sensible quality; as the surface by reason of colour. Yet they are not acci-

dental sensibles, for they produce a certain variety in the change of the senses. For sense is changed differently by a large and by a small surface, since whiteness itself is said to be great or small, and therefore is divided according to its proper subject.

Reply Obj. 3. As the Philosopher seems to say,[3] the sense of touch is generically one, but is divided into several specific senses, and for this reason it extends to various contrarieties; which senses, however, are not separate from one another in their organ, but are spread throughout the whole body, so that their distinction is not evident. But taste, which perceives the sweet and the bitter, accompanies touch in the tongue, but not in the whole body; so it is easily distinguished from touch. We might also say that all those contrarieties agree, each in some proximate genus, and all in a common genus, which is the object of touch according to its common notion. Such common genus is, however, unnamed, just as the proximate genus of hot and cold is unnamed.

Reply Obj. 4. The sense of taste, according to a saying of the Philosopher,[4] is a kind of touch existing in the tongue only. It is not distinct from touch in genus, but only from the species of touch distributed in the body. But if touch is one sense only, on account of the common notion of its object, we must say that taste is distinguished from touch by reason of a different notion of change. For touch involves a natural, and not only a spiritual, change in its organ, by reason of the quality which is its proper object. But the organ of taste is not necessarily changed by a natural change according to the quality which is its proper object, so that the tongue itself becomes sweet or bitter, but by reason of a preceding quality on which is based the flavour, which quality is moisture, the object of touch.

ARTICLE 4. *Whether the Interior Senses Are Suitably Distinguished?*

We proceed thus to the Fourth Article: It would seem that the interior senses are not suitably distinguished.

Objection 1. For the common is not divided against the proper. Therefore the common sense should not be numbered among the interior sensitive powers in addition to the proper exterior senses.

Obj. 2. Further, there is no need to assign an interior power of apprehension when the proper and exterior sense suffices. But the proper and

---

[1] *Physics*, VIII, 7 (260ª28).
[2] Aristotle, VII, 2 (244ᵇ12).

[3] *Soul*, II, 11 (422ᵇ17).
[4] *Ibid.*, II, 9 (421ª18); also II, 11 (423ª17).

exterior senses suffice for us to judge of sensible things, for each sense judges of its proper object. In like manner they seem to suffice for the perception of their own actions, for since the action of the sense is, in a way, between the power and its object, it seems that sight must be much more able to perceive its own vision, as being nearer to it, than the colour; and in like manner with the other senses. Therefore for this there is no need to assign an interior power, called the common sense.

Obj. 3. Further, according to the Philosopher[1] the imagination and the memory are passions of the "first sensitive." But passion is not divided against its subject. Therefore memory and imagination should not be assigned as powers distinct from the senses.

Obj. 4. Further, the intellect depends on the senses less than any power of the sensitive part. But the intellect knows nothing but what it receives from the senses; hence we read[2] that "those who lack one sense lack one kind of knowledge." Therefore much less should we assign to the sensitive part a power which they call the estimative power, for the perception of intentions which the sense does not perceive.

Obj. 5. Further, the action of the cogitative power, which consists in comparing, uniting, and dividing, and the action of the reminiscence, which consists in the use of a kind of syllogism for the sake of inquiry, is not less distant from the actions of the estimative and memorative powers, than the action of the estimative is from the action of the imagination. Therefore either we must add the cogitative and reminiscing to the estimative and memorative powers, or the estimative and memorative powers should not be made distinct from the imagination.

Obj. 6. Further, Augustine (*Gen. ad lit.* xii, 6, 7, 24)[3] describes "three kinds of vision; namely, corporeal, which is an action of the sense, spiritual, which is an action of the imagination or phantasy, and intellectual, which is an action of the intellect." Therefore there is no interior power between the sense and intellect besides the imagination.

On the contrary, Avicenna (*De Anima* iv, 1)[4] assigns five interior sensitive powers; namely, common sense, phantasy, imagination, and the estimative and memorative powers.

I answer that, As nature does not fail in necessary things, there must be as many actions of

the sensitive soul as suffice for the life of a perfect animal. If any of these actions cannot be reduced to one principle, they must be assigned to different powers, since a power of the soul is nothing else than the proximate principle of the soul's operation.

Now we must observe that for the life of a perfect animal, the animal should apprehend a thing not only at the actual time of sensation, but also when it is absent. Otherwise, since animal motion and action follow apprehension, an animal would not be moved to seek something absent, the contrary of which we may observe specially in perfect animals, which are moved by progression, for they are moved towards something apprehended and absent. Therefore an animal through the sensitive soul must not only receive the species of sensible things, when it is actually changed by them, but it must also retain and preserve them. Now to receive and retain are, in corporeal things, reduced to diverse principles; for moist things are apt to receive, but retain with difficulty, while it is the reverse with dry things. Therefore, since the sensitive power is the act of a corporeal organ, it follows that the power which receives the species of sensible things must be distinct from the power which preserves them.

Again we must observe that if an animal were moved by pleasing and disagreeable things only as affecting the sense, there would be no need to suppose that an animal has a power besides the apprehension of those forms which the senses perceive, and in which the animal takes pleasure, or from which it shrinks with horror. But the animal needs to seek or to avoid certain things not only because they are pleasing or otherwise to the senses, but also on account of other advantages and uses, or disadvantages; just as the sheep runs away when it sees an approaching wolf not on account of its colour or shape, but as a natural enemy; and again a bird gathers together straws, not because they are pleasant to the sense, but because they are useful for building its nest. Animals, therefore, need to perceive such intentions, which the exterior sense does not perceive. And some distinct principle is necessary for this, since the perception of sensible forms comes by a sensible change, which is not the case with the perception of the intentions spoken of.

Thus, therefore, for the reception of sensible forms, the "proper sense" and the "common sense" are appointed, and of their distinction we shall speak further on (Ans. 1, 2). But for the retention and preservation of these forms, the

---

[1] *Memory and Reminiscence,* 1 (450a10).
[2] Aristotle, *Posterior Analytics,* 1, 18 (81a38).
[3] PL 34, 458, 459, 474.
[4] (17va); also 1, 5 (5rb).

phantasy or imagination is appointed, which is as it were a storehouse of forms received through the senses. Furthermore, for the apprehension of intentions which are not received through the senses, the estimative power is appointed; and for the preservation of them, the memorative power, which is a storehouse of such intentions. A sign of this we have in the fact that the principle of memory in animals is found in some such intention, for instance, that something is harmful or otherwise. And the very notion of the past, which memory considers, is to be reckoned among these intentions.

Now, we must observe that as to sensible forms there is no difference between man and other animals; for they are similarly changed by the exterior sensible. But there is a difference as to the above intentions. For other animals perceive these intentions only by some natural instinct, but man perceives them by means of a kind of comparing. Therefore the power which in other animals is called the natural estimative, in man is called the cogitative, which by some sort of gathering together and comparison discovers these intentions.[1] Therefore it is also called "the particular reason," to which medical men assign a certain particular organ, namely, the middle part of the head;[2] for it compares individual intentions, just as the intellectual reason compares universal intentions. As to the memorative power, man has not only memory, as other animals have in the sudden recollection of the past, but also reminiscence, by syllogistically, as it were, seeking for a recollection of the past by the application of individual intentions.

Avicenna, however,[3] assigns between the estimative and the imaginative, a fifth power, which combines and divides imaginary forms; as when from the imaginary form of gold, and the imaginary form of a mountain, we compose the one form of a golden mountain, which we have never seen. But this operation is not to be found in animals other than man, in whom for this purpose the imaginative power suffices. To man also does Averroes attribute this action in his book *De sensu et sensibilibus.*[4]

So there is no need to assign more than four interior powers of the sensitive part—namely, the common sense, the imagination, and the estimative and memorative powers.

Reply Obj. 1. The interior sense is called common not by predication, as if it were a genus, but as the common root and principle of the exterior senses.

Reply Obj. 2. The proper sense judges of the proper sensible by discerning it from other things which come under the same sense; for instance, by discerning white from black or green. But neither sight nor taste can discern white from sweet, because what discerns between two things must know both. Therefore the discerning judgment must be assigned to the common sense, to which, as to a common term, all apprehensions of the senses must be referred, and by which, again, all the intentions of the senses are perceived; as when someone sees that he sees. For this cannot be done by the proper sense, which only knows the form of the sensible by which it is changed, in which change the action of sight is completed, and from which change follows another in the common sense which perceives the act of vision.

Reply Obj. 3. As one power arises from the soul by means of another, as we have seen above (Q. LXXVII, A. 7), so also the soul is the subject of one power through another. In this way the imagination and the memory are called passions of the "first sensitive."

Reply Obj. 4. Although the operation of the intellect has its origin in the senses, yet, in the thing apprehended through the senses, the intellect knows many things which the senses cannot perceive. In like manner does the estimative power, though in a less perfect manner.

Reply Obj. 5. The cogitative and memorative powers in man owe their excellence not to that which is proper to the sensitive part, but to a certain affinity and proximity to the universal reason, which, so to speak, overflows into them. Therefore they are not distinct powers, but the same, yet more perfect than in other animals.

Reply Obj. 6. Augustine calls that vision spiritual which is effected by the likenesses of bodies in the absence of bodies. Hence it is clear that it is common to all interior apprehensions.

---

[1] CP. Alexander of Hales, *Summa Theol.*, I–II, n. 357 (QR II, 434); Albert, *In De An.*, III, 2, 19 (BO V, 367). This doctrine is arabic in origin. Cf. Alfarabi, *Philosophische Abhandlungen* (DI 122.5); Averroes, *Colliget*, II, 20 (X, 30F).

[2] Avicenna, *De An.*, I, 5 (5rb); Averroes, *loc. cit.*; Alexander of Hales, *op. cit.*, I–II, n. 359 (QR II, 435).

[3] *De An.*, IV, 1 (17va).

[4] VI, 2 (16 I).

QUESTION LXXIX
OF THE INTELLECTUAL POWERS
(*In Thirteen Articles*)

THE next question concerns the intellectual powers, under which head there are thirteen points of inquiry: (1) Whether the intellect is a power of the soul, or its essence? (2) If it be a power, whether it is a passive power? (3) If it is a passive power, whether there is an agent intellect? (4) Whether it is something in the soul? (5) Whether the agent intellect is one in all? (6) Whether memory is in the intellect? (7) Whether the memory is distinct from the intellect? (8) Whether the reason is a distinct power from the intellect? (9) Whether the superior and inferior reason are distinct powers? (10) Whether the intelligence is a power distinct from the intellect? (11) Whether the speculative and practical intellect are different powers? (12) Whether *synderesis* is a power of the intellectual part? (13) Whether the conscience is a power of the intellectual part?

ARTICLE 1. *Whether the Intellect Is a Power of the Soul?*

We proceed thus to the First Article: It would seem that the intellect is not a power of the soul, but the essence of the soul.

Objection 1. For the intellect seems to be the same as the mind. Now the mind is not a power of the soul, but the essence, for Augustine says (*De Trin.* ix, 2):[1] "Mind and spirit are not relative things, but denominate the essence." Therefore the intellect is the essence of the soul.

Obj. 2. Further, different genera of the soul's powers are not united in some one power, but only in the essence of the soul. Now the appetitive and the intellectual are different genera of the soul's powers as the Philosopher says,[2] but they are united in the mind, for Augustine (*De Trin.* x, 11)[3] places the intelligence and will in the mind. Therefore the mind and intellect of man is the very essence of the soul and not one of its powers.

Obj. 3. Further, according to Gregory, in a homily for the Ascension (xxix. *in Ev.*),[4] "man understands with the angels." But angels are called Minds and Intellects. Therefore the mind and intellect of man are not a power of the soul, but the soul itself.

Obj. 4. Further, a substance is intellectual by the fact that it is immaterial. But the soul is immaterial through its essence. Therefore it seems that the soul must be intellectual through its essence.

On the contrary, The Philosopher assigns intellect as a power of the soul.[5]

I answer that, In accordance with what has been already shown (Q. LIV, A. 3; Q. LXXVII, A.

1) it is necessary to say that the intellect is a power of the soul, and not the very essence of the soul. For the essence of that which operates is the immediate principle of operation, only when operation itself is its being; for as power is related to operation as its act, so is essence to being. But the act of understanding is His very Being in God alone. Therefore in God alone is His intellect His essence, while in other intellectual creatures the intellect is a power.

Reply Obj. 1. Sense is sometimes taken for the power, and sometimes for the sensitive soul; for the sensitive soul takes its name from its chief power, which is sense. And in like manner the intellectual soul is sometimes called intellect, as from its chief power; and thus we read[6] that "the intellect is a substance." And in this sense also Augustine says that the mind is a species or essence (*De Trin.* ix, 2; xiv, 16).[7]

Reply Obj. 2. The appetitive and intellectual powers are different genera of powers in the soul by reason of the different natures of their objects. But the appetitive power agrees partly with the intellectual power and partly with the sensitive in its mode of operation either through a corporeal organ or without it; for appetite follows apprehension. And in this way Augustine puts the will in the mind, and the Philosopher, in the reason.[8]

Reply Obj. 3. In the angels there is no other power than the intellect, and the will, which follows the intellect. And for this reason an angel is called a Mind or an Intellect; because his whole power consists in this. But the soul has many other powers, such as the sensitive and nutritive powers, and therefore the comparison fails.

Reply Obj. 4. The immateriality of the created intelligent substance is not its intellect, but through its immateriality it has the power of understanding. Hence it follows not that the intellect is the substance of the soul, but that it is its virtue and power.

ARTICLE 2. *Whether the Intellect Is a Passive Power?*

We proceed thus to the Second Article: It would seem that the intellect is not a passive power.

Objection 1. For everything is passive by its matter, and acts by its form. But the intellectual power results from the immateriality of the in-

---

[1] PL 42, 962.   [2] *Soul,* II, 3 (414ᵃ31).
[3] PL 42, 983.   [4] PL 76, 1214.
[5] *Soul,* II, 3 (414ᵃ32).

[6] *Ibid.,* I, 4 (408ᵇ18).
[7] PL 42, 962, 1053.
[8] *Soul,* III, 9 (432ᵇ5).

telligent substance. Therefore it seems that the intellect is not a passive power.

Obj. 2. Further, the intellectual power is incorruptible, as we have said above (Q. LXXV, A. 6). But "if the intellect is passive, it is corruptible."[1] Therefore the intellectual power is not passive.

Obj. 3. Further, the "agent is nobler than the patient," as Augustine[2] and Aristotle[3] say. But all the powers of the vegetative part are active; yet they are the lowest among the powers of the soul. Much more, therefore, all the intellectual powers, which are the highest, are active.

On the contrary, The Philosopher says[4] that "to understand is in a way to be passive."

I answer that, To be passive may be taken in three ways. First, in its most strict sense, when from a thing is taken something which belongs to it by virtue either of its nature, or of its proper inclination, as when water loses coolness by heating, and as when a man becomes ill or sad. Secondly, less strictly, a thing is said to be passive when something, whether suitable or unsuitable, is taken away from it. And in this way not only he who is ill is said to be passive, but also he who is healed; not only he that is sad, but also he that is joyful, or whatever way he be altered or moved. Thirdly, in a wide sense a thing is said to be passive, from the very fact that what is in potency to something receives that to which it was in potency without being deprived of anything. And accordingly, whatever passes from potency to act may be said to be passive, even when it is perfected. And thus with us to understand is to be passive. This is clear from the following reason. For the intellect, as we have seen above (Q. LXXVIII, A. 1), has an operation extending to universal being. We may therefore see whether the intellect be in act or potency by observing first of all the nature of the relation of the intellect to universal being. For we find an intellect whose relation to universal being is that of the act of all being, and such is the Divine intellect, which is the Essence of God, in which originally and virtually, all being pre-exists as in its first cause. And therefore the Divine intellect is not in potency, but is pure act. But no created intellect can be an act in relation to the whole universal being; otherwise it would have to be an infinite being. Therefore no created intellect is the act of all things intelligible by reason of its very

being, but is compared to these intelligible things as a potency to act.

Now, potency has a twofold relation to act. There is a potency which is always perfected by its act; as the matter of the heavenly bodies (Q. LVIII, A. 1). And there is another potency which is not always in act, but proceeds from potency to act; as we observe in things that are corrupted and generated. Therefore the angelic intellect is always in act as regards those things which it can understand, by reason of its nearness to the first intellect, which is pure act, as we have said above. But the human intellect, which is the lowest in the order of intellects and the most removed from the perfection of the Divine intellect, is in potency with regard to things intelligible, and is at first "like a clean tablet on which nothing is written," as the Philosopher says.[5] This is made clear from the fact that at first we are only in potency to understand, and afterwards we are made to understand actually. And so it is evident that with us to understand is in a way to be passive, taking passion in the third sense. And consequently the intellect is a passive power.

Reply Obj. 1. This objection is verified of passion in the first and second senses, which belong to primary matter. But in the third sense passion is in anything which is reduced from potency to act.

Reply Obj. 2. Passive intellect is the name given by some[6] to the sensitive appetite, in which are the passions of the soul; which appetite is also called "rational by participation, because it obeys the reason."[7] Others[8] give the name of passive intellect to the cogitative power, which is called the particular reason. And in each case passive may be taken in the two first senses, according as this so-called intellect is the act of a corporeal organ. But the intellect which is in potency to things intelligible and which for this reason Aristotle calls "the possible intellect"[9] is not passive except in the third sense, for it is not an act of a corporeal organ. Hence it is incorruptible.

Reply Obj. 3. The agent is nobler than the patient if the action and the passion are referred to the same thing, but not always, if they refer to different things. Now the intellect is a passive power in regard to the whole universal being, while the vegetative power is active in regard to

---

[1] *Ibid.*, III, 4 (430ᵃ1).
[2] *Gen. ad lit.*, XII, 16 (PL 34, 467).
[3] *Soul*, III, 5 (430ᵃ18).
[4] *Ibid.*, III, 4 (429ᵇ24).

[5] *Ibid.*, III, 4 (430ᵃ1).
[6] Themistius, *In De An.*, III, v (CG v 101.5); cf. Averroes, *In de An.*, III, 20 (VI, 2–163E).
[7] Aristotle, *Ethics*, I, 13 (1102ᵇ25).
[8] Cf. Averroes, *In de An.*, III, 20 (VI, 2–164c).
[9] *Soul*, III, 4 (429ᵃ22).

some particular thing, namely, the body as united to the soul. Therefore nothing prevents such a passive force being nobler than such an active one.

ARTICLE 3. *Whether There Is an Agent Intellect?*

We proceed thus to the Third Article: It would seem that there is no agent intellect.

Objection 1. For as the senses are to things sensible, so is our intellect to things intelligible. But because sense is in potency to things sensible we do not say there is "an agent sense," but only a passive sense. Therefore, since our intellect is in potency to things intelligible, it seems that we cannot say that there is an agent intellect, but only a possible intellect.[1]

Obj. 2. Further, if we say that also in the senses there is something active, such as light,[2] on the contrary, light is required for sight, in so far as it makes the medium to be actually luminous; for colour of its own nature moves the luminous medium. But in the operation of the intellect there is no medium that has to be brought into act. Therefore there is no necessity for an agent intellect.

Obj. 3. Further, the likeness of the agent is received into the patient according to the mode of the patient. But the possible intellect is an immaterial power. Therefore its immateriality suffices for forms to be received into it immaterially. Now a form is intelligible in act from the very fact that it is immaterial. Therefore there is no need to posit an agent intellect to make the species actually intelligible.[3]

On the contrary, The Philosopher says,[4] "As in every nature, so in the soul is there something by which it becomes all things, and something by which it makes all things." Therefore we must admit an agent intellect.

I answer that, According to the opinion of Plato, there is no need for an agent intellect in order to make things actually intelligible, although perhaps in order to provide intellectual light to the intellect, as will be explained further on (A. 4, Q. LXXXIV, A. 6). For Plato supposed[5] that the forms of natural things subsisted apart from matter, and consequently that they are intelligible, since a thing is actually intelligible from the very fact that it is immaterial. And he called such forms "species" or "ideas," from a

participation of which he said that even corporeal matter was formed, in order that individuals might be naturally established in their proper genera and species,[6] and that our intellect was formed by such participation in order to have knowledge of the genera and species of things.[7] But since Aristotle did not allow that forms of natural things subsist apart from matter,[8] and as forms existing in matter are not actually intelligible, it follows that the natures or forms of the sensible things which we understand are not actually intelligible. Now nothing is reduced from potency to act except by something in act; just as the senses are made actual by what is actually sensible. We must therefore assign on the part of the intellect some power to make things actually intelligible, by the abstraction of the species from material conditions. And such is the necessity for positing an agent intellect.

Reply Obj. 1. Sensible things are found in act outside the soul, and hence there is no need for an agent sense. And thus it is clear that in the nutritive part all the powers are active, whereas in the sensitive part all are passive; but in the intellectual part, there is something active and something passive.

Reply Obj. 2. There are two opinions as to the effect of light. For some say[9] that light is required for sight, in order to make colours actually visible. And according to this the agent intellect is required for understanding, in like manner and for the same reason as light is required for seeing. But in the opinion of others, light is required for sight "not for the colours to become actually visible, but in order that the medium may become actually luminous," as the Commentator says.[10] And according to this, Aristotle's comparison of the agent intellect to light[11] is verified in this, that as it is required for understanding, so is light required for seeing; but not for the same reason.

Reply Obj. 3. Given the agent, it may well happen that its likeness is received variously into various things, on account of their dispositions. But if the agent does not pre-exist, the disposition of the recipient has nothing to do with the matter. Now the intelligible in act is not something existing in nature, if we consider the

---

[1] An argument of William of Paris, *De An.,* 7, 4 (II, 207). See Gilson, AHDLM (1926) p. 59.

[2] William of Paris, *loc. cit.;* Gilson, *op. cit.,* p. 60.

[3] William of Paris, *op. cit.,* 7, 5 (II, 210); Gilson, *op. cit.,* p. 61.

[4] *Soul,* III, 5 (430ª10).   [5] See above, Q. VI, A. 4.

[6] Cf. Aristotle, *Metaphysics* I, 9 (991ᵇ3); *Phaedo* (100). See also above, Q. X, A. 3.

[7] See below, Q. LXXXIV, AA. 1, 4.

[8] Cf. *Metaphysics,* III, 4 (999ᵇ18); VIII, 3 (1043ᵇ19).

[9] Avempace, according to Averroes, *In de An.,* II, 67 (VI, 2–84E).

[10] *In de An.,* II, comm. 67 (VI, 2–84E).

[11] *Soul,* III, 5 (430ª15); cf. Averroes, *op. cit.*

nature of things sensible, which do not subsist apart from matter. And therefore in order to understand them, the immaterial nature of the possible intellect would not suffice but for the presence of the agent intellect, which makes things actually intelligible by way of abstraction.

ARTICLE 4. *Whether the Agent Intellect Is Something in the Soul?*

We proceed thus to the Fourth Article: It would seem that the agent intellect is not something in the soul.

Objection 1. For the effect of the agent intellect is to give light for the purpose of understanding. But this is done by something higher than the soul, according to John 1. 9, *He was the true light that enlighteneth every man coming into this world.* Therefore the agent intellect is not something in the soul.[1]

Obj. 2. Further, the Philosopher says[2] of the agent intellect, "that is does not sometimes understand and sometimes not understand." But our soul does not always understand: sometimes it understands, and sometimes it does not understand. Therefore the agent intellect is not something in our soul.[3]

Obj. 3. Further, agent and patient suffice for action. If, therefore, the possible intellect, which is a passive power, is something belonging to the soul; and also the agent intellect, which is an active power, it follows that man would always be able to understand when he wished, which is clearly false. Therefore the agent intellect is not something in our soul.[4]

Obj. 4. Further, the Philosopher says[5] that "the agent intellect is a substance in actual being." But nothing can be in potency and in act with regard to the same thing. If, therefore, the possible intellect, which is in potency to all things intelligible, is something in the soul, it seems impossible for the agent intellect to be also something in our soul.

Obj. 5. Further, if the agent intellect is something in the soul, it must be a power. For it is neither a passion nor a habit, since habits and passions do not have the character of agents in regard to the passivity of the soul, but rather passion is the very action of the passive power, while habit is something which results from acts. But every power flows from the essence of the soul. It would therefore follow that the agent intellect flows from the essence of the soul. And thus it would not be in the soul by way of participation from some higher intellect, which is unfitting. Therefore the agent intellect is not something in our soul.

On the contrary, The Philosopher says[6] that it is necessary for these differences, namely, the possible and agent intellect, to be in the soul.

I answer that, The agent intellect, of which the Philosopher speaks, is something in the soul. In order to make this evident, we must observe that above the intellectual soul of man we must suppose a superior intellect, from which the soul acquires the power of understanding. For what is such by participation, and what is subject to motion, and what is imperfect always requires the pre-existence of something essentially such, immovable and perfect. Now the human soul is called intellectual by reason of a participation in intellectual power, a sign of which is that it is not wholly intellectual but only in part. Moreover it reaches to the understanding of truth by arguing, with a kind of reasoning and movement. Again it has an imperfect understanding, both because it does not understand everything, and because, in those things which it does understand, it passes from potency to act. Therefore there must be some higher intellect, by which the soul is helped to understand.

Therefore some held[7] that this intellect, substantially separate, is the agent intellect, which by lighting up the phantasms as it were, makes them to be actually intelligible. But, even supposing the existence of such a separate agent intellect, it would still be necessary to assign to the human soul some power participating in that superior intellect, by which power the human soul makes things actually intelligible. Just as in other perfect natural things, besides the universal active causes, each one is endowed with its proper powers derived from those universal causes; for the sun alone does not generate man, but in man is the power of begetting man, and in like manner with other perfect animals. Now among these lower things nothing is more perfect than the human soul. Therefore we must say that in the soul is some power derived from a higher intellect, whereby it is able to light up the phantasms.

---

[1] An argument of William of Paris, *De An.*, 7, 6 (II, 211). See Gilson, AHDLM (1926) p. 63.

[2] *Soul*, III, 5 (430ª22).

[3] Cf. William of Paris, *op. cit.*, 7, 3 (II, 206); Gilson, *loc. cit.*

[4] Cf. William of Paris, *op. cit.*, 7, 4 (II, 208); Gilson, *op. cit.*, p. 64.

[5] *Soul*, III, 5 (430ª18).

[6] *Ibid.*, (430ª13).

[7] Alexander of Aphrodisias, *De intellectu et Intellecto* (TH 76); Averroes, *In de An.*, III, 18 (VI, 161E); 19 (VI, 162A); Avicenna, *De An.*, V, 5 (25rb); *Meta.*, IX, 3 (104rb). For William of Paris, Roger Bacon, John Peckham, and others on this point, cf. Gilson, AHDLM (1926), p. 80.

And we know this by experience, since we perceive that we abstract universal forms from their particular conditions, which is to make them actually intelligible. Now no action belongs to anything except through some principle formally inherent in it, as we have said above of the potential intellect (Q. LXXVI, A. 1). Therefore the power which is the principle of this action must be something in the soul. For this reason Aristotle compared[1] the agent intellect to light, which is something received into the air, while Plato compared the separate intellect impressing the soul to the sun, as Themistius says in his commentary on the third book of the *Soul*.[2]

But the separate intellect, according to the teaching of our faith, is God Himself, Who is the soul's Creator, and only happiness, as will be shown later on (Q. XC, A. 3; Part I.-II., Q. III, A. 7).And so the human soul derives its intellectual light from Him, according to Ps. 4. 7, *The light of Thy countenance, O Lord, is signed upon us.*

Reply Obj. 1. That true light enlightens as a universal cause, from which the human soul derives a particular power, as we have explained.

Reply Obj. 2. The Philosopher says those words not of the agent intellect, but of the intellect in act, of which he had already said: "Knowledge in act is the same as the thing." Or, if we refer those words to the agent intellect, then they are said because it is not owing to the agent intellect that sometimes we do, and sometimes we do not understand, but to the intellect which is in potency.

Reply Obj. 3. If the relation of the agent intellect to the possible intellect were that of the active object to a power, as, for instance, of the visible in act to the sight, it would follow that we could understand all things instantly, since the agent intellect is that which makes all things in act. But the agent intellect is not like an object, rather is it that whereby the objects are made to be in act, for which, besides the presence of the agent intellect, we require the presence of phantasms, the good disposition of the sensitive powers, and practice in this sort of operation, since through one thing understood, other things come to be understood, as from terms are made propositions, and from first principles, conclusions. From this point of view it matters not whether the agent intellect is something belonging to the soul, or something separate from the soul.

Reply Obj. 4. The intellectual soul is indeed

actually immaterial, but it is in potency to determinate species of things. On the other hand, though, phantasms are actual likenesses of certain species, but are immaterial in potency. And so nothing prevents one and the same soul, in so far as it is actually immaterial, having one power by which it makes things actually immaterial by abstraction from the conditions of individual matter, which power is called the agent intellect; and another power, receptive of such species, which is called the possible intellect by reason of its being in potency to such species.

Reply Obj. 5. Since the essence of the soul is immaterial, created by the supreme intellect, nothing prevents that power which it participates from the supreme intellect, and whereby it abstracts from matter, flowing from the essence of the soul, in the same way as its other powers.

ARTICLE 5. *Whether the Agent Intellect Is One in All?*

We proceed thus to the Fifth Article: It would seem that there is one agent intellect in all.

Objection 1. For what is separate from the body is not multiplied according to the number of bodies. But "the agent intellect is separate," as the Philosopher says.[3] Therefore it is not multiplied in the many human bodies, but is one for all men.

Obj. 2. Further, the agent intellect is the cause of the universal, which is one in many. But that which is the cause of unity is still more itself one. Therefore the agent intellect is the same in all.

Obj. 3. Further, all men agree in the first intellectual concepts. But to these they assent by the agent intellect. Therefore all agree in one agent intellect.

On the contrary, The Philosopher says[4] that "the agent intellect is as a light." But light is not the same in the various things enlightened. Therefore the same agent intellect is not in various men.

I answer that, The truth about this question depends on what we have already said (A. 4). For if the agent intellect were not something belonging to the soul, but were some separate substance, there would be one agent intellect for all men. And this is what they mean who hold that there is one agent intellect for all.[5] But if the agent intellect is something belonging to the soul, as one of its powers, we are bound to say

---

[1] *Soul,* III, 5 (430ª15).
[2] CG V, 3–103.35; *Republic* (508).

[3] *Soul,* III, 5 (430ª17).
[4] *Ibid.* (430ª15).
[5] See above, A. 4.

that there are as many agent intellects as there are souls, which are multiplied according to the number of men, as we have said above (Q. LXXVI, A. 2). For it is impossible that one same power belong to various substances.

Reply Obj. 1. The Philosopher proves that the agent intellect is separate by the fact that the possible intellect is separate; because, as he says,[1] "the agent is more noble than the patient." Now the possible intellect is said to be separate because it is not the act of any corporeal organ. And in the same sense the agent intellect is also called separate; but not as a separate substance.

Reply Obj. 2. The agent intellect is the cause of the universal, by abstracting it from matter. But for this purpose it need not be the same intellect in all intelligent beings; but it must be one in its relationship to all those things from which it abstracts the universal, with respect to which things the universal is one. And this befits the agent intellect since it is immaterial.

Reply Obj. 3. All things which are of one species enjoy in common the action which accompanies the nature of the species, and consequently the power which is the principle of such action, but not in such a way that that power is identical in all. Now to know the first intelligible principles is the action belonging to the human species. And so all men must enjoy in common the power which is the principle of this action, and this power is the agent intellect. But there is no need for it to be identical in all. Yet it must be derived by all from one principle. And thus the possession by all men in common of the first principles proves the unity of the separate intellect, which Plato compares to the sun, but not the unity of the agent intellect, which Aristotle compares to light.

ARTICLE 6. *Whether Memory Is In the Intellectual Part of the Soul?*

We proceed thus to the Sixth Article: It would seem that memory is not in the intellectual part of the soul.

Objection 1. For Augustine says (*De Trin.* xii, 2, 8)[2] that to the higher part of the soul belong those things "which are not common to man and beast." But memory is common to man and beast, for he says (*ibid.* 2) that "beasts can sense corporeal things through the senses of the body, and commit them to memory." Therefore memory does not belong to the intellectual part of the soul.

Obj. 2. Further, memory is of the past. But

[1] *Soul*, III, 5 (430ª18).   [2] PL 42, 999, 1005.

the past is said of something with regard to a fixed time. Memory, therefore, knows a thing under a condition of a fixed time, which involves knowledge under the conditions of *here* and *now*. But this is not the province of the intellect, but of the sense. Therefore memory is not in the intellectual part, but only in the sensitive part.

Obj. 3. Further, in the memory are preserved the species of those things of which we are not actually thinking. But this cannot happen in the intellect, because the intellect is reduced to act by the fact that it is informed by the intelligible species. Now the intellect in act implies understanding in act. and therefore the intellect actually understands all things of which it has the species. Therefore the memory is not in the intellectual part.

On the contrary, Augustine says (*De Trin.* x, 11)[3] that "memory, understanding, and will are one mind."

I answer that, Since it is of the nature of the memory to preserve the species of those things which are not actually apprehended, we must first of all consider whether the intelligible species can thus be preserved in the intellect, because Avicenna held that this was impossible.[4] For he admitted that this could happen in the sensitive part, as to some powers, since they are acts of corporeal organs, in which certain species may be preserved apart from actual apprehension. But in the intellect, which has no corporeal organ, nothing but what is intelligible exists. And so every thing of which the likeness exists in the intellect must be actually understood. Thus, therefore, according to him, as soon as we cease to understand something actually, the species of that thing ceases to be in our intellect, and if we wish to understand that thing anew, we must turn to the agent intellect, which he held to be a separate substance, in order that the intelligible species may thence flow again into our possible intellect. And from the practice and habit of turning to the agent intellect there is formed, according to him, a certain aptitude in the possible intellect for turning to the agent intellect, which aptitude he calls the habit of science. According, therefore, to this supposition, nothing is preserved in the intellectual part that is not actually understood, and so it would not be possible to admit memory in the intellectual part.

But this opinion is clearly opposed to the teaching of Aristotle. For he says[5] that, "when the possible intellect is identified with each thing

[3] PL 42, 983.   [4] *De An.,* v, 6 (26rb).
[5] *Soul*, III, 4 (429ᵇ5).

as knowing it, it is said to be in act," and that "this happens when it can operate of itself. And, even then, it is in potency, but not absolutely, as before learning and discovering." Now, the possible intellect is said to be each thing inasmuch as it receives the intelligible species of each thing. To the fact, therefore, that it receives the species of intelligible things it owes its being able to operate when it wills, but not so that it be always operating; for even then is it in potency in a certain sense, though otherwise than before the act of understanding—namely, in the sense that whoever has habitual knowledge is in potency to actual consideration.

The foregoing opinion is also opposed to reason. For what is received into something is received according to the mode of the recipient. But the intellect is of a more stable nature, and is more immovable than corporeal matter. If, therefore, corporeal matter holds the forms which it receives, not only while it actually does something through them, but also after ceasing to act through them, much more does the intellect receive the species unchangeably and lastingly, whether it receive them from things sensible or derive them from some superior intellect. Thus, therefore, if we take memory only for the power of retaining species, we must say that it is in the intellectual part.

But if in the notion of memory we include its object as something past, then the memory is not in the intellectual, but only in the sensitive part, which apprehends individual things. For past, as past, since it signifies being under a condition of fixed time, is something individual.

Reply Obj. 1. Memory, if considered as retentive of species, is not common to us and other animals. For species are not retained in the sensitive part of the soul only, but rather in the body and soul united, since the memorative power is the act of some organ. But the intellect in itself is retentive of species, apart from the association of any corporeal organ. And so the Philosopher says[1] that "the soul is the seat of the species, not the whole soul, but the intellect."

Reply Obj. 2. The condition of past may be referred to two things—namely, to the object which is known, and to the act of knowledge. These two are found together in the sensitive part, which apprehends something from the fact of its being changed by a present sensible; and so at the same time an animal remembers to have sensed before in the past, and to have sensed some past sensible thing. But as concerns the intellectual part, the past is acidental, and

[1] *Soul*, III, 4 (429ᵃ27).

is not in itself a part of the object of the intellect. For the intellect understands man, as man; and to man, as man, it is accidental that he exist in the present, past, or future. But on the part of the act, the condition of past, even as such, may be understood to be in the intellect, as well as in the senses. Because our soul's act of understanding is an individual act, existing in this or that time, according as a man is said to understand now, or yesterday, or tomorrow. And this is not incompatible with the intellectual nature, for such an act of understanding, though something individual, is yet an immaterial act, as we have said above of the intellect (Q. LXXVI, A. 1); and therefore, as the intellect understands itself, though it be itself an individual intellect, so also it understands its act of understanding, which is an individual act, in the past, present, or future. In this way, then, the notion of memory, in as far as it regards past events, is preserved in the intellect, according as it understands that it previously understood; but not in the sense that it understands the past as something *here* and *now*.

Reply Obj. 3. The intelligible species are sometimes in the intellect only in potency, and then the intellect is said to be in potency. Sometimes the intelligible species is in the intellect as regards the ultimate completion of the act, and then it understands in act. And sometimes the intelligible species is in a middle state, between potency and act, and then we have habitual knowledge. In this way the intellect retains the species even when it does not understand in act.

ARTICLE 7. *Whether the Intellectual Memory Is a Power Distinct From the Intellect?*

We proceed thus to the Seventh Article: It would seem that the intellectual memory is distinct from the intellect.

Objection 1. For Augustine (*De Trin.* x, 11)[2] assigns to the mind memory, understanding, and will. But it is clear that the memory is a distinct power from the will. Therefore it is also distinct from the intellect.

Obj. 2. Further, the reason of distinction among the powers in the sensitive part is the same as in the intellectual part. But memory in the sensitive part is distinct from sense, as we have said (Q. LXXVIII, A. 4). Therefore memory in the intellectual part is distinct from the intellect.

Obj. 3. Further, according to Augustine (*De Trin.* x, 11; xi, 7),[3] memory, understanding, and

[2] PL 42, 983; cf. XIV, 7 (1043).
[3] PL 42, 983, 993.

will are equal to one another, and one arises from the other. But this could not be if memory and intellect were the same power. Therefore they are not the same power.

On the contrary, From its nature the memory is the treasury or storehouse of species. But the Philosopher[1] attributes this to the intellect, as we have said (A. 6 Ans. 1). Therefore the memory is not another power from the intellect.

I answer that, As has been said above (Q. LXXXVII, A. 3), the powers of the soul are distinguished by the different aspects of their objects, since each power is defined in reference to that thing to which it is directed and which is its object. It has also been said above (Q. LIX, A. 4) that if any power by its nature be directed to an object according to the common aspect of the object, that power will not be differentiated according to the individual differences of that object; just as the power of sight, which regards its object under the common aspect of colour is not differentiated by differences of black and white. Now, the intellect regards its object under the common aspect of being, since the possible intellect is that which becomes all things. And so the possible intellect is not differentiated by any difference of being. Nevertheless there is a distinction between the power of the agent intellect and of the possible intellect, because as regards the same object, the active power which makes the object to be in act must be distinct from the passive power, which is moved by the object existing in act. Thus the active power is compared to its object as a being in act is to a being in potency, whereas the passive power, on the contrary, is compared to its cbject as a being in potency is to a being in act.

Therefore there can be no other difference of powers in the intellect, but that of possible and agent. And so it is clear that memory is not a distinct power from the intellect, for it belongs to the nature of a passive power to retain as well as to receive.

Reply Obj. 1. Although it is said (3 *Sent.,* D, 1) that memory, intellect, and will are three powers, this is not in accordance with the meaning of Augustine, who says expressly (*De Trin.* xiv)[2] that "if we take memory, intelligence, and will as always present in the soul, whether we actually reflect upon them or not, they seem to pertain to the memory only. And by intelligence I mean that by which we understand when ac-

tually thinking; and by will I mean that love or affection which unites the child and its parent." From this it is clear that Augustine does not take the above three for three powers, but by memory he understands the soul's habit of retention, by intelligence, the act of the intellect, and by will the act of the will.

Reply Obj. 2. Past and present may differentiate the sensitive powers, but not the intellectual powers, for the reason given above.

Reply Obj. 3. Intelligence arises from memory, just as act from habit; and in this way it is equal to it, but not as a power to a power.

ARTICLE 8. *Whether the Reason Is a Power Distinct From the Intellect?*

We proceed thus to the Eighth Article: It would seem that the reason is a power distinct from the intellect.

Objection 1. For it is stated in *De Spiritu et Anima*[3] that "when we wish to rise from lower things to higher, first the sense comes to our aid, then imagination, then reason, then the intellect." Therefore the reason is distinct from the intellect, just as imagination is from sense.

Obj. 2. Further, Boëthius says (*De Consol.* iv, 6),[4] that intellect is compared to reason, as eternity to time. But it does not pertain to the same power to be in eternity and to be in time. Therefore reason and intellect are not the same power.

Obj. 3. Further, man has intellect in common with the angels, and sense in common with the brutes. But reason, which is proper to man, from which he is called a rational animal, is a power distinct from sense. Therefore is it equally true to say that it is distinct from the intellect, which properly belongs to the angel. Hence they are called intellectual.

On the contrary, Augustine says (*Gen. ad lit.* iii, 20)[5] that "that in which man excels irrational animals is reason, or mind, or intelligence, or whatever appropriate name we like to give it." Therefore reason, intellect, and mind are one power.

I answer that, Reason and intellect in man cannot be distinct powers. We shall understand this clearly if we consider their respective actions. For to understand is simply to apprehend intelligible truth, and to reason is to advance from one thing understood to another, so as to know an intelligible truth. And therefore angels

---

[1] *Soul,* III, 4 (429[a]27).
[2] Chap. 7 (PL 42, 1043).

[3] Pseudo-Augustine (Alcher of Clairvaux). Chap. 11 (PL 40, 780).
[4] PL 63, 818.
[5] PL 34, 292.

who, according to their nature, possess perfect knowledge of intelligible truth, have no need to advance from one thing to another, but apprehend the truth simply and without mental discursion, as Dionysius says (*Div. Nom.* vii).[1] But man arrives at the knowledge of intelligible truth by advancing from one thing to another, and therefore he is called rational. Reasoning, therefore, is compared to understanding as movement is to rest, or acquisition to possession, of which one belongs to the perfect, the other to the imperfect. And since movement always proceeds from something immovable and ends in something at rest, hence it is that human reasoning, by way of inquiry and discovery, advances from certain things simply understood— namely, the first principles; and, again, by way of judgment returns by analysis to first principles, in the light of which it examines what it has found. Now it is clear that rest and movement are not to be referred to different powers, but to one and the same, even in natural things, since by the same nature a thing is moved towards a certain place, and rests in that place. Much more, therefore, by the same power do we understand and reason. And so it is clear that in man reason and intellect are the same power.

Reply Obj. 1. That enumeration is made according to the order of actions, not according to the distinction of powers. Moreover, that book is not of great authority.

Reply Obj. 2. The answer is clear from what we have said. For eternity is compared to time as immovable to movable. And thus Boëthius compared the intellect to eternity, and reason to time.

Reply Obj. 3. Other animals are so much lower than man that they cannot attain to the knowledge of truth, which reason seeks. But man attains, although imperfectly, to the knowledge of intelligible truth, which angels know. Therefore in the angels the power of knowledge is not of a different genus from that which is in the human reason, but is compared to it as the perfect to the imperfect.

ARTICLE 9. *Whether the Higher and Lower Reason Are Distinct Powers?*

We proceed thus to the Ninth Article: It would seem that the higher and lower reason are distinct powers.

Objection 1. For Augustine says (*De Trin.* xii, 4),[2] that the image of the Trinity is in the higher part of the reason, and not in the lower.

But the parts of the soul are its powers. Therefore the higher and lower reason are two powers.

Obj. 2. Further, nothing arises from itself. Now, the lower reason arises from the higher, and is ruled and directed by it. Therefore the higher reason is another power from the lower.

Obj. 3. Further, the Philosopher says[3] that the scientific part of the soul, by which the soul knows necessary things, is another principle, and another part from the opinionative and reasoning part by which it knows contingent things. And he proves this from the principle that "for those things which are generically different, generically different parts of the soul are ordained." Now contingent and necessary are generically different, as corruptible and incorruptible. Since, therefore, necessary is the same as eternal, and temporal the same as contingent, it seems that what the Philosopher calls the scientific part must be the same as the higher reason, which, according to Augustine[4] is intent on "the consideration and consultation of things eternal"; and that what the Philosopher calls the reasoning or opinionative part is the same as the lower reason, which, according to Augustine, is intent on the disposal of temporal things. Therefore the higher reason is another power than the lower.

Obj. 4. Further, Damascene says (*De Fid. Orth.* ii)[5] that "opinion rises from imagination; then the mind by judging of the truth or error of the opinion discerns the truth; whence *mens* (mind) is derived from *metiendo* (measuring). And therefore the intellect regards those things which are already subject to judgment and true decision." Therefore the opinionative power, which is the lower reason, is distinct from the mind and the intellect, by which we may understand the higher reason.

On the contrary, Augustine says (*De Trin.* xii, 4)[6] that the higher and lower reason are only distinct by their functions. Therefore they are not two powers.

I answer that, The higher and lower reason, as they are understood by Augustine, can in no way be two powers of the soul. For he says that the higher reason is "that which is intent on the contemplation and consultation of things eternal,"[7] since in contemplation it sees them in themselves, and in consultation it takes its rules of action from them. But he calls the lower reason "that which is intent on the disposal of

[3] *Ethics,* VI, 1 (1139ᵃ6).
[4] *De Trin.,* XII, 7 (PL 42, 1005).
[5] Chap. 22 (PG 94, 941).
[6] PL 42, 1000.
[7] *Op. cit.,* XII, 7 (PL 42, 1005).

[1] Sect. 2 (PG 3, 868).
[2] PL 42, 1000.

temporal things." Now these two—namely, eternal and temporal—are related to our knowledge in this way, that one of them is the means of knowing the other. For by way of discovery we come through knowledge of temporal things to that of things eternal, according to the words of the Apostle (Rom. i. 20), *The invisible things of God are clearly seen, being understood by the things that are made;* while by way of judgment, from eternal things already known, we judge of temporal things, and according to rules of things eternal we dispose of temporal things.

But it may happen that the medium and what is attained thereby belong to different habits, just as the first indemonstrable principles belong to the habit of intellect, whereas the conclusions which we draw from them belong to the habit of science. And so it happens that from the principles of geometry we draw a conclusion in another science—for example, perspective. But both medium and term pertain to the same power of reason. For the act of the reason is, as it were, a movement from one thing to another. But the same movable thing passes through the medium and reaches the end. And hence the higher and lower reasons are one and the same power. But according to Augustine[1] they are distinguished by the functions of their actions, and according to their various habits, for wisdom is attributed to the higher reason, science to the lower.

Reply Obj. 1. We can speak of parts, in whatever way a thing is divided. And so far as reason is divided according to its various acts, the higher and lower reason are called parts; but not because they are different powers.

Reply Obj. 2. The lower reason is said to flow from the higher, or to be ruled by it, in so far as the principles made use of by the lower reason are drawn from and directed by the principles of the higher reason.

Reply Obj. 3. The scientific part, of which the Philosopher speaks, is not the same as the higher reason, for necessary truths are found even among temporal things, of which natural science and mathematics treat. And the opinionative and ratiocinative part is more limited than the lower reason, for it regards only things contingent. Neither must we say, without any qualification, that a power by which the intellect knows necessary things is distinct from a power by which it knows contingent things, because it knows both under the same objective aspect—namely, under the aspect of being and

truth. Thus it perfectly knows necessary things, which have perfect being in truth, since it penetrates to their very quiddity, from which it demonstrates their proper accidents. On the other hand, it knows contingent things, but imperfectly, just as they have but imperfect being and truth. Now perfect and imperfect in the action do not vary the power, but they vary the actions as to the mode of acting, and consequently the principles of the actions and the habits themselves. And therefore the Philosopher postulates two lesser parts of the soul—namely, the scientific and the ratiocinative, not because they are two powers, but because they are distinct according to a different aptitude for receiving various habits, concerning the variety of which he inquires. For contingent and necessary, though differing according to their proper genera, nevertheless agree in the common aspect of being, which the intellect considers, and to which they are variously compared as perfect and imperfect.

Reply Obj. 4. That distinction given by Damascene is according to the variety of acts, not according to the variety of powers. For opinion signifies an act of the intellect which leans to one side of a contradiction, though with fear of the other. But to judge or measure (*mensurare*) is an act of the intellect applying principles which are certain to examine propositions. From this is taken the word *mens* (mind). Lastly, to understand is to adhere to the formed judgment with approval.

ARTICLE 10. *Whether Intelligence Is a Power Distinct From Intellect?*

We proceed thus to the Tenth Article: It would seem that the intelligence is another power than the intellect.

Objection 1. For we read in *De Spiritu et Anima*[2] that "when we rise from lower to higher things, first the sense comes to our aid, then imagination, then reason, then intellect, and afterwards intelligence." But imagination and sense are distinct powers. Therefore also intellect and intelligence are distinct.

Obj. 2. Further, Boëthius says (*De Consol.* v, 4)[3] that "sense considers man in one way, imagination in another, reason in another, intelligence in another." But intellect is the same power as reason. Therefore, it seems, intelligence is a distinct power from intellect, as reason is a distinct power from imagination or sense.

---

[1] *Op. cit.,* XII, 4, 14 (PL 42, 1000, 1009).

[2] Pseudo-Augustine. (Alcher of Clairvaux) chap. 11 (PL 40, 780).

[3] PL 63, 849.

Obj. 3. Further, "actions come before powers," as the Philosopher says.[1] But intelligence is an act separate from others attributed to the intellect. For Damascene says (*De Fid. Orth.* ii)[2] that "the first movement is called intelligence; but that intelligence which is about a certain thing is called intention; that which remains and conforms the soul to that which is understood is called cogitation, and cogitation when it remains in the same man, examining and judging of itself, is called phronesis (that is, wisdom), and phronesis if dilated makes thought, that is, orderly internal speech; from which, they say, comes speech expressed by the tongue." Therefore it seems that intelligence is some special power.

On the contrary, The Philosopher says[3] that "intelligence is of indivisible things in which there is nothing false." But the knowledge of these things belongs to the intellect. Therefore the intelligence is not another power than the intellect.

I answer that, This word intelligence properly signifies the intellect's very act, which is to understand. However, in some works translated from the Arabic, the separate substances[4] which we call angels are called Intelligences, and perhaps for this reason, that such substances are always actually understanding. But in works translated from the Greek,[5] they are called Intellects or Minds. Thus intelligence is not distinct from intellect, as power is from power, but as act is from power. And such a division is recognized even by the philosophers.[6] For sometimes they assign four intellects—namely, the agent and possible intellects, the intellect in habit, and the actual intellect. Of these four the agent and possible intellects are different powers, just as in all things the active power is distinct from the passive. But three of these are distinguished as three states of the possible intellect, which is sometimes in potency only, and thus it is called possible; sometimes it is in the first act, which is knowledge, and thus it is called intellect in habit; and sometimes

it is in the second act, which is to consider, and thus it is called intellect in act, or actual intellect.

Reply Obj. 1. If this authority is accepted, intelligence there means the act of the intellect. And thus it is divided against intellect as act against power.

Reply Obj. 2. Boëthius takes intelligence as meaning that act of the intellect which transcends the act of the reason. And so he also says that reason alone belongs to the human race, as intelligence alone belongs to God, for it belongs to God to understand all things without any investigation.

Reply Obj. 3. All those acts which Damascene enumerates belong to one power—namely, the intellectual power. For this power first of all apprehends something absolutely; and this act is called intelligence. Secondly, it directs what it apprehends to the knowledge of something else, or to some operation; and this is called intention. And when it goes on in search of what it intends, it is called cogitation. When, by reference to something known for certain, it examines what it has cogitated, it is said to know or to be wise, which belongs to phronesis or wisdom; for "it belongs to the wise man to judge," as the Philosopher says.[7] And when once it has obtained something for certain, as being fully examined, it thinks about the means of making it known to others; and this is the ordering of interior speech, from which proceeds external speech. For not every difference of acts makes the powers vary, but only what cannot be reduced to the one same principle, as we have said above (Q. LXXVIII, A. 4).

ARTICLE 11. *Whether the Speculative and Practical Intellects Are Distinct Powers?*

We proceed thus to the Eleventh Article: It would seem that the speculative and practical intellects are distinct powers.

Objection. 1. For the apprehensive and moving are different kinds of powers, as is clear from the book on the *Soul.*[8] But the speculative intellect is merely an apprehensive power, while the practical intellect is a moving power. Therefore they are distinct powers.

Obj. 2. Further, the different nature of the object differentiates the power. But the object of the speculative intellect is truth, and of the practical is good, which differ in nature. Therefore the speculative and practical intellect are distinct powers.

---

[1] *Soul,* II, 4 (415ᵃ18).

[2] Chap. 22 (PG 94, 941).

[3] *Soul,* III, 6 (430ᵃ26).

[4] Cf. Avicenna, *Meta.,* X, 1 (107va); Averroes. *Destruct. Destruct.,* disp. 16 (IX, 122F). Also Maimonides, *Guide,* II, 6 (FR 160).

[5] In Dionysius. See above, Q. LIV, A. 3, Ans. I.

[6] Albert the Great, *Summa de Creatur.,* pt. II, Q. 54, A. 1 (BO XXV, 449), attributes this division to Algazel and Avicenna. Cf. Alexander of Aphrodisias, *De Intellectu et Intellecto* (TH 74); Alfarabi, *De Intellectu et Intellecto* (GI 117.82); Avicenna, *De An.,* I, 5 (5vb); cf. Gilson, AHDLM (1929), p. 7; p. 53.

[7] *Metaphysics,* I, 2 (982ᵃ18).

[8] Aristotle, II, 3 (414ᵃ31).

Obj. 3. Further, in the intellectual part, the practical intellect is compared to the speculative, as the estimative is to the imaginative power in the sensitive part. But the estimative differs from the imaginative as power from power, as we have said above (Q. LXXVIII, A. 4). Therefore also the speculative intellect differs from the practical.

On the contrary, The speculative intellect by extension becomes practical.[1] But one power is not changed into another. Therefore the speculative and practical intellects are not distinct powers.

I answer that, The speculative and practical intellects are not distinct powers. The reason of which is that, as we have said above (Q. LXXVII, A. 3), what is accidental to the nature of the object of a power does not differentiate that power. For it is accidental to a thing coloured to be man, or to be great or small; hence all such things are apprehended by the same power of sight. Now, to a thing apprehended by the intellect, it is accidental whether it be directed to operation or not, and it is according to this the speculative and practical intellects differ. For it is the speculative intellect which directs what it apprehends, not to operation, but to the consideration of truth, while the practical intellect is that which directs what it apprehends to operation. And this is what the Philosopher says,[2] that "the speculative differs from the practical in its end." Hence each is named from its end: the one speculative, the other practical —that is, operative.

Reply Obj. 1. The practical intellect is a moving power not as executing movement, but as directing towards it; and this belongs to it according to its mode of apprehension.

Reply Obj. 2. Truth and good include one another; for truth is something good, otherwise it would not be desirable; and good is something true, otherwise it would not be intelligible. Therefore just as the object of the appetite may be something true, as having the aspect of good, for example, when some one desires to know the truth, so the object of the practical intellect is good directed to operation, and under the aspect of truth. For the practical intellect knows truth, just as the speculative, but it directs the known truth to operation.

Reply Obj. 3. Many differences differentiate the sensitive powers which do not differentiate the intellectual powers, as we have said above (A. 7, Ans. 2, Q. LXXVII, A. 3, Ans. 4).

---

[1] Aristotle, *Soul,* III, 10 (433ª14).
[2] *Ibid.*

ARTICLE 12. *Whether Synderesis Is a Special Power of the Soul Distinct From the Others?*

We proceed thus to the Twelfth Article: It would seem that synderesis is a special power, distinct from the others.

Objection 1. For those things which fall under one division seem to be of the same genus. But in the gloss of Jerome on Ezech. 1. 6[3] synderesis is divided against the irascible, the concupiscible, and the rational, which are powers. Therefore synderesis is a power.

Obj. 2. Further, opposite things are of the same genus. But synderesis and sensuality seem to be opposed to one another because synderesis always inclines to good, while sensuality always inclines to evil; hence it is signified by the serpent, as is clear from Augustine (*De Trin.* xii, 12, 13).[4] It seems, therefore, that synderesis is a power just as sensuality is.

Obj. 3. Further, Augustine says (*De Lib. Arb.* ii, 10)[5] that in the natural power of judgment there are certain "rules and seeds of virtue, both true and unchangeable." And this is what we call synderesis. Since, therefore, the unchangeable rules which guide our judgment belong to the reason as to its higher part, as Augustine says (*De Trin.* xii, 2,)[6] it seems that synderesis is the same as reason. And thus it is a power.

On the contrary, According to the Philosopher[7] "rational powers regard opposite things." But synderesis does not regard opposites, but inclines to good only. Therefore synderesis is not a power. For if it were a power it would be a rational power, since it is not found in brute animals.

I answer that, Synderesis is not a power but a habit, though some held[8] that it is "a power higher than reason," while others said[9] that it is "reason itself, not as reason, but as a nature." In order to make this clear we must observe that, as we have said above (A. 8), man's act of reasoning, since it is a kind of movement, proceeds from the understanding of certain things—namely, those which are naturally known without any investigation on the part of reason, as from an immovable principle,—and ends also at the understanding, since by means

---

[3] *Glossa ordin.,* (IV, 210E). Jerome, *In Ezech.* I, on 1.6 (PL 25, 22).
[4] PL 42, 1007, 1009.
[5] PL 32, 1256.   [6] PL 42, 999.
[7] *Metaphysics,* IX, 2 (1046ᵇ5).
[8] Wm. of Auxerre, *Summa Aurea,* II, 12, 1 (fol. 65 vb), who is followed by Roland of Cremana and John of Rochelle. (See text cited by Lottin, RNP (1926) p. 446).
[9] Cf. Alexander of Hales, *Sum. Theol.,* I-II, n. 418 (QR II, 493)—See Lottin, RNP (1927) p. 265.

of those principles naturally known we judge of those things which we have discovered by reasoning. Now it is clear that, as the speculative reason reasons about speculative things, so the practical reason reasons about practical things. Therefore we must have bestowed on us by nature not only speculative principles, but also practical principles. Now the first speculative principles bestowed on us by nature do not belong to a special power, but to a special habit, which is called "the understanding of principles," as the Philosopher explains.[1] And so also the first practical principles, bestowed on us by nature, do not belong to a special power, but to a special natural habit, which we call synderesis. And so synderesis is said to stir up to good, and to murmur at evil, since through first principles we proceed to discover, and judge of what we have discovered. It is therefore clear that synderesis is not a power, but a natural habit.

Reply Obj. 1. The division given by Jerome is taken from the variety of acts, and not from the variety of powers; and various acts can belong to one power.

Reply Obj. 2. In like manner, the opposition of sensuality to synderesis is an opposition of acts, and not of the different species of one genus.

Reply Obj. 3. Those unchangeable notions are the first practical principles, concerning which no one errs; and they are attributed to reason as to a power, and to synderesis as to a habit. And thus we judge naturally both by our reason and by synderesis.

ARTICLE 13. *Whether Conscience Is a Power?*

We proceed thus to the Thirteenth Article: It would seem that conscience is a power.

Objection 1. For Origen says[2] that conscience is "a correcting and guiding spirit accompanying the soul, by which it is led away from evil and made to cling to good." But in the soul, spirit designates a power—either the mind itself, according to the text (Eph. 4. 13), *Be ye renewed in the spirit of your mind*—or the imagination, from which imaginary vision is called "spiritual," as Augustine says (*Gen. ad lit.* vii, 7, 24).[3] Therefore conscience is a power.

Obj. 2. Further, nothing is a subject of sin except a power of the soul. But conscience is a subject of sin; for it is said of some that *their mind and conscience are defiled* (Titus 1. 15). Therefore it seems that conscience is a power.

Obj. 3. Further, conscience must of necessity be either an act, a habit, or a power. But it is not an act, for thus it would not always exist in man. Nor is it a habit, for conscience is not one thing but many, since we are directed in our actions by many habits of knowledge. Therefore conscience is a power.

On the contrary, Conscience can be laid aside. But a power cannot be laid aside. Therefore conscience is not a power.

I answer that, Properly speaking conscience is not a power, but an act. This is evident both from the very name and from those things which in the common way of speaking are attributed to conscience. For conscience, according to the very nature of the word, implies the relation of knowledge to something; for conscience may be resolved into *cum alio scientia* [that is, knowledge applied to an individual case]. But the application of knowledge to something is done by some act. And thus, from this explanation of the name it is clear that conscience is an act.

The same is manifest from those things which are attributed to conscience. For conscience is said to witness, to bind, or stir up, and also to accuse, torment, or rebuke. And all these follow the application of knowledge or science to what we do, which application is made in three ways. One way in so far as we recognize that we have done or not done something: *Thy conscience knoweth that thou hast often spoken evil of others* (Eccles. 7. 23), and according to this, conscience is said to witness. In another way, so far as through the conscience we judge that something should be done or not done, and in this sense, conscience is said to stir up or to bind. In the third way, so far as by conscience we judge that something done is well done or ill done, and in this sense conscience is said to excuse, accuse, or torment. Now, it is clear that all these things follow the actual application of knowledge to what we do. Therefore, properly speaking, conscience denominates an act. But since habit is a principle of act, sometimes the name conscience is given to the first natural habit—namely, synderesis: thus Jerome calls synderesis conscience (Gloss. Ezech. 1. 6);[4] Basil,[5] the "natural power of judgment," and Damascene[6] says that it is the "law of our intellect." For it is customary for causes and effects to be called after one another.

Reply Obj. 1. Conscience is called a spirit, so

---

[1] *Ethics*, VI, 6 (1141ª7).
[2] *Commentary on Rom.*, 2.15 (PG 14, 892).
[3] PL 34, 459, 474.

[4] *Glossa ordin.* (IV, 210F); Jerome, *In Ezech.* I, on 1.6 (PL 25, 22).
[5] Hom. XII, *In Princ. Prov.* (PG 31, 404).
[6] *De Fide Orth.*, IV. 22 (PG 94, 1089).

far as spirit is the same as mind, because conscience is a certain pronouncement of the mind.

Reply Obj. 2. The conscience is said to be defiled, not as a subject, but as the thing known is in knowledge; in so far, that is, as someone knows he is defiled.

Reply Obj. 3. Although an act does not always remain in itself, yet it always remains in its cause, which is power and habit. Now all the habits by which conscience is formed, although many, nevertheless have their efficacy from one first principle, the habit of first principles, which is called synderesis. And for this special reason, this habit is sometimes called conscience, as we have said above.

QUESTION LXXX
OF THE APPETITIVE POWERS IN GENERAL
(*In Two Articles*)

NEXT we consider the appetitive powers, concerning which there are four heads of consideration: first, the appetitive powers in general; second, sensuality (Q. LXXXI); third, the will (Q. LXXXII); fourth, free choice (Q. LXXXIII). Under the first there are two points of inquiry. (1) Whether the appetite should be considered a special power of the soul? (2) Whether the appetite should be divided into intellectual and sensitive as distinct powers?

ARTICLE 1. *Whether the Appetite Is a Special Power of the Soul?*

We proceed thus to the First Article: It would seem that the appetite is not a special power of the soul.

Objection 1. For no power of the soul is to be assigned for those things which are common to animate and to inanimate things. But to desire is common to animate and inanimate things, since "the good is what all desire" as the Philosopher says.[1] Therefore the appetite is not a special power of the soul.

Obj. 2. Further, powers are differentiated by their objects. But what we desire is the same as what we know. Therefore the appetitive power is not distinct from the apprehensive power.

Obj. 3. Further, the common is not divided from the proper. But each power of the soul desires some particular desirable thing—namely, its own suitable object. Therefore, with regard to this object which is the desirable in general we should not assign some particular power distinct from the others, called the appetitive power.

[1] *Ethics*, I, 1 (1094ᵃ3).

On the contrary, The Philosopher distinguishes[2] the appetitive from the other powers. Damascene also (*De Fid. Orth.* ii, 22)[3] distinguishes the appetitive from the cognitive powers.

I answer that, It is necessary to assign an appetitive power to the soul. To make this evident, we must observe that some inclination follows every form; for example, fire, by its form, is inclined to rise, and to generate its like. Now, the form is found to be more perfect in those things which participate knowledge than in those which lack knowledge. For in those which lack knowledge, the form is found to determine each thing only to its own being—that is, to the being natural to each. Therefore this natural form is followed by a natural inclination, which is called the natural appetite. But in those things which have knowledge, each one is determined to its own natural being by its natural form, in such a manner that it is nevertheless receptive of the species of other things; for example, sense receives the species of all things sensible, and the intellect, of all things intelligible, and thus the soul of man is, in a way, all things by sense and intellect. And thus those things that have knowledge, in a way, approach to a likeness to God, "in Whom all things pre-exist," as Dionysius says (*Div. Nom.* v).[4]

Therefore, as forms exist in those things that have knowledge in a higher manner and above the manner of natural forms, so must there be in them an inclination surpassing the natural inclination, which is called the natural appetite. And this superior inclination belongs to the appetitive power of the soul, through which the animal is able to desire what it apprehends, and not only that to which it is inclined by its natural form. And so it is necessary to assign an appetitive power to the soul.

Reply Obj. 1. To desire is found in things which have knowledge above the common manner in which it is found in all things, as we have said above. Therefore it is necessary to assign to the soul a particular power.

Reply Obj. 2. What is apprehended and what is desired are the same in subject, but differ in aspect; for a thing is apprehended as a sensible or intelligible being, whereas it is desired as suitable or good. Now, it is diversity of aspect in the objects, and not material diversity, which demands a diversity of powers.

Reply Obj. 3. Each power of the soul is a

[2] *Soul*, II, 3 (414ᵃ31); cf. also III, 10 (433ᵃ9).
[3] PG 94, 941.
[4] Sect. 5 (PG 3, 820).

form or nature, and has a natural inclination to something. Therefore each power desires by the natural appetite that object which is suitable to itself. Above this natural appetite is the animal appetite, which follows the apprehension, and by which something is desired not as suitable to the act of this or that power, such as sight for seeing, or sound for hearing, but as suitable absolutely to the animal.

ARTICLE 2. *Whether the Sensitive and Intellectual Appetites Are Distinct Powers?*

We proceed thus to the Second Article: It would seem that the sensitive and intellectual appetites are not distinct powers.

Objection 1. For powers are not differentiated by accidental differences, as we have seen above (Q. LXXVII, A. 3). But it is accidental to the desirable object whether it be apprehended by the sense or by the intellect. Therefore the sensitive and intellectual appetites are not distinct powers.

Obj. 2. Further, intellectual knowledge is of universals, and so it is distinct from sensitive knowledge, which is of individual things. But there is no place for this distinction in the appetitive part, for since the appetite is a movement of the soul to individual things, it seems that every act of the appetite regards an individual thing. Therefore the intellectual appetite should not be distinguished from the sensitive.

Obj. 3. Further, as under the apprehensive power, the appetitive is subordinate as a lower power, so also is the moving power. But the moving power which in man follows the intellect is not distinct from the moving power which in animals follows sense. Therefore, for a like reason, neither is there distinction in the appetitive part.

On the contrary, The Philosopher distinguishes[1] a twofold appetite, and says[2] that the higher appetite moves the lower.

I answer that, We must say that the intellectual appetite is a distinct power from the sensitive appetite. For the appetitive power is a passive power, which is naturally moved by the thing apprehended, "and thus the desirable thing apprehended is a mover which is not moved, while the appetite is a mover moved," as the Philosopher says.[3] Now things passive and movable are differentiated according to the distinction of the corresponding active and moving principles, because the moving principle must

be proportionate to the movable, and the active to the passive; indeed, the passive power itself has its very nature from its relation to its active principle. Therefore, since what is apprehended by the intellect and what is apprehended by sense are generically different, consequently the intellectual appetite is distinct from the sensitive.

Reply Obj. 1. It is not accidental to the thing desired to be apprehended by the sense or the intellect; on the contrary, this belongs to it *per se,* for the desirable thing does not move the appetite except as it is apprehended. And so differences in the thing apprehended are of themselves differences of the desirable thing. And so the appetitive powers are distinct according to the distinction of the things apprehended, as according to their proper objects.

Reply Obj. 2. The intellectual appetite, though it tends to things which are singular outside the soul, yet tends to them according to some universal aspect, as when it desires something because it is good. Hence the Philosopher says[4] that hatred can pertain to a universal, as when "we hate every kind of thief." In the same way by the intellectual appetite we may desire the immaterial good, which is not apprehended by sense, such as knowledge, the virtues and the like.

Reply Obj. 3. As the Philosopher says,[5] a universal opinion does not move except by means of a particular opinion; and in like manner the higher appetite moves by means of the lower. And therefore there are not two distinct moving powers following the intellect and the sense.

QUESTION LXXXI
OF SENSUALITY
(*In Three Articles*)

NEXT we have to consider sensuality, concerning which there are three points of inquiry: (1) Whether sensuality is only an appetitive power? (2) Whether it is divided into irascible and concupiscible as distinct powers? (3) Whether the irascible and concupiscible powers obey reason?

ARTICLE 1. *Whether Sensuality Is Only Appetitive?*

We proceed thus to the First Article: It would seem that sensuality is not only appetitive, but also cognitive.

Objection 1. For Augustine says (*De Trin.* xii, 12)[6] that "the sensual movement of the soul

---

[1] *Soul,* III, 9 (432[b]5); also III, 10 (433[a]23).
[2] *Ibid.,* III, 11 (434[a]12).
[3] *Ibid.,* III, 10 (433[b]16); *Metaphysics,* XII, 7 (1072[a]26).

[4] *Rhetoric,* II, 4 (1382[a]5).
[5] *Soul,* III, 11 (434[a]16).   [6] PL 42, 1007.

which is directed to the bodily senses is common to us and beasts." But the bodily senses belong to the apprehensive powers. Therefore sensuality is a cognitive power.

Obj. 2. Further, things which come under one division seem to be of one genus. But Augustine (*De Trin.* xii, *loc. cit.*) divides sensuality against the higher and lower reason, which pertain to knowledge. Therefore sensuality also is a cognitive power.

Obj. 3. Further, in man's temptations sensuality stands in the place of the serpent. But in the temptation of our first parents the serpent presented himself as one giving information and proposing sin, which belong to the cognitive power. Therefore sensuality is a cognitive power.

On the contrary, Sensuality is defined as "the appetite of things pertaining to the body."[1]

I answer that, The name sensuality seems to be taken from the sensual movement, of which Augustine speaks (*De Trin.* xii, 12, 13),[2] just as the name of a power is taken from its act; for instance, sight from seeing. Now the sensual movement is an appetite following sensitive apprehension. For the act of the apprehensive power is not so properly called a movement as the act of the appetite, since the operation of the apprehensive power is completed in the very fact that the thing apprehended is in the one that apprehends, while the operation of the appetitive power is completed in the fact that he who desires is borne towards the thing desirable. Therefore the operation of the apprehensive power is likened to rest, whereas the operation of the appetitive power is rather likened to movement. Therefore by sensual movement we understand the operation of the appetitive power, so that sensuality is the name of the sensitive appetite.

Reply Obj. 1. By saying that the sensual movement of the soul is directed to the bodily senses, Augustine does not give us to understand that the bodily senses are included in sensuality, but rather that the movement of sensuality is a certain inclination to the bodily senses, since we desire things which are apprehended through the bodily senses. And thus the bodily senses appertain to sensuality as a kind of preliminary.

Reply Obj. 2. Sensuality is divided against higher and lower reason, as having in common with them the act of movement; for the apprehensive power, to which belong the higher and lower reason, is a moving power, as is appetite, to which appertains sensuality.

Reply Obj. 3. The serpent not only showed and proposed sin, but also incited to the commission of sin. And in this sensuality is signified by the serpent.

ARTICLE 2. *Whether the Sensitive Appetite Is Divided Into the Irascible and Concupiscible As Distinct Powers?*

We proceed thus to the Second Article: It would seem that the sensitive appetite is not divided into the irascible and concupiscible as distinct powers.

Objection 1. For the same power of the soul regards "both sides of a contrariety, as sight regards both black and white," according to the Philosopher.[3] But suitable and harmful are contraries. Since, then, the concupiscible power regards what is suitable, while the irascible is concerned with what is harmful, it seems that irascible and concupiscible are the same power in the soul.

Obj. 2. Further, the sensitive appetite regards only what is suitable according to the senses. But such is the object of the concupiscible power. Therefore there is no sensitive appetite differing from the concupiscible.

Obj. 3. Further, hatred is in the irascible part; for Jerome says on Matt. 13. 33:[4] "We ought to have the hatred of vice in the irascible power." But hatred is contrary to love, and is in the concupiscible part. Therefore the concupiscible and irascible are the same powers.

On the contrary, Gregory of Nyssa (Nemesius, *De Natura Hominis*)[5] and Damascene (*De Fid. Orth.* ii, 12)[6] assign two powers to the sensitive appetite, the irascible and the concupiscible parts.

I answer that, The sensitive appetite is one generic power, and is called sensuality; but it is divided into two powers, which are species of the sensitive appetite—the irascible and the concupiscible. In order to make this clear, we must observe that in natural corruptible things there is needed an inclination not only to the acquisition of what is suitable and to the avoiding of what is harmful, but also to resistance against corruptive and contrary agencies which are a hindrance to the acquisition of what is suitable, and are productive of harm. For example, fire has a natural inclination not only

---

[1] Cf. Peter Lombard, *Sent.*, II, d. XXIV, 4 (QR I, 421).
[2] PL 42, 1007, 1009.
[3] *Soul*, II, 11 (422[b]23).
[4] Bk. I (PL 26, 94).
[5] Chaps. 16, 17 (PG 40, 672, 676).
[6] PG 94, 928.

to rise from a lower position, which is unsuitable to it, towards a higher position which is suitable, but also to resist whatever destroys or hinders its action. Therefore, since the sensitive appetite is an inclination following sensitive apprehension, as natural appetite is an inclination following the natural form, there must be two appetitive powers in the sensitive part—one through which the soul is inclined absolutely to seek what is suitable according to the senses, and to fly from what is hurtful, and this is called the concupiscible; and another by which an animal resists these attacks that hinder what is suitable and inflict harm, and this is called the irascible. And so we say that its object is something arduous, because its tendency is to overcome and rise above obstacles.

Now these two are not to be reduced to one principle, for sometimes the soul busies itself with unpleasant things against the inclination of the concupiscible appetite in order that, following the impulse of the irascible appetite, it may fight against obstacles. Hence also the passions of the irascible appetite seem to go against the passions of the concupiscible appetite, since concupiscence, on being roused, diminishes anger, and anger being roused, diminishes concupiscence in many cases. This is clear also from the fact that the irascible is, as it were, the champion and defender of the concupiscible, when it rises up against what hinders the acquisition of the suitable things which the concupiscible desires, or against what inflicts harm, from which the concupiscible flies. And for this reason all the passions of the irascible appetite rise from the passions of the concupiscible appetite and terminate in them; for instance, anger rises from sadness, and having wrought vengeance, terminates in joy. For this reason also the quarrels of animals are about things concupiscible—namely, food and sex, as the Philosopher says.[1]

Reply Obj. 1. The concupiscible power regards both what is suitable and what is unsuitable. But the object of the irascible power is to resist the onslaught of the unsuitable.

Reply Obj. 2. As in the apprehensive powers of the sensitive part there is an estimative power, which perceives those things which do not change the senses, as we have said above (Q. LXXVIII, A. 2), so also in the sensitive appetite there is a certain appetitive power which regards something as suitable not because it pleases the senses, but because it is useful to the animal for self-defence; and this is the irascible power.

Reply Obj. 3. Hatred belongs absolutely to the concupiscible appetite, but by reason of the strife which arises from hatred, it may pertain to the irascible appetite.

ARTICLE 3. *Whether the Irascible and Concupiscible Appetites Obey Reason?*

We proceed thus to the Third Article: It would seem that the irascible and concupiscible appetites do not obey reason.

Objection 1. For irascible and concupiscible are parts of sensuality. But sensuality does not obey reason; hence it is signified by the serpent, as Augustine says (*De Trin.* xii, 12, 13).[2] Therefore the irascible and concupiscible appetites do not obey reason.

Obj. 2. Further, what obeys a certain thing does not resist it. But the irascible and concupiscible appetites resist reason: according to the Apostle (Rom. 7. 23): *I see another law in my members fighting against the law of my mind.* Therefore the irascible and concupiscible appetites do not obey reason.

Obj. 3. Further, as the appetitive power is inferior to the rational part of the soul, so also is the sensitive power. But the sensitive part of the soul does not obey reason, for we neither hear nor see just when we wish. Therefore, in like manner, neither do the powers of the sensitive appetite, the irascible and concupiscible, obey reason.

On the contrary, Damascene says (*De Fid. Orth.* ii, 12)[3] that "the part of the soul which is obedient and amenable to reason is divided into concupiscence and anger."

I answer that, In two ways the irascible and concupiscible powers obey the higher part, in which are the intellect or reason, and the will: first, as to the reason, secondly as to the will. They obey the reason in their own acts, because in other animals the sensitive appetite is naturally moved by the estimative power; for instance, a sheep, esteeming the wolf as an enemy, is afraid. In man the estimative power, as we have said above (Q. LXXVIII, A. 4), is replaced by the cogitative power, which is called by some the particular reason, because it compares individual intentions.[4] Thus in man the sensitive appetite is naturally moved by this particular reason. But this same particular reason is naturally guided and moved according to the uni-

---

[1] *History of Animals,* VIII, 1 (589ᵃ2); cf. VII, 18 (571ᵇ8); IX, 1 (608ᵇ19).

[2] PL 42, 1007, 1009.

[3] PG 94, 928.

[4] Cf. above, Q. LXXVIII, A. 4.

versal reason and so, in syllogistic reasoning particular conclusions are drawn from universal propositions. Therefore it is clear that the universal reason directs the sensitive appetite, which is divided into concupiscible and irascible, and this appetite obeys it. But because to draw particular conclusions from universal principles is not the work of the intellect, as such, but of the reason, hence it is that the irascible and concupiscible are said to obey the reason rather than to obey the intellect. Anyone can experience this in himself, for by applying certain universal considerations, anger or fear or the like may be modified or excited.

To the will also is the sensitive appetite subject in execution, which is accomplished by the moving power. For in other animals movement follows at once the concupiscible and irascible appetites; for instance, the sheep, fearing the wolf, flies at once, because it has no superior counteracting appetite. On the contrary, man is not moved at once, according to the irascible and concupiscible appetites, but he awaits the command of the will, which is the superior appetite. For wherever there is order among a number of moving powers, the second only moves by virtue of the first; and so the lower appetite is not sufficient to cause movement unless the higher appetite consents. And this is what the Philosopher says,[1] that the higher appetite moves the lower appetite, as the higher sphere moves the lower. In this way, therefore, the irascible and concupiscible are subject to reason.

Reply Obj. 1. Sensuality is signified by the serpent in what is proper to it as a sensitive power. But the irascible and concupiscible powers denominate the sensitive appetite rather on the part of the act, to which they are led by the reason, as we have said.

Reply Obj. 2. As the Philosopher says,[2] "We observe in an animal a despotic and a politic principle, for the soul dominates the body by a despotic power; but the intellect dominates the appetite by a politic and royal power." For that power is called despotic whereby a man rules his slaves, who have not the right to resist in any way the orders of the one that commands them, since they have nothing of their own. But that power is called politic and royal by which a man rules over free subjects, who, though subject to the government of the ruler, have nevertheless something of their own, by reason of which they can resist the orders of him who commands. And so, the soul is said to rule the

body by a despotic power because the members of the body cannot in any way resist the sway of the soul, but at the soul's command both hand and foot, and whatever member is naturally moved by voluntary movement, are moved at once. But the intellect or reason is said to rule the irascible and concupiscible by a politic power, because the sensitive appetite has something of its own, by virtue of which it can resist the commands of reason. For the sensitive appetite is naturally moved not only by the estimative power in other animals, and in man by the cogitative power which the universal reason guides, but also by the imagination and sense. And so it is that we experience that the irascible and concupiscible powers do resist reason, since we sense or imagine something pleasant, which reason forbids, or unpleasant, which reason commands. And so from the fact that the irascible and concupiscible resist reason in something we must not conclude that they do not obey.

Reply Obj. 3. The exterior senses require for action exterior sensible things, whereby they are changed, and the presence of which is not ruled by reason. But the interior powers, both appetitive and apprehensive, do not require exterior things. Therefore they are subject to the command of reason, which can not only incite or modify the affections of the appetitive power, but can also form the phantasms of the imagination.

QUESTION LXXXII
OF THE WILL
(In Five Articles)

WE next consider the will. Under this head there are five points of inquiry: (1) Whether the will desires something of necessity? (2) Whether it desires everything of necessity? (3) Whether it is a higher power than the intellect? (4) Whether the will moves the intellect? (5) Whether the will is divided into irascible and concupiscible?

ARTICLE 1. *Whether the Will Desires Something of Necessity?*

We proceed thus to the First Article: It would seem that the will desires nothing of necessity.

Objection 1. For Augustine says[3] that if anything is necessary it is not voluntary. But whatever the will desires is voluntary. Therefore nothing that the will desires is desired of necessity.

---

[1] *Soul*, III, 11 (434ª12).   [2] *Politics*, I, 5 (1254b2).

[3] *City of God*, v, 10 (PL 41, 152).

Obj. 2. Further, "the rational powers," according to the Philosopher,[1] "extend to opposite things." But the will is a rational power, because, as he says,[2] "the will is in the reason." Therefore the will extends to opposite things, and therefore it is determined to nothing of necessity.

Obj. 3. Further, by the will we are masters of our own actions. But we are not masters of that which is of necessity. Therefore the act of the will cannot be necessitated.

On the contrary, Augustine says (*De Trin.* xiii, 4)[3] that "all desire happiness with one will." Now if this were not necessary, but contingent, there would at least be a few exceptions. Therefore the will desires something of necessity.

I answer that, The word necessity is employed in many ways. For that which cannot not be is necessary. Now that a thing must be may belong to it by an intrinsic principle: either material, as when we say that everything composed of contraries is of necessity corruptible; or formal, as when we say that it is necessary for the three angles of a triangle to be equal to two right angles. And this is natural and absolute necessity. In another way, that a thing must be, belongs to it by reason of something extrinsic, which is either the end or the agent. On the part of the end, as when without it the end is not to be attained or so well attained; for instance, food is said to be necessary for life, and a horse is necessary for a journey. This is called necessity of end, and sometimes also utility. On the part of the agent, a thing must be, when someone is forced by some agent, so that he is not able to do the contrary. This is called necessity of coercion.

Now this necessity of coercion is altogether contrary to the will. For we call that violent which is against the inclination of a thing. But the very movement of the will is an inclination to something. Therefore, as a thing is called natural because it is according to the inclination of nature, so a thing is called voluntary because it is according to the inclination of the will. Therefore, just as it is impossible for a thing to be at the same time violent and natural, so it is impossible for a thing to be absolutely coerced or violent, and voluntary.

But necessity of end is not contrary to the will when the end cannot be attained except in one way; thus from the will to cross the sea arises in the will the necessity to wish for a ship.

In like manner neither is natural necessity contrary to the will. Indeed, more than this, for as the intellect of necessity adheres to the first principles, the will must of necessity adhere to the last end, which is happiness, since the end is in practical matters what the principle is in speculative matters, as is stated in the *Physics.*[4] For what befits a thing naturally and immovably must be the root and principle of all else pertaining to it, since the nature of a thing is the first in everything, and every movement arises from something immovable.

Reply Obj. 1. The words of Augustine are to be understood of the necessity of coercion. But natural necessity does not take away the liberty of the will, as he says himself.[5]

Reply Obj. 2. The will, so far as it desires a thing naturally, corresponds rather to the intellect as regards natural principles than to the reason, which extends to opposite things. Therefore in this respect it is rather an intellectual than a rational power.

Reply Obj. 3. We are masters of our own actions by reason of our being able to choose this or that. But choice regards not the end, but "the means to the end," as the Philosopher says.[6] Thus the desire of the ultimate end does not regard those actions of which we are masters.

ARTICLE 2. *Whether the Will Desires of Necessity, Whatever It Desires?*

We proceed thus to the Second Article: It would seem that the will desires all things of necessity, whatever it desires.

Objection 1. For Dionysius says (*Div. Nom.* iv)[7] that "evil is outside the scope of the will." Therefore the will tends of necessity to the good which is proposed to it.

Obj. 2. Further, the object of the will is compared to the will as the mover to the thing movable. But the movement of the movable necessarily follows the mover. Therefore it seems that the will's object moves it of necessity.

Obj. 3. Further, as the thing apprehended by sense is the object of the sensitive appetite, so the thing apprehended by the intellect is the object of the intellectual appetite, which is called the will. But what is apprehended by the sense moves the sensitive appetite of necessity; for Augustine says (*Gen. ad lit.* ix, 14)[8] that "animals are moved by things seen." Therefore it

---

[1] *Metaphysics,* IX, 2 (1046[b]5).
[2] *Soul,* III, 9 (432[b]5).
[3] PL 42, 1018.

[4] Aristotle, II, 9 (200[a]21).
[5] *Loc. cit.*
[6] *Ethics,* III, 2 (1111[b]27).
[7] Sect. 32 (PG 3, 732).
[8] PL 34, 402.

seems that whatever is apprehended by the intellect moves the will of necessity.

On the contrary, Augustine says (*Retract.* i, 9)[1] that "it is the will by which we sin and live well," and so the will extends to opposite things. Therefore it does not desire of necessity all things whatsoever it desires.

I answer that, The will does not desire of necessity whatsoever it desires. In order to make this evident we must observe that as the intellect naturally and of necessity adheres to the first principles, so the will adheres to the last end, as we have said already (A. 1). Now there are some things intelligible which have not a necessary connection with the first principles, such as contingent propositions, the denial of which does not involve a denial of the first principles. And to such the intellect does not assent of necessity. But there are some propositions which have a necessary connection with the first principles, such as demonstrable conclusions, a denial of which involves a denial of the first principles. And to these the intellect assents of necessity, when once it is aware, through demonstration, of the necessary connection of these conclusions with the principles; but it does not assent of necessity until through the demonstration it recognizes the necessity of such connection. It is the same with the will. For there are certain individual goods which have not a necessary connection with happiness, because without them a man can be happy, and to such the will does not adhere of necessity. But there are some things which have a necessary connection with happiness, by means of which things man adheres to God, in Whom alone true happiness consists. Nevertheless, until through the certitude of the Divine Vision the necessity of such connection be shown, the will does not adhere to God of necessity, nor to those things which are of God. But the will of the man who sees God in His Essence of necessity adheres to God, just as now we desire of necessity to be happy. It is therefore clear that the will does not desire of necessity whatever it desires.

Reply Obj. 1. The will can tend to nothing except under the aspect of good. But because good is of many kinds, for this reason the will is not of necessity determined to one.

Reply Obj. 2. The mover of necessity causes movement in the thing movable when the power of the mover exceeds the thing movable. so that its entire capacity (*possibilitas*) is subject to the mover. But as the capacity of the will regards the universal and perfect good, its capaci-

ty is not subjected to any individual good. And therefore it is not of necessity moved by it.

Reply Obj. 3. The sensitive power does not compare different things with each other, as reason does, but it apprehends absolutely some one thing. Therefore, according to that one thing, it moves the sensitive appetite in a determinate way. But the reason is a power that compares several things together. Therefore from several things the intellectual appetite—that is, the will —may be moved, but not of necessity from one thing.

ARTICLE 3. *Whether the Will Is a Higher Power Than the Intellect?*

We proceed thus to the Third Article: It would seem that the will is a higher power than the intellect.

Objection 1. For the object of the will is good and the end. But the end is the first and highest cause. Therefore the will is the first and highest power.

Obj. 2. Further, in the order of natural things we observe a progress from imperfect things to perfect. And this also appears in the powers of the soul, for sense precedes the intellect, which is more noble. Now the act of the will, in the natural order, follows the act of the intellect. Therefore the will is a more noble and perfect power than the intellect.

Obj. 3. Further, habits are proportioned to their powers as perfections to what they make perfect. But the habit which perfects the will— namely, charity—is more noble than the habits which perfect the intellect, for it is written (I Cor. 13. 2): *If I should know all mysteries, and if I should have all faith, and have not charity, I am nothing.* Therefore the will is a higher power than the intellect.

On the contrary, The Philosopher holds the intellect to be the highest power of the soul.[2]

I answer that, The superiority of one thing over another can be considered in two ways: absolutely and relatively. Now a thing is considered to be such absolutely which is considered such in itself, but relatively as it is such with regard to something else. If therefore the intellect and will be considered with regard to themselves, then the intellect is the higher power. And this is clear if we compare their respective objects to one another. For the object of the intellect is more simple and more absolute than the object of the will, since the object of the intellect is the very notion of good as desirable; and the good as desirable, the notion of which is

---

[1] PL 32, 596; cf. also *City of God,* v, 10 (PL 41, 152).   [2] *Ethics,* x, 7 (1177[a]20).

in the intellect, is the object of the will. Now the more simple and the more abstract a thing is, the nobler and higher it is in itself; and therefore the object of the intellect is higher than the object of the will. Therefore, since the proper nature of a power is in its order to its object, it follows that the intellect in itself and absolutely is higher and nobler than the will.

But relatively and by comparison with something else, we find that the will is sometimes higher than the intellect, from the fact that the object of the will occurs in something higher than that in which occurs the object of the intellect. Thus, for instance, I might say that hearing is relatively nobler than sight, in so far as something in which there is sound is nobler than something in which there is colour, though colour is nobler and simpler than sound. For, as we have said above (Q. XVI, A. 1; Q. XXVII, A. 4), the action of the intellect consists in this—that the notion of the thing understood is in the one who understands, while the act of the will consists in this—that the will is inclined to the thing itself as it is in itself. And therefore the Philosopher says in the *Metaphysics*[1] that good and evil, which are objects of the will, are in things, but truth and error, which are objects of the intellect, are in the mind. When, therefore, the thing in which there is good is nobler than the soul itself, in which is the idea understood, by comparison with such a thing the will is higher than the intellect. But when the thing which is good is less noble than the soul, then even in comparison with that thing the intellect is higher than the will. Therefore the love of God is better than the knowledge of God; but, on the contrary, the knowledge of corporeal things is better than the love of them. Absolutely, however, the intellect is nobler than the will.

Reply Obj. 1. The aspect of cause is perceived by comparing one thing to another, and in such a comparison the notion of good is found to be nobler; but truth signifies something, more absolute, and extends to the notion of good itself; thus, even good is something true. But, again, truth is something good, according as the intellect is a thing, and truth its end. And among other ends this is the most excellent, as also is the intellect among the other powers.

Reply Obj. 2. What precedes in order of generation and time is less perfect, for in one and the same thing potency precedes act, and imperfection precedes perfection. But what precedes absolutely and in the order of nature is more perfect, for thus act precedes potency. And in this

way the intellect precedes the will, as the moving power precedes the thing movable, and as the active precedes the passive; for good which is understood moves the will.

Reply Obj. 3. This reason is verified of the will as compared with what is above the soul. For charity is the virtue by which we love God.

ARTICLE 4. *Whether the Will Moves the Intellect?*

We proceed thus to the Fourth Article: It would seem that the will does not move the intellect.

Objection 1. For what move excels and precedes what is moved, because what moves is an agent, and "the agent is nobler than the patient," as Augustine says (*Gen. ad lit.* xii, 16),[2] and the Philosopher.[3] But the intellect excels and precedes the will, as we have said above (A. 3). Therefore the will does not move the intellect.

Obj. 2. Further, what moves is not moved by what is moved, except perhaps accidentally. But the intellect moves the will, because the good apprehended by the intellect moves without being moved, whereas the appetite moves and is moved. Therefore the intellect is not moved by the will.

Obj. 3. Further, we can will nothing but what we understand. If, therefore, in order to understand, the will moves by willing to understand, that act of the will must be preceded by another act of the intellect, and this act of the intellect by another act of the will, and so on indefinitely, which is impossible. Therefore the will does not move the intellect.

On the contrary, Damascene says (*De Fid. Orth.* ii, 26):[4] "It is in our power whether to learn an art or not." But a thing is in our power by the will, and we learn art by the intellect. Therefore the will moves the intellect.

I answer that, A thing is said to move in two ways. First, as an end, for instance, when we say that the end moves the doer. In this way the intellect moves the will, because the good understood is the object of the will, and moves it as an end. Secondly, a thing is said to move as an agent, as what alters moves what is altered, and what impels moves what is impelled. In this way the will moves the intellect, and all the powers of the soul, as Anselm says (Eadmer, *De Similitudinibus*).[5] The reason is, because wherever we have order among a number of active powers,

---

[1] VI, 4 (1027[b]25).

[2] PL 34, 467.

[3] *Soul*, III, 5 (430[a]18).

[4] PG 94, 960.

[5] Chap. 2 (PL 159, 605).

that power which regards the universal end moves the powers which regard particular ends. And we may observe this both in nature and in political things. For the heaven, which aims at the universal preservation of things subject to generation and corruption moves all inferior bodies, each of which aims at the preservation of its own species or of the individual. The king also, who aims at the common good of the whole kingdom, by his rule moves all the governors of cities, each of whom rules over his own particular city. Now the object of the will is good and the end in general, and each power is directed to some suitable good proper to it, as sight is directed to the perception of colour, and the intellect to the knowledge of truth. Therefore the will as an agent moves all the powers of the soul to their respective acts, except the natural powers of the vegetative part, which are not subject to our choice.

Reply Obj. 1. The intellect may be considered in two ways: as apprehensive of universal being and truth, and as a thing and a particular power having a determinate act. In like manner also the will may be considered in two ways: according to the common nature of its object—that is to say, as appetitive of universal good—and as a determinate power of the soul having a determinate act. If, therefore, the intellect and will be compared with one another under the aspect of the universality of their respective objects, then, as we have said above (A. 3), the intellect is higher and nobler absolutely than the will. If, however, we take the intellect according to the common nature of its object and the will as a determinate power, then again the intellect is higher and nobler than the will, because under the notion of being and truth which the intellect apprehends is contained both the will itself, and its act, and its object. Thus the intellect understands the will, and its act, and its object, just as it understands other special things, as stone or wood, which are contained in the common notion of being and truth. But if we consider the will as regards the common nature of its object, which is good, and the intellect as a thing and a special power, then the intellect itself, and its act, and its object, which is truth, each of which is some special good, are contained under the common notion of good. And in this way the will is higher than the intellect, and can move it. From this we can easily understand why these powers include one another in their acts, because the intellect understands that the will wills, and the will wills the intellect to understand. In the same way good is contained in truth, inasmuch

as it is an understood truth, and truth in good, inasmuch as it is a desired good.

Reply Obj. 2. The intellect moves the will in one sense, and the will moves the intellect in another, as we have said above.

Reply Obj. 3. There is no need to go on indefinitely, but we must stop at the intellect as preceding all the rest. For every movement of the will must be preceded by apprehension, whereas every apprehension is not preceded by an act of the will; but the principle of counselling and understanding is an intellectual principle higher than our intellect—namely, God—as also Aristole says,[1] and in this way he explains that there is no need to proceed to infinity.

ARTICLE 5. *Whether We Should Distinguish Irascible and Concupiscible Parts in the Superior Appetite?*

We proceed thus to the Fifth Article: It would seem that we ought to distinguish irascible and concupiscible parts in the superior appetite, which is the will.

Objection 1. For the concupiscible power is so called from *concupiscere,* to desire, and the irascible part from *irasci,* to be angry. But there is a concupiscence which cannot belong to the sensitive appetite, but only to the intellectual, which is the will, as the concupiscence of wisdom, of which it is said (Wisd. 6. 21): *The concupiscence of wisdom bringeth to the eternal kingdom.* There is also a certain anger which cannot belong to the sensitive appetite, but only to the intellectual, as when our anger is directed against vice. Hence Jerome commenting on Matt. 13. 33[2] warns us to have the hatred of vice in the irascible part. Therefore we should distinguish irascible and concupiscible parts in the intellectual soul as well as in the sensitive.

Obj. 2. Further, as is commonly said, charity is in the concupiscible, and hope in the irascible part. But they cannot be in the sensitive appetite, because their objects are not sensible, but intellectual. Therefore we must assign an irascible and a concupiscible power to the intellectual part.

Obj. 3. Further, it is said (*De Spiritu et Anima*)[3] that "the soul has these powers"—namely, the irascible, concupiscible, and rational—"before it is united to the body." But no power of the sensitive part belongs to the soul alone, but to the soul and body united, as we have said

---

[1] *Eudemian Ethics*, VII, 14 (1248ᵃ26).
[2] Bk I. (PL 26, 94).
[3] Pseudo-Augustine (Alcher of Clairvaux), Chap. 16 (PL 40, 791).

above (Q. LXXVIII, AA. 5, 8). Therefore the irascible and concupiscible powers are in the will, which is the intellectual appetite.

On the contrary, Gregory of Nyssa (Nemesius, *De Nat. Hom.*)[1] says that the irrational part of the soul is divided into the desiring and irascible, and Damascene says the same (*De Fid. Orth.* ii, 12).[2] And the Philosopher says[3] that "the will is in the reason, while in the irrational part of the soul are concupiscence and anger, or desire and wrath."

I answer that, The irascible and concupiscible are not parts of the intellectual appetite, which is called the will. Because, as was said above (Q. LIX, A. 4; Q. LXXIX, A. 7), a power which is directed to an object according to some common notion is not differentiated by special differences which are contained under that common notion. For instance, because sight regards the visible thing under the common notion of something coloured, the visual power is not multiplied according to the different kinds of colour; but if there were a power regarding white as white, and not as something coloured, it would be distinct from a power regarding black as black.

Now the sensitive appetite does not consider the common notion of good, because neither do the senses apprehend the universal. And therefore the parts of the sensitive appetite are differentiated by the different notions of particular good; for the concupiscible is related to its proper notion of good, as something pleasant to the senses and suitable to nature, whereas the irascible is related to the notion of good as something that wards off and repels what is hurtful. But the will regards good according to the common notion of good, and therefore in the will, which is the intellectual appetite, there is no differentiation of appetitive powers, so that there be in the intellectual appetite an irascible power distinct from a concupsicible power; just as neither on the part of the intellect are the apprehending powers multiplied, although they are on the part of the senses.

Reply Obj. 1. Love, concupiscence, and the like can be understood in two ways. Sometimes they are taken as passions—arising, that is, with a certain disturbance of the soul. And thus they are commonly understood, and in this sense they are only in the sensitive appetite. They may, however, be taken in another way, as far as they are simple affections without passion or disturbance of the soul, and thus they are acts of the will. And in this sense, too, they are attributed to the angels and to God. But if taken in this sense, they do not belong to different powers, but only to one power, which is called the will.

Reply Obj. 2. The will itself may be said to be irascible, as far as it wills to repel evil not from any sudden movement of a passion, but from a judgment of the reason. And in the same way the will may be said to be concupiscible on account of its desire for good. And thus in the irascible and concupiscible are charity and hope ––that is, in the will as ordered to such acts. And in this way, too, we may understand the words quoted (*De Spiritu et Anima*), that the irascible and concupiscible powers are in the soul before it is united to the body (as long as we understand priority of nature, and not of time), although there is no need to have faith in what that book says. And so the *answer to the third objection* is clear.

QUESTION LXXXIII
OF FREE CHOICE
(*In Four Articles*)

WE now inquire concerning free choice. Under this head there are four points of inquiry: (1) Whether man has free choice? (2) What is free choice—a power, an act, or a habit? (3) If it is a power, is it appetitive or cognitive? (4) If it is appetitive, is it the same power as the will, or distinct?

ARTICLE 1. *Whether Man Has Free Choice?*

We proceed thus to the First Article: It would seem that man has not free choice.

Objection 1. For whoever has free choice does what he wills. But man does not what he wills, for it is written (Rom. 7. 19): *For the good which I will I do not, but the evil which I will not, that I do.* Therefore man has not free choice.

Obj. 2. Further, whoever has free choice has in his power to will or not to will, to do or not to do. But this is not in man's power, for it is written (Rom. 9. 16): *It is not of him that willeth* —namely, to will—*nor of him that runneth*— namely, to run. Therefore man has not free choice.

Obj. 3. Further "what is free is cause of itself," as the Philosopher says.[4] Therefore what is moved by another is not free. But God moves the will, for it is written (Prov. 21. 1): *The heart of the king is in the hand of the Lord;*

---

[1] Chap. 16 (PG 40, 672), also chap. 17 (676).
[2] PG 94, 928.
[3] *Soul*, III, 9 (432[b]5).
[4] *Metaphysics*, I, 2 (982[b]26).

whithersoever He will He shall turn it; and (Phil. 2. 13): *It is God Who worketh in you both to will and to accomplish.* Therefore man has not free choice.

Obj. 4. Further, whoever has free choice is master of his own actions. But man is not master of his own actions: for it is written (Jer. 10. 23): *The way of a man is not his: neither is it in a man to walk.* Therefore man has not free choice.

Obj. 5. Further, the Philosopher says,[1] "According as each one is, such does the end seem to him." But it is not in our power to be of one quality or another, for this comes to us from nature. Therefore it is natural to us to follow some particular end, and therefore we do not do so from free choice.

On the contrary, It is written (Ecclus. 15. 14): *God made man from the beginning, and left him in the hand of his own counsel;* and the gloss adds[2]: That is "of his free choice."

I answer that, Man has free choice. Otherwise counsels, exhortations, commands, prohibitions, rewards and punishments would be in vain. In order to make this evident, we must observe that some things act without judgment, as a stone moves downwards; and in like manner all things which lack knowledge. And some act from judgment, but not a free judgment; as brute animals. For the sheep, seeing the wolf, judges it a thing to be shunned, from a natural and not a free judgment, because it judges, not from an act of comparison, but from natural instinct. And the same thing is to be said of any judgment of brute animals. But man acts from judgment because by his knowing power he judges that something should be avoided or sought. But because this judgment, in the case of some particular act, is not from a natural instinct, but from some act of comparison in the reason, therefore he acts from free judgment and retains the power of being inclined to various things. For reason in contingent matters may follow opposite courses, as we see in dialectic syllogisms and rhetorical arguments. Now particular operations are contingent, and therefore in such matters the judgment of reason may follow opposite courses, and is not determined to one. And since man is rational man must have free choice.

Reply Obj. 1. As we have said above (Q. LXXXI, A. 3, Ans. 2), the sensitive appetite, though it obeys the reason, yet in a given case can resist by desiring what the reason forbids. This is therefore the good which man does not

when he wishes—namely, not to desire against reason, as Augustine says.[3]

Reply Obj. 2. Those words of the Apostle are not to be taken as though man does not wish or does not run of his free choice, but because the free choice is not sufficient for this unless it be moved and helped by God.

Reply Obj. 3. Free choice is the cause of its own movement, because by his free choice man moves himself to act. But it does not of necessity belong to liberty that what is free should be the first cause of itself, as neither for one thing to be cause of another need it be the first cause. God, therefore, is the first cause, Who moves causes both natural and voluntary. And just as by moving natural causes He does not prevent their acts being natural, so by moving voluntary causes He does not deprive their actions of being voluntary, but rather is He the cause of this very thing in them; for He operates in each thing according to its own nature.

Reply Obj. 4. "Man's way" is said "not to be his" in the execution of his choice, in which he may be impeded, whether he will or not. The choice itself, however, is in us, but presupposes the help of God.

Reply Obj. 5. Quality in man is of two kinds: natural and coming from without. Now the natural quality may be in the intellectual part or in the body and its powers. From the very fact, therefore, that man is such by virtue of a natural quality which is in the intellectual part, he naturally desires his last end, which is happiness. Which, indeed, is a natural desire, and is not subject to free choice, as is clear from what we have said above (Q. LXXXII, AA. 1, 2). But on the part of the body and its powers man may be such by virtue of a natural quality, in so far as he is of such a temperament or disposition due to any impression whatever produced by corporeal causes, which cannot affect the intellectual part, since it is not the act of a corporeal organ. And such as a man is by virtue of a corporeal quality, such also does his end seem to him, because from such a disposition a man is inclined to choose or reject something. But these inclinations are subject to the judgment of reason, which the lower appetite obeys, as we have said (Q. LXXXI, A. 3). And so this is in no way prejudicial to free choice.

The qualities that come from without are habits and passions, by virtue of which a man is inclined to one thing rather than to another. And

---

[1] *Ethics,* III, 5 (1114ᵃ32).
[2] *Glossa interl.* (III, 401V); cf. *Glossa ordin.* (III, 401E).
[3] *Serm. ad Popul.,* CLIV, 3 (PL 38, 834). Cf. *Glossa interl.,* on Rom. 7.19 (VI, 17r); cf. also *Glossa ordin.,* on Rom. 7.23 (VI, 17F).

yet even these inclinations are subject to the judgment of reason. Such qualities, too, are subject to reason, as it is in our power either to acquire them, whether by causing them or disposing ourselves to them, or to reject them. And so there is nothing in this that is contrary to the freedom of choice.

ARTICLE 2. *Whether Free Choice Is a Power?*

We proceed thus to the Second Article: It would seem that free choice is not a power.

Objection 1. For free choice is nothing but a free judgment. But judgment denominates an act, not a power. Therefore free choice is not a power.

Obj. 2. Further, free choice is defined as "the faculty of the will and reason."[1] But faculty denominates a facility of power, which is due to a habit. Therefore free choice is a habit. Moreover Bernard says (*De Gratia et Lib. Arb.* 1, 2)[2] that free choice is "the soul's habit of disposing of itself." Therefore it is not a power.

Obj. 3. Further, no natural power is forfeited through sin. But free choice is forfeited through sin, for Augustine says[3] that "man, by abusing free choice, loses both it and himself." Therefore free choice is not a power.

On the contrary, Nothing but a power, it seems, is the subject of a habit. But free choice is the subject of grace, by the help of which it chooses what is good. Therefore free choice is a power.

I answer that, Although free choice in its strict sense denotes an act, in the common manner of speaking we call free choice that which is the principle of the act by which man judges freely. Now in us the principle of an act is both power and habit; for we say that we know something both by knowledge and by the intellectual power. Therefore free choice must be either a power[4] or a habit,[5] or a power with a habit.[6] That it is neither a habit nor a power together with a habit, can be clearly proved in two ways. First of all, because, if it is a habit, it must be a natural habit; for it is natural to man to have a free choice. But there is no natural habit in us with

respect to those things which come under free choice; for we are naturally inclined to those things of which we have natural habits—for instance, to assent to first principles, while those things to which we are naturally inclined are not subject to free choice, as we have said of the desire of happiness (Q. LXXXII, AA. 1, 2). And so it is against the very notion of free choice that it should be a natural habit. And that it should be a non-natural habit is against its nature. Therefore in no sense is it a habit.

Secondly, this is clear because "habits are defined as that by reason of which we are well or ill disposed with regard to actions and passions"[7]; for by temperance we are well-disposed as regards concupiscences, and by intemperance ill-disposed; and by knowledge we are well-disposed to the act of the intellect when we know the truth, and by the contrary habit ill-disposed. But free choice is indifferent to good or evil choice; hence it is impossible for free choice to be a habit. Therefore it is a power.

Reply Obj. 1. It is not unusual for a power to be named from its act. And so from this act, which is a free judgment, is named the power which is the principle of this act. Otherwise, if free choice denominated an act, it would not always remain in man.

Reply Obj. 2. Faculty sometimes denominates a power ready for operation, and in this sense faculty is used in the definition of free choice. But Bernard takes habit not as divided against power, but as signifying a certain aptitude by which a man has some sort of relation to an act. And this may be both by a power and by a habit, for by a power man is, as it were, empowered to do the action, and by the habit he is apt to act well or ill.

Reply Obj. 3. Man is said to have lost free choice by falling into sin, not as to natural liberty, which is freedom from coercion, but as regards freedom from fault and unhappiness. Of this we shall treat later in the treatise on Morals in the second part of this work (Part I.-II. Q. LXXXV ff.; Q. CIX).

ARTICLE 3. *Whether Free Choice Is an Appetitive Power?*

We proceed thus to the Third Article: It would seem that free choice is not an appetitive, but a cognitive power.[8]

Objection 1. For Damascene (*De Fid. Orth.*

---

[1] Peter Lombard, *Sent.,* II, d. 24, chap. 3 (QR 1–421). Wm. of Auxerre, St. Thomas (*De Ver.* Q. 24, A. 4, arg. 1) and many others attributed this definition to St. Augustine. Cf. Lottin, *La Théorie* (p. 49).

[2] PL 182, 1002.

[3] *Enchiridion,* Chap. 30 (PL 40, 246).

[4] According to Albert, *Summa de Creat.,* II, 70, A. 2 (BO XXXV, 575). See Lottin, *La Théorie* (p. 110).

[5] According to Bonaventure, *In Sent.,* II, d. 25, pt. 1, A. 1, Q. 4 (QR II, 601). See Lottin, *La Théorie* (p. 119).

[6] According to Alexander of Hales, *Summa Theol.,* I-II, u. 390. (QR II, 486). See Lottin, *La Théorie* (p. 80).

[7] *Ethics,* II, 5 (1105^{b}25).

[8] Praepositinus, Wm. of Auxerre, Roland of Cremona held this doctrine. Cf. Lottin, *La Théorie* (p. 37, 51, 55). For the contrary doctrine, cf. Bonaventure, *In Sent.,* II, d. 25, pt. 1, A. 1, Q. 6 (QR II, 605). Cf. Lottin (p. 121).

ii, 27)[1] says that "free choice straightway accompanies the rational nature." But reason is a cognitive power. Therefore free choice is a cognitive power.

Obj. 2. Further, free choice is so called as though it were a free judgment. But to judge is an act of a cognitive power. Therefore free choice is a cognitive power.

Obj. 3. Further, the principal function of the free choice is to choose. But choice seems to belong to knowledge, because it implies a certain comparison of one thing to another, which belongs to the cognitive power. Therefore free choice is a cognitive power.

On the contrary, The Philosopher says[2] that choice is "the desire of those things which are in us." But desire is an act of the appetitive power. Therefore choice is also. But free choice is that by which we choose. Therefore free choice is an appetitive power.

I answer that, The proper act of free choice is election. For we say that we have a free choice because we can take one thing while refusing another, and this is to choose. Therefore we must consider the nature of free choice by considering the nature of choice. Now two things come together in choice: one on the part of the cognitive power, the other on the part of the appetitive power. On the part of the cognitive power, counsel is required, by which we judge one thing to be preferred to another; and on the part of the appetitive power it is required that the appetite should accept the judgment of counsel. Therefore Aristotle[3] leaves it in doubt whether choice belongs principally to the appetitive or the cognitive power, since he says that choice is "either an appetitive intellect or an intellectual appetite." But he inclines to its being an intellectual appetite when he describes choice as "a desire proceeding from counsel."[4] And the reason of this is because the proper object of choice is the means to the end, and this, as such, is in the nature of that good which is called useful; therefore since good, as such, is the object of the appetite, it follows that choice is principally an act of the appetitive power. And thus free choice is an appetitive power.

Reply Obj. 1. The appetitive powers accompany the apprehensive, and in this sense Damascene says that free choice straightway accompanies the rational power.

Reply Obj. 2 Judgment, as it were, concludes

and determines counsel. Now counsel is determined, first, by the judgment of reason, secondly, by the acceptation of the appetite; hence the Philosopher says[5] that, "having formed a judgment by counsel, we desire in accordance with that counsel." And in this sense choice itself is a judgment from which free choice takes its name.

Reply Obj. 3. This comparison which is implied in the name choice belongs to the preceding counsel, which is an act of reason. For though the appetite does not make comparisons, yet since it is moved by the apprehensive power which does compare, it has some likeness of comparison by choosing one in preference to another.

ARTICLE 4. *Whether Free Choice Is a Power Distinct From the Will?*

We proceed thus to the Fourth Article: It would seem that free choice is a power distinct from the will.[6]

Objection 1. For Damascene says (*De Fid. Orth.* ii, 22)[7] that Θέλησις is one thing and βούλησις another. But Θέλησις is the will, while βούλησις seems to be the free choice, because βούλησις according to him, is the will as concerning an object by way of comparison between two things. Therefore it seems that free choice is a distinct power from the will.

Obj. 2. Further, powers are known by their acts. But election, which is the act of free choice, is distinct from the will, because "the will regards the end, whereas choice regards the means to the end."[8] Therefore free choice is a distinct power from the will.

Obj. 3. Further, the will is the intellectual appetite. But on the part of the intellect there are two powers—the agent and the possible. Therefore, also on the part of the intellectual appetite there must be another power besides the will. And it seems that this can only be free choice. Therefore free choice is a distinct power from the will.

On the contrary, Damascene says (*De Fid. Orth.* iii, 14)[9] free choice is nothing else than the will.

I answer that, The appetitive powers must be proportionate to the apprehensive powers, as we

---

[5] *Ibid.*

[6] This is the teaching of Albert the Great. Cf. *Summa de Creaturis*, II, Q. 70, A. 2 (BO XXXV, 577); *In Sent.*, II, d. 24, A. 5 (BO XXVII, 402). See Lottin, *La Théorie* (p. 113; p. 134).

[7] PG 94, 944.

[8] *Ethics*, III, 2 (1111[b]26).

[9] PG 94, 1037.

---

[1] PG 94, 949.

[2] *Ethics*, III, 3 (1113[a]11).

[3] *Ibid.*, VI, 2 (1139[b]4).

[4] *Ibid.*, III, 3 (1113[a]11).

have said above (Q. LXIV, A. 2; Q. LXXX, A. 2). Now, as on the part of the intellectual apprehension we have intellect and reason, so on the part of the intellectual appetite we have will, and free choice which is nothing else but the power of choice. And this is clear from their relations to their respective objects and acts. For the act of understanding implies the simple acceptance of something; hence we say that we understand first principles, which are known of themselves without any comparison. But to reason, properly speaking, is to come from one thing to the knowledge of another; and so, properly speaking, we reason about conclusions, which are known from the principles. In like manner on the part of the appetite to will implies the simple appetite for something; hence the will is said to regard the end, which is desired for itself. But to choose is to desire something for the sake of obtaining something else, and so, properly speaking, it regards the means to the end. Now, just as in matters of knowledge, the principles are related to the conclusion to which we assent on account of the principles, so, in appetitive matters, the end is related to the means, which is desired on account of the end. Hence it is evident that as the intellect is to reason, so is the will to the power of choice, that is, to free choice. But it has been shown above (Q. LXXIX, A. 8) that it belongs to the same power both to understand and to reason, even as it belongs to the same power to be at rest and to be in movement. Therefore it belongs also to the same power to will and to choose, and on this account the will and the free choice are not two powers, but one.

Reply Obj. 1. βούλησις is distinct from Θέλησις on account of a distinction not of powers, but of acts.

Reply Obj. 2. Choice and will—that is, the act of willing—are different acts; yet they belong to the same power, as also to understand and to reason, as we have said.

Reply Obj. 3. The intellect is compared to the will as moving the will. And therefore there is no need to distinguish in the will an agent and a possible will.

QUESTION LXXXIV

How the Soul While United to the Body Understands Corporeal Things Beneath It

(*In Eight Articles*)

We now have to consider the acts and habits of the soul in regard to the intellectual and the appetitive powers, for the other powers of the soul do not come directly under the consideration of the theologian. Furthermore, the acts of the appetitive part of the soul come under the consideration of the science of morals; and so we shall treat of them in the second part of this work, to which the consideration of moral matters belongs. But of the acts of the intellectual part we shall treat now. First, we shall consider the acts, secondly, the habits.

In treating of these acts we shall proceed in the following order. First, we shall inquire how the soul understands when united to the body; secondly, how it understands when separated from the body (Q. LXXXIX).

The former of these inquiries will be threefold: (1) How the soul understands bodies which are beneath it. (2) How it understands itself and things contained in itself (Q. LXXXVII). (3) How it understands immaterial substances, which are above it (Q. LXXXVIII).

In treating of the knowledge of corporeal things there are three points to be considered: (1) Through what does the soul know them? (2) How and in what order does it know them? (Q. LXXXV). (3) What does it know in them? (Q. LXXXVI).

Under the first head there are eight points of inquiry: (1) Whether the soul knows bodies through the intellect? (2) Whether it understands them through its essence, or through some species? (3) If through some species, whether the species of all things intelligible are naturally innate in the soul? (4) Whether these species are derived by the soul from certain separate immaterial forms? (5) Whether our soul sees in the eternal ideas all that it understands? (6) Whether it acquires intellectual knowledge from the senses? (7) Whether the intellect can, through the species of which it is possessed, actually understand, without turning to the phantasms? (8) Whether the judgment of the intellect is hindered by an obstacle in the sensitive powers?

ARTICLE 1. *Whether the Soul Knows Bodies Through the Intellect?*

We proceed thus to the First Article: It would seem that the soul does not know bodies through the intellect.

Objection 1. For Augustine says (*Soliloq.* ii, 4)[1] that "bodies cannot be understood by the intellect, nor indeed anything corporeal unless it can be perceived by the senses." He says also (*Gen. ad lit.* xii, 24)[2] that intellectual vision is

[1] PL 32, 888.   [2] PL 34, 474.

of those things that are in the soul by their essence. But such are not bodies. Therefore the soul cannot know bodies through the intellect.

Obj. 2. Further. as sense is to the intelligible, so is the intellect to the sensible. But the soul can by no means, through the senses, understand spiritual things, which are intelligible. Therefore by no means can it, through the intellect, know bodies, which are sensible.

Obj. 3. Further, the intellect is concerned with things that are necessary and unchangeable. But all bodies are movable and changeable. Therefore the soul cannot know bodies through the intellect.

On the contrary, Science is in the intellect. If, therefore, the intellect does not know bodies, it follows that there is no science of bodies; and thus natural science, which treats of movable bodies, is destroyed.

I answer, In order to make this question clear, that the early philosophers. who inquired into the natures of things, thought there was nothing in the world save bodies.[1] And because they observed that all bodies are movable, and considered them to be always in a state of flux, they were of opinion that we can have no certain knowledge of the truth of things. For what is in a continual state of flux cannot be grasped with certitude, for it passes away before the mind can form a judgment of it, according to the saying of Heraclitus, that "it is not possible twice to touch a drop of water in a passing torrent," as the Philosopher relates.[2]

After these came Plato, who, wishing to save the certitude of our knowledge of truth through the intellect, maintained that, besides these things corporeal. there is another genus of beings, separate from matter and movement, which beings he called species or ideas, by participation of which each one of these singular and sensible things is said to be either a man, or a horse, or the like.[3] And so he said that sciences and definitions, and whatever pertains to the act of the intellect, are not referred to these sensible bodies, but to those beings immaterial and separate,[4] so that according to this the soul does not understand these corporeal things, but the separate species of these corporeal things.

Now this may be shown to be false for two reasons. First, because. since those species are immaterial and immovable, knowledge of move-

ment and matter would be excluded from science (which knowledge is proper to natural science), and likewise all demonstration through moving and material causes. Secondly, because it seems ridiculous, when we seek for knowledge of things which are clear to us, to introduce other beings, which cannot be the substance of those others, since they differ from them in being; so that granted that we have a knowledge of those separate substances, we cannot for that reason claim to form a judgment concerning these sensible things.

Now it seems that Plato strayed from the truth[5] because, having considered that all knowledge takes place through some kind of likeness,[6] he thought that the form of the thing known must of necessity be in the knower in the same manner as in the thing known. Then he considered that the form of the thing understood is in the intellect under conditions of universality, immateriality, and unchangeableness, which is apparent from the very operation of the intellect, which understands in a universal way, and under a certain manner of necessity; for the mode of action corresponds to the mode of the agent's form. And therefore he thought that the things which we understand must subsist in themselves under the same conditions of immateriality and unchangeableness.

But there is no necessity for this. For even in sensible things it is to be observed that the form is otherwise in one sensible than in another; for instance, whiteness may be of great intensity in one, and of a less intensity in another, and in one we find whiteness with sweetness, in another without sweetness. In the same way the sensible form is conditioned differently in the thing which is outside the soul, and in the sense which receives the forms of sensible things without matter such as the colour of gold without receiving gold. So also the intellect, according to its own mode, receives under conditions of immateriality and unchangeableness the species of material and changeable bodies; for the received is in the receiver according to the mode of the receiver. We must conclude, therefore, that through the intellect the soul knows bodies by a knowledge which is immaterial, universal, and necessary.

Reply Obj. 1. These words of Augustine are to be understood as referring to those things by which the intellect knows, but not to what it knows. For the intellect knows bodies by under-

---

[1] Cf. Q. XLIV, A. 2.

[2] *Metaphysics*, IV, 5 (1010ᵃ14).

[3] Cf. Aristotle, *Metaphysics*, I, 6, 9 (987ᵇ6; 992ᵇ7); *Theaetetus* (156).

[4] See below, A. 3, obj. 3; cf. also Avicenna, *Meta.*, VII, 2 (96ra).

[5] Cf. Avicenna, *Meta.*, VII, 3 (96rb); St. Thomas, *In Meta.*, I, 10.

[6] Cf. Aristotle, *Soul*, I, 2 (404ᵇ17).

standing them, not indeed through bodies, nor through material and corporeal likenesses, but through immaterial and intelligible species, which can be in the soul by their own essence.

Reply Obj. 2. As Augustine says,[1] it is not correct to say that as the sense knows only bodies so the intellect knows only spiritual things; for it follows that God and the angels would not know corporeal things. The reason of this diversity is that the lower power does not extend to those things that belong to the higher power, whereas the higher power does in a more excellent manner those things which belong to the lower power.

Reply Obj. 3. Every movement presupposes something immovable, for when a change of quality occurs the substance remains unmoved, and when there is a change of substantial form, matter remains unmoved. Moreover the dispositions of mutable things are themselves immovable; for instance, though Socrates be not always sitting, yet it is unchangeably true that whenever he does sit he remains in one place. For this reason there is nothing to hinder our having an unchangeable science of movable things.

ARTICLE 2. *Whether the Soul Understands Corporeal Things Through Its Essence?*

We proceed thus to the Second Article: It would seem that the soul understands corporeal things through its essence.

Objection 1. For Augustine says (*De Trin.* x, 5)[2] that the soul "collects and lays hold of the images of bodies which are formed in the soul and of the soul, for in forming them it gives them something of its own substance." But the soul understands bodies by likenesses of bodies. Therefore the soul knows bodies through its essence, which it employs for the formation of such likenesses, and from which it forms them.

Obj. 2. Further, the Philosopher says[3] that "the soul, after a fashion, is everything." Since, therefore, like is known by like, it seems that the soul knows corporeal things through itself.

Obj. 3. Further, the soul is superior to corporeal creatures. Now lower things are in higher things in a more eminent way than in themselves, as Dionysius says (*Cæl. Hier.* xii).[4] Therefore all corporeal creatures exist in a more excellent way in the soul than in themselves. Therefore the soul can know corporeal creatures through its essence.

On the contrary, Augustine says (*De Trin.* ix,

3)[5] that "the mind gathers knowledge of corporeal things through the bodily senses." But the soul itself cannot be known through the bodily senses. Therefore it does not know corporeal things through its own substance.

I answer that, The ancient philosophers held that the soul knows bodies through its essence. For it was instilled in the minds of all in common that "like is known by like."[6] But they thought that the form of the thing known is in the knower in the same mode as in the thing known. The Platonists however were of a contrary opinion. For Plato, having observed that the intellectual soul is immaterial,[7] and has an immaterial mode of knowledge,[8] held that the forms of things known subsist immaterially.[9] While the earlier natural philosophers, observing that things known are corporeal and material, held that things known must exist materially even in the soul that knows them. And therefore, in order to ascribe to the soul a knowledge of all things, they held that it has a nature in common with all things.[10] And because the nature of a result is determined by its principles, they ascribed to the soul the nature of a principle, so that those who thought fire to be the principle of all, held that the soul had the nature of fire, and in like manner as to air and water.[11] Lastly, Empedocles, who posited four material elements and two principles of movement, said that the soul was composed of these.[12] Consequently, since they held that things exist in the soul materially, they maintained that all the soul's knowledge is material, thus failing to discern intellect from sense.[13]

But this opinion will not hold. First, because in the material principle of which they spoke the various results do not exist save in potency. But a thing is not known according as it is in potency, but only according as it is in act, as is shown in the *Metaphysics*;[14] hence neither is a power known except through its act. It is therefore insufficient to ascribe to the soul the nature of the principles of things in order to explain the fact that it knows all things, unless we further

---

[1] *City of God,* XXII, 29 (PL 41, 800).   [2] PL 42, 977.
[3] *Soul,* III, 8 (431^{b}21).   [4] Sect. 2 (PG 3, 293).
[5] PL 42, 963.   [6] Cf. Aristotle, *Soul,* I, 5 (409^{b}24).
[7] See Nemesius, *De Nat. Hom.,* 2 (PG 40, 572); Augustine, *City of God,* VIII, 5 (PL 41, 230).
[8] Cf. Aristotle, *Metaphysics,* I, 6 (987^{b}6).
[9] See above, A. 1.
[10] Cf. Aristotle, *Soul,* I, 5 (409^{b}24).
[11] Cf. Aristotle, *Soul,* I, 2 (405^{a}5); Nemesius, *De Nat. Hom.,* 2 (PG 40, 536). Macrobius, *In Somn. Scip.,* I, 14 (DD 48^a).
[12] Cf. Aristotle, *Generation and Corruption,* I, 1 (314^{a}16); *Soul,* I, 5 (410^{a}3).
[13] Cf. Aristotle, *Soul,* III, 3 (427^{a}21).
[14] Aristotle, IX, 9 (1051^{a}29).

admit in the soul the natures and forms of each individual result, for instance, of bone, flesh, and the like; thus does Aristotle argue against Empedocles.[1] Secondly, because if it were necessary for the thing known to exist materially in the knower, there would be no reason why things which subsist materially outside the soul should lack knowledge; why, for instance, if by fire the soul knows fire, that fire also which is outside the soul should not have knowledge of fire.

We must conclude, therefore, that material things known must exist in the knower not materially, but immaterially. The reason of this is because the act of knowledge extends to things outside the knower, for we also know the things that are outside us. Now by matter the form of a thing is determined to some one thing. Therefore it is clear that knowledge is in inverse ratio to materiality. And consequently things that are not receptive of forms save materially, have no power of knowledge whatever—such as plants, as the Philosopher says.[2] But the more immaterially a thing has the form of the thing known, the more perfect is its knowledge. Therefore the intellect which abstracts the species not only from matter, but also from the individuating conditions of matter, has more perfect knowledge than the senses, which receive the form of the thing known, without matter indeed, but subject to material conditions. Moreover, among the senses, sight has the most perfect knowledge because it is the least material, as we have remarked above (Q. LXXVIII, A. 3), while among intellects the more perfect is the more immaterial.

It is therefore clear from the foregoing that if there be an intellect which knows all things by its essence, then its essence must have all things in itself immaterially; thus the early philosophers held that the essence of the soul, that it may know all things, is actually composed of the principles of all material things. Now it is proper to God that His Essence comprise all things immaterially, as effects pre-exist virtually in their cause. God alone, therefore, understands all things through His Essence; but neither the human soul nor the angels can do so.

Reply Obj. 1. Augustine in that passage is speaking of an imaginary vision, which takes place through the images of bodies. To the formation of such images the soul gives something of its substance, just as a subject is given in order to be informed by some form. In this way the soul makes such images from itself; not that the soul or some part of the soul be turned into

this or that image, but just as we say that a body is made into something coloured because of its being informed with colour. That this is the sense, is clear from what follows. For he says that the soul "keeps something"—namely, not informed with such image—"which is able freely to judge of the species of these images," and that "this is the mind or intellect." And he says that the part which is informed with these images—namely, the imagination—is common to us and beasts.

Reply Obj. 2. Aristotle did not hold that the soul is actually composed of all things, as did the earlier philosopher. He said that "the soul is all things, after a fashion," in so far as it is in potency to all things—through the senses, to all things sensible—through the intellect, to all things intelligible.

Reply Obj. 3. Every creature has a finite and determinate being. And so although the essence of the higher creature has a certain likeness to the lower creature, according as they have something in common generically, yet it has not a complete likeness of it, because it is determined to a certain species other than the species of the lower creature. But the Divine Essence, as the universal principle of all things, is a perfect likeness of whatever may be found in things created.

ARTICLE 3. *Whether the Soul Understands All Things Through Innate Species?*

We proceed thus to the Third Article: It would seem that the soul understands all things through innate species.

Objection 1. For Gregory says, in a homily for the Ascension (xxix *in Ev.*),[3] that "man has understanding in common with the angels." But angels understand all things through innate forms; hence in the book *De Causis*[4] it is said that "every intelligence is full of forms." Therefore the soul also has innate species of things, by means of which it understands corporeal things.

Obj. 2. Further, the intellectual soul is more excellent than corporeal primary matter. But primary matter was created by God under the forms to which it is in potency. Therefore much more is the intellectual soul created by God under intelligible species. And so the soul understands corporeal things through innate species.

Obj. 3. Further, no one can answer the truth except concerning what he knows. But even a person untaught and devoid of acquired knowledge answers the truth to every question if put

---

[1] *Soul*, I, 5 (409[b]23).   [2] *Ibid.*, II, 12 (424[a]32).   [3] PL 76, 1214.   [4] Sect. 9 (BA 178).

to him in orderly fashion, as we find related in the *Meno* of Plato,[1] concerning a certain individual. Therefore we have some knowledge of things even before we acquire science, which would not be the case unless we had innate species. Therefore the soul understands corporeal things through innate species.

On the contrary, The Philosopher, speaking of the intellect, says[2] that it is like "a tablet on which nothing is written."

I answer that, Since form is the principle of action, a thing must be related to the form which is the principle of an action as it is to that action; for instance, if upward motion is from lightness, then that which only potentially moves upwards must be only potentially light, but that which actually moves upwards must be actually light. Now we observe that man sometimes is only a potential knower, both as to sense and as to intellect. And he is reduced from such potency to act: to the act of sensation through the action of the sensibles on his senses; to the act of understanding by instruction or dicovery. Hence we must say that the cognitive soul is in potency both to the likenesses which are the principles of sensing, and to those which are the principles of understanding. For this reason Aristotle (*ibid.*) held that the intellect by which the soul understands has no innate species, but is at first in potency to all such species.

But since that which has a form actually is sometimes unable to act according to that form on account of some hindrance, as a light thing may be hindered from moving upwards, for this reason Plato held[3] that naturally man's intellect is filled with all intelligible species, but that, by being united to the body, it is hindered from the realization of its act. But this seems to be wrong. First, because, if the soul has a natural knowledge of all things, it seems impossible for the soul so far to forget this natural knowledge as not to know that it has it. For no man forgets what he knows naturally; that, for instance, every whole is larger than the part, and the like. And especially unreasonable does this seem if we suppose that it is natural to the soul to be united to the body, as we have established above (Q. LXXVI, A. I), for it is unreasonable that the natural operation of a thing be totally hindered by that which belongs to it naturally. Secondly, the falseness of this opinion is clearly proved from the fact that if a sense be wanting, the

[1] *Meno*, 82; cf. Cicero, *Tuscul.*, 24 (DD 635); Augustine, *De Trin.*, II, 15 (PL 42, 1011).
[2] *Soul*, III, 4 (430ª1).
[3] Cf. Aristotle, *Metaphysics*, I, 9 (993ª1); see also Q. LXXXIX, A. I.

knowledge of what is apprehended through that sense is wanting also; for instance, a man who is born blind can have no knowledge of colours. This would not be the case if the soul had innate species of all intelligible things. We must therefore conclude that the soul does not know corporeal things through innate species.

Reply Obj. 1. Man indeed has intelligence in common with the angels, but not in the same degree of perfection; just as the lower grades of bodies, which merely exist, according to Gregory (*loc. cit.*), have not the same degree of perfection as the higher bodies. For the matter of the lower bodies is not totally completed by its form, but is in potency to forms which it has not; but the matter of heavenly bodies is totally completed by its form, so that it is not in potency to any other form, as we have said above (Q. LXVI, A. 2). In the same way the angelic intellect is perfected by intelligible species, in accordance with its nature, whereas the human intellect is in potency to such species.

Reply Obj. 2. Primary matter has substantial being through its form, and consequently it had to be created under some form; otherwise it would not be in act. But when once it exists under one form it is in potency to others. On the other hand, the intellect does not receive substantial being through the intelligible species, and therefore there is no comparison.

Reply Obj. 3. If questions be put in an orderly fashion they proceed from universal self-evident principles to what is particular. Now by such a process knowledge is produced in the mind of the learner. Therefore when he answers the truth to a subsequent question, this is not because he had knowledge previously, but because he thus learns for the first time. For it does not matter whether the teacher proceeds from universal principles to conclusions by questioning or by asserting, for in either case the mind of the listener is assured of what follows by that which preceded.

ARTICLE 4. *Whether the Intelligible Species Flow into the Soul from Certain Separate Forms?*

We proceed thus to the Fourth Article: It would seem that the intelligible species flow into the soul from some separate forms.

Objection 1. For whatever is such by participation is caused by what is such essentially; for instance, that which is on fire is reduced to fire as its cause. But the intellectual soul according as it is actually understanding, participates the intelligibles themselves, for, in a way, the intellect in act is the thing understood in act. Therefore what in itself and in its essence is understood in act is the cause that the intellectual soul actually understands. Now that which in its essence is actually understood is a form existing without matter. Therefore the intelligible species, by which the soul understands, are caused by certain separate forms.

Obj. 2. Further, the intelligible is to the intellect as the sensible is to the sense. But the sensible species which are in the senses, and by which we sense, are caused by the sensibles which exist actually outside the soul. Therefore the intelligible species, by which our intellect understands, are caused by some things actually intelligible existing outside the soul. But these can be nothing else than forms separate from matter. Therefore the intelligible forms of our intellect flow from some separate substances.

Obj. 3. Further, whatever is in potency is reduced to act by something in act. If, therefore, our intellect, previously in potency, afterwards actually understands, this must be caused by some intellect which is always in act. But this is a separate intellect. Therefore the intelligible species by which we actually understand are caused by some separate substances.

On the contrary, If this were true we should not need the senses in order to understand. And this is proved to be false especially from the fact that if a man be wanting in a sense, he cannot have any knowledge of the sensibles corresponding to that sense.

I answer that, Some have held that the intelligible species of our intellect proceed from certain separate forms or substances. And this in two ways. For Plato, as we have said (A. 1), held that the forms of sensible things subsist by themselves without matter; for instance, the form of a man which he called *per se* man, and the form or idea of a horse which he called *per se* horse, and so forth. He said therefore that these forms are participated both by our soul and by corporeal matter: by our soul, for knowing, and by corporeal matter for being;[1] so that just as corporeal matter by participating the idea of a stone becomes this stone, so our intellect, by participating the idea of a stone, is made to understand a stone. Now participation of an idea takes place by some likeness of the idea in the participator, just as a model is participated by a copy.[2] So just as he held that the sensible

forms, which are in corporeal matter, flow from the ideas as certain likenesses of them, so he held that the intelligible species of our intellect are likenesses of the ideas, flowing from them.[3] And for this reason, as we have said above (A. 1), he referred sciences and definitions to those ideas.

But since it is contrary to the nature of sensible things that their forms should subsist without matter, as Aristotle proves in many ways,[4] Avicenna,[5] setting this opinion aside, held that the intelligible species of all sensible things, instead of subsisting in themselves without matter, preexist immaterially in the separate intellects, from the first of which, he said, such species are derived by a second, and so on to the last separate intellect which he called the agent intellect, from which, according to him,[6] intelligible species flow into our souls, and sensible forms into corporeal matter. And so Avicenna agrees with Plato in this, that the intelligible species of our intellect flow from certain separate forms; but these Plato held to subsist of themselves, while Avicenna placed them in the agent intelligence. They differ, too, in this respect, that Avicenna held that the intelligible species do not remain in our intellect after it has ceased actually to understand, and that it needs to turn (to the agent intellect) in order to receive them anew.[7] Consequently he does not hold that the soul has innate knowledge, as Plato, who held that the participated ideas remain immovably in the soul.[8]

But in this opinion no sufficient reason can be assigned for the soul being united to the body. For it cannot be said that the intellectual soul is united to the body for the sake of the body; for neither is form for the sake of matter, nor is the mover for the sake of the moved, but rather the reverse. Especially does the body seem necessary to the intellectual soul for the latter's proper operation which is to understand, since as to its being the soul does not depend on the body. But if the soul by its very nature had an inborn aptitude for receiving intelligible species through the influence of only certain separate principles and were not to receive them from the senses, it would not need the body in order to understand. And so it would be united to the body to no purpose.

---

[3] For the expression "flow from" (*effluere*), see Plotinus, II *Ennead*, 1; also Avicenna, *De An.* v, 5 (25rb); *Meta.*, IX, 4 (105ra). [4] *Metaphysics*, VII, 14 (1039ª24).

[5] *De Anima*, v, 5 (25rb).

[6] *De Anima* v, 6 (26rb); *Meta.*, IX, 5 (105rb); cf. above, Q. LXV, A. 4. [7] *De Anima, loc. cit.*; cf. *Contra Gent.*, II, 74.

[8] Cf. Aristotle, *Metaphysics*, I, 7 (988ᵇ3); *Topics*, II, 7 (113ª27).

---

[1] Cf. Aristotle, *Metaphysics*, I, 9 (991ᵇ3); *Phaedo* (100); Augustine, QQ. LXXXIII, Q. 46 (PL 40, 30).

[2] Cf. Aristotle, *Metaphysics*, I, 9 (991ª21); *Timaeus* (28, 30).

But if it be said that our soul needs the senses in order to understand through being in some way awakened by them to the consideration of those things the intelligible species of which it receives from the separate principles,[1] even this seems an insufficient explanation. For this awakening does not seem necessary to the soul except in as far as it is overcome by "sluggishness," as the Platonists expressed it,[2] and by "forgetfulness," through its union with the body; and thus the senses would be of no use to the intellectual soul except for the purpose of removing the obstacle which the soul encounters through its union with the body.[3] Consequently the reason of the union of the soul with the body still remains to be sought.

And if it be said with Avicenna that the senses are necessary to the soul because by them it is roused to turn to the agent intelligence from which it receives the species, neither is this a sufficient explanation. Because if it is natural for the soul to understand through species which flow from the agent intelligence, it follows that at times the soul of an individual wanting in one of the senses can turn to the agent intelligence, either from the inclination of its very nature, or through being roused by another sense, in order to receive the species of the things sensible for which the sense is wanting. And thus a man born blind could have knowledge of colours, which is clearly untrue. We must therefore conclude that the intelligible species by which our soul understands do not flow from separate forms.

Reply Obj. 1. The intelligible species which are participated by our intellect are reduced, as to their first cause, to a first principle which is by its essence intelligible—namely, God. But they proceed from that principle by means of the forms of sensible and material things, from which we gather knowledge, as Dionysius says (*Div. Nom.* vii).[4]

Reply Obj. 2. Material things, as to the being which they have outside the soul, may be actually sensible, but not actually intelligible. Therefore there is no comparison between sense and intellect.

Reply Obj. 3. Our possible intellect is reduced from potency to act by some being in act, that is, by the agent intellect, which is a power of the soul as we have said (Q. LXXIX, A. 4), and not by a separate intellect, as proximate cause, although possibly as a remote cause.

ARTICLE 5. *Whether the Intellectual Soul Knows Material Things in the Eternal Types?*

We proceed thus to the Fifth Article: It would seem that the intellectual soul does not know material things in the eternal types.

Objection 1. For that in which anything is known must itself be known more and previously. But the intellectual soul of man, in the present state of life, does not know the eternal types; for it does not know God in Whom the eternal types exist, but is united to God as to the unknown, as Dionysius says (*Myst. Theolog.* i).[5] Therefore the soul does not know all in the eternal types.

Obj. 2. Further, it is written (Rom. 1. 20) that the *invisible things of God are clearly seen . . . by the things that are made*. But among the invisible things of God are the eternal types. Therefore the eternal types are known through material creatures and not the converse.

Obj. 3. Further, the eternal types are nothing other than ideas, for Augustine says (QQ. LXXXIII, *qu.* 46)[6] that "ideas are unchanging types of things existing in the Divine mind." If therefore we say that the intellectual soul knows all things in the eternal types, we come back to the opinion of Plato[7] who said that all knowledge is derived from them.

On the contrary, Augustine says,[8] "If we both see that what you say is true, and if we both see that what I say is true, where do we see this, I pray? Neither do I see it in you, nor do you see it in me, but we both see it in the unchangeable truth which is above our minds." Now the unchangeable truth is contained in the eternal types. Therefore the intellectual soul knows all true things in the eternal types.

I answer that, As Augustine says,[9] "If those who are called philosophers said by chance anything that was true and consistent with our faith, we must claim it from them as from unjust possessors. For some of the doctrines of the heathens are spurious imitations or superstitious inventions, which we must be careful to avoid when we renounce the society of the heathens." Consequently whenever Augustine, who was imbued with the doctrines of the Platonists, found in their teaching anything consistent with faith, he adopted it; and those things which he found contrary to faith he amended. Now Plato held, as we have said above (A. 4), that the forms of

---

[1] Cf. Wm. of Paris, *De Univ.*, II–II, 76 (II, 876); III–II, 3 (II, 959); cf. Plato, *Republic* (523).

[2] Pseudo-Augustine (Alcher of Clairvaux), *De Spir. et An.*, I. (PL 40, 781).   [3] See below, Q. LXXXIX, A. 1.

[4] Sect. 2 (PG 3, 886).

[5] Sect. 3 (PG 3, 1001); cf. *De Div. Nom.*, I, 1 (PG 3, 585).

[6] PL 40, 30.   [7] See above, AA. 1, 4.

[8] *Confessions*, XII, 35 (PL 32, 840).

[9] *Christian Doctrine*, II, 40 (PL 34, 63).

things subsist of themselves apart from matter; and these he called ideas, by participation of which he said that our intellect knows all things, so that just as corporeal matter by participating the idea of a stone becomes a stone, so our intellect, by participating the same idea, has knowledge of a stone. But since it seems contrary to faith that forms of things should subsist of themselves outside the things themselves and apart from matter, as the Platonists held, asserting that *per se* life or *per se* wisdom are creative substances, as Dionysius relates (*Div. Nom.* xi),[1] therefore Augustine (QQ. LXXXIII, *loc. cit.*), for the ideas defended by Plato, substituted the types of all creatures existing in the Divine mind, according to which types all things are made, and are known to the human soul.

When, therefore, the question is asked: Does the human soul know all things in the eternal types? we must reply that one thing is said to be known in another in two ways. First, as in an object itself known, as one may see in a mirror the images of things reflected there. In this way the soul, in the present state of life, cannot see all things in the eternal types, but the blessed know all things thus in the eternal types, for they see God, and all things in Him. Secondly, one thing is said to be known in another as in a principle of knowledge; thus we might say that we see in the sun what we see by the sun. And in this way we must say that the human soul knows all things in the eternal types, since by participation of these types we know all things. For the intellectual light itself which is in us is nothing other than a participated likeness of the uncreated light, in which are contained the eternal types. Hence it is written (Ps. 4. 6, 7), *Many say; who showeth us good things?* which question the Psalmist answers, *The light of Thy countenance, O Lord, is signed upon us,* as though he were to say: By the seal of the Divine light in us, all things are made known to us.

But since besides the intellectual light which is in us, intelligible species, which are derived from things, are required in order for us to have knowledge of material things, therefore this same knowledge is not due merely to a participation of the eternal types, as the Platonists held, maintaining that the mere participation of ideas sufficed for knowledge.[2] And so Augustine says (*De Trin.* iv, 16):[3] "Although the philosophers prove by convincing arguments that all things

occur in time according to the eternal types, were they able to see in the eternal types, or to find out from them how many kinds of animals there are and the origin of each? Did they not seek for this information from the story of times and places?"

But that Augustine did not understand all things to be known in their eternal types or in the unchangeable truth, as though the eternal types themselves were seen, is clear from what he says (QQ. LXXXIII, *loc. cit.*)—namely, that "not each and every rational soul can be said to be worthy of that vision," namely, of the eternal types, "but only those that are holy and pure," such as the souls of the blessed.

From what has been said *the objections* are easily solved.

ARTICLE 6. *Whether Intellectual Knowledge Is Derived From Sensible Things?*

We proceed thus to the Sixth Article: It would seem that intellectual knowledge is not derived from sensible things.

Objection 1. For Augustine says (QQ. LXXXIII., *qu.* 9)[4] that "we cannot expect to learn the fulness of truth from the senses of the body." This he proves in two ways. First, because "whatever the bodily senses reach, is continually being changed; and what is never the same cannot be perceived." Secondly, because "whatever we perceive by the body, even when not present to the senses, may be present to the imagination, as when we are asleep or angry; yet we cannot discern by the senses whether what we perceive be the sensible object, or the deceptive image thereof. Now nothing can be perceived which cannot be distinguished from its counterfeit." And so he concludes that we cannot expect to learn the truth from the senses. But intellectual knowledge apprehends the truth. Therefore intellectual knowledge cannot be looked for from the senses.

Obj. 2. Further, Augustine says (*Gen. ad lit.* xii, 16):[5] "We must not think that the body can make any impression on the spirit, as though the spirit were to supply the place of matter in regard to the body's action; for that which acts is in every way more excellent than that which it acts on." Hence he concludes that the body does not cause its image in the spirit, but the spirit causes it in itself. Therefore intellectual knowledge is not derived from sensible things.

Obj. 3. Further, an effect does not surpass the power of its cause. But intellectual knowl-

---

[1] Sect. 6 (PG 3,956).
[2] See above AA. 1, 4; also below, Q. LXXXVII, A. 1. Cf. the teaching of Bonaventure, *Quaest. Disp. de Scientia Christi*, Q. 4 (QR VI7).   [3] PL 42, 902.
[4] PL 40, 13.   [5] PL 34, 467.

edge extends beyond sensible things, for we understand some things which cannot be perceived by the senses. Therefore intellectual knowledge is not derived from sensible things.

On the contrary, The Philosopher says[1] that the beginning of our knowledge is from the senses.

I answer that, On this point the philosophers held three opinions. For Democritus held that "all knowledge is caused by images issuing from the bodies we think of and entering into our souls," as Augustine says in his letter to Dioscorus (cxviii, 4).[2] And Aristotle says[3] that Democritus held that knowledge is caused by "a discharge of images." And the reason for this opinion was that both Democritus and the other early naturalists did not distinguish between intellect and sense, as Aristotle relates.[4] Consequently, since the sense is changed by the sensible, they thought that all our knowledge is affected by this change alone brought about by sensible things. Democritus held this change to be caused by a discharge of images.

Plato, on the other hand, held that the intellect is distinct from the senses,[5] and that it is an immaterial power not making use of a corporeal organ for its action. And since the incorporeal cannot be changed by the corporeal, he held that intellectual knowledge is not brought about by sensible things affecting the intellect, but by separate intelligible forms being participated by the intellect, as we have said above (AA. 4, 5). Moreover he held that sense is a power operating of itself. Consequently neither is sense, since it is a spiritual power, changed by the sensible, but the sensible organs are changed by the sensible, the result being that the soul is in a way roused to form within itself the species of the sensible. Augustine seems to touch on this opinion (*Gen. ad lit.* xii, 24)[6] where he says that "the body feels not, but the soul through the body, which it makes use of as a kind of messenger, for reproducing within itself what is announced from without." Thus according to Plato, neither does intellectual knowledge proceed from sensible knowledge, nor sensible knowledge wholly from sensible things, but these rouse the sensible soul to the sentient act, while the senses rouse the intellect to the act of understanding.

Aristotle chose a middle course. For with Plato he agreed that intellect and sense are dif-

ferent.[7] But he held that the sense does not have its proper operation without the co-operation of the body, so that "to feel is not an act of the soul alone," but of the composite.[8] And he held the same in regard to all the operations of the sensitive part. Since, therefore, it is not unreasonable that the sensible things which are outside the soul should produce some effect in the composite, Aristotle agreed with Democritus in this, that the operations of the sensitive part are caused by the impression of the sensible on the sense: not by a discharge, as Democritus said, but by some kind of operation. For Democritus maintained that every operation is by way of a discharge of atoms, as we gather from the book on *Generation and Corruption*.[9] But Aristotle held that the intellect has an operation which is independent of the body's co-operation.[10] Now nothing corporeal can make an impression on the incorporeal. And therefore in order to cause the intellectual operation, according to Aristotle, the impression of sensible bodies does not suffice, but something more noble is required, for "the agent is more noble than the patient," as he says.[11] Not, indeed, in the sense that the intellectual operation is effected in us by the mere impression of some superior beings, as Plato held, but that the higher and more noble agent which he calls the agent intellect, of which we have spoken above (Q. LXXIX, AA. 3, 4), causes the phantasms received from the senses to be actually intelligible, by way of abstraction.

According to this opinion, then, on the part of the phantasms intellectual knowledge is caused by the senses. But since the phantasms cannot of themselves change the possible intellect, and require to be made actually intelligible by the agent intellect, it cannot be said that sensible knowledge is the total and perfect cause of intellectual knowledge, but rather that it is in a way the matter of the cause.

Reply Obj. 1. These words of Augustine mean that we must not expect truth wholly from the senses. For the light of the agent intellect is needed, through which we know the truth unchangeably in changeable things, and discern things themselves from their likeness.

Reply Obj. 2. In this passage Augustine speaks not of intellectual but of imaginary knowledge. And since, according to the opinion of Plato, the imagination has an operation which belongs to the soul only, Augustine, in order to

[1] *Metaphysics,* I, 1 (981ᵃ2); *Posterior Analytics,* II, 19 (100ᵃ3).   [2] PL 33, 446.
[3] *Prophesying,* 2 (464ᵃ5).   [4] *Soul,* III, 3 (427ᵃ17).
[5] See above, Q. LXXV, A. 3.   [6] PL 34, 475.

[7] *Soul,* III, 3 (427ᵇ6).   [8] *Sleep,* 1 (454ᵃ7).
[9] Aristotle, I, 8 (324ᵇ25).   [10] *Soul,* III, 4 (429ᵃ24).
[11] *Soul,* III, 5 (430ᵃ18).

show that corporeal likenesses are impressed on the imagination not by bodies but by the soul, uses the same argument as Aristotle does in proving that the agent intellect must be separate, namely, because "the agent is more noble than the patient." And without doubt, according to the above opinion, in the imagination there must be not only a passive but also an active power. But if we hold, according to the opinion of Aristotle, that the action of the power of imagination is an action of the composite,[1] there is no difficulty; because the sensible body is more noble than the organ of the animal, in so far as it is compared to it as a being in act to a being in potency, even as the thing actually coloured is compared to the pupil which is potentially coloured. It may, however, be said, that although the first change of the imagination is through the movement of the sensible, since "fancy is movement produced in accordance with sensation,"[2] nevertheless there is in man an operation which by dividing and composing forms images of various things, even of things not perceived by the senses. And Augustine's words may be taken in this sense.

Reply Obj. 3. Sensitive knowledge is not the entire cause of intellectual knowledge. And therefore it is not strange that intellectual knowledge should extend further than sensitive knowledge.

ARTICLE 7. *Whether the Intellect Can Actually Understand Through the Intelligible Species of Which It Is Possessed, Without Turning to the Phantasms?*

We proceed thus to the Seventh Article: It would seem that the intellect can actually understand through the intelligible species of which it is possessed, without turning to the phantasms.

Objection 1. For the intellect is made actual by the intelligible species by which it is informed. But if the intellect is in act, it understands. Therefore the intelligible species suffices for the intellect to understand actually, without turning to the phantasms.

Obj. 2. Further, the imagination is more dependent on the senses than the intellect on the imagination. But the imagination can actually imagine in the absence of the sensible. Therefore much more can the intellect understand without turning to the phantasms.

Obj. 3. There are no phantasms of incorporeal things, for the imagination does not transcend time and space. If, therefore, our intel-

lect cannot understand anything actually without turning to the phantasms, it follows that it cannot understand anything incorporeal. Which is clearly false, for we understand truth, and God, and the angels.

On the contrary, The Philosopher says[3] that "the soul understands nothing without a phantasm."

I answer that, In the present state of life in which the soul is united to a passible body, it is impossible for our intellect to understand anything actually except by turning to the phantasms. And of this there are two indications. First of all because the intellect, being a power that does not make use of a corporeal organ, would in no way be hindered in its act through the lesion of a corporeal organ if for its act there were not required the act of some power that does make use of a corporeal organ. Now sense, imagination and the other powers belonging to the sensitive part, make use of a corporeal organ. Therefore it is clear that for the intellect to understand actually, not only when it acquires fresh knowledge, but also when it uses knowledge already acquired, there is need for the act of the imagination and of the other powers. For when the act of the imagination is hindered by a lesion of the corporeal organ, for instance, in a case of frenzy, or when the act of the memory is hindered, as in the case of lethargy, we see that a man is hindered from actually understanding things of which he had a previous knowledge. Secondly, anyone can experience this of himself, that when he tries to understand something, he forms certain phantasms to serve him by way of examples, in which as it were he examines what he is striving to understand. It is for this reason that when we wish to make someone understand something, we lay examples before him, from which he can form phantasms for the purpose of understanding.

Now the reason of this is that the power of knowledge is proportioned to the thing known. Thus the proper object of the angelic intellect, which is entirely separate from a body, is an intelligible substance separate from a body, and through such intelligible substances it knows material things. On the other hand, the proper object of the human intellect, which is united to a body, is a quiddity or nature existing in corporeal matter, and through such natures of visible things it rises even to some knowledge of things invisible. Now it belongs to such a nature to exist in an individual, and

[1] *Soul,* I, 1 (403ª5).   [2] *Ibid.,* III, 3 (429ª1).   [3] *Ibid.,* III, 7 (431ª16).

this cannot be apart from corporeal matter; for instance, it belongs to the nature of a stone to be in this stone, and to the nature of a horse to be in this horse, and so forth. And so the nature of a stone or any material thing cannot be known completely and truly, except according as it is known as existing in the individual. Now we apprehend the individual through the senses and the imagination. And, therefore, for the intellect to understand actually its proper object, it must of necessity turn to the phantasms in order to examine the universal nature existing in the individual. But if the proper object of our intellect were a separate form, or if, as the Platonists say,[1] the natures of sensible things subsisted apart from the individual, there would be no need for the intellect to turn to the phantasms whenever it understands.

Reply Obj. 1. The species preserved in the possible intellect exist there habitually when it does not understand them actually, as we have said above (Q. LXXIX, A. 6). Hence in order for us to understand actually, the fact that the species are preserved is not enough. We need further to make use of them in a manner befitting the things of which they are the species, which things are natures existing in individuals.

Reply Obj. 2. Even the phantasm is the likeness of an individual thing; therefore the imagination does not need any further likeness of the individual, whereas the intellect does.

Reply Obj. 3. Incorporeal things, of which there are no phantasms, are known to us by comparison with sensible bodies of which there are phantasms. Thus we understand truth by considering a thing of which we examine the truth; and God, as Dionysius says (*Div. Nom.* i),[2] we know as cause, by way of excess and by way of remotion. Other incorporeal substances we know in the present state of life only by way of remotion or by some comparison to corporeal things. And, therefore, when we understand something about these things, we need to turn to phantasms of bodies, although there are no phantasms of the things themselves.

ARTICLE 8. *Whether the Judgment of the Intellect Is Hindered through Suspension of the Senses?*

We proceed thus to the Eighth Article: It would seem that the judgment of the intellect is not hindered by suspension of the senses.

Objection 1. For the superior does not depend on the inferior. But the judgment of the intel-

lect is higher than the senses. Therefore the judgment of the intellect is not hindered through suspension of the senses.

Obj. 2. Further, to syllogize is an act of the intellect. But during sleep the senses are suspended, as is said in the book on *Sleep*,[3] and yet it sometimes happens that we syllogize while asleep. Therefore the judgment of the intellect is not hindered through suspension of the senses.

On the contrary, What a man does while asleep, against the moral law, is not imputed to him as a sin, as Augustine says (*Gen. ad lit.* xii, 15).[4] But this would not be the case if man, while asleep, had free use of his reason and intellect. Therefore the judgment of the intellect is hindered by suspension of the senses.

I answer that, As we have said above (A. 7; Q. XII, AA. 4, 11), our intellect's proper and proportionate object is the nature of a sensible thing. Now a perfect judgment concerning anything cannot be formed, unless all that pertains to that thing is known; especially if that which is the term and end of judgment is not known. Now the Philosopher says[5] that "as the end of a practical science is the work to be done, so the end of natural science is that which is perceived principally through the senses"; for the smith does not seek knowledge of a knife except for the purpose of the work to be done, in order that he may produce a certain individual knife; and in like manner the natural philosopher does not seek to know the nature of a stone and of a horse save for the purpose of knowing the natures of those things which he perceives with his senses. Now it is clear that a smith cannot judge perfectly of a knife unless he knows the work that must be done, and in like manner the natural philosopher cannot judge perfectly of natural things unless he knows sensible things. But in the present state of life whatever we understand we know by comparison to natural sensible things. Consequently it is not possible for our intellect to form a perfect judgment while the senses are suspended, through which sensible things are known to us.

Reply Obj. 1. Although the intellect is superior to the senses, nevertheless in a manner it receives from the senses, and its first and principal objects are founded in sensible things. And therefore suspension of the senses necessarily involves a hindrance to the judgment of the intellect.

Reply Obj. 2. The senses are suspended in

---

[1] See above, AA. 1, 4.
[2] Sect. 5 (PG 3, 593).
[3] Chap. 1 (454^{b}13).
[4] PL 34, 466.
[5] *Heavens*, III, 7 (306^{a}16).

the sleeper through certain evaporations and the escape of certain exhalations, as we read in the book on *Sleep*.[1] And, therefore, according to the disposition of such evaporation, the senses are more or less suspended. For when the motion of the vapors is considerable, not only are the senses suspended, but also the imagination, so that there are no phantasms; and this happens especially when a man falls asleep after eating and drinking copiously. If, however, the motion of the vapors be somewhat less, phantasms appear, but distorted and without order; thus it happens in a case of fever. And if the motion be still more attenuated, the phantasms will have a certain order; thus especially does it happen towards the end of sleep, in sober men and those who are gifted with a strong imagination. If the motion of the vapors is very slight, not only does the imagination retain its freedom, but also the common sense is partly freed, so that sometimes while asleep a man may judge that what he sees is a dream, discerning, as it were, between things and their likenesses. Nevertheless, the common sense remains partly suspended, and therefore, although it discriminates some likenesses from the reality, yet is it always deceived in some particular. Therefore, while man is asleep, according as sense and imagination are free, so the judgment of his intellect is unfettered, though not entirely. Consequently, if a man syllogizes while asleep, when he wakes up he invariably recognizes a flaw in some respect.

QUESTION LXXXV
OF THE MODE AND ORDER OF
UNDERSTANDING
(*In Eight Articles*)

WE come now to consider the mode and order of understanding. Under this head there are eight points of inquiry: (1) whether our intellect understands by abstracting the species from the phantasms? (2) Whether the intelligible species abstracted from the phantasms are what our intellect understands, or that whereby it understands? (3) Whether our intellect naturally first understands the more universal? (4) Whether our intellect can know many things at the same time? (5) Whether our intellect understands by composing and dividing? (6) Whether the intellect can err? (7) Whether one intellect can understand the same thing better than another? (8) Whether our intellect understands the indivisible before the divisible?

[1] Aristotle, 3 (456ᵇ17).

ARTICLE 1. *Whether Our Intellect Understands Corporeal and Material Things by Abstraction from Phantasms?*

We proceed thus to the First Article: It would seem that our intellect does not understand corporeal and material things by abstraction from the phantasms.

Objection. 1. For the intellect is false if it understands a thing other than it is. Now the forms of material things do not exist abstracted from the particular things whose likenesses are the phantasms. Therefore, if we understand material things by abstraction of the species from the phantasm, there will be falsity in the intellect.

Obj. 2. Further, material things are natural things which include matter in their definition. But nothing can be understood apart from that which enters into its definition. Therefore material things cannot be understood apart from matter. Now matter is the principle of individuation. Therefore material things cannot be understood by abstraction of the universal from the particular, which is to abstract the intelligible species from the phantasm.

Obj. 3. Further, the Philosopher says[2] that "the phantasm is to the intellectual soul what colour is to the sight." But seeing is not caused by abstraction of species from colour, but by colour impressing itself on the sight. Therefore neither does the act of understanding take place by abstraction of something from the phantasm, but by the phantasm impressing itself on the intellect.

Obj. 4. Further, the Philosopher says[3] there are two things in the intellectual soul—the possible intellect and the agent intellect. But it does not pertain to the possible intellect to abstract the intelligible species from the phantasm, but to receive them when abstracted. Neither does it seem to pertain to the agent intellect, which is related to the phantasm, as light is to colour, since light does not abstract anything from colour, but rather flows into it. Therefore in no way do we understand by abstraction from phantasms.

Obj. 5. Further, the Philosopher says[4] that "the intellect understands the species in the phantasm," and not, therefore, by abstraction.

On the contrary, The Philosopher says[5] that "things are intelligible in proportion as they are separable from matter." Therefore material things must be understood according as they are

[2] *Soul*, III, 7 (431ᵃ14).   [3] *Ibid.*, III, 5 (430ᵃ14).
[4] *Ibid.*, III, 7 (431ᵇ2).   [5] *Ibid.*, III, 4 (429ᵇ21).

abstracted from matter and from material likenesses, namely, phantasms.

I answer that, As stated above (Q. LXXXIV, A.
7), the object of knowledge is proportionate to
the power of knowledge. Now there are three
grades of knowing powers. For one knowing
power, namely, the sense, is the act of a corporeal organ. And therefore the object of every
sensitive power is a form as existing in corporeal matter. And since such matter is the principle of individuality, therefore every power
of the sensitive part can only have knowledge
of the individual. There is another grade of
knowing power which is neither the act of a
corporeal organ, nor in any way connected with
corporeal matter; such is the angelic intellect,
the object of whose knowing power is therefore
a form subsisting apart from matter, for though
angels know material things, yet they do not
contemplate them save in something immaterial, namely, either in themselves or in God.
But the human intellect holds a middle place,
for it is not the act of an organ, yet it is a
power of the soul which is the form of the
body, as is clear from what we have said above
(Q. LXXVI, A. 1). And therefore it is proper to
it to know a form existing individually in corporeal matter, but not as existing in this individual matter. But to know what is in individual matter, not as existing in such matter,
is to abstract the form from individual matter
which is represented by the phantasms. Therefore we must say that our intellect understands
material things by abstracting from the phantasms, and through material things thus considered we acquire some knowledge of immaterial things, just as, on the contrary, angels
know material things through the immaterial.

But Plato, considering only the immateriality
of the human intellect, but not the fact that it
is in some way united to the body, held that
the objects of the intellect are separate ideas,
and that we understand not by abstraction, but
by participating things abstract, as stated above
(Q. LXXXIV, A. 1).

Reply Obj. 1. Abstraction may occur in two
ways: First, by way of composition and division,
as when we understand that one thing does not
exist in some other, or that it is separate from
it. Secondly, by way of simple and absolute
consideration, as when we understand one thing
without considering the other. Thus for the intellect to abstract one from another things
which are not really abstract from one another,
does, in the first mode of abstraction, imply
falsehood. But, in the second mode of abstrac-

tion, for the intellect to abstract things which
are not really abstract from one another does
not involve falsehood, as clearly appears in the
case of the senses. For if we understood or said
that colour is not in a coloured body, or that
it is separate from it, there would be error in
this opinion or assertion. But if we consider
colour and its properties, without reference to
the apple which is coloured, or if we express in
word what we thus understand, there is no error
in such an opinion or assertion, because apple
is not in the notion of colour, and therefore
colour can be understood independently of the
apple. Likewise, the things which belong to the
notion of the species of a material thing, such
as a stone, or a man, or a horse, can be thought
of apart from the individualizing principles
which do not belong to the notion of the species.
This is what we mean by abstracting the universal from the particular, or the intelligible
species from the phantasm; that is, by considering the nature of the species apart from its individual principles, which are represented by
the phantasms. If, therefore, the intellect is
said to be false when it understands a thing
otherwise than as it is, that is so, if the word
"otherwise" refers to the thing understood; for
the intellect is false when it understands a thing
otherwise than as it is, and so the intellect would
be false if it abstracted the species of a stone
from its matter in such a way as to understand
the species not to be in matter, as Plato held.[1]
But it is not so, if the word "otherwise" be
taken as referring to the one who understands.
For it is quite true that the mode of understanding, in one who understands, is not the same as
the mode of a thing in being, since the thing
understood is immaterially in the one who understands, according to the mode of the intellect, and not materially, according to the mode
of a material thing.

Reply Obj. 2. Some have thought[2] that the
species of a natural thing is a form only, and
that matter is not part of the species. If that
were so, matter would not enter into the definition of natural things. Therefore it must be
said otherwise, that matter is twofold: common,
and signate or individual; common, such as
flesh and bone, and individual, as this flesh and
these bones. The intellect therefore abstracts
the species of a natural thing from the individual sensible matter, but not from the common sensible matter; for example, it abstracts

---

[1] See above, Q. LXXXIV, A. 4.
[2] Averroes, *In Meta.,* VII, 21 (VIII, 171I); 34 (184D).
Cf. St. Thomas, *In Meta.,* VII, 9.

the species of man from *this flesh and these bones,* which do not belong to the notion of the species, but to the individual,[1] and need not be considered in the species; the species of man however cannot be abstracted by the intellect from *flesh and bones.*

Mathematical species, however, can be abstracted by the intellect from sensible matter, not only from individual, but also from common matter, though not from common intelligible matter, but only from individual matter. For sensible matter is corporeal matter as subject to sensible qualities, such as being cold or hot, hard or soft, and the like, while intelligible matter is substance as subject to quantity. Now it is manifest that quantity is in substance before sensible qualities are. Hence quantities, such as number, dimension, and figures, which are the terminations of quantity, can be considered apart from sensible qualities, and this is to abstract them from sensible matter; but they cannot be considered without understanding the substance which is subject to the quantity, for that would be to abstract them from common intelligible matter. Yet they can be considered apart from this or that substance, for that is to abstract them from individual intelligible matter.

But some things can be abstracted even from common intelligible matter, such as being, unity, potency and act, and the like, which can be without matter, as is plain regarding immaterial things. Because Plato failed to consider the twofold kind of abstraction, as above explained (ANS. 1), he held that all those things which we have stated to be abstracted by the intellect are abstract in reality.[2]

Reply Obj. 3. Colours, as being in individual corporeal matter, have the same mode of existence as the power of sight, and therefore they can impress their likeness on the sight. But phantasms, since they are likenesses of individuals and exist in corporeal organs, have not the same mode of existence as the human intellect, as is clear from what we have said, and therefore have not the power of themselves to make an impression on the possible intellect. This is done by the power of the agent intellect which by turning towards the phantasm produces in the possible intellect a certain likeness which represents the thing of which it is the phantasm only so far as regards the nature of the species. It is thus that the intelligible species is said to be abstracted from the phantasm, not

that the numerically same form which previously was in the phantasm is subsequently in the possible intellect, in the way in which a body is taken from one place and transferred to another.

Reply Obj. 4. The phantasm, is both illuminated by the agent intellect and, beyond this, the intelligible species is abstracted from it by the power of the agent intellect. The agent intellect illuminates the phantasm because just as the sensitive part acquires a greater power by its conjunction with the intellect, so by the power of the agent intellect the phantasms are made more fit for the abstraction from them of intelligible intentions. Furthermore the agent intellect abstracts the intelligible species from the phantasm, since by the power of the agent intellect we are able to take into our consideration apart from individual conditions the natures of species, in accordance with whose likenesses the possible intellect is informed.

Reply Obj. 5. Our intellect both abstracts the intelligible species from the phantasms, in so far as it considers the natures of things universally, and nevertheless understands these natures in the phantasms, since it cannot understand the things of which it abstracts the species without turning to the phantasms, as we have said above (Q. LXXXIV, A. 7).

ARTICLE 2. *Whether the Intelligible Species Abstracted from the Phantasm Is Related to Our Intellect As That Which Is Understood?*

We proceed thus to the Second Article: It would seem that the intelligible species abstracted from the phantasm is related to our intellect as that which is understood.

Objection 1. For the understood in act is in the one who understands, since the understood in act is the intellect itself in act. But nothing of what is understood is in the intellect actually understanding save the abstracted intelligible species. Therefore this species is what is actually understood.

Obj. 2. Further, what is actually understood must be in something; otherwise it would be nothing. But it is not in the thing which is outside the soul, for, since the thing which is outside the soul is material, nothing therein can be what is actually understood. Therefore what is actually understood is in the intellect. Consequently it can be nothing else than the above mentioned intelligible species.

Obj. 3. Further, the Philosopher says[3] that "words are signs of the passions in the soul."

---

[1] Aristotle, *Metaphysics,* VII, 10 (1035ᵇ28).
[2] See Q. LXXXIV, A. 1; also Q. L, A. 2.

[3] *Interpretation,* 1 (16ᵃ3).

But words signify the things understood, for we express by word what we understand. Therefore these passions of the soul, namely, the intelligible species, are what is actually understood.

On the contrary, The intelligible species is to the intellect what the sensible image is to the sense. But the sensible image is not what is perceived, but rather that by which sense perceives. Therefore the intelligible species is not what is understood, but that by which the intellect understands.

I answer that, Some have asserted that our intellectual powers know only the impression made on them,[1] as, for example, that sense is cognizant only of the impression made on its own organ. According to this theory, the intellect understands only its own impression, namely, the intelligible species which it has received, so that this species is what is understood.

This is, however, manifestly false for two reasons. First, because the things we understand and the objects of science are the same. Therefore if what we understand is merely the intelligible species in the soul, it would follow that every science would not be concerned with things outside the soul, but only with the intelligible species within the soul; thus, according to the teaching of the Platonists all science is about ideas, which they held to be actually understood.[2] Secondly, it is untrue because it would lead to the opinion of the philosophers of antiquity who maintained that "whatever seems, is true,"[3] and that consequently contradictories are true simultaneously. For if the power knows its own impression only, it can judge of that only. Now a thing seems according to the impression made on the knowing power. Consequently the knowing power will always judge of its own impression as such, and so every judgment will be true; for instance, if taste perceived only its own impression, when anyone with a healthy taste judges that honey is sweet, he would judge truly; and likewise if anyone with a corrupt taste judges that honey is bitter, this would be true, for each would judge according to the impression on his taste. Thus every opinion would be equally true; in fact, every sort of apprehension.

Therefore it must be said that the intelligible species is related to the intellect as that by which it understands, which is proved thus.

There is a twofold action,[4] one which remains in the agent, for instance, to see and to understand, and another which passes into an external thing, for instance, to heat and to cut; and each of these actions proceeds in virtue of some form. And as the form from which an act tending to something external proceeds is the likeness of the object of the action, as heat in the heater is a likeness of the thing heated, so the form from which an action remaining in the agent proceeds is the likeness of the object. Hence that by which the sight sees is the likeness of the visible thing; and the likeness of the thing understood, that is, the intelligible species, is the form by which the intellect understands. But since the intellect is turned back (*reflectitur*) upon itself, by the same reflection it understands both its own act of understanding and the species by which it understands. Thus the intelligible species is that which is understood secondarily, but that which is primarily understood is the thing, of which the intelligible species is the likeness.

This also appears from the opinion of the ancient philosophers,[5] who said that "like is known by like." For they said that the soul knows the earth outside itself by the earth within itself; and so of the rest. If, therefore, we take the species of the earth instead of the earth, according to Aristotle,[6] who says that "a stone is not in the soul, but the likeness of the stone," it follows that the soul knows the things which are outside of it, by means of its intelligible species.

Reply Obj. 1. The thing understood is in the one who understands by its own likeness, and it is in this sense that we say that the thing actually understood is the intellect in act, because the likeness of the thing understood is the form of the intellect, just as the likeness of a sensible thing is the form of the sense in act. Hence it does not follow that the intelligible species abstracted is what is actually understood, but rather that it is the likeness of it.

Reply Obj. 2. In these words "the thing actually understood" there is a twofold meaning: the thing which is understood, and the fact that it is understood. In like manner the words "abstract universal" imply two things, the nature of a thing and its abstraction or universality. Therefore the nature itself to which it falls to be understood, or to be abstracted, or to bear the intention of universality is only in individ-

---

[1] Protagoras and Heraclitus; cf. Aristotle, *Metaphysics,* IX, 3 (1047ª6); IV, 3 (1005ᵇ25). Cf. St. Thomas, *In Meta.,* IX, 3; IV, 6.

[2] Cf. Q. LXXXIV, AA. 1, 4.

[3] Cf. Aristotle, *Metaphysics,* IV, 5 (1009ª8).

[4] *Metaphysics,* IX, 8 (1050ª23).

[5] Empedocles and Plato, in Aristotle, *Soul,* I, 5 (409ᵇ26); I, 2 (404ᵇ17).   [6] *Soul,* III, 8 (431ᵇ29).

uals; but that it is understood, abstracted, or bears the intention of universality is in the intellect. We see something similar to this in the senses. For the sight sees the colour of the apple apart from its smell. If therefore it be asked where is the colour which is seen apart from the smell, it is clear that the colour which is seen is only in the apple; but that it is perceived apart from the smell is owing to the sight, since the likeness of colour and not of smell is in the sight. In like manner the humanity which is understood is only in this or that man, but that humanity is apprehended without the individual conditions, that is, that it is abstracted and consequently considered as universal, happens to humanity according as it is perceived by the intellect, in which there is a likeness of the specific nature, but not of the individual principles.

Reply Obj. 3. There are two operations in the sensitive part. One in regard to change only, and thus the operation of the senses takes place by the senses being changed by the sensible. The other is formation, according as the imagination forms for itself an image of an absent thing, or even of something never seen. Both of these operations are found in the intellect. For in the first place there is the passion of the possible intellect as informed by the intelligible species; and then the possible intellect thus informed forms a definition, or a division, or a composition, which is expressed by a word. Thus the notion signified by a word is its definition, and a proposition signifies the intellect's division or composition. Words do not therefore signify the intelligible species themselves, but that which the intellect forms for itself for the purpose of judging of external things.

ARTICLE 3. *Whether the More Universal Is First in Our Intellectual Knowledge?*

We proceed thus to the Third Article: It would seem that the more universal is not first in our intellectual knowledge.

Objection 1. For what is first and more known in its own nature is secondarily and less known in relation to ourselves. But universals come first as regards their nature, because that is first which does not involve the existence of its correlative. Therefore the universals are secondarily known as regards our intellect.

Obj. 2. Further, the composite precedes the simple in relation to us. But universals are the more simple. Therefore they are known secondarily by us.

Obj. 3. Further, the Philosopher says[1] that

[1] *Physics*, I, I (184ᵇ11).

the object defined comes in our knowledge before the parts of its definition. But the more universal is part of the definition of the less universal, as animal is part of the definition of man. Therefore the universals are secondarily known by us.

Obj. 4. Further, we know causes and principles by their effects. But universals are principles. Therefore universals are secondarily known by us.

On the contrary, "We must proceed from the universal to the singular."[2]

I answer that, In our knowledge there are two things to be considered. First, that intellectual knowledge in some degree arises from sensible knowledge. And, because sense has singular things for its object, and intellect has the universal for its object, it follows that our knowledge of the former comes before our knowledge of the latter. Secondly, we must consider that our intellect proceeds from a state of potency to a state of act. But everything which proceeds from potency to act comes first to an incomplete act, which is midway between potency and act, before achieving the perfect act. The perfect act of the intellect is complete knowledge, when the thing is distinctly and determinately known, whereas the incomplete act is imperfect knowledge, when the thing is known indistinctly, and as it were confusedly. A thing thus imperfectly known, is known relatively in act and in some measure in potency, and hence the Philosopher says,[3] that "what is manifest and certain is known to us at first confusedly; afterwards we know it by distinguishing its principles and elements." Now it is evident that to know something that comprises many things without proper knowledge of each thing contained in it is to know that thing confusedly. In this way we can have knowledge not only of the universal whole, which contains parts potentially, but also of the integral whole; for each whole can be known confusedly, without its parts being known. But to know distinctly what is contained in the universal whole is to know the less common, as to know animal indistinctly is to know it as animal, whereas to know animal distinctly is to know it as rational or irrational animal, that is, to know a man or a lion; therefore our intellect knows animal before it knows man, and the same reason holds in comparing anything more universal with the less universal.

Moreover, as sense, like the intellect, proceeds from potency to act, the same order of

[2] *Ibid.,* (184ᵃ23).
[3] *Ibid.,* (184ᵃ21).

knowledge appears in the senses. For by sense we judge of the more common before the less common, in reference both to place and time; in reference to place, when a thing is seen afar off it is seen to be a body before it is seen to be an animal, and to be an animal before it is seen to be a man, and to be a man before it is seen to be Socrates or Plato; and the same is true as regards time, for a child can distinguish man from not man before he distinguishes this man from that, and therefore "children at first call all men fathers, and later on distinguish each one from the others."[1]

The reason of this is clear, because he who knows a thing indistinctly is in a state of potency as regards knowing its principle of distinction, just as he who knows genus is in a state of potency as regards knowing difference. Thus it is evident that indistinct knowledge is midway between potency and act. We must therefore conclude that knowledge of the singular and individual is prior, as regards us, to the knowledge of the universal, just as sensible knowledge is prior to intellectual knowledge. But in both sense and intellect the knowledge of the more common precedes the knowledge of the less common.

Reply Obj. 1. The universal can be considered in two ways. First, the universal nature may be considered together with the intention of universality. And since the intention of universality, namely, the relation of one and the same to many, is due to intellectual abstraction, the universal thus considered must be a secondary consideration. Hence it is said[2] that the "universal animal is either nothing or something secondary." But according to Plato, who held that universals are subsistent,[3] the universal considered thus would be prior to the particular, for the latter, according to him, are only participations of the subsistent universals which he called ideas.

Secondly, the universal can be considered in the nature itself—for instance, animality or humanity as existing in the individual. And thus we must distinguish two orders of nature: one, by way of generation and time; and thus the imperfect and the potential come first. In this way the more common comes first in the order of nature, as appears clearly in the generation of man and animal; for "the animal is generated before man," as the Philosopher says.[4] The other order is the order of perfection or of the intention of nature. For instance, act considered absolutely is naturally prior to potency, and the perfect to the imperfect; thus the less common comes naturally before the more common, as man comes before animal. For the intention of nature does not stop at the generation of animal, but goes on to the generation of man.

Reply Obj. 2. The more common universal may be compared to the less common, as the whole and as the part. As the whole, considering that in the more universal is potentially contained not only the less universal, but also other things, as in animal is contained not only man but also horse. As part, considering that the less common contains in its notion not only the more common, but also other things as *man* contains not only animal but also rational. Therefore animal in itself comes into our knowledge before man, but man comes before animal considered as part of the same notion.

Reply Obj. 3. A part can be known in two ways. First, absolutely, considered in itself; and thus nothing prevents the parts being known before the whole, as stones are known before a house is known. Secondly, as belonging to a certain whole; and thus we must know the whole before its parts. For we know a house in a confused way before we know its individual parts. So likewise the elements of a definition absolutely considered are known before the thing defined is known; otherwise the thing defined would not be made known by them. But as parts of the definition they are known after. For we know man in a confused way as man before we know how to distinguish all that belongs to the notion of man.

Reply Obj. 4. The universal, as understood with the intention of universality, is, indeed, in a way, a principle of knowledge, in that the intention of universality results from the mode of understanding which is by way of abstraction. But what is a principle of knowledge is not of necessity a principle of being, as Plato thought,[5] since at times we know a cause through its effect, and substance through accidents. Therefore the universal thus considered, according to the opinion of Aristotle, is neither a principle of being, nor a substance, as he makes clear.[6] But if we consider the generic or specific nature itself as existing in the singular, thus in a way it is in the nature of a formal principle in regard to the singulars, for the singular is the result of matter, while the notion of species is from the form. But the generic nature is compared to the

---

[1] *Physics*, I, 1 (184[b]12). [2] Aristotle, *Soul*, I, 1 (402[b]7).
[3] See above, Q. LXXXIV, A. 1.
[4] *Generation of Animals*, II, 3 (736[b]2).

[5] See above, Q. LXXXIV, A. 1.
[6] *Metaphysics*, VII, 13 (1038[b]8).

specific nature rather after the fashion of a material principle, because the generic nature is taken from that which is material in a thing, while the notion of species is taken from that which is formal; thus the notion of animal is taken from the sensitive part, while the notion of man is taken from the intellectual part. Thus it is that the ultimate intention of nature is to the species and not to the individual, nor to the genus, because the form is the end of generation, while matter is for the sake of the form. Neither is it necessary that, as regards us, knowledge of any cause or principle should be secondary, since at times through sensible causes we become acquainted with unknown effects, and sometimes conversely.

ARTICLE 4. *Whether We Can Understand Many Things at the Same Time?*

We proceed thus to the Fourth Article: It would seem that we can understand many things at the same time.

Objection 1. For intellect is above time, whereas the succession of before and after belongs to time. Therefore the intellect does not understand different things in succession, but at the same time.

Obj. 2. Further, there is nothing to prevent different forms not opposed to each other from actually being in the same subject, as, for instance, colour and smell are in the apple. But intelligible species are not opposed to each other. Therefore there is nothing to prevent the same intellect being in act as regards different intelligible species, and thus it can understand many things at the same time.

Obj. 3. Further, the intellect understands a whole at the same time, such as a man or a house. But a whole contains many parts. Therefore the intellect understands many things at the same time.

Obj. 4. Further, we cannot know the difference between two things unless we know both at the same time,[1] and the same is to be said of any other comparison. But our intellect knows the difference between one thing and another. Therefore it knows many things at the same time.

On the contrary, It is said[2] that "understanding is of one thing only, science is of many."

I answer that, The intellect can, indeed, understand many things as one, but not as many; that is to say, by one but not by many intelligible species. For the mode of every action follows the form which is the principle of that action. Therefore whatever things the intellect can understand under one species it can understand at the same time; hence it is that God sees all things at the same time, because He sees all in one, that is, in His Essence. But whatever things the intellect understands under different species, it does not understand at the same time. The reason of this is that it is impossible for one and the same subject to be perfected at the same time by many forms of one genus and diverse species, just as it is impossible for one and the same body at the same time to have different colours or different shapes. Now all intelligible species belong to one genus, because they are the perfections of one intellectual power; although the things of which they are the species belong to different genera. Therefore it is impossible for one and the same intellect to be perfected at the same time by different intelligible species so as actually to understand different things.

Reply Obj. 1. The intellect is above that time which is the measure of the movement of corporeal things. But the multitude itself of intelligible species causes a certain change of intelligible operations, according as one operation succeeds another. And this change is called time by Augustine, who says (*Gen. ad lit.* viii, 20, 22),[3] that "God moves the spiritual creatures through time."

Reply Obj. 2. Not only is it impossible for opposite forms to exist at the same time in the same subject, but neither can any forms belonging to the same genus, even though they are not opposed to one another, as is clear from the examples of colours and shapes.

Reply Obj. 3. Parts can be understood in two ways. First, in a confused way, as existing in the whole, and thus they are known through the one form of the whole, and so are known together. In another way they are known distinctly; thus each is known by its species, and so they are not understood at the same time.

Reply Obj. 4. When the intellect knows the difference or comparison between one thing and another, it knows both under the aspect of their difference or comparison; just as it knows the parts under the aspect of the whole, as we have said above (ad 3).

ARTICLE 5. *Whether Our Intellect Understands by Composition and Division?*

We proceed thus to the Fifth Article: It would seem that our intellect does not understand by composition and division.

---

[1] Aristotle, *Soul*, III, 2 (426ᵇ22).
[2] Aristotle, *Topics*, II, 10 (114ᵇ34).
[3] PL. 34, 388, 389.

Objection 1. For composition and division are only of many. But the intellect cannot understand many things at the same time. Therefore it cannot understand by composition and division.

Obj. 2. Further, every composition and division implies past, present, or future time. But the intellect abstracts from time, as also from other individual conditions. Therefore the intellect does not understand by composition and division.

Obj. 3. Further, the intellect understands things by assimilation to them. But composition and division are not in things, for nothing is in things but the thing signified by the predicate and the subject, which is one and the same if the composition is true, for *man* is truly what *animal* is. Therefore the intellect does not act by composition and division.

On the contrary, Words signify the conceptions of the intellect, as the Philosopher says.[1] But in words we find composition and division, as appears in affirmative and negative propositions. Therefore the intellect acts by composition and division.

I answer that, That human intellect must of necessity understand by composition and division. For since the intellect passes from potency to act, it has a likeness to things which are generated, which do not attain to perfection all at once but acquire it by degrees. And likewise the human intellect does not acquire perfect knowledge of the thing by the first apprehension; but it first apprehends something about the thing, such as its quiddity, and this is its first and proper object; and then it understands the properties, accidents, and the various relations of the essence. Thus it necessarily compares one thing with another by composition or division; and from one composition and division it proceeds to another, which is to reason.

But the angelic and the Divine intellect, like all incorruptible things, have their perfection at once from the beginning. Hence the angelic and the Divine intellect have the entire knowledge of a thing at once and perfectly; and hence also in knowing the quiddity of a thing they know at once whatever we can know by composition, division, and reasoning. Therefore the human intellect knows by composition, division, and reasoning. But the Divine and the angelic intellect know, indeed, composition, division, and reasoning, not by the process itself, but by understanding the simple quiddity.

Reply Obj. 1. Composition and division of the intellect are made by differentiating and comparing. Hence the intellect knows many things when it composes and divides, just as when it knows the difference and comparison of things.

Reply Obj. 2. Although the intellect abstracts from the phantasms, it does not understand actually without turning to the phantasms, as we have said (A. 1, and Q. LXXXIV, A. 7). And as regards turning to the phantasms, composition and division of the intellect involve time.

Reply Obj. 3. The likeness of a thing is received into the intellect according to the mode of the intellect, and not according to the mode of the thing. Therefore something on the part of the thing corresponds to the composition and division of the intellect, but it does not exist in the same way in the intellect and in the thing. For the proper object of the human intellect is the quiddity of a material thing, which falls under the senses and the imagination. Now in a material thing there is a twofold composition. First, there is the composition of form with matter, and to this corresponds that composition of the intellect by which the universal whole is predicated of its part; for the genus is derived from common matter, while the difference that completes the species is derived from the form, and the particular from individual matter. The second composition is of accident with subject, and to this composition corresponds that composition of the intellect by which accident is predicated of subject, as when we say "the man is white." Nevertheless composition of the intellect differs from composition of things; for in the latter the components are diverse, whereas composition of the intellect is a sign of the identity of the components. For the composition of the intellect does not assert that man is whiteness, but the assertion, "the man is white, means that "the man is something having whiteness," and the subject, which is a man, is identified with a subject having whiteness. It is the same with the composition of form and matter, for animal signifies that which has a sensitive nature; rational, that which has an intellectual nature; man, that which has both; and Socrates that which has all these things together with individual matter. And according to this kind of identity our intellect composes one thing with another by the act of predication.

ARTICLE 6. *Whether the Intellect Can Be False?*

We proceed thus to the Sixth Article: It would seem that the intellect can be false.

Objection 1. For the Philosopher says[2] that

[1] *Interpretation,* 1 (16ᵃ3).

[2] *Metaphysics,* VI, 4 (1027ᵇ27).

"truth and falsehood are in the mind." But the mind and intellect are the same, as is shown above (Q. LXXII). Therefore falsehood is in the intellect.

Obj. 2. Further, opinion and reasoning belong to the intellect. But falsehood is found in both. Therefore falsehood can be in the intellect.

Obj. 3. Further, sin is in the intellectual part. But sin involves falsehood, for *those err that work evil* (Prov. 14. 22). Therefore falsehood can be in the intellect.

On the contrary, Augustine says (QQ. LXXXIII, qu. 32),[1] that "everyone who is deceived, does not rightly understand that wherein he is deceived." And the Philosopher says[2] that "the intellect is always true."

I answer that, The Philosopher[3] compares intellect with sense on this point. For sense is not deceived in its proper object, as sight in regard to colour, save accidentally through some hindrance occurring to the organ—for example, the taste of a fever-stricken person judges a sweet thing to be bitter, through his tongue being vitiated by ill humours. Sense, however, may be deceived as regards common sensibles, as size or figure; when, for example, it judges the sun to be only a foot in diameter, whereas in reality it exceeds the earth in size. Much more is sense deceived concerning accidental sensibles, as when it judges that vinegar is honey by reason of the colour being the same. The reason of this is evident; for every power, as such, is *per se* directed to its proper object, and things of this kind are always the same. Hence, so long as the power exists, its judgment concerning its own proper object does not fail. Now the proper object of the intellect is the quiddity of a thing; and hence, properly speaking, the intellect is not at fault concerning this quiddity. But it may go astray as regards what surrounds the essence or quiddity of the thing, when it refers one thing to another, or in composition or division, or also in reasoning. Therefore, also in regard to those propositions, which are understood as soon as the meanings of their terms are understood, the intellect cannot err, as in the case of first principles from which arises the infallibility of truth, with regard to the certitude of scientific conclusions.

The intellect, however, may be accidentally deceived in the quiddity of composite things, not by the defect of its organ, for the intellect is not a power using an organ, but on the part of the composition affecting the definition, when, for instance, the definition of a thing is false in relation to something else, as the definition of a circle applied to a triangle; or when a definition is false in itself as involving the composition of things incompatible, as, for instance, to describe anything as a rational winged animal. Hence as regards simple things in whose definition composition does not enter, we cannot be deceived unless, indeed, we understand nothing whatever about them, as is said the *Metaphysics*.[4]

Reply Obj. 1. The Philosopher says that falsehood is in the mind in regard to composition and division. The same answer applies to the *second objection* concerning opinion and reasoning, and to the *third objection,* concerning the error of the sinner, who errs in the practical judgment of the object of desire. But in the absolute consideration of the quiddity of a thing and of those things which are known thereby, the intellect is never deceived. In this sense are to be understood the authorities quoted in proof of *the opposite conclusion.*

ARTICLE 7. *Whether One Person Can Understand One and the Same Thing Better Than Another Can?*

We proceed thus to the Seventh Article: It would seem that one person cannot understand one and the same thing better than another can.

Objection 1. For Augustine says (QQ. LXXXIII, qu. 32),[5] "Whoever understands a thing otherwise than as it is does not understand it at all. Hence it is clear that there is a perfect understanding, than which none other is more perfect; and therefore there are not infinite degrees of understanding a thing, nor can one person understand a thing better than another can."

Obj. 2. Further, the intellect is true in its act of understanding. But truth, being a certain equality between thought and thing, is not subject to more or less; for a thing cannot be said to be more or less equal. Therefore a thing cannot be more or less understood.

Obj. 3. Further, the intellect is that which most pertains to form in man. But different forms cause different species. Therefore if one man understands better than another, it would seem that they do not belong to the same species.

On the contrary, Experience shows that some understand more deeply than do others, as one who carries a conclusion to its first principles and ultimate causes understands it more deeply

---

[1] PL 40, 22.   [2] *Soul,* III, 10 (433ª26).
[3] *Ibid.,* III, 6 (430ᵇ29).

[4] Aristotle, IX, 10 (1052ª1).
[5] PL 40, 22.

than the one who reduces it only to its proximate causes.

I answer that, To say that a thing is understood more by one than by another may be taken in two senses. First, so that the word *more* be taken as determining the act of understanding as regards the thing understood; and thus, one cannot understand the same thing more than another, because to understand it otherwise than as it is, either better or worse, would entail being deceived, and such a one would not understand it, as Augustine argues (*loc. cit.*). In another sense the word *more* can be taken as determining the act of understanding on the part of him who understands; and so one may understand the same thing better than someone else, through having a greater power of understanding, just as a man may see a thing better with his bodily sight, whose power is greater, and whose sight is more perfect. The same applies to the intellect in two ways. First, as regards the intellect itself, which is more perfect. For it is plain that the better the disposition of a body, the better the soul allotted to it, which clearly appears in things of different species. And the reason for this is that act and form are received into matter according to matter's capacity. Hence because some men have bodies of better disposition, their souls have a greater power of understanding. Thus it is said[1] that we see that those who have delicate flesh are of apt mind. Secondly, this occurs in regard to the lower powers of which the intellect has need in its operation, for those in whom the imaginative, cogitative and remembering powers are of better disposition are better disposed to understand.

The *reply to the first objection* is clear from the above; likewise the *reply to the second,* for the truth of the intellect consists in the intellect understanding a thing as it is.

Reply Obj. 3. The difference of form which is due only to the different disposition of matter causes not a specific but only a numerical difference; for different individuals have different forms, diversified according to the difference of matter.

ARTICLE 8. *Whether the Intellect Understands the Indivisible Before the Divisible?*

We proceed thus to the Eighth Article: It would seem that the intellect understands the indivisible before the divisible.

Objection 1. For the Philosopher says[2] that we understand and know from the knowledge of principles and elements. But principles are indivisible, and elements are of divisible things. Therefore the indivisible is known to us before the divisible.

Obj. 2. Further, the definition of a thing contains what is known previously, for a "definition proceeds from the first and more known," as is said in the *Topics.*[3] But the indivisible is part of the definition of the divisible, as a point comes into the definition of a line; for as Euclid says,[4] a line is length without breadth, the extremities of which are points. Also unity comes into the definition of number, for "number is multitude measured by one," as is said in the *Metaphysics.*[5] Therefore our intellect understands the indivisible before the divisible.

Obj. 3. Further, Like is known by like. But the indivisible is more like to the intellect than is the divisible, because "the intellect is simple."[6] Therefore our intellect first knows the indivisible.

On the contrary, It is said[7] that "the indivisible becomes known as a privation." But privation is known secondarily. Therefore likewise is the indivisible.

I answer that, The object of our intellect in its present state is the quiddity of a material thing, which it abstracts from the phantasms, as above stated (Q. LXXXIV, A. 7). And since that which is known first and of itself by our knowing power is its proper object, we must consider its relationship to that quiddity in order to discover in what order the indivisible is known. Now the indivisible is threefold, as is said in the book on the *Soul.*[8] First, the continuous is indivisible, since actually it is undivided although potentially divisible; and this indivisible is known to us before its division, which is a division into parts, because confused knowledge is prior to distinct knowledge, as we have said above (A. 3). Secondly, the indivisible is called so in relation to species, as the essence of man is something indivisible. This way, also, the indivisible is understood before its division into essential parts, as we have said above (*ibid.*); and again before the intellect composes and divides by affirmation and negation. The reason of this is that both these kinds of indivisible are understood by the intellect of itself, as its proper object. The third kind of indivisible is what is altogether indivisible, as a point and unity, which cannot be divided either actually or potentially.

---

[1] Aristotle, *Soul,* II, 9 (421[a]25).
[2] *Physics,* I, 1 (184[a]12).
[3] Aristotle, VI, 4 (141[a]32).
[4] *Geom.,* trans. of Boëthius, I (PL 63, 1307).
[5] Aristotle, X, 6 (1057[a]3).
[6] Aristotle, *Soul,* III, 4 (429[a]18; [b]23).
[7] *Ibid.,* III, 6 (430[b]21).   [8] Aristotle, III, 6 (430[b]6).

And this indivisible is known secondarily, through the privation of divisibility. Hence a point is defined by way of privation as "that which has no parts,"[1] and in like manner "the notion of one is that it is indivisible," as stated in the *Metaphysics*.[2] And the reason of this is that this indivisible has a certain opposition to corporeal reality, which is the quiddity which the intellect seizes primarily and *per se*.

But if our intellect understood by participation of separate indivisible (forms), as the Platonists maintained,[3] it would follow that an indivisible of this kind is understood primarily, for according to the Platonists what is first is first participated by things.[4]

Reply Obj. 1. In the acquisition of knowledge, principles and elements are not always first, for sometimes from sensible effects we arrive at the knowledge of principles and intelligible causes. But in perfected knowledge, the knowledge of effects always depends on the knowledge of principles and elements; for as the Philosopher says in the same passage that we consider ourselves to know, when we can resolve principles into their causes.

Reply Obj. 2. A point is not included in the definition of a line in general, for it is manifest that in an infinite line and in a circular line there is no point, save potentially. Euclid defines a finite straight line, and therefore he places a point in the definition of a line as the limit in the definition of that which is limited. But unity is the measure of number. Therefore it is included in the definition of a measured number. But it is not included in the definition of the divisible, but rather conversely.

Reply Obj. 3. The likeness through which we understand is the species of the known in the knower. Therefore a thing is known first, not on account of a natural likeness to the knowing power, but on account of a relation of agreement between the knowing power and the object; otherwise sight would perceive hearing rather than colour.

QUESTION LXXXVI
WHAT OUR INTELLECT KNOWS IN
MATERIAL THINGS
(In Four Articles)

WE now have to consider what our intellect knows in material things. Under this head there

are four points of inquiry: (1) Whether it knows singulars? (2) Whether it knows infinite things? (3) Whether it knows contingent things? (4) Whether it knows future things?

ARTICLE 1. *Whether Our Intellect Knows Singulars?*

We proceed thus to the First Article: It would seem that our intellect knows singulars.

Objection 1. For whoever knows composition knows the terms of composition. But our intellect knows this composition: "Socrates is a man," for it pertains to the intellect to form a proposition. Therefore our intellect knows this singular, Socrates.

Obj. 2. Further, the practical intellect directs to action. But actions are concerned with singular things. Therefore the intellect knows the singular.

Obj. 3. Further, our intellect understands itself. But in itself it is a singular, otherwise it would have no action, for actions pertain to singulars. Therefore our intellect knows singulars.

Obj. 4. Further, a superior power can do whatever is done by an inferior power. But sense knows the singular. Much more, therefore, can the intellect know it.

On the contrary, The Philosopher says[5] that "the universal is known by reason, and the singular is known by sense."

I answer that, Our intellect cannot know the singular in material things directly and primarily. The reason of this is that the principle of singularity in material things is individual matter, while our intellect, as we have said above (Q. LXXXV, A. 1), understands by abstracting the intelligible species from such matter. Now what is abstracted from individual matter is the universal. Hence our intellect knows directly the universal only. But indirectly, and as it were by a kind of turning back (reflectio), it can know the singular, because, as we have said above (Q. LXXXV, A. 7), even after abstracting the intelligible species, the intellect, in order to understand actually, needs to turn to the phantasms in which it understands the species, as is said in the book on the *Soul*.[6] Therefore it understands the universal directly through the intelligible species, and indirectly the singulars represented by the phantasms. And thus it forms the proposition, "Socrates is a man." From this the *reply to the first objection* is clear.

Reply Obj. 2. The choice of a particular thing to be done is, as it were, the conclusion of a syl-

---

[1] Euclid, *Geom.*, trans. of Boëthius, Bk. 1 (PL 63, 1307).
[2] Aristotle, x, 1 (1052[b]16).
[3] Cf. Q. LXXXIV, AA. 1, 4; Q. LXXXVII, A. 1.
[4] Cf. *Liber de Causis*, 1 (BA 163.3).

[5] *Physics*, I, 5 (189[a]5).   [6] Aristotle, III, 7 (431[b]2)

logism formed by the practical intellect, as is said in the *Ethics*.[1] But a singular proposition cannot be directly concluded from a universal proposition except through the medium of a singular proposition. Therefore the universal principle of the practical intellect does not move save through the medium of a particular apprehension of the sensitive part, as is said in the book on the *Soul*.[2]

Reply Obj. 3. Intelligibility is incompatible with the singular not as such, but as material, for nothing can be understood otherwise than immaterially. Therefore if there be an immaterial singular such as the intellect, there is no reason why it should not be intelligible.

Reply Obj. 4. The higher power can do what the lower power can, but in a more eminent way. And so what the sense knows materially and concretely, which is to know the singular directly, the intellect knows immaterially and in the abstract, which is to know the universal.

ARTICLE 2. *Whether Our Intellect Can Know the Infinite Things?*

We proceed thus to the Second Article: It would seem that our intellect can know infinite things.

Objection 1. For God excels all infinite things. But our intellect can know God, as we have said above (Q. XII, A. 1). Much more, therefore, can our intellect know all other infinite things.

Obj. 2. Further, our intellect can naturally know genera and species. But there is an infinity of species in some genera, as in number, proportion, and figure. Therefore our intellect can know infinite things.

Obj. 3. Further, if one body can coexist with another in the same place, there is nothing to prevent an infinite number of bodies being in one place. But one intelligible species can exist with another in the same intellect, for many things can be known habitually at the same time. Therefore our intellect can have an habitual knowledge of an infinite number of things.

Obj. 4. Further, as the intellect is not a power of corporeal matter, as we have said (Q. LXXVI, A. 1), it appears to be an infinite power. But an infinite power has a capacity for an infinite number of things. Therefore our intellect can know infinite things.

On the contrary, It is said[3] that "the infinite, considered as such, is unknown."

I answer that, Since a power is proportioned to its object, the intellect must be related to the infinite in the same way as its object, which is the quiddity of a material thing, is related to it. Now in material things the infinite does not exist actually, but only in potency, in so far as one thing succeeds another, as is said.[4] Therefore infinity is potentially in our intellect through its considering successively one thing after another, because our intellect never understands so many things, that it cannot understand more.

On the other hand, our intellect cannot understand the infinite either actually or habitually. Not actually, for our intellect cannot know actually at the same time, except what it knows through one species. But the infinite is not represented by one species, for if it were it would be something whole and complete. Consequently it cannot be understood except by a successive consideration of one part after another, as is clear from its definition:[5] for "the infinite is that from which, however much we may take, there always remains something to be taken." Thus the infinite could not be known actually, unless all its parts were counted, which is impossible.

For the same reason we cannot have habitual knowledge of the infinite, because in us habitual knowledge results from actual consideration, since by understanding we acquire knowledge, as is said in the *Ethics*.[6] And so it would not be possible for us to have a habit of an infinity of things distinctly known unless we had already considered the entire infinity of them, counting them according to the succession of our knowledge, which is impossible. And therefore neither actually or habitually can our intellect know the infinite, but only potentially, as explained above.

Reply Obj. 1. As we have said above (Q. VII, A. 1), God is called infinite, because He is a form unlimited by matter, whereas in material things the term infinite is applied to that which is deprived of any formal termination. And because form is known in itself, whereas matter cannot be known without form, it follows that the material infinite is in itself unknowable. But the formal infinite, God, is of Himself known; but He is unknown to us by reason of the defect of our intellect, which in its present state has a natural aptitude for material things only. Therefore we cannot know God in our present life except through material effects. In the future life this defect of intellect will be removed by the state of glory, when we shall be able to see the

[1] Aristotle, VII, 3 (1147ᵃ28).
[2] Aristotle, III, 11 (434ᵃ16).
[3] Aristotle, *Physics*, I, 4 (187ᵇ7).
[4] *Ibid.*, III, 5 (204ᵃ20).
[5] *Ibid.*, 6 (207ᵃ7).
[6] Aristotle, II, 1 (1103ᵃ33).

Essence of God Himself, though without being able to comprehend Him.

Reply Obj. 2. Our intellect naturally knows species abstracted from phantasms; therefore it cannot know actually or habitually species of numbers or figures that have not been imagined, except in a general way and in their universal principles. And this is to know them potentially and confusedly.

Reply Obj. 3. If two or more bodies were in the same place, there would be no need for them to occupy the place successively in order for the things placed to be counted according to this succession of occupation. But the intelligible species enter into our intellect successively, since many things cannot be actually understood at the same time. And therefore there must be a determinate and not an infinite number of species in our intellect.

Reply Obj. 4. Our intellect knows the infinite after the manner in which it is infinite in power. For its power is indeed infinite in so far as it is not determined by corporeal matter. Moreover it can know the universal, which is abstracted from individual matter, and which consequently is not limited to one individual, but, considered in itself, extends to an infinite number of individuals.

ARTICLE 3. *Whether Our Intellect Can Know Contingent Things?*

We proceed thus to the Third Article: It would seem that the intellect cannot know contingent things.

Objection 1. Because, as the Philosopher says,[1] the objects of understanding, wisdom and knowledge are not contingent, but necessary things.

Obj. 2. Further, as stated in the *Physics*,[2] "what sometimes is and sometimes is not, is measured by time." Now the intellect abstracts from time, and from other material conditions. Therefore, as it is proper to a contingent thing at one time to be and at another not to be, it seems that contingent things are not known by the intellect.

On the contrary, All knowledge is in the intellect. But some sciences are of contingent things, as the moral sciences, the objects of which are human acts subject to free choice; and, again, the natural sciences in as far as they are drawn from things subject to generation and corruption. Therefore the intellect knows contingent things.

[1] *Ethics,* VI, 6 (1040[b]31).
[2] Aristotle, IV, 12 (221[b]29).

I answer that, Contingent things can be considered in two ways: either as contingent, or as containing some element of necessity, since every contingent thing has in it something necessary. For example, that Socrates runs, is in itself contingent; but the relation of running to motion is necessary, for it is necessary that Socrates move if he runs. Now contingency arises from matter, for contingency is a potency to be or not to be, and potency pertains to matter. But necessity results from form, because whatever is consequent on form is of necessity in the subject. But matter is the principle of individuation, whereas the universal comes from the abstraction of the form from the particular matter. Moreover it was laid down above (A. 1) that the intellect of itself and directly is related to the universal, while the sense is related to the singular, which in a certain way also is indirectly related to the intellect, as we have said above (*ibid.*). Therefore the contingent, considered as such, is known directly by sense and indirectly by the intellect, while the universal and necessary principles of contingent things are known by the intellect. Hence if we consider the objects of science in their universal principles, then all science is of necessary things. But if we consider the things themselves, then some sciences are of necessary things, some of contingent things.

From which *the replies to the objections* are clear.

ARTICLE 4. *Whether Our Intellect Can Know the Future Things?*

We proceed thus to the Fourth Article: It would seem that our intellect knows future things.

Objection 1. For our intellect knows by means of intelligible species abstracted from the *here* and *now,* and hence related indifferently to all time. But it can know the present. Therefore it can know future things.

Obj. 2. Further, man, while his senses are suspended, can know some future things, as in sleep, and in frenzy. But the intellect is freer and more vigorous when removed from sense. Therefore the intellect of its own nature can know the future.

Obj 3. The intellectual knowledge of man is superior to any knowledge of brutes. But some animals know the future; thus crows by their frequent cawing foretell rain. Therefore much more can the intellect know the future.

On the contrary, It is written (Eccles. 8. 6, 7), *There is great affliction for man, because he is ignorant of things past; and things to come he cannot know by any messenger.*

I answer that, We must apply the same distinction to the knowledge of future things, as we applied above (A. 3) to the knowledge of contingent things. For future things considered as subject to time are singular, and the human intellect knows t'iem by reflexion only, as stated above (A. 1). But the principles of future things may be universal; and thus they may enter the domain of the intellect and become the objects of science.

Speaking, however, of the knowledge of the future in a general way, we must observe that the future may be known in two ways: either in itself, or in its cause. The future cannot be known in itself save by God alone, to Whom even that is present which in the course of events is future, since from eternity His glance embraces the whole course of time, as we have said above when treating of God's knowledge (Q. XIV, A. 13). But according as it exists in its cause, the future can be known by us also. And if, indeed, the cause be such as to have a necessary connection with its future result, then the future is known with scientific certitude, just as the astronomer foresees the future eclipse. If, however, the cause be such as to produce a certain result more frequently than not, then the future can be known more or less conjecturally, according as its cause is more or less inclined to produce the effect.

Reply Obj. 1. This argument is true of that knowledge which is drawn from universal causal principles; from these the future may be known after the manner of the order of effects to their cause.

Reply Obj. 2. As Augustine says in the twelfth book of the *Confessions*,[1] the soul has a certain power of forecasting, so that by its very nature it can know the future; hence when withdrawn from corporeal sense, and, as it were, turned back upon itself, it shares in the knowledge of the future. Such an opinion would be reasonable if we were to admit that the soul receives knowledge by participating the ideas as the Platonists maintained,[2] because in that case the soul by its nature would know the universal causes of all effects, and would only be impeded in its knowledge by the body; and hence when withdrawn from the bodily senses it would know the future.

But since it is connatural to our intellect to know things not in this way, but by receiving its knowledge from the senses, it is not natural for the soul to know the future when withdrawn from the senses; rather does it know the future by the impression of superior spiritual and corporeal causes. By the impression of spiritual causes when by Divine power the human intellect is enlightened through the ministry of angels, and the phantasms are directed to the knowledge of future events; or, by the influence of demons when the imagination is moved regarding the future known to the demons, as explained above (Q. LVII, A. 3). The soul is naturally more inclined to receive these impressions of spiritual causes when it is withdrawn from the senses, as it is then nearer to the spiritual world, and freer from external distractions. The same may also come from superior corporeal causes. For it is clear that superior bodies influence inferior bodies. Hence, in consequence of the sensitive powers being acts of corporeal organs, the influence of the heavenly bodies causes the imagination to be affected. and so, as the heavenly bodies cause many future events, the imagination receives certain signs of some such events. These signs are perceived more at night and while we sleep than in the daytime and while we are awake, because, as stated in *Prophesying*,[3] "impressions made by day are evanescent. The night air is calmer, when silence reigns, hence bodily impressions are made in sleep, when slight internal movements are felt more than in wakefulness, and such movements produce in the imagination phantasms from which the future may be foreseen."

Reply Obj. 3. Brute animals have no power above the imagination to regulate the phantasms, as man has his reason, and therefore their imagination follows entirely the influence of the heavenly bodies. Thus from such animals' movements some future things, such as rain and the like, may be better known rather than from human movements directed by the counsel of reason. Hence the Philosopher says[4] that some who are most imprudent are most far-seeing; for their intelligence is not burdened with cares, but is as it were barren and bare of all anxiety, moving at the caprice of whatever is brought to bear on it.

QUESTION LXXXVII

HOW THE INTELLECTUAL SOUL KNOWS ITSELF AND ALL WITHIN ITSELF

(*In Four Articles*)

WE have now to consider how the intellectual soul knows itself and all within itself. Under this

---

[1] Cf. *De Gen. ad lit.*, XII, 13 (PL 34, 464).
[2] Cf. Q. LXXXIV, AA. 1, 4; Q. LXXXVII, A. 1.
[3] Aristotle, 2 (464ᵃ12).
[4] *Ibid.*, (464ᵃ18).

head there are four points of inquiry: (1) Whether the soul knows itself by its own essence? (2) Whether it knows its own habits? (3) How does the intellect know its own act? (4) How does it know the act of the will?

ARTICLE 1. *Whether the Intellectual Soul Knows Itself by Its Essence?*

We proceed thus to the First Article: It would seem that the intellectual soul knows itself by its own essence.

Objection 1. For Augustine says (*De Trin.* ix, 3),[1] that "the mind knows itself by itself, because it is incorporeal."

Obj. 2. Further, both angels and human souls belong to the genus of intellectual substance. But an angel understands itself by its own essence. Therefore likewise does the human soul.

Obj. 3. Further, "in things void of matter, the intellect and that which is understood are the same."[2] But the human mind is without matter, for it is not the act of a body, as stated above (Q. LXXVI, A. 1). Therefore the intellect and what is understood are the same in the human mind; and therefore the human mind understands itself by its own essence.

On the contrary, It is said[3] that the intellect understands itself in the same way as it understands other things. But it understands other things not by their essence, but by their likenesses. Therefore it does not understand itself by its own essence.

I answer that, Everything is knowable so far as it is in act, and not according as it is in potency,[4] for a thing is a being, and is true, and therefore knowable, according as it is actual. This is quite clear as regards sensible things, for the eye does not see what is potentially coloured, but what is actually coloured. In like manner it is clear that the intellect, so far as it knows material things, does not know save what is in act, and hence it does not know primary matter except as proportionate to form, as is stated in the *Physics.*[5] Consequently immaterial substances are intelligible by their own essence, according as each one is actual by its own essence.

Therefore the Essence of God, which is pure and perfect act, is absolutely and perfectly in itself intelligible; and hence God by His own Essence knows not only Himself, but all other things also. The angelic essence belongs, indeed, to the genus of intelligible things as act, but not as a pure act, nor as a complete act, and hence

the angel's act of understanding is not completed by his essence. For although an angel understands himself by his own essence, still he cannot understand all things by his own essence, but he knows things other than himself by their likenesses. Now the human intellect is only a being in potency in the genus of intelligible beings, just as primary matter is in potency in the genus of sensible beings; and hence it is called "possible."[6] Therefore considered in its essence the human mind is potentially understanding. Hence it has in itself the power to understand, but not to be understood, except as it is made actual. For even the Platonists asserted[7] that an order of intelligible beings existed above the order of intellects, since the intellect understands only by participation of the intelligible; for they said that the participator is below what it participates.

If, therefore, the human intellect, as the Platonists held,[8] became actual by participating separate intelligible forms, it would understand itself by such participation of incorporeal beings. But as in this life our intellect naturally has material and sensible things for its proper object, as stated above (Q. LXXXIV, A. 7), it understands itself according as it is made actual by the species abstracted from sensible things through the light of the agent intellect, which actuates the intelligibles themselves, and by their instrumentality, the possible intellect. Therefore the intellect knows itself not by its essence, but by its act.

This happens in two ways. In the first place, in a particular manner, as when Socrates or Plato perceives that he has an intellectual soul because he perceives that he understands. In the second place, in a universal manner, as when we consider the nature of the human mind from the act of understanding. It is true, however, that the judgment and worth of this knowledge, whereby we know the nature of the soul, comes to us according to the derivation of our intellectual light from the Divine Truth which contains the types of all things as above stated (Q. LXXXIV, A. 5). Hence Augustine says (*De Trin.* ix, 6):[9] "We gaze on the inviolable truth whence we can as perfectly as possible define, not what each man's mind is, but what it ought to be in the light of the eternal types."

---

[1] PL 42, 963.   [2] Aristotle, *Soul,* III, 4 (430ª3).
[3] *Ibid.*   [4] Aristotle, *Metaphysics,* IX, 9 (1051ª29).
[5] Aristotle, I, 7 (191ª8).

[6] Cf. Aristotle, *Soul,* III, 4 (428ª22).
[7] See Dionysius, *De Div. Nom.,* IV, 1 (PG 3, 693); *Liber de Causis,* 9 (BA. 173); Proclus, *Inst. Theol.,* 163, 164 (DD c 111).
[8] See previous note. Cf. also Bonaventure, *In Sent.,* II, d. 39, A. 1, Q. 2 (QR II, 904). Cf. Luyckx, *Die Erkenntnislehre* (p. 171-200).   [9] PL 42, 966.

There is, however, a difference between these two kinds of knowledge, and it consists in this that the mere presence of the mind suffices for the first; for the mind itself is the principle of action whereby it perceives itself, and hence it is said to know itself by its own presence. But as regards the second kind of knowledge, the mere presence of the mind does not suffice, and there is further required a careful and subtle inquiry. Hence many are ignorant of the soul's nature, and many have erred about it. So Augustine says (*De Trin.* x, 9),[1] concerning such inquiry about the mind: "Let the mind strive not to see itself as if it were absent, but to discern itself as present"—that is, to know how it differs from other things, which is to know its quiddity and nature.

Reply Obj. 1. The mind knows itself by means of itself because at length it acquires knowledge of itself, though led to it by its own act; for it is itself that it knows, since it loves itself, as he says in the same passage. For a thing can be called self-evident in two ways: either because we can know it by nothing else except itself, as first principles are called self-evident; or because it is not accidentally knowable, just as colour is visible of itself, whereas substance is visible accidentally.

Reply Obj. 2. The essence of an angel is as an act in the genus of intelligible things, and therefore it is both intellect and the thing understood. Hence an angel apprehends his own essence through itself; not so the human mind, which is either altogether in potency with respect to the intelligible,—as is the possible intellect,—or is the act of the intelligibles which are abstracted from the phantasms,—as is the agent intellect.

Reply Obj. 3. This saying of the Philosopher is universally true in every kind of intellect. For as the sense in act is the sensible by reason of the likeness of the sensible which is the form of the sense in act, so likewise the intellect in act is the thing understood in act, by reason of the likeness of the thing understood, which is the form of the intellect in act. So the human intellect, which becames actual by the species of the object understood, is itself understood by the same species as by its own form. Now to say that in "things without matter the intellect and what is understood are the same," is equal to saying that as regards things actually understood the intellect and what is understood are the same. For a thing is actually understood in that it is immaterial. But a distinction must be drawn, since the essences of some things are

without matter, as the separate substances called angels, each of which is understood and understands, whereas there are other things whose essences are not without matter, but only the likenesses abstracted from them. Hence the Commentator says (*De Anima*, iii)[2] that the proposition quoted is true only of separate substances; because in a sense it is verified in their regard, and not in regard of other substances, as already stated (ANS. 2).

ARTICLE 2. *Whether Our Intellect Knows the Habits of the Soul by Their Essence?*

We proceed thus to the Second Article: It would seem that our intellect knows the habits of the soul by their essence.

Objection 1. For Augustine says (*De Trin.* xiii, 1):[3] *Faith is not seen in the heart wherein it abides, as the soul of a man may be seen by another from the movement of the body; but we know most certainly that it is there, and conscience proclaims its existence.* And the same applies to the other habits of the soul. Therefore the habits of the soul are not known by their acts, but by themselves.

Obj. 2. Further, material things outside the soul are known by their likeness being present in the soul, and are said therefore to be known by their likenesses. But the soul's habits are present by their essence in the soul. Therefore the habits of the soul are known by their essence.

Obj. 3. Further, whatever is the cause of a thing being such is still more so. But habits and intelligible species cause things to be known by the soul. Therefore they are still more known by the soul in themselves.

On the contrary, Habits like powers are the principles of acts. But as is said,[4] "acts and operations are logically prior to powers." Therefore in the same way they are prior to habits; and thus habits, like the powers, are known by their acts.

I answer that, A habit is a kind of medium between pure power and pure act. Now, it has been said (A. 1) that nothing is known except as it is actual. Therefore so far as a habit fails in being a perfect act, it falls short in being of itself knowable, and can be known only by its act. Thus, for example, anyone knows he has a habit from the fact that he can produce the act proper to that habit; or he may inquire into the nature and character of the habit by considering the act. The first kind of knowledge of the habit arises from its being present, for the very fact of its presence causes the act whereby it is known. The second kind of knowledge of the habit arises from a careful inquiry, as is explained above of the mind (A. 1).

Reply Obj. 1. Although faith is not known by outward movements of the body, it is perceived by him in whom it resides, by the interior act of the heart. For no one knows that he has faith unless he perceives that he believes.

Reply Obj. 2. Habits are present in our intellect, not as its object, since, in the present state of life, our intellect's object is the nature of a material thing as stated above (Q. LXXXIV, A. 7), but as that by which it understands.

Reply Obj. 3. The axiom, whatever is the cause of a thing being such, is still more so, is true of things that are of the same order, for instance, of the same kind of cause; for example, we may say that health is desirable on account of life, and therefore life is more desirable still. But if we take things of different orders the axiom is not true: for we may say that health is caused by medicine, but it does not follow that medicine is more desirable than health, for health belongs to the order of final causes, whereas medicine belongs to the order of efficient causes. So of two things which belong per se to the order of the objects of knowledge, the one which is the cause of the other being known is the more known, as principles are more known than conclusions. But habit as such does not belong to the order of objects of knowledge; nor are things known on account of the habit, as on account of an object known, but as on account of a disposition or form by which the subject knows. And therefore the argument does not prove.

ARTICLE 3. *Whether Our Intellect Knows Its Own Act?*

We proceed thus to the Third Article: It would seem that our intellect does not know its own act.

Objection 1. For what is known is the object of the knowing power. But the act differs from the object. Therefore the intellect does not know its own act.

Obj. 2. Further, whatever is known is known by some act. If, then, the intellect knows its own act, it knows it by some act, and again it knows that act by some other act; this is to proceed indefinitely, which seems impossible.

Obj. 3. Further, the intellect has the same relation to its act as sense has to its act. But the proper sense does not sense its own act, for this belongs to the common sense, as stated in the book on the *Soul*.[1] Therefore neither does the intellect understand its own act.

On the contrary, Augustine says (*De Trin.* x, 11),[2] "I understand that I understand."

I answer that, As stated above (AA. 1, 2) a thing is known according as it is in act. Now the ultimate perfection of the intellect is its operation, for this is not an act tending to something else in which lies the perfection of the work accomplished, as building is the perfection of the thing built, but it remains in the agent as its perfection and act, as is said in the *Metaphysics*.[3] Therefore the first thing understood of the intellect is its own act of understanding. This occurs in different ways with different intellects. For there is an intellect, namely, the Divine, which is Its own act of understanding, so that in God the understanding of His understanding and the understanding of His Essence, are one and the same act, because His Essence is His act of understanding. But there is another intellect, the angelic, which is not its own act of understanding, as we have said above (Q. LXXIX, A. 1), and yet the first object of its act of understanding is the angelic essence. And so although there is a logical distinction between the act whereby the angel understands that he understands, and that whereby he understands his essence, yet he understands both by one and the same act; because to understand his own essence is the proper perfection of his essence, and by one and the same act is a thing together with its perfection understood. And there is yet another, namely, the human intellect, which neither is its own act of understanding, nor is its own essence the first object of its act of understanding, for this object is something extrinsic, namely, the nature of a material thing. And therefore that which is first known by the human intellect is an object of this kind, and that which is known secondarily is the act by which that object is known; and through the act the intellect itself is known, the perfection of which is this very act of understanding. For this reason did the Philosopher assert that objects are known before acts, and acts before powers.[4]

Reply Obj. 1. The object of the intellect is something common, namely, being and the true, in which also the act of understanding is com-

[1] Aristotle, III, 2 (425ᵇ12).

[2] PL 42, 983. For the various interpretations of this passage in Bonaventure, see Luyckx, *Die Erkenntnislehre* (p. 171).

[3] Aristotle, IX, 8 (1050ᵃ36).

[4] *Soul*, II, 4 (415ᵃ16).

prised. Therefore the intellect can understand its own act. But not primarily, since the first object of our intellect, in this state of life, is not every being and everything true, but being and true, as considered in material things, as we have said above (Q. LXXXIV, A. 7), from which it acquires knowledge of all other things.

Reply Obj. 2. The act of understanding of the human intellect is not the act and perfection of the nature understood, as if the nature of the material thing and the act of understanding could be understood by one act; just as a thing and its perfection are understood by one act. Hence the act whereby the intellect understands a stone is distinct from the act whereby it understands that it understands a stone, and so on. Nor is there any difficulty in the intellect being potentially infinite, as explained above (Q. LXXXVI, A. 2).

Reply Obj. 3. The proper sense senses by reason of the change in the material organ caused by the external sensible. A material thing, however, cannot change itself, but one is changed by another, and therefore the act of the proper sense is perceived by the common sense. The intellect, on the contrary, does not understand by the material change of an organ; and so there is no comparison.

ARTICLE 4. *Whether the Intellect Understands the Act of the Will?*

We proceed thus to the Fourth Article: It would seem that the intellect does not understand the act of the will.

Objection 1. For nothing is known by the intellect unless it be in some way present in the intellect. But the act of the will is not in the intellect, since the will and the intellect are distinct powers. Therefore the act of the will is not known by the intellect.

Obj. 2. Further, the act is specified by the object. But the object of the will is not the same as the object of the intellect. Therefore the act of the will is specifically distinct from the object of the intellect, and therefore the act of the will is not known by the intellect.

Obj. 3. Augustine says[1] of the soul's affections that they are known "neither by images as bodies are known, nor by their presence, like the arts, but by certain notions." Now it does not seem that there can be in the soul any notions of things, other than the essences of things known or their likenesses. Therefore it seems impossible for the intellect to know the affections of the soul which are the acts of the will.

On the contrary, Augustine says (*De Trin.* x, 11),[2] "I understand that I will."

I answer that, As stated above (Q. LIX, A. 1), the act of the will is nothing but an inclination consequent on the form understood, just as the natural appetite is an inclination consequent on the natural form. Now the inclination of a thing resides in it according to the mode of being of the thing; and hence the natural inclination resides in a natural thing naturally, and the inclination called the sensible appetite is in the sensible thing sensibly; and likewise the intelligible inclination, which is the act of the will, is in the intelligent subject intelligibly, as in its principle and proper subject. Hence the Philosopher expresses himself thus, that "the will is in the reason."[3] Now whatever is intelligibly in an intelligent subject is understood by that subject. Therefore the act of the will is understood by the intellect, both in so far as one knows that one wills, and in so far as one knows the nature of this act, and consequently, the nature of its principle which is the habit or power.

Reply Obj. 1. This argument would hold good if the will and the intellect were in different subjects, just as they are distinct powers, for then whatever was in the will would not be in the intellect. But as both are rooted in the same substance of the soul, and since one is in a certain way the principle of the other, consequently what is in the will is, in a certain way, also in the intellect.

Reply Obj. 2. The good and the true which are the objects of the will and of the intellect differ logically, but one is contained in the other, as we have said above (Q. LXXXII, A. 4, ANS. 1; Q. XVI, A. 4, ANS. 1); for the true is a certain good, and the good is a certain true. Therefore what pertains to the will falls under the intellect, and what pertains to the intellect can fall under the will.

Reply Obj. 3. The affections of the soul are in the intellect not by likeness only, as are bodies, nor by being present in their subject, as the arts, but as the thing caused is in its principle, which contains some notion of the thing caused. And so Augustine says that the soul's affections are in the memory by certain notions.

QUESTION LXXXVIII

HOW THE HUMAN SOUL KNOWS WHAT IS ABOVE ITSELF

(*In Three Articles*)

WE must now consider how the human soul knows what is above itself, namely, immaterial

[1] *Confessions*, x, 20 (PL 32, 790). [2] PL 42, 983. [3] *Soul*, III, 9 (432b5).

substances. Under this head there are three points of inquiry: (1) Whether the human soul in the present state of life can understand the immaterial substances called angels, in themselves? (2) Whether it can arrive at the knowledge of them by the knowledge of material things? (3) Whether God is what is first known by us?

ARTICLE 1. *Whether the Human Soul in the Present State of Life Can Understand Immaterial Substances in Themselves?*

We proceed thus to the First Article: It would seem that the human soul in the present state of life can understand immaterial substances in themselves.

Objection 1. For Augustine (*De Trin.* ix, 3)[1] says: "As the mind itself acquires the knowledge of corporeal things by means of the corporeal senses, so it gains from itself the knowledge of incorporeal things." But these are immaterial substances. Therefore the human mind understands immaterial substances.

Obj. 2. Further, like is known by like. But the human mind is more akin to immaterial than to material things, since its own nature is immaterial, as is clear from what we have said above (Q. LXXVI, A. 1). Since then our mind understands material things, much more does it understand immaterial things.

Obj. 3. Further, the fact that things which are in themselves most sensible are not most sensed by us comes from sense being corrupted by their very excellence. But the excellence of the intelligible thing does not corrupt the intellect, as is stated in the book on the *Soul*.[2] Therefore things which are in themselves in the highest degree intelligible are likewise to us most intelligible. As material things, however, are intelligible only so far as we make them actually so by abstracting them from matter, it is clear that those substances are more intelligible in themselves whose nature is immaterial. Therefore they are much more known to us than are material things.

Obj. 4. Further, the Commentator says[3] that nature would be frustrated in its end were we unable to understand abstract substances, because it would have made what in itself is naturally intelligible not to be understood at all. But in nature nothing is idle or purposeless.

Therefore immaterial substances can be understood by us.

Obj. 5. Further, as sense is to the sensible, so is intellect to the intelligible. But our sight can see all things corporeal, whether superior and incorruptible, or lower and corruptible. Therefore our intellect can understand all intelligible substances, even the superior and immaterial.

On the contrary, It is written (Wisd. 9. 16): *The things that are in heaven who shall search out?* But these substances are said to be in heaven, according to Matthew 18. 10, *Their angels in heaven,* etc. Therefore immaterial substances cannot be known by human investigation.

I answer that, In the opinion of Plato, immaterial substances are not only understood by us, but are the objects we understand first of all. For Plato taught that immaterial subsisting forms, which he called Ideas, are the proper objects of our intellect, and are thus first and *per se* understood by us[4]; and, further, that material things are known by the soul according as imagination and sense are mixed up with the intellect.[5] Hence the more purified the intellect is, the more clearly does it perceive the intelligible truth of immaterial things.[6]

But in Aristotle's opinion,[7] which experience corroborates, our intellect in its present state of life has a natural relationship to the natures of material things, and therefore it can only understand by turning to the phantasms, as we have said above (Q. LXXXIV, A. 7). Thus it clearly appears that immaterial substances which do not fall under sense and imagination, cannot first and *per se* be known by us according to the mode of knowledge which experience proves us to have.

Nevertheless Averroës (*Comment. De Anima,* iii)[8] teaches that in this present life man can in the end arrive at the knowledge of separate substances because it is continous with or united to some separate substance, which he calls the agent intellect, which, since it is a separate substance itself, naturally understands separate substances. Hence, when it is perfectly united to us so that by its means we are able to understand perfectly, we also shall be able to understand separate substances, as in the present life through the possible intellect united to us we can understand material things.

[1] PL 42, 963. Cf. Bonaventure's interpretation of this text: *Quaest. Disp. de Scientia Christi,* IV, 3. (QR V, 21, 24); also, *In Sent.,* I, d. III, p. 1, A. 1, Q. 1 (QR I, 68).
[2] Aristotle, III, 4 (429^b2).
[3] *In Meta.,* II, comm. 1 (VIII, 29c).

[4] Cf. Q. LXXXIV, A. 4.
[5] Cf. Macrobius, *In Somn. Scip.,* I, 12, 14 (DD 41b; 46b).
[6] Cf. Cicero, *Tuscul.,* I, 30 (DD III, 640); *Phaedo* (80); Augustine, QQ. LXXXIII, Q. 46 (PL 40, 30).
[7] *Soul,* III, 7 (431^a16).   [8] Comm. 36, PT. V (VI, 2, 183c).

Now he held that the agent intellect is united to us, thus. Since we understand by means of both the agent intellect and contemplated intelligible objects, as, for instance, we understand conclusions by principles understood, it is clear that the active intellect must be compared to the objects understood either as the principal agent is to the instrument, or as form to matter. For an action is ascribed to two principles in one of these two ways: to a principal agent and to an instrument, as cutting to the workman and the saw; to a form and its subject, as heating to heat and fire. In both these ways the agent intellect can be related to the intelligible object as perfection is to the perfectible, and as act is to potency. Now a subject is made perfect and receives its perfection at one and the same time, as the reception of what is actually visible synchronizes with the reception of light in the eye. Therefore the possible intellect receives the intelligible object and the agent intellect together. And the more numerous the intelligible objects received, so much the nearer do we come to the point of perfect union between ourselves and the agent intellect, so much so that when we shall have understood all the intelligible objects, the agent intellect will become one with us, and by its instrumentality we shall understand all things material and immaterial And in this he places the ultimate happiness of man.[1] Nor, as regards the present inquiry, does it matter whether the possible intellect in that state of happiness understands separate substances by the agent intellect, as he himself maintains, or whether (as he says Alexander holds)[2] the possible intellect can never understand separate substances (because according to him it is corruptible), but man rather understands separate substances by means of the agent intellect.

This opinion, however, is untrue. First, because, supposing the active intellect to be a separate substance, we could not formally understand through it, for that by which an agent acts formally is its form and act, since every agent acts according to its actuality, as was said of the possible intellect (Q. LXXVI, A. I).

This opinion is untrue secondly because in the above explanation, the agent intellect, supposing it to be a separate substance, would not be joined to us in its substance, but only in its light, as participated in things understood, and would

not extend to the other acts of the agent intellect so as to enable us to understand immaterial substances; just as when we see colours illuminated by the sun we are not united to the substance of the sun so as to act like the sun, but its light only is united to us, that we may see the colours.

This opinion is untrue thirdly, because granted that, as above explained, the agent intellect were united to us in substance, still it is not said that it is wholly united to us in regard to one intelligible object, or two, but rather in regard to all the contemplated intelligible objects. But all such objects together do not equal the power of the agent intellect, as it is a much greater thing to understand separate substances than to understand all material things. Hence it is clear that the knowledge of all material things would not make the agent intellect to be so united to us as to enable us by its means to understand separate substances.

This opinion is untrue fourthly, because it is hardly possible for anyone in this world to understand all material things, and thus no one, or very few, could reach to perfect happiness; which is against what the Philosopher says,[3] that "happiness is a kind of common good, communicable to all capable of virtue." Further, it is unreasonable that only the few of any species attain to the end of the species.

Fifthly, the Philosopher expressly says[4] that "happiness is an operation according to perfect virtue"; and after enumerating many virtues in the tenth book,[5] he concludes that ultimate happiness consisting in the knowledge of the highest things intelligible is attained through the virtue of wisdom, which in the sixth chapter.[6] he had named as the "chief of the speculative sciences." Hence Aristotle clearly places the ultimate happiness of man in the knowledge of separate substances, obtainable by speculative science, and not by a continuation with the agent intellect, as some imagined.

Sixthly, as was shown above (Q. LXXIX, A. 4), the agent intellect is not a separate substance, but a power of the soul, extending itself actively to the same objects to which the possible intellect extends receptively; because, as is stated,[7] the possible intellect is "all things potentially," and the agent intellect is "all things in act." Therefore both intellects, according to the present state of life, extend to material things

---

[1] *De An. Beat.*, I (IX, 148b). For the same doctrine, cf. Avicenna, *De An.*, V, 6 (26 va).

[2] Alexander of Aphrodisias. Cf. Averroes, *In De An.*, III, 36. (VI, 2, 176B).

[3] *Ethics.* I, 9 (1099b18).

[4] *Ibid.*, I, 10 (1101a14).

[5] *Ibid.*, X, 7, 8 (1177a21; 1179a30).

[6] *Ibid.*, VI, 7 (1141a20).

[7] Aristotle, *Soul*, III, 5 (430a14).

only, which are made actually intelligible by the agent intellect, and are received in the possible intellect. Hence in the present state of life we cannot understand separate immaterial substances in themselves, either by the possible or by the agent intellect.

Reply Obj. 1. Augustine may be taken to mean that the knowledge of incorporeal things in the mind can be gained by the mind itself. This is so true that philosophers also say that the knowledge concerning the soul is a principle for the knowledge of separate substances.[1] For by knowing itself it attains to some knowledge of incorporeal substances, such as is within its compass; not that the knowledge of itself gives it a perfect and absolute knowledge of them.

Reply Obj. 2. The likeness of nature is not a sufficient reason of knowledge; otherwise what Empedocles said would be true—that the soul needs to have the nature of all in order to know all.[2] But knowledge requires that the likeness of the thing known be in the knower, as a kind of form thereof. Now our possible intellect, in the present state of life, is such that it can be informed with likenesses abstracted from phantasms, and therefore it knows material things rather than immaterial substances.

Reply Obj. 3. There must be some proportion between the object and the knowing power, such as of the active to the passive, and of perfection to the perfectible. Hence that sensible objects of great intensity are not grasped by the senses is due not merely to the fact that they corrupt the organ, but also to their being disproportionate to the sensitive power. And thus it is that immaterial substances are disproportionate to our intellect in our present state of life, so that it cannot understand them.

Reply Obj. 4. This argument of the Commentator fails in several ways. First, because if separate substances are not understood by us it does not follow that they are not understood by any intellect, for they are understood by themselves, and by one another.

Secondly, to be understood by us is not the end of separate substances, while only that is vain and purposeless which fails to attain its end. It does not follow, therefore, that immaterial substances are purposeless, even if they are not understood by us at all.

Reply Obj. 5. Sense knows bodies, whether superior or inferior, in the same way, that is, by the sensible acting on the organ. But we do not understand material and immaterial substances in the same way. The former we understand by way of abstraction, which is impossible in the case of the latter, for there are no phantasms of what is immaterial.

ARTICLE 2. *Whether Our Intellect Can Arrive at the Understanding of Immaterial Substances through Its Knowledge of Material Things?*

We proceed thus to the Second Article: It would seem that our intellect can arrive at the understanding of immaterial substances through the knowledge of material things.

Objection 1. For Dionysius says (*Cæl. Hier.* i)[3] that "the human mind cannot be raised up to immaterial contemplation of the heavenly hierarchies unless it is led thereto by material guidance according to its own nature." Therefore we can be led by material things to know immaterial substances.

Obj. 2. Further, science is in the intellect. But there are sciences and definitions of immaterial substances, for Damascene defines an angel (*De Fid. Orth.* ii, 3);[4] and we find angels treated of both in theology and philosophy. Therefore immaterial substances can be understood by us.

Obj. 3. Further, the human soul belongs to the genus of immaterial substances. But it can be understood by us through its act, by which it understands material things. Therefore also other immaterial substances can be understood by us through their effects in material things.

Obj. 4. Further, the only cause which cannot be comprehended through its effects is that which is infinitely distant from them, and this is proper to God alone. Therefore other created immaterial substances can be understood by us through material things.

On the contrary, Dionysius says (*Div. Nom.* i)[5] that "intelligible things cannot be understood through sensible things, nor composite things through simple, nor incorporeal through corporeal."

I answer that, Averroës says (*De Anima,* iii)[6] that a philosopher named Avempace taught that by the understanding of natural substances we can be led, according to true philosophical principles, to the understanding of immaterial substances. For since the nature of our intellect is to abstract the quiddity of

---

[1] Averroes, *In De An.,* I, 2 (VI, 2, 1F); III, 5 (VI, 2, 151E). Cf. St. Thomas, *In De An.,* I, 1.
[2] Cf. Aristotle, *Soul,* I, 2 (404^{b}11).
[3] Sect. 3 (PG 3, 124).
[4] PG 94, 865.
[5] PG 3, 588.
[6] Comm. 36, Pt. III (VI, 2, 180E).

material things from matter, anything material residing in that abstracted quiddity can again be abstracted and as the process of abstraction cannot go on for ever, it must arrive at length at the understanding of some quiddity which would be absolutely without matter; and this would be the understanding of immaterial substance.

Now this opinion would be true, if immaterial substances were the forms and species of these material things, as the Platonists supposed.[1] But supposing, on the contrary, that immaterial substances differ altogether from the quiddity of material things, it follows that however much our intellect abstract the quiddity of material things from matter, it could never arrive at anything like immaterial substance. Therefore we are not able perfectly to understand immaterial substances through material substances.

Reply Obj. 1. From material things we can rise to some kind of knowledge of immaterial things, but not to the perfect knowledge of them. For there is no proper and adequate proportion between material and immaterial things, and the likenesses drawn from material things for the understanding of immaterial things are very dissimilar from them, as Dionysius says (*Cæl. Hier.* ii).[2]

Reply Obj. 2. Science treats of higher things principally by way of remotion. Thus Aristotle explains[3] the heavenly bodies by denying to them the properties of inferior bodies. Hence it follows that much less can immaterial substances be known by us in such a way that we apprehend their quiddity; but we may have a scientific knowledge of them by way of remotion and by their relation to material things.

Reply Obj. 3. The human soul understands itself through its own act of understanding, which is proper to it, showing perfectly its power and nature. But the power and nature of immaterial substances cannot be perfectly known through this act, nor through anything else in material things, because there is no proportion between the latter and the power of the former.

Reply Obj. 4. Created immaterial substances are not in the same natural genus as material substances, for they do not agree in power or in matter; but they belong to the same logical genus, because even immaterial substances are in the predicament of Substance, as their quiddity is distinct from their being. But God has

nothing in common with material things, as regards either natural genus or logical genus, because God is in no way in a genus, as stated above (Q. III, A. 5). Hence through the likenesses of material things we can know something positive concerning the angels, according to some common notion, though not according to the specific nature. But we cannot acquire any such knowledge at all about God.

ARTICLE 3. *Whether God Is the First Thing Known by the Human Mind?*

We proceed thus to the Third Article: It would seem that God is the first thing known by the human mind.

Objection 1. For that object in which all others are known and by which we judge others, is the first thing known to us; as light is to the eye, and first principles to the intellect. But we know all things in the light of the first truth, and judge of all things thereby, as Augustine says (*De Trin.* xii, 2; *De Vera Rel.* xxxi).[4] Therefore God is the first object known to us.

Obj. 2. Further, whatever causes a thing to be such is more so. But God is the cause of all our knowledge, for He is *the true light which enlighteneth every man that cometh into this world* (John 1. 9). Therefore God is what is first and most known to us.

Obj. 3. Further, what is first known in the image is the exemplar to which the image is formed. But in our mind is "the image of God," as Augustine says (*De Trin.* xii, 4).[5] Therefore God is the first thing known to our mind.

On the contrary, No man hath seen God at any time (John 1. 18).

I answer that, Since the human intellect in the present state of life cannot understand even created immaterial substances (A. 1), much less can it understand the essence of the uncreated substance. Hence it must be said absolutely that God is not the first object of our knowledge. Rather do we know God through creatures, according to the Apostle (Rom. 1. 20), *the invisible things of God are clearly seen, being understood by the things that are made,* while the first object of our knowledge in this life is the quiddity of a material thing, which is the proper object of our intellect, as appears above in many passages (Q. LXXXIV, A. 7; Q. LXXXV, A. 8; Q. LXXXVII, A. 2, Ans. 2).

Reply Obj. 1. We see and judge of all things

---

[1] Cf. Q. LXXXIV, A. 1.
[2] Sect. 2 (PG 3, 137).
[3] *Heavens*, I, 3 (269ᵇ18).

[4] PL 42, 999; PL 34, 147. Also, *Confessions*, XII, 35 (PL 32, 840). On this doctrine, cf. Luyckx, *Die Erkenntnislehre* (p. 242-253).
[5] PL 42, 1000.

in the light of the first truth, in so far as the light itself of our mind, whether natural or freely given, is nothing else than the impression of the first truth upon it, as stated above, (Q. XII, A. 11, ANS. 3; Q. LXXXIV, A. 5). Hence, as the light itself of our intellect is not the thing it understands, but that by which it understands, much less can it be said that God is the first thing known by our intellect.

Reply Obj. 2. The axiom, Whatever causes a thing to be such is more so, must be understood of things belonging to one and the same order, as explained above (Q. LXXXVII, A. 2, ANS. 3). Other things than God are known because of God, not as if He were the first known thing, but because He is the first cause of our power of knowledge.

Reply Obj. 3. If there existed in our souls a perfect image of God, as the Son is the perfect image of the Father, our mind would know God at once. But the image in our mind is imperfect. Hence the argument does not prove.

QUESTION LXXXIX

OF THE KNOWLEDGE OF THE SEPARATED SOUL

(*In Eight Articles*)

WE must now consider the knowledge of the separated soul. Under this head there are eight points of inquiry: (1) Whether the soul separated from the body can understand? (2) Whether it understands separate substances? (3) Whether it understands all natural things? (4) Whether it understands singulars? (5) Whether the habits of knowledge acquired in this life remain? (6) Whether the soul can use the habit of knowledge acquired in this life? (7) Whether local distance impedes the separated soul's knowledge? (8) Whether souls separated from the body know what happens here?

ARTICLE 1. *Whether the Separated Soul Can Understand Anything?*

We Proceed thus to the First Article: It would seem that the soul separated from the body can understand nothing at all.

Objection 1. For the Philosopher says[1] that "the understanding is corrupted together with its interior principle." But by death all human interior principles are corrupted. Therefore also the intellect itself is corrupted.

Obj. 2. Further, the human soul is hindered from understanding when the senses are bound,

and by a disordered imagination, as explained above (Q. LXXXIV, AA. 7, 8). But death destroys the senses and imagination, as we have shown above (Q. LXXVII, A. 8). Therefore after death the soul understands nothing.

Obj. 3. Further, if the separated soul can understand, this must be by means of some species. But it does not understand by means of innate species, because from the first, it is like a tablet on which nothing is written. Nor does it understand by species abstracted from things, for it does not then possess organs of sense and imagination which are necessary for the abstraction of species. Nor does it understand by means of species formerly abstracted and retained in the soul, for if that were so, a child's soul after death would have no means of understanding at all. Nor does it understand by means of intelligible species divinely infused, for such knowledge would not be natural, such as we treat of now, but the effect of grace. Therefore the soul apart from the body understands nothing.

On the contrary, The Philosopher says,[2] "If the soul had no proper operation, it could not be separated from the body." But the soul is separated from the body. Therefore it has a proper operation, and above all, that which consists in understanding. Therefore the soul can understand when it is apart from the body.

I answer that, The difficulty in solving this question arises from the fact that the soul united to the body can understand only by turning to the phantasms, as experience shows. If this did not proceed from the soul's very nature, but accidentally through its being bound up with the body, as the Platonists said,[3] the difficulty would vanish, for in that case when the hindrance of the body was once removed,[4] the soul would return to its own nature, and would understand intelligible things simply, without turning to the phantasms, as is the case with other separate substances. In that case, however, the union of soul and body would not be for the soul's good, for evidently it would understand worse in the body than out of it, but for the good of the body, which would be unreasonable, since matter exists on account of the form, and not the form for the sake of the matter. But if we admit that the nature of the

---

[1] *Soul,* I, 4 (408ᵇ24).

[2] *Ibid.*, I, 1 (403ᵃ11).
[3] Cf. Cicero, *Tuscul.*, I, 31 (DD III, 640); *Phaedo* (67); Macrobius, *In Somn. Scip.*, I, 14 (DD 45b); cf. also Augustine, *City of God*, XIII, 16 (PL 41, 389); Wm. of Paris, *De Univ.*, II-II, 65, 73. (II 861, 873.)
[4] Cf. Cicero, *op. cit.*, I, 34 (DD 636); *Phaedo* (65); cf. also Avicenna, *De An.*, V, 5 (25va).

soul requires it to understand by turning to the phantasms, it will seem, since the death of the body does not change its nature, that it can then naturally understand nothing, as the phantasms are wanting to which it may turn.

To solve this difficulty we must consider that as nothing acts except so far as it is actual, the mode of action in every agent follows from its mode of being. Now the soul has one mode of being when joined to the body, and another when separated from it, its nature remaining always the same. But this does not mean that its union with the body is an accidental thing, for, on the contrary, such a union belongs to it by reason of its nature, just as the nature of a light object is not changed whether it is in its proper place, which is natural to it, or outside its proper place, which is foreign to its nature. The soul, therefore, when united to the body, appropriately to that mode of existence has a mode of understanding by turning to corporeal phantasms, which are in corporeal organs; but when it is separated from the body, it is fitting to it to have a mode of understanding by turning to absolutely intelligible objects, as is proper to other separate substances. Hence it is as natural for the soul to understand by turning to the phantasms as it is for it to be joined to the body. But to be separated from the body is not in accordance with its nature, and likewise to understand without turning to the phantasms is not natural to it, and hence it is united to the body in order that it may have an existence and an operation suitable to its nature. But here again a difficulty arises. For since a thing is always ordered to what is best, and since it is better to understand by turning to absolutely intelligible things than by turning to the phantasms, God should have made the soul's nature so that the nobler way of understanding would have been natural to it, and it would not have needed the body for that purpose.

In order to resolve this difficulty we must consider that while it is true that it is nobler in itself to understand by turning to something higher than to understand by turning to phantasms, nevertheless such a mode of understanding was not so perfect as regards what was possible to the soul. This will appear if we consider that every intellectual substance possesses the power of understanding by the influx of the Divine light, which is one and simple in its first principle, and the further off intellectual creatures are from the first principle so much the more is the light divided and diversified, as is the case with lines radiating from the centre of

a circle. Hence it is that God by His own Essence understands all things, while the superior intellectual substances understand by means of many forms, which nevertheless are fewer and more universal and bestow a deeper comprehension of things, because of the efficaciousness of the intellectual power of such natures. But the inferior intellectual natures possess a greater number of forms, which are less universal, and bestow a lower degree of comprehension in proportion as they recede from the intellectual power of the higher natures. If, therefore, the inferior substances received forms in the same degree of universality as the superior substances, since they are not so strong in understanding, the knowledge which they would derive through them would be imperfect and of a general and confused nature. We can see this to a certain extent in man, for those who are of weaker intellect fail to acquire perfect knowledge through the universal conceptions of those who have a better understanding, unless things are explained to them singly and in detail. Now it is clear that in the natural order human souls hold the lowest place among intellectual substances. But the perfection of the universe required various grades of being. If, therefore, God had willed human souls to understand in the same way as separate substances, it would follow that human knowledge, so far from being perfect, would be confused and general. Therefore to make it possible for human souls to possess perfect and proper knowledge, they were so made that their nature required them to be joined to bodies, and thus to receive a proper knowledge of sensible things from the sensible things themselves; thus we see in the case of uneducated men that they have to be taught by sensible examples.

It is clear then that it was for the soul's good that it was united to a body, and that it understands by turning to the phantasms. Nevertheless it is possible for it to exist apart from the body, and also to understand in another way.

Reply Obj. 1. The Philosopher's words carefully examined will show that he said this on the previous supposition[1] that understanding is a movement of body and soul as united, just as sensation is, for he had not as yet explained the difference between intellect and sense. We may also say that he is referring to the way of understanding by turning to phantasms. This is also the meaning of the second objection.

Reply Obj. 3. The separated soul does not understand by way of innate species, nor by spe-

[1] *Soul*, I, 4 (408^{b}6).

cies abstracted in that state, nor only by retained species, and this the objection proves;
but the soul in that state understands by means
of participated species arising from the influx
of the Divine light, shared by the soul as by
other separate substances though, in a lesser
degree. Hence as soon as it ceases to act by
turning to the body, the soul turns at once to
the superior things; nor is this way of knowledge unnatural, for God is the author of the
influx both of the light of grace and of the light
of nature.

ARTICLE 2. *Whether the Separated Soul Under-stands Separate Substances?*

We proceed thus to the Second Article: It
would seem that the separated soul does not understand separate substances.

Objection 1. For the soul is more perfect
when joined to the body than when separated
from it, since it is naturally a part of human nature, and every part of a whole is more perfect
when it exists in that whole. But the soul joined
to the body does not understand separate substances, as shown above (Q. LXXXVIII, A. 1).
Therefore much less is it able to do so when separated from the body.

Obj. 2. Further, whatever is known is known
either by its presence or by its species. But separate substances cannot be known to the soul by
their presence, for God alone can enter into the
soul; nor by means of species abstracted by the
soul from an angel, for an angel is more simple
than a soul. Therefore the separated soul cannot
at all understand separate substances.

Obj. 3. Further, some philosophers said[1] that
the ultimate happiness of man consists in the
knowledge of separate substances. If, therefore,
the separated soul can understand separate substances, its happiness would be secured by its
separation alone, which cannot reasonably be
said.

On the contrary, Souls apart from the body
know other separated souls, as we see in the
case of the rich man in hell, who saw Lazarus
and Abraham (Luke 16. 23). Therefore separated souls see the devils and the angels.

I answer that, As Augustine says (*De Trin.*
ix, 3),[2] "our mind acquires the knowledge of incorporeal things by itself"—that is, by knowing
itself (Q. LXXXVIII, A. 1, Ans. 1). Therefore
from the knowledge which the separated soul
has of itself, we can judge how it knows other
separate things. Now it was said above (A. 1),

[1] See Q. LXXXVIII, A. 1.
[2] PL 42, 963.

that as long as it is united to the body the soul
understands by turning to phantasms, and therefore it does not understand itself save through
becoming actually understanding by means of
species abstracted from phantasms; for thus it
understands itself through its own act, as shown
above (Q. LXXXVII, A. 1). When, however, it is
separated from the body, it understands no
longer by turning to phantasms, but by turning
to those things which are intelligible in themselves; hence in that state it understands itself
through itself. Now, every separate substance
understands what is above itself and what is
below itself, according to the mode of its substance, for a thing is understood according as it
is in the one who understands, while one thing
is in another according to the nature of that in
which it is. And the mode of being of a separated soul is inferior to that of an angel, but is
the same as that of other separated souls. Therefore the soul apart from the body has perfect
knowledge of other separate souls, but it has an
imperfect and defective knowledge of the angels
so far as its natural knowledge is concerned.
But the knowledge of glory is otherwise.

Reply Obj. 1. The separated soul is, indeed,
less perfect considering its nature in which it
communicates with the nature of the body; but
it has a greater freedom of understanding, since
the weight and care of the body is a hindrance
to the clearness of its understanding in the present life.

Reply Obj. 2. The separated soul understands
the angels by means of divinely impressed likenesses, which, however, fail to give perfect representation of them, since the nature of the soul
is inferior to that of an angel.

Reply Obj. 3. Man's ultimate happiness consists not in the knowledge of any separate substances whatsoever, but in the knowledge of
God, Who is seen only by grace. The knowledge
of other separate substances if perfectly understood gives great happiness, though not final
and ultimate happiness. But the separated soul
does not understand them perfectly, as was
shown above in this article.

ARTICLE 3. *Whether the Separated Soul Knows All Natural Things?*

We proceed thus to the Third Article: It
would seem that the separated soul knows all
natural things.

Objection 1. For the types of all natural
things exist in separate substances. Therefore,
as separated souls know separate substances,
they also know all natural things.

Obj. 2. Further, whoever understands the greater intelligible will be able much more to understand the lesser intelligible. But the separated soul understands immaterial substances, which are in the highest degree of intelligibility. Therefore much more can it understand all natural things which are in a lower degree of intelligibility.

On the contrary, The devils have a more vigorous natural knowledge than the separated soul; yet they do not know all natural things, but have to learn many things by long experience, as Isidore says.[1] Therefore neither can the separated soul know all natural things.

Further, if the soul as soon as separated gained knowledge of all natural things, the efforts of men to know would be in vain. But this cannot be admitted. Therefore the separated soul does not know all natural things.

I answer that, As stated above (A. 1), the separated soul, like the angels, understands by means of species received from the influx of the Divine light. Nevertheless, as the soul by nature is inferior to an angel, to whom this kind of knowledge is natural, the soul apart from the body does not receive perfect knowledge through such species, but only a general and confused kind of knowledge. Separated souls, therefore, have the same relation through such species to imperfect and confused knowledge of natural things as the angels have to the perfect knowledge of them. Now angels through such species know all natural things perfectly, because all that God has produced in the respective natures of natural things has been produced by Him in the angelic intelligence, as Augustine says (*Gen. ad. lit.* ii, 8).[2] Hence it follows that separated souls know all natural things not with a certain and proper knowledge, but in a general and confused manner.

Reply Obj. 1. Even an angel does not understand all natural things through his substance, but through certain species, as stated above (Q. LV, A. 1; Q. LXXXVII, A. 1). So it does not follow that the soul knows all natural things because it knows separate substances.

Reply Obj. 2. As the soul separated from the body does not perfectly understand separate substances, so neither does it know all natural things perfectly, but it knows them confusedly, as explained above in this article.

Reply Obj. 3. Isidore speaks of the knowledge of future things which neither angels, nor demons, nor separated souls know except so far as

[1] *Sent.,* I, 10 (PL 83, 556).
[2] PL 34, 269.

future things pre-exist in their causes or are known by Divine revelation. But we are here treating of the knowledge of natural things.

Reply Obj. 4. Knowledge acquired here by study is proper and perfect; the knowledge of the separated soul is confused. Hence it does not follow that to study in order to learn is useless.

ARTICLE 4. *Whether the Separated Soul Knows Singulars?*

We proceed thus to the Fourth Article: It would seem that the separated soul does not know singulars.

Objection 1. For no knowing power besides the intellect remains in the separated soul, as is clear from what has been said above (Q. LXXXVII, A. 8). But the intellect cannot know singulars, as we have shown (Q. LXXXVI, A. 1). Therefore the separated soul cannot know singulars.

Obj. 2. Further, the knowledge of the singular is more determinate than knowledge of the universal. But the separated soul has no determinate knowledge of the species of natural things, and therefore much less can it know singulars.

Obj. 3. Further, if it knew the singulars other than by sense, by equal reason it would know all singulars. But it does not know all singulars. Therefore it knows none.

On the contrary, The rich man in hell said: *I have five brethren* (Luke 16. 28).

I answer that, Separated souls know some singulars, but not all, not even all present singulars. To understand this we must consider that there is a twofold way of knowing things, one by means of abstraction from phantasms, and in this way singulars cannot be directly known by the intellect, but only indirectly, as stated above (Q. LXXXVI, A. 1). The other way of understanding is by the infusion of species by God, and in that way it is possible for the intellect to know singulars. For as God knows all things, universal and singular, by His Essence, as the cause of universal and individual principles (Q. XIV, A. 11; Q. LVII, A. 2), so likewise separate substances can know singulars by species which are a kind of participated likeness of the Divine Essence.

There is a difference, however, between angels and separated souls in the fact that through these species the angels have a perfect and proper knowledge of things, whereas separated souls have only a confused knowledge. Hence the angels, by reason of the efficacy of their intellect, through these species know not only the specific natures of things but also the singulars contained in those species; but separated souls by these species know only those singulars to which they are in a certain way determined by former knowledge in this life, or by some affection, or by natural aptitude, or by the disposition of the Divine order; because whatever is received into anything is determined in it according to the mode of the receiver.

Reply Obj. 1. The intellect does not know the singular by way of abstraction; neither does the separated soul know it thus, but as explained above.

Reply Obj. 2. The knowledge of the separated soul is limited to those species or individuals to which the soul has some kind of determinate relation, as we have said.

Reply Obj. 3. The separated soul has not the same relation to all singulars, but one relation to some and another to others. Therefore there is not the same reason why it should know all singulars.

ARTICLE 5. *Whether the Habit of Knowledge Acquired in This Life Remains in the Separated Soul?*

We proceed thus to the Fifth Article: It would seem that the habit of knowledge (*scientia*) acquired in this life does not remain in the soul separated from the body.

Objection 1. For the Apostle says: *Knowledge shall be destroyed* (I Cor. 13. 8).

Obj. 2. Further, some in this world who are less good enjoy knowledge denied to others who are better. If, therefore, the habit of knowledge remained in the soul after death, it would follow that some who are less good would, even in the future life, excel some who are better, which seems unfitting.

Obj. 3. Further, separated souls will possess knowledge by an influx of the Divine light. Supposing, therefore, that knowledge here acquired remained in the separated soul, it would follow that two forms of the same species would coexist in the same subject, which is impossible.

Obj. 4. Further, the Philosopher says[1] that "a habit is a quality hard to remove; yet sometimes knowledge is destroyed by sickness or the like." But in this life there is no change so thorough as death. Therefore it seems that the habit of knowledge is destroyed by death.

On the contrary, Jerome says (*Ep.* liii, *ad Paulinum*),[2] "Let us learn on earth that kind

of knowledge which will remain with us in heaven."

I answer that, Some say that the habit of knowledge resides not in the intellect itself, but in the sensitive powers, namely, the imaginative, cogitative, and remembering, and that the intelligible species are not kept in the possible intellect.[3] If this were true, it would follow that when the body is destroyed by death, knowledge acquired here would also be entirely destroyed.[4]

But, since knowledge resides in the intellect, which is "the abode of species," as the Philosopher says,[5] the habit of knowledge acquired in this life must be partly in the sensitive powers mentioned above, and partly in the intellect. This can be seen by considering the very actions from which the habit of science is acquired. For habits are like the actions whereby they are acquired.[6] Now the actions of the intellect, by which science is acquired in this life, are performed by the mind turning to the phantasms in the sensitive powers mentioned above. Hence through such acts the possible intellect acquires a certain facility in considering the species received, and the above mentioned lower powers acquire a certain aptitude in helping the action of the intellect when it turns to them to consider the intelligible object. But as the intellectual act resides chiefly and formally in the intellect itself, whilst it resides materially and dispositively in the lower powers, the same distinction is to be applied to habit.

Knowledge, therefore, acquired in the present life does not remain in the separated soul as regards what belongs to the lower powers; but as regards what belongs to the intellect itself, it must remain. Because, as the Philosopher says,[7] a form may be corrupted in two ways: first, per se, when corrupted by its contrary, as heat, by cold; and, secondly, accidentally when its subject is corrupted. Now it is evident that human knowledge is not corrupted through corruption of the subject, for the intellect is incorruptible, as above stated (Q. LXXIX, A. 2, Ans. 2; Q. LXXV, A. 6). Neither can the intelligible species in the possible intellect be corrupted by their contrary, for there is no contrary to intelligible intentions, above all as regards simple understanding by which what a thing is, is understood. But contrariety may exist in the intellect as regards mental composition

---

[1] *Categories,* 8 (8^{b}28).
[2] PL 22, 549.
[3] Avicenna, *De An.,* v, 6 (26 va).
[4] Cf. Dominic Gundisalinus, *De An.,* 10 (MK 97.12).
[5] *Soul,* III, 4 (429^{a}27).
[6] *Ethics,* II, 1 (1103^{b}21).
[7] *Longevity,* 2 (465^{a}19).

and division, or also reasoning, in so far as what is false in a proposition or argument is contrary to truth. And thus knowledge sometimes is corrupted by its contrary when a false argument leads anyone away from the knowledge of truth. For this reason the Philosopher in the above work[1] mentions two ways in which knowledge is corrupted *per se:* namely, forgetfulness on the part of the remembering power, and deception on the part of a false argument. But these have no place in the separated soul. Therefore we must conclude that the habit of knowledge, so far as it is in the intellect, remains in the separated soul.

Reply Obj. 1. The Apostle is not speaking of knowledge as a habit, but as to the act of knowing; and hence he says, in proof of the assertion quoted, *Now, I know in part.*

Reply Obj. 2. As a less good man may exceed a better man in bodily stature, so the same kind of many may have a habit of knowledge in the future life which a better man may not have. Such knowledge, however, cannot be compared with the other prerogatives enjoyed by the better man.

Reply Obj. 3. These two kinds of knowledge are not of the same species, so there is no impossibility.

Reply Obj. 4. This objection considers the corruption of knowledge on the part of the sensitive powers.

ARTICLE 6. *Whether the Act of Knowledge Acquired in This Life Remains in the Separated Soul?*

We proceed thus to the Sixth Article: It would seem that the act of knowledge (*scientia*) acquired in this life does not remain in the separated soul.

Objection 1. For the Philosopher says[2] that "when the body is corrupted, the soul neither remembers nor loves." But to consider what is previously known is an act of memory. Therefore the separated soul cannot have an act of knowledge acquired in this life.

Obj. 2. Further, intelligible species cannot have greater power in the separated soul than they have in the soul united to the body. But in this life we cannot understand by intelligible species without turning to phantasms, as shown above (Q. LXXXIV, A. 7). Therefore the separated soul cannot do so, and thus it cannot understand at all by intelligible species acquired in this life.

1 *Longevity,* 2 (465[a]23).
2 *Soul,* I, 4 (408[b]27).

Obj. 3. Further, the Philosopher says[3] that habits produce acts similar to those whereby they are acquired. But the habit of knowledge is acquired in this life by acts of the intellect turning to phantasms. Therefore it cannot produce any other acts. These acts, however, are not adapted to the separated soul. Therefore the soul in the state of separation will not have any act of knowledge acquired in this life.

On the contrary, It was said to Dives in hell (Luke 16. 25): *Remember thou didst receive good things in thy lifetime.*

I answer that, In an act two things are to be considered, its species and its mode. Its species comes from the object, to which the knowing power is directed by the species, which is the object's likeness, while the mode is gathered from the power of the agent. Thus that a person see a stone is due to the species of the stone in his eye, but that he see it clearly is due to the eye's visual power. Therefore as the intelligible species remain in the separated soul, as stated above (A. 5), and since the state of the separated soul is not the same as it is in this life, it follows that through the intelligible species acquired in this life the soul apart from the body can understand what it understood formerly, but in a different way; not by turning to phantasms, but by a mode suited to a soul existing apart from the body. Thus the act of knowledge acquired in this life remains in the separated soul, but in a different way.

Reply Obj. 1. The Philosopher speaks of remembrance according as memory belongs to the sensitive part, but not as belonging in a way to the intellect, as explained above (Q. LXXIX, A. 6).

Reply Obj. 2. The different mode of understanding is produced by the different state of the soul which understands, and not by difference in power of species.

Reply Obj. 3. The acts by which a habit is acquired are like the acts caused by that habit in species, but not in mode. For example, to do just things, but not in justly, that is, with pleasure, causes the habit of political justice, by which we act with pleasure.

ARTICLE 7. *Whether Local Distance Impedes the Knowledge in the Separated Soul?*

We proceed thus to the Seventh Article: It would seem that local distance impedes the separated soul's knowledge.

Objection 1. For Augustine says (*De Cura*

3 *Ethics,* II, 1 (1103[b]21).

pro Mort. xiii),[1] that "the souls of the dead are where they cannot know what is done here." But they know what is done among themselves. Therefore local distance impedes the knowledge in the separated soul.

Obj. 2. Further, Augustine says (*De Divin. Dæmon,* iii),[2] that "the demons' rapidity of movement enables them to tell things unknown to us." But agility of movement would be useless in that respect unless their knowledge was impeded by local distance, which, therefore, is a much greater hindrance to the knowledge of the separated soul, whose nature is inferior to the demon's.

Obj. 3. Further, as there is distance of place, so is there distance of time. But distance of time impedes knowledge in the separated soul, for the soul does not know future things. Therefore it seems that distance of place also impedes its knowledge.

On the contrary, It is written (Luke 16. 23), that Dives, *lifting up his eyes when he was in torment, saw Abraham afar off.* Therefore local distance does not impede knowledge in the separated soul.

I answer that, Some have held that the separated soul knows the singular by abstraction from the sensible.[3] If that were so, it could be said that local distance would impede its knowledge, for either the sensible would need to act upon the soul, or the soul upon the sensible, and in either case a determinate distance would be necessary. This is, however, impossible, because abstraction of the species from the sensible is done through the senses and other sensible powers which do not remain actually in the soul apart from the body. But the soul when separated understands singulars by species derived from the Divine light, which is indifferent to what is near or distant. Hence knowledge in the separated soul is not hindered by local distance.

Reply Obj. 1. Augustine says that the souls of the departed cannot see what is done here, not because they are *there,* as if impeded by local distance, but for some other cause, as we shall explain (A. 8).

Reply Obj. 2. Augustine speaks there in accordance with the opinion that demons have bodies naturally united to them,[4] and so have sensitive powers, which require a determinate

distance. In the same book[5] he expressly sets down this opinion, though apparently rather by way of narration than of assertion, as we may gather from The *City of God.*[6]

Reply Obj. 3. Future things, which are distant in time, do not actually exist, and therefore are not knowable in themselves, because so far as a thing falls short of being, so far does it fall short of being knowable. But what is locally distant exists actually, and is knowable in itself. Hence we cannot argue from distance of time to distance of place.

ARTICLE 8. *Whether Separated Souls Know What Takes Place on Earth?*

We proceed thus to the Eighth Article: It would seem that separated souls know what takes place on earth.

Objection 1. For otherwise they would have no care for it, as they have, according to what Dives said (Luke 16. 27, 28), *I have five brethren . . . he may testify unto them, lest they also come into the place of torments.* Therefore separated souls know what passes on earth.

Obj. 2. Further, the dead often appear to the living, asleep or awake, and warn them of what takes place here; as Samuel appeared to Saul (I Kings 28. 11). But this could not be unless they knew what takes place here. Therefore they know what takes place on earth.

Obj. 3. Further, separated souls know what happens among themselves. If, therefore, they do not know what takes place among us, it must be by reason of local distance; which has been shown to be false (A. 7).

On the contrary, It is written (Job 14. 21): *He will not understand whether his children come to honour or dishonour.*

I answer that, By natural knowledge, of which we are treating now, the souls of the dead do not know what passes on earth. This follows from what has been laid down (A. 4), since the separated soul has knowledge of singulars through being in a way determined to them, either by some vestige of previous knowledge or affection, or by the Divine order. Now the souls of the dead are in a state of separation from the living, both by Divine order and by their mode of being, whilst they are joined to the world of incorporeal spiritual substances; and hence they are ignorant of what goes on among us. And Gregory gives the reason thus: "The dead do not know how the living act, for the life of the spirit is far from the life of the flesh; and so, as

---

[1] PL 40, 605.   [2] PL 40, 584.
[3] Cf. Cassiodorus, *De An.,* 2 (PL 70, 1286); Pseudo-Augustine (Alcher of Clairvaux), *De Spir. et An.,* 30 (PL 40, 800). Cf. also Bonaventure, *In Sent.,* IV, d. 50, Pt. 2, A. 1, Q. 1 (QR IV, 1046).
[4] Cf. Q. LI. A. 1, ADS. 1.

[5] *De Div. Dæmon,* 3 (PL 40, 584).
[6] XXI, 10 (PL 41, 724).

corporeal things differ from incorporeal in genus, so they are distinct in knowledge" (*Moral.* xii)[1] Augustine seems to say the same (*De Cura pro Mort.* xiii),[2] when he asserts that, "the souls of the dead have no concern in the affairs of the living."

Gregory and Augustine, however, seem to be divided in opinion as regards the souls of the blessed in heaven, for Gregory continues the passage above quoted: "The case of the holy souls is different, for since they see the light of Almighty God, we cannot believe that external things are unknown to them." But Augustine (*De Cura pro Mort.* xiii)[3] expressly says that the dead, even the saints, do not know what is done by the living or by their own children, as a gloss quotes on the text, *Abraham hath not known us* (Isa. 63. 16).[4] He confirms this opinion by saying that he was not visited nor consoled in sorrow by his mother, as when she was alive, and he could not think it possible that she was less kind when in a happier state; and again by the fact that the Lord promised to King Josias that he should die, lest he should see his people's afflictions (IV Kings 22. 20). Yet Augustine says this in doubt, and premises, "Let every one take, as he pleases, what I say." Gregory, on the other hand, is positive, since he says, "We cannot believe." His opinion, indeed, seems to be the more probable one,—that the souls of the blessed who see God do know all that passes here. For they are equal to the angels, of whom Augustine says that they know what happens among those living on earth.[5] But as the souls of the blessed are most perfectly united to Divine justice, they do not suffer from sorrow, nor do they interfere in mundane affairs, except in accordance with Divine justice.

Reply Obj. 1. The souls of the dead may care for the living, even if ignorant of their state, just as we care for the dead by offering prayers on their behalf, though we are ignorant of their state. Moreover, the affairs of the living can be made known to them not in themselves, but through the souls who come to them from this life, or by angels and demons, or even "by the revelation of the Holy Ghost," as Augustine says in the same book.[6]

Reply Obj. 2. That the dead appear to the living in any way whatever is either by the special dispensation of God, in order that the souls of

the dead may intervene in affairs of the living,—and this is to be accounted as miraculous; or, else such apparitions occur through the instrumentality of bad or good angels, without the knowledge of the departed, as may likewise happen when in sleep the living appear, without their own knowledge, to others living, as Augustine says in the same book.[7] And so it may be said of Samuel that he appeared through Divine revelation, according to Ecclus. 46. 23, *he slept, and told the king the end of his life.* Or, again, we can say that this apparition was procured by the demons if the authority of Ecclesiasticus be set aside through not being received by the Jews as canonical Scripture.

Reply Obj. 3. This kind of ignorance does not proceed from the obstacle of local distance, but from the cause mentioned above.

QUESTION XC
OF THE FIRST PRODUCTION OF MAN'S SOUL
(*In Four Articles*)

AFTER the foregoing we must consider the first production of man, concerning which there are four subjects of treatment: (1) The production of man himself. (2) The end of this production (Q. XCIII). (3) The state and condition of the first man (Q. XCIV). (4) The place of his abode (Q. CII). Concerning the production of man, there are three things to be considered: (1) The production of man's soul. (2) The production of man's body (Q. XCI). (3) The production of the woman (Q. XCII).

Under the first head there are four points of inquiry: (1) Whether man's soul was something made, or was of the Divine substance? (2) Whether, if made, it was created? (3) Whether it was made by means of the angels? (4) Whether it was made before the body?

ARTICLE 1. *Whether the Soul Was Made, or Was of God's Substance?*

We proceed thus to the First Article: It would seem that the soul was not made, but was of God's substance.

Objection 1. For it is written (Gen. 2. 7): *God formed man of the slime of the earth, and breathed into his face the breath of life, and man was made a living soul.* But he who breathes sends forth something of himself. Therefore the soul, by which man lives, is of the Divine substance.

Obj. 2. Further, as explained above (Q. LXXV,

---

[1] Chap. 21 (PL 75, 999).
[2] PL 40, 604; also, chap. 16 (PL 40, 607).
[3] PL 40, 604.
[4] *Glossa interl.* (IV, 102V).
[5] *De Cura pro Mort.*, 15 (PL 40, 605).
[6] Chap. 15 (PL 40, 606).
[7] Chap. 12 (PL 40, 600).

A. 5), the soul is a simple form. But a form is an act. Therefore the soul is of God's substance.

Obj. 3. Further, things that exist and do not differ are the same. But God and the mind exist, and in no way differ, for they could only be differentiated by certain differences, and thus would be composite. Therefore God and the human mind are the same.

On the contrary, Augustine (*De Orig. Animæ* iii. 15)[1] mentions certain opinions which he calls "exceedingly and evidently perverse, and contrary to the Catholic Faith," among which the first is the opinion that "God made the soul not out of nothing, but from Himself."

I answer that, To say that the soul is of the Divine substance involves a manifest improbability. For, as is clear from what has been said (Q. LXXVII, A. 2; Q. LXXIX, A. 2; Q. LXXXIV, A. 6), the human soul is sometimes in a state of potency to the act of understanding, acquires its knowledge somehow from things, and has various powers; all of which are foreign to the Divine Nature, Which is a pure act, receiving nothing from any other, and admitting of no variety in itself, as we have proved (Q. III, AA. 1, 7; Q. IX, A. 1).

This error seems to have originated from two opinions of the ancients. For those who first began to observe the natures of things, being unable to rise above their imagination, supposed that nothing but bodies existed.[2] Therefore they said that God was a body,[3] which they considered to be the principle of other bodies. And since they held that the soul was of the same nature as that body which they regarded as the first principle, as is stated in the book on the *Soul*,[4] it followed that the soul was of the substance of God. According to this supposition, also, the Manichæans, thinking that God was a corporeal light, held that the soul was part of that light, bound up with the body.[5]

Then a further step in advance was made, and some apprehended the being of something incorporeal, not apart from the body, but the form of a body,[6] so that Varro said, "God is a soul governing the world by movement and reason," as Augustine relates.[7] So some supposed man's soul to be part of that all-embracing soul,[8] just

as man is a part of the whole world; for they were unable to go so far as to distinguish the different degrees of spiritual substance, except according to the distinction of bodies.

But, all these theories are impossible, as proved above (Q. III, AA. 1, 8; and Q. LXXV, A. 1), and therefore it is evidently false that the soul is of the substance of God.

Reply Obj. 1. The term "breathe" is not to be taken in the corporeal sense; but as regards the act of God, to breathe (*spirare*), is the same as to make a spirit. Moreover, even in the corporeal sense, man by breathing does not send forth anything of his own substance, but an extraneous thing.

Reply Obj. 2. Although the soul is a simple form in its essence, yet it is not its own being, but is a being by participation, as above explained (Q. LXXV, A. 5, Ans. 4). Therefore it is not a pure act like God.

Reply Obj. 3. That which differs, properly speaking, differs by something; therefore we seek for difference where we find also resemblance. For this reason things which differ must in some way be compound, since they differ in something, and in something resemble each other. In this sense, although all that differ are diverse, yet all things that are diverse do not differ, as is stated in the *Metaphysics*.[9] For simple things differ in themselves and not by other different things out of which they are composed. For instance, a man and a horse differ by the difference of rational and irrational, but we cannot say that these again differ by some further difference.

ARTICLE 2. *Whether the Soul Was Produced in Being by Creation?*

We proceed thus to the Second Article: It would seem that the soul was not produced in being by creation.

Objection. 1. For that which has in itself something material is produced from matter. But the soul has something material in itself, since it is not a pure act. Therefore the soul was made of matter, and hence it was not created.

Obj. 2. Further, every act of matter is drawn out of the potency of that matter; for since matter is in potency to act, any act pre-exists in matter potentially. But the soul is the act of corporeal matter, as is clear from its definition.[10] Therefore the soul is drawn out of the potency of matter.

Obj. 3. Further, the soul is a form. Therefore,

---

[1] PL 44, 522.   [2] Cf. Q. XLIV, A. 2.

[3] Cf. Q. II, A. 1, Ans. 2 (note).   [4] Aristotle, I, 2 (405ª3).

[5] Cf. Augustine, *De Haeres*, XLVI (PL 42, 35); *Gen. ad litt.*, VII, 11 (PL 34, 361).

[6] Cf. Q. XLIV, A. 2.

[7] *City of God*, VII, 6 (PL 41, 199); cf. also IV, 31 (PL 41, 138).

[8] Macrobius, *In Somn. Scip.*, I, 14 (DD 45b); Plato, according to Albert the Great, in *De Mot. An.*, I, 1 (BO IX, 258).

[9] Aristotle, V, 9 (1018ª11).

[10] Aristotle, *Soul*, II, 1 (412ª27).

if the soul is created, by equal reason all other forms are created. Thus no forms would come into being by generation; which is not true.

On the contrary, It is written (Gen. 1. 27): *God created man to His own image*. But man is in the image of God in his soul. Therefore the soul was created.

I answer that, The rational soul can be made only by creation, which is not true of other forms. The reason is because since to be made is the way to being, a thing must be made in such a way as is suitable to its mode of being. Now that properly is said to be which itself has being, subsisting as it were in its own being. Therefore only substances are properly and truly called beings. But an accident does not have being, but something is by it, and so far is it called a being; for instance, whiteness is called a being because by it something is white. Hence it is said in the *Metaphysics*[1] that an accident should be described as of a being rather than as a being. The same is to be said of all other non-subsistent forms. Therefore, properly speaking, it does not pertain to any non-existing form to be made, but they are said to be made through the composite substances being made. On the other hand, the rational soul is a subsistent form, as above explained (Q. LXXV, A. 2). And so it properly pertains to it to be and to be made. And since it cannot be made of pre-existing (*præjacens*) matter, neither corporeal because in this way it would be a corporeal nature; nor spiritual, which would involve the transmutation of one spiritual substance into another, we must conclude that it cannot exist except by creation.

Reply Obj. 1. The soul's simple essence is as the material element, while its participated being is its formal element, which participated being necessarily exists at the same time with the soul's essence, because being naturally follows the form. The same reason holds if the soul is supposed to be composed of some spiritual matter, as some maintain;[2] because that matter is not in potency to another form, just as the matter of a celestial body is not; otherwise the soul would be corruptible. Therefore the soul cannot in any way be made of pre-existent matter.

Reply Obj. 2. The drawing out of act from the potency of matter is nothing else but something becoming actual that previously was in potency. But since the rational soul does not depend in its being on corporeal matter, but has subsistent being, and exceeds the capacity of corporeal

matter, as we have seen (Q. LXXV, A. 2), for this reason it is not drawn out from the potency of matter.

Reply Obj. 3. As we have said, there is no comparison between the rational soul and other forms.

ARTICLE 3. *Whether the Rational Soul Is Produced by God Immediately?*

We proceed thus to the Third Article: It would seem that the rational soul is not immediately made by God, but by the instrumentality of the angels.

Objection 1. For spiritual things have more order than corporeal things. But inferior bodies are produced by means of the superior, as Dionysius says (*Div. Nom.* iv).[3] Therefore also the inferior spirits, who are the rational souls, are produced by means of the superior spirits, the angels.

Obj. 2. Further, the end corresponds to the beginning of things, for God is the beginning and end of all. Therefore the issue of things from their beginning corresponds to their going back to their end. But "lower things are brought back by the higher," as Dionysius says (*Eccl. Hier.* v);[4] therefore also the lower come into being through the higher, and souls by angels.

Obj. 3. Further, "The perfect is that which can produce its like," as is stated in the fourth book on *Meteorology*.[5] But spiritual substances are much more perfect than corporeal. Therefore, since bodies produce their like in their own species, much more are angels able to produce something specifically inferior to themselves; and such is the rational soul.

On the contrary, It is written (Gen. 2. 7) that God Himself *breathed into the face of man the breath of life*.

I answer that, Some have held that angels, acting by the power of God, produce rational souls.[6] But this is quite impossible, and is against faith. For it has been proved (A. 2) that the rational soul cannot be produced except by creation. Now, God alone can create, for the first agent alone can act without presupposing anything, while the second cause always presupposes something derived from the first cause, as above explained (Q. LXV, A. 3). And every agent

---

[1] Aristotle, VII, 1 (1028ª25).
[2] Cf. Q. L, A. 2; Q. LXXV, A. 6.

[3] Sect. 4 (PG 3, 697).   [4] Sect. 4 (PG 3, 504).
[5] Aristotle, 3 (380ª14).
[6] Avicenna, *Meta.*, IX, 4 (104 vb); cf. Algazel, in Averroes, *Dest. Dest.*, 3 (IX, 52E); *Liber de Causis*, 3 (BA 166.2); cf. Augustine, *De Haeres.*, 59 (PL 42, 41). Albert the Great, in *Summa de Creatur.*, attributes this position to Gundissalinus; cf. Gundissalinus, *De An.*, 5 (MK 51.10).

that presupposes something to its act, acts by making a change in it. Therefore everything else acts by producing a change, but God alone acts by creation. Since, therefore, the rational soul cannot be produced by a change in matter, it cannot be produced except immediately by God.

Thus the *replies to the objections* are clear. For that bodies produce their like or something inferior to themselves, and that the higher things lead back the inferior,—all these things are effected through a certain transmutation.

ARTICLE 4. *Whether the Human Soul Was Produced Before the Body?*

We proceed thus to the Fourth Article: It would seem that the human soul was made before the body.

Objection 1. For the work of creation preceded the work of distinction and adornment, as shown above (Q. LXVI, A. 1; Q. LXX, A. 1). But the soul was produced in being by creation, whereas the body was made at the end of the work of adornment as was maintained above (Q. LXXII). Therefore the soul of man was made before the body.

Obj. 2. Further, the rational soul has more in common with the angels than with the brute animals. But angels were created before bodies, or at least, at the beginning with corporeal matter, while the body of man was formed on the sixth day, when also the animals were made. Therefore the soul of man was created before the body.

Obj. 3. Further, the end is proportioned to the beginning. But in the end the soul outlasts the body. Therefore in the beginning it was created before the body.

On the contrary, The proper act is produced in its proper potency. Therefore, since the soul is the proper act of the body, the soul was produced in the body.

I answer that, Origen (*Peri Archon,* i)[1] held that not only the soul of the first man, but also the souls of all men were created at the same time as the angels, before their bodies. For he thought that all spiritual substances, whether souls or angels, are equal in their natural condition, and differ only by merit, so that some of them—namely, the souls of men or of heavenly bodies—are united to bodies while others remain in their different orders entirely free from matter. Of this opinion we have already spoken (Q. XLVII, A. 2), and so we need say nothing about it here.

[1] Chaps. 6, 8, 9 (PG 11, 166, 178, 229).

Augustine, however (*Gen. ad lit.* vii, 24),[2] says that the soul of the first man was created at the same time as the angels, before the body, for another reason. For he supposes that the body of man, during the work of the six days, was produced not actually, but only in their causal principles; which cannot be said of the soul, because neither was it made of any preexisting corporeal or spiritual matter, nor could it be produced from any created principle. Therefore it seems that the soul itself, during the work of the six days when all things were made, was created, together with the angels, and that afterwards, by its own will, was joined to the service of the body. But he does not say this by way of assertion, as his words prove. For he says (*loc. cit.*):[3] "We may believe, if neither Scripture nor reason forbid, that man was made on the sixth day, in the sense that his body was created as to its causal principle in the elements of the world, but that the soul was already created."

Now this could be upheld by those who hold that the soul has of itself a complete species and nature, and that it is not united to the body as its form, but as its ruler.[4] But if the soul is united to the body as its form, and is naturally a part of human nature, this supposition is altogether impossible. For it is clear that God made the first things in their perfect natural state, according as the species of each required. Now the soul, as a part of human nature, has its natural perfection only as united to the body. Therefore it would have been unfitting for the soul to be created without the body.

Therefore, if we admit the opinion of Augustine about the work of the six days (Q. LXXIV, A. 2), we may say that the human soul preceded in the work of the six days by a certain generic likeness, so far as it has intellectual nature in common with the angels, but was itself created at the same time as the body. According to other saints,[5] both the body and soul of the first man were produced in the work of the six days.

Reply Obj. 1. If the soul by its nature were a complete species, so that it might be created in itself, this reason would prove that the soul was created in itself in the beginning. But as the soul is naturally the form of the body, it was necessarily created not separately but in the body.

Reply Obj. 2. The same observation applies to the second objection. For if the soul had a spe-

[2] PL 34 (368); cf. also Chap. 28 (370).
[3] Bk. VII, Chap. 4 (PL 34, 368).
[4] Cf. Q. LXXVI, A. 1.
[5] Cf. Q. LXXIV, A. 2.

cies of itself it would have something still more in common with the angels. But, as the form of the body, it belongs to the genus of animal, as a formal principle.

Reply Obj. 3. That the soul remains after the body is due to a defect of the body, namely, death. Which defect was not due when the soul was first created.

QUESTION XCI
THE PRODUCTION OF THE FIRST MAN'S BODY
(In Four Articles)

WE have now to consider the production of the first man's body. Under this head there are four points of inquiry: (1) The matter from which it was produced. (2) The author by whom it was produced. (3) The disposition it received in its production. (4) The mode and order of its production.

ARTICLE 1. *Whether the Body of the First Man Was Made of the Slime of the Earth?*

We proceed thus to the First Article: It would seem that the body of the first man was not made of the slime of the earth.

Objection 1. For it is an act of greater power to make something out of nothing than out of something, because non-being is further from act than being in potency. But since man is the most excellent of God's lower creatures, it was fitting that in the production of man's body the power of God should be most clearly shown. Therefore it should not have been made of the slime of the earth, but out of nothing.

Obj. 2. Further, the heavenly bodies are nobler than earthly bodies. But the human body has the greatest nobility, since it is perfected by the noblest form, which is the rational soul. Therefore it should not be made of an earthly body, but of a heavenly body.

Obj. 3. Further, fire and air are nobler bodies than earth and water, as is clear from their subtlety. Therefore, since the human body is most noble, it should rather have been made of fire and air than of the slime of the earth.

Obj. 4. Further, the human body is composed of the four elements. Therefore it was not made of the slime of the earth, but of the four elements.

On the contrary, It is written (Gen. 2. 7): *God made man of the slime of the earth.*

I answer that, As God is perfect in His works, He bestowed perfection on all of them according to their manner: *God's works are perfect*

(Deut. 32. 4). He Himself is absolutely perfect by the fact that "all things are pre-contained in Him, not as component parts, but as united in one simple whole," as Dionysius says (*Div. Nom.* v),[1] in the same way as various effects pre-exist in their cause, according to its single power. This perfection is bestowed on the angels, since all things which are produced by God in nature through various forms come under their knowledge. But on man this perfection is bestowed in an inferior way. For he does not possess a natural knowledge of all natural things, but is in a manner composed of all things, since he has in himself a rational soul of the genus of spiritual substances, and in likeness to the heavenly bodies he is removed from contraries by an equable temperament. As to the elements, he has them in their very substance, yet in such a way that the higher elements, fire and air, predominate in him by their power; for life is mostly found where there is heat, which is from fire, and where there is moisture, which is of the air. But the inferior elements abound in man by their substance; otherwise the mingling of elements would not be evenly balanced, unless the inferior elements, which have the less power, predominated in quantity. Therefore the body of man is said to have been formed from the slime of the earth; because earth and water mingled are called slime, and for this reason man is called "a little world,"[2] because all creatures of the world are in a way to be found in him.

Reply Obj. 1. The power of the Divine Creator was manifested in man's body when its matter was produced by creation. But it was fitting that the human body should be made of the four elements that man might have something in common with the inferior bodies, as being something between spiritual and corporeal substances.

Reply Obj. 2. Although the heavenly body is absolutely nobler than the earthly body, yet for the acts of the rational soul the heavenly body is less adapted. For the rational soul receives the knowledge of truth in a certain way through the senses, the organs of which cannot be formed of a heavenly body which is impassible. Nor is it true that something of the fifth essence enters materially into the composition of the human body, as some say,[3] who suppose that the soul is

---

[1] Sect. 9 (PG 3, 825).

[2] Cf. Aristotle, *Physics*, VIII, 2 (252ᵇ26); Macrobius, *In Somn. Scip.*, II, 12 (DD 98b); Nemesius, *De Nat. Hom.*, I (PG 40, 533); cf. also Part I-II, Q. XVII, A. 8, obj. 2 (note).

[3] Cf. Q. LXXVI, A. 7.

united to the body by means of light. For, first of all, what they say is false—that light is a body. Secondly, it is impossible for something to be taken from the fifth essence, or from a heavenly body, and to be mingled with the elements, since a heavenly body is impassible. Therefore it does not enter into the composition of mixed bodies, except as in the effects of its power.

Reply Obj. 3. If fire and air, whose action is of greater power, predominated also in quantity in the human body, they would entirely draw the rest into themselves, and there would be no equality in the mingling, such as is required in the composition of man for the sense of touch, which is the foundation of the other senses. For the organ of any particular sense must not actually have the contraries of that of which that sense has the perception, but only potentially; either in such a way that it is entirely lacking in the whole genus of such contraries,—thus, for instance, the pupil of the eye is without colour, so as to be in potency to all colours, which is not possible in the organ of touch, since it is composed of the very elements whose qualities are perceived by that sense; or so that the organ is a medium between two contraries, as must be the case with regard to touch; for the medium is in potency to the extremes.

Reply Obj. 4. In the slime of the earth are earth and water binding the earth together. Of the other elements, Scripture makes no mention, because they are less in quantity in the human body, as we have said; and because also in the account of the Creation no mention is made of fire and air, which are not perceived by senses of primitive men such as those to whom the Scripture was immediately addressed.

ARTICLE 2. *Whether the Human Body Was Immediately Produced by God?*

We proceed thus to the Second Article: It would seem that the human body was not produced by God immediately.

Objection 1. For Augustine says (*De Trin.* iii, 4),[1] that "corporeal things are disposed by God through the angels." But the human body was made of corporeal matter, as stated above (A. 1). Therefore it was produced by the instrumentality of the angels, and not immediately by God.

Obj. 2. Further, whatever can be made by a created power, is not necessarily produced immediately by God. But the human body can be produced by the created power of a heavenly

body, for even certain animals are produced from putrefaction by the active power of a heavenly body, and Albumazar says that man is not generated where heat and cold are extreme, but only in temperate regions.[2] Therefore the human body was not necessarily produced immediately by God.

Obj. 3. Further, nothing is made of corporeal matter except by some material change. But all corporeal change is caused by a movement of a heavenly body, which is the first movement. Therefore, since the human body was produced from corporeal matter, it seems that a heavenly body had part in its production.

Obj. 4. Further, Augustine says (*Gen. ad lit.* vii, 24)[3] that man's body was made during the work of the six days, according to the causal principles which God inserted in corporeal creatures, and that it was actually produced afterwards. But what pre-exists in the corporeal creature by reason of causal principles can be produced by some corporeal body. Therefore the human body was produced by some created power, and not immediately by God.

On the contrary, It is written (Ecclus. 17. 1): *God created man out of the earth.*

I answer that, The first formation of the human body could not be by the instrumentality of any created power, but was immediately from God. Some, indeed, supposed that the forms which are in corporeal matter are derived from some immaterial forms;[4] but the Philosopher refutes this opinion,[5] for the reason that "forms cannot be made in themselves, but only in the composite," as we have explained (Q. LXV, A. 4).[6] And because the agent must be like its effect, it is not fitting that a pure form, not existing in matter, should produce a form which is in matter, and which is only made by the fact that the composite is made. So a form which is in matter can only be the cause of another form that is in matter according as composite is made by composite. Now God, though He is absolutely immaterial, alone can by His own power produce matter by creation. Therefore He alone can produce a form in matter without the aid of any preceding material form. For this reason the angels cannot transform a body except by making use of seminal principles, as Augustine says (*De Trin.* iii).[7] Therefore as no pre-existing

---

[1] PL 42, 873.

[2] Cf. Duhem, *Le Système du Monde* (II, 369).
[3] PL 34, 368.
[4] Cf. Q. XLV, A. 8; Q. LXV, A. 4; Q. CXV, A. I.
[5] *Metaphysics*, VII, 8 (1033[b]16).
[6] Cf. also Q. XLV, A. 8; Q. XC, A. 2.
[7] Chaps. 8, 9 (PL 42, 876, 878).

body had been formed whereby another body of the same species could be generated, the first human body was of necessity made immediately by God.

Reply Obj. 1. Although the angels are the ministers of God as regards what they do in bodies, yet God does something in bodies beyond the angels' power, as, for instance, raising the dead, or giving sight to the blind, and by this power He formed the body of the first man from the slime of the earth. Nevertheless the angels could act as ministers in the formation of the body of the first man, in the same way as they will do at the last resurrection, by collecting the dust.

Reply Obj. 2. Perfect animals, produced from seed, cannot be made by the sole power of a heavenly body, as Avicenna imagined,[1] although the power of a heavenly body may assist by co-operation in the work of natural generation; for the Philosopher says,[2] "man and the sun beget man from matter." For this reason, a place of moderate temperature is required for the production of man and other perfect animals. But the power of heavenly bodies suffices for the production of some imperfect animals from properly disposed matter; for it is clear that more conditions are required to produce a perfect than an imperfect thing.

Reply Obj. 3. The movement of the heavens causes natural changes, but not changes that surpass the order of nature, and are caused by the Divine Power alone, as for the dead to be raised to life, or the blind to see, like to which also is the making of man from the slime of the earth.

Reply Obj. 4. A thing may be said to preexist in the causal principles of creatures in two ways. First, both in active and in passive potency, so that not only can it be produced out of pre-existing matter, but also that some pre-existing creature can produce it. Secondly, in passive potency only; that is, that out of pre-existing matter it can be produced by God. In this sense, according to Augustine, the human body pre-existed in the works produced according to the causal principles.

ARTICLE 3. *Whether the Body of Man Was Given a Fitting Disposition?*

We proceed thus to the Third Article: It would seem that the body of man was not given a fitting disposition.

Objection 1. For since man is the noblest of

animals, his body ought to be the best disposed in what is proper to an animal, that is, in sense and movement. But some animals have sharper senses and quicker movement than man; thus dogs have a keener smell, and birds move more swiftly. Therefore man's body was not aptly disposed.

Obj. 2. Further, the perfect is what lacks nothing. But the human body lacks more than the body of other animals, for these are provided with covering and natural arms of defence, in which man is lacking. Therefore the human body is very imperfectly disposed.

Obj. 3. Further, man is more distant from plants than he is from the brutes. But plants are erect in stature, while brutes are prone in stature. Therefore man should not be of erect stature.

On the contrary, It is written (Eccles. 7. 30): *God made man right.*

I answer that, All natural things were produced by the Divine art, and so may be called God's works of art. Now every artist intends to give to his work the best disposition; not absolutely the best, but the best as regards the proposed end. And even if this entails some defect, the artist does not care. Thus, for instance, when a man makes himself a saw for the purpose of cutting, he makes it of iron, which is suitable for the object in view; and he does not prefer to make it of glass, though this be a more beautiful material, because this very beauty would be an obstacle to the end he has in view. Thus, therefore, God gave to each natural being the best disposition; not absolutely so, but in view of its proper end. This is what the Philosopher says,[3] "And because it is better so, not absolutely, but for each one's substance."

Now the proximate end of the human body is the rational soul and its operations, since matter is for the sake of the form, and instruments are for the action of the agent. I say, therefore, that God fashioned the human body in that disposition which was best, as most suited to such a form and to such operations. And if there seems to be some defect in the disposition of the human body, it is well to observe that such defect arises as a necessary result of the matter, from the conditions required in the body in order to make it suitably proportioned to the soul and its operations.

Reply Obj. 1. The sense of touch, which is the foundation of the other senses, is more perfect in man than in any other animal, and for this reason man must have the most equable tem-

---

[1] Cf. Q. LXXI, Ans. 1.
[2] *Physics*, II, 2 (194^{b}13).
[3] *Ibid.*, II, 7 (198^{b}8).

perament of all animals. Moreover man excels all other animals in the interior sensitive powers, as is clear from what we have said above (Q. LXXVIII, A. 4). But by a kind of necessity, man falls short of the other animals in some of the exterior senses; thus of all animals he has the least sense of smell. For man of all animals needs the largest brain as compared to the body, both for his greater freedom of action in the interior powers required for the intellectual operations, as we have seen above (Q. LXXXIV, A. 7), and in order that the low temperature of the brain may modify the heat of the heart, which has to be considerable in man for him to be able to stand up erect. So that the size of the brain, by reason of its humidity, is an impediment to the smell, which requires dryness. In the same way, we may suggest a reason why some animals have a keener sight, and a more acute hearing than man; namely, on account of a hindrance to his senses arising necessarily from the perfect equability of his temperament. The same reason suffices to explain why some animals are more rapid in movement than man, since this excellence of speed is inconsistent with the equability of the human temperament.

Reply Obj. 2. Horns and claws, which are the weapons of some animals, and toughness of hide and quantity of hair or feathers, which are the clothing of animals, are signs of an abundance of the earthly element, which does not agree with the equability and softness of the human temperament. Therefore such things do not suit the nature of man. Instead of these, he has reason and hands whereby he can make himself arms and clothes, and other necessaries of life, of infinite variety. And so the hand is called by Aristotle[1] "the organ of organs." Moreover this was more becoming to the rational nature, which is capable of conceiving an infinite number of things so as to make for itself an infinite number of instruments.

Reply Obj. 3. An upright stature was becoming to man for four reasons. First, because the senses are given to man, not only for the purpose of procuring the necessaries of life for which they are bestowed on other animals, but also for the purpose of knowledge. Hence, whereas the other animals take delight in the objects of the senses only as ordered to food and sex, man alone takes pleasure in the beauty of sensible objects for its own sake. Therefore, as the senses are situated chiefly in the face, other animals have the face turned to the ground, as it were for the purpose of seeking food and pro-

curing a livelihood; but man has his face erect, in order that by the senses, and chiefly by sight, which is more subtle and penetrates further into the differences of things, he may freely survey the sensible objects around him, both heavenly and earthly, so as to gather intelligible truth from all things. Secondly, for the greater freedom of the acts of the interior powers; the brain, wherein these actions are, in a way, performed, not being low down, but lifted up above other parts of the body. Thirdly, because if man's stature were prone to the ground he would need to use his hands as fore-feet, and thus their utility for other purposes would cease. Fourthly, because if man's stature were prone to the ground and he used his hands as fore-feet, he would be obliged to take hold of his food with his mouth. Thus he would have a protruding mouth, with thick and hard lips, and also a hard tongue, so as to keep it from being hurt by exterior things, as we see in other animals. Moreover, such an attitude would quite hinder speech, which is reason's proper operation.

Nevertheless, though of erect nature, man is far above plants. For man's superior part, his head, is turned towards the superior part of the world, and his inferior part is turned towards the inferior world; and therefore he is perfectly disposed as to the general situation of his body. Plants have the superior part turned towards the lower world, since their roots correspond to the mouth, and their inferior parts towards the upper world. But brute animals have a middle disposition, for the superior part of the animal is that by which it takes food, and the inferior part that by which it rids itself of the surplus.

ARTICLE 4. *Whether the Production of the Human Body Is Fittingly Described in Scripture?*

We proceed thus to the Fourth Article: It would seem that the production of the human body is not fittingly described in Scripture (Gen. 1. 26; 2. 7).

Objection 1. For, as the human body was made by God, so also were the other works of the six days. But in the other works it is written, *God said; Let it be made, and it was made.* Therefore the same should have been said of man.

Obj. 2. Further, the human body was made by God immediately, as explained above (A. 2). Therefore it was not fittingly said, *Let us make man.*

Obj. 3. Further, the form of the human body is the soul itself which is the breath of life. Therefore, having said, *God made man of the*

---

[1] *Soul*, III, 8 (432[a]1).

slime of the earth, he should not have added: *And He breathed into him the breath of life.*

Obj. 4. Further, the soul, which is the breath of life, is in the whole body, and chiefly in the heart. Therefore it was not fittingly said: *He breathed into his face the breath of life.*

Obj. 5. Further, the male and female sex belong to the body, while the image of God belongs to the soul. But the soul, according to Augustine (*Gen. ad lit.* vii, 24),[1] was made before the body. Therefore having said: *To His image He made them,* he should not have added, *male and female He created them.*

On the contrary, Is the authority of Scripture.

Reply Obj. 1. As Augustine observes (*Gen. ad lit.* vi, 12),[2] man surpasses other things not in the fact that God Himself made man, as though He did not make other things; since it is written (Ps. 101. 26), *The work of Thy hands is the heaven,* and elsewhere (Ps. 94. 5), *His hands laid down the dry land,* but in this, that man is made to God's image. Yet in describing man's production, Scripture uses a special way of speaking to show that other things were made for man's sake. For we are accustomed to do with more deliberation and care what we have chiefly in mind.

Reply Obj. 2. We must not imagine that when God said *Let us make man,* He spoke to the angels, as some were perverse enough to think.[3] But by these words is signified the plurality of the Divine Person, Whose image is more clearly expressed in man.

Reply Obj. 3. Some have thought that man's body was formed first in priority of time, and that afterwards the soul was infused into the formed body.[4] But it is against the notion of the perfection of the first production of things, that God should have made either the body without the soul, or the soul without the body, since each is a part of human nature. This is especially unfitting as regards the body, for the body depends on the soul, and not the soul on the body.

To remove the difficulty some have said that the words, *God made man,* must be understood of the production of the body with the soul, and that the subsequent words, *and He breathed into his face the breath of life,* should be understood of the Holy Ghost; just as the Lord breathed on

His Apostles, saying, *Receive ye the Holy Ghost* (John 20. 22).[5] But this explanation, as Augustine says,[6] is excluded by the very words of Scripture. For we read further on, *And man was made a living soul,* which words the Apostle (I Cor. 15. 45) refers not to spiritual life, but to animal life. Therefore, by breath of life we must understand the soul, so that the words, *He breathed into his face the breath of life,* are a sort of exposition of what goes before; for the soul is the form of the body.

Reply Obj. 4. Since vital operations are more clearly seen in man's face, on account of the senses which are there expressed, therefore Scripture says that the breath of life was breathed into man's face.

Reply Obj. 5. According to Augustine (*Gen. ad lit.* iv, 34),[7] the works of the six days were done all at one time. And so according to him, man's soul, which he holds to have been made with the angels, was not made before the sixth day; but on the sixth day both the soul of the first man was made actually, and his body in its causal principles. But other doctors hold that on the sixth day both body and soul of man were actually made.[8]

QUESTION XCII
THE PRODUCTION OF THE WOMAN
(*In Four Articles*)

WE must next consider the production of the woman. Under this head there are four points of inquiry: (1) Whether the woman should have been made in that first production of things? (2) Whether the woman should have been made from man? (3) Whether of man's rib? (4) Whether the woman was made immediately by God?

ARTICLE 1. *Whether the Woman Should Have Been Made in the First Production of Things?*

We proceed thus to the First Article: It would seem that the woman should not have been made in the first production of things.

Objection 1. For the Philosopher says[9] that "the female is a misbegotten male." But nothing misbegotten or defective should have been in the first production of things. Therefore woman should not have been made at that first production.

---

[1] PL 34, 368. Also chap. 28 (370).
[2] PL 34, 362.
[3] Cf. Peter Lombard, *Sent.,* II, XVI, 2 (QR I, 379). Cf. also Augustine, *City of God,* XVI, 6 (PL 41, 484).
[4] Cf. Peter Lombard, *loc. cit.;* Augustine, *Gen. ad lit.,* VII, 24 (PL 34, 368); Hugh of St. Victor, *De Sacram.,* I, VI, 3 (PL 176, 275); cf. also Portalié, DTC, art. on Augustine (I, 2350).

[5] Cf. Augustine, *City of God,* XIII, 24 (PL 41. 398); *Gen. contra Manich.,* II, 8 (PL 34, 201).
[6] *City of God,* XIII, 24 (PL 41, 401).
[7] PL 34, 319.
[8] Cf. Q. XC, A. 4.
[9] *Generation of Animals,* II, 3 (737ª27).

Obj. 2. Further, subjection and lessening were a result of sin, for to the woman was it said after sin (Gen. 3. 16): *Thou shalt be under the man's power;* and Gregory says that, "Where there is no sin, there is no inequality."[1] But woman is naturally of less strength and dignity than man, for the agent is always more honourable than the patient, as Augustine says (*Gen. ad lit.* xii, 16).[2] Therefore woman should not have been made in the first production of things before sin.

Obj. 3. Further, occasions of sin should be cut off. But God foresaw that the woman would be an occasion of sin to man. Therefore He should not have made woman.

On the contrary, It is written (Gen. 2. 18): *It is not good for man to be alone; let us make him a helper like to himself.*

I answer that, It was necessary for woman to be made, as the Scripture says, as a helper to man; not, indeed, as a helpmate in other works, as some say,[3] since man can be more efficiently helped by another man in other works, but as a helper in the work of generation. This can be made clear if we observe the mode of generation carried out in various living things. Some living things do not possess in themselves the power of generation, but are generated by an agent of another species, such as some plants and animals by the influence of the heavenly bodies, from some fitting matter and not from seed. Others possess the active and passive generative power together, as we see in plants which are generated from seed. For the noblest vital function in plants is generation, and so we observe that in these the active power of generation invariably accompanies the passive power. Among perfect animals the active power of generation belongs to the male sex, and the passive power to the female. And as among animals there is a vital operation nobler than generation, to which their life is principally directed, therefore the male sex is not found in continual union with the female in perfect animals, but only at the time of coition; so that we may consider that by coition the male and female become one, just as in plants they are always united, although in some cases one of them preponderates, and in some the other. But man is yet further ordered to a still nobler vital action, and that is to understand. Therefore there was greater reason for the distinction of these two forces in man, so that the female should be produced separately

[1] *Moral.*, XXI, 15 (PL 76, 203).
[2] PL 34, 467.
[3] Cf. Augustine, *Gen. ad lit.*, IX, 3 (PL 34, 395); *City of God*, XIV, 21 (PL 41, 429).

from the male, although they are carnally united for generation. Therefore directly after the formation of woman, it was said: *And they shall be two in one flesh* (Gen. 2. 24).

Reply Obj. 1. As regards the particular nature, woman is defective and misbegotten, for the active force in the male seed tends to the production of a perfect likeness in the masculine sex, while the production of woman comes from defect in the active force or from some material indisposition, or even from some external change, such as that of a south wind, which is moist, as the Philosopher observes.[4] On the other hand, in relation to the universal nature, woman is not misbegotten, but is included in nature's intention as ordered to the work of generation. Now the universal intention of nature depends on God, Who is the universal Author of nature. Therefore, in producing nature, God formed not only the male but also the female.

Reply Obj. 2. Subjection is twofold. One is servile, by virtue of which a superior makes use of a subject for his own benefit, and this kind of subjection began after sin. There is another kind of subjection, which is called economic or civil, whereby the superior makes use of his subjects for their own benefit and good; and this kind of subjection existed even before sin. For good order would have been wanting in the human family if some were not governed by others wiser than themselves. So by such a kind of subjection woman is naturally subject to man, because in man the discretion of reason predominates. Nor is inequality among men excluded by the state of innocence, as we shall prove (Q. XCVI, A. 3).

Reply Obj. 3. If God had deprived the world of all those things which proved an occasion of sin, the universe would have been imperfect. Nor was it fitting for the common good to be destroyed in order that individual evil might be avoided, especially as God is so powerful that He can direct any evil to a good end.

ARTICLE 2. *Whether Woman Should Have Been Made from Man?*

We proceed thus to the Second Article: It would seem that woman should not have been made from man.

Objection 1. For sex belongs both to man and animals. But in the other animals the female was not made from the male. Therefore neither should it have been so with man.

Obj. 2. Further, things of the same species are of the same matter. But male and female are of

[4] *Generation of Animals*, IV, 2 (766[b]33).

the same species. Therefore, as man was made of the slime of the earth, so woman should have been made of the same, and not from man.

Obj. 3. Further, woman was made to be a helpmate to man in the work of generation. But close relationship makes a person unfit for that office; hence near relations are debarred from intermarriage, as is written (Lev. 18. 6). Therefore woman should not have been made from man.

On the contrary, It is written (Ecclus. 17. 5): *He created of him,* that is, out of man, *a helpmate like to himself,* that is, woman.

I answer that, When all things were first formed, it was more suitable for the woman to be made from the man than (for the female to be from the male) in other animals. First, in order thus to give the first man a certain dignity, so that just as God is the principle of the whole universe, so the first man, in likeness to God, was the principle of the whole human race. And so Paul says that *God made the whole human race from one* (Acts 17. 26). Secondly, that man might love woman all the more, and cleave to her more closely, knowing her to be fashioned from himself. Hence it is written (Gen. 2. 23, 24): *She was taken out of man, wherefore a man shall leave father and mother, and shall cleave to his wife.* This was most necessary as regards the human race, in which the male and female live together for life, which is not the case with other animals. Thirdly, because, as the Philosopher says,[1] "the human male and female are united not only for generation, as with other animals, but also for the purpose of domestic life, in which each has his or her particular duty, and in which the man is the head of the woman." Therefore it was suitable for the woman to be made out of man, as out of her principle. Fourthly, there is a sacramental reason for this. For by this is signified that the Church takes her origin from Christ. Therefore the Apostle says (Eph. 5. 32): *This is a great sacrament; but I speak in Christ and in the Church.*

Reply Obj. 1 is clear from the foregoing.

Reply Obj. 2. Matter is that from which something is made. Now created nature has a determinate principle; and since it is determined to one thing, it has also a determinate mode of proceeding. Therefore from determinate matter it produces something in a determinate species. On the other hand, the Divine Power, being infinite, can produce things of the same species out of any matter, such as a man from the slime of the earth, and a woman from a man.

_____
[1] *Ethics,* VIII, 12 (1162[a]19).

Reply Obj. 3. A certain affinity arises from natural generation, and this is an impediment to matrimony. Woman, however, was not produced from man by natural generation, but by the Divine Power alone. Hence Eve is not called the daughter of Adam; and so this argument does not prove.

ARTICLE 3. *Whether the Woman Was Fittingly Made from the Rib of Man?*

We proceed thus to the Third Article: It would seem that the woman should not have been formed from the rib of man.

Objection 1. For the rib was much smaller than the woman's body. Now from a smaller thing a larger thing can only be made either by addition (and then the woman ought to have been described as made out of that which was added, rather than out of the rib itself), or by rarefaction, because, as Augustine says (*Gen. ad lit.* x):[2] "A body cannot increase in bulk except by rarefaction." But the woman's body is not more rarefied than man's—at least, not in the proportion of a rib to Eve's body. Therefore Eve was not formed from a rib of Adam.

Obj. 2. Further, in those things which were first created there was nothing superfluous. Therefore a rib of Adam belonged to the integrity of his body. So, if a rib was removed, his body remained imperfect, which is unreasonable to suppose.

Obj. 3. Further, a rib cannot be removed from man without pain. But there was no pain before sin. Therefore it was not right for a rib to be taken from the man, that Eve might be made from it.

On the contrary, It is written (Gen. 2. 22): *God built the rib, which He took from Adam, into a woman.*

I answer that, It was right for the woman to be made from a rib of man. First, to signify the social union of man and woman, for the woman should neither use authority over man, and so she was not made from his head; nor was it right for her to be subject to man's contempt as his slave, and so she was not made from his feet. Secondly, for the sacramental signification; for from the side of Christ sleeping on the Cross the Sacraments flowed—namely, blood and water—on which the Church was established.

Reply Obj. 1. Some say that the woman's body was formed by a material increase, without anything being added, in the same way as

_____
[2] Chap. 26 (PL 34, 428).

our Lord multiplied the five loaves.[1] But this is quite impossible. For such an increase of matter would either be by a change of the very substance of matter itself, or by a change of its dimensions. Not by change of the substance of the matter, both because matter, considered in itself, is altogether unchangeable, since it has a potential existence, and has nothing but the character of being a subject, and because multiplication and size are extraneous to the essence of matter itself. Therefore multiplication of matter is quite unintelligible, as long as the matter itself remains the same without anything added to it, unless it receives greater dimensions. This implies rarefaction, which is for the same matter to receive greater dimensions, as the Philosopher says.[2] To say, therefore, that matter is multiplied, without being rarefied, is to combine contradictories—namely, the definition with the absence of the thing defined.

Therefore, as no rarefaction is apparent in such multiplication of matter, we must admit an addition of matter, either by creation or, which is more probable, by conversion. Hence Augustine says (*Tract.* xxiv, *in Joan.*)[3] that "Christ filled five thousand men with five loaves in the same way as from a few seeds He produces the harvest of corn"—that is, by conversion of the nourishment. Nevertheless, we say that the crowds were fed with five loaves, or that woman was made from the rib, because an addition was made to the already existing matter of the loaves and of the rib.

Reply Obj. 2. The rib belonged to the integral perfection of Adam, not as an individual, but as the principle of the human race; just as the semen belongs to the perfection of the begetter, and is released by a natural and pleasurable operation. Much more, therefore, was it possible that by the Divine power the body of the woman should be produced from the man's rib without pain.

From this it is clear how to answer the *third objection.*

ARTICLE 4. *Whether the Woman Was Formed Immediately by God?*

We proceed thus to the Fourth Article: It would seem that the woman was not formed immediately by God.

Objection 1. For no individual is produced immediately by God from another individual

alike in species. But the woman was made from a man who is of the same species. Therefore she was not made immediately by God.

Obj. 2. Further, Augustine (*De Trin.* iii, 4)[4] says that corporeal things are governed by God through the angels. But the woman's body was formed from corporeal matter. Therefore it was made through the ministry of the angels, and not immediately by God.

Obj. 3. Further, those things which pre-exist in creatures as to their causal principles are produced by the power of some creature, and not immediately by God. But the woman's body was produced in its causal principles among the first created works, as Augustine says (*Gen. ad lit.* ix, 15).[5] Therefore it was not produced immediately by God.

On the contrary, Augustine says, in the same work:[6] "God alone, to Whom all nature owes its existence, could form or build up the woman from the man's rib."

I answer that, As was said above (A. 2, Ans. 2), the natural generation of every species is from some determinate matter. Now the matter from which man is naturally begotten is the human semen of man or woman. Therefore from any other matter an individual of the human species cannot naturally be generated. Now God alone, the Author of nature, can produce a thing in being outside the ordinary course of nature. Therefore God alone could produce either a man from the slime of the earth, or a woman from the rib of man.

Reply Obj. 1. This argument is verified when an individual is begotten, by natural generation, from that which is like it in the same species.

Reply Obj. 2. As Augustine says (*Gen. ad lit.* ix, 15),[7] we do not know whether the angels were employed by God in the formation of the woman; but it is certain that, as the body of man was not formed by the angels from the slime of the earth, so neither was the body of the woman formed by them from the man's rib.

Reply Obj. 3. As Augustine says (*ibid.* 18):[8] "The first creation of things did not demand that woman should be made thus; it made it possible for her to be thus made." Therefore the body of the woman did indeed pre-exist in these causal principles, in the things first created; not as regards active potency, but as regards a potency ordered to the active potency of the Creator.

[1] Hugh of St. Victor, *De Sacram.*, I, vi, 36 (PL 176, 284); Peter Lombard, *Sent.*, ii, d. 18, chap. 4 (QR i, 389).

[2] *Physics*, IV, 9 (217ᵃ25).

[3] PL 35, 1593.

[4] PL 42, 873.   [5] PL 34, 404.

[6] PL 34, 403.   [7] PL 34, 404.

[8] PL 34, 407.

QUESTION XCIII

THE END OR TERM OF THE PRODUCTION OF MAN

(*In Nine Articles*)

WE now treat of the end or term of man's production, according as he is said to be made to the image and likeness of God. There are under this head nine points of inquiry: (1) Whether the image of God is in man? (2) Whether the image of God is in irrational creatures? (3) Whether the image of God is in the angels more than in man? (4) Whether the image of God is in every man? (5) Whether the image of God is in man by comparison with the Essence, or with all the Divine Persons, or with one of them? (6) Whether the image of God is in man, as to his mind only? (7) Whether the image of God is in man's power or in his habits and acts? (8) Whether the image of God is in man by comparison with every object? (9) Of the difference between image and likeness.

ARTICLE 1. *Whether the Image of God Is in Man?*

We proceed thus to the First Article: It would seem that the image of God is not in man.

Objection 1. For it is written (Isa. 40. 18): *To whom have you likened God? or what image will you make for Him?*

Obj 2. Further, to be the image of God is the property of the First-Begotten, of Whom the Apostle says (Col. 1. 15): *Who is the image of the invisible God, the First-Born of every creature.* Therefore the image of God is not to be found in man.

Obj. 3. Further, Hilary says (*De Synod.*)[1] that "an image is of the same species as that which it represents"; and he also says[2] that "an image is the undivided and united likeness of one thing adequately representing another." But there is no species common to both God and man, nor can there be an equality between God and man. Therefore there can be no image of God in man.

On the contrary, It is written (Gen. 1. 26): *Let Us make man to Our own image and likeness.*

I answer that, As Augustine says (QQ. LXXXIII, qu. 74):[3] "Where an image exists, there immediately is likeness; but where there is likeness, there is not necessarily an image." Hence it is

[1] PL 10, 490.
[2] *De Synod.*, (PL 10, 490).
[3] PL 40, 85.

clear that likeness pertains to the notion of image, and that an image adds something to the notion of likeness—namely, that it is copied from something else. For an image is called so because it is produced as an imitation of something else; and so, for instance, an egg, however much like and equal to another egg, is not called an image; for, as Augustine says (*ibid.*): copied from it.

But equality does not belong to the notion of an image; for, as Augustine says (*ibid.*): "Where there is an image there is not necessarily equality," as we see in a person's image reflected in a glass. Yet this pertains to the notion of a perfect image, for in a perfect image nothing is wanting that is to be found in that of which it is a copy. Now it is manifest that in man there is some likeness to God, copied from God as from an exemplar. Yet this likeness is not one of equality, for such an exemplar infinitely excels its copy. Therefore there is in man a likeness to God; not, indeed, a perfect likeness, but imperfect. And Scripture implies the same when it says that man was made "to" God's likeness, for the preposition "to" signifies a certain approach, as of something at a distance.

Reply Obj. 1. The Prophet speaks of bodily images made by man. Therefore he says pointedly: *What image will you make for Him?* But God made a spiritual image to Himself in man.

Reply Obj. 2. The First-Born of creatures is the perfect Image of God, reflecting perfectly that of which He is the Image, and so He is said to be the Image, and never to the Image. But man is said to be both image by reason of the likeness, and to the image by reason of the imperfect likeness. And since the perfect likeness to God cannot be except in identity of nature, the Image of God exists in His first-born Son; as the image of the king is in his son, who is of the same nature as himself; but it exists in man as in an alien nature, as the image of the king is in a silver coin, as Augustine explains in *De decem Chordis* (*Serm.* ix).[4]

Reply Obj. 3. As unity means absence of division, a species is said to be the same in so far as it is one. Now a thing is said to be one not only numerically, specifically, or generically, but also according to a certain analogy or proportion. In this sense a creature is one with God, or like to Him; but when Hilary says "of a thing which adequately represents another," this pertains to the notion of a perfect image.

[4] Chap. 8 (PL 38, 82).

ARTICLE 2. *Whether the Image of God Is To Be Found in Irrational Creatures?*

We proceed thus to the Second Article: It would seem that the image of God is to be found in irrational creatures.

Objection 1. For Dionysius says (*Div. Nom.* ii):[1] "Effects are contingent images of their causes." But God is the cause not only of rational, but also of irrational creatures. Therefore the image of God is to be found in irrational creatures.

Obj. 2. Further, the more distinct a likeness is, the nearer it approaches to the nature of an image. But Dionysius says (*Div. Nom.* iv)[2] that the solar ray has a very great likeness to the Divine goodness. Therefore it is made to the image of God.

Obj 3. Further, the more perfect anything is in goodness, the more it is like God. But the whole universe is more perfect in goodness than man; for though each individual thing is good, all things together are called *very good* (Gen. 1. 31). Therefore the whole universe is to the image of God, and not only man.

Obj. 4. Further, Boëthius (*De Consol.* iii, 9)[3] says of God: "Holding the world in His mind, and forming it into His image." Therefore the whole world is to the image of God, and not only the rational creature.

On the contrary, Augustine says (*Gen. ad lit.* vi, 12):[4] "Man's excellence consists in the fact that God made him to His own image by giving him an intellectual mind, which raises him above the beasts of the field." Therefore things without intellect are not made to God's image.

I answer that, Not every likeness, not even what is copied from something else, is sufficient to make an image; for if the likeness be only generic, or existing by virtue of some common accident, this does not suffice for one thing to be the image of another. For instance, a worm, though it may originate from man, cannot be called man's image merely because of the generic likeness. Nor, if anything is made white like something else, can we say that it is therefore the image of that thing; for whiteness is an accident common to many species. But the notion of an image requires likeness in species; thus the image of the king exists in his son, or, at least, in some accident proper to the species, and chiefly in the shape; thus, we speak of a man's image in copper. And so Hilary says pointedly[5] that "an image is of the same species."

Now it is clear that specific likeness follows the ultimate difference. But some things are like God first and most commonly because they exist; secondly, because they live; and thirdly because they know or understand; and these last, as Augustine says (QQ. LXXXIII; qu. 51),[6] "approach so near to God in likeness, that among all creatures nothing comes nearer to Him." It is clear, therefore, that intellectual creatures alone, properly speaking, are made to God's image.

Reply Obj. 1. Everything imperfect is a participation of what is perfect. Therefore even what falls short of the notion of an image, so far as it possesses any sort of likeness to God, participates in some degree the notion of an image. So Dionysius says that effects are "contingent images" of their causes; that is, as much as they happen (*contingit*) to be so, but not absolutely.

Reply Obj. 2. Dionysius compares the solar ray to Divine goodness as regards its causality, not as regards its natural dignity which is required in the notion of an image.

Reply Obj. 3. The universe is more perfect in goodness than the intellectual creature as regards extension and diffusion; but intensively and collectively the likeness to the Divine goodness is found rather in the intellectual creature, which is capable of the highest good. Or else we may say that a part is not rightly divided against the whole, but only against another part. Therefore, when we say that the intellectual nature alone is to the image of God, we do not mean that the universe in any part is not to God's image, but that the other parts are excluded.

Reply Obj. 4. Boëthius here uses the word image to express the likeness which the product of an art bears to the species of the art in the mind of the artist. Thus every creature is an image of its exemplary type in the Divine mind. We are not, however, using the word image in this sense; but as it implies a likeness in nature, that is, inasmuch as all things, as being, are like the First Being, as living, like to the First Life, and as intelligent, like to the Supreme Wisdom.

ARTICLE 3. *Whether the Angels Are More to the Image of God Than Man Is?*

We proceed thus to the Third Article: It would seem that the angels are not more to the image of God than man is.

Objection 1. For Augustine says in a sermon *de Imagine*[7] that God granted to no other crea-

---

[1] Sect. 8 (PG 3, 645).   [2] Sect. 4 (PG 3, 697).
[3] PL 63, 759.   [4] PL 34, 348.   [5] *De Synod.* (PL 10, 490).
[6] PL 40, 32.   [7] *Sermo ad Popul.,* XLIII, 2 (PL 38, 255).

ture besides man to be to His image. Therefore it is not true to say that the angels are more than man to the image of God.

Obj. 2. Further, according to Augustine (QQ. LXXXIII; *qu.* 51),[1] "man is so much to God's image that God did not make any creature to be between Him and man, and therefore nothing is more akin to Him." But a creature is called God's image so far as it is akin to God. Therefore the angels are not more to the image of God than man.

Obj. 3. Further, a creature is said to be to God's image so far as it is of an intellectual nature. But the intellectual nature does not admit of intensity or lessening, for it is not an accidental thing, since it is a substance. Therefore the angels are not more to the image of God than man.

On the contrary, Gregory says (*Hom. in Evang.* xxxiv):[2] "The angel is called a 'seal of resemblance' (Ezech. 28. 12) because in him the resemblance of the Divine image is wrought with greater expression."

I answer that, We may speak of God's image in two ways. First, we may consider in it that in which the notion of image chiefly consists, that is, the intellectual nature. Thus the image of God is more in the angels than in man, because their intellectual nature is more perfect, as is clear from what has been said (Q. LVIII, A. 3; Q. LXXIX, A. 8). Secondly, we may consider the image of God in man as regards that in which its notion secondarily consists, according as there is found in man a certain imitation of God, consisting in the fact that man proceeds from man, as God from God; and also in the fact that the whole human soul is in the whole body, and again, in every part, as God is in regard to the whole world. In these and the like things the image of God is more perfect in man than it is in the angels. But these do not of themselves belong to the notion of the Divine image in man, unless we presuppose the first imitation, which is in the intellectual nature; otherwise even brute animals would be to God's image. Therefore, as in their intellectual nature, the angels are more to the image of God than man is, we must grant that, absolutely speaking, the angels are more to the image of God than man is, but that man is relatively more like to God.

Reply Obj. 1. Augustine excludes the inferior creatures bereft of reason from the image of God; but not the angels.

[1] PL 40, 33.
[2] PL 76, 1250.

Reply Obj. 2. As fire is said to be specifically the most subtle of bodies, while, nevertheless, one kind of fire is more subtle than another, so we say that nothing is more like to God than the human soul according to the genus of intellectual nature, because as Augustine had said previously, "things which have knowledge are so near to Him in likeness that of all creatures none are nearer." Therefore this does not mean that the angels are not more to God's image.

Reply Obj. 3. When we say that "substance does not admit of more or less,"[3] we do not mean that one species of substance is not more perfect than another, but that one and the same individual does not participate in its specific nature at one time more than at another; nor do we mean that a species of substance is shared among different individuals in a greater or lesser degree.

ARTICLE 4. *Whether the Image of God Is Found in Every Man?*

We proceed thus to the Fourth Article: It would seem that the image of God is not found in every man.

Objection 1. For the Apostle says that *man is the image of God, but woman is the image* (Vulg., *glory*) *of man* (I Cor. 11. 7). Therefore, as woman is an individual of the human species, it is clear that every individual is not an image of God.

Obj. 2. Further, the Apostle says (Rom. 8. 29): *Whom God foreknew, He also predestinated to be made conformable to the image of His Son.* But all men are not predestined. Therefore all men have not the conformity of image.

Obj. 3. Further, likeness belongs to the notion of image, as above explained (A. 1). But by sin man becomes unlike God. Therefore he loses the image of God.

On the contrary, it is written (Ps. 38. 7): *Surely man passeth as an image.*

I answer that, Since man is said to be the image of God by reason of his intellectual nature, he is the most perfectly like God according to that in which he can best imitate God in his intellectual nature. Now the intellectual nature imitates God chiefly in this, that God understands and loves Himself. And so we see that the image of God is in man in three ways. First, because man possesses a natural aptitude for understanding and loving God; and this aptitude consists in the very nature of the mind,

[3] Aristotle, *Categories,* 5 (3^{b}33); cf. Boëthius, *In Cat. Arist.,* 1 (PL 64, 197).

which is common to all men. Secondly, because man actually or habitually knows and loves God, though imperfectly; and this image consists in the conformity of grace. Thirdly, because man knows and loves God perfectly; and this image consists in the likeness of glory. Therefore on the words, *The light of Thy countenance, O Lord, is signed upon us* (Ps. 4. 7), the gloss distinguishes a threefold image, of creation, of re-creation, and of likeness.[1] The first is found in all men, the second only in the just, the third only in the blessed.

Reply Obj. 1. The image of God, in its principal signification, namely the intellectual nature, is found both in man and in women. Hence after the words, *To the image of God He created him,* it is added, *Male and female He created them* (Gen. 1. 27). Moreover it is said "them," in the plural, as Augustine (*Gen. ad lit.* iii, 22)[2] remarks, lest it should be thought that both sexes were united in one individual. But in a secondary sense the image of God is found in man, and not in woman, for man is the beginning and end of woman, just as God is the beginning and end of every creature. So when the Apostle had said that *man is the image and glory of God, but woman is the glory of man,* he adds his reason for saying this: *For man is not of woman, but woman of man; and man was not created for woman, but woman for man.*

Reply Objs. 2 and 3. These reasons refer to the image which consists in the conformity of grace and glory.

ARTICLE 5. *Whether the Image of God Is in Man According to the Trinity of Persons?*

We proceed thus to the Fifth Article: It would seem that the image of God is not in man as to the Trinity of Persons.

Objection 1. For Augustine says (Fulgentius, *De Fide ad Petrum,* i):[3] "One in essence is the Godhead of the Holy Trinity; and one is the image to which man was made." And Hilary (*De Trin.* v)[4] says: "Man is made to the image of that which is common in the Trinity." Therefore the image of God in man is of the Divine Essence, and not of the Trinity of Persons.

Obj. 2. Further, it is said (*De Eccl. Dogmat.*)[5] that the image of God in man is to be referred to "eternity." Damascene also says

(*De Fid. Orth.* ii, 12)[6] that the image of God in man belongs to him as an intelligent being endowed with free choice and self-movement. Gregory of Nyssa (*De Homin. Opificio,* xvi)[7] also asserts that, when Scripture says that man was made to the image of God, "it means that human nature was made a participator of all good: for the Godhead is the fulness of goodness." Now all these things belong more to the unity of the Essence than to the distinction of the Persons. Therefore the image of God in man regards, not the Trinity of Persons, but the unity of the Essence.

Obj. 3. Further, an image leads to the knowledge of that of which it is the image. Therefore, if there is in man the image of God as to the Trinity of Persons, since man can know himself by his natural reason, it follows that by his natural knowledge man could know the Trinity of the Divine Persons; which is untrue, as was shown above (Q. XXXII, A. 1).

Obj. 4. Further, the name of Image is not applicable to any of the Three Persons, but only to the Son; for Augustine says (*De Trin.* vi, 2)[8] that "the Son alone is the image of the Father." Therefore, if in man there were an image of God as regards the Person, this would not be an image of the Trinity, but only of the Son.

On the contrary, Hilary says (*De Trin.* iv):[9] The plurality of the Divine Persons is shown from the fact that man is said to have been made to the image of God.

I answer that, as we have seen (Q. XL, A. 2), the distinction of the Divine Persons is only according to origin, or, rather, relations of origin. Now the mode of origin is not the same in all things, but in each thing is adapted to the nature of that thing, animated things being produced in one way, and inanimate in another, animals in one way, and plants in another. And so it is manifest that the distinction of the Divine Persons is suitable to the Divine Nature; and therefore to be to the image of God by imitation of the Divine Nature does not exclude being to the same image by the representation of the Divine Persons, but rather one follows from the other. We must, therefore, say that in man there exists the image of God, both as regards the Divine Nature and as regards the Trinity of Persons; for also in God Himself there is one Nature in Three Persons.

Thus it is clear how to solve *the first two objections.*

---

[1] *Glossa ordin.* (III, 92A); *Gloss* of Peter Lombard (PL 113, 88).
[2] PL 34, 294.   [3] PL 65, 674.
[4] PL 10, 134.
[5] Gennadius, chap. 88 (PL 58, 1000).
[6] PG 94, 920.   [7] PG 44, 184.
[8] PL 42, 925.
[9] PL 10, 111.

Reply Obj. 3. This argument would be true if the image of God in man represented God in a perfect manner. But, as Augustine says (*De Trin.* xv),[1] there is a great difference between the trinity within ourselves and the Divine Trinity. Therefore, as he there says[2]: "We see, rather than believe, the trinity which is in ourselves; but we believe rather than see that God is Trinity."

Reply Obj. 4. Some have said that in man there is an image of the Son only. Augustine rejects this opinion (*De Trin.* xii, 6).[3] First, because as the Son is like the Father by a likeness of essence, it would follow of necessity if man were made in likeness to the Son that he is made to the likeness of the Father. Secondly, because if man were made only to the image of the Son, the Father would not have said, *Let Us make man to* Our *own image and likeness,* but *To Thy image.*

When, therefore, it is written, *He made him to the image of God,* the sense is not that the Father made man to the image of the Son only, Who is God, as some explained it, but that the Divine Trinity made man to Its image, that is, of the whole Trinity.

When it is said that God *made man to His image,* this can be understood in two ways. First, so that this preposition "to" points to the term of the making, and then the sense is, "Let Us make man in such a way that Our image may be in him." Secondly, this preposition "to" may point to the exemplary cause, as when we say, "This book is made (like) to that one." Thus the image of God is the very Essence of God, Which is incorrectly called an image according as image is put for the exemplar. Or, as some say, the Divine Essence is called an image because thereby one Person imitates another.[4]

ARTICLE 6. *Whether the Image of God Is in Man As Regards the Mind Only?*

We proceed thus to the Sixth Article: It would seem that the image of God is not only in man's mind.

Objection 1. For the Apostle says (I Cor. 11. 7) that *the man is the image . . . of God.* But man is not only mind. Therefore the image of God is to be observed not only in his mind.

Obj. 2. Further, it is written (Gen. 1. 27): *God created man to His own image; to the image of God He created him; male and female He created them.* But the distinction of male and female is in the body. Therefore the image of God is also in the body, and not only in the mind.

Obj. 3. Further, an image seems to apply principally to the shape of a thing. But shape belongs to the body. Therefore the image of God is to be seen in man's body also, and not only in his mind.

Obj. 4. Further, according to Augustine (*Gen. ad lit.* xii, 7, 24)[5] there is a threefold vision in us, corporeal, spiritual, or imaginary, and intellectual. Therefore, if in the intellectual vision that belongs to the mind there exists in us a trinity by reason of which we are made to the image of God, for the like reason there must be another trinity in the others.

On the contrary, The Apostle says (Eph. 4. 23, 24): *Be renewed in the spirit of your mind, and put on the new man.* From this we are given to understand that our renewal which consists in putting on the new man, belongs to the mind. Now, he says (Col. 3. 10): *Putting on the new* man; *him who is renewed unto knowledge* of God, *according to the image of Him that created him,* where the renewal which consists in putting on the new man is ascribed to the image of God. Therefore to be to the image of God belongs to the mind only.

I answer that, While in all creatures there is some kind of likeness to God, in the rational creature alone we find a likeness of image as we have explained above (AA. 1, 2); but in other creatures we find a likeness by way of a trace. Now the intellect or mind is that in which the rational creature excels other creatures; and so this image of God is not found even in the rational creature except in the mind, while in the other parts which the rational creature may happen to possess, we find the likeness of a trace, as in other things to which, in reference to such parts, the rational creature can be likened. We may easily understand the reason of this if we consider the way in which a trace and the way in which an image, represents anything. An image represents something by likeness in species, as we have said (A. 2), while a trace represents something by way of an effect, which represents the cause in such a way as not to attain to the likeness of species. For imprints which are left by the movements of animals are called traces; so also ashes are a trace of fire, and desolation of the land a trace of a hostile army.

---

[1] Chaps. 20, 23 (PL 42, 1088, 1090).
[2] PL 42, 1064.   [3] PL 42, 1001.
[4] Cf. Hilary, *De Trin.*, IV (PL 10, 111); Peter Lombard, *Sent.*, I, II, 4 (QR I, 24).
[5] PL 34, 459, 474.

Therefore we may observe this difference between rational creatures and others, both as to the representation of the likeness of the Divine Nature in creatures, and as to the representation in them of the uncreated Trinity. For as to the likeness of the Divine Nature, rational creatures seem to attain, after a fashion, to the representation of the species, since they imitate God, not only in being and life, but also in intelligence, as above explained (A. 2); but other creatures do not understand, although we observe in them a certain trace of the Intellect that created them if we consider their disposition.

Likewise, as the uncreated Trinity is distinguished by the procession of the Word from the Speaker, and of Love from both of these, as we have seen (Q. XXVIII, A. 3), so we may say that in rational creatures in whom we find a procession of the word in the intellect, and a procession of the love in the will, there exists an image of the uncreated Trinity by a certain representation of the species. In other creatures, however, we do not find the principle of the word, and the word, and love; but we do see in them a certain trace of the existence of these in the Cause that produced them. For the fact that a creature has a modified and finite substance proves that it proceeds from a principle, while its species points to the word of the maker, just as the shape of a house points to the concept of the architect; and order points to the maker's love by reason of which he directs the effect to good, as also the use of the house points to the will of the architect.

So we find in man a likeness to God by way of an image in his mind, but in the other parts of his being by way of a trace.

Reply Obj. 1. Man is called the image of God not that he is essentially an image, but that the image of God is impressed on his mind; just as a coin is an image of the king, as having the image of the king. Therefore there is no need to consider the image of God as existing in every part of man.

Reply Obj. 2. As Augustine says (*De Trin.* xii, 5),[1] some have thought that the image of God was not in man individually, but severally. They held that "the man represents the Person of the Father; those born of man denote the person of the Son; and that the woman is a third person in likeness to the Holy Ghost, since she so proceeded from man as not to be his son or daughter." All of this is manifestly absurd: first, because it would follow that the

Holy Ghost is the principle of the Son, as the woman is the principle of the man's offspring; secondly, because one man would be only the image of one Person; thirdly, because in that case Scripture should not have mentioned the image of God in man until after the birth of the offspring. Therefore we must understand that when Scripture had said, *to the image of God He created him,* it added, *male and female He created them,* not to imply that the image of God came through the distinction of sex, but that the image of God is common to both sexes, since it is in the mind, wherein there is no distinction of sexes. And so the Apostle (Col. 3. 10), after saying, *According to the image of Him that created him,* added, *Where there is neither male nor female* (Vulg., *neither Gentile nor Jew*).[2]

Reply Obj. 3. Although the image of God in man is not to be found in his bodily shape, yet because "the body of man alone among terrestrial animals is not inclined prone to the ground, but is adapted to look upward to heaven, for this reason we may rightly say that it is made to God's image and likeness, rather than the bodies of other animals," as Augustine remarks (Q. LXXXIII; *qu.* 51).[3] But this is not to be understood as though the image of God were in man's body, but in the sense that the very shape of the human body represents the image of God in the soul by way of a trace.

Reply Obj. 4. Both in the corporeal and in the imaginary vision we may find a trinity, as Augustine says (*De Trin.* xi, 2).[4] For in corporeal vision there is first the species of the exterior body; secondly, the act of vision, which occurs by the impression on the sight of a certain likeness of that species; thirdly, the intention of the will applying the sight to see, and to rest on what is seen.

Likewise, in the imaginary vision we find first the species kept in the memory; secondly, the vision itself, which takes place when the power of vision of the soul, that is, the power of imagination, is informed by the species; and thirdly, we find the intention of the will joining both together. But each of these trinities falls short of the Divine image. For the species of the external body is extrinsic to the essence of the soul, while the species in the memory, though not extrinsic to the soul, comes to it from without; and thus in both cases the species falls short of representing the connaturality

---

[1] PL 42, 1000.

[2] Cf. Gal. 3.28.

[3] PL 40, 33.

[4] PL 42, 985.

and co-eternity of the Divine Persons. The corporeal vision, too, does not proceed only from the species of the external body, but from this, and, at the same time, from the sense of the seer; in like manner imaginary vision is not only from the species which is preserved in the memory, but also from the imagination. For these reasons the procession of the Son from the Father alone is not suitably represented. Lastly the intention of the will joining the two together does not proceed from them either in corporeal or spiritual vision. Therefore the procession of the Holy Ghost from the Father and the Son is not thus properly represented.

ARTICLE 7. *Whether the Image of God Is to Be Found in the Acts of the Soul?*

We proceed thus to the Seventh Article: It would seem that the image of God is not found in the acts of the soul.

Objection 1. For Augustine says[1] that "man was made to God's image, inasmuch as we are and know that we are, and love this being and knowledge." But to be does not signify an act. Therefore the image of God is not to be found in the soul's acts.

Obj. 2. Further, Augustine (*De Trin.* ix, 12)[2] assigns God's image in the soul to these three things—"mind, knowledge, and love." But mind does not signify an act, but rather the power or the essence of the intellectual soul. Therefore the image of God does not extend to the acts of the soul.

Obj. 3. Further, Augustine (*De Trin.* x, 12)[3] assigns the image of the Trinity in the soul to "memory, understanding, and will." But these three are "natural powers of the soul," as the Master of the Sentences says (1 *Sent.* D. iii).[4] Therefore the image of God is in the powers, and does not extend to the acts of the soul.

Obj. 4. Further, the image of the Trinity always remains in the soul. But an act does not always remain. Therefore the image of God does not extend to the acts.

On the contrary, Augustine (*De Trin.* xi, 2 seqq.)[5] assigns the trinity in the lower part of the soul, in relation to the actual vision, whether sensible or imaginative. Therefore, also, the trinity in the mind, by reason of which man is like God's image, must be referred to actual vision.

I answer that, As above explained (A. 2), a certain representation of the species belongs to the notion of an image. Hence, if the image of the Divine Trinity is to be found in the soul, we must look for it where the soul approaches the nearest (so far as this is possible) to a representation of the species of the Divine Persons. Now the Divine Persons are distinct from each other by reason of the procession of the Word from the Speaker, and the procession of Love joining Both. But in our soul word "cannot exist without actual thought," as Augustine says (*De Trin.* xiv, 7).[6] Therefore, first and chiefly, the image of the Trinity is to be found in the acts of the mind, that is, namely, as from the knowledge which we possess, by thinking we form an internal word, and thence break forth into love. But, since the principles of acts are the habits and powers, and everything exists virtually in its principle, therefore, secondarily and as though consequently, the image of the Trinity may be considered as existing in the powers, and still more in the habits, according as the acts exist virtually in them.

Reply Obj. 1. Our being bears the image of God so far as it is proper to us, and excels that of the other animals, in so far as we are endowed with a mind. Therefore, this trinity is the same as that which Augustine mentions (*De Trin.* ix, 12),[7] and which consists in "mind, knowledge, and love."

Reply Obj. 2. Augustine observed this trinity first in the mind. But because the mind, though it knows itself entirely in a certain degree, yet also in a way does not know itself—namely, as being distinct from others (and thus also it seeks itself, as Augustine subsequently proves —*De Trin.* x);[8] therefore, since knowledge is not wholly equal to the mind, he takes three things in the soul which are proper to the mind, namely, memory, understanding, and will, which everyone knows he has, and assigns the image of the Trinity preeminently to these three, as though the first ascription were in part deficient.

Reply Obj. 3. As Augustine proves (*De Trin.* xiv, 7),[9] we may be said to understand, will, or to love certain things, both when we actually think of them, and when we do not think of them. When they are not under our actual consideration, they belong to memory only, which, in his opinion, is nothing else than habitual re-

---

[1] *City of God,* XI, 26 (PL 41, 339).
[2] PL 42, 972.   [3] PL 42, 984.
[4] Chap. 2 (QR 1, 35).
[5] PL 42, 985.

[6] PL 42, 1043.
[7] PL 42, 972.
[8] Chaps. 4, 8 (PL 42, 976, 979).
[9] PL 42, 1042.

tention of knowledge and love.[1] "But since," as he says,[2] "a word cannot be there without actual thought (for we think everything that we say, even if we speak with that interior word belonging to no nation's tongue), this image chiefly consists in these three things, memory, understanding, and will. And by understanding I mean here that whereby we understand with actual thought; and by will, love, or dilection I mean that which unites this child with its parent." From which it is clear that he places the image of the Divine Trinity more in actual understanding and will than in these as existing in the habitual retention of the memory, although even thus the image of the Trinity exists in the soul in a certain degree, as he says in the same place. Thus it is clear that memory, understanding, and will are not three powers as stated in the *Sentences*.

Reply Obj. 4. Someone might answer by referring to Augustine's statement (*De Trin.* xiv, 6),[3] that "the mind ever remembers itself, ever understands itself, ever loves itself," which some take to mean that the soul ever actually understands, and loves itself.[4] But he excludes this interpretation by adding that "it does not always think of itself as actually distinct from other things." Thus it is clear that the soul always understands and loves itself, not actually but habitually, though we might say that by perceiving its own act, it understands itself whenever it understands anything. But since it is not always actually understanding, as in the case of sleep, we must say that these acts, although not always actually existing in themselves, yet always exist in their principles, the habits and powers. And so, Augustine says (*De Trin.* xiv, 4):[5] "If the rational soul is made to the image of God in the sense that it can make use of reason and intellect to understand and consider God, then the image of God was in the soul from the beginning of its existence."

ARTICLE 8. *Whether the Image of the Divine Trinity Is in the Soul Only By Comparison With God as Its Object?*

We proceed thus to the Eighth Article: It would seem that the image of the Divine Trinity is in the soul not only by comparison with God as its object.

[1] Cf. Q. LXXIX., A. 7, 1. Ans.
[2] *De Trin.*, XIV, 7 (PL 42, 1043).
[3] PL 42, 1042; cf. also X, 12 (984).
[4] Cf. Bonaventure, *In Sent.*, I, III, P. 2, A. 2, Q. 1 (QR 1, 88). Albert the Great also seems to hold this opinion—cf. *In Sent.*, I, d. 3, A. 20 (BO XXV, 119); A. 27 (BO XXV, 126). [5] PL 42, 1040.

Objection 1. For the image of the Divine Trinity is to be found in the soul, as shown above (A. 7), according as the word in us proceeds from the speaker, and love from both. But this is to be found in us as regards any object. Therefore the image of the Divine Trinity is in our mind as regards any object.

Obj. 2. Further, Augustine says (*De Trin.* xii, 4)[6] that "when we seek trinity in the soul, we seek it in the whole of the soul, without separating the process of reasoning in temporal matters from the consideration of things eternal." Therefore the image of the Trinity is to be found in the soul, even as regards temporal objects.

Obj. 3. Further, it is by grace that we can know and love God. If, therefore, the image of the Trinity is found in the soul by reason of the memory, understanding, and will or love of God, this image is not in man by nature but by grace, and thus will not be common to all.

Obj. 4. Further, the saints in heaven are most perfectly conformed to the image of God by the vision of glory. And so it is written (II Cor. 3. 18): *We . . . are transformed into the same image from glory to glory.* But temporal things are known by the vision of glory. Therefore the image of God exists in us even according to temporal things.

On the contrary, Augustine says (*De Trin.* xiv, 12):[7] "The image of God exists in the mind not because it has a remembrance of itself, loves itself, and understands itself but because it can also remember, understand, and love God by Whom it was made." Much less, therefore, is the image of God in the soul, in respect of other objects.

I answer that, As above explained (AA. 2, 7), image means a likeness which in some degree, however small, attains to a representation of the species. Therefore we need to seek in the image of the Divine Trinity in the soul some kind of representation of the species of the Divine Persons, so far as this is possible to a creature. Now the Divine Persons, as above stated (AA. 6, 7), are distinguished from each other according to the procession of the word from the speaker, and the procession of love from both. Moreover the Word of God is born of God by the knowledge of Himself, and Love proceeds from God according as He loves Himself. But it is clear that diversity of objects diversifies the species of word and love; for the word conceived in the heart of man of a stone

[6] PL 42, 1000.
[7] PL 42, 1048.

is specifically different from that conceived of a horse, while also the love regarding each of them is specifically different. Hence we refer the Divine image in man to the verbal concept born of the knowledge of God, and to the love derived therefrom. Thus the image of God is found in the soul according as the soul turns to God, or possesses a nature that enables it to turn to God. Now the mind may turn towards an object in two ways: directly and immediately, or indirectly and mediately; as, for instance, when anyone sees a man reflected in a looking-glass he may be said to be turned towards that man. So Augustine says (*De Trin.* xiv, 8),[1] that "the mind remembers itself, understands itself, and loves itself. If we perceive this, we perceive a trinity, not, indeed God, but, nevertheless, rightly called the image of God." But this is due to the fact, not that the mind is turned to itself absolutely, but that thereby it can furthermore turn to God, as appears from the authority quoted above (Arg. *On the contrary*).

Reply Obj. 1. For the notion of an image it is not enough that something proceed from another, but it is also necessary to observe what proceeds and from what it proceeds; namely, that what is Word of God proceeds from knowledge of God.

Reply Obj. 2. In all the soul we may see a kind of trinity, not, however, as though besides the doing of temporal things and the contemplation of eternal things "any third thing should be required to make up the trinity," as he adds in the same passage. But in that part of the reason which is concerned with temporal things, "although a trinity may be found, yet the image of God is not to be seen there," as he says further on, because this knowledge of temporal things comes to the soul from without. Moreover even the habits by which temporal things are known are not always present, but sometimes they are actually present, and sometimes present only in memory even after they begin to exist in the soul. Such is clearly the case with faith, which comes to us temporally for this present life, while in the future life faith will no longer exist, but only the remembrance of faith.

Reply Obj. 3. The meritorious knowledge and love of God can be in us only by grace. Yet there is a certain natural knowledge and love as seen above (Q. XII, A. 12; Q. LVI, A. 3; Q. LX, A. 5). This, too, is natural, that the mind in order to understand God can make use of reason, in which sense we have already said (A. 7, ad 4) that the image of God abides always in the soul; "whether this image of God be so expunged," as it were clouded, "as almost to amount to nothing," as in those who have not the use of reason, "or obscured and disfigured," as in sinners, "or clear and beautiful," as in the just as Augustine says (*De Trin.* xiv).[2]

Reply Obj. 4. By the vision of glory temporal things will be seen in God Himself, and such a vision of things temporal will belong to the image of God. This is what Augustine means when he says[3] that "in that nature to which the mind will blissfully adhere, whatever it sees it will see as unchangeable;" for in the Uncreated Word are the types of all creatures.

ARTICLE 9. *Whether Likeness Is Properly Distinguished from Image?*

We proceed thus to the Ninth Article: It would seem that likeness is not properly distinguished from image.

Objection 1. For genus is not properly distinguished from species. Now, likeness is to image as genus to species, because, "where there is image, forthwith there is likeness, but not conversely" as Augustine says (QQ. LXXXIII; *qu.* 74).[4] Therefore likeness is not properly to be distinguished from image.

Obj. 2. Further, the notion of image consists not only in the representation of the Divine Persons, but also in the representation of the Divine Essence, to which representation belong immortality and indivisibility. So it is not right to say that "the likeness is in the essence because it is immortal and indivisible, whereas the image is in other things" (2 *Sent.*, d. XVI).[5]

Obj. 3. Further, the image of God in man is threefold,—the image of nature, of grace and of glory, as above explained (A. 4). But innocence and justice belong to grace. Therefore it is incorrectly said (*ibid.*) that "the image is taken from the memory, the understanding, and the will, while the likeness is from innocence and justice."

Obj. 4. Further, knowledge of truth belongs to the intellect, and love of virtue to the will, and these two things are parts of the image. Therefore it is incorrect to say (*ibid.*) that "the image consists in the knowledge of truth, and the likeness in the love of virtue."

On the contrary, Augustine says (QQ. LXXXIII; *qu.* 51):[6] "Some consider that these

---

[2] Chap. 4 (PL 42, 1040).
[3] *De Trin.*, XIV, 14 (PL 42, 1051).   [4] PL 40, 85.
[5] Peter Lombard (QR 1, 381).   [6] PL 40, 33.

[1] PL 42, 1044.

two were mentioned not without reason, namely 'image' and 'likeness,' since, if they meant the same, one would have sufficed."

I answer that, Likeness is a kind of unity, for oneness in quality causes likeness, as the Philosopher says.[1] Now, since "one" is a transcendental, it is both common to all, and applicable to each single thing, just as the good and the true. Therefore, just as the good can be compared to any individual thing both as preliminary and as subsequent to it, as signifying some perfection in it, so also in the same way there is a kind of comparison between likeness and image. For the good comes before man, since man is an individual good; and, again, the good is subsequent to man, since we may say in a special way of a certain man that he is good by reason of his perfect virtue. In like manner, likeness may be considered as preliminary to image, according as it is something more common than image, as we have said above (A. 1); and again, it may be considered as subsequent to image, according as it signifies a certain perfection of image. For we say that an image is like or unlike what it represents according as the representation is perfect or imperfect.

Thus likeness may be distinguished from image in two ways. First as preliminary to it and existing in more things, and in this sense likeness concerns things which are more common than the properties of an intellectual nature in which the image is properly to be seen. In this sense it is stated (QQ. LXXXIII; *qu.* 51)[2] that "the spirit" (namely, the mind) "without doubt was made to the image of God. But the other parts of man," namely, those belonging to the soul's inferior powers, or even to the body, "are in the opinion of some made to God's likeness." In this sense he says (*De Quant. Animæ* ii)[3] that the likeness of God is found in the soul's incorruptibility; for corruptible and incorruptible are differences of universal being. But likeness may be considered in another way, as signifying the expression and perfection of the image. In this sense Damascene says (*De Fid. Orth,* ii, 12)[4] that "the image implies an intelligent being, endowed with free choice and self-movement, whereas likeness implies a likeness of power, as far as this may be possible in man." In the same sense likeness is said to belong to the love of virtue, for there is no virtue without love of virtue.

Reply Obj. 1. Likeness is not distinct from image in the common notion of likeness (for thus it is included in the notion of image), but so far as any likeness falls short of the notion of image, or again, as it perfects the notion of image.

Reply Obj. 2. The soul's essence belongs to the image as representing the Divine Essence in those things which are proper to the intellectual nature, but not in those conditions which follow on being in general, such as to be simple and indissoluble.

Reply Obj. 3. Even certain virtues are natural to the soul, at least, in their seeds, by reason of which we may say that a natural likeness exists in the soul. Nor is it unfitting to use the term image from one point of view, and from another the term likeness.

Reply Obj. 4. Love of the word, which is knowledge loved, pertains to the notion of image; but love of virtue pertains to likeness, as virtue itself pertains to likeness.

QUESTION XCIV

OF THE STATE AND CONDITION OF THE FIRST MAN AS REGARDS HIS INTELLECT

(*In Four Articles*)

WE next consider the state or condition of the first man; first, as regards his soul; secondly, as regards his body (Q. XCVII). Concerning the first there are two things to be considered: (1) The condition of man as to his intellect; (2) the condition of man as to his will (Q. XCV).

Under the first head there are four points of inquiry: (1) Whether the first man saw the God through His Essence? (2) Whether he could see the separate substances, that is, the angels? (3) Whether he possessed all knowledge? (4) Whether he could err or be deceived?

ARTICLE 1. *Whether the First Man Saw God Through His Essence?*

We proceed thus to the First Article: It would seem that the first man saw God through His Essence.

Objection 1. For man's happiness consists in the vision of the Divine Essence. But the first man, "while established in Paradise, led a life of happiness in the enjoyment of all things," as Damascene says (*De Fid. Orth.* ii, 11).[5] And Augustine says,[6] "If man was gifted with the same disposition as now, how happy must he have been in Paradise, that place of ineffable happiness!" Therefore the first man in Paradise saw God through His Essence.

---

[1] *Metaphysics,* v, 15 (1021ᵃ11). [2] Augustine (PL 40, 33). [3] PL 32, 1037. [4] PG 94, 920.

[5] PG 94, 912. [6] *City of God,* XIV, 10 (PL 41, 417).

Obj. 2. Further, Augustine says[1] that the first man "lacked nothing which his good-will might obtain." But our good-will can obtain nothing better than the vision of the Divine Essence. Therefore man saw God through His Essence.

Obj. 3. Further, the vision of God in His Essence is that in which God is seen without a medium or enigma. But man in the state of innocence saw God immediately, as the Master of the Sentences asserts (4 *Sent.*, D. i).[2] He also saw without an enigma, for an enigma implies obscurity, as Augustine says (*De Trin.* xv, 9).[3] Now, obscurity resulted from sin. Therefore man in the primitive state saw God through His Essence.

On the contrary, The Apostle says (I Cor. 15. 46): *That was not first which is spiritual, but that which is natural.* But to see God through His Essence is most spiritual. Therefore the first man in the primitive state of his animal life did not see God through His Essence.

I answer that, The first man did not see God through His Essence if we consider the ordinary state of that life; unless, perhaps, it be said that he saw God in ecstasy, when *God cast a deep sleep upon Adam* (Gen. 2. 21). The reason is because, since the Divine Essence is Happiness itself, the intellect of a man who sees the Divine Essence has the same relation to God as a man has to happiness. Now it is clear that man cannot willingly be turned away from happiness, since naturally and necessarily he desires it, and shuns unhappiness. Therefore no one who sees the Essence of God can willingly turn away from God, which means to sin. Hence all who see God through His Essence are so firmly established in the love of God, that for eternity they are not able to sin. Therefore, as Adam did sin, it is clear that he did not see God through His Essence.

Nevertheless he knew God with a more perfect knowledge than we do now. Thus in a sense his knowledge was midway between our knowledge in the present state and the knowledge we shall have in heaven, when we see God through His Essence. To make this clear, we must consider that the vision of God through His Essence is contra-distinguished from the vision of God through His creatures. Now the higher the creature is, and the more like it is to God, the more clearly is God seen in it; for instance, a man is seen more clearly through a mirror in which his image is the more clearly expressed.

Thus God is seen in a much more perfect manner through His intelligible effects than through those which are only sensible or corporeal. But in his present state man is impeded as regards the full and clear consideration of intelligible creatures, because he is distracted by and occupied with sensible things. Now, it is written (Eccles. 7. 30): *God made man right.* And man was made right by God in this sense, that in him the lower powers were subjected to the higher, and the higher nature was made so as not to be impeded by the lower. Therefore the first man was not impeded by exterior things from a clear and steady contemplation of the intelligible effects which he perceived by the radiation of the first truth, whether by a natural or by a freely given knowledge. Hence Augustine says (*Gen. ad lit,* xi. 33)[4] that, "perhaps God used to speak to the first man as He speaks to the angels, by shedding on his mind a ray of the unchangeable truth, yet without bestowing on him the experience of which the angels are capable in the participation of the Divine Essence." Therefore, through these intelligible effects of God, man knew God then more clearly than we know Him now.

Reply Obj. 1. Man was happy in Paradise but not with that perfect happiness to which he was destined, which consists in the vision of the Divine Essence. He was, however, endowed with "a life of happiness in a certain measure," as Augustine says (*ibid.,* 18),[5] so far as he was gifted with natural integrity and perfection.

Reply Obj. 2. A good will is a well-ordered will; but the will of the first man would have been ill-ordered had he willed to have, while in the state of merit, what had been promised to him as a reward.

Reply Obj. 3. A medium is twofold; one through which, and, at the same time, in which, something is seen, as, for example, a man is seen through a mirror, and is seen with the mirror. Another kind of medium is that by which we attain to the knowledge of something unknown, such as the medium in a demonstration. God was seen without this second kind of medium, but not without the first kind. For there was no need for the first man to attain to the knowledge of God by demonstration drawn from an effect, such as we need, since he knew God simultaneously in His effects, especially in the intelligible effects, according to his capacity. Again, we must remark that the obscurity which is implied in the word enigma may be of two kinds. First, so far as every creature is some-

---

[1] *City of God,* XIV,10, (PL 41, 417)
[2] Chap. 5 (QR II, 747).　　　[3] PL 42, 1069.
[4] PL 34, 447.　　　[5] PL 34, 438.

thing obscure when compared with the immensity of the Divine splendour; and thus Adam saw God in an enigma, because he saw Him in a created effect. Secondly, we may take obscurity as an effect of sin, so far as man is impeded in the consideration of intelligible things by being preoccupied with sensible things; in which sense Adam did not see God in an enigma.

ARTICLE 2. *Whether Adam in the State of Innocence Saw the Angels Through Their Essence?*

We proceed thus to the Second Article: It would seem that Adam, in the state of innocence, saw the angels through their essence.

Objection 1. For Gregory says (*Dialog.* iv, 1)[1]: "In Paradise man was accustomed to enjoy the words of God and by purity of heart and loftiness of vision to have the company of the good angels."

Obj. 2. Further, the soul in the present state is impeded from the knowledge of separate substances by union with a corruptible body which *is a load upon the soul,* as is written Wisdom 9. 15. Therefore the separate soul can see separate substances, as above explained (Q. LXXXIX, A. 2). But the body of the first man was not a load upon his soul, for the body was not corruptible. Therefore he was able to see separate substances.

Obj. 3. Further, one separate substance knows another separate substance by knowing itself (*De Causis*, xiii).[2] But the soul of the first man knew itself. Therefore it knew separate substances.

On the contrary, The soul of Adam was of the same nature as ours. But our souls cannot now understand separate substances. Therefore neither could Adam's soul.

I answer that, The state of the human soul may be distinguished in two ways. First, from a diversity of mode in its natural being; and in this way the state of the separate soul is distinguished from the state of the soul joined to the body. Secondly, the state of the soul is distinguished in relation to integrity and corruption, the state of natural being remaining the same; and thus the state of innocence is distinct from the state of man after sin. For man's soul, in the state of innocence, was adapted to perfect and govern the body just as it is now, and so the first man is said to have been made into a *living soul,* that is, a soul giving life to the body,—namely animal life. But he was endowed with integrity as to this life in that the body was entirely subject to the soul, hindering

it in no way, as we have said above (A. 1). Now it is clear from what has been already said (Q. LXXXIV, A. 7; Q. LXXXV, A. 1; Q. LXXXIX, A. 1) that since the soul is adapted to perfect and govern the body, as regards animal life, it is fitting that it should have that mode of understanding which is by turning to phantasms. Therefore this mode of understanding was fitting to the soul of the first man also.

Now, according to this mode of understanding, there are three degrees of movement in the soul, as Dionysius says (*Div. Nom.* iv).[3] The first is by the soul passing from exterior things to concentrate its powers on itself; the second is by the soul ascending so as to be associated with superior powers joined together in union, namely the angels; the third is when the soul is led on yet further to the supreme good, that is, to God.

In virtue of the first movement of the soul from exterior things to itself, the soul's knowledge is perfected. This is because the intellectual operation of the soul has a natural order to external things, as we have said above (Q. LXXXVII, A. 3), and so by the knowledge of them, our intellectual operation can be known perfectly, as an act through its object. And through the intellectual operation itself, the human intellect can be known perfectly, as a power through its proper act. But in the second movement we do not find perfect knowledge. Because, since the angel does not understand by turning to phantasms, but by a far more excellent process, as we have said above (Q. LV, A. 2), the above-mentioned mode of knowledge, by which the soul knows itself, is not sufficient to lead it to the knowledge of an angel. Much less does the third movement lead to perfect knowledge, for even the angels themselves, by the fact that they know themselves, are not able to arrive at the knowledge of the Divine Substance, by reason of its surpassing excellence.

Thus therefore the soul of the first man could not see the angels in their essence. Nevertheless he had a more excellent mode of knowledge regarding the angels than we possess, because his knowledge of intelligible things within him was more certain and fixed than our knowledge. And it was on account of this excellence of knowledge that Gregory says that "he enjoyed the company of the angelic spirits."

This makes clear the *reply to the first objection.*

Reply Obj. 2. That the soul of the first man

fell short of the knowledge regarding separate substances was not owing to the fact that the body was a load upon it, but to the fact that its connatural object fell short of the excellence of separate substances. We, in our present state, fall short on account of both these reasons.

Reply Obj. 3. The soul of the first man was not able to arrive at knowledge of separate substances by means of its self-knowledge, as we have shown above, for even each separate substance knows others in its own measure.

ARTICLE 3. *Whether the First Man Knew All Things?*

We proceed thus to the Third Article: It would seem that the first man did not know all things.

Objection 1. For if he had such knowledge it would be either by acquired species, or by connatural species, or by infused species. Not, however, by acquired species, for this kind of knowledge is caused by experience, as stated in the *Metaphysics,*[1] and the first man had not then gained experience of all things. Nor through connatural species, because he was of the same nature as we are, and our soul, as Aristotle says,[2] is "like a clean tablet on which nothing is written." And if his knowledge came by infused species, it would have been of a different kind from ours, which we acquire from things themselves.

Obj. 2. Further, individuals of the same species have the same way of arriving at perfection. Now other men have not from the beginning, knowledge of all things, but they acquire it in the course of time according to their capacity. Therefore neither did Adam know all things when he was first created.

Obj. 3. Further, the present state of life is given to man in order that his soul may advance in knowledge and merit; indeed, the soul seems to be united to the body for that purpose. Now man would have advanced in merit in that state of life, and therefore also in knowledge. Therefore he was not endowed with knowledge of all things.

On the contrary, Man named the animals (Gen. 2. 20). But names should be adapted to the nature of things. Therefore Adam knew the animals' natures, and in like manner he was possessed of the knowledge of all other things.

I answer that, In the natural order, perfection comes before imperfection, as act precedes potency, for whatever is in potency is made actual only by some being in act. And since

[1] Aristotle, I, 1 (980b28).　　[2] *Soul,* III, 4 (430a1).

God created the first things not only for their own existence, but also that they might be the principles of other things, so creatures were produced in their perfect state to be the principles as regards others. Now man can be the principle of another man not only by generation of the body, but also by instruction and government. Hence, as the first man was produced in his perfect state, as regards his body, for the work of generation, so also was his soul established in a perfect state to instruct and govern others.

Now no one can instruct others unless he has knowledge, and so the first man was established by God in such a manner as to have knowledge of all those things for which man has a natural aptitude. And such are whatever are virtually contained in the first self-evident principles, that is, whatever truths man is naturally able to know. Moreover, in order to direct his own life and that of others, man needs to know not only those things which can be naturally known, but also things surpassing natural knowledge, because the life of man is ordered to a supernatural end; just as it is necessary for us to know the truths of faith in order to direct our own lives. Therefore the first man was endowed with such a knowledge of these supernatural truths as was necessary for the direction of human life in that state. But those things which cannot be known by merely human effort, and which are not necessary for the direction of human life, were not known by the first man; such as the thoughts of men, future contingent events, and some individual facts, as for instance the number of pebbles in a stream, and the like.

Reply Obj. 1. The first man had knowledge of all things by divinely infused species. Yet his knowledge was not different from ours, as the eyes which Christ gave to the man born blind were not different from those given by nature.

Reply Obj. 2. To Adam, as being the first man, was due a degree of perfection which was not due to other men, as is clear from what is above explained.

Reply Obj. 3. Adam would have advanced in natural knowledge, not in the number of things known, but in the manner of knowing, because what he knew speculatively he would subsequently have known by experience. But as regards supernatural knowledge, he would also have advanced as regards the number of things known, by further revelation, just as the angels advance by further enlightenment. Moreover there is no comparison between advance in knowledge and advance in merit, since one man cannot be a principle of merit to another, although he can be to another a principle of knowledge.

ARTICLE 4. *Whether Man in His First State Could Be Deceived?*

We proceed thus to the Fourth Article: It would seem that man in his primitive state could have been deceived.

Objection 1. For the Apostle says (I *Tim.* 2. 14) that *the woman being seduced was in the transgression.*

Obj. 2. Further, the Master says (2 *Sent.*, D. xxi)[1] that, "the woman was not frightened at the serpent speaking, because she thought that he had received the faculty of speech from God." But this was untrue. Therefore before sin the woman was deceived.

Obj. 3. Further, it is natural that the farther off anything is from us, the smaller it seems to be. Now, the nature of the eyes is not changed by sin. Therefore this would have been the case in the state of innocence. Therefore man would have been deceived in the size of what he saw, just as he is deceived now.

Obj. 4. Further, Augustine says (*Gen. ad lit.* xii, 2)[2] that, in sleep the soul adheres to the likenesses of things as if they were the things themselves. But in the state of innocence man would have eaten and consequently have slept and dreamed. Therefore he would have been deceived, adhering to likenesses as to realities.

Obj. 5. Further, the first man would have been ignorant of other men's thoughts, and of future contingent events, as stated above (A. 3). So if anyone had told him what was false about these things, he would have been deceived.

On the contrary, Augustine says (*De Lib. Arb.* iii, 18):[3] "To regard what is true as false, is not natural to man as created, but is a punishment of man condemned."

I answer that, in the opinion of some,[4] deception may mean two things; namely, any slight surmise, in which one adheres to what is false, as though it were true, but without the assent of belief; or it may mean a firm belief. Thus before sin Adam could not be deceived in either of these ways as regards those things to which his knowledge extended; but as regards things to which his knowledge did not ex-

tend, he might have been deceived, if we take deception in the wide sense of the term for any surmise without assent of belief. This opinion was held with the idea that it is not harmful to man to entertain a false opinion in such matters, and that provided he does not assent rashly, he is not to be blamed.

Such an opinion, however, is not fitting as regards the integrity of the primitive state of life, because, as Augustine says,[5] in that state of life "sin was avoided without struggle, and while it remained so, no evil could exist." Now it is clear that as truth is the good of the intellect, so falsehood is its evil, as the Philosopher says.[6] So that, as long as the state of innocence continued, it was impossible for the human intellect to assent to falsehood as if it were truth. For as some perfections, such as clarity, were lacking in the bodily members of the first man, though no evil could be therein, so there could be in his intellect the absence of some knowledge, but no false opinion.

This is clear also from the very rectitude of the primitive state, by virtue of which, while the soul remained subject to God, the lower powers in man were subject to the higher, and were no impediment to their action. And from what has preceded (Q. LXXXV, A. 6),[7] it is clear that as regards its proper object the intellect is always true; and hence it is never deceived of itself, but whatever deception occurs must be ascribed to some lower power, such as the imagination or the like. Hence we see that when the natural power of judgment is free we are not deceived by such images, but only when it is not free, as is the case in sleep. Therefore it is clear that the rectitude of the primitive state was incompatible with deception of the intellect.

Reply Obj. 1. Though the woman was deceived before she sinned in deed, still it was not till she had already sinned by interior pride. For Augustine says (*Gen. ad lit.* xi, 30)[8] that, "the woman could not have believed the words of the serpent had she not already acquiesced in the love of her own power, and in a presumption of self-conceit."

Reply Obj. 2. The woman thought that the serpent had received this power of speaking, not as acting in accordance with nature, but by virtue of some supernatural operation. We need not, however, follow the Master of the Sentences in this point.

Reply Obj. 3. Were anything presented to the

---

[1] Chap. 4 (QR 1, 405).   [2] PL 34, 455.   [3] PL 32, 1296.
[4] Anonymously mentioned in Bonaventure, *In Sent.*, II, d. 23, A. 2, Q. 2 (QR II, 540); cf. also Alexander of Hales, *Summa Theol.*, I-II, n. 520 (QR II, 773).

[5] *City of God*, XIV, 10 (PL 41, 417).
[6] *Ethics*, VI, 2 (1139ᵃ28).
[7] Cf. also Q. XVII, A. 3.   [8] PL 34, 445.

imagination or sense of the first man not in accordance with the nature of things, he would not have been deceived, for his reason would have enabled him to judge the truth.

Reply Obj. 4. A man is not accountable for what occurs during sleep, as he has not then the use of his reason, which is man's proper act.

Reply Obj. 5. If anyone had said something untrue as regards future contingencies, or as regards secret thoughts, man in the primitive state would not have believed it was so, but he might have believed that such a thing was possible, which would not have been to entertain a false opinion.

It might also be said that he would have been divinely guided from above, so as not to be deceived in a matter to which his knowledge did not extend.

If any object, as some do,[1] that he was not guided, when tempted, though he was then most in need of guidance, we reply that man had already sinned in his heart, and that he failed to have recourse to the Divine aid.

QUESTION XCV

OF THE THINGS PERTAINING TO THE FIRST MAN'S WILL—NAMELY, GRACE AND JUSTICE

(In Four Articles)

WE next consider what belongs to the will of the first man, concerning which there are two points for treatment: (1) The grace and justice of the first man; (2) the use of justice as regards his dominion over other things.

Under the first head there are four points of inquiry: (1) Whether the first man was created in grace? (2) Whether in the state of innocence he had passions of the soul? (3) Whether he had all virtues? (4) Whether what he did would have been as meritorious as now?

ARTICLE 1. *Whether the First Man Was Created in Grace?*

We proceed thus to the First Article: It would seem that the first man was not created in grace.

Objection 1. For the Apostle, distinguishing between Adam and Christ, says (I Cor. 15. 45): *The first Adam was made into a living soul; the last Adam into a quickening spirit.* But the spirit is quickened by grace. Therefore Christ alone was made in grace.

Obj. 2. Further, Augustine says (QQ. *Vet. et*

Nov. Test., qu. 123)[2] that "Adam did not possess the Holy Ghost." But whoever possesses grace has the Holy Ghost. Therefore Adam was not created in grace.

Obj. 3. Further, Augustine says (*De Correp. et Grat.* x)[3] that "God so ordered the life of angels and men as to show first what they could do by free choice, then what they can do by His grace, and by the discernment of justice." God thus first created men and angels in the state of natural freedom of choice only, and afterwards bestowed grace on them.

Obj. 4. Further, the Master says (2 *Sent.*, D. XXIV):[4] "When man was created he was given sufficient help to stand, but not sufficient to advance." But whoever has grace can advance by merit. Therefore the first man was not created in grace.

Obj. 5. Further, the reception of grace requires the consent of the receiver, since thereby a kind of spiritual marriage takes place between God and the soul. But this consent presupposes existence. Therefore man did not receive grace in the first moment of his creation.

Obj. 6. Further, nature is more distant from grace than grace is from glory, which is but grace consummated. But in man grace precedes glory. Therefore much more did nature precede grace.

On the contrary, Man and angel are both ordered to grace. But the angels were created in grace, for Augustine says,[5] "God at the same time fashioned their nature and endowed them with grace." Therefore man also was created in grace.

I answer that, Some say[6] that the first man was not created in grace, but that it was bestowed on him subsequently before sin, and many authorities of the Saints declare[7] that man possessed grace in the state of innocence.

But the very rectitude of the primitive state, with which man was endowed by God, seems to require that, as others say,[8] he was created in grace, according to Eccles. 7. 30, *God made man right.* For this rectitude consisted in his

---

[1] Cf. Peter Lombard, *Sent.*, II, d. 23, chap. 1 (QR 1, 417); cf. also Augustine, *Gen. ad lit.*, XI, 10 (PL 34, 434).

[2] Ambrosiaster (PL 35, 2371).
[3] PL 44, 932.   [4] Chap. 1 (QR 1, 419).
[5] City of God, XII, 9 (PL 41, 357).
[6] William of Auxerre, *Summa Aurea*, II, 1, 1 (fol. 35 rb); Alexander of Hales, *Summa Theol.*, I-II, n. 505 (QR II, 279); Bonaventure, *In Sent.*, II, d. 29, A. 2, Q. 2 (QR II, 703). See also Kors, *La Justice Primitive* (p. 61).
[7] Cf. Jerome, *In Ephes.*, III, on 4.30 (PL 26, 546); Augustine, *City of God*, XIII, 13 (PL 41, 386); Basil, *Contra Eunom.*, V (PG 29, 728).
[8] Praepositinus, *Summa* (fol. 77rb); Albert the Great, *In Sent.*, II, d. 3, A. 12. (BO XXVII, 85), Cf. Kors, *La Justice Primitive* (p. 62).

reason being subject to God, the lower powers to reason, and the body to the soul. And the first subjection was the cause of both the second and the third, for while reason was subject to God, the lower powers remained subject to reason, as Augustine says.[1] Now it is clear that such a subjection of the body to the soul and of the lower powers to reason, was not from nature; otherwise it would have remained after sin, since even in the demons the natural gifts remained after sin, as Dionysius declares (*Div. Nom.* iv).[2] Hence it is clear that also the primitive subjection by virtue of which reason was subject to God was not a merely natural gift, but a supernatural endowment of grace. For it is not possible that the effect should be of greater efficiency than the cause. Hence Augustine says[3] that, "as soon as they disobeyed the Divine command, and forfeited Divine grace, they were ashamed of their nakedness, for they felt the impulse of disobedience in the flesh, as though it were a punishment corresponding to their own disobedience." Hence if the loss of grace dissolved the obedience of the flesh to the soul, we may gather that the inferior powers were subjected to the soul through grace existing therein.

Reply Obj. 1. The Apostle in these words means to show that there is a spiritual body, if there is an animal body, because the spiritual life of the body began in Christ, who is *the firstborn of the dead* (Col. 1. 18), as the body's animal life began in Adam. From the Apostle's words, therefore, we cannot gather that Adam had no spiritual life in his soul, but that he had not spiritual life as regards the body.

Reply Obj. 2. As Augustine says in the same passage, it is not disputed that Adam, like other just souls, was in some degree gifted with the Holy Ghost; but he did not possess the Holy Ghost, "as the faithful possess Him now," who are admitted to eternal happiness directly after death.

Reply Obj. 3. This passage from Augustine does not assert that angels or men were created with natural freedom of choice before they possessed grace, but that God shows first what their free choice could do before being confirmed in grace, and what they acquired afterwards by being so confirmed.

Reply Obj. 4. The Master here speaks according to the opinion of those who held that man was not created in grace, but only in a state of nature. We may also say that, though man was created in grace, yet it was not by virtue of the nature in which he was created that he could advance by merit, but by virtue of the grace which was added.

Reply Obj. 5. As the motion of the will is not continuous there is nothing against the first man having consented to grace even in the first moment of his existence.

Reply Obj. 6. We merit glory by an act of grace, but we do not merit grace by an act of nature. Hence the comparison fails.

ARTICLE 2. *Whether Passions Existed in the Soul of the First Man?*

We proceed thus to the Second Article: It would seem that the first man's soul had no passions.

Objection 1. For by the passions of the soul *the flesh lusteth against the spirit* (Gal. 5. 17). But this did not happen in the state of innocence. Therefore in the state of innocence there were no passions of the soul.

Obj. 2. Further, Adam's soul was nobler than his body. But his body was impassible. Therefore no passions were in his soul.

Obj. 3. Further, the passions of the soul are restrained by the moral virtues. But in Adam the moral virtues were perfect. Therefore the passions were entirely excluded from him.

On the contrary, Augustine says[4] that "in our first parents there was undisturbed love of God," and other passions of the soul.

I answer that, The passions of the soul are in the sensual appetite, the object of which is good and evil. Therefore some passions of the soul are directed to what is good, as love and joy; others to what is evil, as fear and sorrow. And since in the primitive state, evil was neither present nor imminent, nor was any good wanting which a good-will could desire to have then, as Augustine says (*ibid.*), therefore Adam had no passion with evil as its object, such as fear, sorrow, and the like. Neither had he passions in respect of good not possessed, but to be possessed now, as burning concupiscence. But those passions which regard present good, as joy and love, or which regard future good to be had at the proper time, as desire and hope that does not cast down, existed in the state of innocence; otherwise, however, than as they exist in ourselves. For our sensual appetite, where the passions reside, is not entirely subject to reason; hence at times our passions forestall and

---

[1] *City of God*, XIII, 13 (PL 41, 386); *De Pecc. Remiss. et Bapt. Parv.*, I, 16 (PL 44, 120).

[2] Sect. 23 (PG 3, 725).

[3] *City of God*, XIII, 13 (PL 41, 386).

[4] *City of God*, XIV, 10 (PL 41, 417).

hinder reason's judgment, at other times they follow after reason's judgment, accordingly as the sensual appetite obeys reason to some extent. But in the state of innocence the inferior appetite was wholly subject to reason, so that in that state the passions of the soul existed only as consequent upon the judgment of reason.

Reply Obj. 1. The flesh lusts against the spirit by the rebellion of the passions against reason, which could not occur in the state of innocence.

Reply Obj. 2. The human body was impassible in the state of innocence as regards the passions which alter the disposition of nature, as will be explained later on (Q. XCVII, A. 2). Likewise the soul was impassible as regards the passions which hinder reason.

Reply Obj. 3. Perfection of moral virtue does not wholly take away the passions, but regulates them; for "the temperate man desires as he ought to desire, and what he ought to desire," as stated in the *Ethics*.[1]

ARTICLE 3. *Whether Adam Had All the Virtues?*

We proceed thus to the Third Article: It would seem that Adam had not all the virtues.

Objection 1. For some virtues are directed to curb the passions. Thus immoderate concupiscence is restrained by temperance, and immoderate fear by fortitude. But in the state of innocence no immoderation existed in the passions. Therefore neither did these virtues then exist.

Obj. 2. Further, some virtues are concerned with the passions which have evil as their object; as meekness with anger, fortitude with fear. But these passions did not exist in the state of innocence, as stated above (A. 2). Therefore neither did those virtues exist then.

Obj. 3. Further, penance is a virtue that regards sin committed. Mercy, too, is a virtue concerned with unhappiness. But in the state of innocence neither sin nor unhappiness existed. Therefore neither did those virtues exist.

Obj. 4. Further, perseverance is a virtue. But Adam did not possess perseverance, as is proved by his subsequent sin. Therefore he did not possess every virtue.

Obj. 5. Further, faith is a virtue. But it did not exist in the state of innocence, for it implies an obscurity of knowledge which seems to be incompatible with the perfection of the primitive state.

On the contrary, Augustine says, in a homily (*Serm. contra Judæos*):[2] "The prince of sin

overcame Adam who was made from the slime of the earth to the image of God, adorned with modesty, restrained by temperance, refulgent with brightness."

I answer that, in the state of innocence man in a certain sense possessed all the virtues; and this can be proved from what precedes. For it was shown above (A. 1) that such was the rectitude of the primitive state that reason was subject to God, and the lower powers to reason. Now the virtues are nothing but those perfections by which reason is directed to God, and the inferior powers regulated according to the dictate of reason, as will be explained in the Treatise on the Virtues (Part I-II, Q. LXIII, A. 2).[3] Therefore the rectitude of the primitive state required that man should in a sense possess every virtue.

It must, however, be noted that some virtues of their very notion do not involve imperfection, such as charity and justice. And these virtues did exist in the primitive state absolutely, both in habit and in act. But other virtues are of such a nature as to imply imperfection either in their act, or on the part of the matter. If such imperfection be consistent with the perfection of the primitive state, such virtues could then exist in that state; as faith, which is of things not seen, and hope which is of things not yet possessed. For the perfection of that state did not extend to the vision of the Divine Essence, and the possession of God with the enjoyment of final Happiness. Hence faith and hope could exist in the primitive state, both as to habit and as to act. But any virtue which implies imperfection incompatible with the perfection of the primitive state could exist in that state as a habit, but not as to the act; for instance, penance, which is sorrow for sin committed, and mercy, which is sorrow for others' unhappiness; because sorrow, guilt, and unhappiness are incompatible with the perfection of the primitive state. Therefore such virtues existed as habits in the first man, but not as to their acts; for he was so disposed that he would repent, if there had been a sin to repent for, and had he seen unhappiness in his neighbour, he would have done his best to remedy it. This is in accordance with what the Philosopher says, "Shame," which regards what is ill done, "may be found in a virtuous man, but only conditionally, as being so disposed that he would be ashamed if he did wrong."[4]

Reply Obj. 1. It is accidental to temperance

[1] Aristotle, III, 12 (1119[b]16).
[2] c. II. Falsely attributed to Augustine (PL 42, 1117). Cf. Peter Lombard, *Sent.,* II, d. 29, chap. 2 (QR 1, 457).
[3] Cf. also Q. LVI, AA. 4, 6.
[4] *Ethics,* IV, 9 (1128[b]29).

and fortitude to subdue superabundant passion, in so far as they are in a subject which happens to have superabundant passions; and yet those virtues are *per se* suited to moderate the passions.

Reply Obj. 2. Passions which have evil for their object were incompatible with the perfection of the primitive state if that evil be in the one affected by the passion, such as fear and sorrow. But passions which relate to evil in another are not incompatible with the perfection of the primitive state, for in that state man could hate the demons' malice, as he could love God's goodness. Thus the virtues which relate to such passions could exist in the primitive state, in habit and in act. Virtues, however, relating to passions which regard evil in the same subject, if relating to such passions only, could not exist in the primitive state in act, but only in habit, as we have said above of penance and of mercy. But there are other virtues which have relation not to such passions only, but to others also; such as temperance, which relates not only to sorrow, but also to joy; and fortitude, which relates not only to fear, but also to daring and hope. Thus the act of temperance could exist in the primitive state, so far as it moderates pleasure; and in like manner fortitude, as moderating daring and hope, but not as moderating sorrow and fear.

Reply Obj. 3 appears from what has been said above.

Reply Obj. 4. Perseverance may be taken in two ways. In one sense as a particular virtue, signifying a habit by which a man makes a choice of persevering in good. In that sense Adam possessed perseverance. In another sense it is taken as a circumstance of virtue, signifying a certain uninterrupted continuation of virtue. In this sense Adam did not possess perseverance.

Reply Obj. 5 appears from what has been said above.

ARTICLE 4. *Whether the Actions of the First Man Were Less Meritorious Than Ours Are?*

We proceed thus to the Fourth Article: It would seem that the actions of the first man were less meritorious than ours are.

Objection 1. For grace is given to us through the mercy of God, Who succours most those who are most in need. Now we are more in need of grace than was man in the state of innocence. Therefore grace is more copiously poured out upon us. And since grace is the source of merit, our actions are more meritorious.

Obj. 2. Further, struggle and difficulty are required for merit; for it is written (II Tim. 2. 5): *He . . . is not crowned except he strive lawfully;* and the Philosopher says,[1] "The object of virtue is the difficult and the good." But there is more strife and difficulty now. Therefore there is greater efficacy for merit.

Obj. 3. Further, the Master says (2 *Sent.*, D. XXIV)[2] that man would not have merited in resisting temptation, whereas he does merit now, when he resists. Therefore our actions are more meritorious than in the primitive state.

On the contrary, if such were the case, man would be better off after sinning.

I answer that, Merit as regards degree may be gauged in two ways. First, in its root, which is grace and charity. Merit thus measured corresponds in degree to the essential reward, which consists in the enjoyment of God; for the greater the charity from which our actions proceed, the more perfectly shall we enjoy God. Secondly, the degree of merit is measured by the degree of the action itself. This degree is of two kinds, absolute and proportional. The widow who put two mites into the treasury performed a deed of absolutely less degree than others who put in great sums. But in proportionate degree the widow gave more, as Our Lord said, because she gave more in proportion to her means. In each of these cases the degree of merit corresponds to the accidental reward, which consists in rejoicing for created good.

We conclude therefore that in the state of innocence man's works were more meritorious than after sin was committed, if we consider the degree of merit on the part of grace, which would have been more copious as meeting with no obstacle in human nature. And in like manner, if we consider the absolute degree of the work done, because, as man would have had greater virtue, he would have performed greater works. But if we consider the proportionate degree, a greater reason for merit exists after sin, on account of man's weakness; because a small deed is more beyond the capacity of one who works with difficulty than a great deed is beyond one who performs it easily.

Reply Obj. 1. After sin man requires grace for more things than before sin, but he does not need grace more, because man even before sin required grace to obtain eternal life, which is the chief reason for the need of grace. But after sin man required grace also for the remission of sin, and for the support of his weakness.

[1] *Ethics*, II, 3 (1105ᵃ9).
[2] Chap. I (QR I, 420).

Reply Obj. 2. Difficulty and struggle belong to the degree of merit according to the proportionate degree of the work done, as explained above. It is also a sign of the will's promptitude that it strive after what is difficult to itself, and the promptitude of the will is caused by the intensity of charity. Yet it may happen that a person performs an easy deed with as prompt a will as another performs an arduous deed, because he is ready to do even what may be difficult to him. But the actual difficulty, by its penal character, enables the deed to satisfy for sin.

Reply Obj. 3. The first man would not have gained merit in resisting temptation, according to the opinion of those who say that he did not possess grace,[1] even as now there is no merit to those who have not grace. But in this point there is a difference, because in the primitive state there was no interior impulse to evil, as in our present state. Hence man was more able then than now to resist temptation even without grace.

QUESTION XCVI

OF THE MASTERSHIP BELONGING TO MAN IN THE STATE OF INNOCENCE

(*In Four Articles*)

WE next consider the mastership which belonged to man in the state of innocence. Under this head there are four points of inquiry: (1) Whether man in the state of innocence was master over the animals? (2) Whether he was master over all creatures? (3) Whether in the state of innocence all men were equal? (4) Whether in that state man would have been master over men?

ARTICLE 1. *Whether Adam in the State of Innocence Had Mastership over the Animals?*

We proceed thus to the First Article: It would seem that in the state of innocence Adam had no mastership over the animals.

Objection 1. For Augustine says (*Gen. ad lit.* ix, 14),[2] that the animals were brought to Adam, under the direction of the angels, to receive their names from him. But the angels need not have intervened thus if man himself were master over the animals. Therefore in the state of innocence man had no mastership of the animals.

Obj. 2. Further, it is unfitting that elements hostile to one another should be brought under the mastership of one. But many animals are hostile to one another, as the sheep and the

wolf. Therefore all animals were not brought under the mastership of man.

Obj. 3. Further, Jerome says[3] that God gave man mastership over the animals, although before sin he had no need of them, for God foresaw that after sin animals would become useful to man. Therefore, at least before sin, it was unfitting for man to make use of his mastership.

Obj. 4. Further, it is proper to a master to command. But a command is not given rightly except to a rational being. Therefore man had no mastership over the irrational animals.

On the contrary, It is written (Gen. 1. 26): *Let him have dominion over the fishes of the sea, and the birds of the air, and the beasts of the earth* (Vulg., *and the whole earth*).

I answer that, As above stated (Q. XCV, A. 1) for his disobedience to God, man was punished by the disobedience of those creatures which should be subject to him. Therefore in the state of innocence, before man had disobeyed, nothing disobeyed him that was naturally subject to him. Now all animals are naturally subject to man. This can be proved in three ways. First, from the order observed by nature. For just as in the generation of things we perceive a certain order of procession of the perfect from the imperfect (thus matter is for the sake of form, and the imperfect form for the sake of the perfect), so also is there order in the use of natural things. Thus the imperfect are for the use of the perfect; as the plants make use of the earth for their nourishment, and animals make use of plants, and man makes use of both plants and animals. Therefore it is in keeping with the order of nature, that man should be master over animals. Hence the Philosopher says[4] that "the hunting of wild animals is just and natural," because man thereby exercises a natural right. Secondly, this is proved from the order of Divine Providence which always governs inferior things by the superior. Therefore, as man, being made to the image of God, is above other animals, these are rightly subject to his government. Thirdly, this is proved from a property of man and of other animals. For we see in the latter a certain participated prudence of natural estimation, in regard to certain particular acts; but man possesses a universal prudence as regards all practical matters. Now whatever is participated is subject to what is essential and universal. Therefore it is clear that the subjection of other animals to man is natural.

Reply Obj. 1. A higher power can do many

---

[1] See above, A. 1. [2] PL 34, 402.

[3] Bede, *Hexaëm*, I, on Gen. 1, 26 (PL 91, 200).

[4] *Politics*, I, 8 (1256ᵇ24).

things that an inferior power cannot do to those which are subject to them. Now an angel is naturally higher than man. Therefore certain things in regard to animals could be done by angels, which could not be done by man; for instance, the rapid gathering together of all the animals.

Reply Obj. 2. In the opinion of some,[1] those animals which now are fierce and kill others, would, in that state, have been tame, not only in regard to man, but also in regard to other animals. But this is quite unreasonable. For the nature of animals was not changed by man's sin, as if those whose nature now it is to devour the flesh of others would then have lived on herbs, as the lion and falcon. Nor does Bede's gloss on Gen. I. 30,[2] say that trees and herbs were given as food to all animals and birds, but to some. Thus there would have been a natural antipathy between some animals. They would not, however, on this account have been excepted from the mastership of man, as neither at present are they for that reason excepted from the mastership of God, Whose Providence has ordained all this. Of this Providence man would have been the executor, as appears even now in regard to domestic animals, since fowls are given by men as food to the trained falcon.

Reply Obj. 3. In the state of innocence man would not have had any bodily need of animals; neither for clothing, since then they were naked and not ashamed, there being no inordinate motions of concupiscence, nor for food, since they fed on the trees of paradise, nor to carry him about, his body being strong enough for that purpose. But man needed animals in order to have experimental knowledge of their natures. This is signified by the fact that God led the animals to man, that he might give them names expressive of their respective natures.

Reply Obj. 4. All animals by their natural estimative sense have a certain participation of prudence and reason; which accounts for the fact that cranes follow their leader, and bees obey their queen. So all animals would have obeyed man of their own accord, as in the present state some domestic animals obey him.

ARTICLE 2. *Whether Man Had Mastership over All Other Creatures?*

We proceed thus to the Second Article: It would seem that in the state of innocence man

would not have had mastership over all other creatures.

Objection 1. For an angel naturally has a greater power than man. But, as Augustine says (*De Trin.* iii, 8),[3] corporeal matter would not have obeyed even the holy angels. Much less therefore would it have obeyed man in the state of innocence.

Obj. 2. Further, the only powers of the soul existing in plants are nutritive, augmentative, and generative. Now these do not naturally obey reason, as we can see in the case of any one man. Therefore, since it is by his reason that man has mastership, it seems that in the state of innocence man had no dominion over plants.

Obj. 3. Further, whosoever is master of a thing, can change it. But man could not have changed the course of the heavenly bodies, for this belongs to God alone, as Dionysius says (*Ep. ad Polycarp*, vii).[4] Therefore man had no dominion over them.

On the contrary, It is written (Gen. I. 26): *That he may have dominion over . . . every creature.*

I answer that, Man in a certain sense contains all things; and so according as he is master of what is within himself, in the same way he can have mastership over other things. Now we may consider four things in man: his reason, which makes him like the angels; his sensitive powers, which make him like the animals; his natural powers, which make him like the plants; and the body itself, wherein he is like inanimate things. Now in man reason has the position of a master and not of a subject. Therefore man had no mastership over the angels in the primitive state; so when we read *all creatures,* we must understand the creatures which are not made to God's image. Over the sensitive powers, such as the irascible and concupiscible, which obey reason in some degree, the soul has mastership by commanding. So in the state of innocence man had mastership over the animals by commanding them. But of the natural powers and the body itself man is master not by commanding, but by using them. Thus also in the state of innocence man's mastership over plants and inanimate things consisted not in commanding or in changing them, but in making use of them without hindrance.

The *answers to the objections* appear from the above.

---

[1] Alexander of Hales, *Summa Theol.*, I-II, n. 522 (QR II, 781). Cf. Peter Lombard, *Sent.*, II, d. 15, chap. 3 (QR I, 374); Bonaventure, *In Sent.*, II, d. 15, A. 2, Q. I (QR II, 383).

[2] *Glossa ordin.*, Gen. I, 30 (I, 28F); *In Pentat.*, on Gen. I, 30 (PL 91, 202).

[3] PL 42, 875.

[4] Sect. 2 (PG 3, 1080).

ARTICLE 3. *Whether Men Were Equal in the State of Innocence?*

We proceed thus to the Third Article: It would seem that in the state of innocence all would have been equal.

Objection 1. For Gregory says (*Moral.* xxi):[1] "Where there is no sin, there is no inequality." But in the state of innocence there was no sin. Therefore all were equal.

Obj. 2. Further, likeness and equality are the reason of mutual love, according to Ecclus. 13. 19, *Every beast loveth its like; so also every man him that is nearest to himself.* Now in that state there was among men an abundance of love, which is the bond of peace. Therefore all were equal in the state of innocence.

Obj. 3. Further, the cause ceasing, the effect also ceases. But the cause of present inequality among men seems to arise, on the part of God, from the fact that He rewards some for merit and punishes others; and on the part of nature, from the fact that some, through a defect of nature, are born weak and deficient, others strong and perfect, which would not have been the case in the primitive state.

On the contrary, It is written (Rom. 13. 1): *The things which are of God, are well ordered* (Vulg., *Those that are, are ordained of God*). But order chiefly consists in inequality; for Augustine says,[2] "Order disposes things equal and unequal in their proper place." Therefore in the primitive state, which was most proper and orderly, inequality would have existed.

I answer that, We must admit that in the primitive state there would have been some inequality, at least as regards sex, because generation depends upon diversity of sex. And likewise as regards age, for some would have been born of others, nor would sexual union have been sterile.

Moreover, as regards the soul, there would have been inequality as to justice and knowledge. For man worked not of necessity, but of his own free choice, by virtue of which man can apply himself, more or less, to action, desire, or knowledge. Hence some would have made a greater advance in justice and knowledge than others.

There might also have been bodily disparity. For the human body was not entirely exempt from the laws of nature, so as not to receive from exterior sources more or less advantage and help, since indeed it was dependent on food with which to sustain life.

So we may say that, according to the climate, or the movement of the stars, some would have been born more robust in body than others, and also greater, and more beautiful, and in all ways better disposed; in such a way, however, in those who were thus surpassed, there would have been no defect or fault either in soul or body.

Reply Obj. 1. By those words Gregory means to exclude such inequality as exists between justice and sin, the result of which is that some are placed in subjection to others as a penalty.

Reply Obj. 2. Equality is the cause of equality in mutual love. Yet between those who are unequal there can be a greater love than between equals, although there may not be an equal response; for a father naturally loves his son more than a brother loves his brother, although the son may not love his father as much as he is loved by him.

Reply Obj. 3. The cause of inequality could be on the part of God; not indeed that He would punish some and reward others, but that He would exalt some above others, so that the beauty of order would the more shine forth among men. Inequality might also arise on the part of nature as above described, without any defect of nature.

ARTICLE 4. *Whether in the State of Innocence Man Would Have Been Master over Man?*

We proceed thus to the Fourth Article: It would seem that in the state of innocence man would not have been master over man.

Objection 1. For Augustine says,[3] "God willed that man, who was endowed with reason and made to His image, should rule over none but irrational creatures; not over men, but over cattle."

Obj. 2. Further, what came into the world as a penalty for sin would not have existed in the state of innocence. But man was made subject to man as a penalty; for after sin it was said to the woman (Gen. 3. 16): *Thou shalt be under thy husband's power.* Therefore in the state of innocence man would not have been subject to man.

Obj. 3. Further, subjection is opposed to liberty. But liberty is one of the chief goods, and would not have been lacking in the state of innocence, "where nothing was wanting that man's good-will could desire," as Augustine says.[4] Therefore man would not have been master over man in the state of innocence.

[1] Chap. 15 (PL 76, 203).
[2] *City of God,* XIX, 13 (PL 41, 640).
[3] *Ibid.,* XIX, 15 (PL 41, 643).
[4] *Ibid.,* XIV, 10 (PL 41, 417).

On the contrary, The condition of man in the state of innocence was not more exalted than the condition of the angels. But among the angels some rule over others; and so one order is called that of Dominations. Therefore it was not against the dignity of the state of innocence that one man should be subject to another.

I answer that, Mastership has a twofold meaning. First, as opposed to slavery, in which sense a master means one to whom another is subject as a slave. In another sense mastership is referred in a general sense to any kind of subject, and in this sense even he who has the office of governing and directing free men can be called a master. In the state of innocence man could have been a master of men, not in the former but in the latter sense.

This distinction is founded on the reason that a slave differs from a free man in that the latter "has the disposal of himself," as is stated in the beginning of the *Metaphysics*,[1] but a slave is ordered to another. So that one man is master of another as his slave when he refers the one whose master he is, to his own—namely, the master's, use. And since every man's proper good is desirable to himself, and consequently it is a grievous matter to anyone to yield to another what ought to be one's own, therefore such dominion implies of necessity a pain inflicted on the subject. And therefore in the state of innocence such a mastership could not have existed between man and man.

But a man is the master of a free subject by directing him either towards his proper welfare, or to the common good. Such a kind of mastership would have existed in the state of innocence between man and man, for two reasons. First, because man is naturally a social animal, and so in the state of innocence he would have led a social life. Now a social life cannot exist among a number of people unless under the headship of one to look after the common good; for many, as such, seek many things, but one attends only to one. Therefore the Philosopher says, in the beginning of the *Politics*,[2] that "wherever many things are directed to one, we shall always find one at the head directing them." Secondly, if one man surpassed another in knowledge and justice, this would not have been fitting unless these gifts conduced to the benefit of others, according to I Pet. 4. 10, *As every man hath received grace, ministering the same one to another.* Therefore Augustine says,[3] "Just men command not by the love of domi-

neering, but by the service of counsel. The natural order of things requires this; and thus did God make man."

From this appear the *replies to the objections* which are founded on the first-mentioned kind of mastership.

QUESTION XCVII
OF THE PRESERVATION OF THE
INDIVIDUAL IN THE PRIMITIVE STATE
(In Four Articles)

WE next consider what belongs to the bodily state of the first man: first, as regards the preservation of the individual; secondly, as regards the preservation of the species (Q. XCVIII).

Under the first head there are four points of inquiry: (1) Whether man in the state of innocence was immortal? (2) Whether he was impassible? (3) Whether he stood in need of food? (4) Whether he would have obtained immortality by the tree of life?

ARTICLE 1. *Whether in the State of Innocence Man Would Have Been Immortal?*

We proceed thus to the First Article: It would seem that in the state of innocence man was not immortal.

Objection 1. For the term mortal belongs to the definition of man. But if you take away the definition, you take away the thing defined. Therefore as long as man was man he could not be immortal.

Obj. 2. Further, "corruptible and incorruptible are generically distinct," as the Philosopher says.[4] But there can be no passing from one genus to another. Therefore if the first man was incorruptible, man could not be corruptible in the present state.

Obj. 3. Further, if man were immortal in the state of innocence, this would have been due either to nature or to grace. Not to nature, for since nature does not change within the same species, he would also have been immortal now. Likewise neither would this be owing to grace, for the first man recovered grace by repentance, according to Wisdom 10. 2: *He brought him out of his sins.* Hence he would have regained his immortality, which is clearly not the case. Therefore man was not immortal in the state of innocence.

Obj. 4. Further, immortality is promised to man as a reward, according to Apoc. 21. 4: *Death shall be no more.* But man was not created in the state of reward, but that he might

---

[1] Aristotle, I, 2 (982[b]26).   [2] I, 5 (1254[a]28).
[3] *City of God,* XIX, 14 (PL 41, 643).
[4] *Metaphysics,* X, 10 (1058[b]28).

deserve the reward. Therefore man was not immortal in the state of innocence.

On the contrary, It is written (Rom. 5. 12): *By sin death came into the world.* Therefore man was immortal before sin.

I answer that, A thing may be incorruptible in three ways. First, on the part of matter; that is to say, either because it possesses no matter, like an angel, or because it possesses matter that is in potency to one form only, like the heavenly bodies. Such things as these are incorruptible by their very nature. Secondly, a thing is incorruptible in its form, because although it is by nature corruptible, yet it has an inherent disposition which preserves it wholly from corruption. And this is called incorruptibility of glory, because, as Augustine says (*Ep. ad Dioscor.*):[1] "God made man's soul of such a powerful nature that from its fulness of beatitude there redounds to the body a fulness of health, with the vigour of incorruption." Thirdly, a thing may be incorruptible on the part of its efficient cause; in this sense man was incorruptible and immortal in the state of innocence. For, as Augustine says (*QQ. Vet. et Nov. Test., qu.* 19):[2] "God made man immortal as long as he did not sin, so that he might achieve for himself life or death." For man's body was indissoluble not by reason of any intrinsic vigour of immortality, but by reason of a supernatural force given by God to the soul, by which it was enabled to preserve the body from all corruption so long as it remained itself subject to God. This entirely agrees with reason, for since the rational soul surpasses the capacity of corporeal matter, as above explained (Q. LXXVI, A. 1), it was most properly endowed at the beginning with the power of preserving the body in a manner surpassing the capacity of corporeal matter.

Reply Obj. 1 and 2. These objections are founded on natural incorruptibility and immortality.

Reply Obj. 3. This power of preserving the body was not natural to the soul, but was the gift of grace. And though man recovered grace as regards remission of guilt and the merit of glory, yet not as regards his lost immortality; for this was reserved for Christ to accomplish, by Whom the defect of nature was to be restored into something better, as we shall explain further on (Part III, Q. XIV, A. 4, ANS. 1).

Reply Obj. 4. The promised reward of the immortality of glory differs from the immortality which was bestowed on man in the state of innocence.

ARTICLE 2. *Whether in the State of Innocence Man Would Have Been Passible?*

We proceed thus to the Second Article: It would seem that in the state of innocence man was passible.

Objection 1. For sensation is a kind of passion. But in the state of innocence man would have been sensitive. Therefore he would have been passible.

Obj. 2. Further, sleep is a kind of passion. Now, man slept in the state of innocence, according to Gen. 2. 21, *God cast a deep sleep upon Adam.* Therefore he would have been passible.

Obj. 3. Further, the same passage goes on to say that He *took a rib out of Adam.* Therefore he was passible even to the degree of the cutting out of part of his body.

Obj. 4. Further, man's body was soft. But a soft body is naturally passible as regards a hard body. Therefore if a hard body had come in contact with the soft body of the first man, the latter would have suffered from the impact. Therefore the first man was passible.

On the contrary, Had man been passible, he would have been also corruptible, because excessive suffering wastes the very substance.

I answer that, Passion may be taken in two senses. First, in its proper sense, and thus a thing is said to suffer when changed from its natural disposition. For passion is the effect of action, and in nature contraries are mutually active or passive, according as one thing changes another from its natural disposition. Secondly, passion can be taken in a general sense for any kind of change, even if pertains to the perfection of nature. Thus "understanding and sensation are said to be passions."[3] In this second sense, man was passible in the state of innocence, and was passible both in soul and body. In the first sense, man was impassible, both in soul and body, as he was likewise immortal; for he could curb his passion, as he could avoid death, so long as he refrained from sin.

Thus it is clear how to *reply to the first two objections*, since sensation and sleep do not remove from man his natural disposition, but are ordered to the good of nature.

Reply Obj. 3. As already explained (Q. XCII, A. 3, ANS. 2), the rib was in Adam as the principle of the human race, as the semen in man, who is a principle through generation. Hence as

---

[1] *Epist.*, 118, chap. 3 (PL 33, 439).
[2] Cf. Ambrosiaster (PL 35, 2227).
[3] Aristotle, *Soul*, III, 4 (429ª13).

man does not suffer any natural deterioration by seminal issue, so neither did he through the separation of the rib.

Reply Obj. 4. Man's body in the state of innocence could be preserved from suffering injury from a hard body partly by the use of his reason, by which he could avoid what was harmful, and partly also by Divine Providence, so preserving him that nothing of a harmful nature could come upon him unawares.

ARTICLE 3. *Whether in the State of Innocence Man Had Need of Food?*

We proceed thus to the Third Article: It would seem that in the state of innocence man did not require food.

Objection 1. For food is necessary for man to restore what he has lost. But Adam's body suffered no loss, because it was incorruptible. Therefore he had no need of food.

Obj. 2. Further, food is needed for nourishment. But nourishment involves passibility. Since, then, man's body was impassible, it does not appear how food could be necessary to him.

Obj. 3. Further, we need food for the preservation of life. But Adam could preserve his life otherwise; for had he not sinned, he would not have died. Therefore he did not require food.

Obj. 4. Further, the consumption of food involves voiding of the surplus, which seems unsuitable to the state of innocence. Therefore it seems that man did not take food in the primitive state.

On the contrary, It is written (Gen. 2. 16): *Of every tree in Paradise ye shall* (Vulg., *thou shalt*) *eat.*

I answer that, In the state of innocence man had an animal life requiring food, but after the resurrection he will have a spiritual life needing no food. In order to make this clear, we must observe that the rational soul is both soul and spirit. It is called a soul by reason of what it possesses in common with other souls—that is, as giving life to the body. And so it is written (Gen. 2. 7): *Man was made into a living soul;* that is, a soul giving life to the body. But the soul is called a spirit according to what properly belongs to itself, and not to other souls, as possessing an intellectual immaterial power.

Thus in the primitive state, the rational soul communicated to the body what belonged to itself as a soul; and so the body was called animal,[1] through having its life from the soul. Now the first principle of life in these lower creatures

as the Philosopher says[2] is the vegetative soul, the operations of which are the use of food, generation, and growth. Therefore such operations befitted man in the state of innocence. But in the final state, after the resurrection, the soul will, to a certain extent, communicate to the body what properly belongs to itself as a spirit: immortality to everyone; to the good, whose bodies will be called *spiritual*,[3] impassibility, glory, and power. So, after the resurrection, man will not require food; though he required it in the state of innocence.

Reply Obj. 1. As Augustine says (QQ. *Vet. et Nov. Test., qu.* 19):[4] "How could man have an immortal body, which was sustained by food? Since an immortal being needs neither food nor drink." For we have explained (A. 1) that the immortality of the primitive state was based on a supernatural force in the soul, and not on any intrinsic disposition of the body. Thus by the action of heat, the body might lose part of its humid qualities; and to prevent the entire consumption of the humour, man was obliged to take food.

Reply Obj. 2. A certain passion and alteration attends nutriment on the part of the food changed into the substance of the thing nourished. So we cannot conclude from this that man's body was passible, but that the food taken was passible; although also this kind of passion conduced to the perfection of the nature.

Reply Obj. 3. If man had not taken food he would have sinned, as he also sinned by taking the forbidden fruit. For he was told at the same time to abstain from the tree of the knowledge of good and evil and to eat of every other tree of Paradise.

Reply Obj. 4. Some say[5] that in the state of innocence man would not have taken more than necessary food, so that there would have been nothing superfluous. But this seems unreasonable, as implying that there would have been no fæcal matter. Therefore there was need for voiding the surplus, yet so disposed by God as to be fitting to the state.

ARTICLE 4. *Whether in the State of Innocence Man Would Have Acquired Immortality by the Tree of Life?*

We proceed thus to the Fourth Article: It would seem that the tree of life could not be the cause of immortality.

Objection. 1. For nothing can act beyond its

---

[1] From *anima*, a soul; cf. I Cor. 15.44 ff.

[2] *Soul*, II. 4 (415^{a}23); also, III, 9 (432^{b}8).   [3] I Cor. 15.44.
[4] Ambrosiaster (PL 35, 2227).   [5] Cf. Alexander of Hales, *Summa Theol.*, I-II, n. 457 (QR II, 592).

own species, for an effect does not exceed its cause. But the tree of life was corruptible; otherwise it could not be taken as food, since food is changed into the substance of the thing nourished as we have said (A. 3, ANS. 2). Therefore the tree of life could not give incorruptibility or immortality.

Obj. 2. Further, effects caused by the powers of plants and other natural agencies are natural. If therefore the tree of life caused immortality, this would have been natural immortality.

Obj. 3. Further, this would seem to be reduced to the ancient fable, that the gods by eating a certain food, became immortal, which the Philosopher ridicules.[1]

On the contrary, It is written (Gen. 3. 22): *Lest perhaps he put forth his hand, and take of the tree of life, and eat, and live for ever.* Further Augustine says (QQ. *Vet. et Nov. Test., qu.* 19):[2] "A taste of the tree of life warded off corruption of the body; and even after sin man would have remained immortal, had he been allowed to eat of the tree of life."

I answer that, The tree of life in a certain way was the cause of immortality, but not absolutely. To understand this, we must observe that in the primitive state man possessed, for the preservation of life, two remedies, against two defects. One of these defects was the loss of moisture by the action of natural heat, which acts as the soul's instrument. As a remedy against such loss man was provided with food taken from the other trees of paradise, as now we are provided with the food which we take for the same purpose. The second defect, as the Philosopher says,[3] arises from the fact that the humour which is caused from extraneous sources, when added to the humour already existing, lessens the specific active power; as water added to wine takes at first the taste of wine, then, as more water is added, the strength of the wine is diminished, till the wine becomes watery. In like manner, we may observe that at first the active force of the species is so strong that it is able to transform so much of the food as is required to replace the lost tissue, as well as what suffices for growth; later on, however, the assimilated food does not suffice for growth, but only replaces what is lost. Last of all, in old age, it does not suffice even for this purpose, whereupon the body declines, and finally breaks up. Against this defect man was provided with a remedy in the tree of life, for its effect was to

strengthen the force of the species against the weakness resulting from the admixture of extraneous nutriment. Therefore Augustine says,[4] "Man had food to appease his hunger, drink to slake his thirst, and the tree of life to banish the breaking up of old age"; and,[5] "The tree of life, like a medicine, warded off all bodily corruption."

Yet it did not absolutely cause immortality. For neither was the soul's intrinsic power of preserving the body due to the tree of life, nor was it able to give the body a disposition to immortality, by which it might become indissoluble; which is clear from the fact that every bodily power is finite, so that the power of the tree of life could not go so far as to give the body the power of living for an infinite time, but only for a definite time. For it is clear that the greater a force is, the more durable is its effect. Therefore, since the power of the tree of life was finite, man's life was to be preserved for a definite time by partaking of it once; and when that time had elapsed, man was to be either transferred to a spiritual life, or had need to eat once more of the tree of life.

From this the *replies to the objections* clearly appear. For the first proves that the tree of life did not absolutely cause immortality, while the others show that it caused incorruption by warding off corruption, according to the explanation above given.

QUESTION XCVIII

OF THE PRESERVATION OF THE SPECIES

(*In Two Articles*)

WE next consider what belongs to the preservation of the species; and, first, of generation; secondly, of the state of the offspring (Q. XCIX). Under the first head there are two points of inquiry: (1) Whether in the state of innocence there would have been generation? (2) Whether generation would have been through coition?

ARTICLE 1. *Whether in the State of Innocence Generation Existed?*

We proceed thus to the First Article: It would seem there would have been no generation in the state of innocence.

Objection 1. For, as stated in the *Physics*,[6] "corruption is contrary to generation." But contraries affect the same subject. And there would have been no corruption in the state of inno-

---

[1] *Metaphysics,* III, 4 (1000ª12).
[2] Ambrosiaster (PL 35, 2227).
[3] *Generation and Corruption,* I, 5 (322ª28).

[4] *City of God,* XIV, 26 (PL 41, 434).
[5] Ambrosiaster, QQ. *Vet. et Nov. Test.,* Q. 19 (PL 35 2228).   [6] Aristotle, V, 5 (229ᵇ12).

cence. Therefore neither would there have been generation.

Obj. 2. Further, the object of generation is the preservation in the species of that which cannot be preserved through the individual. Therefore there is no generation in those individual things which last for ever. But in the state of innocence man would have lived for ever. Therefore in the state of innocence there would have been no generation.

Obj. 3. Further, by generation man is multiplied. But the multiplication of masters requires the division of property, to avoid confusion of mastership. Therefore, since man was made master of the animals, it would have been necessary to make a division of overlordship when the human race increased by generation. This is against the natural law, according to which all things are in common, as Isidore says (*Etym.* v, 4).[1] Therefore there would have been no generation in the state of innocence.

On the contrary, It is written (Gen. 1. 28): *Increase and multiply, and fill the earth.* But this increase could not come about save by generation, since the original number of mankind was two only. Therefore there would have been generation in the state of innocence.

I answer that, In the state of innocence there would have been generation of offspring for the multiplication of the human race; otherwise man's sin would have been very necessary, in order that such a great blessing be its result. We must, therefore, observe that man, by his nature, is established as it were midway between corruptible and incorruptible creatures, his soul being naturally incorruptible, while his body is naturally corruptible. We must also observe that nature's purpose appears to be different as regards corruptible and incorruptible things. For that seems to be the direct purpose of nature, which is invariable and perpetual, while what is only for a time is seemingly not the chief purpose of nature, but, as it were, subordinate to something else; otherwise, when it ceased to exist, nature's purpose would become void.

Therefore, since in things corruptible none is everlasting and permanent except the species, it follows that the chief purpose of nature is the good of the species, for the preservation of which natural generation is ordained. On the other hand, incorruptible substances survive not only in the species, but also in the individual; and so even the individuals are included in the chief purpose of nature.

Hence it pertains to man to beget offspring,

[1] PL 82, 199.

on the part of the naturally corruptible body. But on the part of the soul, which is incorruptible, it is fitting that the multitude of individuals should be the direct purpose of nature, or rather of the Author of nature, Who alone is the Creator of the human soul. Therefore, to provide for the multiplication of the human race, He established the begetting of offspring even in the state of innocence.

Reply Obj. 1. In the state of innocence the human body was in itself corruptible, but it could be preserved from corruption by the soul. Therefore, since generation belongs to things corruptible, man was not to be deprived of it.

Reply Obj. 2. Although generation in the state of innocence might not have been required for the preservation of the species, yet it would have been required for the multiplication of the individual.

Reply Obj. 3. In our present state a division of possessions is necessary on account of the multiplicity of masters, since community of possession is a source of strife, as the Philosopher says.[2] In the state of innocence, however, the will of men would have been so ordered that without any danger of strife they would have used in common, according to each one's need, those things of which they were masters—a state of things to be observed even now among many good men.

ARTICLE 2. *Whether in the State of Innocence There Would Have Been Generation by Coition?*

We proceed thus to the Second Article: It would seem that generation by coition would not have existed in the state of innocence.

Objection 1. For, as Damascene says (*De Fid. Orth.* ii, 11),[3] the first man in the terrestrial Paradise was "like an angel." But in the future state of the resurrection, when men will be like to the angels, *they shall neither marry nor be married,* as it is written Matt. 22. 30. Therefore neither in Paradise would there have been generation by coition.

Obj. 2. Further, our first parents were created at the age of perfect development. Therefore, if generation by coition had existed before sin, they would have had intercourse while still in Paradise, which was not the case according to Scripture (Gen. 4. 1).

Obj. 3. Further, in carnal intercourse, more than at any other time, man becomes like the beasts, on account of the vehement delight which he takes therein; and so continency, by

[2] *Politics,* II, 5 (1263[a]21).   PG 94, 916.

which man refrains from such pleasures, is praiseworthy. But man is compared to beasts by reason of sin, according to Psalm 48. 13: *Man, when he was in honour, did not understand; he is compared to senseless beasts, and is become like to them*. Therefore, before sin, there would have been no such intercourse of man and woman.

Obj. 4. Further, in the state of innocence there would have been no corruption. But virginal integrity is corrupted by intercourse. Therefore there would have been no such thing in the state of innocence.

On the contrary, God made man and woman before sin (Gen. 1. 2.). But nothing is void in God's works. Therefore, even if man had not sinned, there would have been such intercourse, to which the distinction of sex is ordained.

Moreover, we are told that woman was made to be a help to man (Gen. 2. 18, 20). But she was not fitted to help man except in generation, because another man would have proved a more effective help in anything else. Therefore there would have been such generation also in the state of innocence.

I answer that, Some of the earlier doctors,[1] considering the nature of concupiscence as regards generation in our present state, concluded that in the state of innocence generation would not have been effected in the same way. Thus Gregory of Nyssa says (*De Hom. Opif.* xvii)[2] that in Paradise the human race would have been multiplied by some other means, just as the angels were multiplied without coition by the operation of the Divine Power. He adds that God made man male and female before sin because He foreknew the mode of generation which would take place after sin, which He foresaw.

But this is unreasonable. For what is natural to man was neither acquired nor forfeited by sin. Now it is clear that generation by coition is natural to man by reason of his animal life, which he possessed even before sin, as above explained (Q. XCVII, A. 3), just as it is natural to other perfect animals, as the corporeal members make it clear. So we cannot allow that these members would not have had a natural use, as other members had, before sin.

Thus, as regards generation by coition, there are, in the present state of life, two things to be considered. One, which comes from nature, is

the union of man and woman; for in every act of generation there is an active and a passive principle. Therefore, since wherever there is distinction of sex, the active principle is male and the passive is female, the order of nature demands that for the purpose of generation there should be concurrence of male and female. The second thing to be observed is a certain deformity of excessive concupiscence, which in the state of innocence would not have existed, when the lower powers were entirely subject to reason. Therefore Augustine says,[3] "We must be far from supposing that offspring could not be begotten without concupiscence. All the bodily members would have been equally moved by the will, without ardent or wanton incentive, with calmness of soul and body."

Reply Obj. 1. In Paradise man would have been like an angel in his spirituality of mind, yet with an animal life in his body. After the resurrection man will be like an angel, spiritualized in soul and body. And so there is no parallel.

Reply Obj. 2. As Augustine says (*Gen. ad lit.* ix, 4),[4] our first parents did not come together in Paradise, because on account of sin they were ejected from Paradise shortly after the creation of the woman; or because, having received the general Divine command relative to generation, they awaited the special command relative to the time.

Reply Obj. 3. Beasts are without reason. In this way man becomes, as it were, like them in coition, because he cannot moderate concupiscence. In the state of innocence nothing of this kind would have happened that was not regulated by reason, not because delight of sense was less, as some say[5] (rather indeed would sensible delight have been the greater in proportion to the greater purity of nature and the greater sensibility of the body), but because the force of concupiscence would not have so inordinately thrown itself into such pleasure, being curbed by reason, whose place it is not to lessen sensual pleasure, but to prevent the force of concupiscence from cleaving to it immoderately. By "immoderately" I mean going beyond the bounds of reason, just as a sober person does not take less pleasure in food taken in moderation than the glutton, but his concupiscence lingers less in such pleasures. This is what Augustine means by the words quoted, which do not exclude intensity of pleasure from the state of innocence, but

---

[1] John Chrysostom, *In Genesim*, XVI (PG 53, 126); XVIII (PG 53, 153); John Damascene, *De Fide Ortho.*, II, 30 (PG 94, 976), IV, 24 (PG 94, 1208).
[2] PG 44, 189.

[3] *City of God*, XIV, 26 (PL 41, 434).   [4] PL 34, 395.
[5] Bonaventure, *In Sent.*, II, d. 20, A. 1, Q. 3 (QR II, 481); cf. also Alexander of Hales, *Summa Theol.*, I-II, n. 496 (QR II, 703).

the ardour of desire and restlessness of the soul. Therefore continence would not have been praiseworthy in the state of innocence, whereas it is praiseworthy in our present state, not because it removes fecundity, but because it excludes disordered desire. In that state fecundity would have been without lust.

Reply Obj. 4. As Augustine says,[1] In that state *intercourse would have been without prejudice to virginal integrity; thus would have remained intact, as it does in the menses. And just as in giving birth the mother was then relieved not by groans of pain, but by the instigations of maturity, so in conceiving, the union was one not of lustful desire, but of deliberate action.*

QUESTION XCIX

OF THE CONDITION OF THE OFFSPRING AS TO THE BODY

(In Two Articles)

WE must now consider the condition of the offspring—first, as regards the body; secondly, as regards justice (Q. CI); thirdly, in knowledge (Q. C). Under the first head there are two points of inquiry: (1) Whether in the state of innocence children would have had full powers of the body immediately after birth? (2) Whether all infants would have been of the male sex?

ARTICLE 1. *Whether in the State of Innocence Children Would Have Had Perfect Strength of Body As To the Use of Its Members Immediately after Birth?*

We proceed thus to the First Article: It would seem that in the state of innocence children would have had perfect strength of the body, as to the use of its members, immediately after birth.

Objection 1. For Augustine says (*De Pecc. Merit. et Remiss.* i, 38):[2] "This weakness of the body befits their weakness of mind." But in the state of innocence there would have been no weakness of mind. Therefore neither would there have been weakness of body in infants.

Obj. 2. Further, some animals at birth have sufficient strength to use their members. But man is nobler than other animals. Therefore much more is it natural to man to have strength to use his members at birth. And thus it appears to be a punishment of sin that he has not that strength.

Obj. 3. Further, inability to secure a proffered pleasure causes affliction. But if children had

not full strength in the use of their limbs, they would often have been unable to procure something pleasurable offered to them. And so they would have been afflicted, which was not possible before sin. Therefore, in the state of innocence, children would not have been deprived of the use of their limbs.

Obj. 4. Further, the weakness of old age seems to correspond to that of infancy. But in the state of innocence there would have been no weakness of old age. Therefore neither would there have been such weakness in infancy.

On the contrary, Everything generated is first imperfect. But in the state of innocence children would have been begotten by generation. Therefore from the first they would have been imperfect in bodily size and power.

I answer that, By faith alone do we hold truths which are above nature, and what we believe rests on authority. Therefore, in making any assertion, we must be guided by the nature of things, except in those things which are above nature, and are made known to us by Divine authority. Now it is clear that it is as natural as it is befitting to the principles of human nature that children should not have sufficient strength for the use of their limbs immediately after birth. Because in proportion to other animals man has naturally a larger brain. Therefore it is natural, on account of the considerable moisture of the brain in children that the nerves which are instruments of movement should not be apt for moving the limbs. On the other hand, no Catholic doubts it possible for a child to have, by Divine power, the use of its limbs immediately after birth.

Now we have it on the authority of Scripture that *God made man right* (Eccles. 7. 30), which rightness, as Augustine says,[3] consists in the perfect subjection of the body to the soul. As, therefore, in the primitive state it was impossible to find in the human limbs anything contrary to man's well-ordered will, so was it impossible for those limbs to fail in executing the will's commands. Now the human will is well ordered when it tends to acts which are befitting to man. But the same acts are not befitting to man at every season of life. We must, therefore, conclude that children would not have had sufficient strength for the use of their limbs for the purpose of performing every kind of act, but only for the acts befitting the state of infancy, such as suckling, and the like.

Reply Obj. 1. Augustine is speaking of the

---

[1] *City of God,* XIV, 26 (PL 41, 434).
[2] PL 44, 150.

[3] *City of God,* XIII, 13 (PL 41, 386); cf. also *De Pecc. Remiss. et Bapt. Parv.,* I, 16 (PL 44, 120).

weakness which we observe in children even as regards those acts which befit the state of infancy, as is clear from his preceding remark that "even when close to the breast, and longing for it, they are more apt to cry than to suckle."

Reply Obj. 2. The fact that some animals have the use of their limbs immediately after birth, is due not to their superiority, since more perfect animals are not so endowed, but to the dryness of the brain and to the operations proper to such animals being imperfect, so that a small amount of strength suffices them.

Reply Obj. 3 is clear from what we have said above. We may add that they would have desired nothing except with an ordered will, and only what was befitting to their state of life.

Reply Obj. 4. In the state of innocence man would have been born, yet not subject to corruption. Therefore in that state there could have been certain infantile defects which result from birth, but not senile defects leading to corruption.

ARTICLE 2. *Whether, in the Primitive State, Women Would Have Been Born?*

We proceed thus to the Second Article: It would seem that in the primitive state woman would not have been born.

Objection 1. For the Philosopher says[1] that "woman is a misbegotten male," as though she were a product outside the purpose of nature. But in that state nothing would have been unnatural in human generation. Therefore in that state women would not have been born.

Obj. 2. Further, every agent produces its like, unless prevented by insufficient power or the improper disposition of matter; thus a small fire cannot burn green wood. But in generation the active force is in the male. Since, therefore, in the state of innocence man's active force was not subject to defect, nor was there improper disposition of matter on the part of the woman, it seems that males would always have been born.

Obj. 3. Further, in the state of innocence generation is ordered to the multiplication of the human race. But the race would have been sufficiently multiplied by the first man and woman from the fact that they would have lived for ever. Therefore, in the state of innocence, there was no need for women to be born.

On the contrary, nature's process in generation would have been in harmony with the manner in which it was established by God. But God established male and female in human nature, as

it is written (Gen. 1. and 2.). Therefore also in the state of innocence male and female would have been born.

I answer that, Nothing belonging to the completeness of human nature would have been lacking in the state of innocence. And as different grades belong to the perfection of the universe, so also diversity of sex belongs to the perfection of human nature. Therefore in the state of innocence, both sexes would have been begotten.

Reply Obj. 1. Woman is said to be a misbegotten male, as being a product outside the purpose of nature considered in the individual case, but not against the purpose of universal nature, as above explained (Q. XCII, A. 1, Ans. 2).

Reply Obj. 2. The generation of woman is not occasioned either by a defect of the active force or by an improper disposition of matter, as the objection supposes, but sometimes by an extrinsic accidental cause; thus the Philosopher says,[2] "The northern wind favours the generation of males, and the southern wind that of females"; sometimes also by some impression in the soul, which may easily have some effect on the body. Especially was this the case in the state of innocence, when the body was more subject to the soul, so that by the mere will of the parent the sex of the offspring might be diversified.

Reply Obj. 3. The offspring would have been begotten to an animal life, as to the use of food and generation. Hence it was fitting that all should generate, and not only the first parents. From this it seems to follow that males and females would have been in equal number.

QUESTION C

OF THE CONDITION OF THE OFFSPRING AS REGARDS JUSTICE

(*In Two Articles*)

WE now have to consider the condition of the offspring as to justice. Under this head there are two points of inquiry: (1) Whether men would have been born in a state of justice? (2) Whether they would have been born confirmed in justice?

ARTICLE 1. *Whether Men Would Have Been Born in a State of Justice?*

We proceed thus to the First Article: It would seem that in the state of innocence men would not have been born in a state of justice.

Objection 1. For Hugh of St. Victor says (*De*

---

[1] *Generation of Animals*, II, 3 (737ª27).

[2] *History of Animals*, VI, 19 (574ª1).

Sacram. i)[1] that before sin, the first man would have begotten children sinless, but not heirs to their father's justice.

Obj. 2. Further, justice is effected by grace, as the Apostle says (Rom. 5. 16, 21). Now grace is not transfused from one to another, for thus it would be natural, but is infused by God alone. Therefore children would not have been born in a state of justice.

Obj. 3. Further, justice is in the soul. But the soul is not transmitted from the parent. Therefore neither would justice have been transmitted from parents to the children.

On the contrary, Anselm says (*De Concep. Virg.* x):[2] "As long as man did not sin, he would have begotten children endowed with justice together with the rational soul."

I answer that, Man naturally begets what is like himself in species. Hence whatever accidental qualities result from the nature of the species must be alike in parent and child, unless nature fails in its operation, which would not have occurred in the state of innocence. But individual accidents do not necessarily exist alike in parent and child. Now original justice, in which the first man was created, was an accident pertaining to the nature of the species, not as caused by the principles of the species, but as a gift conferred by God on the entire human nature. This is clear from the fact that opposites are of the same genus; and original sin, which is opposed to original justice, is called the sin of nature, and so it is transmitted from the parent to the offspring. And for this reason also, the children would have been like their parents as regards original justice.

Reply Obj. 1. These words of Hugh are to be understood as referring not to the habit of justice, but to the execution of its act.

Reply Obj. 2. Some say[3] that children would have been born not with the justice of grace, which is the principle of merit, but with original justice. But since the root of original justice, which conferred rectitude on the first man when he was made, consists in the supernatural subjection of the reason to God, which subjection results from sanctifying grace, as above explained (Q. XCV, A. 1), we must conclude that if children were born in original justice, they would also have been born in grace; thus we have said above that the first man was created in grace (*ibid.*). This grace, however, would not

have been natural, for it would not have been transfused by virtue of the semen, but would have been conferred on man immediately on his receiving a rational soul. In the same way the rational soul, which is not transmitted by the parent, is infused by God as soon as the human body is disposed to receive it.

From this the *reply to the third objection* is clear.

ARTICLE 2. *Whether in the State of Innocence Children Would Have Been Born Confirmed in Justice?*

We proceed thus to the Second Article: It would seem that in the state of innocence children would have been born confirmed in justice.

Objection 1. For Gregory says (*Moral.* iv)[4] on the words of Job 3. 13: *For now I should have been asleep,* etc.: "If no sinful corruption had infected our first parent, he would not have begotten 'children of hell'; no children would have been born of him but such as were destined to be saved by the Redeemer." Therefore all would have been born confirmed in justice.

Obj. 2. Further, Anselm says (*Cur Deus Homo* i, 18)[5] that if our first parents "had lived so as not to yield to temptation, they would have been confirmed in grace, so that with their offspring they would have been unable to sin any more." Therefore the children would have been born confirmed in justice.

Obj. 3. Further, good is stronger than evil. But by the sin of the first man there resulted, in those born of him, the necessity of sin. Therefore, if the first man had persevered in justice, his descendants would have derived from him the necessity of preserving justice.

Obj. 4. Further, the angels who remained faithful to God, while the others sinned, were at once confirmed in justice, so as to be unable henceforth to sin. In like manner, therefore, man would have been confirmed in justice if he had persevered. But he would have begotten children like himself. Therefore they also would have been born confirmed in justice.

On the contrary, Augustine says,[6] "Happy would have been the whole human race if neither they"—that is, our first parents—"had committed any evil to be transmitted to their descendants, nor any of their race had committed any sin for which they would have been condemned." From these words we gather that even if our first parents had not sinned, any of

[1] VI, 24 (PL 176, 278).

[2] PL 158, 444.

[3] Alexander of Hales, *Summa Theol.,* I-II, n. 499 (QR II, 712); n. 500 (QR II, 714).

[4] Chap. 31 (PL 75, 671).

[5] PL 158, 387.

[6] *City of God,* XIV, 10 (PL 41, 417).

their descendants might have done evil, and therefore they would not have been born confirmed in justice.

I answer that, It does not seem possible that in the state of innocence children would have been born confirmed in justice. For it is clear that at their birth they would not have had greater perfection than their parents at the time of begetting. Now the parents, as long as they begot children, would not have been confirmed in justice. For the rational creature is confirmed in justice through the Happiness given by the clear vision of God; and when once it has seen God, it cannot but cleave to Him Who is the essence of goodness, from which no one can turn away, since nothing is desired or loved but under the aspect of good. I say this according to the general law, for it may be otherwise in the case of special privilege, such as we believe was granted to the Virgin Mother of God. And as soon as Adam had attained to that happy state of seeing God in His Essence, he would have become spiritual in soul and body, and his animal life would have ceased, in which alone there is generation. Hence it is clear that children would not have been born confirmed in justice.

Reply Obj. 1. If Adam had not sinned, he would not have begotten children of hell in the sense that they would contract from him sin which is the cause of hell. Yet by sinning of their own free choice they could have become children of hell. If, however, they did not become children of hell by falling into sin, this would not have been owing to their being confirmed in justice, but to Divine Providence preserving them free from sin.

Reply Obj. 2. Anselm does not say this by way of assertion, but only as an opinion, which is clear from his mode of expression as follows: "It seems that if they had lived," etc.

Reply Obj. 3. This argument is not conclusive, though Anselm seems to have been influenced by it, as appears from his words quoted above. For the necessity of sin incurred by the descendants would not have been such that they could not return to justice, which is the case only with the damned. Therefore neither would the parents have transmitted to their descendants the necessity of not sinning, which is only in the blessed.

Reply Obj. 4. There is no comparison between man and the angels; for man's free choice is changeable, both before and after choice, whereas the angel's is not changeable, as we have said above in treating of the angels (Q. LXIV, A. 2).

QUESTION CI

OF THE CONDITION OF THE OFFSPRING AS REGARDS KNOWLEDGE

(*In Two Articles*)

WE next consider the condition of the offspring as to knowledge. Under this head there are two points of inquiry: (1) Whether in the state of innocence children would have been born with perfect knowledge? (2) Whether they would have had perfect use of reason at the moment of birth?

ARTICLE 1. *Whether in the State of Innocence Children Would Have Been Born with Perfect Knowledge?*

We proceed thus to the First Article: It would seem that in the state of innocence children would have been born with perfect knowledge.

Objection 1. For Adam would have begotten children like himself. But Adam was gifted with perfect knowledge (Q. XCIV, A. 3). Therefore children would have been born of him with perfect knowledge.

Obj. 2. Further, ignorance is a result of sin, as Bede says[1] (*cf.* Part I-II, Q. LXXXV, AA. 1, 3). But ignorance is privation of knowledge. Therefore before sin children would have had perfect knowledge as soon as they were born.

Obj. 3. Further, children would have been gifted with justice from birth. But knowledge is required for justice, since it directs our actions. Therefore they would also have been gifted with knowledge.

On the contrary, The human soul is naturally "like a blank tablet on which nothing is written," as the Philosopher says.[2] But the nature of the soul is the same now as it would have been in the state of innocence. Therefore the souls of children would have been without knowledge at birth.

I answer that, As above stated (Q. XCIX, A. 1), as regards belief in matters which are above nature, we rely on authority alone; and so, when authority is wanting, we must be guided by the ordinary course of nature. Now it is natural for man to acquire knowledge through the senses, as above explained (Q. LV, A. 2; Q. LXXXIV, A. 7), and the soul is united to the body because it needs it for its proper operation. And this would not be so if the soul were endowed at

[1] BEDE, *In Luc.*, III, on 10.30 (PL 92, 469); cf. also *Glossa ordin.*, on Luke, 10.30 (v, 153A).

[2] *Soul*, III, 4 (430ᵃ1).

birth with knowledge not acquired through the sensitive powers. We must conclude then, that in the state of innocence children would not have been born with perfect knowledge, but in course of time they would have acquired knowledge without difficulty by discovery or learning.

Reply Obj. 1. The perfection of knowledge was an individual accident of our first parent, so far as he was established as the father and instructor of the whole human race. Therefore he begot children like himself, not in that respect, but only in those accidents which were natural or conferred freely on the whole nature.

Reply Obj. 2. Ignorance is privation of knowledge due at some particular time, and this would not have been in children from their birth, for they would have possessed the knowledge due to them at that time. Hence, no ignorance would have been in them, but only nescience in regard to certain matters. Such nescience was even in the holy angels, according to Dionysius (*Cœl. Hier.* vii).[1]

Reply Obj. 3. Children would have had sufficient knowledge to direct them to deeds of justice, in which men are guided by universal principles of what is right; and this knowledge of theirs would have been much more complete than what we have now by nature, as likewise their knowledge of other universal principles.

ARTICLE 2. *Whether Children Would Have Had Perfect Use of Reason at Birth?*

We proceed thus to the Second Article: It would seem that children would have had perfect use of reason at birth.

Objection 1. For that children have not perfect use of reason in our present state is due to the soul being weighed down by the body, which was not the case in paradise, because, as it is written, *The corruptible body is a load upon the soul* (Wisd. 9. 15). Therefore, before sin and the corruption which resulted from sin, children would have had the perfect use of reason at birth.

Obj. 2. Further, some animals at birth have the use of their natural powers, as the lamb at once flies from the wolf. Much more, therefore, would men in the state of innocence have had perfect use of reason at birth.

On the contrary, In all things produced by generation nature proceeds from the imperfect to the perfect. Therefore children would not have had the perfect use of reason from the very outset.

[1] Sect. 3 (PG 3, 209).

I answer that, As above stated (Q. LXXXIV, A. 7), the use of reason depends in a certain manner on the use of the sensitive powers. Therefore, while the senses are tied and the interior sensitive powers hampered, man has not the perfect use of reason, as we see in those who are asleep or delirious. Now the sensitive powers are powers of corporeal organs. And therefore, so long as the organs are hindered, the action of the powers is of necessity hindered also, and likewise, consequently, the use of reason. Now children are hindered in the use of these powers on account of the moisture of the brain; therefore they have perfect use neither of these powers nor of reason. Therefore, in the state of innocence, children would not have had the perfect use of reason, which they would have enjoyed later on in life. Yet they would have had a more perfect use than they have now, as to matters regarding that particular state, as explained above regarding the use of their limbs (Q. XCIX, A. 1).

Reply Obj. 1. The corruptible body is a load upon the soul because it hinders the use of reason even in those matters which belong to man at all ages.

Reply Obj. 2. Even other animals have not at birth such a perfect use of their natural powers as they have later on. This is clear from the fact that birds teach their young to fly; and the like may be observed in other animals. Moreover a special impediment exists in man from the copious moisture of the brain, as we have said above (Q. XCIX, A. 1).

QUESTION CII

OF MAN'S ABODE, WHICH IS PARADISE

(*In Four Articles*)

WE next consider man's abode, which is paradise. Under this head there are four points of inquiry: (1) Whether paradise is a corporeal place? (2) Whether it is a place suitable for human habitation? (3) For what purpose was man placed in paradise? (4) Whether he should have been created in paradise?

ARTICLE 1. *Whether Paradise Is a Corporeal Place?*

We proceed thus to the First Article: It would seem that paradise is not a corporeal place.

Objection 1. For Bede says[2] that paradise reaches "to the lunar circle." But no earthly place answers that description, both because it

[2] Cf. *Glossa ordin.*, on Gen. 2.8 (1, 36F); cf. also Peter Lombard, *Sent.*, II, d. 17, chap. 5 (QR 1, 386).

is contrary to the nature of the earth to be raised up so high, and because beneath the moon is the region of fire, which would consume the earth. Therefore paradise is not a corporeal place.

Obj. 2. Further, Scripture mentions four rivers as rising in paradise (Gen. 2. 10). But the rivers there mentioned have visible sources elsewhere, as is clear from the Philosopher.[1] Therefore paradise is not a corporeal place.

Obj. 3. Further, although men have explored the entire habitable world, yet none have made mention of the place of paradise.[2] Therefore apparently it is not a corporeal place.

Obj. 4. Further, the tree of life is described as growing in paradise. But the tree of life is a spiritual thing, for it is written of Wisdom that *She is a tree of life to them that lay hold on her* (Prov. 3. 18). Therefore paradise also is not a corporeal, but a spiritual place.

Obj. 5. Further, if paradise be a corporeal place, the trees also of paradise must be corporeal. But it seems they were not, for corporeal trees were produced on the third day, while the planting of the trees of paradise is recorded after the work of the six days. Therefore paradise was not a corporeal place.

On the contrary, Augustine says (*Gen. ad lit.* viii, 1):[3] "Three general opinions prevail about paradise. Some understand a place merely corporeal; others a place entirely spiritual; while others, whose opinion, I confess, pleases me, hold that paradise was both corporeal and spiritual."

I answer that, As Augustine says,[4] "Nothing prevents us from holding, within proper limits, a spiritual paradise, so long as we believe in the truth of the events narrated as having there occurred." For whatever Scripture tells us about paradise is set down as matter of history, and wherever Scripture makes use of this method, we must hold to the historical truth of the narrative as a foundation of whatever spiritual explanation we may offer. And so paradise, as Isidore says (*Etym.* xiv, 3),[5] "is a place situated in the east, its name being the Greek for garden." It was fitting that it should be in the east, for it is to be believed that it was situated in the most excellent part of the earth. Now the east is the right hand of the heavens, as the Philosopher explains,[6] and the right hand is nobler than the

left; hence it was fitting that God should place the earthly paradise in the east.

Reply Obj. 1. Bede's assertion is untrue, if taken in its obvious sense. It may, however, be explained to mean that paradise reaches to the moon not literally, but figuratively; because, as Isidore says (*loc. cit.*), the atmosphere there is of "a continually even temperature," and in this respect it is like the heavenly bodies, which are without opposing elements. Mention, however, is made of the moon rather than of other bodies, because of all the heavenly bodies the moon is nearest to us, and is, moreover, the most akin to the earth; hence it is observed to be overshadowed by clouds so as to be almost obscured. Others say[7] that paradise reached to the moon—that is, to the middle space of the air, where rain, and wind, and the like arise, because the moon is said to have influence on such changes. But in this sense it would not be a fit place for human dwelling, through being uneven in temperature, and not attuned to the human temperament, as is the lower atmosphere in the neighbourhood of the earth.

Reply Obj. 2. Augustine says (*Gen. ad lit.* viii, 7):[8] "It is probable that man has no idea where paradise was, and that the rivers, whose sources are said to be known, flowed for some distance underground, and then sprang up elsewhere. For who is not aware that such is the case with some other streams?"

Reply Obj. 3. The situation of paradise is shut off from the habitable world by mountains, or seas, or some torrid region, which cannot be crossed; and so people who have written about places make no mention of it.

Reply Obj. 4. The tree of life is a material tree, and called so because its fruit was endowed with a life-preserving power, as above stated (Q. XCVII, A. 4). Yet it had a spiritual signification, just as the rock in the desert was of a material nature, and yet signified Christ (I Cor. 10. 4). In like manner the tree of the knowledge of good and evil was a material tree, so called in view of future events, because, after eating of it, man was to learn, by experience of the consequent punishment, the difference between the good of obedience and the evil of rebellion. It may also be said to signify spiritually the free choice, as some say.[9]

Reply Obj. 5. According to Augustine (*Gen.*

---

[1] *Meteorology,* I, 13 (350[b]18).

[2] See Albert, *De Nat. Locorum,* I, 6 (BO IX, 527) III, I (BO IX, 566). Cf. Brunet and Mieli, *Histoire des Sciences,* pp. 684, 1041.

[3] PL 34, 371.   [4] *City of God,* XIII, 21 (PL 41, 395).

[5] PL 82, 496.   [6] *Heavens,* II, 2 (285[b]16).

[7] *Glossa ordin.,* on Gen. 2.8 (I, 36F); Peter Lombard, *Sent.,* II, d. 17, chap. 5 (QR I, 386); Peter the Eater, *Hist. Schol., lib Gen.,* 13 (PL 198, 1067).

[8] PL 34, 378.

[9] Augustine, *City of God,* XIII, 21 (PL 41, 395); Bede, *In Pentat.,* I, on Gen. 2.8 (PL 91, 208).

ad lit. v, 4; viii, 3),[1] the plants were not actually produced on the third day, but in their seminal principles; but, after the work of the six days, the plants, both of paradise and others, were actually produced. According to other holy writers,[2] we ought to say that all the plants were actually produced on the third day, including the trees of paradise. And what is said of the trees of paradise being planted after the work of the six days is to be understood, they say, by way of recapitulation. And so our text reads: *The Lord God had planted a paradise of pleasure from the beginning* (Gen. 2. 8).

ARTICLE 2. *Whether Paradise Was a Place Adapted To Be the Abode of Man?*

We proceed thus to the Second Article: It would seem that paradise was not a place adapted to be the abode of man.

Objection 1. For man and angels are similarly ordered to happiness. But the angels from the very beginning of their existence were made to dwell in the abode of the blessed—that is, the empyrean heaven. Therefore the place of man's habitation should have been there also.

Obj. 2. Further, if some definite place were required for man's abode, this would be required on the part either of the soul or of the body. If on the part of the soul, the place would be in heaven, which is adapted to the nature of the soul, since the desire of heaven is implanted in all. On the part of the body, there was no need for any other place than the one provided for other animals. Therefore paradise was not at all adapted to be the abode of man.

Obj. 3. Further, a place which contains nothing is useless. But after sin, paradise was not occupied by man. Therefore if it were adapted as a dwelling-place for man, it seems that God made paradise to no purpose.

Obj. 4. Further, since man is of an even temperament, a fitting place for him should be of even temperature. But paradise was not of an even temperature, for it is said to have been on the equator[3]—a situation of extreme heat, since twice in the year the sun passes vertically over the heads of its inhabitants.[4] Therefore paradise was not a fit dwelling-place for man.

On the contrary, Damascene says (*De Fid. Orth.* ii, 11):[5] "Paradise was a divinely ordered

[1] PL 34, 324, 371.

[2] Cf. Q. LXIX, A. 2.

[3] Albert the Great, *Summa de Creatur.*, II, Q. 79, A I (BO XXXV, 640). *In Sent.*, II, d. 17, A. 4 (BO XXVII, 304); Bonaventure, *In Sent.*, II, d. 17, dub. 3 (QR II, 427).

[4] Cf. Albert, *De Nat. Locorum*, I, 6 (BO IX, 539).

[5] PG 94, 913.

region, and worthy of him who was made to God's image."

I answer that, as above stated (Q. XCVII, A. 1), Man was incorruptible and immortal not because his body had a disposition to incorruptibility, but because in his soul there was a power preserving the body from corruption. Now the human body may be corrupted from within or from without. From within, the body is corrupted by the consumption of the humours, and by old age, as above explained (*ibid.*, A. 4), and man was able to ward off such corruption by food. Among those things which corrupt the body from without, the chief seems to be an atmosphere of unequal temperature, and to such corruption a remedy is found in an atmosphere of equable nature. In paradise both conditions were found; because, as Damascene says (*loc. cit.*): "Paradise was permeated with the all-pervading brightness of a temperate, pure, and exquisite atmosphere, and decked with ever-flowering plants." And so it is clear that paradise was most fit to be a dwelling-place for man, and in keeping with his original state of immortality.

Reply Obj. 1. The empyrean heaven is the highest of corporeal places, and is outside the region of change. By the first of these two conditions, it is a fitting abode for the angelic nature; for, as Augustine says (*De Trin.* iii),[6] God rules corporeal creatures through spiritual creatures. Hence it is fitting that the spiritual nature should be established above the entire corporeal nature, as presiding over it. By the second condition, it is a fitting abode for the state of happiness, which is endowed with the highest degree of stability. Thus the abode of happiness was suited to the very nature of the angel; therefore he was created there. But it is not suited to man's nature, since man is not set as a ruler over the entire corporeal creation; it is a fitting abode for man in regard only to his happiness. Therefore he was not placed from the beginning in the empyrean heaven, but was destined to be transferred there in the state of his final Happiness.

Reply Obj. 2. It is ridiculous to assert that any particular place is natural to the soul or to any spiritual substances, though some particular place may have a certain fitness in regard to spiritual substances. For the earthly paradise was a place adapted to man as regards both his body and his soul—that is, in so far as in his soul was the force which preserved the human body from corruption. This could not be said of the

[6] Chap. 4 (PL 42, 873).

other animals. Therefore, as Dasmascene says (*loc. cit.*): "No irrational animal inhabited paradise"; although, by a certain dispensation, the animals were brought there by God to Adam; and the serpent was able to trespass there through the work of the devil.

Reply Obj. 3. Paradise did not become useless through being unoccupied by man after sin, just as immortality was not conferred on man in vain, though he was to lose it. For thereby we learn God's kindness to man, and what man lost by sin. Moreover, some say that Enoch and Elias still dwell in that paradise.[1]

Reply Obj. 4. Those who say that paradise was on the equinoctial line are of opinion that such a situation is most temperate, on account of the unvarying equality of day and night; that it is never too cold there, because the sun is never too far off, and never too hot, because, although the sun passes over the heads of the inhabitants, it does not remain long in that position. However, Aristotle expressly says that such a region is uninhabitable on account of the heat.[2] This seems to be more probable, because, even those regions where the sun does not pass vertically overhead are extremely hot on account of the mere proximity of the sun. But whatever be the truth of the matter, we must hold that paradise was situated in a most temperate situation, whether on the equator or elsewhere.

ARTICLE 3. *Whether Man Was Placed in Paradise to Work It and Keep It?*

We proceed thus to the Third Article: It would seem that man was not placed in paradise to work and keep it.

Objection 1. For what was brought on him as a punishment of sin would not have existed in paradise in the state of innocence. But the cultivation of the soil was a punishment of sin (Gen. 3. 17). Therefore man was not placed in paradise to work and keep it.

Obj. 2. Further, there is no need of a keeper when there is no fear of trespass with violence. But in paradise there was no fear of trespass with violence. Therefore there was no need for man to keep paradise.

Obj. 3. Further, if man was placed in paradise to work and keep it, man would apparently have been made for the sake of paradise, and not contrariwise; which seems to be false. There-

fore man was not placed in paradise to work and keep it.

On the contrary, It is written (Gen. 2. 15): *The Lord God took man and placed him in the paradise of pleasure, to dress and keep it.*

I answer that, As Augustine says (*Gen. ad lit.* viii, 10),[3] these words of Genesis may be understood in two ways. First, in the sense that God placed man in paradise that He might Himself work in man and keep him, by sanctifying him (for if this work cease, man at once relapses into darkness, as the air grows dark when the light ceases to shine), and by keeping man from all corruption and evil. Secondly, that man might work and keep paradise, which working would not have involved labour, as it did after sin, but would have been pleasant on account of man's practical knowledge of the powers of nature. Nor would man have kept paradise against a trespasser, but he would have striven to keep paradise for himself lest he should lose it by sin. All of this was for man's good; and so paradise was ordered to man's benefit, and not conversely.

From this the *Replies to the Objections* are made clear.

ARTICLE 4. *Whether Man Was Created in Paradise?*

We proceed thus to the Fourth Article: It would seem that man was created in paradise.

Objection 1. For the angel was created in his dwelling-place—namely, the empyrean heaven. But before sin paradise was a fitting abode for man. Therefore it seems that man was created in paradise.

Obj. 2. Further, other animals remain in the place where they are produced, as the fish in water, and walking animals on the earth from which they were made. Now man would have remained in paradise after he was created (Q. XCVII, A. 4). Therefore he was created in paradise.

Obj. 3. Further, woman was made in paradise. But man is greater than woman. Therefore much more should man have been made in paradise.

On the contrary, It is written (Gen. 2. 15): *God took man and placed him in paradise.*

I answer that, Paradise was a fitting abode for man as regards the incorruptibility of the primitive state. Now this incorruptibility was man's not by nature, but by a supernatural gift of God. Therefore that this might be attributed to the grace of God, and not to human nature, God

---

[1] Augustine, *Gen. ad lit.*, IX, 6 (PL 34, 396); *Contra Julian.*, VI, 30 (PL 45, 1581); this opinion can be found generally throughout the Fathers.

[2] *Meteorology*, II, 5 (362[b]25).

[3] PL 34, 380.

made man outside of paradise, and afterwards placed him there to live there during the whole of his animal life; and, having attained to the spiritual life, to be transferred to heaven.

Reply Obj. 1. The empyrean heaven was a fitting abode for the angels as regards their nature, and therefore they were created there.

In the same way I *reply to the second objec-tion,* for those places befit those animals in their nature.

Reply Obj. 3. Woman was made in paradise not by reason of her own dignity, but on account of the dignity of the principle from which her body was formed. For the same reason the children would have been born in paradise, where their parents were already.

TREATISE ON THE DIVINE GOVERNMENT

QUESTION CIII

OF THE GOVERNMENT OF THINGS IN GENERAL

(In Eight Articles)

HAVING considered the creation of things and their distinction, we now consider in the third place their government and (1) the government of things in general; (2) in particular, the effects of this government (Q. CIV). Under the first head there are eight points of inquiry: (1) Whether the world is governed by someone? (2) What is the end of this government? (3) Whether the world is governed by one? (4) Of the effects of this government? (5) Whether all things are subject to Divine government? (6) Whether all things are immediately governed by God? (7) Whether the Divine government is frustrated in anything? (8) Whether anything is contrary to the Divine Providence?

ARTICLE 1. *Whether the World Is Governed by Anyone?*

We proceed thus to the First Article: It would seem that the world is not governed by anyone.

Objection 1. For it pertains to those things which move or work for an end to be governed. But natural things which make up the greater part of the world do not move, or work for an end, for they have no knowledge of their end. Therefore the world is not governed.

Obj. 2. Further, those things are governed which are moved towards some thing. But the world does not appear to be so directed, but has stability in itself. Therefore it is not governed.

Obj. 3. Further, what is necessarily determined by its own nature to one particular thing does not require any external principle of government. But the principal parts of the world are by a certain necessity determined to something particular in their actions and movements. Therefore the world does not require to be governed.

On the contrary, It is written (Wisd. 14. 3): *But Thou, O Father, governest all things by Thy Providence.* And Boëthius says (*De Con-*

sol. iii, 9):[1] Thou Who governest this universe by mandate eternal."

I answer that, Certain philosophers of old denied the government of the world, saying that all things happened by chance.[2] But such an opinion can be shown to be impossible in two ways. First, by observation of things themselves. For we observe that in nature things happen always or nearly always for the best, which would not be the case unless some sort of providence directed nature towards good as an end, which is to govern. Therefore the unfailing order we observe in things is a sign of their being governed. For instance, if we enter a well-ordered house we gather from it the intention of him who put it in order, as Cicero says (*De Nat. Deorum*, ii),[3] quoting Aristotle. Secondly, this is clear from a consideration of Divine goodness, which, as we have said above (Q. XLIV, A. 4; Q. LXV, A. 2), was the cause of the production of things in being. For as it pertains to the best to produce the best, it is not fitting that the supreme goodness of God should produce things without giving them their perfection. Now a thing's ultimate perfection consists in the attainment of its end. Therefore it pertains to the Divine goodness, to lead things to their end just as it brought things into being. And this is to govern.

Reply Obj. 1. A thing moves or operates for an end in two ways. First, in moving itself to the end, as man and other rational creatures; and such things have knowledge of their end, and of the means to the end. Secondly, a thing is said to move or operate for an end, as though moved or directed to it by another, as an arrow directed to the target by the archer, who knows the end unknown to the arrow. Therefore, as the movement of the arrow towards a definite end shows clearly that it is directed by someone with knowledge, so the unvarying course of natural things which are without knowledge, shows clearly that the world is governed by some reason.

Reply Obj. 2. In all created things there is a stable element, at least primary matter, and

[1] PL 63, 758.
[2] Democritus and Epicurus; cf. Q. XXII, A. 2.
[3] Chap. 5 (DD IV, 111).

something belonging to movement, according as under movement we include operation. And things need governing as to both, because even that which is stable, since it is created from nothing, would return to nothingness were it not sustained by a governing hand, as will be explained later (Q. CIV, A. 1).

Reply Obj. 3. The natural necessity inherent in those beings which are determined to a particular thing is a kind of impression from God, directing them to their end; as the necessity whereby an arrow is moved so as to fly towards a certain point is an impression from the archer, and not from the arrow. But there is a difference, since that which creatures receive from God is their nature, while that which natural things receive from man over and above their nature is somewhat violent. Therefore, as the violent necessity in the movement of the arrow shows the action of the archer, so the natural necessity of things shows the government of Divine Providence.

ARTICLE 2. *Whether the End of the Government of the World Is Something Outside the World?*

We proceed thus to the Second Article: It would seem that the end of the government of the world is not something existing outside the world.

Objection 1. For the end of the government of a thing is that to which the thing governed is brought. But that to which a thing is brought is some good in the thing itself; thus a sick man is brought back to health, which is something good in him. Therefore the end of the government of things is some good not outside, but within the things themselves.

Obj. 2. Further, the Philosopher says,[1] "Some ends are an operation; some are a work" —that is, produced by an operation. But nothing can be produced by the whole universe outside itself, and operation exists in the agent. Therefore nothing extrinsic can be the end of the government of things.

Obj. 3. Further, the good of the multitude seems to consist in order, and peace which is "the tranquillity of order," as Augustine says.[2] But the world is composed of a multitude of things. Therefore the end of the government of the world is the peaceful order in things themselves. Therefore the end of the government of the world is not an extrinsic good.

On the contrary, It is written (Prov. 16. 4):

[1] *Ethics,* I, 1 (1094ª4).
[2] *City of God,* XIX, 13 (PL 41, 640).

The Lord hath made all things for Himself. But God is outside the entire order of the universe. Therefore the end of all things is some good extrinsic to them.

I answer that, As the end of a thing corresponds to its beginning, it is not possible to be ignorant of the end of things if we know their beginning. Therefore, since the beginning of all things is something outside the universe, namely, God, as is clear from what has been expounded above (Q. XLIV, A. 1), we must conclude that the end of all things is some extrinsic good. This can be proved by reason. For it is clear that good has the nature of an end; therefore, a particular end of anything consists in some particular good, while the universal end of all things is the universal good. But the universal good is that which is good of itself by virtue of its essence, which is the very essence of goodness, whereas a particular good is good by participation. Now it is manifest that in the whole created universe there is not a good which is not such by participation. Therefore that good which is the end of the whole universe must be a good outside the universe.

Reply Obj. 1. We may acquire some good in many ways: first, as a form existing in us, such as health or knowledge; secondly, as something done by us, as a builder attains his end by building a house; thirdly, as something good possessed or acquired by us, as the buyer of a field attains his end when he enters into possession. Therefore nothing prevents something outside the universe being the good to which it is directed.

Reply Obj. 2. The Philosopher is speaking of the ends of the arts. For the end of some arts consists in the operation itself, as the end of a harpist is to play the harp, while the end of other arts consists in something produced, as the end of a builder is not the act of building, but the house he builds. Now it may happen that something extrinsic is the end not only as made, but also as possessed or acquired, or even as represented, as if we were to say that Hercules is the end of the statue made to represent him. Therefore we may say that some good outside the whole universe is the end of the government of the universe, as something possessed and represented; for each thing tends to participate in it, and to imitate it as far as is possible.

Reply Obj. 3. A good existing in the universe, namely, the order of the universe itself, is an end of the universe; this, however, is not its ultimate end, but is ordered to the extrinsic good as to the ultimate end, just as "the order in an army is ordered to the general," as stated in the *Metaphysics*.[1]

ARTICLE 3. *Whether the World Is Governed by One?*

We proceed thus to the Third Article: It would seem that the world is not governed by one.

Objection 1. For we judge the cause by the effect. Now, we see in the government of the universe that things are not moved and do not operate uniformly, but some contingently and some of necessity and according to other differences. Therefore the world is not governed by one.

Obj. 2. Further, things which are governed by one do not act against each other, except by the incapacity or unskilfulness of the ruler, which cannot apply to God. But created things do not agree together, and fight against each other, as is evident in the case of contraries. Therefore the world is not governed by one.

Obj. 3. Further, in nature we always find what is the better. But it *is better that two should be together than one* (Eccles. 4. 9). Therefore the world is not governed by one, but by many.

On the contrary, We confess our belief in one God and one Lord, according to the words of the Apostle (I Cor. 8. 6): *To us there is but one God, the Father . . . and one Lord,* and both of these pertain to government. For to the Lord belongs dominion over subjects, and the name of God is taken from Providence as stated above (Q. XIII, A. 8). Therefore the world is governed by one.

I answer that, We must of necessity say that the world is governed by one. For since the end of the government of the world is that which is essentially good, which is the greatest good, the government of the world must be the best kind of government. Now the best government is government by one. The reason of this is that government is nothing but the directing of the things governed to the end, which consists in some good. But unity belongs to the notion of goodness, as Boëthius proves (*De Consol.* iii, 11),[2] from the fact that, as all things desire good, so do they desire unity, without which they could not be. For a thing so far exists as it is one. And so we observe that things resist division, as far as they can, and the dissolution of a thing arises from some defect in it. Therefore

the intention of a ruler over a multitude is unity, or peace. Now the cause per se of unity is one. For it is clear that several cannot be the cause of unity or concord, except so far as they are united. Furthermore, what is one in itself is a more apt and a better cause of unity than several things united. Therefore a multitude is better governed by one than by several. From this it follows that the government of the world, since it is the best form of government, must be by one. This is expressed by the Philosopher:[3] "Things refuse to be ill governed; and multiplicity of authorities is a bad thing; therefore there should be one ruler."

Reply Obj. 1. Movement is the act of a thing moved, caused by the mover. Therefore dissimilarity of movements is caused by diversity of things moved, which diversity is required for the perfection of the universe (Q. XLVII, AA. 1, 2; Q. XLVIII, A. 2), and not by a diversity of governors.

Reply Obj. 2. Although contraries do not agree with each other in their proximate ends, nevertheless they agree in the ultimate end, so far as they are included in the one order of the universe.

Reply Obj. 3. If we consider individual goods, then two are better than one. But if we consider the essential good, then no addition of good is possible.

ARTICLE 4. *Whether the Effect of Government Is One or Many?*

We proceed thus to the Fourth Article: It would seem that there is but one effect of the government of the world, and not many.

Objection 1. For the effect of government is that which is caused in the things governed. This is one, namely, the good which consists in order, as may be seen in the example of an army. Therefore the government of the world has but one effect.

Obj. 2. Further, from one there naturally proceeds but one. But the world is governed by one as we have proved (A. 3). Therefore also the effect of this government is but one.

Obj. 3. Further, if the effect of government is not one by reason of the unity of the Governor, it must be many by reason of the many things governed. But these are too numerous to be counted. Therefore we cannot assign any definite number to the effects of government.

On the contrary, Dionysius says (*Div. Nom.* xii):[4] "God contains all and fills all by His

---

[1] Aristotle, XII, 10 (1075ª15).

[2] PL 63, 771.

[3] *Metaphysics*, XII, 10 (1076ª3).

[4] Sect. 2 (PG 3, 969).

providence and perfect goodness." But government belongs to providence. Therefore there are certain definite effects of the Divine government.

I answer that, The effect of any action may be judged from its end, because it is by action that the attainment of the end is effected. Now the end of the government of the world is the essential good, to the participation and imitation of which all things tend. Consequently the effect of the government of the world may be taken in three ways. First, on the part of the end itself; and in this way there is but one effect, that is, assimilation to the supreme good. Secondly, the effect of the government of the world may be considered on the part of those things by means of which the creature is made like to God. Thus there are, in general, two effects of the government. For the creature is made like God in two things: first, with regard to this, that God is good; and so the creature becomes like Him by being good. And secondly, with regard to this, that God is the cause of goodness in others; and so the creature becomes like God by moving others to be good. Thus there are two effects of government, the preservation of things in their goodness, and the moving of things to good. Thirdly, we may consider the effects of the government of the world in particular things; and in this way they are without number.

Reply Obj. 1. The order of the universe includes both the preservation of the different things created by God and their movement. As regards these two things we find order among them, according as one is better than another, and as one is moved by another.

From what has been said above, we can gather the *replies to the other two objections.*

ARTICLE 5. *Whether All Things Are Subject to the Divine Government?*

We proceed thus to the Fifth Article: It would seem that not all things are subject to the Divine government.

Objection 1. For it is written (Eccles. 9. 11): *I saw that under the sun the race is not to the swift, nor the battle to the strong, nor bread to the wise, nor riches to the learned, nor favour to the skilful, but time and chance in all.* But things subject to the Divine government are not ruled by chance. Therefore those things which are under the sun are not subject to the Divine government.

Obj. 2. Further, the Apostle says (I Cor. 9. 9): *God hath no care for oxen.* But he that governs has care for the things he governs. Therefore all things are not subject to the Divine government.

Obj. 3. Further, what can govern itself does not need to be governed by another. But the rational creature can govern itself, since it is master of its own act, and acts of itself, and is not made to act by another, which seems proper to things which are governed. Therefore all things are not subject to the Divine government.

On the contrary, Augustine says,[1] "Not only heaven and earth, not only man and angel, even the bowels of the lowest animal, even the wing of the bird, the flower of the plant, the leaf of the tree, hath God endowed with every fitting detail of their nature." Therefore all things are subject to His government.

I answer that, God the ruler of things for the same reason as He is their cause, because the same being gives existence as gives perfection, and this belongs to government. Now God is the cause not indeed only of some particular kind of being, but of the whole universal being, as proved above (Q. XLIV, AA. 1, 2). Therefore, as there can be nothing which is not created by God, so there can be nothing which is not subject to His government. This can also be proved from the nature of the end of government. For a man's government extends over all those things which come under the end of his government. Now the end of the Divine government is the Divine goodness, as we have shown (A. 2). Therefore, as there can be nothing that is not ordered to the Divine goodness as its end, as is clear from what we have said above (Q. XLIV, A. 4; Q. LXV, A. 2), so it is impossible for anything to escape from the Divine government.

Foolish therefore was the opinion of those who said that the corruptible lower world,[2] or individual things,[3] or that even human affairs,[4] were not subject to the Divine government. These are represented as saying, *God hath abandoned the earth* (Ezech. 9. 9).

Reply Obj. 1. These things are said to be under the sun which are generated and corrupted according to the sun's movement. In all such things we find chance. Not that everything which occurs in such things is by chance, but that in each one there is an element of chance.

---

[1] *City of God,* v, 11 (PL 41, 154).
[2] Cf. Q. XXII, A, 2.
[3] Cf. Q. LVII, A. 2.
[4] Cf. Augustine, *City of God,* v, 9 (PL 41, 148), where he argues against Cicero.

And the very fact that an element of chance is found in those things proves that they are subject to government of some kind. For unless corruptible things of this kind were governed by a higher being, they would tend to nothing definite, especially those which possess no kind of knowledge. So nothing in them would happen unintentionally, which constitutes the nature of chance. Therefore to show how things happen by chance and yet according to the ordering of a higher cause, he does not say absolutely that he observes chance in all things, but *time and chance*, that is to say, that defects may be found in these things according to some order of time.

Reply Obj. 2. Government implies a certain change effected by the governor in the things governed. Now every movement is "the act of a movable thing, caused by the moving principle," as is laid down in the *Physics*.[1] And every act is proportioned to that of which it is an act. Consequently, various movable things must be moved variously, even as regards movement by one and the same mover. Thus by the one art of the Divine governor, various things are variously governed according to their variety. Some, according to their nature, act of themselves, having dominion over their actions; and these are governed by God, not only in this, that they are moved by God Himself, Who works in them interiorly, but also in this, that they are induced by Him to do good and to fly from evil, by precepts and prohibitions, rewards and punishments. But irrational creatures which do not act but are acted upon, are not thus governed by God. Hence, when the Apostle says that *God hath no care for oxen*, he does not wholly withdraw them from the Divine government, but only as regards the way in which rational creatures are governed.

Reply Obj. 3. The rational creature governs itself by its intellect and will, both of which require to be governed and perfected by the Divine intellect and will. Therefore above the government by which the rational creature governs itself as master of its own act, it requires to be governed by God.

ARTICLE 6. *Whether All Things Are Immediately Governed by God?*

We proceed thus to the Sixth Article: It would seem that all things are governed by God immediately.

[1] Aristotle, III, 3 (202ᵃ14).

Objection 1. For Gregory of Nyssa (Nemesius, *De Nat. Hom.*)[2] reproves the opinion of Plato who divides providence into three parts. The first he ascribes to the supreme god, who watches over heavenly things and all universals; the second providence he attributes to the secondary deities, who go the round of the heavens to watch over things subject to generation and corruption; while he ascribes a third providence to certain spirits who are guardians on earth of human actions. Therefore it seems that all things are immediately governed by God.

Obj. 2. Further, it is better that a thing be done by one, if possible, than by many, as the Philosopher says.[3] But God can by Himself govern all things without any intermediary cause. Therefore it seems that He governs all things immediately.

Obj. 3. Further, in God nothing is defective or imperfect. But it seems to be imperfect in a ruler to govern by means of others. Thus an earthly king, by reason of his not being able to do everything himself, and because he cannot be everywhere at the same time, requires to govern by means of ministers. Therefore God governs all things immediately.

On the contrary, Augustine says (*De Trin.* iii, 4):[4] "As the lower and grosser bodies are ruled in a certain orderly way by bodies of greater subtlety and power, so all bodies are ruled by the rational spirit of life, and the sinful and unfaithful spirit is ruled by the good and just spirit of life, and this spirit by God Himself."

I answer that, In government there are two things to be considered: the principle of government, which is providence itself; and the execution of the design. As to the principle of government, God governs all things immediately, but as to its execution, He governs some things by means of others.

The reason of this is that as God is the very essence of goodness, so everything must be attributed to God in its highest degree of goodness. Now the highest degree of goodness in any practical order, or plan, or knowledge (and such is the principle of government) consists in knowing the individuals acted upon; as the best physician is not the one who can only give his attention to general principles, but who can consider the least details; and so on in other things. Therefore we must say that in God is

[2] Chap. 44 (PG 40, 794).
[3] *Physics*, VIII, 6 (259ᵃ8). [4] PL 42, 873.

the principle of the government of all things, even of the very least.

But since things which are governed should be brought to perfection by government, this government will be so much the better in the degree the things governed are brought to perfection. Now it is a greater perfection for a thing to be good in itself and also the cause of goodness in others, than only to be good in itself. Therefore God so governs things that He makes some of them to be causes of others in government; as a master, who not only imparts knowledge to his pupils, but also makes them teachers of others.

Reply Obj. 1. Plato's opinion is to be rejected, because he held that God did not govern all things immediately, even in the principle of government; this is clear from the fact that he divided providence, which is the principle of government, into three parts.

Reply Obj. 2. If God governed alone, things would be deprived of the perfection of causality. Therefore all that is effected by many would not be better accomplished by one.

Reply Obj. 3. That an earthly king should have ministers to execute his laws is a sign not only of his being imperfect, but also of his dignity, because by the ordering of ministers the kingly power is brought into greater evidence.

ARTICLE 7. *Whether Anything Can Happen outside the Order of the Divine Government?*

We proceed thus to the Seventh Article: It would seem possible that something may occur outside the order of the Divine government.

Objection 1. For Boëthius says (*De Consol.* iii, 12)[1] that "God disposes all for good." Therefore, if nothing happens outside the order of the Divine government, it would follow that no evil exists.

Obj. 2. Further, nothing that is in accordance with the pre-ordination of a ruler occurs by chance. Therefore, if nothing occurs outside the order of the Divine government, it follows that there is nothing fortuitous and casual.

Obj. 3. Further, the order of Divine government is certain and unchangeable, because it is in accordance with the eternal design. Therefore, if nothing happens outside the order of the Divine government, it follows that all things happen by necessity, and nothing is contingent, which is false. Therefore it is possible for something to occur outside the order of the Divine government.

[1] PL 63, 779.

On the contrary, It is written (Esth. 13. 9): *O Lord, Lord, almighty King, all things are in Thy power, and there is none that can resist Thy will.*

I answer that, It is possible for an effect to come about outside the order of some particular cause, but not outside the order of the universal cause. The reason of this is that no effect results outside the order of a particular cause, except through some other impeding cause, which other cause must itself be reduced to the first universal cause; just as indigestion may occur outside the order of the nutritive power by some such impediment as the coarseness of the food, which again is to be reduced to some other cause, and so on till we come to the first universal cause. Therefore as God is the first universal cause, not of one genus only, but of all being, it is impossible for anything to happen outside the order of the Divine government. But from the very fact that from one point of view something seems to evade the order of Divine providence considered in regard to one particular cause, it must necessarily come back to that order as regards some other cause.

Reply Obj. 1. There is nothing wholly evil in the world, for evil is always founded on good, as shown above (Q. XLVIII, A. 3). Therefore something is said to be evil through its escaping from the order of some particular good. If it wholly escaped from the order of the Divine government, it would wholly cease to exist.

Reply Obj. 2. Things are said to be fortuitous as regards some particular cause from the order of which they escape. But as to the order of Divine providence, "nothing in the world happens by chance," as Augustine declares (QQ. LXXXIII, qu. 24).[2]

Reply Obj. 3. Certain effects are said to be contingent as compared to their proximate causes, which may fail in their effects; but not as though anything could happen entirely outside the order of Divine government. The very fact that something occurs outside the order of some proximate cause, is owing to some other cause, itself subject to the Divine government.

ARTICLE 8. *Whether Anything Can Resist the Order of the Divine Government?*

We proceed thus to the Eighth Article: It would seem possible that some resistance can be made to the order of the Divine government.

Objection 1. For it is written (Isa. 3. 8):

[2] PL 40, 17.

Their tongue and their devices are against the Lord.

Obj. 2. Further, a king does not justly punish those who do not rebel against his commands. Therefore if no one rebelled against God's commands, no one would be justly punished by God.

Obj. 3. Further, everything is subject to the order of the Divine government. But some things oppose others. Therefore some things rebel against the order of the Divine government.

On the contrary, Boëthius says (*De Consol.* iii, 12):[1] "There is nothing that can desire to or is able to resist this sovereign good. It is this sovereign good therefore that ruleth all mightily and ordereth all sweetly, as is said (Wisd. 8.) of Divine wisdom.

I answer that, We may consider the order of Divine providence in two ways: in general, according as it proceeds from the governing cause of all; and in particular, according as it proceeds from some particular cause which executes the order of the Divine government.

Considered in the first way, nothing can resist the order of the Divine government. This can be proved in two ways. First, from the fact that the order of the Divine government is wholly directed to good, and everything by its own operation and effort tends to good only; "for no one acts intending evil," as Dionysius says (*Div. Nom.* iv).[2] Secondly from the fact that, as we have said above (A. 1, Ans. 3; A. 5, Ans. 2), every inclination of anything, whether natural or voluntary, is nothing but a kind of impression from the first mover, just as the inclination of the arrow towards a fixed point is nothing but an impulse received from the archer. Therefore every agent, whether natural or free, attains to its divinely appointed end, as though of its own accord. For this reason God is said *to order all things sweetly.* (Wisd. 8. 1).

Reply Obj. 1. Some are said to think or speak, or act against God, not that they entirely resist the order of the Divine government, for even the sinner intends the attainment of a certain good, but because they resist some particular good, which is fitting to their nature or state. Therefore they are justly punished by God.

Reply Obj. 2 is clear from the above.

Reply Obj. 3. From the fact that one thing opposes another, it follows that some one thing can resist the order of a particular cause, but not that order which depends on the universal cause of all things.

[1] PL 63, 779.
[2] Sect. 31 (PG 3, 732).

QUESTION CIV

THE SPECIAL EFFECTS OF THE DIVINE GOVERNMENT

(*In Four Articles*)

WE next consider the effects of the Divine government in particular, concerning which four points of inquiry arise: (1) Whether creatures need to be kept in being by God? (2) Whether they are immediately preserved by God? (3) Whether God can reduce anything to nothingness? (4) Whether anything is reduced to nothingness?

ARTICLE 1. *Whether Creatures Need to Be Kept in Being by God?*

We proceed thus to the First Article: It would seem that creatures do not need to be kept in being by God.

Objection 1. For what cannot not-be, does not need to be kept in being, just as that which cannot depart, does not need to be kept from departing. But some creatures by their very nature cannot not-be. Therefore not all creatures need to be kept in being by God. The middle proposition is proved thus. That which is included in a thing per se is necessarily in that thing, and its contrary cannot be in it; thus a multiple of two must necessarily be even, and cannot possibly be an odd number. Now being follows *per se* upon form, because everything is an actual being so far as it has form. But some creatures are subsistent forms, as we have said of the angels (Q. L, AA. 2, 5), and thus to be is in them per se. The same reasoning applies to those creatures whose matter is in potency to one form only, as explained above of heavenly bodies (Q. LXVI, A. 2). Therefore such creatures as these have in their nature to be necessarily, and cannot not-be; for there can be no potency to not-being, either in the form which per se follows on being, or in matter existing under a form which it cannot lose, since it is not in potency to any other form.

Obj. 2. Further, God is more powerful than any created agent. But a created agent, even after ceasing to act, can cause its effect to be preserved in being. Thus the house continues to stand after the builder has ceased to build, and water remains hot for some time after the fire has ceased to heat. Much more, therefore, can God cause His creature to be kept in being after He has ceased to create it.

Obj. 3. Further, nothing violent can occur without some active cause. But tendency to not-being is unnatural and violent to any creature, since all creatures naturally desire to be. Therefore no creature can tend to not-being except through some active cause of corruption. Now there are creatures of such a nature that nothing can cause them to corrupt, such as spiritual substances and heavenly bodies. Therefore such creatures cannot tend to not-being even if God were to withdraw His action.

Obj. 4. Further, if God keeps creatures in being, this is done by some action. Now every action of an agent, if that action be efficacious, produces something in the effect. Therefore the preserving power of God must produce something in the creature. But this does not seem to be the case, because this action does not give being to the creature, since being is not given to that which already is; nor does it add anything new to the creature, because either God would not keep the creature in being continually, or He would be continually adding something new to the creature; either of which is unreasonable. Therefore creatures are not kept in being by God.

On the contrary, It is written (Heb. 1. 3): *Upholding all things by the word of His power.*

I answer that, Both reason and faith bind us to say that creatures are kept in being by God. To make this clear, we must consider that a thing is preserved by another in two ways. First, indirectly, and accidentally; thus a person is said to preserve anything by removing the cause of its corruption, as a man may be said to preserve a child whom he guards from falling into the fire. In this way God preserves some things, but not all, for there are some things of such a nature that nothing can corrupt them, so that it is not necessary to keep them from corruption. Secondly, a thing is said to preserve another *per se* and directly, namely, when what is preserved depends on the preserver in such a way that it cannot exist without it. In this manner all creatures need to be preserved by God. For the being of every creature depends on God, so that not for a moment could it subsist, but would fall into nothingness were it not kept in being by the operation of the Divine power, as Gregory says (*Moral.* xvi).[1]

This is made clear as follows. Every effect depends on its cause, so far as it is its cause. But we must observe that an agent is the cause of the becoming of its effect, but not directly of its being. This may be seen both in artificial and in natural things. For the builder causes the house in its becoming, but he is not the direct cause of

[1] Chap. 37 (PL 75, 1143).

its being. For it is clear that the being of the house is a result of its form, which consists in the putting together and arrangement of the materials, and results from the natural qualities of certain things. Thus a cook dresses the food by applying the natural activity of fire; in the same way a builder constructs a house, by making use of cement, stones, and wood which are able to be put together in a certain order and to preserve it. Therefore the being of a house depends on the nature of these materials, just as its becoming depends on the action of the builder. The same principle applies to natural things. For if an agent is not the cause of a form as such, neither will it be directly the cause of being which results from that form, but it will be the cause of the effect in its becoming only.

Now it is clear that of two things in the same species one cannot *per se* cause the other's form as such, since it would then be the cause of its own form, since it is of the same nature in both. But it can be the cause of this form according as it is in matter—in other words, it may be the cause that this matter receives this form. And this is to be the cause of becoming, as when man begets man, and fire causes fire. Thus whenever a natural effect is such that it has an aptitude to receive from its active cause an impression specifically the same as in that active cause, then the becoming of the effect, but not its being, depends on the agent.

Sometimes, however, the effect does not have this aptitude to receive the impression of its cause in the same way as it exists in the agent, as may be seen clearly in all agents which do not produce an effect of the same species as themselves. Thus the heavenly bodies cause the generation of inferior bodies which differ from them in species. Such an agent can be the cause of a form as such, and not merely as existing in this matter. Consequently it is not merely the cause of becoming but also the cause of being.

Therefore as the becoming of a thing cannot continue when that action of the agent ceases which causes the becoming of the effect, so neither can the being of a thing continue after that action of the agent has ceased, which is the cause of the effect not only in becoming but also in being. This is why hot water retains heat after the cessation of the fire's action, while, on the contrary, the air does not continue to be lit up, even for a moment, when the sun ceases to act upon it, because the matter of water is susceptive of the fire's heat in the same way as it exists in the fire. Therefore if it were to be reduced to the perfect form of fire, it would retain that form always; but if it has the form of fire imperfectly in some rudimentary way, the heat will remain for a time only, by reason of the imperfect participation of the principle of heat. On the other hand, air is not of such a nature as to receive light in the same way as it exists in the sun, that is, it is not of such a nature as to receive the form of the sun, which is the principle of light. Therefore, since it has no root in the air, the light ceases with the action of the sun.

Now every creature may be compared to God, as the air is to the sun which enlightens it. For as the sun possesses light by its nature, and as the air is enlightened by sharing the sun's light, though it does not share in its nature, so God alone is Being by virtue of His own Essence, since His Essence is His Being. But every creature has being by participation, so that its essence is not its existence. Therefore, as Augustine says (*Gen. ad lit.* iv, 12):[1] "If the ruling power of God were withdrawn from His creatures, their nature would at once cease, and all nature would collapse." In the same work (viii, 12)[2] he says: "As the air becomes light by the presence of the sun, so is man enlightened by the presence of God, and in His absence returns at once to darkness."

Reply Obj. 1. Being follows per se from the form of a creature given the influence of the Divine action, just as light results from the diaphanous nature of the air, given the action of the sun. Therefore the potency to not-being in spiritual creatures and heavenly bodies is rather in God, Who can withdraw His influence, than in the form or matter of those creatures.

Reply Obj. 2. God cannot impart to a creature conservation in being after the cessation of the Divine influence, just as neither can He make it not to have received its being from Himself. For the creature needs to be preserved by God in so far as the being of an effect depends on the cause of its being. So that there is no comparison with an agent that is not the cause of being, but only of becoming.

Reply Obj. 3. This argument holds in regard to that preservation which consists in the removal of corruption; but all creatures do not need to be preserved thus, as stated above.

Reply Obj. 4. The preservation of things by God is not through any new action but through a continuation of that action by which He gives being, which action is without either motion or

[1] PL 34, 304.
[2] PL 34, 383.

time; so also the preservation of light in the air is by the continual influence of the sun.

ARTICLE 2. *Whether God Preserves Every Creature Immediately?*

We proceed thus to the Second Article: It would seem that God preserves every creature immediately.

Objection 1. For God creates and preserves things by the same action, as above stated (A. 1, Ans. 4). But God created all things immediately. Therefore He preserves all things immediately.

Obj. 2. Further, a thing is nearer to itself than to another. But it cannot be given to a creature to preserve itself; much less therefore can it be given to a creature to preserve another. Therefore God preserves all things without any intermediate cause preserving them.

Obj. 3. Further, an effect is kept in being by the cause, not only of its becoming, but also of its being. But all created causes do not seem to cause their effects except in their becoming, for they cause only by moving, as above stated (Q. XLV, A. 3). Therefore they do not cause so as to keep their effects in being.

On the contrary, A thing is kept in being by that which gives it being. But God gives being to things by means of certain intermediate causes. Therefore He also keeps things in being by means of certain causes.

I answer that, As stated above (A. 1), a thing keeps another in being in two ways. First, indirectly and accidentally, by removing or hindering the action of a corrupting cause. Secondly, directly and *per se*, by the fact that on it depends the other's being, as the being of the effect depends on the cause. And in both ways a created thing keeps another in being. For it is clear that even in corporeal things there are many causes which hinder the action of corrupting agents, and for that reason are called preservatives; just as salt preserves meat from putrefaction, and in like manner with many other things. It happens also that an effect depends on a creature as to its being. For when we have a series of ordered causes, it necessarily follows that while the effect depends first and principally on the first cause, it also depends in a secondary way on all the middle causes. Therefore the first cause is the principal cause of the preservation of the effect, which is to be referred to the middle causes in a secondary way; and all the more so, as the middle cause is higher and nearer to the first cause.

For this reason, even in things corporeal, the

preservation and persistence of things is ascribed to the higher causes. Thus the Philosopher says[1] that the first, namely the diurnal, movement is the cause of the continuation of things generated; but the second movement, which is from the zodiac, is the cause of diversity owing to generation and corruption. In like manner astrologers[2] ascribe to Saturn, the highest of the planets, those things which are permanent and fixed. So we conclude that God keeps certain things in being by means of certain causes.

Reply Obj. 1. God created all things immediately, but in the creation itself He established an order among things, so that some depend on others by which they are preserved in being, though He remains the principal cause of their preservation.

Reply Obj. 2. Since an effect is preserved by its proper cause on which it depends, so, just as no effect can be its own cause, though it can produce another effect, no effect can be endowed with the power of self-preservation, but only with the power of preserving another.

Reply Obj. 3. No created nature can be the cause of another, as regards the latter acquiring a new form, or disposition, except by virtue of some change; for the created nature acts always on something presupposed. But after causing the form or disposition in the effect, without any fresh change in the effect, the cause preserves that form or disposition; just as we must allow some change to have taken place in the air, when it is lit up anew, while the preservation of the light is without any further change in the air due to the presence of the source of light.

ARTICLE 3. *Whether God Can Annihilate Anything?*

We proceed thus to the Third Article: It would seem that God cannot annihilate anything.

Objection 1. For Augustine says (QQ. LXXXIII, qu. 21)[3] that "God is not the cause of anything tending to non-being." But He would be such a cause if He were to annihilate anything. Therefore He cannot annihilate anything.

Obj. 2. Further, by His goodness God is the cause why things exist, since, as Augustine says,[4] "Because God is good, we exist." But God can-

not not be good. Therefore He cannot cause things to cease to exist, which would be the case were He to annihilate anything.

Obj. 3. Further, if God were to annihilate anything it would be by His action. But this cannot be, because the term of every action is some being. Hence even the action of a corrupting cause has its term in something generated; for when one thing is generated another undergoes corruption. Therefore God cannot annihilate anything.

On the contrary, It is written (Jer. 10. 24): *Correct me, O Lord, but yet with judgment; and not in Thy fury, lest Thou bring me to nothing.*

I answer that, Some have held that God, in giving being to creatures, acted from natural necessity.[5] If this were true, God could not annihilate anything, since His nature cannot change. But, as we have said above (Q. XIX, A. 4), such an opinion is false, and absolutely contrary to the Catholic Faith, which confesses that God created things by a free will, according to Ps. 134. 6: *Whatsoever the Lord pleased, He hath done.* Therefore that God gives being to a creature depends on His will; nor does He preserve things in being otherwise than by continually pouring out being into them, as we have said. Therefore, just as before things existed, God was free not to give them being, and so not to make them, so after they have been made, He is free not to give them being, and thus they would cease to exist; and this would be to annihilate them.

Reply Obj. 1. Non-being has no cause *per se;* for nothing is a cause except in so far as it is a being, and a being essentially as such is a cause of being. Therefore God cannot cause a thing to tend to non-being, but a creature has this tendency of itself, since it is produced from nothing. But accidentally God can be the cause of things being reduced to nothing, by withdrawing His action from them.

Reply Obj. 2. God's goodness is the cause of things, not as though by natural necessity, because the Divine goodness does not depend on creatures, but on a free will. Therefore, as without prejudice to His goodness, He might not have produced things in being, so, without prejudice to His goodness He might not preserve things in being.

Reply Obj. 3. If God were to annihilate anything, this would not imply an action on God's part, but a mere cessation of His action.

[1] *Metaphysics*, XII, 6 (1072ᵃ9); cf. *Generation and Corruption*, II, 10 (336ᵃ31): cf. also Q. LXVIII, A. 2, Ans. 3).

[2] Cf. Averroes, *In Meta.*, XII, 44 (VIII, 327G); cf. Albumasar, in Duhem, *Le Systeme du Monde* (II, 376).

[3] PL 40, 16.

[4] *Christian Doctrine*, I, 32 (PL 34, 32).

[5] Cf. Q. XXV, A. 5.

ARTICLE 4. *Whether Anything Is Annihilated?*

We proceed thus to the Fourth Article: It would seem that something is annihilated.

Objection 1. For the end corresponds to the beginning. But in the beginning there was nothing but God. Therefore all things must tend to this end, that there shall be nothing but God. Therefore creatures will be reduced to nothing.

Obj. 2. Further, every creature has a finite power. But no finite power extends to the infinite. And so the Philosopher proves[1] that "a finite power cannot move in infinite time." Therefore a creature cannot last for an infinite duration, and so at some time it will be reduced to nothing.

Obj. 3. Further, forms and accidents have no matter as part of themselves. But at some time they cease to exist. Therefore they are reduced to nothing.

On the contrary, It is written (Eccles. 3. 14): *I have learned that all the works that God hath made continue for ever.*

I answer that, Some of those things which God does in creatures occur in accordance with the natural course of things; others happen miraculously, and not in accordance with the natural order, as will be explained (Q. CV, A. 6). Now whatever God wills to do according to the natural order of things may be observed from their nature; but those things which occur miraculously are ordered for the manifestation of grace, according to the Apostle, *To each one is given the manifestation of the Spirit, unto profit* (I Cor. 12. 7); and subsequently he mentions, among others, the working of miracles.

Now the nature of creatures shows that none of them is annihilated. For, either they are immaterial, and therefore have no potency to non-being; or they are material, and then they continue to exist, at least in matter, which is incorruptible, since it is the subject of generation and corruption. Moreover, the annihilation of things does not pertain to the manifestation of grace, since rather the power and goodness of God are manifested by the preservation of things in being. Therefore we must conclude by denying absolutely that anything at all will be annihilated.

Reply Obj. 1. That things were brought into being from a state of non-being clearly shows the power of Him Who made them. But that they should be reduced to nothing would obcure that manifestation, since the power of God is conspicuously shown in His preserving all things in being, according to the Apostle; *Upholding all things by the word of His power* (Heb. 1. 3).

Reply Obj. 2. A creature's potency to being is merely receptive; the active power belongs to God Himself, from Whom being is derived. Therefore the infinite duration of things is a consequence of the infinity of the Divine power. To some things, however, is given a determinate power of duration for a certain time, so far as they may be hindered from receiving the influx of being which comes from Him by some contrary agent whose finite power they cannot resist for an infinite but only for a fixed time. So things which have no contrary, although they have a finite power, continue to exist for ever.

Reply Obj. 3. Forms and accidents are not complete beings, since they do not subsist, but each one of them is something of a being and so is called a being, because something is by it. Yet so far as their mode of existence is concerned, they are not entirely reduced to nothingness; not that any part of them survives, but that they remain in the potency of the matter, or of the subject.

QUESTION CV

OF THE CHANGE OF CREATURES BY GOD

(In Eight Articles)

WE now consider the second effect of the Divine government, that is, the change of creatures; and first, the change of creatures by God; secondly, the change of one creature by another (Q. CVI).

Under the first head there are eight points of inquiry: (1) Whether God can move immediately the matter to the form? (2) Whether He can immediately move a body? (3) Whether He can move the intellect? (4) Whether He can move the will? (5) Whether God works in every worker? (6) Whether He can do anything outside the order given to things? (7) Whether all that God does is miraculous? (8) Of the diversity of miracles.

ARTICLE 1. *Whether God Can Move the Matter Immediately to the Form?*

We proceed thus to the First Article: It would seem that God cannot move the matter immediately to receive the form.

Objection 1. For, as the Philosopher proves,[2] nothing can bring a form into any particular matter except that form which is in matter, because, like begets like. But God is not a form in

[1] *Physics,* VIII, 10 (266[a]12).

[2] *Metaphysics,* VII, 8 (1033[b]23).

matter. Therefore He cannot cause a form in matter.

Obj. 2. Further, any agent inclined to several effects will produce none of them, unless it is determined to a particular one by some other cause; for, as the Philosopher says,[1] a universal opinion does not move the mind except by means of some particular apprehension. But the Divine power is the universal cause of all things. Therefore it cannot produce any particular form except by means of a particular agent.

Obj. 3. As universal being depends on the first universal cause, so determinate being depends on determinate particular causes, as we have seen above (Q. CIV, A. 2). But the determinate being of a particular thing is from its own form. Therefore the forms of things are produced by God only by means of particular causes.

On the contrary, It is written (Gen. 2. 7): *God formed man of the slime of the earth.*

I answer that, God can move matter immediately to a form, because a being in passive potency can be reduced to act by the active power which extends over that potency. Therefore, since the Divine power extends over matter, as produced by God, it can be reduced to act by the Divine power. And this is what is meant by matter being moved to a form, for a form is nothing else but the act of matter.

Reply Obj. 1. An effect is likened to the active cause in two ways. First, according to the same species; as man is generated by man, and fire by fire. Secondly, by being virtually contained in the cause; as the form of the effect is virtually contained in its cause. Thus animals produced by putrefaction, and plants, and minerals are like the sun and stars, by whose power they are produced. In this way the effect is like its active cause as regards all that over which the power of that cause extends. Now the power of God extends to both matter and form, as we have said above (Q. XIV, A. 11; Q. XLIV, A. 2). Therefore if a composite thing be produced, it is likened to God by way of a virtual inclusion; and it is likened to the composite generator by a likeness of species. Therefore just as the composite generator can move matter to a form by generating a composite thing like itself, so also can God. But no other form not existing in matter can do this, because the power of no other separate substance extends over matter. Hence angels and demons operate on visible matter not by imprinting forms in matter, but by making use of corporeal elements.

[1] *Soul,* III, 11 (434ª16).

Reply Obj. 2. This argument would hold if God were to act of natural necessity. But since He acts by His will and intellect, which knows the particular and not only the universal natures of all forms, it follows that He can imprint this or that form on matter in a determinate way.

Reply Obj. 3. The fact that secondary causes are ordered to determinate effects is due to God. Therefore since God orders other causes to determinate effects He can also produce determinate effects by Himself without any other cause.

ARTICLE 2. *Whether God Can Move a Body Immediately?*

We proceed thus to the Second Article: It would seem that God cannot move a body immediately.

Objection 1. For as "the mover and the moved must exist simultaneously," as the Philosopher says,[2] it follows that there must be some contact between the mover and the moved. But there can be no contact between God and a body, for Dionysius says (*Div. Nom.* i):[3] "There is no contact with God." Therefore God cannot move a body immediately.

Obj. 2. Further, God is the mover unmoved. But such also is the desirable object when apprehended. Therefore God moves as the object of desire and apprehension. But He cannot be apprehended except by the intellect, which is neither a body nor a corporeal power. Therefore God cannot move a body immediately.

Obj. 3. Further, the Philosopher proves[4] that an infinite power moves instantaneously. But it is impossible for a body to be moved in one instant; for since every movement is between opposites, it follows that two opposites would exist at once in the same subject, which is impossible. Therefore a body cannot be moved immediately by an infinite power. But God's power is infinite, as we have explained above (Q. XXV, A. 2). Therefore God cannot move a body immediately.

On the contrary, God produced the works of the six days immediately, among which is included the movements of bodies, as is clear from Gen. 1. 9: *Let the waters be gathered together into one place.* Therefore God can move a body immediately.

I answer that, It is erroneous to say that God cannot Himself produce all the determinate ef-

[2] *Physics,* VII, 2 (243ª4).
[3] Sect. 5 (PG 3, 593).
[4] *Physics,* VIII, 10 (266ª31).

fects which are produced by any created cause.[1] Therefore, since bodies are moved immediately by created causes, we cannot possibly doubt that God can move immediately any bodies whatever. This indeed follows from what is above stated (A. I). For every movement of any body whatever either results from a form, as the movements of things heavy and light result from the form which they have from their generating cause, for which reason the generator is called the mover, or else tends to a form, as heating tends to the form of heat. Now it belongs to the same cause, to imprint a form, to dispose to that form, and to give the movement which results from that form; for fire not only generates fire, but it also heats and moves things upwards. Therefore, as God can imprint form immediately in matter, it follows that He can move any body whatever in respect of any movement whatever.

Reply Obj. 1. There are two kinds of contact: corporeal contact, when two bodies touch each other; and virtual contact, as the cause of sadness is said to touch the one made sad. According to the first kind of contact, God, since He is incorporeal, neither touches, nor is touched. But according to virtual contact He touches creatures by moving them, but He is not touched, because the natural power of no creature can reach up to Him. Thus did Dionysius understand the words, "There is no contact with God"; that is, in such a way that God Himself would be touched.

Reply Obj. 2. God moves as the object of desire and understanding. But it does not follow that He always moves as being desired and understood by that which is moved, but as being desired and known by Himself. For He does all things for His own goodness.

Reply Obj. 3. The Philosopher intends to prove[2] that the power of the first mover is not a power of size, by the following argument. The power of the first mover is infinite (which he proves from the fact that the first mover can move in infinite time).[3] Now an infinite power, if it were a power of size, would move without time, which is impossible; therefore the infinite power of the first mover must be in something which is not measured by size. From this it is clear that for a body to be moved without time can only be the result of an infinite power. The

reason is that every power which has size moves in its entirety, since it moves by the necessity of its nature. But an infinite power surpasses out of all proportion any finite power. Now the greater the power of the mover, the greater is the speed of the movement. Therefore, since a finite power moves in a determinate time, it follows that an infinite power does not move in any time, for between one time and any other time there is some proportion. On the other hand, a power which is without size is the power of an intelligent being, which operates in its effects according to what is fitting to them; and therefore, since it cannot be fitting for a body to be moved without time, it does not follow that it moves without time.

ARTICLE 3. *Whether God Moves the Created Intellect Immediately?*

We proceed thus to the Third Article: It would seem that God does not immediately move the created intellect.

Objection 1. For the action of the intellect proceeds from that in which it resides, since it does not pass into external matter, as stated in the *Metaphysics*.[4] But the action of what is moved by another does not proceed from that in which it is, but from the mover. Therefore the intellect is not moved by another; and so apparently God cannot move the created intellect.

Obj. 2. Further, anything which has in itself a sufficient principle of movement is not moved by another. But the movement of the intellect is its act of understanding, in the sense in which we say that to understand or to feel is a kind of movement, as the Philosopher says.[5] But the intellectual light which is natural to the soul is a sufficient principle of understanding. Therefore it is not moved by another.

Obj. 3. Further, as the senses are moved by the sensible, so the intellect is moved by the intelligible. But God is not intelligible to us, and exceeds the capacity of our intellect. Therefore God cannot move our intellect.

On the contrary, The teacher moves the intellect of the one taught. But it is written (Ps. 93. 10) that God *teaches man knowledge.* Therefore God moves the human intellect.

I answer that, As in corporeal movement that is called the mover which gives the form that is the principle of movement, so that is said to move the intellect which is the cause of the form that is the principle of the intellectual op-

---

[1] Cf. St. Thomas, *Op.* X, A. I, *Op.* XI, A. 13. Cf. also in Chenu, *Milanges Mandonnet* (I, 91) and Destrez, *Mélanges Mandonnet* (I, 103).

[2] *Physics,* VIII, 10 (266ᵃ10).

[3] *Ibid.* (267ᵇ25).

[4] Aristotle, IX, 8 (1050ᵃ36).

[5] *Soul,* III, 7 (431ᵃ6).

eration, called the movement of the intellect. Now there is a twofold principle of intellectual operation in the intelligent being, one which is the intellectual power itself, which principle exists also in the one who understands in potentiality, and the other which is the principle of actual understanding, namely, the likeness of the thing understood in the one who understands. So a thing is said to move the intellect, whether it gives to him who understands the power of understanding, or impresses on him the likeness of the thing understood.

Now God moves the created intellect in both ways. For He is the First immaterial Being, and since intellectuality is a result of immateriality, it follows that He is the First intelligent Being. Therefore since in each order the first is the cause of all that follows, we must conclude that from Him proceeds all intellectual power. In like manner, since He is the First Being, and all other beings pre-exist in Him as in their First Cause, it follows that they exist intelligibly in Him, after the mode of His own Nature. For as the intelligible types of everything exist first of all in God, and are derived from Him by other intellects in order that these may actually understand, so also are they derived by creatures that they may subsist. Therefore God moves the created intellect in this way, since He gives it the power of understanding, whether natural, or superadded, and impresses on the created intellect the intelligible species, and maintains and preserves both power and species in being.

Reply Obj. 1. The intellectual operation is performed by the intellect in which it exists, as by a secondary cause; but it proceeds from God as from its first cause. For the power to understand is given by Him to the one who understands.

Reply Obj. 2. The intellectual light together with the likeness of the thing understood is a sufficient principle of understanding, but it is a secondary principle, and depends upon the First Principle.

Reply Obj. 3. The intelligible moves our intellect, in so far as, in a certain way, it impresses on it its own likeness, by means of which the intellect is able to understand it. But the likenesses which God impresses on the created intellect are not sufficient to enable the created intellect to understand Him through His Essence, as we have seen above (Q. XII, A. 2; Q. LVI, A. 3). Hence He moves the created intellect, and yet He cannot be intelligible to it, as we have explained (Q. XII, A. 4).

ARTICLE 4. *Whether God Can Move the Created Will?*

We proceed thus to the Fourth Article: It would seem that God cannot move the created will.

Objection 1. For whatever is moved from without, is forced. But the will cannot be forced. Therefore it is not moved from without. And therefore cannot be moved by God.

Obj. 2. Further, God cannot make contradictories to be true at the same time. But this would follow if He moved the will, for to be voluntarily moved means to be moved from within, and not by another. Therefore God cannot move the will.

Obj. 3. Further, movement is attributed to the mover rather than to the one moved. Therefore homicide is not ascribed to the stone, but to the thrower. Therefore, if God moves the will, it follows that voluntary actions are not imputed to man for reward or blame. But this is false. Therefore God does not move the will.

On the contrary, It is written (Phil. 2. 13) : *It is God who worketh in us* (Vulgate,—*you*) *both to will and to accomplish.*

I answer that, As the intellect is moved by the object and by the giver of the power of understanding, as stated above (A. 3), so is the will moved by its object, which is the good, and by Him who creates the power of willing. Now the will can be moved by some good as its object, but sufficiently and efficaciously by God alone. For nothing can move a movable thing sufficiently unless the active power of the mover surpasses or at least equals the passive power of the thing movable. Now the passive power of the will extends to the universal good, for its object is the universal good, just as the object of the intellect is universal being. But every created good is some particular good. God alone is the universal good. Therefore He alone fills the capacity of the will, and moves it sufficiently as its object. In like manner the power of willing is caused by God alone. For to will is nothing but to be inclined towards the object of the will, which is universal good. But to incline towards the universal good belongs to the First Mover, to Whom the ultimate end is proportioned; just as in human affairs to him that presides over the community belongs the directing of his subjects to the common good. Therefore in both ways it belongs to God to move the will, but especially in the second way by inclining it in an interior way.

Reply Obj. 1. A thing moved by another is

forced if moved against its own inclination; but if it is moved by another giving to it its own inclination, it is not forced. For example, when a heavy body is made to move downwards by that which produced it, it is not forced. In like manner God, while moving the will, does not force it, because He gives the will its own inclination.

Reply Obj. 2. To be moved voluntarily is to be moved from within, that is, by an interior principle. Yet this interior principle may be caused by an exterior principle, and so to be moved from within is not contrary to being moved by another.

Reply Obj. 3. If the will were so moved by another as in no way to be moved from within itself, the act of the will would not be held accountable for reward or blame. But since its being moved by another does not prevent its being moved from within itself, as we have stated (*ad* 2), it does not thereby forfeit the reason for merit or demerit.

ARTICLE 5. *Whether God Works in Every Agent?*

We proceed thus to the Fifth Article: It would seem that God does not work in every agent.

Objection 1. For we must not attribute any insufficiency to God. If therefore God works in every agent, He works sufficiently in each one. Hence it would be superfluous for the created agent to work at all.

Obj. 2. Further, the same work cannot proceed at the same time from two sources, just as neither one and the same movement can belong to two movable things. Therefore if the creature's operation is from God operating in the creature, it cannot at the same time proceed from the creature. And so no creature works at all.

Obj. 3. Further, the maker is the cause of the operation of the thing made, as giving it the form by which it operates. Therefore, if God is the cause of the operation of things made by Him, this would be in so far as He gives them the power of operating. But this is in the beginning, when He makes them. Thus it seems that God does not operate any further in the operating creature.

On the contrary, It is written (Isa. 26. 12): *Lord, Thou hast wrought all our works in* (Vulgate,—*for*) *us.*

I answer that, Some have understood God to work in every agent in such a way that no created power has any effect in things, but that God alone is the immediate cause of everything wrought;[1] for instance, that it is not fire that gives heat, but God in the fire, and so forth. But this is impossible. First, because the order of cause and effect would be taken away from created things. This would imply lack of power in the Creator, for it is due to the power of the cause that it bestows active power on its effect. Secondly, because the active powers which are seen to exist in things would be bestowed on things to no purpose if these wrought nothing through them. Indeed, all things created would seem, in a way, to be purposeless if they lacked an operation proper to them, since the purpose of everything is its operation. For the less perfect is always for the sake of the more perfect. And consequently as the matter is for the sake of the form, so the form which is the first act, is for the sake of its operation, which is the second act; and thus operation is the end of the creature. We must therefore understand that God works in things in such a manner that things nevertheless have their proper operation.

In order to make this clear, we must observe that although there are four kinds of causes, matter is not a principle of action, but is the subject that receives the effect of action. On the other hand, the end, the agent, and the form, are principles of action, but in a certain order. For the first principle of action is the end, which moves the agent; the second is the agent; the third is the form of that which the agent applies to action (although the agent also acts through its own form), as may be clearly seen in things made by art. For the craftsman is moved to action by the end, which is the thing wrought, for instance a chest or a bed; and applies to action the axe which cuts through its being sharp.

Thus then does God work in every worker, according to these three things. First as an end. For since every operation is for the sake of some good, real or apparent, and since nothing is good either really or apparently, except in as far as it participates in a likeness to the Supreme Good, which is God, it follows that God Himself is the cause of every operation as its end. Again it is to be observed that where there are several agents in order, the second always acts in virtue of the first, for the first agent moves the second to act. And thus all agents act in virtue of God Himself, and in this way He is the cause of action in every agent. Thirdly, we must observe that God not only moves things to operate, by applying as it were their forms and powers to operation, just as the workman ap-

---

[1] Cf. Q. XLV, A. 8; Q. CXV, A. 1. Cf. also Averroes, *In Meta.,* IX, 7 (VIII, 231H); XII, 18 (VIII, 305F).

plies the axe to cut (who nevertheless oftentimes does not give the axe its form), but He also gives created agents their forms and preserves them in being. Therefore He is the cause of action not only by giving the form which is the principle of action, as the generator is said to be the cause of movement in things heavy and light, but also as preserving the forms and powers of things, just as the sun is said to be the cause of the manifestation of colours, since it gives and preserves the light by which colours are made manifest. And since the form of a thing is within the thing, and all the more as it approaches nearer to the First and Universal Cause, and because in all things God Himself is properly the cause of universal being which is innermost in all things, it follows that in all things God works inwardly. For this reason in Holy Scripture the operations of nature are attributed to God as operating in nature, according to Job 10. 11: *Thou hast clothed me with skin and flesh: Thou hast put me together with bones and sinews.*

Reply Obj. 1. God works sufficiently in things as First Agent, but it does not follow from this that the operation of secondary agents is superfluous.

Reply Obj. 2. One action does not proceed from two agents of the same order. But nothing hinders the same action from proceeding from a primary and a secondary agent.

Reply Obj. 3. God not only gives things their form, but He also preserves them in being, and applies them to act, and is moreover the end of every action, as explained above.

ARTICLE 6. *Whether God Can Do Anything Outside the Established Order of Things?*

We proceed thus to the Sixth Article: It would seem that God cannot do anything outside the established order of nature.

Objection 1. For Augustine (*Contra Faust.* xxvi, 3)[1] says: "God the Maker and Creator of each nature, does nothing against nature." But that which is outside the natural order seems to be against nature. Therefore God can do nothing outside the natural order.

Obj. 2. Further, as the order of justice is from God, so is the order of nature. But God cannot do anything outside the order of justice, for then He would do something unjust. Therefore He cannot do anything outside the established order of things.

Obj. 3. Further, God established the order of nature. Therefore if God does anything outside

[1] PL 42, 480.

the order of nature, it would seem that He is changeable, which cannot be said.

On the contrary, Augustine says (*Contra Faust.* xxvi, *ibid.*):[2] "God sometimes does things which are contrary to the ordinary course of nature."

I answer that, From each cause there results a certain order to its effects, since every cause is a principle. And so, according to the multiplicity of causes, there results a multiplicity of orders, subjected one to the other, as cause is subjected to cause. And so a higher cause is not subjected to a cause of a lower order, but conversely. An example of this may be seen in human affairs. On the father of a family depends the order of the household, which order is contained in the order of the city, which order again depends on the ruler of the city, while this last order depends on that of the king, by whom the whole kingdom is ordered.

If therefore we consider the order of things depending on the first cause, God cannot do anything against this order; for, if He did so, He would act against His foreknowledge, or His will, or His goodness. But if we consider the order of things depending on any secondary cause, then God can do something outside this order; for He is not subject to the order of secondary causes, but, on the contrary, this order is subject to Him, as proceeding from Him, not by a natural necessity, but by the choice of His own will, for He could have created another order of things. Therefore God can do something outside this order created by Him, when He chooses, for instance by producing the effects of secondary causes without them, or by producing certain effects to which secondary causes do not extend. So Augustine says (*Contra Faust.* xxvi, *ibid.*): "God acts against the wonted course of nature, but by no means does He act against the supreme law, because He does not act against Himself."

Reply Obj. 1. In natural things something may happen outside this natural order in two ways. It may happen by the action of an agent which did not give them their natural inclination; as, for example, when a man moves upwards a heavy body, which does not owe to him its natural inclination to move downwards; and that would be against nature. It may also happen by the action of the agent on whom the natural inclination depends; and this is not against nature, as is clear in the ebb and flow of the tide, which is not against nature, although it is against the natural movement of water in a downward direction, for it is owing to the influ-

[2] PL 42, 481.

ence of a heavenly body, on which the natural inclination of lower bodies depends. Therefore since the order of nature is given to things by God, if He does anything outside this order, it is not against nature. And so Augustine says (*ibid.*): "That is natural to each thing which is caused by Him from Whom is all measure, number, and order in nature."

Reply Obj. 2. The order of justice arises by relation to the First Cause, Who is the rule of all justice; and therefore God can do nothing against this order.

Reply Obj. 3. God fixed a certain order in things in such a way that at the same time He reserved to Himself whatever He intended to do otherwise than by a particular cause. So when He acts outside this order, He does not change.

ARTICLE 7. *Whether Whatever God Does Outside the Natural Order Is Miraculous?*

We proceed thus to the Seventh Article: It would seem that not everything which God does outside the natural order of things is miraculous.

Objection 1. For the creation of the world, and of souls, and the justification of the unrighteous, are done by God outside the natural order, for they are not accomplished by the action of any natural cause. Yet these things are not called miracles. Therefore not everything that God does outside the natural order is a miracle.

Obj. 2. Further, a miracle is "something difficult, which seldom occurs, surpassing the power of nature, and going so far beyond our hopes as to compel our astonishment."[1] But some things outside the order of nature are not difficult, for they occur in small things, such as the recovery of jewels and the healing of the sick. Nor are they of rare occurrence, since they happen frequently, as when the sick were placed in the streets, to be healed by the shadow of Peter (Acts 5. 15). Nor do they surpass the power of nature, as when people are cured of a fever. Nor are they beyond our hopes, since we all hope for the resurrection of the dead, which nevertheless will be outside the course of nature. Therefore not all things that are outside the course of nature are miraculous.

Obj. 3. Further, the word miracle is derived from admiration. Now admiration concerns things manifest to the senses. But sometimes things happen outside the order of nature, which are not manifest to the senses, as when the Apostles were endowed with knowledge without

studying or being taught. Therefore not everything that occurs outside the order of nature is miraculous.

On the contrary, Augustine says (*Contra Faust.* xxvi, 3):[2] "Where God does anything against that order of nature which we know and are accustomed to observe, we call it a miracle."

I answer that, The word miracle is derived from admiration, which arises when an effect is manifest, and its cause is hidden, as when a man sees an eclipse of the sun without knowing its cause, as the Philosopher says in the beginning of his *Metaphysics*.[3] Now the cause of an effect which makes its appearance may be known to one, but unknown to others. And so a thing is wonderful to one man, and not at all to others; as an eclipse is to a rustic, but not to an astronomer. Now a miracle is called so as being full of wonder, and as having a cause absolutely hidden from all; and this cause is God. Therefore those things which God does outside those causes which we know, are called miracles.

Reply Obj. 1. Creation, and the justification of the unrighteous, though done by God alone, are not, properly speaking, miracles, because they are not of a nature to proceed from any other cause. So they do not occur outside the order of nature, since they do not belong to that order.

Reply Obj. 2. A difficult thing is called a miracle not on account of the excellence of the thing in which it is done, but because it surpasses the power of nature; likewise a thing is called unusual not because it does not often happen, but because it is outside the usual natural course of things. Furthermore, a thing is said to be above the power of nature not only by reason of the substance of the thing done, but also on account of the manner and order in which it is done. Again, a miracle is said to go beyond the hope of nature, not beyond the hope of grace, which hope comes from faith, by which we believe in the future resurrection.

Reply Obj. 3. The knowledge of the Apostles, although not manifest in itself, yet was made manifest in its effect, from which it was shown to be wonderful.

ARTICLE 8. *Whether One Miracle Is Greater Than Another?*

We proceed thus to the Eighth Article: It would seem that one miracle is not greater than another.

---

[1] Augustine, *De utilitate credendi*, XVI (PL 42, 90).   [2] PL 42, 481.   [3] I, 2 (982ᵇ16).

Objection 1. For Augustine says (*Epist. ad Volusian.* cxxxvii):[1] "In miraculous deeds, the whole measure of the deed is the power of the doer." But by the same power of God all miracles are done. Therefore one miracle is not greater than another.

Obj. 2. Further, the power of God is infinite. But the infinite exceeds the finite beyond all proportion; and therefore no more reason exists to wonder at one of its effects than at another. Therefore one miracle is not greater than another.

On the contrary, The Lord says, speaking of miraculous works (John 14. 12): *The works that I do, he also shall do, and greater than these shall he do.*

I answer that, Nothing is called a miracle by comparison with the Divine Power, because no action is of any account compared with the power of God, according to Isa. 40. 15: *Behold the Gentiles are as a drop from a bucket, and are counted as the smallest grain of a balance.* But a thing is called a miracle by comparison with the power of nature which it surpasses. So the more the power of nature is surpassed, the greater is the miracle.

Now the power of nature is surpassed in three ways. First, in the substance of the deed, for instance, if two bodies occupy the same place, or if the sun goes backwards, or if a human body is glorified. Nature is absolutely unable to do such things, and these hold the highest rank among miracles. Secondly, a thing surpasses the power of nature not in the deed, but in that in which it is done, such as the raising of the dead, and giving sight to the blind, and the like. For nature can give life, but not to the dead, and nature can give sight, but not to the blind. And such hold the second rank in miracles. Thirdly, a thing surpasses nature's power in the measure and order in which it is done, as when a man is cured of a fever suddenly, without treatment or the usual process of nature; or as when the air is suddenly condensed into rain, by Divine power without a natural cause, as occurred at the prayers of Samuel and Elias.[2] And these hold the lowest place in miracles. Moreover, each of these kinds has various degrees, according to the different ways in which the power of nature is surpassed.

From this it is clear how to *reply to the objections,* arguing as they do from the Divine power.

[1] Chap. 2 (PL 33, 519).
[2] II Kings, 12.18; III Kings, 18.44.

QUESTION CVI

How one creature moves another

(In Four Articles)

WE next consider how one creature moves another. This consideration will be threefold. (1) How the angels who are purely spiritual creatures move; (2) How bodies move (Q. CXV); (3) How man moves, who is composed of a spiritual and a corporeal nature (Q. CXVII).

Concerning the first point, there are three things to be considered: (1) How an angel acts on an angel; (2) How an angel acts on a corporeal nature (Q. CX); (3) How an angel acts on man (Q. CXI).

The first of these raises the question of the enlightenment and speech of the angels (Q. CVII); and of their mutual ordering, both of the good and of the bad angels (Q. CVIII; Q. CIX).

Concerning their enlightenment there are four points of inquiry: (1) Whether one angel moves the intellect of another by enlightenment? (2) Whether one angel moves the will of another? (3) Whether an inferior angel can enlighten a superior angel? (4) Whether a superior angel enlightens an inferior angel in all that he knows himself?

ARTICLE 1. *Whether One Angel Enlightens Another?*

We proceed thus to the First Article: It would seem that one angel does not enlighten another.

Objection 1. For the angels possess now the same Happiness which we hope to obtain. But one man will not then enlighten another, according to Jer. 31. 34: *They shall teach no more every man his neighbour, and every man his brother.* Therefore neither does an angel enlighten another now.

Obj. 2. Further, light in the angels is threefold: of nature, of grace, and of glory. But an angel is enlightened in the light of nature, by the Creator; in the light of grace, by the Justifier; in the light of glory by the Beatifier; all of which comes from God. Therefore one angel does not enlighten another.

Obj. 3. Further, light is a form in the mind. But the rational mind is "informed by God alone, without created intervention," as Augustine says (QQ. LXXXIII, *qu.* 51).[3] Therefore one angel does not enlighten the mind of another.

On the contrary, Dionysius says (*Cæl. Hier.* viii)[4] that "the angels of the second hierarchy

[3] PL 40, 33.   [4] Sect. 1 (PG 3, 240).

are cleansed, enlightened and perfected by the angels of the first hierarchy."

I answer that, One angel enlightens another. To make this clear, we must observe that intellectual light is nothing else than a manifestation of truth, according to Eph. 5. 13: *All that is made manifest is light.* Hence to enlighten means nothing else but to communicate to others the manifestation of the known truth; according to the Apostle (Eph. 3. 8): *To me the least of all the saints is given this grace . . . to enlighten all men, that they may see what is the dispensation of the mystery which hath been hidden from eternity in God.* Therefore one angel is said to enlighten another by manifesting the truth which he knows himself. Hence Dionysius says (*Cæl. Hier.* vii):[1] "Theologians plainly show that the orders of the heavenly beings are taught Divine science by the higher minds."

Now since two things co-operate in understanding, as we have said (Q. CV, A. 3), namely, the intellectual power, and the likeness of the thing understood, and in both of these one angel can announce the known truth to another. First, by strengthening his intellectual power. For just as the power of an imperfect body is strengthened by the neighbourhood of a more perfect body,—for instance, the less hot is made hotter by the presence of what is hotter, so the intellectual power of an inferior angel is strengthened by the superior angel turning to him. For in spiritual things, for one thing to turn to another corresponds to neighbourhood in corporeal things. Secondly, one angel manifests the truth to another as regards the likeness of the thing understood. For the superior angel receives the knowledge of truth by a kind of universal conception, which the inferior angel's intellect is not sufficiently powerful to seize, for it is natural to him to receive truth in a more particular manner. Therefore the superior angel distinguishes, in a way, the truth which he conceives universally, so that it can be grasped by the inferior angel; and thus he proposes it to his knowledge. Thus it is with us that the teacher, in order to adapt himself to others, divides into many points the knowledge which he possesses in the universal. This is thus expressed by Dionysius (*Cæl. Hier.* xv):[2] "Every intellectual substance with provident power divides and multiplies the uniform knowledge bestowed on it by one nearer to God, so as to lead its inferiors upwards by analogy."

Reply Obj. 1. All the angels, both inferior and superior, see the Essence of God immediately, and in this respect one does not teach another. It is of this truth that the prophet speaks; and so he adds: *They shall teach no more every man his brother, saying: Know the Lord: for all shall know Me, from the least of them even to the greatest.* But all the types of the Divine works, which are known in God as in their cause, God knows in Himself, because He comprehends Himself; but of others who see God, each one knows the more types the more perfectly he sees God. Hence a superior angel knows more about the types of the Divine works than an inferior angel, and concerning these the former enlightens the latter; and as to this Dionysius says (*Div. Nom.* iv),[3] that the angels "are enlightened by the types of existing things."

Reply Obj. 2. An angel does not enlighten another by giving him the light of nature, grace, or glory, but by strengthening his natural light, and by manifesting to him the truth of things pertaining to the state of nature, of grace, and of glory, as explained above.

Reply Obj. 3. The rational mind is formed immediately by God, either as the image from the exemplar, because it is made to the image of God alone; or as the subject by the ultimate perfecting form. For the created mind is always considered to be unformed, unless it adheres to the first truth, while other kinds of enlightenment that proceed from man or angel are, as it were, dispositions to this ultimate form.

ARTICLE 2. *Whether One Angel Moves Another Angel's Will?*

We proceed thus to the Second Article: It would seem that one angel can move another angel's will.

Objection 1. Because, according to Dionysius,[4] as one angel enlightens another, so does he cleanse and perfect another. But cleansing and perfecting seem to belong to the will, for the former seems to point to the stain of sin which pertains to the will, while to be perfected is to obtain an end, which is the object of the will. Therefore an angel can move another angel's will.

Obj. 2. Further, as Dionysius says (*Cæl. Hier.* vii)[5] that the names of the angels designate their properties. Now the Seraphim are called so because they kindle or give heat, and this is by love which belongs to the will. Therefore one angel moves another angel's will.

[1] Sect. 3 (PG 3, 209).
[2] Sect. 3 (PG 3, 332).
[3] Sect. 1 (PG 3, 693). [4] *Cæl. Hier.*, VIII, 1 (PG 3, 240).
[5] Sect. 1 (PG 3, 205).

Obj. 3. Further, the Philosopher says[1] that the higher appetite moves the lower. But as the intellect of the superior angel is higher, so also is his will. It seems, therefore, that the superior angel can change the will of another angel.

On the contrary, To him it belongs to change the will to whom it belongs to bestow justice, for justice is the rightness of the will. But God alone bestows justice. Therefore one angel cannot change another angel's will.

I answer that, As was said above (Q. CV, A. 4), the will is changed in two ways, on the part of the object, and on the part of the power. On the part of the object, both the good itself which is the object of the will moves the will, as the desirable object moves the appetite, and he who points out the object, as, for instance, one who proves something to be good. But as we have said above (*ibid.*), other goods in a measure incline the will, yet nothing sufficiently moves the will save the universal good, and that is God. And this good He alone shows, that it may be seen in its essence by the blessed, Who, when Moses asked: *Show me Thy glory,* answered: *I will show thee all good* (Exod. 33. 18, 19). Therefore an angel does not move the will sufficiently, either as the object or as showing the object. But he inclines the will as something lovable, and as manifesting some created good ordered to God's goodness. And thus he can incline the will to the love of the creature or of God, by way of persuasion.

But on the part of the power the will cannot be moved at all save by God. For the operation of the will is a certain inclination of the willer to the thing willed. And He alone can change this inclination Who bestowed on the creature the power to will; just as that agent alone can change the natural inclination which can give the power which the natural inclination follows. Now God alone gave to the creature the power to will, because He alone is the author of the intellectual nature. Therefore an angel cannot move another angel's will.

Reply Obj. 1. Cleansing and perfecting are to be understood according to the mode of enlightenment. And since God enlightens by changing the intellect and will, He cleanses by removing defects of intellect and will, and perfects according to the end of the intellect and will. But the enlightenment caused by an angel concerns the intellect, as explained above (A. 1). Therefore an angel is to be understood as cleansing from the defect of nescience in the intellect, and as perfecting by the achievement of the end

of the intellect, and this is the knowledge of truth. Thus Dionysius says (*Eccl. Hier.* vi)[2] that "in the heavenly hierarchy the cleansing of the inferior essence is an enlightening on things unknown, that leads them to more perfect knowledge." For instance, we might say that corporeal sight is cleansed by the removal of darkness, enlightened by the diffusion of light, and perfected by being brought to the knowledge of the coloured thing.

Reply Obj. 2. One angel can induce another to love God by persuasion, as explained above.

Reply Obj. 3. The Philosopher speaks of the lower sensitive appetite, which can be moved by the superior intellectual appetite, because it belongs to the same nature of the soul, and because the inferior appetite is a power in a corporeal organ. But this does not apply to the angels.

ARTICLE 3. *Whether an Inferior Angel Can Enlighten a Superior Angel?*

We proceed thus to the Third Article: It would seem that an inferior angel can enlighten a superior angel.

Objection 1. For the ecclesiastical hierarchy is derived from, and represents the heavenly hierarchy; and hence the heavenly Jerusalem is called *our mother* (Gal. 4. 26). But in the Church even superiors are enlightened and taught by their inferiors, as the Apostle says (I Cor. 14. 31): *You may all prophesy one by one, that all may learn and all may be exhorted.* Therefore, likewise in the heavenly hierarchy the superiors can be enlightened by inferiors.

Obj. 2. Further, as the order of corporeal substances depends on the will of God, so also does the order of spiritual substances. But, as was said above (Q. CV, A. 6), God sometimes acts outside the order of corporeal substances. Therefore he also sometimes acts outside the order of spiritual substances, by enlightening inferiors otherwise than through their superiors. Therefore in that way the inferiors enlightened by God can enlighten superiors.

Obj. 3. Further, one angel enlightens the other to whom he turns, as was above explained (A. 1). But since this turning to another is voluntary, the highest angel can turn to the lowest, passing over the others. Therefore he can enlighten him immediately, and thus the latter can enlighten his superiors.

On the contrary, Dionysius says that "this is the Divine unalterable law, that inferior things

[1] *Soul,* III, 11 (434ª13).   [2] Part III (PG 3, 537).

are led to God by the superior" (*Cæl. Hier.* iv; *Eccl. Hier.* v).[1]

I answer that, The inferior angels never enlighten the superior, but are always enlightened by them. The reason is, because, as explained above (Q. CV, A. 6), one order is under another, as cause is under cause; and hence as cause is ordered to cause, so is order to order. Therefore there is no incongruity if at times something is done outside the order of the inferior cause to be ordered to the superior cause, as in human affairs the command of the lesser ruler is passed over from obedience to the prince. So it happens that God works miraculously outside the order of corporeal nature in order that men may be ordered to the knowledge of Him. But the passing over of the order that is due to spiritual substances in no way pertains to the ordering of men to God, since the angelic operations are not made known to us, as are the operations of sensible bodies. Thus the order which belongs to spiritual substances is never passed over by God, so that the inferiors are always moved by the superior, and not conversely.

Reply Obj. 1. The ecclesiastical hierarchy imitates the heavenly in some degree, but not by a perfect likeness. For in the heavenly hierarchy the entire principle of order is nearness to God, so that those who are the nearer to God are the more sublime in degree, and more clear in knowledge; and on that account the superiors are never enlightened by the inferiors. But in the ecclesiastical hierarchy, sometimes those who are the nearer to God in sanctity are in the lowest degree, and are not outstanding in knowledge. And some also are eminent in one kind of knowledge, and fail in another. And on that account superiors may be taught by inferiors.

Reply Obj. 2. As explained above, there is no similarity between what God does outside the order of corporeal nature, and that of spiritual nature. Hence the argument does not hold.

Reply Obj. 3. An angel turns voluntarily to enlighten another angel, but the angel's will is always regulated by the Divine law which established the order in the angels.

ARTICLE 4. *Whether the Superior Angel Enlightens the Inferior As Regards All He Himself Knows?*

We proceed thus to the Fourth Article: It would seem that the superior angel does not enlighten the inferior concerning all he himself knows.

Objection 1. For Dionysius says (*Cæl. Hier.*

xii),[2] that the superior angels have a more universal knowledge, and the inferior a more particular and inferior knowledge. But more is contained under a universal knowledge than under a particular knowledge. Therefore not all that the superior angels know is known by the inferior through the enlightenment by the former.

Obj. 2. Further, the Master of the *Sentences* says (II, XI)[3] that the superior angels had long known the Mystery of the Incarnation, but that the inferior angels did not know it until it was accomplished. Thus we find that on some of the angels inquiring, as it were, in ignorance: *Who is this King of glory?* other angels, who knew, answered: *The Lord of Hosts, He is the King of glory,* as Dionysius expounds (*Cæl. Hier.* vii).[4] But this would not be if the superior angels enlightened the inferior concerning all they know themselves. Therefore they do not do so.

Obj. 3. Further, if the superior angels enlighten the inferior about all they know, nothing that the superior angels know would be unknown to the inferior angels. Therefore the superior angels could communicate nothing more to the inferior, which appears open to objection. Therefore the superior angels enlighten the inferior in all things.

On the contrary, Gregory says:[5] "In that heavenly country, though there are some excellent gifts, yet nothing is held individually." And Dionysius says: "Each heavenly essence communicates to the inferior the understanding derived from the superior" (*Cæl. Hier.* xv),[6] as quoted above (A. 1).

I answer that, Every creature participates in the Divine goodness, so as to diffuse the good it possesses to others, for it is of the nature of good to communicate itself to others. Hence also corporeal agents give their likeness to others so far as they can. So the more an agent is established in the share of the Divine goodness, so much the more does it strive to transmit its perfections to others as far as possible. Hence the Blessed Peter admonishes those who by grace share in the Divine goodness, saying: *As every man hath received grace, ministering the same one to another; as good stewards of the manifold grace of God* (I Pet. 4. 10). Much more therefore do the holy angels, who enjoy the fulness of participation of the Divine goodness impart the same to those below them.

---

[2] Sect. 2 (PG 3, 293).
[3] QR 1, 356.
[4] Sect. 3 (PG 3, 209).
[5] Cf. Gregory, Hom. XXXIV *in Ev.* (PL 76, 1255); cf. also Peter Lombard, *Sent.,* II, d. 9, chap. 3 (QR 1, 346).
[6] Sect. 3 (PG 3, 332).

[1] Sect. 3 (PG 3, 181); Pt. 1 (PG 3, 504).

Nevertheless this gift is not received so excellently by the inferior as by the superior angels, and therefore the superior always remain in a higher order, and have a more perfect knowledge, just as the master understands the same thing more fully than the pupil who learns from him.

Reply Obj. 1. The knowledge of the superior angels is said to be more universal as regards the more eminent mode of understanding.

Reply Obj. 2. The Master's words are not to be so understood as if the inferior angels were entirely ignorant of the Mystery of the Incarnation, but that they did not know it as fully as the superior angels, and that they progressed in the knowledge of it afterwards when the Mystery was accomplished.

Reply Obj. 3. Till the Judgment Day some new things are always being revealed by God to the highest angels concerning the course of the world, and especially the salvation of the elect. Hence there is always something for the superior angels to make known to the inferior.

QUESTION CVII
THE SPEECH OF THE ANGELS
(*In Five Articles*)

WE now consider the speech of the angels. Here there are five points of inquiry: (1) Whether one angel speaks to another? (2) Whether the inferior speaks to the superior. (3) Whether an angel speaks to God? (4) Whether the angelic speech is subject to local distance? (5) Whether the speech of one angel to another is known to all?

ARTICLE 1. *Whether One Angel Speaks to Another?*

We proceed thus to the First Article: It would seem that one angel does not speak to another.

Objection 1. For Gregory says (*Moral.* xviii)[1] that, in the state of the resurrection "each one's body will not hide his mind from his fellows." Much less, therefore, is one angel's mind hidden from another. But speech manifests to another what lies hidden in the mind. Therefore it is not necessary that one angel should speak to another.

Obj. 2. Further, speech is twofold: interior, whereby one speaks to oneself, and exterior, whereby one speaks to another. But exterior speech takes place by some sensible sign, as by voice, or gesture, or some bodily member, as the tongue, or the fingers, and this cannot apply to

[1] Chap. 48 (PL 76, 84).

the angels. Therefore one angel does not speak to another.

Obj. 3. Further, the speaker incites the hearer to listen to what he says. But it does not appear that one angel incites another to listen, for this happens among us by some sensible sign. Therefore one angel does not speak to another.

On the contrary, The Apostle says (I Cor. 13. 1): *If I speak with the tongues of men and of angels.*

I answer that, The angels speak in a certain way. But, as Gregory says (*Moral.* ii):[2] "It is fitting that our mind, rising above the properties of bodily speech, should be lifted to the sublime and unknown ways of interior speech."

To understand how one angel speaks to another, we must consider that, as we explained above (Q. LXXXII, A. 4) when treating of the actions and powers of the soul, the will moves the intellect to its operation. Now an intelligible object is present to the intellect in three ways. First, habitually, or in the memory, as Augustine says (*De Trin.* xiv, 6, 7).[3] Secondly, as actually considered or conceived. Thirdly, as related to something else. And it is clear that the intelligible object passes from the first to the second stage by the command of the will, and hence in the definition of habit these words occur: "which anyone uses when he wills."[4] So likewise the intelligible object passes from the second to the third stage by the will. For by the will the concept of the mind is ordered to something else, as, for instance, either to the performing of an action, or to being made known to another. Now when the mind turns itself to the actual consideration of any habitual knowledge, then a person speaks to himself; for the concept of the mind is called the interior word. And by the fact that the concept of the angelic mind is ordered to be made known to another by the will of the angel himself, the concept of one angel is made known to another; and in this way one angel speaks to another. For to speak to another means nothing other than to make known the mental concept to another.

Reply Obj. 1. Our mental concept is hidden by a twofold obstacle. The first is in the will, which can retain the mental concept within, or can direct it externally. In this way God alone can see the mind of another, according to I Cor. 2. 11: *What man knoweth the things of a man, but the spirit of a man that is in him?* The other obstacle by which the mind of man is shut off from another one's knowledge, comes from the

[2] Chap. 7 (PL 75, 559).   [3] PL 42, 1042, 1043.
[4] Averroes, *In De An.,* II, 18 (VI, 2, 161E).

denseness of the body; and so it happens that even when the will directs the concept of the mind to make itself known, it is not at once made known to another, but some sensible sign must be used. Gregory alludes to this fact when he says (*Moral.* ii):[1] "To other eyes we seem to stand aloof as it were behind the wall of the body; and when we wish to make ourselves known, we go out as it were by the door of the tongue to show what we really are." But an angel has no such obstacle, and so he can make his concept known to another at once.

Reply Obj. 2. External speech, made by the voice, is a necessity for us on account of the obstacle of the body. Hence it does not befit an angel, but only interior speech belongs to him; and this includes not only the interior speech by mental concept, but also its being ordered to another's knowledge by the will. So the tongue of an angel is called metaphorically the angel's power, whereby he manifests his concept.

Reply Obj. 3. There is no need to draw the attention of the good angels, since they always see each other in the Word, for as one always sees the other, so he always sees what is ordered to himself. But because even in the state of nature they were able to speak to each other, and even now the bad angels speak to each other, we must say that the intellect is moved by the intelligible object just as sense is affected by the sensible object. Therefore, as sense is aroused by the sensible object, so the mind of an angel can be aroused to attention by some intelligible power.

ARTICLE 2. *Whether the Inferior Angel Speaks to the Superior?*

We proceed thus to the Second Article: It would seem that the inferior angel does not speak to the superior.

Objection 1. For on the text (I Cor. 13. 1), *If I speak with the tongues of men and of angels*, a gloss remarks[2] that the speech of the angels is an enlightenment whereby the superior enlightens the inferior. But the inferior never enlightens the superior, as was above explained (Q. CVI, A. 3). Therefore neither do the inferior speak to the superior.

Obj. 2. Further, as was said above (Q. CVI, A. 1), to enlighten means merely to make known to one being what is known to another, and this is to speak. Therefore to speak and to enlighten are the same. And so the same conclusion follows.

¹ Chap. 7 (PL 75, 559).
² *Glossa ordin.*, (VI, 53E); *Glossa* Lombardi (PL 191, 1658).

Obj. 3. Further, Gregory says (*Moral.* ii):[3] "God speaks to the angels by the very fact that He shows to their hearts His hidden and invisible things." But this is to enlighten them. Therefore, whenever God speaks, He enlightens. In the same way every angelic speech is an enlightening. Therefore an inferior angel can in no way speak to a superior angel.

On the contrary, According to the exposition of Dionysius (*Cæl. Hier.* vii),[4] the inferior angels said to the superior: *Who is this King of Glory?* (Ps. 23.10)

I answer that, The inferior angels can speak to the superior. To make this clear, we must consider that every angelic enlightening is an angelic speech; but on the other hand, not every speech is an enlightening; because, as we have said (A. 1), for one angel to speak to another angel means nothing else but that by his own will he directs his concept in such a way that it becomes known to the other. Now what the mind conceives may be reduced to a twofold principle: to God Himself, Who is the first truth; and to the will of the one who understands, whereby we actually consider anything. But because truth is the light of the intellect, and God Himself is the rule of all truth, the manifestation of what is conceived by the mind, as depending on the first truth, is both speech and enlightenment as, for example, when one man says to another: "Heaven was created by God" or, "Man is an animal." The manifestation, however, of what depends on the will of the one who understands cannot be called an enlightenment, but is only a speech; for instance, when one says to another: "I wish to learn this; I wish to do this or that." The reason is that the created will is not a light, nor a rule of truth, but participates of light. Hence to communicate what comes from the created will is not, as such, an enlightening. For to know what you may will, or what you may understand, does not belong to the perfection of my intellect, but only to know the truth in reality.

Now it is clear that the angels are called superior or inferior by comparison with this principle, God; and therefore enlightenment, which depends on the principle which is God, is conveyed only by the superior angels to the inferior. But as regards the will as the principle, he who wills is first and supreme, and therefore the manifestation of what belongs to the will is conveyed to others by the one who wills. In that manner both the superior angels speak to the inferior, and the inferior speak to the superior.

³ Chap. 7 (PL 75, 559).   ⁴ Sect. 3 (PG 3, 209).

From this the *replies to the first and second objections clearly appear.*

Reply Obj. 3. Every speech of God to the angels is an enlightening because, since the will of God is the rule of truth, it pertains to the perfection and enlightenment of the created mind to know even what God wills. But the same does not apply to the will of the angels, as was explained above.

ARTICLE 3. *Whether an Angel Speaks to God?*

We proceed thus to the Third Article: It would seem that an angel does not speak to God.

Objection 1. For speech makes known something to another. But an angel cannot make known anything to God, who knows all things. Therefore an angel does not speak to God.

Obj. 2. Further, to speak is to order the concept of the intellect in reference to another, as was shown above (A. 1). But an angel always orders his mental concept to God. So if an angel speaks at any time to God, he always speaks to God; which in some way appears to be unreasonable, since an angel sometimes speaks to another angel. Therefore it seems that an angel never speaks to God.

On the contrary, It is written (Zach. 1. 12): *The angel of the Lord answered and said: O Lord of hosts, how long wilt Thou not have mercy on Jerusalem.* Therefore an angel speaks to God.

I answer that, As was said above (AA. 1, 2), the angel speaks by ordering his mental concept to something else. Now one thing is ordered to another in a twofold manner. In one way for the purpose of giving one thing to another, as in natural things the agent is ordered to the patient, and in human speech the teacher is ordered to the learner. And in this sense an angel in no way speaks to God either of what concerns the truth, or of whatever depends on the created will, because God is the principle and source of all truth and of all will. In another way one thing is ordered to another to receive something, as in natural things the passive is ordered to the agent, and in human speech the disciple to the master. And in this way an angel speaks to God, either by consulting the Divine will of what ought to be done, or by admiring the Divine excellence which he can never comprehend. Thus Gregory says (*Moral.* ii)[1] that "the angels speak to God, when by contemplating what is above themselves they rise to a movement of admiration."

Reply Obj. 1. Speech is not always for the

[1] Chap. 7 (PL 75, 560).

purpose of making something known to another, but is sometimes finally ordered to the purpose of manifesting something to the speaker himself, as when the disciples ask instruction from the master.

Reply Obj. 2. The angels are always speaking to God in the sense of praising and admiring Him and His works; but they speak to Him by consulting Him about what ought to be done whenever they have to perform any new work, concerning which they desire enlightenment.

ARTICLE 4. *Whether Local Distance Influences the Angelic Speech?*

We proceed thus to the Fourth Article: It would seem that local distance affects the angelic speech.

Objection 1. For as Damascene says (*De Fid. Orth.* 1, 13):[2] "An angel works where he is." But speech is an angelic operation. Therefore, as an angel is in a determinate place, it seems that an angel's speech is limited by the bounds of that place.

Obj. 2. Further, a speaker cries out on account of the distance of the hearer. But it is said of the Seraphim that *they cried one to another* (Isa. 6. 3). Therefore in the angelic speech local distance has some effect.

On the contrary. It is said that the rich man in hell spoke to Abraham, notwithstanding the local distance (Luke 16. 24). Much less therefore does local distance impede the speech of one angel to another.

I answer that, The angelic speech consists in an intellectual operation, as explained above (AA. 1, 2, 3). And the intellectual operation of an angel abstracts from place and time. For even our own intellectual operation takes place by abstraction from the here and now, except accidentally on the part of the phantasms, which do not exist at all in an angel. But as regards whatever is abstracted from place and time, neither difference of time nor local distance has any influence whatever. Hence in the angelic speech local distance is no impediment.

Reply Obj. 1. The angelic speech, as above explained (A. 1, ANS. 2), is interior, but perceived, nevertheless, by another; and therefore it exists in the angel who speaks, and consequently where the angel is who speaks. But just as local distance does not prevent one angel seeing another, so neither does it prevent an angel perceiving what is ordered to him on the part of another. And this is to perceive his speech.

Reply Obj. 2. The cry mentioned is not a

[2] PG 94, 853.

bodily voice raised by reason of the local distance, but is taken to signify the importance of what is said, or the intensity of the affection, according to what Gregory says (*Moral.* ii) :[1] "The less one desires, the less one cries out."

ARTICLE 5. *Whether All the Angels Know What One Speaks to Another?*

We proceed thus to the Fifth Article: It would seem that all the angels know what one speaks to another.

Objection 1. For unequal local distance is the reason why all men do not know what one man says to another. But in the angelic speech local distance has no effect, as above explained (A. 4). Therefore all the angels know what one speaks to another.

Obj. 2. Further, all the angels have the intellectual power in common. So if the mental concept of one ordered to another is known by one, it is for the same reason known by all.

Obj. 3. Further, enlightenment is a kind of speech. But the enlightenment of one angel by another extends to all the angels, because, as Dionysius says (*Cæl. Hier.* xv) :[2] "Each one of the heavenly essences communicates what he learns to the others." Therefore the speech of one angel to another extends to all.

On the contrary, One man can speak to another alone; much more can this be the case among the angels.

I answer that, As above explained (AA. 1, 2), the mental concept of one angel can be perceived by another when the angel who possesses the concept refers it by his will to another. Now a thing can be ordered through some cause to one thing and not to another. Consequently the concept of one (angel) may be known by one and not by another. And therefore an angel can perceive the speech of one angel to another while others do not, not through the obstacle of local distance, but on account of the will so ordering, as explained above (AA. 1, 2).

From this appear the *replies to the first and second objections.*

Reply Obj. 3. Enlightenment is of those truths that emanate from the first rule of truth, which is the principle common to all the angels; and in that way enlightenments are common to all. But speech may be of something ordered to the principle of the created will, which is proper to each angel. And in this way it is not necessary that these speeches should be common to all.

---

[1] Chap. 7 (PL 75, 560).
[2] Sect. 3 (PG 3, 332).

QUESTION CVIII
OF THE ANGELIC DEGREES OF HIERARCHIES AND ORDERS
(*In Eight Articles*)

WE next consider the degrees of the angels in their hierarchies and orders; for it was said above (Q. CVI, A. 3), that the superior angels enlighten the inferior angels; and not conversely.

Under this head there are eight points of inquiry: (1) Whether all the angels belong to one hierarchy? (2) Whether in one hierarchy there is only one order? (3) Whether in one order there are many angels? (4) Whether the distinction of hierarchies and orders is natural? (5) Of the names and properties of each order. (6) Of the comparison of the orders to one another. (7) Whether the orders will outlast the Day of Judgment? (8) Whether men are taken up into the angelic orders?

ARTICLE 1. *Whether All the Angels Are of One Hierarchy?*

We proceed thus to the First Article: It would seem that all the angels belong to one hierarchy.

Objection 1. For since the angels are supreme among creatures, it is evident that they are ordered for the best. But the best ordering of a multitude is for it to be governed by one authority, as the Philosopher shows.[3] Therefore as a hierarchy is nothing but a sacred principality, it seems that all the angels belong to one hierarchy.

Obj. 2. Further, Dionysius says (*Cæl. Hier,* iii)[4] that "hierarchy is order, knowledge, and action." But all the angels agree in one order towards God, Whom they know, and by Whom in their actions they are ruled. Therefore all the angels belong to one hierarchy.

Obj. 3. Further, the sacred principality called hierarchy is to be found among men and angels. But all men are of one hierarchy. Therefore likewise all the angels are of one hierarchy.

On the contrary, Dionysius (*Cæl. Hier.* vi)[5] distinguishes three hierarchies of angels.

I answer that, Hierarchy means a sacred principality, as above explained (obj. 1). Now principality includes two things: the ruler himself and the multitude ordered under the ruler. Therefore because there is one God, the ruler not only of all the angels but also of men and

---

[3] *Metaphysics,* XII, 10 (1076ª4); cf. *Ethics,* VIII, 10 (1160ª35); *Politics,* IV, 2 (1289ª40).
[4] Sect. 1 (PG 3, 164).
[5] Sect. 2 (PG 3, 200).

all creatures; so there is one hierarchy, not only of all the angels, but also of all rational creatures, who can be participators of sacred things, according as Augustine says,[1] "There are two cities, that is, two societies, one of the good angels and men, the other of the wicked." But if we consider the principality on the part of the multitude ordered under the ru'er, then principality is said to be one according as the multitude can be subject in one way to the government of the ruler. And those that cannot be governed in the same way by a ruler belong to different principalities. Thus, under one king there are different cities, which are governed by different laws and administrators. Now it is evident that men do not perceive the Divine enlightenments in the same way as do the angels; for the angels receive them in their intelligible purity, whereas men receive them under sensible likeness, as Dionysius says (*Cæl. Hier.* 1).[2] Therefore there must be a distinction between the human and the angelic hierarchy.

In the same manner we distinguish three angelic hierarchies. For it was shown above (Q. LV, A. 3), in treating of the angelic knowledge, that the superior angels have a more universal knowledge of the truth than the inferior angels. This universal knowledge has three grades among the angels. For the types of things, concerning which the angels are enlightened, can be considered in a threefold manner. First as proceeding from God as the first universal principle. And this mode of knowledge belongs to the first hierarchy, connected immediately with God, and, "as it were, placed in the vestibule of God," as Dionysius says (*Cæl. Hier.* vii).[3] Secondly, according as these types depend on the universal created causes which in some way are already multiplied; and this mode belongs to the second hierarchy. Thirdly, according as these types are applied to particular things as depending on their causes; and this mode belongs to the lowest hierarchy. All this will appear more clearly when we treat of each of the orders (A. 6). In this way are the hierarchies distinguished on the part of the multitude of subjects.

Hence it is clear that those err and speak against the meaning of Dionysius. For in the Divine Persons there exists, indeed, a natural order, but there is no hierarchical order, for as Dionysius says (*Cæl. Hier.* iii):[4] "The hierarchical order is so directed that some be

cleansed, enlightened, and perfected; and that others cleanse, enlighten, and perfect." And far be it from us to apply this to the Divine Persons.

Reply Obj. 1. This objection holds good as concerns the relation of the ruler to the principality, since the multitude is best ruled by one ruler, as the Philosopher asserts in those passages.

Reply Obj. 2. As regards knowing God Himself, Whom all see in one way—that is, in His Essence—there is no hierarchical distinction among the angels; but there is such a distinction as regards the types of created things, as explained above.

Reply Obj. 3. All men are of one species, and have one connatural mode of understanding, which is not the case in the angels. And hence the same argument does not apply to both.

ARTICLE 2. *Whether There Are Several Orders in One Hierarchy?*

We proceed thus to the Second Article: It would seem that in the one hierarchy there are not several orders.

Objection 1. For when a definition is multiplied, the thing defined is also multiplied. But hierarchy is order, as Dionysius says (*Cæl. Hier.* iii).[5] Therefore, if there are many orders, there is not one hierarchy only, but many.

Obj. 2. Further, different orders are different grades, and grades among spirits are constituted by different spiritual gifts. But among the angels all the spiritual gifts are common to all, for amongst them nothing is possessed individually. Therefore there are not different orders of angels.

Obj. 3. Further, in the ecclesiastical hierarchy the orders are distinguished according to the actions of cleansing, enlightening, and perfecting. For the order of deacons is cleansing, the order of priests is enlightening, and of bishops perfecting, as Dionysius says (*Eccl. Hier.* v).[6] But each of the angels cleanses, enlightens, and perfects. Therefore there is no distinction of orders among the angels.

On the contrary. The Apostle says (Eph. 1. 20, 21) that *God has set the Man Christ above all principality and power, and virtue, and dominion,* which are the various orders of the angels, and some of them belong to one hierarchy, as will be explained (A. 6).

I answer that, As explained above (A. 1), one hierarchy is one principality—that is, one multi-

---

[1] *City of God,* XII, 1 (PL 41, 349).
[2] Sect. 2 (PG 3, 140).
[3] Sect. 2 (PG 3, 208).
[4] Sect. 2 (PG 3, 165).

[5] Sect. 1 (PG 3, 164).
[6] Pt. 1, Sect. 6 (PG 3, 505).

tude ordered in one way under the governance of a ruler. Now such a multitude would not be ordered, but confused, if there were not in it different orders. So the nature of a hierarchy requires diversity of orders.

This diversity of order arises from the diversity of offices and actions, as appears in one city where there are different orders according to the different actions. For there is one order of those who judge, and another of those who fight, and another of those who labour in the fields, and so forth.

But although one city thus comprises several orders, all may be reduced to three, when we consider that every multitude has a beginning, a middle, and an end. So in every city, a threefold order of men is to be seen, some of whom are supreme, as the nobles; others are the last, as the common people, while others hold a place between these, as the middle-class (*populus honorabilis*). In the same way we find in each angelic hierarchy the orders distinguished according to their actions and offices, and all this diversity is reduced to three—namely, to the summit, the middle, and the base. And so in every hierarchy Dionysius places three orders (*Cæl. Hier.* vi). [1]

Reply Obj. 1. Order is twofold. In one way it is taken as the order comprehending in itself different grades, and in that way a hierarchy is called an order. In another way one grade is called an order, and in that sense the several orders of one hierarchy are so called.

Reply Obj. 2. All things are possessed in common by the angelic society, some things, however, being held more excellently by some than by others. Each gift is more perfectly possessed by the one who can communicate it than by the one who cannot communicate it; just as the hot thing which can communicate heat is more perfect than what is unable to give heat. And the more perfectly anyone can communicate a gift, the higher grade he occupies, as he is in the more perfect grade of mastership who can teach a higher science. By this likeness we can reckon the variety of grades or orders among the angels, according to their different offices and actions.

Reply Obj. 3. The inferior angel is superior to the highest man of our hierarchy, according to the words, *He that is the lesser in the kingdom of heaven, is greater than he*—namely, John the Baptist, than whom *there hath not risen a greater among them that are born of women* (Matt. 11. 11). Hence the lesser angel of the heavenly hierarchy can not only cleanse,

[1] PG 3, 200.

but also enlighten and perfect, and in a higher way than can the orders of our hierarchy. Thus the heavenly orders are not distinguished by reason of these, but by reason of other different acts.

ARTICLE 3. *Whether There Are Many Angels in One Order?*

We proceed thus to the Third Article: It seems that there are not many angels in one order.

Objection 1. For it was shown above (Q. L, A. 4), that all the angels are unequal. But equals belong to one order. Therefore there are not many angels in one order.

Obj. 2. Further, it is superfluous for a thing to be done by many which can be done sufficiently by one. But that which belongs to one angelic office can be done sufficiently by one angel, by so much the more sufficiently than the one sun does what belongs to the office of the sun, according as the angel is more perfect than a heavenly body. If, therefore, the orders are distinguished by their offices, as stated above (A. 2), several angels in one order would be superfluous.

Obj. 3. Further, it was said above (obj. 1), that all the angels are unequal. Therefore, if several angels (for instance, three or four), are of one order, the lowest one of the superior order will be more akin to the highest of the inferior order than with the highest of his own order. And thus he does not seem to be more of one order with the latter than with the former. Therefore there are not many angels of one order.

On the contrary, It is written: *The Seraphim cried to one another* (Isa. 6. 3). Therefore there are many angels in the one order of the Seraphim.

I answer that, Whoever knows anything perfectly is able to distinguish its acts, powers, and nature, down to the minutest details, but he who knows a thing in an imperfect manner can only distinguish it in a general way, and only as regards a few points. Thus, one who knows natural things imperfectly can distinguish their orders in a general way, placing the heavenly bodies in one order, inanimate inferior bodies in another, plants in another, and animals in another. But he who knows natural things perfectly is able to distinguish different orders in the heavenly bodies themselves, and in each of the other orders.

Now our knowledge of the angels is imperfect, as Dionysius says (*Cæl. Hier.* vi). [2] Hence

[2] Sect. 1 (PG 3, 200).

we can only distinguish the angelic offices and orders in a general way, so as to place many angels in one order. But if we knew the offices and distinctions of the angels perfectly, we should know perfectly that each angel has his own office and his own order among things, and much more so than any star, though this be hidden from us.

Reply Obj. 1. All the angels of one order are in some way equal in a common likeness according to which they are placed in that order, but absolutely speaking they are not equal. Hence Dionysius says (*Cæl. Hier.* x)[1] that in one and the same order of angels there are those who are first, middle, and last.

Reply Obj. 2. That special distinction of orders and offices according to which each angel has his own office and order is hidden from us.

Reply Obj. 3. As in a surface which is partly white and partly black the two parts on the borders of white and black are more akin as regards their position than any other two white parts, but are less akin in quality, so two angels who are on the boundary of two orders are more akin in propinquity of nature than one of them is akin to the others of its own order, but less akin in their fitness for similar offices, which fitness, indeed, extends to a definite limit.

ARTICLE 4. *Whether the Distinction of Hierarchies and Orders Comes from the Angelic Nature?*

We proceed thus to the Fourth Article: It would seem that the distinction of hierarchies and of orders is not from the nature of the angels.

Objection 1. For hierarchy is a sacred principality, and Dionysius places in its definition that "it approaches a resemblance to God, as far as may be" (*Cæl. Hier.* iii).[2] But sanctity and resemblance to God is in the angels by grace, and not by nature. Therefore the distinction of hierarchies and orders in the angels is by grace, and not by nature.

Obj. 2. Further, "the Seraphim are called burning or kindling," as Dionysius says (*Cæl. Hier.* vii).[3] This pertains to charity which comes not from nature but from grace; for *it is poured forth in our hearts by the Holy Ghost Who is given to us* (Rom. 5. 5), which is said not only of holy men, but also of the holy angels, as Augustine says.[4] Therefore the angelic orders are not from nature, but from grace.

Obj. 3. Further, the ecclesiastical hierarchy is copied from the heavenly. But the orders among men are not from nature, but by the gift of grace; for it is not a natural gift for one to be a bishop, and another a priest, and another a deacon. Therefore neither in the angels are the orders from nature, but from grace only.

On the contrary, The Master says (ii, d, 9)[5] that an angelic order is a multitude of heavenly spirits who are likened to each other by some gift of grace, just as they agree also in the participation of natural gifts. Therefore the distinction of orders among the angels is not only by gifts of grace, but also by gifts of nature.

I answer that, The order of government, which is the order of a multitude under authority, is derived from its end. Now the end of the angels may be considered in two ways. First, according to the power of nature, as, for example, that they may know and love God by natural knowledge and love; and according to their relation to this end the orders of the angels are distinguished by natural gifts. Secondly, the end of the angelic multitude can be taken from what is above their natural powers, which consists in the vision of the Divine Essence, and in the unchangeable enjoyment of His goodness, to which end they can reach only by grace. And hence as regards this end, the orders in the angels are adequately distinguished by the gifts of grace, but dispositively by natural gifts, because the angels are given gratuitous gifts according to the capacity of their natural gifts, which is not the case with men, as explained above (Q. LXII, A. 6). Hence among men the orders are distinguished according to the gratuitous gifts only, and not according to natural gifts.

From the above the *replies to the objections* are evident.

ARTICLE 5. *Whether the Orders of the Angels Are Properly Named?*

We proceed thus to the Fifth Article: It would seem that the orders of the angels are not properly named.

Objection 1. For all the heavenly spirits are called Angels and Virtues heavenly powers.[6] But common names should not be appropriated to individuals. Therefore the orders of the Angels and Virtues are ineptly named.

Obj. 2. Further, it is proper to God alone to be Lord, according to the words, *Know ye that the Lord He is God* (Ps. 99. 3). Therefore one

---

[1] Sect. 2 (PG 3, 273).   [2] Sect. 1 (PG 3, 164).
[3] Sect. 1 (PG 3, 205).
[4] *City of God*, XII, 9 (PL 41, 357).
[5] Chap. 2 (QR I, 345).
[6] Dionysius, *Cæl. Hier.*, 5 (PG 3, 196).

order of the heavenly spirits is not properly called Dominations.

Obj. 3. Further, the name Domination seems to imply government, and likewise the names Principalities and Powers. Therefore these three names do not seem to be properly applied to three orders.

Obj. 4. Further, archangels are as it were princes of the angels. Therefore this name ought not to be given to any other order than to the Principalities.

Obj. 5. Further, the name Seraphim is derived from ardour, which pertains to charity, and the name Cherubim from knowledge. But charity and knowledge are gifts common to all the angels. Therefore they ought not to be names of any particular orders.

Obj. 6. Further, Thrones are seats. But from the fact that God knows and loves the rational creature He is said to sit within it. Therefore there ought not to be any order of Thrones besides the Cherubim and Seraphim. Therefore it appears that the orders of angels are not properly named.

On the contrary is the authority of Holy Scripture wherein they are so named. For the name Seraphim is found in Isaias 6. 2; the name Cherubim in Ezechiel 1. (*cf.* 10. 15, 20); Thrones in Colossians 1. 16; Dominations, Virtues, Powers, and Principalities are mentioned in Ephesians 1. 21; the name Archangels in the canonical epistle of St. Jude (9), and the name Angels is found in many places of Scripture.

I answer that, As Dionysius says (*Cœl. Hier.* vii),[1] in the names of the angelic orders it is necessary to observe that "the proper name of each order expresses its property." Now to see what is the property of each order, we must consider that in ordered things something may be found in a threefold manner: by way of property, by way of excess, and by way of participation. A thing is said to be in another by way of property if it is adequate and proportionate to its nature; by excess when an attribute is less than that to which it is attributed, but is possessed thereby in an eminent manner, as we have stated (Q. XIII, A. 2) concerning all the names which are attributed to God; by participation, when an attribute is possessed by something not fully but partially—thus holy men are called gods by participation. Therefore, if anything is to be called by a name designating its property, it ought not to be named from what it participates imperfectly, nor from that which it possesses in excess, but from that which is

[1] Sect. 1 (PG 3, 205).

equal to it. For instance, when we wish properly to name a man, we should call him a rational substance, but not an intellectual substance, which is the proper name of an angel, because simple intelligence belongs to an angel as a property, and to a man by participation. Nor do we call him a sensible substance, which is the proper name of a brute animal; because sense is less than the property of a man, and belongs to man in a more excellent way than to other animals.

So we must consider that in the angelic orders all spiritual perfections are common to all the angels, and that they are all more abundantly in the superior than in the inferior angels. Further, as in these perfections there are grades, the superior perfection belongs to the superior order as its property, but to the inferior by participation. And conversely the inferior perfection belongs to the inferior order as its property, and to the superior by way of excess. And thus the superior order is named from the superior perfection.

So in this way Dionysius (*Cœl. Hier.* vii)[2] explains the names of the orders according as they befit the spiritual perfections they signify. Gregory, on the other hand, in expounding these names (*Hom.* xxxiv *in Evang.*)[3] seems to regard more the exterior ministrations. For he says that "angels are called so as announcing the least things; and the archangels in the greatest; by the virtues miracles are wrought; by the powers hostile powers are repulsed; and the principalities preside over the good spirits themselves."

Reply Obj. 1. Angel means messenger. So all the heavenly spirits, so far as they make known Divine things, are called angels. But the superior angels enjoy a certain excellence, as regards this manifestation, from which the superior orders are named. The lowest order of angels possess no excellence above the common manifestation, and therefore it is named from manifestation only; and thus the common name remains as it were proper to the lowest order, as Dionysius says (*Cœl. Hier.* v).[4] Or we may say that the lowest order can be specially called the order of Angels because they announce things to us immediately.

Virtue can be taken in two ways. First, commonly, considered as the medium between the essence and the operation, and in that sense all

[2] Sect. 1 (PG 3, 205). Cf. Also, Chap. VIII, 1; IX, 1 (PG 3, 237, 257).
[3] PL 76, 1250.
[4] PG 3, 196.

the heavenly spirits are called heavenly Virtues, as also "heavenly essences."[1] Secondly, as meaning a certain excellence of strength; and thus it is the proper name of an angelic order. Hence Dionysius says (*Cæl. Hier.* viii)[2] that "the name 'virtues' signifies a certain virile and immovable strength," first, in regard of all those Divine operations which befit them, secondly, in regard to receiving Divine gifts. Thus it signifies that they undertake fearlessly the Divine behests appointed to them; and this seems to imply strength of mind.

Reply Obj. 2. As Dionysius says (*Div. Nom.* xii):[3] "Domination is attributed to God in a special manner, by way of excess: but the Divine word gives the more illustrious heavenly princes the name of Lord by participation, through whom the inferior angels receive the Divine gifts." Hence Dionysius also states (*Cæl. Hier.* viii)[4] that "the name Domination means first a certain liberty, free from servile condition and common subjection, such as that of plebeians, and from tyrannical oppression, endured sometimes even by the great. Secondly, it signifies a certain rigid and inflexible supremacy which does not bend to any servile act, or to the act of those who are subject to or oppressed by tyrants. Thirdly, it signifies the desire and participation of the true dominion which belongs to God." Likewise the name of each order signifies the participation of what belongs to God, as the name Virtues signifies the participation of the Divine virtue; and the same principle applies to the rest.

Reply Obj. 3. The names Domination, Power, and Principality belong to government in different ways. The place of a lord is only to prescribe what is to be done. So Gregory says (*In Evang.* II, hom. xxxiv),[5] that "some companies of the angels, because others are subject in obedience to them, are called dominations." The name Power points out a kind of order, according to what the Apostle says, *He that resisteth the power, resisteth the ordination of God* (Rom. 13. 2). And so Dionysius says (*Cæl. Hier.* viii)[6] that the name Power signifies a kind of ordination both as regards the reception of Divine things, and as regards the Divine actions performed by superiors towards inferiors by leading them to things above. Therefore, to the

order of Powers it belongs to regulate what is to be done by those who are subject to them. "To preside (*principari*)," as Gregory says (*loc. cit.*) "is to be first among others," as being first in carrying out what is ordered to be done. And so Dionysius says (*Cæl. Hier.* ix)[7] that the name of Principalities signifies one who leads in a sacred order. For those who lead others, being first among them, are properly called princes, according to the words, *Princes went before joined with singers* (Ps. 67. 26).

Reply Obj. 4. The Archangels, according to Dionysius (*Cæl. Hier.* ix),[8] are between the Principalities and the Angels. A medium compared to one extreme seems like the other, as participating in the nature of both extremes; thus tepid seems cold compared to hot, and hot compared to cold. So the Archangels are called the angel princes, because they are princes as regards the Angels, and angels as regards the Principalities. But according to Gregory (*loc. cit.*) they are called "Archangels, because they preside over the one order of the Angels, announcing as it were, great things. And the Principalities are called so as presiding over all the heavenly Virtues who fulfil the Divine commands."

Reply Obj. 5. The name Seraphim does not come from charity only, but from the excess of charity, expressed by the word ardour or fire. Hence Dionysius (*Cæl. Hier.* vii)[9] expounds the name Seraphim according to the properties of fire, containing an excess of heat. Now in fire we may consider three things. First, the movement which is upwards and continuous. This signifies that they are borne inflexibly towards God. Secondly, the active force which is heat, which is not found in fire absolutely, but exists with a certain acuity, as being of most penetrating action, and reaching even to the smallest things, and as it were, with superabundant fervour. And by this is signified the action of these angels, exercised powerfully upon those who are subject to them, rousing them to a like fervour, and cleansing them wholly by their heat. Thirdly, we consider in fire its brightness, which signifies that these angels have in themselves an inextinguishable light, and that they also perfectly enlighten others.

In the same way the name Cherubim comes from a certain excess of knowledge; hence it is interpreted fulness of knowledge. Dionysius (*Cæl. Hier.* vii)[10] expounds this in regard to

---

[1] Dionysius, *Cæl. Hier.*, 5 (PG 3, 196).
[2] Sect. 1 (PG 3, 237).
[3] Sect. 2 (PG 3, 969;) sect. 4 (PG 3, 972).
[4] Sect. 1 (PG 3, 237).
[5] PL 76, 1251.
[6] Sect. 1 (PG 3, 240).

[7] Sect. 1 (PG 3, 257).   [8] *Ibid.*
[9] Sect. 1 (PG 3, 205).
[10] *Ibid.*

four things: the perfect vision of God; the full reception of the Divine Light; their contemplation in God of the beauty of the Divine order; and in regard to the fact that possessing this knowledge fully, they pour it forth copiously upon others.

Reply Obj. 6. The order of the Thrones excels the inferior orders as having an immediate knowledge of the types of the Divine works. But the Cherubim have the excellence of knowledge and the Seraphim the excellence of ardour. And although these two excellent attributes include the third, yet the gift belonging to the Thrones does not include the other two; and so the order of the Thrones is distinguished from the orders of the Cherubim and the Seraphim. For it is a common rule in all things that the excellence of the inferior is contained in the superior, but not conversely. But Dionysius (*ibid.*) explains the name Thrones by its relation to material seats, in which we may consider four things. First, the site; because seats are raised above the earth, and so the angels who are called Thrones are raised up to the immediate knowledge of the types of things in God. Secondly, because in material seats is displayed strength, since a person sits firmly on them. But here the reverse is the case, for the angels themselves are made firm by God. Thirdly, because the seat receives him who sits there, and he can be carried upon it; and so the angels receive God in themselves, and in a certain way bear Him to the inferior creatures. Fourthly, because in its shape, a seat is open on one side to receive the sitter; and thus are the angels promptly open to receive God and to serve Him.

ARTICLE 6. *Whether the Grades of the Orders Are Properly Assigned?*

We proceed thus to the Sixth Article: It would seem that the grades of the orders are not properly assigned.

Objection 1. For the order of prelates is the highest. But the names of Dominations, Principalities, and Powers of themselves imply precedence. Therefore these orders ought to be supreme.

Obj. 2. Further, the nearer an order is to God, the higher it is. But the order of Thrones is the nearest to God; for nothing is nearer to the sitter than the seat. Therefore the order of the Thrones is the highest.

Obj. 3. Further, knowledge comes before love, and intellect is higher than will. Therefore the order of Cherubim seems to be higher than the Seraphim.

Obj. 4. Further, Gregory (*In Evang. II,* hom. xxxiv)[1] places the Principalities above the Powers. These therefore are not placed immediately above the Archangels, as Dionysius says (*Cæl. Hier.* ix).[2]

On the contrary, Dionysius (*ibid.* vi),[3] places in the highest hierarchy the Seraphim as the first, the Cherubim as the middle, the Thrones as the last; in the middle heirarchy he places the Dominations, as the first, the Virtues in the middle, the Powers last; in the lowest heirarchy the Principalities first, then the Archangels, and lastly the Angels.

I answer that, The grades of the angelic orders are assigned by Gregory (*loc. cit.*) and Dionysius (*Cæl. Hier. ibid.*), who agree as regards all except the Principalities and Virtues. For Dionysius places the Virtues beneath the Dominations, and above the Powers; the Principalities beneath the Powers and above the Archangels. Gregory, however, places the Principalities between the Dominations and the Powers; and the Virtues between the Powers and the Archangels. Each of these placings may claim authority from the words of the Apostle, who (Eph. 1. 20, 21) enumerates the middle orders, beginning from the lowest, saying that *God set Him,* that is, Christ, *on His right hand in the heavenly places above all Principality and Power, and Virtue, and Domination.* Here he places Virtues between Powers and Dominations, according to the placing of Dionysius. Writing however to the Colossians (1. 16), numbering the same orders from the highest, he says: *Whether Thrones, or Dominations, or Principalities, or Powers, all things were created by Him and in Him.* Here he places the Principalities between Dominations and Powers, as does also Gregory.

Let us then first examine the reason for the ordering of Dionysius, in which we see, that, as said above (A. 1), the highest hierarchy contemplates the types of things in God Himself, the second in the universal causes, and the third in their application to particular effects. And because God is the end not only of the angelic ministrations, but also of the whole creation, it pertains to the first hierarchy to consider the end. To the middle one pertains the universal disposition of what is to be done. And to the last pertains the application of this disposition to the effect, which is the carrying out of the work. For it is clear that these three things exist

---

[1] PL 76, 1249.
[2] Sect. 1 (PG 3, 257); cf. also VI, 2 (PG 3, 200).
[3] Sect. 2 (PG 3, 200).

in every kind of operation. So Dionysius,[1] considering the properties of the orders as derived from their names, places in the first hierarchy those orders the names of which are taken from their relation to God, the Seraphim, Cherubim, and Thrones. And he places in the middle hierarchy those orders whose names denote a certain kind of common government or disposition, —the Dominations, Virtues, and Powers. And he places in the third hierarchy the orders whose names denote the execution of the work, the Principalities, Angels and Archangels.

As regards the end, three things may be considered. For first we consider the end, then we acquire perfect knowledge of the end, thirdly, we fix our intention on the end; of these the second is an addition to the first, and the third an addition to both. And because God is the end of creatures, as the leader is the end of an army, as the Philosopher says,[2] so a somewhat similar order may be seen in human affairs. For there are some who enjoy the dignity of being able with familiarity to approach the king or leader; others in addition are privileged to know his secrets; and others above these always keep near him, in a close union. According to this likeness, we can understand the disposition in the orders of the first hierarchy; for the Thrones are raised up so as to be the familiar recipients of God in themselves, in the sense of knowing immediately the types of things in Himself; and this is proper to the whole of the first hierarchy. The Cherubim know the Divine secrets supereminently. And the Seraphim excel in what is the supreme excellence of all, in being united to God Himself. And all this is in such a manner that the whole of this hierarchy can be called the Thrones; as, from what is common to all the heavenly spirits together, they are all called Angels.

As regards government, three things are comprised in its notion. The first which is to appoint those things which are to be done, and this belongs to the Dominations. The second is to give the power of carrying out what is to be done, which belongs to the Virtues. The third is to order how what has been commanded or decided to be done can be carried out by others, which belongs to the Powers.

The execution of the angelic ministrations consists in announcing Divine things. Now in the execution of any action there are beginners and leaders; as in singing, the precentors; and in war, generals and officers. This pertains to the Principalities. There are others who simply execute what is to be done; and these are the Angels. Others hold a middle place; and these are the Archangels, as above explained (A. 5, ANS. 4).

This explanation of the orders is a reasonable one. For the highest in an inferior order always has affinity to the lowest in the higher order, just as the lowest animals are near to the plants. Now the first order is that of the Divine Persons, which terminates in the Holy Ghost, Who is Love proceeding, with Whom the highest order of the first hierarchy has affinity, named as it is from the fire of love. The lowest order of the first hierarchy is that of the Thrones, who in their own order are akin to the Dominations. For the Thrones, according to Gregory (*op. cit.*),[3] are called so "because through them God accomplishes His judgments," since they are enlightened by Him in a manner adapted to the immediate enlightening of the second hierarchy, to which pertains the disposition of the Divine ministrations.—The order of the Powers is akin to the order of the Principalities. For as it belongs to the Powers to impose order on those subject to them, this ordering is plainly shown at once in the name of Principalities, who, as presiding over the government of peoples and kingdoms (which occupies the first and principal place in the Divine ministrations), are the first in their execution; for the good of a nation is more divine than the good of one man. And hence it is written, *The prince of the kingdom of the Persians resisted me* (Dan. 10. 13).

The disposition of the orders which is mentioned by Gregory is also reasonable. For since the Dominations appoint and order what belongs to the Divine ministrations, the orders subject to them are arranged according to the disposition of those things in which the Divine ministrations are effected. Still, as Augustine says (*De Trin.* iii),[4] "bodies are ruled in a certain order; the inferior by the superior; and all of them by the spiritual creature, and the bad spirit by the good spirit." So the first order after the Dominations is called that of Principalities, who rule even over good spirits. Then the Powers, who coerce the evil spirits, even as evildoers are coerced by earthly powers, as it is written (Rom. 13. 3, 4). After these come the Virtues, who have power over corporeal nature in the working of miracles; after these are the Angels and the Archangels, who announce to men either great things above reason, or small things within the scope of reason.

[1] *Ibid.* Cf. also VIII, 1; IX, 1 (PG 3, 237, 257).
[2] *Metaphysics*, XII, 10 (1075ᵃ15).
[3] PL 76, 1252.   [4] Chap. 4 (PL 42, 873).

Reply Obj. 1. The angels' subjection to God is greater than their presiding over inferior things, and the latter is derived from the former. Thus the orders which derive their name from presiding are not the first and highest, but rather the orders deriving their name from their nearness and relation to God.

Reply Obj. 2. The nearness to God designated by the name of the Thrones, belongs also to the Cherubim and Seraphim, and in a more excellent way, as explained above.

Reply Obj. 3. As explained above (Q. XXVII, A. 3), knowledge takes place according as the thing known is in the knower, but love according as the lover is united to the object loved. Now higher things are in a nobler way in themselves than in lower things, but lower things are in higher things in a nobler way than they are in themselves. Therefore to know lower things is better than to love them; and to love the higher things, God above all, is better than to know them.

Reply Obj. 4. A careful comparison will show that little or no difference exists in reality between the dispositions of the orders according to Dionysius and Gregory. For Gregory expounds[1] the name Principalities from their "presiding over good spirits," which also agrees with the Virtues according as this name expresses a certain strength, giving efficacy to the inferior spirits in the execution of the Divine ministrations. Again, according to Gregory, the Virtues seem to be the same as the Principalities of Dionysius. For to work miracles holds the first place in the Divine ministrations, since thus the way is prepared for the announcements of the archangels and the angels.

ARTICLE 7. *Whether the Orders Will Outlast the Day of Judgment?*

We proceed thus to the Seventh Article: It would seem that the orders of angels will not outlast the Day of Judgment.

Objection 1. For the Apostle says (I Cor. 15. 24), that Christ will *bring to naught all principality and power, when He shall have delivered up the kingdom to God and the Father;* and this will be in the final consummation. Therefore for the same reason all other orders will be abolished in that state.

Obj. 2. Further, to the office of the angelic orders it belongs to cleanse, enlighten, and perfect. But after the Day of Judgment one angel will not cleanse, enlighten, or perfect another, because they will not advance any more in knowl-

edge. Therefore the angelic orders would remain for no purpose.

Obj. 3. Further, the Apostle says of the angels (Heb. 1. 14), that *they are all ministering spirits, sent to minister to them who shall receive the inheritance of salvation;* from this it appears that the angelic offices are ordered for the purpose of leading men to salvation. But all the elect are in pursuit of salvation until the Day of Judgment. Therefore the angelic offices and orders will not outlast the Day of Judgment.

On the contrary, It is written (Judg. 5. 20): *Stars remaining in their order and courses,* which is applied to the angels.[2] Therefore the angels will ever remain in their orders.

I answer that, In the angelic orders we may consider two things, the distinction of grades, and the execution of their offices. The distinction of grades among the angels takes place according to the difference of grace and nature, as above explained (A. 4). And these differences will always remain in the angels, for these differences of natures cannot be taken from them unless they themselves be corrupted. The difference of glory will also remain always in them according to the difference of preceding merit. As to the execution of the angelic offices, it will to a certain degree remain after the Day of Judgment, and to a certain degree will cease. It will cease accordingly as their offices are directed towards leading others to their end, but it will remain, accordingly as it harmonizes with the attainment of the end. Thus also the various ranks of soldiers have different duties to perform in battles and in triumph.

Reply Obj. 1. The principalities and powers will come to an end in that final consummation as regards their office of leading others to their end, because when the end is attained, it is no longer necessary to tend towards the end. This is clear from the words of the Apostle, *When He shall have delivered up the kingdom of God and the Father,* that is, when He shall have led the faithful to the enjoyment of God Himself.

Reply Obj. 2. The actions of angels over the other angels are to be considered according to a likeness to our own intellectual actions. In ourselves we find many intellectual actions which are ordered according to the order of cause and effect, as when we gradually arrive at one conclusion by many middle terms. Now it is manifest that the knowledge of a conclusion depends on all the preceding middle terms not only in the new acquisition of knowledge, but also as

---

[1] *In Evang.* II, hom. XXXIV (PL 76, 1251).

[2] *Glossa interl.* (II, 38r).

regards the keeping of the knowledge acquired. A proof of this is that when anyone forgets any of the preceding middle terms he can have opinion or belief about the conclusion, but not knowledge, because he is ignorant of the order of the causes. So, since the inferior angels know the types of the Divine works by the light of the superior angels, their knowledge depends on the light of the superior angels not only as regards the acquisition of knowledge, but also as regards the preserving of the knowledge possessed. So, although after the Judgment the inferior angels will not progress in the knowledge of some things, still this will not prevent their being enlightened by the superior angels.

Reply Obj. 3. Although after the Day of Judgment men will not be led any more to salvation by the ministry of the angels, still those who are already saved will be enlightened through the angelic ministry.

ARTICLE 8. *Whether Men Are Taken up into the Angelic Orders?*

We proceed thus to the Eighth Article: It would seem that men are not taken up into the orders of the angels.

Objection 1. For the human hierarchy is stationed beneath the lowest heavenly hierarchy, as the lowest under the middle hierarchy and the middle beneath the first. But the angels of the lowest hierarchy are never transferred into the middle, or the first. Therefore neither are men transferred to the angelic orders.

Obj. 2. Further, certain offices belong to the orders of the angels, as to guard, to work miracles, to coerce the demons, and the like, which do not appear to pertain to the souls of the saints. Therefore they are not transferred to the angelic orders.

Obj. 3. Further, as the good angels lead on to good, so do the demons to what is evil. But it is erroneous to say that the souls of bad men are changed into demons, for Chrysostom rejects this (*Hom.* xxviii *in Matt.*).[1] Therefore it does not seem that the souls of the saints will be transferred to the orders of angels.

On the contrary, The Lord says of the saints that, *they will be as the angels of God* (Matt. 22. 30).

I answer that, As above explained (AA. 4, 7), the orders of the angels are distinguished according to the conditions of nature and according to the gifts of grace. Considered only as regards the grade of nature, men can in no way be assumed into the angelic orders, for the natural

distinction will always remain. In view of this distinction, some asserted[2] that men can in no way be transferred to an equality with the angels. But this is erroneous, contradicting as it does the promise of Christ saying that the children of the resurrection will be equal to the angels in heaven (Luke 20. 36). For whatever belongs to nature is as the material part in the notion of order, whilst that which perfects is from grace which depends on the liberty of God, and not on the order of nature. Therefore by the gift of grace men can merit glory in such a degree as to be equal to the angels, in each of the angelic grades; and this implies that men are taken up into the orders of the angels. Some, however, say[3] that not all who are saved are assumed into the angelic orders, but only virgins or the perfect, and that the others will constitute their own order, corresponding as it were to the whole society of the angels. But this is against what Augustine says,[4] that there will not be two societies of men and of angels, but only one; because the happiness of all is to cleave to God alone.

Reply Obj. 1. Grace is given to the angels in proportion to their natural gifts. This, however, does not apply to men, as above explained (A. 4; Q. LXII, A. 6). So, as the inferior angels cannot be transferred to the natural grade of superior, neither can they be transferred to the superior grade of grace. Men however can ascend to the grade of grace, but not of nature.

Reply Obj. 2. The angels according to the order of nature are between us and God; and therefore according to the common law not only human affairs are administered by them, but also all corporeal matters. But holy men even after this life are of the same nature with ourselves. And hence according to the common law they do not administer human affairs, "nor do they interfere in the things of the living," as Augustine says (*De cura pro mortuis* xiii, xvi).[5] Still, by a certain special dispensation it is sometimes granted to some of the saints to exercise these offices, by working miracles, by coercing the demons, or by doing something of that kind, as Augustine says (*ibid.*, xvi).

Reply Obj. 3. It is not erroneous to say that men are transferred to the penalty of demons;

---

[1] PG 57, 354.

[2] Eustratius, *In Eth.*, VI, VI (CG XX, 318.1). Cf. Albert the Great, *In Eth.*, VI, VI, 18 (BO VII, 433).

[3] Cf. Bonaventure, *In Sent.*, II, d. IX, A. I, Q. 7 (QR II, 254). Cf. also Gregory, *In Evang.*, II, hom. XXXIV (PL 76, 1249, 1252); Peter Lombard, *Sent.*, II, d. IX, chap. 6 (QR I, 349).

[4] *City of God*, XII, 9 (PL 41, 357).

[5] PL 40, 604, 607.

but some erroneously stated that the demons are nothing but souls of the dead,[1] and it is this that Chrysostom rejects.

QUESTION CIX
The ordering of the bad angels
(In Four Articles)

WE now consider the ordering of the bad angels, concerning which there are four points of inquiry: (1) Whether there are orders among the demons? (2) Whether among them there is precedence? (3) Whether one enlightens another? (4) Whether they are subject to the precedence of the good angels?

ARTICLE 1. *Whether There Are Orders Among the Demons?*

We proceed thus to the First Article: It would seem that there are no orders among the demons.

Objection 1. For order pertains to the notion of good, as also mode, and species, as Augustine says (*De Nat. Boni,* iii);[2] and on the contrary, disorder pertains to the notion of evil. But there is nothing disorderly in the good angels. Therefore in the bad angels there are no orders.

Obj. 2. Further, the angelic orders are contained under a hierarchy. But the demons are not in a hierarchy, which is a holy principality, for they are empty of all holiness. Therefore among the demons there are no orders.

Obj. 3. Further, the demons fell from every one of the angelic orders, as is commonly supposed. Therefore, if some demons are said to belong to an order, as falling from that order, it would seem necessary to give them the names of each of those orders. But we never find that they are called Seraphim, or Thrones, or Dominations. Therefore on the same ground they are not to be placed in any other order.

On the contrary, The Apostle says (Eph. 6. 12): *Our wrestling . . . is against principalities and powers, against the rulers of the world of this darkness.*

I answer that, As explained above (Q. CVIII, AA. 4, 7, 8), order in the angels is considered both according to the grade of nature, and according to that of grace. Now grace has a twofold state, the imperfect, which is that of merit, and the perfect, which is that of consummate glory.

[1] Cf. John Chrysostom, *In Math.,* hom. XXVIII (PG 57, 353). Augustine in *De Haeres,* 86 (PL 42, 47), ascribes this doctrine to Tertullian.   [2] PL 42, 553.

If therefore we consider the angelic orders in the light of the perfection of glory, then the demons are not in the angelic orders, and never were. But if we consider them in relation to imperfect grace, in that view the demons were at that time in the orders of angels, but fell away from them, according to what was said above (Q. LXII, A. 3), that all the angels were created in grace. But if we consider them in the light of nature, in that view they are still in those orders, because they have not lost their natural gifts, as Dionysius says (*Div. Nom.* iv).[3]

Reply Obj. 1. Good can exist without evil, but evil cannot exist without good (Q. XLIX, A. 3); so there is order in the demons, in so far as they possess a good nature.

Reply Obj. 2. If we consider the ordering of the demons on the part of God Who orders them, it is sacred, for He uses the demons for Himself. But on the part of the demons' will it is not a sacred thing, because they abuse their nature for evil.

Reply Obj. 3. The name Seraphim is given from the ardour of charity, and the name Thrones from the Divine indwelling, and the name Dominations imports a certain liberty, all of which are opposed to sin. And therefore these names are not given to the angels who sinned.

ARTICLE 2. *Whether Among the Demons There Is Precedence?*

We proceed thus to the Second Article: It would seem that there is no precedence among the demons.

Objection 1. For every precedence is according to some order of justice. But the demons are wholly fallen from justice. Therefore there is no precedence among them.

Obj. 2. Further, there is no precedence where obedience and subjection do not exist. But these cannot be without concord, which is not to be found among the demons, according to the text, *Among the proud there are always contentions* (Prov. 13. 10). Therefore there is no precedence among the demons.

Obj. 3. If there be precedence among them it is either according to nature, or according to their sin or punishment. But it is not according to their nature, for subjection and service do not come from nature, but from subsequent sin. Neither is it according to sin or punishment, because in that case the superior demons who have sinned the most grievously would be subject to the inferior. Therefore there is no precedence among the demons.

[3] Sect. 23 (PG 3, 725).

On the contrary, On I Cor. 15. 24 the gloss says:[1] "While the world lasts, angels will preside over angels, men over men, and demons over demons."

I answer that, Since action follows the nature of a thing, where natures are ordered, actions also must be ordered to each other. Thus it is in corporeal things, for as the inferior bodies by natural order are below the heavenly bodies, their actions and movements are subject to the actions and movements of the heavenly bodies. Now it is plain from what we have said (A. 1), that the demons are by natural order subject to others. And hence their actions are subject to the action of those above them. And this is what we mean by precedence, namely, that the action of the subject should be under the action of a superior. So the natural disposition itself of the demons requires that there should be precedence among them. This agrees too with Divine wisdom, which leaves nothing unordered, which *reacheth from end to end mightily, and ordereth all things sweetly* (Wisd. 8. 1).

Reply Obj. 1. The authority of the demons is not founded on their justice, but on the justice of God ordering all things.

Reply Obj. 2. The concord of the demons, whereby some obey others, does not arise from mutual friendships, but from their common wickedness, whereby they hate men, and fight against God's justice. For it is proper to wicked men to join and subject themselves to those whom they see to be stronger, in order to carry out their own wickedness.

Reply Obj. 3. The demons are not equal in nature; and so among them there exists a natural precedence, which is not the case with men, who are naturally equal. That the inferior are subject to the superior is not for the benefit of the superior, but rather to their detriment, because since to do evil belongs in a pre-eminent degree to unhappiness, it follows that to take the lead in evil is to be more unhappy.

ARTICLE 3. *Whether There Is Enlightenment in the Demons?*

We proceed thus to the Third Article: It would seem that enlightenment is in the demons.

Objection 1. For enlightenment means the manifestation of the truth. But one demon can manifest truth to another, because the superior excel in natural knowledge. Therefore the superior demons can enlighten the inferior.

[1] *Glossa ordin.* (VI, 58B); *Glossa* Lombardi (PL 191, 1679).

Obj. 2. Further, a body abounding in light can enlighten a body deficient in light, as the sun enlightens the moon. But the superior demons abound in the participation of natural light. Therefore it seems that the superior demons can enlighten the inferior.

On the contrary, Enlightenment is not without cleansing and perfecting, as stated above (Q. CVI, A. 1). But to cleanse does not befit the demons, according to the words: *What can be made clean by the unclean?* (Ecclus. 34. 4). Therefore neither can they enlighten.

I answer that, There can be no enlightenment properly speaking among the demons. For, as above explained (Q. CVII, A. 2), enlightenment, properly speaking, is the manifestation of the truth in reference to God, Who enlightens every intellect. Another kind of manifestation of the truth is speech, as when one angel manifests his concept to another. Now the demon's perversity does not lead one to order another to God, but rather to lead away from the Divine order; and so one demon does not enlighten another. But one can make known his mental concept to another by way of speech.

Reply Obj. 1. Not every kind of manifestation of the truth is enlightenment, but only that which is above described.

Reply Obj. 2. According to what pertains to natural knowledge, there is no necessary manifestation of the truth either in the angels, or in the demons, because, as expounded above (Q. LV, A. 2; Q. LVIII, A. 2; Q. LXXIX, A. 2), they know from the first all that pertains to their natural knowledge. So the greater fulness of natural light in the superior demons does not prove that they can enlighten others.

ARTICLE 4. *Whether the Good Angels Have Precedence over the Bad Angels?*

We proceed thus to the Fourth Article: It would seem that the good angels have no precedence over the bad angels.

Objection 1. For the angels' precedence is especially connected with enlightenment. But the bad angels, since they are darkness, are not enlightened by the good angels. Therefore the good angels do not rule over the bad.

Obj. 2. Further, superiors are responsible as regards negligence for the evil deeds of their subjects. But the demons do much evil. Therefore if they are subject to the good angels, it seems that negligence is to be charged to the good angels, which cannot be admitted.

Obj. 3. Further, the angels' precedence follows upon the order of nature, as explained above (A. 2). But if the demons fell from every order, as is commonly said, many of the demons are superior to many good angels in the natural order. Therefore the good angels have no precedence over all the bad angels.

On the contrary, Augustine says (*De Trin.* iii),[1] that "the treacherous and sinful spirit of life is ruled by the rational, pious, and just spirit of life"; and Gregory says (*Hom.* xxxiv)[2] that "the Powers are the angels to whose charge are subjected the hostile powers."

I answer that, The whole order of precedence is first and originally in God, and it is shared by creatures accordingly as they are the nearer to God. For those creatures, which are more perfect and nearer to God have the power to act on others. Now the greatest perfection and that which brings them nearest to God belongs to the creatures who enjoy God, as the holy angels, of which perfection the demons are deprived. And therefore the good angels have precedence over the bad, and these are ruled by them.

Reply Obj. 1. Many things concerning Divine mysteries are made known by the holy angels to the bad angels, whenever the Divine justice requires the demons to do anything, whether for the punishment of the evil, or for the trial of the good, as in human affairs the judge's assessors make known his sentence to the executioners. This revelation, if compared to the angelic revealers, can be called an enlightenment, since they order it to God. But it is not an enlightenment on the part of the demons, for these do not order it to God, but to the fulfilment of their own wickedness.

Reply Obj. 2. The holy angels are the ministers of the Divine wisdom. Hence as the Divine wisdom permits some evil to be done by bad angels or men, for the sake of the good that is drawn out of it, so also the good angels do not entirely restrain the bad from inflicting harm.

Reply Obj. 3. An angel who is inferior in the natural order presides over demons, although these may be naturally superior, because the power of Divine justice to which the good angels cleave is stronger than the natural power of the angels. Hence likewise among men, *the spiritual man judgeth all things* (I Cor. 2. 15), and the Philosopher says[3] that "the virtuous man is the rule and measure of all human acts."

[1] Chap. 4 (PL 42, 873).
[2] PL 76, 1251.
[3] *Ethics*, x, 5 (1176ª17).

QUESTION CX
How angels rule over bodies
(*In Four Articles*)

WE now consider how the angels rule over corporeal creatures. Under this head there are four points of inquiry: (1) Whether the corporeal creature is governed by the angels? (2) Whether the corporeal creature obeys the mere will of the angels? (3) Whether the angels by their own power can immediately move bodies locally? (4) Whether the good or bad angels can work miracles?

ARTICLE 1. *Whether the Corporeal Creature Is Governed by the Angels?*

We proceed thus to the First Article: It would seem that the corporeal creature is not governed by the angels.

Objection 1. For whatever possesses a determinate mode of action does not need to be governed by any superior power. For we must be governed lest we do what we ought not. But corporeal things have their actions determined by the nature divinely bestowed upon them. Therefore they do not need the government of angels.

Obj. 2. Further, the lowest beings are ruled by the superior. But some corporeal things are inferior and others are superior. Therefore they need not be governed by the angels.

Obj. 3. Further, the different orders of the angels are distinguished by different offices. But if corporeal creatures were ruled by the angels, there would be as many angelic offices as there are species of things. So also there would be as many orders of angels as there are species of things, which is against what is laid down above (Q. CVIII, A. 2). Therefore the corporeal creature is not governed by angels.

On the contrary, Augustine says (*De Trin.* iii, 4)[4] that "all bodies are ruled by the rational spirit of life"; and Gregory says (*Dial.* iv, 6),[5] that "in this visible world nothing takes place without the agency of the invisible creature."

I answer that, It is generally found both in human affairs and in natural things that every particular power is governed and ruled by the universal power; as, for example, the bailiff's power is governed by the power of the king. Among the angels also, as explained above (Q. LV, A. 3; Q. CVIII, A. 1), the superior angels who preside over the inferior possess a more universal knowledge. Now it is manifest that the

[4] PL 42, 873.
[5] PL 77, 329.

power of any individual body is more particular than the power of any spiritual substance. For every corporeal form is a form individualized by matter, and determined to the here and now; but immaterial forms are absolute and intelligible. Therefore, as the inferior angels who have the less universal forms, are ruled by the superior, so are all corporeal things ruled by the angels. This is not only laid down by the holy doctors, but also by all philosophers who admit the existence of incorporeal substances.[1]

Reply Obj. 1. Corporeal things have determinate actions, but they exercise such actions only according as they are moved, because it is proper to a body not to act unless moved. Hence a corporeal creature must be moved by a spiritual creature.

Reply Obj. 2. The reason alleged is according to the opinion of Aristotle who laid down[2] that the heavenly bodies are moved by spiritual substances, the number of which he endeavoured to assign according to the number of motions apparent in the heavenly bodies. But he did not say that there were any spiritual substances with immediate rule over the inferior bodies, except perhaps human souls. And this was because he did not consider that any operations were exercised in the inferior bodies except the natural ones for which the government of the heavenly bodies sufficed. But because we assert that many things are done in the inferior bodies besides the natural corporeal actions, for which the movements of the heavenly bodies are not sufficient, therefore in our opinion we must assert that the angels possess an immediate rule not only over the heavenly bodies, but also over the inferior bodies.

Reply Obj. 3. Philosophers have held different opinions about immaterial substances. For Plato laid down that immaterial substances were types and species of sensible bodies, and that some were more universal than others; and so he held that immaterial substances preside immediately over all sensible bodies, and different ones over different bodies.[3] But Aristotle held that immaterial substances are not the species of sensible bodies, but something higher and more universal; and so he did not attribute to them any immediate presiding over single bodies, but only over the universal agents, the heavenly bodies.[4] Avicenna followed a middle

course.[5] For he agreed with Plato in supposing some spiritual substance to preside immediately in the sphere of active and passive elements, because, as Plato also said, he held that the forms of these sensible things are derived from immaterial substances. But he differed from Plato because he supposed only one immaterial substance to preside over all inferior bodies, which he called the agent intelligence.

The holy doctors held with the Platonists that different spiritual substances were placed over corporeal things. For Augustine says (QQ. LXXXIII, *qu.* 79):[6] Every visible thing in this world has an angelic power placed over it. And Damascene says (*De Fid. Orth.* ii, 4):[7] "The devil was one of the angelic powers who presided over the terrestrial order"; and Origen says on the text, *When the ass saw the angel* (Num. 22. 23), that "the world has need of angels who preside over beasts, and over the birth of animals, and trees, and plants, and over the increase of all other things" (*Hom.* xiv *in Num.*).[8] The reason of this, however, is not that one kind of angel is more fitted by his nature to preside over animals than over plants, because each angel, even the least, has a higher and more universal power than any kind of corporeal thing. The reason is to be sought in the order of Divine wisdom, Who places different rulers over different things. Nor does it follow that there are more than nine orders of angels, because, as above expounded (Q. CVIII, A. 2), the orders are distinguished by their general offices. Hence as according to Gregory[9] "all the angels whose proper office is to preside over the demons are of the order of the Powers, so to the order of the Virtues do those angels seem to belong who preside over purely corporeal creatures; for by their ministration miracles are sometimes performed."

ARTICLE 2. *Whether Corporeal Matter Obeys the Mere Will of an Angel?*

We proceed thus to the Second Article: It would seem that corporeal matter obeys the mere will of an angel.

Objection 1. For the power of an angel excels the power of the soul. But corporeal matter certainly obeys a conception of the soul, for the body of man is changed by a conception of the soul as regards heat and cold, and sometimes

---

[1] See below, ANS. 3; cf. Destrez, Mél. Mandonnet (I, 128); Chenu, Mél. Mandonnet (I, 195).

[2] *Metaphysics*, XII, 8 (1073ª32).

[3] Cf. Q. LXXXIV, AA. 1, 4; Q. LXV, A. 4; Q. XXII, A. 2.

[4] *Metaphysics*, VII, 8 (1033b27); XII, 8 (1073ª32); cf. also Maimonides, *Guide*, XVII (FR 282).

[5] *Meta.*, IX, 3 (104rb); 4 (104vb); cf. also Q. LXV, A. 4; Q. LXXXIV, A. 4.

[6] PL 40, 90.

[7] PG 94, 873.

[8] PG 12, 680.

[9] *In Evang.*, II, hom. 34 (PL 76, 1251).

even as regards health and sickness. Therefore much more is corporeal matter changed by a conception of an angel.

Obj. 2. Further, whatever can be done by an inferior power, can be done by a superior power. Now the power of an angel is superior to corporeal power. But a body by its power is able to transform corporeal matter, as appears when fire begets fire. Therefore much more efficaciously can an angel by his power transform corporeal matter.

Obj. 3. Further, all corporeal nature is under angelic administration, as appears above (A. 1), and thus it appears that bodies are as instruments to the angels, for an instrument is essentially a mover moved. Now in effects there is something that is due to the power of their principal agents, and which cannot be due to the power of the instrument, and it is this that takes the principal place in the effect. For example, digestion is due to the force of natural heat, which is the instrument of the nutritive soul, but that living flesh is thus generated is due to the power of the soul. Again the cutting of the wood is from the saw, but that it assumes at length the form of a bed is due to the power of the craftsman. Therefore the substantial form which takes the principal place in the corporeal effects, is due to the angelic power. Therefore matter obeys the angels in receiving its form.

On the contrary, Augustine says,[1] "It is not to be thought that this visible matter obeys these rebel angels; for it obeys God alone."

I answer that, The Platonists asserted[2] that the forms which are in matter are caused by immaterial forms, because they said that the material forms are participations of immaterial forms. Avicenna followed them in this opinion to some extent, for he said that "all forms which are in matter, proceed from the concept of the intelligence," and that "corporeal agents only dispose [matter] for the forms."[3] They seem to have been deceived on this point, through supposing a form to be something made *per se*, so that it would be the effect of a formal principle. But, as the Philosopher proves,[4] what is made, properly speaking, is the composite; for this, properly speaking, is what subsists. But the form is called a being not as that which is, but as that by which something is; and consequently neither is a form, properly speaking,

made; for that is made which is, since to be made is nothing but the way to being.

Now it is manifest that what is made is like to the maker, because every agent makes its like. So whatever makes natural things, has a likeness to the composite; either because it is composite itself, as when fire begets fire, or because the whole composite as to both matter and form is within its power, which is proper to God. Therefore every informing of matter is either immediately from God, or from some corporeal agent, but not immediately from an angel.

Reply Obj. 1. Our soul is united to the body as the form, and so it is not surprising for the body to be formally changed by the soul's conception, especially as the movement of the sensitive appetite, which is accompanied with a certain bodily change, is subject to the command of reason. An angel, however, has not the same relation with natural bodies, and hence the argument does not hold.

Reply Obj. 2. Whatever an inferior power can do, a superior power can do, not in the same way, but in a more excellent way; for example, the intellect can know sensible things in a more excellent way than sense knows them. So an angel can change corporeal matter in a more excellent way than can corporeal agents, that is by moving the corporeal agents themselves, as being the superior cause.

Reply Obj. 3. There is nothing to prevent some natural effect taking place by angelic power for which the power of corporeal agents would not suffice. This, however, is not to obey an angel's will (as neither does matter obey the mere will of a cook, when by regulating the fire according to the prescription of the art he produces a dish that the fire could not have produced by itself), since to reduce matter to the act of the substantial form does not exceed the power of a corporeal agent; for it is natural for like to make like.

ARTICLE 3. *Whether Bodies Obey the Angels as Regards Local Motion?*

We proceed thus to the Third Article: It would seem that bodies do not obey the angels in local motion.

Objection 1. For the local motion of natural bodies follows on their forms. But the angels do not cause the forms of natural bodies, as stated above (A. 2; Q. LXV, A. 4; Q. XCI, A. 2). Therefore neither can they cause in them local motion.

---

[1] *De Trin*., III, 8 (PL 42, 875).   [2] Cf. Q. LXV, A. 4.
[3] *Meta*., IX, 3 (103vb); cf. Q. LXXXIV, A. 4.
[4] *Metaphysics*, VII, 8 (1033^{b}17).

Obj. 2. Further, the Philosopher proves[1] that "local motion is the first of all movements." But the angels cannot cause other movements by a formal change of the matter. Therefore neither can they cause local motion.

Obj. 3. Further, the corporeal members obey the conception of the soul as regards local movement, as having in themselves some principle of life. In natural bodies, however, there is no vital principle. Therefore they do not obey the angels in local motion.

On the contrary, Augustine says (*De Trin.* iii, 8, 9)[2] that the angels use corporeal seed to produce certain effects. But they cannot do this without causing local movement. Therefore bodies obey them in local motion.

I answer that, As Dionysius says (*Div. Nom.* vii):[3] "Divine wisdom has joined the ends of the first to the principles of the second." Hence it is clear that the inferior nature at its highest point reaches to the superior nature. Now corporeal nature is below the spiritual nature. But among all corporeal movements the most perfect is local motion, as the Philosopher proves.[4] The reason of this is that what is moved locally is not as such in potency to anything intrinsic, but only to something extrinsic—that is, to place. Therefore the corporeal nature has a natural aptitude to be moved immediately by the spiritual nature as regards place. Hence also the philosophers asserted[5] that the supreme bodies are moved locally by the spiritual substances. And so we see that the soul moves the body first and chiefly by a local motion.

Reply Obj. 1. There are in bodies other local movements besides those which result from the forms; for instance, the ebb and flow of the sea does not follow from the substantial form of the water, but from the influence of the moon. And much more can local movements result from the power of spiritual substances.

Reply Obj. 2. The angels, by causing local motion, as the first motion, can thereby cause other movements; that is, by employing corporeal agents to produce these effects, as a workman employs fire to soften iron.

Reply Obj. 3. The power of an angel is not so limited as is the power of the soul. Hence the moving power of the soul is limited to the body united to it, which is vivified by it, and by which it can move other things. But an angel's power is not limited to any body. Hence it can move locally bodies not joined to it.

ARTICLE 4. *Whether Angels Can Work Miracles?*

We proceed thus to the Fourth Article: It would seem that the angels can work miracles.

Objection 1. For Gregory says (*Hom.* xxxiv *in Ev.*):[6] "Those spirits are called virtues by whom signs and miracles are usually done."

Obj. 2. Further, Augustine says (QQ. LXXXIII.; *qu.* 79)[7] that " magicians work miracles by private contract; good Christians by public justice, bad Christians by the signs of public justice." But magicians work miracles because "they are heard by the demons," as he says elsewhere in the same work.[8] Therefore the demons can work miracles. Therefore much more can the good angels.

Obj. 3. Further, Augustine says in the same work (*ibid.*) that "it is not absurd to believe that all the things we see happen may be brought about by the lower powers that dwell in our atmosphere." But when an effect of natural causes is produced outside the order of natural cause, we call it a miracle, as, for instance, when anyone is cured of a fever without the operation of nature. Therefore the angels and demons can work miracles.

Obj. 4. Further, superior power is not subject to the order of an inferior cause. But corporeal nature is inferior to an angel. Therefore an angel can work outside the order of corporeal agents, which is to work miracles.

On the contrary, It is written of God (Ps. 135. 4): *Who alone doth great wonders.*

I answer that, A miracle properly so called is when something is done outside the order of nature. But it is not enough for a miracle if something is done outside the order of any particular nature; for otherwise anyone would perform a miracle by throwing a stone upwards, as such a thing is outside the order of the stone's nature. So for something to be called a miracle it is required that it be against the order of the whole created nature. But God alone can do this, because, whatever an angel or any other creature does by its own power, is according to the order of created nature, and thus it is not a miracle. Hence God alone can work miracles.

Reply Obj. 1. Some angels are said to work miracles either because God works miracles at their request, in the same way as holy men are said to work miracles, or because they exercise

---

[1] *Physics*, VIII, 7 (260ᵃ28).   [2] PL 42, 875, 878.
[3] Sect. 3 (PG 3, 872). [4] *Op. cit.* (261ᵃ14). [5] Cf. Q. LVII, A. 2.
[6] PL 76, 1251.   [7] PL 40, 92.
[8] Cf. *Liber* XXI *Sent.,* 4; among the suppositious works of St. Augustine. (PL 40, 726).

a kind of ministry in the miracles which take place, as in collecting the dust in the general resurrection, or by doing something of that kind.

Reply Obj. 2. Properly speaking, as said above, miracles are those things which are done outside the order of the whole of created nature. But as we do not know all the power of created nature, it follows that when anything is done outside the order of created nature by a power unknown to us, it is called a miracle as regards ourselves. So when the demons do anything of their own natural power, these things are called miracles not in an absolute sense, but in reference to ourselves. In this way the magicians work miracles through the demons; and these are said to be done "by private contract," since every power of the creature, in the universe, may be compared to the power of a private person in a city. Hence when a magician does anything by compact with the devil, this is done as it were by private contract. On the other hand, the Divine justice is in the whole universe as the public law is in the city. Therefore good Christians, so far as they work miracles by Divine justice, are said to work miracles "by public justice"; but bad Christians "by the signs of public justice," as by invoking the name of Christ, or by making use of other sacred signs.

Reply Obj. 3. Spiritual powers are able to effect whatever happens in this visible world by employing corporeal seeds by local movement.

Reply Obj. 4. Although the angels can do something which is outside the order of corporeal nature, yet they cannot do anything outside the whole created order, which is essential to a miracle, as explained above.

QUESTION CXI

THE ACTION OF THE ANGELS ON MAN

(In Four Articles)

WE now consider the action of the angels on man, and inquire: (1) How far they can change them by their own natural power. (2) How they are sent by God to the ministry of men (Q. CXII). (3) How they guard and protect men (Q. CXIII). Under the first head there are four points of inquiry: (1) Whether an angel can enlighten the human intellect? (2) Whether he can change man's will? (3) Whether he can change man's imagination? (4) Whether he can change man's senses?

ARTICLE 1. *Whether an Angel Can Enlighten Man?*

We proceed thus to the First Article: It would seem that an angel cannot enlighten man.

Objection 1. For man is enlightened by faith. Hence Dionysius (*Eccl. Hier.* iii)[1] attributes enlightenment to baptism, as the sacrament of faith. But faith is immediately from God, according to Eph. 2. 8: *By grace you are saved through faith, and that not of yourselves, for it is the gift of God.* Therefore man is not enlightened by an angel, but immediately by God.

Obj. 2. Further, on the words, *God hath manifested it to them* (Rom. 1. 19), the gloss observes[2] that "not only natural reason availed," for the manifestation of Divine truths to men, "but God also revealed them by His work," that is, by His creature. But both are immediately from God—that is, natural reason and the creature. Therefore God enlightens man immediately.

Obj. 3. Further, whoever is enlightened is aware of being enlightened. But man is not aware of being enlightened by angels. Therefore he is not enlightened by them.

On the contrary, Dionysius says (*Cæl. Hier.* iv)[3] that the revelation of Divine things reaches men through the ministry of the angels. But such revelation is an enlightenment, as we have stated (Q. CVI, A. 1; Q. CVII, A. 2). Therefore men are enlightened by the angels.

I answer that, Since the order of Divine Providence disposes that lower things be subject to the actions of higher, as explained above (Q. CIX, A. 2), just as the inferior angels are enlightened by the superior, so men, who are inferior to the angels, are enlightened by them.

The modes of each of these kinds of enlightenment are in one way alike and in another way unlike. For, as was shown above (Q. CVI, A. 1), the enlightenment which consists in making known Divine truth has two functions: namely, according as the inferior intellect is strengthened by the action of the superior intellect, and according as the intelligible species which are in the superior intellect are proposed to the inferior so as to be grasped by it. This takes place in the angels when the superior angel divides his universal concept of the truth according to the capacity of the inferior angel, as explained above (*ibid.*).

[1] Sect. 3 (PG 3, 397); cf. also II, 1 (PG 3, 392).
[2] *Glossa ordin.* (VI, 5B); *Glossa* Lombardi (PL 191, 1326).
[3] Sect. 2 (PG 3, 180).

The human intellect, however, cannot grasp the universal truth itself unveiled, because its nature requires it to understand by turning to the phantasms, as above explained (Q. LXXXIV, A. 7). So the angels propose the intelligible truth to men under the likenesses of sensible things, according to what Dionysius says (*Cæl. Hier.* i),[1] that, "It is impossible for the divine ray to shine on us, otherwise than shrouded by the variety of the sacred veils." On the other hand, the human intellect as the inferior, is strengthened by the action of the angelic intellect. And in these two ways man is enlightened by an angel.

Reply Obj. 1. Two dispositions come together in the virtue of faith. First, the habit of the intellect by which it is disposed to obey the will tending to Divine truth. For the intellect assents to the truth of faith not as convinced by the reason, but as commanded by the will; hence Augustine says,[2] "No one believes except willingly." In this respect faith comes from God alone. Secondly, faith requires that what is to be believed be proposed to the believer, which is accomplished by man, according to Rom. 10. 17, *Faith cometh by hearing;* but principally, however, by the angels, by whom Divine things are revealed to men. Hence the angels have some part in the enlightenment of faith. Moreover, men are enlightened by the angels not only concerning what is to be believed, but also as regards what is to be done.

Reply Obj. 2. Natural reason, which is immediately from God, can be strengthened by an angel, as we have said above. Again, the more the human intellect is strengthened, so much higher an intelligible truth can be elicited from the species derived from creatures. Thus man is assisted by an angel so that he may obtain from creatures a more perfect knowledge of God.

Reply Obj. 3. Intellectual operation and enlightenment can be understood in two ways. First, on the part of the thing understood. Thus whoever understands or is enlightened, knows that he understands or is enlightened, because he knows that the thing is made known to him. Secondly, on the part of the principle. And in this case it does not follow that whoever understands a truth knows what the intellect is, which is the principle of the intellectual operation. In like manner not everyone who is enlightened by an angel knows that he is enlightened by him.

[1] Sect. 2 (PG 3, 121).
[2] *In Joann.* VI, 44, tract. XXVI (PL 35, 1607).

ARTICLE 2. *Whether the Angels Can Change the Will of Man?*

We proceed thus to the Second Article: It would seem that the angels can change the will of man.

Objection 1. For, upon the text, *Who maketh His angels spirits and His ministers a flame of fire* (Heb. 1. 7), the gloss notes[3] that "they are fire, as being spiritually fervent, and as burning away our vices." This could not be, however, unless they changed the will. Therefore the angels can change the will.

Obj. 2. Further, Bede says (*Super Matt.* 15. 11),[4] that the devil does not send wicked thoughts, but kindles them. Damascene, however, says that he also sends them, for he remarks that "every malicious act and unclean passion is contrived by the demons and put into men" (*De Fid. Orth.* ii, 4):[5] In like manner also the good angels introduce and kindle good thoughts. But this could only be if they changed the will. Therefore the will is changed by them.

Obj. 3. Further, the angel, as above explained, enlightens the human intellect by means of the phantasms. But as the imagination which serves the intellect can be changed by an angel, so can the sensitive appetite which serves the will, because it also is a power using a corporeal organ. Therefore as the angel enlightens the mind, so can he change the will.

On the contrary, To change the will belongs to God alone, according to Prov. 21. 1: *The heart of the king is in the hand of the Lord, whithersoever He will He shall turn it.*

I answer that, The will can be changed in two ways. First, from within. And in this way, since the movement of the will is nothing but the inclination of the will to the thing willed, God alone can thus change the will, because He gives the power of such an inclination to the intellectual nature. For as the natural inclination is from God alone Who gives the nature, so the inclination of the will is from God alone, Who causes the will.

Secondly, the will is moved from without. As regards an angel, this can be only in one way, —by the good apprehended by the intellect. Hence in as far as anyone may be the cause why anything be apprehended as a desirable good, so far does he move the will. In this way also God

[3] *Glossa* Lombardi (PL 192, 410); *Ibid.*, on Ps. 103.4 (PL 191, 929); cf. Also *Glossa ordin.* (VI 135A); Augustine, *Enarr. in Psalm.*, Ps. 103.4, Serm. 1 (PL 37, 1349).
[4] PL 92, 75; Cf. *Glossa ordin.*, on Matt. 15.11 (V, 49E).
[5] PG 94, 877.

alone can move the will efficaciously; but an angel and man move the will by way of persuasion, as above explained (Q. CVI, A. 2).

In addition to this manner the human will can be moved from without in another way; namely, by the passion residing in the sensitive appetite. Thus by concupiscence or anger the will is inclined to will something. In this manner the angels, as being able to rouse these passions, can move the will, not however by necessity, for the will always remains free to consent to, or to resist, the passion.

Reply Obj. 1. Those who act as God's ministers, either men or angels, are said to burn away vices, and to incite to virtue by way of persuasion.

Reply Obj. 2. The demon cannot put thoughts in our minds by causing them from within, since the act of the knowing power is subject to the will; nevertheless the devil is called the kindler of thoughts, inasmuch as he incites to thought, by the desire of the things thought of, by way of persuasion, or by rousing the passions. Damascene calls this kindling "a putting in," because such a work is accomplished within. But good thoughts are attributed to a higher principle, namely, God, though they may be procured by the ministry of the angels.

Reply Obj. 3. The human intellect in its present state can understand only by turning to the phantasms. But the human will can will something following the judgment of reason rather than the passion of the sensitive appetite. Hence the comparison does not hold.

ARTICLE 3. *Whether an Angel Can Change Man's Imagination?*

We proceed thus to the Third Article: It would seem that an angel cannot change man's imagination.

Objection 1. For the phantasy, as is said in the book on the *Soul,*[1] is "a motion caused by the sense in act." But if this motion were caused by an angel, it would not be caused by the sense in act. Therefore it is contrary to the nature of the phantasy, which is the act of the imaginative power, to be changed by an angel.

Obj. 2. Further, since the forms in the imagination are spiritual, they are nobler than the forms existing in sensible matter. But an angel cannot impress forms upon sensible matter (Q. CX, A. 2). Therefore he cannot impress forms on the imagination, and so he cannot change it.

Obj. 3. Further, Augustine says (*Gen. ad lit.* xii, 12):[2] "One spirit by intermingling with another can communicate his knowledge to the other spirit by these images, so that the latter either understands it himself, or accepts it as understood by the other." But it does not seem that an angel can be mingled with the human imagination, nor that the imagination can seize the intelligibles, which are what the angel knows. Therefore it seems that an angel cannot change the imagination.

Obj. 4. Further, in the imaginative vision man cleaves to the likenesses of the things as to the things themselves. But in this there is deception. So as a good angel cannot be the cause of deception, it seems that he cannot cause the imaginative vision by changing the imagination.

On the contrary, Those things which are seen in dreams are seen by imaginative vision. But the angels reveal things in dreams, as appears from Matt. 1. 20; 2. 13, 19 in regard to the angel who appeared to Joseph in dreams. Therefore an angel can move the imagination.

I answer that, Both a good and a bad angel by their own natural power can move the human imagination. This may be explained as follows. For it was said above (Q. CX, A. 3), that corporeal nature obeys the angel as regards local movement, so that whatever can be caused by the local movement of bodies is subject to the natural power of the angels. Now it is manifest that imaginative apparitions are sometimes caused in us by the local movement of animal spirits and humours. Hence Aristotle says,[3] when assigning the cause of visions in dreams, that "when an animal sleeps, the blood descends in abundance to the sensitive principle, and movements descend with it"; that is, the impressions left from the movements of sensible things, which movements are preserved in the animal spirits, "and move the sensitive principle," so that a certain appearance ensues, as if the sensitive principle were being then changed by the external objects themselves. Indeed, the disturbance of the spirits and humours may be so great that such appearances may even occur to those who are awake, as is seen in mad people, and the like. So, as this happens by a natural disturbance of the humours, and sometimes also by the will of man who voluntarily imagines what he previously experienced, so also the same may be done by the power of a good or a bad angel, sometimes with alienation from the bodily senses, sometimes without such alienation.

Reply Obj. 1. The principle of the imagination is from the sense in act. For we cannot imagine what we have never perceived by the

---

[1] Aristotle, III, 3 (429[a]1).   [2] PL 34. 464.   [3] *Sleep,* 3 (461[b]11).

senses, either wholly or partly; as a man born blind cannot imagine colour. Sometimes, however, the imagination is informed in such a way that the act of the imaginative movement arises from the impressions preserved within, as we have said above.

Reply Obj. 2. An angel changes the imagination, not indeed by the impression of an imaginative form in no way previously received from the senses (for he cannot make a man born blind imagine colour), but by local movement of the spirits and humours, as explained above.

Reply Obj. 3. The commingling of the angelic spirit with the human imagination is not a mingling of essences, but by reason of an effect which he produces in the imagination in the way stated above, so that he shows man what he [the angel] knows, but not in the way he knows.

Reply Obj. 4. An angel causing an imaginative vision, sometimes enlightens the intellect at the same time, so that it knows what these images signify, and then there is no deception. But sometimes by the angelic operation the likeness of things only appear in the imagination. But neither then is deception caused by the angel, but by the defect in the intellect of him to whom such things appear. Thus neither was Christ a cause of deception when He spoke many things to the people in parables, which He did not explain to them.

ARTICLE 4. *Whether an Angel Can Change the Human Senses?*

We proceed thus to the Fourth Article: It seems that an angel cannot change the human senses.

Objection 1. For the sensitive operation is a vital operation. But such an operation does not come from an extrinsic principle. Therefore the sensitive operation cannot be caused by an angel.

Obj. 2. Further, the sensitive operation is nobler than the nutritive. But the angel cannot change the nutritive power, nor other natural forms. Therefore neither can he change the sensitive power.

Obj. 3. Further, the senses are naturally moved by the sensible objects. But an angel cannot change the order of nature (Q. CX, A. 4). Therefore an angel cannot change the senses, but these are changed always by the sensible object.

On the contrary, The angels who overturned Sodom, *struck the people of Sodom with blindness* or ἀορασία,[1] *so that they could not find the door* (Gen. 19. 11). The same is recorded of the Syrians whom Eliseus led into Samaria (IV Kings 6. 18).

I answer that, The senses may be changed in a twofold manner. From without, as when they are changed by the sensible object. And from within, for we see that the senses are changed when the spirits and humours are disturbed; as for example, a sick man's tongue, charged with choleric humour, tastes everything as bitter, and the like with the other senses. Now an angel, by his natural power, can work a change in the senses both ways. For an angel can offer the senses a sensible object from without, formed by nature or by the angel himself, as when he assumes a body, as we have said above (Q. LI, A. 2). Likewise he can move the spirits and humours from within, as above remarked (A. 3), by which the senses are changed in various ways.

Reply Obj. 1. The principle of the sensitive operation cannot be without the interior principle which is the sensitive power; but this interior principle can be moved in many ways by the exterior principle, as explained above.

Reply Obj. 2. By the interior movement of the spirits and humours an angel can do something towards changing the act of the nutritive power, and also of the appetitive and sensitive power, and of any other power using a corporeal organ.

Reply Obj. 3. An angel can do nothing outside the entire order of creatures, but he can outside some particular order of nature, since he is not subject to that order. Thus in some special way an angel can work a change in the senses outside the common way of nature.

QUESTION CXII
THE MISSION OF THE ANGELS
(*In Four Articles*)

WE next consider the mission of the angels. Under this head arise four points of inquiry: (1) Whether any angels are sent on works of ministry? (2) Whether all are sent? (3) Whether those who are sent stand before God. (4) From what orders they are sent.

ARTICLE 1. *Whether the Angels Are Sent on Works of Ministry?*

We proceed thus to the First Article: It would

---

[1] These are the only two passages in the Greek version where the word ἀορασία appears. It expresses, in fact, the effect produced on the people of Sodom—namely, dazzling (French version, *éblouissement*), which the Latin *cæcitas* (blindness) does not necessarily imply.

seem that the angels are not sent on works of ministry.

Objection 1. For every mission is to some determinate place. But intellectual actions do not determine a place, for intellect abstracts from the here and now. Since therefore the angelic actions are intellectual, it appears that the angels are not sent to perform their own actions.

Obj. 2. Further, the empyrean heaven is the place that befits the angelic dignity. Therefore if they are sent to us in ministry, it seems that something of their dignity would be lost, which is not fitting.

Obj. 3. Further, external occupation hinders the contemplation of wisdom; hence it is said: *He that is less in action, shall receive wisdom* (Ecclus. 38. 25). So if some angels are sent on external ministrations, they would seemingly be hindered from contemplation. But the whole of their happiness consists in the contemplation of God. So if they were sent, their happiness would be lessened, which is unfitting.

Obj. 4. Further, to minister is the part of an inferior. Hence it is written (Luke 22. 27): *Which is the greater, he that sitteth at table, or he that serveth? is not he that sitteth at table?* But the angels are naturally greater than we are. Therefore they are not sent to administer to us.

On the contrary, It is written (Exod. 23. 20): *Behold I will send My angels who shall go before thee.*

I answer that, From what has been said above (Q. CVIII, A. 6), it may be shown that some angels are sent in ministry by God. For, as we have already stated (Q. XLIII, A. 1), in treating of the mission of the Divine Persons, he is said to be sent who in any way proceeds from another so as to begin to be where he was not, or to be in another way where he already was. Thus the Son, or the Holy Ghost is said to be sent as proceeding from the Father by origin, and begins to be in a new way by grace or by the nature assumed, where He was before by the presence of His Godhead. For it is proper to God to be present everywhere, because, since He is the universal agent, His power reaches to all being, and hence He exists in all things (Q. VIII, A. 1).

An angel's power, however, as a particular agent, does not reach to the whole universe, but reaches to one thing in such a way as not to reach another. And so he is *here* in such a manner as not to be *there*. But it is clear from what was above stated (Q. CX, A. 1), that the corporeal creature is governed by the angels. Hence, whenever an angel has to perform any

work concerning a corporeal creature, the angel applies himself anew to that body by his power, and in that way begins to be there afresh. Now all this takes place by Divine command. Hence it follows that an angel is sent by God.

Yet the action performed by the angel who is sent proceeds from God as from its first principle, at Whose nod and by Whose authority the angels work; and is reduced to God as to its last end. Now this is what is meant by a minister, for a minister is an intelligent instrument; but an instrument is moved by another, and its action is ordered to another. Hence angels' actions are called ministries; and for this reason they are said to be sent in ministry.

Reply Obj. 1. An operation can be intellectual in two ways. In one way, as dwelling in the intellect itself, as contemplation. Such an operation does not require to be in a place; indeed, as Augustine says (*De Trin.* iv, 20):[1] "Even we ourselves as mentally tasting something eternal, are not in this world." In another sense an action is said to be intellectual because it is regulated and commanded by some intellect. In that sense the intellectual operations evidently have sometimes a determinate place.

Reply Obj. 2. The empyrean heaven belongs to the angelic dignity by way of fitness, since it is fitting that the higher body should be appointed to that nature which occupies a rank above bodies. Yet an angel does not derive his dignity from the empyrean heaven. So when he is not actually in the empyrean heaven, nothing of his dignity is lost, as neither does a king lessen his dignity when not actually sitting on his regal throne, which suits his dignity.

Reply Obj. 3. In ourselves the purity of contemplation is obscured by exterior occupation because we give ourselves to action through the sensitive powers, the action of which when it is intense impedes the action of the intellectual powers. An angel, on the contrary, regulates his exterior actions by the intellectual operation alone. Hence it follows that his external occupations in no respect impede his contemplation, because, given two actions, one of which is the rule and the reason of the other, one does not hinder but helps the other. Therefore Gregory says (*Moral.* ii)[2] that "the angels do not go abroad in such a manner as to lose the delights of inward contemplation."

Reply Obj. 4. In their external actions the angels chiefly minister to God, and secondarily to us; not because we are superior to them, abso-

---

[1] PL 42, 907.
[2] Chap. 3 (PL 75, 556).

lutely speaking, but because, since every man or angel by cleaving to God is made one spirit with God, he is thereby superior to every creature. Hence the Apostle says (Phil. 2. 3): *Esteeming others better than themselves.*

ARTICLE 2. *Whether All the Angels Are Sent in Ministry?*

We proceed thus to the Second Article: It would seem that all the angels are sent in ministry.

Objection 1. For the Apostle says (Heb. 1. 14): *All are ministering spirits, sent to minister* (Vulg., *Are they not all . . .?*).

Obj. 2. Further, among the orders, the highest is that of the Seraphim, as stated above (Q. CVIII, A. 6). But a Seraph was sent to purify the lips of the prophet (Isa. 6. 6, 7). Therefore much more are the inferior orders sent.

Obj. 3. Further, the Divine Persons infinitely excel all the angelic orders. But the Divine Persons are sent. Therefore much more are even the highest angels sent.

Obj. 4. Further, if the superior angels are not sent to the external ministries, this can only be because the superior angels execute the Divine ministries by means of the inferior angels. But as all the angels are unequal, as stated above (Q. L, A. 4), each angel has an angel inferior to himself except the last one. Therefore only the last angel would be sent in ministry, which contradicts the words, *Thousands of thousands ministered to Him* (Dan. 7. 10).

On the contrary, Gregory says (*Hom.* xxxiv *in Ev.*),[1] quoting the statement of Dionysius (*Cæl. Hier.* xiii),[2] that "the higher ranks fulfil no exterior service."

I answer that, As appears from what has been said above (Q. CVI, A. 3; Q. CX, A. 1), the order of Divine Providence has so disposed not only among the angels, but also in the whole universe, that inferior things are administered by the superior. By the Divine dispensation, however, this order is sometimes departed from as regards corporeal things for the sake of a higher order, that is, according as it is suitable for the manifestation of grace. That the man born blind was enlightened (John, 9.1), that Lazarus was raised from the dead (John 11. 43), was accomplished immediately by God without the action of the heavenly bodies. Moreover both good and bad angels can work some effect in these bodies independently of the heavenly bodies, by the condensation of the clouds into

rain, and by producing some such effects. Nor can anyone doubt that God can immediately reveal things to men without the help of the angels, and the superior angels without the inferior. From this standpoint some have said[3] that according to the general law the superior angels are not sent, but only the inferior, yet that sometimes, by Divine dispensation, the superior angels also are sent.

This, however, does not seem to be reasonable, because the angelic order is according to the gifts of grace. Now the order of grace has no order above itself for the sake of which it should be passed over, as the order of nature is passed over for the sake of grace. It may likewise be observed that the order of nature in the working of miracles is passed over for the strengthening of faith, which purpose would receive no additional strength if the angelic order were passed over, since this could not be perceived by us. Further, there is nothing in the Divine ministries above the capacity of the inferior orders. Hence Gregory says (*loc. cit.*) that "those who announce the highest things are called archangels. For this reason the archangel Gabriel was sent to the Virgin Mary." And yet, as he says further on, this was the greatest of all the Divine ministries. Thus with Dionysius (*Cæl. Hier.* xiii)[4] we must say, without any distinction, that the superior angels are never sent to the external ministry.

Reply Obj. 1. As in the missions of the Divine Persons there is a visible mission, in regard to the corporeal creature, and an invisible mission, in regard to a spiritual effect, so likewise in the angelic missions there is an external mission, in respect of some administration of corporeal things—and on such a mission not all the angels are sent,—and an interior mission, in respect of some intellectual effect, just as one angel enlightens another—and in this way all the angels are sent.

It may also be said that the Apostle wishes to prove that Christ is greater than the angels who were chosen as the messengers of the law, in order that He might thus show the excellence of the new over the old law. Hence there is no need to apply this to any other angels besides those who were sent to give the law.

Reply Obj. 2. According to Dionysius (*ibid.*), the angel who was sent to purify the prophet's lips was one of the inferior order, but was called a *Seraph,* that is, burning in an equivocal sense, because he came to burn the lips of the prophet.

---

[1] PL 76, 1254.
[2] Sect. 2 (PG 3, 300).

[3] Dionysius, *Cæl. Hier.*, XIII, 2 (PG 3, 300).
[4] *Ibid.*

It may also be said that the superior angels communicate their own proper gifts whereby they are named, through the ministry of the inferior angels. Thus one of the Seraphim is described as purifying by fire the prophet's lips, not as if he did so immediately, but because an inferior angel did so by his power, just as the Pope is said to absolve a man when he gives absolution by means of someone else.

Reply Obj. 3. The Divine Persons are not sent in ministry, but are said to be sent in an equivocal sense, as appears from what has been said (Q. XLIII, A. 1).

Reply Obj. 4. Many grades exist in the Divine ministries. Hence there is nothing to prevent angels though unequal from being sent immediately in ministry, in such a manner however that the superior are sent to the higher ministries, and the lower to the inferior ministries.

ARTICLE 3. *Whether All the Angels Who Are Sent Stand Before God?*

We proceed thus to the Third Article: It would seem that the angels who are sent also stand before God (*assistant*).

Objection 1. For Gregory says (*Hom.* xxxiv *in Ev.*):[1] "So the angels are sent and stand before God; for, though the angelic spirit is limited, yet the supreme Spirit, God, is not limited."

Obj. 2. Further, the angel was sent to administer to Tobias. Yet he said, *I am the angel Raphael, one of the seven who stand before the Lord* (Tob. 12. 15). Therefore the angels who are sent stand before God.

Obj. 3. Further, every holy angel is nearer to God than Satan is. Yet Satan stood before God, according to Job. 1. 6: *When the sons of God came to stand before the Lord, Satan also was present among them.* Therefore much more do the angels who are sent to minister stand before God.

Obj. 4. Further, if the inferior angels do not stand before God, the reason is because they receive the Divine enlightenment not immediately, but through the superior angels. But every angel receives the Divine enlightenment from a superior, except the one who is highest of all. Therefore only the highest angel would stand before God, which is contrary to the text of Dan. 7. 10: *Ten thousand times a hundred thousand stood before Him.* Therefore the angels who are sent also stand before God.

On the contrary, Gregory says, on Job. 25. 3:

Is there any numbering of His soldiers? (*Moral.* xvii):[2] "Those powers stand before God who do not go forth as messengers to men." Therefore those who are sent in ministry do not assist.

I answer that, The angels are spoken of as being present before and administering, after the likeness of those who attend upon a king, some of whom ever wait upon him, and hear his commands immediately, while others there are to whom the royal commands are conveyed by those who are in attendance—for instance, those who are placed at the head of the administration of various cities. These are said to administer, not to wait upon.

We must therefore observe that all the angels gaze upon the Divine Essence immediately; in regard to which all, even those who minister, are said to stand before God. Hence Gregory says (*Moral.* ii)[3] that "those who are sent on the external ministry of our salvation can always be present before or see the face of the Father." Yet not all the angels can perceive the secrets of the Divine mysteries in the clearness itself of the Divine Essence, but only the superior angels who announce them to the inferior. And in that respect only the superior angels belonging to the highest hierarchy are said to be present before God, those, according to Dionysius,[4] whose special prerogative it is to be enlightened immediately by God.

From this appears the *reply to the first and second objections,* which are based on the first mode of attending.

Reply Obj. 3. Satan is not described as having stood before God, but as present among those who stood before God; for, as Gregory says (*Moral.* ii),[5] "though he has lost happiness still he has retained a nature like to the angels."

Reply Obj. 4. All the attendants see some things immediately in the glory of the Divine Essence, and so it may be said that it is the prerogative of the whole of the highest hierarchy to be immediately enlightened by God. But the higher ones among them see more than is seen by the inferior; some of whom enlighten others, as also among those who attend upon the king, one knows more of the king's secrets than another.

ARTICLE 4. *Whether All the Angels of the Second Hierarchy Are Sent?*

We proceed thus to the Fourth Article: It

---

[1] PL 76, 1255.
[2] Chap. XIII (PL 76, 20).   [3] Chap. III (PL 76, 556).
[4] *Cæl. Hier.*, VII, 3 (PG 3, 209).
[5] Chap. 4 (PL 75, 557).

would seem that all the angels of the second hierarchy are sent.

Objection 1. For all the angels either attend, or minister, according to Daniel 7. 10. But the angels of the second hierarchy do not stand before God, for they are enlightened by the angels of the first hierarchy, as Dionysius says (*Cæl. Hier.* viii).[1] Therefore all the angels of the second hierarchy are sent in ministry.

Obj. 2. Further, Gregory says (*Moral.* xvii)[2] that "there are more who minister than who stand before the throne." This would not be the case if the angels of the second hierarchy were not sent in ministry. Therefore all the angels of the second hierarchy are sent to minister.

On the contrary, Dionysius says (*Cæl. Hier.* viii)[3] that "the Dominations are above all subjection." But to be sent implies subjection. Therefore the Dominations are not sent to minister.

I answer that, As above stated (A. 1), to be sent to external ministry properly belongs to an angel according as he acts by Divine command in respect of any corporeal creature, which is part of the execution of the Divine ministry. Now the angelic properties are manifested by their names, as Dionysius says (*Cæl. Hier.* vii).[4] And therefore the angels of those orders are sent to external ministry whose names signify some kind of administration. But the name Dominations does not signify any such administration, but only disposition and command in administering. On the other hand, the names of the inferior orders imply administration, for the Angels and Archangels are called so from announcing; the Virtues and Powers are called so in respect of some act; and it is right that the Prince, according to what Gregory says (*Hom.* xxxiv *in Ev.*),[5] "be first among the workers." Hence it belongs to these five orders to be sent to external ministry, but not to the four superior orders.

Reply Obj. 1. The Dominations are counted amongst the ministering angels, not as exercising but as disposing and commanding what is to be done by others. Thus an architect does not put his hands to the production of his art, but only disposes and orders what others are to do.

Reply Obj. 2. A twofold reason may be given in assigning the number of the attending and ministering angels. For Gregory says that those

who minister are more numerous than those who attend, because he takes the words (Dan. 7. 10) *thousands of thousands ministered to Him,* not in a multiple but in a partitive sense, to mean thousands out of thousands. Thus the number of those who minister is indefinite, and signifies excess; but the number of attendants is finite as in the words added, *and ten thousand times a hundred thousand assisted Him.* This explanation rests on the opinion of the Platonists,[6] who said that the nearer things are to the one first principle, the smaller they are in number, just as the nearer a number is to unity, the lesser it is than multitude. This opinion is verified as regards the number of orders, as six administer and three stand before the throne.

Dionysius, however (*Cæl. Hier.* xiv)[7] declares that the multitude of angels surpasses all the multitude of material things; so that, just as the superior bodies exceed the inferior in magnitude to an immeasurable degree, so the superior incorporeal natures surpass all corporeal natures in multitude, because whatever is better is more intended and more multiplied by God. Hence, as the attendants are superior to the ministers there will be more attendants than ministers. In this way, the words "thousands of thousands" are taken by way of multiplication, to signify a thousand times a thousand. And because ten times a hundred is a thousand, if it were said "ten times a hundred thousand" it would mean that there are as many attendants as ministers. But since it is written "ten thousand times a hundred thousand," we are given to understand that the attendants are much more numerous than the ministers. Nor is this said to signify that this is the precise number of angels, but rather that it is much greater, in that it exceeds all material multitude. This is signified by the multiplication together of the greatest numbers, namely ten, a hundred, and a thousand, as Dionysius remarks in the same passage.

QUESTION CXIII

OF THE GUARDIANSHIP OF THE GOOD ANGELS AND THEIR WARFARE AGAINST THE EVIL ANGELS

(*In Eight Articles*)

WE next consider the guardianship exercised by the good angels, and their warfare against the

---

[1] Sect. 1 (PG 3, 240).
[2] Chap. 13 (PL 75, 20).
[3] Sect. 1 (PG 3, 237).
[4] Sect. 1 (PG 3, 205). Cf. also VIII, 1 (PG 3, 237).
[5] PL 76, 1251.

[6] *Lib. de Causis,* 4 (BA 166.23); Proclus, *Inst. Theol.,* prop. 5 (DD LII); Dionysius, *De Div. Nom.,* XIII, 2 (PG 3, 280); Avicenna, *Meta.,* IX, 4 (104vb).
[7] PG 3, 321.

evil angels (Q. CXIV). Under the first head eight points of inquiry arise: (1) Whether men are guarded by the angels? (2) Whether to each man is assigned a single guardian angel? (3) Whether the guardianship belongs only to the lowest order of angels? (4) Whether it is fitting for each man to have an angel guardian? (5) When does an angel's guardianship of a man begin? (6) Whether the angel guardians always watch over men? (7) Whether the angel grieves over the loss of the one guarded? (8) Whether rivalry exists among the angels as regards their guardianship?

ARTICLE 1. *Whether Men Are Guarded By the Angels?*

We proceed thus to the First Article: It would seem that men are not guarded by the angels.

Objection 1. For guardians are assigned to some because they either do not know how, or are not able, to guard themselves, as children and the sick. But man is able to guard himself by his free choice, and knows how by his natural knowledge of natural law. Therefore man is not guarded by an angel.

Obj. 2. Further, a strong guard makes a weaker one superfluous. But men are guarded by God, according to Ps. 120. 4: *He shall neither slumber nor sleep, that keepeth Israel.* Therefore man does not need to be guarded by an angel.

Obj. 3. Further, the loss of the guarded comes back to the negligence of the guardian; hence it was said to a certain one: *Keep this man; and if he shall slip away, thy life shall be for his life* (III Kings 20. 39). Now many perish daily through falling into sin, whom the angels could help by visible appearance, or by miracles, or in some such way. The angels would therefore be negligent if men are given to their guardianship. But that is clearly false. Therefore the angels are not the guardians of men.

On the contrary, It is written (Ps. 90. 11): *He hath given His angels charge over thee, to keep thee in all thy ways.*

I answer that, According to the plan of Divine Providence, we find that in all things the movable and changeable are moved and regulated by the immovable and unchangeable, as all corporeal things by immovable spiritual substances, and the inferior bodies by the superior which are unchangeable in substance. We ourselves also are regulated as regards conclusions, about which we may have various opinions, by the principles which we hold in an invariable

manner. It is moreover manifest that as regards things to be done human knowledge and affection can vary and fail from good in many ways. And so it was necessary that angels should be assigned for the guardianship of men, in order to regulate them and move them to good.

Reply Obj. 1. By free choice man can avoid evil to a certain degree, but not in any sufficient degree, for he is weak in affection towards good on account of the manifold passions of the soul. Likewise universal natural knowledge of the law, which by nature belongs to man, to a certain degree directs man to good, but not in a sufficient degree, because in the application of the universal principles of law to particular works man happens to be deficient in many ways. Hence it is written (Wisd. 9. 14): *The thoughts of mortal men are fearful, and our counsels uncertain.* Thus man needs to be guarded by the angels.

Reply Obj. 2. Two things are required for a good action. First, that the affection be inclined to good, which is effected in us by the habit of moral virtue. Secondly, that reason should discover the proper ways to carry out the good of virtue. This the Philosopher attributes[1] to prudence. As regards the first, God guards man immediately by pouring into him grace and virtues. As regards the second, God guards man as his universal teacher, Whose precepts reach man by the medium of the angels, as above stated (Q. CXI, A. 1).

Reply Obj. 3. As men depart from the natural instinct of good by reason of a sinful passion, so also do they depart from the instigation of the good angels, which takes place invisibly when they enlighten man that he may do what is right. Hence that men perish is not to be ascribed to the negligence of the angels but to the malice of men. That they sometimes appear to men visibly outside the ordinary course of nature comes from a special grace of God, as likewise that miracles occur outside the order of nature.

ARTICLE 2. *Whether Each Man Is Guarded By an Angel?*

We proceed thus to the Second Article: It would seem that each man is not guarded by an angel.

Objection 1. For an angel is stronger than a man. But one man suffices to guard many men. Therefore much more can one angel guard many men.

Obj. 2. Further, the lower things are brought

[1] *Ethics*, VI, 12 (1144[a]8).

to God through the medium of the higher, as Dionysius says (*Cæl. Hier.* iv).[1] But as all the angels are unequal (Q. L, A. 4), there is only one angel between whom and men there is no medium. Therefore there is only one angel who immediately keeps men.

Obj. 3. Further, the greater angels are deputed to the greater offices. But it is not a greater office to keep one man more than another, since all men are naturally equal. Since therefore of all the angels one is greater than another, as Dionysius says (*Cæl. Hier.* x),[2] it seems that different men are not guarded by different angels.

On the contrary, On the text, *Their angels in heaven,* etc. (Matt. 8. 10), Jerome says:[3] "Great is the dignity of souls, for each one to have an angel assigned to guard it from its birth."

I answer that, Each man has a guardian angel appointed to him. The reason for this is that the guardianship of angels belongs to the execution of Divine Providence concerning men. But God's providence acts differently as regards men and as regards other corruptible creatures, for they are related differently to incorruptibility. For men are not only incorruptible in the common species, but also in the proper forms of each individual, which are the rational souls, which cannot be said of other incorruptible things. Now it is manifest that the providence of God is chiefly exercised towards what remains for ever; but as regards things which pass away, the providence of God acts so as to order them to the things which are perpetual. Thus the providence of God is related to each man as it is to every genus or species of things corruptible. But, according to Gregory (*Hom.* xxxiv *in Ev.*),[4] "the different orders are assigned to the different genera of things, for instance the Powers to coerce the demons, the Virtues to work miracles in things corporeal." And it is probable that the different species are presided over by different angels of the same order. Hence it is also reasonable to suppose that different angels are appointed to the guardianship of different men.

Reply Obj. 1. A guardian may be assigned to a man for two reasons. First, since a man is an individual, and thus to one man one guardian is due; and sometimes several are appointed to guard one. Secondly, since a man is part of a community. And thus one man is appointed as

guardian of a whole community, to whom it pertains to deal with what concerns each man in his relation to the whole community, such as external deeds, which are sources of strength or weakness to others. But guardian angels are given to men also as regards invisible and hidden things, concerning the salvation of each one in his own regard. Hence individual angels are appointed to guard individual men.

Reply Obj. 2. As above stated (Q. CXII, A. 3, ANS. 4), all the angels of the first hierarchy are, as to some things, enlightened by God directly; but, as to other things, only the superior are directly enlightened by God, and these reveal them to the inferior. And the same also applies to the inferior orders. For a lower angel is enlightened in some respects by one of the highest, and in other respects by the one immediately above him. Thus it is possible that some one angel enlightens a man immediately, and yet has other angels beneath him whom he enlightens.

Reply Obj. 3. Although men are equal in nature, still inequality exists among them, according as Divine Providence orders some to the greater, and others to the lesser things, according to Ecclus. 33. 11, 12: *With much knowledge the Lord hath divided them, and diversified their ways: some of them hath He blessed and exalted, and some of them hath He cursed and brought low.* Thus it is a greater office to guard one man than another.

ARTICLE 3. *Whether to Guard Men Belongs Only to the Lowest Order of Angels?*

We proceed thus to the Third Article: It would seem that the guardianship of men does not belong only to the lowest order of the angels.

Objection 1. For Chrysostom says[5] that the text (Matt. 18. 10), *Their angels in heaven,* etc., "is to be understood not of any angels, but of the highest." Therefore the superior angels guard men.

Obj. 2. Further, the Apostle says that angels *are sent to minister for them who shall receive the inheritance of salvation* (Heb. 1. 14), and thus it seems that the mission of the angels is directed to the guardianship of men. But five orders are sent in external ministry (Q. CXII, A. 4). Therefore all the angels of the five orders are appointed to the guardianship of men.

Obj. 3. Further, for the guardianship of men it seems especially necessary to coerce the demons, which pertains most of all to the Powers,

---

[1] Sect. 3 (PG 3, 181).
[2] Sect. 2, 3 (PG 3, 273).
[3] Bk. III (PL 26, 135).
[4] PL 76, 1251.

[5] *In Matt.,* hom. LIX (PG 58, 579).

according to Gregory (*Hom.* xxxiv *in Ev.*),[1] and to work miracles, which pertains to the Virtues. Therefore these orders are also appointed to the work of guardianship, and not only the lowest order.

On the contrary, In the Psalm (90) the guardianship of men is attributed to the angels, who belong to the lowest order, according to Dionysius (*Cæl. Hier.* ix).[2]

I answer that, As above stated (A. 2, Ans. 1), man is guarded in two ways. In one way by particular guardianship, according as to each man an angel is appointed to guard him; and such guardianship belongs to the lowest order of the angels, whose place it is, according to Gregory,[3] "to announce the lesser things." For it seems to be the least of the angelic offices to procure what concerns the salvation of only one man. The other kind of guardianship is universal, multiplied according to the different orders. For the more universal an agent is, the higher it is. Thus the guardianship of the human race belongs to the order of Principalities, or perhaps to the Archangels, whom we call the angel princes. Hence, Michael, whom we call an archangel, is also styled *one of the princes* (Dan. 10. 13). Moreover all corporeal natures are guarded by the Virtues, and likewise the demons by the Powers, and the good spirits by the Principalities, according to Gregory's opinion (*op. cit.*).[4]

Reply Obj. 1. The words of Chrysostom can be taken to mean the highest in the lowest order of angels. For, as Dionysius says (*Cæl. Hier.* x)[5] in each order there are first, middle, and last. It is, however, probable that the greater angels are appointed to keep those chosen by God for the higher degree of glory.

Reply Obj. 2. Not all the angels who are sent have a particular guardianship of individual men, but some orders have a universal guardianship, greater or less, as explained above.

Reply Obj. 3. Even inferior angels exercise the office of the superior, in so far as they share in their gifts, and they are executors of the superiors' power. And in this way all the angels of the lowest order can coerce the demons, and work miracles.

ARTICLE 4. *Whether Angels Are Appointed to the Guardianship of All Men?*

We proceed thus to the Fourth Article: It would seem that angels are not appointed to the guardianship of all men.

Objection 1. For it is written of Christ (Phil. 2. 7) that He was *made in the likeness of men, and in habit found as a man.* If therefore angels are appointed to the guardianship of all men, Christ also would have had a guardian angel. But this is not fitting, for Christ is greater than all the angels. Therefore angels are not appointed to the guardianship of all men.

Obj. 2. Further, Adam was the first of all men. But it was not fitting that he should have a guardian angel, at least in the state of innocence, for then he was not beset by any dangers. Therefore angels are not appointed to the guardianship of all men.

Obj. 3. Further, angels are appointed to the guardianship of men that they may take them by the hand and guide them to eternal life, encourage them to good works, and protect them against the assaults of the demons. But men who are foreknown to damnation never attain to eternal life. Infidels also, though at times they perform good works, do not perform them well, for they have not a right intention; for "faith directs the intention" as Augustine says (*Enarr.* ii *in* Ps. 31).[6] Moreover, the coming of Antichrist will be *according to the working of Satan,* as it is written (II Thess. 2. 9). Therefore angels are not appointed to the guardianship of all men.

On the contrary is the authority of Jerome quoted above (A. 2),[7] for he says that "each soul has an angel appointed to guard it."

I answer that, Man while in this state of life, is, as it were, on a road by which he should journey towards heaven. On this road man is threatened by many dangers both from within and from without, according to Ps. 161. 4: *In this way wherein I walked, they have hidden a snare for me.* And therefore as guardians are appointed for men who have to pass by an unsafe road, so an angel guardian is assigned to each man as long as he is a wayfarer. When, however, he arrives at the end of life he no longer has a guardian angel, but in the kingdom he will have an angel to reign with him, in hell a demon to punish him.

Reply Obj. 1. Christ as man was guided immediately by the Word of God. Therefore He did not need to be guarded by an angel. Again as regards His soul, He was one comprehending, although in regard to His passible body, he was a wayfarer. In this latter respect it was right that He should have, not a guardian angel as

---

[1] PL 76, 1251.   [2] Sect. 2 (PG 3, 260).
[3] *Op. cit.* (PL 76, 1250).
[4] PL 76, 1251.
[5] Sect. 2 (PG 3, 273).
[6] PL 36, 259.   [7] *In Matt.*, III, on 18.10 (PL 26, 135).

superior to Him, but a ministering angel as inferior to Him. And so it is written (Matt. 4. 11) that *angels came and ministered to Him.*

Reply Obj. 2. In the state of innocence man was not threatened by any peril from within, because all was well ordered within him, as we have said above (Q. XCV, AA. 1, 3). But peril threatened from without on account of the snares of the demons, as was proved by the event. For this reason he needed a guardian angel.

Reply Obj. 3. Just as the foreknown, the infidels, and even Antichrist, are not deprived of the interior help of natural reason, so neither are they deprived of that exterior help granted by God to the whole human race,—namely the guardianship of the angels. And although this help which they receive does not result in their deserving eternal life by good works, it does nevertheless conduce to their being protected from certain evils which would hurt both themselves and others. For even the demons are held off by the good angels, lest they hurt as much as they will to do. In like manner Antichrist will not do as much harm as he would wish.

ARTICLE 5. *Whether an Angel Is Appointed to Guard a Man from His Birth?*

We proceed thus to the Fifth Article: It would seem that an angel is not appointed to guard a man from his birth.

Objection 1. For angels are *sent to minister for them who shall receive the inheritance of salvation,* as the Apostle says (Heb. 1. 14). But men begin to receive the inheritance of salvation when they are baptized. Therefore an angel is appointed to guard a man from the time of his baptism, not of his birth.

Obj. 2. Further, men are guarded by angels in as far as angels enlighten and instruct them. But children are not capable of instruction as soon as they are born, for they do not have the use of reason. Therefore angels are not appointed to guard children as soon as they are born.

Obj. 3. Further, a child has a rational soul for some time before birth, just as well as after. But it does not appear that an angel is appointed to guard a child before its birth, for they are not then admitted to the sacraments of the Church. Therefore angels are not appointed to guard men from the moment of their birth.

On the contrary, Jerome says[1] that "each soul has an angel appointed to guard it from its birth."

I answer that, As Origen observes (*Tract.* xiii *super Matt.*)[2] there are two opinions on this

matter. For some have held that the guardian angel is appointed at the time of baptism, others, that he is appointed at the time of birth. The latter opinion Jerome approves (*loc. cit.*), and with reason. For those benefits which are conferred by God on man as a Christian, such as receiving the Eucharist, and the like, begin with his baptism. But those which are conferred by God on man as a rational being, are bestowed on him at his birth, for it is then that he receives that nature. Among the latter benefits we must count the guardianship of angels, as we have said above (AA. 1, 4). Therefore from the very moment of his birth man has an angel guardian appointed to him.

Reply Obj. 1. Angels are sent to minister, and efficaciously, only for those who will receive the inheritance of salvation, if we consider the ultimate effect of their guardianship, which is the realizing of that inheritance. Nevertheless, the angelic ministrations are not withdrawn from others, although they are not so efficacious as to bring them to salvation. Still, they are efficacious in so far as they ward off many evils.

Reply Obj. 2. Guardianship is ordered to enlightenment by instruction as to its ultimate and principal effect. Nevertheless it has many other effects consistent with childhood; for instance to ward off the demons, and to prevent both bodily and spiritual harm.

Reply Obj. 3. As long as the child is in the mother's womb it is not entirely separate, but by reason of a certain intimate tie, is still part of her, just as the fruit while hanging on the tree is part of the tree. And therefore it can be said with some degree of probability, that the angel who guards the mother guards the child while in the womb. But at its birth, when it becomes separate from the mother, an angel guardian is appointed to it, as Jerome, quoted above, says.

ARTICLE 6. *Whether the Angel Guardian Ever Forsakes a Man?*

We proceed thus to the Sixth Article: It would seem that the angel guardian sometimes forsakes the man whom he is appointed to guard.

Objection 1. For it is said (Jer. 51. 9) in the person of the angels: *We would have cured Babylon, but she is not healed: let us forsake her.* And (Isa. 5. 5) it is written: *I will take away the hedge*—that is, the guardianship of the angels (gloss)[3]—*and it shall be wasted.*

Obj. 2. Further, God's guardianship excels that of the angels. But God forsakes man at

---

[1] *In Matt.*, III, on 18.10 (PL 26, 135).   [2] PG 13, 1165.   [3] *Glossa interl.*, on Isa., 5.5 (IV, 141).

times, according to Ps. 21. 2: *O God, my God, look upon me: why hast Thou forsaken me?* Much rather therefore does an angel guardian forsake man.

Obj. 3. Further, according to Damascene (*De Fide Orth.* ii, 3),[1] "When the angels are here with us, they are not in heaven." But sometimes they are in heaven. Therefore sometimes they forsake us.

On the contrary, The demons are ever assailing us, according to I Pet. 5. 8: *Your adversary the devil, as a roaring lion, goeth about, seeking whom he may devour.* Much more therefore do the good angels ever guard us.

I answer that, As appears above (A. 2), the guardianship of the angels is an effect of Divine Providence in regard to man. Now it is evident that neither man, nor anything at all, is entirely withdrawn from the providence of God; for in as far as a thing participates being, so far is it subject to the providence that extends over all being. God indeed is said to forsake man, according to the ordering of His providence, but only in so far as He allows man to suffer some defect of punishment or of fault. In like manner it must be said that the angel guardian never forsakes a man entirely, but sometimes he leaves him in some particular, for instance by not preventing him from being subject to some trouble, or even from falling into sin, according to the ordering of Divine judgments. In this sense Babylon and the House of Israel are said to have been forsaken by the angels, because their angel guardians did not prevent them from being subject to tribulation.

From this the answers are clear to the *first and second objections.*

Reply Obj. 3. Although an angel may forsake a man sometimes as regards place, he does not for that reason forsake him as to the effect of his guardianship. For even when he is in heaven he knows what is happening to man; nor does he need time for his local motion, for he can be with man in an instant.

ARTICLE 7. *Whether Angels Grieve for the Ills of Those Whom They Guard?*

We proceed thus to the Seventh Article: It would seem that angels grieve for the ills of those whom they guard.

Objection 1. For it is written (Isa. 33. 7): *The angels of peace shall weep bitterly.* But weeping is a sign of grief and sorrow. Therefore angels grieve for the ills of those whom they guard.

Obj. 2. Further, according to Augustine,[2] "sorrow is for those things that happen against our will." But the loss of the man whom he has guarded is against the guardian angel's will. Therefore angels grieve for the loss of men.

Obj. 3. Further, as sorrow is contrary to joy, so penance is contrary to sin. But angels rejoice about one sinner doing penance, as we are told, Luke 15. 7. Therefore they grieve for the just man who falls into sin.

Obj. 4. Further, on Numbers 18. 12: *Whatsoever first-fruits they offer,* etc., the gloss of Origen says:[3] "The angels are brought to judgment as to whether men have fallen through their negligence or through their own fault." But it is reasonable for anyone to grieve for the ills which have brought him to judgment. Therefore angels grieve for men's sins.

On the contrary, Where there is grief and sorrow, there is not perfect happiness. And so it is written (Apoc. 21. 4): *Death shall be no more, nor mourning, nor crying, nor sorrow.* But the angels are perfectly happy. Therefore they have no cause for grief.

I answer that, Angels do not grieve, either for sins or for the pains inflicted on men. For grief and sorrow, according to Augustine (*loc. cit.*) are for those things which occur against our will. But nothing happens in the world contrary to the will of the angels and the other blessed, because their will cleaves entirely to the ordering of Divine justice, while nothing happens in the world save what is effected or permitted by Divine justice. Therefore absolutely speaking, nothing occurs in the world against the will of the blessed. For as the Philosopher says[4] that is called absolutely voluntary, which a man wills in a particular case, and at a particular time, having considered all the circumstances. But considered universally, such a thing would not be voluntary; thus for example, the sailor does not will the casting of his cargo into the sea, considered universally and absolutely, but he wills it on account of the threatened danger of his life. And so this is voluntary rather than involuntary, as stated in the same passage. Therefore universally and absolutely speaking, the angels do not will sin and the pains inflicted on its account, but they do will the fulfilment of the ordering of Divine justice in this matter, in respect of which some are subjected to pains and are allowed to fall into sin.

Reply Obj. 1. These words of Isaias may be

---

[1] PG 94, 869.

[2] *City of God,* XIV, 15 (PL 41, 424).
[3] *In Num.,* hom. XI (PG 12, 647).
[4] *Ethics,* III, I (1110[a]9).

understood of the angels, that is, the messengers, of Ezechias, who wept on account of the words of Rabsaces, as related Isa. 37. 2 seqq. This would be the literal sense. According to the allegorical sense the angels of peace are the apostles and preachers who weep for men's sins. If this passage be expounded of the blessed angels according to the anagogical sense, then the expression is metaphorical, and signifies that, universally speaking, the angels will the salvation of mankind. For it is in this manner that we attribute passions to God and the angels.

The *reply to the second objection* appears from what has been said.

Reply Obj. 3. Both in man's repentance and in man's sin there is one reason for the angel's joy, namely the fulfilment of the ordering of the Divine Providence.

Reply Obj. 4. The angels are brought into judgment for the sins of men, not as guilty, but as witnesses to convict man of weakness.

ARTICLE 8. *Whether There Can Be Strife or Discord among the Angels?*

We proceed thus to the Eighth Article: It would seem that there can not be strife or discord among the angels.

Objection 1. For it is written (Job 25. 2): *Who maketh peace in His high places.* But strife is opposed to peace. Therefore among the high angels there is no strife.

Obj. 2. Further, where there is perfect charity and just authority there can be no strife. But all this exists among the angels. Therefore there is no strife among the angels.

Obj. 3. Further, if we say that angels strive for those whom they guard, one angel must take one side, and another angel the opposite side. But if one side has justice the other side lacks justice. It will follow therefore, that a good angel is a furtherer of injustice, which is unfitting. Therefore there is no strife among good angels.

On the contrary, It is written (Dan. 10. 13): *The prince of the kingdom of the Persians resisted me one and twenty days.* But this prince of the Persians was the angel appointed to the guardianship of the kingdom of the Persians. Therefore one good angel resists the others, and thus there is strife among them.

I answer that, The raising of this question is occasioned by this passage of Daniel.[1] Jerome explains it[2] by saying that the prince of the king-

dom of the Persians is the angel who opposed the setting free of the people of Israel, for whom Daniel was praying, his prayers being offered to God by Gabriel. And this resistance of his may have been caused by some prince of the demons having led the Jewish captives in Persia into sin, which sin was an impediment to the efficacy of the prayer which Daniel put up for that same people.

But according to Gregory (*Moral.* xvii),[3] the prince of the kingdom of Persia was a good angel appointed to the guardianship of that kingdom. To see therefore how one angel can be said to resist another, we must note that the Divine judgments in regard to various kingdoms and various men are executed by the angels. Now in their actions the angels are ruled by the Divine decree. But it happens at times in various kingdoms or various men there are contrary merits or demerits, so that one of them is subject to or placed over another. As to what is the ordering of Divine wisdom on such matters, the angels cannot know it unless God reveal it to them, and so they need to consult Divine wisdom concerning these things. And so according as they consult the Divine will concerning various contrary and opposing merits, they are said to resist one another; not that their wills are in opposition, since they are all of one mind as to the fulfilment of the Divine decree, but that the things about which they seek knowledge are in opposition.

From this *the answers to the objections* are clear.

QUESTION CXIV
OF THE ASSAULTS OF THE DEMONS
(In Five Articles)

WE now consider the assaults of the demons. Under this head there are five points of inquiry: (1) Whether men are assailed by the demons? (2) Whether to tempt is proper to the devil? (3) Whether all the sins of men are to be set down to the assaults or temptations of the demons? (4) Whether they can work true miracles for the purpose of leading men astray? (5) Whether the demons who are overcome by men are hindered from making further assaults?

ARTICLE 1. *Whether Men Are Assailed by the Demons?*

We proceed thus to the First Article: It would seem that men are not assailed by the demons.

---

[1] Cf. Alexander of Hales, *Summa Theol.*, I–II, n. 223 (QR II, 277); cf. also William of Auxerre, *Summa Aurea*, II, 4, Q. 8 (fol. 46a).

[2] *In Dan.*, on 10.13 (PL 25, 581).

[3] Chap. 12 (PL 76, 19).

Objection 1. For angels are sent by God to guard man. But demons are not sent by God, for the demons' intention is the loss of souls, whereas God's intention is the salvation of souls. Therefore demons are not assigned to assail man.

Obj. 2. Further, it is not a fair fight for the weak to be set against the strong, and the ignorant against the astute. But men are weak and ignorant, whereas the demons are strong and astute. It is not therefore to be permitted by God, the author of all justice, that men should be assailed by demons.

Obj. 3. Further, the assaults of the flesh and the world are enough for man's exercise. But God permits His elect to be assailed that they may be exercised. Therefore there is no need for them to be assailed by the demons.

On the contrary, The Apostle says (Eph. 6. 12): *Our wrestling is not against flesh and blood; but against Principalities and Powers, against the rulers of the world of this darkness, against the spirits of wickedness in the high places.*

I answer that, Two things may be considered in the assault of the demons—the assault itself, and its ordering. The assault itself is due to the malice of the demons, who through envy endeavour to hinder man's progress, and through pride usurp a semblance of Divine power, by appointing certain ministers to assail man, as the angels of God in their various offices minister to man's salvation. But the ordering of the assault is from God, Who knows how to make orderly use of evil by ordering it to good. On the other hand, in regard to the angels, both their guardianship and its ordering are to be referred to God as their first author.

Reply Obj. 1. The wicked angels assail men in two ways. First, by instigating them to sin. And thus they are not sent by God to assail us, but are sometimes permitted to do so according to God's just judgments. But sometimes their assault is a punishment to man. And thus they are sent by God, as the lying spirit was sent to punish Achab, King of Israel, as is related in III Kings (22. 20). For punishment is referred to God as its first author. Nevertheless the demons who are sent to punish, do so with an intention other than that for which they are sent; for they punish from hatred or envy, although they are sent by God on account of His justice.

Reply Obj. 2. In order that the conditions of the fight be not unequal, there is as regards man the promised recompense, to be gained principally through the grace of God, secondarily through the guardianship of the angels. And so (IV Kings 6. 16), Eliseus said to his servant: *Fear not, for there are more with us than with them.*

Reply Obj. 3. The assault of the flesh and the world would suffice for the exercise of human weakness, but it does not suffice for the demons' malice, which makes use of both the above in assailing men. But by the Divine ordering this tends to the glory of the elect.

ARTICLE 2. *Whether to Tempt Is Proper to the Devil?*

We proceed thus to the Second Article: It would seem that to tempt is not proper to the devil.

Objection 1. For God is said to tempt, according to Genesis 22. 1, *God tempted Abraham.* Moreover man is tempted by the flesh and the world. Again, man is said to tempt God, and to tempt man. Therefore it is not proper to the devil to tempt.

Obj. 2. Further, to tempt is a sign of ignorance. But the demons know what happens among men. Therefore the demons do not tempt.

Obj. 3. Further, temptation is the road to sin. Now sin dwells in the will. Since therefore the demons cannot change man's will, as appears from what has been said above (Q. CXI, A. 2), it seems that it is not in their province to tempt.

On the contrary, It is written (I Thess. 3. 5): *Lest perhaps he that tempteth should have tempted you:* to which the gloss adds,[1] "that is, the devil, whose office it is to tempt."

I answer that, To tempt is, properly speaking, to make trial of something. Now we make trial of something in order to know something about it. Hence the immediate end of every tempter is knowledge. But sometimes another end, either good or bad, is sought to be acquired through that knowledge; a good end, when, for instance, one desires to know of someone, what sort of a man he is as to knowledge, or virtue, with a view to his advancement; a bad end, when that knowledge is sought with the purpose of deceiving or ruining him.

From this we can gather how various beings are said to tempt in various ways. For man is said to tempt sometimes indeed merely for the sake of knowing something; and for this reason it is a sin to tempt God. For man, being uncertain as it were, presumes to make an experiment of God's power. Sometimes too he tempts

---

[1] *Glossa inter.* (VI, 110 v); *Glossa* Lombardi (PL 192, 297).

in order to help, sometimes in order to hurt. The devil, however, always tempts in order to hurt by urging man into sin. In this sense it is said to be his proper office to tempt; for though at times man tempts thus, he does this as minister of the devil. God is said to tempt that He may know, in the same sense as that is said to know which makes others to know. Hence it is written (Deut. 13. 3): *The Lord your God trieth you, that it may appear whether you love Him.*

The flesh and the world are said to tempt as the instruments or matter of temptations, since one can know what sort of a man someone is, according as he follows or resists the desires of the flesh, and according as he despises worldly advantages and adversity; of which things the devil also makes use in tempting.

Thus the *reply to the first objection* is clear.

Reply Obj. 2. The demons know what happens outwardly among men, but the inward disposition of man God alone knows, Who is the *weigher of spirits* (Prov. 16. 2). It is this disposition that makes man more prone to one vice than to another. Hence the devil tempts in order to explore this inward disposition of man, so that he may tempt him to that vice to which he is most prone.

Reply Obj. 3. Although a demon cannot change the will, yet, as stated above (Q. CXI, A. 3), he can change the lower powers of man, in a certain degree, by which powers, though the will cannot be forced, it can nevertheless be inclined.

ARTICLE 3. *Whether All Sins Are Due to the Temptation of the Devil?*

We proceed thus to the Third Article: It would seem that all sins are due to the temptation of the devil.

Objection 1. For Dionysius says (*Div. Nom.* iv)[1] that "the multitude of demons is the cause of all evils, both to themselves and to others." And Damascene says (*De Fide Orth.* ii, 4)[2] that "all malice and all uncleanness have been devised by the devil."

Obj. 2. Further, of every sinner can be said what the Lord said of the Jews (John 8. 44): *You are of your father the devil.* But this was in as far as they sinned through the devil's instigation. Therefore every sin is due to the devil's instigation.

Obj. 3. Further, as angels are appointed to guard men, so demons are appointed to assail men. But every good thing we do is due to the

suggestion of the good angels, because the Divine gifts are borne to us by the angels. Therefore all the evil we do, is due to the instigation of the devil.

On the contrary, It is written (*De Eccl. Dogmat.*):[3] "Not all our evil thoughts are stirred up by the devil, but sometimes they arise from the movement of our free choice."

I answer that, One thing can be the cause of another in two ways, directly and indirectly. Indirectly as when an agent is the cause of a disposition to a certain effect, it is said to be the occasional and indirect cause of that effect. For instance, we might say that he who dries the wood is the cause of the wood burning. In this way we must admit that the devil is the cause of all our sins, because it was he who instigated the first man to sin, from whose sin there resulted a proneness to sin in the whole human race. And we must take the words of Damascene and Dionysius in this sense.

But a thing is said to be the direct cause of something, when its action tends to it directly. And in this way the devil is not the cause of every sin. For all sins are not committed at the devil's instigation, but some are due to the freedom of choice and the corruption of the flesh. For, as Origen says (*Peri Archon,* iii),[4] even if there were no devil, men would have the desire for food and love and such pleasures, with regard to which many disorders may arise unless those desires be curbed by reason, especially if we presuppose the corruption of our natures. Now it is in the power of free choice to curb this appetite and keep it in order. Consequently there is no need for all sins to come from the instigation of the devil. But those sins which are from his instigation man perpetrates "through being deceived by the same blandishments as were our first parents," as Isidore says.[5]

Thus the *answer to the first objection* is clear.

Reply Obj. 2. When man commits sin without being instigated to it by the devil, he nevertheless becomes a child of the devil, in so far as he imitates him who was the first to sin.

Reply Obj. 3. Man can of his own accord fall into sin, but he cannot advance in merit without the Divine assistance, which is borne to man by the ministry of the angels. For this reason the angels take part in all our good works, though all our sins are not due to the demons' instigation. Nevertheless there is no kind of sin which is not sometimes due to the demons' suggestion.

---

[1] Sect. 18 (PG 3, 716).   [2] PG 94, 877.

[3] Gennadius, Chap. 82 (PL 58, 999).
[4] Chap. 2 (PG 11, 305).
[5] *Sent.,* III, 5 (PL 83, 664).

ARTICLE 4. *Whether Demons Can Lead Men Astray by Means of True Miracles?*

We proceed thus to the Fourth Article: It would seem that the demons cannot lead men astray by means of true miracles.

Objection 1. For the activity of the demons will show itself especially in the works of Antichrist. But as the Apostle says (II Thess. 2. 9), his *coming is according to the working of Satan, in all power, and signs, and lying wonders.* Much the more therefore at other times do the demons perform only by lying wonders.

Obj. 2. Further, true miracles are wrought by some corporeal change. But demons are unable to change the nature of a body. For Augustine says,[1] "I cannot believe that the human body can receive the limbs of a beast by means of a demon's art or power." Therefore the demons cannot work true miracles.

Obj. 3. Further, an argument which may prove both ways is useless. If therefore true miracles can be wrought by demons to persuade one of what is false, they will be useless to confirm the teaching of faith. This is unfitting, for it is written (Mark 16. 20): *The Lord working withal, and confirming the word with signs that followed.*

On the contrary, Augustine says (QQ. LXXXIII):[2] "Often by means of the magic art miracles are wrought like those which are wrought by the servants of God."

I answer that, As is clear from what has been said above (Q. CX, A. 4), if we take a miracle in the strict sense, the demons cannot work miracles, nor can any creature, but God alone, since in the strict sense a miracle is something done outside the order of the entire created nature, under which order every power of a creature is contained. But sometimes miracles may be taken in a wide sense for whatever exceeds the human power and experience. And thus demons can work miracles, that is, things which rouse man's astonishment, by reason of their being beyond his power and outside his sphere of knowledge. For even a man by doing what is beyond the power and knowledge of another leads him to marvel at what he has done, so that in a way he seems to that man to have worked a miracle.

It is to be noted, however, that although these works of demons which appear marvellous to us are not real miracles, they are sometimes never-theless something real. Thus the magicians of Pharaoh by the demons' power produced real serpents and frogs (Exod. 7.12; 8.7). And "when fire came down from heaven and at one blow consumed Job's servants and sheep; when the storm struck down his house and with it his children—these were the work of Satan, not phantoms," as Augustine says.[3]

Reply Obj. 1. As Augustine says in the same place, the works of Antichrist may be called lying signs, "either because he will deceive men's senses by means of phantoms, so that he will not really do what he will seem to do; or because, if he work real prodigies, they will lead those into falsehood who believe in him."

Reply Obj. 2. As we have said above (Q. CX, A. 2), corporeal matter does not obey either good or bad angels at their will, in such a way as to enable the demons by their power to transmute matter from one form to another. But they can employ certain seeds that exist in the elements of the world in order to produce these effects, as Augustine says (*De Trin.* iii, 8, 9).[4] Therefore it must be admitted that all the transformations of corporeal things which can be produced by certain natural powers, to which we must assign the seeds mentioned above, can be produced by the operation of the demons by the employment of these seeds, as when certain things are transformed into serpents or frogs, which can be produced by putrefaction. But those transformations which cannot be produced by the power of nature cannot in reality be effected by the operation of the demons; for instance, that the human body be changed into the body of a beast, or that the body of a dead man return to life. And if at times something of this sort seems to be effected by the operation of demons, it is not real but according to appearance only.

Now this may happen in two ways. First, from within. In this way a demon can work on man's imagination and even on his corporeal senses, so that something seems otherwise than it is, as explained above (Q. CXI, AA. 3, 4). It is said indeed that this can be done sometimes by the power of certain bodies. Secondly, from without. For just as he can from the air form a body of any form and shape, and assume it so as to appear in it visibly, so, in the same way he can clothe any corporeal thing with any corporeal form, so as to appear there. This is what Augustine says:[5] "Man's imagination, which,

[1] *City of God,* XVIII, 18 (PL 41, 575).
[2] *Lib.* XXI, *Sent.,* 4, among the supposititious works of St. Augustine. (PL 40, 726).
[3] *City of God,* XX, 19 (PL 41, 687).
[4] PL 42, 875, 877.
[5] *City of God,* XVIII, 18 (PL 41, 575).

whether thinking or dreaming, takes the forms of an innumerable number of things, appears to other men's senses, as it were embodied in the semblance of some animal." This is not to be understood as though the imagination itself or the images formed in it were identified with that which appears embodied to the senses of another man, but that the demon, who forms an image in a man's imagination, can offer the same picture to another man's senses.

Reply Obj. 3. As Augustine says (QQ. LXXXIII, *qu.* 79):[1] "When magicians do what holy men do, they do it for a different end and by a different law. The former do it for their own glory, the latter, for the glory of God; the former, by certain private compacts, the latter by the evident assistance and command of God, to Whom every creature is subject."

ARTICLE 5. *Whether a Demon Who Is Overcome by Man, Is for This Reason Hindered from Making Further Assaults?*

We proceed thus to the Fifth Article: It would seem that a demon who is overcome by a man, is not for that reason hindered from any further assault.

Objection 1. For Christ overcame the tempter most effectively. Yet afterwards the demon assailed Him by instigating the Jews to kill Him. Therefore it is not true that the devil when conquered ceases his assaults.

Obj. 2. Further, to inflict punishment on one who has been worsted in a fight, is to incite him to a sharper attack. But this does not accord with God's mercy. Therefore the conquered demons are not prevented from further assaults.

On the contrary, It is written (Matt. 4. 11): *Then the devil left Him,* that is, Christ Who overcame.

I answer that, Some say[2] that when once a demon has been overcome he can no more tempt any man at all, neither to the same nor to any other sin. And others say[3] that he can tempt others, but not the same man. This seems more probable as long as we understand it to be so for a certain definite time. And so it is written (Luke 4. 13): *All temptation being ended, the devil departed from Him for a time.* There are two reasons for this. One is on the part of God's clemency. For as Chrysostom says (*Super*

[1] PL 40, 92.

[2] Origen, *In Lib. Jesu Nave,* xv (PG 12, 903), cited in Peter Lombard, *Sent.,* ii, d. vi, chap. 7 (QR i, 333).

[3] Anonymously mentioned by Albert the Great, *In Sent.* ii, d. vi, A. 9 (BO xxvii, 138). Cf. also Alexander of Hales, *Summa Theol.,* ii–ii, 105 (QR iii, 124); also Origen, *In Lib. Jesu Nave,* xv (PG 12, 903).

Matt. Hom. v),[4] "the devil does not tempt man for just as long as he likes, but for as long as God allows; for although He allows him to tempt for a short time, He orders him off on account of our weakness." The other reason is taken from the astuteness of the devil. As to this, Ambrose says[5] on Luke 4. 13: "The devil is afraid of persisting, because he shrinks from frequent defeat." That the devil does nevertheless sometimes return to the assault, is apparent from Matthew 12. 44: *I will return into my house from whence I came out.*

From what has been said, *the objections* can easily be solved.

QUESTION CXV

OF THE ACTION OF THE CORPOREAL CREATURE

(In Six Articles)

WE have now to consider the action of the corporeal creature (Q. CXVI), and fate, which is ascribed to certain bodies. Concerning corporeal actions there are six points of inquiry: (1) Whether a body can be active? (2) Whether there exist in bodies certain seminal principles? (3) Whether the heavenly bodies are the causes of what is done here by the inferior bodies? (4) Whether they are the cause of human acts? (5) Whether demons are subject to their influence? (6) Whether the heavenly bodies impose necessity on those things which are subject to their influence?

ARTICLE 1. *Whether a Body Can Be Active?*

We proceed thus to the First Article: It would seem that no bodies are active.

Objection 1. For Augustine says,[6] "There are things that are acted upon, but do not act; such are bodies: there is one Who acts but is not acted upon; this is God: there are things that both act and are acted upon; these are the spiritual substances."

Obj. 2. Further, every agent except the first agent requires in its work a subject susceptible of its action. But "there is no substance below the corporeal substance which can be receptive of the latter's action, since it belongs to the lowest degree in beings."[7] Therefore corporeal substance is not active.

Obj. 3. Further, every corporeal substance is limited by quantity. But quantity hinders sub-

[4] In the *Opus Imperfectum,* among his supposititious works.

[5] PL 15, 1707.   [6] *City of God,* v, 9 (PL 41, 151).

[7] Avicebron, *Fons Vitae,* ii, 9 (BK 40.22) on this and the following, cf. Gilson, AHDLM (1926), p. 29–33.

stance from movement and action, because it surrounds it and penetrates it, just as a cloud hinders the air from receiving light. A sign of this is that the more a body increases in quantity, the heavier it is and the more difficult to move.[1] Therefore no corporeal substance is active.

Obj. 4. Further, the power of action in every agent is according to its nearness to the first active cause. But "bodies, being most composite, are most remote from the first active cause, which is most simple."[2] Therefore no bodies are active.

Obj. 5. Further, if a body is an agent, the term of its action is either a substantial, or an accidental form. But it is not a substantial form, for it is not possible to find in a body any principle of action save an active quality, which is an accident, and an accident cannot be the cause of a substantial form, since the cause is always more excellent than the effect. Likewise, neither is it an accidental form, for an accident does not extend beyond its subject, as Augustine says (*De Trin.* ix, 4).[3] Therefore no bodies are active.

On the contrary, Dionysius says (*Cæl. Hier.* xv)[4] that among other qualities of corporeal fire, "it shows its greatness in its action and power on that of which it lays hold."

I answer that, It is apparent to the senses that some bodies are active. But concerning the action of bodies there have been three errors. For some denied all action to bodies. This is the opinion of Avicebron in his book on *The Fount of Life,* where, by the arguments mentioned above, he endeavours to prove that no bodies act, but that all the actions which seem to be the actions of bodies are the actions of "some spiritual power that penetrates all bodies."[5] Thus, according to him, it is not fire that heats, but a spiritual power which penetrates by means of the fire. And this opinion seems to be derived from that of Plato. For Plato held that all forms existing in corporeal matter are participated, and determined and limited to this nature, and that separate forms are absolute and as it were universal.[6] Therefore he said that these separate forms are the causes of forms that exist in matter.[7] Therefore since the form which is in corporeal matter is determined to

this matter individualized by quantity, Avicebron held[8] that the corporeal form is held fast and confined by quantity, as the principle of individuation, so as to be unable by action to extend to any other matter; and that the spiritual and immaterial form alone, which is not confined by quantity, can flow forth in action on something else.

But this does not prove that the corporeal form is not an agent, but that it is not a universal agent. For in proportion as a thing is participated, so, of necessity, must that which is proper to it be participated; thus the participation of visibility is in proportion to the participation of light. But to act, which is nothing else than to make something to be in act, is essentially proper to an act as such; and thus every agent produces its like. So therefore that a thing is an indeterminate and universal agent comes from the fact that it is a form not determined by matter subject to quantity; but that it is a limited and particular agent comes from the fact that it is determined to this matter. And so if the form of fire were separate, as the Platonists supposed, it would be, in a fashion, the cause of every burning. But this form of fire which is in this corporeal matter, is the cause of this burning which passes from this body to that. Hence such an action is effected by the contact of two bodies.

But this opinion of Avicebron goes further than that of Plato. For Plato held only substantial forms to be separate,[9] while he reduced accidents to the material principles which are the great and the small, which he considered to be the first contraries,[10] just as others considered them to be the rare and the dense.[11] Consequently both Plato and Avicenna, who follow him to a certain extent, held that corporeal agents act through their accidental forms, by disposing matter for the substantial form, but that the ultimate perfection attained by the introduction of the substantial form is due to an immaterial principle. And this is the second opinion concerning the action of bodies, of which we have spoken above when treating of the creation (Q. XLV, A. 8).[12]

The third opinion is that of Democritus, who held that action takes place through the flowing out of atoms from the corporeal agent, while passion consists in the reception of the atoms in the pores of the passive body. This opinion is

---

[1] *Fons Vitae,* chaps. 9, 10 (BK 41).   [2] *Ibid.*
[3] PL 42, 963; cf. Maimonides, *Guide,* I, 73 (FR 124).
[4] Sect. 2 (PG 3, 329).
[5] *Fons Vitae,* II, 10 (BK 42.1).
[6] Cf. Q. LXXXIV, A. I.
[7] Cf. St. Thomas, *De Potent.,* III, 8; Averroes, *In Meta.,* XII, 8 (VIII, 305E).

[8] *Fons Vitae,* II, 9, 10 (BK 41).
[9] Cf. Aristotle, *Metaphysics,* I, 9 (990[b]29).
[10] Cf. Aristotle, *Physics,* I, 4 (187[a]17).
[11] Cf. Aristotle, *Ibid.,* (187[a]15).
[12] Cf. also Q. LXV, A. 4.

disproved by Aristotle.[1] For it would follow that a body would not be passive as a whole, and that the quantity of the active body would be diminished through its action, which things are manifestly untrue.

We must therefore say that a body acts according as it is in act, on another body according as it is in potency.

Reply Obj. 1. This passage of Augustine is to be understood of the whole corporeal nature considered as a whole, which thus has no nature inferior to it, on which it can act, in the way the spiritual nature acts on the corporeal, and the uncreated nature on the created. Nevertheless one body is inferior to another, according as it is in potency to that which the other has in act.

From this follows the solution of the second objection. But it must be observed, when Avicebron argues thus,[2] "There is a mover who is not moved, namely, the first maker of all; therefore, on the other hand, there exists something moved which is purely passive," that this is to be conceded. But this latter is prime matter, which is a pure potency, just as God is pure act. Now a body is composed of potency and act, and therefore it is both active and passive.

Reply Obj. 3. Quantity does not entirely hinder the corporeal form from action, as stated above, but from being a universal agent, in so far as a form is individualized through being in matter subject to quantity. The proof taken from the weight of bodies is not to the purpose. First, because addition of quantity is not the cause of weight, as is proved.[3] Secondly, it is false that weight retards movement; on the contrary, the heavier a thing, the more it moves with its own movement. Thirdly, because action is not effected by local movement, as Democritus held, but by something being reduced from potency to act.

Reply Obj. 4. A body is not that which is most distant from God, for it participates something of a likeness to the Divine Being, according as it has a form. That which is most distant from God is prime matter, which is in no way active, since it is a pure potency.

Reply Obj. 5. The term of a body's action is both an accidental form and a substantial form. For the active quality, such as heat, although itself an accident, acts nevertheless by virtue of the substantial form, as its instrument, and so its action can terminate in a substantial form. Thus natural heat, as the instrument of the soul,

has an action terminating in the generation of flesh. But it produces an accident by its own power. Nor is it against the nature of an accident to surpass its subject in acting, but that it surpass it in being, unless indeed one were to imagine that an accident transfers its identical self from the agent to the patient, in the way that Democritus explained action by a procession of atoms.

ARTICLE 2. *Whether There Are Any Seminal Principles in Corporeal Matter?*

We proceed thus to the Second Article: It would seem that there are no seminal principles in corporeal matter.

Objection 1. For principle (*ratio*) implies something of a spiritual order. But in corporeal matter nothing exists spiritually, but only materially, that is, according to the mode of that in which it is. Therefore there are no seminal principles in corporeal matter.

Obj. 2. Further, Augustine (*De Trin.* iii, 8, 9)[4] says that demons produce certain results by employing with a hidden movement certain seeds, which they know to exist in matter. But bodies, not principles, are what can be employed with local movement. Therefore it is unreasonable to say that there are seminal principles in corporeal matter.

Obj. 3. Further, seeds are active principles. But there are no active principles in corporeal matter, since, as we have said above, it does not pertain to matter to act (A. 1, ANS. 2, 4). Therefore there are no seminal principles in corporeal matter.

Obj. 4. Further, there are said to be certain causal principles (Augustine, *De Gen. ad lit.* vi, 14)[5] which seem to suffice for the production of things. But seminal principles are not causal principles, for miracles are outside the scope of seminal principles, but not of causal principles. Therefore it is unreasonable to say that there are seminal principles in corporeal matter.

On the contrary, Augustine says (*De Trin.* iii, 8):[6] "Of all the things which are generated in a corporeal and visible fashion, certain seeds lie hidden in the corporeal things of this world."

I answer that, It is customary to name things after what is more perfect, as the Philosopher says.[7] Now in the whole corporeal nature, living bodies are the most perfect, and so the word nature has been transferred from living things to

---

[1] *Generation and Corruption*, I, 8 (325ᵃ23).
[2] *Fons Vitae*, II, 10 (BK 42.7).
[3] Aristotle, *Heavens*, IV, 2 (308ᵇ5).

[4] PL 42, 876, 878.
[5] PL 34, 349; cf. also Bonaventure, *In Sent.*, II, d. 18, A. 1, Q. 2 (QR II, 438).
[6] PL 42, 875.   [7] *Soul*, II, 4 (416ᵇ23).

all natural things. For the word itself, nature, as the Philosopher says,[1] was first applied to signify the generation of living things, which is called nativity. And because living things are generated from a principle united to them, as fruit from a tree, and the offspring from the mother, to whom it is united, consequently the word nature has been applied to every principle of movement existing in that which is moved. Now it is manifest that the active and passive principles of the generation of living things are the seeds from which living things are generated. Therefore Augustine fittingly gave the name of seminal principles (*seminales rationes*) to all those active and passive powers which are the principles of natural generation and movement.[2]

These active and passive powers may be considered in several orders. For in the first place, as Augustine says (*Gen. ad lit.* vi, 10),[3] they are principally and originally in the Word of God, as exemplar ideas. Secondly, they are in the elements of the world, where they were produced altogether at the beginning, as in universal causes. Thirdly, they are in those things which, in the succession of time, are produced by universal causes, for instance in this plant, and in that animal, as in particular causes. Fourthly, they are in the seeds produced from animals and plants. And these again are related to further particular effects, as the primordial universal causes to the first effects produced.

Reply Obj. 1. These active and passive powers (virtues) of natural things, though not called principles (*rationes*) by reason of their being in corporeal matter, can nevertheless be called so in respect of their origin, according as they are the effect of the exemplar ideas (*rationes ideales*).

Reply Obj. 2. These active and passive principles are in certain parts of corporeal things, and when they are employed with local movement for the production of certain results, we speak of the demons as employing seeds.

Reply Obj. 3. The seed of the male is the active principle in the generation of an animal. But that can be called seed also which the female contributes as the passive principle. And thus the word seed covers both active and passive principles.

Reply Obj. 4. From the words of Augustine when speaking of these seminal principles, it is easy to gather that they are also causal principles, just as seed is a kind of cause; for he says

(*De Trin.* iii, 9)[4] that, "as a mother is pregnant with the unborn offspring, so is the world itself pregnant with the causes of unborn beings." Nevertheless, the exemplar ideas can be called causal principles, but not, strictly speaking, seminal principles, because seed is not a separate principle, and because miracles are not wrought outside the scope of causal principles. Likewise neither are miracles wrought which are outside the scope of the passive principles so implanted in the creature that the latter can be used to any purpose that God commands. But miracles are said to be wrought outside the scope of the natural active principles, and the passive potencies which are ordered to such active principles, and this is what is meant when we say that they are wrought outside the scope of seminal principles.

ARTICLE 3. *Whether the Heavenly Bodies Are the Cause of What Is Produced in Bodies Here Below?*

We proceed thus to the Third Article: It would seem that the heavenly bodies are not the cause of what is produced in bodies here below.

Objection 1. For Damascene says (*De Fide Orth.* ii, 7):[5] "We say that they," namely, the heavenly bodies, "are not the cause of generation or corruption; they are rather signs of storms and atmospheric changes."

Obj. 2. Further, for the production of anything, an agent and matter suffice. But in things here below there is passive matter; and there are contrary agents—heat and cold, and the like. Therefore for the production of things here below there is no need to ascribe causality to the heavenly bodies.

Obj. 3. Further, the agent produces its like. Now we see that everything which is produced here below is produced through the action of heat and cold, moisture and dryness, and other such qualities, which do not exist in the heavenly bodies. Therefore the heavenly bodies are not the cause of what is produced here below.

Obj. 4. Further, Augustine says,[6] "Nothing is more corporeal than sex." But sex is not caused by the heavenly bodies; a sign of this is that of twins born under the same constellation, one may be male, the other female. Therefore the heavenly bodies are not the cause of things produced in bodies here below.

On the contrary, Augustine says (*De Trin.* iii, 4):[7] "Bodies of a grosser and inferior nature are ruled in a certain order by those of a more sub-

---

[1] *Metaphysics*, v, 4 (1014[b]16).
[2] *De Trin.*, III, 8 (PL 42, 875).   [3] PL 34, 346.
[4] PL 42, 878.   [5] PG 94, 983.
[6] *City of God*, v, 6 (PL 41, 146).   [7] PL 42, 873.

tle and powerful nature." And Dionysius (*Div. Nom.* iv)[1] says that "the light of the sun conduces to the generation of sensible bodies, moves them to life, gives them nourishment, growth, and perfection."

I answer that, Since every multitude proceeds from unity, and since what is immovable is always in the same way of being, while what is moved has many ways of being, it must be observed that throughout the whole of nature, all movement proceeds from the immovable. Therefore the more immovable certain things are, the more are they the cause of those things which are most movable. Now the heavenly bodies are of all bodies the most immovable, for they are not moved save locally. Therefore the movements of bodies here below, which are various and multiform, must be reduced to the movement of the heavenly bodies, as to their cause.

Reply Obj. 1. These words of Damascene are to be understood as denying that the heavenly bodies are the first cause of generation and corruption here below; for this was affirmed by those who held that the heavenly bodies are gods.

Reply Obj. 2. The active principles of bodies here below are only the active qualities of the elements, such as hot and cold and the like. If therefore the substantial forms of inferior bodies were not diversified save according to accidents of that kind, the principles of which the early natural philosophers held to be the rare and the dense,[2] there would be no need to suppose some principle above these inferior bodies, for they would be of themselves sufficient to act. But to anyone who considers the matter rightly, it is clear that those accidents are merely material dispositions in regard to the substantial forms of natural bodies. Now matter is not of itself sufficient to act. And therefore it is necessary to suppose some active principle above these material dispositions.

This is why the Platonists maintained the existence of separate species, by participation of which the inferior bodies receive their substantial forms.[3] But this does not seem enough. For the separate species, since they are supposed to be immovable, would always have the same mode of being, and consequently there would be no variety in the generation and corruption of inferior bodies, which is clearly false.

Therefore it is necessary, as the Philosopher says,[4] to suppose a movable active principle,

which by reason of its presence or absence causes variety in the generation and corruption of inferior bodies. And such are the heavenly bodies. Consequently whatever generates here below moves to the production of the species as the instrument of a heavenly body. Thus the Philosopher says that "man and the sun generate man."[5]

Reply Obj. 3. The heavenly bodies have not a specific likeness to the bodies here below. Their likeness consists in this, that by reason of their universal power, whatever is generated in inferior bodies, is contained in them. In this way also we say that all things are like God.

Reply Obj. 4. The actions of heavenly bodies are variously received in inferior bodies, according to the various dispositions of matter. Now it happens at times that the matter in the human conception is not wholly disposed to the male sex. Therefore it is formed sometimes into a male, sometimes into a female. Augustine quotes this as an argument against divination by stars, because the effects of the stars are varied even in corporeal things, according to the various dispositions of matter.

ARTICLE 4. *Whether the Heavenly Bodies Are the Cause of Human Actions?*

We proceed thus to the Fourth Article: It would seem that the heavenly bodies are the cause of human actions.

Objection 1. For since the heavenly bodies are moved by spiritual substances, as stated above (Q. CX, A. 3), they act by their power as their instruments. But those spiritual substances are superior to our souls. Therefore it seems that they can cause impressions on our souls, and thus cause human actions.

Obj. 2. Further, everything multiform is reducible to a uniform principle. But human actions are various and multiform. Therefore it seems that they are reducible to the uniform movements of heavenly bodies, as to their principles.

Obj. 3. Further, astrologers often foretell the truth concerning the outcome of wars, and other human actions, of which the intellect and will are the principles. But they could not do this by means of the heavenly bodies, unless these were the cause of human actions. Therefore the heavenly bodies are the cause of human actions.

On the contrary, Damascene says (*De Fide Orth.* ii, 7)[6] that "the heavenly bodies are by no means the cause of human actions."

---

[1] Sect. 4 (PG 3, 700).
[2] Cf. Aristotle, *Physics*, I, 4 (187ª15).   [3] Cf. above, A. 1.
[4] *Generation and Corruption*, II, 10 (336ª15).
[5] *Physics*, II, 2 (194b13).   [6] PG 94, 893.

I answer that, The heavenly bodies can directly and of themselves act on bodies, as stated above (A. 3). They can act directly indeed on those powers of the soul which are the acts of corporeal organs, but accidentally, because the acts of such powers must be hindered by obstacles in the organs; thus an eye when disturbed cannot see well. Therefore if the intellect and will were powers tied to corporeal organs, as some maintained,[1] holding that intellect does not differ from sense, it would follow of necessity that the heavenly bodies are the cause of human choice and action. It would also follow that man is led by natural instinct to his actions, just as other animals, in which there are no powers other than those which are bound up with corporeal organs; for whatever is done here below in virtue of the action of heavenly bodies, is done naturally. It would therefore follow that man has no free choice, and that he would have determinate actions, like other natural things. All of which is manifestly false, and contrary to the way men act.

It must be observed, however, that indirectly and accidentally, the impressions of heavenly bodies can reach the intellect and will, in so far, namely, as both intellect and will receive something from the inferior powers which are bound up with corporeal organs. But in this the intellect and will are differently situated. For the intellect of necessity receives from the inferior apprehensive powers; therefore if the imaginative, cogitative, or memorative powers be disturbed, the action of the intellect is of necessity disturbed also. The will, on the contrary, does not of necessity follow the inclination of the lower appetite; for although the irascible and concupiscible passions have a certain force in inclining the will, nevertheless the will retains the power of following the passions or repressing them. Therefore the impressions of the heavenly bodies, by virtue of which the inferior powers can be changed, has less influence on the will, which is the proximate cause of human actions, than on the intellect.

To maintain therefore that heavenly bodies are the cause of human actions is proper to those who hold that intellect does not differ from sense. And so some of these said that "such is the will of men, as is the day which the father of men and of gods brings on" (*Odyssey* xviii, 136). Since, therefore, it is manifest that intel-

lect and will are not acts of corporeal organs, it is impossible that heavenly bodies be the cause of human actions.

Reply Obj. 1. The spiritual substances that move the heavenly bodies do indeed act on corporeal things by means of the heavenly bodies; but they act immediately on the human intellect by enlightening it. On the other hand, they cannot compel the will, as stated above (Q. CXI, A. 2).

Reply Obj. 2. Just as the multiformity of corporeal movements is reducible to the uniformity of the heavenly movement as to its cause, so the multiformity of actions proceeding from the intellect and the will is reduced to a uniform principle which is the Divine intellect and will.

Reply Obj. 3. The majority of men follow their passions, which are movements of the sensitive appetite, in which movements heavenly bodies can co-operate; but few are wise enough to resist these passions. Consequently astrologers are able to foretell the truth in the majority of cases, especially in a general way. But not in particular cases, for nothing prevents man resisting his passions by his free-will. And so the astrologers themselves say that the wise man is stronger than the stars,[3] in so far as, that is, he conquers his passions.

ARTICLE 5. *Whether Heavenly Bodies Can Act on the Demons?*

We proceed thus to the Fifth Article: It would seem that heavenly bodies can act on the demons.

Objection 1. For the demons, according to certain phases of the moon, can harass men, who on that account are called lunatics, as appears from Matthew 4. 24 and 17. 14. But this would not be if they were not subject to the heavenly bodies. Therefore the demons are subject to them.

Obj. 2. Further, necromancers observe certain constellations in order to invoke the demons. But these would not be invoked through the heavenly bodies unless they were subject to them. Therefore they are subject to them.

Obj. 3. Further, heavenly bodies are more powerful than inferior bodies. But the demons are confined to certain inferior bodies, namely, "herbs, stones, animals, and to certain sounds and words, forms and figures," as Porphyry

---

[1] Cf. Aristotle, *Soul*, III, 3 (427ª21).
[2] This quotation is found in Aristotle, *Soul*, III, 3 (427ª 26), in the translation ascribed to Boëthius by St. Thomas (*In De An.*, III, 4).

[3] Ptolemy, *Centiloquium*, 4–8 (46vb–47rb); cf. *Quadripartitum*, I, 3 (2v); see also Albert the Great, *In Sent.*, II d. 15, A. 4 (BO XXVII, 276).

says, quoted by Augustine.[1] Much more therefore are the demons subject to the action of heavenly bodies.

On the contrary, The demons are superior, in the order of nature, to the heavenly bodies. But the agent is superior to the patient, as Augustine says (*Gen. ad lit.* xii, 16).[2] Therefore the demons are not subject to the action of heavenly bodies.

I answer that, There have been three opinions about the demons. In the first place the Peripatetics denied the existence of demons, and held that what is ascribed to the demons, according to the necromantic art, is effected by the power of the heavenly bodies. This is what Augustine relates[3] as having been held by Porphyry, namely, that "on earth men fabricate certain powers useful in producing certain effects of the stars." But this opinion is manifestly false. For we know by experience that many things are done by demons, for which the power of heavenly bodies would in no way suffice; for instance, that a man in a state of delirium should speak an unknown tongue, recite poetry and authors of whom he has no previous knowledge, that necromancers make statues to speak and move, and other like things.

For this reason the Platonists were led to hold that "demons are animals with an aerial body and a passive soul," as Apuleius says, quoted by Augustine.[4]

And this is the second of the opinions mentioned above, according to which it could be said that demons are subject to heavenly bodies in the same way as we have said man is subject to them (A. 4). But this opinion is proved to be false from what we have said above (Q. LI, A. 1), for we hold that demons are spiritual substances not united to bodies. Hence it is clear that they are subject to the action of heavenly bodies neither essentially nor accidentally, neither directly nor indirectly.

Reply Obj. 1. That demons harass men according to certain phases of the moon happens in two ways. Firstly, they do so in order to defame God's creature, namely, the moon, as Jerome (*In Matt.* 4. 24)[5] and Chrysostom (*Hom.* lvii *in Matt.*)[6] say. Secondly, because as they are unable to effect anything save by means of the natural forces, as stated above (Q. CXIV, A. 4, ANS. 2) they take into account the aptitude of bodies for the intended result. Now it is manifest that "the brain is the most moist of all the parts of the body," as Aristotle says.[7] Therefore it is the most subject to the action of the moon, the property of which is to move what is moist. And it is precisely in the brain that animal forces culminate. Therefore the demons, according to certain phases of the moon, disturb man's imagination, when they observe that the brain is so disposed.

Reply Obj. 2. Demons when summoned through certain constellations, come for two reasons. First, in order to lead man into the error of believing that there is a certain divinity in the stars. Secondly, because they consider that under certain constellations corporeal matter is better disposed for the result for which they are summoned.

Reply Obj. 3. As Augustine says,[8] "the demons are enticed through various kinds of stones, herbs, trees, animals, songs, rites, not as an animal is enticed by food, but as a spirit by signs"; that is to say, in so far as these things are offered to them in token of the honour due to God, of which they are covetous.

ARTICLE 6. *Whether Heavenly Bodies Impose Necessity on Things Subject to Their Action?*

We proceed thus to the Sixth Article: It would seem that heavenly bodies impose necessity on things subject to their action.

Objection 1. For given a sufficient cause, the effect follows of necessity. But heavenly bodies are a sufficient cause of their effects. Since, therefore, heavenly bodies, with their movements and dispositions, are necessary beings, it seems that their effects follow of necessity.

Obj. 2. Further, an agent's effect results of necessity in matter, when the power of the agent is such that it can subject the matter to itself entirely. But the entire matter of inferior bodies is subject to the power of heavenly bodies, since this is a higher power than theirs. Therefore the effect of the heavenly bodies is of necessity received in corporeal matter.

Obj. 3. Further, if the effect of the heavenly body does not follow of necessity, this is due to some hindering cause. But any corporeal cause that might possibly hinder the effect of a heavenly body, must of necessity be reducible to some heavenly principle, since the heavenly bodies are the causes of all that takes place here below. Therefore, since also that heavenly principle is necessary, it follows that the effect of the heavenly body is necessarily hindered. Con-

---

[1] *City of God,* x, 11 (PL 41, 290).   [2] PL 34, 467.
[3] *Loc. cit.,* x, 11 (PL 41, 290).
[4] *City of God,* VIII, 16 (PL 41, 241).
[5] PL 26, 34.   [6] PG 58, 562.

[7] *Parts of Animals,* II, 7 (652^{a}27); *Sleep,* 3 (457^{b}29).
[8] *City of God,* XXI, 6 (PL 41, 717).

sequently it would follow that all that takes place here below happens of necessity.

On the contrary, The Philosopher says,[1] "It is not incongruous that many of the signs observed in bodies of occurrences in the heavens, such as rain and wind, should not be fulfilled." Therefore not all the effects of heavenly bodies take place of necessity.

I answer that, This question is partly solved by what was said above (A. 4), and in part presents some difficulty. For it was shown that although the action of heavenly bodies produces certain inclinations in corporeal nature, the will nevertheless does not of necessity follow these inclinations. Therefore there is nothing to prevent the effect of heavenly bodies being hindered by the action of the will, not only in man himself, but also in other things to which human action extends.

But in natural things there is no such principle, endowed with freedom to follow or not to follow the impressions produced by heavenly agents. Therefore it seems that in such things at least, everything happens of necessity according to the reasoning of some of the ancients,[2] who supposing that everything that is, has a cause, and that, given the cause, the effect follows of necessity, concluded that all things happen of necessity. This opinion as to this double supposition, is refuted by Aristotle.[3]

For in the first place it is not true that, given any cause whatever, the effect must follow of necessity. For some causes are so ordered to their effects as to produce them not of necessity but in the majority of cases, and in the minority to fail in producing them. But that such causes do fail in the minority of cases is due to some hindering cause; consequently the above-mentioned difficulty seems not to be avoided, since the cause in question is hindered of necessity.

Therefore we must say, in the second place, that everything that is a being *per se,* has a cause; but what is accidentally has not a cause, because it is not truly a being, since it is not truly one. For (that a thing is) *white* has a cause, likewise (that a man is) *musical* has a cause, but (that a being is) *white-musical* has not a cause, because it is not truly a being, nor truly one. Now it is manifest that a cause which hinders the action of a cause so ordered to its effect as to produce it in the majority of cases, clashes sometimes with this cause by accident;

and so the clashing of these two causes, in so far as it is accidental, has no cause. Consequently what results from this clashing of causes is not to be reduced to a further pre-existing cause, from which it follows of necessity. For instance, that some terrestrial body take fire in the higher regions of the air and fall to the earth is caused by some heavenly power; again, that there be on the surface of the earth some combustible matter, is reducible to some heavenly principle. But that the burning body should alight on this matter and set fire to it is not caused by a heavenly body, but is accidental. Consequently not all the effects of heavenly bodies result of necessity.

Reply Obj. 1. The heavenly bodies are causes of effects that take place here below, through the means of particular inferior causes, which can fail in their effects in the minority of cases.

Reply Obj. 2. The power of a heavenly body is not infinite. Therefore it requires a determinate disposition in matter, both as to local distance and as to other conditions, in order to produce its effect. Therefore as local distance hinders the effect of a heavenly body (for the sun has not the same effect in heat in Dacia as in Ethiopia), so the density of matter, its low or high temperature or other such disposition, can hinder the effect of a heavenly body.

Reply Obj. 3. Although the cause that hinders the effect of another cause can be reduced to a heavenly body as its cause, nevertheless the clashing of two causes, being accidental, is not reduced to the causality of a heavenly body, as stated above.

QUESTION CXVI
OF FATE
(*In Four Articles*)

WE come now to the consideration of fate. Under this head there are four points of inquiry: (1) Is there such a thing as fate? (2) Where is it? (3) Is it unchangeable? (4) Are all things subject to fate?

ARTICLE 1. *Whether There Be Such a Thing as Fate?*

We proceed thus to the First Article: It would seem that fate is nothing.

Objection 1. For Gregory says in a homily for the Epiphany (*Hom.* xi *in Ev.*):[4] "Far be it from the hearts of the faithful to think that fate is anything real."

Obj. 2. Further, what happens by fate is not

---

[1] *Prophesying*, 2 (463[b]22).   [2] Avicenna, *Sufficientia*, I, 13 (21ra); *Meta.*, I, 7 (73ra); cf. St. Thomas, *In Meta.*, VI, 3.   [3] *Metaphysics*, VI, 3 (1027[a]31).   [4] PL 76, 1112.

unforeseen, for as Augustine says,[1] "fate is understood to be derived from the verb '*fari*' which means to speak"; as though things were said to happen by fate which are "fore-spoken" by one who decrees them to happen. Now what is foreseen is neither lucky nor chance-like. If therefore things happen by fate, there will be neither luck nor chance in the world.

On the contrary, What does not exist cannot be defined. But Boëthius (*De Consol.* iv, 6)[2] defines fate thus: "Fate is a disposition inherent to changeable things, by which Providence connects each one with its proper order."

I answer that, In this world some things seem to happen by luck or chance. Now it happens sometimes that something is lucky or chance-like, as compared to inferior causes, which, if compared to some higher cause, is directly intended. For instance, if two servants are sent by their master to the same place, the meeting of the two servants in regard to themselves is by chance; but as referred to the master, who had ordered it, it is directly intended.

So there were some who refused to refer to a higher cause such events which take place here below by luck or chance. These denied the existence of fate and Providence, as Augustine relates of Tully.[3] And this is contrary to what we have said above about Providence (Q. XXII, A. 2).

On the other hand, some have considered that everything that takes place here below by luck or by chance, whether in natural things or in human affairs, is to be reduced to a superior cause, namely, the heavenly bodies.[4] According to these fate is nothing else than "a disposition of the stars under which each one is begotten or born."[5]

But this will not hold. First, as to human affairs, because we have proved above (Q. CXV, A. 4) that human actions are not subject to the action of heavenly bodies, save accidentally and indirectly. Now the cause of fate, since it has the ordering of things that happen by fate, must of necessity be directly and of itself the cause of what takes place. Secondly, as to all things that happen accidentally, for it has been said (*ibid.* A. 6) that what is accidental is, properly speaking, neither a being, nor a unity. But every action of nature terminates in some one thing. Therefore it is impossible for that which is acci-

dental to be the effect *per se* of an active natural principle. No natural cause can therefore have for its proper effect that a man intending to dig a grave finds a treasure. Now it is manifest that a heavenly body acts after the manner of a natural principle, and so its effects in this world are natural. It is therefore impossible that any active power of a heavenly body be the cause of what happens by accident here below, whether by luck or by chance.

We must therefore say that what happens here by accident, both in natural things and in human affairs, is reduced to a pre-ordaining cause, which is Divine Providence. For nothing hinders that which happens by accident being considered as one by an intellect. Otherwise the intellect could not form this proposition: "The digger of a grave found a treasure." And just as an intellect can apprehend this so can it effect it. For instance, someone who knows of a place where a treasure is hidden, might instigate a rustic, ignorant of this, to dig a grave there. Consequently, nothing hinders what happens here by accident, by luck or by chance, being reduced to some ordering cause which acts by the intellect, especially the Divine intellect. For God alone can change the will, as shown above (Q. CV, A. 4).[6] Consequently the ordering of human actions, the principle of which is the will, must be ascribed to God alone.

So therefore since all that happens here below is subject to Divine Providence, as being pre-ordained, and as it were fore-spoken, we can admit the existence of fate; although the holy doctors avoided the use of this word, on account of those who twisted its application to a certain force in the position of the stars. Hence Augustine says,[7] "If anyone ascribes human affairs to fate, meaning thereby the will or power of God, let him keep to his opinion, but hold his tongue." For this reason Gregory denies the existence of fate; and so the first objection's solution is manifest.

Reply Obj. 2. Nothing hinders certain things happening by luck or by chance, if compared to their proximate causes, but not if compared to Divine Providence, in accordance with which "nothing happens at random in the world," as Augustine says (QQ. LXXXIII., *qu.* 24).[8]

ARTICLE 2. *Whether Fate Is in Created Things?*

We proceed thus to the Second Article: It would seem that fate is not in created things.

---

[1] *City of God*, v, 9 (PL 41, 150).   [2] PL 63, 815.
[3] *City of God*, v, 9 (PL 41, 148); cf. Cicero, *De Divin.*, II, 5, 10 (DD IV, 218, 221).
[4] Posidonius and the Astrologers, in Augustine, *City of God*, v, 7 (PL 41, 147).
[5] Cf. Augustine, *City of God*, v, 1 (PL 41, 141).

[6] Cf. also Q. CVI, A. 2; Q. CXV, A. 2.
[7] *City of God*, v, 1 (PL 41, 141).
[8] PL 40, 17.

Objection 1. For Augustine says[1] that "the Divine will or power is called fate." But the Divine will or power is not in creatures, but in God. Therefore fate is not in creatures but in God.

Obj. 2. Further, fate is compared to things that happen by fate, as their cause, as the very use of the word shows. But the universal cause that of itself effects what takes place by accident here below is God alone, as stated above (A. 1). Therefore fate is in God, and not in creatures.

Obj. 3. Further, if fate is in creatures it is either a substance or an accident, and whichever it is it must be multiplied according to the number of creatures. Since, therefore, fate seems to be one thing only, it seems that fate is not in creatures, but in God.

On the contrary, Boëthius says (*De Consol.* iv, 6):[2] "Fate is a disposition inherent to changeable things."

I answer that, As is clear from what has been stated above (Q. XXII, A. 3; Q. CIII, A. 6), Divine Providence produces effects through mediate causes. We can therefore consider the ordering of the effects in two ways. First, as being in God Himself, and thus the ordering of the effects is called Providence. But if we consider this ordering as being in the mediate causes ordered by God to the production of certain effects, thus it has the nature of fate. This is what Boëthius says (*De Consol.* iv):[3] "Fate is worked out when Divine Providence is served by certain spirits, whether by the soul, or by all nature itself which obeys Him, whether by the heavenly movements of the stars, whether by the angelic power, or by the ingenuity of the demons, whether by some of these, or by all, the chain of fate is forged." Of each of these things we have spoken above (A. 1; Q. CIV, A. 2; Q. CX, A. 1; Q. CXIII, Q. CXIV). It is therefore manifest that fate is in the created causes themselves, as ordered by God to the production of their effects.

Reply Obj. 1. The ordering itself of second causes, which Augustine calls the "series of causes,"[4] has not the nature of fate, except as dependent on God. Therefore the Divine power or will can be called fate as being the cause of fate. But essentially fate is the very disposition or series, that is, the order, of second causes.

Reply Obj. 2. Fate has the nature of a cause,

just as much as the second causes themselves, the ordering of which is called fate.

Reply Obj. 3. Fate is called a disposition, not that disposition which is a species of quality, but in the sense in which it signifies order, which is not a substance, but a relation. And if this order be considered in relation to its principle, it is one, and thus fate is one. But if it be considered in relation to its effects, or to the mediate causes, this fate is multiple. In this sense the poet wrote: "Thy fate draws thee."[5]

ARTICLE 3. *Whether Fate Is Unchangeable?*

We proceed thus to the Third Article: It seems that fate is not unchangeable.

Objection 1. For Boëthius says (*De Consol.* iv, 6):[6] "As reasoning is to the intellect, as the begotten is to that which is, as time to eternity, as the circle to its centre, so is the fickle chain of fate to the unwavering simplicity of Providence."

Obj. 2. Further, the Philosopher says[7]: "If we be moved, what is in us is moved." But fate is "a disposition inherent to changeable things," as Boëthius says (*loc. cit.*).[8] Therefore fate is changeable.

Obj. 3. Further, if fate is unchangeable, what is subject to fate happens unchangeably and of necessity. But things ascribed to fate seem principally to be contingencies. Therefore there would be no contingencies in the world, but all things would happen of necessity.

On the contrary, Boëthius says (*ibid.*)[9] that fate is an unchangeable disposition.

I answer that, The disposition of second causes which we call fate, can be considered in two ways. First, in regard to the second causes themselves which are thus disposed or ordered; secondly, in regard to the first principle, namely, God, by Whom they are ordered. Some, therefore, have held[10] that the series itself or disposition of causes is in itself necessary, so that all things would happen of necessity, for the reason that each effect has a cause, and given a cause the effect must follow of necessity. But this is false, as proved above (Q. CXV, A. 6).

Others, on the other hand, held that fate is changeable, even as dependent on Divine Providence. Therefore the Egyptians said that fate could be changed by certain sacrifices, as Gregory of Nyssa says (Nemesius, *De Homine*).[11]

---

[1] *City of God,* v, 1 (PL 41, 141).
[2] PL 63, 815.   [3] *Ibid.*
[4] *City of God,* v, 8 (PL 41, 148).
[5] Hildebertus Cenomanensis, *Versus de Excidio Troiae* (PL 171, 1449D).
[6] PL 63, 817.   [7] *Topics,* II, 7 (113ᵃ29).
[8] PL 63, 815.   [9] PL 63, 816.
[10] Cf. above, Q. CXV, A. 6.
[11] Chap. 36 (PG 40, 745).

This too has been disproved above for the reason that it is contrary to the unchangeable character of Divine Providence.[1]

We must therefore say that fate, considered in regard to second causes, is changeable, but as subject to Divine Providence, it derives a certain unchangeableness, not of absolute but of conditional necessity. In this sense we say that this conditional is true and necessary: "If God foreknew that this would happen, it will happen." Therefore Boëthius, having said that the chain of fate is fickle, shortly afterwards adds, —"which, since it is derived from an unchangeable Providence, must also itself be unchangeable."

From this the answers to the objections are clear.

ARTICLE 4. *Whether All Things Are Subject to Fate?*

We proceed thus to the Fourth Article: It seems that all things are subject to fate.

Objection 1. For Boëthius says (*De Consol.* iv, 6):[2] "The chain of fate moves the heaven and the stars, tempers the elements to one another, and models them by a reciprocal transformation. By fate all things that are born into the world and perish are renewed in a uniform progression of offspring and seed." Nothing therefore seems to be excluded from the domain of fate.

Obj. 2. Further, Augustine says[3] that "fate is something real, as referred to the Divine will and power." But the Divine will is cause of all things that happen, as Augustine says (*De Trin.* iii, 1, *seqq.*).[4] Therefore all things are subject to fate.

Obj. 3. Further, Boëthius says (*loc. cit.*)[5] that fate is "a disposition inherent to changeable things." But all creatures are changeable, and God alone is truly unchangeable, as stated above (Q. IX, A. 2). Therefore fate is in all things.

On the contrary, Boëthius says (*De Consol.* iv, 6)[6] that "some things subject to Providence are above the ordering of fate."

I answer that, As stated above (A. 2), fate is the ordering of second causes to effects foreseen by God. Whatever, therefore, is subject to second causes, is subject also to fate. But whatever is done immediately by God, since it is not subject to second causes, neither is it subject

to fate; such are creation, the glorification of spiritual substances, and the like. And this is what Boëthius says (*loc. cit.*), namely, that "those things which are nigh to God have a state of immobility, and exceed the changeable order of fate." Hence it is clear that "the further a thing is from the First Mind, the more it is involved in the chain of fate," since so much the more it is bound up with second causes.

Reply Obj. 1. All the things mentioned in this passage are done by God by means of second causes; for this reason they are contained in the order of fate. But it is not the same with everything else, as stated above.

Reply Obj. 2. Fate is to be referred to the Divine will and power as to its first principle. Consequently it does not follow that whatever is subject to the Divine will or power is subject also to fate, as already stated.

Reply Obj. 3. Although all creatures are in some way changeable, yet some of them do not proceed from changeable created causes. And these, therefore, are not subject to fate, as stated above.

QUESTION CXVII

OF THINGS PERTAINING TO THE ACTION OF MAN

(In Four Articles)

WE have next to consider those things which pertain to the action of man, who is composed of a created corporeal and spiritual nature. In the first place we shall consider the action of man, and secondly the propagation of man from man (Q. CXVIII). As to the first, there are four points of inquiry: (1) Whether one man can teach another, as being the cause of his knowledge? (2) Whether man can teach an angel? (3) Whether by the power of his soul man can change corporeal matter? (4) Whether the separate soul of man can move bodies by local movement?

ARTICLE 1. *Whether One Man Can Teach Another?*

We proceed thus to the First Article: It would seem that one man cannot teach another.

Objection 1. For the Lord says (Matt. 23. 8): *Be not you called Rabbi,* on which the gloss of Jerome says,[7] "Lest you give to men the honour due to God." Therefore to be a master is properly an honour due to God. But it belongs to a master to teach. Therefore man cannot teach, and this is proper to God.

---

[1] Cf. Q. XXIII, A. 8.   [2] PL 63, 817.
[3] *City of God,* v, 1 (PL 41, 141); cf. also v, 8 (PL 41, 148).
[4] PL 42, 871; *Enchiridion,* chap. 95 (PL 40, 276).
[5] PL 63, 815.   [6] PL 63, 816.
[7] *Glossa interl.* (V, 71r).

Obj. 2. Further, if one man teaches another, this is only in so far as he acts through his own knowledge, so as to cause knowledge in the other. But a quality through which anyone acts so as to produce his like is an active quality. Therefore it follows that knowledge is an active quality just as heat is.

Obj. 3. Further, for knowledge we require intellectual light, and the species of the thing understood. But a man cannot cause either of these in another man. Therefore a man cannot by teaching cause knowledge in another man.

Obj. 4. Further, the teacher does nothing in regard to a disciple save to propose to him certain signs, so as to signify something by words or gestures. But it is not possible to teach anyone so as to cause knowledge in him, by putting signs before him. For these are signs either of things that he knows or of things he does not know. If of things that he knows, he to whom these signs are proposed is already in the possession of knowledge, and does not acquire it from the master. If they are signs of things that he does not know, he can learn nothing from them. For instance, if one were to speak Greek to a man who only knows Latin, he would learn nothing thereby. Therefore in no way can a man cause knowledge in another by teaching him.

On the contrary, The Apostle says (I Tim. 2. 7): *Whereunto I am appointed a preacher and an apostle . . . a doctor of the Gentiles in faith and truth.*

I answer that, On this question there have been various opinions. For Averroes, commenting on the third book on the *Soul*,[1] maintains that all men have one possible intellect in common, as stated above (Q. LXXVI, A. 2). From this it followed that the same intelligible species belong to all men. Consequently he held that one man does not cause another to have a knowledge distinct from that which he has himself, but that he communicates the identical knowledge which he has himself, by moving him to order rightly the phantasms in his soul, so that they be rightly disposed for intelligible apprehension. This opinion is true so far as knowledge is the same in disciple and master, if we consider the identity of the thing known, for the same truth of the thing is known by both of them. But so far as he maintains that all men have but one possible intellect and the same intelligible species, differing only as to various phantasms, his opinion is false, as stated above (Q. LXXVI, A. 2).

Besides this, there is the opinion of the Pla-

tonists, who held that our souls are possessed of knowledge from the very beginning, through the participation of separate forms, as stated above (Q. LXXXIV, AA. 3, 4), but that the soul is hindered, through its union with the body, from the free consideration of those things which it knows. According to this, the disciple does not acquire fresh knowledge from his master, but is roused by him to consider what he knows, so that to learn would be nothing else than to remember. In the same way they held[2] that natural agents only dispose (matter) to receive forms, which matter acquires by a participation of separate species. But against this we have shown above (Q. LXXIX, A. 2; Q. LXXXIV, A. 3) that the possible intellect of the human soul is in pure potency to intelligibles, as Aristotle says.[3]

We must therefore decide the question differently, by saying that the teacher causes knowledge in the learner by reducing him from potency to act, as the Philosopher says.[4] In order to make this clear, we must observe that of effects proceeding from an exterior principle, some proceed from the exterior principle alone; as for instance the form of a house is caused to be in matter by art alone. But other effects proceed sometimes from an exterior principle, sometimes from an interior principle; thus health is caused in a sick man, sometimes by an exterior principle, namely by the medical art, sometimes by an interior principle, as when a man is healed by the force of nature. In these latter effects two things must be noticed. First, that art in its work imitates nature, for just as nature heals a man by alteration, digestion, rejection of the matter that caused the sickness, so does art. Secondly, we must remark that the exterior principle, art, acts not as principal agent, but as helping the principal agent, which is the interior principle, by strengthening it, and by furnishing it with instruments and assistance, of which nature makes use in producing the effect. Thus the physician strengthens nature, and employs food and medicine, of which nature makes use for the intended end.

Now knowledge is acquired in man both from an interior principle, as is clear in one who procures knowledge by his own search, and from an exterior principle, as is clear in one who learns (by instruction). For in every man there is a certain principle of knowledge, namely the light of the agent intellect, through which certain

---

[1] Comm. 5, *digressio*, p. v (VI, 2, 146F).

[2] Plato and Avicenna; cf. above, Q. CXV, A. I.

[3] *Soul*, III, 4 (429ᵇ30).

[4] *Physics*, VIII, 4 (225ᵇ1).

universal principles of all the sciences are naturally understood as soon as proposed to the intellect. Now when anyone applies these universal principles to certain particular things, the memory or experience of which he acquires through the senses, then by his own search advancing from the known to the unknown, he obtains knowledge of what he knew not before. Therefore anyone who teaches leads the disciple from things known by the latter to the knowledge of things previously unknown to him, according to what the Philosopher says,[1] "All teaching and all learning proceed from previous knowledge."

Now the master leads the disciple from things known to knowledge of the unknown in a twofold manner. First, by proposing to him certain helps or means of instruction, which his intellect can use for the acquisition of science. For instance, he may put before him certain less universal propositions, of which nevertheless the disciple is able to judge from previous knowledge; or he may propose to him some sensible examples, either by way of likeness or of opposition, or something of the sort, from which the intellect of the learner is led to the knowledge of truth previously unknown. Secondly, by strengthening the intellect of the learner; not, indeed, by some active power as of a higher nature, as explained above (Q. CVI, A. 1; Q. CXI, A. 1) of the angelic enlightenment, because all human intellects are of one grade in the natural order, but in so far as he proposes to the disciple the order of principles to conclusions, because he does not have sufficient powers of comparison to be able to draw the conclusions from the principles. Hence the Philosopher says[2] that "a demonstration is a syllogism that causes knowledge." In this way a demonstrator causes his hearers to know.

Reply Obj. 1. As stated above, the teacher only brings exterior help, as the physician who heals. But just as the inward nature is the principal cause of the healing, so the interior light of the intellect is the principal cause of knowledge. But both of these are from God. Therefore as of God is it written: *Who healeth all thy diseases* (Ps. 102. 3), so of Him is it written: *He that teacheth man knowledge* (Ps. 93. 10), since *the light of His countenance is signed upon us* (Ps. 4. 7), through which light all things are shown to us.

Reply Obj. 2. As Averroes argues[3], the teacher does not cause knowledge in the disciple after the manner of a natural agent. Therefore knowledge need not be an active quality, but is the principle by which one is directed in teaching, just as art is the principle by which one is directed in working.

Reply Obj. 3. The master does not cause the intellectual light in the disciple, nor does he cause the intelligible species directly, but he moves the disciple by teaching, so that the latter, by the power of his intellect, forms intelligible concepts, the signs of which are proposed to him from without.

Reply Obj. 4. The signs proposed by the master to the disciple are of things known in a universal and confused manner, but not known in particular and distinctly. Therefore when anyone acquires knowledge by himself, he cannot be called self-taught, or be said to have been his own master, because perfect knowledge did not precede in him, such as is required in a master.

ARTICLE 2. *Whether Man Can Teach the Angels?*

We proceed thus to the Second Article: It would seem that men can teach angels.

Objection 1. For the Apostle says (Eph. 3, 10): *That the manifold wisdom of God may be made known to the principalities and powers in the heavenly places through the Church.* But the Church is the union of all the faithful. Therefore some things are made known to angels through men.

Obj. 2. Further, the superior angels, who are enlightened immediately concerning Divine things by God, can instruct the inferior angels, as stated above (Q. CVI, A. 1; Q. CXII, A. 3). But some men are instructed immediately concerning Divine things by the Word of God, as appears principally of the apostles from Heb. 1. 1, 2: *Last of all, in these days (God) hath spoken to us by His Son.* Therefore some men have been able to teach the angels.

Obj. 3. Further, the inferior angels are instructed by the superior. But some men are higher than some angels, since some men are taken up to the highest angelic orders, as Gregory says in a homily (*Hom. xxxiv in Ev.*).[4] Therefore some of the inferior angels can be instructed by men concerning Divine things.

On the contrary, Dionysius says (*Div. Nom.* iv)[5] that every Divine enlightenment is borne to men by the ministry of the angels. Therefore angels are not instructed by men concerning Divine things.

---

[1] *Posterior Analytics*, I, 1 (71^{a}1).
[2] *Ibid.*, I, 2 (71^{b}17).
[3] *In De An.*, III, 5, digressio, pt. v (VI, 2, 152D).

[4] PL 76, 1252.   [5] Sect. 2 (PG 3, 180).

I answer that, As stated above (Q. CVII, A. 2), the inferior angels can indeed speak to the superior angels, by making their thoughts known to them; but concerning Divine things superior angels are never enlightened by inferior angels. Now it is manifest that in the same way as inferior angels are subject to the superior, the highest men are subject even to the lowest angels. This is clear from Our Lord's words (Matt. II. II): *There hath not risen among them that are born of women a greater than John the Baptist; yet he that is lesser in the kingdom of heaven is greater than he.* Therefore angels are never enlightened by men concerning Divine things. But men can by means of speech make known to angels the thoughts of their hearts, because it belongs to God alone to know the heart's secrets.

Reply Obj. 1. Augustine (*Gen. ad lit.* v, 19)[1] thus explains this passage of the Apostle, who in the preceding verses says: *"To me, the least of all the saints, is given this grace . . . to enlighten all men, that they may see what is the dispensation of the mystery which hath been hidden from eternity in God.*—Hidden, yet so that 'the multiform wisdom of God' was made known to the principalities and powers in the heavenly places—that is, through the Church." As though he were to say: This mystery was hidden from men, but not from the Church in heaven, which is contained in the principalities and powers who knew it "from all ages, but not before all ages: because the Church was at first there, where after the resurrection this Church composed of men will be gathered together."

It can also be explained otherwise that "what is hidden, is known by the angels, not only in God, but also here when it takes place and is made public," as Augustine says further on (*ibid.*). Thus when the mysteries of Christ and the Church were fulfilled by the apostles, some things concerning these mysteries became apparent to the angels which were hidden from them before. In this way we can understand what Jerome says (*Comment. in Ep. ad Eph., loc. cit.*),—that from the preaching of the apostles the angels learnt certain mysteries; that is to say, through the preaching of the apostles, the mysteries were realized in the things themselves. Thus by the preaching of Paul the Gentiles were converted, of which mystery the Apostle is speaking in the passage quoted.

Reply Obj. 2. The apostles were instructed immediately by the Word of God, not according to His Divinity, but according as He spoke in His human nature. Hence the argument does not prove.

Reply Obj. 3. Certain men even in this state of life are greater than certain angels, not actually, but virtually, in so far as they have such great charity that they can merit a higher degree of happiness than that possessed by certain angels. In the same way we might say that the seed of a great tree is virtually greater than a small tree, though actually it is much smaller.

ARTICLE 3. *Whether Man by the Power of His Soul Can Change Corporeal Matter?*

We proceed thus to the Third Article: It would seem that man by the power of his soul can change corporeal matter.

Objection 1. For Gregory says (*Dialog.* ii, 30):[2] "Saints work miracles, sometimes by prayer, sometimes by their power. Thus Peter, by prayer, raised the dead Tabitha to life, and by his reproof delivered to death the lying Ananias and Saphira." But in the working of miracles a change is wrought in corporeal matter. Therefore men, by the power of the soul, can change corporeal matter.

Obj. 2. Further, on these words (Gal. 3. 1): *Who hath bewitched you, that you should not obey the truth?* the gloss says[3] that "some have blazing eyes, who by a single look bewitch others, especially children." But this would not be unless the power of the soul could change corporeal matter. Therefore man can change corporeal matter by the power of his soul.

Obj. 3. Further, the human body is nobler than other inferior bodies. But by the apprehension of the human soul the human body is changed to heat and cold, as appears when a man is angry or afraid; indeed this change sometimes goes so far as to bring on sickness and death. Much more, then, can the human soul by its power change corporeal matter.

On the contrary, Augustine says (*De Trin.* iii, 8):[4] "Corporeal matter obeys God alone at will."

I answer that, As stated above (Q. CX, A. 2), corporeal matter is not changed to (the reception of) a form save either by some agent composed of matter and form, or by God Himself, in Whom both matter and form pre-exist virtually, as in the primordial cause of both. Therefore of the angels also we have stated (*ibid.*) that they cannot change corporeal matter by their natural power, except by employing cor-

---

[1] PL 34, 335.

[2] PL 66, 188.

[3] *Glossa ordin.* (VI, 82A); *Glossa* Lombardi (PL 192, 117). cf. Jerome, *In 1 Gal.* on 3.1 (PL 26, 372).

[4] PL 42, 875.

poreal agents for the production of certain effects. Much less therefore can the soul, by its natural power, change corporeal matter, except by means of bodies.

Reply Obj. 1. The saints are said to work miracles by the power of grace, not of nature. This is clear from what Gregory says in the same place: "Those who are sons of God, in power, as John says,—what wonder is there that they should work miracles by that power?"

Reply Obj. 2. Avicenna assigns the cause of bewitchment to the fact that corporeal matter has a natural tendency to obey spiritual substance rather than natural contrary agents.[1] Therefore when the soul is of strong imagination, it can change corporeal matter. This he says is the cause of the "evil eye."

But it has been shown above (Q. CX, A. 2) that corporeal matter does not obey spiritual substances at will, but the Creator alone. Therefore it is better to say, that by a strong imagination the spirits of the body united to that soul are changed, which change in the spirits takes place especially in the eyes, to which the more subtle spirits can reach. And the eyes infect the air which is in contact with them to a certain distance, in the same way as a new and clear mirror contracts a tarnish from the look of a woman in menstruation, as Aristotle says.[2]

Hence then when a soul is vehemently moved to wickedness, as occurs mostly in little old women, according to the above explanation, the countenance becomes venomous and hurtful, especially to children, who have a tender and most impressionable body. It is also possible that by God's permission, or from some hidden deed, the spiteful demons co-operate in this, as the witches may have some compact with them.

Reply Obj. 3. The soul is united to the body as its form, and the sensitive appetite, which obeys the reason in a certain way, as stated above (Q. LXXXI, A. 3), is the act of a corporeal organ. Therefore at the apprehension of the human soul, the sensitive appetite must be moved with an accompanying corporeal operation. But the apprehension of the human soul does not suffice to work a change in exterior bodies, except by means of a change in the body united to it, as stated above (ANS. 2).

ARTICLE 4. *Whether the Separated Human Soul Can Move Bodies at Least Locally?*

We proceed thus to the Fourth Article: It seems that the separated human soul can move bodies at least locally.

Objection 1. For a body naturally obeys a spiritual substance as to local motion, as stated above (Q. CX, A. 3). But the separated soul is a spiritual substance. Therefore it can move exterior bodies by its command.

Obj. 2. Further, in the *Itinerary* of Clement it is said[3] in the narrative of Nicetas to Peter, that Simon Magus, by sorcery retained power over the soul of a child that he had slain, and that through this soul he worked magical wonders. But this could not have been without some corporeal change at least as to place. Therefore the separated soul has the power to move bodies locally.

On the contrary, the Philosopher says[4] that the soul cannot move any other body whatsoever but its own.

I answer that, The separated soul cannot by its natural power move a body. For it is manifest that, even while the soul is united to the body, it does not move the body unless it is endowed with life, so that if one of the members become lifeless, it does not obey the soul as to local motion. Now it is also manifest that no body is quickened by the separated soul. Therefore within the limits of its natural power the separated soul cannot command the obedience of a body, though, by the power of God, it can exceed those limits.

Reply Obj. 1. There are certain spiritual substances whose powers are not determined to certain bodies. Such are the angels who are naturally unfettered by a body; consequently various bodies may obey them as to movement. But if the moving power of a separated substance is naturally determined to move a certain body, that substance will not be able to move a body of higher degree, but only one of lower degree; thus according to philosophers the mover of the lower heaven cannot move the higher heaven.[5] Therefore, since the soul is by its nature determined to move the body of which it is the form, it cannot by its natural power move any other body.

Reply Obj. 2. As Augustine[6] and Chrysostom (*Hom.* xxviii *in Matt.*)[7] say, the demons often pretend to be the souls of the dead, in order to confirm the error of the Gentiles, who believed this. It is therefore credible that Simon Magus was deceived by some demon who pretended to be the soul of the child whom the magician had slain.

---

[1] *De An.,* IV, 4 (20vb).   [2] *Sleep,* 2 (459b26).

[3] *De Gestis S. Petri,* XXVII (PG 2, 492).
[4] *Soul,* I, 3 (407b19).
[5] Cf. Q. LVII, A. 2; Q. LII, A. 2.
[6] *City of God,* X, 11 (PL 41, 290).
[7] PG 57, 353.

QUESTION CXVIII

Of the production of man from man as to the soul

(*In Three Articles*)

WE now consider the production of man from man: first, as to the soul; secondly, as to the body. (Q. CXIX).

Under the first head there are three points of inquiry: (1) Whether the sensitive soul is transmitted with the semen? (2) Whether the intellectual soul is thus transmitted? (3) Whether all souls were created at the same time?

ARTICLE 1. *Whether the Sensitive Soul Is Transmitted with the Semen?*

We proceed thus to the First Article: It would seem that the sensitive soul is not transmitted with the semen, but created by God.

Objection 1. For every perfect substance not composed of matter and form that begins to exist, acquires existence not by generation but by creation, for nothing is generated save from matter. But the sensitive soul is a perfect substance, otherwise it could not move the body; and since it is the form of a body, it is not composed of matter and form. Therefore it begins to exist not by generation but by creation.

Obj. 2. Further, in living things the principle of generation is the generating power, which, since it is one of the powers of the vegetative soul, is of a lower order than the sensitive soul. Now nothing acts beyond its species. Therefore the sensitive soul cannot be caused by the animal's generating power.

Obj. 3. Further, the generator begets its like, so that the form of the generator must be actually in the cause of generation. But neither the sensitive soul itself nor any part of it is actually in the semen, for no part of the sensitive soul is elsewhere than in some part of the body. But in the semen there is not even a particle of the body, because there is not a particle of the body which is not made from the semen and by its power. Therefore the sensitive soul is not produced through the semen.

Obj. 4. Further, if there be in the semen any principle productive of the sensitive soul, this principle either remains after the animal is begotten, or it does not remain. Now it cannot remain. For either it would be identified with the sensitive soul of the begotten animal, which is impossible, for thus there would be identity between begetter and begotten, maker and made; or it would be distinct from it, and again this

is impossible, for it has been proved above (Q. LXXVI, A. 4) that in one animal there is but one formal principle, which is the soul. If on the other hand this principle does not remain, this again seems to be impossible, for thus an agent would act to its own destruction, which is impossible. Therefore the sensitive soul cannot be generated from the semen.

On the contrary, The power in the semen is to the animal generated from semen, as the power in the elements of the world is to animals produced from these elements,—for instance by putrefaction. But in the latter animals the soul is produced by the power that is in the elements, according to Genesis 1. 20: *Let the waters bring forth the creeping creatures having life.* Therefore also the souls of animals generated from semen are produced by the seminal power.

I answer that, Some have held that the sensitive souls of animals are created by God.[1] This opinion would hold if the sensitive soul were subsistent, having being and operation of itself. For thus, as having being and operation of itself, to be made would be proper to it. And since a simple and subsistent thing cannot be made except by creation, it would follow that the sensitive soul would come into being by creation.

But this principle is false,—namely, that being and operation are proper to the sensitive soul, as has been made clear above (Q. LXXV, A. 3), for then it would not cease to exist when the body perishes. Since, therefore, it is not a subsistent form, its relation to existence is that of the corporeal forms, to which being does not belong as proper to them, but which are said to be in so far as the subsistent composites exist through them.

And so to be made is proper to composites. And since the generator is like the generated, it follows of necessity that both the sensitive soul, and all other like forms are naturally brought into being by certain corporeal agents that reduce the matter from potency to act, through some corporeal power of which they are possessed.

Now the more powerful an agent, the greater the scope of its action. For instance, the hotter a body, the greater the distance to which its heat carries. Therefore bodies not endowed with life, which are the lowest in the order of nature, generate their like, not through some medium, but by themselves; thus fire by itself generates fire. But living bodies, as being more powerful, act so as to generate their like, both without

---

[1] Plato, according to Averroes, *In Meta.*, VII, 31 (VIII 180K); cf. St. Thomas, *De Pot.*, III, 11; *In De An.*, I, 10.

and with a medium. Without a medium—in the work of nutrition, in which flesh generates flesh; with a medium—in the act of generation, because the seed of the animal or plant derives a certain active force from the soul of the generator, just as the instrument derives a certain moving power from the principal agent. And as it matters not whether we say that something is moved by the instrument or by the principal agent, so neither does it matter whether we say that the soul of the generated is caused by the soul of the generator, or by some seminal power derived from it.

Reply Obj. 1. The sensitive soul is not a perfect self-subsistent substance. We have spoken of this above (Q. LXXV, A. 3), nor need we repeat it here.

Reply Obj. 2. The generating power begets not only by its own power, but by that of the whole soul, of which it is a power. Therefore the generating power of a plant generates a plant, and that of an animal begets an animal. For the more perfect the soul is, to so much a more perfect effect is its generating power ordered.

Reply Obj. 3. This active force which is in the semen, and which is derived from the soul of the generator, is, as it were, a certain movement of this soul itself; nor is it the soul or a part of the soul, save virtually. Thus the form of a bed is not in the saw or the axe, but a certain movement towards that form. Consequently there is no need for this active force to have an actual organ; but it is based on the (vital) spirit in the semen which is frothy, as is attested by its whiteness. In the spirit, moreover, there is a certain heat derived from the power of the heavenly bodies, by virtue of which the inferior bodies also act towards the production of the species as stated above (Q. CXV, A. 3, ANS. 2). And since in this (vital) spirit, the power of the soul is concurrent with the power of a heavenly body, it has been said that "man and the sun generate man"[1] Moreover, elemental heat is employed instrumentally by the soul's power, as also by the nutritive power, as stated.[2]

Reply Obj. 4. In perfect animals, generated by coition, the active force is in the semen of the male, as the Philosopher says,[3] but the fœtal matter is provided by the female. In this matter the vegetable soul exists from the very beginning, not as to the second act, but as to the first act, as the sensitive soul is in one who

sleeps. But as soon as it begins to attract nourishment, then it already operates in act. This matter therefore is transmuted by the power which is in the semen of the male, until it is actually informed by the sensitive soul; but not as though the force itself which was in the semen becomes the sensitive soul, for in this way the generator and generated would be identical, and this would be more like nourishment and growth than generation, as the Philosopher says.[4] And after the sensitive soul by the power of the active principle in the semen has been produced in one of the principal parts of the thing generated, then the sensitive soul of the offspring begins to work towards the perfection of its own body, by nourishment and growth. As to the active power which was in the semen, it ceases to be, when the semen is dissolved and its (vital) spirit vanishes. Nor is there anything unreasonable in this, because this force is not the principal but the instrumental agent, and the movement of an instrument ceases when once the effect has been produced.

ARTICLE 2. *Whether the Intellectual Soul Is Produced From the Semen?*

We proceed thus to the Second Article: It would seem that the intellectual soul is produced from the semen.

Objection 1. For it is written (Gen. 46. 26): *All the souls that came out of Jacob's thigh, sixty-six.* But nothing is produced from the thigh of a man, except as caused by the semen. Therefore the intellectual soul is produced from the semen.

Obj. 2. Further, as shown above (Q. LXXVI, A. 3), the intellectual, sensitive, and nutritive souls are, in substance, one soul in man. But the sensitive soul in man is generated from the semen, as in other animals. And so the Philosopher says[5] that "the animal and the man are not made at the same time," but first of all the animal is made having a sensitive soul. Therefore also the intellectual soul is produced from the semen.

Obj. 3. Further, it is one and the same agent whose action is directed to the matter and to the form. Otherwise from the matter and the form there would not result something absolutely one. But the intellectual soul is the form of the human body, which is formed by the power of the semen. Therefore the intellectual soul also is produced by the power of the semen.

Obj. 4. Further, man begets his like in spe-

---

[1] Aristotle, *Physics*, II, 2 (194^{b}13).
[2] Aristotle, *Soul*, II, 4 (416^{a}9; ^{a}28).
[3] *Generation of Animals*, II, 4 (740^{b}24).

[4] *Generation and Corruption*, I, 5 (321^{a}22).
[5] *Generation of Animals*, II, 3 (736^{b}2).

cies. But the human species is constituted by the rational soul. Therefore the rational soul is from the begetter.

Obj. 5. Further, it cannot be said that God co-operates in sin. But if the rational soul be created by God, sometimes God co-operates in the sin of adultery, since sometimes offspring is begotten of illicit intercourse. Therefore the rational soul is not created by God.

On the contrary, It is written in *De Eccl. Dogmat.* xiv[1] that "the rational soul is not engendered by coition."

I answer that, It is impossible for an active power existing in matter to extend its action to the production of an immaterial effect. Now it is manifest that the intellectual principle in man transcends matter, for it has an operation in which the body takes no part whatever. It is therefore impossible for the seminal power to produce the intellectual principle.

Again, the seminal power acts by virtue of the soul of the begetter, according as the soul of the begetter is the act of the body, making use of the body in its operation. Now the body has nothing whatever to do in the operation of the intellect. Therefore the power of the intellectual principle, as intellectual, cannot reach to the semen. Hence the Philosopher says,[2] "It follows that the intellect alone comes from without."

Again, since the intellectual soul has a vital operation independent of the body, it is subsistent, as proved above (Q. LXXV, A. 2). Therefore to be and to be made are proper to it. Moreover, since it is an immaterial substance it cannot be caused through generation, but only through creation by God. Therefore to hold that the intellectual soul is caused by the begetter is nothing else than to hold the soul to be non-subsistent, and consequently to perish with the body. It is therefore heretical to say that the intellectual soul is transmitted with the semen.

Reply Obj. 1. In the passage quoted, the part is put instead of the whole, the soul for the whole man, by the figure of synecdoche.

Reply Obj. 2. Some say that the vital functions observed in the embryo are not from its soul, but from the soul of the mother,[3] or from the formative power of the semen,[4] Both of these explanations are false, for vital functions such as feeling, nourishment, and growth cannot be from an extrinsic principle. Consequently it must be said that the soul is in the embryo, the nutritive soul from the beginning, then the sensitive, lastly the intellectual soul.

Therefore some say that in addition to the vegetative soul which existed first, another, namely, the sensitive soul supervenes;[5] and in addition to this, again another, namely the intellectual soul. Thus there would be in man three souls of which one would be in potency to another. This has been disproved above (Q. LXXVI, A. 3).

Therefore others say[6] that the same soul which was at first merely vegetative, afterwards through the action of the seminal power, becomes a sensitive soul. And finally this same soul becomes intellectual, not indeed through the active seminal power, but by the power of a higher agent, namely God enlightening it from without. For this reason the Philosopher says that the intellect comes from without.[7]—But this will not hold. First, because no substantial form is susceptive of more or less, but addition of greater perfection constitutes another species, just as the addition of unity constitutes another species of number. Now it is not possible for the same identical form to belong to different species. Secondly, because it would follow that the generation of an animal would be a continuous movement, proceeding gradually from the imperfect to the perfect, as happens in alteration. Thirdly, because it would follow that the generation of a man or an animal is not generation absolutely, because its subject would be a being in act. For if the vegetative soul is from the beginning in the matter of offspring, and is subsequently gradually brought to perfection, there will be addition of further perfection without corruption of the preceding perfection. And this is contrary to the nature of generation properly so called. Fourthly, because either that which is caused by the action of God is something subsistent, and then it must be essentially distinct from the pre-existing form, which was non-subsistent (and we shall then come back to the opinion of those who held the existence of several souls in the body)—or else it is not subsistent, but a perfection of the pre-

---

[1] Gennadius, 14 (PL 58, 984).

[2] *Generation of Animals,* II, 3 (736b27).

[3] Alexander of Hales, *Summa Theol.,* I–II, 489 (QR II, 683); cf. Aristotle, *Generation of Animals,* II, 1 (733b32); Albert the Great, *In de An.,* XVI, 1, 2 (BO XII, 136).

[4] Avicenna, *De An.,* xv, 2 (6orb); cf. also Averroes, *In De Gen. Anim.,* II, 3 (VI, 3, 75c).

[5] Cf. Q. LXXVI, A. 3; also Avicebron, *Fons Vitae,* III, 46 (BK 181.14); cf. also St. Thomas, *Quodl.,* XI, A. 5; Robert Kilwardby, in Denifle, *Chartularium,* n. 474 (I, 559), and John Peckham, *Ibid.,* n. 517 (I, 624).

[6] Albert the Great, *In de An.,* XVI, 1, 11 (BO XII, 157); *Summa de Creatur.,* II, 17.3 (BO XXXV, 155).

[7] *Generation of Animals,* II, 3 (736b27).

existing soul; and from this it follows of necessity that the intellectual soul perishes with the body, which cannot be admitted.

There is again another explanation, according to those who held that all men have but one intellect in common: but this has been disproved above (Q. LXXVI, A. 2).[1]

We must therefore say that since the generation of one thing is the corruption of another, it follows of necessity that both in men and in other animals, when a more perfect form supervenes the previous form is corrupted, yet so that the succeeding form contains the perfection of the previous form, and something in addition. It is in this way that through many generations and corruptions we arrive at the ultimate substantial form, both in man and other animals. This indeed is apparent to the senses in animals generated from putrefaction. We conclude therefore that the intellectual soul is created by God at the end of human generation, and this soul is at the same time sensitive and nutritive, the pre-existing forms being corrupted.

Reply Obj. 3. This argument holds in the case of different agents not ordered to one another. But where there are many agents ordered to one another, nothing hinders the power of the higher agent from reaching to the ultimate form, while the powers of the inferior agents extend only to some disposition of matter. Thus in the generation of an animal, the seminal power disposes the matter, but the power of the soul gives the form. Now it is manifest from what has been said above (Q. CV, A. 5; Q. CX, A. 1) that the whole of corporeal nature acts as the instrument of a spiritual power, especially of God. Therefore nothing hinders the formation of the body from being due to a corporeal power, while the intellectual soul is from God alone.

Reply Obj. 4 Man begets his like in so far as by his seminal power the matter is disposed for the reception of a certain species of form.

Reply Obj. 5. In the action of the adulterer, what is of nature is good; in this God co-operates. But what there is of inordinate lust is evil, and in this God does not co-operate.

ARTICLE 3. *Whether Human Souls Were Created All Together at the Beginning of the World?*

We proceed thus to the Third Article: It would seem that human souls were created all together at the beginning of the world.

[1] Cf. Albert, *De Nat. et Orig. An.*, tr. 1, 5 (BO IX, 390), where he refers to Abubacer.

Objection 1. For it is written (Gen. 2. 2): *God rested Him from all His work which He had done.* This would not be true if He created new souls every day. Therefore all souls were created at the same time.

Obj. 2. Further, spiritual substances before all others pertain to the perfection of the universe. If therefore souls were created with the bodies, every day innumerable spiritual substances would be added to the perfection of the universe and so, at the beginning the universe would have been imperfect. This is contrary to Genesis 2. 2, where it is said that *God ended all His work.*

Obj. 3. Further, the end of a thing corresponds to its beginning. But the intellectual soul remains when the body perishes. Therefore it began to exist before the body.

On the contrary, it is said (*De Eccl. Dogmat.* xiv, xviii)[2] that "the soul is created together with the body."

I answer that, Some have maintained that it is accidental to the intellectual soul to be united to the body, asserting that the soul is of the same condition as those spiritual substances which are not united to a body.[3] These, therefore, stated that the souls of men were created together with the angels at the beginning. But this statement is false. First, in the very principle on which it is based. For if it were accidental to the soul to be united to the body, it would follow that man who results from this union is a being by accident, or that the soul is a man, which is false, as proved above (Q. LXXV, A. 4). Moreover, that the human soul is not of the same nature as the angels is proved from the different mode of understanding, as shown above (Q. LV, A. 2; Q. LXXXV, A. 1); for man understands through receiving from the senses, and turning to phantasms, as stated above (Q. LXXXV, A. 1). For this reason the soul needs to be united to the body, which is necessary to it for the operation of the sensitive part. But this cannot be said of an angel.

Secondly, this position can be proved to be false in itself. For if it is natural to the soul to be united to the body, it is unnatural to it to be without a body, and as long as it is without a body it does not have its natural perfection. Now it was not fitting that God should begin His work with things imperfect and unnatural, for He did not make man without a hand or a foot, which are natural parts of a man. Much

[2] Gennadius, (PL 58, 984, 985).

[3] Origen, *Peri Archon*, I, 6, 8 (PG 11, 166, 178); II, 9 (PG 11. 229).

less, therefore, did He make the soul without the body.

But if someone say that it is not natural to the soul to be united to the body, we must seek reason why it is united to a body. And the reason must be either because the soul so willed, or for some other reason. That the soul willed it seems incongruous. First, because it would be unreasonable of the soul to wish to be united to the body, if it did not need the body; for if it did need it, it would be natural for it to be united to it, since nature does not fail in what is necessary. Secondly, because there would be no reason why, having been created from the beginning of the world, the soul should, after such a long time, come to wish to be united to the body. For a spiritual substance is above time, and superior to the heavenly revolutions. Thirdly, because it would seem that this body was united to this soul by chance, since for this union to take place two wills would have to concur—namely, that of the soul which comes, and that of the begetter. If, however, this union be neither voluntary nor natural on the part of the soul, then it must be the result of some violent cause, and would be to the soul something of a penal and afflicting character. This is in keeping with the opinion of Origen, who held that souls were embodied in punishment of sin. Since, therefore, all these opinions are unreasonable, we must confess absolutely that souls were not created before bodies, but are created at the same time as they are infused into them.

Reply Obj. 1. God is said to have rested on the seventh day, not from all work, since we read (John 5. 17): *My Father worketh until now,* but from the creation of any new genera and species, which did not in some way pre-exist in the first works. For in this sense, the souls which are created now, pre-existed, as to the likeness of the species, in the first works, which included the creation of Adam's soul.

Reply Obj. 2. Something can be added every day to the perfection of the universe, as to the number of individuals, but not as to the number of species.

Reply Obj. 3. That the soul remains without the body is due to the corruption of the body, which was a result of sin. Consequently it was not fitting that God should make the soul without the body from the beginning; for as it is written (Wisd. 1. 13, 16): *God made not death . . . but the wicked with works and words have called it to them.*

QUESTION CXIX

Of the propagation of man as to the body

(*In Two Articles*)

We now consider the propagation of man as to the body. Concerning this there are two points of inquiry: (1) Whether any part of the food is changed into true human nature? (2) Whether the semen, which is the principle of human generation, is produced from the surplus food?

Article 1. *Whether Some Part of the Food Is Changed into True Human Nature?*

We proceed thus to the First Article: It would seem that none of the food is changed into true human nature.

Objection 1. For it is written (Matt. 15. 17): *Whatsoever entereth into the mouth, goeth into the belly, and is cast out into the privy.* But what is cast out is not changed into the reality of human nature. Therefore none of the food is changed into true human nature.

Obj. 2. Further, the Philosopher distinguishes flesh according to species from flesh according to matter, and says that the latter comes and goes.[1] Now what is formed from food comes and goes. Therefore what is produced from food is flesh according to matter, not to according species. But what pertains to true human nature pertains to the species. Therefore the food is not changed into true human nature.

Obj. 3. Further, the radical humour seems to belong to the reality of human nature, and if it is lost, it cannot be recovered, according to physicians.[2] But it could be recovered if the food were changed into the humour. Therefore food is not changed into true human nature.

Obj. 4. Further, if the food were changed into true human nature, whatever is lost in man could be restored. But man's death is due only to the loss of something. Therefore man would be able by taking food to insure himself forever against death.

Obj. 5. Further, if the food is changed into true human nature, there is nothing in man which may not disappear or be repaired, for what is generated in a man from his food can both disappear and be repaired. If therefore a man lived long enough, it would follow that in the end nothing would be left in him of what be-

[1] *Generation and Corruption,* I, 5 (321^{b}21).

[2] Avicenna. Cf. in Bonaventure, *Opera Omnia, In Sent.,* II, p. 736, notes 2 and 3.

longed to him, materially at the beginning. Consequently he would not be numerically the same man throughout his life, since for the thing to be numerically the same, identity of matter is necessary. But this is incongruous. Therefore the food is not changed into true human nature.

On the contrary, Augustine says (*De Vera Relig.* xl):[1] "The bodily food when corrupted, that is, having lost its form, is changed into the texture of the members." But the texture of the members pertains to true human nature. Therefore the food is changed into the reality of human nature.

I answer that, According to the Philosopher,[2] "The relation of a thing to truth is the same as its relation to being." Therefore that belongs to the true nature of any thing which enters into the constitution of that nature. But nature can be considered in two ways, first, in general according to the notion of the species; secondly, as it is in this individual. And while the form and the common matter belong to a thing's true nature considered in general, individual signate matter and the form individualized by that matter belong to the true nature considered in this particular individual. Thus a soul and body belong to the true human nature in general, but to the true human nature of Peter and Martin belong this soul and this body.

Now there are certain things whose form cannot exist save in one signate matter; thus the form of the sun cannot exist save in the matter in which it actually is. And in this sense some have said that the human form cannot exist but in a certain signate matter, which, they said, was given that form at the very beginning in the first man.[3] So that whatever may have been added to that which was derived by posterity from the first parent does not belong to the truth of human nature, as not receiving in truth the form of human nature.

But, said they, that matter which, in the first man, was the subject of the human form, was multiplied in itself, and in this way the multitude of human bodies is derived from the body of the first man. According to these, the food is not changed into true human nature. We take food, they stated, in order to help nature to resist the action of natural heat, and prevent the consumption of the radical humour, just as lead or tin is mixed with silver to prevent its being consumed by fire.

But this is unreasonable in many ways. First, because it comes to the same thing that a form can be produced in another matter, or that it can cease to be in its proper matter. Therefore all things that can be generated are corruptible, and conversely. Now it is manifest that the human form can cease to exist in this matter which is its subject; otherwise the human body would not be corruptible. Consequently it can begin to exist in another matter, something else being changed into true human nature. Secondly, because in all beings whose entire matter is found in one individual there is only one individual in the species, as is clearly the case with the sun, moon and the like. Thus there would only be one individual of the human species. Thirdly, because multiplication of matter cannot be understood otherwise than either in respect of quantity only, as in things which are rarefied, so that their matter increases in dimensions, or in respect of the substance itself of the matter. But as long as the substance alone of matter remains, it cannot be said to be multiplied, for multitude cannot consist in the addition of a thing to itself, since of necessity it can only result from division. Therefore some other substance must be added to matter, either by creation, or by something else being changed into it. Consequently no matter can be multiplied save either by rarefaction, as when air is made from water, or by the change of some other thing, as fire is multiplied by the addition of wood, or lastly by the creation of matter. Now it is manifest that the multiplication of matter in the human body does not occur by rarefaction, for thus the body of a man of perfect age would be more imperfect than the body of a child. Nor does it occur by creation of new matter, for, according to Gregory (*Moral.* xxxii):[4] "All things were created together as to the substance of matter, but not as to the specific form." Consequently the multiplication of the human body can only be the result of the food being changed into the true human body. Fourthly, because, since man does not differ from animals and plants in regard to the vegetative soul, it would follow that the bodies of animals and plants do not increase through a change of nourishment into the body so nourished, but through some kind of multiplication. Nor can this multiplication be natural, since the matter cannot naturally extend beyond a certain fixed quantity. Nor again does anything increase naturally save either by rarefaction or the change of something else into it. Conse-

---

[1] PL 34, 155.

[2] *Metaphysics,* II, 1 (993^{b}30).

[3] Peter Lombard, *Sent.,* II, d. 30, chap. 14 (QR 1, 467); also, Ps. Hugh of St. Victor, *Summae Sent.,* III, 10 (PL 176, 105).

[4] Chap. 12 (PL 76, 644).

quently the whole process of generation and nourishment, which are called natural powers, would be miraculous. And this cannot be admitted.

And so others have said that the human form can indeed begin to exist anew in some other matter if we consider the human nature in general, but not if we consider it as it is in this individual.[1] For in the individual the form remains confined to a certain determinate matter, on which it is first imprinted at the generation of that individual, so that it never leaves that matter until the ultimate dissolution of the individual. And this matter, say they, principally belongs to the true human nature. But since this matter does not suffice for the requisite quantity, some other matter must be added, through the change of food into the substance of the individual partaking of it, in such a quantity as suffices for the increase required. And this matter, they state, belongs secondarily to the true human nature, because it is not required for the primary being of the individual, but for the quantity due to him. And if anything further is produced from the food, this does not belong to true human nature, properly speaking.

However, this also is inadmissible. First, because this opinion judges of living bodies in the same way as of inanimate bodies, in which, although there be a power of generating their like in species, there is not the power of generating their like in the individual (which power in living bodies is the nutritive power). Nothing, therefore, would be added to living bodies by their nutritive power, if their food were not changed into their true nature. Secondly, because the active seminal power is a certain impression derived from the soul of the begetter, as stated above (Q. CXVIII, A. 1). Hence it cannot have a greater power in acting than the soul from which it is derived. If, therefore, by the seminal power a certain matter truly assumes the form of human nature, much more can the soul, by the nutritive power, imprint the true form of human nature on the food which is assimilated. Thirdly, because food is needed not only for growth, (otherwise at the term of growth, food would no longer be necessary) but also to renew that which is lost by the action of natural heat. But there would be no renewal, unless what is formed from the food took the place of what is lost. Therefore just as that

which was there previously belonged to true human nature, so also does that which is generated from the food.

Therefore, according to others,[2] it must be said that the food is really changed into the true human nature by reason of its assuming the specific form of flesh, bones and the like parts. This is what the Philosopher says,[3] that is, that food nourishes in so far as it is potentially flesh.

Reply Obj. 1. Our Lord does not say that the whole of what enters into the mouth, but all,—because something from every kind of food is cast out into the privy. It may also be said that whatever is generated from food can be dissolved by natural heat, and be cast aside through the pores, as Jerome expounds the passage.[4]

Reply Obj. 2. By flesh belonging to the species, some have understood that which first receives the human species, which is derived from the begetter; and this, they say, lasts as long as the individual does.[5] By flesh belonging to the matter these understand what is generated from food; and this, they say, does not always remain, but as it comes, so it goes. But this is contrary to the mind of Aristotle. For he says there,[6] that "just as in things which have their species in matter,"—for instance, wood or stone —"so in flesh, there is something belonging to the species, and something belonging to matter." Now it is clear that this distinction has no place in inanimate things, which are not generated seminally, or nourished. Again, since what is generated from food is united to the body so nourished, by mixing with it, just as water is mixed with wine, as the Philosopher says there by way of example,[7] it follows that that which is added, and that to which it is added, cannot be of different natures, since they are already made one by a true mixture. Therefore there is no reason for saying that one is destroyed by natural heat, while the other remains.

It must therefore be said that this distinction of the Philosopher is not of different kinds of flesh, but of the same flesh considered from different points of view. For if we consider the flesh according to the species, that is, according to that which is formal in it, then it remains always, because the nature of flesh always remains together with its natural disposition. But

---

[1] Cf. Bonaventure, *In Sent.*, II, d. 30, A. 3, Q. 1 (QR II, 730); Q. 2 (QR II, 735). Cf. also the reference to Alexander the Commentator in Averroes, *In De Gener.*, I, 38 (v, 358F).

[2] Averroes, *In De Gener.*, I, 38 (v, 358H).
[3] *Soul*, II, 4 (416^{b}10); cf. *Generation and Corruption*, I, 5 (322^{a}27).
[4] *In Matt.*, Bk. II (PL 26, 112).
[5] Bonaventure, *In Sent.*, II. d. 30, A. 3, Q. 2 (QR II, 735).
[6] *Generation and Corruption*, I, 5 (321^{b}20).
[7] *Ibid.* (322^{a}9).

if we consider flesh according to matter, then it does not remain, but is gradually destroyed and renewed, just as in the fire of a furnace, the form of fire remains, but the matter is gradually consumed, and other matter is substituted in its place.

Reply Obj. 3. The radical humour is said to comprise whatever the power of the species is founded on. If this is taken away it cannot be renewed, as when a man's hand or foot is amputated. But the nutritive humour is that which has not yet received perfectly the specific nature, but is on the way there; for example the blood, and the like. Therefore if such as these are taken away, the power of the species remains in its root, which is not destroyed.

Reply Obj. 4. Every power of a passible body is weakened by continuous action, because such agents are also acted upon. Therefore the transforming power is strong at first so as to be able to transform not only enough for the renewal of what is lost, but also for growth. Later on it can only transform enough for the renewal of what is lost, and then growth ceases. At last it cannot even do this, and then begins decline. Finally, when this virtue fails altogether, the animal dies. Thus the power of wine that transforms the water added to it, is weakened by further additions of water, so as to become at length watery, as the Philosopher says by way of example.[1]

Reply Obj. 5. As the Philosopher says,[2] when a certain matter is directly transformed into fire, then fire is said to be generated anew; but when matter is transformed into a fire already existing, then fire is said to be fed. And so if the entire matter together loses the form of fire, and another matter transformed into fire, there will be another distinct fire. But if, while one piece of wood is gradually burning, another piece is laid on, and so on until the first piece is entirely consumed, the same identical fire will remain all the time, because that which is added passes into what pre-existed. It is the same with living bodies, in which by means of nourishment that is restored which was consumed by natural heat.

ARTICLE 2. *Whether the Semen Is Produced from Surplus Food?*

We proceed thus to the Second Article: It would seem that the semen is not produced from the surplus food, but from the substance of the begetter.

Objection 1. For Damascene says (*De Fide*

Orth. i, 8)[3] that generation is "a work of nature, producing, from the substance of the begetter, that which is begotten." But that which is generated is produced from the semen. Therefore the semen is produced from the substance of the begetter.

Obj. 2. Further, the son is like his father in respect of that which he receives from him. But if the semen from which something is generated is produced from the surplus food, a man would receive nothing from his grandfather and his ancestors in whom the food never existed. Therefore a man would not be more like to his grandfather or ancestors than to any other men.

Obj. 3. Further, the food of the generator is sometimes the flesh of cows, pigs and like. If, therefore, the semen were produced from surplus food, the man begotten of such semen would be more akin to the cow and the pig than to his father or other relations.

Obj. 4. Further, Augustine says (*Gen. ad lit.* x, 20)[4] that we were in Adam "not only by seminal principle, but also in the very substance of the body." But this would not be if the semen were produced from surplus food. Therefore the semen is not produced from surplus food.

On the contrary, The Philosopher proves in many ways[5] that "the semen is surplus food."

I answer that, This question depends in some way on what has been stated above (A. 1; Q. CXVIII, A. 1). For if there is in human nature a power for the communication of its form to alien matter not only in another, but also in its own subject, it is clear that the food which at first is dissimilar becomes at length similar through the form communicated to it. Now it is the order of nature that a thing should be reduced from potency to act gradually. Hence in things generated we observe that at first each is imperfect and is afterwards perfected. But it is clear that the common is to the proper and determinate, as imperfect is to perfect. Therefore we see that in the generation of an animal, the animal is generated first, then the man or the horse. So therefore food first of all receives a certain common virtue in regard to all the parts of the body, and is subsequently determinate to this or that part.

Now it is not possible that the semen be a kind of solution from what is already transformed into the substance of the members. For this solution, if it does not retain the nature of the member it is taken from, would no longer be

---

[1] *Generation and Corruption*, I, 5 (322ᵃ31).
[2] *Ibid.* (322ᵃ14).

[3] PG 94, 813.   [4] PL 34, 424.
[5] *Generation of Animals*, I, 18 (726ᵃ26).

of the nature of the begetter, and would be as it were already on the way to corruption; and consequently it would not have the power of transforming something else into the likeness of that nature. But if it retained the nature of the member it is taken from, then it is limited to a determinate part of the body, and it would not have the power of moving towards (the production of) the whole nature, but only the nature of that part. Unless one were to say that the solution is taken from all the parts of the body, and that it retains the nature of each part. Thus the semen would be as a kind of small animal in act, and generation of animal from animal would be a mere division, as mud is generated from mud, and as animals which continue to live after being cut in two. This, however, cannot be admitted.

It remains to be said, therefore, that the semen is not something cut off from what was the actual whole. Rather is it the whole, though potentially, having the power, derived from the soul of the begetter, to produce the whole body, as stated above (A. 1; Q. CVIII, A. 1). Now that which is in potency to the whole is that which is generated from the food before it is transformed into the substance of the members. Therefore the semen is taken from this. In this sense the nutritive power is said to serve the generative power, because what is transformed by the nutritive power is employed as semen by the generative power. A sign of this, according to the Philosopher,[1] is that animals of great size, which require much food, have little semen in proportion to the size of their bodies, and generate seldom; and in like manner fat men, and for the same reason.

Reply Obj. 1. Generation is from the sub-

[1] *Generation of Animals*, I, 18 (725ᵃ28).

stance of the begetter in animals and plants, in so far as the semen owes its power to the form of the begetter, and in so far as it is in potency to the substance.

Reply Obj. 2. The likeness of the begetter to the begotten is on account not of the matter, but of the form of the agent that generates its like. And so in order for a man to be like his grandfather, there is no need that the corporeal seminal matter should have been in the grandfather, but that there be in the semen a power derived from the soul of the grandfather through the father.

In like manner the *third objection* is answered. For kinship is not according to matter, but rather according to the derivation of the form.

Reply Obj. 4. These words of Augustine are not to be understood as though the immediate seminal principle, or the corporeal substance from which this individual was formed were actually in Adam, but that both were in Adam according to origin. For even the corporeal matter, which is supplied by the mother and which he calls the corporeal substance, is originally derived from Adam; and likewise the active seminal power of the father, which is the immediate seminal principle of this man.

But Christ is said to have been in Adam according to the corporeal substance, not according to the seminal principle. Because the matter from which His Body was formed, and which was supplied by the Virgin Mother, was derived from Adam; but the active power was not derived from Adam, because His Body was not formed by the seminal power of a man, but by the operation of the Holy Ghost. For such a birth was becoming to Him, WHO IS ABOVE ALL GOD FOR EVER BLESSED. Amen.

SECOND PART

❖❖❖❖❖❖❖❖❖❖❖

Part I of the Second Part

PROLOGUE

SINCE, as Damascene states (*De Fide Orthod.* ii, 12),[1] man is said to be made to God's image, in so far as the image implies an intelligent being endowed with free choice and self-movement, now that we have treated of the exemplar, that is, of God, and of those things which came forth from the power of God in accordance with His will, it remains for us to treat of His image, that is, man, according as he too is the principle of his actions, as having free choice and control of his actions.

TREATISE ON THE LAST END

QUESTION I
OF MAN'S LAST END
(In Eight Articles)

IN this matter we shall consider first the last end of human life, and secondly, those things by means of which man may advance towards this end, or stray from it (Q. VI); for the end is the rule of whatever is ordered to the end. And since the last end of human life is stated to be Happiness, we must consider (1) the last end in general; (2) Happiness (Q. II).

Under the first head there are eight points of inquiry: (1) Whether it pertains to man to act for an end? (2) Whether this is proper to the rational nature? (3) Whether a man's actions are specified by the end? (4) Whether there is any last end of human life? (5) Whether one man can have several last ends? (6) Whether man orders all things to the last end? (7) Whether all men have the same last end? (8) Whether all other creatures agree with man in that last end?

ARTICLE 1. *Whether It Is Proper to Man To Act for an End?*

We proceed thus to the First Article: It seems unfitting for man to act for an end.

[1] PG 94, 920.

Objection 1. For a cause is naturally first. But an end, in its very name, has the nature of something that is last. Therefore an end does not have the nature of a cause. But that for which a man acts, is the cause of his action, since this preposition "for" indicates a relation of causality. Therefore it is not proper to man to act for an end.

Obj. 2. Further, that which is itself the last end is not for the sake of an end. But in some cases the last end is an action, as the Philosopher states.[2] Therefore man does not do everything for an end.

Obj. 3. Further, a man seems to act for an end whenever he acts deliberately. But man does many things without deliberation, sometimes not even thinking of what he is doing; for instance when one moves one's foot or hand or scratches one's beard while intent on something else. Therefore man does not do everything for an end.

On the contrary, All things contained in a genus are derived from the principle of that genus. Now the end is the principle in human operations, as the Philosopher states.[3] Therefore it is proper to man to do everything for an end.

I answer that, Of actions done by man those alone are properly called "human" which are

[2] *Ethics,* I, 9 (1094[a]4). [3] *Physics,* II. 9 (200[a]34).

proper to man as man. Now man differs from irrational creatures in this, that he is master of his actions. And so those actions alone are properly called human of which man is master. Now man is master of his actions through his reason and will; hence, too, free choice is called "the power of will and reason."[1] Therefore those actions are properly called human which proceed from a deliberate will. And if any other actions are found in man, they can be called actions "of a man," but not properly "human" actions, since they do not pertain to man as man. Now it is clear that whatever actions proceed from a power are caused by that power in accordance with the nature of its object. But the object of the will is the end and the good. Therefore all human actions must be for an end.

Reply Obj. 1. Although the end is last in the order of execution, yet it is first in the order of the agent's intention. And it is in this way that it has the nature of a cause.

Reply Obj. 2. If any human action be the last end, it must be voluntary; otherwise it would not be human, as stated above. Now an action is voluntary in one of two ways: first, because it is commanded by the will, for example, to walk, or to speak; secondly, because it is elicited by the will, for instance the very act of willing. Now it is impossible for the very act elicited by the will to be the last end. For the object of the will is the end, just as the object of sight is colour; therefore just as the first visible cannot be the act of seeing, because every act of seeing is of some visible object; so the first appetible, that is, the end, cannot be the act itself of willing. Consequently it follows that if a human action be the last end, it must be an action commanded by the will, so that even in this case some action of man, at least the act of willing, is for the end. Therefore whatever a man does it is true to say that man acts for an end, even when he does that action in which the last end consists.

Reply Obj. 3. Actions of this kind are not properly human actions, since they do not proceed from deliberation of the reason, which is the proper principle of human actions. Therefore they have a kind of imagined end, but not one that is fixed by reason.

ARTICLE 2. *Whether It Is Proper to the Rational Nature to Act for an End?*

We proceed thus to the Second Article: It seems that it is proper to the rational nature to act for an end.

---

¹ Cf. Peter Lombard, *Sent.*, ii, d. 24, chap.3 (QR i, 421).

Objection 1. For man, to whom it pertains to act for an end, never acts for an unknown end. On the other hand, there are many things that have no knowledge of an end, either because they are altogether without knowledge, as insensible creatures, or because they do not apprehend the aspect of end, as irrational animals. Therefore it seems proper to the rational nature to act for an end.

Obj. 2. Further, to act for an end is to order one's action to an end. But this is the work of reason. Therefore it does not befit things that lack reason.

Obj. 3. Further, the good and the end is the object of the will. But "the will is in the reason."[2] Therefore to act for an end belongs to none but a rational nature.

On the contrary, The Philosopher proves[3] that "not only intellect but also nature acts for an end."

I answer that, Every agent, of necessity, acts for an end. For if in a number of causes ordered to one another the first be removed, the others must of necessity be removed also. Now the first of all causes is the final cause. The reason of which is that matter does not strive after form, save in so far as it is moved by an agent; for nothing reduces itself from potency to act. But an agent does not move except out of intention for an end. For if the agent were not determined to some effect, it would not do one thing rather than another; consequently in order that it produce a determinate effect, it must, of necessity, be determined to some certain one, which has the nature of an end. And just as this determination is effected in the rational nature by the rational appetite, which is called the will, so in other things it is caused by their natural inclination, which is called the natural appetite.

Nevertheless, it must be observed that a thing tends to an end by its action or movement in two ways: first, as a thing moving itself to the end,—as for instance man; secondly, as a thing moved by another to the end, as an arrow tends to a determinate end through being moved by the archer, who directs his action to the end. Therefore those things that have reason move themselves to an end, because they have dominion over their actions through their free choice which is the power of will and reason. But those things that lack reason tend to an end by natural inclination, as being moved by another and not by themselves, since they do not know the nature of an end, and consequently cannot order

---

² *Soul,* iii, 9 (432ᵇ5). ³ *Physics,* ii, 5 (196ᵇ21).

anything to an end, but can be ordered to an end only by another. For the entire irrational nature is related to God as an instrument to the principal agent, as stated above (Part I, Q. XXII, A. 2, reply 4; Q. CIII, A. 1, reply 3). Consequently it is proper to the rational nature to tend to an end as moving (agens) and leading itself to the end; but it is proper to the irrational nature to tend to an end as moved or led by another, whether it apprehend the end, as do irrational animals, or do not apprehend it, as is the case of those things which are altogether lacking in knowledge.

Reply Obj. 1. When a man of himself acts for an end, he knows the end, but when he is moved or led by another, for instance, when he acts at another's command, or when he is moved under another's compulsion, it is not necessary that he should know the end. And it is thus with irrational creatures.

Reply Obj. 2. To order towards an end pertains to that which directs itself to an end, whereas to be ordered to an end belongs to that which is directed by another to an end. And this can belong to an irrational nature, but by reason of some one possessed of reason.

Reply Obj. 3. The object of the will is the end and the good in universal. Consequently there can be no will in those things that lack reason and intellect, since they cannot apprehend the universal; but they have a natural appetite or a sensitive appetite, determined to some particular good. Now it is clear that particular causes are moved by a universal cause; thus the governor of a city, who intends the common good, moves by his command all the particular departments of the city. Consequently all things that lack reason are of necessity moved to their particular ends by some rational will which extends to the universal good, namely by the Divine will.

ARTICLE 3. *Whether Human Acts Are Specified By Their End?*

We proceed thus to the Third Article: It seems that human acts are not specified by their end.

Objection 1. For the end is an extrinsic cause. But everything is specified by an intrinsic principle. Therefore human acts are not specified by their end.

Obj. 2. Further, that which gives a thing its species should exist before it. But the end comes last in being. Therefore a human act does not derive its species from the end.

Obj. 3. Further, one thing cannot be in more than one species. But one and the same act may happen to be ordered to various ends. Therefore the end does not give the species to human acts.

On the contrary, Augustine says (*De Mor. Eccl. et Manich.* ii, 13) :[1] "According as their end is worthy of blame or praise, so are our deeds worthy of blame or praise."

I answer that, Each thing receives its species in respect of an act and not in respect of potency; therefore things composed of matter and form are established in their respective species by their own forms. And this is also to be observed in proper movements. For since movements are, in a way, divided into action and passion, each of these receives its species from an act; action indeed from the act which is the principle of acting, and passion from the act which is the term of the movement. And so heating as an action is nothing other than a certain movement proceeding from heat, while heating as a passion is nothing other than a movement towards heat; and it is the definition that shows the specific nature. And either way, human acts, whether they be considered as actions or as passions, receive their species from the end. For human acts can be considered in both ways, since man moves himself, and is moved by himself. Now it has been stated above (A. 1) that acts are called human in so far as they proceed from a deliberate will. Now the object of the will is the good and the end. And hence it is clear that the principle of human acts, in so far as they are human, is the end. In like manner it is their term, for the human act terminates at that which the will intends as the end; thus in natural agents the form of the thing generated is conformed to the form of the generator. And since, as Ambrose says (*Prolog. super Luc.*)[2] "morality is said properly of man," moral acts properly speaking receive their species from the end, for moral acts are the same as human acts.

Reply Obj. 1. The end is not altogether extrinsic to the act, because it is related to the act as principle or term; and it is just this that is characteristic of an act, namely, to proceed from something considered as action, and to proceed towards something considered as passion.

Reply Obj. 2. The end, in so far as it pre-exists in the intention, pertains to the will, as stated above (A. 1, reply 1). And it is thus that it gives the species to the human or moral act.

Reply Obj. 3. One and the same act, in so far as it proceeds once from the agent, is ordered but to one proximate end, from which it has its species, but it can be ordered to several remote

[1] PL 32, 1356.   [2] PL 15, 1612.

ends, of which one is the end of the other. It is possible, however, that an act which is one in respect of its natural species is ordered to several ends of the will; thus this act, to kill a man, which is but one act in respect of its natural species, can be ordered, as to an end, to the safeguarding of justice, and to the satisfying of anger, the result being that there would be several acts in different species of morality, since in one way there will be an act of virtue, in another, an act of vice. For a movement does not receive its species from that which is its term accidentally, but only from that which is its *per se* term. Now moral ends are accidental to a natural thing, and conversely the character of a natural end is accidental to morality. Consequently there is no reason why acts which are the same considered in their natural species should not be different considered in their moral species, and conversely.

ARTICLE 4. *Whether There Is One Last End of Human Life?*

We proceed thus to the Fourth Article: It would seem that there is no last end of human life, but that we proceed to infinity in ends.

Objection 1. For good, according to its very notion spreads itself abroad, as Dionysius states (*Div. Nom.* iv).[1] Consequently if that which proceeds from good is itself good, the latter must diffuse some other good. so that the diffusion of good goes on to infinity. But good has the nature of an end. Therefore there is an infinite series of ends.

Obj. 2. Further, things pertaining to the reason can be multiplied to infinity; thus mathematical quantities have no limit. For the same reason the species of numbers are infinite, since given any number the reason can think of one yet greater. But desire of the end is consequent on the apprehension of the reason. Therefore it seems that there is also an infinite series of ends.

Obj. 3. Further, the good and the end is the object of the will. But the will can turn back on itself an infinite number of times, for I can will something, and will to will it, and so on infinitely. Therefore there is an infinite series of ends of the human will, and there is no last end of the human will.

On the contrary, The Philosopher says[2] that "to suppose a thing to be infinite is to eliminate the good." But the good is that which has the nature of an end. Therefore it is contrary to the nature of an end to proceed to infinity. Therefore it is necessary to fix one last end.

[1] Sect. 20 (PG 3, 719). Cf. also sects. 1, 4 (694, 698).
[2] *Metaphysics*, II, 2 (994^{b}12).

I answer that, Absolutely speaking, it is not possible to proceed infinitely in the matter of ends, from any point of view. For in whatsoever things there is an essential order of one to another, if the first be removed those that are ordered to the first must of necessity be removed also. Thus the Philosopher proves[3] that "we cannot proceed to infinity in causes of movement," because then there would be no first mover, without which neither can the others move, since they move only through being moved by the first mover. Now there is to be observed a twofold order in ends, the order of intention, and the order of execution, and in either of these orders there must be something first. For that which is first in the order of intention is the principle, as it were, moving the appetite; consequently, if you remove this principle there will be nothing to move the appetite. On the other hand, the principle in execution is that in which work has its beginning, and if this principle is taken away, no one will begin to work. Now the principle in the intention is the last end, while the principle in execution is the first of the things which are ordered to the end. Consequently, on neither side is it possible to go on to infinity, since if there were no last end nothing would be desired, nor would any action have its term, nor would the intention of the agent be at rest; while if there is no first thing among those that are ordered to the end, none would begin to work at anything, and counsel would have no term, but would continue infinitely.

On the other hand, we may have an infinity of things that are ordered to one another not essentially but accidentally, for accidental causes are not determinate. And in this way it happens that there is an accidental infinity of ends and of things ordered to the end.

Reply Obj. 1. The very nature of good is that something flows from it, but not that it proceeds from something else. Since, therefore, good has the nature of end, and the first good is the last end, this argument does not prove that there is no last end, but that from the end already supposed we may proceed downwards infinitely towards those things that are ordered to the end. And this would be true if we considered but the power of the First Good, which is infinite. But, since the First Good diffuses itself according to the intellect, to which it is proper to flow forth into its effects according to a certain determined form it follows that there is a certain measure to the flow of good things from the First Good from Which all other goods share

[3] *Physics*, VIII, 5 (256^{a}17).

the power of diffusion. Consequently the diffusion of good does not proceed indefinitely, but, as it is written (Wisd. 11. 21), God disposes all things *in number, weight and measure.*

Reply Obj. 2. In things which are of themselves reason begins from principles that are known naturally, and advances to some term. And so the Philosopher proves[1] that there is no infinite process in demonstrations, because there we find a process of things having an essential, not an accidental, connection with one another. But in those things which are accidentally connected nothing hinders the reason from proceeding indefinitely. Now it is accidental to a stated quantity or number, as such, that quantity or unity be added to it. Therefore in things of this kind nothing hinders the reason from an infinite process.

Reply Obj. 3. This multiplication of acts of the will turning back on itself is accidental to the order of ends. This is clear from the fact that in regard to one and the same end the will turns back on itself indifferently once or several times.

ARTICLE 5. *Whether One Man Can Have Several Last Ends?*

We proceed thus to the Fifth Article: It would seem possible for one man's will to be directed at the same time to several things, as last ends.

Objection 1. For Augustine says[2] that some held man's last end to consist in four things, namely, "in pleasure, repose the gifts of nature, and virtue." But these are clearly more than one thing. Therefore one man can place the last end of his will in many things.

Obj. 2. Further, things not in opposition to one another do not exclude one another. Now there are many things which are not in opposition to one another. Therefore the supposition that one thing is the last end of the will does not exclude others.

Obj. 3. Further, by the fact that it places its last end in one thing, the will does not lose its freedom. But before it placed its last end in that thing, for example, pleasure, it could place it in something else, for example, riches. Therefore even after having placed his last end in pleasure, a man can at the same time place his last end in riches. Therefore it is possible for one man's will to be directed at the same time to several things, as last ends.

On the contrary, That in which a man rests as

in his last end is master of his affections, since he takes from this his entire rule of life. Hence of gluttons it is written (Phil. 3. 19): *Whose god is their belly,* namely, because they place their last end in the pleasures of the belly. Now according to Matt. 6. 24, *No man can serve two masters,* such, that is, as are not ordered to one another. Therefore it is impossible for one man to have several last ends not ordered to one another.

I answer that, It is impossible for one man's will to be directed at the same time to diverse things, as to so many last ends. Three reasons may be assigned for this. First, because since everything desires its own perfection a man desires for his ultimate end that which he desires as his perfect and crowning good. Hence Augustine says,[3] "In speaking of the end of good we mean now not that it passes away so as to be no more, but that it is perfected so as to be complete." It is therefore necessary for the last end so to fill man's appetite that nothing is left beside it for man to desire. And this is not possible if something else be required for his perfection. Consequently it is not possible for the appetite so to tend to two things as though each were its perfect good.

The second reason is because just as in the process of reasoning the principle is that which is naturally known, so in the process of the rational appetite, which is the will, the principle must be that which is naturally desired. Now this must be one, since nature tends to one thing only. But the principle in the process of the rational appetite is the last end. Therefore that to which the will tends under the aspect of last end, must be one.

The third reason is because since voluntary actions receive their species from the end, as stated above (A. 3), they must receive their genus from the last end, which is common to them all, just as natural things are placed in a genus according to a common form. Since, then, all things that can be desired by the will, belong, as such, to one genus, the last end must be one. And all the more because in every genus there is one first principle, and the last end has the nature of a first principle, as stated above.

Now as the last end of man, taken absolutely as man, is to the whole human race, so is the last end of any individual man to that individual man. Therefore, just as of all men there is naturally one last end, so the will of an individual man must be fixed on one last end.

Reply Obj. 1. All these several things were

---

[1] *Posterior Analytics,* I, 3 (72^{b}7); cf. I, 22 (84^{a}11).
[2] *City of God,* XIX, 1 (PL 41, 622); cf. also XIX, 4 (PL 41, 627).
[3] *City of God,* XIX, 1 (PL 41, 621).

considered as one perfect good made up from them by those who placed in them the last end.

Reply Obj. 2. Although it is possible to find several things which are not in opposition to one another, yet it is contrary to the perfect good that anything besides be required for that thing's perfection.

Reply Obj. 3. The power of the will does not extend to making opposites to be at the same time. Which would be the case were it to tend to several diverse objects as last ends, as has been shown above (REPLY 2).

ARTICLE 6. *Whether Man Wills All That He Wills for the Last End?*

We proceed thus to the Sixth Article: It would seem that man does not will all things whatsoever he wills for the last end.

Objection 1. For things ordered to the last end are said to be serious things, as being useful. But jests are distinguished from serious things. Therefore what man does in jest, he does not order to the last end.

Obj. 2. Further, the Philosopher says at the beginning of his *Metaphysics*[1] that the speculative sciences are sought for their own sake. Now it cannot be said that each speculative science is the last end. Therefore man does not desire all things whatsoever he desires for the last end.

Obj. 3. Further, whoever orders something to an end, thinks of that end. But man does not always think of the last end in all that he desires or does. Therefore man neither desires nor does all for the last end.

On the contrary, Augustine says,[2] "That is the end of our good, for the sake of which we love other things, whereas we love it for its own sake."

I answer that, Man must, of necessity, desire all things whatsoever he desires for the last end. This is evident for two reasons. First, because whatever man desires he desires it under the aspect of good. And if he does not desire it as his perfect good, which is the last end, he must, of necessity, desire it as tending to the perfect good, because the beginning of anything is always ordered to its completion, as is clearly the case in effects both of nature and of art. Therefore every beginning of perfection is ordered to complete perfection which is achieved through the last end. Secondly, because the last end stands in the same relation in moving the appetite as the first mover in other movements. Now it is clear that secondary moving causes do not

move except according as they are moved by the first mover. Therefore secondary objects of the appetite do not move the appetite, except as ordered to the first object of the appetite, which is the last end.

Reply Obj. 1. Actions done jestingly are not ordered to any extrinsic end but merely to the good of the jester, in so far as they afford him pleasure or relaxation. But man's perfect good is his last end.

Reply Obj. 2. The same applies to speculative science, which is desired as the investigator's good, included in complete and perfect good, which is the ultimate end.

Reply Obj. 3. One need not always be thinking of the last end whenever one desires or does something; but the force of the first intention, which is in respect of the last end, persists in every desire directed to any object whatever, even though one's thoughts be not actually directed to the last end. Thus while walking along the road one does not need to be thinking of the end at every step.

ARTICLE 7. *Whether All Men Have the Same Last End?*

We proceed thus to the Seventh Article: It would seem that all men have not the same last end.

Objection 1. For before all else the unchangeable good seems to be the last end of man. But some turn away from the unchangeable good, by sinning. Therefore all men have not the same last end.

Obj. 2. Further, man's entire life is ruled according to his last end. If, therefore, all men had the same last end, they would not have various pursuits in life. Which is evidently false.

Obj. 3. Further, the end is the term of action. But actions are of individuals. Now although men agree in their specific nature, yet they differ in things pertaining to individuals. Therefore all men have not the same last end.

On the contrary, Augustine says (*De Trin.* xiii, 3)[3] that all men agree in desiring the last end, which is happiness.

I answer that, We can speak of the last end in two ways: first, considering the notion of last end; secondly, considering the thing in which the aspect of last end is found. So, then, as to the notion of last end, all agree in desiring the last end, since all desire the fulfilment of their perfection, and it is in this that the last end consists, as stated above (A. 5). But as to the thing in which this notion is realized, all men are not

---

[1] 1, 2 (982[a]14; [a]28).
[2] *City of God,* XIX, 1 (PL 41, 621).
[3] PL 42, 1018.

agreed as to their last end, since some desire riches as their consummate good; some, pleasure; others, something else. Thus to every taste the sweet is pleasant; but to some, the sweetness of wine is most pleasant, to others, the sweetness of honey, or of something similar. Yet that sweet is absolutely the best of all pleasant things in which he who has the best taste takes most pleasure. In like manner that good is most complete which the man with well-disposed affections desires for his last end.

Reply Obj. 1. Those who sin turn from that in which their last end really consists, but they do not turn away from the intention of the last end, which intention they mistakenly seek in other things.

Reply Obj. 2. Various pursuits in life are found among men by reason of the various things in which men seek to find their last end.

Reply Obj. 3. Although actions are of individuals, yet their first principle of action is nature, which tends to one thing, as stated above (A. 5).

ARTICLE 8. *Whether Other Creatures Concur in That Last End?*

We proceed thus to the Eighth Article: It would seem that all other creatures concur in man's last end.

Objection 1. For the end corresponds to the beginning. But man's beginning—that is, God—is also the beginning of all else. Therefore all other things concur in man's last end.

Obj. 2. Further, Dionysius says (*Div. Nom.* iv)[1] that God turns all things to Himself as to their last end. But He is also man's last end, because He alone is to be enjoyed by man. Therefore other things, too, concur in man's last end.

Obj. 3. Further, man's last end is the object of the will. But the object of the will is the universal good, which is the end of all. Therefore all must concur in man's last end.

On the contrary, man's last end is happiness, which all men desire, as Augustine says (*De Trin.* xiii, 3, 4).[2] But "happiness is not possible for animals bereft of reason," as Augustine says.[3] Therefore other things do not concur in man's last end.

I answer that, As the Philosopher says,[4] the end is twofold,—the end for which and the end by which; namely, the thing itself in which is found the aspect of good, and the use or acqui-

[1] Sect. 4 (PG 3, 700).
[2] Chap. 3 (PL 42, 1018); cf. also *City of God*, XIX, 1 (PL 41, 621).
[3] QQ. LXXXIII., Q. 5 (PL 40, 12).
[4] *Physics*, II, 2 (194ᵃ35); cf. also *Soul*, II, 4 (415ᵇ2; ᵇ20).

sition of that thing. Thus we say that the end of the movement of a weighty body is either a lower place as thing, or to be in a lower place, as use; and the end of the miser is money as thing, or possession of money as use.

If, therefore, we speak of man's last end and mean the thing which is the end, then all other things concur in man's last end, since God is the last end of man and of all other things. If, however, we speak of man's last end and mean the attainment of the end, then irrational creatures have no part with man in this end. For man and other rational creatures reach their last end by knowing and loving God, and this is not possible to other creatures, which attain their last end in so far as they share in the Divine likeness, according as they are, or live, or even know.

Hence it is evident how *the objections* are solved, since happiness means the attainment of the last end.

QUESTION II
OF THOSE THINGS IN WHICH MAN'S HAPPINESS CONSISTS
(*In Eight Articles*)

WE have now to consider happiness: and (1) in what it consists; (2) what it is (Q. III); (3) how we can obtain it (Q. V).

Concerning the first there are eight points of inquiry: (1) Whether happiness consists in wealth? (2) Whether in honour? (3) Whether in fame or glory? (4) Whether in power? (5) Whether in any good of the body? (6) Whether in pleasure? (7) Whether in any good of the soul? (8) Whether in any created good?

ARTICLE 1. *Whether Man's Happiness Consists in Wealth?*

We proceed thus to the First Article: It seems that man's happiness consists in wealth.

Objection 1. For since happiness is man's last end, it must consist in that which has the greatest hold on man's affections. Now this is wealth, for it is written (Eccles. 10. 19): *All things obey money.* Therefore man's happiness consists in wealth.

Obj. 2. Further, according to Boëthius (*De Consol.* iii, 2),[5] happiness is "a state of life made perfect by the aggregate of all good things." Now money seems to be the means of possessing all things, for, as the Philosopher says,[6] money was invented that it might be a sort of guarantee for the acquisition of what-

[5] PL 63, 724.   [6] *Ethics*, v, 5 (1133ᵇ12).

ever man desires. Therefore happiness consists in wealth.

Obj. 3. Further, since the desire for the sovereign good never fails, it seems to be infinite. But this is the case with riches more than anything else, since *a covetous man shall not be satisfied with riches* (Eccles. 5. 9). Therefore happiness consists in wealth.

On the contrary, Man's good consists in retaining happiness rather than in giving it up. But as Boëthius says (*De Consol.* ii, 5),[1] "wealth shines in giving rather than in hoarding, for the miser is hateful whereas the generous man is applauded." Therefore man's happiness does not consist in wealth.

I answer that, It is impossible for man's happiness to consist in wealth. For wealth is twofold, as the Philosopher says,[2] natural and artificial. Natural wealth is that which serves man as a remedy for his natural wants, such as food, drink, clothing, conveyances, dwellings, and things of this kind, while artificial wealth is that which is not a direct help to nature, as money, but is invented by the art of man for the convenience of exchange and as a measure of things saleable.

Now it is evident that man's happiness cannot consist in natural wealth. For wealth of this kind is sought as a support of human nature; consequently it cannot be man's last end, but rather is ordered to man as to its end. Therefore in the order of nature, all such things are below man, and made for him, according to Ps. 8. 8: *Thou hast subjected all things under his feet.*

And as to artificial wealth, it is not sought save for the sake of natural wealth, since man would not seek it except that by its means he procures for himself the necessaries of life. Consequently much less does it have the character of the last end. Therefore it is impossible for happiness, which is the last end of man, to consist in wealth.

Reply Obj. 1. All material things obey money so far as the multitude of fools is concerned, who know no other than material goods, which can be obtained for money. But we should take our judgment of human goods not from the foolish but from the wise, just as it is for a person whose sense of taste is in good order to judge whether a thing is palatable.

Reply Obj. 2. All things saleable can be had for money, but not spiritual things, which cannot be sold. Hence it is written (Prov. 17. 16):

What doth it avail a fool to have riches, seeing he cannot buy wisdom?

Reply Obj. 3. The desire for natural riches is not infinite, because they suffice for nature in a certain measure. But the desire for artificial wealth is infinite, for it is the servant of disordered concupiscence, which is not curbed, as the Philosopher makes clear.[3] Yet this desire for wealth is infinite otherwise than the desire for the sovereign good. For the more perfectly the sovereign good is possessed, the more is it loved and other things despised, because the more we possess it, the more we know it. Hence it is written (Ecclus. 24. 29): *They that eat me shall yet hunger.* Whereas in the desire for wealth and for whatsoever temporal goods, the contrary is the case, for when we already possess them, we despise them and seek others, which is the sense of Our Lord's words (John 4. 13): *Whosoever drinketh of this water,* by which temporal goods are signified, *shall thirst again.* The reason of this is that we realize more their insufficiency when we possess them: and this very fact shows that they are imperfect, and that the sovereign good does not consist in them.

ARTICLE 2. *Whether Man's Happiness Consists in Honours?*

We proceed thus to the Second Article: It seems that man's happiness consists in honours.

Objection 1. For "happiness or bliss is the reward of virtue," as the Philosopher says.[4] But honour more than anything else seems to be that by which virtue is rewarded, as the Philosopher says.[5] Therefore happiness consists especially in honours.

Obj. 2. Further, that which belongs to God and to beings of great excellence seems especially to be happiness, which is the perfect good. But that is honour, as the Philosopher says.[6] Moreover, the Apostle says (I Tim. 1. 17): *To . . . the only God be honour and glory.* Therefore happiness consists in honour.

Obj. 3. Further, that which man desires above all is happiness. But nothing seems more desirable to man than honour, since man suffers loss in all other things lest he should suffer loss of honour. Therefore happiness consists in honour.

On the contrary, Happiness is in the happy. But honour "is not in the honoured, but rather in him who honours," and who offers deference to the person honoured, as the Philosopher

[1] PL 63, 690.
[2] *Politics,* I, 9 (1257ᵃ4).
[3] *Ibid.* (1258ᵃ1).
[4] *Ethics,* I, 9 (1099ᵇ16).
[5] *Ibid.,* IV, 3 (1123ᵇ35).
[6] *Ibid.,* IV, 3 (1123ᵇ20).

says.[1] Therefore happiness does not consist in honour.

I answer that, It is impossible for happiness to consist in honour. For honour is given to a man on account of some excellence in him, and consequently it is a sign and testimony of the excellence that is in the person honoured. Now a man's excellence is in proportion to his happiness, which is man's perfect good; and to its parts, that is those goods by which he has a certain share of happiness. And therefore honour can result from happiness, but happiness cannot principally consist therein.

Reply Obj. 1. As the Philosopher says,[2] honour is not that reward of virtue, for which the virtuous work, but they receive honour from men by way of reward, as from those who have nothing greater to offer. But virtue's true reward is happiness itself, for which the virtuous work, whereas if they worked for honour, it would no longer be virtue, but ambition.

Reply Obj. 2. Honour is due to God and to beings of great excellence as a sign or testimony of excellence already existing, not that honour makes them excellent.

Reply Obj. 3. That man desires honour above all else arises from his natural desire for happiness, from which honour results, as stated above. And so man seeks to be honoured especially by the wise, on whose judgment he believes himself to be excellent or happy.

ARTICLE 3. *Whether Man's Happiness Consists in Fame or Glory?*

We proceed thus to the Third Article: It seems that man's happiness consists in glory.

Objection 1. For happiness seems to consist in that which is paid to the saints for the trials they have undergone in the world. But this is glory, for the Apostle says (Rom. 8. 18) *The sufferings of this time are not worthy to be compared with the glory to come, that shall be revealed in us.* Therefore happiness consists in glory.

Obj. 2. Further, good pours itself out, as stated by Dionysius (*Div. Nom.* iv).[3] But man's good is spread abroad in the knowledge of others by glory more than by anything else, since, according to Ambrose (Augustine,—*Contra Maxim. Arian.* ii),[4] glory consists "in being well known and praised." Therefore man's happiness consists in glory.

Obj. 3. Further, happiness is the most enduring good. Now this seems to be fame or glory, because by this men attain to eternity after a fashion. Hence Boëthius says (*De Consol.* ii, 7):[5] "You seem to beget unto yourselves eternity, when you think of your fame in future time." Therefore man's happiness consists in fame or glory.

On the contrary, Happiness is man's true good. But it happens that fame or glory is false, for as Boëthius says (*De Consol.* iii, 6),[6] "Many owe their renown to the lying reports spread among the people. Can anything be more shameful? For those who receive false fame must blush at their own praise." Therefore man's happiness does not consist in fame or glory.

I answer that, Man's happiness cannot consist in human fame or glory. For glory consists "in being well known and praised," as Ambrose (Augustine, *loc. cit.*) says. Now the thing known is related to human knowledge otherwise than to God's knowledge, for human knowledge is caused by the things known, whereas God's knowledge is the cause of the things known. Therefore the perfection of human good, which is called happiness, cannot be caused by human knowledge, but rather human knowledge of another's happiness proceeds from, and, in a fashion, is caused by, human happiness itself, whether incomplete or perfect. Consequently man's happiness cannot consist in fame or glory. On the other hand, man's good depends on God's knowledge as its cause. And therefore man's happiness depends, as on its cause, on the glory which man has with God; according to Ps. 90. 15, 16: *I will deliver him, and I will glorify him; I will fill him with length of days, and I will show him my salvation.*

Furthermore, we must observe that human knowledge often fails, especially in contingent singulars, such as are human acts. For this reason human glory is frequently deceptive. But since God cannot be deceived, His glory is always true; hence it is written (II Cor. 10. 18): *He . . . is approved . . . whom God commendeth.*

Reply Obj. 1. The Apostle speaks, then, not of the glory which is with men, but of the glory which is from God, with His angels. Hence it is written (Mark 8. 38): *The Son of Man shall confess him in the glory of His Father, before His angels.*[7]

Reply Obj. 2. A man's good which, through fame or glory, is in the knowledge of many, if

---

[1] *Ethics,* 1, 5 (1005ᵇ24).   [2] *Ibid.*
[3] Sect. 20 (PG 3, 719); cf. sects. 1, 4 (694, 698).
[4] Chap. 13 (PL 42, 770).

[5] PL 63, 711.   [6] PL 63, 745.
[7] St. Thomas joins Mark 8. 38 with Luke 12. 8, owing to a possible variant in his text, or to the fact that he was quoting from memory.

this knowledge be true, must be derived from good existing in the man himself, and hence it presupposes perfect or incomplete happiness. But if the knowledge be false, it does not harmonize with the thing, and thus good does not exist in him who is looked upon as famous. Hence it follows that fame can in no way make man happy.

Reply Obj. 3. Fame has no stability; in fact, it is easily ruined by false report. And if sometimes it endures, this is by accident. But happiness endures of itself, and for ever.

ARTICLE 4. *Whether Man's Happiness Consists in Power?*

We proceed thus to the Fourth Article: It seems that happiness consists in power.

Objection 1. For all things desire to become like God, as to their last end and first beginning. But men who are in power seem, on account of the similarity of power, to be most like God; hence also in Scripture they are called gods (Exod. 12. 8),—*Thou shalt not speak ill of the gods.* Therefore happiness consists in power.

Obj. 2. Further, happiness is the perfect good. But the highest perfection for man is to be able to rule others, which belongs to those who are in power. Therefore happiness consists in power.

Obj. 3. Further, since happiness is supremely desirable, it is contrary to that which is before all to be shunned. But, more than anything else, men shun servitude, which is contrary to power. Therefore happiness consists in power.

On the contrary, Happiness is the perfect good. But power is most imperfect. For as Boëthius says (*De Consol.* iii, 4),[1] "the power of man cannot relieve the gnawings of care, nor can it avoid the thorny path of anxiety"; and further on: "Think you a man is powerful who is surrounded by attendants, whom he inspires with fear indeed, but whom he fears still more?" Therefore happiness does not consist in power.

I answer that, It is impossible for happiness to consist in power, and this for two reasons. First because power has the nature of a principle, as is stated in the *Metaphysics*,[2] whereas happiness has the nature of last end. Secondly, because power has relation to good and evil, whereas happiness is man's proper and perfect good. Therefore some happiness might consist rather in the good use of power, which is through virtue, rather than in power itself.

Now four general reasons may be given to prove that happiness consists in none of the foregoing external goods. First, because, since

happiness is man's supreme good, it is incompatible with any evil. Now all the foregoing can be found both in good and in evil men. Secondly, because since it is the nature of happiness "to be self-sufficient," as stated in the *Ethics*,[3] having gained happiness man cannot lack any needed good. But after acquiring any one of the foregoing, man may still lack many goods that are necessary to him; for instance, wisdom, bodily health, and the like. Thirdly, because, since happiness is the perfect good, no evil can accrue to anyone from it. This cannot be said of the foregoing, for it is written (Eccles. 5. 12) that *riches* are sometimes *kept to the hurt of the owner;* and the same may be said of the other three. Fourthly, because man is ordered to happiness through principles that are within him, since he is naturally ordered to happiness. Now the four goods mentioned above are due rather to external causes, and in most cases to fortune, for which reason they are called goods of fortune. Therefore it is evident that happiness in no way consists in the foregoing.

Reply Obj. 1. God's power is His goodness; hence He cannot use His power otherwise than well. But it is not so with men. Consequently it is not enough for man's happiness that he become like God in power, unless he become like Him in goodness also.

Reply Obj. 2. Just as it is a very good thing for a man to make good use of power in ruling many, so is it a very bad thing if he makes a bad use of it. And so it is that power is towards good and evil.

Reply Obj. 3. Servitude is a hindrance to the good use of power; therefore is it that men naturally shun it, not because man's supreme good consists in power.

ARTICLE 5. *Whether Man's Happiness Consists in Any Bodily Good?*

We proceed thus to the Fifth Article: It would seem that man's happiness consists in bodily goods.

Objection 1. For it is written (Ecclus. 30. 16): *There are no riches above the riches of the health of the body.* But happiness consists in that which is best. Therefore it consists in the health of the body.

Obj. 2. Further, Dionysius says (*Div. Nom.* v),[4] that to be is better than to live, and to live is better than all that follows. But for man's being and living, the health of the body is necessary. Since, therefore, happiness is man's su-

---

[1] PL 63, 741.   [2] Aristotle, V, 12 (1019a15).

[3] Aristotle, I, 7 (1097b8).

[4] Sect. 2 (PG 3. 872).

preme good, it seems that health of the body belongs more than anything else to happiness.

Obj. 3. Further, the more universal a thing is, the higher the principle from which it depends, because the higher a cause is, the greater the scope of its power. Now just as the causality of the efficient cause consists in its flowing into something, so the causality of the end consists in its drawing the appetite. Therefore, just as the First Efficient Cause is that which flows into all things, so the last end is that which attracts the desire of all. But being itself is that which is most desired by all. Therefore man's happiness consists most of all in things pertaining to his being, such as the health of the body.

On the contrary, Man surpasses all other animals in regard to happiness. But in bodily goods he is surpassed by many animals; for instance, by the elephant in longevity, by the lion in strength, by the stag in fleetness. Therefore man's happiness does not consist in goods of the body.

I answer that, It is impossible for man's happiness to consist in the goods of the body, and this for two reasons. First, because if a thing be ordered to another as to its end, the last end of that thing cannot consist in the preservation of its own being. Hence a captain does not intend, as a last end, the preservation of the ship entrusted to him, since a ship is ordered to something else as an end, namely, to navigation. Now just as the ship is entrusted to the captain that he may steer its course, so man is given over to his will and reason, according to Ecclus. 15. 14: *God made man from the beginning and left him in the hand of his own counsel.* Now it is evident that man is ordered to something as his end, since man is not the supreme good. Therefore the last end of man's reason and will cannot be the preservation of man's being.

Secondly, because, granted that the end of man's will and reason be the preservation of man's being, it could not be said that the end of man is some good of the body. For man's being consists in soul and body; and though the being of the body depends on the soul, yet the being of the human soul depends not on the body, as shown above (Part I, Q. LXXV, A. 2); and the very body is for the sake of the soul, as matter for its form, and the instruments for the man that puts them into motion, that by their means he may do his work. And so all goods of the body are ordered to the goods of the soul, as to their end. Consequently happiness, which is man's last end, cannot consist in goods of the body.

Reply Obj. 1. Just as the body is ordered to the soul, as its end, so are external goods ordained to the body itself. And therefore it is with reason that the good of the body is preferred to external goods, which are signified by riches, just as the good of the soul is preferred to all bodily goods.

Reply Obj. 2. Being taken absolutely, as including all perfection of being, surpasses life and all the perfections consequent upon it; for thus being itself includes all these. And in this sense Dionysius speaks. But if we consider being itself as participated in this or that thing, which does not possess the whole perfection of being but has imperfect being, such as the being of any creature, then it is evident that being itself together with an additional perfection is more excellent. Hence in the same passage Dionysius says that things that live are better than things that exist, and intelligent better than living things.

Reply Obj. 3. Since the end corresponds to the beginning, this argument proves that the last end is the first beginning of being, in Whom every perfection of being is, Whose likeness, according to their perfection, some desire as to being only, some as to living being, some as to being which is living, intelligent and happy. And this belongs to few.

ARTICLE 6. *Whether Man's Happiness Consists in Pleasure?*

We proceed thus to the Sixth Article: It seems that man's happiness consists in pleasure.

Objection 1. For since happiness is the last end, it is not desired for something else, but other things for it. But this answers to pleasure more than to anything else, "for it is absurd to ask anyone what is his motive in wishing to be pleased."[1] Therefore happiness consists principally in pleasure and delight.

Obj. 2. Further, "the first cause goes more deeply into the effect than the second cause" (*De Causis,* i).[2] Now the influence of the end consists in its attracting the appetite. Therefore it seems that that which moves most the appetite answers to the notion of the last end. Now this is pleasure, and a sign of this is that delight so far absorbs man's will and reason that it causes him to despise other goods. Therefore it seems that man's last end, which is happiness, consists principally in pleasure.

Obj. 3. Further, since desire is for good, it seems that what all desire is best. But all desire delight, both wise and foolish, and even irra-

[1] *Ethics,* x, 2 (1172^{b}22).   [2] BA 163.

tional creatures. Therefore delight is the best of all. Therefore happiness, which is the supreme good, consists in pleasure.

On the contrary, Boëthius says (*De Consol.* iii, 7):[1] "Any one that chooses to look back on his past excesses, will perceive that pleasures have a sad ending; and if they can render a man happy, there is no reason why we should not say that the very beasts are happy too."

I answer that, "Because bodily delights are more generally known, the name of pleasure has been appropriated to them,"[2] although other delights excel them; and yet happiness does not consist in them. Because in every thing, that which pertains to its essence is distinct from its proper accident; thus in man it is one thing that he is a mortal rational animal, and another that he is an animal capable of laughter. We must therefore consider that every delight is a kind of proper accident resulting from happiness or from some part of happiness, since the reason that a man is delighted is that he has some fitting good, either in reality, or in hope, or at least in memory. Now a fitting good, if indeed it be the perfect good, is precisely man's happiness; and if it is imperfect, it is a share of happiness, either proximate, or remote, or at least apparent. Therefore it is evident that neither is delight, which results from the perfect good, the very essence of happiness, but something resulting from it as its proper accident.

But bodily pleasure cannot result from the perfect good even in that way. For it results from a good apprehended by sense, which is a power of the soul, which power makes use of the body. Now good pertaining to the body and apprehended by sense cannot be man's perfect good. For since the rational soul excels the proportion of corporeal matter, that part of the soul which is independent of a corporeal organ has a certain infinity in regard to the body and those parts of the soul which are tied down to the body, just as immaterial things are in a way infinite as compared to material things, since a form is, after a fashion, contracted and bounded by matter, so that a form which is independent of matters is, in a way, infinite. Therefore sense, which is a power of the body, knows the singular, which is determinate through matter, whereas the intellect, which is a power independent of matter, knows the universal, which is abstracted from matter, and contains under it an infinite number of singulars. Consequently it is evident that good which is fitting to the body, and which

[1] PL 63, 749.   [2] *Ethics*, VII, 13 (1153[b]33).

causes bodily delight through being apprehended by sense, is not man's perfect good, but is very small as compared with the good of the soul. Hence it is written (Wisd. 7. 9) that *all gold in comparison of her, is as a little sand*. And therefore bodily pleasure is neither happiness itself nor a proper accident of happiness.

Reply Obj. 1. It comes to the same whether we desire good, or desire delight, which is nothing else than the appetite's rest in good; thus it is owing to the same natural force that a weighty body is borne downwards and that it rests there. Consequently just as good is desired for itself, so delight is desired for itself and not for anything else, if the preposition "for" denote the final cause. But if it denote the formal or rather the moving cause, then delight is desirable for something else, that is, for the good, which is the object of that delight, and consequently is its principle, and gives it its form; for the reason that delight is desired is that it is rest in the thing desired.

Reply Obj. 2. The vehemence of desire for sensible delight arises from the fact that operations of the senses, through being the principles of our knowledge, are more perceptible. And so it is that sensible pleasures are desired by the majority.

Reply Obj. 3. All desire delight in the same way as they desire good, and yet they desire delight by reason of the good and not conversely, as stated above (reply 1). Consequently it does not follow that delight is the supreme and per se good, but that every delight results from some good, and that some delight results from that which is the per se and supreme good.

ARTICLE 7. *Whether Some Good of the Soul Constitutes Man's Happiness?*

We proceed thus to the Seventh Article: It seems that some good of the soul constitutes man's happiness.

Objection 1. For happiness is man's good. Now this is threefold, external goods, goods of the body, and goods of the soul. But happiness does not consist in external goods, nor in goods of the body, as shown above (AA. 4, 5). Therefore it consists in goods of the soul.

Obj. 2. Further, we love that for which we desire good more than the good that we desire for it; thus we love a friend for whom we desire money more than we love money. But whatever good a man desires, he desires it for himself. Therefore he loves himself more than all other goods. Now happiness is what is loved above all, which is evident from the fact that for its sake all else is loved and desired. Therefore happiness consists in some good of man himself; not, however, in goods of the body. Therefore it consists in goods of the soul.

Obj. 3. Further, perfection is something belonging to that which is perfected. But happiness is a perfection of man. Therefore happiness is something belonging to man. But it is not something belonging to the body, as shown above (A. 5). Therefore it is something belonging to the soul; and thus it consists in goods of the soul.

On the contrary. As Augustine says,[1] "that which constitutes the life of happiness is to be loved for its own sake." But man is not to be loved for his own sake, but whatever is in man is to be loved for God's sake. Therefore happiness consists in no good of the soul.

I answer that, As stated above (Q. 1, A. 8), the end is twofold: namely, the thing itself, which we desire to attain, and the use, namely, the attainment or possession of that thing. If, then, we speak of man's last end as to the thing itself which we desire as last end, it is impossible for man's last end to be the soul itself or something belonging to it. Because the soul, considered in itself, is as something existing in potency; for it becomes knowing actually, from being potentially knowing and actually virtuous, from being potentially virtuous. Now since potency is for the sake of act as for its fulfilment, that which in itself is in potency cannot have the character of last end. Therefore the soul itself cannot be its own last end.

In like manner neither can anything belonging to it, whether power, habit, or act. For that good which is the last end is the perfect good fulfilling the desire. Now man's appetite, otherwise the will, is for the universal good. And any good inherent to the soul is a participated good, and consequently a particularized good. Therefore none of them can be man's last end.

But if we speak of man's last end, with respect to its attainment or possession, or as to any use whatever of the thing itself desired as an end, in this way something of man, in respect of his soul, belongs to his last end, since man attains happiness through his soul. Therefore the thing itself which is desired as end is that which constitutes happiness, and makes man happy; but the attainment of this thing is called happiness. Consequently we must say that happiness is something belonging to the soul, but that which constitutes happiness is something outside the soul.

[1] *Christian Doctrine,* I, 22 (PL 34, 26).

Reply Obj. 1. According as this division includes all goods that man can desire, the good of the soul is not only power, habit, or act, but also the object of these, which is something outside. And in this way nothing hinders us from saying that what constitutes happiness is a good of the soul.

Reply Obj. 2. As far as the proposed objection is concerned, happiness is loved above all, as the good desired, whereas a friend is loved as that to which good is desired; and thus, too, man loves himself. Consequently it is not the same kind of love in both cases. As to whether man loves anything to a greater degree than himself with the love of friendship, there will be occasion to inquire when we treat of Charity.

Reply Obj. 3. Happiness itself, since it is a perfection of the soul, is a good inhering in the soul; but that which constitutes happiness, namely what makes man happy, is something outside his soul, as stated above.

ARTICLE 8. *Whether Any Created Good Constitutes Man's Happiness?*

We proceed thus to the Eighth Article: It seems that some created good constitutes man's happiness.

Objection 1. For Dionysius says (*Div. Nom.* vii)[2] that "Divine wisdom unites the ends of first things to the beginnings of second things," from which we may gather that the summit of a lower nature touches the base of the higher nature. But man's highest good is happiness. Since then the angel is above man in the order of nature, as stated in the First Part (Q. CXI, A. 1; Q. CVIII, AA. 2, 8; Q. CXI, A. 1), it seems that man's happiness consists in man somehow reaching to the angel.

Obj. 2. Further, the last end of each thing is that which, in relation to it, is perfect; hence the part is for the whole, as for its end. But the universe of creatures which is called the macrocosm, is compared to man who is called the microcosm,[3] as perfect to imperfect. Therefore man's happiness consists in the whole universe of creatures.

Obj. 3. Further, man is made happy by that in which his natural desire takes its rest. But man's desire does not reach out to a good surpassing his capacity. Since then man's capacity does not include that good which surpasses the limits of all creation, it seems that man can be made happy by some created good. Consequently some created good constitutes man's happiness.

On the contrary, Augustine says,[4] "As the soul

[2] Sect. 3 (PG 3, 872).   [3] *Physics,* VIII, 2 (252^{b}24).
[4] *City of God,* XIX, 26 (PL 41, 656).

is the life of the body, so God is man's life of happiness; of Whom it is written": *Happy is that people whose God is the Lord* (Ps. 143 15).

I answer that, It is impossible for any created good to constitute man's happiness. For happiness is the perfect good, which, quiets the appetite altogether since it would not be the last end if something yet remained to be desired. Now the object of the will, that is, of man's appetite, is the universal good, just as the object of the intellect is the universal true. Hence it is evident that nothing can quiet man's will except the universal good. This is to be found not in any creature, but in God alone, because every creature has goodness by participation. Therefore God alone can satisfy the will of man, according to the words of Ps. 102. 5: *Who satisfieth thy desire with good things.* Therefore God alone constitutes man's happiness.

Reply Obj. 1. The summit of man does indeed touch the base of the angelic nature, by a kind of likeness; but man does not rest there as in his last end, but reaches out to the universal fount itself of good, which is the common object of happiness of all the blessed, as being the infinite and perfect good.

Reply Obj. 2. If a whole be not the last end, but ordered to a further end, then the last end of its part is not the whole itself, but something else. Now the universe of creatures, to which man is related as part to whole, is not the last end, but is ordered to God, as to its last end. Therefore the last end of man is not the good of the universe, but God Himself.

Reply Obj. 3. Created good is not less than that good of which man is capable, as of something intrinsic and inherent to him, but it is less than the good of which he is capable as of an object, and which is infinite. And the participated good which is in an angel, and in the whole universe, is a finite and restricted good.

QUESTION III
WHAT IS HAPPINESS
(In Eight Articles)

We have now to consider (1) what happiness is, and (2) what things are required for it (Q. IV).

Concerning the first there are eight points of inquiry: (1) Whether happiness is something uncreated? (2) If it be something created, whether it is an operation? (3) Whether it is an operation of the sensitive, or only of the intellectual part? (4) If it be an operation of the

intellectual part, whether it is an operation of the intellect, or of the will? (5) If it be an operation of the intellect, whether it is an operation of the speculative or of the practical intellect? (6) If it be an operation of the speculative intellect, whether it consist in the considerations of speculative sciences? (7) Whether it consists in the consideration of separate substances, namely, angels? (8) Whether it consists in the sole contemplation of God seen in His Essence?

ARTICLE 1. *Whether Happiness Is Something Uncreated?*

We proceed thus to the First Article: It seems that happiness is something uncreated.

Objection 1. For Boëthius says (*De Consol.* iii, 10):[1] "We must confess that God is happiness itself."

Obj. 2. Further, happiness is the supreme good. But it pertains to God to be the supreme good. Since, then, there are not several supreme goods, it seems that happiness is the same as God.

Obj. 3. Further, happiness is the last end, to which man's will tends naturally. But man's will should tend to nothing else as an end, but to God, Who alone is to be enjoyed, as Augustine says.[2] Therefore happiness is the same as God.

On the contrary, Nothing made is uncreated. But man's happiness is something made, because according to Augustine,[3] "Those things are to be enjoyed, which make us happy." Therefore happiness is not something uncreated.

I answer that, As stated above (Q. I, A. 8; Q. II, A. 7), our end is twofold. First, there is the thing itself which we desire to attain; thus for the miser, the end is money. Secondly there is the attainment or possession, the use or enjoyment of the thing desired; thus we may say that the end of the miser is the possession of money, and the end of the intemperate man is to enjoy something pleasurable. In the first sense, then, man's last end is the uncreated good, namely God, Who alone, of His infinite goodness can perfectly satisfy man's will. But in the second way, man's last end is something created, existing in him, and this is nothing else than the attainment or enjoyment of the last end. Now the last end is called happiness. If, therefore, we consider man's happiness in its cause or object, then it is something uncreated; but if we con-

---

[1] PL 63, 766.
[2] *Christian Doctrine,* I, 5, 22 (PL 34, 21, 26).
[3] *Ibid.,* I, 3 (PL 34, 20).

sider it as to the very essence of happiness, then it is something created.

Reply Obj. 1. God is happiness by His Essence, for He is happy not by acquisition or participation of anything else, but by His Essence. On the other hand, men are happy, as Boethius says (*loc. cit.*) by participation, just as they are called gods, by participation. And this participation of happiness, in respect of which man is said to be happy, is something created.

Reply Obj. 2. Happiness is called man's supreme good because it is the attainment or enjoyment of the supreme good.

Reply Obj. 3. Happiness is said to be the last end in the same way as the attainment of the end is called the end.

ARTICLE 2. *Whether Happiness Is an Operation?*

We proceed thus to the Second Article: It would seem that happiness is not an operation.

Objection 1. For the Apostle says (Rom. 6. 22): *You have your fruit unto sanctification, and the end, life everlasting.* But life is not an operation, but the very being of living things. Therefore the last end, which is happiness, is not an operation.

Obj. 2. Further, Boethius says (*De Consol.* iii, 2)[1] that happiness is "a state made perfect by the aggregate of all good things." But state does not indicate operation. Therefore happiness is not an operation.

Obj. 3. Further, happiness signifies something existing in the happy one, since it is man's final perfection. But the meaning of operation does not imply anything existing in the operator, but rather something proceeding from it. Therefore happiness is not an operation.

Obj. 4. Further, happiness remains in the happy one. Now operation does not remain, but passes. Therefore happiness is not an operation.

Obj. 5. Further, to one man there is one happiness. But operations are many. Therefore happiness is not an operation.

Obj. 6. Further, happiness is in the happy one uninterruptedly. But human operation is often interrupted; for instance, by sleep, or some other occupation, or by cessation. Therefore happiness is not an operation.

On the contrary, The Philosopher says[2] that "happiness is an operation according to perfect virtue."

I answer that, In so far as man's happiness is something created, existing in him, we must

say that it is an operation. For happiness is man's supreme perfection. Now each thing is perfect in so far as is actual, for potency without act is imperfect. Consequently happiness must consist in man's last act. But it is evident that operation is the last act of the operator, and so the Philosopher calls it second act,[3] because that which has a form can be potentially operating, just as he who knows is potentially considering. And hence it is that in other things, too, "each thing is said to be for its operation."[4] Therefore man's happiness must of necessity consist in an operation.

Reply Obj. 1. Life is taken in two senses. First for the very being of the living. And thus happiness is not life, since it has been shown (Q. II, A. 5) that the being of a man, no matter in what it may consist, is not that man's happiness; for of God alone is it true that His Being is His happiness. Secondly, life means the operation of the living, by which operation the principle of life is made actual; thus we speak of active and contemplative life, or of a life of pleasure. And in this sense eternal life is said to be the last end, as is clear from John 17. 3: *This is life everlasting, that they may know Thee, the only true God.*

Reply Obj. 2. Boëthius, in defining happiness, considered happiness in general, for considered thus it is the perfect common good; and he signified this by saying that happiness is "a state made perfect by the aggregate of all good things," thus implying nothing other than that the happy man is in a state of perfect good. But Aristotle expressed the very essence of happiness, showing by what man is established in this state, and that it is by some kind of operation.[5] And so it is that he also proves happiness to be "the perfect good."[6]

Reply Obj. 3. As stated in the *Metaphysics*[7] action is twofold. One proceeds from the agent into outward matter, such as to burn and to cut. And such an operation cannot be happiness, for such an operation is an action and a perfection not of the agent but rather of the patient, as is stated in the same passage. The other is an action that remains in the agent, such as to feel, to understand, and to will, and such an action is a perfection and an act of the agent. And such an operation can be happiness.

Reply Obj. 4. Since happiness signifies some final perfection, according as various things

[1] PL 63, 724.
[2] *Ethics*, I, 13 (1102ª5); also, I, 7 (1098ª16).
[3] *Soul*, II, 1 (412ª23).
[4] *Heavens*, II, 3 (286ª8).
[5] *Ethics*, I, 7, 13 (1098ª16; 1102ª5).
[6] *Ibid.*, I, 7 (1097ª29).
[7] Aristotle, IX, 8 (1050ª30).

capable of happiness can attain to various degrees of perfection, so must there be various
meanings applied to happiness. For in God there
is happiness essentially, since His very Being is
His operation, whereby He enjoys no other than
Himself. In the happy angels, the final perfection is in respect of some operation, by which
they are united to the Uncreated Good, and this
operation of theirs is one only and everlasting.
But in men, according to their present state of
life, the final perfection is in respect of an operation whereby man is united to God; but this
operation neither can be continual, nor, consequently, is it one only, because operation is multiplied by being interrupted. And for this reason in the present state of life, perfect happiness cannot be attained by man. Hence the
Philosopher, in placing man's happiness in this
life,[1] says that it is imperfect, and after a long
discussion, concludes: "We call men happy,
but only as men." But God has promised us perfect happiness, when we shall be *as the angels
. . . in heaven* (Matt. 22. 30).

Consequently in regard to this perfect happiness, the objection fails, because in that state of
happiness, man's mind will be united to God by
one, continual, everlasting operation. But in the
present life, in as far as we fall short of the unity
and continuity of that operation, we fall short
of perfect happiness. Nevertheless it is a participation of happiness, and so much the greater
as the operation can be more continuous and
more one. Consequently the active life, which is
busy with many things, has less of the character
of happiness than the contemplative life, which
is busied with one thing, that is, the contemplation of truth. And if at any time man is not actually engaged in this operation, yet since he can
always easily turn to it, and since he orders the
very cessation, for example, sleep or other natural occupations to the aforesaid operation, the
latter seems, as it were, continuous.

From these remarks the *replies to objections
5 and 6 are evident.*

ARTICLE 3. *Whether Happiness Is an Operation
of the Sensitive Part, or of the Intellectual
Part Only?*

We proceed thus to the Third Article: It
seems that happiness consists in an operation of
the senses only.

Objection 1. For there is no more excellent
operation in man than that of the senses, except
the intellectual operation. But in us the intellectual operation depends on the sensitive, since

[1] *Ethics,* I, 10 (1101ᵃ20).

"we cannot understand without a phantasm."[2]
Therefore happiness consists in an operation of
the senses also.

Obj. 2. Further, Boëthius says (*De Consol.*
iii. 2)[3] that happiness is "a state made perfect
by the aggregate of all good things." But some
goods are sensible, which we attain by the operation of the senses. Therefore it seems that
the operation of the senses is needed for happiness.

Obj. 3. Further, "happiness is the perfect
good," as we find proved in the *Ethics,*[4] which
would not be true, were not man perfected
thereby in all his parts. But some parts of the
soul are perfected by sensitive operations.
Therefore sensitive operation is required for
happiness.

On the contrary, Irrational animals have the
sensitive operation in common with us, but they
have not happiness in common with us. Therefore happiness does not consist in a sensitive
operation.

I answer that, A thing may pertain to happiness in three ways: (1) essentially, (2) antecedently, (3) consequently. Now the operation
of sense cannot pertain to happiness essentially.
For man's happiness consists essentially in his
being united to the Uncreated Good, Which is
his last end, as shown above (A. 1), to Which
man cannot be united by an operation of his
senses. Again, in like manner, because, as shown
above (Q. II, A. 5), man's happiness does not
consist in goods of the body, which goods alone,
however, we attain through the operation of the
senses.

Nevertheless the operations of the senses can
pertain to happiness, both antecedently and consequently: antecedently, in respect of imperfect happiness, such as can be had in this life,
since the operation of the intellect demands a
previous operation of the sense; consequently,
in that perfect happiness which we await in
heaven, because at the resurrection, from the
very happiness of the soul, as Augustine says
(*Ep. ad Dioscor.*)[5] the body and the bodily
senses will receive a certain overflow, so as to
be perfected in their operations, a point which
will be explained further on when we treat of the
resurrection (Part III, Suppl. Q. LXXXII). But
then the operation by which man's mind is
united to God will not depend on the senses.

Reply Obj. 1. This objection proves that the
operation of the senses is required antecedently

[2] *Soul,* III, 7 (431ᵃ16).   [3] PL 63, 724.
[4] Aristotle, I, 7 (1097ᵃ29).
[5] *Epist.,* 118, chap. 3 (PL 33, 439).

for imperfect happiness, such as can be had in this life.

Reply Obj. 2. Perfect happiness, such as the angels have, includes the aggregate of all good things, by being united to the universal source of all good,—not that it requires each individual good. But in this imperfect happiness, we need the aggregate of those goods that suffice for the most perfect operation of this life.

Reply Obj. 3. In perfect happiness the entire man is perfected, but in the lower part of his nature, by an overflow from the higher. However in the imperfect happiness of this life, it is otherwise; we advance from the perfection of the lower part to the perfection of the higher part.

ARTICLE 4. *Whether, if Happiness Is in the Intellectual Part, It Is an Operation of the Intellect or of the Will?*

We proceed thus to the Fourth Article: It would seem that happiness consists in an act of the will.

Objection 1. For Augustine says[1] that man's happiness consists in peace; therefore it is written (Ps. 147. 3): *Who hath placed peace in thy end* (Douay,— *borders*). But peace pertains to the will. Therefore man's happiness is in the will.

Obj. 2. Further, happiness is the supreme good. But good is the object of the will. Therefore happiness consists in an operation of the will.

Obj. 3. Further, the last end corresponds to the first mover; thus the last end of the whole army is victory, which is the end of the leader, who moves all the men. But the first mover in regard to operations is the will, because it moves the other powers, as we shall state further on (Q. IX, AA. 1, 3). Therefore happiness pertains to the will.

Obj. 4. Further, if happiness be an operation, it must be man's most excellent operation. But the love of God, which is an act of the will, is a more excellent operation than knowledge, which is an operation of the intellect, as the Apostle declares (I Cor. 13.). Therefore it seems that happiness consists in an act of the will.

Obj. 5. Further, Augustine says (*De Trin.* xiii, 5)[2] that "happy is he who has whatever he desires, and desires nothing amiss." And a little further on he adds:[3] "He is almost happy who desires well, whatever he desires, for good things make a man happy, and such a man already possesses some good—namely, a good will." Therefore happiness consists in an act of the will.

On the contrary, Our Lord said (John 17. 3): *This is eternal life: that they may know Thee, the only true God.* Now eternal life is the last end, as stated above (A. 2, REPLY 1). Therefore man's happiness consists in the knowledge of God, which is an act of the intellect.

I answer that, As stated above (Q. II, A. 6) two things are needed for happiness: the one, which is the essence of happiness; the other, which is, as it were, its proper accident, that is, the delight joined to it. I say, then, that as to the very essence of happiness, it is impossible for it to consist in an act of the will. For it is evident from what has been said (AA. 1, 2; Q. II, A. 7) that happiness is the attainment of the last end. But the attainment of the end does not consist in the act of the will itself. For the will is directed to the end, both absent, when it desires it, and present, when it is delighted by resting in it. Now it is evident that the desire itself of the end is not the attainment of the end, but is a movement towards the end, while delight comes to the will from the end being present; and a thing, conversely, is not made present by the fact that the will delights in it. Therefore, that the end be present to him who desires it must be due to something else than an act of the will.

This is evidently the case in regard to sensible ends. For if the acquisition of money were through an act of the will, the covetous man would have it from the very moment that he wished for it. But at that moment it is far from him; and he attains it by grasping it in his hand, or in some like manner, and then he delights in the money acquired. And so it is with an intelligible end. For at first we desire to attain an intelligible end; we attain it, through its being made present to us by an act of the intellect; and then the delighted will rests in the end when it is attained.

So, therefore, the essence of happiness consists in an act of the intellect; but the delight that results from happiness pertains to the will. In this sense Augustine says[4] that "happiness is joy in truth," because, namely, joy itself is the consummation of happiness.

Reply Obj. 1. Peace pertains to man's last end, not as though it were the very essence of happiness, but because it is antecedent and consequent to it: antecedent, in so far as all those things are removed which disturb and hinder

---

[1] *City of God,* XIX, 10, 11 (PL 41, 636, 637).
[2] PL 42, 1020.   [3] Chap. 6 (PL 42, 1020).   [4] *Confessions,* X, 33 (PL 32, 793).

man in attaining the last end; consequent, since, when man has attained his last end, he remains at peace, his desire being at rest.

Reply Obj. 2. The will's first object is not its act, just as the first object of the sight is not vision, but a visible thing. Therefore, from the very fact that happiness pertains to the will, as the will's first object, it follows that it does not pertain to it as its act.

Reply Obj. 3. The intellect apprehends the end before the will does, yet motion towards the end begins in the will. And therefore to the will belongs that which last of all follows the attainment of the end, namely, delight or enjoyment.

Reply Obj. 4. Love ranks above knowledge in moving, but knowledge precedes love in attaining, for "naught is loved save what is known," as Augustine says (*De Trin.* x).[1] Consequently we first attain an intelligible end by an act of the intellect, just as we first attain a sensible end by an act of sense.

Reply Obj. 5. He who has whatever he desires, is happy because he has what he desires, and this indeed is by something other than the act of his will. But to desire nothing amiss is needed for happiness, as a necessary disposition thereto. And a good will is reckoned among the good things which make a man happy, since it is an inclination of the will; just as a movement is reduced to the genus of its term, for instance, alteration to the genus quality.

ARTICLE 5. *Whether Happiness Is an Operation of the Speculative, or of the Practical Intellect?*

We proceed thus to the Fifth Article: It seems that happiness is an operation of the practical intellect.

Objection 1. For the last end of every creature consists in becoming like God. But man is like God by his practical intellect, which is the cause of things understood, rather than by his speculative intellect, which derives its knowledge from things. Therefore man's happiness consists in an operation of the practical intellect rather than of the speculative.

Obj. 2. Further, happiness is man's perfect good. But the practical intellect is ordered to the good rather than the speculative intellect, which is ordered to the true. Hence we are said to be good according to the perfection of the practical intellect, but not according to the perfection of the speculative intellect, according to which we are said to be knowing or understanding. Therefore man's happiness consists in an act of

[1] PL 42, 973.

the practical intellect rather than of the speculative.

Obj. 3. Further, happiness is a good of man himself. But the speculative intellect is more concerned with things outside man, whereas the practical intellect is concerned with things pertaining to man himself, namely, his operations and passions. Therefore man's happiness consists in an operation of the practical intellect rather than of the speculative.

On the contrary, Augustine says (*De Trin.* i, 8)[2] that "contemplation is promised us as being the goal of all our actions, and the everlasting perfection of our joys."

I answer that, Happiness consists in an operation of the speculative rather than of the practical intellect. This is evident for three reasons. First because if man's happiness is an operation, it must be man's highest operation. Now man's highest operation is that of his highest power in respect of its highest object, and his highest power is the intellect, whose highest object is the Divine Good, which is the object not of the practical, but of the speculative intellect. Consequently happiness consists principally in such an operation, namely, in the contemplation of Divine things. And since "that seems to be each man's self, which is best in him," according to the *Ethics*,[3] therefore such an operation is most proper to man and most delightful to him.

Secondly, it is evident from the fact that contemplation is sought principally for its own sake. But the act of the practical intellect is not sought for its own sake but for the sake of the action, and these very actions are ordered to some end. Consequently it is evident that the last end cannot consist in the active life, which pertains to the practical intellect.

Thirdly, it is again evident, from the fact that in the contemplative life man has something in common with things above him, namely, with God and the angels, to whom he is made like by happiness. But in things pertaining to the active life other animals also have something in common with man, although imperfectly.

Therefore the last and perfect happiness, which we await in the life to come, consists entirely in contemplation. But imperfect happiness, such as can be had here, consists first and principally in contemplation, but secondarily, in an operation of the practical intellect ordering human actions and passions, as stated in the *Ethics*.[4]

[2] PL 42, 831.
[3] Aristotle, IX, 8 (1169ª2); X, 7 (1178ª2).
[4] Aristotle, X, 7, 8 (1177ª12; 1178ª9).

Reply Obj. 1. The asserted likeness of the practical intellect to God is one of proportionality; that is to say, it stands in relation to what it knows as God does to what He knows. But the likeness of the speculative intellect to God is one of union or informing, which is a much greater likeness. And yet it may be answered that, in regard to the principal thing known, which is His Essence, God has not practical but only speculative knowledge.

Reply Obj. 2. The practical intellect is ordered to good which is outside of it, but the speculative intellect has good within it, namely, the contemplation of truth. And if this good be perfect, the whole man is perfected and made good by it. The practical intellect does not have such a good but it orders man to it.

Reply Obj. 3. This argument would hold if man himself were his own last end, for then the consideration and ordering of his actions and passions would be his happiness. But since man's last end is something outside of him, namely, God, to Whom we reach out by an operation of the speculative intellect, therefore man's happiness consists in an operation of the speculative intellect rather than of the practical intellect.

ARTICLE 6. *Whether Happiness Consists in the Consideration of Speculative Sciences?*

We proceed thus to the Sixth Article: It seems that man's happiness consists in the consideration of speculative sciences.

Objection 1. For the Philosopher says[1] that "happiness is an operation according to perfect virtue." And in distinguishing the virtues, he gives no more than three speculative virtues,— science, wisdom and understanding,[2] which all belong to the consideration of speculative sciences. Therefore man's final happiness consists in the consideration of speculative sciences.

Obj. 2. Further, that which all desire for its own sake seems to be man's final happiness. Now such is the consideration of speculative sciences, because, as stated in the *Metaphysics*,[3] "all men naturally desire to know"; and, a little further on it is stated[4] that speculative sciences are sought for their own sakes. Therefore happiness consists in the consideration of speculative sciences.

Obj. 3. Further, happiness is man's final perfection. Now everything is perfected according as it is reduced from potency to act. But the hu-

man intellect is reduced to act by the consideration of speculative sciences. Therefore it seems that in the consideration of these sciences, man's final happiness consists.

On the contrary, It is written (Jer. 9. 23): *Let not the wise man glory in his wisdom,* and this is said in reference to speculative sciences. Therefore man's final happiness does not consist in the consideration of these.

I answer that, As stated above (A. 2, REPLY 4), man's happiness is twofold, one perfect, the other imperfect. And by perfect happiness we are to understand that which attains to the true notion of happiness; and by imperfect happiness that which does not attain to it, but partakes of some particular likeness of happiness. Thus perfect prudence is in man, with whom is the notion of things to be done; while imperfect prudence is in certain irrational animals, who are possessed of certain particular instincts in respect of works similar to works of prudence.

Accordingly perfect happiness cannot consist essentially in the consideration of speculative sciences. To prove this, we must observe that the consideration of a speculative science does not extend beyond the scope of the principles of that science, since the entire science is virtually contained in its principles. Now the first principles of speculative sciences are received through the senses, as the Philosopher clearly states at the beginning of the *Metaphysics*,[5] and at the end of the *Posterior Analytics*.[6] Therefore the entire consideration of speculative sciences cannot extend further than knowledge of sensibles can lead. Now man's final happiness, which is his final perfection, cannot consist in the knowledge of sensibles. For a thing is not perfected by something lower, except in so far as the lower partakes of something higher. Now it is evident that the form of a stone or of any sensible, is lower than man. Consequently the intellect is not perfected by the form of a stone, as such, but in so far as it partakes of a certain likeness to that which is above the human intellect, namely, the intelligible light, or something of the kind. Now whatever is by something else is reduced to that which is of itself. Therefore man's final perfection must be through knowledge of something above the human intellect. But it has been shown (Part I, Q. LXXXVIII, A. 2) that man cannot acquire through sensibles the knowledge of separate substances, which are above the human intellect. Consequently it follows that man's happiness cannot consist in the consideration of speculative sciences. However,

---

[1] *Ethics,* I, 13 (1102a5).
[2] *Ibid.,* VI, 3, 7 (1139b16; 1141a19).
[3] Aristotle, I, 1 (980a21). [4] *Ibid.,* I, 2 (982a14; a28).
[5] I, 1 (980b29). [6] II, 19 (100a6).

just as in sensible forms there is a participation of some likeness of higher substances, so the consideration of speculative sciences is a certain participation of true and perfect happiness.

Reply Obj. 1. In his book on *Ethics* the Philosopher treats of imperfect happiness, such as can be had in this life, as stated above (A. 2, REPLY 4).

Reply Obj. 2. Not only is perfect happiness naturally desired, but also any likeness or participation of it.

Reply Obj. 3. Our intellect is reduced to act, in a fashion, by the consideration of speculative sciences, but not to its final and complete act.

ARTICLE 7. *Whether Happiness Consists in the Knowledge of Separate Substances, Namely, Angels?*

We proceed thus to the Seventh Article: It seems that man's happiness consists in the knowledge of separate substances, namely, angels.

Objection 1. For Gregory says in a homily (xxvi):[1] It avails nothing to take part in the feasts of men, if we fail to take part in the feasts of angels," by which he means final happiness. But we can take part in the feasts of the angels by contemplating them. Therefore it seems that man's final happiness consists in contemplating the angels.

Obj. 2. Further, the final perfection of each thing is for it to be united to its principle; hence a circle is said to be a perfect figure, because it has the same beginning and end. But the beginning of human knowledge is from the angels, by whom men are enlightened, as Dionysius says (*Cæl. Hier.* iv).[2] Therefore the perfection of the human intellect consists in contemplating the angels.

Obj. 3. Further, each nature is perfect when united to a higher nature, just as the final perfection of a body is to be united to the spiritual nature. But above the human intellect, in the natural order, are the angels. Therefore the final perfection of the human intellect is to be united to the angels by contemplation.

On the contrary, It is written (Jerem. 9. 24): *Let him that glorieth, glory in this, that he understandeth and knoweth Me.* Therefore man's final glory or happiness consists only in the knowledge of God.

I answer that, As stated above (A. 6), man's perfect happiness consists not in that which perfects the intellect by some participation, but in

that which is so by its essence. Now it is evident that whatever perfects a power does so in so far as it has the character of the proper object of that power. Now the proper object of the intellect is the true. Therefore the contemplation of whatever has participated truth does not perfect the intellect with its final perfection. Since, therefore, the order of things is the same in being and in truth,[3] whatever are beings by participation are true by participation. Now angels have being by participation, because in God alone is His Being His Essence, as shown in the First Part (Q. XLIV, A. 1; Q. III, A. 4). It follows that God alone is truth by His Essence, and that contemplation of Him makes man perfectly happy. However, there is no reason why we should not admit a certain imperfect happiness in the contemplation of the angels; and higher indeed than in the consideration of speculative science.

Reply Obj. 1. We shall take part in the feasts of the angels by contemplating not only the angels, but also, together with them God Himself.

Reply Obj. 2. According to those that hold human souls to be created by the angels, it seems fitting enough that man's happiness should consist in the contemplation of the angels, in the union, as it were, of man with his beginning.[4] But this is erroneous, as stated in the First Part (Q. XC, A. 3). Therefore the final perfection of the human intellect is by union with God, Who is the first principle both of the creation of the soul and of its enlightenment. But the angel enlightens as a minister, as stated in the First Part (Q. CXI, A. 2 REPLY 2). Consequently, by his ministration he helps man to attain to happiness, but he is not the object of man's happiness.

Reply Obj. 3. The lower nature may reach the higher in two ways. First, according to a degree of the participating power, and thus man's final perfection will consist in his attaining to a contemplation such as that of the angels. Secondly, as the object is attained by the power, and thus the final perfection of each power is to attain that in which the notion of its object is found to the full degree.

ARTICLE 8. *Whether Man's Happiness Consists in the Vision of the Divine Essence?*

We proceed thus to the Eighth Article: It seems that man's happiness does not consist in the vision of the Divine Essence.

---

[1] *In Evang.,* II (PL 76, 1202).
[2] Sect. 2 (PG 3, 180).

[3] Aristotle, *Metaphysics,* II, 1 (993[b]30).
[4] *Liber de Causis,* 3 (BA 166.2); Avicenna, *Meta.,* IX, 4 (104vb), *De An.,* V, 6 (26va).

Objection 1. For Dionysius says (*Myst. Theol.* i)[1] that by that which is highest in his intellect man is united to God as to something altogether unknown. But that which is seen in its essence is not altogether unknown. Therefore the final perfection of the intellect, namely, happiness, does not consist in God being seen in His Essence.

Obj. 2. Further, the higher perfection belongs to the higher nature. But to see His own Essence is the perfection proper to the Divine intellect. Therefore the final perfection of the human intellect does not reach to this, but consists in something less.

On the contrary, It is written (I John 3. 2): *When He shall appear, we shall be like to Him; and* (Vulg., *because*) *we shall see Him as He is.*

I answer that, Final and perfect happiness can consist in nothing else than the vision of the Divine Essence. To make this clear, two points must be observed. First, that man is not perfectly happy, so long as something remains for him to desire and seek; secondly, that the perfection of any power is determined by the nature of its object. Now "the object of the intellect is what a thing is, that is, the essence of a thing," according to the book on the *Soul.*[2] Therefore the intellect attains perfection in so far as it knows the essence of a thing. If therefore an intellect know the essence of some effect in which it is not possible to know the essence of the cause, that is, to know of the cause "what it is," that intellect cannot be said to reach that cause absolutely, although it may be able to gather from the effect the knowledge that the cause is. Consequently, when man knows an effect, and knows that it has a cause, there naturally remains in man the desire to know about that cause, "what it is." And this desire is one of wonder, and causes inquiry, as is stated in the beginning of the *Metaphysics.*[3] For instance, if a man, knowing the eclipse of the sun, consider that it must be due to some cause, and know not what that cause is, he wonders about it, and from wondering proceeds to inquire. Nor does this inquiry cease until he arrive at a knowledge of the essence of the cause.

If therefore the human intellect, knowing the essence of some created effect, knows no more of God than that He is, the perfection of that intellect does not yet reach absolutely the First Cause, but there remains in it the natural desire to seek the cause. And so it is not yet perfectly happy. Consequently, for perfect happiness the intellect needs to reach the very Essence of the First Cause. And thus it will have its perfection through union with God as with that object in which alone man's happiness consists, as stated above (AA. 1, 7; Q. II, A. 8).

Reply Obj. 1. Dionysius speaks of the knowledge of wayfarers journeying towards happiness.

Reply Obj. 2. As stated above (Q. 1, A. 8), the end has a twofold acceptation. First, as to the thing itself which is desired, and in this way, the same thing is the end of the higher and of the lower nature, and indeed of all things, as stated above (*ibid.*). Secondly, as to the attainment of this thing, and thus the end of the higher nature is different from that of the lower, according to their respective relations to that thing. So then the happiness of God, Who, in understanding his Essence comprehends It, is higher than that of a man or angel who sees It indeed, but does not comprehend It.

QUESTION IV

OF THOSE THINGS THAT ARE REQUIRED FOR HAPPINESS

(*In Eight Articles*)

WE have now to consider those things that are required for happiness, and concerning this there are eight points of inquiry: (1) Whether delight is required for happiness? (2) Which is of greater account in happiness, delight or vision? (3) Whether comprehension is required? (4) Whether rectitude of the will is required? (5) Whether the body is necessary for man's happiness? (6) Whether any perfection of the body is necessary? (7) Whether any external goods are necessary? (8) Whether the fellowship of friends is necessary?

ARTICLE 1. *Whether Delight Is Required for Happiness?*

We proceed thus to the First Article: It seems that delight is not required for happiness.

Objection 1. For Augustine says (*De Trin.* i, 8)[4] that "vision is the entire reward of faith." But "the prize or reward of virtue is happiness," as the Philosopher clearly states.[5] Therefore nothing besides vision is required for happiness.

Obj. 2. Further, "happiness is the most self-sufficient of all goods," as the Philosopher declares.[6] But that which needs something else is

---

[1] Sect. 3 (PG 3, 1001).
[2] Aristotle, III, 6 (430ᵇ27).
[3] Aristotle, I, 2 (982ᵇ12; 983ᵃ12).

[4] PL 42, 831; cf. also *Enarr. in Ps.* 90.16, serm. 2 (PL 37, 1170).
[5] *Ethics,* I, 9 (1099ᵇ16).   [6] *Ibid.,* I, 7 (1097ᵇ8).

not self-sufficient. Since then the essence of happiness consists in seeing God, as stated above (Q. III, A. 8), it seems that delight is not necessary for happiness.

Obj. 3. Further, "the operation of bliss or happiness should be unhindered."[1] But delight hinders the operation of the intellect, since it destroys the estimation of prudence.[2] Therefore delight is not necessary for happiness.

On the contrary, Augustine says[3] that "happiness is joy in truth."

I answer that, One thing may be necessary for another in four ways. First, as a preamble or preparation to it; thus instruction is necessary for science. Secondly, as perfecting it; thus the soul is necessary for the life of the body. Thirdly, as helping it from without; thus friends are necessary for some undertaking. Fourthly, as something concomitant; thus we might say that heat is necessary for fire. And in this way delight is necessary for happiness. For it is caused by the appetite being at rest in the good attained. Therefore, since happiness is nothing else but the attainment of the Sovereign Good, it cannot be without concomitant delight.

Reply Obj. 1. From the very fact that a reward is given to anyone, the will of him who deserves it is at rest, and in this consists delight. Consequently, delight is included in the very notion of reward.

Reply Obj. 2. The very sight of God causes delight. Consequently, he who sees God cannot need delight.

Reply Obj. 3. Delight that is attendant upon the operation of the intellect does not hinder it, but rather perfects it, as stated in the *Ethics,*[4] since what we do with delight we do with greater care and perseverance. On the other hand, delight which is extraneous to the operation is a hindrance to it: sometimes by distracting the attention, because, as already observed, we are more attentive to those things that delight us, and when we are very attentive to one thing, we must be less attentive to another; and sometimes on account of opposition; thus a sensual delight that is contrary to reason, hinders the estimation of prudence more than it hinders the estimation of the speculative intellect.

ARTICLE 2. *Whether in Happiness Vision Ranks Before Delight?*

We proceed thus to the Second Article: It would seem that in happiness, delight ranks before vision.

Objection 1. For "delight is the perfection of operation."[5] But perfection ranks before the thing perfected. Therefore delight ranks before the operation of the intellect, that is, vision.

Obj. 2. Further, that by reason of which a thing is desirable, is itself yet more desirable. But operations are desired on account of the delight they afford; hence, too, nature has adjusted delight to those operations which are necessary for the preservation of the individual and of the species, lest animals should neglect such operations. Therefore, in happiness, delight ranks before the operation of the intellect, which is vision.

Obj. 3. Further, vision corresponds to faith, while delight or enjoyment corresponds to charity. But charity ranks before faith, as the Apostle says (I Cor. 13. 13). Therefore delight or enjoyment ranks before vision.

On the contrary, The cause is greater than its effect. But vision is the cause of delight. Therefore vision ranks before delight.

I answer that, The Philosopher discusses this question,[6] and leaves it unsolved. But if one consider the matter carefully, the operation of the intellect which is vision, must rank before delight. For delight consists in a certain repose of the will. Now that the will finds rest in anything can only be on account of the goodness of that thing in which it reposes. If therefore the will reposes in an operation, the will's repose is caused by the goodness of the operation. Nor does the will seek good for the sake of repose, for thus the very act of the will would be the end, which has been disproved above (Q. 1, A. 1, REPLY 2; Q. III, A. 4), but it seeks to be at rest in the operation, because that operation is its good. Consequently it is evident that the operation in which the will reposes ranks before the resting of the will therein.

Reply Obj. 1. As the Philosopher says,[7] "delight perfects operation as grace perfects youth, because it is a result of youth." Consequently delight is a perfection attendant upon vision, but not a perfection by which vision is made perfect in its own species.

Reply Obj. 2. The apprehension of the senses does not attain to the universal notion of good, but to some particular good which is delightful. And consequently, according to the sensitive appetite which is in animals, operations are sought for the sake of delight. But the intellect apprehends the universal notion of good, the attainment of which results in delight; hence its pur-

---

[1] *Ethics,* VII, 1 (1153^{b}16).   [2] *Ibid.,* VI, 5 (1140^{b}12).
[3] *Confessions,* X, 33 (PL 32, 793). [4] *Ethics,* X, 4 (1174^{b}23).

[5] *Ibid.* (1174^{b}23; ^{b}31).
[6] *Ibid.* (1175^{a}18).   [7] *Ibid.* (1174^{b}31).

pose is directed to good rather than to delight. And so it is that the Divine intellect, which is the Author of nature, adjusted delights to operations for the sake of the operations. Nor should we form our estimate of things absolutely according to the order of the sensitive appetite, but rather according to the order of the intellectual appetite.

Reply Obj. 3. Charity does not seek the good loved for the sake of delight; it is only by way of consequence that charity delights in the good gained which it loves. Thus delight does not answer to charity as its end, but vision does, by which the end is first made present to charity.

Article 3. *Whether Comprehension Is Necessary for Happiness?*

We proceed thus to the Third Article: It seems that comprehension is not necessary for happiness.

Objection 1. For Augustine says (*Ad Paulinam de Videndo Deum;—De Verbis Evang., Serm.* CXVII, 3):[1] "To reach God with the mind is great happiness, to comprehend Him is impossible." Therefore happiness is without comprehension.

Obj. 2. Further, happiness is the perfection of man as to his intellectual part, in which there are no other powers than the intellect and will, as stated in the First Part (QQ. LXXIX *and foll.*). But the intellect is sufficiently perfected by seeing God, and the will by enjoying Him. Therefore there is no need for comprehension as a third.

Obj. 3. Further, happiness consists in an operation. But operations are determined by their objects, and there are two universal objects, the true and the good, of which the true corresponds to vision, and good to delight. Therefore there is no need for comprehension as a third.

On the contrary, The Apostle says (I Cor. 9. 24): *So run that you may comprehend* (Douay, *—obtain*). But happiness is the goal of the spiritual race; hence he says (II Tim. 4. 7, 8): *I have fought a good fight, I have finished my course, I have kept the faith; as to the rest there is laid up for me a crown of justice.* Therefore comprehension is necessary for Happiness.

I answer that, Since Happiness consists in gaining the last end, those things that are required for Happiness must be gathered from the way in which man is ordered to an end. Now man is ordered to an intelligible end partly through his intellect, and partly through his

[1] PL 38, 633.

will: through his intellect in so far as a certain imperfect knowledge of the end pre-exists in the intellect; through the will, first by love which is the will's first movement towards anything, secondly, by a real relation of the lover to the thing loved, which relation may be threefold. For sometimes the thing loved is present to the lover, and then it is no longer sought for. Sometimes it is not present, and it is impossible to attain it, and then, too, it is not sought for. But sometimes it is possible to attain it, yet it is raised above the power of the attainer, so that he cannot have it at once; and this is the relation of one that hopes to that which he hopes for, and this relation alone causes a search for the end.

To these three, there are a corresponding three in Happiness itself. For perfect knowledge of the end corresponds to imperfect knowledge; presence of the end corresponds to the relation of hope; but delight in the end now present results from love, as already stated (A. 2, reply 3). And therefore these three must come together in Happiness: namely, vision, which is perfect knowledge of the intelligible end; comprehension, which implies presence of the end; and delight or enjoyment, which implies repose of the lover in the thing loved.

Reply Obj. 1. Comprehension is twofold. First, inclusion of the comprehended in the one comprehending; and thus whatever is comprehended by the finite is itself finite. And so God cannot be comprehended in this way by a created intellect. Secondly, comprehension means nothing but the holding of something already present and possessed; thus one who runs after another is said to comprehend ("catch") him when he lays hold on him. And in this sense comprehension is necessary for Happiness.

Reply Obj. 2. Just as hope and love pertain to the will, because it is the same person that loves a thing, and that tends towards it while not possessed, so, too, comprehension and delight belong to the will, since it is the same person that possesses a thing and reposes in it.

Reply Obj. 3. Comprehension is not an operation distinct from vision, but a certain relation to the end already gained. Therefore even vision itself, or the thing seen according as it is present, is the object of comprehension.

Article 4. *Whether Rectitude of the Will Is Necessary for Happiness?*

We proceed thus to the Fourth Article: It seems that rectitude of the will is not necessary for Happiness.

Objection 1. For Happiness consists essentially in an operation of the intellect, as stated above (Q. III, A. 4). But rectitude of the will, by reason of which men are said to be clean of heart, is not necessary for the perfect operation of the intellect; for Augustine says (*Retract.* i, 4):[1] "I do not approve of what I said in a prayer: O God, Who didst will none but the clean of heart to know the truth. For it can be answered that many who are not clean of heart, know many truths." Therefore rectitude of the will is not necessary for Happiness.

Obj. 2. Further, what precedes does not depend on what follows. But the operation of the intellect precedes the operation of the will. Therefore Happiness, which is the perfect operation of the intellect, does not depend on rectitude of the will.

Obj. 3. Further, that which is ordered to another as its end is not necessary when the end is already gained; as a ship, for instance, after arrival in port. But rectitude of the will, which is by reason of virtue, is ordered to Happiness as its end. Therefore, when Happiness is once obtained, rectitude of the will is no longer necessary.

On the contrary, It is written (Matt. 5. 8): *Blessed are the clean of heart; for they shall see God;* and (Heb. 12. 14): *Follow peace with all men, and holiness; without which no man shall see God.*

I answer that, Rectitude of the will is necessary for Happiness both antecedently and concomitantly. Antecedently, because rectitude of the will consists in being duly ordered to the last end. Now the end in comparison to what is ordered to the end is as form compared to matter. Therefore, just as matter cannot receive a form unless it be properly disposed to it, so nothing gains an end unless it is properly ordered to it. And therefore none can obtain Happiness without rectitude of the will. Concomitantly, because as stated above (Q. III, A. 8), final Happiness consists in the vision of the Divine Essence, Which is the very essence of goodness. So that the will of him who sees the Essence of God of necessity loves whatever he loves in subordination to God, just as the will of him who does not see God's Essence of necessity loves whatever he loves under that common notion of good which he knows. And this is precisely what makes the will right. Therefore it is evident that Happiness cannot be without a right will.

Reply Obj. 1. Augustine is speaking of the
[1] PL 32, 589.

knowledge of that truth which is not the very Essence of goodness.

Reply Obj. 2. Every act of the will is preceded by an act of the intellect, but a certain act of the will precedes a certain act of the intellect. For the will tends to the final act of the intellect which is happiness. And consequently right inclination of the will is required antecedently for happiness, just as the arrow must take a right course in order to strike the target.

Reply Obj. 3. Not everything that is ordered to the end ceases with the getting of the end, but only that which involves imperfection, such as movement. Hence the instruments of movement are no longer necessary when the end has been gained, but the due order to the end is necessary.

ARTICLE 5. *Whether the Body Is Necessary for Man's Happiness?*

We proceed thus to the Fifth Article: It seems that the body is necessary for Happiness.

Objection 1. For the perfection of virtue and grace presupposes the perfection of nature. But Happiness is the perfection of virtue and grace. Now the soul, without the body, does not have the perfection of nature, since the body is naturally a part of human nature and every part is imperfect while separated from its whole. Therefore the soul cannot be happy without the body.

Obj. 2. Further, Happiness is a perfect operation, as stated above (Q. III, AA. 2,5). But perfect operation follows perfect being, since nothing operates except in so far as it is an actual being. Since, therefore, the soul does not have perfect being while it is separated from the body, just as neither does a part while separate from its whole, it seems that the soul cannot be happy without the body.

Obj. 3. Further, Happiness is the perfection of man. But the soul without the body is not man. Therefore Happiness cannot be in the soul separated from the body.

Obj. 4. Further, according to the Philosopher,[2] "the operation of bliss, in which operation happiness consists, is not hindered." But the operation of the separate soul is hindered, because, as Augustine says (*Gen. ad lit.* xii, 35)[3] the soul "has a natural desire to rule the body, the result of which is that it is held back, so to speak, from tending with all its might to the heavenward journey," that is, to the vision of the Divine Essence. Therefore the soul cannot be happy without the body.

[2] *Ethics,* VII, 13 (1153[b]16).   [3] PL 34, 483.

Obj. 5. Further, Happiness is the sufficient good and lulls desire. But this cannot be said of the separated soul, for it yet desires to be united to the body, as Augustine says (*ibid.*). Therefore the soul is not happy while separated from the body.

Obj. 6. Further, in Happiness man is equal to the angels. But the soul without the body is not equal to the angels, as Augustine says (*ibid.*). Therefore it is not happy.

On the contrary, It is written (Apoc. 14. 13): *Happy* (Douay,—*blessed*) *are the dead who die in the Lord.*

I answer that, Happiness is twofold: the one is imperfect and is had in this life; the other is perfect, consisting in the vision of God. Now it is evident that the body is necessary for the happiness of this life. For the happiness of this life consists in an operation of the intellect, either speculative or practical. And the operation of the intellect in this life cannot be without a phantasm, which is only in a bodily organ, as was shown in the First Part (Q. LXXXIV, AA. 6, 7). Consequently that happiness which can be had in this life, depends, in a way, on the body.

But as to perfect Happiness, which consists in the vision of God, some have maintained that it is not possible to the soul separated from the body,[1] and have said that the souls of saints, when separated from their bodies, do not attain to that Happiness until the Day of Judgment, when they will receive their bodies back again. And this is shown to be false, both by authority and by reason. By authority, since the Apostle says (II Cor. 5. 6): *While we are in the body, we are absent from the Lord;* and he points out the reason of this absence, saying: *For we walk by faith and not by sight.* Now from this it is clear that so long as we walk by faith and not by sight, bereft of the vision of the Divine Essence, we are not present to the Lord. But the souls of the saints, separated from their bodies, are in God's presence; and so the text continues: *But we are confident and have a good will to be absent . . . from the body, and to be present with the Lord.* From this it is evident that the souls of the saints, separated from their bodies, *walk by sight,* seeing the Essence of God, in whom is true Happiness.

Again this is made clear by reason. For the intellect does not need the body for its operation save on account of the phantasms, in which it looks on the intelligible truth, as stated in the First Part (Q. LXXXIV, A. 7). Now it is evident

[1] Cf. Part I, Q. LXIV, A. 4, Reply 3, note.

that the Divine Essence cannot be seen by means of phantasms, as stated in the First Part (Q. XII, A. 3). Therefore, since man's perfect Happiness consists in the vision of the Divine Essence, it does not depend on the body. Consequently, the soul can be happy without the body.

We must, however, notice that something may pertain to a thing's perfection in two ways. First, as constituting its essence; thus the soul is necessary for man's perfection. Secondly, as necessary for its well-being; thus, beauty of body and keenness of wit belong to man's perfection. Therefore though the body does not belong in the first way to the perfection of human Happiness, yet it does in the second way. For since operation depends on a thing's nature, the more perfect is the soul in its nature, the more perfectly it has its proper operation, wherein its Happiness consists. Hence Augustine, after inquiring (*Gen. ad lit.* xii, 35)[2] "whether that perfect Happiness can be ascribed to the souls of the dead separated from their bodies," answers that "they cannot see the Unchangeable Substance, as the blessed angels see It; either for some other more hidden reason, or because they have a natural desire to rule the body."

Reply Obj. 1. Happiness is the perfection of the soul on the part of the intellect, in respect of which the soul transcends the organs of the body; but not according as the soul is the natural form of the body. Therefore the soul retains that natural perfection in respect of which Happiness is due to it, though it does not retain that natural perfection in respect of which it is the form of the body.

Reply Obj. 2. The relation of the soul to being is not the same as that of other parts, for the being of the whole is not that of any individual part. Therefore, either the part ceases altogether to be, when the whole is destroyed, just as the parts of an animal, when the animal is destroyed; or, if they remain, they have another actual being, just as a part of a line has another being from that of the whole line. But the human soul retains the being of the composite after the destruction of the body, and this because the being of the form is the same as that of its matter, and this is the being of the composite. Now the soul subsists in its own being, as stated in the First Part (Q. LXXV, A. 2). It follows, therefore, that after being separated from the body it has perfect being, and that consequently it can have a perfect operation, although it has not the perfect specific nature.

Reply Obj. 3. Happiness belongs to man in re-

[2] PL 34, 483.

spect of his intellect, and, therefore, since the intellect remains, it can have Happiness. Thus the teeth of an Ethiopian, in respect of which he is said to be white, can retain their whiteness, even after extraction.

Reply Obj. 4. One thing is hindered by another in two ways. First, by way of contrariety, just as cold hinders the action of heat, and such a hindrance to operation is contrary to Happiness. Secondly, by way of some kind of defect, because, namely, that which is hindered does not have all that is necessary to make it perfect in every way, and such a hindrance to operation is not contrary to Happiness, but prevents it from being perfect in every way. And thus it is that separation from the body is said to hold the soul back from tending with all its might to the vision of the Divine Essence. For the soul desires to enjoy God in such a way that the enjoyment also may overflow into the body, as far as possible. And therefore, as long as it enjoys God, without the fellowship of the body, its appetite is at rest in that which it has, in such a way that it would still wish the body to attain to its share.

Reply Obj. 5. The desire of the separated soul is entirely at rest, as regards the thing desired, since it has that which suffices its appetite. But it is not wholly at rest as regards the desirer, since it does not possess that good in every way that it would wish to possess it. Consequently, after the body has been resumed, Happiness increases not in intensity, but in extent.

Reply Obj. 6. The passage quoted to the effect that "the souls of the departed see not God as the angels do," is not to be understood as referring to inequality of quantity, because even now some souls of the Blessed are raised to the higher orders of angels, thus seeing God more clearly than the lower angels. But it refers to inequality of proportion, because the angels, even the lowest, have every perfection of Happiness that they ever will have, whereas the separated souls of the saints have not.

ARTICLE 6. *Whether Perfection of the Body Is Necessary for Happiness?*

We proceed thus to the Sixth Article: It seems that perfection of the body is not necessary for man's perfect Happiness.

Objection 1. For perfection of the body is a bodily good. But it has been shown above (Q. II) that Happiness does not consist in bodily goods. Therefore no perfect disposition of the body is necessary for man's Happiness.

Obj. 2. Further, man's Happiness consists in

the vision of the Divine Essence, as shown above (Q. III, A. 8). But the body has no part in this operation, as shown above (A. 5). Therefore no disposition of the body is necessary for Happiness.

Obj. 3. Further, the more the intellect is abstracted from the body the more perfectly it understands. But Happiness consists in the most perfect operation of the intellect. Therefore the soul should be abstracted from the body in every way. Therefore, in no way is a disposition of the body necessary for Happiness.

On the contrary, Happiness is the reward of virtue; therefore it is written (John 13. 17): *You shall be blessed, if you do them.* But the reward promised to the saints is not only that they shall see and enjoy God, but also that their bodies shall be well-disposed; for it is written (Isa. 66. 14): *You shall see and your heart shall rejoice, and your bones shall flourish like a herb.* Therefore good disposition of the body is necessary for Happiness.

I answer that, If we speak of that happiness which man can acquire in this life, it is evident that a well-disposed body is of necessity required for it. For "this happiness consists," according to the Philosopher,[1] "in an operation according to perfect virtue"; and it is clear that man can be hindered, by indisposition of the body, from every operation of virtue.

But speaking of perfect Happiness, some have maintained that no disposition of body is necessary for Happiness; indeed, that it is necessary for the soul to be entirely separated from the body. Hence Augustine[2] quotes the words of Porphyry who said that "for the soul to be happy, it must be severed from everything corporeal." But this is unfitting. For since it is natural to the soul to be united to the body, it is not possible for the perfection of the soul to exclude its natural perfection.

Consequently, we must say that perfect disposition of the body is necessary, both antecedently and consequently, for that Happiness which is in all ways perfect.—Antecedently, because, as Augustine says (*Gen. ad lit.* xii, 35),[3] "if the body be such that the governance thereof is difficult and burdensome, like unto flesh which is corruptible and weighs upon the soul, the mind is turned away from that vision of the highest heaven." And so he concludes that, "when this body will no longer be 'animal,' but 'spiritual,' then will it be equalled to the angels, and that will be its glory, which erstwhile was

---

[1] *Ethics,* I, 13 (1102ᵃ5).
[2] *City of God,* XXII, 26 (PL41, 794).   [3] PL 34, 483.

its burden."—Consequently, because from the Happiness of the soul there will be an overflow on to the body, so that this too will obtain its perfection. Hence Augustine says (*Ep. ad Dioscor.*)[1] that "God gave the soul such a powerful nature that from its exceeding fulness of happiness the vigour of incorruption overflows into the lower nature."

Reply Obj. 1. Happiness does not consist in bodily good as its object, but bodily good can add a certain grace and perfection to Happiness.

Reply Obj. 2. Although the body has no part in that operation of the intellect whereby the Essence of God is seen, yet it might prove a hindrance to it. Consequently, perfection of the body is necessary, lest it hinder the mind from being lifted up.

Reply Obj. 3. The perfect operation of the intellect requires indeed that the intellect be abstracted from this corruptible body which weighs upon the soul, but not from the spiritual body, which will be wholly subject to the spirit. On this point we shall treat in the Third Part of this work (Suppl., Q. LXXXII).

ARTICLE 7. *Whether Any External Goods Are Necessary for Happiness?*

We proceed thus to the Seventh Article: It seems that external goods also are necessary for Happiness.

Objection 1. For that which is promised the saints for reward belongs to Happiness. But external goods are promised the saints; for instance, food and drink, wealth, and a kingdom; for it is said (Luke 22. 30): *That you may eat and drink at My table in My kingdom;* and (Matt. 6. 20): *Lay up to yourselves treasures in heaven;* and (Matt. 25. 34): *Come, ye blessed of my Father, possess you the kingdom.* Therefore external goods are necessary for Happiness.

Obj. 2. Further, according to Boëthius (*De Consol.* iii, 2)[2], happiness is "a state made perfect by the aggregate of all good things." But "some of man's goods are external, although they be of least account," as Augustine says (*De Lib. Arb.* ii, 19).[3] Therefore they too are necessary for Happiness.

Obj. 3. Further, Our Lord said (Matt. 5. 12): *Your reward is very great in heaven.* But to be in heaven implies being in a place. Therefore at least external place is necessary for Happiness.

[1] *Epist.*, 118, chap. 3 (PL 33, 439).
[2] PL 63, 724.   [3] PL 32, 1267.

On the contrary, It is written (Ps. 72. 25): *For what have I in heaven? and besides Thee what do I desire upon earth?* As though to say: "I desire nothing but this,—*It is good for me to adhere to my God.*" Therefore nothing outside God is necessary for Happiness.

I answer that, For imperfect happiness, such as can be had in this life, external goods are necessary, not as belonging to the essence of happiness, but by serving as instruments to happiness, "which consists in an operation of virtue," as stated in the *Ethics.*[4] For man needs, in this life, the necessaries of the body, both for the operation of contemplative virtue, and for the operation of active virtue, for which latter he needs also many other things by means of which to perform its operations.

On the other hand, such goods as these are in no way necessary for perfect Happiness, which consists in seeing God. The reason of this is that all external goods of this kind are requisite either for the support of the animal body, or for certain operations which belong to human life, which we perform by means of the animal body. But that perfect Happiness which consists in seeing God will be either in the soul separated from the body, or in the soul united to the body then no longer animal but spiritual. Consequently these external goods are in no way necessary for that Happiness, since they are ordered to the animal life.—And, since, in this life, the happiness of contemplation, as being more God-like, approaches nearer than the happiness of action to the likeness of that perfect Happiness, therefore it stands in less need of these goods of the body, as stated in the *Ethics.*[5]

Reply Obj. 1. All those material promises contained in Holy Scripture are to be understood metaphorically, since Scripture is accustomed to express spiritual things under the form of things corporeal, in order that "from things we know, we may rise to the desire of things unknown," as Gregory says (*Hom.* xi. *in Ev.*).[6] Thus food and drink signify the delight of Happiness; wealth, the sufficiency of God for man; the kingdom, the lifting up of man to union with God.

Reply Obj. 2. These goods that serve for the animal life are incompatible with that spiritual life in which perfect Happiness consists. Nevertheless in that Happiness there will be the aggregate of all good things, because whatever

[4] Aristotle, I, 13 (1102ᵃ5).
[5] Aristotle, X, 8 (1178ᵇ1).
[6] Bk. II (PL 76, 1114).

good there be in these things, we shall possess it all in the Supreme Fount of goodness.

Reply Obj. 3. According to Augustine (*De Serm. Dom. in Monte*, i, 5),[1] it is not a material heaven that is described as the reward of the saints, but a heaven raised on the height of spiritual goods. Nevertheless a bodily place, namely, the empyrean heaven, will be appointed to the Blessed, not as a need of Happiness, but by reason of a certain fitness and adornment.

ARTICLE 8. *Whether the Fellowship of Friends Is Necessary for Happiness?*

We proceed thus to the Eighth Article: It seems that friends are necessary for Happiness.

Objection 1. For future Happiness is frequently designated by Scripture under the name of glory. But glory consists in man's good being brought to the notice of many. Therefore the fellowship of friends is necessary for Happiness.

Obj. 2. Further, Boëthius says[2] that "there is no delight in possessing any good whatever, without someone to share it with us." But delight is necessary for Happiness. Therefore fellowship of friends is also necessary.

Obj. 3. Further, charity is perfected in Happiness. But charity includes the love of God and of our neighbour. Therefore it seems that fellowship of friends is necessary for Happiness.

On the contrary, It is written (Wisd. 7. 11): *All good things came to me together with her,* that is, with divine wisdom, which consists in contemplating God. Consequently nothing else is necessary for Happiness.

I answer that, If we speak of the happiness of this life, the happy man needs friends, as the Philosopher says,[3] not, indeed, to make use of them, since he suffices himself, nor to delight in them, since he possesses perfect delight in the operation of virtue, but for the purpose of a good operation, namely, that he may do good to them, that he may delight in seeing them do good, and again that he may be helped by them in his good work. For in order that man may do well, whether in the works of the active life, or in those of the contemplative life, he needs the fellowship of friends.

But if we speak of perfect Happiness which will be in our heavenly Fatherland, the fellowship of friends is not essential to Happiness,

since man has the entire fulness of his perfection in God. But the fellowship of friends conduces to the well-being of Happiness. Hence Augustine says (*Gen. ad lit.* viii, 25)[4] that "the spiritual creatures receive no other interior aid to happiness than the eternity, truth, and charity of the Creator. But if they can be said to be helped from without, perhaps it is only by this that they see one another and rejoice in God, at their fellowship."

Reply Obj. 1. That glory which is essential to Happiness is that which man has not with man but with God.

Reply Obj. 2. This saying is to be understood of the possession of good that does not fully satisfy. This does not apply to the question under consideration, because man possesses in God a sufficiency of every good.

Reply Obj. 3. Perfection of charity is essential to Happiness, as to the love of God, but not as to the love of our neighbour. And so if there were but one soul enjoying God, it would be happy, though having no neighbour to love. But supposing one neighbour to be there, love of him results from perfect love of God. Consequently, friendship is, as it were, concomitant with perfect Happiness.

QUESTION V
OF THE ATTAINMENT OF HAPPINESS
(*In Eight Articles*)

WE must now consider the attainment of Happiness. Under this heading there are eight points of inquiry: (1) Whether man can attain Happiness? (2) Whether one man can be happier than another? (3) Whether any man can be happy in this life? (4) Whether Happiness once had can be lost? (5) Whether man can attain Happiness by means of his natural powers? (6) Whether man attains Happiness through the action of some higher creature? (7) Whether any actions of man are necessary in order that man may obtain Happiness of God? (8) Whether every man desires Happiness?

ARTICLE 1. *Whether Man Can Attain Happiness?*

We proceed thus to the First Article: It seems that man cannot attain Happiness.

Objection 1. For just as the rational nature is above the sensible nature, so the intellectual is above the rational, as Dionysius declares (*Div. Nom.* iv, vi, vii)[5] in several passages. But ir-

---

[1] PL 34, 1237.

[2] Cf. Seneca, *Ad Lucilium*, Epist., VI (DD 532).

[3] *Ethics*, IX, 9 (1169[b]22).

[4] PL 34, 391.

[5] PG 3, 693, 856, 868.

rational animals that have the sensitive nature only, cannot attain the end of the rational nature. Therefore neither can man, who is of rational nature, attain the end of the intellectual nature, which is Happiness.

Obj. 2. Further, True Happiness consists in seeing God, Who is pure Truth. But from his very nature, man considers truth in material things; hence "he understands the intelligible species in the phantasm."[1] Therefore he cannot attain Happiness.

Obj. 3. Further, Happiness consists in attaining the Sovereign Good. But we cannot arrive at the top without surmounting the middle. Since, therefore, the angelic nature through which man cannot mount is midway between God and human nature, it seems that he cannot attain Happiness.

On the contrary, It is written (Ps. 93. 12): *Blessed is the man whom Thou shalt instruct, O Lord.*

I answer that, Happiness is the attainment of the Perfect Good. Whoever, therefore, is capable of the Perfect Good can attain Happiness. Now, that man is capable of the Perfect Good, is proved both because his intellect can apprehend the universal and perfect good, and because his will can desire it. And therefore man can attain Happiness. This can be proved again from the fact that man is capable of seeing God, as stated in the First Part (Q. XII, A. 1), in which vision, as we stated above (Q. III, A. 8) man's perfect Happiness consists.

Reply Obj. 1. The rational exceeds the sensitive nature otherwise than the intellectual surpasses the rational. For the rational exceeds the sensitive nature in respect of the object of its knowledge, since the senses have no knowledge whatever of the universal, whereas the reason does have knowledge of the universal. But the intellectual surpasses the rational nature as to the mode of knowing intelligible truth, for the intellectual nature grasps at once the truth which the rational nature reaches by the inquiry of reason, as was made clear in the First Part (Q. LVIII, A. 3; Q. LXXIX, A. 8). Therefore reason arrives by a kind of movement at that which the intellect apprehends. Consequently the rational nature can attain Happiness, which is the perfection of the intellectual nature, but otherwise than the angels. Because the angels attained it at once after the beginning of their knowledge, whereas man attains it after a time. But the sensitive nature can attain this end in no way.

Reply Obj. 2. To man in the present state of life the natural way of knowing intelligible truth is by means of phantasms. But after this state of life, he has another natural way, as was stated in the First Part (Q. LXXXIV, A. 7; Q. LXXXIX, A. 1).

Reply Obj. 3. Man cannot surmount the angels in the degree of nature, so as to be above them naturally. But he can surmount them by an operation of the intellect, by understanding that there is above the angels something that makes men happy, and that when he has attained it, he will be perfectly happy.

ARTICLE 2. *Whether One Man Can Be Happier Than Another?*

We proceed thus to the Second Article: It seems that one man cannot be happier than another.

Objection 1. For "Happiness is the reward of virtue," as the Philosopher says.[2] But equal reward is given for all the works of virtue, because it is written (Matt. 20. 10) that all who laboured in the vineyard *received every man a penny;* for, as Gregory says (*Hom.* xix *in Evang.*),[3] "each was equally rewarded with eternal life." Therefore one man cannot be happier than another.

Obj. 2. Further, Happiness is the supreme good. But nothing can surpass the supreme. Therefore one man's Happiness cannot be surpassed by another's.

Obj. 3. Further, since Happiness is the perfect and sufficient good it brings rest to man's desire. But his desire is not at rest if he yet lacks some good that can be had. And if he lack nothing that he can get, there can be no still greater good. Therefore either man is not happy; or, if he be happy, no other Happiness can be greater.

On the contrary, It is written (John 14. 2): *In My Father's house there are many mansions;* which, according to Augustine (*Tract.* lxvii)[4] signify "the various dignities of merits in the eternal life." But the dignity of eternal life which is given according to merit is Happiness itself. Therefore there are various degrees of Happiness, and Happiness is not equally in all.

I answer that, As stated above (Q. I, A. 8; Q. II, A. 7), in the notion of Happiness there are two things, namely, the last end itself, which is the Sovereign Good, and the attainment or enjoyment of that same Good. As to that Good it-

---

[1] *Soul,* III, 7 (431[b]2).

[2] *Ethics,* I, 9 (1099[b]16).

[3] Bk. 1 (PL 76, 1156).

[4] *In Joann.,* on 14.2 (PL 35, 1812).

self Which is the object and cause of Happiness, one Happiness cannot be greater than another, since there is but one Sovereign Good, namely, God, by enjoying Whom, men are made happy. But as to the attainment or enjoyment of this Good, one man can be happier than another because the more a man enjoys this Good the happier he is. Now, that one man enjoys God more than another happens through his being better disposed or ordered to the enjoyment of Him. And in this sense one man can be happier than another.

Reply Obj. 1. The one penny signifies that Happiness is one in its object. But the many mansions signify the manifold Happiness in the different degrees of enjoyment.

Reply Obj. 2. Happiness is said to be the supreme good, because it is the perfect possession or enjoyment of the Supreme Good.

Reply Obj. 3. None of the Blessed lacks any desirable good, since they have the Infinite Good Itself, Which is "the good of all good," as Augustine says (*Enarr. in* Ps. 134).[1] But one is said to be happier than another by reason of different participation of the same good. And the addition of other goods does not increase Happiness; hence Augustine says,[2] "He who knows Thee, and others besides, is not the happier for knowing them, but is happy for knowing Thee alone."

ARTICLE 3. *Whether One Can Be Happy in This Life?*

We proceed thus to the Third Article: It would seem that Happiness can be had in this life.

Objection 1. For it is written (Ps. 118. 1): *Blessed are the undefiled in the way, who walk in the law of the Lord.* But this happens in this life. Therefore one can be happy in this life.

Obj. 2. Further, imperfect participation in the Sovereign Good does not destroy the nature of Happiness, otherwise one would not be happier than another. But men can participate in the Sovereign Good in this life by knowing and loving God, although imperfectly. Therefore man can be happy in this life.

Obj. 3. Further, what is said by many cannot be altogether false, since what is in many, comes, apparently, from nature, and nature does not fail altogether. Now many say that Happiness can be had in this life, as appears from Ps. 143. 15: *They have called the people happy that hath these things,* that is to say, the

good things of this life. Therefore one can be happy in this life.

On the contrary, It is written (Job 14. 1): *Man born of a woman, living for a short time, is filled with many miseries.* But Happiness excludes misery. Therefore man cannot be happy in this life.

I answer that, A certain participation of Happiness can be had in this life, but perfect and true Happiness cannot be had in this life. This may be seen from a twofold consideration.

First, from the general notion of happiness. For since happiness is a perfect and sufficient good, it excludes every evil, and fulfils every desire. But in this life every evil cannot be excluded. For this present life is subject to many unavoidable evils: to ignorance on the part of the intellect, to disordered affection on the part of the appetite, and to many penalties on the part of the body, as Augustine sets forth in the *City of God.*[3] Likewise neither can the desire for good be satiated in this life. For man naturally desires the good which he has to be abiding. Now the goods of the present life pass away, since life itself passes away, which we naturally desire to have, and would wish to hold abidingly, for man naturally shrinks from death. Therefore it is impossible to have true Happiness in this life.

Secondly, from a consideration of that in which Happiness specially consists, namely, the vision of the Divine Essence, which man cannot obtain in this life, as was shown in the First Part (Q. XII, A. 2). Hence it is evident that none can attain true and perfect Happiness in this life.

Reply Obj. 1. Some are said to be happy in this life, either on account of the hope of obtaining Happiness in the life to come, according to Rom. 8. 24: *We are saved by hope;* or on account of a certain participation of Happiness, by reason of a kind of enjoyment of the Sovereign Good.

Reply Obj. 2. The imperfection of participated Happiness is due to one of two causes. First, on the part of the object of Happiness, which is not seen in Its Essence. And this imperfection takes away the character of true Happiness. Secondly, the imperfection may be on the part of the participator, who indeed attains the object of Happiness, in itself, namely God, but imperfectly in comparison with the way in which God enjoys Himself. This imperfection does not destroy the true notion of Happiness; because, since Happiness is an opera-

---

[1] PL 37, 1741.

[2] *Confessions,* v. 5 (PL 32, 708).

[3] XIX, 4 (PL 41, 628).

tion, as stated above (Q. III, A. 2), the true notion of Happiness is taken from the object, which specifies the act, and not from the subject.

Reply Obj. 3. Men consider that there is some kind of happiness to be had in this life on account of a certain likeness to true Happiness. And thus they do not fail altogether in their estimate.

ARTICLE 4. *Whether Happiness Once Had Can Be Lost?*

We proceed thus to the Fourth Article: It would seem that Happiness can be lost.

Objection 1. For Happiness is a perfection. But every perfection is in the thing perfected according to the mode of the latter. Since then man is, by his nature, changeable, it seems that Happiness is participated by man in a changeable manner. And consequently it seems that man can lose Happiness.

Obj. 2. Further, Happiness consists in an act of the intellect, and the intellect is subject to the will. But the will can be directed to opposites. Therefore it seems that it can desist from the operation whereby man is made happy; and thus man will cease to be happy.

Obj. 3. Further, the end corresponds to the beginning. But man's Happiness has a beginning, since man was not always happy. Therefore it seems that it has an end.

On the contrary, It is written (Matt. 25. 46) of the just that *they shall go . . . into life everlasting,* which, as stated above (A. 2), is the Happiness of the saints. Now what is eternal does not cease. Therefore Happiness cannot be lost.

I answer that, If we speak of imperfect happiness, such as can be had in this life, in this sense it can be lost. This is clear of contemplative happiness, which is lost either by forgetfulness, for instance, when knowledge is lost through sickness; or again by certain occupations, whereby a man is altogether withdrawn from contemplation.

This is also clear of active happiness, since man's will can be changed so as to fall to vice from the virtue in whose act that happiness principally consists. If, however, the virtue remain unimpaired, outward changes can indeed disturb such happiness, in so far as they hinder many acts of virtue; but they cannot take it away altogether, because there still remains an act of virtue, as long as man bears these trials in a praiseworthy manner. And since the happiness of this life can be lost, which seems to be

against the notion of happiness, therefore the Philosopher stated that some are happy in this life not absolutely, but as men, whose nature is subject to change.[1]

But if we speak of that perfect Happiness which we await after this life, it must be observed that Origen (*Peri Archon,* ii),[2] following the error of certain Platonists,[3] held that man can become unhappy after the final Happiness.

This, however, is evidently false, for two reasons. First, from the general notion of happiness. For since happiness is the perfect and sufficient good, it must set man's desire at rest and exclude every evil. Now man naturally desires to hold to the good that he has, and to have the surety of his holding; otherwise he must of necessity be troubled with the fear of losing it, or with the sorrow of knowing that he will lose it. Therefore it is necessary for true Happiness that man have the assured opinion of never losing the good that he possesses. If this opinion be true, it follows that he never will lose happiness; but if it be false, it is in itself an evil that he should have a false opinion, because the false is the evil of the intellect, just as the true is its good, as stated in the *Ethics.*[4] Consequently he will no longer be truly happy if evil is in him.

Secondly, it is again evident if we consider the special notion of Happiness. For it has been shown above (Q. III, A. 8) that man's perfect Happiness consists in the vision of the Divine Essence. Now it is impossible for anyone seeing the Divine Essence to wish not to see It. Because every good that one possesses and yet wishes to be without is either insufficient, something more sufficing being desired in its stead; or else has some inconvenience attached to it, by reason of which it becomes wearisome. But the vision of the Divine Essence fills the soul with all good things, since it unites it to the source of all goodness; hence it is written (Ps. 16. 15): *I shall be satisfied when Thy glory shall appear;* and (Wisd. 7. 11): *All good things came to me together with her,* that is, with the contemplation of wisdom. In like manner neither has it any inconvenience attached to it, because it is written of the contemplation of wisdom (Wisd. 8. 16): *Her conversation hath no bitterness, nor her company any tediousness.* It is thus evident that the happy man cannot forsake Happiness of his own will.

[1] *Ethics,* I, 10 (1101ᵃ19).
[2] Jerome's translation, Bk. I., chaps. 5, 6 (PG 11, 164 167, note 70).
[3] See Jerome, *Epist.,* 124 *Ad Avitum,* chap. 2 (PL 22 1066). Cf. also Augustine, *City of God,* X, 30 (PL 41, 309).
[4] Aristotle, VI, 2 (1139ᵃ26).

Moreover, neither can he lose Happiness through God taking it away from him. Because, since the withdrawal of Happiness is a punishment, it cannot be enforced by God, the just Judge, except for some fault; and he that sees the Essence of God cannot fall into a fault, since rightness of the will, of necessity, results from that vision as was shown above (Q. IV, A. 4). Nor again can it be withdrawn by any other agent. Because the mind that is united to God is raised above all other things, and consequently no other agent can sever the mind from that union. Therefore it seems unreasonable that as time goes on, man should pass from happiness to misery, and contrariwise, because such vicissitudes of time can only be for such things as are subject to time and movement.

Reply Obj. 1. Happiness is consummate perfection, which excludes every defect from the happy. And therefore whoever has happiness has it altogether unchangeably. This is done by the Divine power, which raises man to the participation of eternity which transcends all change.

Reply Obj. 2. The will can be directed to opposites in things which are ordered to the end; but it is ordered of natural necessity to the last end. This is evident from the fact that man is unable not to wish to be happy.

Reply Obj. 3. Happiness has a beginning owing to the condition of the participator; but it has no end by reason of the condition of the good in whose participation man is made happy. Hence the beginning of happiness is from one cause, its endlessness is from another.

ARTICLE 5. *Whether Man Can Attain Happiness by His Natural Powers?*

We proceed thus to the Fifth Article: It seems that man can attain Happiness by his natural powers.

Objection 1. For nature does not fail in necessary things. But nothing is so natural to man as that by which he attains the last end. Therefore this is not lacking to human nature. Therefore man can attain Happiness by his natural powers.

Obj. 2. Further, since man is more noble than irrational creatures, it seems that he must be more self-sufficient. But irrational creatures can attain their end by their natural powers. Much more therefore can man attain Happiness by his natural powers.

Obj. 3. Further, "Happiness is a perfect operation," according to the Philosopher.[1] Now the beginning of a thing and its perfecting pertain

[1] *Ethics,* VII, 13 (1153[b]16).

to the same principle. Since, therefore, the imperfect operation, which is as it were the beginning in human operations, is subject to man's natural power, by which he is master of his own actions, it seems that he can attain to perfect operation, that is, Happiness, by his natural powers.

On the contrary, Man is naturally the principle of his action by his intellect and will. But final Happiness prepared for the saints surpasses the intellect and will of man; for the Apostle says (I Cor. 2, 9): *Eye hath not seen, nor ear heard, neither hath it entered into the heart of man, what things God hath prepared for them that love Him.* Therefore man cannot attain Happiness by his natural powers.

I answer that, Imperfect happiness that can be had in this life can be acquired by man by his natural powers, in the same way as virtue, in whose operation it consists; on this point we shall speak further on (Q. LXIII). But man's perfect Happiness, as stated above (Q. III, A. 8), consists in the vision of the Divine Essence. Now the vision of God's Essence surpasses the nature not only of man, but also of every creature, as was shown in the First Part (Q. XII, A. 4). For the natural knowledge of every creature is in keeping with the mode of its substance; thus it is said of the intelligence (*De Causis*)[2] that it knows things that are above it, and things that are below it, according to the mode of its substance. But every knowledge that is according to the mode of created substance falls short of the vision of the Divine Essence, which infinitely surpasses all created substance. Consequently neither man, nor any creature, can attain final Happiness by his natural powers.

Reply Obj. 1. Just as nature does not fail man in necessaries, although it has not provided him with weapons and clothing as it provided other animals, because it gave him reason and hands, with which he is able to get these things for himself, so neither did it fail man in things necessary, by not giving him the means to attain Happiness, since this was impossible. But it did give him free choice, with which he can turn to God, that He may make him happy. "For what we do by means of our friends, is done, in a sense, by ourselves."[3]

Reply Obj. 2. The nature that can attain perfect good, although it needs help from without in order to attain it, is of more noble condition than a nature which cannot attain perfect good but attains some imperfect good, although it

[2] Sect. 7 (BA 170).
[3] *Ethics,* III, 3 (1112[b]27).

need no help from without in order to attain it, as the Philosopher says.[1] Thus he is better disposed to health who can attain perfect health, even though by means of medicine, than he who can attain but imperfect health without the help of medicine. And therefore the rational creature, which can attain the perfect good of Happiness, but needs the Divine assistance for the purpose, is more perfect than the irrational creature, which is not capable of attaining this good, but attains some imperfect good by its natural powers.

Reply Obj. 3. When imperfect and perfect are of the same species, they can be caused by the same power. But this does not follow of necessity, if they be of different species, for not everything that can cause the disposition of matter can confer the final perfection. Now the imperfect operation, which is subject to man's natural power, is not of the same species as that perfect operation which is man's happiness, since operation takes its species from its object. Consequently the argument does not prove.

ARTICLE 6. *Whether Man Attains Happiness through the Action of Some Higher Creature?*

We proceed thus to the Sixth Article: It seems that man can be made happy through the action of some higher creature, namely, an angel.

Objection 1. For since we observe a twofold order in things—one, of the parts of the universe to one another, the other, of the whole universe to a good which is outside the universe; the former order is ordered to the second as to its end.[2] Thus the order of the parts of an army to each other is dependent on the order of the whole army to the general. But the order of the parts of the universe to each other consists in the higher creatures acting on the lower, as stated in the First Part (Q. CIX, A. 2),[3] while happiness consists in the order of man to a good which is outside the universe, that is, God. Therefore man is made happy through a higher creature, namely, an angel, acting on him.

Obj. 2. Further, that which is such in potency can be reduced to act by that which is such actually; thus what is potentially hot is made actually hot by something that is actually hot. But man is potentially happy. Therefore he can be made actually happy by an angel who is actually happy.

Obj. 3. Further, Happiness consists in an operation of the intellect, as stated above (Q. III, A. 4). But an angel can enlighten man's intellect, as shown in the First Part (Q. CXI, A. 1). Therefore an angel can make a man happy.

On the contrary, It is written (Ps. 83. 12): *The Lord will give grace and glory.*

I answer that, Since every creature is subject to the laws of nature from the very fact that its power and action are limited, that which surpasses created nature cannot be done by the power of any creature. Consequently if anything need to be done that is above nature, it is done by God immediately, such as raising the dead to life, restoring sight to the blind, and the like. Now it has been shown above (A. 5) that Happiness is a good surpassing created nature. Therefore it is impossible that it be bestowed through the action of any creature, but man is made happy by God alone, if we speak of perfect Happiness. If, however, we speak of imperfect happiness, the same is to be said of it and of the virtue in whose exercise it consists.

Reply Obj. 1. It often happens in the case of active powers ordered to one another that it belongs to the highest power to reach the last end, while the lower powers contribute to the attainment of that last end, by causing a disposition to it; thus it pertains to the art of sailing, which governs the art of ship-building, to use a ship for the end for which it was made. Thus, too, in the order of the universe, man is indeed helped by angels in the attainment of his last end, in respect of certain preliminary dispositions to that end; but he attains the last end itself through the First Agent, which is God.

Reply Obj. 2. When a form exists in something according to its natural and perfect being, it can be the principle of action on something else; for instance, a hot thing heats through fire. But if a form exist in something imperfectly and not according to its natural being, it cannot be the principle by which it is communicated to something else; thus the intention of colour which is in the pupil, cannot make a thing white; nor indeed can anything illuminated or heated give heat or light to something else, for if they could, illumination and heating would go on to infinity. But the light of glory, by which God is seen, is in God perfectly according to its natural being; but in any creature, it is imperfectly and according to the being of likeness or participation. Consequently no creature can communicate its Happiness to another.

Reply Obj. 3. A happy angel enlightens the intellect of a man or of a lower angel, as to certain notions of the Divine works, but not as to

[1] *Heavens*, II, 12 (292ᵃ22).
[2] *Metaphysics*, XII, 10 (1075ᵃ11).
[3] Cf. also, Q. XIX, A. 5 reply 2; Q. XLVIII, A. 1, reply 5.

the vision of the Divine Essence, as was stated in the First Part (Q. CVI, A. 1), since in order to see this, all are immediately enlightened by God.

ARTICLE 7. *Whether Any Good Works Are Necessary that Man May Receive Happiness from God?*

We proceed thus to the Seventh Article: It seems that no works of man are necessary that he may obtain Happiness from God.

Objection 1. For since God is an agent of infinite power, He requires before acting, neither matter, nor disposition of matter, but can immediately produce the whole effect. But man's works, since they are not required for Happiness as its efficient cause, as stated above (A. 6), can be required only as dispositions to Happiness. Therefore God Who does not require dispositions before acting bestows Happiness without any previous works.

Obj. 2. Further, just as God is the immediate cause of Happiness, so is He the immediate cause of nature. But when God first established nature, He produced creatures without any previous disposition or action on the part of the creature, but made each one perfect at once in its species. Therefore it seems that He bestows Happiness on man without any previous works.

Obj. 3. Further, the Apostle says (Rom. 4. 6) that Happiness is of the man *to whom God reputeth justice without works.* Therefore no works of man are necessary for attaining Happiness.

On the contrary, It is written (John 13. 17): *If you know these things, you shall be blessed if you do them.* Therefore Happiness is obtained through works.

I answer that, Rightness of the will, as stated above (Q. IV, A. 4), is necessary for Happiness, since it is nothing else than the due order of the will to the last end; and it is therefore necessary for obtaining the last end, just as the right disposition of matter, in order to receive the form. But this does not prove that any work of man need precede his Happiness, for God could make a will which has a right tendency to the end which at the same time attains the end; just as sometimes He disposes matter and at the same time introduces the form. But the order of Divine wisdom demands that it should not be thus; for as it is stated in the book on the *Heavens,*[1] "Of those things that have a natural capacity for the perfect good, one has it without movement, some by one movement, some

by several." Now to possess the perfect good without movement, belongs to that which has it naturally, and to have Happiness naturally belongs to God alone. Therefore it belongs to God alone not to be moved towards Happiness by any previous operation. Now since Happiness surpasses every created nature, no mere creature can fittingly gain Happiness, without the movement of operation, whereby it tends to it. But the angel, who is above man in the natural order, obtained it according to the order of Divine wisdom by one movement of a meritorious work, as was explained in the First Part (Q. LXII, A. 5); man however obtains it by many movements of works which are called merits. Hence also according to the Philosopher,[2] "happiness is the reward of works of virtue."

Reply Obj. 1. Works are necessary to man in order to gain Happiness not on account of the insufficiency of the Divine power which bestows Happiness, but that the order in things be observed.

Reply Obj. 2. God produced the first creatures so that they were perfect at once without any previous disposition or operation of the creature because He instituted the individuals of the various species, that through them nature might be propagated to their progeny. And in like manner, because Happiness was to be bestowed on others through Christ, Who is God and Man, *Who,* according to Heb. 2. 10, *had brought many children into glory,* therefore, from the very beginning of His conception His soul was happy, without any preceding meritorious operation. But this is peculiar to Him, for Christ's merit avails baptized children for the gaining of Happiness, though they have no merits of their own, because by Baptism they are made members of Christ.

Reply Obj. 3. The Apostle is speaking of the Happiness of Hope, which is bestowed on us by sanctifying grace, which is not given on account of previous works. For grace is not a term of movement, as Happiness is; rather is it the principle of the movement that tends towards Happiness.

ARTICLE 8. *Whether Every Man Desires Happiness?*

We proceed thus to the Eighth Article: It seems that not all desire Happiness.

Objection 1. For no man can desire what he knows not, since the good apprehended is the object of the appetite.[3] But many do not know

---

[1] Aristotle, II. 12 (292ª22).

[2] *Ethics,* I, 9 (1099ᵇ16).
[3] *Soul,* III, 10 (433ª27; ᵇ12).

what Happiness is. This is evident from the fact that, as Augustine says (*De Trin.* xiii, 4),[1] "some thought that Happiness consists in pleasures of the body; some, in a power of the soul; some, in other things." Therefore not all desire Happiness.

Obj. 2. Further, the essence of Happiness is the vision of the Divine Essence, as stated above (Q. III, A. 8). But some consider it impossible for man to see the Divine Essence,[2] and so they do not desire it. Therefore all men do not desire Happiness.

Obj. 3. Further, Augustine says (*De Trin.* xiii, 5)[3] that "happy is he who has all he desires, and desires nothing amiss." But all do not desire this; for some desire certain things amiss, and yet they wish to desire such things. Therefore all do not desire Happiness.

On the contrary, Augustine says (*De Trin.* xiii, 3):[4] "If that actor had said: 'You all wish to be happy; you do not wish to be unhappy,' he would have said that which none would have failed to acknowledge in his will." Therefore everyone desires to be happy.

I answer that, Happiness can be considered in two ways. First according to the general notion of happiness; and thus, of necessity, every man desires happiness. For the general notion of happiness consists in the perfect good, as stated above (AA. 3, 4). But since good is the object of the will, the perfect good of a man is that which entirely satisfies his will. Consequently to desire happiness is nothing else than to desire that one's will be satisfied. And this everyone desires. Secondly we may speak of Happiness according to its special notion, as to that in which it consists. And thus all do not know Happiness, because they do not know in what thing the general notion of happiness is found. And consequently, in this respect, not all desire it. Therefore the *reply to the first Objection* is clear.

Reply Obj. 2. Since the will follows the apprehension of the intellect or reason, just as it happens that where there is no real distinction there may be a distinction according to the consideration of reason, so does it happen that one and the same thing is desired in one way, and not desired in another. So that happiness may be considered under the aspect of final and perfect good, which is the general notion of happiness; and thus the will naturally and of necessity tends to it, as stated above. Again it can be considered under other special aspects, either on the part of the operation itself, or on the part of the operating power, or on the part of the object; and thus the will does not tend to it of necessity.

Reply Obj. 3. This definition of Happiness given by some,[5]—Happy is the man that has all he desires, or, whose every wish is fulfilled, is a good and adequate definition if it be understood in a certain way, but an inadequate definition if understood in another. For if we understand it absolutely of all that man desires by his natural appetite, thus it is true that he who has all that he desires, is happy, since nothing satisfies man's natural desire except the perfect good which is Happiness. But if we understand it of those things that man desires according to the apprehension of the reason, in this way it does not pertain to Happiness to have certain things that man desires; rather does it belong to unhappiness, in so far as the possession of such things hinders man from having all that he desires naturally; just as reason also sometimes accepts as true things that are a hindrance to the knowledge of truth. And it was through taking this into consideration that Augustine added so as to include perfect Happiness,—that "he desires nothing amiss," although the first part suffices if rightly understood, that is to say, that "happy is he who has all he desires."

---

[1] PL 42, 1018; cf. also *City of God*, XVIII, 41 (PL 41, 601).

[2] Almaric of Bène; cf. Capelle, *Amaury de Bène*, p. 105; cf. William of Paris (Denifle, *Chartularium*, n. 128–1, 170). See Motte, RSPT (1933) pp. 27–46.

[3] PL 42, 1020.

[4] PL 42, 1018.

[5] Cf. Augustine, *De Trin.*, XIII, 5 (PL 42, 1020); Peter Lombard, *Sent.*, IV, d. 49, chap. 1 (QR II, 1029).

TREATISE ON HUMAN ACTS

I. Of those Acts Which are Proper to Man

(a) The Nature of Voluntary Acts in General

QUESTION VI

Of the voluntary and the involuntary

(In Eight Articles)

Since therefore Happiness must be gained by means of certain acts, we are obliged consequently to consider human acts, in order to know by what acts we may obtain Happiness, and by what acts we are prevented from obtaining it. But because operations and acts are concerned with things singular, consequently all practical knowledge is incomplete unless it take account of things in detail. The study of Morals, therefore, since it treats of human acts, should consider first the universal principles, and secondly matters of detail Part II-II.

In treating of the universal principles, the points that offer themselves for our consideration are—(1) human acts themselves; (2) their principles (Q. XLIX). Now of human acts some are proper to man; others are common to man and animals. And since Happiness is man's proper good, those acts which are proper to man have a closer connection with Happiness than have those which are common to man and the other animals. First, then, we must consider those acts which are proper to man; secondly, those acts which are common to man and the other animals, and are called Passions (Q. XXII). The first of these points offers a twofold consideration: (1) What makes a human act? (2) What distinguishes human acts (Q. XVIII)?

And since those acts are properly called human which are voluntary, because the will is the rational appetite, which is proper to man, we must consider acts in so far as they are voluntary.

First, then, we must consider the voluntary and involuntary in general; secondly, those acts which are voluntary, as being elicited by the will, and as issuing from the will immediately (Q. VIII); thirdly, those acts which are voluntary, as being commanded by the will, which issue from the will through the medium of the other powers (Q. XVII).

And because voluntary acts have certain circumstances, according to which we form our judgment concerning them, we must first consider the voluntary and the involuntary, and afterwards, the circumstances of those acts which are found to be voluntary or involuntary (Q. VII). Under the first head there are eight points of inquiry: (1) Whether there is anything voluntary in human acts? (2) Whether in irrational animals? (3) Whether there can be voluntariness without any action? (4) Whether violence can be done to the will? (5) Whether violence causes involuntariness? (6) Whether fear causes involuntariness? (7) Whether concupiscence causes involuntariness? (8) Whether ignorance causes involuntariness?

ARTICLE 1. Whether There Is Anything Voluntary in Human Acts?

We proceed thus to the First Article: It seems that there is nothing voluntary in human acts.

Objection 1. For "that is voluntary which has its principle within itself," as Gregory of Nyssa (Nemesius, De Natura Hom. xxxii),[1] Damascene (De Fide Orthod. ii, 24),[2] and Aristotle[3] declare. But the principle of human acts is not in man himself, but outside him, since man's appetite is moved to act by the appetible object which is outside him, and is as "a mover unmoved."[4] Therefore there is nothing voluntary in human acts.

Obj. 2. Further, the Philosopher proves[5] that in animals no new act arises that is not preceded by a motion from without. But all human acts are new, since none is eternal. Consequently, the principle of all human acts is from with-

[1] PG 40, 728.
[2] PG 94, 953.
[3] Ethics, III, 1 (1111ᵃ23).
[4] Aristotle, Soul, III, 4 (433ᵇ11).
[5] Physics, VIII, 2 (253ᵃ11).

out, and therefore there is nothing voluntary in them.

Obj. 3. Further, he that acts voluntarily can act of himself. But this is not true of man; for it is written (John 15. 5): *Without Me you can do nothing.* Therefore there is nothing voluntary in human acts.

On the contrary, Damascene says (*De Fide Orthod.* ii)[1] that "the voluntary is an act consisting in a rational operation." Now such are human acts. Therefore there is something voluntary in human acts.

I answer that, There must be something voluntary in human acts. In order to make this clear, we must take note that the principle of some acts or movements is within the agent, or that which is moved and that the principle of some movements or acts is outside. For when a stone is moved upwards, the principle of this movement is outside the stone; but when it is moved downwards, the principle of this movement is in the stone. Now of those things that are moved by an intrinsic principle, some move themselves, some not. For since every agent or thing moved acts or is moved for an end, as stated above (Q. 1, A. 2), those are perfectly moved by an intrinsic principle whose intrinsic principle is one not only of movement but of movement for an end. Now in order for a thing to be done for an end some knowledge of the end is necessary. Therefore, whatever so acts or is so moved by an intrinsic principle that it has some knowledge of the end, has within itself the principle of its act, so that it not only acts, but acts for an end. On the other hand, if a thing has no knowledge of the end, even though it have an intrinsic principle of action or movement, nevertheless the principle of acting or being moved for an end is not in that thing, but in something else, by which the principle of its action towards an end is imprinted on it. Therefore things of this kind are not said to move themselves, but to be moved by others. But those things which have a knowledge of the end are said to move themselves because there is in them a principle by which they not only act but also act for an end. And consequently, since both are from an intrinsic principle, namely, that they act and that they act for an end, the movements of such things are said to be voluntary, for the word voluntary implies that their movements and acts are from their own inclination. Hence it is that, according to the definitions of Aristotle, Gregory of Nyssa, and Damascene (obj. 1), the voluntary is defined not

only as having "a principle within" the agent, but also as implying "knowledge." Therefore, since man especially knows the end of his work, and moves himself, in his acts especially is the voluntary to be found.

Reply Obj. 1. Not every principle is a first principle. Therefore, although it is essential to the voluntary act that its principle be within the agent, nevertheless it is not contrary to the nature of the voluntary act that this intrinsic principle be caused or moved by an extrinsic principle, because it is not essential to the voluntary act that its intrinsic principle be a first principle. Yet again it must be observed that a principle of movement may happen to be first in a genus, but not first absolutely; thus in the genus of things subject to alteration, the first mover is a heavenly body, which nevertheless is not the first mover absolutely, but is moved locally by a higher mover. And so the intrinsic principle of the voluntary act, which is the knowing and appetitive power, is the first principle in the genus of appetitive movement, although it is moved by an extrinsic principle according to other species of movement.

Reply Obj. 2. New movements in animals are indeed preceded by a motion from without; and this in two respects. First, in so far as by means of an extrinsic motion an animal's senses are confronted with something sensible, which, on being apprehended, moves the appetite. Thus a lion, on seeing a stag in movement and coming towards him, begins to be moved towards the stag. Secondly, in so far as some extrinsic motion produces a physical change in an animal's body, as in the case of cold or heat; and through the body being thus changed by the motion of an outward body, the sensitive appetite which is the power of a bodily organ, is also moved indirectly; thus it happens that through some alteration in the body the appetite is roused to the desire of something. But this is not contrary to the nature of voluntariness, as stated above (REPLY 1), for such movements caused by an extrinsic principle are of another genus of movement.

Reply Obj. 3. God moves man to act not only by proposing the appetible to the senses, or by effecting a change in his body, but also by moving the will itself, because every movement either of the will or of nature, proceeds from God as the First Mover. And just as it is not incompatible with nature that the natural movement be from God as the First Mover, since nature is an instrument of God moving it, so it is not contrary to the notion of a voluntary act that it proceed from God in so far as the will is moved by God. Nevertheless both natural and voluntary movements have this in common, that it is essential that they should proceed from a principle within the agent.

ARTICLE 2. *Whether There Is Anything Voluntary in Irrational Animals?*

We proceed thus to the Second Article: It seems that there is nothing voluntary in irrational animals.

Objection 1. For a thing is called "voluntary" from *voluntas* (will). Now since the will is "in the reason,"[1] it cannot be in irrational animals. Therefore neither is there anything voluntary in them.

Obj. 2. Further, according as human acts are voluntary, man is said to be master of his actions. But irrational animals are not masters of their actions; for "they act not; rather are they acted upon," as Damascene says (*De Fide Orthod.* ii).[2] Therefore there is no such thing as a voluntary act in irrational animals.

Obj. 3. Further, Damascene says (*ibid.*)[3] that "voluntary acts lead to praise and blame." But neither praise nor blame is due to the acts of irrational animals. Therefore such acts are not voluntary.

On the contrary, The Philosopher says[4] that "both children and irrational animals participate in the voluntary." The same is said by Damascene (*loc. cit.*) and Gregory of Nyssa.[5]

I answer that, As stated above (A. 1), it is essential to the voluntary act that its principle be within the agent, together with some knowledge of the end. Now knowledge of the end is twofold: perfect and imperfect. Perfect knowledge of the end consists in not only apprehending the thing which is the end, but also in knowing it under the aspect of end, and the relationship of the means to that end. And such knowledge belongs only to the rational nature. But imperfect knowledge of the end consists in mere apprehension of the end, without knowing it under the aspect of end, or the relationship of an act to the end. Such knowledge of the end is exercised by irrational animals through their senses and their natural estimative power.

Consequently perfect knowledge of the end leads to the perfect voluntary act according as, having apprehended the end, a man can, from deliberating about the end and the means to it, be moved, or not moved, to gain that end. But

[1] Aristotle, *Soul,* III, 9 (432ᵇ5).   [2] Chap. 27 (PG 94, 960).
[3] Chap. 24 (PG 94, 953).   [4] *Ethics,* III, 2 (1111ᵇ8).
[5] Nemesius, *De Nat. Hom.,* XXXII (PG 40, 729).

imperfect knowledge of the end leads to the imperfect voluntary act, according as the agent apprehends the end, but does not deliberate, and is moved to the end at once. Therefore the voluntary act in its perfection belongs to none but the rational nature; but the imperfect voluntary act pertains to even irrational animals.

Reply Obj. 1. The will is the name of the rational appetite, and consequently it cannot be in things devoid of reason. But the word "voluntary" is derived from *voluntas* (will), and can be extended to those things in which there is some participation of will, by way of likeness. It is thus that voluntary action is attributed to irrational animals, in so far as they are moved to an end through some kind of knowledge.

Reply Obj. 2. The fact that man is master of his actions is due to his being able to deliberate about them, for since the deliberating reason is indifferently disposed to opposite things, the will can be inclined to either. But it is not thus that voluntariness is in irrational animals, as stated above.

Reply Obj. 3. Praise and blame are the result of the voluntary act, in which the perfect notion of voluntariness is to be found, such as is not to be found in irrational animals.

ARTICLE 3. *Whether There Can Be Voluntariness Without Any Act?*

We proceed thus to the Third Article: It seems that voluntariness cannot be without any act.

Objection 1. For that is voluntary which proceeds from the will. But nothing can proceed from the will except through some act, at least an act of the will. Therefore there cannot be voluntariness without act.

Obj. 2. Further, just as one is said to wish by an act of the will, so when the act of the will ceases, one is said not to wish. But not to wish causes involuntariness, which is opposed to voluntariness. Therefore there can be nothing voluntary when the act of the will ceases.

Obj. 3. Further, knowledge is essential to the voluntary, as stated above (AA. 1, 2). But knowledge involves an act. Therefore voluntariness cannot be without some act.

On the contrary, the word "voluntary" is applied to that of which we are masters. Now we are masters in respect of to act and not to act, to will and not to will. Therefore just as to act and to will are voluntary, so also are not to act and not to will.

I answer that, Voluntary is what proceeds from the will. Now one thing proceeds from another in two ways. First, directly, in which sense something proceeds from another inasmuch as this other acts; for instance, heating from heat. Secondly, indirectly in which sense something proceeds from another through this other not acting; thus the sinking of a ship is set down to the helmsman, from his having ceased to steer. But we must take note that the cause of what follows from want of action is not always the agent as not acting, but only then when the agent can and ought to act. For if the helmsman were unable to steer the ship, or if the ship's helm be not entrusted to him, the sinking of the ship would not be set down to him, although it might be due to his absence from the helm.

Since, then, the will by willing and acting, is able, and sometimes ought, to hinder not-willing and not-acting, this not-willing and not-acting is imputed to the will as though arising from it. And thus it is that we can have the voluntary without an act; sometimes without outward act, but with an interior act, for instance, when one wills not to act; and sometimes without even an interior act, as when one does not will to act.

Reply Obj. 1. We apply the word "voluntary" not only to that which proceeds from the will directly, as from its action, but also to that which proceeds from it indirectly as from its inaction.

Reply Obj. 2. "Not to wish" is said in two senses. First, as though it were one word, and the infinitive of "I-do-not-wish." Consequently just as when I say "I do not wish to read," the sense is, "I wish not to read," so "not to wish to read" is the same as "to wish not to read," and in this sense "not to wish" implies involuntariness. Secondly it is taken as a sentence, and then no act of the will is affirmed. And in this sense "not to wish" does not cause involuntariness.

Reply Obj. 3. Voluntariness requires an act of knowledge in the same way as it requires an act of will; namely, in order that it be in one's power to consider, to wish, and to act. And then, just as not to wish, and not to act, when it is time to wish and to act, is voluntary, so is it voluntary not to consider.

ARTICLE 4. *Whether Violence Can Be Done to the Will?*

We proceed thus to the Fourth Article: It seems that violence can be done to the will.

Objection 1. For everything can be compelled by that which is more powerful. But there is something, namely, God, that is more powerful than the human will. Therefore it can be compelled, at least by Him.

Obj. 2. Further, every passive subject is compelled by its active principle when it is changed by it. But the will is a passive force, "for it is a mover moved."[1] Therefore, since it is sometimes moved by its active principle, it seems that sometimes it is compelled.

Obj. 3. Further, violent movement is that which is contrary to nature. But the movement of the will is sometimes contrary to nature, as is clear of the will's movement to sin, which is contrary to nature, as Damascene says (*De Fide Orthod.* iv, 20).[2] Therefore the movement of the will can be compelled.

On the contrary, Augustine says[3] that what is done by the will is not done of necessity. Now, whatever is done under compulsion is done of necessity. Consequently what is done by the will cannot be compelled. Therefore the will cannot be compelled to act.

I answer that, The act of the will is twofold: one is its immediate act, as it were, elicited by it, namely, to wish; the other is an act of the will commanded by it, and put into execution by means of some other power, such as to walk and to speak, which are commanded by the will to be executed by means of the power of movement.

As regards the commanded acts of the will, then, the will can suffer violence, in so far as violence can prevent the exterior members from executing the will's command. But as to the will's own proper act, violence cannot be done to the will.

The reason of this is that the act of the will is nothing else than an inclination proceeding from the interior principle of knowledge, just as the natural appetite is an inclination proceeding from an interior principle without knowledge. Now what is compelled or violent is from an exterior principle. Consequently it is contrary to the notion of the will's own act that it should be subject to compulsion or violence, just as it is also contrary to the notion of the natural inclination or movement of a stone that it should be borne upwards. For a stone may have an upward movement from violence, but that this violent movement be from its natural inclination is impossible. In like manner a man may be dragged by force, but it is contrary to the very notion of violence that he be thus dragged of his own will.

[1] Aristotle, *Soul*, III, 10 (433^{a}9; ^{b}16).
[2] PG 94, 1196.   [3] *City of God*, V, 10 (PL 41, 152).

Reply Obj. 1. God Who is more powerful than the human will, can move the will of man, according to Prov. 21. 1: *The heart of the king is in the hand of the Lord; whithersoever He will He shall turn it.* But if this were by compulsion, it would no longer be by an act of the will, nor would the will itself be moved, but something else against the will.

Reply Obj. 2. It is not always a violent movement when a passive subject is changed by its active principle, but only when this is done against the interior inclination of the passive subject. Otherwise every alteration and generation of simple bodies would be unnatural and violent, whereas they are natural by reason of the natural interior aptitude of the matter or subject to such a disposition. In like manner when the will is moved according to its own inclination by the appetible object, this movement is not violent but voluntary.

Reply Obj. 3. That to which the will tends by sinning, although in reality, it is evil and contrary to the rational nature, nevertheless is apprehended as something good and suitable to nature in so far as it is suitable to man by reason of some pleasurable sensation or some corrupt habit.

Article 5. *Whether Violence Causes Involuntariness?*

We proceed thus to the Fifth Article: It seems that violence does not cause involuntariness.

Objection 1. For we speak of voluntariness and involuntariness in respect of the will. But violence cannot be done to the will, as shown above (A. 4). Therefore violence cannot cause involuntariness.

Obj. 2. Further, that which is done involuntarily is done with grief, as Damascene (*De Fide Orthod.* ii)[1] and the Philosopher[2] say. But sometimes a man suffers compulsion without being grieved thereby. Therefore violence does not cause involuntariness.

Obj. 3. Further, what is from the will cannot be involuntary. But some violent actions proceed from the will, for instance, when a man with a heavy body goes upwards, or when a man contorts his limbs in a way contrary to their natural flexibility. Therefore violence does not cause involuntariness.

On the contrary, The Philosopher[3] and Damascene (*loc. cit.*) say that "things done under compulsion are involuntary."

[1] Chap. 24 (PG 94, 953).
[2] *Ethics,* III, 1 (1111^{b}20).   [3] *Ibid.* (1109^{b}35).

I answer that, Violence is directly opposed to the voluntary, as likewise to the natural. For the voluntary and the natural have this in common, that both are from an intrinsic principle, whereas violence is from an extrinsic principle. And for this reason, just as in things devoid of knowledge, violence effects something against nature, so in things endowed with knowledge, it effects something against the will. Now that which is against nature is said to be unnatural; and in like manner that which is against the will is said to be involuntary. Therefore violence causes involuntariness.

Reply Obj. 1. The involuntary is opposed to the voluntary. Now it has been said (A. 4) that not only the act, which proceeds immediately from the will, is called voluntary, but also the act commanded by the will. Consequently, as to the act which proceeds immediately from the will, violence cannot be done to the will, as stated above (*ibid.*). But as to the commanded act, the will can suffer violence, and consequently in this respect violence causes involuntariness.

Reply Obj. 2. As that is said to be natural which is according to the inclination of nature, so that is said to be voluntary which is according to the inclination of the will. Now a thing is said to be natural in two ways. First, because it is from nature as from an active principle; thus it is natural for fire to produce heat. Secondly, according to a passive principle, because, namely, there is an innate inclination to receive an action from an extrinsic principle; thus the movement of the heavens is said to be natural by reason of the natural aptitude in a heavenly body to receive such movement, although the cause of that movement is a voluntary agent. In like manner an act is said to be voluntary in two ways. First, in regard to action, for instance, when one wishes to act; secondly, in regard to passion, as when one wishes to be acted upon by another. Hence when action is brought to bear on something by an extrinsic agent, as long as the will to suffer that action remains in the passive subject there is not violence absolutely, for although the patient does nothing by way of action, he does something by being willing to suffer. Consequently this cannot be called involuntary.

Reply Obj. 3. As the Philosopher says,[4] the movement of an animal by which at times an animal is moved against the natural inclination of the body, although it is not natural to the body, is nevertheless somewhat natural to the

[4] *Physics,* VIII, 4 (254^{b}14).

animal, to which it is natural to be moved according to its appetite. Accordingly this is violent not absolutely, but relatively. The same remark applies in the case of one who contorts his limbs in a way that is contrary to their natural disposition. For this is violent relatively, that is, as to that particular limb, but not absolutely, that is, as to the man himself.

ARTICLE 6. *Whether Fear Causes Involuntariness Simply?*

We proceed thus to the Sixth Article: It seems that fear causes involuntariness simply.

Objection 1. For just as is violence with respect to that which is contrary to the will at the time, so is fear with respect to a future evil which is contrary to the will. But violence causes involuntariness absolutely. Therefore fear too causes involuntariness absolutely.

Obj. 2. Further, that which is such of itself, remains such, whatever be added to it; thus what is hot of itself, as long as it remains, is still hot, whatever be added to it. But that which is done through fear is involuntary in itself. Therefore, even with the addition of fear, it is involuntary.

Obj. 3. Further, that which is such, subject to a condition, is such relatively; but what is such without any condition, is such absolutely; thus what is necessary, subject to a condition, is necessary relatively: but what is necessary absolutely, is necessary simply. But that which is done through fear is absolutely involuntary, and is not voluntary save under a condition, namely, in order that the evil feared may be avoided. Therefore that which is done through fear, is involuntary simply.

On the contrary, Gregory of Nyssa[1] and the Philosopher[2] say that such things as are done through fear are voluntary rather than involuntary.

I answer that, As the Philosopher says[3] and likewise Gregory of Nyssa in his book on Man (Nemesius, *loc. cit.*), such things as are done through fear are of a mixed character, being partly voluntary and partly involuntary. For that which is done through fear, considered in itself, is not voluntary; but it becomes voluntary in this particular case, in order, namely, to avoid the evil feared.

But if the matter be considered rightly, such things are voluntary rather than involuntary; for they are voluntary absolutely, but involuntary relatively. For a thing is said to be abso-

lutely, according as it is in act; but according as it is only in the apprehension, it is not absolutely, but relatively. Now that which is done through fear is in act in so far as it is done. For, since acts are concerned with singulars, and the singular, as such, is here and now, that which is done is in act, in so far as it is here and now and under other individuating circumstances. And that which is done through fear, is voluntary, in so far as it is here and now, that is to say, in so far as in this instance it hinders a greater evil which was feared; thus the throwing of the cargo into the sea becomes voluntary during the storm, through fear of the danger. And so it is clear that it is voluntary absolutely. And hence it is that what is done out of fear possesses the character of being voluntary, because its principle is within. But if we consider what is done through fear as being outside this particular case, and according as it is averse to the will, this is merely something existing in our reason. And consequently what is done through fear is involuntary, considered in that respect, that is to say, outside the actual circumstances of the case.

Reply Obj. 1. Things done through fear and compulsion differ not only according to present and future time, but also in this, that the will does not consent, but is moved entirely counter to that which is done through compulsion, whereas what is done through fear becomes voluntary because the will is moved towards it, although not for its own sake, but on account of something else, that is, in order to avoid an evil which is feared. For the conditions of a voluntary act are satisfied if it be done on account of something else voluntary, since the voluntary is not only what we will for its own sake, as an end, but also what we will for the sake of something else, as an end. It is clear therefore that in what is done from compulsion, the will does nothing inwardly; but in what is done through fear, the will does something. Accordingly, as Gregory of Nyssa (Nemesius, *loc. cit.*) says, in order to exclude things done through fear, a violent action is defined as not only one, "the principle of which is from without," but with the addition, "in which he that suffers violence in no way concurs," because the will of him that is in fear does concur somewhat in that which he does through fear.

Reply Obj. 2. Things that are such absolutely remain such, whatever be added to them, for instance, a cold thing, or a white thing; but things that are such relatively, vary according as they are compared with different things. For what is

[1] Nemesius, *De Nat. Hom.*, xxx (PG 40, 721).
[2] *Ethics*, III, 1 (1110ᵇ12).   [3] *Ibid.*

big in comparison with one thing is small in comparison with another. Now a thing is said to be voluntary, not only for its own sake, as it were absolutely, but also for the sake of something else, as it were relatively. Accordingly, nothing prevents a thing which was not voluntary in comparison with one thing from becoming voluntary when compared with another.

Reply Obj. 3. That which is done through fear is voluntary without any condition, that is to say, according as it is actually done; but it is involuntary under a certain condition, that is, if such a fear were not threatening. Consequently, this argument proves rather the opposite.

ARTICLE 7. *Whether Concupiscence Causes Involuntariness?*

We proceed thus to the Seventh Article: It would seem that concupiscence causes involuntariness.

Objection 1. For just as fear is a passion, so is concupiscence. But fear causes involuntariness to a certain extent. Therefore concupiscence does so too.

Obj. 2. Further, just as the timid man through fear acts counter to that which he proposed, so does the incontinent, through concupiscence. But fear causes involuntariness to a certain extent. Therefore concupiscence does so also.

Obj. 3. Further, knowledge is necessary for voluntariness. But concupiscence impairs knowledge; for the Philosopher says[1] that delight, or the lust of pleasure, destroys the judgment of prudence. Therefore concupiscence causes involuntariness.

On the contrary, Damascene says (*De Fide Orthod.* ii, 24):[2] "The involuntary act deserves mercy or indulgence, and is done with regret." But neither of these can be said of that which is done out of concupiscence. Therefore concupiscence does not cause involuntariness.

I answer that, Concupiscence does not cause involuntariness, but rather makes something to be voluntary. For a thing is said to be voluntary from the fact that the will is moved to it. Now concupiscence inclines the will to desire the object of concupiscence. Therefore the effect of concupiscence is to make something to be voluntary rather than involuntary.

Reply Obj. 1. Fear regards evil, but concupiscence regards good. Now evil of itself is counter to the will, whereas good harmonizes with the will. Therefore fear is more inclined than concupiscence to cause involuntariness.

Reply Obj. 2. He who acts from fear remains

¹ *Ethics,* VI, 5 (1140ᵇ12).   ² PG 94, 953.

averse in his will to that which he does, considered in itself. But he that acts from concupiscence, for example, an incontinent man, does not retain his former will whereby he repudiated the object of his concupiscence; for his will is changed, so that he desires that which previously he repudiated. Accordingly, that which is done out of fear is involuntary to a certain extent, but that which is done from concupiscence is in no way involuntary. For the man who yields to concupiscence acts counter to that which he purposed at first, but not counter to that which he desires now; but the timid man acts counter to that which in itself he desires now.

Reply Obj. 3. If concupiscence were to destroy knowledge altogether, as happens with those whom concupiscence has rendered mad, it would follow that concupiscence would take away voluntariness. And yet, properly speaking, it would not result in the act being involuntary, because in things bereft of reason, there is neither voluntary nor involuntary. But sometimes in those actions which are done from concupiscence, knowledge is not completely destroyed, because the power of knowing is not taken away entirely, but only the actual consideration in some particular possible act. Nevertheless, this itself is voluntary, according as by voluntary we mean that which is in the power of the will, as not to act and not to will, and in like manner not to consider; for the will can resist the passion, as we shall state later on (Q. X, A. 3; Q. LXXVII, A. 7).

ARTICLE 8. *Whether Ignorance Causes Involuntariness?*

We proceed thus to the Eighth Article: It seems that ignorance does not cause involuntariness.

Objection 1. For the "involuntary act deserves pardon," as Damascene says (*De Fide Orthod.* ii, 24).[3] But sometimes that which is done through ignorance does not deserve pardon, according to I Cor. 14. 38: *If any man know not, he shall not be known.* Therefore ignorance does not cause involuntariness.

Obj. 2. Further, every sin implies ignorance, according to Prov. 14. 22: *They err, that work evil.* If, therefore, ignorance causes involuntariness, it would follow that every sin is involuntary, which is opposed to the saying of Augustine, that "every sin is voluntary" (*De Vera Relig.* xiv).[4]

Obj. 3. Further, "involuntariness is not without sadness," as Damascene says (*loc. cit.*).

³ PG 94, 953.   ⁴ PL 34, 133.

But some things are done out of ignorance, but without sadness; for instance, a man may kill a foe, whom he wishes to kill, thinking at the time that he is killing a stag. Therefore ignorance does not cause involuntariness.

On the contrary, Damascene (*loc. cit.*) and the Philosopher[1] say that "what is done through ignorance is involuntary."

I answer that, Ignorance causes involuntariness, by the very fact that it excludes knowledge, which is a necessary condition of voluntariness, as was declared above (A. 1). But not every kind of ignorance deprives one of this knowledge. Accordingly, we must take note that ignorance has a threefold relationship to the act of the will: in one way, concomitantly; in another, consequently; in a third way, antecedently. Ignorance is concomitant to the act when a person is ignorant of what he is doing but would do it just the same if he knew. For then, ignorance does not induce one to wish this to be done, but it just happens that a thing is at the same time done and not known; thus in the example given (obj. 3) a man did indeed wish to kill his foe, but killed him in ignorance, thinking to kill a stag. And ignorance of this kind, as the Philosopher states,[2] does not cause involuntariness, since it is not the cause of anything that is averse to the will; but it causes non-voluntariness, since that which is unknown cannot be actually willed.

Ignorance is consequent to the act of the will in so far as ignorance itself is voluntary and this happens in two ways, in accordance with the two kinds of voluntary acts mentioned above. (A. 3). First, because the act of the will is brought to bear on the ignorance, as when a man wishes not to know, that he may have an excuse for sin, or that he may not be withheld from sin, according to Job 21.14: *We desire not the knowledge of Thy ways.* And this is called "affected ignorance." Secondly, ignorance is said to be voluntary with respect to that which one can and ought to know, for in this sense not to act and not to will are said to be voluntary, as stated above (A. 3). And ignorance of this kind happens either when one does not actually consider what one can and ought to consider, which is called "ignorance of evil choice," and arises from some passion or habit; or it happens when one does not take the trouble to acquire the knowledge which one ought to have in which sense, ignorance of the general principles of law, which one ought to know, is voluntary, as being

due to negligence. Accordingly if, in either of these ways, ignorance is voluntary, it cannot cause involuntariness simply. Nevertheless, it causes involuntariness relatively, since it precedes the movement of the will towards the act, which movement would not be, if there were knowledge.

Ignorance is antecedent to the act of the will when it is not voluntary, and yet is the cause of man's willing what he would not will otherwise. Thus a man may be ignorant of some circumstance of his act which he was not bound to know, the result being that he does that which he would not do if he knew of that circumstance; for instance, a man, after taking proper precaution, may not know that someone is coming along the road, so that he shoots an arrow and slays a passer-by. Such ignorance causes involuntariness absolutely.

From this may be gathered the *solution of the objections.* For the first objection deals with ignorance of what a man is bound to know. The second, with ignorance of choice, which is voluntary to a certain extent, as stated above. The third, of that ignorance which is concomitant with the act of the will.

QUESTION VII
OF THE CIRCUMSTANCES OF HUMAN ACTS
(In Four Articles)

WE must now consider the circumstances of human acts, under which head there are four points of inquiry: (1) What is a circumstance? (2) Whether a theologian should take note of the circumstances of human acts? (3) How many circumstances are there? (4) Which are the most important of them?

ARTICLE 1. *Whether a Circumstance Is an Accident of a Human Act?*

We proceed thus to the First Article: It would seem that a circumstance is not an accident of a human act.

Objection 1. For Tully says (*De Invent. Rhetor.* i)[3] that a circumstance is that from which an orator adds authority and strength to his argument. But oratorical arguments are derived principally from things pertaining to the substance of a thing, such as the definition, the genus, the species, and the like, from which also Tully declares that an orator should draw his arguments.[4] Therefore a circumstance is not an accident of a human act.

---

[1] *Ethics,* III, 1 (1110ᵃ1).
[2] *Ibid.* (1110ᵇ25).
[3] Chap. 17 (DD I, 99).
[4] *Top.,* III (DD I, 491).

Obj. 2. Further, "to be in" is proper to an accident. But that which surrounds (*circumstat*) is rather out than in. Therefore the circumstances are not accidents of human acts.

Obj. 3. Further, an accident has no accident. But human acts themselves are accidents. Therefore the circumstances are not accidents of acts.

On the contrary, The particular conditions of any singular thing are called its individuating accidents. But the Philosopher calls the circumstances particular things, *i.e.,* the particular conditions of each act.[1] Therefore the circumstances are individual accidents of human acts.

I answer that, Since, according to the Philosopher,[2] words are the signs of what we understand, it must be that in naming things we follow the process of intellectual knowledge. Now our intellectual knowledge proceeds from the better known to the less known. Accordingly with us, names of more known things are transferred so as to signify things less known; and hence it is that, as stated in the *Metaphysics*,[3] the notion of distance has been transferred from things that are apart locally, to all kinds of opposition, and in like manner words that signify local movement are employed to designate all other movements, because bodies which are circumscribed by place, are best known to us. And hence it is that the word "circumstance" has passed from things in place to human acts.

Now in things in place, that is said to surround something which is outside it, but touches it, or is near to it in place. Accordingly, whatever conditions are outside the substance of an act and yet in some way touch the human act are called circumstances. Now what is outside a thing's substance but pertains to that thing, is called its accident. Therefore the circumstances of human acts should be called their accidents.

Reply Obj. 1. The orator gives strength to his argument, in the first place, from the substance of the act, and, secondly, from the circumstances of the act. Thus a man becomes indictable, first, through being guilty of murder; secondly, through having done it deceitfully, or from motives of greed, or at a holy time or place, and so forth. And so in the passage quoted, it is said pointedly that the orator "adds strength to his argument," as though this were something secondary.

Reply Obj. 2. A thing is said to be an accident of something in two ways. First, from being in

that thing; thus, whiteness is said to be an accident of Socrates. Secondly, because it is together with that thing in the same subject; thus, whiteness is an accident of music, in so far as they meet in the same subject, so as to touch one another, as it were. And in this sense circumstances are said to be the accidents of human acts.

Reply Obj. 3. As stated above (reply 2), an accident is said to be the accident of an accident, from the fact that they meet in the same subject. But this happens in two ways. First, in so far as two accidents are both related to the same subject without any relation to one another, as whiteness and music in Socrates. Secondly, when such accidents are related to one another, as when the subject receives one accident by means of the other; for instance, a body receives colour by means of its surface. And in this way also one accident is said to be in another; for we speak of colour as being in the surface.

Accordingly, circumstances are related to acts in both these ways. For some circumstances that have a relation to acts pertain to the agent otherwise than through the act, such as place and condition of person; but others belong to the agent by reason of the act, as for example the manner in which the act is done.

ARTICLE 2. *Whether Theologians Should Take Note of the Circumstances of Human Acts?*

We proceed thus to the Second Article: It seems that theologians should not take note of the circumstances of human acts.

Objection 1. Because theologians do not consider human acts otherwise than according to their quality of good or evil. But it seems that circumstances cannot give quality to human acts, for a thing is never qualified, formally speaking, by that which is outside it, but by that which is in it. Therefore theologians should not take note of the circumstances of acts.

Obj. 2. Further, circumstances are the accidents of acts. But one thing may be subject to an infinity of accidents; hence the Philosopher says[4] that "no art or science considers accidental being," except the art of sophistry. Therefore the theologian has not to consider circumstances.

Obj. 3. Further, the consideration of circumstances belongs to the rhetorician. But rhetoric is not a part of theology. Therefore it is not a theologian's business to consider circumstances.

On the contrary, Ignorance of circumstances

---

[1] *Ethics,* III, I (1110b33).
[2] *Interpretation,* I (16a3).
[3] Aristotle, X, 4 (1055a9).

[4] *Metaphysics,* VI, 2 (1026b3).

causes an act to be involuntary, according to Damascene (*De Fide Orthod.* ii)[1] and Gregory of Nyssa (Nemesius,—*De Nat. Hom.* xxxi).[2] But involuntariness excuses from sin, the consideration of which belongs to the theologian. Therefore circumstances also should be considered by the theologian.

I answer that, Circumstances come under the consideration of the theologians for a threefold reason. First, because the theologian considers human acts in so far as man is thereby ordered to Happiness. Now, everything that is ordered to an end should be proportionate to that end. But acts are made proportionate to an end by means of a certain commensurateness, which results from the due circumstances. Hence the theologian has to consider the circumstances. Secondly, because the theologian considers human acts according as they are found to be good or evil, better or worse, and this diversity depends on circumstances, as we shall see further on (Q. XVIII, AA. 10, 11; Q. LXXIII, A. 7). Thirdly, because the theologian considers human acts under the aspect of merit and demerit, which is proper to human acts; and for this it is requisite that they be voluntary. Now a human act is judged to be voluntary or involuntary according to knowledge or ignorance of circumstances, as stated above (cf. Q. VI, A. 8). Therefore the theologian has to consider circumstances.

Reply Obj. 1. Good ordered to the end is said to be useful, and this implies some kind of relation; therefore the Philosopher says[3] that "good in relation to something, is the useful." Now, in the genus "relation" a thing is denominated not only according to that which is inherent in the thing, but also according to that which is extrinsic to it, as may be seen in the expressions right and left, equal and unequal, and the like. Accordingly, since the goodness of acts consists in their usefulness to the end, nothing hinders their being called good or bad according to their proportion to extrinsic things adjacent to them.

Reply Obj. 2. Accidents which are altogether accidental are neglected by every art, by reason of their uncertainty and infinity. But accidents of this kind are not what we call circumstances, because circumstances, although, as stated above (A. 1), they are extrinsic to the act, nevertheless are in a kind of contact with it, by being related to it. Proper accidents, however, come under the consideration of art.

Reply Obj. 3. The consideration of circum-

stances belongs to the moralist, the politician, and the rhetorician. To the moralist, in so far as with respect to circumstances we find or lose the mean of virtue in human acts and passions. To the politician and to the rhetorician, in so far as circumstances make acts to be worthy of praise or blame, of excuse or indictment. In different ways, however, because where the rhetorician persuades, the politician judges. To the theologian this consideration belongs in all the ways mentioned, since to him all the other arts are subservient; for he has to consider virtuous and vicious acts, just as the moralist does, and with the rhetorician and politician he considers acts according as they are deserving of reward or punishment.

ARTICLE 3. *Whether the Circumstances Are Properly Set Forth in the Third Book of Ethics?*

We proceed thus to the Third Article: It would seem that the circumstances are not properly set forth in the *Ethics*.[4]

Objection 1. For a circumstance of an act is described as something outside the act. Now time and place answer to this description. Therefore there are only two circumstances, namely, when and where.

Obj. 2. Further, we judge from the circumstances whether a thing is well or ill done. But this belongs to the mode of an act. Therefore all the circumstances are included under one, which is the mode of acting.

Obj. 3. Further, circumstances are not part of the substance of an act. But the causes of an act seem to belong to its substance. Therefore no circumstance should be taken from the cause of the act itself. Accordingly, neither "who," nor "why," nor "about what," are circumstances, since "who" refers to the efficient cause, "why" to the final cause, and "about what" to the material cause.

On the contrary is the authority of the Philosopher in the *Ethics*.[5]

I answer that, Tully, in his Rhetoric (*De Invent. Rhetor.* i),[6] gives seven circumstances, which are contained in this verse:

Quis, quid, ubi, quibus auxiliis, cur, quomodo, quando—

Who, what, where, by what aids, why, how, and when.

For in acts we must take note of who did it, by what aids or instruments he did it, what he did, where he did it, why he did it, how and when he did it. But Aristotle in the *Ethics*[7]

---

[1] Chap. 24 (PG 94, 953).   [2] PG 40, 724.
[3] *Ethics*, I, 6 (1096ª26).

[4] Aristotle, III, 1 (1111ª3).   [5] III, 1 (1111ª3).
[6] Chap. 24 (DD I, 104).   [7] *Loc. Cit.*

added yet another, namely, about what, which Tully included in the circumstance what.

The reason of this enumeration may be set down as follows. For a circumstance is described as something outside the substance of the act, and yet in a way touching it. Now this happens in three ways: first, in so far as it touches the act itself; secondly, in so far as it touches the cause of the act; thirdly, in so far as it touches the effect. It touches the act itself either by way of measure, as time and place, or by way of qualifying the act, as the mode of acting. It touches the effect when we consider what is done. It touches the cause of the act, as to the final cause, by the circumstance why; as to the material cause, or object, in the circumstance about what; as to the principal efficient cause, in the circumstance who; and as to the instrumental agent cause, in the circumstance by what aids.

Reply Obj. 1. Time and place surround (*circumstant*) the act by way of measure, but the others surround the act by touching it in any other way, while at the same time they are extrinsic to the substance of the act.

Reply Obj. 2. This mode "well" or "ill" is not a circumstance, but results from all the circumstances. But the mode which pertains to a quality of the act is a special circumstance; for instance, that a man walk fast or slowly, that he strike hard or gently, and so forth.

Reply Obj. 3. A condition of the cause, on which the substance of the act depends, is not a circumstance but an additional condition. Thus, in regard to the object, it is not a circumstance of theft that the object is another's property, for this belongs to the substance of the act, but that it be great or small. And the same applies to the other causes. For the end that specifies the act is not a circumstance, but some additional end. Thus, that a valiant man act valiantly for the sake of the good of the virtue of fortitude is not a circumstance, but rather if he act valiantly for the sake of the delivery of the state, or of Christendom, or some such purpose. The same is to be said with regard to the circumstance what; for that a man by pouring water on someone should happen to wash him is not a circumstance of the washing, but that in doing so he give him a chill, or scald him, heal him or harm him, these are circumstances.

ARTICLE 4. *Whether the Most Important Circumstances Are "Why" and "In What the Act Consists?"*

We proceed thus to the Fourth Article: It would seem that these are not the most impor-

tant circumstances, namely, "why" and those "in which the act is," as stated in the *Ethics*.[1]

Objection 1. For those "in which the act is" seem to be place and time, and these do not seem to be the most important of the circumstances, since, of them all, they are the most extrinsic to the act. Therefore "those things in which the act is" are not the most important circumstances.

Obj. 2. Further, the end of a thing is extrinsic to it. Therefore it is not the most important circumstance.

Obj. 3. Further, that which holds the foremost place in regard to each thing is its cause and its form. But the cause of an act is the person that does it, while the form of an act is the manner in which it is done. Therefore these two circumstances seem to be of the greatest importance.

On the contrary, Gregory of Nyssa[2] says that "the most important circumstances are why it is done and what is done."

I answer that, As stated above (Q. I, A. I), acts are properly called human according as they are voluntary. Now, the motive and object of the will is the end. Therefore that circumstance is the most important of all which touches the act on the part of the end, namely, the circumstance "why"; and the second in importance is that which touches the very substance of the act, namely, the circumstance "what he did." As to the other circumstances, they are more or less important according as they more or less approach to these.

Reply Obj. 1. By those things "in which the act is" the Philosopher does not mean time and place, but those circumstances that are joined to the act itself. Therefore Gregory of Nyssa, as though he were explaining the dictum of the Philosopher, instead of the latter's term,—"in which the act is," said, "what is done."

Reply Obj. 2. Although the end is not part of the substance of the act, yet it is the most important cause of the act, since it moves the agent to act. Therefore the moral act is specified chiefly by the end.

Reply Obj. 3. The person that does the act is the cause of that act in so far as he is moved to it by the end; and it is chiefly in this respect that he is ordered to the act; but the other conditions of the person have not such an important relation to the act. As to the mode, it is not the substantial form of the act, for in an act the

[1] Aristotle, III, I (1111ª18).
[2] Nemesius, *De Nat. Hom.*, XXXI (PG 40, 728).

substantial form depends on the object and term or end; but it is, as it were, a certain accidental quality of the act.

QUESTION VIII

OF THE WILL, IN REGARD TO WHAT IT WILLS

(In Three Articles)

WE must now consider the different acts of the will; and in the first place, those acts which belong to the will itself immediately, as being elicited by the will; secondly, those acts which are commanded by the will (Q. XVII).

Now the will is moved to the end, and to the means to the end. We must therefore consider (1) Those acts of the will by which it is moved to the end; and (2) those whereby it is moved to the means (Q. XIII). And since it seems that there are three acts of the will in reference to the end; namely, volition, enjoyment, and intention, we must consider (1) Volition; (2) enjoyment (Q. XI); (3) intention (Q. XII).—Concerning the first, three things must be considered: (1) Of what things is the will? (2) By what is the will moved (Q. IX)? (3) How is it moved (Q. X)?

Under the first head there are three points of inquiry: (1) Whether the will is of good only? (2) Whether it is of the end only, or also of the means? (3) If in any way it is of the means, whether it is moved to the end and to the means by the one movement?

ARTICLE 1. *Whether the Will Is of Good Only?*

We proceed thus to the First Article: It seems that the will is not of good only.

Objection 1. For the same power regards opposites; for instance, sight regards white and black. But good and evil are opposites. Therefore the will is not only of good, but also of evil.

Obj. 2. Further, rational powers can be directed to opposite purposes, according to the Philosopher.[1] But the will is a rational power, since it is "in the reason," as is stated in the book of the *Soul*.[2] Therefore the will can be directed to opposites. And consequently its volition is not confined to good, but extends to evil.

Obj. 3. Further, good and being are convertible. But will is directed not only to beings, but also to non-beings. For sometimes we will not

[1] *Metaphysics*, IX, 2 (1046ᵇ8).
[2] Aristotle, III, 9 (432ᵇ5).

to walk, or not to speak; and again at times we will future things, which are not actual beings. Therefore the will is not of good only.

On the contrary, Dionysius says (*Div. Nom.* iv)[3] that "evil is outside the scope of the will," and that "all things desire good."[4]

I answer that, The will is a rational appetite. Now every appetite is only of something good. The reason of this is that the appetite is nothing else than an inclination of a person desirous of a thing towards that thing. Now every inclination is to something like and suitable to the thing inclined. Since, therefore, everything, in so far as it is being and substance, is a good, it must be that every inclination is to something good. And hence it is that the Philosopher says[5] that "the good is that which all desire."

But it must be noted that since every inclination follows from a form, the natural appetite results from a form existing in nature, while the sensitive appetite, as also the intellectual or rational appetite, which we call the will, follows from an apprehended form. Therefore, just as the natural appetite tends to good existing in a thing, so the animal or voluntary appetite tends to a good which is apprehended. Consequently, in order that the will tend to anything, it is requisite, not that this be good in very truth, but that it be apprehended under the aspect of good. Therefore the Philosopher says[6] that "the end is a good, or an apparent good."

Reply Obj. 1. The same power regards opposites, but it is not referred to them in the same way. Accordingly, the will is referred both to good and to evil, but to good, by desiring it, to evil by shunning it. Therefore the actual desire of good is called "volition,"[7] meaning thereby the act of the will; for it is in this sense that we are now speaking of the will. On the other hand, the shunning of evil is better described as "nolition." Therefore, just as volition is of good, so nolition is of evil.

Reply Obj. 2. A rational power is not directed to any opposite whatsoever, but to those which are contained under its proper object, for no power seeks other than its proper object. Now, the object of the will is good. And so the will can be directed to such opposites as are contained under good, such as to be moved, or to be at rest, to speak or to be silent, and the like, for the will can be directed to either under the aspect of good.

[3] Sect. 32 (PG 3, 732).   [4] Sect. 10 (PG 3, 708).
[5] *Ethics*, I, 1 (1094ᵃ3).   [6] *Physics*, II, 3 (195ᵃ26).
[7] In Latin,—*voluntas*. To avoid confusion with *voluntas* (the will) St. Thomas adds a word of explanation, which in the translation may appear superfluous.

Reply Obj. 3. That which is not a being in nature is considered as a being in the reason, and thus negations and privations are said to be "beings of reason." In this way, too, future things, in so far as they are apprehended, are beings. Accordingly, in so far as things of this kind are beings, they are apprehended under the aspect of good; and it is thus that the will is directed to them. Therefore the Philosopher says[1] that to lack evil has the nature of a good.

ARTICLE 2. *Whether Volition Is of the End Only, or Also of the Means?*

We proceed thus to the Second Article: It seems that volition is not of the means, but of the end only.

Objection 1. For the Philosopher says[2] that "volition is of the end, while choice is of the means."

Obj. 2. Further, "For objects differing in genus there are corresponding different powers of the soul."[3] Now, the end and the means are in different genera of good, because the end, which is either the virtuous good (*bonum honestum*) or the good of pleasure, is in the genus quality, or action, or passion; but "the good which is useful, and is directed to an end, is in the genus relation."[4] Therefore, if volition is of the end, it is not of the means.

Obj. 3. Further, habits are proportionate to powers, since they are perfections of them. But in those habits which are called practical arts, the end belongs to one, and the means to another art; thus the use of a ship, which is its end, belongs to the (art of the) helmsman; but the building of the ship, which is directed to the end, belongs to the art of the shipwright. Therefore, since volition is of the end, it is not of the means.

On the contrary, In natural things, a thing passes through the middle space and arrives at the term by the same power. But the means are a kind of middle space, through which one arrives at the end or term. Therefore, if volition is of the end, it is also of the means.

I answer that, The word *voluntas* sometimes designates the power of the will, sometimes its act.[5] Accordingly, if we speak of the will as a power, it extends both to the end and to the means. For every power extends to those things in which may be found the nature of its object in any way whatever; thus the sight extends to all things whatsoever that are in

any way coloured. Now the aspect of good, which is the object of the power of will, may be found not only in the end but also in the means.

If, however, we speak of the will in regard to its act, then, properly speaking, volition is of the end only. Because every act denominated from a power designates the simple act of that power; thus to understand designates the simple act of the understanding. Now the simple act of a power is directed towards what is in itself the object of that power. But that which is good and willed for itself is the end. Therefore volition, properly speaking, is of the end itself. On the other hand, the means are good and willed not for themselves, but as related to the end. Therefore the will is directed to them only in so far as it is directed to the end, so that what it wills in them is the end. Thus, to understand, is properly directed to things that are known in themselves, that is, principles; but we do not speak of understanding with regard to things known through principles except is so far as we see the principles in those things. "For in morals the end is what principles are in speculative science."[6]

Reply Obj. 1. The Philosopher is speaking of the will in reference to the simple act of the will, not in reference to the power of the will.

Reply Obj. 2. There are different powers for objects that differ in genus and are of equal degree; for instance, sound and colour are different genera of sensibles, to which are referred hearing and sight. But the useful and the virtuous are related to one another not in an equal degree, but as that which is of itself, and that which is in relation to another. Now objects of this kind are always referred to the same power; for instance, the power of sight perceives both colour and light by which colour is seen.

Reply Obj. 3. Not everything that diversifies habits diversifies the powers, since habits are certain determinations of powers to certain special acts. Moreover, every practical art considers both the end and the means. For the art of the helmsman does indeed consider the end, as that which it effects; and the means, as that which it commands. On the other hand, the shipbuilding art considers the means as that which it effects; but it considers that which is the end, as that to which it orders what it effects. And again, in every practical art there is an end proper to it, and means that belong properly to that art.

---

[1] *Ethics*, v, 1 (1129b8).   [2] *Ibid.*, iii, 2 (1111b26).
[3] *Ibid.*, vi, 1 (1139a8).   [4] *Ibid.*, i, 6 (1096a26).
[5] Cf. A. 1, note.
[6] Cf. Aristotle, *Ethics*, vii, 8 (1151a16).

ARTICLE 3. *Whether the Will Is Moved by the Same Act to the End and to the Means?*

We proceed thus to the Third Article: It would seem that the will is moved by the same act, to the end and to the means.

Objection 1. Because according to the Philosopher,[1] "where one thing is on account of another there is only one." But the will does not will the means save on account of the end. Therefore it is moved to both by the same act.

Obj. 2. Further, the end is the reason for willing the means, just as light is the reason of seeing colours. But light and colours are seen by the same act. Therefore the movement of the will, whereby it wills the end and the means is one and the same.

Obj. 3. Further, the movement which tends through the middle space to the term is one and the same natural movement. But the means are related to the end as the middle space is to the term. Therefore the movement of the will whereby it is directed to the end and to the means is one and the same.

On the contrary, Acts are diversified according to their objects. But the end is a different species of good from the means, which are a useful good. Therefore the will is not moved to both by the same act.

I answer that, Since the end is willed in itself, whereas the means, as such, are only willed for the end, it is evident that the will can be moved to the end, as such, without being moved to the means; but it cannot be moved to the means, as such, unless it is moved to the end. Accordingly the will is moved to the end in two ways: first, to the end absolutely and in itself; secondly, as the reason for willing the means. Hence it is evident that the will is moved by one and the same movement,—to the end, as the reason for willing the means, and to the means themselves. But the act whereby the will is moved to the end absolutely is another act. And sometimes this act precedes the other in time; for example, when a man first wills to have health, and afterwards, deliberating by what means to be healed, wills to send for the doctor to heal him. The same happens in regard to the intellect: for at first a man understands the principles in themselves; but afterwards he understands them in the conclusions, according as he assents to the conclusions on account of the principles.

Reply Obj. 1. This argument holds in respect of the will being moved to the end as the reason for willing the means.

---
[1] *Topics*, III, 2 (117ᵃ18).

Reply Obj. 2. Whenever colour is seen, by the same act the light is seen; but the light can be seen without the colour being seen. In like manner whenever a man wills the means, by the same act he wills the end; but not conversely.

Reply Obj. 3. In the execution of a work, the means are as the middle-space, and the end, as the term. Therefore just as natural movement sometimes stops in the middle and does not reach the term, so sometimes one is busy with the means, without gaining the end. But in willing it is the reverse, for the will through (willing) the end comes to will the means, just as the intellect arrives at the conclusions through the principles which are called means. Hence it is that sometimes the intellect understands a mean and does not proceed from it to the conclusion. And in like manner the will sometimes wills the end and yet does not proceed to will the means.

The solution to the argument in the contrary sense is clear from what has been said above (A. 2 Ans. 2). For the useful and the virtuous are not species of good in an equal degree, but are as that which is for its own sake and that which is for the sake of something else; and so the act of the will can be directed to one and not to the other, but not conversely.

QUESTION IX

Of what moves the will

(*In Six Articles*)

We must now consider what moves the will, and under this head there are six points of inquiry: (1) Whether the will is moved by the intellect? (2) Whether it is moved by the sensitive appetite? (3) Whether the will moves itself? (4) Whether it is moved by an intrinsic principle? (5) Whether it is moved by a heavenly body? (6) Whether the will is moved by God alone as by an extrinsic principle?

ARTICLE 1. *Whether the Will Is Moved by the Intellect?*

We proceed thus to the First Article: It would seem that the will is not moved by the intellect.

Objection 1. For Augustine says on Ps. 118. 20:[2] *My soul hath coveted to long for Thy justifications*, "The intellect flies ahead, the desire follows sluggishly or not at all; we know what is good, but deeds delight us not." But it would not be so, if the will were moved by the intellect, because movement of the moveable results

---
[2] *Enarr. in Ps.*, Serm. 8 (PL 37, 1552).

from motion of the mover. Therefore the intellect does not move the will.

Obj. 2. Further, the intellect in presenting the desirable thing to the will stands in relation to the will as the imagination in representing the desirable thing to the sensitive appetite. But the imagination, in presenting the desirable thing, does not move the sensitive appetite; indeed sometimes our imagination affects us no more than what is set before us in a picture, and moves us not at all.[1] Therefore neither does the intellect move the will.

Obj. 3. Further, the same is not mover and moved in respect of the same thing. But the will moves the intellect, for we use our intellect when we will. Therefore the intellect does not move the will.

On the contrary, The Philosopher says[2] that the desirable thing is "a mover not moved," but the will is "a mover moved."

I answer that, A thing requires to be moved by something in so far as it is in potency to several things; for that which is in potency must be reduced to act by something actual, and to do this is to move. Now a power of the soul is seen to be in potency to different things in two ways: first, with regard to acting and not acting; secondly, with regard to this or that action. Thus the sight sometimes sees actually, and sometimes does not see; and sometimes it sees white, and sometimes black. It needs a mover therefore in two respects: namely, as to the exercise or use of the act, and as to the determination of the act. The first of these is on the part of the subject, which is sometimes acting, sometimes not acting, while the other is on the part of the object, by reason of which the act is specified.

The motion of the subject itself is due to some agent. And since every agent acts for an end, as was shown above (Q. I, A. 2), the principle of this motion lies in the end. And hence it is that the art which is concerned with the end, by its command moves the art which is concerned with the means, " just as the art of sailing commands the art of shipbuilding."[3] Now good in general, which has the nature of an end, is the object of the will. Consequently, in this respect, the will moves the other powers of the soul to their acts, for we make use of the other powers when we will. For the end and perfection of every other power is included under the object of the will as some particular good, and always the act or power to which the universal

end belongs moves to their acts the acts or powers to which belong the particular ends included in the universal end. Thus the leader of an army, who intends the common good—that is, the order of the whole army—by his command moves one of the captains, who intends the order of one company.

On the other hand, the object moves by determining the act, after the manner of a formal principle, by which in natural things actions are specified, as heating by heat. Now the first formal principle is universal being and truth, which is the object of the intellect. And therefore by this kind of motion the intellect moves the will, as presenting its object to it.

Reply Obj. 1. The passage quoted proves not that the intellect does not move, but that it does not move of necessity.

Reply Obj. 2. Just as the imagination of a form without estimation of fitness or harmfulness does not move the sensitive appetite, so neither does the apprehension of the true without the aspect of goodness and desirability. Hence it is not the speculative intellect that moves, but the practical intellect.[4]

Reply Obj. 3. The will moves the intellect as to the exercise of its act, since even the true itself which is the perfection of the intellect is included in the universal good, as a particular good. But as to the determination of the act, which the act derives from the object, the intellect moves the will, since the good itself is apprehended under a special aspect as contained in the universal true. It is therefore evident that the same is not mover and moved in the same respect.

ARTICLE 2. *Whether the Will Is Moved by the Sensitive Appetite?*

We proceed thus to the Second Article: It would seem that the will cannot be moved by the sensitive appetite.

Objection 1. For "to move and to act is more excellent than to be passive," as Augustine says (*Gen. ad lit.* xii, 16).[5] But the sensitive appetite is less excellent than the will which is the intellectual appetite, just as sense is less excellent than intellect. Therefore the sensitive appetite does not move the will.

Obj. 2. Further, no particular power can produce a universal effect. But the sensitive appetite is a particular power, because it follows the particular apprehension of sense. Therefore it cannot cause the movement of the will, which

---

[1] *Soul,* III, 3 (427[b]23).   [2] *Ibid.,* III, 6 (433[b]10).
[3] *Physics,* II, 2 (194[b]5).

[4] *Soul,* III, 9 (432[b]26); III, 10 (433[a]17).
[5] PL 34, 467.

movement is universal, as following the universal apprehension of the intellect.

Obj. 3. Further, as is proved in the *Physics*,[1] the mover is not moved by that which it moves, in such a way that there be reciprocal motion. But the will moves the sensitive appetite, in so far as the sensitive appetite obeys the reason. Therefore the sensitive appetite does not move the will.

On the contrary, It is written (James 1. 14): *Every man is tempted by his own concupiscence, being drawn away and allured.* But man would not be drawn away by his concupiscence unless his will were moved by the sensitive appetite, in which concupiscence resides. Therefore the sensitive appetite moves the will.

I answer that, As stated above (A. 1), that which is apprehended under the aspect of good and fitting moves the will by way of object. Now, that a thing appear to be good and fitting, happens from two causes: namely, from the condition either of the thing proposed, or of the one to whom it is proposed. But fitness is spoken of by way of relation; and so it depends on both extremes. And hence it is that taste, according as it is variously disposed, takes to a thing in various ways, as being fitting or unfitting. Therefore as the Philosopher says,[2] "According as a man is, such does the end seem to him."

Now it is evident that man is changed to a certain disposition according to a passion of the sensitive appetite. Therefore according as man is affected by a passion, something seems to him fitting which does not seem so when he is not so affected; thus that seems good to a man when angered which does not seem good when he is calm. And in this way the sensitive appetite moves the will on the part of the object.

Reply Obj. 1. Nothing hinders that which is better absolutely and in itself from being less excellent in a certain respect. Accordingly the will is absolutely more excellent than the sensitive appetite, but in respect of the man in whom a passion is predominant, in so far as he is subject to that passion, the sensitive appetite is more excellent.

Reply Obj. 2. Men's acts and choices are in reference to singulars. Therefore from the very fact that the sensitive appetite is a particular power, it has great influence in disposing man so that something seems to him such or otherwise, in particular cases.

Reply Obj. 3. As the Philosopher says,[3] the reason, in which resides the will, moves by its command the irascible and concupiscible powers, not, indeed, by a despotic rule, as a slave is moved by his master, but by a royal and political rule, as free men are ruled by their governor, and can nevertheless act counter to his commands. Hence both irascible and concupiscible can move counter to the will, and accordingly nothing hinders the will from being moved by them at times.

ARTICLE 3. *Whether the Will Moves Itself?*

We proceed thus to the Third Article: It would seem that the will does not move itself.

Objection 1. For every mover, as such, is in act, but what is moved is in potency, since "movement is the act of that which is in potency, as such."[4] Now the same thing is not in potency and in act in respect of the same. Therefore nothing moves itself. Neither, therefore, can the will move itself.

Obj. 2. Further, the movable is moved on the mover being present. But the will is always present to itself. If, therefore, it moved itself, it would always be moving itself, which is clearly false.

Obj. 3. Further, the will is moved by the intellect, as stated above (A. 1). If, therefore, the will move itself, it would follow that the same thing is at once moved immediately by two movers, which seems unreasonable. Therefore the will does not move itself.

On the contrary, The will is mistress of its own act, and to it belongs to will and not to will. But this would not be so had it not the power to move itself to will. Therefore it moves itself.

I answer that, As stated above (A. 1), it pertains to the will to move the other powers, by reason of the end which is the will's object. Now, as stated above (Q. VIII, A. 2), the end is in things desirable, what the principle is in things intelligible. But it is evident that the intellect, through its knowledge of the principle, reduces itself from potency to act, as to its knowledge of the conclusions; and thus it moves itself. And, in like manner, the will, through willing the end, moves itself to will the means.

Reply Obj. 1. It is not in respect of the same that the will moves itself and is moved, and so neither is it in act and in potency in respect of the same. But in so far as it actually wills the end, it reduces itself from potency to act with

---

[1] Aristotle, VIII, 5 (257^{b}23).
[2] *Ethics*, III, 5 (1114^{a}32).
[3] *Politics*, I, 5 (1254^{b}5).
[4] Aristotle, *Physics*, III, 1 (201^{a}10).

regard to the means, so that it actually wills them.

Reply Obj. 2. The power of the will is always actually present to itself, but the act of the will, by which it wills an end, is not always in the will. And this is the way it moves itself. Accordingly it does not follow that it is always moving itself.

Reply Obj. 3. The will is moved by the intellect otherwise than by itself. By the intellect it is moved on the part of the object, whereas it is moved by itself as to the exercise of its act, in respect of the end.

ARTICLE 4. *Whether the Will Is Moved by an Exterior Principle?*

We proceed thus to the Fourth Article: It would seem that the will is not moved by anything exterior.

Objection 1. For the movement of the will is voluntary. But it pertains to the notion of the voluntary act that it be from an intrinsic principle, just as it pertains to the notion of the natural act. Therefore the movement of the will is not from anything exterior.

Obj. 2. Further, the will cannot suffer violence, as was shown above (Q. VI, A. 4). But "the violent act is one the principle of which is outside the agent."[1] Therefore the will cannot be moved by anything exterior.

Obj. 3. Further, that which is sufficiently moved by one mover does not need to be moved by another. But the will moves itself sufficiently. Therefore it is not moved by anything exterior.

On the contrary, The will is moved by the object, as stated above (A. 1). But the object of the will can be something exterior offered to the sense. Therefore the will can be moved by something exterior.

I answer that, As far as the will is moved by the object, it is evident that it can be moved by something exterior. But in so far as it is moved to the exercise of its act, we must again hold it to be moved by some exterior principle.

For everything that is at one time an agent actually, and at another time an agent in potency, needs to be moved by a mover. Now it is evident that the will begins to will something, whereas previously it did not will it. Therefore it must, of necessity, be moved by something to will it. And, indeed, it moves itself, as stated above (A. 3.), in so far as through willing the end it reduces itself to the act of willing the means. Now it cannot do this without the aid of counsel. For when a man wills to be healed, he

begins to reflect how this can be attained, and through this reflection he comes to the conclusion that he can be healed by a physician, and he wills this. But since he did not always actually will to have health, he must, of necessity, have begun, through something moving him, to will to be healed. And if the will moved itself to will this, it must of necessity have done this with the aid of counsel following some previous volition. But this process could not go on to infinity. Therefore we must of necessity suppose that the will advanced to its first movement in virtue of the impulse of some exterior mover, as Aristotle concludes in a chapter of the *Eudemian Ethics.*[2]

Reply Obj. 1. It pertains to the notion of the voluntary act that its principle be within the agent, but it is not necessary that this inward principle be the first principle unmoved by another. And so though the voluntary act has an inward proximate principle, nevertheless its first principle is from without. Thus, too, the first principle of the natural movement is from without, that, namely, which moves nature.

Reply Obj. 2. For an act to be violent it is not enough that its principle be extrinsic, but we must add "without the concurrence of him that suffers violence." This does not happen when the will is moved by an exterior principle, for it is the will that wills, though moved by another. But this movement would be violent if it were counter to the movement of the will, which in the present case is impossible, since then the will would will and not will the same thing.

Reply Obj. 3. The will moves itself sufficiently in one respect, and in its own order, that is to say as proximate agent; but it cannot move itself in every respect, as we have shown. Therefore it needs to be moved by another as first mover.

ARTICLE 5. *Whether the Will Is Moved by a Heavenly Body?*

We proceed thus to the Fifth Article: It seems that the human will is moved by a heavenly body.

Objection 1. For all various and multiform movements are reduced, as to their cause, to a uniform movement which is that of the heavens, as is proved in the *Physics.*[3] But human movements are various and multiform, since they begin to be, whereas previously they were not. Therefore they are reduced, as to their cause, to the movement of the heavens, which is uniform according to its nature.

[1] Aristotle, *Ethics,* III, 1 (1110[a]1).

[2] VII, 14 (1248[a]14).

[3] Aristotle, VIII, 9 (265[a]27); cf. IV, 14 (223[b]18).

Obj. 2. Further, according to Augustine (*De Trin.* iii, 4)[1] "the lower bodies are moved by the higher." But the movements of the human body, which are caused by the will, could not be reduced to the movement of the heavens, as to their cause, unless the will too were moved by the heavens. Therefore the heavens move the human will.

Obj. 3. Further, by observing the heavenly bodies astrologers foretell the truth about future human acts, which are caused by the will. But this would not be so if the heavenly bodies could not move man's will. Therefore the human will is moved by a heavenly body.

On the contrary, Damascene says (*De Fide Orthod.* ii, 7)[2] that the heavenly bodies are not the causes of our acts. But they would be, if the will, which is the principle of human acts, were moved by the heavenly bodies. Therefore the will is not moved by the heavenly bodies.

I answer that, It is evident that the will can be moved by the heavenly bodies in the same way as it is moved by its exterior object, that is to say, in so far as exterior bodies, which move the will through being offered to the senses, and also the organs themselves of the sensitive powers, are subject to the movements of the heavenly bodies.

But some have maintained that heavenly bodies have an influence on the human will in the same way as some exterior agent moves the will, as to the exercise of its act.[3] But this is impossible. For "the will," as stated in the book on the *Soul,*[4] "is in the reason." Now the reason is a power of the soul, not bound to a bodily organ. And so it follows that the will is a power absolutely incorporeal and immaterial. But it is evident that no body can act on what is incorporeal, but rather the reverse; because things incorporeal and immaterial have a power more formal and more universal than any corporeal things whatever. Therefore it is impossible for a heavenly body to act directly on the intellect or the will. For this reason Aristotle[5] ascribed to those who held that intellect does not differ from sense the theory that "such is the will of men as is the day which the father of men and of gods brings on"[6] (referring to Jupiter, by whom they understand the entire heavens). For all the sensitive powers, since they are acts of bodily organs, can be moved accidentally by the heavenly

bodies—that is, through those bodies (whose acts they are) being moved.

But since it has been stated (A. 2) that the intellectual appetite is moved, in a fashion, by the sensitive appetite, the movements of the heavenly bodies have an indirect bearing on the will, in so far as the will happens to be moved by the passions of the sensitive appetite.

Reply Obj. 1. The multiform movements of the human will are reduced to some uniform cause, which, however, is above the intellect and will. This can be said not of any body, but of some superior immaterial substance. Therefore there is no need for the movement of the will to be referred to the movement of the heavens as to its cause.

Reply Obj. 2. The movements of the human body are reduced, as to their cause, to the movement of a heavenly body in so far as the disposition suitable to a particular movement is somewhat due to the influence of heavenly bodies; also, in so far as the sensitive appetite is stirred by the influence of heavenly bodies; and again, in so far as exterior bodies are moved in accordance with the movement of heavenly bodies, at whose presence the will begins to will or not to will something; for instance, when the body is chilled, we begin to wish to make the fire. But this movement of the will is on the part of the object offered from without, not on the part of an inward impulse.

Reply Obj. 3. As stated above (cf. Part I, Q. LXXXIV, AA. 6, 7) the sensitive appetite is the act of a bodily organ. Therefore there is no reason why man should not be prone to anger or concupiscence, or some like passion, by reason of the influence of heavenly bodies, just as by reason of his natural make-up. But the majority of men are led by the passions, which the wise alone resist. Consequently, in the majority of cases predictions about human acts, gathered from the observation of heavenly bodies, are fulfilled. Nevertheless, as Ptolemy says (*Centiloquium* v),[7] "the wise man governs the stars," which is as though to say that by resisting his passions, he opposes his will, which is free and in no way subject to the movement of the heavens, to effects of this nature of the heavenly bodies.

Or, as Augustine says (*Gen. ad lit.* ii, 17)[8]: "We must confess that when the truth is foretold by astrologers, this is due to some most hidden inspiration, to which the human mind

[1] PL 42, 873.

[2] PG 94, 893.

[3] Cf. Denifle, *Chartularium,* n. 432 (I, 487).

[4] Aristotle, III, 9 (432^{b}5).

[5] *Soul,* III, 3 (427^{a}25).

[6] *Odyssey,* XVIII, 136.

[7] Cf. *Quadripartitum,* I, 3; cf. Also Albert, *In Sent.,* II, d. xv, A. 4 (BO XXVII, 276).

[8] PL 34, 278.

is subject without knowing it. And since this is done in order to deceive man, it must be the work of the lying spirits."

ARTICLE 6. *Whether the Will Is Moved by God Alone, as Exterior Principle?*

We proceed thus to the Sixth Article: It would seem that the will is not moved by God alone as exterior principle.

Objection 1. For it is natural that the inferior be moved by its superior, just as the lower bodies are moved by the heavenly bodies. But there is something which is higher than the will of man and below God, namely, the angel. Therefore man's will can be moved by an angel also, as exterior principle.

Obj. 2. Further, the act of the will follows the act of the intellect. But man's intellect is reduced to act not by God alone, but also by the angel who enlightens it, as Dionysius says (*Cæl. Hier.* iv).[1] For the same reason, therefore, the will also is moved by an angel.

Obj. 3. Further, God is not cause of other than good things, according to Gen. 1. 31: *God saw all the things that He had made, and they were very good.* If therefore man's will were moved by God alone, it would never be moved to evil, and yet "it is the will whereby we sin and whereby we do right," as Augustine says (*Retract.* i, 9).[2]

On the contrary, It is written (Phil. 2. 13): *It is God Who worketh in us* (Vulg.,—*you*) *both to will and to accomplish.*

I answer that, The movement of the will is from within, as also is the movement of nature. Now although it is possible for something to move a natural thing without being the cause of the nature of the thing moved, yet that alone which is in some way the cause of a thing's nature can cause a natural movement in that thing. For a stone is moved upwards by a man, who is not the cause of the stone's nature; but the natural movement of the stone is caused by no other than the cause of its nature. Hence it is said in the *Physics*[3] that the being who generates them moves heavy and light things according to place. And so man endowed with a will is sometimes moved by something that is not his cause; but that his voluntary movement be from an exterior principle that is not the cause of his will is impossible.

Now the cause of the will can be none other than God. And this is evident for two reasons.

---

[1] Sect. 2 (PG 3, 180).
[2] PL 32, 596.
[3] Aristotle, VIII, 4 (255[b]35).

First, because the will is a power of the rational soul, which is caused by God alone, by creation, as was stated in the First Part (Q. XC, A. 2). Secondly, it is evident from the fact that the will is ordered to the universal good. Therefore nothing else can be the cause of the will, except God Himself, Who is the universal good, while every other good is good by participation, and is some particular good; and a particular cause does not give a universal inclination. Hence neither can prime matter, which is potency to all forms, be created by some particular agent.

Reply Obj. 1. An angel is not above man in such a way as to be the cause of his will in the way that the heavenly bodies are the causes of natural forms from which result the natural movements of natural bodies.

Reply Obj. 2. Man's intellect is moved by an angel on the part of the object, which by the power of the angelic light is proposed to man's knowledge. And in this way the will also can be moved by a creature from without, as stated above (A. 4).

Reply Obj. 3. God moves man's will as the Universal Mover to the universal object of the will, which is the good. And without this universal motion, man cannot will anything. But man determines himself by his reason to will this or that, which is true or apparent good. Nevertheless, sometimes God moves some specially to the willing of something determinate, which is good, as in the case of those whom He moves by grace, as we shall state later on (Q. CIX, A. 2).

QUESTION X

OF THE MANNER IN WHICH THE WILL IS MOVED

(*In Four Articles*)

WE must now consider the manner in which the will is moved. Under this head there are four points of inquiry: (1) Whether the will is moved to anything naturally? (2) Whether it is moved of necessity by its object? (3) Whether it is moved of necessity by the lower appetite? (4) Whether it is moved of necessity by the exterior mover which is God?

ARTICLE 1. *Whether the Will Is Moved to Anything Naturally?*

We proceed thus to the First Article: It seems that the will is not moved to anything naturally.

Objection 1. For the natural agent is divided against the voluntary agent, as stated at the beginning of the second book of the *Physics*.[1] Therefore the will is not moved to anything naturally.

Obj. 2. Further, that which is natural is in a thing always, as being hot is in fire. But no movement is always in the will. Therefore no movement is natural to the will.

Obj. 3. Further, nature is determined to one thing, whereas the will is referred to opposites. Therefore the will wills nothing naturally.

On the contrary, The movement of the will follows the act of the intellect. But the intellect understands some things naturally. Therefore the will, too, wills some things naturally.

I answer that, As Boëthius says (*De Duabus Nat.*),[2] and the Philosopher also,[3] the word nature is used in a manifold sense. For sometimes it stands for the intrinsic principle in movable things. In this sense nature is either matter or the material form, as stated in the *Physics*.[4] In another sense nature stands for any substance, or even for any being. And in this sense, that is said to be natural to a thing which befits it in respect of its substance. And this is that which of itself is in a thing. Now all things that do not of themselves belong to the thing in which they are, are reduced to something which belongs of itself to that thing, as to their principle. Therefore, taking nature in this sense, it is necessary that the principle of whatever belongs to a thing be a natural principle. This is evident in regard to the intellect, for the principles of intellectual knowledge are naturally known. In like manner the principle of voluntary movements must be something naturally willed.

Now this is the good in general, to which the will tends naturally, as does each power to its object; and again it is the last end, which stands in the same relation to things desirable, as the first principles of demonstrations to things intelligible; and, speaking generally, it is all those things which belong to the willer according to his nature. For it is not only things pertaining to the power of the will that the will desires, but also that which pertains to each power, and to the entire man. Therefore man wills naturally not only the object of the will, but also other things that are appropriate to the other powers, such as the knowledge of truth, which befits the intellect, and to be and to live and other like things which regard the natural well-being, all of which are included in the object of the will as so many particular goods.

Reply Obj. 1. The will is distinguished from nature as one kind of cause from another, for some things happen naturally and some are done voluntarily. There is, however, another manner of causing that is proper to the will, which is mistress of its act, besides the manner proper to nature, which is determined to one thing. But since the will is founded on some nature, it is necessary that the movement proper to nature be shared by the will, to some extent, just as what belongs to a previous cause is shared by a subsequent cause. Because in every thing, being itself which is from nature, precedes volition, which is from the will. And hence it is that the will wills something naturally.

Reply Obj. 2. In the case of natural things, that which is natural as a result of the form only is always in them actually, as heat is in fire. But that which is natural as a result of matter is not always in them actually, but sometimes only in potency, because form is act, whereas matter is potency. Now "movement is the act of that which is in potency."[5] Therefore that which pertains to or results from movement in regard to natural things is not always in them. Thus fire does not always move upwards, but only when it is outside its own place.[6] And in like manner it is not necessary that the will (which is reduced from potency to act when it wills something), should always be in the act of willing, but only when it is in a certain determinate disposition. But God's will, which is pure act, is always in the act of willing.

Reply Obj. 3. To every nature there is one thing corresponding, proportioned to that nature. For to nature considered as a genus there corresponds something one generically; and to nature as species there corresponds something one specifically; and to the individualized nature there corresponds some one individual. Since, therefore, the will is an immaterial power, like the intellect, some one common thing corresponds naturally to it, which is the good; just as to the intellect there corresponds some one common thing, which is the true, or being, or what a thing is. And under good in general are included many particular goods, to none of which is the will determined.

ARTICLE 2. *Whether the Will Is Moved of Necessity by Its Object?*

We proceed thus to the Second Article: It

[1] Aristotle, II, 1 (192^{b}8); II, 5 (196^{b}21).
[2] Chap. 1 (PL 64, 1341).
[3] *Metaphysics*, V, 4 (1014^{b}16). [4] Aristotle, II, 1 (193^{a}28).

[5] Aristotle, *Physics*, III, 1 (201^{a}10).
[6] The Aristotelian theory was that fire's proper place is the fiery heaven, that is, the Empyrean.

seems that the will is moved of necessity by its object.

Objection 1. For the object of the will is compared to the will as mover to movable, as stated in the book on the *Soul*.[1] But a mover, if it be sufficient, moves the movable of necessity. Therefore the will can be moved of necessity by its object.

Obj. 2. Further, just as the will is an immaterial power, so is the intellect, and both powers are ordered to a universal object, as stated above (A. 1. Reply 3). But the intellect is moved of necessity by its object; therefore the will also, by its object.

Obj. 3. Further, whatever one wills, is either the end or something ordered to an end. But it seems that one wills an end necessarily, because it is like the principle in speculative matters, to which principle one assents of necessity. Now the end is the reason for willing the means, and so it seems that we will the means also necessarily. Therefore the will is moved of necessity by its object.

On the contrary, The rational powers, according to the Philosopher,[2] are directed to opposites. But the will is a rational power, since it is "in the reason," as stated in the book on the *Soul*.[3] Therefore the will is directed to opposites. Therefore it is not moved of necessity to either of the opposites.

I answer that, The will is moved in two ways: first, as to the exercise of its act; secondly, as to the specification of its act, which is from the object. As to the first way, no object moves the will necessarily, for no matter what the object be, it is in man's power not to think of it, and consequently not to will it actually.

But as to the second manner of motion, the will is moved by one object necessarily, by another not. For in the movement of a power by its object, we must consider under what aspect the object moves the power. For the visible moves the sight under the aspect of colour actually visible. Therefore if colour be offered to the sight, it moves the sight necessarily, unless one turns one's eyes away, which pertains to the exercise of the act. But if the sight were confronted with something not in all respects coloured actually, but only so in some respects, and in other respects not, the sight would not of necessity see such an object, for it might look at that part of the object which is not actually coloured, and thus it would not see it. Now just as

the actually coloured is the object of sight, so is good the object of the will. Therefore if the will be offered an object which is good universally and from every point of view, the will tends to it of necessity, if it wills anything at all, since it cannot will the opposite. If, on the other hand, the will is offered an object that is not good from every point of view, it will not tend to it of necessity. And since lack of any good whatever is a non-good, consequently that good alone which is perfect and lacking in nothing is such a good that the will cannot not-will it; and this is Happiness. But any other particular goods, in so far as they are lacking in some good, can be regarded as non-goods, and from this point of view, they can be set aside or approved by the will, which can tend to one and the same thing from various points of view.

Reply Obj. 1. The sufficient mover of a power is none but that object that in every respect presents the aspect of the mover of that power. If, on the other hand, it is lacking in any respect, it will not move of necessity, as stated above.

Reply Obj. 2. The intellect is moved of necessity by an object which is such as to be always and necessarily true, but not by that which may be either true or false—namely, by that which is contingent, as we have said of the good.

Reply Obj. 3. The last end moves the will necessarily, because it is the perfect good, and in like manner whatever is ordered to that end, and without which the end cannot be attained, such as to be and to live, and the like. But other things without which the end can be gained are not necessarily willed by one who wills the end, just as he who assents to the principle does not necessarily assent to the conclusions without which the principles can still be true.

ARTICLE 3. *Whether the Will Is Moved, of Necessity, by the Lower Appetite?*

We proceed thus to the Third Article: It would seem that the will is moved of necessity by a passion of the lower appetite.

Objection 1. For the Apostle says (Rom. 7. 19): *The good which I will I do not; but the evil which I will not, that I do,* and this is said by reason of concupiscence, which is a passion. Therefore the will is moved of necessity by a passion.

Obj. 2. Further, as stated in the *Ethics*,[4] "according as a man is, such does the end seem to him." But it is not in the power of the will to cast aside a passion at once. Therefore it is not

---

[1] Aristotle, III, 10 (433[b]10).
[2] *Metaphysics*, IX, 2 (1046[b]8).
[3] III, 9 (432[b]5).
[4] Aristotle, III, 5 (1114[a]32).

in the power of the will not to will that to which the passion inclines him.

Obj. 3. Further, a universal cause is not applied to a particular effect except by means of a particular cause; therefore the universal reason does not move save by means of a particular estimation, as stated in the book on the *Soul*.[1] But as the universal reason is to the particular estimation, so is the will to the sensitive appetite. Therefore the will is not moved to will something particular except through the sensitive appetite. Therefore, if the sensitive appetite happen to be disposed to something, by reason of a passion, the will cannot be moved in a contrary sense.

On the contrary, It is written (Gen. 4. 7): *Thy lust* (Vulg.—*The lust thereof*) *shall be under thee, and thou shalt have dominion over it.* Therefore man's will is not moved of necessity by the lower appetite.

I answer that, As stated above (Q. IX, A. 2), the passion of the sensitive appetite moves the will, in so far as the will is moved by its object, inasmuch as, namely, man through being disposed in such and such a way by a passion, judges something to be fitting and good, which he would not judge thus were it not for the passion. Now this influence of a passion on man occurs in two ways. First, so that his reason is wholly bound, so that he has not the use of reason, as happens in those who through a violent access of anger or concupiscence become furious or insane, just as they may from some other bodily disorder; for passions of this kind do not take place without some change in the body. And of such the same is to be said as of irrational animals, which follow of necessity the impulse of their passions; for in them there is no movement of reason, nor, consequently, of will.

Sometimes, however, the reason is not entirely engrossed by the passion, so that the judgment of reason retains, to a certain extent, its freedom; and thus the movement of the will remains in a certain degree. Accordingly in so far as the reason remains free, and not subject to the passion, to this extent also the will's movement, which also remains, does not tend of necessity to that to which the passion inclines it. Consequently, either there is no movement of the will in that man, and the passion alone holds its sway, or if there be a movement of the will, it does not necessarily follow the passion.

Reply Obj. 1. Although the will cannot prevent the movement of concupiscence from arising, of which the Apostle says: *The evil which I will not, that I do*—that is, *I desire,* yet it is in the power of the will not to will to desire, or not to consent to concupiscence. And thus it does not necessarily follow the movement of concupiscence.

Reply Obj. 2. Since there is in man a twofold nature, intellectual and sensitive, sometimes man is disposed in a certain way uniformly in respect of his whole soul, either because the sensitive part is wholly subject to his reason as in the virtuous, or because reason is entirely engrossed by passion, as in a madman. But sometimes, although reason is clouded by passion, yet something of the reason remains free. And in respect of this, man can either repel the passion entirely, or at least hold himself in check so as not to be led away by the passion. For when thus disposed, since man is variously disposed according to the various parts of the soul, a thing appears to him otherwise according to his reason than it does according to a passion.

Reply Obj. 3. The will is moved not only by the universal good apprehended by the reason, but also by good apprehended by sense. Therefore he can be moved to some particular good independently of a passion of the sensitive appetite. For we will and do many things without passion, and through choice alone, as is most evident in those cases in which reason resists passion.

ARTICLE 4. *Whether the Will Is Moved of Necessity by the Exterior Mover Which Is God?*

We proceed thus to the Fourth Article: It would seem that the will is moved of necessity by God.

Objection 1. For every agent that cannot be resisted moves of necessity. But God cannot be resisted, because His power is infinite; therefore it is written (Rom. 9. 19); *Who resisteth His will?* Therefore God moves the will of necessity.

Obj. 2. Further, the will is moved of necessity to whatever it wills naturally, as stated above (A. 2. REPLY 3). But "whatever God does in a thing is natural to it," as Augustine says (*Contra Faust.* xxvi, 3).[2] Therefore the will wills of necessity everything to which God moves it.

Obj. 3. Further, a thing is possible if nothing impossible follows from its being supposed. But something impossible follows from the supposition that the will does not will that to which

---

[1] Aristotle, III, 11 (434ᵃ19).

[2] PL. 42, 480.

God moves it, because in that case God's operation would be ineffectual. Therefore it is not possible for the will not to will that to which God moves it. Therefore it wills it of necessity.

On the contrary, It is written (Ecclus. 15. 14): *God made man from the beginning, and left him in the hand of his own counsel.* Therefore He does not of necessity move man's will.

I answer that, As Dionysius says (*Div. Nom.* iv)[1] it pertains "to Divine providence not to destroy but to preserve the nature of things." Therefore it moves all things in accordance with their conditions, so that from necessary causes, through the Divine motion, effects follow of necessity; but from contingent causes, effects follow contingently. Since, therefore, the will is an active principle, not determined to one thing, but having an indifferent relation to many things, God so moves it that He does not determine it of necessity to one thing, but its movement remains contingent and not necessary, except in those things to which it is moved naturally.

Reply Obj. 1. The Divine will extends not only to the doing of something by the thing which He moves, but also to its being done in a way which is fitting to the nature of that thing. And therefore it would be more contrary to the Divine motion for the will to be moved of necessity, which is not fitting to its nature, than for it to be moved freely, which is fitting to its nature.

Reply Obj. 2. That is natural to a thing, which God makes to be natural to it. Thus something is fitting to a thing, according as God wishes it to be fitting to it. Now He does not wish that whatever He works in things should be natural to them, for instance, that the dead should rise again. But this He does wish to be natural to each thing,—that it be subject to the Divine power.

Reply Obj. 3. If God moves the will to anything, it is impossible to hold that the will be not moved to it. But it is not impossible absolutely. Consequently it does not follow that the will is moved by God necessarily.

(b) *The Nature of Elicited Voluntary Acts*

QUESTION XI

OF ENJOYMENT, WHICH IS AN ACT OF THE WILL

(*In Four Articles*)

WE must now consider enjoyment (fruition), concerning which there are four points of inquiry: (1) Whether to enjoy is an act of the appetitive power? (2) Whether it belongs to the rational creature alone, or also to irrational animals? (3) Whether enjoyment is only of the last end? (4) Whether it is only of the end possessed?

ARTICLE 1. *Whether to Enjoy Is an Act of the Appetitive Power?*

We proceed thus to the First Article: It would seem that to enjoy belongs not only to the appetitive power.

Objection 1. For to enjoy [*frui*] seems nothing else than to lay hold of the fruit. But it is the intellect, in whose act Happiness consists, as shown above (Q. III, A. 4), that receives the fruit of human life, which is Happiness. Therefore to enjoy is not an act of the appetitive power, but of the intellect.

Obj. 2. Further, each power has its proper end, which is its perfection; thus the end of

sight is to know the visible, of the hearing, to perceive sounds, and so forth. But the end of a thing is its fruit. Therefore to enjoy belongs to each power, and not only to the appetite.

Obj. 3. Further, enjoyment implies a certain delight. But sensible delight belongs to sense, which delights in its object; and for the same reason, intellectual delight belongs to the apprehensive, and not to the appetitive power.

On the contrary, Augustine says,[2] "To enjoy is to adhere lovingly to something for its own sake." But love belongs to the appetitive power. Therefore also to enjoy is an act of the appetitive power.

I answer that, Fruitio (enjoyment) and *fructus* (fruit) seem to refer to the same, the one being derived from the other; which from which, matters not for our purpose, though it seems probable that the one which is more clearly known, was first named. Now those things are most manifest to us which appeal most to the senses, and so it seems that the word "fruition" is derived from sensible fruits. But sensible fruit is that which we expect the tree to produce in the last place, and in which a certain sweetness is to be perceived. Hence fruition seems to have relation to love, or to the delight which one has

[1] Sect. 33 (PG 3, 733).

[2] *Christian Doctrine,* I, 4 (PL 34, 20); *De Trin.,* X, 10, 11 (PL 42, 981, 982).

in realizing the longed-for term, which is the end. Now the end and the good is the object of the appetitive power. Therefore it is evident that fruition[1] is the act of the appetitive power.

Reply Obj. 1. Nothing hinders one and the same thing from belonging, under different aspects, to different powers. Accordingly the vision of God, as vision, is an act of the intellect; but as a good and an end, is the object of the will. And it is according to the latter that the enjoyment of the vision of God is realized. The intellect attains this end as the executive power, but the will as the power which moves towards the end and enjoys the end attained.

Reply Obj. 2. The perfection and end of every other power is contained in the object of the appetitive power as the proper is contained in the common, as stated above (Q. IX, A. 1). Hence the perfection and end of each power, in so far as it is a good, belongs to the appetitive power. Thus the appetitive power moves the other powers to their ends, and itself realizes the end when each of them reaches the end.

Reply Obj. 3. In delight there are two things: perception of what is fitting—and this pertains to the apprehensive power; and satisfaction in that which is offered as fitting—and this pertains to the appetitive power, in which the notion of delight is realized.

ARTICLE 2. *Whether to Enjoy Belongs to the Rational Creature Alone, or Also to Irrational Animals?*

We proceed thus to the Second Article: It would seem that to enjoy belongs to men alone.

Objection 1. For Augustine says[2] that "it is given to us men to enjoy and to use." Therefore other animals cannot enjoy.

Obj. 2. Further, to enjoy relates to the last end. But irrational animals cannot attain to the last end. Therefore it is not for them to enjoy.

Obj. 3. Further, just as the sensitive appetite is beneath the intellectual appetite, so is the natural appetite beneath the sensitive. If, therefore, to enjoy belongs to the sensitive appetite, it seems that for the same reason it can belong to the natural appetite. But this is evidently false, since the latter cannot delight in anything. Therefore the sensitive appetite cannot enjoy, and accordingly enjoyment is not possible for irrational animals.

On the contrary, Augustine says (QQ. LXXXIII,

qu. 30):[3] "It is not so absurd to suppose that even beasts enjoy their food and any bodily pleasure."

I answer that, As was stated above (A. 1) to enjoy is not the act of the power that achieves the end as executor, but of the power that commands the achievement; for we have said that it belongs to the appetitive power. Now things that do not have knowledge have indeed a power of achieving an end by way of execution, as that by which a heavy body has a downward tendency, and a light body has an upward tendency. Yet the power of command in respect of the end is not in them, but in some higher nature, which moves all nature by its command, just as in things endowed with knowledge the appetite moves the other powers to their acts. Therefore it is clear that things void of knowledge, although they attain an end, have no enjoyment of the end. This is only for those that are endowed with knowledge.

Now knowledge of the end is twofold: perfect and imperfect. Perfect knowledge of the end is that whereby not only is that known which is the end and the good, but also the universal nature of the end and the good; and such knowledge belongs to the rational nature alone. On the other hand, imperfect knowledge is that by which the end and the good are known in the particular. Such knowledge is in irrational animals, whose appetitive powers do not command with freedom, but are moved according to a natural instinct to whatever they apprehend. Consequently, enjoyment belongs to the rational nature in a perfect degree; to irrational animals, imperfectly; to other creatures, not at all.

Reply Obj. 1. Augustine is speaking there of perfect enjoyment.

Reply Obj. 2. Enjoyment need not be of the last end absolutely, but of that which each one chooses for his last end.

Reply Obj. 3. The sensitive appetite follows knowledge, but not the natural appetite, especially in things void of knowledge.

Reply Obj. 4. Augustine is speaking there of imperfect enjoyment. This is clear from his way of speaking, for he says that "it is not so absurd to suppose that even beasts enjoy," that is, as it would be, if one were to say that they use.

ARTICLE 3. *Whether Enjoyment Is Only of the Last End?*

We proceed thus to the Third Article: It seems that enjoyment is not only of the last end.

---

[1] *Fruitio* is translated in general throughout this work as "enjoyment."

[2] *Christian Doctrine,* I, 22 (PL 34, 26).

[3] PL 40, 19.

Objection 1. For the Apostle says (*Philem.* 20): *Yea, brother, may I enjoy thee in the Lord.* But it is evident that Paul had not placed his last end in a man. Therefore to enjoy is not only of the last end.

Obj. 2. Further, what we enjoy is the fruit. But the Apostle says (*Gal.* 5. 22): *The fruit of the Spirit is charity, joy, peace,* and other like things, which are not in the nature of the last end. Therefore enjoyment is not only of the last end.

Obj. 3. Further, the acts of the will reflect on themselves; for I will to will, and I love to love. But to enjoy is an act of the will, since "it is the will with which we enjoy," as Augustine says (*De Trin.* x. 10).[1] Therefore a man enjoys his enjoyment. But the last end of man is not enjoyment, but the uncreated good alone, which is God. Therefore enjoyment is not only of the last end.

On the contrary, Augustine says (*De Trin.* x. 11):[2] "A man does not enjoy that which he desires for the sake of something else." But the last end alone is that which man does not desire for the sake of something else. Therefore enjoyment is of the last end alone.

I answer that, As stated above (A. 1) the notion of fruit implies two things: first that it should come last; secondly, that it should calm the appetite with a certain sweetness and delight. Now a thing is last either absolutely or relatively; absolutely, if it be referred to nothing else; relatively, if it is the last in a particular series. Therefore that which is last absolutely, and in which one delights as in the last end, is properly called fruit, and this it is that one is properly said to enjoy. But that which is delightful not in itself, but is desired only as referred to something else, for example, a bitter potion for the sake of health, cannot in any way be called fruit. And that which has something delightful about it, to which a number of preceding things are referred, may indeed be called fruit in a certain manner, but we cannot be said to enjoy it properly or as though it answered perfectly to the notion of fruit. Hence Augustine says (*De Trin.* x, 10)[3] that "we enjoy what we know, when the delighted will is at rest therein." But its rest is not absolute save in the possession of the last end, for as long as something is looked for, the movement of the will remains in suspense, although it has reached something. Thus in local movement, although any point between the two terms is a beginning and an end, yet it is not

considered as an actual end, except when the movement stops there.

Reply Obj. 1. As Augustine says,[4] "if he had said, 'May I enjoy thee,' without adding 'in the Lord,' he would seem to have set the end of his love in him. But since he added that he set his end in the Lord, he implied his desire to enjoy Him," as if we were to say that he expressed his enjoyment of his brother not as a term but as a means.

Reply Obj. 2. Fruit bears one relation to the tree that bore it, and another to man that enjoys it. To the tree indeed that bore it, it is compared as effect to cause; to the one enjoying it, as the final object of his longing and the consummation of his delight. Accordingly these fruits mentioned by the Apostle are called so because they are certain effects of the Holy Ghost in us, and so they are called *fruits of the Spirit,* but not as though we are to enjoy them as our last end. Or we may say with Ambrose[5] that they are called fruits "because we should desire them for their own sake," not indeed as though they were not ordered to Happiness, but because they are in themselves of such a character that we ought to find pleasure in them.

Reply Obj. 3. As stated above (Q. I, A. 8; Q. II, A. 7), we speak of an end in a twofold sense: first, as being the thing itself; secondly, as the attainment of it. These are not, of course, two ends, but one end, considered in itself and in its relation to something else. Accordingly God is the last end as that which is ultimately sought for, while the enjoyment is as the attainment of this last end. And so, just as God is not one end and the enjoyment of God another, so it is the same enjoyment by which we enjoy God, and by which we enjoy our enjoyment of God. And the same applies to created happiness which consists in enjoyment.

ARTICLE 4. *Whether Enjoyment Is Only of the End Possessed?*

We proceed thus to the Fourth Article: It would seem that enjoyment is only of the end possessed.

Objection 1. For Augustine says (*De Trin.* x, 11)[6] that "to enjoy is to use joyfully, with the joy, not of hope, but of possession." But so long as a thing is not had, there is joy, not of possession but of hope. Therefore enjoyment is only of the end possessed.

---

[1] PL 42, 981.   [2] PL 42, 983.
[3] PL 42, 981.

[4] *Christian Doctrine,* I, 33 (PL 34, 33).
[5] Cf. *Glossa interl.,* on Gal. 5.22 (VI, 87v); *Glossa* Lombardi, on Gal. 5.22 (PL 192, 160); *Sent.,* I, I, 3 (QR I, 19); cf. also Ambrose, *In Gal.* 5.22 (PL 17, 389).   [6] PL 42, 982.

Obj. 2. Further, as stated above (A. 3), enjoyment is not properly otherwise than of the last end, because this alone gives rest to the appetite. But the appetite has no rest save in the possession of the end. Therefore enjoyment, properly speaking, is only of the end possessed.

Obj. 3. Further, to enjoy is to lay hold of the fruit. But one does not lay hold of the fruit until one is in possession of the end. Therefore enjoyment is only of the end possessed.

On the contrary, "To enjoy is to adhere lovingly to something for its own sake," as Augustine says.[1] But this is possible, even in regard to a thing which is not in our possession. Therefore it is possible to enjoy the end even though it be not possessed.

I answer that, To enjoy implies a certain relation of the will to the last end, according as the will possesses something as a last end. Now an end is possessed in two ways; perfectly and imperfectly. Perfectly, when it is possessed not only in intention but also in reality; imperfectly, when it is possessed in intention only. Perfect enjoyment, therefore, is of the end already possessed. But imperfect enjoyment is also of the end possessed, not really, but only in intention.

Reply Obj. 1. Augustine speaks there of perfect enjoyment.

Reply Obj. 2. The will is hindered in two ways from being at rest. First on the part of the object, by reason of its not being the last end, but ordered to something else. Secondly on the part of the one who desires the end, by reason of his not being yet in possession of it. Now it is the object that specifies an act. But on the agent depends the manner of acting, whether it be perfect or imperfect, according to the condition of the agent. Therefore enjoyment of anything but the last end is not enjoyment properly speaking, as falling short of the nature of enjoyment. But enjoyment of the last end not yet possessed, is enjoyment properly speaking, but imperfect, on account of the imperfect way in which it is possessed.

Reply Obj. 3. One is said to lay hold of or to have an end, not only in reality, but also in intention, as stated above.

QUESTION XII
OF INTENTION
(*In Five Articles*)

WE must now consider Intention, concerning which there are five points of inquiry: (1) Whether intention is an act of the intellect or

[1] *Christian Doctrine*, I, 4 (PL 34, 20).

of the will? (2) Whether it is only of the last end? (3) Whether one can intend two things at the same time? (4) Whether intention of the end is the same act as volition of the means? (5) Whether intention is appropriate to irrational animals?

ARTICLE 1. *Whether Intention Is an Act of the Intellect or of the Will?*

We proceed thus to the First Article: It seems that intention is an act of the intellect, and not of the will.

Objection 1. For it is written (Matt. 6. 22): *If thy eye be single, thy whole body shall be lightsome,* where, according to Augustine (*De Serm. Dom. in Monte* ii)[2] "the eye signifies intention." But since the eye is the instrument of sight, it signifies the apprehensive power. Therefore intention is not an act of the appetitive but of the apprehensive power.

Obj. 2. Further, Augustine says (*ibid.*) that Our Lord spoke of intention as a light, when He said (Matt. 6. 23): *If the light that is in thee be darkness,* etc. But light pertains to knowledge. Therefore intention does too.

Obj. 3. Further, intention implies a kind of ordering to an end. But to order is an act of reason. Therefore intention belongs not to the will but to the reason.

Obj. 4. Further, an act of the will is either of the end or of the means. But the act of the will in respect of the end is called volition, or enjoyment; with regard to the means, it is choice, from which intention is distinct. Therefore it is not an act of the will.

On the contrary, Augustine says (*De Trin.* xi, 4, 8, 9)[3] that "the intention of the will unites the sight to the object seen; and the images retained in the memory, to the penetrating gaze of the soul's inner thought." Therefore intention is an act of the will.

I answer that, Intention, as the very word denotes, means to tend to something. Now both the action of the mover and the movement of the thing moved tend to something. But that the movement of the thing moved tends to anything is due to the action of the mover. Consequently intention belongs first and principally to that which moves to the end; hence we say that an architect or anyone who is in authority, by his command moves others to that which he intends. Now the will moves all the other powers of the soul to the end, as shown above (Q. IX, A. 1). Therefore it is evident that intention, properly speaking, is an act of the will.

[2] Chap. 13 (PL 34, 1289).   [3] PL 42. 990, 994, 996.

Reply Obj. 1. The eye designates intention figuratively, not because intention has reference to knowledge, but because it presupposes knowledge, which proposes to the will the end to which the latter moves. Thus we foresee with the eye where we should tend with our bodies.

Reply Obj. 2. Intention is called a light because it is manifest to him who intends. And so works are called darkness, because a man knows what he intends, but does not know what the result may be, as Augustine expounds (*loc. cit.*).

Reply Obj. 3. The will does not order, but tends to something according to the order of reason. Consequently this word "intention" indicates an act of the will, presupposing the act by which the reason orders something to the end.

Reply Obj. 4. Intention is an act of the will in regard to the end. Now the will stands in a threefold relation to the end. First, absolutely. And in this way we have volition, whereby we will absolutely to have health and so forth. Secondly, it considers the end, as its place of rest. And in this way enjoyment regards the end. Thirdly, it considers the end as the term towards which something is ordered; and thus intention regards the end. For when we speak of intending to have health, we mean not only that we will to have it, but that we will to have it by means of something else.

ARTICLE 2. *Whether Intention Is Only of the Last End?*

We proceed thus to the Second Article: It seems that intention is only of the last end.

Objection 1. For it is said in the book of Prosper's *Sentences:*[1] "The intention of the heart is a cry to God." But God is the last end of the human heart. Therefore intention always regards the last end.

Obj. 2. Further, intention regards the end as the term, as stated above (A. 1. Reply 4). But a term is something last. Therefore intention always regards the last end.

Obj. 3. Further, just as intention regards the end, so does enjoyment. But enjoyment is always of the last end. Therefore intention is too.

On the contrary, There is but one last end of human wills, namely, Happiness, as stated above (Q. 1, A. 7). If, therefore, intention were only of the last end, men would not have different intentions, which is evidently false.

I answer that, As stated above (A. 1. Reply 4), intention regards the end as a term of the

movement of the will. Now a term of movement may be taken in two ways. First, the very last term, when the movement comes to a stop; this is the term of the whole movement. Secondly, some point midway, which is the beginning of one part of the movement, and the end or term of the other. Thus in the movement from A to C through B, C is the last term, while B is a term, but not the last. And intention can be of both. Consequently though intention is always of the end, it need not be always of the last end.

Reply Obj. 1. The intention of the heart is called a cry to God, not that God is always the object of intention, but because He knows our intention.—Or because, when we pray, we direct our intention to God, which intention has the force of a cry.

Reply Obj. 2. A term is something last, not always in respect of the whole, but sometimes in respect of a part.

Reply Obj. 3. Enjoyment implies rest in the end, and this pertains to the last end alone. But intention implies movement towards an end, not rest. Therefore the comparison proves nothing.

ARTICLE 3. *Whether One Can Intend Two Things at the Same Time?*

We proceed thus to the Third Article: It would seem that one cannot intend several things at the same time.

Objection 1. For Augustine says (*De Serm. Dom. in Monte,* ii, 14, 17)[2] that man's intention cannot be directed at the same time to God and to bodily benefits. Therefore, for the same reason, neither to any other two things.

Obj. 2. Further, intention designates a movement of the will towards a term. Now there cannot be several terms in the same direction of one movement. Therefore the will cannot intend several things at the same time.

Obj. 3. Further, intention presupposes an act of reason or of the intellect. But "it is not possible to understand several things at the same time," according to the Philosopher.[3] Therefore neither is it possible to intend several things at the same time.

On the contrary, Art imitates nature. Now nature intends two purposes by means of one instrument; thus "the tongue is for the purpose of taste and speech."[4] Therefore, for the same reason, art or reason can at the same time

---

[1] *Sent.,* 100 (PL51, 441).
[2] PL 34, 1290, 1294.
[3] *Topics,* II, 10 (114^{b}35).
[4] *Soul,* II, 8 (420^{b}18).

direct one thing to two ends, so that one can intend several ends at the same time.

I answer that, The expression "two things" may be taken in two ways: they may be ordered to one another or not so ordered. And if they are ordered to one another, it is evident, from what has been said, that a man can intend many things at the same time. For intention is not only of the last end, as stated above (A. 2), but also of an intermediary end. Now a man intends at the same time both the proximate and the last end, as for example, the mixing of a medicine and the giving of health.

But if we take two things that are not ordered to one another, in this way also a man can intend several things at the same time. This is evident from the fact that a man prefers one thing to another because it is the better of the two. Now one of the reasons for which one thing is better than another is that it is available for more purposes, and so one thing can be chosen in preference to another, because of the greater number of purposes for which it is available. And so it is evident that a man can intend several things at the same time.

Reply Obj. 1. Augustine means to say that man cannot at the same time direct his intention to God and to bodily benefits, as to two last ends, since, as stated above (Q. I, A. 5), one man cannot have several last ends.

Reply Obj. 2. There can be several terms ordered to one another, of the same movement and in the same direction, but not unless they are ordered to one another. At the same time it must be observed that what is not one in reality can be taken as one by the reason. Now intention is a movement of the will to something already ordered by the reason, as stated above (A. I. Reply 3). Therefore where we have many things in reality, we may take them as one term of intention, in so far as the reason takes them as one; either because two things meet for the integrity of one whole, as a proper measure of heat and cold conduce to health, or because two things are included in one which may be intended. For instance, the acquiring of wine and clothing is included in wealth, as in something common to both. And so nothing hinders the man who intends to acquire wealth from intending both the others.

Reply Obj. 3. As stated in the First Part (Q. XII, A. 10; Q. LVIII, A. 2; Q. LXXXV, A. 4), it is possible to understand several things at the same time, in so far as, in some way, they are one.

ARTICLE 4. *Whether Intention of the End Is the Same Act as the Volition of the Means?*

We proceed thus to the Fourth Article: It seems that the intention of the end and the volition of the means are not one and the same movement.

Objection 1. For Augustine says (*De Trin.* xi)[1] that "the will to see the window has for its end the seeing of the window, and is another act from the will to see, through the window, the passers-by." But that I should will to see the passers-by through the window belongs to intention; but that I will to see the window belongs to the volition of the means. Therefore intention of the end and the willing of the means are distinct movements of the will.

Obj. 2. Further, acts are distinct according to their objects. But the end and the means are different objects. Therefore the intention of the end and the willing of the means are different movements of the will.

Obj. 3. Further, the willing of the means is called choice. But choice and intention are not the same. Therefore intention of the end and the willing of the means are not the same movement of the will.

On the contrary, The means in relation to the end are as the mid-space to the term. Now it is all the same movement that passes through the mid-space to the term, in natural things. Therefore in things pertaining to the will, the intention of the end is the same movement as the willing of the means.

I answer that, The movement of the will to the end and to the means can be considered in two ways. First, according as the will is moved to each absolutely and in itself. And thus there are absolutely two movements of the will to them. Secondly, it may be considered accordingly as the will is moved to the means for the sake of the end, and in this way the movement of the will to the end and its movement to the means are one and the same thing. For when I say: I wish to take medicine for the sake of health, I signify no more than one movement of my will. And this is because the end is the reason for willing the means. Now the object, and that by reason of which it is an object, come under the same act; thus it is the same act of sight that perceives colour and light, as stated above (Q. VIII, A. 3. Reply 2). And the same applies to the intellect, for if it consider principle and conclusion absolutely, it considers

[1] PL 42, 992.

each by a distinct act; but when it assents to the conclusion on account of the principles, there is but one act of the intellect.

Reply Obj. 1. Augustine is speaking of seeing the window and of seeing, through the window, the passers-by, according as the will is moved to either absolutely.

Reply Obj. 2. The end, considered as a thing, and the means to that end, are distinct objects of the will. But in so far as the end is the reason for willing the means, they are one and the same object.

Reply Obj. 3. A movement which is one as to the subject, may differ, according to reason, as to its beginning and end, as in the case of ascent and descent.[1] Accordingly, in so far as the movement of the will is to the means, as ordered to the end, it is called choice; but the movement of the will to the end as acquired by the means, is called intention. A sign of this is that we can have intention of the end without having determined the means which are the object of choice.

ARTICLE 5. *Whether Intention Is Appropriate to Irrational Animals?*

We proceed thus to the Fifth Article: It would seem that irrational animals intend the end.

Objection 1. For in things lacking reason nature stands further apart from the rational nature than does the sensitive nature in irrational animals. But nature intends the end even in things void of reason, as is proved in the *Physics*.[2] Much more, therefore, do irrational animals intend the end.

Obj. 2. Further, just as intention is of the end, so is enjoyment. But enjoyment is in irrational animals, as stated above (Q. XI, A. 2). Therefore intention is too.

Obj. 3. Further, to intend an end belongs to one who acts for an end, since to intend is nothing else than to tend to something. But irrational animals act for an end, for an animal is moved either to seek food, or to do something of the kind. Therefore irrational animals intend an end.

On the contrary, Intention of an end implies ordering something to an end, which pertains to reason. Since therefore irrational animals do not have reason, it seems that they do not intend an end.

I answer that, As stated above (A. 1), to intend is to tend to something, and this pertains

[1] Aristotle, *Physics*, III, 3 (202ᵃ19).
[2] Aristotle, II, 8 (199ᵇ30).

to the mover and to the moved. According, therefore, as that which is moved to an end by another is said to intend the end; in this way nature is said to intend an end as being moved to its end by God, just as the arrow is moved by the archer. And in this way irrational animals intend an end, in so far as they are moved to something by natural instinct. The other way of intending an end belongs to the mover, according as he orders the movement of something, either his own or another's, to an end. This belongs to reason alone. And so irrational animals do not intend an end in this way, which is to intend properly and principally, as stated above (A. 1).

Reply Obj. 1. This argument takes intention in the sense of being moved to an end.

Reply Obj. 2. Enjoyment does not imply the ordering of one thing to another, as intention does, but absolute repose in the end.

Reply Obj. 3. Irrational animals are moved to an end, not as though they thought that they can gain the end by this movement, for this belongs to the one that intends; but through desiring the end by natural instinct, they are moved to an end, moved, as it were, by another, like other things that are moved naturally.

QUESTION XIII

OF CHOICE, WHICH IS AN ACT OF THE WILL IN RELATION TO THE MEANS

(In Six Articles)

WE must now consider the acts of the will in relation to the means. There are three of them: to choose, to consent, and to use. And choice is preceded by counsel. First of all, then, we must consider choice; secondly, counsel (Q. XIV); thirdly, consent (Q. XV); fourthly, use (Q. XVI).

Concerning choice there are six points of inquiry: (1) Of what power is it the act; of the will or of the reason? (2) Whether choice is to be found in irrational animals? (3) Whether choice is only of the means, or sometimes also of the end? (4) Whether choice is only of things that we do ourselves? (5) Whether choice is only of possible things? (6) Whether man chooses of necessity or freely?

ARTICLE 1. *Whether Choice Is an Act of Will or of Reason?*

We proceed thus to the First Article: It would seem that choice is an act, not of will but of reason.

Objection 1. For choice implies comparison,

by which one is given preference to another. But to compare is an act of reason. Therefore choice is an act of reason.

Obj. 2. Further, it pertains to the same power to form a syllogism and to draw the conclusion. But, in practical matters, it is the reason that forms syllogisms. Since therefore choice is a kind of conclusion in practical matters, as stated in the *Ethics*[1] it seems that it is an act of reason.

Obj. 3. Further, ignorance does not pertain to the will but to the knowing power. Now "there is an ignorance of choice", as is stated in the *Ethics*.[2] Therefore it seems that choice does not belong to the will but to the reason.

On the contrary, The Philosopher says[3] that "choice is the desire of things in our own power." But desire is an act of will. Therefore choice is too.

I answer that, The word choice implies something belonging to the reason or intellect, and something belonging to the will; for the Philosopher says[4] that "choice is either intellect influenced by appetite or appetite influenced by intellect." Now whenever two things concur to make one, one of them serves as form for the other. Hence Gregory of Nyssa (Nemesius, *De Nat. Hom.* xxxiii)[5] says that "choice is neither desire only, nor counsel only, but a combination of the two. For just as we say that an animal is composed of soul and body, and that it is neither a mere body, nor a mere soul, but both, so is it with choice."

Now we must observe, as regards the acts of the soul, that an act belonging essentially to some power or habit, receives a form or species from a higher power or habit, according as the lower is ordered by the higher. For if a man were to perform an act of fortitude for the love of God, that act is materially an act of fortitude, but formally, an act of charity. Now it is evident that, in a sense, reason precedes the will and orders its act, that is in so far as the will tends to its object according to the order of reason, since the apprehensive power presents the object to the appetite. Accordingly, that act by which the will tends to something proposed to it as good, is, from the fact that it is ordered to the end by the reason, materially an act of the will, but formally an act of the reason. Now in matters of this kind the substance of the act is as the matter in relation to the order imposed by the higher power. There-

fore choice is substantially not an act of the reason but of the will, for choice is accomplished by a certain movement of the soul towards the good which is chosen. Consequently it is evidently an act of the appetitive power.

Reply Obj. 1. Choice implies a previous comparison, but not as though it consisted in the comparison itself.

Reply Obj. 2. It is true that it is for the reason to draw the conclusion of a practical syllogism; and it is called a decision or judgment, to be followed by choice. And for this reason the conclusion seems to belong to the act of choice, as to that which results from it.

Reply Obj. 3. In speaking of ignorance of choice, we do not mean that choice is a sort of knowledge, but that there is ignorance of what ought to be chosen.

ARTICLE 2. *Whether Choice Is to Be Found in Irrational Animals?*

We proceed thus to the Second Article: It would seem that irrational animals are able to choose.

Objection 1. For choice is "the desire of certain things on account of an end," as stated in the *Ethics*.[6] But irrational animals desire something on account of an end, since they act for an end and from desire. Therefore choice is in irrational animals.

Obj. 2. Further, the very word *electio* (choice) seems to signify the taking of something in preference to others. But irrational animals take something in preference to others, for we can easily see for ourselves that a sheep will eat one grass and refuse another. Therefore choice is in irrational animals.

Obj. 3. Further, according to the *Ethics*,[7] "it is from prudence that a man makes a good choice of means." But prudence is found in irrational animals; hence it is said in the beginning of the *Metaphysics*[8] that "those animals which, like bees, cannot hear sounds, are prudent without learning it." We see this plainly, in wonderful cases of sagacity manifested in the works of various animals, such as bees, spiders, and dogs. For a hound in following a stag, on coming to a cross-road, tries by scent whether the stag has passed by the first or the second road, and if he find that the stag has not passed there, being thus assured, takes to the third road without trying the scent, as though he were reasoning by way of exclusion, arguing

---

[1] Aristotle, III, 3 (1113ª4).
[2] Aristotle, III, 1 (1110ᵇ31).   [3] *Ethics*, III, 3 (1113ª9).
[4] *Ibid.*, VI, 2 (1139ᵇ4).   [5] PG 40, 732.

[6] Aristotle, III, 2, 3 (1111ᵇ27; 1113ª11).
[7] Aristotle, VI, 12 (1144ª8).
[8] Aristotle, I, 1 (980ᵇ22).

that the stag must have passed by this way, since he did not pass by the others, and there is no other road. Therefore it seems that irrational animals are able to choose.

On the contrary, Gregory of Nyssa says[1] that "children and irrational animals act willingly but not from choice." Therefore choice is not in irrational animals.

I answer that, Since choice is the taking of one thing in preference to another, it must of necessity be in respect of several things that can be chosen. Consequently in those things which are altogether determined to one thing there is no place for choice. Now the difference between the sensitive appetite and the will is that, as stated above (Q. I, A. 2. reply 3), the sensitive appetite is determined to one particular thing, according to the order of nature; but the will, although determined to one thing in general, namely, the good, according to the order of nature, is nevertheless indeterminate in respect of particular goods. Consequently choice belongs properly to the will, and not to the sensitive appetite which is all that irrational animals have. Therefore irrational animals are not able to choose.

Reply Obj. 1. Not every desire of one thing on account of an end is called choice, but there must be a certain discrimination of one thing from another. And this cannot be except when the appetite can be moved to several things.

Reply Obj. 2. An irrational animal takes one thing in preference to another because its appetite is naturally determined to that thing. Therefore as soon as an animal, whether by its sense or by its imagination, is offered something to which its appetite is naturally inclined, it is moved to that alone, without making any choice. Just as fire is moved upwards and not downwards, without its making any choice.

Reply Obj. 3. As stated in the *Physics,*[2] "movement is the act of the movable, caused by a mover." Therefore the power of the mover appears in the movement of that which it moves. Accordingly, in all things moved by reason, the order of reason which moves them is evident, although the things themselves are void of reason; for an arrow through the motion of the archer goes straight towards the target, as though it were endowed with reason to direct its course. The same may be seen in the movements of clocks and all engines put together by the art of man. Now as artificial

things are in comparison to human art, so are all natural things in comparison to the Divine art. And accordingly order is to be seen in things moved by nature, just as in things moved by reason, as is stated in the *Physics.*[3] And thus it is that in the works of irrational animals we notice certain marks of sagacity, in so far as they have a natural inclination to set about their actions in a most orderly manner through being ordered by the Supreme art. For which reason, too, certain animals are called prudent or sagacious, and not because they reason or exercise any choice about things. This is clear from the fact that all that share in one nature invariably act in the same way.

ARTICLE 3. *Whether Choice Is Only of the Means, or Sometimes Also of the End?*

We proceed thus to the Third Article: It seems that choice is not only of the means.

Objection 1. For the Philosopher says[4] that "virtue makes us choose rightly; but it is not the part of virtue, but of some other power to direct rightly those things which are to be done for its sake." But that for the sake of which something is done is the end. Therefore choice is of the end.

Obj. 2. Further, choice implies preference of one thing to another. But just as there can be preference of means, so can there be preference of ends. Therefore choice can be of ends, just as it can be of means.

On the contrary, The Philosopher says[5] that "volition is of the end, but choice, of the means."

I answer that, As already stated (A. I. REPLY 2), choice results from the decision or judgment which is, as it were, the conclusion of a practical syllogism. Hence that which is the conclusion of a practical syllogism, falls under choice. Now in practical things the end stands in the position of a principle, not of a conclusion, as the Philosopher says.[6] Therefore the end, as such, is not a matter of choice.

But just as in speculative knowledge nothing hinders the principle of one demonstration or of one science from being the conclusion of another demonstration or science, although the first indemonstrable principle cannot be the conclusion of any demonstration or science, so too that which is the end in one operation may be ordered to something as an end. And in this

---

[1] Nemesius, *De Nat. Hom.,* XXXIII (PG 40, 732).
[2] Aristotle, III, 3 (202ᵃ13).
[3] Aristotle, II, 5 (196ᵇ17).
[4] *Ethics,* VI, 12 (1144ᵃ20).
[5] *Ibid.,* III, 2 (1111ᵇ26).
[6] *Physics,* II, 9 (200ᵃ20).

way it is a matter of choice. Thus in the work of a physician, health is the end, and so it is not a matter of choice for a physician, but a matter of principle. Now the health of the body is ordered to the good of the soul, so that with one who has charge of the soul's health, health or sickness may be a matter of choice; for the Apostle says (II Cor. 12. 10): *For when I am weak, then am I powerful.* But the last end is in no way a matter of choice.

Reply Obj. 1. The proper ends of virtues are ordered to Happiness as to their last end. And thus it is that they can be a matter of choice.

Reply Obj. 2. As stated above (Q. I, A. 5), there is but one last end. Accordingly wherever there are several ends, they can be the subject of choice, in so far as they are ordered to a further end.

ARTICLE 4. *Whether Choice Is of Those Things Only That Are Done by Us?*

We proceed thus to the Fourth Article: It seems that choice is not only in respect of human acts.

Objection 1. For choice regards the means. Now, "not only acts, but also the organs, are means."[1] Therefore choice is not only concerned with human acts.

Obj. 2. Further, action is distinct from contemplation. But choice has a place even in contemplation, in so far as one opinion is preferred to another. Therefore choice is not concerned with human acts alone.

Obj. 3. Further, men are chosen for certain posts, whether secular or ecclesiastical, by those who exercise no action in their regard. Therefore choice is not concerned with human acts alone.

On the contrary, The Philosopher says[2] that "no man chooses save what he thinks he can do himself."

I answer that, Just as intention is of the end, so is choice of the means. Now the end is either an action or a thing. And when the end is a thing, some human action must intervene, either in so far as man produces the thing which is the end, as the physician produces health (and so the production of health is said to be the end of the physician), or in so far as man, in some fashion, uses or enjoys the thing which is the end; thus for the miser, money or the possession of money is the end. The same is to be said of the means. For the means must needs

[1] *Physics*, II, 3 (195ᵃ1).
[2] *Ethics*, III, 2 (1111ᵇ25).

be either an action, or a thing, with some action intervening by which man either makes the thing which is the means, or puts it to some use. And thus it is that choice is always in regard to human acts.

Reply Obj. 1. The organs are ordered to the end, inasmuch as man makes use of them for the sake of the end.

Reply Obj. 2. In contemplation itself there is the act of the intellect assenting to this or that opinion. What is put in contradistinction to contemplation is exterior action.

Reply Obj. 3. When a man chooses someone for a bishopric or some high position in the state, he chooses to name that man to that post. Otherwise, if he had no right to act in the appointment of the bishop or official, he would have no right to choose. Likewise, whenever we speak of one thing being chosen in preference to another, it is in conjunction with some action of the chooser.

ARTICLE 5. *Whether Choice Is Only of Possible Things?*

We proceed thus to the Fifth Article: It seems that choice is not only of possible things.

Objection 1. For choice is an act of the will, as stated above (A. 1). Now "there is a willing of possibilities and impossibilities."[3] Therefore there is also a choice of impossibilities.

Obj. 2. Further, choice is of things done by us, as stated above (A. 4.) Therefore it does not matter, as far as the act of choosing is concerned, whether one choose that which is impossible absolutely or that which is impossible to the chooser. Now it often happens that we are unable to accomplish what we choose, so that this proves to be impossible to us. Therefore choice is of the impossible.

Obj. 3. Further, to try to do a thing is to choose to do it. But the blessed Benedict says (*Regula* lxviii)[4] that if the superior command what is impossible, it should be attempted. Therefore choice can be of the impossible.

On the contrary, The Philosopher says[5] that "there is no choice of impossibilities."

I answer that, As stated above (A. 4), our choice is always concerned with our actions. Now whatever is done by us, is possible to us. Therefore we must say that choice is only of possible things.

Moreover, the reason for choosing a thing

[3] *Ibid.*, III, 2 (1111ᵇ22).
[4] PL 66, 917.
[5] *Ethics*, III, 2 (1111ᵇ20).

is that it leads to an end. But what is impossible cannot lead to an end. A sign of this is that when men in taking counsel together come to something that is impossible to them, they depart, as being unable to proceed with the business.

Again, this is evident if we examine the process of the reason that precedes. For the means, which are the object of choice, are to the end as the conclusion is to the principle. Now it is clear that an impossible conclusion does not follow from a possible principle. Therefore an end cannot be possible, unless the means be possible. Now no one is moved to the impossible. Consequently no one would tend to the end, save for the fact that the means appear to be possible. Therefore the impossible is not the object of choice.

Reply Obj. 1. The will stands between the intellect and the external action, for the intellect proposes to the will its object, and the will itself causes the external action. Hence the beginning of the movement in the will is to be found in the intellect, which apprehends something as universal good; but the term or perfection of the will's act is to be observed in its relation to the action by which a man tends to the attainment of a thing; for the movement of the will is from the soul to the thing. Consequently the perfection of the act of the will is in respect of something that is good for one to do. Now this cannot be something impossible. Therefore the complete act of the will is only in respect of what is possible and good for him that wills. But the incomplete act of the will is in respect of the impossible, and by some is called "velleity," because, namely, one would will (*vellet*) such a thing, were it possible. But choice is an act of the will already determined to something to be done by the chooser. And therefore it can only be of what is possible.

Reply Obj. 2. Since the object of the will is the apprehended good, we must judge of the object of the will according as it it apprehended. And so, just as sometimes the will tends to something which is apprehended as good, and yet is not really good, so is choice sometimes made of something apprehended as possible to the chooser, and yet impossible to him.

Reply Obj. 3. The reason for this is that the subject should not rely on his own judgment to decide whether a certain thing is possible, but in each case should stand by his superior's judgment.

ARTICLE 6. *Whether Man Chooses of Necessity or Freely?*

We proceed thus to the Sixth Article: It seems that man chooses of necessity.

Objection 1. For the end stands in relation to the things that can be chosen as the principle to that which follows from the principles, as declared in the *Ethics.*[1] But conclusions follow of necessity from their principles. Therefore man is moved of necessity from the end to the choice.

Obj. 2. Further, as stated above (A. 1. REPLY 2), choice follows the reason's judgment of what is to be done. But reason judges of necessity about some things, on account of the necessity of the premises. Therefore it seems that choice also follows of necessity.

Obj. 3. Further, if two things are absolutely equal, man is not moved to one more than to the other. Thus if a hungry man, as Plato says,[2] be confronted on either side with two portions of food equally appetizing and at an equal distance, he is not moved towards one more than to the other; and he finds the reason of this in the immobility of the earth in the middle of the world as it is said in the book on the *Heavens.*[3] Now much less can that be chosen which is less desirable than that which is equally so. Therefore if two or more things are available, of which one appears to be more desirable, it is impossible to choose any of the others. Therefore that which appears to hold the first place is chosen of necessity. But every act of choosing is in regard to something that seems in some way better. Therefore every choice is made necessarily.

On the contrary, Choice is an act of a rational power, which according to the Philosopher,[4] stands in relation to opposites.

I answer that, Man does not choose of necessity. And this is because that which is possible not to be, is not of necessity. Now the reason why it is possible not to choose, or to choose, may be gathered from a twofold power in man. For man can will and not will, act and not act; again, he can will this or that, and do this or that. The reason of this is seated in the very power of the reason. For the will can tend to whatever the reason can apprehend as good. Now the reason can apprehend as good, not only this, namely, to will or to act, but also this,

---

[1] Aristotle, VII, 8 (1151ª16).

[2] *Timaeus* (63); *Phaedo* (108); cf. Averroes, *In de Cælo*, II, 90 (V, 157c). See also Duhem, *Le Système du Monde.* (I, 85).

[3] Aristotle, II, 13 (295ᵇ12; ᵇ25); cf. St. Thomas, *In de Cælo*, II, 25.

[4] *Metaphysics*, IX, 2 (1046ᵇ8).

namely, not to will or not to act. Again, in all particular goods, the reason can consider an aspect of some good and the lack of some good, which has the aspect of evil; and in this respect, it can apprehend any single one of such goods as to be chosen or to be avoided. The perfect good alone, which is Happiness, cannot be apprehended by the reason under the aspect of evil, or as lacking in any way. Consequently man wills Happiness of necessity, nor can he will not to be happy, or to be unhappy. Now since choice is not of the end, but of the means, as stated above (A. 3), it is not of the perfect good, which is Happiness, but of other particular goods. Therefore man chooses not of necessity but freely.

Reply Obj. 1. The conclusion does not always of necessity follow from the principles, but only when the principles cannot be true if the conclusion is not true. In like manner, the end does not always necessitate in man the choosing of the means, because the means are not always such that the end cannot be gained without them; of, if they be such, they are not always considered in that light.

Reply Obj. 2. The reason's decision or judgment of what is to be done is about contingent things that are possible to us. In such matters the conclusions do not follow of necessity from principles that are absolutely necessary, but from such as are so conditionally; as, for instance, If he runs, he is in motion.

Reply Obj. 3. If two things be proposed as equal under one aspect, nothing hinders us from considering in one of them some particular point of superiority, so that the will has a bent towards that one rather than towards the other.

QUESTION XIV
OF COUNSEL, WHICH PRECEDES CHOICE
(*In Six Articles*)

WE must now consider counsel; concerning which there are six points of inquiry: (1) Whether counsel is an inquiry? (2) Whether counsel is of the end or only of the means? (3) Whether counsel is only of things that we do? (4) Whether counsel is of all things that we do? (5) Whether the process of counsel is one of resolution? (6) Whether the process of counsel is infinite?

ARTICLE 1. *Whether Counsel Is an Inquiry?*

We proceed thus to the First Article: It seems that counsel is not an inquiry.

Objection 1. For Damascene says (*De Fide Orth*. ii)[1] that "counsel is an appetite." But inquiry is not an act of the appetite. Therefore counsel is not an inquiry.

Obj. 2. Further, inquiry is a discursive act of the intellect, for which reason it is unbecoming to God, Whose knowledge is not discursive, as we have shown in the First Part (Q. XIV, A. 7). But counsel is ascribed to God, for it is written (Eph. 1. 11) that *He worketh all things according to the counsel of His will*. Therefore counsel is not inquiry.

Obj. 3. Further, inquiry is of doubtful matters. But counsel is given in matters that are certainly good; thus the Apostle says (I Cor. 7. 25): *Now concerning virgins I have no commandment of the Lord: but I give counsel*. Therefore, counsel is not an inquiry.

On the contrary, Gregory of Nyssa says[2]: "Every counsel is an inquiry; but not every inquiry is a counsel."

I answer that, Choice, as stated above (Q. XIII, A. 1. REPLY 2; A. 3), follows the judgment of the reason about what is to be done. Now there is much uncertainty in things that have to be done, because actions are concerned with contingent singulars, which by reason of their changeability, are uncertain. Now in things doubtful and uncertain the reason does not pronounce judgment without previous inquiry. Therefore the reason must of necessity institute an inquiry before deciding on the objects of choice, and this inquiry is called counsel. Hence the Philosopher says[3] that choice is "the desire of what has been already counselled."

Reply Obj. 1. When the acts of two powers are ordered to one another, in each of them there is something belonging to the other power. Consequently each act can be named from either power. Now it is evident that the act of the reason giving direction as to the means, and the act of the will tending to these means according to the reason's direction, are ordered to one another. Consequently there is to be found something of the reason, namely, order, in that act of the will, which is choice. And in counsel, which is an act of reason, there is to be found something of the will,—both as matter (since counsel is of what man wills to do),—and as motive (because it is from willing the end, that man is moved to take counsel in regard to the means). And therefore, just as the Philosopher says[4] that "choice is intellect influenced by ap-

---

[1] Chap. 22 (PG 94, 945).
[2] Nemesius, *De Nat. Hom.*, XXXIV (PG 40, 736).
[3] *Ethics*, III, 2, 3 (1112^{a}15, 1113^{a}11).
[4] *Ibid.*, VI, 2 (1139^{b}4).

petite," thus pointing out that both concur in the act of choosing, so Damascene says (loc. cit.) that "counsel is appetite based on inquiry," so as to show that counsel belongs, in a way, both to the will, on whose behalf and by whose impulse the inquiry is made, and to the reason that makes the inquiry.

Reply Obj. 2. The things that we say of God must be understood without any of the defects which are to be found in us. Thus in us science is of conclusions derived by reasoning from causes to effects, but science when said of God, means certain knowledge of all effects in the First Cause, without any reasoning process. In like manner we ascribe counsel to God, as to the certainty of His decision or judgment, which certainty in us arises from the inquiry of counsel. But such inquiry has no place in God, and therefore in this respect it is not ascribed to God. In which sense Damascene says (loc. cit.): "God takes not counsel: those only take counsel who lack knowledge."

Reply Obj. 3. It may happen that things which are most certainly good in the opinion of wise and spiritual men are not certainly good in the opinion of many, or at least of carnal-minded men. Consequently in such things counsel may be given.

ARTICLE 2. Whether Counsel Is of the End, or Only of the Means?

We proceed thus to the Second Article: It would seem that counsel is not only of the means but also of the end.

Objection 1. For whatever is doubtful, can be the subject of inquiry. Now in things to be done by man there happens sometimes a doubt as to the end and not only as to the means. Since therefore inquiry as to what is to be done is counsel, it seems that counsel can be of the end.

Obj. 2. Further, the matter of counsel is human actions. But some human actions are ends, as stated in the Ethics.[1] Therefore counsel can be of the end.

On the contrary, Gregory of Nyssa says[2] that "counsel is not of the end, but of the means."

I answer that, The end is the principle in practical matters, because the nature of the means is to be found in the end. Now the principle cannot be called in question, but must be presupposed in every inquiry. Since therefore counsel is an inquiry, it is not of the end but only of the means. Nevertheless it may happen that what is the end in regard to some things is

ordered to something else; just as also what is the principle of one demonstration is the conclusion of another. And consequently that which is looked upon as the end in one inquiry may be looked upon as the means in another. And thus it will become an object of counsel.

Reply Obj. 1. That which is looked upon as an end is already determined. Consequently as long as there is any doubt about it, it is not looked upon as an end. Therefore if counsel is taken about it, it will be counsel not about the end, but about the means.

Reply Obj. 2. Counsel is about operations, in so far as they are ordered to some end. Consequently if any human act be an end, it will not, as such, be the matter of counsel.

ARTICLE 3. Whether Counsel Is Only of Things That We Do?

We proceed thus to the Third Article: It seems that counsel is not only of things that we do.

Objection 1. For counsel implies some kind of bringing together. But it is possible for many to compare things that are not subject to movement, and are not the result of our actions, such as the natures of various things. Therefore counsel is not only of things that we do.

Obj. 2. Further, men sometimes seek counsel about things that are laid down by law; hence we speak of counsel at law. And yet those who seek counsel thus have nothing to do in making the laws. Therefore counsel is not only of things that we do.

Obj. 3. Further, some are said to take consultation about future events, which, however, are not in our power. Therefore counsel is not only of things that we do.

Obj. 4. Further, if counsel were only of things that we do, no one would take counsel about what another does. But this is clearly untrue. Therefore counsel is not only of things that we do.

On the contrary, Gregory of Nyssa (Nemesius,—De Nat. Hom. xxxiv)[3] says: "We take counsel of things that take place within us and that we are able to do."

I answer that, Counsel properly implies a conference held between several. The very word (consilium) denotes this, for it means a sitting together (considium), from the fact that many sit together in order to confer with one another. Now we must take note that in contingent particular cases, in order that anything be known for certain it is necessary to take several condi-

---

[1] Aristotle, I, 1 (1094^a4).
[2] Nemesius, De Nat. Hom., XXXIV (PG 40, 740).
[3] PG 40, 737.

tions or circumstances into consideration, which it is not easy for one to consider, but are considered by several with greater certainty, since what one takes note of escapes the notice of another. But in necessary and universal things, our view is brought to bear on matters much more absolute and simple, so that one man by himself may be more adequate to consider these things. Therefore the inquiry of counsel is concerned, properly speaking, with contingent singulars. Now the knowledge of the truth in such matters does not rank so high as to be desirable of itself, as is the knowledge of things universal and necessary, but it is desired as being useful towards action, because actions bear on things singular and contingent. Consequently, properly speaking, counsel is about things done by us.

Reply Obj. 1. Counsel implies comparison, not of any kind, but about what is to be done, for the reason given above.

Reply Obj. 2. Although that which is laid down by the law is not due to the action of him who seeks counsel, nevertheless it directs him in his action, since the mandate of the law is one reason for doing something.

Reply Obj. 3. Counsel is not only about what is done, but also about whatever has relation to what is done. And for this reason we speak of consulting about future events, in so far as man is induced to do or omit something, through the knowledge of future events.

Reply Obj. 4. We seek counsel about the actions of others in so far as they are, in some way, one with us; either by union of affection—thus a man is solicitous about what concerns his friend, as though it concerned himself; or after the manner of an instrument, for the principal agent and the instrument are, in a way, one cause, since one acts through the other; thus the master takes counsel about what he would do through his servant.

ARTICLE 4. *Whether Counsel Is About All Things That We Do?*

We proceed thus to the Fourth Article: It seems that counsel is about all things that we have to do.

Objection 1. For choice is the desire of what is counselled as stated above (A. 1). But choice is about all things that we do. Therefore counsel is too.

Obj. 2. Further, counsel implies the reason's inquiry. But whenever we do not act through the impulse of passion we act in virtue of the reason's inquiry. Therefore there is counsel about everything that we do.

Obj. 3. Further, the Philosopher says[1] that "if it appears that something can be done by more means than one, we take counsel by inquiring whereby it may be done most easily and best; but if it can be accomplished by one means, how it can be done by this." But whatever is done, is done by one means or by several. Therefore counsel takes place in all things that we do.

On the contrary, Gregory of Nyssa (Nemesius,—*De Nat. Hom.* xxxiv)[2] says that "counsel has no place in things that are done according to science or art."

I answer that, Counsel is a kind of inquiry, as stated above (A. 1). But we are accustomed to inquire about things that admit of doubt; hence the process of inquiry, which is called an argument, is a reason that certifies to something that admitted of doubt. Now, that something in relation to human acts, admits of no doubt, arises from a twofold source. First, because certain determinate ends are gained by certain determinate means, as happens in the arts which are governed by certain fixed rules of action. Thus a writer does not take counsel how to form his letters, for this is determined by art. Secondly, from the fact that it matters little whether it is done this or that way. This occurs in trivial matters, which help or hinder but little towards the end aimed at; and reason accounts them as nothing. Consequently there are two things of which we do not take counsel, although they are ordered to the end, as the Philosopher says;[3] namely, trivial things, and those which have a fixed way of being done, as in works produced by art, with the exception of those arts that admit of conjecture, such as medicine, commerce, and the like, as Gregory of Nyssa says (Nemesius,—*loc. cit.*).

Reply Obj. 1. Choice presupposes counsel by reason of its judgment or decision. Consequently when the judgment or decision is evident without inquiry there is no need for the inquiry of counsel.

Reply Obj. 2. In matters that are evident the reason makes no inquiry, but judges at once. Consequently there is no need of counsel in all that is done by reason.

Reply Obj. 3. When a thing can be accomplished by one means, but in different ways, doubt may arise, just as when it can be accomplished by several means. And hence the need of counsel. But when not only the means but also the way of using the means, is fixed, then there is no need of counsel.

[1] *Ethics,* III, 3 (1112^{b}16).   [2] PG 40, 740.
[3] *Ethics,* III, 3 (1112^{b}9).

ARTICLE 5. *Whether the Process of Counsel Is One of Resolution?*

We proceed thus to the Fifth Article: It seems that the process of counsel is not one of resolution.

Objection 1. For counsel is about things that we do. But the process of our actions is not one of resolution, but rather one of composition, namely, from the simple to the composite. Therefore counsel does not always proceed by way of resolution.

Obj. 2. Further, counsel is an inquiry of the reason. But reason proceeds from things that precede to things that follow, according to the more appropriate order. Since then, the past precedes the present, and the present precedes the future, it seems that in taking counsel one should proceed from the past and present to the future, which is not the order of resolution. Therefore the process of counsel is not one of resolution.

Obj. 3. Further, counsel is only of such things as are possible to us, according to the *Ethics*.[1] But the question as to whether a certain thing is possible to us depends on what we are able or unable to do in order to gain such and such an end. Therefore the inquiry of counsel should begin from things present.

On the contrary, The Philosopher says[2] that "he who takes counsel seems to inquire and resolve."

I answer that, In every inquiry one must begin from some principle. And if this principle precedes both in knowledge and in being, the process is not one of resolution, but rather of composition, because to proceed from cause to effect is to proceed by way of composition, since causes are more simple than effects. But if that which precedes in knowledge is later in the order of being, the process is one of resolution, as when our judgment deals with clearly known effects, which we resolve into their simple causes. Now the principle in the inquiry of counsel is the end, which precedes indeed in intention, but comes afterwards in being. Hence the inquiry of counsel must be one of resolution, beginning, that is to say, from that which is intended in the future, and continuing until it arrives at that which is to be immediately done.

Reply Obj. 1. Counsel is indeed about action. But the notion of action is taken from the end, and consequently the order of reasoning about actions is contrary to the order of actions.

[1] Aristotle, III, 3 (1112[b]26).
[2] *Ethics*, III, 3 (1112[b]20).

Reply Obj. 2. Reason begins with that which is first according to reason, but not always with that which is first in point of time.

Reply Obj. 3. We should not want to know whether something to be done for an end be possible, if it were not suitable for gaining that end. Hence we must first inquire whether it be conducive to the end before considering whether it be possible.

ARTICLE 6. *Whether the Process of Counsel Is Infinite?*

We proceed thus to the Sixth Article: It seems that the process of counsel is infinite.

Objection 1. For counsel is an inquiry about the particular things with which action is concerned. But singulars are infinite. Therefore the process of counsel is infinite.

Obj. 2. Further, the inquiry of counsel has to consider not only what is to be done, but how to avoid obstacles. But every human action can be hindered, and an obstacle can be removed by some human reason. Therefore the inquiry about removing obstacles can go on infinitely.

Obj. 3. Further, the inquiry of demonstrative science does not go on infinitely, because one can come to principles that are self-evident, which are absolutely certain. But certainty of this kind is not to be had in contingent singulars, which are variable and uncertain. Therefore the inquiry of counsel goes on infinitely.

On the contrary, "No one is moved to that which he cannot possibly reach."[3] But it is impossible to pass through the infinite. If therefore the inquiry of counsel is infinite, no one would begin to take counsel. Which is clearly untrue.

I answer that, The inquiry of counsel is actually finite on both sides, on that of its principle and on that of its term. For a twofold principle is available in the inquiry of counsel. One is proper to it, and belongs to the very genus of things pertaining to operation; this is the end, which is not the matter of counsel, but is taken for granted as its principle, as stated above (A. 2). The other principle is taken from another genus, so to speak; thus in demonstrative sciences one science postulates certain things from another, without inquiring into them. Now these principles which are taken for granted in the inquiry of counsel are any facts received through the senses—for instance, that this is bread or iron; and also what is known in a universal manner either through speculative or through practical science; for instance, that adultery is

[3] Aristotle, *Heavens*, I, 7 (274[b]17).

forbidden by God, or that man cannot live without suitable nourishment. Of such things counsel makes no inquiry. But the term of inquiry is that which we are able to do at once. For just as the end has the character of a principle, so the means have the character of a conclusion. Therefore that which presents itself as to be done first, has the character of an ultimate conclusion at which the inquiry comes to an end. Nothing however prevents counsel from being infinite potentially, since an infinite number of things may present themselves to be inquired into by means of counsel.

Reply Obj. 1. Singulars are infinite, not actually, but only potentially.

Reply Obj. 2. Although human action can be hindered, the hindrance is not always present. Consequently it is not always necessary to take counsel about removing the obstacle.

Reply Obj. 3. In contingent singulars, something may be taken for certain, not absolutely, indeed, but for the time being, and as far as it concerns the work to be done. Thus that Socrates is sitting is not a necessary statement, but that he is sitting, as long as he continues to sit, is necessary. And this can be held with certainty.

QUESTION XV

OF CONSENT, WHICH IS AN ACT OF THE WILL IN RELATION TO THE MEANS

(In Four Articles)

WE must now consider consent, concerning which there are four points of inquiry: (1) Whether consent is an act of the appetitive or of the apprehensive power? (2) Whether it is appropriate to irrational animals? (3) Whether it is directed to the end or to the means? (4) Whether consent to an act pertains to the higher part of the soul only?

ARTICLE 1. *Whether Consent Is an Act of the Appetitive or of the Apprehensive Power?*

We proceed thus to the First Article: It seems that consent belongs only to the apprehensive part of the soul.

Objection 1. For Augustine (*De Trin.* xii)[1] ascribes consent to the higher reason. But the reason is an apprehensive power. Therefore consent belongs to an apprehensive power.

Obj. 2. Further, consent is "co-sense." But sense is an apprehensive power. Therefore consent is the act of an apprehensive power.

Obj. 3. Further, just as assent is an application of the intellect to something, so is consent. But assent pertains to the intellect, which is an apprehensive power. Therefore consent also belongs to an apprehensive power.

On the contrary, Damascene says (*De Fide Orthod.* ii)[2] that "if a man judge without love for that of which he judges, there is no decision," that is, consent. But to love pertains to the appetitive power. Therefore consent does also.

I answer that, Consent implies application of sense to something. Now it is proper to sense to take cognizance of things present, for the imagination apprehends the likeness of corporeal things even in the absence of the things of which they bear the likeness, while the intellect apprehends universal notions, which it can apprehend indifferently, whether the singulars be present or absent. And since the act of an appetitive power is a kind of inclination to the thing itself, the application of the appetitive power to the thing, in so far as it cleaves to it, gets by a kind of likeness, the name of sense, since it acquires an experience as it were, of the thing to which it cleaves, in so far as it is satisfied in it. Hence it is written (Wisd. 1. 1): *Think of (Sentite) the Lord in goodness.* And on these grounds consent is an act of the appetitive power.

Reply Obj. 1. As stated in the treatise on the *Soul*,[3] "the will is in the reason." Hence, when Augustine ascribes consent to the reason, he takes reason as including the will.

Reply Obj. 2. Sense, properly speaking, belongs to the apprehensive faculty; but by way of likeness, in so far as it implies seeking acquaintance, it pertains to the appetitive power, as stated above.

Reply Obj. 3. To assent (*assentire*) is, so to speak, to feel towards something (*ad aliud sentire*); and thus it implies a certain distance from that to which assent is given. But to consent (*consentire*) is to feel with, and this implies a certain union to the object of consent. Hence the will, to which it pertains to tend to the thing itself, is more properly said to consent; but the intellect, whose act does not consist in a movement towards the thing, but rather the reverse, as we have stated in the First Part (Q. XVI, A. 1; Q. XXVII, A. 4; Q. LIX, A. 2), is more properly said to assent; although one word is customarily used for the other. We may also say that the intellect assents, in so far as it is moved by the will.

[1] Chap. 12 (PL 42, 1007).
[2] Chap. 22 (PG 94, 945).
[3] Aristotle, III, 9 (432^{b}5).

ARTICLE 2. *Whether Consent Is Appropriate to Irrational Animals?*

We proceed thus to the Second Article: It seems that consent is appropriate to irrational animals.

Objection 1. For consent implies a determination of the appetite to one thing. But the appetite of irrational animals is determined to one thing. Therefore consent is to be found in irrational animals.

Obj. 2. Further, if you remove what is first, you remove what follows. But consent precedes the accomplished act. If therefore there were no consent in irrational animals, there would be no act accomplished, which is clearly false.

Obj. 3. Further, men are sometimes said to consent to do something through some passion; desire, for instance, or anger. But irrational animals act through passion. Therefore they consent.

On the contrary, Damascene says (*De Fide Orthod.* ii)[1] that "after judging, man approves and embraces the judgment of his counselling, and this is called the decision," that is, consent. But counsel is not in irrational animals. Therefore neither is consent.

I answer that, Consent, properly speaking, is not in irrational animals. The reason of this is that consent implies an application of the appetitive movement to something as to be done. Now to apply the appetitive movement to the doing of something pertains to the subject in whose power it is to move the appetite. Thus to touch a stone is an action suitable to a stick, but to apply the stick so that it touch the stone, pertains to one who has the power of moving the stick. But irrational animals have not the command of the appetitive movement, for this is in them through natural instinct. Hence in the irrational animal, there is indeed the movement of appetite, but it does not apply that movement to some particular thing. And hence it is that the irrational animal is not properly said to consent. This is proper to the rational nature alone, which has the command of the appetitive movement, and is able to apply or not to apply it to this or that thing.

Reply Obj. 1. In irrational animals the determination of the appetite to a particular thing is merely passive. But consent implies a determination of the appetite which is active rather than merely passive.

Reply Obj. 2. If the first be removed, then what follows is removed, provided that, properly

speaking, it follow from that only. But if something can follow from several things, it is not removed by the fact that one of them is removed. Thus if hardening is the effect of heat and of cold (since bricks are hardened by fire, and frozen water is hardened by the cold), then by removing heat it does not follow that there is no hardening. Now the accomplishment of an act follows not only from consent, but also from the impulse of the appetite, such as is found in irrational animals.

Reply Obj. 3. The man who acts through passion is able not to follow the passion. But irrational animals do not have that power. Hence the comparison fails.

ARTICLE 3. *Whether Consent Is Directed to the End or to the Means?*

We proceed thus to the Third Article: It would seem that consent is directed to the end.

Objection 1. Because that on account of which a thing is such is still more such. But it is on account of the end that we consent to the means. Therefore, still more do we consent to the end.

Obj. 2. Further, the act of the intemperate man is his end, just as the act of the virtuous man is his end. But the intemperate man consents to his own act. Therefore consent can be directed to the end.

Obj. 3. Further, desire of the means is choice, as stated above (Q. XIII, A. 1). If therefore consent were only directed to the means it would in no way differ from choice. And this is proved to be false by the authority of Damascene who says (*De Fide Orthod.* ii, 22)[2] that after the approval which he calls the decision, comes the choice. Therefore consent is not only directed to the means.

On the contrary, Damascene says (*ibid.*) that the decision, that is, the consent, takes place "when man approves and embraces the judgment of his counsel." But counsel is only about the means. Therefore the same applies to consent.

I answer that, Consent is the application of the appetitive movement to something that is already in the power of him who causes the application. Now the order of action is this: first there is the apprehension of the end; then the desire of the end; then the counsel about the means; then the desire of the means. Now the appetite tends to the last end naturally, and therefore the application of the appetitive movement to the apprehended end has not the

[1] Chap. 22 (PG 94, 945).

[2] PG 94, 945.

nature of consent, but of simple volition. But as to those things which come under consideration after the last end, in so far as they are directed to the end, they come under counsel; and so consent can be applied to them, in so far as the appetitive movement is applied to the judgment resulting from counsel. But the appetitive movement to the end is not applied to counsel, but rather counsel is applied to it, because counsel presupposes the desire of the end. On the other hand, the desire of the means presupposes the decision of counsel. And therefore the application of the appetitive movement to counsel's decision is consent, properly speaking. Consequently, since counsel is only about the means, consent, properly speaking, is of nothing else but the means.

Reply Obj. 1. Just as the knowledge of conclusions through the principles is science, while the knowledge of the principles is not science, but something higher, namely, understanding, so we consent to the means on account of the end, in respect of which our act is not consent, but something greater, namely, volition.

Reply Obj. 2. Delight in his act, rather than the act itself, is the end of the intemperate man, and for sake of this delight he consents to that act.

Reply Obj. 3. Choice includes something that consent does not have, namely, a certain relation to something to which something else is preferred. And therefore after consent there still remains a choice. For it may happen that by aid of counsel several means have been found which lead to the end, and through each of these meeting with approval, consent has been given to each. But after approving of many, we have given our preference to one by choosing it. But if only one meets with approval, then consent and choice do not differ in reality, but only in our way of looking at them, so that we call it consent, according as we approve of doing that thing, but choice according as we prefer it to those that do not meet with our approval.

ARTICLE 4. *Whether Consent to the Act Pertains Only to the Higher Part of the Soul?*

We proceed thus to the Fourth Article: It would seem that consent to the act does not always pertain to the higher reason.

Objection 1. For *delight follows action, and perfects it, just as beauty perfects youth.*[1] But consent to delight pertains to the lower reason,

as Augustine says (*De Trin.* xii, 12).[2] Therefore consent to the act does not pertain only to the higher reason.

Obj. 2. Further, an act to which we consent is said to be voluntary. But it pertains to many powers to produce voluntary acts. Therefore the higher reason is not alone in consenting to the act.

Obj. 3. Further, the higher reason is that which is intent on "the contemplation and consultation of things eternal," as Augustine says (*De Trin.* xii. 7).[3] But man often consents to an act not for eternal, but for temporal reasons, or even on account of some passion of the soul. Therefore consent to an act does not pertain to the higher reason alone.

On the contrary, Augustine says (*De Trin.* xii, 12):[4] It is impossible for man to make up his mind to commit a sin, unless that mental faculty which has the sovereign power of urging his members to act, or restraining them from act, yield to the evil deed and become its slave."

I answer that, The final decision belongs to him who holds the highest place, and to whom it pertains to judge of the others. For as long as judgment about some matter remains to be pronounced, the final decision has not been given. Now it is evident that it pertains to the higher reason to judge of all, since it is by the reason that we judge of sensible things; and of things pertaining to human principles we judge according to Divine principles, which is the function of the higher reason. Therefore as long as a man is uncertain whether he should resist or not, according to Divine principles, no judgment of the reason can be considered in the light of a final decision. Now the final decision of what is to be done is consent to the act. Therefore consent to the act pertains to the higher reason, but in that sense in which the reason includes the will, as stated above (A. 1. REPLY 1).

Reply Obj. 1. Consent to delight in the work done belongs to the higher reason, as also does consent to the work, but consent to delight in thought belongs to the lower reason, just as to the lower reason it belongs to think. Nevertheless the higher reason exercises judgment on the fact of thinking or not thinking, considered as an action, and in like manner on the delight that results. But in so far as the act of thinking is considered as ordered to a further act, it pertains to the lower reason. For that which is ordered to something else, pertains to a lower art

---

[1] Aristotle, *Ethics,* x, 4 (1174ᵇ31); οἷον τοῖς ἀκμαίοις ἡ ὥρα ; as youthful vigour perfects a man in his prime.

[2] PL 42, 1008.   [3] PL 42, 1005.
[4] PL 42, 1008.

or power than does the end to which it is ordered. Hence the art which is concerned with the end is called the master (archetectonic) or principal art.

Reply Obj. 2. Since actions are called voluntary from the fact that we consent to them, it does not follow that consent is an act of each power, but of the will which is in the reason, as stated above (A. 1. Reply 1), and from which the voluntary act is named.

Reply Obj. 3. The higher reason is said to consent not only because it always moves to act according to the eternal ideas, but also because it does not dissent according to those same ideas.

QUESTION XVI
OF USE, WHICH IS AN ACT OF THE
WILL IN RELATION TO THE MEANS
(*In Four Articles*)

WE must now consider use, concerning which there are four points of inquiry: (1) Whether use is an act of the will? (2) Whether it is to be found in irrational animals? (3) Whether it is of the means only, or the end also? (4) Of the relation of use to choice.

ARTICLE 1. *Whether Use Is an Act of the Will?*

We proceed thus to the First Article: It seems that use is not an act of the will.

Objection 1. For Augustine says[1] that "to use is to refer that which is the object of use to the obtaining of something else." But to refer something to another is an act of the reason to which it pertains to compare and to order. Therefore use is an act of the reason and not of the will.

Obj. 2. Further, Damascene says (*De Fide Orthod.* ii)[2] that "man goes forward to the operation, and this is called impulse; then he makes use (of the powers) and this is called use." But operation belongs to the executive power, and the act of the will does not follow the act of the executive power. On the contrary execution comes last. Therefore use is not an act of the will.

Obj. 3. Further, Augustine says,[3] "All things that were made were made for man's use, because reason with which man is endowed uses all things by its judgment of them." But judgment of things created by God pertains to the speculative reason, which seems to be altogether

[1] *Christian Doctrine,* I, 4 (PL 34, 20).
[2] Chap. 22 (PG 94, 945).
[3] QQ. LXXXIII, Qu. 30 (PL 40, 20).

distinct from the will, which is the principle of human acts. Therefore use is not an act of the will.

On the contrary, Augustine says (*De Trin.* x):[4] "To use is to apply something in the power of the will."

I answer that, The use of a thing implies the application of that thing to an operation. Hence the operation to which we apply a thing is called its use; thus the use of a horse is to ride, and the use of a stick is to strike. Now we apply to an operation not only the interior principles of action, namely, the powers of the soul or the members of the body, as the intellect to understand and the eye to see, but also external things, as a stick to strike. But it is evident that we do not apply external things to an operation save through the interior principles, which are either the powers of the soul, or the habits of those powers, or the organs which are parts of the body. Now it has been shown above (Q. IX, A. 1) that it is the will which moves the soul's powers to their acts, and this is to apply them to operation. Hence it is evident that first and principally use belongs to the will as first mover, to the reason, as directing, and to the other powers as executing the operation, which powers are compared to the will which applies them to act, as the instruments are compared to the principal agent. Now action is properly ascribed not to the instrument, but to the principal agent, as building is ascribed to the builder but not to his tools. Hence it is evident that use is, properly speaking, an act of the will.

Reply Obj. 1. Reason does indeed refer one thing to another, but the will tends to that which is referred by the reason to something else. And in this sense to use is to refer one thing to another.

Reply Obj. 2. Damascene is speaking of use in so far as it belongs to the executive powers.

Reply Obj. 3. Even the speculative reason is applied by the will to the act of understanding or judging. Consequently the speculative reason is said to use, in so far as it is moved by the will, in the same way as the other executive powers.

ARTICLE 2. *Whether Use Is to Be Found in Irrational Animals?*

We proceed thus to the Second Article: It would seem that use is to be found in irrational animals.

Objection 1. For it is better to enjoy than to use, because, as Augustine says (*De Trin.* x, 10):[5] "We use things by referring them to some-

[4] Chap. 11 (PL 42, 982).   [5] PL 42, 981

thing else which we are to enjoy." But enjoyment is to be found in irrational animals, as stated above (Q. XI, A. 2). Much more, therefore, is it possible for them to use.

Obj. 2. Further, to apply the members to action is to use them. But irrational animals apply their members to action; for instance, their feet, to walk, their horns, to strike. Therefore it is possible for irrational animals to use.

On the contrary, Augustine says (QQ. LXXXIII, *qu.* 30):[1] "None but a rational animal can make use of a thing."

I answer that, as stated above (A. I), to use is to apply an active principle to action. Thus to consent is to apply the appetitive movement to the desire of something, as stated above (Q. XV, AA. I, 2, 3). Now he alone who has the disposal of a thing, can apply it to something else, and this pertains to him alone who knows how to refer it to something else, which is an act of the reason. And therefore none but a rational animal consents and uses.

Reply Obj. 1. To enjoy implies the absolute movement of the appetite to the appetible, but to use implies a movement of the appetite to something as ordered to something else. If therefore we compare use and enjoyment in respect of their objects, enjoyment is better than use, because that which is desirable absolutely is better than that which is desirable only as ordered to something else. But if we compare them in respect of the apprehensive power that precedes them, greater excellence is required on the part of use, because to direct one thing to another is an act of reason, but to apprehend something absolutely is within the capacity even of sense.

Reply Obj. 2. Animals by means of their members do something from natural instinct, not through knowing the relation of their members to these operations. Therefore, properly speaking, they do not apply their members to action, nor do they use them.

ARTICLE 3. *Whether Use Can Be Also of the Last End?*

We proceed thus to the Third Article: It seems that use can be also of the last end.

Objection 1. For Augustine says (*De Trin.* x):[2] "Whoever enjoys, uses." But man enjoys the last end. Therefore he uses the last end.

Obj. 2. Further, "to use is to apply something in the power of the will" (*ibid.*). But the last end, more than anything else, is the object of

the will's application. Therefore it can be the object of use.

Obj. 3. Further, Hilary says (*De Trin.* ii)[3] that "Eternity is in the Father, Likeness in the Image," that is, in the Son, "Use in the Gift," that is, in the Holy Ghost. But the Holy Ghost, since He is God, is the last end. Therefore the last end can be the object of use.

On the contrary, Augustine says,[4] "No one rightly uses God, but he enjoys Him." But God alone is the last end. Therefore we cannot use the last end.

I answer that, Use, as stated above (A. I), implies the application of one thing to another. Now that which is applied to another is regarded in the light of means to an end; and consequently use always is of the means. For this reason things are adapted to a certain end are said to be useful; in fact their very usefulness is sometimes called use.

It must, however, be observed that the last end may be taken in two ways: first, absolutely; secondly, in respect of an individual. For since the end, as stated above (Q. I, A. 8; Q. II, A. 7), signifies sometimes the thing itself, and sometimes the attainment or possession of that thing (thus the miser's end is either money or the possession of it), it is evident that, absolutely speaking, the last end is the thing itself; for the possession of money is good only in so far as there is some good in money. But in regard to the individual, the obtaining of money is the last end, for the miser would not seek for money, save that he might have it. Therefore, absolutely and properly speaking, a man enjoys money, because he places his last end in it; but in so far as he seeks to possess it, he is said to use it.

Reply Obj. 1. Augustine is speaking of use in general, in so far as it implies the relation of an end to the enjoyment which a man seeks in that end.

Reply Obj. 2. The end is applied to the purpose of the will, that the will may rest in it. Consequently this rest in the end, which is the enjoyment of the end, is in this sense called use of the end. But the means are applied to the will's purpose not only in being used as means, but as ordered to something else in which the will finds rest.

Reply Obj. 3. The words of Hilary refer to use as applicable to rest in the last end; just as, speaking in a general sense, one may be said to use the end for the purpose of attaining it, as

---

[1] PL, 40, 19
[2] Chap. 11 (PL 42, 982).
[3] PL 10, 51.
[4] QQ. LXXXIII, Qu. 30 (PL 40, 20).

stated above. Hence Augustine says (*De Trin.* vi, 10)[1] that "this love, delight, felicity, or happiness, is called use by him."

ARTICLE 4. *Whether Use Precedes Choice?*

We proceed thus to the Fourth Article: It would seem that use precedes choice.

Objection 1. For nothing follows after choice, except execution. But use, since it pertains to the will, precedes execution. Therefore it precedes choice also.

Obj. 2. Further, the absolute precedes the relative. Therefore the less relative precedes the more relative. But choice implies two relations: one, of the thing chosen, in relation to the end; the other, of the thing chosen, in respect of that to which it is preferred. But use implies relation to the end only. Therefore use precedes choice.

Obj. 3. Further, the will uses the other powers in so far as it moves them. But the will moves itself too, as stated above (Q. IX, A. 3). Therefore it uses itself, by applying itself to act. But it does this when it consents. Therefore there is use in consent. But consent precedes choice, as stated above (Q. XV, A. 3. Reply 3). Therefore use does also.

On the contrary, Damascene says (*De Fide Orthod.* ii)[2] that "the will after choosing has an impulse to the operation, and afterwards it uses (the powers)." Therefore use follows choice.

I answer that, The will has a twofold relation to the thing willed. One, according as the thing willed is, in a way, in the willing subject, by a kind of proportion or order to the thing willed. And so those things that are naturally proportioned to a certain end are said to desire that end naturally. Yet to have an end thus is to have it imperfectly. Now every imperfect thing tends to perfection. And therefore both the natural and the voluntary appetite tend to have the end in reality, and this is to have it perfectly. This is the second relation of the will to the thing willed.

Now the thing willed is not only the end, but also the means. And the last act that pertains to the first relation of the will to the means, is choice, for there the will becomes fully proportioned, by willing the means fully. Use, on the other hand, pertains to the second relation of the will, in respect of which it tends to the realization of the thing willed. Therefore it is evident that use follows choice, provided that by use we mean the will's use of the executive power in moving it. But since the will, in a way, moves the reason also, and uses it, we may take the use of the means as consisting in the consideration of the reason, according as it refers the means to the end. In this sense use precedes choice.

Reply Obj. 1. The motion of the will to the execution of the work precedes execution but follows choice. And so, since use belongs to that very motion of the will, it stands between choice and execution.

Reply Obj. 2. What is essentially relative is after the absolute, but the thing to which relation is referred need not come after. Indeed, the more a cause precedes, the more numerous the effects to which it has relation.

Reply Obj. 3. Choice precedes use, if they are referred to the same object. But nothing hinders the use of one thing preceding the choice of another. And since the acts of the will react on one another, in each act of the will we can find both consent and choice and use, so that we may say that the will consents to choose, and consents to consent, and uses itself in consenting and choosing. And such acts as are ordered to that which precedes, precede also.

(c) *The Nature of Commanded Voluntary Acts*

QUESTION XVII
OF THE ACTS COMMANDED BY THE WILL
(*In Nine Articles*)

WE must now consider the acts commanded by the will, under which head there are nine points of inquiry: (1) Whether command is an act of the will or of the reason? (2) Whether command pertains to irrational animals? (3) Of the order between command and use. (4) Whether command and the commanded act are one act or distinct? (5) Whether the act of the will is commanded? (6) Whether the act of the reason is commanded? (7) Whether the act of the sensitive appetite is commanded? (8) Whether the act of the vegetal soul is commanded? (9) Whether the acts of the external members are commanded?

ARTICLE 1. *Whether Command Is an Act of the Reason or of the Will?*

We proceed thus to the First Article: It seems that command is not an act of the reason but of the will.

[1] PL 42, 932.   [2] Chap. 22 (PG 94, 945).

Objection 1. For command is a kind of motion; because Avicenna says[1] that there is a fourfold way of moving, by perfecting, by disposing, by commanding, and by counselling. But it pertains to the will to move all the other powers of the soul, as stated above (Q. IX, A. 1). Therefore command is an act of the will.

Obj. 2. Further, just as to be commanded pertains to that which is subject, so to command seems to pertain to that which is most free. But the root of liberty is especially in the will. Therefore to command pertains to the will.

Obj. 3. Further, command is followed at once by act. But the act of the reason is not followed at once by act, for he who judges that a thing should be done, does not do it at once. Therefore command is not an act of the reason, but of the will.

On the contrary, Gregory of Nyssa[2] and the Philosopher[3] say that "the appetite obeys reason." Therefore command is an act of the reason.

I answer that, Command is an act of the reason, presupposing, however, an act of the will. In proof of this, we must take note that since the acts of the reason and of the will can be brought to bear on one another, in so far as the reason reasons about willing, and the will wills to reason, the result is that the act of the reason precedes the act of the will, and conversely. And since the power of the preceding act continues in the act that follows, it happens sometimes that there is an act of the will in so far as it retains in itself something of an act of the reason, as we have stated in reference to use (Q. XVI, A. 1) and choice (Q. XIII, A. 1); and conversely, that there is an act of the reason in so far as it retains in itself something of an act of the will.

Now, command is essentially indeed an act of the reason, for the commander orders the one commanded to do something, by way of intimation or declaration, and to order thus by intimating or declaring is an act of the reason. Now the reason can intimate or declare something in two ways. First, absolutely. And this intimation is expressed by a verb in the indicative mood, as when one person says to another: "This is what you should do." Sometimes, however, the reason intimates something to a man by moving him to it; and this intimation is expressed by a verb in the imperative mood, as when it is said to someone: "Do this." Now the first mover

among the powers of the soul to the doing of an act is the will, as stated above (Q. IX, A. 1).[4] Since, therefore, the second mover does not move save in virtue of the first mover, it follows that the very fact that the reason moves by commanding is due to the power of the will. Consequently it follows that command is an act of the reason, presupposing an act of the will, in virtue of which the reason, by its command, moves to the execution of the act.

Reply Obj. 1. To command is to move, not anyhow, but by intimating and declaring to another; and this is an act of the reason.

Reply Obj. 2. The root of liberty is the will as its subject, but it is the reason as its cause. For the will can tend freely towards various objects, owing to the fact that the reason can have various conceptions of good. Hence philosophers define free choice as being "a free judgment arising from reason,"[5] implying that reason is the cause of liberty.

Reply Obj. 3. This argument proves that command is an act of reason not absolutely, but with a kind of motion, as stated above.

ARTICLE 2. *Whether Command Pertains to Irrational Animals?*

We proceed thus to the Second Article: It seems that command pertains to irrational animals.

Objection 1. Because, according to Avicenna,[6] "the power that commands movement is the appetite, and the power that executes movement is in the muscles and nerves." But both powers are in irrational animals. Therefore command is to be found in irrational animals.

Obj. 2. Further, the condition of a slave is that of one who receives commands. But the body is compared to the soul as a slave to his master, as the Philosopher says.[7] Therefore the body is commanded by the soul, even in irrational animals, since they are composed of soul and body.

Obj. 3. Further, by commanding, man has an impulse towards an action. But "impulse to action is to be found in irrational animals," as Damascene says (*De Fide Orthod.* ii).[8] Therefore command is to be found in irrational animals.

On the contrary, Command is an act of reason, as stated above (A. 1). But in irrational

---

[1] *Suffic.*, I, 10 (19ra).
[2] Nemesius, *De Nat. Hom.*, XVI, (PG 40, 672).
[3] *Ethics*, I, 13 (1102[b]26).
[4] Cf. also Part I, Q. LXXXII, A. 4.
[5] Boëthius, *Maior Comm. in De Interp. Arist.*, Bk. III, Prol. (PL 64, 492). Cf. Peter Lombard, *Sent.*, II, d. 25, chap. I. (QR I, 428).
[6] *De An.*, I, 5 (4vb).   [7] *Politics*, I, 5 (1254[b]4).
[8] Chap. 22 (PG 94, 945).

animals there is no reason. Neither, therefore, is there command.

I answer that, To command is nothing other than to direct someone to do something, by a certain motion of intimation. Now to direct (ordinare) is the proper act of the reason. Therefore it is impossible that irrational animals should command in any way, since they are devoid of reason.

Reply Obj. 1. The appetitive power is said to command movement in so far as it moves the commanding reason. But this is only in man. In irrational animals the appetitive power is not, properly speaking, a commanding faculty, unless command be taken in a wide sense for motion.

Reply Obj. 2. The body of the irrational animal is able to obey, but its soul is not able to command, because it is not able to direct. Consequently there is no aspect there of commander and commanded, but only of mover and moved.

Reply Obj. 3. Impulse to action is in irrational animals otherwise than in man. For the impulse of man to action arises from the directing reason, and so his impulse has the character of command. On the other hand, the impulse of the irrational animals arises from natural instinct, because as soon as they apprehend the fitting or the unfitting, their appetite is moved naturally to pursue or to avoid. Therefore they are directed by another to act, and they themselves do not direct themselves to act. Consequently there is impulse in them but not command.

ARTICLE 3. *Whether Use Precedes Command?*

We proceed thus to the Third Article: It would seem that use precedes command.

Objection 1. For command is an act of the reason presupposing an act of the will, as stated above (A. 1). But, as we have already shown (Q. XVI, A. 1), use is an act of the will. Therefore use precedes command.

Obj. 2. Further, command is one of those things that are ordered to the end. But use is of those things that are ordered to the end. Therefore it seems that use precedes command.

Obj. 3. Further, every act of a power moved by the will is called use, because the will uses the other powers, as stated above (Q. XVI, A. 1). But command is an act of the reason as moved by the will, as stated above (A. 1). Therefore command is a kind of use. Now the common precedes the proper. Therefore use precedes command.

On the contrary, Damascene says (*De Fide*

Orthod. ii)[1] that impulse to action precedes use. But impulse to operation is given by command. Therefore command precedes use.

I answer that, Use of that which is directed to the end, in so far as it is in the reason referring this to the end, precedes choice, as stated above (Q. XVI, A. 4). Therefore much more does it precede command. On the other hand, use of that which is directed to the end, in so far as it is subject to the executive power, follows command, because use in the user is united to the act of the thing used; for one does not use a stick before doing something with the stick. But command is not simultaneous with the act of the thing to which the command is given, for it naturally precedes its fulfilment, sometimes, indeed, by priority of time. Consequently it is evident that command precedes use.

Reply Obj. 1. Not every act of the will precedes this act of the reason which is command, but an act of the will precedes, namely, choice, and an act of the will follows, namely, use. Because after counsel's decision, which is reason's judgment, the will chooses; and after choice, the reason commands that power which has to do what was chosen; and then, last of all, someone's will begins to use, by executing the command of reason. Sometimes it is another's will, when one commands another; sometimes the will of the one that commands, when he commands himself to do something.

Reply Obj. 2. Just as act ranks before power, so does the object rank before the act. Now the object of use is that which is directed to the end. Consequently, from the fact that command is directed to the end, one should conclude that command precedes, rather than that it follows use.

Reply Obj. 3. Just as the act of the will in using the reason for the purpose of command precedes the command, so also we may say that this act whereby the will uses the reason is preceded by a command of reason, because the acts of these powers react on one another.

ARTICLE 4. *Whether Command and the Commanded Act Are One Act, or Distinct?*

We proceed thus to the Fourth Article: It would seem that the commanded act is not one with the command itself.

Objection 1. For the acts of different powers are themselves distinct. But the commanded act belongs to one power, and the command to another, since one is the power that commands,

---

[1] Chap. 22 (PG 94, 945). Cf. Albert, *Summa de Creatura*, Pt. II, Q. 69, A. 2 (BO XXXV, 567).

and the other is the power that receives the command. Therefore the commanded act is not one with the command.

Obj. 2. Further, whatever things can be separated from one another, are distinct, for nothing is separated from itself. But sometimes the commanded act is separated from the command, for sometimes the command is given, and the commanded act does not follow. Therefore command is a distinct act from the act commanded.

Obj. 3. Further, whatever things are related to one another as before and after, are distinct. But command naturally precedes the commanded act. Therefore they are distinct.

On the contrary, The Philosopher says[1] that "where one thing is by reason of another, there is but one." But there is no commanded act unless by reason of the command. Therefore they are one.

I answer that, Nothing prevents certain things being distinct in one respect, and one in another respect. Indeed, every multitude is one in some respect, as Dionysius says (*Div. Nom.* xiii).[2] But a difference is to be observed in this, that some are many absolutely, and one in a particular respect, while with others it is the reverse. Now *one* is predicated in the same way as *being.* And substance is being absolutely, while accident or being of reason is a being only in a certain respect. And so those things that are one in substance are one absolutely, though many in a certain respect. Thus, in the genus substance, the whole composed of its integral or essential parts, is one absolutely, because the whole is being and substance absolutely, and the parts are beings and substances in the whole. But those things which are distinct in substance, and one according to an accident, are distinct absolutely, and one in a certain respect. Thus many men are one people, and many stones are one heap, which is unity of composition or order. In like manner also many individuals that are one in genus or species are many absolutely, and one in a certain respect, since to be one in genus or species is to be one according to the consideration of the reason.

Now just as in the genus of natural things, a whole is composed of matter and form (for example, man, who is one natural being, though he has many parts, is composed of soul and body), so in human acts, the act of a lower power is in the position of matter in regard to the act of a higher power, in so far as the lower power acts in virtue of the higher power moving it; for thus also the act of the first mover is as the form in regard to the act of its instrument. Hence it is evident that command and the commanded act are one human act, just as a whole is one, yet, in its parts, many.

Reply Obj. 1. If the distinct powers are not ordered to one another, their acts are different absolutely. But when one power is the mover of the other, then their acts are, in a way, one, since "the act of the mover and the act of the thing moved are one act."[3]

Reply Obj. 2. The fact that command and the commanded act can be separated from one another shows that they are many in parts. Because the parts of a man can be separated from one another, and yet they form one whole.

Reply Obj. 3. In those things that are many in parts, but one as a whole, nothing hinders one part from preceding another. Thus the soul, in a way, precedes the body, and the heart, the other members.

ARTICLE 5. *Whether the Act of the Will Is Commanded?*

We proceed thus to the Fifth Article: It would seem that the act of the will is not commanded.

Objection 1. For Augustine says,[4] "The mind commands the mind to will, and yet it does not." But to will is the act of the will. Therefore the act of the will is not commanded.

Obj. 2. Further, to receive a command belongs to one who can understand the command. But the will cannot understand the command, for the will differs from the intellect, to which it pertains to understand. Therefore the act of the will is not commanded.

Obj. 3. Further, if one act of the will is commanded, for the same reason all are commanded. But if all the acts of the will are commanded, we must proceed to infinity, because the act of the will precedes the act of reason commanding, as stated above (A. 1). For if that act of the will be also commanded, this command will be preceded by another act of the reason, and so on to infinity. But to proceed to infinity is not possible. Therefore the act of the will is not commanded.

On the contrary, Whatever is in our power is subject to our command. But the acts of the will, most of all, are in our power, since all our acts are said to be in our power in so far as they are voluntary. Therefore the acts of the will are commanded by us.

[1] *Topics,* III, 2 (1117[a]18).   [2] Sect. 2 (PG 3, 977).
[3] Aristotle, *Physics,* III, 3 (202[a]18; [b]20).
[4] *Confessions,* VIII, 21 (PL 32, 758).

I answer that, As stated above (A. 1), command is nothing other than the act of the reason directing, with a certain motion, something to act. Now it is evident that the reason can direct the act of the will, for just as it can judge it to be good to will something so it can direct by commanding man to will. From this it is evident that an act of the will can be commanded.

Reply Obj. 1. As Augustine says,[1] when the mind commands itself perfectly to will, then already it wills. But that sometimes it commands and wills not, is due to the fact that it commands imperfectly. Now imperfect command arises from the fact that the reason is moved by opposite motives to command or not to command; and so it fluctuates between the two, and fails to command perfectly.

Reply Obj. 2. Just as each of the members of the body works not for itself alone but for the whole body, as, for example the eye sees for the whole body, so is it with the powers of the soul. For the intellect understands not for itself alone, but for all the powers, and the will wills not only for itself, but for all the powers too. Therefore man, in so far as he is endowed with intellect and will, commands the act of the will for himself.

Reply Obj. 3. Since command is an act of the reason, that act is commanded which is subject to reason. Now the first act of the will is not due to the direction of the reason but to the instigation of nature, or of a higher cause, as stated above (Q. IX, A. 4). Therefore there is no need to proceed to infinity.

ARTICLE 6. *Whether the Act of the Reason Is Commanded?*

We proceed thus to the Sixth Article: It seems that the act of the reason cannot be commanded.

Objection 1. For it seems impossible for a thing to command itself. But it is the reason that commands, as stated above (A. 1). Therefore the act of the reason is not commanded.

Obj. 2. Further, that which is through its essence is different from that which is by participation. But the power whose act is commanded by reason is rational by participation, as stated in the *Ethics.*[2] Therefore the act of that power which is essentially rational is not commanded.

Obj. 3. Further, that act is commanded which is in our power. But to know and judge the truth, which is the act of reason, is not always in our power. Therefore the act of the reason cannot be commanded.

[1] *Confessions*, VIII, 21 (PL 32, 758).
[2] Aristotle, I, 13 (1102^{b}13; ^{b}26).

On the contrary, That which we do of our free choice, can be done by our command. But the acts of the reason are accomplished through free choice, for Damascene says (*De Fide Orthod.* ii, 22)[3] that "by his free choice man inquires, considers, judges, disposes." Therefore the acts of the reason can be commanded.

I answer that, Since the reason turns back on itself, just as it directs the acts of other powers, so it can direct its own act. Consequently its act can be commanded. But we must take note that the act of the reason may be considered in two ways. First, as to the exercise of the act. And considered thus, the act of the reason can always be commanded, as when one is told to be attentive, and to use one's reason. Secondly, as to the object, in respect of which two acts of the reason have to be noticed. One is the act by which it apprehends the truth about something. This act is not in our power, because it happens in virtue of a natural or supernatural light. Consequently in this respect, the act of the reason is not in our power and cannot be commanded. The other act of the reason is that by which it assents to what it apprehends. If, therefore, that which the reason apprehends is such that it naturally assents to it, for example, the first principles, it is not in our power to assent or dissent; for with such things assent follows naturally, and consequently, properly speaking, is not subject to our command. But some things which are apprehended do not convince the intellect to such an extent as not to leave it free to assent or dissent, or at least suspend its assent or dissent, on account of some cause or other. And in such things assent or dissent is in our power, and is subject to our command.

Reply Obj. 1. Reason commands itself, just as the will moves itself, as stated above (Q. IX, A. 3), that is to say, in so far as each power turns back upon its own act, and from one thing tends to another.

Reply Obj. 2. On account of the difference of objects subject to the act of the reason, nothing prevents the reason from participating in itself, just as the knowledge of principles is participated in the knowledge of the conclusions.

The *reply to the third objection* is evident from what has been said.

ARTICLE 7. *Whether the Act of the Sensitive Appetite Is Commanded?*

We proceed thus to the Seventh Article: It seems that the act of the sensitive appetite is not commanded.

[3] PG 94, 945.

Objection 1. For the Apostle says (*Rom.* 7. 15): *For I do not that good which I will,* and a gloss explains this by saying[1] that man lusts, although he wills not to lust. But to lust is an act of the sensitive appetite. Therefore the act of the sensitive appetite is not subject to our command.

Obj. 2. Further, corporeal matter obeys God alone as to change of form, as was shown in the First Part (Q. LXV, A. 4; Q. XCI, A. 2; Q. CX, A. 2). But the act of the sensitive appetite is accompanied by a formal change of the body, consisting in heat or cold. Therefore the act of the sensitive appetite is not subject to man's command.

Obj. 3. Further, the proper moving principle of the sensitive appetite is something apprehended by sense or imagination. But it is not always in our power to apprehend something by sense or imagination. Therefore the act of the sensitive appetite is not subject to our command.

On the contrary, Gregory of Nyssa (Nemesius,—*De Nat. Hom.* xvi)[2] says: "That which obeys reason is twofold, the concupiscible and the irascible," which belong to the sensitive appetite. Therefore the act of the sensitive appetite is subject to the command of reason.

I answer that, An act is subject to our command in so far as it is in our power, as stated above (A. 5). Consequently in order to understand in what manner the act of the sensitive appetite is subject to the command of reason, we must consider in what manner it is in our power. Now it must be observed that the sensitive appetite differs from the intellectual appetite, which is called the will, in the fact that the sensitive appetite is the power of a corporeal organ, while the will is not. Again, every act of a power that uses a corporeal organ depends not only on a power of the soul, but also on the disposition of that corporeal organ; thus the act of vision depends on the power of sight, and on the condition of the eye, which is a help or a hindrance to that act. Consequently the act of the sensitive appetite depends not only on the appetitive power, but also on the disposition of the body.

But the activity of any power of the soul follows apprehension. And the apprehension of the imagination, since it is a particular apprehension, is regulated by the apprehension of reason, which is universal; just as a particular active power is regulated by a universal active power. Consequently in this respect the act of the sensitive appetite is subject to the command of reason. On the other hand, condition (*qualitas*) and disposition of the body is not subject to the command of reason. And consequently in this respect, the movement of the sensitive appetite is hindered from being wholly subject to the command of reason.

Moreover it happens sometimes that the movement of the sensitive appetite is aroused suddenly in consequence of an apprehension of the imagination or sense. And then such movement occurs without the command of reason, although reason could have prevented it, had it foreseen. Hence the Philosopher says[3] that "the reason governs the irascible and concupiscible not by a despotic supremacy," which is that of a master over his slave, "but by a politic or royal supremacy," which is the way the free are governed, who are not wholly subject to command.

Reply Obj. 1. That man lusts, although he wills not to lust, is due to a disposition of the body by which the sensitive appetite is hindered from perfect compliance with the command of reason. Hence the Apostle adds (*ibid.*): *I see another law in my members, fighting against the law of my mind.* This may also happen through a sudden movement of concupiscence, as stated above.

Reply Obj. 2. The condition (*qualitas*) of the body stands in a twofold relation to the act of the sensitive appetite. First, as preceding it; thus a man may be disposed in one way or another, in respect of his body, to this or that passion. Secondly, as consequent to it; thus a man becomes heated through anger. Now the condition that precedes, is not subject to the command of reason, since it is due either to nature, or to some previous movement, which cannot quiet down at once. But the condition that is consequent, follows the command of reason, since it results from the local movement of the heart, which has various movements according to the various acts of the sensitive appetite.

Reply Obj. 3. Since the external sensible is necessary for the apprehension of the senses, it is not in our power to apprehend anything by the senses, unless the sensible be present; and this presence of the sensible is not always in our power. For it is then that man can use his senses if he will to do so, unless there be some obstacle on the part of the organ. On the other hand, the apprehension of the imagination is

---

[1] *Glossa ordin.,* Rom. 7.15 (VI, 17B). Augustine, *Contra Julian.,* III, 26 (PL 44, 734).

[2] PG 40, 672.

[3] *Politics,* I, 5 (1254[b]5).

subject to the ordering of reason, in proportion to the strength or weakness of the imaginative power. For that man is unable to imagine the things that reason considers, is either because they cannot be imagined, such as incorporeal things, or because of the weakness of the imaginative power, due to some organic indisposition.

ARTICLE 8. *Whether the Act of the Vegetal Soul Is Commanded?*

We proceed thus to the Eighth Article: It seems that the acts of the vegetal soul are subject to the command of reason.

Objection 1. For the sensitive powers are of higher rank than the vegetal powers. But the powers of the sensitive soul are subject to the command of reason. Much more, therefore, are the powers of the vegetal soul.

Obj. 2. Further, "man is called a little world,"[1] because "the soul is in the body, just as God is in the world."[2] But God is in the world in such a way that everything in the world obeys His command. Therefore all that is in man, even the powers of the vegetal soul, obey the command of reason.

Obj. 3. Further, praise and blame are awarded only to such acts as are subject to the command of reason. But in the acts of the nutritive and generative power, there is room for praise and blame, virtue and vice, as in the case of gluttony and lust, and their opposite virtues. Therefore the acts of these powers are subject to the command of reason.

On the contrary, Gregory of Nyssa says[3] that "the nutritive and generative power is one over which the reason has no control."

I answer that, Some acts proceed from the natural appetite, others from the animal, or from the intellectual appetite, for every agent desires an end in some way. Now the natural appetite does not follow from some apprehension, as do the animal and the intellectual appetite. But the reason commands by way of an apprehensive power. And so those acts that proceed from the intellective or the animal appetite can be commanded by the reason, but not those acts that proceed from the natural appetite. And such are the acts of the vegetal soul; hence Gregory of Nyssa (Nemesius,—*loc. cit.*)

---

[1] Aristotle, *Physics*, VIII, 2 (252b26).
[2] This interpretation is given on the supposed authority of Augustine (Alcher of Clairvaux), *De Spir. et An.*, 35 (PL 40, 805). Cf. Albert the Great, *Summa de Creat.*, II, 3, A. 1 (BO XXXV, 28); also Bonaventure, *In Sent.*, III, d. II, A. 1, Q. 2 (QR III, 40).
[3] Nemesius, *De Nat. Hom.*, XXII (PG 40, 692).

says that "generation and nutrition belong to what are called natural powers." Consequently the acts of the vegetal soul are not subject to the command of reason.

Reply Obj. 1. The more immaterial an act is, the more noble it is, and the more is it subject to the command of reason. Hence the very fact that the acts of the vegetal soul do not obey reason shows that they rank lowest.

Reply Obj. 2. The comparison holds in a certain respect, because, namely, as God moves the world, so the soul moves the body. But it does not hold in every respect, for the soul did not create the body out of nothing, as God created the world, for which reason the world is wholly subject to His command.

Reply Obj. 3. Virtue and vice, praise and blame are not due to the acts themselves of the nutritive and generative power, that is, digestion, and formation of the human body, but rather to the acts of the sensitive part that are ordered to the acts of generation and nutrition; for example the desire for pleasure in the act of taking food or in the act of generation, and their right or wrong use.

ARTICLE 9. *Whether the Acts of the External Members Are Commanded?*

We proceed thus to the Ninth Article: It seems that the members of the body do not obey reason as to their acts.

Objection 1. For it is evident that the members of the body are more distant from the reason than the powers of the vegetal soul. But the powers of the vegetal soul do not obey reason, as stated above (A. 8). Therefore much less do the members of the body obey.

Obj. 2. Further, the heart is the principle of animal movement. But the movement of the heart is not subject to the command of reason, for Gregory of Nyssa (Nemesius,—*De Nat. Hom.* xxii)[4] says that "the pulse is not controlled by reason." Therefore the movement of the bodily members is not subject to the command of reason.

Obj. 3. Further, Augustine says[5] that the movement of the genital members "is sometimes inopportune and not desired; sometimes when sought it fails, and whereas the heart is warm with desire, the body remains cold." Therefore the movements of the members are not obedient to reason.

On the contrary, Augustine says,[6] "The mind commands a movement of the hand, and so

---

[4] PG 40, 693.   [5] *City of God*, XIV, 16 (PL 41, 425).
[6] *Confessions*, VIII, 21 (PL 32, 758).

ready is the hand to obey, that scarcely can one discern obedience from command."

I answer that, The members of the body are organs of the soul's powers. Consequently according as the powers of the soul stand in respect of obedience to reason, so do the members of the body stand in respect of obedience to reason. Since then the sensitive powers are subject to the command of reason, while the natural powers are not, therefore all movements of members that are moved by the sensitive powers are subject to the command of reason, but those movements of members that arise from the natural powers are not subject to the command of reason.

Reply Obj. 1. The members do not move themselves but are moved through the powers of the soul; of these powers, some are closer to reason than are the powers of the vegetal soul.

Reply Obj. 2. In things pertaining to intellect and will that which is according to nature, from which all other things are derived, stands first. Thus from the knowledge of principles that are naturally known is derived knowledge of the conclusions, and from volition of the end naturally desired is derived the choice of the means. So also in bodily movements the principle is according to nature. Now the principle of bodily movements begins with the movement of the heart. Consequently the movement of the heart is according to nature, and not according to the will, for like a proper accident, it results from life, which follows from the union of soul and body. Thus the movement of heavy and light things results from their substantial form, for which reason they are said to be moved by their generator, as the Philosopher states.[1] And so this movement is called vital. For which reason Gregory of Nyssa (Nemesius,—*loc. cit.*) says

that, just as the movement of generation and nutrition does not obey reason, so neither does the pulse which is a vital movement. By the pulse he means the movement of the heart which is indicated by the pulse veins.

Reply Obj. 3. As Augustine says[2] it is in punishment of sin that the movement of these members does not obey reason, in this sense, that the soul is punished for its rebellion against God by the insubmission of that member by which original sin is transmitted to posterity.

But because, as we shall state later on (Q. LXXXV, A. 1. Reply 3), the effect of the sin of our first parent was that his nature was left to itself, through the withdrawal of the supernatural gift which God had bestowed on man, we must consider the natural cause of this particular member's non-submission to reason. This is stated by Aristotle,[3] who says that "the movements of the heart and of the organs of generation are involuntary," and that the reason of this is as follows. These members are stirred at the occasion of some apprehension, in so far as the intellect and imagination represent such things as arouse the passions of the soul, of which passions these movements are a consequence. But they are not moved at the command of the reason or intellect, because there is required for these movements a certain natural change of heat and cold, which change is not subject to the command of reason. This is the case with these two organs in particular, because each is as it were a separate animal being, in so far as it is a principle of life; and the principle is virtually the whole. For the heart is the principle of the senses, and from the organ of generation proceeds the seminal principle, which is virtually the entire animal. Consequently they have their proper movements naturally, because principles must be natural, as stated above (ANS. 2).

(d) *The Division of Human Acts*

QUESTION XVIII

OF THE GOOD AND EVIL OF HUMAN ACTS, IN GENERAL

(In Eleven Articles)

WE must now consider the good and evil of human acts. First, how a human act is good or evil; secondly, what results from the good or evil of a human act, as merit or demerit, sin and guilt (Q. XXI).

Under the first head there will be a threefold

consideration. The first will be of the good and evil of human acts, in general; the second, of the good and evil of internal acts (Q. XIX); the third, of the good and evil of external acts (Q. XX).

Concerning the first there are eleven points of inquiry: (1) Whether every human action is good, or are there evil actions? (2) Whether the good or evil of a human action is derived from its object? (3) Whether it is derived from

[1] *Physics,* VIII, 4 (255[b]35).
[2] *City of God,* XIV, 17, 20 (PL 41, 425, 428).
[3] *Motion of Animals,* 11 (703[b]5).

a circumstance? (4) Whether it is derived from the end? (5) Whether a human action is good or evil in its species? (6) Whether an act has the species of good or evil from its end? (7) Whether the species derived from the end is contained under the species derived from the object, as under its genus, or conversely? (8) Whether any act is indifferent in its species? (9) Whether an individual act can be indifferent? (10) Whether a circumstance places a moral act in the species of good or evil? (11) Whether every circumstance that makes an act better or worse, places the moral action in the species of good or evil?

ARTICLE 1. *Whether Every Human Action Is Good, or Are There Evil Actions?*

We proceed thus to the First Article: It seems that every human action is good, and that none is evil.

Objection 1. For Dionysius says (*Div. Nom.* iv)[1] that evil does not act, except through the power of the good. But no evil is done through the power of the good. Therefore no action is evil.

Obj. 2. Further, nothing acts except in so far as it is in act. Now a thing is evil not according as it is in act, but according as its potency is deprived of act, while in so far as its potency is perfected by act, it is good, as stated in the *Metaphysics.*[2] Therefore nothing acts in so far as it is evil, but only according as it is good. Therefore every action is good, and none is evil.

Obj. 3. Further, evil cannot be a cause, except accidentally, as Dionysius declares (*Div. Nom.* iv).[3] But every action has some effect which is proper to it. Therefore no action is evil, but every action is good.

On the contrary, Our Lord said (John 3. 20): *Every one that doth evil, hateth the light.* Therefore some actions of man are evil.

I answer that, We must say of good and evil in actions just what we say of good and evil in things, because such as everything is such is the act that it produces. Now in things, each one has as much of good as it has of being, since good and being are convertible, as was stated in the First Part (Q. V, AA. 1, 3). But God alone has the whole fulness of His Being in a unified and simple way, while every other thing has its proper fulness of being according to a certain multiplicity. And so it happens with some things that they have being in some respect and yet they are lacking in the fulness of being due to

them. Thus the fulness of human being requires a composite of soul and body, having all the powers and instruments of knowledge and movement. Therefore if any man is lacking in any of these, he is lacking in something due to the fulness of his being. So that as much as he has of being, so much has he of goodness, while so far as he is lacking in the fulness of his being, so far is he lacking in goodness, and is said to be evil. Thus a blind man is possessed of goodness from the fact that he lives, and yet it is an evil for him to be without sight. But if anything were without either being or goodness, it could not be said to be either evil or good. But since this same fulness of being is of the very nature of good, if a thing be lacking in its due fulness of being, it is not said to be good absolutely, but in a certain respect, in so far as it is a being, although it can be called a being absolutely, and a non-being in a certain respect, as was stated in the First Part (Q. V, A. 1. reply 1).

We must therefore say that every action has goodness in so far as it has being, but it is lacking in goodness in so far as it is lacking in something of the fulness of being due to a human action, and thus it is said to be evil; for instance if it lacks the quantity determined by reason, or its due place, or something of the kind.

Reply Obj. 1. Evil acts through the power of a deficient good. For if there were nothing of good there, there would be neither being nor possibility of action. On the other hand if good were not deficient, there would be no evil. Consequently the action done is a deficient good, which is good in a certain respect, but evil absolutely.

Reply Obj. 2. Nothing hinders a thing from being in act in a certain respect, so that it can act, and in a certain respect deficient in act, so as to cause a deficient act. Thus a blind man has in act the power of walking by which, he is able to walk; but in so far as he is deprived of sight he suffers a defect in walking by stumbling when he walks.

Reply Obj. 3. An evil action can have a proper effect, according to the goodness and being that it has. Thus adultery is the cause of human generation, in so far as it implies union of male and female, but not in so far as it lacks the order of reason.

ARTICLE 2. *Whether the Good or Evil of a Man's Action Is Derived from Its Object?*

We proceed thus to the Second Article: It seems that the good or evil of an action is not derived from its object.

---

[1] Sect. 20 (PG 3, 717). [2] Aristotle, IX, 9 (1051ª4; ª29).
[3] Sect. 20, 32 (PG 3, 717, 732).

Objection 1. For the object of an action is a thing. But evil is not in things, but in the sinner's use of them, as Augustine says.[1] Therefore the good or evil of a human action is not derived from its object.

Obj. 2. Further, the object is compared to the action as its matter. But the goodness of a thing is not from its matter, but rather from the form, which is an act. Therefore good and evil in actions is not derived from their object.

Obj. 3. Further, the object of an active power is compared to the action as effect to cause. But the goodness of a cause does not depend on its effect, but rather the contrary. Therefore good or evil in actions is not derived from their object.

On the contrary, It is written (Osee 9. 10): *They became abominable as those things which they loved.* Now man becomes abominable to God on account of the malice of his action. Therefore the malice of his action is according to the evil objects that man loves. And the same applies to the goodness of his action.

I answer that, as stated above (A. 1) the good or evil of an action, as of other things, depends on its fulness of being or its lack of that fulness. Now the first thing that pertains to the fulness of being seems to be that which gives a thing its species. And just as a natural thing has its species from its form, so an action has its species from its object, as also movement from its term. And therefore just as the primary goodness of a natural thing is derived from its form, which gives it its species, so the primary goodness of a moral action is derived from its suitable object. Hence some call such an action "good in its genus";[2] for instance, to make use of what is one's own. And just as, in natural things, the primary evil is when a generated thing does not realize its specific form (for instance, if instead of a man, something else be generated), so the primary evil in moral actions is that which is from the object, for instance, to take what belongs to another. And this action is said to be evil in its genus, genus here standing for species, just as we apply the term mankind to the whole human species.

Reply Obj. 1. Although external things are good in themselves, nevertheless they have not always a due proportion to this or that action. And so, in so far as they are considered as objects of such actions, they have not the nature of goodness.

Reply Obj. 2. The object is not the matter

out of which, but the matter about which, and in a certain way has the character of form, in so far as it gives (the act) its species.

Reply Obj. 3. The object of the human action is not always the object of an active power. For the appetitive power is, in a way, passive, in so far as it is moved by the appetible object; and yet it is a principle of human actions. Nor again have the objects of the active powers always the nature of an effect, but only when they are already transformed; thus food when transformed is the effect of the nutritive power, but food before being transformed stands in relation to the nutritive power as the matter about which it exercises its operation. Now since the object is in some way the effect of the active power, it follows that it is the term of its action, and consequently that it gives it its form and species, since movement derives its species from its terms. Moreover, although the goodness of an action is not caused by the goodness of its effect, yet an action is said to be good from the fact that it can produce a good effect. Consequently the very proportion of an action to its effect is the measure of its goodness.

ARTICLE 3. *Whether Man's Action Is Good or Evil from a Circumstance?*

We proceed thus to the Third Article: It seems that an action is not good or evil from a circumstance.

Objection 1. For circumstances stand around (*circumstant*) an act, as existing outside it, as stated above (Q. VII, A. 1). But "good and evil are in things themselves," as is stated in the *Metaphysics*.[3] Therefore an action does not derive goodness or malice from a circumstance.

Obj. 2. Further, the goodness or malice of an act is considered principally in the doctrine of morals. But since circumstances are accidents of acts, it seems that they are outside the scope of art, because "no art takes notice of what is accidental."[4] Therefore the goodness or malice of an action is not taken from a circumstance.

Obj. 3. Further, that which belongs to a thing in respect of its substance, is not attributed to it in respect of an accident. But good and evil belong to an action in respect of its substance, because an action can be good or evil in its genus as stated above (A. 2). Therefore an action is not good or bad from a circumstance.

On the contrary, the Philosopher says[5] that "a virtuous man acts as he should, and when he

---

[1] *Christian Doctrine*, III, 12 (PL 34, 73).
[2] Peter Lombard; cf. *Sent.*, II, d. 36, chap. 6 (QR I, 504)
[3] Aristotle, VI, 4 (1027b25).
[4] Aristotle, *Metaphysics*, VI, 2 (1026b4).
[5] *Ethics* II, 3 (1104b26).

should, and so on in respect of the other circumstances." Therefore, on the other hand, the vicious man, in the matter of each vice, acts when he should not, or where he should not, and so on with the other circumstances. Therefore human actions are good or evil according to circumstances.

I answer that, In natural things, it is to be noted that the whole fulness of perfection due to a thing is not from the substantial form that gives it its species, for a thing derives much from supervening accidents, as man does from shape, colour, and the like. And if any one of these accidents be out of due proportion, evil is the result. So is it with action. For the fulness of its goodness does not consist wholly in its species, but also in certain additions which accrue to it by reason of certain accidents. And its due circumstances are of this character. Therefore if something be wanting that is requisite as a due circumstance the action will be evil.

Reply Obj. 1. Circumstances are outside an action in so far as they are not part of its essence; but they are in an action as its accidents. Thus, too, accidents in natural substances are outside the essence.

Reply Obj. 2. Every accident is not accidentally in its subject, for some are proper accidents, and of these every art takes notice. And thus it is that the circumstances of actions are considered in the doctrine of morals.

Reply Obj. 3. Since good and being are convertible, according as being is predicated of substance and of accident, so is good predicated of a thing both in respect of its essential being, and in respect of its accidental being; and this, both in natural things and in moral actions.

ARTICLE 4. *Whether a Human Action Is Good or Evil from Its End?*

We proceed thus to the Fourth Article: It would seem that the good and evil in human actions are not from the end.

Objection 1. For Dionysius says (*Div. Nom.* iv)[1] that "nothing acts with a view to evil." If therefore an action were good or evil from its end, no action would be evil. Which is clearly false.

Obj. 2. Further, the goodness of an action is something in the action. But the end is an extrinsic cause. Therefore an action is not said to be good or bad according to its end.

Obj. 3. Further, a good action may happen to be ordered to an evil end, as when a man gives an alms from vainglory; and conversely, an evil action may happen to be ordered to a good end, as a theft committed in order to give something to the poor. Therefore an action is not good or evil from its end.

On the contrary, Boëthius says (*De Differ. Topic.* ii)[2] that "if the end is good, the thing is good"; and if the end be evil, the thing also is evil.

I answer that, The disposition of things as to goodness is the same as their disposition as to being. Now in some things the being does not depend on another, and in these it suffices to consider their being absolutely. But there are things the being of which depends on something else, and hence in their regard we must consider their being in its relation to the cause on which it depends. Now just as the being of a thing depends on the agent and the form, so the goodness of a thing depends on its end. Hence in the Divine Persons, Whose goodness does not depend on another, the measure of goodness is not taken from the end. But human actions, and other things, the goodness of which depends on something else, have a measure of goodness from the end on which they depend, besides that goodness which is in them absolutely.

Accordingly a fourfold goodness may be considered in a human action. First, that which, as an action, it derives from its genus; because as much as it has of action and being so much has it of goodness, as stated above (A. 1). Secondly, it has goodness according to its species, which is derived from its suitable object. Thirdly, it has goodness from its circumstances, in respect, as it were, of its accidents. Fourthly, it has goodness from its end, to which it is related as to the cause of its goodness.

Reply Obj. 1. The good in view of which one acts is not always a true good, but sometimes it is a true good, sometimes an apparent good. And in the latter event, an evil action results from the end in view.

Reply Obj. 2. Although the end is an extrinsic cause, nevertheless due proportion to the end, and relation to the end, are inherent to the action.

Reply Obj. 3. Nothing hinders an action that is good in one of the ways mentioned above from lacking goodness in another way. And thus it may happen that an action which is good in its species or in its circumstances, is ordered to an evil end, or vice versa. However, an action is not good absolutely, unless it is good in all those ways, since "evil results from any single defect, but good from the complete cause," as Dionysius says (*Div. Nom.* iv).[3]

---

[1] Sects. 19, 31 (PG 3, 716, 732).

[2] PL 64, 1189.   [3] Sect. 30 (PG 3, 729).

ARTICLE 5. *Whether a Human Action Is Good or Evil in Its Species?*

We proceed thus to the Fifth Article: It would seem that good and evil in moral acts do not make a difference of species.

Objection 1. For the existence of good and evil in actions is in conformity with their existence in things, as stated above (A. 1). But good and evil do not make a specific difference in things; for a good man is specifically the same as a bad man. Therefore neither do they make a specific difference in actions.

Obj. 2. Further, since evil is a privation, it is a non-being. But non-being cannot be a difference, according to the Philosopher.[1] Since therefore the difference constitutes the species, it seems that an action is not constituted in a species through being evil. Consequently good and evil do not diversify the species of human actions.

Obj. 3. Further, acts that differ in species produce different effects. But the same specific effect results from a good and from an evil action; thus a man is born of adulterous or of lawful wedlock. Therefore good and evil actions do not differ in species.

Obj. 4. Further, actions are sometimes said to be good or bad from a circumstance, as stated above (A. 3). But since a circumstance is an accident, it does not give an action its species. Therefore human actions do not differ in species on account of their goodness or malice.

On the contrary, According to the Philosopher,[2] "like habits produce like actions." But a good and a bad habit differ in species, as liberality and prodigality. Therefore also good and bad actions differ in species.

I answer that, Every action derives its species from its object, as stated above (A. 2). Hence it follows that a difference of object causes a difference of species in actions. Now, it must be observed that a difference of objects causes a difference in actions according as the latter are referred to one active principle, and does not cause a difference in actions according as they are referred to another active principle. Because nothing accidental constitutes a species, but only that which is essential, and a difference of object may be essential in reference to one active principle, and accidental in reference to another. Thus to know colour and to know sound differ essentially in reference to sense, but not in reference to the intellect.

Now in human actions, good and evil are predicated in reference to the reason, because as Dionysius says (*Div. Nom.* iv),[3] the good of man is to be in accordance with reason, and "evil is to be against reason." For that is good for a thing which suits it in regard to its form; and evil, that which is against the order of its form. It is therefore evident that the difference of good and evil considered in reference to the object has a direct relation to reason; that is to say, according as the object is suitable or unsuitable to reason. Now certain actions are called human or moral according as they proceed from the reason. And so it is evident that good and evil diversify the species in moral actions, since essential differences cause a difference of species.

Reply Obj. 1. Even in natural things, good and evil (in so far as something is according to nature, and something against nature), diversify the natural species; for a dead body and a living body are not of the same species. In like manner, good, in so far as it is in accord with reason, and evil, in so far as it is against reason, diversify the moral species.

Reply Obj. 2. Evil implies not absolute privation, but privation affecting some potentiality. For an action is said to be evil in its species not because it has no object at all, but because it has an object in disaccord with reason; for instance, to appropriate another's property. Therefore in so far as the object is something positive, it can constitute the species of an evil act.

Reply Obj. 3. The conjugal act and adultery, as related to reason, differ specifically and have effects specifically different, because the one deserves praise and reward, and the other blame and punishment. But as related to the generative power, they do not differ in species. And thus they have one specific effect.

Reply Obj. 4. A circumstance is sometimes taken as the essential difference of the object, according as it is related to reason; and then it can specify a moral act. And this must be so whenever a circumstance changes an action from good to evil; for a circumstance would not make an action evil except through being contrary to reason.

ARTICLE 6. *Whether an Action Has the Species of Good or Evil from Its End?*

We proceed thus to the Sixth Article: It would seem that the good and evil which are from the end do not diversify the species of actions.

[1] *Metaphysics*, III, 3 (988ᵇ22). [2] *Ethics*, II, 1 (1103ᵇ21). [3] Sect. 32 (PG 3, 732).

Objection 1. For actions derive their species from the object. But the end is outside the notion of the object. Therefore the good and evil which are from the end do not diversify the species of an action.

Obj. 2. Further, that which is accidental does not constitute the species, as stated above (A. 5). But it is accidental to an action to be ordered to some particular end; for instance, to give alms from vainglory. Therefore actions are not diversified as to species according to the good and evil which are from the end.

Obj. 3. Further, acts that differ in species, can be ordered to the same end; thus actions of various virtues and vices can be ordered to the end of vainglory. Therefore the good and evil which are taken from the end do not diversify the species of action.

On the contrary, It has been shown above (Q. I, A. 3) that human actions derive their species from the end. Therefore good and evil which are taken from the end diversify the species of actions.

I answer that, Certain acts are called human in so far as they are voluntary, as stated above (Q. I, A. I). Now, in a voluntary act, there is a twofold act, namely, the interior act of the will, and the external act, and each of these acts has its object. The end is properly the object of the interior act of the will, while the object of the external action is that on which the action is brought to bear. Therefore just as the external act takes its species from the object on which it bears, so the interior act of the will takes its species from the end, as from its proper object.

Now that which is on the part of the will is formal in relation to that which is on the part of the external action, because the will uses the limbs to act, as instruments; nor have external actions any measure of morality, except in so far as they are voluntary. Consequently the species of a human act is considered formally with regard to the end, but materially with regard to the object of the external act. Hence the Philosopher says[1] that "he who steals that he may commit adultery, is, strictly speaking, more adulterer than thief."

Reply Obj. 1. The end also has the character of an object, as stated above.[2]

Reply Obj. 2. Although it is accidental to the external action to be ordered to some particular end, it is not accidental to the interior act of the will, which act is related to the external act, as form to matter.

[1] *Ethics,* V, 2 (1130ᵃ24).
[2] Ans; cf. also Q. I, AA. I, 3.

Reply Obj. 3. When many actions, differing in species, are ordered to the same end, there is indeed a diversity of species on the part of the external actions, but unity of species on the part of the internal action.

ARTICLE 7. *Whether the Species Derived from the End Is Contained Under the Species Derived from the Object, as Under Its Genus, or Conversely?*

We proceed thus to the Seventh Article: It seems that the species of goodness derived from the end is contained under the species of goodness derived from the object, as a species is contained under its genus, as for instance, when a man commits a theft in order to give an alms.

Objection 1. For an action takes its species from its object, as stated above (A. 6). But it is impossible for a thing to be contained under another species if this species be not contained under the proper species of that thing, because the same thing cannot be contained in different species that are not subalterns. Therefore the species which is taken from the end is contained under the species which is taken from the object.

Obj. 2. Further, the last difference always constitutes the last species. But the difference derived from the end seems to come after the difference derived from the object, because the end is something last. Therefore the species derived from the end is contained under the species derived from the object, as the last species.

Obj. 3. Further, the more formal a difference is, the more particular (*specialis*) it is because difference is related to genus, as form to matter. But the species derived from the end, is more formal than that which is derived from the object, as stated above (A. 6). Therefore the species derived from the end is contained under the species derived from the object, as the most particular species is contained under the subaltern genus.

On the contrary, Each genus has its determinate differences. But an action of one same species on the part of its object can be ordered to an infinite number of ends; for instance, theft can be ordered to an infinite number of good and bad ends. Therefore the species derived from the end is not contained under the species derived from the object, as under its genus.

I answer that, The object of the external act can stand in a twofold relation to the end of the will. First, as being of itself ordered to it; thus to fight well is of itself ordered to victory. Secondly, as being ordered to it accidentally; thus to take what belongs to another is ordered accidentally to the giving of alms. Now the differences that divide a genus and constitute the species of that genus, must, as the Philosopher says,[1] divide that genus essentially; and if they belong to it accidentally, the division is incorrect, as for example if one were to say: "Animals are divided into rational and irrational; and the irrational into animals with wings, and animals without wings"; for "winged" and "wingless" are not essential determinations of irrational being. But the following division would be correct: "Some animals have feet, some have no feet; and of those that have feet, some have two feet, some four, some many," because these are an essential determination of the prior difference. Accordingly when the object is not essentially ordered to the end, the specific difference derived from the object is not an essential determination of the species derived from the end, nor conversely. Therefore one of these species is not under the other. But then the moral action is contained under two species that are disparate, as it were. Consequently we say that he that commits theft for the sake of adultery, is guilty of a twofold malice in one action. On the other hand, if the object is essentially ordered to the end, one of these differences is an essential determination of the other. Therefore one of these species will be contained under the other.

It remains to be considered which of the two is contained under the other. In order to make this clear, we must first of all observe that the more particular the form is from which a difference is taken, the more specific is the difference. Secondly, that the more universal an agent is, the more universal a form does it cause. Thirdly, that the more remote an end is, the more universal the agent to which it corresponds; thus victory, which is the last end of the army, is the end intended by the commander in chief, while the right ordering of this or that regiment is the end intended by one of the lower officers. From all this it follows that the specific difference derived from the end, is more general, and that the difference derived from an object which is essentially ordered to that end is a specific difference in relation to the former. For the will, whose proper object is the end, is the universal mover in respect of all the powers of the soul, whose proper objects are the objects of their particular acts.

Reply Obj. 1. One and the same thing, considered in its substance, cannot be in two species, one of which is not subordinate to the oth-

er. But in respect of those things which are superadded to the substance, one thing can be contained under different species. Thus one and the same fruit, as to its colour, is contained under one species, namely, white; and, as to its odor, under the species of sweet-smelling things. In like manner an action which, as to its substance, is in one natural species, considered in respect to the moral conditions that are added to it can belong to two species, as stated above (Q. I, A. 3. REPLY 3).

Reply Obj. 2. The end is last in execution, but first in the intention of the reason, according to which moral actions receive their species.

Reply Obj. 3. Difference is compared to genus as form to matter, in so far as it actualizes the genus. On the other hand, the genus is considered as more formal than the species, according as it is something more absolute and less contracted. Hence also the parts of a definition are reduced to the genus of formal cause, as is stated in the *Physics*.[2] And in this sense the genus is the formal cause of the species, and so much the more formal as it is more universal.

ARTICLE 8. *Whether Any Action Is Indifferent in Its Species?*

We proceed thus to the Eighth Article: It would seem that no action is indifferent in its species.

Objection 1. For evil is the privation of good, according to Augustine (*Enchirid.* xi).[3] But privation and habit are immediate contraries, according to the Philosopher.[4] Therefore there is no such thing as an action that is indifferent in its species, as though it were between good and evil.

Obj. 2. Further, human actions derive their species from their end or object, as stated above (A. 6; Q. I, A. 3). But every end and every object is either good or bad. Therefore every human action is good or evil according to its species. None, therefore, is indifferent in its species.

Obj. 3. Further, as stated above (A. I), an action is said to be good when it has its due perfection of goodness; and evil, when it lacks that perfection. But every action must either have the entire fulness of its goodness, or lack it in some respect. Therefore every action must needs be either good or bad in its species, and none is indifferent.

On the contrary, Augustine says (*De Serm. Dom. in Mont.* ii, 18),[5] that there are certain

---

[1] *Metaphysics*, VII, 12 (1038ᵃ9).

[2] Aristotle, II, 3 (194ᵇ26).   [3] PL 40, 236.
[4] *Categories*, 10 (12ᵇ26).
[5] PL 34, 1296.

deeds of a middle kind, "which can be done with a good or evil mind," of which it is rash to form a judgment. Therefore some actions are indifferent according to their species.

I answer that, As stated above (AA. 2, 5), every action takes its species from its object, and human action, which is called moral, takes its species from the object, in relation to the principle of human actions, which is the reason. Therefore if the object of an action includes something in accord with the order of reason, it will be a good action according to its species; for instance, to give alms to a person in want. On the other hand, if it includes something contrary to the order of reason, it will be an evil act according to its species; for instance, to steal, which is to take what belongs to another. But it may happen that the object of an action does not include something pertaining to the order of reason; for instance, to pick up a straw from the ground, to walk in the fields, and the like, and such actions are indifferent according to their species.

Reply Obj. 1. Privation is twofold. One is total privation of being (*privatum esse*), and this leaves nothing, but takes all away. Thus blindness takes away sight altogether, darkness, light, and death, life. Between this privation and the contrary habit, there can be no medium in respect of the proper subject. The other is privation in process (*privari*); thus sickness is privation of health, not that it takes health away altogether, but that it is a kind of road to the entire loss of health, occasioned by death. And since this sort of privation leaves something, it is not always the immediate contrary of the opposite habit. In this way evil is a privation of good, as Simplicius says in his commentary on the *Categories,*[1] because it does not take away all good, but leaves some. Consequently there can be something between good and evil.

Reply Obj. 2. Every object or end has some goodness or malice, at least natural; but this does not imply moral goodness or malice, which is considered in relation to the reason, as stated above, and which is what we are now concerned with.

Reply Obj. 3. Not everything belonging to an action belongs also to its species. And so although an action's specific nature may not contain all that belongs to the full complement of its goodness, it is not therefore an action specifically bad, nor is it specifically good. Thus a man in regard to his species is neither virtuous nor wicked.

[1] *In Cat.,* X (CG VIII, 388.7).

ARTICLE 9. *Whether an Individual Action Can Be Indifferent?*

We proceed thus to the Ninth Article: It seems that an individual action can be indifferent.

Objection 1. For there is no species that does not, or cannot, contain an individual. But an action can be indifferent in its species, as stated above (A. 8). Therefore an individual action can be indifferent.

Obj. 2. Further, "individual actions cause like habits," as stated in *Ethics.*[2] But a habit can be indifferent. For the Philosopher says[3] that those who are of an even temper and prodigal disposition are not evil; and yet it is evident that they are not good, since they depart from virtue; and thus they are indifferent in respect of a habit. Therefore some individual actions are indifferent.

Obj. 3. Further, moral good pertains to virtue, while moral evil pertains to vice. But it happens sometimes that a man fails to order a specifically indifferent action to a vicious or virtuous end. Therefore an individual action may happen to be indifferent.

On the contrary, Gregory says in a homily (vi *in Evang.*).[4] "An idle word is one that lacks either the usefulness of rectitude or the motive of just necessity or pious utility." But an idle word is an evil, because *men . . . shall render an account of it in the day of judgment* (Matt. 12. 36), while if it does not lack the motive of just necessity or pious utility, it is good. Therefore every word is either good or bad. For the same reason every other action is either good or bad. Therefore no individual action is indifferent.

I answer that, It sometimes happens that an action is indifferent in its species, but considered in the individual it is good or evil. And the reason of this is because a moral action, as stated above (A. 3), derives its goodness not only from its object, from which it takes its species, but also from the circumstances, which are its accidents, as it were; just as something belongs to a man by reason of his individual accidents which does not belong to him by reason of his species. And every individual action must have some circumstance that makes it good or bad, at least in respect of the intention of the end. For since it belongs to the reason to direct, if an action that proceeds from deliberate reason be not directed to the due end, it is, by that fact alone, contrary to reason, and has the character

[2] Aristotle, II, 1 (1103[b]21).
[3] *Ethics,* IV, 1 (1121[a]26).　　[4] PL 76, 1098.

of evil. But if it be directed to a due end it is in accord with reason, and so it has the character of good. Now it must be either directed or not directed to a due end. Consequently every human action that proceeds from deliberate reason, if it be considered in the individual, must be good or bad.

If, however, it does not proceed from deliberate reason, but from some act of the imagination, as when a man strokes his beard, or moves his hand or foot, such an action, properly speaking, is not moral or human, since this depends on the reason. Hence it will be indifferent, as standing apart from the genus of moral actions.

Reply Obj. 1. For an action to be indifferent in its species can be understood in several ways. First in such a way that its indifference is drawn from its very species; and in this respect the objection proves. But no action can be specifically indifferent in this way, since no object of human action is such that it cannot be ordered to good or evil, either through its end or through a circumstance. Secondly, an action may be indifferent in its species from the fact that as far as its species is concerned, it is neither good nor bad. Therefore it can be made good or bad by something else. Thus man, as far as his species is concerned, is neither white nor black. Nor is it a condition of his species that he should not be black or white, but blackness or whiteness is superadded to man by other principles than those of his species.

Reply Obj. 2. The Philosopher states[1] that a man is evil, properly speaking, if he be hurtful to others. And accordingly he says[2] that the prodigal is not evil, because he hurts none save himself. And the same applies to all others who are not hurtful to their neighbors. But we say here that evil, in general, is all that is repugnant to right reason. And in this sense every individual action is either good or bad, as stated above.

Reply Obj. 3. Whenever an end is intended by deliberate reason, it pertains either to the good of some virtue or to the evil of some vice. Thus, if a man's action is directed to the support or repose of his body, it is also directed to the good of virtue, provided he direct his body itself to the good of virtue. The same clearly applies to other actions.

ARTICLE 10. *Whether a Circumstance Places a Moral Action in the Species of Good or Evil?*

We proceed thus to the Tenth Article: It seems that a circumstance cannot place a moral action in the species of good or evil.

[1] *Ethics,* IV, 1 (1121ᵃ29).   [2] *Ibid* (1121ᵃ26).

Objection 1. For the species of an action is taken from its object. But circumstances differ from the object. Therefore circumstances do not give an action its species.

Obj. 2. Further, circumstances are as accidents in relation to the moral action, as stated above (Q. VII, A. 1). But an accident does not constitute the species. Therefore a circumstance does not constitute a species of good or evil.

Obj. 3. Further, one thing is not in several species. But one action has several circumstances. Therefore a circumstance does not place a moral action in a species of good or evil.

On the contrary, Place is a circumstance. But place puts a moral action in a certain species of evil; for theft of a thing from a holy place is a sacrilege. Therefore a circumstance makes a moral action to be specifically good or bad.

I answer that, Just as the species of natural things are constituted by their natural forms, so the species of moral actions are constituted by forms as conceived by the reason, as is evident from what was said above (A. 5). But since nature is determined to one thing, nor can a process of nature go on to infinity, there must be some ultimate form constituting a specific difference beyond which no further specific difference is possible. Hence it is that in natural things, that which is accidental to a thing cannot be taken as a difference constituting the species. But the process of reason is not determined to any one thing, for at any point it can still proceed further. And consequently that which, in one action, is taken as a circumstance added to the object that specifies the action, can again be taken by the directing reason as the principal condition of the object that determines the action's species. Thus to take another's property is specified by reason of the property being another's, and in this respect it is placed in the species of theft; and if we consider that action also in its bearing on place or time, then this will be an additional circumstance. But since the reason can direct as to place, time, and the like, it may happen that the condition as to place, in relation to the object, is considered as being in disaccord with reason; for instance, reason forbids injury to be done to a holy place. Consequently to steal from a holy place has a special contrariness to the order of reason. And thus place, which was first of all considered as a circumstance, is considered here as the principal condition of the object, and as itself contrary to reason. And in this way, whenever a circumstance has a special relation to reason, either for or against, it must specify the moral action, either as good or bad.

Reply Obj. 1. A circumstance, in so far as it specifies an action, is considered as a condition of the object, as stated above, and as being, as it were, a specific difference of it.

Reply Obj. 2. A circumstance, so long as it is but a circumstance, does not specify an action, since thus it is a mere accident, but when it becomes a principal condition of the object, then it does specify the action.

Reply Obj. 3. Not every circumstance places the moral action in the species of good or evil, since not every circumstance implies accord or disaccord with reason. Consequently, although one action may have many circumstances, it does not follow that it is in many species. Nevertheless there is no reason why one action should not be in several, even disparate, moral species, as said above (A. 7. Reply 1; Q. 1, A. 3. Reply 3).

ARTICLE 11. *Whether Every Circumstance That Makes an Action Better or Worse Places a Moral Action in a Species of Good or Evil?*

We proceed thus to the Eleventh Article: It would seem that every circumstance relating to good or evil specifies an action.

Objection 1. For good and evil are specific differences of moral actions. Therefore that which causes a difference in the goodness or malice of a moral action causes a specific difference, which is the same as to make it differ in species. Now that which makes an action better or worse makes it differ in goodness and malice. Therefore it causes it to differ in species. Therefore every circumstance that makes an action better or worse constitutes a species.

Obj. 2. Further, an additional circumstance either has in itself the character of goodness or malice, or it has not. If not, it cannot make the action better or worse, because what is not good cannot make a greater good, and what is not evil cannot make a greater evil. But if it has in itself the character of good or evil, for this very reason it has a certain species of good or evil. Therefore every circumstance that makes an action better or worse constitutes a new species of good or evil.

Obj. 3. Further, according to Dionysius (*Div. Nom.* iv),[1] "evil is caused by each single defect." Now every circumstance that increases malice has a special defect. Therefore every such circumstance adds a new species of sin. And for the same reason, every circumstance

[1] Sect. 30 (PG 3, 729).

that increases goodness seems to add a new species of goodness; just as every unity added to a number makes a new species of number, for the good consists in number, weight, and measure (Part I, Q. V, A. 5).

On the contrary, More and less do not change a species. But more and less is a circumstance of additional goodness or malice. Therefore not every circumstance that makes a moral action better or worse places it in a species of good or evil.

I answer that, As stated above (A. 10), a circumstance gives the species of good or evil to a moral action, in so far as it concerns a special order of reason. Now it happens sometimes that a circumstance does not concern a special order of reason in respect of good or evil, except on the supposition of another previous circumstance, from which the moral action takes its species of good or evil. Thus to take something in a large or small quantity does not concern the order of reason in respect of good or evil, unless a certain other condition is presupposed, from which the action takes its malice or goodness; for instance, if what is taken belongs to another, which makes the action to be discordant with reason. Therefore to take what belongs to another in a large or small quantity does not change the species of the sin. Nevertheless it can aggravate or diminish the sin. The same applies to other evil or good actions. Consequently not every circumstance that makes a moral action better or worse changes its species.

Reply Obj. 1. In things which can be more or less intense the difference of more or less does not change the species. Thus by differing in whiteness through being more or less white a thing is not changed in regard to its species of colour. In like manner that which makes an action to be more or less good or evil does not make the action differ in species.

Reply Obj. 2. A circumstance that aggravates a sin or adds to the goodness of an action, sometimes has no goodness or malice in itself, but in regard to some other condition of the action, as stated above. Consequently it does not add a new species, but adds to the goodness or malice derived from this other condition of the action.

Reply Obj. 3. A circumstance does not always involve a distinct defect of its own; sometimes it causes a defect in reference to something else. In like manner a circumstance does not always add further perfection, except in reference to something else. And, to the extent that it does, although it may add to the goodness or malice, it does not always change the species of good or evil.

QUESTION XIX
OF THE GOODNESS AND MALICE
OF THE INTERIOR ACT OF THE WILL
(In Ten Articles)

WE must now consider the goodness of the interior act of the will, under which head there are ten points of inquiry: (1) Whether the goodness of the will depends on the object? (2) Whether it depends on the object alone? (3) Whether it depends on reason? (4) Whether it depends on the eternal law? (5) Whether erring reason binds? (6) Whether the will is evil if it follows the erring reason against the law of God? (7) Whether the goodness of the will in regard to the means depends on the intention of the end? (8) Whether the degree of goodness or malice in the will depends on the degree of good or evil in the intention? (9) Whether the goodness of the will depends on its conformity to the Divine Will? (10) Whether it is necessary for the human will in order to be good to be conformed to the Divine Will as regards the thing willed?

ARTICLE 1. *Whether the Goodness of the Will Depends on the Object?*

We proceed thus to the First Article: It would seem that the goodness of the will does not depend on the object.

Objection 1. For the will cannot be directed otherwise than to what is good, for "evil is outside the scope of the will," as Dionysius says (*Div. Nom.* iv).[1] If therefore the goodness of the will were to be judged from the object, it would follow that every act of the will is good, and none bad.

Obj. 2. Further, good is first of all in the end. Therefore the goodness of the end, as such, does not depend on any other. But, according to the Philosopher,[2] "goodness of action is the end, but goodness of making is never the end," because the latter is always ordered to the thing made, as to its end. Therefore the goodness of the act of the will does not depend on any object.

Obj. 3. Further, according as a thing is, so does it make a thing to be. But the object of the will is good by reason of the goodness of *nature*. Therefore it cannot give *moral* goodness to the will. Therefore the moral goodness of the will does not depend on the object.

[1] Sect. 32 (PG 3, 732).
[2] *Ethics*, VI, 5 (1140b6).

On the contrary, The Philosopher says[3] that "justice is that habit from which men wish for just things," and accordingly, virtue is a habit from which men wish for good things. But a good will is one which is in accordance with virtue. Therefore the goodness of the will is from the fact that a man wills that which is good.

I answer that, Good and evil are essential differences of the act of the will. Because good and evil of themselves pertain to the will, just as truth and falsehood pertain to reason, the act of which is divided essentially by the difference of truth and falsehood, according as an opinion is said to be true or false. Consequently good and evil acts of the will are acts differing in species. Now the specific difference in acts is according to objects, as stated above (Q. XVIII, A. 5). Therefore good and evil in the acts of the will is derived properly from the objects.

Reply Obj. 1. The will is not always directed to what is truly good, but sometimes to the apparent good, which has indeed some measure of good, but not of a good that is absolutely suitable to be desired. Hence it is that the act of the will is not always good, but sometimes evil.

Reply Obj. 2. Although an action can, in a certain way, be man's last end, nevertheless such action is not an act of the will, as stated above (Q. I, A. I. reply 2).

Reply Obj. 3. Good is presented by the reason to the will as its object, and in so far as it is in accord with reason, it enters the moral order, and causes moral goodness in the act of the will. For reason is the principle of human and moral acts, as stated above (Q. XVIII, A. 5).

ARTICLE 2. *Whether the Goodness of the Will Depends on the Object Alone?*

We proceed thus to the Second Article: It seems that the goodness of the will does not depend on the object alone.

Objection 1. For the end has a closer relationship to the will than to any other power. But the acts of the other powers derive goodness not only from the object but also from the end, as we have shown above (Q. XVIII, A. 4). Therefore the act also of the will derives goodness not only from the object but also from the end.

Obj. 2. Further, the goodness of an action is derived not only from the object but also from the circumstances, as stated above (Q. XVIII, A. 3). But according to the difference of circumstances there may be a difference of goodness and malice in the act of the will; for instance, if a man will, when he ought, where he ought, as

[3] *Ibid.*, V, 1 (1129a9).

much as he ought, and how he ought, or if he will as he ought not. Therefore the goodness of the will depends not only on the object, but also on the circumstances.

Obj. 3. Further, ignorance of circumstances excuses malice of the will, as stated above (Q. VI, A. 8). But it would not be so unless the goodness or malice of the will depended on the circumstances. Therefore the goodness and malice of the will depend on the circumstances, and not only on the object.

On the contrary, An action does not take its species from the circumstances as such, as stated above (Q. XVIII, A. 10. Reply 2). But good and evil are specific differences of the act of the will, as stated above (A. 1). Therefore the goodness and malice of the will depend not on the circumstances but on the object alone.

I answer that, In every genus, the more a thing is first, the more simple it is, and the fewer the principles of which it consists; thus primary bodies are simple. Hence it is to be observed that the first things in every genus, are, in some way, simple and consist of one principle. Now the principle of the goodness and malice of human actions is taken from the act of the will. Consequently the goodness and malice of the act of the will depend on some one thing, while the goodness and malice of other acts may depend on several things.

Now that one thing which is the principle in each genus is not something accidental to that genus but something essential to it, because whatever is accidental is reduced to something essential, as to its principle. Therefore the goodness of the will's act depends on that one thing alone, which of itself causes goodness in the act; and that one thing is the object, and not the circumstances, which are accidents, as it were, of the act.

Reply Obj. 1. The end is the object of the will, but not of the other powers. Hence, in regard to the act of the will, the goodness derived from the object does not differ from that which is derived from the end, as they differ in the acts of the other powers, except perhaps accidentally, in so far as one end depends on another, and one act of the will on another.

Reply Obj. 2. Given that the act of the will is fixed on some good, no circumstance can make that act bad. Consequently when it is said that a man wills a good when he ought not, this can be understood in two ways. First, so that this circumstance is referred to the thing willed. And in this way the act of the will is not fixed on something good, since to will to do something

when it ought not to be done is not to will something good. Secondly, so that the circumstance is referred to the act of willing. And thus, it is impossible to will something good when one ought not to, because one ought always to will what is good; unless, perhaps, accidentally, in so far as a man by willing some particular good, is prevented from willing at the same time another good which he ought to will at that time. And then evil results not from his willing that particular good but from his not willing the other. The same applies to the other circumstances.

Reply Obj. 3. Ignorance of circumstances excuses malice of the will, in so far as the circumstance affects the thing willed; that is to say, in so far as a man is ignorant of the circumstances of the act which he wills.

ARTICLE 3. *Whether the Goodness of the Will Depends on Reason?*

We proceed thus to the Third Article: It seems that the goodness of the will does not depend on reason.

Objection 1. For what comes first does not depend on what follows. But the good pertains to the will before it belongs to reason, as is clear from what has been said above (Q. IX, A. 1). Therefore the goodness of the will does not depend on reason.

Obj. 2. Further, the Philosopher says[1] that "the goodness of the practical intellect is a truth that is in conformity with right desire." But right desire is a good will. Therefore the goodness of the practical reason depends on the goodness of the will, rather than conversely.

Obj. 3. Further, the mover does not depend on that which is moved, but vice versa. But the will moves the reason and the other powers, as stated above (Q. IX, A. 1). Therefore the goodness of the will does not depend on reason.

On the contrary, Hilary says (*De Trin.* x) :[2] "It is an unruly will that persists in its desires in opposition to reason." But the goodness of the will consists in not being unruly. Therefore the goodness of the will depends on its being subject to reason.

I answer that, As stated above (AA. 1, 2), the goodness of the will depends properly on the object. Now the will's object is proposed to it by reason. Because the good understood is the proportionate object of the will, while sensitive or imaginary good is proportionate not to the will but to the sensitive appetite, for the will can tend to the universal good, which reason apprehends, but the sensitive appetite tends only to

[1] *Ethics,* VI, 2 (1139^{a}29).   [2] PL 10, 344.

the particular good, apprehended by the sensitive power. Therefore the goodness of the will depends on reason, in the same way as it depends on the object.

Reply Obj. 1. The good considered as such, that is, as desirable, pertains to the will before pertaining to the reason. But considered as true it pertains to the reason, before, under the aspect of goodness, pertaining to the will, because the will cannot desire a good that is not previously apprehended by reason.

Reply Obj. 2. The Philosopher speaks there of the practical intellect, in so far as it counsels and reasons about the means; for in this respect it is perfected by prudence. Now in regard to the means, the rectitude of the reason depends on its conformity with the desire of a due end. Nevertheless the very desire of the due end presupposes a right apprehension of the end, which is through reason.

Reply Obj. 3. The will moves the reason in one way, and the reason moves the will in another, namely, on the part of the object, as stated above (Q. IX, A. 1).

ARTICLE 4. *Whether the Goodness of the Will Depends on the Eternal Law?*

We proceed thus to the Fourth Article: It would seem that the goodness of the human will does not depend on the eternal law.

Objection 1. Because to one thing there is one rule and one measure. But the rule of the human will, on which its goodness depends, is right reason. Therefore the goodness of the will does not depend on the eternal law.

Obj. 2. Further, "a measure is homogeneous with the thing measured."[1] But the eternal law is not homogeneous with the human will. Therefore the eternal law cannot be the measure on which the goodness of the human will depends.

Obj. 3. Further, a measure should be most certain. But the eternal law is unknown to us. Therefore it cannot be the measure on which the goodness of our will depends.

On the contrary, Augustine says (*Contra Faust.* xxii)[2] that "sin is a deed, word or desire against the eternal law." But malice of the will is the root of sin. Therefore, since malice is contrary to goodness, the goodness of the will depends on the eternal law.

I answer that, Wherever a number of causes are subordinate to one another, the effect depends more on the first than on the second cause, since the second cause acts only in virtue

of the first. Now that human reason is the rule of the human will, from which the human will derives its goodness, is from the eternal law, which is the Divine Reason. Hence it is written (Ps. 4. 6, 7): *Many say: Who showeth us good things? The light of Thy countenance, O Lord, is signed upon us*, as though to say: "The light of our reason is able to show us good things, and guide our will, in so far as it is the light of (that is, derived from) Thy countenance." It is therefore evident that the goodness of the human will depends on the eternal law much more than on human reason. And when human reason fails we must have recourse to the Eternal Reason.

Reply Obj. 1. To one thing there are not several proximate measures; but there can be several measures subordinate to one another.

Reply Obj. 2. A proximate measure is homogeneous with the thing measured; a remote measure is not.

Reply Obj. 3. Although the eternal law is unknown to us according as it is in the Divine Mind, nevertheless, it becomes known to us somewhat, either by natural reason which is derived from it as its proper image, or by some sort of additional revelation.

ARTICLE 5. *Whether the Will Is Evil When It Is at Variance with Erring Reason?*

We proceed thus to the Fifth Article: It would seem that the will is not evil when it is at variance with erring reason.

Objection 1. Because the reason is the rule of the human will, in so far as it is derived from the eternal law, as stated above (A. 4). But erring reason is not derived from the eternal law. Therefore erring reason is not the rule of the human will. Therefore the will is not evil if it be at variance with erring reason.

Obj. 2. Further, according to Augustine,[3] the command of a lower authority does not bind if it be contrary to the command of a higher authority, for instance, if a proconsul command something that is forbidden by the emperor. But erring reason sometimes proposes what is against the command of a higher power, namely, God Whose power is supreme. Therefore the dictate of an erring reason does not bind. Consequently the will is not evil if it be at variance with erring reason.

Obj. 3. Further, every evil will is reducible to some species of malice. But the will that is at variance with erring reason is not reducible to some species of malice. For instance, if a man's reason err in telling him to commit fornication,

---

[1] Aristotle, *Metaphysics*, x, 1 (1053ª24).

[2] Chap. 27 (PL 42, 418).

[3] *Serm. ad Popul.*, Serm. LXII, 8 (PL 38, 421).

his will in not willing to do so cannot be reduced to any species of malice. Therefore the will is not evil when it is at variance with erring reason.

On the contrary, As stated in the First Part (Q. LXXIX, A. 13), conscience is nothing else than the application of knowledge to some action. Now knowledge is in the reason. Therefore when the will is at variance with erring reason, it is against conscience. But every such will is evil, for it is written (Rom. 14. 23): *All that is not of faith*—that is, all that is against conscience—*is sin.* Therefore the will is evil when it is at variance with erring reason.

I answer that, Since conscience is a kind of dictate of the reason (for it is an application of knowledge to action, as was stated in the First Part, Q. LXXIX, A. 13), to inquire whether the will is evil when it is at variance with erring reason, is the same as to inquire whether an erring conscience binds. On this matter, some distinguished three kinds of actions: for some are good generically, some are indifferent, and some are evil generically.[1] And they say that if reason or conscience tell us to do something which is good generically, there is no error. And in like manner if it tell us not to do something which is evil generically, since it is the same reason that prescribes what is good and forbids what is evil. On the other hand if a man's reason or conscience tell him that he is bound by precept to do what is evil in itself, or that what is good in itself, is forbidden, then his reason or conscience errs. In like manner if a man's reason or conscience tell him that what is indifferent in itself, for instance to raise a straw from the ground, is forbidden or commanded, his reason or conscience errs. They say, therefore, that reason or conscience when erring in matters of indifference, either by commanding or by forbidding them, binds, so that the will which is at variance with that erring reason is evil and sinful. But they say that when reason or conscience errs in commanding what is evil in itself, or in forbidding what is good in itself, it does not bind. And so in such cases the will which is at variance with erring reason or conscience is not evil.

But this is unreasonable. For in matters of indifference the will that is at variance with erring reason or conscience is evil in some way on account of the object, on which the goodness or malice of the will depends; not indeed on account of the object according as it is in its own nature, but according as it is accidentally apprehended by reason as something evil to do or to avoid. And since the object of the will is that which is proposed by the reason, as stated above (A. 3), from the very fact that a thing is proposed by the reason as being evil, the will by tending to it becomes evil. And this is the case not only in indifferent matters, but also in those that are good or evil in themselves. For not only indifferent matters can receive the character of goodness or malice accidentally, but also that which is good can receive the character of evil, or that which is evil can receive the character of goodness, on account of the reason apprehending it as such. For instance, to refrain from fornication is good, yet the will does not tend to this good except in so far as it is proposed by the reason. If, therefore, the erring reason propose it as an evil, the will tends to it as to something evil. Consequently the will is evil, because it wills evil, not indeed that which is evil in itself, but that which is evil accidentally, through being apprehended as such by the reason. In like manner, to believe in Christ is good in itself, and necessary for salvation, but the will does not tend to this, except in so far as it is proposed by the reason. Consequently if it be proposed by the reason as something evil, the will tends to it as to something evil—not as if it were evil in itself, but because it is evil accidentally, through the apprehension of the reason. Hence the Philosopher says[2] that "properly speaking the incontinent man is one who does not follow right reason; but accidentally, he is also one who does not follow false reason." We must therefore conclude that, absolutely speaking, every will at variance with reason, whether right or erring, is always evil.

Reply Obj. 1. Although the judgment of an erring reason is not derived from God, yet the erring reason puts forward its judgment as being true, and consequently as being derived from God, from Whom is all truth.

Reply Obj. 2. The saying of Augustine holds good when it is known that the inferior authority prescribes something contrary to the command of the higher authority. But if a man were to believe the command of the proconsul to be the command of the emperor, in scorning the command of the proconsul he would scorn the command of the emperor. In like manner if a man were to know that human reason was dictating something contrary to God's commandment, he would not be bound to abide by reason; but then reason would not be entirely erroneous. But when erring reason proposes some-

---

[1] Bonaventure, *In Sent.*, II, d. 39, A. 1, Q. 3 (QR II, 906); see also Alexander of Hales, *Summa Theol.*, I–II, n. 388 (QR III, 388).

[2] *Ethics,* VII, 9 (1151ᵃ33).

thing as being commanded by God, then to scorn the dictate of reason is to scorn the commandment of God.

Reply Obj. 3. Whenever reason apprehends something as evil, it apprehends it under some aspect of evil; for instance, as being something contrary to a divine precept, or as giving scandal, or for some such reason. And then that evil is reduced to that species of malice.

ARTICLE 6. *Whether the Will Is Good When It Abides by Erring Reason?*

We proceed thus to the Sixth Article: It seems that the will is good when it abides by erring reason.

Objection 1. For just as the will when at variance with the reason tends to that which reason judges to be evil, so, when in accord with the reason it tends to what reason judges to be good. But the will is evil when it is at variance with reason, even when erring. Therefore even when it abides by erring reason the will is good.

Obj. 2. Further, the will is always good when it abides by the commandment of God and the eternal law. But the eternal law and God's commandment are proposed to us by the apprehension of the reason, even when it errs. Therefore the will is good even when it abides by erring reason.

Obj. 3. Further, the will is evil when it is at variance with erring reason. If, therefore, the will is evil also when it abides by erring reason, it seems that the will is always evil when in conjunction with erring reason, so that in such a case a man would be in two minds, and, of necessity, would sin, which is unreasonable. Therefore the will is good when it abides by erring reason.

On the contrary, The will of those who slew the apostles was evil. And yet it was in accord with their erring reason, according to John 16. 2: *The hour cometh, that whosoever killeth you, will think that he doth a service to God.* Therefore the will can be evil when it abides by erring reason.

I answer that, Just as the previous question is the same as inquiring whether an erring conscience binds, so this question is the same as inquiring whether an erring conscience excuses. Now this question depends on what has been said above about ignorance. For it was said (Q. VI, A. 8) that ignorance sometimes causes an act to be involuntary, and sometimes not. And since moral good and evil consist in action in so far as it is voluntary, as was stated above (A. 2), it is evident that when ignorance causes an

act to be involuntary it takes away the character of moral good and evil; but not, when it does not cause the act to be involuntary. Again, it has been stated above (Q. VI, A. 8) that when ignorance is in any way willed, either directly or indirectly, it does not cause the act to be involuntary. And I call that ignorance directly voluntary, to which the act of the will tends; and that ignorance indirectly voluntary, which is due to negligence, by reason of a man not wishing to know what he ought to know, as stated above (Q. VI, A. 8).

If then reason or conscience err with an error that is voluntary, either directly, or through negligence, so that one errs about what one ought to know, then such an error of reason or conscience does not excuse the will that abides by that erring reason or conscience from being evil. But if the error arise from ignorance of some circumstance, and without any negligence, so that it cause the act to be involuntary, then that error of reason or conscience excuses the will that abides by that erring reason from being evil. For instance, if erring reason tell a man that he should go to another man's wife, the will that abides by that erring reason is evil, since this error arises from ignorance of the Divine Law, which he is bound to know. But if a man's reason errs in mistaking another for his wife, and if he wish to give her her right when she asks for it, his will is excused from being evil, because this error arises from ignorance of a circumstance, which ignorance excuses, and causes the act to be involuntary.

Reply Obj. 1. As Dionysius says (*Div. Nom.* iv),[1] "good results from the entire cause, evil from each particular defect." Consequently, in order that the thing to which the will tends be called evil, it suffices either that it be evil in itself, or that it be apprehended as evil. But in order for it to be good, it must be good in both ways.

Reply Obj. 2. The eternal law cannot err, but human reason can. Consequently the will that abides by human reason is not always right, nor is it always in accord with the eternal law.

Reply Obj. 3. Just as in syllogistic arguments, granted one absurdity, others must follow, so in moral matters, given one absurdity, others must follow too. Thus suppose a man to seek vainglory, he will sin, whether he does his duty for vainglory, or whether he omit to do it. Nor is he in two minds about the matter, because he can put aside his evil intention. In like manner, if we suppose a man's reason or conscience to

[1] Sect. 30 (PG 3, 729).

err through inexcusable ignorance, then evil must result in the will. Nor is this man in two minds, because he can lay aside his error, since his ignorance is vincible and voluntary.

ARTICLE 7. *Whether the Goodness of the Will, as Regards the Means, Depends on the Intention of the End?*

We proceed thus to the Seventh Article: It seems that the goodness of the will does not depend on the intention of the end.

Objection 1. For it has been stated above (A. 2) that the goodness of the will depends on the object alone. But as regards the means, the object of the will is one thing, and the end intended is another. Therefore in such matters the goodness of the will does not depend on the intention of the end.

Obj. 2. Further, to wish to keep God's commandment, belongs to a good will. But this can be referred to an evil end, for instance to vainglory or covetousness, by willing to obey God for the sake of temporal gain. Therefore the goodness of the will does not depend on the intention of the end.

Obj. 3. Further, just as good and evil diversify the will, so do they diversify the end. But malice of the will does not depend on the malice of the end intended; for a man who wills to steal in order to give alms has an evil will, although he intends a good end. Therefore neither does the goodness of the will depend on the goodness of the end intended.

On the contrary, Augustine says that God rewards the intention.[1] But God rewards a thing because it is good. Therefore the goodness of the will depends on the intention of the end.

I answer that, The intention may stand in a twofold relation to the act of the will; first, as preceding it, secondly as following it. The intention precedes the act of the will causally when we will something because we intend a certain end. And then the order to the end is considered as the reason of the goodness of the thing willed; for instance, when a man wills to fast for God's sake, because the act of fasting has the character of good from the very fact that it is done for God's sake. Therefore, since the goodness of the will depends on the goodness of the thing willed, as stated above (AA. 1, 2), it must of necessity depend on the intention of the end.

On the other hand, intention follows the act of the will when it is added to a preceding act of the will; for instance, a man may will to do

something, and may afterwards refer it to God. And then the goodness of the previous act of the will does not depend on the subsequent intention, except in so far as that act is repeated with the subsequent intention.

Reply Obj. 1. When the intention is the cause of the act of willing, the order to the end is considered as the reason of the goodness of the object, as stated above.

Reply Obj. 2. The act of the will cannot be said to be good if an evil intention is the cause of willing. For when a man wills to give an alms for the sake of vainglory, he wills that which is good in itself, under the aspect of evil; and therefore, as willed by him, it is evil. Therefore his will is evil. If, however, the intention is subsequent to the act of the will, then the latter may be good, and the intention does not spoil that act of the will which preceded, but that which is repeated.

Reply Obj. 3. As we have already stated (A. 6, REPLY 1), "evil results from each particular defect, but good from the whole and entire cause." Hence, whether the will tend to what is evil in itself, even under the aspect of good, or to the good under the aspect of evil, it will be evil in either case. But in order for the will to be good, it must tend to the good under the aspect of good; in other words, it must will the good for the sake of the good.

ARTICLE 8. *Whether the Degree of Goodness or Malice in the Will Depends on the Degree of Good or Evil in the Intention?*

We proceed thus to the Eighth Article: It seems that the degree of goodness in the will depends on the degree of good in the intention.

Objection 1. Because on Matt. 12. 35 (Luke 6. 45), *A good man out of the good treasure of his heart, bringeth forth that which is good,* the gloss says: "A man does as much good as he intends."[2] But the intention gives goodness not only to the external action, but also to the act of the will, as stated above (A. 7). Therefore the goodness of a man's will is according to the goodness of his intention.

Obj. 2. Further, if you add to the cause, you add to the effect. But the goodness of the intention is the cause of the good will. Therefore a man's will is good according as his intention is good.

Obj. 3. Further, in evil actions, a man sins in proportion to his intention. For if a man were to throw a stone with a murderous intention, he would be guilty of murder. Therefore, for the

---

[1] *Confessions,* XIII, 41 (PL 32, 863).

[2] *Glossa interl.* (V, 43r).

same reason, in good actions, the will is good in proportion to the good intended.

On the contrary, The intention can be good, while the will is evil. Therefore, for the same reason, the intention can be better, and the will less good.

I answer that, In regard to both the act and the intention of the end, we may consider a two-fold quantity. One, on the part of the object, by reason of a man willing or doing a good that is greater. The other, taken from the intensity of the act, according as a man wills or acts intensely; and this is more on the part of the agent.

If then we speak of these respective quantities from the point of view of the object, it is evident that the quantity in the act does not depend on the quantity in the intention. With regard to the external act this may happen in two ways. First, through the object that is ordered to the intended end not being proportionate to that end; for instance, if a man were to give ten pounds, he could not realize his intention if he intended to buy a thing worth a hundred pounds. Secondly, on account of the obstacles that may supervene in regard to the exterior action, which obstacles we are unable to remove; for instance, a man intends to go to Rome, and encounters obstacles, which prevent him from going. On the other hand, with regard to the interior act of the will, this happens in only one way, because the interior acts of the will are in our power, though the external actions are not. But the will can will an object that is not proportionate to the intended end, and thus the will that tends to that object considered absolutely is not so good as the intention. Yet because the intention also belongs, in a way, to the act of the will,—in so far, namely, as it is the reason for the act, therefore the quantity of goodness in the intention overflows upon the act of the will; that is to say, in so far as the will wills some great good for an end, although that by which it wills to gain so great a good is not proportionate to that good.

But if we consider the quantity in the intention and in the act according to their respective intensity, then the intensity of the intention redounds upon the interior act and the exterior act of the will, since the intention stands in relation to them as a kind of form, as is clear from what was said above (Q. XII, A. 4; Q. XVIII, A. 6). And yet considered materially, while the intention is intense, the interior or exterior act may be not so intense (materially speaking); for instance, when a man does not will with as much intensity to take medicine as he wills to regain health. Nevertheless the very fact of intending health intensely, redounds, as a formal principle, upon the intense willing of medicine.

We must observe, however, that the intensity of the interior or exterior act may be referred to the intention as its object; for instance when a man intends to will intensely, or to do something intensely. And yet it does not follow that he wills or acts intensely, because the quantity of goodness in the interior or exterior act does not depend on the quantity of the good intended, as was shown above (A. 7). And hence it is that a man does not merit as much as he intends to merit, because the quantity of merit is measured by the intensity of the act, as we shall show later on (Q. XX, A. 4; Q. CXIV, A. 4).

Reply Obj. 1. This gloss speaks of good as in the estimation of God, Who considers principally the intention of the end. And so another gloss says on the same passage that "the treasure of the heart is the intention, according to which God judges our works."[1] For the goodness of the intention, as stated above, redounds in a certain way upon the goodness of the will, which makes the eternal act also meritorious in God's sight.

Reply Obj. 2. The goodness of the intention is not the whole cause of a good will. Hence the argument does not prove.

Reply Obj. 3. The mere malice of the intention suffices to make the will evil; and therefore too, the will is as evil as the intention is evil. But the same reasoning does not apply to goodness, as stated above. (REPLY 2).

ARTICLE 9. *Whether the Goodness of the Will Depends on Its Conformity to the Divine Will?*

We proceed thus to the Ninth Article: It would seem that the goodness of the human will does not depend on its conformity to the Divine will.

Objection 1. Because it is impossible for man's will to be conformed to the Divine will, as appears from the word of Isaias (55. 9): *As the heavens are exalted above the earth, so are My ways exalted above your ways, and My thoughts above your thoughts.* If therefore goodness of the will depended on its conformity to the Divine will, it would follow that it is impossible for man's will to be good. Which is inadmissible.

[1] *Glossa ordin.,* on Matt. 12.35 (v, 43A); also cf. Rabanus Maurus, *In Matt.* IV, on 12.35 (PL 107, 931).

Obj. 2. Further, just as our wills arise from the Divine will, so does our knowledge flow from the Divine knowledge. But our knowledge does not require to be conformed to God's knowledge, since God knows many things that we do not know. Therefore there is no need for our will to be conformed to the Divine will.

Obj. 3. Further, the will is a principle of action. But our action cannot be conformed to God's. Therefore neither can our will be conformed to His.

On the contrary, It is written (Matt. 26. 39): *Not as I will, but as Thou wilt,* which words He said, because He wishes man to be upright and to tend to God as Augustine expounds in the *Enchiridion.*[1] But the rectitude of the will is its goodness. Therefore the goodness of the will depends on its conformity to the Divine will.

I answer that, As stated above (A. 7), the goodness of the will depends on the intention of the end. Now the last end of the human will is the Sovereign Good, namely, God, as stated above (Q. I, A. 8; Q. III, A. 1). Therefore the goodness of the human will requires it to be ordered to the Sovereign Good, that is, to God.

Now this Good is primarily and essentially related to the Divine will, as its proper object. Again that which is primary in any genus is the measure and rule of all that belongs to that genus. Moreover, everything is right and good in so far as it comes up to its proper measure. Therefore in order that man's will be good it must be conformed to the Divine will.

Reply Obj. 1. The human will cannot be conformed to the will of God so as to equal it, but only so as to imitate it. In like manner human knowledge is conformed to the Divine knowledge, in so far as it knows truth. And human action is conformed to the Divine, in so far as it is right for the agent—and this is by way of imitation, not by way of equality.

From the above may be gathered the *replies to the Second and Third Objections.*

ARTICLE 10. *Whether It Is Necessary for the Human Will, in Order to Be Good, To Be Conformed to the Divine Will, as Regards the Thing Willed?*

We proceed thus to the Tenth Article: It seems that the human will need not always be conformed to the Divine will, as regards the thing willed.

Objection 1. For we cannot will what we do not know since the good apprehended is the object of the will. But in many things we do not know what God wills. Therefore the human will cannot be conformed to the Divine will as to the thing willed.

Obj. 2. Further, God wills to damn the man whom He foresees about to die in mortal sin. If therefore man were bound to conform his will to the Divine will in the point of the thing willed, it would follow that a man is bound to will his own damnation. Which is inadmissible.

Obj. 3. Further, no one is bound to will what is against filial piety. But if man were to will what God wills, this would sometimes be contrary to filial piety, for instance, when God wills the death of a father. If his son were to will it also, it would be against filial piety. Therefore man is not bound to conform his will to the Divine will, as to the thing willed.

On the contrary, (1) On Ps. 32. 1, *Praise becometh the upright,* a gloss says: "That man has an upright heart, who wills what God wills."[2] But everyone is bound to have an upright heart. Therefore everyone is bound to will what God wills.

(2) Moreover, the will takes its form from the object, as does every act. If therefore man is bound to conform his will to the Divine will, it follows that he is bound to conform it as to the thing willed.

(3) Moreover, opposition of wills arises from men willing different things. But whoever has a will in opposition to the Divine will, has an evil will. Therefore whoever does not conform his will to the Divine will, as to the thing willed, has an evil will.

I answer that, As is evident from what has been said above (AA. 3, 5), the will tends to its object according as it is proposed by the reason. Now a thing may be considered in various ways by the reason, so as to appear good from one point of view, and not good from another point of view. And therefore if a man's will wills a thing to be, according as it appears to be good, his will is good; and the will of another man, who wills that thing not to be, according as it appears evil, is also good. Thus a judge has a good will, in willing a thief to be put to death, because this is just; while the will of another for example, the thief's wife or son, who wishes him not to be put to death, in so far as killing is a natural evil, is also good.

Now since the will follows the apprehension of the reason or intellect, the more universal the aspect of the apprehended good, the more

---

[1] *Enarr. in Psalm,* Ps. 32.1 (PL 36, 278).

[2] *Glossa ordin.* (III, 130A); *Glossa* Lombardi (PL 191, 325); Augustine, *Enarr. in Psalm,* Ps. 32.1 (PL 36, 277).

universal the good to which the will tends. This is evident in the example given above, because the judge has care of the common good, which is justice, and therefore he wishes the thief's death, which has the aspect of good in relation to the common estate; but the thief's wife has to consider the private good of the family, and from this point of view she wishes her husband, the thief, not to be put to death. Now the good of the whole universe is that which is apprehended by God, Who is the Maker and Governor of all things. Hence whatever He wills, He wills it under the aspect of the common good; this is His own Goodness, which is the good of the whole universe. On the other hand, the apprehension of a creature, according to its nature, is of some particular good, proportionate to that nature. Now a thing may happen to be good under a particular aspect, and yet not good under a universal aspect, or vice verse, as stated above. And therefore it comes to pass that a certain will is good from willing something considered under a particular aspect, which nevertheless God does not will, under a universal aspect, and vice versa. And hence too it is that various wills of various men can be good in respect of opposite things, according as, under various aspects, they wish a particular thing to be or not to be.

But a man's will is not right in willing a particular good unless he refer it to the common good as an end, since even the natural appetite of each part is ordered to the common good of the whole. Now it is the end that supplies the formal reason, as it were, of willing whatever is directed to the end. Consequently, in order that a man will some particular good with a right will, he must will that particular good materially, and the Divine and universal good formally. Therefore the human will is bound to be conformed to the Divine will as to that which is willed formally, for it is bound to will the Divine and universal good; but not as to that which is willed materially, for the reason given above.

At the same time in both these respects, the human will is conformed to the Divine, in a certain degree. Because in so far as it is conformed to the Divine will in the common aspect of the thing willed, it is conformed to it in the point of the last end. While, in so far as it is not conformed to the Divine will in the thing willed materially, it is conformed to that will considered as efficient cause, since the proper inclination consequent to nature, or to the particular apprehension of some particular thing, comes to a thing from God as its efficient cause. Hence it is customary to say that a man's will, in this respect, is conformed to the Divine will, because it wills what God wishes him to will.

There is yet another kind of conformity in respect of the formal cause, consisting in man's willing something from charity, as God wills it. And this conformity is also reduced to the formal conformity, that is in respect of the last end, which is the proper object of charity.

Reply Obj. 1. We can know in a general way what God wills. For we know that whatever God wills, He wills it under the aspect of good. Consequently whoever wills a thing under any aspect of good, has a will conformed to the Divine will, as to the character of the thing willed. But we do not know what God wills in particular, and in this respect we are not bound to conform our will to the Divine will.

But in the state of glory, every one will see in each thing that he wills the relation of that thing to what God wills in that particular matter. Consequently he will conform his will to God in all things not only formally, but also materially.

Reply Obj. 2. God does not will the damnation of a man under that aspect, nor a man's death under that aspect because, *He wills all men to be saved* (I Tim. 2. 4), but He wills such things under the aspect of justice. Therefore in regard to such things it suffices for man to will the upholding of God's justice and of the natural order.

From this the *reply to the Third Objection* is evident.

To the first argument advanced in a contrary sense, it should be said that a man who conforms his will to God's as far as the reason of the thing willed is concerned, wills what God wills more than the man who conforms his will to God's, in the point of the very thing willed; because the will tends more to the end than to that which is on account of the end.

To the second, it must be replied that the species and form of an act are taken from the object considered formally rather than from the object considered materially.

To the third, it must be said that there is no opposition of wills when several people desire different things, but not under the same aspect. But there is opposition of wills, when under one and the same aspect, one man wills a thing which another wills not. But there is no question of this here.

QUESTION XX

OF GOODNESS AND MALICE IN EXTERNAL HUMAN ACTIONS

(*In Six Articles*)

WE must now consider goodness and malice as to external actions, under which point there are six points of inquiry: (1) Whether goodness and malice is first in the act of the will or in the external action? (2) Whether the whole goodness or malice of the external action depends on the goodness of the will? (3) Whether the goodness and malice of the interior act are the same as those of the external action? (4) Whether the external action adds any goodness or malice to that of the interior act? (5) Whether the consequences of an external action increase its goodness or malice? (6) Whether one and the same external action can be both good and evil?

ARTICLE 1. *Whether Goodness or Malice Is First in the Act of the Will, or in the Eternal Action?*

We proceed thus to the First Article: It seems that good and evil are in the external action prior to being in the act of the will.

Objection 1. For the will derives goodness from its object, as stated above (Q. XIX, AA. 1, 2). But the external action is the object of the interior act of the will; for a man is said to will to commit a theft, or to will to give an alms. Therefore good and evil are in the external action, prior to being in the act of the will.

Obj. 2. Further, good belongs first to the end, since what is directed to the end receives the aspect of good from its relation to the end. Now while the act of the will cannot be an end, as stated above (Q. I, A. 1. reply 2), the act of another power can be an end. Therefore good is in the act of some other power prior to being in the act of the will.

Obj. 3. Further, the act of the will is related to the external action as its form, as stated above (Q. XVIII, A. 6). But that which is formal is subsequent, since form comes to matter. Therefore good and evil are in the external action prior to being in the act of the will.

On the contrary, Augustine says (*Retract.* i, 9)[1] that "it is by the will that we sin, and that we live rightly." Therefore moral good and evil are first in the will.

I answer that, External actions may be said to be good or bad in two ways. First, in regard

to their genus, and the circumstances connected with them; thus the giving of alms, if the required conditions be observed, is said to be good. Secondly, a thing is said to be good or evil from its relation to the end; thus the giving of alms for vainglory is said to be evil. Now, since the end is the will's proper object, it is evident that this aspect of good or evil which the external action derives from its relation to the end is to be found first of all in the act of the will, and from there it passes to the external action. On the other hand, the goodness or malice which the external action has of itself, on account of its being about due matter and its being attended by due circumstances, is not derived from the will, but rather from the reason. Consequently, if we consider the goodness of the external action in so far as it comes from reason's ordering and apprehension, it is prior to the goodness of the act of the will. But if we consider the external action in so far as it is in the execution of the action done, it is subsequent to the goodness of the will, which is its principle.

Reply Obj. 1. The exterior action is the object of the will in so far as it is proposed to the will by the reason, as a good apprehended and ordered by the reason; and thus it is prior to the good in the act of the will. But in so far as it is found in the execution of the action, it is an effect of the will, and is subsequent to the will.

Reply Obj. 2. The end precedes in the order of intention, but follows in the order of execution.

Reply Obj. 3. A form as received into matter is subsequent to matter in the order of generation, although it precedes it in the order of nature. But according as it is in the active cause, it precedes in every way. Now the will is related to the exterior action as its efficient cause. And so the goodness of the act of the will, as existing in the active cause, is the form of the exterior action.

ARTICLE 2. *Whether the Whole Goodness and Malice of the External Action Depend on the Goodness of the Will?*

We proceed thus to the Second Article: It would seem that the whole goodness and malice of the external action depend on the goodness of the will.

Objection 1. For it is written (Matt. 7. 18): *A good tree cannot bring forth evil fruit, neither can an evil tree bring forth good fruit.* But, according to the gloss,[2] the tree signifies the will,

---

[1] PL 32, 596.

[2] *Glossa ordin.,* on Matt. 7.18 (v, 29B); Augustine, *Contra Julian.,* i, 8 (PL 44, 667).

and fruit signifies works. Therefore, it is impossible for the interior act of the will to be good, and the external action evil, or vice versa.

Obj. 2. Further, Augustine says (*Retract.* i, 9)[1] that there is no sin without the will. If therefore there is no sin in the will, there will be none in the external action. And so the whole goodness or malice of the external action depends on the will.

Obj. 3. Further, the good and evil of which we are speaking now are differences of the moral act. Now differences make an essential division in a genus, according to the Philosopher.[2] Since therefore an act is moral from being voluntary, it seems that goodness and malice in an act are derived from the will alone.

On the contrary, Augustine says (*Contra Mendac.* vii)[3] that "there are some actions which neither a good end nor a good will can make good."

I answer that, As stated above (A. 1), we may consider a twofold goodness or malice in the external action: one in respect of due matter and circumstances; the other in respect of the order to the end. And the goodness which is in respect of the order to the end depends entirely on the will. But the goodness which is in respect of due matter or circumstances depends on the reason, and on this goodness depends the goodness of the will, in so far as the will tends towards it.

Now it must be observed, as was noted above (Q. XIX, A. 6. Reply 1), that for a thing to be evil, one single defect suffices. But for it to be good absolutely, it is not enough for it to be good in one point only, it must be good in every respect. If therefore the will be good both from its proper object and from its end, it follows that the external action is good. But if the will be good from its intention of the end, this is not enough to make the external action good; and if the will be evil either by reason of its intention of the end, or by reason of the act willed, it follows that the external action is evil.

Reply Obj. 1. If the good tree be taken to signify the good will, it must be in so far as the will derives goodness from the act willed and from the end intended.

Reply Obj. 2. A man sins by his will not only when he wills an evil end, but also when he wills an evil act.

Reply Obj. 3. Voluntariness applies not only to the interior act of the will, but also to external actions, according as they proceed from

the will and the reason. Consequently the difference of good and evil is applicable to both the interior and external act.

ARTICLE 3. *Whether the Goodness and Malice of the External Action Are the Same As Those of the Interior Act?*

We proceed thus to the Third Article: It would seem that the goodness and malice of the interior act of the will are not the same as those of the external action.

Objection 1. For the principle of the interior act is the interior apprehensive or appetitive power of the soul, while the principle of the external action is the power that accomplishes the movement. Now where the principles of action are different, the actions themselves are different. Moreover, it is the action which is the subject of goodness or malice, and the same accident cannot be in different subjects. Therefore the goodness of the interior act cannot be the same as that of the external action.

Obj. 2. Further, "A virtue makes that which has it good, and renders its action good also."[4] But the intellectual virtue in the commanding power is distinct from the moral virtue in the power commanded, as is declared in the *Ethics.*[5] Therefore the goodness of the interior act, which belongs to the commanding power, is distinct from the goodness of the external action, which belongs to the power commanded.

Obj. 3. Further, the same thing cannot be cause and effect, since nothing is its own cause. But the goodness of the interior act is the cause of the goodness of the external action, or *vice versa,* as stated above (AA. 1, 2). Therefore it is not the same goodness in each.

On the contrary, It was shown above (Q. XVIII, A. 6) that the act of the will is the form, as it were, of the external action. Now that which results from the material and formal element is one thing. Therefore there is but one goodness of the internal and external act.

I answer that, As stated above (Q. XVII, A. 4), the interior act of the will, and the external action, considered morally, are one act. Now it happens sometimes that one and the same individual act has several aspects of goodness or malice, and sometimes that it has but one. Hence we must say that sometimes the goodness of the interior act is the same as that of the external action, and sometimes not. For as we have already said (AA. 1, 2), these two goodnesses or malices, of the internal and external

---

[1] PL 32, 596.   [2] *Metaphysics,* VII, 12 (1038ᵃ9).
[3] PL 40, 528.

[4] Aristotle, *Ethics,* II, 6 (1106ᵃ15).
[5] Aristotle, I, 13 (1103ᵃ3).

acts, are ordered to one another. Now it may happen, in things that are ordered to something else, that a thing is good merely from being ordered to another; thus a bitter draught is good merely because it procures health. Therefore there are not two goodnesses, one the goodness of health, and the other the goodness of the draught, but one and the same. On the other hand it happens sometimes that that which is ordered to another has some aspect of goodness in itself, besides the fact of its being ordered to some other good; thus a palatable medicine can be considered in the light of a pleasurable good, besides of being conducive to health.

We must therefore say that when the external action derives goodness or malice from its relation to the end only, then there is but one and the same goodness of the act of the will which of itself regards the end and of the external action, which regards the end through the medium of the act of the will. But when the external action has goodness or malice of itself, that is, in regard to its matter and circumstances, then the goodness of the external action is distinct from that goodness of the will which is taken from the end; yet so that the goodness of the end passes into the external action, and the goodness of the matter and circumstances passes into the act of the will, as stated above (AA. 1, 2).

Reply Obj. 1. This argument proves that the internal and external actions are different in the natural order; yet distinct as they are in that respect, they combine to form one thing in the moral order, as stated above (Q. XVII, A. 4).

Reply Obj. 2. As stated in the *Ethics*,[1] a moral virtue is ordered to the act of that virtue, which act is the end, as it were, of that virtue; but prudence, which is in the reason, is ordered to things directed to the end. For this reason different virtues are necessary. But right reason in regard to the very end of a virtue has no other goodness than the goodness of that virtue, in so far as the goodness of the reason is participated in each virtue.

Reply Obj. 3. When a thing is derived by one thing from another, as from a univocal agent cause, then it is not the same in both; thus when a hot thing heats, the heat of the thing heating is distinct from the heat of the thing heated, although it is the same specifically. But when a thing is derived by one thing from another according to analogy or proportion, then it is one and the same in both; thus the healthi-

ness which is in medicine or urine is derived from the healthiness of the animal's body; nor is health as applied to urine and medicine, distinct from health as applied to the body of an animal, of which health medicine is the cause, and urine the sign. It is in this way that the goodness of the external action is derived from the goodness of the will, and vice versa; namely, according to the order of one to the other.

ARTICLE 4. *Whether the External Action Adds Any Goodness or Malice to That of the Interior Act?*

We proceed thus to the Fourth Article: It would seem that the external action does not add any goodness or malice to that of the interior action.

Objection 1. For Chrysostom says (*Hom.* xix *in Matt.*):[2] "It is the will that is rewarded for doing good, or punished for doing evil." Now works are the witnesses of the will. Therefore God seeks for works not on His own account, in order to know how to judge, but for the sake of others, that all may understand how just He is. But good or evil is to be estimated according to God's judgment rather than according to the judgment of man. Therefore the external action adds no goodness or malice to that of the interior act.

Obj 2. Further, the goodness and malice of the interior and external acts are one and the same, as stated above (A. 3). But increase is the addition of one thing to another. Therefore the external action does not add to the goodness or malice of the interior act.

Obj. 3. Further, the entire goodness of created things does not add to the Divine Goodness, because it is entirely derived from it. But sometimes the entire goodness of the external action is derived from the goodness of the interior act, and sometimes conversely, as stated above (AA. 1, 2). Therefore neither of them adds to the goodness or malice of the other.

On the contrary, Every agent intends to attain good and avoid evil. If therefore by the external action no further goodness or malice is added, it is to no purpose that he who has a good or an evil will does a good deed or refrains from an evil deed. Which is unreasonable.

I answer that, If we speak of the goodness which the external action derives from the will tending to the end, then the external action adds nothing to this goodness, unless it happen

---

[1] Aristotle, VI, 12 (1144ᵃ8).

[2] PG 57, 274.

that the will in itself is made better in good things, or worse in evil things. This, it seems, may happen in three ways. First in point of number. If, for instance, a man wishes to do something with a good or an evil end in view, and does not do it then, but afterwards wills and does it, the act of his will is doubled, and a double good, or a double evil is the result. Secondly, in point of extension. If, for instance, a man wishes to do something for a good or an evil end, and is hindered by some obstacle, while another man perseveres in the movement of the will until he accomplish it in deed, it is evident that the will of the latter is more lasting in good or evil, and, in this respect, is better or worse. Thirdly, in point of intensity. For there are certain external actions, which, in so far as they are pleasurable or painful, are such as naturally to make the will more intense or more remiss. And it is evident that the more intensely the will tends to good or evil, the better or worse it is.

On the other hand, if we speak of the goodness which the external action derives from its matter and due circumstances, thus it stands in relation to the will as its term and end. And in this way it adds to the goodness or malice of the will, because every inclination or movement is perfected by attaining its end or reaching its term. Therefore the will is not perfect, unless it be such that, given the opportunity, it realizes the operation. But if this prove impossible, as long as the will is perfect, so as to realize the operation if it could, the lack of perfection derived from the external action, is involuntary absolutely. Now just as the involuntary deserves neither punishment nor reward in the accomplishment of good or evil deeds, so neither does it lessen reward or punishment if a man through absolute involuntariness fail to do good or evil.

Reply Obj. 1. Chrysostom is speaking of the case where a man's will is complete, and does not refrain from the deed save through the impossibility of achievement.

Reply Obj. 2. This argument applies to that goodness which the external action derives from the will as tending to the end. But the goodness which the external action takes from its matter and circumstances is distinct from that which it derives from the end; but it is not distinct from that which it has from the very act willed, to which it stands in the relation of measure and cause, as stated above (AA. 1, 2).

From this the *reply to the Third Objection* is evident.

ARTICLE 5. *Whether the Consequences of the External Action Increase Its Goodness or Malice?*

We proceed thus to the Fifth Article: It would seem that the consequences of the external action increase its goodness or malice.

Objection 1. For the effect pre-exists virtually in its cause. But the consequences result from the action as an effect from its cause. Therefore they pre-exist virtually in actions. Now a thing is judged to be good or bad according to its virtue, since "a virtue makes that which has it to be good."[1] Therefore the consequences increase the goodness or malice of an action.

Obj. 2. Further, the good actions of his hearers are consequences resulting from the words of a preacher. But such goods as these redound to the merit of the preacher, as is evident from Phil. 4. 1: *My dearly beloved brethren, my joy and my crown.* Therefore the consequences of an action increase its goodness or malice.

Obj. 3. Further, punishment is not increased, unless the fault increases, and so it is written (Deut. 25. 2): *According to the measure of the sin shall the measure also of the stripes be.* But the punishment is increased on account of the consequences; for it is written (Exod. 21. 29): *But if the ox was wont to push with his horn yesterday and the day before, and they warned his master, and he did not shut him up, and he shall kill a man or a woman, then the ox shall be stoned, and his owner also shall be put to death.* But he would not have been put to death if the ox, although he had not been shut up, had not killed a man. Therefore the consequences increase the goodness or malice of an action.

Obj. 4. Further, if a man do something which may cause death, by striking, or by sentencing, and if death does not ensue, he does not contract irregularity;[2] but he would if death were to ensue. Therefore the consequences of an action increase its goodness or malice.

On the contrary, The consequences do not make an action that was evil to be good, nor one that was good to be evil. For instance, if a man give an alms to a poor man who makes bad use of the alms by committing a sin, this does not undo the good done by the giver; and, in like manner, if a man bear patiently a wrong done to him, the wrongdoer is not on that account excused. Therefore the consequences of an action do not increase its goodness or malice.

---

[1] *Ethics*, II, 6 (1106ª15).

[2] Irregularity—"Infraction of the rule as to entrance into or exercise of Holy Orders"—O.E.D.

I answer that, The consequences of an action are either foreseen or not. If they are foreseen, it is evident that they increase the goodness or malice. For when a man foresees that many evils may follow from his action, and yet does not therefore desist from it, this shows his will to be all the more inordinate.

But if the consequences are not foreseen, we must make a distinction. Because if they follow from the nature of the action, and in the majority of cases, in this respect, the consequences increase the goodness or malice of that action; for it is evident that an action is better in kind, if better results can follow from it, and worse, if it is of a nature to produce worse results. On the other hand, if the consequences follow by accident and seldom, then they do not increase the goodness or malice of the action, because we do not judge of a thing according to that which belongs to it by accident, but only according to that which belongs to it of itself.

Reply Obj. 1. The virtue of a cause is measured by the effect that flows from the nature of the cause, not by that which results by accident.

Reply Obj. 2. The good actions done by the hearers result from the preacher's words as an effect that flows from their very nature. Hence they redound to the merit of the preacher and, especially when such is his intention.

Reply Obj. 3. The consequences for which that man is ordered to be punished, both follow from the nature of the cause, and are supposed to be foreseen. For this reason they are considered as punishable.

Reply Obj. 4. This argument would prove if irregularity were the result of the fault. But it is not the result of the fault, but of the fact, and of the obstacle to the reception of a sacrament.

ARTICLE 6. *Whether One and the Same External Action Can Be Both Good and Evil?*

We proceed thus to the Sixth Article: It would seem that one and the same external action can be both good and evil.

Objection 1. For "movement, if continuous, is one and the same."[1] But one continuous movement can be both good and bad; for instance, a man may go to Church continuously, intending at first vainglory, and afterwards the service of God. Therefore one and the same action can be both good and evil.

Obj. 2. Further, according to the Philoso-

[1] Aristotle, *Physics,* v, 4 (228ᵃ20).

pher,[2] "action and passion are one act." But the passion may be good, as Christ's was, and the action evil, as that of the Jews. Therefore one and the same act can be both good and evil.

Obj. 3. Further, since a servant is an instrument, as it were, of his master, the servant's action is his master's, just as the action of a tool is the workman's action. But it may happen that the servant's action result from his master's good will, and is therefore good, and from the evil will of the servant, and is therefore evil. Therefore the same action can be both good and evil.

On the contrary, The same thing cannot be the subject of contraries. But good and evil are contraries. Therefore the same action cannot be both good and evil.

I answer that, Nothing hinders a thing from being one in so far as it is in one genus, and manifold in so far as it is referred to another genus. Thus a continuous surface is one, considered as in the genus of quantity; and yet it is manifold, considered as to the genus of colour, if it be partly white and partly black. And accordingly, nothing hinders an action from being one, considered in the natural order, which nevertheless, is not one, considered in the moral order, and vice versa, as we have stated above (Q. XVIII, A. 7. REPLY 1). For continuous walking is one action, considered in the natural order, but it may resolve itself into many actions, considered in the moral order, if a change take place in the walker's will, for the will is the principle of moral actions. If therefore we consider an action in the moral order, it is impossible for it to be morally both good and evil. But if it be one as to natural and not moral unity, it can be both good and evil.

Reply Obj. 1. This continual movement which proceeds from various intentions, although it is one in the natural order, is not one in the point of moral unity.

Reply Obj. 2. Action and passion belong to the moral order, in so far as they are voluntary. And therefore in so far as they are voluntary in respect of wills that differ, they are two distinct things, and good can be in one of them, while evil is in the other.

Reply Obj. 3. The action of the servant, in so far as it proceeds from the will of the servant, is not the master's action, but only in so far as it proceeds from the master's command. And so the evil will of the servant does not make the action evil in this respect.

[2] *Physics,* III, 3 (202ᵃ18).

QUESTION XXI

Of the consequences of human actions by reason of their goodness and malice

(*In Four Articles*)

We have now to consider the consequences of human actions by reason of their goodness and malice, and under this head there are four points of inquiry: (1) Whether a human action is right or sinful by reason of its being good or evil? (2) Whether it thus deserves praise or blame? (3) Whether accordingly, it is meritorious or demeritorious? (4) Whether it is accordingly meritorious or demeritorious before God?

ARTICLE 1. *Whether a Human Action Is Right or Sinful, in so Far as It Is Good or Evil?*

We proceed thus to the First Article: It seems that a human action is not right or sinful, in so far as it is good or evil.

Objection 1. For "monsters are the sins of nature."[1] But monsters are not actions, but things engendered outside the order of nature. Now things that are produced according to art and reason imitate those that are produced according to nature.[2] Therefore an action is not sinful by reason of its being disordered and evil.

Obj. 2. Further, sin, as stated in the *Physics*,[3] occurs in nature and art, when the end intended by nature or art is not attained. But the goodness or malice of a human action depends, before all, on the intention of the end, and on its achievement. Therefore it seems that the malice of an action does not make it sinful.

Obj. 3. Further, if the malice of an action makes it sinful, it follows that wherever there is evil, there is sin. But this is false, since punishment is not a sin, although it is an evil. Therefore an action is not sinful by reason of its being evil.

On the contrary, As shown above (Q. XIX, A. 4), the goodness of a human action depends principally on the Eternal Law, and consequently its malice consists in its being in disaccord with the Eternal Law. But this is the very nature of sin; for Augustine says (*Contra Faust.* xxii)[4] that "sin is a word, deed, or desire, in opposition to the Eternal Law." Therefore a human action is sinful by reason of its being evil.

[1] Aristotle, *Physics*, II, 8 (199^b4).
[2] *Ibid.*, (199^a16).   [3] *Ibid.*, (199^a33).
[4] Chap. 27 (PL 42, 418).

I answer that, Evil is more comprehensive than sin, as also is good than right. For every privation of good, in whatever subject, is an evil; but sin consists properly in an action done for a certain end, and lacking due order to that end. Now the due order to an end is measured by some rule. In things that act according to nature, this rule is the natural power that inclines them to that end. When therefore an action proceeds from a natural power, in accord with the natural inclination to an end, then the action is said to be right, since the means does not exceed its limits, that is, the action does not swerve from the order of its active principle to the end. But when an action strays from this rightness, it comes under the notion of sin.

Now in those things that are done by the will, the proximate rule is the human reason, while the supreme rule is the Eternal Law. When, therefore, a human action tends to the end, according to the order of reason and of the Eternal Law, then that action is right; but when it turns aside from that rightness, then it is said to be a sin. Now it is evident from what has been said (Q. XIX, AA. 3, 4) that every voluntary action that turns aside from the order of reason and of the Eternal Law, is evil, and that every good action is in accord with reason and the Eternal Law. Hence it follows that a human action is right or sinful by reason of its being good or evil.

Reply Obj. 1. Monsters are called sins in so far as they result from a sin in nature's action.

Reply Obj. 2. The end is twofold; the last end, and the proximate end. In the sin of nature, the action does indeed fail in respect of the last end, which is the perfection of the thing generated; but it does not fail in respect of any proximate end whatever, since when nature works it forms something. In like manner, the sin of the will always fails as regards the last end intended, because no voluntary evil action can be ordered to happiness, which is the last end; and yet it does not fail in respect of some proximate end, which is intended and achieved by the will. Therefore also, since the very intention of this end is ordered to the last end, this same intention may be right or sinful.

Reply Obj. 3. Each thing is ordered to its end by its action, and therefore sin, which consists in straying from the order to the end, consists properly in an action. On the other hand, punishment regards the person of the sinner, as was stated in the First Part (Q. XLVIII, A. 5. Reply 4; A. 6. Reply 3).

ARTICLE 2. *Whether a Human Action Deserves Praise or Blame, by Reason of Its Being Good or Evil?*

We proceed thus to the Second Article: It would seem that a human action does not deserve praise or blame by reason of its being good or evil.

Objection 1. For "sin happens even in things done by nature."[1] And yet natural things are not deserving of praise or blame.[2] Therefore a human action does not deserve blame by reason of its being evil or sinful; and, consequently, neither does it deserve praise by reason of its being good.

Obj. 2. Further, just as sin occurs in moral actions, so does it happen in the productions of art, because as stated in the *Physics*,[3] "it is a sin in a grammarian to write badly, and in a doctor to give the wrong medicine." But the artist is not blamed for making something bad, because the artist's work is such that he can produce a good or a bad thing, just as he wishes. Therefore it seems that neither is there any reason for blaming a moral action in the fact that it is evil.

Obj. 3. Further, Dionysius says (*Div. Nom.* iv)[4] that "evil is weak and powerless." But weakness or inability either takes away or diminishes guilt. Therefore a human action does not incur guilt from being evil.

On the contrary, The Philosopher says[5] that virtuous deeds deserve praise, while deeds that are opposed to virtue deserve censure and blame. But good actions are virtuous, because "virtue makes that which has it good, and makes its operation good" as stated in the *Ethics*.[6] And so actions opposed to virtue are evil. Therefore a human action deserves praise or blame through being good or evil.

I answer that, Just as evil is more comprehensive than sin, so is sin more comprehensive than blame (culpa). For an action is said to deserve praise or blame from its being imputed to the agent; for to praise or to blame means nothing else than to impute to someone the malice or goodness of his action. Now an action is imputed to an agent when it is in his power, so that he has dominion over it. And this is the case in all voluntary acts, because it is through

---

[1] Aristotle, *Physics*, II, 8 (199ᵃ35).
[2] Aristotle, *Ethics*, III, 5 (1144ᵃ23).
[3] Aristotle, II, 8 (199ᵃ33).
[4] Sect. 31 (PG 3, 732).
[5] *Virtues and Vices*, I (1249ᵃ28); cf. *Ethics*, III, I (1109 ᵇ31); IV, 5 (1127ᵇ4).
[6] Aristotle, II, 6 (1106ᵃ15).

his will that man has dominion over his actions, as was made clear above (Q. I, AA. I, 2). Hence it follows that good or evil, in voluntary actions alone, renders them worthy of praise or blame; and in actions of this kind, evil, sin and guilt are one and the same thing.

Reply Obj. 1. Natural actions are not in the power of the natural agent, since the action of nature is determined to one thing. And, therefore, although there be sin in natural actions, there is no blame.

Reply Obj. 2. Reason stands in different relations to the productions of art and to moral actions. In matters of art, reason is directed to a particular end, which is something devised by reason, while in moral matters, it is directed to the general end of all human life. Now a particular end is ordered to the general end. Since therefore sin is a departure from the order to the end, as stated above (A. I), sin may occur in two ways in a production of art. First, by a departure from the particular end intended by the artist, and this sin will be proper to the art; for instance, if an artist produce a bad thing while intending to produce something good, or produce something good while intending to produce something bad. Secondly, by a departure from the general end of human life, and then he will be said to sin if he intend to produce a bad work, and does so in effect, so that another is thus deceived. But this sin is not proper to the artist as such, but as a man. Consequently for the former sin the artist is blamed as an artist, while for the latter he is blamed as a man. On the other hand, in moral matters, where we take into consideration the order of reason to the general end of human life, sin and evil are always due to a departure from the order of reason to the general end of human life. Therefore man is blamed for such a sin both as man and as a moral being. Hence the Philosopher says[7] that "in art, he who sins voluntarily is preferable"; but in prudence, as in the moral virtues, which prudence directs, he is less preferable.

Reply Obj. 3. Weakness that occurs in voluntary evils is subject to man's power, and so it neither takes away nor diminishes guilt.

ARTICLE 3. *Whether a Human Action Is Meritorious or Demeritorious, In So Far As It Is Good or Evil?*

We proceed thus to the Third Article: It would seem that a human action is not meritorious or demeritorious on account of its goodness or malice.

---

[7] *Ethics*, VI, 5 (1140ᵇ22).

Objection 1. For we speak of merit or demerit in relation to retribution, which has no place save in matters relating to another person. But good or evil actions are not all related to another person, for some are related to the person of the agent. Therefore not every good or evil human action is meritorious or demeritorious.

Obj. 2. Further, no one deserves punishment or reward for doing as he chooses with that of which he is master; thus if a man destroys what belongs to him, he is not punished, as if he had destroyed what belongs to another. But man is master of his own actions. Therefore a man does not merit punishment or reward through putting his action to a good or evil purpose.

Obj. 3. Further, if a man acquire some good for himself, he does not on that account deserve to be benefited by another man, and the same applies to evil. Now a good action is itself a kind of good and perfection of the agent, while a disordered action is his evil. Therefore a man does not merit or demerit from the fact that he does a good or an evil deed.

On the contrary, It is written (Isa. 3. 10, 11): *Say to the just man that it is well; for he shall eat the fruit of his doings. Wo to the wicked unto evil; for the reward of his hands shall be given him.*

I answer that, We speak of merit and demerit in relation to retribution rendered according to justice. Now, retribution according to justice is rendered to a man by reason of his having done something to another's advantage or hurt. It must, moreover, be observed that every individual member living in a society is, in a way, a part and member of the whole society. Therefore, any good or evil done to the member of a society, redounds on the whole society; thus, who hurts the hand, hurts the man. When, therefore, anyone does good or evil to another individual, there is a twofold measure of merit or demerit in his action: first, in respect of the retribution owed to him by the individual to whom he has done good or harm; secondly, in respect of the retribution owed to him by the whole of society. Now when a man orders his action directly for the good or evil of the whole society, retribution is owed to him, before and above all, by the whole society; secondarily, by all the parts of society. But when a man does that which conduces to his own benefit or disadvantage, then again is retribution owed to him, in so far as this too affects the community, according as he is a part of society, although retribution is not due to him, in so far as it conduces to the good or harm of an individual, who

is identical with the agent; unless, perhaps, he owe retribution to himself, by a sort of resemblance, in so far as man is said to be just to himself.

It is therefore evident that a good or evil action deserves praise or blame, in so far as it is in the power of the will; that it is right or sinful, according as it is ordered to the end; and that its merit or demerit depends on the recompense for justice or injustice towards another.

Reply Obj. 1. Sometimes a man's good or evil actions, although not ordered to the good or evil of another individual, are nevertheless ordered to the good or evil of that other which is the community.

Reply Obj. 2. Man is master of his actions; and yet, in so far as he belongs to another, that is, the community, of which he forms part, he merits or demerits, in so far as he disposes his actions well or ill; just as if he were to dispense well or ill other belongings of his in respect of which he is bound to serve the community.

Reply Obj. 3. This very good or evil which a man does to himself by his action redounds to the community, as stated above.

ARTICLE 4. *Whether a Human Action Is Meritorious or Demeritorious before God, According as It Is Good or Evil?*

We proceed thus to the Fourth Article: It would seem that man's actions, good or evil, are not meritorious or demeritorious in the sight of God.

Objection 1. Because, as stated above (A. 3), merit and demerit imply relation to retribution for good or harm done to another. But a man's action, good or evil, does no good or harm to God; for it is written (Job 35. 6, 7): *If thou sin, what shalt thou hurt Him? . . . And if thou do justly, what shalt thou give Him?* Therefore a human action, good or evil, is not meritorious or demeritorious in the sight of God.

Obj. 2. Further, an instrument acquires no merit or demerit in the sight of him that uses it, because the entire action of the instrument belongs to the user. Now when man acts he is the instrument of the Divine power which is the principal cause of his action; hence it is written (Isa. 10. 15): *Shall the axe boast itself against him that cutteth with it? Or shall the saw exalt itself against him by whom it is drawn?* where man while acting is evidently compared to an instrument. Therefore man merits or demerits nothing in God's sight, by good or evil deeds.

Obj. 3. Further, a human action acquires

merit or demerit through being ordered to someone else. But not all human actions are ordered to God. Therefore not every good or evil action acquires merit or demerit in God's sight.

On the contrary, It is written (Eccles. 12. 14): *All things that are done, God will bring into judgment . . . whether it be good or evil.* Now judgment implies retribution, in respect of which we speak of merit and demerit. Therefore every human action, both good and evil, has the character of merit or demerit in God's sight.

I answer that, A man's action, as stated above (A. 3), acquires merit or demerit through being ordered to someone else, either by reason of himself, or by reason of the community; and in each way, our actions, good and evil, acquire merit or demerit in the sight of God. On the part of God Himself, in so far as He is man's last end; and it is our duty to refer all our actions to the last end, as stated above (Q. XIX, A. 10). Consequently whoever does an evil deed, not referable to God, does not give God the honour due to Him as our last end. On the part of the whole community of the universe, because in every community, he who governs the community, cares, first of all, for the common good; and so it is his business to award retribution for such things as are done well or ill in the community. Now God is the governor and ruler of the whole universe, as stated in the First Part (Q. CIII, A. 5), and especially of rational creatures. Consequently it is evident that human actions acquire merit or demerit in reference to Him; otherwise it would follow that human actions are no business of God's.

Reply Obj. 1. God in Himself neither gains nor loses anything by the action of man. But man, for his part, takes something from God, or offers something to Him, when he observes or does not observe the order instituted by God.

Reply Obj. 2. Man is so moved as an instrument by God, that at the same time he moves himself by his free choice, as was explained above (Q. IX, A. 6. Reply 3). Consequently, by his action he acquires merit or demerit in God's sight.

Reply Obj. 3. Man is not ordered to the body politic according to all that he is and has; and so it does not follow that every action of his acquires merit or demerit in relation to the body politic. But all that man is, and can, and has, must be ordered to God; and therefore every action of man, whether good or bad, acquires merit or demerit in the sight of God, from the very character itself of the act.

2. OF THE PASSIONS, WHICH ARE ACTS COMMON TO MAN AND OTHER ANIMALS

(a) *In General*

QUESTION XXII

OF THE SUBJECT OF THE SOUL'S PASSIONS

(In Three Articles)

WE must now consider the passions of the soul: first, in general; secondly, in particular (Q. XXVI). Taking them in general, there are four things to be considered: (1) Their subject; (2) The difference between them (Q. XXIII); (3) Their mutual relationship (Q. XXV); (4) Their malice and goodness (Q. XXIV).

Under the first head there are three points of inquiry: (1) Whether there is any passion in the soul? (2) Whether passion is in the appetitive rather than in the apprehensive part? (3) Whether passion is in the sensitive appetite rather than in the intellectual appetite, which is called the will?

ARTICLE 1. *Whether Any Passion Is in the Soul?*

We proceed thus to the First Article: It seems that there is no passion in the soul.

Objection 1. Because to be passive is proper to matter. But the soul is not composed of matter and form, as stated in the First Part (Q. LXXV, A. 5). Therefore there is no passion in the soul.

Obj. 2. Further, passion is movement, as is stated in the *Physics.*[1] But the soul is not moved, as is proved in the book on the *Soul.*[2] Therefore passion is not in the soul.

Obj. 3. Further, passion is the road to corruption; for "every passion, when increased, alters the substance," as is stated in the *Topics.*[3] But

[1] Aristotle, III, 3 (202ª25).
[2] Aristotle, I, 3 (406ª12).
[3] Aristotle, VI, 6 (145ª3).

the soul is incorruptible. Therefore no passion is in the soul.

On the contrary, The Apostle says (Rom. 7. 5): *When we were in the flesh, the passions of sins which were by the law, did work in our members.* Now sins are, properly speaking, in the soul. Therefore passions also, which are described as being *of sins,* are in the soul.

I answer that, The word *passive* is used in three ways. First, in a general way, according as whatever receives something is passive, even though nothing is taken from it; thus we may say that the air is passive when it is lit up. But this is to be perfected rather than to be passive. Secondly, the word passive is employed in its proper sense, when something is received, while something else is taken away, and this happens in two ways. For sometimes that which is lost is unsuitable to the thing; thus when an animal's body is healed, it is said to be passive, because it receives health, and loses sickness. At other times the contrary occurs; thus to ail is to be passive, because the ailment is received and health is lost. And here we have passion in its most proper acceptation. For a thing is said to be passive from its being drawn to the agent, and when a thing recedes from what is suitable to it, then especially does it appear to be drawn to something else. Moreover in the treatise on *Generation and Corruption,*[1] it is stated that when a more excellent thing is generated from a less excellent, we have generation absolutely, and corruption relatively. But the reverse is the case, when from a more excellent thing a less excellent is generated. In these three ways it happens that passions are in the soul. For in the sense of reception only, we speak of "feeling and understanding as being a kind of passion."[2] But passion accompanied by the loss of something is only in respect of a bodily change; and so passion properly so called cannot be in the soul, save accidentally, in so far, namely, as the composite is passive. But here again we find a difference, because when this change is for the worse, it has more of the nature of a passion than when it is for the better; hence sorrow is more properly a passion than joy.

Reply Obj. 1. It is proper to matter to be passive in such a way as to lose something and to be changed; hence this is found only in those things that are composed of matter and form. But to be passive according as it implies reception only need not be in matter but can be in anything that is in potency. Now, though the soul is not composed of matter and form, yet it has something of potentiality, in respect of which it is fitting to it to receive or to be passive, according as the act of understanding is a kind of passion, as stated in the book on the *Soul.*[3]

Reply Obj. 2. Although it does not belong to the soul in itself to be passive and to be moved, yet it belongs to it accidentally, as stated in the book on the *Soul.*[4]

Reply Obj. 3. This argument is true of passion accompanied by change to something worse. And passion, in this sense, is not found in the soul, except accidentally; but the composite, which is corruptible, admits of it by reason of its own nature.

ARTICLE 2. *Whether Passion Is in the Appetitive Rather Than in the Apprehensive Part?*

We proceed thus to the Second Article: It would seem that passion is in the apprehensive part of the soul rather than in the appetitive.

Objection 1. Because that which is first in any genus, seems to rank first among all things that are in that genus, and to be their cause, as is stated in the *Metaphysics.*[5] Now passion is found to be in the apprehensive before being in the appetitive part. For the appetitive part is not affected unless there be a previous passion in the apprehensive part. Therefore passion is in the apprehensive part more than in the appetitive.

Obj. 2. Further, what is more active seems to be less passive; for action is contrary to passion. Now the appetitive part is more active than the apprehensive. Therefore it seems that passion is more in the apprehensive part.

Obj. 3. Further, just as the sensitive appetite is the power of a corporeal organ, so is the power of sensitive apprehension. But passion in the soul occurs, properly speaking, in respect of a bodily change. Therefore passion is not more in the appetitive than in the apprehensive part.

On the contrary, Augustine says[6] that "the movements of the soul, which the Greeks call πάθη, are styled by some of our writers, Cicero for instance,[7] disturbances; by some, affections or emotions; while others rendering the Greek more accurately, call them passions." From this it is evident that the passions of the soul are the same as affections. But affections manifestly pertain to the appetitive, and not to the ap-

---

[1] Aristotle, I, 3 (318^{b}2).
[2] Aristotle, *Soul,* I, 5 (410^{a}25).

[3] Aristotle, III, 4 (429^{b}25).   [4] Aristotle, I, 3 (406^{b}5).
[5] Aristotle, II, 1 (993^{b}24).
[6] *City of God,* IX, 4 (PL 41, 258).   [7] *Tusc.,* IV, 5.

prehensive part. Therefore the passions are in the appetitive rather than in the apprehensive part.

I answer that, As we have already stated (A. 1) the word passion implies that the patient is drawn to that which belongs to the agent. Now the soul is drawn to a thing by the appetitive power rather than by the apprehensive power, because the soul has, through its appetitive power, an order to things as they are in themselves. Hence the Philosopher says[1] that "good and evil," that is, the objects of the appetitive power, "are in things themselves." On the other hand the apprehensive power is not drawn to a thing as it is in itself, but knows it according to an intention of the thing, which intention it has in itself, or receives in its own way. Hence, we find it stated[2] that "the true and the false," which pertain to knowledge, "are not in things, but in the mind." Consequently it is evident that the notion of passion is found rather in the appetitive than in the apprehensive part.

Reply Obj. 1. In things relating to perfection the case is the opposite, in comparison to things that pertain to defect. Because in things relating to perfection, intensity is in proportion to the approach to one first principle, to which the nearer a thing approaches, the more intense it is. Thus the intensity of a thing possessed of light depends on its approach to something endowed with light in a supreme degree, to which the nearer a thing approaches, the more light it possesses. But in things that relate to defect, intensity depends not on approach to something supreme but in receding from that which is perfect, because in this consists the very notion of privation and defect. Therefore the less a thing recedes from that which stands first, the less intense it is; and the result is that at first we always find some small defect, which afterwards increases as it goes on. Now passion pertains to defect, because it belongs to a thing according as it is in potency. Therefore in those things that approach to the Supreme Perfection, namely, to God, there is but little potency and passion; while in other things, consequently, there is more. Hence also, in the supreme power, that is, the apprehensive, power of the soul, passion is found less than in the other powers.

Reply Obj. 2. The appetitive power is said to be more active because it is, more than the apprehensive power, the principle of the exterior action; and this from the very fact that it is

more passive through being related to things as they are in themselves, since it is through the external action that we attain to things.

Reply Obj. 3. As stated in the First Part (Q. LXXVIII, A. 3), the organs of the soul can be changed in two ways. First, by a spiritual change, in respect of which the organ receives an intention of the thing. And this is essential to the act of the sensitive power of apprehension; thus the eye is changed by the visible thing, not by being coloured, but by receiving an intention of colour. But the organs are receptive of another natural change, which affects their natural disposition; for instance, when they become hot or cold, or undergo some similar change. And this kind of change is accidental to the act of the sensitive power of apprehension; for instance, if the eye be wearied through gazing intently at something, or be overcome by the intensity of the object. On the other hand, this kind of change is essential to the act of the sensitive appetite; and so the material element in the definitions of the movements of the appetitive part is the natural change of the organ; for instance, anger is said to be "a kindling of the blood about the heart."[3] Hence it is evident that the notion of passion is found more in the act of the sensitive appetite than in that of the sensitive apprehension, although both are actions of a corporeal organ.

ARTICLE 3. *Whether Passion Is in the Sensitive Appetite Rather Than in the Intellectual Appetite, Which Is Called the Will?*

We proceed thus to the Third Article: It would seem that passion is not more in the sensitive than in the intellectual appetite.

Objection 1. For Dionysius declares (*Div. Nom.* ii)[4] Hierotheus "to be taught by a kind of yet more Godlike instruction; not only by learning Divine things, but also by suffering (*patiens*) them." But the sensitive appetite cannot suffer Divine things, since its object is the sensible good. Therefore passion is in the intellectual appetite, just as it is also in the sensitive appetite.

Obj. 2. Further, the more powerful the active force, the more intense the passion. But the object of the intellectual appetite, which is the universal good, is a more powerful active force than the object of the sensitive appetite, which is a particular good. Therefore passion is found

---

[1] *Metaphysics*, VI, 4 (1027[b]25).
[2] *Ibid.*

[3] Aristotle, *Soul*, I, 1 (403[a]31); cf. below, Q. XLVIII, A. 2, Arg. on the Contrary; Damascene, *De Fide Orth.*, II, 16 (PG 94, 932).
[4] Sect. 9 (PG 3, 648).

more in intellectual than in the sensitive appetite.

Obj. 3. Further, joy and love are said to be passions. But these are to be found in the intellectual and not only in the sensitive appetite; otherwise they would not be ascribed by the Scriptures to God and the angels. Therefore the passions are not more in the sensitive than in the intellectual appetite.

On the contrary, Damascene says (*De Fide Orthod.* ii, 22),[1] while describing the animal passions: "Passion is a movement of the sensitive appetite when we imagine good or evil; in other words, passion is a movement of the irrational soul, when we think of good or evil."

I answer that, As stated above (A. 1) passion is properly to be found where there is corporeal change. This corporeal change is found in the act of the sensitive appetite, and is not only spiritual, as in the sensitive apprehension, but also natural. Now there is no need for corporeal change in the act of the intellectual appetite because this appetite is not the power of a corporeal organ. It is therefore evident that the notion of passion is found more properly in the act of the sensitive appetite than in that of the intellectual appetite; and this is again evident from the definitions of Damascene quoted above.

Reply Obj. 1. By suffering Divine things is meant being well affected towards them, and united to them by love, and this takes place without any alteration in the body.

Reply Obj. 2. Intensity of passion depends not only on the power of the agent, but also on the possibility of the patient, because things that are disposed to passion suffer much even from petty agents. Therefore although the object of the intellectual appetite has greater activity than the object of the sensitive appetite, yet the sensitive appetite is more passive.

Reply Obj. 3. When love and joy and the like are ascribed to God or the angels, or to man in respect of his intellectual appetite, they signify simple acts of the will having like effects, but without passion. Hence Augustine says:[2] "The holy angels feel no anger while they punish . . ., no fellow-feeling with misery while they relieve the unhappy; and yet ordinary human speech is accustomed to ascribe to them also these passions by name, because, although they have none of our weakness, their acts bear a certain resemblance to ours."

[1] PG 94, 941; cf. also Nemesius, *De Nat. Hom.*, 16 (PG 40, 673).
[2] *City of God*, IX, 5 (PL 41, 261).

QUESTION XXIII

HOW THE PASSIONS DIFFER FROM ONE ANOTHER

(*In Four Articles*)

WE must now consider how the passions differ from one another, and under this head there are four points of inquiry: (1) Whether the passions of the concupiscible part are different from those of the irascible part? (2) Whether the contrariety of passions in the irascible part is based on the contrariety of good and evil? (3) Whether there is any passion that has no contrary? (4) Whether, in the same power there are any passions differing in species but not contrary to one another?

ARTICLE 1. *Whether the Passions of the Concupiscible Part Are Different From Those of the Irascible Part?*

We proceed thus to the First Article: It seems that the same passions are in the irascible and concupiscible parts.

Objection 1. For the Philosopher says[3] that "the passions of the soul are those which are followed by joy or sorrow." But joy and sorrow are in the concupiscible part. Therefore all the passions are in the concupiscible part, and not some in the irascible, others in the concupiscible part.

Obj. 2. Further, on the words of Matt. 13. 33, *The kingdom of heaven is like to leaven,* etc., the gloss of Jerome says:[4] "We should have prudence in the reason; hatred of vice, in the irascible part; desire of virtue, in the concupiscible part." But hatred is in the concupiscible part, as also is love, of which it is the contrary, as is stated in the *Topics.*[5] Therefore the same passion is in the concupiscible and irascible parts.

Obj. 3. Further, passions and actions differ specifically according to their objects. But the objects of the irascible and concupiscible passions are the same, namely, good and evil. Therefore the same passions are in the irascible and concupiscible parts.

On the contrary, The acts of different powers differ in species; for instance, to see, and to hear. But the irascible and the concupiscible are two powers into which the sensitive appetite is divided, as stated in the First Part (Q. LXXXI, A. 2). Therefore, since the passions are movements of the sensitive appetite, as stated above (Q.

[3] *Ethics*, II, 5 (1105[b]23).
[4] PL 26, 94; *Glossa ordin.* (V, 46A).
[5] Aristotle, II, 7 (113[b]1).

XXII, A. 3), the passions of the irascible part are specifically distinct from those of the concupiscible part.

I answer that, The passions of the irascible part differ in species from those of the concupiscible part. For since different powers have different objects, as stated in the First Part (Q. LXXVII, A. 3), the passions of different powers must of necessity be referred to different objects. Much more, therefore, do the passions of different powers differ in species, since a greater difference in the object is required to diversify the species of the powers than to diversify the species of passions or actions. For just as in the physical order, diversity of genus arises from diversity in the potency of matter, while diversity of species arises from diversity of form in the same matter, so in the acts of the soul, those that belong to different powers differ not only in species but also in genus, while acts and passions which concern different special objects, included under the one common object of a single power, differ as the species of that genus.

In order, therefore, to discern which passions are in the irascible and which in the concupiscible part, we must take the object of each of these powers. For we have stated in the First Part (Q. LXXXI, A. 2) that the object of the concupiscible power is sensible good or evil taken absolutely, that is, the pleasurable or the painful. But, since the soul must, of necessity, experience difficulty or struggle at times in acquiring some such good, or in avoiding some such evil, in so far as such good or evil is more than our animal nature can easily acquire or avoid, therefore this very good or evil, according as it is of an arduous or difficult character, is the object of the irascible part. Therefore whatever passions look to good or evil absolutely belong to the concupiscible part; for instance, joy, sorrow, love, hatred and the like. But those passions which have to do with good or bad as arduous, through being difficult to obtain or avoid, belong to the irascible part; such are daring, fear, hope and the like.

Reply Obj. 1. As stated in the First Part (Q. LXXXI, A. 2), the irascible power is bestowed on animals in order to remove the obstacles that hinder the concupiscible power from tending towards its object, either by making some good difficult to obtain, or by making some evil hard to avoid. The result is that all the irascible passions terminate in the concupiscible passions, and thus it is that the passions which are in the irascible part are followed by joy and sorrow which are in the concupiscible part.

Reply Obj. 2. Jerome ascribes hatred of vice to the irascible part, not by reason of hatred, which is properly a concupiscible passion, but on account of the struggle, which pertains to the irascible power.

Reply Obj. 3. Good, in so far as it is delightful, moves the concupiscible power. But if it prove difficult to obtain, from this very fact it has a certain contrariety to the concupiscible power, and hence the need of another power tending to that good. The same applies to evil. And this power is the irascible power. Consequently the concupiscible passions are specifically different from the irascible passions.

ARTICLE 2. *Whether the Contrariety of the Irascible Passions Is Based on the Contrariety of Good and Evil?*

We proceed thus to the Second Article: It seems that the contrariety of the irascible passions is based on no other contrariety than that of good and evil.

Objection 1. For the irascible passions are ordered to the concupiscible passions, as stated above (A. 1, Ans. 1). But the contrariety of the concupiscible passions is no other than that of good and evil; as for instance, love and hatred, joy and sorrow. Therefore the same applies to the irascible passions.

Obj. 2. Further, passions differ according to their objects, just as movements differ according to their terms. But there is no other contrariety of movements except that of the terms, as is stated in the *Physics.*[1] Therefore there is no other contrariety of passions save that of the objects. Now the object of the appetite is good or evil. Therefore in no appetitive power can there be contrariety of passions other than that of good and evil.

Obj. 3. Further, "every passion of the soul is by way of approach and withdrawal," as Avicenna declared in his sixth book of the *Physics.*[2] Now approach is caused by the aspect of good, withdrawal, by the aspect of evil, since just as "the good is what all desire,"[3] so evil is what all shun. Therefore, in the passions of the soul there can be no other contrariety than that of good and evil.

On the contrary, Fear and daring are contrary to one another, as stated in the *Ethics.*[4] But fear and daring do not differ in respect of good and evil, because each looks to some kind of evil. Therefore not every contrariety of the irascible passions is that of good and evil.

[1] Aristotle, V, 5 (229ᵃ30).   [2] *De An.,* II, 3 (8ra).
[3] *Ethics,* I, 1 (1094ᵃ3).   [4] Aristotle, III, 7 (1116ᵃ3).

I answer that, "Passion is a kind of movement," as stated in the *Physics.*[1] Therefore contrariety of passions must be based on contrariety of movements or changes. Now there is a twofold contrariety in changes and movements, as stated in the *Physics.*[2] One is according to approach and withdrawal in respect of the same term, and this contrariety belongs properly to changes, that is, to generation, which is a change to being; and to corruption, which is change from being. The other contrariety is according to opposition of terms, and belongs properly to movements; thus whitening, which is movement from black to white, is contrary to blackening, which is movement from white to black.

Accordingly there is a twofold contrariety in the passions of the soul: one, according to contrariety of objects, that is, of good and evil; the other, according to approach and withdrawal in respect of the same term. In the concupiscible passions the former contrariety alone is to be found; namely, that which is based on the objects. But in the irascible passions we find both forms of contrariety. The reason of this is that the object of the concupiscible power, as stated above (A. 1), is sensible good or evil considered absolutely. Now good, as such, cannot be a term from which, but only a term to which, since nothing shuns good as such, but on the contrary, all things desire it. In like manner, nothing desires evil, as such, but all things shun it. And so evil cannot have the aspect of a term to which, but only of a term from which. Accordingly every concupiscible passion in respect of good, tends to it, as love, desire and joy, while every concupiscible passion in respect of evil, tends from it, as hatred, avoidance or dislike, and sorrow. Therefore, in the concupiscible passions there can be no contrariety of approach and withdrawal in respect of the same object.

On the other hand, the object of the irascible power is sensible good or evil, considered not absolutely, but under the aspect of difficulty or arduousness as we have said above (A. 1). Now the good which is difficult or arduous, considered as good, is of such a nature as to produce in us a tendency to it, which tendency pertains to the passion of hope; but, considered as arduous or difficult, it makes us turn from it, and this pertains to the passion of despair. In like manner the arduous evil, considered as an evil, has the aspect of something to be shunned, and this belongs to the passion of fear. But it also contains a reason for tending to it, as attempting something arduous, in order to escape being

subject to evil, and this tendency is called daring. Consequently in the irascible passions we find contrariety in respect of good and evil (as between hope and fear), and also contrariety according to approach and withdrawal in respect of the same term (as between daring and fear).

From what has been said the *replies to the objections* are evident.

ARTICLE 3. *Whether Any Passion of the Soul Has No Contrary?*

We proceed thus to the Third Article: It would seem that every passion of the soul has a contrary.

Objection 1. For every passion of the soul is either in the irascible or in the concupiscible part, as stated above (A. 1). But both kinds of passions have their respective modes of contrariety. Therefore every passion of the soul has its contrary.

Obj. 2. Further, every passion of the soul has either good or evil for its object; for these are universally the objects of the appetitive part. But a passion having good for its object is contrary to a passion having evil for its object. Therefore every passion has a contrary.

Obj. 3. Further, every passion of the soul is in respect of approach or withdrawal, as stated above (A. 2). But every approach has a corresponding contrary withdrawal, and vice versa. Therefore every passion of the soul has a contrary.

On the contrary, Anger is a passion of the soul. But no passion is set down as being contrary to anger, as stated in the *Ethics.*[3] Therefore not every passion has a contrary.

I answer that, The passion of anger is peculiar in this, that it cannot have a contrary, either according to approach and withdrawal, or according to the contrariety of good and evil. For anger is caused by a difficult evil already present, and when such an evil is present, the appetite must either succumb, so that it does not go beyond the limits of sadness, which is a concupiscible passion; or else it has a movement of attack on the hurtful evil, which movement is that of anger. But it cannot have a movement of withdrawal, because the evil is supposed to be already present or past. Thus no passion is contrary to the movement of anger according to contrariety of approach and withdrawal.

In like manner neither can there be according to contrariety of good and evil. Because the opposite of present evil is good obtained, which can no longer have the aspect of arduousness or

[1] Aristotle, III, 3 (202ª25).   [2] Aristotle, V, 5 (229ª20).   [3] Aristotle, IV, 5 (1125ᵇ26).

difficulty. Nor, when once good is obtained, does there remain any other movement except the appetite's repose in the good obtained; and this repose belongs to joy, which is a passion of the concupiscible faculty.

Accordingly no movement of the soul can be contrary to the movement of anger, and nothing else than cessation from its movement is its contrary. Thus the Philosopher says[1] that "calm is contrary to anger," by opposition not of contrariety but of negation or privation.

From what has been said the *replies to the objections* are evident.

ARTICLE 4. *Whether in the Same Power There Are Any Passions Specifically Different, but Not Contrary to One Another?*

We proceed thus to the Fourth Article: It seems that there cannot be in the same power specifically different passions that are not contrary to one another.

Objection 1. For the passions of the soul differ according to their objects. Now the objects of the soul's passions are good and evil, and on this distinction is based the contrariety of the passions. Therefore no passions of the same power that are not contrary to one another differ specifically.

Obj. 2. Further, difference of species implies a difference of form. But every difference of form is in respect of some contrariety, as stated in the *Metaphysics*.[2] Therefore passions of the same power that are not contrary to one another do not differ specifically.

Obj. 3. Further, since every passion of the soul consists in approach or withdrawal in respect of good or evil, it seems that every difference in the passions of the soul must arise from the difference of good and evil, or from the difference of approach and withdrawal, or from degrees in approach or withdrawal. Now the first two differences cause contrariety in the passions of the soul, as stated above (A. 2). But the third difference does not diversify the species, for thus the species of the soul's passions would be infinite. Therefore it is not possible for passions of the same power to differ in species without being contrary to one another.

On the contrary, Love and joy differ in species, and are in the concupiscible power; and yet they are not contrary to one another; rather, in fact, one causes the other. Therefore in the same power there are passions that differ in species without being contrary to one another.

I answer that, Passions differ according to

their active causes, which are the objects of the soul's passions. Now active causes are differentiated in two ways. First, in respect of their species or nature; thus fire differs from water. Secondly in respect of a difference in their active powers. And the difference of active or moving causes, in respect of their moving powers, can be applied to the passions of the soul, according to the likeness to natural agents. For every mover, in a fashion, either draws the patient to itself, or drives it back. Now in drawing it to itself, it does three things in the patient. Because, in the first place, it gives the patient an inclination or aptitude to tend to the mover; thus a light body, which is above, bestows lightness on the body generated, so that it has an inclination or aptitude to be above. Secondly, if the generated body be outside its proper place, the mover gives it movement towards that place. Thirdly, it makes it to rest when it shall have come to its proper place, since to the same cause both rest in a place and the movement to that place are due. The same applies to the cause of repulsion.

Now, in the movements of the appetitive part, good has, as it were, a power of attraction, while evil has a power of repulsion. Primarily, therefore, good causes, in the appetitive power, a certain inclination, aptitude or connaturalness for good; and this belongs to the passion of love, the corresponding contrary of which is hatred in respect of evil. Secondly, if the good be not yet possessed, it causes in the appetite a movement towards the attainment of the good loved, and this pertains to the passion of desire or concupiscence; and contrary to it, in respect of evil, is the passion of aversion or dislike. Thirdly, when the good is obtained, it causes the appetite to rest, as it were, in the good obtained, and this pertains to the passion of delight or joy; the contrary of which, in respect of evil, is sorrow or sadness.

On the other hand, in the irascible passions, the aptitude, or inclination to seek good, or to shun evil, is presupposed as arising from the concupiscible part, which regards good or evil absolutely. And in respect of good not yet obtained, we have hope and despair. In respect of evil not yet present we have fear and daring. But in respect of good obtained there is no irascible passion, because it no longer has the character of something arduous, as stated above (A. 3). But evil already present gives rise to the passion of anger.

Accordingly it is clear that in the concupiscible part there are three pairs of passions; namely, love and hatred, desire and aversion, joy and sadness. In like manner there are three groups in the irascible part; namely, hope and despair, fear and daring, and anger which has no contrary passion.

Consequently there are altogether eleven passions differing specifically, six in the concupiscible part, and five in the irascible; and under these all the passions of the soul are contained.

From this the *replies to the objections* are evident.

QUESTION XXIV

OF GOOD AND EVIL IN THE PASSIONS OF THE SOUL

(In Four Articles)

WE must now consider good and evil in the passions of the soul, and under this head there are four points of inquiry: (1) Whether moral good and evil can be found in the passions of the soul? (2) Whether every passion of the soul is morally evil? (3) Whether every passion increases or decreases the goodness or malice of an act? (4) Whether any passion is good or evil specifically?

ARTICLE 1. *Whether Moral Good and Evil Can Be Found in the Passions of the Soul?*

We proceed thus to the First Article: It seems that no passion of the soul is morally good or evil.

Objection 1. For moral good and evil are proper to man, since morals are properly predicated of man," as Ambrose says (*Super Luc., Prolog.*).[1] But passions are not proper to man, for he has them in common with other animals. Therefore no passion of the soul is morally good or evil.

Obj. 2. Further, the good or evil of man consists in being in accord, or in disaccord with reason, as Dionysius says (*Div. Nom.* iv).[2] Now the passions of the soul are not in the reason, but in the sensitive appetite, as stated above (Q. XXII, A. 3). Therefore they do not pertain to human, that is, moral, good or evil.

Obj. 3. Further, the Philosopher says[3] that "we are neither praised nor blamed for our passions." But we are praised and blamed for moral good and evil. Therefore the passions are not morally good or evil.

On the contrary, Augustine says while speaking of the passions of the soul: "They are evil if our love is evil; good if our love is good."[4]

[1] PL 15, 1612.   [2] Sect. 32 (PG 3, 733).
[3] *Ethics*, II, 5 (1105[b]31).
[4] *City of God*, XIV, 7 (PL 41, 410).

I answer that, We may consider the passions of the soul in two ways: first, in themselves; secondly, as being subject to the command of the reason and will. If then the passions be considered in themselves, namely, as movements of the irrational appetite, thus there is no moral good or evil in them, since this depends on the reason, as stated above (Q. XVIII, A. 5). If, however, they be considered as subject to the command of the reason and will, then moral good and evil are in them. For the sensitive appetite is nearer than the outward members to the reason and will, and yet the movements and actions of the outward members are morally good or evil according as they are voluntary. Much more, therefore, may the passions, in so far as they are voluntary, be called morally good or evil. And they are said to be voluntary either from being commanded by the will or from not being checked by the will.

Reply Obj. 1. These passions, considered in themselves, are common to man and other animals; but, as commanded by the reason, they are proper to man.

Reply Obj. 2. Even the lower appetitive powers are called rational, in so far as "they partake of reason in some sort."[5]

Reply Obj. 3. The Philosopher says that we are neither praised nor blamed for our passions considered absolutely; but he does not exclude their becoming worthy of praise or blame, in so far as they are subordinate to reason. Hence he continues: "For the man who fears or is angry, is not praised . . . or blamed, but the man who fears or is angry in a certain way, that is, according to, or against reason."

ARTICLE 2. *Whether Every Passion of the Soul Is Evil Morally?*

We proceed thus to the Second Article: It would seem that all the passions of the soul are morally evil.

Objection 1. For Augustine says that "some call the soul's passions diseases or disturbances of the soul."[6] But every disease or disturbance of the soul is morally evil. Therefore every passion of the soul is evil morally.

Obj. 2. Further, Damascene says (*De Fide Orthod.* ii, 22)[7] that "movement in accord with nature is an operation, but movement contrary to nature is passion." But in movements of the soul, what is against nature has the character of sin and moral evil; hence he says elsewhere[8]

[5] Aristotle, *Ethics*, I, 13 (1102[b]13).
[6] *City of God*, XIV, 5, 9 (PL 41, 408, 415).
[7] PG 94, 941.   [8] *Ibid*, II, 4 (PG 94, 876).

that "the devil turned from that which is in accord with nature to that which is against nature." Therefore these passions are morally evil.

Obj. 3. Further, whatever leads to sin has an aspect of evil. But these passions lead to sin; and thus they are called *the passions of sins* (Rom. 7. 5). Therefore it seems that they are morally evil.

On the contrary, Augustine says[1] that "all these emotions are right in those whose love is rightly placed. . . . For they fear to sin, they desire to persevere; they grieve for sin, they rejoice in good works."

I answer that, On this question the opinion of the Stoics differed from that of the Peripatetics, for the Stoics held that all passions are evil, while the Peripatetics maintained that moderate passions are good.[2] This difference, although it appears great in words, is nevertheless, in reality, none at all, or but little, if we consider the intent of either school. For the Stoics did not discern between sense and intellect, and consequently neither between the intellectual and sensitive appetite.[3] Hence they did not discriminate the passions of the soul from the movements of the will, in so far as the passions of the soul are in the sensitive appetite, while the simple movements of the will are in the intellectual appetite; but every rational movement of the appetitive part they called will, while they called passion a movement that exceeds the limits of reason. Therefore Tully, following their opinion (*Tusc.* iii, 4)[4] calls all passions diseases of the soul, from which he argues that those who are diseased are unsound, and that those who are unsound are wanting in sense. Hence we speak of those who are wanting in sense as being unsound (*insanus*).

On the other hand, the Peripatetics give the name of passions to all the movements of the sensitive appetite. And so they esteem them good when they are checked by reason, and evil when they are unchecked by reason. Hence it is evident that Tully was wrong in disapproving (*ibid.*) of the Peripatetic doctrine of a mean in the passions, when he says that "every evil, though moderate, should be shunned; for, just as a body, though it be moderately ailing, is not sound, so, this mean in the diseases or passions of the soul is not sound." For passions are not called diseases or disturbances of the soul save when they are unchecked by reason.

Hence the *reply to the first objection* is evident.

Reply Obj. 2. In every passion there is an increase or decrease in the natural movement of the heart, according as the heart is moved more or less intensely by contraction and dilatation; and hence it derives the character of passion. But there is no need for passion to deviate always from the order of natural reason.

Reply Obj. 3. The passions of the soul, in so far as they are contrary to the order of reason, incline us to sin; but in so far as they are controlled by reason, they pertain to virtue.

ARTICLE 3. *Whether Passion Increases or Decreases the Goodness or Malice of an Act?*

We proceed thus to the Third Article: It seems that every passion always decreases the goodness of a moral action.

Objection 1. For anything that hinders the judgment of reason, on which depends the goodness of a moral act, consequently decreases the goodness of the moral act. But every passion hinders the judgment of reason; for Sallust says (*Catilin.*):[5] "All those that take counsel about matters of doubt, should be free from hatred, anger, friendship and pity." Therefore passion decreases the goodness of a moral act.

Obj. 2. Further, the more a man's action is like to God, the better it is; hence the Apostle says (Eph. 5. 1): *Be ye followers of God, as most dear children.* But "God and the holy angels feel no anger when they punish . . . no fellow-feeling with misery when they relieve the unhappy," as Augustine says.[6] Therefore it is better to do deeds of this kind without than with a passion of the soul.

Obj. 3. Further, just as moral evil depends on subordination to reason, so also does moral good. But moral evil is lessened by passion, for he sins less who sins from passion than he who sins deliberately. Therefore he does a better deed who does well without passion than he who does with passion.

On the contrary, Augustine says[7] that the passion of pity "is obedient to reason, when pity is bestowed without violating right, as when the poor are relieved, or the penitent forgiven." But nothing that is obedient to reason lessens the moral good. Therefore a passion of the soul does not lessen moral good.

I answer that, Since the Stoics held[8] that every passion of the soul is evil, they consequently

---

[1] *City of God,* XIV, 9 (PL 41, 413).

[2] Cf. Augustine, *City of God,* IX, 4, 5 (PL 41, 258, 261); Cicero, *De Finibus,* III, 12, 13 (DD III, 551, 552).

[3] Cf. Nemesius, *De Nat. Hom.,* 6 (PG 40, 633); Augustine, *Epist.,* CXVIII, 3 (PL 33, 440).　　　[4] DD IV, 3.

[5] Chap. 51 (BU 47).

[6] *City of God,* IX, 5 (PL 41, 261).

[7] *Ibid.*　　　[8] Cf. Cicero, *Tuscul.,* III, 4 (DD IV, 2).

held that every passion of the soul lessens the goodness of an act, since the admixture of evil either destroys good altogether, or makes it to be less good. And this is true indeed, if by passions we understand none but the disorderly movements of the sensitive appetite, considered as disturbances or diseases. But if we give the name of passions absolutely to all the movements of the sensitive appetite, then it pertains to the perfection of man's good that his passions be moderated by reason. For since man's good is founded on reason as its root, that good will be all the more perfect according as it extends to more things pertaining to man. Therefore no one questions the fact that it pertains to the perfection of moral good that the actions of the outward members be controlled by the law of reason. Hence, since the sensitive appetite can obey reason, as stated above (q. xvii, a. 7), it pertains to the perfection of moral or human good that the passions themselves also should be controlled by reason.

Accordingly just as it is better that man should both will good and do it in his external act, so also does it pertain to the perfection of moral good, that man should be moved to good not only in respect of his will, but also in respect of his sensitive appetite; according to Ps. 83. 3: *My heart and my flesh have rejoiced in the living God*, where by *heart* we are to understand the intellectual appetite, and by *flesh* the sensitive appetite.

Reply Obj. 1. The passions of the soul may stand in a twofold relation to the judgment of reason. First, antecedently, and thus, since they obscure the judgment of reason, on which the goodness of the moral act depends, they diminish the goodness of the act; for it is more praiseworthy to do a work of charity from the judgment of reason than from the mere passion of pity. In the second place, consequently, and this in two ways. First, by way of superabundance, because, namely, when the higher part of the soul is intensely moved to anything, the lower part also follows that movement; and thus the passion that results in consequence, in the sensitive appetite, is a sign of the intensity of the will, and so indicates greater moral goodness. Secondly, by way of choice; when, namely, a man, by the judgment of his reason, chooses to be affected by a passion in order to work more promptly with the co-operation of the sensitive appetite. And thus a passion of the soul increases the goodness of an action.

Reply Obj. 2. In God and the angels there is no sensitive appetite, nor again bodily members, and so in them good does not depend on the right ordering of passions or of bodily actions, as it does in us.

Reply Obj. 3. A passion that tends to evil and precedes the judgment of reason diminishes sin; but if it be consequent in either of the ways mentioned above (ans. 1), it aggravates the sin, or else it is a sign of its being more grievous.

ARTICLE 4. *Whether Any Passion Is Good or Evil in Its Species?*

We proceed thus to the Fourth Article: It seems that no passion of the soul is morally good or evil according to its species.

Objection 1. For moral good and evil depend on reason. But the passions are in the sensitive appetite, so that accordance with reason is accidental to them. Since, therefore, nothing accidental belongs to a thing's species, it seems that no passion is good or evil according to its species.

Obj. 2. Further, acts and passions take their species from their object. If, therefore, any passion were good or evil according to its species, it would follow that those passions are specifically good, the object of which is good, such as love, desire and joy; and that those passions are specifically evil, the object of which is evil, such as hatred, fear and sadness. But this is clearly false. Therefore no passion is good or evil according to its species.

Obj. 3. Further, there is no species of passion that is not to be found in other animals. But moral good is in man alone. Therefore no passion of the soul is good or evil according to its species.

On the contrary, Augustine says[1] that pity pertains to virtue. Moreover, the Philosopher says[2] that shame is a praiseworthy passion. Therefore some passions are good or evil according to their species.

I answer that, We ought, it seems, to apply to passions what has been said in regard to acts (q. xviii, aa. 5, 6; q. xx, a. 1)—namely, that the species of a passion, as the species of an act, can be considered from two points of view. First, according to its natural genus; and thus moral good and evil do not pertain to the species of an act or passion. Secondly, according to its moral genus, according as it is voluntary and controlled by reason. In this way moral good and evil can pertain to the species of a passion, in so far as the object to which a passion tends, is, of itself, in harmony or in discord with reason, as

[1] *City of God*, ix, 5 (PL 41, 260).
[2] *Ethics*, ii, 7 (1108ª32).

is clear in the case of shame which is base fear, and of envy which is sorrow for another's good; for thus passions pertain to the same species as the external act.

Reply Obj. 1. This argument considers the passions in their natural species, in so far as the sensitive appetite is considered in itself. But in so far as the sensitive appetite obeys reason, good and evil of reason are no longer accidentally in the passions of the appetite, but *per se.*

Reply Obj. 2. Passions having a tendency to good are themselves good if they tend to that which is truly good, and in like manner if they turn away from that which is truly evil. On the other hand, those passions which consist in aversion from good and a tendency to evil are themselves evil.

Reply Obj. 3. In irrational animals the sensitive appetite does not obey reason. Nevertheless, in so far as they are led by a kind of natural estimative power, which is subject to a higher, that is, the Divine, reason, there is a certain likeness of moral good in them, in regard to the soul's passions.

QUESTION XXV

OF THE ORDER OF THE PASSIONS TO ONE ANOTHER

(In Four Articles)

WE must now consider the order of the passions to one another, and under this head there are four points of inquiry: (1) The order of the irascible passions to the concupiscible passions. (2) The order of the concupiscible passions among themselves. (3) The order of the irascible passions among themselves. (4) The four principal passions.

ARTICLE 1. *Whether the Irascible Passions Precede the Concupiscible Passions, or Vice Versa?*

We proceed thus to the First Article: It seems that the irascible passions precede the concupiscible passions.

Objection 1. For the order of the passions is that of their objects. But the object of the irascible faculty is the difficult good, which seems to be the highest good. Therefore the irascible passions seem to precede the concupiscible passions.

Obj. 2. Further, the mover precedes that which is moved. But the irascible part is compared to the concupiscible, as mover to that which is moved; for it is given to animals, for the purpose of removing the obstacles that hin-

der the concupiscible part from enjoying its object, as stated above (Q. XXIII, A. 1. REPLY 1; Part 1, Q. LXXXI, A. 2). Now that which removes an obstacle, is a kind of mover.[1] Therefore the irascible passions precede the concupiscible passions.

Obj. 3. Further, joy and sadness are concupiscible passions. But joy and sadness succeed to the irascible passions; for the Philosopher says[2] that "retaliation causes anger to cease, because it produces pleasure instead of the previous pain." Therefore the concupiscible passions follow the irascible passions.

On the contrary, The concupiscible passions look to the absolute good, while the irascible passions look to a restricted, namely, the difficult, good. Since, therefore, the absolute good precedes the restricted good, it seems that the concupiscible passions precede the irascible.

I answer that, In the concupiscible passions there is more diversity than in the passions of the irascible part. For in the former we find something relating to movement—for instance, desire; and something belonging to repose, for instance, joy and sadness. But in the irascible passions there is nothing pertaining to repose, and only that which belongs to movement. The reason of this is that when we find rest in a thing, we no longer look upon it as something difficult or arduous, which is the object of the irascible part.

Now since rest is the end of movement, it is first in the order of intention, but last in the order of execution. If, therefore, we compare the passions of the irascible part with those concupiscible passions that denote rest in good, it is evident that in the order of execution the irascible passions take precedence of the like passions of the concupiscible part; thus hope precedes joy, and hence causes it, according to the Apostle (Rom. 12. 12): *Rejoicing in hope.* But the concupiscible passion which denotes rest in evil, namely, sadness, comes between two irascible passions. For it follows fear, since we become sad when we are confronted by the evil that we feared; while it precedes the movement of anger, since the movement towards revenge that results from sadness is the movement of anger. And because it is looked upon as a good thing to pay back the evil done to us, when the angry man has achieved this he rejoices. Thus it is evident that every passion of the irascible part terminates in a concupiscible passion denoting rest, namely, either in joy or in sadness. But if we compare the irascible passions to

[1] *Physics,* VIII, 4 (255[b]24).   [2] *Ethics,* IV, 5 (1126[a]21).

those concupiscible passions that denote movement, then it is clear that the latter take precedence, because the passions of the irascible part add something to those of the concupiscible part, just as the object of the irascible adds the aspect of arduousness or difficulty to the object of the concupiscible part. Thus hope adds to desire a certain effort, and a certain raising of the soul to the realization of the arduous good. In like manner fear adds to flight or detestation a certain depression of the soul, on account of difficulty in shunning the evil.

Accordingly the passions of the irascible part stand between those concupiscible passions that denote movement towards good or evil and those concupiscible passions that denote rest in good or evil. And it is therefore evident that the irascible passions both arise from and terminate in the passions of the concupiscible part.

Reply Obj. 1. This argument would prove, if the notion of the object of the concupiscible part were something contrary to the arduous, just as the notion of the object of the irascible power is that which is arduous. But because the object of the concupiscible power is good absolutely, it naturally precedes the object of the irascible part, as the common precedes the proper.

Reply Obj. 2. The remover of an obstacle is not a per se but an accidental mover, while we are speaking here of passions as directly ordered to one another. Moreover, the irascible passion removes the obstacle that hinders the concupiscible from resting in its object. And so it only follows that the irascible passions precede those concupiscible passions that denote rest.

The third objection leads to the same conclusion.

ARTICLE 2. *Whether Love Is the First of the Concupiscible Passions?*

We proceed thus to the Second Article: It would seem that love is not the first of the concupiscible passions.

Objection 1. For the concupiscible power is called so from concupiscence, which is the same passion as desire. But "things are named from their chief characteristic."[1] Therefore desire takes precedence of love.

Obj. 2. Further, love implies a certain union, since it is "a uniting and binding force," as Dionysius states (*Div. Nom.* iv).[2] But concupiscence or desire is a movement towards union with the thing coveted or desired. Therefore desire precedes love.

---

[1] Aristotle, *Soul*, II, 4 (416^{b}23).   [2] Sect. 12 (PG 3, 709).

Obj. 3. Further, the cause precedes its effect. But pleasure is sometimes the cause of love, since some love on account of pleasure.[3] Therefore pleasure precedes love, and consequently love is not the first of the concupiscible passions.

On the contrary, Augustine says[4] that all the passions are caused by love, since "love yearning for the beloved object, is desire; and, having and enjoying it, is joy." Therefore love is the first of the concupiscible passions.

I answer that, Good and evil are the object of the concupiscible part. Now good naturally precedes evil, since evil is the privation of good. Therefore all the passions, the object of which is good, are naturally before those the object of which is evil,—that is to say, each precedes its contrary passion, because the quest of a good is the reason for shunning the opposite evil.

Now good has the aspect of an end, and the end is indeed first in the order of intention, but last in the order of execution. Consequently the order of the concupiscible passions can be considered either in the order of intention or in the order of sequence. In the order of sequence, the first place belongs to that which occurs first in the thing that tends to the end. Now it is evident that whatever tends to an end, has, in the first place, an aptitude or proportion to that end, for nothing tends to a disproportionate end; secondly, it is moved to that end; thirdly, it rests in the end, after having attained it. And this very aptitude or proportion of the appetite to good is love, which is satisfaction in good, while movement towards good is desire or concupiscence, and rest in good is joy or pleasure. Accordingly in this order, love precedes desire, and desire precedes pleasure. But in the order of intention, it is the reverse, because the pleasure intended causes desire and love. For pleasure is the enjoyment of the good, which enjoyment is, in a way, the end, just as the good itself is, as stated above (Q. XI, A. 3. REPLY 3).

Reply Obj. 1. We name a thing as we know it, for words are signs of thoughts, as the Philosopher states.[5] Now in most cases we know a cause by its effect. But the effect of love, when the object loved is possessed, is pleasure; when it is not possessed, it is desire or concupiscence. And, as Augustine says,[6] "we feel love more, when we lack that which we love." Consequently of all the concupiscible passions, concupis-

---

[3] Aristotle, *Ethics*, VIII, 3, 4 (1156^{a}12; ^{a}31; 1156^{b}33).
[4] *City of God*, XIV, 7 (PL 41, 410).
[5] *Interpretation*, 1 (16^{a}3).
[6] *De Trin.*, X, 12 (PL 42, 984).

cence is felt most; and for this reason the power is named after it.

Reply Obj. 2. The union of lover and the thing loved is twofold. There is real union, consisting in the joining of one with the other. This union pertains to joy or pleasure, which follows desire. There is also an affective union, consisting in an aptitude or proportion, in so far as one thing, from the very fact of its having an aptitude for and an inclination to another, partakes of it; and love implies such a union. This union precedes the movement of desire.

Reply Obj. 3. Pleasure causes love in so far as it precedes love in the order of intention.

ARTICLE 3. *Whether Hope Is the First of the Irascible Passions?*

We proceed thus to the Third Article: It would seem that hope is not the first of the irascible passions.

Objection 1. For the irascible part is denominated from anger. Since, therefore, things are named from their chief characteristic, it seems that anger precedes and surpasses hope.

Obj. 2. Further, the object of the irascible part is something arduous. Now it seems more arduous to strive to overcome a contrary evil that threatens soon to overtake us, which pertains to daring, or an evil actually present, which pertains to anger, than to strive absolutely to obtain some good. Again, it seems more arduous to strive to overcome a present evil than a future evil. Therefore anger seems to be a stronger passion than daring, and daring, than hope. And consequently it seems that hope does not surpass them.

Obj. 3. Further, when a thing is moved towards an end, the movement of withdrawal precedes the movement of approach. But fear and despair imply withdrawal from something, while daring and hope imply approach towards something. Therefore fear and despair precede hope and daring.

On the contrary, The nearer a thing is to the first, the more it precedes others. But hope is nearer to love, which is the first of the passions. Therefore hope is the first of the passions in the irascible part.

I answer that, As stated above (A. 1) all the irascible passions imply movement towards something. Now this movement in the irascible part towards something may be due to two causes: one is the mere aptitude or proportion to the end, and this pertains to love or hatred; the other is the presence of good or evil, and this pertains to sadness or joy. As a matter of fact, the presence of good produces no passion in the irascible, as stated above (Q. XXIII, AA. 3, 4), but the presence of evil gives rise to the passion of anger.

Since then in the order of generation or sequence, proportion or aptitude to the end precedes the achievement of the end, it follows that, of all the irascible passions, anger is the last in the order of generation. And among the other passions of the irascible part which imply a movement arising from love of good or hatred of evil, those whose object is good, namely, hope and despair, must naturally precede those whose object is evil, namely, daring and fear. And yet so that hope precedes despair, since hope is a movement towards good as such, which is of its very nature attractive, so that hope tends to good directly; but despair is a movement away from good, a movement which is consistent with good, not as such, but in respect of something else, and so its tendency from good is accidental, as it were. In like manner fear, through being a movement from evil, precedes daring. And that hope and despair naturally precede fear and daring is evident from this,—that as the desire of good is the reason for avoiding evil, so hope and despair are the reason for fear and daring, because daring arises from the hope of victory, and fear arises from the despair of overcoming. Lastly, anger arises from daring, for no one is angry while seeking vengeance, unless he dare to avenge himself, as Avicenna observes in the sixth book of his *Physics*.[1] Accordingly, it is evident that hope is the first of all the irascible passions.

And if we wish to know the order of all the passions in the way of generation, love and hatred are first; desire and aversion, second; hope and despair, third; fear and daring, fourth; anger, fifth; sixth and last, joy and sadness, which follow from all the passions, as stated in the *Ethics*,[2] yet so that love precedes hatred; desire precedes aversion; hope precedes despair; fear precedes daring; and joy precedes sadness, as may be gathered from what has been stated above. (A.A. 1, 2, 3).

Reply Obj. 1. Because anger arises from the other passions, as an effect from the causes that precede it, the power takes its name from anger as being more manifest than the other passions.

Reply Obj. 2. It is not the arduousness but the good that is the reason for approach or desire. Consequently hope which looks to good

---

[1] *De An.*, IV, 6 (22ra).

[2] Aristotle, II, 5 (1105^{b}23).

more directly, takes precedence, although at times daring or even anger looks to something more arduous.

Reply Obj. 3. The movement of the appetite is primarily and per se towards the good as to its proper object, and its movement from evil results from this. For the movement of the appetitive part is in proportion not to natural movement, but to the intention of nature, which intends the end before intending the removal of a contrary, which removal is desired only for the sake of obtaining the end.

Article 4. *Whether These Are the Four Principal Passions—Joy, Sadness, Hope and Fear?*

We proceed thus to the Fourth Article: It seems that joy, sadness, hope and fear are not the four principal passions.

Objection 1. For Augustine omits hope and puts desire in its place.[1]

Obj. 2. Further, there is a twofold order in the passions of the soul: the order of intention, and the order of sequence or generation. The principal passions should therefore be taken, either in the order of intention, and thus joy and sadness, which are the final passions, will be the principal passions; or in the order of sequence or generation, and thus love will be the principal passion. Therefore joy and sadness, hope and fear should in no way be called the four principal passions.

Obj. 3. Further, just as daring is caused by hope, so fear is caused by despair. Either, therefore, hope and despair, should be accounted as principal passions, since they cause others, or hope and daring from being akin to one another.

On the contrary, Boëthius in enumerating the four principal passions, says:[2]

> Banish joys: banish fears:
> Away with hope: away with tears.

I answer that, These four are commonly called the principal passions.[3] Two of them, namely, joy and sadness, are said to be principal, because in them all the other passions have their completion and end; and so they arise from all the other passions, as is stated in the *Ethics.*[4] Fear and hope are principal passions, not because they complete the others absolutely, but because they complete them as re-

gards the movement of the appetite towards something, for in respect of good, movement begins in love, goes forward to desire, and ends in hope; while in respect of evil, it begins in hatred, goes on to aversion, and ends in fear. Hence it is customary[5] to distinguish these four passions in relation to the present and the future, for movement regards the future, while rest is in something present. Therefore joy relates to present good, sadness relates to present evil, hope regards future good, and fear, future evil.

As to the other passions that concern good or evil, present or future, they all culminate in these four. For this reason have some said that these four are the principal passions, because they are general passions. And this is true, provided that by hope and fear we understand the common tendency of the appetite to desire or aversion for something.

Reply Obj. 1. Augustine puts desire or covetousness in place of hope, in so far as they seem to regard the same thing, namely, some future good.

Reply Obj. 2. These are called principal passions in the order of intention and completion. And though fear and hope are not the last passions absolutely, yet they are the last of those passions that tend towards something as future. Nor can the argument be pressed any further except in the case of anger. Yet neither can anger be reckoned a principal passion, because it is an effect of daring, which cannot be a principal passion, as we shall state further on (*Reply Obj.* 3).

Reply Obj. 3. Despair implies movement away from good, and this is, as it were, accidental. And daring implies movement towards evil, and this too is accidental. Consequently these cannot be principal passions, because that which is accidental cannot be said to be principal. And so neither can anger be called a principal passion, because it arises from daring.

QUESTION XXVI

Of the Passions of the Soul in Particular, and First, of Love

(In Four Articles)

We have now to consider the soul's passions in particular, and (1) The passions of the concupiscible part; (2) The passions of the irascible part (Q. XL).

[1] *City of God,* xiv, 3, 7 (PL 41, 406, 410).
[2] *De Consol.,* i, 7 (PL 63, 657).
[3] According to the doctrine of the Stoics; cf. Cicero, *De Finibus,* iii, 10 (DD iii, 550); Nemesius, *De Nat. Hom.,* 17 (PG 40, 676); cf. Jerome, *In Ezech.,* i, on 1.7; Bonaventure, *In Sent.,* iii, d. 26, A. 2, Q. 5 (QR iii, 579); Albert, *In Sent.,* iii, d. 26, A. 1 (BO xxviii, 490).
[4] Aristotle, ii, 5 (1105ᵇ23).
[5] Amongst the Stoics; cf. Cicero, *Tuscul.,* iv, 6 (DD iv, 27); Nemesius, *De Nat. Hom.,* 17 (PG 40, 676); Damascene, *De Fide Orthod.,* ii, 12 (PG 94, 929).

The first of these considerations will be threefold, since we shall consider (1) Love and hatred; (2) Desire and aversion (Q. XXX); (3) Pleasure and sadness (Q. XXXI).

Concerning love, three points must be considered: (1) Love itself; (2) The cause of love (Q. XXVII); (3) The effects of love (Q. XXVIII). Under the first head there are four points of inquiry: (1) Whether love is in the concupiscible power? (2) Whether love is a passion? (3) Whether love is the same as dilection? (4) Whether love is properly divided into love of friendship, and love of concupiscence?

ARTICLE 1. *Whether Love Is in the Concupiscible Power?*

We proceed thus to the First Article: It seems that love is not in the concupiscible power.

Objection 1. For it is written (Wis. 8. 2): *Her,* namely, wisdom, *have I loved, and have sought her out from my youth.* But the concupiscible power, being a part of the sensitive appetite, cannot tend to wisdom, which is not apprehended by the senses. Therefore love is not in the concupiscible power.

Obj. 2. Further, love seems to be identified with every passion, for Augustine says:[1] "Love, yearning for the object beloved, is desire; having and enjoying it, is joy; fleeing what is contrary to it, is fear; and feeling what is contrary to it, is sadness." But not every passion is in the concupiscible power; indeed, fear, which is mentioned in this passage, is in the irascible power. Therefore we must not say absolutely that love is in the concupiscible power.

Obj. 3. Further, Dionysius (*Div. Nom* iv)[2] mentions a "natural love." But natural love seems to pertain rather to the natural powers, which belong to the vegetal soul. Therefore love is not absolutely in the concupiscible power.

On the contrary, The Philosopher says that "love is in the concupiscible power."[3]

I answer that, Love is something pertaining to the appetite, since good is the object of both. Therefore love differs according to the difference of appetites. For there is an appetite which arises from an apprehension existing, not in the subject of the appetite, but in some other, and this is called the natural appetite. Because natural things seek what is suitable to them according to their nature, by reason of an apprehension which is not in them, but in the

Author of their nature, as stated in the First Part (Q. VI, A. 1. Reply 2; Q. CIII, A. 1. Reply 1, 3). And there is another appetite arising from an apprehension in the subject of the appetite, but from necessity and not from free choice. Such is, in irrational animals, the sensitive appetite, which, however, in man, has a certain share of liberty, in so far as it obeys reason. Again, there is another appetite following from an apprehension in the subject of the appetite according to free choice. And this is the rational or intellectual appetite, which is called the will.

Now in each of these appetites, the name love is given to the principle of movement towards the end loved. In the natural appetite the principle of this movement is the appetitive subject's connaturalness with the thing to which it tends, and may be called natural love; thus the connaturalness of a heavy body for the centre is by reason of its weight and may be called natural love. In like manner the aptitude of the sensitive appetite or of the will to some good, that is to say, its very satisfaction in good, is called sensitive love, or intellectual or rational love. So that sensitive love is in the sensitive appetite, just as intellectual love is in the intellectual appetite. And it belongs to the concupiscible power, because it has to do with good absolutely, and not under the aspect of difficulty, which is the object of the irascible faculty.

Reply Obj. 1. The words quoted refer to intellectual or rational love.

Reply Obj. 2. Love is spoken of as being fear, joy, desire and sadness, not essentially but causally.

Reply Obj. 3. Natural love is not only in the powers of the vegetal soul, but in all the soul's powers, and also in all the parts of the body, and universally in all things, because, as Dionysius says (*Div. Nom.* iv),[4] "Beauty and goodness are beloved by all things," since each single thing has a connaturalness with that which is naturally suitable to it.

ARTICLE 2. *Whether Love Is a Passion?*

We proceed thus to the Second Article: It would seem that love is not a passion. For no power is a passion.

Objection 1. But every love is a power, as Dionysius says (*Div. Nom.* iv).[5] Therefore love is not a passion.

Obj. 2. Further, love is a kind of union or

---

[1] *City of God,* XIV, 7 (PL 41, 410).
[2] Sect. 15 (PG 3, 713).
[3] *Topics,* II, 7 (113b2).

[4] Sect. 10 (PG 3, 708).
[5] Sect. 15 (PG 3, 713).

bond, as Augustine says (*De Trin.* vii, 10).[1] But a union or bond is not a passion, but rather a relation. Therefore love is not a passion.

Obj. 3. Further, Damascene says (*De Fide Orthod.* ii, 22)[2] that "passion is a movement." But love does not imply the movement of the appetite; for this is desire, of which movement love is the principle. Therefore love is not a passion.

On the contrary, The Philosopher says that "love is a passion."[3]

I answer that, Passion is the effect of the agent on the patient. Now a natural agent produces a twofold effect on the patient: for in the first place it gives it the form, and secondly it gives it the movement that results from the form. Thus the generator gives the generated body both weight and the movement resulting from weight, so that weight, from being the principle of movement to the place which is connatural to that body by reason of its weight, can, in a way, be called natural love. In the same way the appetible thing gives the appetite, first, a certain adaptation to itself, which consists in satisfaction in that thing; and from this follows movement towards the appetible thing. For the appetitive movement is circular, as stated in the book on the *Soul*,[4] because the appetible thing moves the appetite, introducing itself, as it were, to its intention, while the appetite moves towards the realization of the appetible thing, so that the movement ends where it began. Accordingly, the first change wrought in the appetite by the appetible thing is called love, and is nothing else than satisfaction in that thing; and from this satisfaction results a movement towards that same thing, and this movement is desire; and lastly, there is rest which is joy. Since, therefore, love consists in a change wrought in the appetite by the appetible thing, it is evident that love is a passion: properly so called, according as it is in the concupiscible part; in a wider and extended sense, according as it is in the will.

Reply Obj. 1. Since power denotes a principle of movement or action, Dionysius calls love a power in so far as it is a principle of movement in the appetite.

Reply Obj. 2. Union belongs to love in so far as by reason of the satisfaction of the appetite, the lover stands in relation to that which he loves as though it were himself or part of himself. Hence it is clear that love is not the very

relation of union, but that union is a result of love. Hence, too, Dionysius says that "love is a unitive force" (*Div. Nom.* iv),[5] and the Philosopher says that "union is the work of love."[6]

Reply Obj. 3. Although love does not denote the movement of the appetite in tending towards the appetible object, yet it denotes that movement by which the appetite is changed by the appetible thing, so as to have satisfaction in it.

ARTICLE 3. *Whether Love Is the Same as Dilection?*

We proceed thus to the Third Article: It seems that love is the same as dilection.

Objection 1. For Dionysius says (*Div. Nom.* iv)[7] that love is to dilection, "as four is to twice two, and as a rectilinear figure is to one composed of straight lines." But these have the same meaning. Therefore love and dilection denote the same thing.

Obj. 2. Further, the movements of the appetite differ by reason of their objects. But the objects of dilection and love are the same. Therefore these are the same.

Obj. 3. Further, if dilection and love differ, it seems that it is chiefly in the fact that "dilection refers to good things, love to evil things, as some have maintained," according to Augustine.[8] But they do not differ thus, because as Augustine says the holy Scripture uses both words in reference to either good or bad things. Therefore love and dilection do not differ; thus indeed Augustine concludes that "it is not one thing to speak of love, and another to speak of dilection."

On the contrary, Dionysius says (*Div. Nom.* iv)[9] that "some holy men have held that love means something more Godlike than dilection does."

I answer that, We find four words referring, in a way, to the same thing: namely love, dilection, charity and friendship. They differ, however, in this, that "friendship," according to the Philosopher,[10] "is like a habit, but love and dilection are expressed by way of act or passion"; and charity can be taken either way.

Moreover these three express act in different ways. For love has a wider signification than the others, since every dilection or charity is love, but not vice versa. Because dilection im-

---

[1] PL 42, 960.   [2] PG 94, 940.
[3] *Ethics,* VIII, 5 (1157[b]28).
[4] Aristotle, III, 10 (433[b]22).

[5] Sect. 12 (PG 3, 709).   [6] *Politics,* II, 4 (1262[b]10).
[7] Sect. 11 (PG 3, 708).
[8] *City of God,* XIV, 7 (PL 41, 410).
[9] Sect. 12 (PG 3, 709).   [10] *Ethics,* VIII, 5 (1157[b]28).

plies, in addition to love, a choice (*electionem*) made beforehand, as the very word denotes; and therefore dilection is not in the concupiscible power, but only in the will, and only in the rational nature. Charity denotes, in addition to love, a certain perfection of love, in so far as that which is loved is held to be of great price, as the word itself implies.[1]

Reply Obj. 1. Dionysius is speaking of love and dilection, in so far as they are in the intellectual appetite; for thus love is the same as dilection.

Reply Obj. 2. The object of love is more general than the object of dilection, because love extends to more than dilection does, as stated above.

Reply Obj. 3. Love and dilection differ, not in respect of good and evil, but as stated in the body of the article. Yet in the intellectual part love is the same as dilection. And it is in this sense that Augustine speaks of love in the passage quoted; hence a little further on he adds that "a right will is a good love, and a wrong will is a bad love." However, the fact that love, which is a concupiscible passion, inclines many to evil, is the reason why some assigned the difference spoken of.[2]

Reply Obj. 4. The reason why some held[3] that, even when applied to the will itself, the word love signifies something more Godlike than dilection, was because love denotes a passion, especially in so far as it is in the sensitive appetite; but dilection presupposes the judgment of reason. But it is possible for man to tend to God by love, being as it were passively drawn by Him, more than he can possibly be drawn to Him by his reason, which pertains to the nature of dilection, as stated above. And consequently love is more Godlike than dilection.

ARTICLE 4. *Whether Love Is Properly Divided into Love of Friendship and Love of Concupiscence?*

We proceed thus to the Fourth Article: It would seem that love is not properly divided into love of friendship and love of concupiscence.[4]

Objection 1. For "love is a passion, while friendship is a habit," according to the Philosopher.[5] But habit cannot be a part of a division of passions. Therefore love is not properly divided into love of concupiscence and love of friendship.

Obj. 2. Further, a thing cannot be divided by another member of the same division; for man is not a member of the same division as animal. But concupiscence is a member of the same division as love, as a passion distinct from love. Therefore concupiscence is not a division of love.

Obj. 3. Further, according to the Philosopher[6] friendship is threefold, that which is founded on usefulness, that which is founded on pleasure, and that which is founded on goodness. But useful and pleasant friendship are not without concupiscence. Therefore concupiscence should not be divided against friendship.

On the contrary, We are said to love certain things, because we desire them; thus "a man is said to love wine, on account of its sweetness which he desires," as stated in the *Topics*.[7] But we have no friendship for wine and the like things, as stated in the *Ethics*.[8] Therefore love of concupiscence is distinct from love of friendship.

I answer that, As the Philosopher says,[9] "to love is to wish good to someone." Hence the movement of love has a twofold tendency: towards the good which a man wishes to someone, whether for himself or for another; and towards that to which he wishes some good. Accordingly, man has love of concupiscence towards the good that he wishes to another, and love of friendship towards him to whom he wishes good.

Now the members of this division are related as primary and secondary, since that which is loved with the love of friendship is love absolutely and for itself; but that which is loved with the love of concupiscence is loved not absolutely and for itself, but for something else. For just as being *per se* is absolutely that which has being, while that which exists in another has relative being, so, because good is convertible with being, the good which itself has goodness is good absolutely; but that which is another's good is a relative good. Consequently the love with which a thing is loved in order that it may have some good, is love absolutely,

---

[1] Referring to the Latin *carus* (dear).

[2] Anonymously mentioned by Augustine, *City of God*, XIV, 7 (PL 41, 410). Cf. Isidore, *Etymol.*, VIII, 2 (PL 82, 296).

[3] Cf. Dionysius, *De Div. Nom.*, IV, 12 (PG 3, 709).

[4] Cf. Albert, *Summa Theol.*, II, 4, Q. XIV, n. 4, A. 2 (BO XXXII, 200); *In Sent.*, III, d. 28, A. 2 (BO XXVIII, 537); Bonaventure, *In Sent.*, II, d. 3, Pt. II, A. 3, Q. 1 (QR II, 125).

[5] *Ethics*, VIII, 5 (1157^{b}28).   [6] *Ibid.*, VIII, 3 (1156^{a}7).

[7] Aristotle, II, 3 (111^{a}3).

[8] Aristotle, VIII, 2 (1155^{b}29).

[9] *Rhetoric*, II 4 (1380^{b}35).

while the love with which a thing is loved that it may be another's good is relative love.

Reply Obj. 1. Love is not divided into friendship and concupiscence, but into love of friendship, and love of concupiscence. For a friend is, properly speaking, one to whom we wish good, while we are said to desire what we wish for ourselves.

Hence the *Reply to the Second Objection* is evident.

Reply Obj. 3. When friendship is based on usefulness or pleasure, a man does indeed wish his friend some good, and in this respect the character of friendship is preserved. But since he refers this good further to his own pleasure or use, the result is that friendship of the useful or pleasant, in so far as it is drawn to the love of concupiscence, loses the character of true friendship.

QUESTION XXVII
OF THE CAUSE OF LOVE
(In Four Articles)

WE must now consider the cause of love, and under this head there are four points of inquiry: (1) Whether good is the only cause of love? (2) Whether knowledge is a cause of love? (3) Whether likeness is a cause of love? (4) Whether any other passion of the soul is the cause of love?

ARTICLE 1. *Whether Good Is the Only Cause of Love?*

We proceed thus to the First Article: It seems that good is not the only cause of love.

Objection 1. For good does not cause love, unless because it is loved. But it happens that evil also is loved, according to Ps. 10. 6: *He that loveth iniquity, hateth his own soul;* otherwise every love would be good. Therefore good is not the only cause of love.

Obj. 2. Further, the Philosopher says[1] that "we love those who acknowledge their evils." Therefore it seems that evil is the cause of love.

Obj. 3. Further, Dionysius says (*Div. Nom.* iv)[2] that "not the good only but also the beautiful is beloved by all."

On the contrary, Augustine says (*De Trin.* viii):[3] "Assuredly, the good alone is beloved." Therefore good alone is the cause of love.

I answer that, As stated above (Q. XXVI, A. 1), Love belongs to the appetitive power which is a passive power. Therefore its object stands

in relation to it as the cause of its movement or act. Therefore the cause of love must properly be the object of love. Now the proper object of love is the good, because, as stated above (Q. XXVI, AA. 1, 2), love implies a certain connaturalness or pleasingness (complacentia) of the lover for the thing loved, and to everything, that thing which is connatural and proportionate to it is a good. It follows, therefore, that good is the proper cause of love.

Reply Obj. 1. Evil is never loved except under the aspect of good, that is to say, in so far as it is good in some respect, and is apprehended as being good absolutely. And thus a certain love is evil in so far as it tends to that which is not absolutely a true good. It is in this way that man loves iniquity, in so far as, by means of iniquity, some good is gained; pleasure, for instance, or money, or the like.

Reply Obj. 2. Those who acknowledge their evils are loved, not for their evils, but because they acknowledge them, for it is a good thing to acknowledge one's faults, in so far as it excludes insincerity or hypocrisy.

Reply Obj. 3. The beautiful is the same as the good, and they differ in aspect only. For since good is what all seek, that which calms the desire is implied in the notion of good, while that which calms the desire by being seen or known pertains to the notion of the beautiful. Consequently those senses especially have to do with the beautiful which are the best avenues of knowledge, namely, sight and hearing, as ministering to reason; for we speak of beautiful sights and beautiful sounds. But in reference to the other objects of the other senses, we do not use the expression beautiful, for we do not speak of beautiful tastes, or of beautiful odours. Thus it is evident that beauty adds to goodness a relation to the knowing power, so that good means that which pleases absolutely the appetite, while the beautiful is something pleasant to apprehend.

ARTICLE 2. *Whether Knowledge Is a Cause of Love?*

We proceed thus to the Second Article: It would seem that knowledge is not a cause of love.

Objection 1. For it is due to love that a thing is sought. But some things are sought without being known, for instance, the sciences; for since "to have them is the same as to know them," as Augustine says,[4] if we knew them we

[1] *Rhetoric,* II, 4 (1381[b]29).
[2] Sect. 10 (PG 3, 708).   [3] PL 42, 949.
[4] QQ. LXXXIII, qu. 35 (PL 40, 24).

should have them, and should not seek them. Therefore knowledge is not the cause of love.

Obj. 2. Further, to love what we know not seems like loving something more than we know it. But some things are loved more than they are known; thus in this life God can be loved in Himself, but cannot be known in Himself. Therefore knowledge is not the cause of love.

Obj. 3. Further, if knowledge were the cause of love, there would be no love where there is no knowledge. But in all things there is love, as Dionysius says (*Div. Nom.* iv);[1] but there is not knowledge in all things. Therefore knowledge is not the cause of love.

On the contrary, Augustine proves (*De Trin.* x, 1)[2] that "none can love what he does not know."

I answer that, As stated above (A. 1), good is the cause of love, as being its object. But good is not the object of the appetite, except as apprehended. And therefore love demands some apprehension of the good that is loved. For this reason the Philosopher says[3] that "bodily sight is the beginning of sensitive love"; and in like manner the contemplation of spiritual beauty or goodness is the beginning of spiritual love. Accordingly knowledge is the cause of love for the same reason as good is, which can be loved only if known.

Reply Obj. 1. He who seeks science is not entirely without knowledge of it, but knows something about it already in some respect, either in a universal way, or in some one of its effects, or from having heard it commended, as Augustine says (*De Trin.* x, 1).[4] But to have it is not to know it in this way, but to know it perfectly.

Reply Obj. 2. Something is required for the perfection of knowledge that is not requisite for the perfection of love. For knowledge pertains to the reason, whose function consists in distinguishing things which in reality are united, and in uniting together, after a fashion, things that are distinct, by comparing one with another. Consequently the perfection of knowledge requires that man should know one by one all that is in a thing, such as its parts, powers, and properties. On the other hand, love is in the appetitive power, which regards a thing as it is in itself; therefore it suffices, for the perfection of love, that a thing be loved according as it is apprehended in itself. Hence it is, therefore, that a thing is loved more than it

is known, since it can be loved perfectly, even without being perfectly known. This is most evident in regard to the sciences, which some love through having a certain summary knowledge of them; for instance, they know that rhetoric is a science that enables man to persuade others, and this is what they love in rhetoric. The same applies to the love of God.

Reply Obj. 3. Even natural love, which is in all things, is caused by a kind of knowledge, not indeed existing in natural things themselves, but in Him Who created their nature, as stated above (Q. XXVI, A. 1; cf. Part I, Q. VI, A. 1. Reply 2).

ARTICLE 3. *Whether Likeness Is a Cause of Love?*

We proceed thus to the Third Article: It would seem that likeness is not a cause of love.

Objection 1. For the same thing is not the cause of contraries. But likeness is the cause of hatred, for it is written (Prov. 13. 10) that *among the proud there are always contentions;* and the Philosopher says[5] that potters quarrel with one another. Therefore likeness is not a cause of love.

Obj. 2. Further, Augustine says[6] that a man loves in another that which he would not be himself; thus he loves an actor, but would not himself be an actor. But it would not be so if likeness were the proper cause of love, for in that case a man would love in another that which he possesses himself, or would like to possess. Therefore likeness is not a cause of love.

Obj. 3. Further, everyone loves that which he needs, even if he have it not; thus a sick man loves health, and a poor man loves riches. But in so far as he needs them and lacks them, he is unlike them. Therefore not only likeness but also unlikeness is a cause of love.

Obj. 4. Further, the Philosopher says[7] that "we love those who bestow money and health on us; and also those who retain their friendship for the dead." But all are not such. Therefore likeness is not a cause of love.

On the contrary, It is written (Ecclus. 13. 19): *Every beast loveth its like.*

I answer that, Likeness, properly speaking, is a cause of love. But it must be observed that likeness between things is twofold. One kind of likeness arises from each thing having the same quality actually; for example, two things hav-

---

[1] Sect. 10 (PG 3, 708).   [2] PL 42, 971.
[3] *Ethics*, IX, 5, 12 (1167ª3; 1171ᵇ29).
[4] PL 42, 974.

[5] *Ethics*, VIII, 1 (1155ª35); cf. *Rhetoric*, II, 4 (1381ᵇ16); *Eudemian Ethics*, VII, 1 (1235ª18).
[6] *Confessions*, IV, 22 (PL 32, 702).
[7] *Rhetoric*, II, 4 (1381ª20; ᵇ24).

ing whiteness are said to be alike. Another kind of likeness arises from one thing having potentially and by way of inclination, a quality which the other has actually; thus we may say that a heavy body existing outside its proper place is like another heavy body that exists in its proper place. Or again, according as potency bears a resemblance to its act, since act is contained, in a manner, in the potency itself.

Accordingly the first kind of likeness causes love of friendship or well-wishing. For the very fact that two men are alike, having, as it were, one form, makes them to be, in a manner, one in that form; thus two men are one thing in the species of humanity, and two white men are one thing in whiteness. Hence the affections of one tend to the other, as being one with him, and he wishes good to him as to himself. But the second kind of likeness causes love of concupiscence, or friendship founded on usefulness or pleasure; because whatever is in potency, as such, has the desire for its act, and it takes pleasure in its realization, if it be a sentient and cognitive being.

Now it has been stated above (Q. XXVI, A. 4), that in the love of concupiscence, the lover, properly speaking, loves himself, in willing the good that he desires. But a man loves himself more than another, because he is one with himself substantially, while with another he is one only in the likeness of some form. Consequently, if this other's likeness to him arising from the participation of a form hinders him from gaining the good that he loves, he becomes hateful to him, not for being like him, but for hindering him from gaining his own good. This is why potters quarrel among themselves, because they hinder one another's gain, and why *there are contentions among the proud,* because they hinder one another in attaining the position they covet.

Hence the *Reply to the First Objection* is evident.

Reply Obj. 2. Even when a man loves in another what he does not love in himself, there is a certain likeness of proportionality, because as the latter is to that which is loved in him, so is the former to that which he loves in himself; for instance, if a good singer love a good writer, we can see a likeness of proportion, according as each one has that which is becoming to him in respect of his art.

Reply Obj. 3. He that loves what he needs bears a likeness to what he loves, as potency bears a likeness to its act, as stated above.

Reply Obj. 4. According to the same likeness

of potency to its act, the illiberal man loves the man who is liberal, in so far as he expects from him something which he desires. The same applies to the man who is constant in his friendship as compared to one who is inconstant. For in either case friendship seems to be based on usefulness. We might also say that although not all men have these virtues in the complete habit, yet they have them according to certain seminal principles in the reason, in force of which principles the man who is not virtuous loves the virtuous man, as being in conformity with his own natural reason.

ARTICLE 4. *Whether Any Other Passion of the Soul Is a Cause of Love?*

We proceed thus to the Fourth Article: It would seem that some other passion can be the cause of love.

Objection 1. For the Philosopher says[1] that some are loved for the sake of the pleasure they give. But pleasure is a passion. Therefore another passion is a cause of love.

Obj. 2. Further, desire is a passion. But we love some because we desire to receive something from them, as happens in every friendship based on usefulness. Therefore another passion is a cause of love.

Obj. 3. Further, Augustine says (*De Trin.* x, 1):[2] "When we have no hope of getting a thing, we love it but half-heartedly or not at all, even if we see how beautiful it is."

On the contrary, All the other emotions of the soul are caused by love, as Augustine says.[3]

I answer that, There is no other passion of the soul that does not presuppose love of some kind. The reason is that every other passion of the soul denotes either movement towards something, or rest in something. Now every movement towards something, or rest in something, arises from some kinship or aptness to that thing; and this pertains to the notion of love. Therefore it is not possible for any other passion of the soul to be universally the cause of every love. But it may happen that some other passion is the cause of some particular love, just as one good is the cause of another.

Reply Obj. 1. When a man loves a thing for the pleasure it affords, his love is indeed caused by pleasure, but that very pleasure is caused, in its turn, by another preceding love; for none takes pleasure save in that which is loved in some way.

Reply Obj. 2. Desire for a thing always pre-

[1] *Ethics,* VIII, 3 (1156ª12).　　[2] PL 42, 973.
[3] *City of God.* XIV, 7 (PL 41, 410).

supposes love for that thing. But desire of one thing can be the cause of another thing being loved; thus he that desires money, for this reason loves him from whom he receives it.

Reply Obj. 3. Hope causes or increases love; both by reason of pleasure, because it causes pleasure, and by reason of desire, because hope strengthens desire, since we do not desire so intensely that which we have no hope of receiving. Nevertheless hope itself is of a good that is loved.

QUESTION XXVIII
OF THE EFFECTS OF LOVE
(In Six Articles)

WE now have to consider the effects of love, under which head there are six points of inquiry: (1) Whether union is an effect of love? (2) Whether mutual indwelling is an effect of love? (3) Whether ecstasy is an effect of love? (4) Whether zeal is an effect of love? (5) Whether love is a passion that is hurtful to the lover? (6) Whether love is cause of all that the lover does?

ARTICLE 1. *Whether Union Is an Effect of Love?*

We proceed thus to the First Article: It would seem that union is not an effect of love.

Objection 1. For absence is contrary to union But love is compatible with absence, for the Apostle says (Gal. 4. 18): *Be zealous for that which is good in a good thing always* (speaking of himself, according to a gloss),[1] *and not only when I am present with you.* Therefore union is not an effect of love.

Obj. 2. Further, every union is either according to essence,—thus form is united to matter, accident to subject, and a part to the whole, or to another part in order to make up the whole —or according to likeness, in genus, species, or accident. But love does not cause union of essence; otherwise love could not be between things essentially distinct. On the other hand, love does not cause union of likeness, but rather is caused by it, as stated above (Q. XXVII, A. 3). Therefore union is not an effect of love.

Obj. 3. Further, the sense in act is the sensible in act, and the intellect in act is the thing actually understood. But the lover in act is not the thing loved in act. Therefore union is the effect of knowledge rather than of love.

On the contrary, Dionysius says (*Div. Nom.* iv)[2] that every love is "a unitive force."

I answer that, The union of lover and the thing loved is twofold. The first is real union; for instance, when the thing loved is present with the lover. The second is union of affection, and this union must be considered in relation to the preceding apprehension; for movement of the appetite follows apprehension. Now love being twofold, namely, love of concupiscence, and love of friendship, each of these arises from a kind of apprehension of the oneness of the thing loved with the lover. For when we love a thing by desiring it, we apprehend it as belonging to our well-being. In like manner when a man loves another with the love of friendship, he wills good to him, just as he wills good to himself; and so he apprehends him as his other self, in so far, namely, as he wills good to him as to himself. Hence a friend is called a man's "other self,"[3] and Augustine says,[4] "Well did one say to his friend: Thou half of my soul."

The first of these unions is caused effectively by love, because love moves man to desire and seek the presence of the being loved, as of something suitable and belonging to him. The second union is caused formally by love, because love itself is this union or bond. In this sense Augustine says (*De Trin.* viii, 10)[5] that "love is a vital principle uniting, or seeking to unite two together, the lover, namely, and the beloved." For in describing it as uniting he refers to the union of affection, without which there is no love; and in saying that it seeks to unite, he refers to real union.

Reply Obj. 1. This argument is true of real union. That is necessary to pleasure as being its cause. Desire implies the real absence of the being loved, but love remains whether the being loved be absent or present.

Reply Obj. 2. Union has a threefold relation to love. There is a union which causes love, and this is substantial union, as regards the love with which one loves oneself; while as regards the love with which one loves other things, it is the union of likeness, as stated above (Q. XXVII, A. 3). There is also a union which is essentially love itself. This union is according to a bond of affection, and is likened to substantial union, in so far as the lover stands to the object of his love as to himself, if it be love of friendship; as to something belonging to himself, if it be love of concupiscence. Again there is a union which is the effect of love. This is real union, which the lover seeks with the object of his love. Moreover

---

[1] *Glossa interl.* (VI, 85v); *Glossa* Lombardi (PL 192, 145).   [2] Sect. 12 (PG 3, 709).

[3] Aristotle, *Ethics*, IX, 4 (1166^{a}31); cf. IX, 9 (1169^{b}6).
[4] *Confessions*, IV, 11 (PL 32, 698).
[5] PL 42, 960.

this union is in keeping with the demands of love, for as the Philosopher relates,[1] "Aristophanes stated that lovers would wish to be united both into one," but since "this would result in either one or both being destroyed," they seek a suitable and becoming union,—to live together, speak together, and be united in other like things.

Reply Obj. 3. Knowledge is perfected by the thing known being united, through its likeness, to the knower. But the effect of love is that the thing itself which is loved, is, in a way, united to the lover, as stated above. Consequently love is more of a unifying force than knowledge.

ARTICLE 2. *Whether Mutual Indwelling Is an Effect of Love?*

We proceed thus to the Second Article: It seems that love does not cause mutual indwelling, so that the lover is in the beloved and vice versa.

Objection 1. For that which is in another is contained by it. But the same thing cannot be both container and contents. Therefore love cannot cause mutual indwelling, so that the lover is in the beloved and vice versa.

Obj. 2. Further, nothing can penetrate within a whole, except by means of a division of the whole. But it is the function of the reason, not of the appetite where love resides, to divide things that are really united. Therefore mutual indwelling is not an effect of love.

Obj. 3. Further, if through love the lover is in the beloved and vice versa, it follows that the beloved is united to the lover in the same way as the lover is united to the beloved. But the union itself is love, as stated above (A. 1). Therefore it follows that the lover is always loved by the object of his love, which is evidently false. Therefore mutual indwelling is not an effect of love.

On the contrary, It is written (I John 4.16): *He that abideth in charity abideth in God, and God in him.* Now charity is the love of God. Therefore, for the same reason, every love makes the beloved to be in the lover, and vice versa.

I answer that, This effect of mutual indwelling may be understood as referring both to the apprehensive and to the appetitive power. For as to the apprehensive power, the beloved is said to be in the lover in so far as the beloved abides in the apprehension of the lover, according to Phil. 1. 7, *For that I have you in my heart.* But the lover is said to be in the beloved according to apprehension in so far as the lover is not satisfied with a superficial apprehension of the beloved, but strives to gain an intimate knowledge of each thing pertaining to the beloved, so as to penetrate into his very soul. Thus it is written concerning the Holy Ghost, Who is God's Love, that He *searcheth all things, yea the deep things of God* (I Cor. 2. 10).

As to the appetitive power, the object loved is said to be in the lover, because it is in his affections by a kind of satisfaction, causing him either to take pleasure in it, or in its good, when present; or, in the absence of the object loved, by his longing, to tend towards it with the love of concupiscence, or towards the good that he wills to the beloved, with the love of friendship, not indeed from any extrinsic cause (as when we desire one thing on account of another, or wish good to another on account of something else), but because the satisfaction in the beloved is rooted in the lover's heart. For this reason we speak of love as being intimate, and of the bowels of charity.

On the other hand, the lover is in the beloved by the love of concupiscence and by the love of friendship, but not in the same way. For the love of concupiscence does not find rest in any external or superficial possession or enjoyment of the beloved, but seeks to possess the beloved perfectly, by penetrating into his heart, as it were. But in the love of friendship the lover is in the beloved in the sense that he regards what is good or evil to his friend, as being so to himself and his friend's will as his own, so that it seems as though he felt the good or suffered the evil in the person of his friend. Hence "it is the way of friends to desire the same things, and to grieve and rejoice at the same," as the Philosopher says.[2] Consequently in so far as he considers what affects his friend as affecting himself, the lover seems to be in the beloved, as though he were become one with him; but in so far as, on the other hand, he wills and acts for his friend's sake as for his own sake, looking on his friend as identified with himself, thus the beloved is in the lover.

In yet a third way, mutual indwelling in the love of friendship can be understood in regard to reciprocal love, in so far as friends return love for love, and desire and do good things for one another.

Reply Obj. 1. The beloved is contained in the lover by being impressed on his affection

---

[1] *Politics,* II, 4 (1262ᵇ11); cf. Plato, *Symposium* (191; 192).

[2] *Ethics,* IX, 3 (1165ᵇ27); *Rhetoric,* II, 4 (1381ᵃ3).

through a kind of tranquil satisfaction. On the other hand, the lover is contained in the beloved because the lover penetrates, so to speak, into the beloved. For nothing hinders a thing from being both container and contents in different ways, just as a genus is contained in its species, and vice versa.

Reply Obj. 2. The apprehension of the reason precedes the movement of love. Consequently, just as the reason divides, so does the movement of love penetrate into the beloved, as was explained above.

Reply Obj. 3. This argument is true of the third kind of mutual indwelling, which is not to be found in every kind of love.

ARTICLE 3. *Whether Ecstasy Is an Effect of Love?*

We proceed thus to the Third Article: It would seem that ecstasy is not an effect of love.

Objection 1. For ecstasy seems to imply loss of reason. But love does not always result in loss of reason, for lovers are masters of themselves at times. Therefore love does not cause ecstasy.

Obj. 2. Further, the lover desires the beloved to be united to him. Therefore he draws the beloved to himself, rather than proceeding to the beloved, going forth out from himself as it were.

Obj. 3. Further, love unites the beloved to the lover, as stated above (A. 1). If, therefore, the lover goes out from himself in order to proceed to the beloved, it follows that the lover always loves the beloved more than himself, which is evidently false. Therefore ecstasy is not an effect of love.

On the contrary, Dionysius says (*Div. Nom.* iv)[1] that "the Divine love produces ecstasy," and that "God Himself suffered ecstasy through love." Since therefore according to the same author (*ibid.*), every love is a participated likeness of the Divine Love, it seems that every love causes ecstasy.

I answer that, To suffer ecstasy means to be placed outside oneself. This happens as to the apprehensive power and as to the appetitive power. As to the apprehensive power, a man is said to be placed outside himself when he is placed outside the knowledge proper to him. This may be due to his being raised to a higher knowledge; thus, a man is said to suffer ecstasy because he is placed outside the connatural apprehension of his sense and reason, when he is raised up so as to comprehend things that surpass sense and reason. Or it may be due to his

[1] Sect. 13 (PG 3, 712).

being cast down into a state of debasement; thus a man may be said to suffer ecstasy when he is overcome by violent passion or madness. As to the appetitive part, a man is said to suffer ecstasy when the appetite is borne towards something else, so that it goes forth out from itself, as it were.

The first of these ecstasies is caused by love by way of disposition, in so far, namely, as love makes the beloved to dwell in the lover's mind, as stated above (A. 2); and the more we give our mind to one thing, the less we think of others. The second ecstasy is caused by love directly; by love of friendship, absolutely, by love of concupiscence, not absolutely but in a relative sense. Because in love of concupiscence, the lover is taken out from himself, in a certain sense; in so far, namely, as not being satisfied with enjoying the good that he has, he seeks to enjoy something outside himself. But since he seeks to have this extrinsic good for himself, he does not go out from himself absolutely, and this affection remains finally within him. On the other hand, in the love of friendship, a man's affection goes out from itself absolutely, because he wishes and does good to his friend, as it were, caring and providing for him, for his sake.

Reply Obj. 1. This argument is true of the first kind of ecstasy.

Reply Obj. 2. This argument applies to love of concupiscence, which, as stated above, does not cause ecstasy absolutely.

Reply Obj. 3. He who loves, goes out from himself, in so far as he wills the good of his friend and works for it. Yet he does not will the good of his friend more than his own good, and so it does not follow that he loves another more than himself.

ARTICLE 4. *Whether Zeal Is an Effect of Love?*

We proceed thus to the Fourth Article: It seems that zeal is not an effect of love.

Objection 1. For zeal is a principle of contention; therefore it is written (I Cor. 3. 3): *Whereas there is among you zeal* (Douay,—*envying*) *and contention,* etc. But contention is contrary to love. Therefore zeal is not an effect of love.

Obj. 2. Further, the object of love is the good, which communicates itself to others. But zeal is opposed to communication, since it seems an effect of zeal that a man refuses to share the object of his love with another; thus husbands are said to be jealous of (*zelare*) their wives because they will not share them with others. Therefore zeal is not an effect of love.

Obj. 3. Further, there is no zeal without hatred, as neither is there without love; for it is written (Ps. 72. 3): *I had a zeal on occasion of the wicked*. Therefore it should not be set down as an effect of love any more than of hatred.

On the contrary, Dionysius says (*Div. Nom.* iv):[1] "God is said to be a Zealot, on account of this great love for all things."

I answer that, Zeal, whatever way we take it arises from the intensity of love. For it is evident that the more intensely a power tends to anything, the more vigorously it withstands opposition or resistance. Since therefore "love is a movement towards the object loved," as Augustine says,[2] an intense love seeks to remove everything that opposes it.

But this happens in different ways according to love of concupiscence and love of friendship. For in love of concupiscence he who desires something intensely is moved against all that hinders his gaining or quietly enjoying the object of his love. It is thus that husbands are said to be jealous of their wives, lest association with others prove a hindrance to their exclusive individual rights. In like manner those who seek to excel are moved against those who seem to excel, as though these were a hindrance to their excelling. And this is the zeal of envy, of which it is written (Ps. 36. 1): *Be not emulous of evil doers, nor envy (zelaveris) them that work iniquity*.

On the other hand, love of friendship seeks the friend's good. Therefore, when it is intense, it causes a man to be moved against everything that opposes the friend's good. In this respect, a man is said to be zealous on behalf of his friend, when he makes a point of repelling whatever may be said or done against his friend's good. In this way, too, a man is said to be zealous on God's behalf, when he endeavours, to the best of his means, to repel whatever is contrary to the honour or will of God; according to III Kings 19. 14: *With zeal have I been zealous for the Lord of hosts*. Again on the words of John 2. 17: *The zeal of Thy house hath eaten me up*, a gloss says[3] that "a man is eaten up with a good zeal, who strives to remedy whatever evil he perceives; and if he cannot, bears with it and laments it."

Reply Obj. 1. The Apostle is speaking in this passage of the zeal of envy, which is indeed the cause of contention, not against the object of love, but for it, and against that which is opposed to it.

Reply Obj. 2. Good is loved in so far as it can be communicated to the lover. Consequently whatever hinders the perfection of this communication becomes hateful. Thus zeal arises from love of good. But through defect of goodness, it happens that certain small goods cannot, in their entirety, be possessed by many at the same time; and from the love of such things arises the zeal of envy. But it does not arise, properly speaking, in the case of those things which in their entirety can be possessed by many; for no one envies another the knowledge of truth, which can be known entirely by many except perhaps one may envy another his superiority in the knowledge of it.

Reply Obj. 3. The very fact that a man hates whatever is opposed to the object of his love is the effect of love. Hence zeal is set down as an effect of love rather than of hatred.

ARTICLE 5. *Whether Love Is a Passion That Wounds the Lover?*

We proceed thus to the Fifth Article: It would seem that love wounds the lover.[4]

Objection 1. For languor denotes a hurt in the one that languishes. But love causes languor, for it is written (Cant. 2. 5): *Stay me up with flowers, compass me about with apples; because I languish with love*. Therefore love is a wounding passion.

Obj. 2. Further, melting is a kind of dissolution. But love melts that in which it is, for it is written (Cant. 5. 6): *My soul melted when my beloved spoke*. Therefore love is a dissolvent and, therefore it is a corruptive and a wounding passion.

Obj. 3. Further, fervour denotes a certain excess of heat, which excess has a corruptive effect. But love causes fervour, for Dionysius (*Cæl. Hier.* vii)[5] in enumerating the properties belonging to the Seraphim's love, includes hot and piercing and most fervent. Moreover it is said of love (Cant. 8. 6) that *its lamps are fire and flames*. Therefore love is a wounding and corruptive passion.

On the contrary, Dionysius says (*Div. Nom.* iv)[6] that "everything loves itself with a love that holds it together," that is, that preserves it. Therefore love is not a wounding passion, but rather one that preserves and perfects.

I answer that, As stated above (Q. XXVI, AA. 1, 2; Q. XXVII, A. 1), love denotes a certain

---

[1] Sect. 13 (PG 3, 712).

[2] QQ. LXXXIII, qu. 35 (PL 40, 23).

[3] *Glossa ordin.,* (v, 193E)—Aug., *In Joann.,* tract x, on 2.17 (PL 35, 1471).

[4] Cf. Hugh of St. Victor, *In Hier. Cæl. S. Dionysii,* vi (PL 175, 1044); see also Rousselot, *Problème de l'amour* (p. 65–69). [5] Sect. 1, (PG3, 205). [6] Sect. 10 (PG3, 708).

adapting of the appetitive power to some good. Now nothing is hurt by being adapted to that which is suitable to it; rather, if possible, it is perfected and bettered. But if a thing be adapted to that which is not suitable to it, it is hurt and made worse by it. Consequently love of a suitable good perfects and betters the lover; but love of a good which is unsuitable to the lover, wounds and worsens him. And so man is perfected and bettered chiefly by the love of God, but is wounded and worsened by the love of sin, according to Osee 9. 10: *They became abominable, as those things which they loved.*

And let this be understood as applying to love in respect to what is formal in it, that is, in regard to the appetite. But in respect to what is material in the passion of love, that is, a certain bodily change, it happens that love is hurtful by reason of this change being excessive, just as it happens in the senses, and in every act of a power of the soul that is exercised through the change of some bodily organ.

In reply to the objections, it is to be observed that four proximate effects may be ascribed to love: namely, melting, enjoyment, languor, and fervour. Of these the first is melting, which is opposed to freezing. For things that are frozen, are closely bound together, so as to be hard to pierce. But it pertains to love that the appetite is fitted to receive the good which is loved, in so far as the object loved is in the lover, as stated above (A. 2). Consequently the freezing or hardening of the heart is a disposition incompatible with love, while melting denotes a softening of the heart, by which the heart shows itself to be ready for the entrance of the beloved. If, then, the beloved is present and possessed, pleasure or enjoyment ensues. But if the beloved be absent, two passions arise: namely, sadness at its absence, which is denoted by languor (hence Tully in *De Tuscul. Quæst.* iii[1] applies the term ailment chiefly to sadness), and an intense desire to possess the beloved, which is signified by fervour. And these are the effects of love considered formally, according to the relation of the appetitive power to its object. But in the passion of love, other effects ensue, proportionate to the above, according to change in the organ.

ARTICLE 6. *Whether Love Is Cause of All That the Lover Does?*

We proceed thus to the Sixth Article: It seems that the lover does not everything from love.

[1] Chap. 11 (DD IV, 7).

Objection 1. For love is a passion, as stated above (Q. XXVI, A. 2). But man does not do everything from passion: some things he does from choice, and some things from ignorance, as stated in the *Ethics.*[2] Therefore man does not everything that he does, from love.

Obj. 2. Further, the appetite is a principle of movement and action in all animals, as stated in the book on the *Soul.*[3] If, therefore, whatever a man does, is done from love, the other passions of the appetitive part are superfluous.

Obj. 3. Further, nothing is produced at one and the same time by contrary causes. But some things are done from hatred. Therefore all things are not done from love.

On the contrary, Dionysius says (*Div. Nom.* iv)[4] that "all things, whatever they do, they do for the love of good."

I answer that, Every agent acts for an end, as stated above (Q. I, A. 2). Now the end is the good desired and loved by each one. Therefore it is evident that every agent, whatever it be, does every action from love of some kind.

Reply Obj. 1. This objection takes love as a passion existing in the sensitive appetite. But here we are speaking of love in a general sense, according as it includes intellectual, rational, animal, and natural love; for it is in this sense that Dionysius speaks of love in chap. iv of *De Divinis Nominibus.*

Reply Obj. 2. As stated above (A. 5) desire, sadness and pleasure, and consequently all the other passions of the soul, result from love. Therefore every act that proceeds from any passion proceeds also from love as from a first cause. And so the other passions, which are proximate causes, are not superfluous.

Reply Obj. 3. Hatred also is caused by love, as we shall state further on (Q. XXIX, A. 2).

QUESTION XXIX
OF HATRED
(*In Six Articles*)

WE must now consider hatred, concerning which there are six points of inquiry: (1) Whether evil is the cause and the object of hatred? (2) Whether love is the cause of hatred? (3) Whether hatred is stronger than love? (4) Whether a man can hate himself (5) Whether a man can hate the truth? (6) Whether a thing can be the object of universal hatred?

[2] Aristotle, v, 8 (1135^{b}21; ^{b}25; 1136^{a}6).
[3] Aristotle, III, 10 (433^{a}21).
[4] Sect. 10 (PG 3, 708).

ARTICLE 1. *Whether Evil Is the Cause and Object of Hatred?*

We proceed thus to the First Article: It seems that evil is not the object and cause of hatred.

Objection 1. For everything that exists, as such, is good. If therefore evil is the object of hatred, it follows that nothing but the lack of something can be the object of hatred, which is clearly untrue.

Obj. 2. Further, hatred of evil is praiseworthy; hence (II Machab. 3. 1) some are praised for that *the laws were very well kept, because of the godliness of Onias the high-priest, and the hatred their souls* (Douay,—*his soul) had of evil.* If, therefore, nothing but evil be the object of hatred, it would follow that all hatred is commendable. And this is clearly false.

Obj. 3. Further, the same thing is not at the same time both good and evil. But the same thing is lovable and hateful to different subjects. Therefore hatred is not only of evil, but also of good.

On the contrary, Hatred is the opposite of love. But the object of love is good, as stated above (Q. XXVI, A. 1; Q. XXVII, A. 1). Therefore the object of hatred is evil.

I answer that, Since the natural appetite is the result of some apprehension (though this apprehension is not in the same subject as the natural appetite), it seems that what applies to the inclination of the natural appetite, applies also to the animal appetite, which does result from an apprehension in the same subject, as stated above (Q. XXVI, A. 1). Now, with regard to the natural appetite, it is evident that just as each thing is naturally attuned and adapted to that which is suitable to it, in which natural love consists, so has it a natural dissonance from that which opposes and destroys it; and this is natural hatred. Hence therefore, in the animal appetite, or in the intellectual appetite, love is a certain harmony of the appetite with that which is apprehended as suitable, while hatred is a certain dissonance of the appetite from that which is apprehended as repugnant and hurtful. Now, just as whatever is suitable, as such, bears the aspect of good, so whatever is repugnant, as such, bears the aspect of evil. And therefore, just as good is the object of love, so evil is the object of hatred.

Reply Obj. 1. Being, as such has not the aspect of incompatibility but only of fittingness, because all things agree in being. But

being, in so far as it is this determinate being, has an aspect of incompatibility to some determinate being. And in this way, one being is hateful to another, and is evil; though not in itself, but by comparison with something else.

Reply Obj. 2. Just as a thing may be apprehended as good, when it is not truly good, so a thing may be apprehended as evil, although it is not truly evil. Hence it happens sometimes that neither hatred of evil nor love of good is good.

Reply Obj. 3. To different things the same thing may be lovable or hateful, in respect of the natural appetite, owing to one and the same thing being naturally suitable to one thing and naturally unsuitable to another; thus heat is accordant with fire and not accordant with water. But in respect of the animal appetite, it is owing to one and the same thing being apprehended by one as good, by another as bad.

ARTICLE 2. *Whether Love Is a Cause of Hatred?*

We proceed thus to the Second Article: It would seem that love is not a cause of hatred.

Objection 1. For "the opposite members of a division are naturally simultaneous."[1] But love and hatred are opposite members of a division, since they are contrary to one another. Therefore they are naturally simultaneous. Therefore love is not the cause of hatred.

Obj. 2. Further, of two contraries, one is not the cause of the other. But love and hatred are contraries. Therefore love is not the cause of hatred.

Obj. 3. Further, that which follows is not the cause of that which precedes. But it seems that hatred precedes love, since hatred implies a turning away from evil, and love implies a turning towards good. Therefore love is not the cause of hatred.

On the contrary, Augustine says[2] that all emotions are caused by love. Therefore hatred also, since it is an emotion of the soul, is caused by love.

I answer that, As stated above (A. 1), love consists in a certain agreement of the lover with the thing loved, while hatred consists in a certain disagreement or dissonance. Now we should consider in each thing what agrees with it, before that which disagrees, since a thing disagrees with another through destroying or hindering that which agrees with it. Consequently love must precede hatred, and nothing is hated save through being contrary to a suit-

[1] Aristotle, *Categories*, 13 (14^b33).
[2] *City of God*, XIV, 7 (PL 41, 410).

able thing which is loved. And hence it is that every hatred is caused by love.

Reply Obj. 1. The opposite members of a division are sometimes naturally simultaneous, both really and logically; for instance, two species of animal, or two species of colour. Sometimes they are simultaneous logically, while, in reality, one precedes, and causes the other; for instance, the species of numbers, figures and movements. Sometimes they are not simultaneous either really or logically; for instance, substance and accident, for substance is in reality the cause of accident, and being is predicated of substance before it is predicated of accident by a priority of reason, because it is not predicated of accident except in so far as the latter is in substance. Now love and hatred are naturally simultaneous logically, but not really. And so nothing hinders love from being the cause of hatred.

Reply Obj. 2. Love and hatred are contraries if considered in respect of the same thing. But if taken in respect of contraries, they are not themselves contrary, but consequent to one another; for it amounts to the same that one love a certain thing, or that one hate its contrary. Thus love of one thing is the cause of one's hating its contrary.

Reply Obj. 3. In the order of execution, the turning away from one term precedes the turning towards the other. But the reverse is the case in the order of intention, since approach to one term is the reason for turning away from the other. Now the appetitive movement pertains rather to the order of intention than to that of execution. Therefore love precedes hatred because each is an appetitive movement.

ARTICLE 3. *Whether Hatred Is Stronger Than Love?*

We proceed thus to the Third Article: It would seem that hatred is stronger than love.

Objection 1. For Augustine says (QQ. LXXXIII, *qu.* 36):[1] "There is no one who does not flee from pain more than he desires pleasure." But flight from pain pertains to hatred, while desire for pleasure belongs to love. Therefore hatred is stronger than love.

Obj. 2. Further, the weaker is overcome by the stronger. But love is overcome by hatred, when, that is to say, love is turned into hatred. Therefore hatred is stronger than love.

Obj. 3. Further, the emotions of the soul are shown by their effects. But man insists more on repelling what is hateful than on seeking

[1] PL 40, 25.

what is pleasant; thus also irrational animals refrain from pleasure for fear of the whip, as Augustine instances (*loc. cit.*). Therefore hatred is stronger than love.

On the contrary, Good is stronger than evil, because evil does nothing except in virtue of good, as Dionysius says (*Div. Nom.* iv).[2] But hatred and love differ according to the difference of good and evil. Therefore hatred is stronger than love.

I answer that, It is impossible for an effect to be stronger than its cause. Now every hatred arises from some love as its cause, as above stated (A. 2). Therefore it is impossible absolutely for hatred to be stronger than love.

But furthermore, love must be stronger, absolutely speaking, than hatred. Because a thing is moved to the end more strongly than to the means. Now turning away from evil is ordered as a means to the gaining of good, as to amend. Therefore, absolutely speaking, the soul's movement in respect of good is stronger than its movement in respect of evil.

Nevertheless hatred sometimes seems to be stronger than love, for two reasons. First, because hatred is more keenly felt than love. For, since the sensitive perception is accompanied by a certain change, when once the change has been received it is not felt so keenly as in the moment of being changed. Hence the heat of a hectic fever, though greater, is nevertheless not felt so much as the heat of a tertian fever, because the heat of the hectic fever is, as it were, habitual and like a second nature. For this reason, love is felt more keenly in the absence of the object loved; thus Augustine says (*De Trin.* x, 12)[3] that "love is felt more keenly when we lack what we love." And for the same reason, the unbecomingness of that which is hated is felt more keenly than the becomingness of that which is loved. Secondly, because comparison is made between a hatred and a love which do not correspond to one another. Because according to different degrees of good there are different degrees of love to which correspond different degrees of hatred. Therefore a hatred that corresponds to a greater love moves us more than a lesser love.

Hence it is clear how to *reply to the First Objection.* For the love of pleasure is less than the love of self-preservation, to which corresponds flight from pain and therefore we flee from pain more than we love pleasure.

Reply Obj. 2. Hatred would never overcome love were it not for the greater love to which

[2] Sect. 20 (PG 3, 717).　　[3] PL 42, 984.

that hatred corresponds. Thus man loves himself more than he loves his friend; and because he loves himself, his friend is hateful to him if he oppose him.

Reply Obj. 3. The reason why we act with greater insistence in repelling what is hateful is because we feel hatred more keenly.

ARTICLE 4. *Whether a Man Can Hate Himself?*

We proceed thus to the Fourth Article: It would seem that a man can hate himself.

Objection 1. For it is written (Ps. 10. 6): *He that loveth iniquity, hateth his own soul.* But many love iniquity. Therefore many hate themselves.

Obj. 2. Further, him we hate, to whom we wish and work evil. But sometimes a man wishes and works evil to himself; for example, a man who kills himself. Therefore some men hate themselves.

Obj. 3. Further, Boëthius says (*De Consol.* ii, 5)[1] that "avarice makes a man hateful"; from this we may conclude that everyone hates a miser. But some men are misers. Therefore they hate themselves.

On the contrary, The Apostle says (Eph. 5. 29) that *no man ever hated his own flesh.*

I answer that, Properly speaking, it is impossible for a man to hate himself. For everything naturally desires good, nor can anyone desire anything for himself, save under the aspect of good; for "evil is outside the scope of the will," as Dionysius says (*Div. Nom.* iv).[2] Now to love a man is to will good to him, as stated above (Q. XXVI, A. 4). Consequently, a man must, of necessity, love himself; and it is impossible for a man to hate himself, properly speaking.

But accidentally it happens that a man hates himself, and this in two ways. First, on the part of the good which a man wills to himself. For it happens sometimes that what is desired as good in some particular respect, is evil absolutely; and in this way, a man accidentally wills evil to himself; and thus hates himself. Secondly, in regard to himself, to whom he wills good. For each thing is that which is predominant in it; hence the state is said to do what the king does, as if the king were the whole state. Now it is clear that man is principally the mind of man. And it happens that some men account themselves as being principally that which they are in their bodily and sensitive nature. And so they love themselves according

to what they take themselves to be, while they hate that which they really are, by desiring what is contrary to reason. And in both these ways, *he that loveth iniquity hateth* not only *his own soul,* but also himself.

From this the *reply to the First Objection* is evident.

Reply Obj. 2. No man wills and works evil to himself, except as he apprehends it under the aspect of good. For even they who kill themselves apprehend death itself as a good, considered as putting an end to some unhappiness or pain.

Reply Obj. 3. The miser hates something accidental to himself, but not for that reason does he hate himself; thus a sick man hates his sickness for the very reason that he loves himself. Or we may say that avarice makes man hateful to others, but not to himself. In fact, it is caused by a disordered self-love, in respect of which man desires temporal goods for himself more than he should.

ARTICLE 5. *Whether a Man Can Hate the Truth?*

We proceed thus to the Fifth Article: It seems that a man cannot hate the truth.

Objection 1. For good, true, and being are convertible. But a man cannot hate good. Neither, therefore, can he hate the truth.

Obj. 2. Further, "All men have a natural desire for knowledge," as stated in the beginning of the *Metaphysics.*[3] But knowledge is only of true things. Therefore truth is naturally desired and loved. But that which is in a thing naturally is always in it. Therefore no man can hate the truth.

Obj. 3. Further, the Philosopher says[4] that "men love those who are straightforward." But there can be no other motive for this save truth. Therefore man loves the truth naturally. Therefore he cannot hate it.

On the contrary, The Apostle says (Gal. 4. 16): *Am I become your enemy because I tell you the truth?*[5]

I answer that, Good, true and being are the same in reality, but differ as considered by reason. For good is considered in the light of something desirable, while being and true are not so considered, for the good is what all things seek. Therefore good, as such, cannot be the object of hatred, neither in the universal

---

[1] PL 63, 690.

[2] Sect. 32 (PG 3, 732).

[3] Aristotle, I, 1 (980[a]21).

[4] *Rhetoric*, II, 4 (1381[b]28).

[5] St. Thomas quotes the passage, probably from memory, as though it were an assertion: *I am become, etc.*

nor in the particular. Being and truth in the universal cannot be the object of hatred because disagreement is the cause of hatred, and agreement is the cause of love, while being and truth are common to all things. But nothing hinders some particular being or some particular truth being an object of hatred, in so far as it is considered as something contrary and repugnant; for contrariness and repugnance are not incompatible with the notion of being and truth, as they are with the notion of good.

Now it may happen in three ways that some particular truth is repugnant or contrary to the good we love. First, according as truth is in things as in its cause and origin. And thus man sometimes hates a particular truth when he wishes that what is true were not true. Secondly, according as truth is in man's knowledge, which hinders him from gaining the object loved; such is the case of those who wish not to know the truth of faith, that they may sin freely; in whose person it is said (Job 21. 14): *We desire not the knowledge of Thy ways.* Thirdly, a particular truth is hated as something repugnant according as it is in the intellect of another man; as, for instance, when a man wishes to remain indolent in his sin, he hates that anyone should know the truth about his sin. In this respect, Augustine says[1] that men "love truth when it enlightens, they hate it when it reproves." This suffices for the *Reply to the First Objection.*

Reply Obj. 2. The knowledge of truth is lovable in itself; hence Augustine says that men love it when it enlightens. But accidentally, the knowledge of truth may become hateful, in so far as it hinders one from accomplishing one's desire.

Reply Obj. 3. The reason why we love those who are straightforward is because they tell the truth, the knowledge of which is lovable for its own sake.

ARTICLE 6. *Whether Anything Can Be an Object of Universal Hatred?*

We proceed thus to the Sixth Article: It seems that a thing cannot be an object of universal hatred.

Objection 1. Because hatred is a passion of the sensitive appetite, which is moved by an apprehension in the senses. But the senses cannot apprehend the universal. Therefore a thing cannot be an object of universal hatred.

Obj. 2. Further, hatred is caused by dissonance; and where there is dissonance, there

is nothing in common. But the notion of universality implies something in common. Therefore nothing can be the object of universal hatred.

Obj. 3. Further, the object of hatred is evil. But "evil is in things, and not in the mind."[2] Since therefore the universal is in the mind only, which abstracts the universal from the particular, it seems that hatred cannot have a universal object.

On the contrary, the Philosopher says[3] that "anger is directed always to something singular, whereas hatred is also directed to a thing in general; for everybody hates the thief and the backbiter."

I answer that, There are two ways of speaking of the universal: first, according as it is under the intention of universality; secondly, as considered in the nature to which the intention is attributed; for it is one thing to consider the universal man, and another to consider man in that which is a man. If, therefore, we take the universal in the first way, no sensitive power, whether of apprehension or of appetite, can attain the universal, because the universal is obtained by abstraction from individual matter, in which every sensitive power is rooted.

Nevertheless the sensitive powers, both of apprehension and of appetite, can tend to something universally. Thus we say that the object of sight is colour considered generically; not that the sight knows universal colour, but because the fact that colour is knowable by the sight is attributed to colour, not as being this particular colour, but because it is colour absolutely. Accordingly hatred in the sensitive part can regard something universally, because this thing, by reason of its common nature, and not merely as an individual, is hostile to the animal—for instance, a wolf in regard to a sheep. Hence a sheep hates the wolf generally. On the other hand, anger is always caused by something in particular because it is caused by some action of the one that hurts us, and actions proceed from individuals. For this reason the Philosopher says[4] that "anger is always directed to something singular, whereas hatred can be directed to a thing in general." But according as hatred is in the intellectual part, since it arises from the universal apprehension of the intellect, it can regard the universal in both ways.

Reply Obj. 1. The senses do not apprehend the universal as such; but they apprehend

[1] *Confessions,* X, 34 (PL 32, 794).

[2] Aristotle, *Metaphysics,* VI, 4 (1027[b]25).
[3] *Rhetoric,* II, 4 (1382[a]4).   [4] *Ibid.*

something to which the character of universality is given by abstraction.

Reply Obj. 2. That which is common to all cannot be a reason of hatred. But nothing hinders a thing from being common to many and dissonant to others, so as to be hateful to them.

Reply Obj. 3. This argument considers the universal under the intention of universality, and thus it does not come under the sensitive apprehension or appetite.

QUESTION XXX
OF CONCUPISCENCE
(*In Four Articles*)

WE have now to consider concupiscence, under which head there are four points of inquiry: (1) Whether concupiscence is in the sensitive appetite only? (2) Whether concupiscence is a special passion? (3) Whether some concupiscences are natural, and some not natural? (4) Whether concupiscence is infinite?

ARTICLE 1. *Whether Concupiscence Is in the Sensitive Appetite Only?*

We proceed thus to the First Article: It seems that concupiscence is not only in the sensitive appetite.

Objection 1. For there is a concupiscence of wisdom, according to Wis. 6. 21: *The concupiscence* (Douay,—*desire*) *of wisdom bringeth to the everlasting kingdom.* But the sensitive appetite can have no tendency to wisdom. Therefore concupiscence is not only in the sensitive appetite.

Obj. 2. Further, the desire for the commandments of God is not in the sensitive appetite; rather the Apostle says (Rom. 7. 18): *There dwelleth not in me, that is to say, in my flesh, that which is good.* But desire for God's commandments falls under concupiscence, according to Ps. 118. 20: *My soul hath coveted (concupivit) to long for thy justification.* Therefore concupiscence is not only in the sensitive appetite.

Obj. 3. Further, proper good to each power is a matter of concupiscence. Therefore concupiscence is in each power of the soul, and not only in the sensitive appetite.

On the contrary, Damascene says (*De Fide Orthod.* ii, 12)[1] that "the irrational part which is subject and amenable to reason, is divided into concupiscence and anger. This is the irrational part of the soul, passive and appetitive."

Therefore concupiscence is in the sensitive appetite.

I answer that, As the Philosopher says,[2] "concupiscence is a desire for that which is pleasant." Now pleasure is twofold, as we shall state later on (Q. XXXI, AA. 3, 4). One is in the intelligible good, which is the good of reason; the other is in good perceptible to the senses. The former pleasure seems to be in the soul alone. But the latter is in both soul and body, because the sense is a power seated in a bodily organ, and so sensible good is the good of the whole composite. Now concupiscence seems to be the desire for this latter pleasure, since it pertains at the same time to both soul and body, as is implied by the very word *concupiscentia* indicates. Therefore, properly speaking, concupiscence is in the sensitive appetite, and in the concupiscible power, which takes its name from it.

Reply Obj. 1. The desire for wisdom, or other spiritual goods is sometimes called concupiscence, either by reason of a certain likeness, or on account of the desire in the higher part of the soul being so intense that it overflows into the lower appetite, so that the latter also, in its own way, tends to the spiritual good, following the lead of the higher appetite, the result being that the body itself tenders its service in spiritual matters, according to Ps. 83. 3: *My heart and my flesh have rejoiced in the living God.*

Reply Obj. 2. Properly speaking, desire may be not only in the lower, but also in the higher appetite. For it does not imply fellowship in craving, as concupiscence does, but simply movement towards the thing desired.

Reply Obj. 3. It pertains to each power of the soul to seek its proper good by the natural appetite, which does not follow from apprehension. But the desire for good by the animal appetite, which follows apprehension, belongs to the appetitive power alone. And to desire a thing under the aspect of a good delightful to the senses, in which concupiscence properly consists, pertains to the concupiscible power.

ARTICLE 2. *Whether Concupiscence Is a Special Passion?*

We proceed thus to the Second Article: It would seem that concupiscence is not a special passion of the concupiscible power.

Objection 1. For passions are distinguished by their objects. But the object of the concupiscible power is something delightful to the senses, and this is also the object of concupis-

---

[1] PG 94, 928; also Nemesius, *De Nat. Hom.*, XVI (PG 40, 672); cf. Aristotle, *Soul*, III, 9 (432[b]6).

[2] *Rhetoric*, I, 11 (1370[a]17).

cence, as the Philosopher declares.[1] Therefore concupiscence is not a special passion of the concupiscible power.

Obj. 2. Further, Augustine says (QQ. LXXXIII, *qu.* 33)[2] that "cupidity is the love of transitory things," so that it is not distinct from love. But all particular passions are distinct from one another. Therefore concupiscence is not a special passion in the concupiscible power.

Obj. 3. Further, to each passion of the concupiscible power there is a particular contrary passion in that power, as stated above (Q. XXIII, A. 4). But no special passion of the concupiscible power is contrary to concupiscence. For Damascene says (*De Fide Orthod.* ii, 12)[3] that "good when desired gives rise to concupiscence, when present, gives joy; in like manner, the evil we apprehend makes us fear, the evil that is present makes us sad," from which we gather that as sadness is contrary to joy, so is fear contrary to concupiscence. But fear is not in the concupiscible, but in the irascible part. Therefore concupiscence is not a special passion of the concupiscible power.

On the contrary, Concupiscence is caused by love, and tends to pleasure, both of which are passions of the concupiscible power. Hence it is distinguished from the other concupiscible passions, as a special passion.

I answer that, As stated above (A. 1; Q. XXIII, A. 1), the good which gives pleasure to the senses is the common object of the concupiscible part. Hence the various concupiscible passions are distinguished according to the differences of that good. Now the diversity of the object can arise from the very nature of the object, or from a diversity in its power of acting. The diversity derived from the nature of the active object causes a material difference of passions, while the difference in regard to its active power causes a formal diversity of passions, in respect of which the passions differ specifically.

Now the character of the moving power of the end or of the good differs according as it is really present, or absent, because, according as it is present, it causes us to find rest in it; but according as it is absent, it causes us to be moved towards it. And so the object of sensible pleasure causes love in so far as, so to speak, it adopts and shapes the appetite to itself; it causes concupiscence in so far as, when absent, it draws the power to itself; and it be-

gets pleasure in so far as, when present, it causes the power to find rest in it. Accordingly, concupiscence is a passion differing in species from both love and pleasure. But concupiscences of this or that pleasurable object differ in number.

Reply Obj. 1. Pleasurable good is the object of concupiscence not absolutely, but considered as absent, just as the sensible, considered as past, is the object of memory. For these particular conditions diversify the species of passions, and even of the powers of the sensitive part, which looks to particular things.

Reply Obj. 2. In the passage quoted we have casual, not essential, predication, for cupidity is not essentially love, but an effect of love. We may also say that Augustine is taking cupidity in a wide sense for any movement of the appetite in respect of good to come, so that it includes both love and hope.

Reply Obj. 3. The passion which is directly contrary to concupiscence has no name, and stands in relation to evil as concupiscence in regard to good. But since, like fear, it regards the absent evil, sometimes it goes by the name of fear, just as hope is sometimes called cupidity. For a small good or evil is accounted as though it were nothing; and consequently every movement of the appetite in future good or evil is called hope or fear, which regard good and evil as arduous.

ARTICLE 3. *Whether Some Concupiscences Are Natural, and Some Not Natural?*

We proceed thus to the Third Article: It would seem that concupiscences are not divided into those which are natural and those which are not.

Objection 1. For concupiscence pertains to the animal appetite, as stated above (A. 1. reply 3). But the natural appetite is divided against the animal appetite. Therefore no concupiscence is natural.

Obj. 2. Further, material difference makes no difference of species, but only numerical difference, a difference which is outside the scope of art. But if some concupiscences are natural, and some not, they differ only in respect of their objects, which amounts to a material difference, and one of number only. Therefore concupiscences should not be divided into those that are natural and those that are not.

Obj. 3. Further, reason is divided against nature, as stated in the *Physics.*[4] If therefore in man there is a concupiscence which is not nat-

[1] *Rhetoric,* I, 11 (1370a16).
[2] PL 40, 23.
[3] PG 94, 929. (See above, Q. XXV, A. 4).
[4] Aristotle, II, 5, 6 (196b22; 198a4).

ural, it must be rational. But this is impossible, because, since concupiscence is a passion, it belongs to the sensitive appetite, and not to the will, which is the rational appetite. Therefore there are no concupiscences which are not natural.

On the contrary, The Philosopher distinguishes[1] natural concupiscences from those that are not natural.

I answer that, As stated above (A. 1), concupiscence is the desire for pleasurable good. Now a thing is pleasurable in two ways. First, because it is suitable to the nature of the animal; for example, food, drink, and the like. And concupiscence of such pleasurable things is said to be natural. Secondly, a thing is pleasurable because it is apprehended as suitable to the animal, as when one apprehends something as good and suitable, and consequently takes pleasure in it. And concupiscence of such pleasurable things is said to be not natural, and is more customarily called cupidity.

Accordingly concupiscences of the first kind, or natural concupiscences, are common to men and other animals, because to both is there something suitable and pleasurable according to nature, and in these all men agree. Therefore the Philosopher[2] calls them common and necessary.—But concupiscences of the second kind are proper to men, to whom it is proper to devise something as good and suitable, beyond that which nature requires. Hence the Philosopher says[3] that "the former concupiscences are irrational, but the latter, rational." And because different men reason differently, therefore the latter are also called[4] peculiar to the individual and acquired, that is, in addition to those that are natural.

Reply Obj. 1. The same thing that is desired by the natural appetite, may be desired by the animal appetite, once it is apprehended. And in this way there may be an animal concupiscence for food, drink and the like, which are objects of the natural appetite.

Reply Obj. 2. The difference between those concupiscences that are natural and those that are not is not merely a material difference; it is also, in a way, formal, in so far as it proceeds from a difference in the active object. Now the object of the appetite is the apprehended good. Hence diversity of the active object follows from diversity of apprehension—according as a thing is apprehended as suitable, either by ab-

solute apprehension, from which arise natural concupiscences, which the Philosopher calls irrational;[5] or by apprehension together with deliberation, from which arise those concupiscences that are not natural, and which for this very reason the Philosopher calls rational.[6]

Reply Obj. 3. Man has not only universal reason, pertaining to the intellectual part, but also particular reason pertaining to the sensitive part, as stated in the First Part (Q. LXXVIII, A. 4; Q. LXXXI, A. 3), so that even rational concupiscence may pertain to the sensitive appetite. Moreover the sensitive appetite can be moved by the universal reason also, through the means of the particular imagination.

ARTICLE 4. *Whether Concupiscence Is Infinite?*

We proceed thus to the Fourth Article: It seems that concupiscence is not infinite.

Objection 1. For the object of concupiscence is good, which has the aspect of an end. But where there is infinity there is no end.[7] Therefore concupiscence cannot be infinite.

Obj. 2. Further, concupiscence is of the suitable good, since it proceeds from love. But the infinite is without proportion, and therefore unsuitable. Therefore concupiscence cannot be infinite.

Obj. 3. Further, there is no passing through infinite things, and thus there is no reaching an ultimate term in them. But the subject of concupiscence is delighted by the fact that he attains the ultimate term. Therefore, if concupiscence were infinite, no delight would ensue.

On the contrary, The Philosopher says[8] that "since concupiscence is infinite, men desire an infinite number of things."

I answer that, As stated above (A. 3), concupiscence is twofold; one is natural, the other is not natural. Natural concupiscence cannot be actually infinite, because it is of that which nature requires; and nature always tends to something finite and fixed. Hence man never desires infinite meat, or infinite drink. But just as in nature there is potential successive infinity, so this kind of concupiscence can be infinite successively; so that, for instance, after getting food, a man may desire food yet again, and so of anything else that nature requires; because these bodily goods, when obtained, do not last for ever, but fail. Hence Our Lord said to the woman of Samaria (John 4. 13): *Whosoever drinketh of this water, shall thirst again.*

---

[1] *Ethics,* III, 11 (1118^b8); *Rhetoric,* I, 11 (1370^a20).
[2] *Ethics, loc. cit.*
[3] *Rhetoric,* I, 11 (1370^a18).   [4] *Ethics, loc. cit.*

[5] *Rhetoric, loc. cit.*   [6] *Rhetoric,* I, 11 (1370^a25).
[7] Aristotle, *Metaphysics,* II, 2 (994^b10).
[8] *Politics,* I, 9 (1258^a1).

But non-natural concupiscence is altogether infinite. Because, as stated above (A. 3) it follows from the reason, and it belongs to the reason to proceed to infinity. Hence he that desires riches may desire to be rich beyond a fixed limit, and absolutely to be as rich as possible.

Another reason may be assigned, according to the Philosopher,[1] why a certain concupiscence is finite, and another infinite. Because concupiscence of the end is always infinite, since the end is desired for its own sake, for instance, health, and thus greater health is more desired, and so on to infinity; just as, if a white thing of itself dilates the sight, that which is more white dilates yet more. On the other hand, concupiscence of the means is not infinite, because the concupiscence of the means is in suitable proportion to the end. Consequently those who place their end in riches have an infinite concupiscence of riches; but those who desire riches on account of the necessities of life, desire a finite measure of riches, sufficient for the necessities of life, as the Philosopher says.[2] The same applies to the concupiscence of any other things.

Reply Obj. 1. Every object of concupiscence is taken as something finite, either because it is finite in reality, as being actually desired at a single time, or because it is finite as apprehended. For it cannot be apprehended as infinite, since "the infinite is that from which, however much we may take, there always remains something to be taken."[3]

Reply Obj. 2. The reason is possessed of infinite power, in a certain sense, in so far as it can consider a thing infinitely, as appears in the addition of numbers and lines. Consequently, the infinite, taken in a certain way, is proportionate to reason. And the universal which the reason apprehends is infinite in a sense, in so far as it contains potentially an infinite number of singulars.

Reply Obj. 3. In order that a man be delighted, there is no need for him to realize all that he desires, for he delights in the realization of each object of his concupiscence.

QUESTION XXXI
OF PLEASURE CONSIDERED IN ITSELF
(In Eight Articles)

WE must now consider pleasure (delectatio) and sadness. Concerning pleasure four things

must be considered: (1) Pleasure in itself (Q. XXXII); (2) The causes of pleasure; (3) Its effects (Q. XXXIII); (4) Its goodness and malice (Q. XXXIV).

Under the first head there are eight points of inquiry: (1) Whether pleasure is a passion? (2) Whether pleasure is subject to time? (3) Whether it differs from joy? (4) Whether it is in the intellectual appetite? (5) Of the pleasures of the higher appetite compared with the pleasures of the lower. (6) Of sensible pleasures compared with one another. (7) Whether any pleasure is non-natural? (8) Whether one pleasure can be contrary to another?

ARTICLE 1. Whether Pleasure Is a Passion?

We proceed thus to the First Article: It would seem that pleasure is not a passion.

Objection 1. For Damascene (De Fide Orthod. ii, 22)[4] distinguishes operation from passion, and says that "operation is a movement in accord with nature, while passion is a movement contrary to nature." But "pleasure is an operation," according to the Philosopher.[5] Therefore pleasure is not a passion.

Obj. 2. Further, to be passive is to be moved, as stated in the Physics.[6] But pleasure does not consist in being moved, but in having been moved for it is caused by good already gained. Therefore pleasure is not a passion.

Obj. 3. Further, pleasure is a kind of a perfection of the one who is delighted "for it perfects operation," as stated in the Ethics.[7] But to be perfected does not consist in being passive or in being changed, as stated in the Physics[8] and the treatise on the Soul.[9] Therefore pleasure is not a passion.

On the contrary, Augustine puts pleasure whether joy or gladness, among the other passions of the soul.[10]

I answer that, The movements of the sensitive appetites are properly called passions, as stated above (Q. XXII, A. 3). Now every emotion arising from a sensitive apprehension is a movement of the sensitive appetite. But this must be in what pleasure consists, since, according to the Philosopher,[11] "Pleasure is a certain

---

[1] Politics, I, 9 (1257^{b}25).   [2] Ibid (1257^{b}30).
[3] Physics, III, 6 (207^{a}7).

[4] PG 94, 941; cf. Nemesius, De Nat. Hom., XVI (PG 40, 673); cf. also Cicero, Tuscul., IV, 21 (DD IV, 35); Diogenes Laertes, De Vita et Mor. Phil., VII, 110 (DD 183).
[5] Ethics, VII, 12 (1153^{b}10); X, 5 (1175^{b}33).
[6] Aristotle, III, 3 (202^{a}25).
[7] Aristotle, X, 4 (1174^{b}23).
[8] Aristotle, VII, 3 (246^{b}2).
[9] Aristotle, II, 5 (417^{b}2).
[10] City of God, IX, 5; XIV, 8 (PL 41, 260, 411).
[11] Rhetoric, I, 11 (1369^{b}33).

movement of the soul and a sensible establishing thereof all at once, in keeping with the nature of the thing."

In order to understand this, we must observe that just as in natural things some happen to attain to their natural perfections, so does this happen in animals. And though movement towards perfection does not occur all at once, yet the attainment of natural perfection does occur all at once. Now there is this difference between animals and other natural things, that when these latter are established in the state becoming their nature, they do not perceive it, while animals do. And from this perception there arises a certain movement of the soul in the sensitive appetite and this movement is called pleasure. Accordingly by saying that pleasure is "a movement of the soul," we designate its genus. By saying that it is "an establishing in keeping with the thing's nature," that is, with that which exists in the thing we assign the cause of pleasure, namely, the presence of a connatural good. By saying that this establishing is "all at once," we mean that this establishing is to be understood not as in the process of establishment, but as in the fact of complete establishment, in the term of the movement, as it were; for pleasure is not a becoming as Plato maintained, but a complete fact, as stated in the *Ethics*.[1] Lastly, by saying that this establishing is "sensible," we exclude the perfections of insensible things in which there is no pleasure. It is therefore evident that, since pleasure is a movement of the animal appetite arising from an apprehension of sense, it is a passion of the soul.

Reply Obj. 1. Connatural operation, which is unhindered, is a second perfection, as stated in the book on the *Soul*,[2] and therefore when a thing is established in its proper connatural and unhindered operation, pleasure follows, which consists in a state of completion, as observed above. Accordingly when we say that pleasure is an operation, we predicate not its essence but its cause.

Reply Obj. 2. A twofold movement is to be observed in an animal: one, according to the intention of the end, and this belongs to the appetite; the other, according to the execution, and this belongs to the external operation. And so, although in him who has already gained the good in which he delights, the movement of execution ceases, by which he tends to the end, yet the movement of the appetitive part does not

cease, since, just as before it desired that which it had not, so afterwards does it delight in that which it possesses. For though pleasure is a certain repose of the appetite, if we consider the presence of the pleasurable good that satisfies the appetite, nevertheless there remains the change made on the appetite by its object, by reason of which pleasure is a kind of movement.

Reply Obj. 3. Although the name of passion is more appropriate to those passions which have a corruptive and evil tendency, such as bodily ailments, and sadness and fear in the soul, yet some passions are ordered to something good, as stated above (Q. XXIII, AA. 1, 4). And in this sense pleasure is called a passion.

ARTICLE 2. *Whether Pleasure Is in Time?*

We proceed thus to the Second Article: It would seem that pleasure is in time.

Objection 1. For "pleasure is a kind of movement," as the Philosopher says.[3] But all movement is in time. Therefore pleasure is in time.

Obj. 2. Further, a thing is said to last long and to be lingering in respect of time. But some pleasures are called lingering. Therefore pleasure is in time.

Obj. 3. Further, the passions of the soul are of one same genus. But some passions of the soul are in time. Therefore pleasure is too.

On the contrary, The Philosopher says[4] that "no one takes pleasure according to time."

I answer that, A thing may be in time in two ways: first, by itself; secondly, by reason of something else, and accidentally as it were. For since time is the measure of successive things, those things are of themselves said to be in time to which, of their very notion, succession or something pertaining to succession belongs; such are movement, repose, speech and the like. On the other hand, those things are said to be in time by reason of something else and not of themselves, to which succession does not belong of their very notion, but which are subject to something successive. Thus the fact of being a man is not of its very notion something successive; for it is not a movement, but the term of a movement or change, namely, of his being begotten. Yet, because human being is subject to changeable causes, in this respect, to be a man is in time.

Accordingly, we must say that pleasure, of itself indeed, is not in time; for it concerns good already gained, which is, as it were, the term of the movement. But if this good gained be sub-

[1] Aristotle, VII, 12 (1153ᵃ13); cf. *Philebus* (53).
[2] Aristotle, II, 1 (412ᵃ10).
[3] *Rhetoric*, I, 11 (1369ᵇ33).
[4] *Ethics*, X, 4 (1174ᵃ17).

ject to change, the pleasure will be in time accidentally; if however it be altogether unchangeable, the pleasure will not be in time, either by reason of itself or accidentally.

Reply Obj. 1. As stated in the book on the *Soul*,[1] movement is twofold. One is "the act of something imperfect," namely, existing in potency as such; this movement is successive and is in time. Another movement is "the act of something perfect," that is, existing in act, for example, to understand, to feel, and to will and the like, and also to delight. This movement is not successive, nor is it of itself in time.

Reply Obj. 2. Pleasure is said to be long lasting or lingering, according as it is accidentally in time.

Reply Obj. 3. Other passions have not for their object a good obtained, as pleasure has. Therefore there is more of the movement of the imperfect in them than in pleasure. And consequently it belongs more to pleasure not to be in time.

ARTICLE 3. *Whether Pleasure Differs From Joy?*

We proceed thus to the Third Article: It would seem that pleasure is altogether the same as joy.

Objection 1. Because the passions of the soul differ according to their objects. But pleasure and joy have the same object, namely, a good obtained. Therefore joy is altogether the same as pleasure.

Obj. 2. Further, one movement does not end in two terms. But one and the same movement, that of concupiscence, ends in joy and pleasure. Therefore pleasure and joy are altogether the same.

Obj. 3. Further, if joy differs from pleasure, it seems that there is equal reason for distinguishing gladness, exultation, and cheerfulness from pleasure, so that they would all be various passions of the soul. But this seems to be untrue. Therefore joy does not differ from pleasure.

On the contrary. We do not speak of joy in irrational animals; but we do speak of pleasure in them. Therefore joy is not the same as pleasure.

I answer that, Joy, as Avicenna states (*De Anima*, iv),[2] is a kind of pleasure. For we must observe that, just as some concupiscences are natural, and some not natural, but consequent to reason, as stated above (Q. XXX, A. 3), so also some pleasures are natural, and some are not natural but rational. Or, as Damascene (*De*

Fide Orthod. ii, 13)[3] and Gregory of Nyssa[4] put it, "some delights are of the body, some are of the soul," which amounts to the same. For we take pleasure both in those things which we desire naturally, when we get them, and in those things which we desire as a result of reason. But we do not speak of joy except when pleasure follows reason; and so we do not ascribe joy to irrational animals, but only pleasure.

Now whatever we desire naturally can also be the object of reasoned desire and pleasure, and consequently whatever can be the object of pleasure, can also be the object of joy in rational beings. And yet everything is not always the object of joy, since sometimes one feels a certain pleasure in the body without rejoicing in it according to reason. And accordingly pleasure extends to more things than does joy.

Reply Obj. 1. Since the object of the appetite of the soul is an apprehended good, diversity of apprehension pertains, in a way, to diversity of the object. And so pleasures of the soul which are also called joys, are distinct from bodily pleasures, which are not called otherwise than pleasures, as we have observed above in regard to concupiscence (Q. XXX, A. 3. REPLY 2).

Reply Obj. 2. A like difference is to be observed in concupiscences also, so that pleasure corresponds to concupiscence, while joy corresponds to desire, which seems to pertain more to animal concupiscence. Hence there is a difference of repose corresponding to the difference of movement.

Reply Obj. 3. These other names pertaining to pleasure are derived from the effects of delight; for *lætitia* (gladness) is derived from the dilatation of the heart, as if one were to say *latitia*;[5] "exultation" is derived from the exterior signs of inward delight, which appear outwardly in so far as the inward joy breaks forth from its bounds;[6] and "cheerfulness" is so called from certain special signs and effects of gladness.[7] Yet all these names seem to pertain to joy; for we do not employ them save in speaking of rational beings.

ARTICLE 4. *Whether Pleasure Is in the Intellectual Appetite?*

We proceed thus to the Fourth Article: It would seem that pleasure is not in the intellectual appetite.

Objection 1. Because the Philosopher says[8]

---

[1] Aristotle, III, 7 (431ª6).   [2] Chap. 5 (21ra).

[3] PG 94, 929.   [4] Nemesius, *De Nat. Hom.*, XVIII (PG 40, 677).   [5] Isidore, *Etymol.*, X, I (PL 82, 383); cf. below, Q. XXX, A. I.   [6] Isidore, *Diff.* I, n. 329 (PL 83, 44). [7] Isidore, *Etymol.*, X, I (PL 82, 380). [8] *Rhetoric*, I, 11 (1369ᵇ33).

that "pleasure is a sensible movement." But sensible movement is not in the intellectual part. Therefore pleasure is not in the intellectual part.

Obj. 2. Further, pleasure is a passion. But every passion is in the sensitive appetite. Therefore pleasure is only in the sensitive appetite.

Obj. 3. Further, pleasure is common to us and to the irrational animals. Therefore it is not elsewhere than in that part which we have in common with irrational animals.

On the contrary, It is written (Ps. 36. 4): *Delight in the Lord.* But the sensitive appetite cannot reach to God; only the intellectual appetite can. Therefore pleasure can be in the intellectual appetite.

I answer that, As stated above (A. 3), a certain pleasure arises from the apprehension of the reason. Now on the reason apprehending something, not only the sensitive appetite is moved, as regards its application to some particular thing, but also the intellectual appetite, which is called the will. And accordingly, in the intellectual appetite or will there is that pleasure which is called joy, but not bodily pleasure. However, there is this difference of pleasure in either power, that pleasure of the sensitive appetite is accompanied by a bodily change, while pleasure of the intellectual appetite is nothing but the simple movement of the will. Hence Augustine says[1] that "desire and joy are nothing else but a volition of consent to the things we wish."

Reply Obj. 1. In this definition of the Philosopher, he uses the word "sensible" in its wide acceptation for any kind of apprehension. For he says[2] that "pleasure is attendant upon every sense, as it is also upon every act of the understanding and speculation."—Or we may say that he is defining pleasure of the sensitive appetite.

Reply Obj. 2. Pleasure has the character of passion, properly speaking, when accompanied by bodily change. It is not thus in the intellectual appetite, but according to simple movement; for thus it is also in God and the angels. Hence the Philosopher says[3] that "God rejoices by one simple act"; and Dionysius says at the end of *De Cœl Hier.,*[4] that "the angels are not susceptible to our passible pleasure, but rejoice together with God with the gladness of incorruption."

Reply Obj. 3. In us there is pleasure not only in common with dumb animals, but also in common with angels. Therefore Dionysius says (*ibid.*) that "holy men often take part in the angelic delights." Accordingly we have pleasure not only in the sensitive appetite, which we have in common with dumb animals, but also in the intellectual appetite, which we have in common with the angels.

ARTICLE 5. *Whether Bodily and Sensible Pleasures Are Greater Than Spiritual and Intellectual Pleasures?*

We proceed thus to the Fifth Article: It would seem that bodily and sensible pleasures are greater than spiritual and intelligible pleasures.

Objection 1. "For all men seek some pleasure," according to the Philosopher.[5] But more seek sensible pleasures, than intelligible spiritual pleasures. Therefore bodily pleasures are greater.

Obj. 2. Further, the greatness of a cause is known by its effect. But bodily pleasures have greater effects, since "they alter the state of the body, and in some they cause madness."[6] Therefore bodily pleasures are greater.

Obj. 3. Further, bodily pleasures need to be tempered and checked, by reason of their vehemence; but there is no need to check spiritual pleasures. Therefore bodily pleasures are greater.

On the contrary, It is written (Ps. 118. 103): *How sweet are thy words on my palate; more than honey to my mouth!* And the Philosopher says[7] that "the greatest pleasure is derived from the operation of wisdom."

I answer that, As stated above (A. 1) pleasure arises from union with a suitable object when it is sensed or known. Now in the operations of the soul, especially of the sensitive and intellectual soul, it must be noted, that, since they do not pass into outward matter, they are acts or perfections of the doer, for instance, to understand, to sense, to will, and the like; because actions which pass into outward matter are actions and perfections rather of the matter transformed; for movement is an act produced by the mover in the thing moved. Accordingly the above mentioned actions of the sensitive and intellectual soul are themselves a certain good of the doer, and are also known by sense and intellect. Therefore from them also pleasure arises, and not only from their objects.

---

[1] *City of God,* XIV, 6 (PL 41, 409).
[2] *Ethics,* X, 4 (1174[b]20).
[3] *Ibid.,* VII, 14 (1154[b]26).
[4] XV, 9 (PG 3, 340).
[5] *Ethics,* X, 2, 4 (1172[b]10; 1175[a]10).
[6] Aristotle, *Ethics,* VII, 3 (1147[a]16).
[7] *Ethics,* X, 7 (1177[a]23).

If therefore we compare intellectual pleasures with sensible pleasures according as we delight in the very actions, for instance in sensitive and in intellectual knowledge, without doubt intellectual pleasures are much greater than sensible pleasures. For man takes much more delight in knowing something, by understanding it, than in knowing something by perceiving it with his sense; both because intellectual knowledge is more perfect and because it is better known, since the intellect reflects on its own act more than sense does. Moreover intellectual knowledge is more loved; for there is no one who would not forfeit his bodily sight rather than his intellectual vision in the way beasts or fools are without the latter, as Augustine says in the *City of God*.[1]

If, however, intellectual spiritual pleasures be compared with sensible bodily pleasures, then, in themselves and absolutely speaking, spiritual pleasures are greater. And this appears from the consideration of the three things needed for pleasure; namely, the good which is brought into conjunction, that to which it is joined, and the union itself. For spiritual good is both greater and more loved than bodily good; a sign of this is that men abstain from even the greatest bodily pleasures, rather than suffer loss of honour which is an intellectual good. Likewise the intellectual part is much more noble and more knowing than the sensitive part. Also the conjunction is more intimate, more perfect and more firm. More intimate, because the senses stop at the outward accidents of a thing, while the intellect penetrates to the essence; for the object of the intellect is what a thing is. More perfect, because the conjunction of the sensible to the sense implies movement, which is an imperfect act; thus sensible pleasures are not wholly together at once, but some part of them is passing away, while some other part is looked forward to as yet to be realized, as is manifest in pleasures of the table and in sexual pleasures. But intelligible things are without movement; hence pleasures of this kind are realized all at once. They are more firm, because the objects of bodily pleasures are corruptible and soon pass away; but spiritual goods are incorruptible.

On the other hand, in relation to us, bodily pleasures are more vehement, for three reasons. First, because sensible things are more known to us than intelligible things. Secondly, because sensible pleasures, through being passions of the sensitive appetite, are accompanied

by some alteration in the body; but this does not occur in spiritual pleasures unless by reason of a certain reaction of the superior appetite on the lower. Thirdly, because bodily pleasures are sought as remedies for bodily defects or troubles, from which various griefs arise. And so bodily pleasures, because they come after griefs of this kind, are felt the more, and consequently are more welcome than spiritual pleasures, which have no contrary griefs, as we shall state further on (Q. XXXV, A. 5).

Reply Obj. 1. The reason why more seek bodily pleasures is because sensible goods are known better and in greater numbers; and, again, because men need pleasures as remedies for many kinds of sorrow and sadness. And since many men cannot attain spiritual pleasures, which are proper to the virtuous, hence it is that they turn aside to seek those of the body.

Reply Obj. 2. Bodily change arises more from bodily pleasures because they are passions of the sensitive appetite.

Reply Obj. 3. Bodily pleasures are realized in the sensitive part which is governed by reason; therefore they need to be tempered and checked by reason. But spiritual pleasures are in the mind, which is itself the rule; hence they are in themselves both sober and moderate.

ARTICLE 6. *Whether the Pleasures of Touch Are Greater Than the Pleasures Afforded By the Other Senses?*

We proceed thus to the Sixth Article: It would seem that the pleasures of touch are not greater than the pleasures afforded by the other senses.

Objection 1. Because the greatest pleasure seems to be that without which all joy is at an end. But such is the pleasure afforded by the sight, according to the words of Tobias 5. 12: *What manner of joy shall be to me, who sit in darkness, and see not the light of heaven?* Therefore the pleasure afforded by the sight is the greatest of sensible pleasures.

Obj. 2. Further, every one finds pleasure in what he loves, as the Philosopher says.[2] But of all the senses the sight is loved most. Therefore the greatest pleasure is that which is afforded by the sight.

Obj. 3. Further, the beginning of friendship which is for the sake of the pleasant is principally sight. But pleasure is the cause of such friendship. Therefore the greatest pleasure seems to be afforded by sight.

---

[1] Cf. *De Trin.*, XIV, 14 (PL 42, 1051).

[2] *Rhetoric*, I, 11 (1370^{b}19); cf. *Ethics*, I, 8 (1099^{a}8).

On the contrary, The Philosopher says[1] that the greatest pleasures are those which are afforded by the touch.

I answer that, As stated above (Q. XXV, A. 2, REPLY 1; Q. XXVII, A. 4, REPLY 1), everything gives pleasure according as it is loved. Now, as stated in the *Metaphysics*,[2] the senses are loved for two reasons: for the purpose of knowledge, and on account of their usefulness. Hence the senses afford pleasure in both these ways. But because it is proper to man to apprehend knowledge itself as something good, it follows that the former pleasures of the senses, that is, those which arise from knowledge, are proper to man; but pleasures of the senses, as loved for their usefulness, are common to all animals.

If therefore we speak of that sensible pleasure which is by reason of knowledge, it is evident that the sight affords greater pleasure than any other sense. On the other hand, if we speak of that sensible pleasure which is by reason of usefulness, then the greatest pleasure is afforded by the touch. For the usefulness of sensible things is gauged by their relation to the preservation of the animal's nature. Now the sensible objects of touch bear the closest relation to this usefulness; for the touch takes cognizance of those things of which an animal consists—namely, of things hot and cold and the like. Therefore in this respect, the pleasures of touch, are greater as being more closely related to the end. For this reason, too, other animals who do not experience sensible pleasure except by reason of usefulness, derive no pleasure from the other senses except as subordinated to the sensible objects of the touch: "for dogs do not take delight in the smell of hares, but in eating them; . . . nor does the lion feel pleasure in the lowing of an ox, but in devouring it."[3]

Since then the pleasure afforded by touch is the greatest in respect of usefulness, and the pleasure afforded by sight the greatest in respect of knowledge, if anyone wish to compare these two he will find that the pleasure of touch is, absolutely speaking, greater than the pleasure of sight, so far as the latter remains within the limits of sensible pleasure. Because it is evident that the natural in any being is also the strongest thing in it. And it is to these pleasures of the touch that the natural concupiscences, such as those of food, sexual union, and the like, are ordered. If, however, we consider the pleasures of sight according as sight is the handmaid of the mind, then the pleasures of sight are

greater, for the same reason that intellectual pleasures are greater than sensible.

Reply Obj. 1. Joy, as stated above (A. 3), denotes animal pleasure; and this belongs principally to the sight. But natural pleasure belongs principally to the touch.

Reply Obj. 2. The sight is loved most on account of knowledge, because "it helps us to distinguish many things" as is stated in the same passage.[4]

Reply Obj. 3. Pleasure causes carnal love in one way; the sight, in another. For pleasure, especially that which is afforded by the touch, is the final cause of the friendship which is for the sake of the pleasant; but the sight is a cause like that from which a movement has its beginning, in so far as the beholder on seeing the lovable object receives an impression of its likeness, which draws him to love it and seek its pleasure.

ARTICLE 7. *Whether Any Pleasure Is Not Natural?*

We proceed thus to the Seventh Article: It would seem that no pleasure is not natural.

Objection 1. For pleasure is to the emotions of the soul what repose is to bodies. But the appetite of a natural body does not rest except in a connatural place. Neither, therefore, can the repose of the animal appetite, which is pleasure, be elsewhere than in something connatural. Therefore no pleasure is non-natural.

Obj. 2. Further, what is against nature is violent. But "whatever is violent causes grief."[5] Therefore nothing which is against nature can give pleasure.

Obj. 3. Further, the fact of being established in one's own nature, if perceived, gives rise to pleasure, as is evident from the Philosopher's definition[6] quoted above (A. 1). But it is natural to every thing to be established in its nature, because that movement is natural which tends to a natural end. Therefore every pleasure is natural.

On the contrary, The Philosopher says[7] that some things are pleasant not from nature but from disease.

I answer that, We speak of that as being natural, which is in accord with nature, as stated in the *Physics*.[8] Now in man nature can be taken in two ways. First, according as intellect

---

[1] *Ethics*, III, 10 (1118ª33).   [2] Aristotle, I, 1 (980ª21).
[3] Aristotle, *Ethics*, III, 10 (1118ª18).

[4] *Metaphysics*, I, 1 (980ª26).
[5] *Ibid.*, V, 5 (1015ª28).
[6] *Rhetoric*, I, 11 (1369ᵇ33).
[7] *Ethics*, VII, 5, 6 (1148ᵇ18; ᵇ27; 1149ᵇ29).
[8] Aristotle, II, 1 (192ᵇ35; 193ª32).

and reason is the principal part of man's nature, since in respect thereof man is constituted in his species. And in this sense, those pleasures may be called natural to man which are derived from things pertaining to man in respect of his reason; for instance, it is natural to man to take pleasure in contemplating the truth and in doing works of virtue. Secondly, nature in man may be taken as divided against reason, and as denoting that which is common to man and other animals, especially that part of man which does not obey reason. And in this sense, that which pertains to the preservation of the body, either as regards the individual, as food, drink, sleep, and the like, or as regards the species, as sexual intercourse, are said to afford man natural pleasure.

Under each kind of pleasures, we find some that are not natural, speaking absolutely, and yet connatural in some respect. For it happens in an individual that some one of the natural principles of the species is corrupted, so that something which is contrary to the specific nature becomes accidentally natural to this individual; thus it is natural to this hot water to give heat. Consequently it happens that something which is not natural to man, either in regard to reason, or in regard to the preservation of the body, becomes connatural to this individual man, on account of there being some corruption of nature in him. And this corruption may be either on the part of the body, for example, from some ailment (thus to a man suffering from fever, sweet things seem bitter, and vice versa)—or from an evil temperament; thus some take pleasure in eating earth and coals and the like; —or on the part of the soul; thus from custom some take pleasure in cannibalism or in the unnatural intercourse of man and beast, or other things of this kind, which are not in accord with human nature.

This suffices for the *answers to the objections.*

ARTICLE 8. *Whether One Pleasure Can Be Contrary to Another?*

We proceed thus to the Eighth Article: It seems that one pleasure cannot be contrary to another.

Objection 1. For the passions of the soul derive their species and contrariety from their objects. Now the object of pleasure is the good. Since therefore good is not contrary to good, but "good is contrary to evil, and evil to evil," as stated in the *Categories,*[1] it seems that one pleasure is not contrary to another.

[1] Aristotle, 11 (13b36).

Obj. 2. Further, "to one thing there is one contrary," as is proved in the *Metaphysics.*[2] But sadness is contrary to pleasure. Therefore pleasure is not contrary to pleasure.

Obj. 3. Further, if one pleasure is contrary to another, this is only on account of the contrariety of the things which give pleasure. But this difference is material and contrariety is a difference of form, as stated in the *Metaphysics.*[3] Therefore there is no contrariety between one pleasure and another.

On the contrary, "Things of the same genus that impede one another are contraries," according to the Philosopher.[4] But some pleasures impede one another, as stated in the *Ethics.*[5] Therefore some pleasures are contrary to one another.

I answer that, Pleasure, in the emotions of the soul, is likened to repose in natural bodies, as stated above (Q. XXIII, A. 4). Now one repose is said to be contrary to another when they are in contrary terms; thus "repose in a high place is contrary to repose in a low place."[6] And so it happens in the emotions of the soul that one pleasure is contrary to another.

Reply Obj. 1. This saying of the Philosopher is to be understood of good and evil as applied to virtues and vices, because one vice may be contrary to another vice, though no virtue can be contrary to another virtue. But in other things nothing prevents one good being contrary to another, such as hot and cold, of which the former is good in relation to fire, the latter, in relation to water. And in this way one pleasure can be contrary to another. That this is impossible with regard to the good of virtue, is due to the fact that virtue's good depends on fittingness in relation to some one thing, namely, reason.

Reply Obj. 2. Pleasure, in the emotions of the soul, is likened to natural repose in bodies; for its object is something suitable and connatural, so to speak. But sadness is like a violent repose, because its object is disagreeable to the animal appetite, just as the place of violent repose is disagreeable to the natural appetite. Now natural repose is contrary both to violent repose of the same body, and to the natural repose of another, as stated in the *Physics.*[7] Therefore pleasure is contrary both to another pleasure and to sadness.

[2] Aristotle, x, 4, 5 (1055a19; 1055b30).
[3] Aristotle, x, 4 (1055a3).
[4] *Physics,* VIII, 8 (262a11); *Metaphysics,* x, 4 (1055a27).
[5] Aristotle, x, 5 (1175b1).
[6] Aristotle, *Physics,* v, 6 (230b11).
[7] Aristotle, v, 6 (230b18; 231a13).

Reply Obj. 3. The things in which we take pleasure, since they are the objects of pleasure, cause not only a material, but also a formal difference, if the aspect of pleasurableness be different. Because difference in the aspect of the object causes a specific difference in acts and passions, as stated above (Q. XXIII, AA. 1, 4; Q. XXX, A. 2).

QUESTION XXXII
OF THE CAUSE OF PLEASURE
(In Eight Articles)

WE must now consider the causes of pleasure; and under this head there are eight points of inquiry: (1) Whether operation is the proper cause of pleasure? (2) Whether movement is a cause of pleasure? (3) Whether hope and memory cause pleasure? (4) Whether sadness causes pleasure? (5) Whether the actions of others are a cause of pleasure to us? (6) Whether doing good to another is a cause of pleasure? (7) Whether likeness is a cause of pleasure? (8) Whether wonder is a cause of pleasure?

ARTICLE 1. *Whether Operation Is the Proper Cause of Pleasure?*

We proceed thus to the First Article: It would seem that operation is not the proper and first cause of pleasure.

Objection 1. For, as the Philosopher says,[1] "pleasure consists in a perception of the senses," since knowledge is requisite for pleasure, as stated above (Q. XXXI, A. 1). But the objects of operations are knowable before the operations themselves. Therefore operation is not the proper cause of pleasure.

Obj. 2. Further, pleasure consists especially in an end gained, since it is this that is chiefly desired. But the end is not always an operation, but is sometimes the effect of the operation. Therefore operation is not the proper and per se cause of pleasure.

Obj. 3. Further, leisure and rest consist in cessation from work, and they are objects of pleasure.[2] Therefore operation is not the proper cause of pleasure.

On the contrary, The Philosopher says[3] that "pleasure is a connatural and uninterrupted operation."

I answer that, As stated above (Q. XXXI, A. 1), two things are requisite for pleasure: namely,

the attainment of the suitable good, and knowledge of this attainment. Now each of these consists in a kind of operation, because actual knowledge is an operation and the attainment of the suitable good is by means of an operation. Moreover, the proper operation itself is a suitable good. Therefore every pleasure must be the result of some operation.

Reply Obj. 1. The objects of operations are not pleasurable except in so far as they are united to us; either by knowledge alone, as when we take pleasure in thinking of or looking at certain things; or in some other way along with knowledge, as when a man takes pleasure in knowing that he has something good,—riches, honour, or the like, which would not be pleasurable unless they were apprehended as possessed. For as the Philosopher observes,[4] "we take great pleasure in looking upon a thing as our own, by reason of the natural love we have for ourselves." Now to have such things is nothing else but to use them or to be able to use them, and this is through some operation. Therefore it is evident that every pleasure is reduced to some operation as its cause.

Reply Obj. 2. Even when the end is not an operation, but the effect of an operation, this effect is pleasant in so far as possessed or effected; and this comes back to use or operation.

Reply Obj. 3. Operations are pleasant in so far as they are proportionate and connatural to the doer. Now, since human power is finite, operation is proportioned to it according to a certain measure. And so if it exceed that measure, it will be no longer proportionate or pleasant, but, on the contrary, painful and irksome. And in this sense, leisure and play and other things pertaining to rest, are pleasant, since they banish sadness which results from labour.

ARTICLE 2. *Whether Movement Is a Cause of Pleasure?*

We proceed thus to the Second Article: It seems that movement is not a cause of pleasure.

Objection 1. Because, as stated above (Q. XXXI, A. 1), the good which is obtained and is actually possessed, is the cause of pleasure. Therefore the Philosopher says[5] that pleasure is not compared with generation, but with the operation of a thing already in existence. Now that which is being moved towards something does not yet have it; but it is, so to speak, being

---

[1] *Rhetoric*, I, 11 (1370[a]27).
[2] *Ibid.* (1370[a]14).
[3] *Ethics*, VII, 12, 13 (1153[a]14; [b]9); X, 4 (1174[b]20).

[4] *Politics*, II, 5 (1263[a]40).
[5] *Ethics*, VII, 12 (1153[a]12).

generated in its regard, since generation or corruption are united to every movement, as stated in the *Physics*.[1] Therefore movement is not a cause of pleasure.

Obj. 2. Further, movement is the chief cause of toil and fatigue in our works. But operations through being toilsome and fatiguing are not pleasant but disagreeable. Therefore movement is not a cause of pleasure.

Obj. 3. Further, movement implies a certain innovation, which is the opposite of custom. But "things which we are accustomed to, are pleasant," as the Philosopher says.[2] Therefore movement is not a cause of pleasure.

On the contrary, Augustine says,[3] "What means this, O Lord my God, whereas Thou art everlasting joy to Thyself, and some things around Thee evermore rejoice in Thee? What means this, that this portion of things ebbs and flows alternately displeased and reconciled?" From these words we gather that man rejoices and takes pleasure in some kind of alternations; and therefore movement seems to cause pleasure.

I answer that, Three things are requisite for pleasure: the one that is pleased, the pleasurable object joined to him, and a third thing, the knowledge of this union. And in respect of these three, movement is pleasant, as the Philosopher says.[4] For as far as we who feel pleasure are concerned, change is pleasant to us because our nature is changeable; and for this reason that which is suitable to us at one time is not suitable at another,—thus to warm himself at a fire is suitable to man in winter and not in summer. Again, on the part of the pleasing good which is united to us, change is pleasant, because the continued action of an agent increases its effect; thus the longer a person remains near the fire, the more he is warmed and dried. Now the natural disposition consists in a certain measure; and therefore when the continued presence of a pleasant object exceeds the measure of one's natural disposition, the removal of that object becomes pleasant. On the part of the knowledge itself (change becomes pleasant) because man desires to know something whole and perfect; when therefore a thing cannot be apprehended all at once as a whole, change in such a thing is pleasant, so that one part may pass and another succeed, and thus the whole be perceived. Hence Augus-

tine says,[5] "Thou wouldst not have the syllables stay, but fly away, that others may come, and thou hear the whole. And so whenever any one thing is made up of many, all of which do not exist together, all would please collectively more than they do severally, if all could be perceived collectively."

If therefore there be any thing whose nature is unchangeable, whose natural disposition cannot be exceeded by the continuation of any pleasing object, and which can behold the whole object of its delight at once,—to such a one change will afford no delight. And the more any pleasures approach to this, the more are they capable of being continual.

Reply Obj. 1. Although the subject of movement does not yet have perfectly that to which it is moved, nevertheless it is beginning to have something of it; and in this respect movement itself has something of pleasure. But it falls short of the perfection of pleasure, because the more perfect pleasures regard things that are unchangeable. Moreover movement becomes the cause of pleasure in so far as thereby something which previously was unsuitable becomes suitable or ceases to be, as stated above.

Reply Obj. 2. Movement causes toil and fatigue when it exceeds our natural disposition. It is not thus that it causes pleasure, but by removing what is contrary to our natural disposition.

Reply Obj. 3. What is customary becomes pleasant, in so far as it becomes natural; for custom is like a second nature. But the movement which gives pleasure is not that which departs from custom, but rather that which prevents the corruption of the natural disposition that might result from continued operation. And thus from the same cause of connaturalness, both custom and movement become pleasant.

ARTICLE 3. *Whether Hope and Memory Cause Pleasure?*

We proceed thus to the Third Article: It seems that memory and hope do not cause pleasure.

Objection 1. Because pleasure is caused by present good, as Damascene says (*De Fide Orthod.* ii).[6] But hope and memory regard what is absent, for memory is of the past, and hope of the future. Therefore memory and hope do not cause pleasure.

Obj. 2. Further, the same thing is not the

---

[1] Aristotle, VIII, 3 (254ᵃ10).
[2] *Rhetoric*, I, 11 (1370ᵇ3; 1371ᵃ24).
[3] *Confessions*, VIII, 8 (PL 32, 752).
[4] *Ethics*. VII, 14 (1154ᵇ28); *Rhetoric*, I, 11 (1371ᵃ25).

[5] *Confessions*, IV, 17 (PL 32, 700).
[6] Chap. 12 (PG 94, 929).

cause of contraries. But hope causes affliction, according to Prov. 13.12: *Hope that is deferred afflicteth the soul.* Therefore hope does not cause pleasure.

Obj. 3. Further, just as hope agrees with pleasure in regarding good, so also do concupiscence and love. Therefore hope should not be assigned as a cause of pleasure, any more than concupiscence or love.

On the contrary, It is written (Rom. 12.12): *Rejoicing in hope;* and (Ps. 76.4): *I remembered God, and was delighted.*

I answer that, Pleasure is caused by the presence of suitable good, in so far as it is sensed, or in any way perceived. Now a thing is present to us in two ways. First, in knowledge, that is, according as the thing known is in the knower by its likeness; secondly, in reality, that is, according as one thing is really joined with another, either actually or potentially according to any kind of union. And since real conjunction is greater than conjunction by likeness, which is the conjunction of knowledge; and again, since actual is greater than potential conjunction, therefore the greatest pleasure is that which arises from sensation which requires the presence of the sensible object. The second place belongs to the pleasure of hope, in which there is pleasurable conjunction, not only in respect of apprehension, but also in respect of the power or possibility of obtaining the pleasurable object. The third place belongs to the pleasure of memory, which has only the conjunction of apprehension.

Reply Obj. 1. Hope and memory are indeed of things which, absolutely speaking, are absent, and yet these are, after a fashion, present, that is, either according to apprehension only; or according to apprehension and power, at least supposed, of attainment.

Reply Obj. 2. Nothing prevents the same thing, in different ways, being the cause of contraries. And so hope, in so far as it implies a present appraising of a future good, causes pleasure; but in so far as it implies absence of that good, it causes affliction.

Reply Obj. 3. Love and concupiscence also cause pleasure. For everything that is loved becomes pleasing to the lover, since love is a kind of union or connaturalness of lover and beloved. In like manner every object of desire is pleasing to the one that desires, since concupiscence is chiefly a desire for pleasure. However hope, as implying a certainty of the real presence of the pleasing good that is not implied either by love or by concupiscence, is

considered in preference to them as causing pleasure; and also in preference to memory, which is of that which has already passed away.

ARTICLE 4. *Whether Sadness Causes Pleasure?*

We proceed thus to the Fourth Article: It would seem that sadness does not cause pleasure.

Objection 1. For nothing causes its own contrary. But sadness is contrary to pleasure. Therefore it does not cause it.

Obj. 2. Further, contraries have contrary effects. But pleasures, when called to mind, cause pleasure. Therefore sad things, when remembered, cause sorrow and not pleasure.

Obj. 3. Further, as sadness is to pleasure, so is hatred to love. But hatred does not cause love, but rather the other way about, as stated above (Q. XXIX, A. 2). Therefore sadness does not cause pleasure.

On the contrary, It is written (Ps. 41. 4): *My tears have been my bread day and night,* where bread denotes the refreshment of pleasure. Therefore tears, which arise from sadness, can give pleasure.

I answer that, Sadness may be considered in two ways: as existing actually, and as existing in the memory, and in both ways sadness can cause pleasure. Because sadness, as actually existing, causes pleasure, since it brings to mind that which is loved, the absence of which causes sadness; and yet the mere thought of it gives pleasure.—The recollection of sadness becomes a cause of pleasure on account of the subsequent deliverance, because absence of evil is looked upon as something good; hence according as a man thinks that he has been delivered from that which caused him sorrow and pain, so much reason has he to rejoice. And so Augustine says in the *City of God*[1] that oftentimes in joy we call to mind sad things . . . and in the season of health we recall past pains without feeling pain, . . . and in proportion are the more filled with joy and gladness; and again he says[2] that "the more peril there was in the battle, so much the more joy will there be in the triumph."

Reply Obj. 1. Sometimes accidentally a thing is the cause of its contrary; thus "that which is cold sometimes causes heat," as stated in the *Physics*.[3] In like manner sadness is the accidental cause of pleasure, in so far as it gives rise to the apprehension of something pleasant.

[1] Cf. Gregory, *Moral.*, IV, 36 (PL 75, 678).
[2] *Confessions*, VIII, 7 (PL 32, 752).
[3] Aristotle, VIII, 1 (251ª31).

Reply Obj. 2. Sad things called to mind cause pleasure, not in so far as they are sad and contrary to pleasant things, but in so far as man is delivered from them. In like manner the recollection of pleasant things, by reason of these being lost, may cause sadness.

Reply Obj. 3. Hatred also can be the accidental cause of love, that is, so far as some love one another because they agree in hating one and the same thing.

ARTICLE 5. *Whether the Actions of Others Are a Cause of Pleasure to Us?*

We proceed thus to the Fifth Article: It seems that the actions of others are not a cause of pleasure to us.

Objection 1. Because the cause of pleasure is our own good when conjoined to us. But the actions of others are not conjoined to us. Therefore they are not a cause of pleasure to us.

Obj. 2. Further, action is the agent's own good. If, therefore, the actions of others are a cause of pleasure to us, for the same reason all goods belonging to others will be pleasing to us, which is evidently untrue.

Obj. 3. Further, action is pleasant through proceeding from an innate habit; hence it is stated in the *Ethics*[1] that "we must regard the pleasure which follows after action, as being the sign of a habit existing in us." But the actions of others do not proceed from habits existing in us, but, sometimes, from habits existing in the agents. Therefore the actions of others are not pleasing to us, but to the agents themselves.

On the contrary, It is written in the second canonical epistle of John (*verse* 4): *I was exceeding glad that I found thy children walking in truth.*

I answer that, As stated above (A. 1; Q. XXXI, A. 1), two things are requisite for pleasure, namely, the attainment of one's proper good, and the knowledge of having obtained it. Therefore the action of another may cause pleasure to us in three ways. First, from the fact that we obtain some good through the action of another. And in this way, the actions of those who do some good to us are pleasing to us, for it is pleasant to be benefited by another. Secondly, from the fact that another's action makes us to know or appreciate our own good; and for this reason men take pleasure in being praised or honoured by others, because, that is, they thus become aware of some good existing in themselves. And since this appreciation receives greater weight from the testimony of good and wise men, therefore men take greater pleasure in being praised and honoured by them. And because a flatterer appears to praise, therefore flattery is pleasing to some. And as love is for something good, while admiration is for something great, so it is pleasant to be loved and admired by others, since a man thus becomes aware of his own goodness or greatness, through their giving pleasure to others. Thirdly, from the fact that another's actions, if they be good, are regarded as one's own good, by reason of the power of love, which makes a man to regard his friend as one with himself. And on account of hatred, which makes one to reckon another's good as being in opposition to oneself, the evil action of an enemy becomes an object of pleasure; and so it is written (I Cor. 13.6) that charity *rejoiceth not in iniquity, but rejoiceth with the truth.*

Reply Obj. 1. Another's action may be joined to me, either by its effect, as in the first way, or by knowledge, as in the second way, or by affection, as in the third way.

Reply Obj. 2. This argument avails for the third mode, but not for the first two.

Reply Obj. 3. Although the actions of another do not proceed from habits that are in me, yet they either produce in me something that gives pleasure; or they make me appreciate or know a habit of mine; or they proceed from the habit of one who is one with me by love.

ARTICLE 6. *Whether Doing Good to Another Is a Cause of Pleasure?*

We proceed thus to the Sixth Article: It seems that doing good to another is not a cause of pleasure.

Objection 1. Because pleasure is caused by one's obtaining one's own good, as stated above (A. 1; Q. XXXI, A. 1). But doing good pertains not to the obtaining but to the spending of one's own good. Therefore it seems to be the cause of sadness rather than of pleasure.

Obj. 2. Further, the Philosopher says[2] that "illiberality is more connatural to man than prodigality." Now it is a mark of prodigality to do good to others, while it is a mark of illiberality to cease from doing good. Since therefore everyone takes pleasure in a connatural operation, as stated in the *Ethics*,[3] it seems that doing good to others is not a cause of pleasure.

Obj. 3. Further, contrary effects proceed from contrary causes. But man takes a natural

[1] Aristotle, II, 3 (1104[b]3).

[2] *Ethics,* IV, 1 (1121[b]14).

[3] Aristotle, VII, 14 (1154[b]20); X, 4 (1174[b]20).

pleasure in certain kinds of ill-doing, such as overcoming, contradicting or scolding others, or, if he be angry, of punishing them, as the Philosopher says.[1] Therefore doing good to others is a cause of sadness rather than of pleasure.

On the contrary, The Philosopher says[2] that "it is most pleasant to give presents or assistance to friends and strangers."

I answer that, Doing good to another may give pleasure in three ways. First, in relation to the effect, which is the good conferred on another. In this respect, since through being united to others by love we look upon their good as being our own, we take pleasure in the good we do to others, especially to our friends, as in our own good. Secondly, in consideration of the end; as when a man, from doing good to another, hopes to get some good for himself, either from God or from man; for hope is a cause of pleasure. Thirdly, in consideration of the principle; and thus, doing good to another can give pleasure in respect of a threefold principle. One is the power of doing good; and in this regard doing good to another becomes pleasant in so far as it arouses in man an imagination of abundant good existing in him, of which he is able to give others a share. Therefore men take pleasure in their children, and in their own works, as being things on which they bestow a share of their own good. Another principle is a man's habitual inclination to do good, by reason of which doing good becomes connatural to him, for which reason the liberal man takes pleasure in giving to others. The third principle is the motive; for instance when a man is moved by one whom he loves to do good to someone. For whatever we do or suffer for a friend is pleasant, because love is the principle cause of pleasure.

Reply Obj. 1. Spending gives pleasure as showing forth one's good. But in so far as it empties us of our own good it may be a cause of sadness; for instance when it is excessive.

Reply Obj. 2. Prodigality is an excessive spending, which is unnatural. Hence prodigality is said to be contrary to nature.

Reply Obj. 3. To overcome, to contradict and to punish, give pleasure, not as tending to another's ill, but as pertaining to one's own good, which man loves more than he hates another's ill. For it is naturally pleasant to overcome, since it makes a man appreciate his own superiority. Therefore all those games in which there is a striving for the mastery, and a possibility of winning it, afford the greatest pleasure; and speaking generally all contests, in so far as they admit hope of victory. To contradict and to scold can give pleasure in two ways. First, as making man imagine himself to be wise and excellent, since it belongs to wise men and elders to reprove and to scold. Secondly, in so far as by scolding and reproving, one does good to another, for this gives one pleasure, as stated above. It is pleasant to an angry man to punish, in so far as he thinks himself to be removing an apparent slight, which seems to be due to a previous hurt; for when a man is hurt by another, he seems to be slighted by him, and therefore he wishes to be quit of this slight by paying back the hurt. And thus it is clear that doing good to another may be of itself pleasant, but doing evil to another is not pleasant, except in so far as it seems to affect one's own good.

ARTICLE 7. *Whether Likeness Is a Cause of Pleasure?*

We proceed thus to the Seventh Article: It would seem that likeness is not a cause of pleasure.

Objection 1. Because ruling and presiding seem to imply a certain unlikeness. But "it is natural to take pleasure in ruling and presiding," as stated in the treatise on *Rhetoric.*[3] Therefore unlikeness, rather than likeness, is a cause of pleasure.

Obj. 2. Further, nothing is more unlike pleasure than sorrow. But those who are burdened by sorrow are most inclined to seek pleasures, as the Philosopher says.[4] Therefore unlikeness, rather than likeness, is a cause of pleasure.

Obj. 3. Further, those who are satiated with certain delights, do not derive pleasure but disgust from them, as when one is satiated with food. Therefore likeness is not a cause of pleasure.

On the contrary, Likeness is a cause of love, as above stated (Q. XXVII, A. 3), and love is the cause of pleasure. Therefore likeness is a cause of pleasure.

I answer that, Likeness is a kind of unity; hence that which is like us, as being one with us, causes pleasure, just as it causes love, as stated above (Q. XXVII, A. 3). And if that which is like us does not hurt our own good, but in-

---

[1] *Rhetoric,* I, 11 (1370^{b}10).
[2] *Politics,* II, 5 (1263^{b}5).
[3] Aristotle, I, 11 (1371^{b}26).
[4] *Ethics,* VII, 14 (1154^{a}27).

crease it, it is pleasurable absolutely; for instance one man in respect of another, one youth in relation to another. But if it be hurtful to our own good, thus accidentally it causes disgust or sadness, not as being like and one with us, but as hurtful to that which is yet more one with us.

Now it happens in two ways that something like is hurtful to our own good. First, by destroying the measure of our own good, by a kind of excess; because good, chiefly bodily good, as health, consists in a certain measure; and thus superfluous food or any bodily pleasure causes disgust. Secondly, by being directly contrary to one's own good; thus a potter dislikes other potters, not because they are potters, but because they deprive him of his own excellence or profits, which he seeks as his own good.

Reply Obj. 1. Since ruler and subject are in communion with one another, there is a certain likeness between them; but this likeness is conditioned by a certain superiority, since ruling and presiding pertain to the excellence of a man's own good; for they belong to men who are wise and better than others, the result being that they give man an idea of his own excellence. Another reason is that by ruling and presiding, a man does good to others, which is pleasant.

Reply Obj. 2. That which gives pleasure to the sorrowful man, though it be unlike sorrow, bears some likeness to the man that is sorrowful, because sorrows are contrary to his own good. And therefore the sorrowful man seeks pleasure as making for his own good, in so far as it is a remedy for its contrary. And this is why bodily pleasures, which are contrary to certain sorrows, are more sought than intellectual pleasures, which have no contrary sorrow, as we shall state later on (Q. XXXV, A. 5). This also explains why all animals naturally desire pleasure, because animals always work through sense and movement. For this reason also young people are most inclined to seek pleasures, on account of the many changes to which they are subject, while yet growing. Moreover this is why the melancholic has a strong desire for pleasures, in order to drive away sorrow, because his body is corroded by a base humour, as stated in the *Ethics.*[1]

Reply Obj. 3. Bodily goods consist in a certain fixed measure. Hence surfeit of such things destroys the proper good, and consequently gives rise to disgust and sorrow, through being contrary to the proper good of man.

[1] Aristotle, VII, 14 (1154b7).

ARTICLE 8. *Whether Wonder Is a Cause of Pleasure?*

We proceed thus to the Eighth Article: It would seem that wonder is not a cause of pleasure.

Objection 1. Because wonder is the act of one who is ignorant of the nature of something, as Damascene says. But knowledge, rather than ignorance, is a cause of pleasure. Therefore wonder is not a cause of pleasure.

Obj. 2. Further, wonder is the beginning of wisdom, being as it were, the road to the search of truth, as stated in the beginning of the *Metaphysics.*[2] But "it is more pleasant to think of what we already know, than to seek for what we know not," as the Philosopher says,[3] since in the latter case we encounter difficulties and hindrances, in the former not; "pleasure however arises from an operation which is unhindered," as stated in the *Ethics.*[4] Therefore wonder hinders rather than causes pleasure.

Obj. 3. Further, everyone takes pleasure in what he is accustomed to; hence the actions of habits acquired by custom, are pleasant. But we wonder at what is unusual as Augustine says (*Tract* xxiv *in Joann.*).[5] Therefore wonder is contrary to the cause of pleasure.

On the contrary, The Philosopher says that wonder is the cause of pleasure.[6]

I answer that, It is pleasant to obtain what one desires, as stated above (Q. XXIII, A. 4), and therefore the greater the desire for the thing loved, the greater the pleasure when it is attained; indeed the very increase of desire brings with it an increase of pleasure, according as it gives rise also to the hope of obtaining that which is loved, since it was stated above (A. 3, REPLY 3) that desire resulting from hope is a cause of pleasure. Now wonder is a kind of desire for knowledge, a desire which comes to man when he sees an effect of which the cause either is unknown to him, or surpasses his knowledge or power of understanding. Consequently wonder is a cause of pleasure in so far as it includes a hope of getting the knowledge which one desires to have. For this reason whatever is wonderful is pleasing, for instance things that are scarce. Also, representations of things, even of those which are not pleasant in themselves, give rise to pleasure; for the soul rejoices in comparing one thing with an-

[2] Aristotle, I, 2 (982b12).
[3] *Ethics,* X, 7 (1177a26).
[4] Aristotle, VII, 12, 13 (1153a14; 1153b11).
[5] PL 35, 1593. [6] *Rhetoric,* I, 11 (1371a31; b4).

other, because comparison of one thing with another is the proper and connatural act of the reason, as the Philosopher says.[1] This again is why "it is more delightful to be delivered from great danger, because it is something wonderful," as stated in the *Rhetoric*.[2]

Reply Obj. 1. Wonder gives pleasure, not because it implies ignorance but in so far as it includes the desire of learning the cause, and in so far as the wonderer learns something new, that is, that the cause is other than he had thought it to be.

Reply Obj. 2. Pleasure includes two things: rest in the good, and perception of this rest. As to the former therefore, since it is more perfect to contemplate the known truth than to seek for the unknown, the contemplation of what we know is in itself more pleasing than the search for what we do not know. Nevertheless, as to the second, it happens that inquiries are sometimes more pleasing accidentally, in so far as they proceed from a greater desire; for greater desire is awakened when we are aware of our ignorance. This is why man takes the greatest pleasure in finding or learning things for the first time.

Reply Obj. 3. It is pleasant to do what we are accustomed to do, since this is connatural to us, as it were. And yet things that are of rare occurrence can be pleasant, either as regards knowledge, from the fact that we desire to know something about them, in so far as they are wonderful; or as regards operation, from the fact that the mind is more inclined by desire to act intensely in things that are new, as stated in the *Ethics*,[3] since more perfect operation causes more perfect pleasure.

QUESTION XXXIII
OF THE EFFECTS OF PLEASURE
(In Four Articles)

WE must now consider the effects of pleasure; and under this head there are four points of inquiry: (1) Whether expansion is an effect of pleasure? (2) Whether pleasure causes thirst or desire for itself? (3) Whether pleasure hinders the use of reason? (4) Whether pleasure perfects operation?

ARTICLE 1. *Whether Expansion Is an Effect of Pleasure?*

We proceed thus to the First Article: It would seem that expansion is not an effect of pleasure.

Objection 1. For expansion seems to pertain more to love, according to the Apostle (II Cor. 6. 11): *Our heart is enlarged.* Therefore it is written (Ps. 118. 96) concerning the precept of charity: *Thy commandment is exceeding broad.* But pleasure is a distinct passion from love. Therefore expansion is not an effect of pleasure.

Obj. 2. Further, when a thing expands it is enabled to receive more. But receiving pertains to desire, which is for something not yet possessed. Therefore expansion seems to belong to desire rather than to pleasure.

Obj. 3. Further, contraction is contrary to expansion. But contraction seems to belong to pleasure, for the hand closes on that which we wish to grasp firmly, and such is the affection of appetite in regard to that which pleases it. Therefore expansion does not pertain to pleasure.

On the contrary, In order to express joy, it is written (Isa. 60. 5): *Thou shalt see and abound, thy heart shall wonder and be enlarged.* Moreover pleasure is called by the name of *laetitia,* as being derived from *dilatatio* (expansion), as stated above (Q. XXXI, A. 3, REPLY 3).

I answer that, Breadth (*latitudo*) is a dimension of bodily magnitude; hence it is not applied to the emotions of the soul except metaphorically. Now expansion denotes a kind of movement towards breadth, and it belongs to pleasure in respect of the two things requisite for pleasure. One of these is on the part of the apprehensive power, which apprehends the union with some suitable good. As a result of this apprehension, man perceives that he has attained a certain perfection, which is a magnitude of the spiritual order; and in this respect man's mind is said to be magnified or expanded by pleasure. The other requisite for pleasure is on the part of the appetitive power, which acquiesces in the pleasurable object, and rests in it, offering, as it were, to enfold it within itself. And thus man's affection is expanded by pleasure, as though it surrendered itself to hold within itself the object of its pleasure.

Reply Obj. 1. In metaphorical expressions nothing hinders one and the same thing from being compared to different things according to different likenesses. And in this way expansion pertains to love by reason of a certain spreading out, in so far as the affection of the lover spreads out to others, so as to care, not only for his own interests, but also for what concerns others. On the other hand expansion pertains to pleasure in so far as a thing becomes more ample in itself so as to become more capacious.

---

[1] *Poetics*, 4 (1448^{b}9); cf. *Rhetoric*, I, 11 (1371^{b}9).
[2] Aristotle, I, 11 (1371^{b}10).   [3] Aristotle, X, 4 (1175^{a}6).

Reply Obj. 2. Desire includes a certain expansion arising from the imagination of the thing desired; but this expansion is much greater in the presence of the pleasurable object, because the mind surrenders itself more to that object when it is already taking pleasure in it than when it desires it before possessing it, since pleasure is the end of desire.

Reply Obj. 3. He that takes pleasure in a thing holds it fast, by clinging to it with all his might; but he opens his heart to it that he may enjoy it perfectly.

ARTICLE 2. *Whether Pleasure Causes Thirst or Desire for Itself?*

We proceed thus to the Second Article: It seems that pleasure does not cause desire for itself.

Objection 1. Because all movement ceases when repose is reached. But pleasure is, as it were, a certain repose of the movement of desire, as stated above (Q. XXIII, A. 4; Q. XXV, A. 2). Therefore the movement of desire ceases when pleasure is reached. Therefore pleasure does not cause desire.

Obj. 2. Further, a thing does not cause its opposite. But pleasure is, in a way, opposite to desire, on the part of the object, since desire regards a good which is not yet possessed, while pleasure regards the good that is possessed. Therefore pleasure does not cause desire for itself.

Obj. 3. Further, distaste is incompatible with desire. But pleasure often causes distaste. Therefore it does not cause desire.

On the contrary, Our Lord said (John 4. 13): *Whosoever drinketh of this water, shall thirst again,* where, according to Augustine (*Tract.* xv *in* Joann.),[1] water denotes pleasures of the body.

I answer that, Pleasure can be considered in two ways: first, as existing in act; secondly, as existing in the memory.—Again thirst, or desire, can be taken in two ways: first, properly, as denoting a desire for something not possessed; secondly, in general, as excluding distaste.

Considered as existing in act, pleasure does not cause thirst or desire for itself, properly speaking, but only accidentally, provided we take thirst or desire as denoting a desire for something not possessed; for pleasure is an emotion of the appetite in respect of something actually present. But it may happen that what is actually present is not perfectly possessed; and this may be on the part of the thing possessed, or on the part of the possessor. On the part of

the thing possessed, this happens through the thing possessed not being a simultaneous whole; therefore one obtains possession of it successively, and while taking pleasure in what one has, one desires to possess the remainder; thus if a man is pleased with the first part of a verse, he desires to hear the second part, as Augustine says.[2] In this way nearly all bodily pleasures cause thirst for themselves, until they are fully realized, because pleasures of this kind arise from some movement, as is evident in pleasures of the table. On the part of the possessor, this happens when a man possesses a thing which is perfect in itself, yet does not possess it perfectly, but obtains possession of it little by little. Thus in this life, a faint perception of Divine knowledge affords us delight, and delight sets up a thirst or desire for perfect knowledge; in which sense we may understand the words of Ecclus. 24. 29: *They that drink me shall yet thirst.*

On the other hand if by thirst or desire we understand the intensity only of the emotion, which excludes distaste, thus more than all others spiritual pleasures cause thirst or desire for themselves. Because bodily pleasures become distasteful by reason of their causing an excess in the natural disposition when they are increased or even when they are protracted, as is evident in the case of pleasures of the table. This is why, when a man arrives at the point of perfection in bodily pleasures, he wearies of them, and sometimes desires another kind. Spiritual pleasures, on the contrary, do not exceed the natural disposition, but perfect nature. Hence when their point of perfection is reached, they then afford the greatest delight; except, perhaps, accidentally, in so far as the work of contemplation is accompanied by some operation of the bodily powers, which tire from protracted activity. And in this sense also we may understand those words of Ecclus. 24. 29: *They that drink me shall yet thirst;* for, even of the angels, who know God perfectly, and delight in Him, it is written (I Pet. 1. 12) that they *desire to look at* Him.

Lastly, if we consider pleasure, not as existing in act, but as existing in the memory, thus it has of itself a natural tendency to cause thirst and desire for itself when, that is, man returns to that disposition in which he was when he experienced the pleasure that is past. But if he be changed from that disposition, the memory of that pleasure does not give him pleasure, but distaste; for instance, the memory of food in

---

[1] PL 35, 1515.

[2] *Confessions,* IV, 17 (PL 32, 700).

respect of a man who has eaten to repletion.

Reply Obj. 1. When pleasure is perfect, then it includes complete rest, and the movement of desire, tending to what was not possessed, ceases. But when it is imperfect, then the movement of desire, tending to what was not possessed, does not cease altogether.

Reply Obj. 2. That which is possessed imperfectly, is possessed in one respect, and in another respect is not possessed. Consequently it may be the object of desire and pleasure at the same time.

Reply Obj. 3. Pleasures cause distaste in one way, desire in another, as stated above.

ARTICLE 3. *Whether Pleasure Hinders the Use of Reason?*

We proceed thus to the Third Article: It seems that pleasure does not hinder the use of reason.

Objection 1. Because repose facilitates very much the due use of reason; hence the Philosopher says[1] that "while we sit and rest the soul becomes knowing and prudent." And it is written (Wisd. 8. 16): *When I go into my house, I shall repose myself with her,* that is, wisdom. But pleasure is a kind of repose. Therefore it helps rather than hinders the use of reason.

Obj. 2. Further, things which are not in the same subject even if they are contraries, do not hinder one another. But pleasure is in the appetitive part, while the use of reason is in the apprehensive part. Therefore pleasure does not hinder the use of reason.

Obj. 3. Further, that which is hindered by another seems in a certain way to be changed by it. But the use of an apprehensive power moves pleasure rather than is moved by it, because it is the cause of pleasure. Therefore pleasure does not hinder the use of reason.

On the contrary, The Philosopher says[2] that pleasure destroys the estimate of prudence.

I answer that, As is stated in the *Ethics,*[3] "appropriate pleasures increase activity . . . but pleasures arising from other sources are impediments to activity." Accordingly there is a certain pleasure that is taken in the very act of reason, as when one takes pleasure in contemplating or in reasoning, and such pleasure does not hinder the act of reason, but helps it, because we are more attentive in doing that which gives us pleasure, and attention helps operation.

[1] *Physics,* VII, 3 (247^b10).
[2] *Ethics,* VI, 5 (1140^b12).
[3] Aristotle, X, 5 (1175^b13).

On the other hand bodily pleasures hinder the use of reason in three ways. First, by distracting the reason. Because, as we have already observed (Q. IV, A. I. REPLY 3), we attend much to that which pleases us. Now when the attention is firmly fixed on one thing, it is either weakened in respect of other things, or it is entirely withdrawn from them; and thus if the bodily pleasure be great, either it entirely hinders the use of reason, by concentrating the mind's attention on itself, or else it hinders it considerably. Secondly, by being contrary to reason. Because some pleasures, especially those that are in excess, are contrary to the order of reason, and in this sense the Philosopher says that bodily pleasures destroy the estimate of prudence, but not the speculative estimate, to which they are not opposed, for instance that the three angles of a triangle are together equal to two right angles. In the first sense, however, they hinder both estimates. Thirdly, by fettering the reason, in so far as bodily pleasure is followed by a certain alteration in the body, greater even than in the other passions, in proportion as the appetite is more vehemently affected towards a present than towards an absent thing. Now such bodily disturbances hinder the use of reason, as may be seen in the case of drunkards, in whom the use of reason is fettered or hindered.

Reply Obj. 1. Bodily pleasure implies indeed repose of the appetite in the object of pleasure, and this repose is sometimes contrary to reason; but on the part of the body it always implies alteration. And in respect of both points, it hinders the use of reason.

Reply Obj. 2. The powers of appetite and of apprehension are indeed distinct parts, but belonging to the one soul. Consequently when the intention of the soul is strongly applied to the act of one part, it is hindered from the contrary act of the other part.

Reply Obj. 3. The use of reason requires the due use of the imagination and of the other sensitive powers, which are exercised through a bodily organ. Consequently alteration in the body hinders the use of reason, because it hinders the acts of the imagination and of the other sensitive powers.

ARTICLE 4. *Whether Pleasure Perfects Operation?*

We proceed thus to the Fourth Article: It seems that pleasure does not perfect operation.

Objection 1. For every human operation depends on the use of reason. But pleasure hinders the use of reason, as stated above (A. 3). Therefore pleasure does not perfect, but weakens human operation.

Obj. 2. Further, nothing perfects itself or its cause. But "pleasure is an operation"[1] that is, either in its essence or in its cause. Therefore pleasure does not perfect operation.

Obj. 3. Further, if pleasure perfects operation, it does so either as end, or as form, or as agent. But not as end, because operation is not sought for the sake of pleasure, but rather the reverse, as stated above (Q. IV, A. 2); nor as agent, because rather is it the operation that causes pleasure; nor again as form, because, according to the Philosopher,[2] "pleasure does not perfect operation, as a habit does." Therefore pleasure does not perfect operation.

On the contrary, The Philosopher says[3] that pleasure perfects operation.

I answer that, Pleasure perfects operation in two ways. First, as an end; not indeed according as an end is that on account of which a thing is, but according as every good which is added to a thing and completes it can be called its end. And in this sense the Philosopher says[4] that "pleasure perfects operation . . . as some end added to it"; that is to say, in so far as to this good, which is operation, there is added another good, which is pleasure, denoting the repose of the appetite in a good that is presupposed. Secondly, as agent; not indeed directly, for the Philosopher says[5] that "pleasure perfects operation, not as a physician makes a man healthy, but as health does." But it does so indirectly, in so far as the agent, through taking pleasure in his action, is more eagerly intent on it, and carries it out with greater care. And in this sense it is said in the *Ethics*[6] that "pleasures increase their appropriate activities, and hinder those that are not appropriate."

Reply Obj. 1. It is not every pleasure that hinders the act of reason, but only bodily pleasure; for this arises, not from the act of reason, but from the act of the concupiscible part, which act is intensified by pleasure. On the contrary, pleasure that arises from the act of reason strengthens the use of reason.

Reply Obj. 2. As stated in the *Physics*,[7] two things may be causes of one another, if one be the efficient, the other the final cause. And in this way operation is the efficient cause of pleas-

ure, while pleasure perfects operation by way of final cause, as stated above.

The *Reply to the Third Objection* is evident from what has been said.

QUESTION XXXIV

OF THE GOODNESS AND MALICE OF PLEASURES

(*In Four Articles*)

WE must now consider the goodness and malice of pleasures, under which head there are four points of inquiry: (1) Whether every pleasure is evil? (2) If not, whether every pleasure is good? (3) Whether any pleasure is the greatest good? (4) Whether pleasure is the measure or rule by which to judge of moral good and evil?

ARTICLE 1. *Whether Every Pleasure Is Evil?*

We proceed thus to the First Article: It seems that every pleasure is evil.

Objection 1. For that which destroys prudence and hinders the use of reason seems to be evil in itself, for man's good is to be in accord with reason, as Dionysius says (*Div. Nom.* iv).[8] But pleasure destroys prudence and hinders the use of reason, and so much the more, as the pleasure is greater. Hence "in sexual pleasures," which are the greatest of all, "it is impossible to understand anything," as stated in the *Ethics.*[9] Moreover, Jerome says in his commentary on Matthew (Origen,—*Hom.* vi *in Num.*)[10] that "at the time of conjugal intercourse, the presence of the Holy Ghost is not vouchsafed, even if it be a prophet that fulfils the conjugal duty." Therefore pleasure is evil in itself, and consequently every pleasure is evil.

Obj. 2. Further, that which the virtuous man shuns, and the ungodly man seeks, seems to be evil in itself, and should be avoided; because, as stated in the *Ethics*,[11] "the virtuous man is a kind of measure and rule of human actions"; and the Apostle says (I Cor. 2. 15): *The spiritual man judgeth all things.* But children and dumb animals, in whom there is no virtue, seek pleasure, but the man who is master of himself does not. Therefore pleasures are evil in themselves and should be avoided.

Obj. 3. Further, "virtue and art are concerned about the difficult and the good."[12] But no art is ordered to pleasure. Therefore pleasure is not something good.

---

[1] Aristotle, *Ethics*, VII, 12, 13 (1153ª10; ᵇ12); X, 5 (1175ᵇ33).

[2] *Ibid.*, X, 4 (1174ᵇ31).

[3] *Ibid.*　[4] *Ibid.*　[5] *Ibid.* (1174ᵇ24).

[6] Aristotle, X, 5 (1175ª36).

[7] Aristotle, II, 3 (195ª8).

[8] Sect. 32 (PG 3, 733).

[9] Aristotle, VII, 11 (1152ᵇ16).

[10] PG 12, 610.

[11] Aristotle, X, 5 (1176ª17); cf. III, 4 (1113ª33); IX, 4 (1166ª12).　[12] Aristotle, *Ethics*, II, 3 (1105ª9).

On the contrary, It is written (Ps. 36. 4): *Delight in the Lord.* Since, therefore, Divine authority leads to no evil, it seems that not every pleasure is evil.

I answer that, As stated in the *Ethics,*[1] some have maintained that all pleasure is evil. The reason seems to have been that they took account only of sensible and bodily pleasures which are more manifest; for, also in other respects, the ancient philosophers did not discriminate between the intelligible and the sensible, nor between intellect and sense.[2] And they held that all bodily pleasures should be accounted as bad, and thus that man, being prone to immoderate pleasures, arrives at the mean of virtue by abstaining from pleasure. But they were wrong in holding this opinion. Because, since none can live without some sensible and bodily pleasure, if they who teach that all pleasures are evil, are found taking pleasure, men will be more inclined to pleasure by following the example of their works instead of listening to the doctrine of their words. For in human actions and passions, in which experience is of great weight, example moves more than words.

We must therefore say that some pleasures are good, and that some are evil. For pleasure is a repose of the appetitive power in some loved good, and resulting from some operation; hence we may assign a twofold reason for this assertion. The first is in respect of the good in which a man reposes with pleasure. For good and evil in the moral order depend on agreement or disagreement with reason, as stated above (Q. XVIII, A. 5), just as in the order of nature, a thing is said to be natural, if it agrees with nature, and unnatural, if it disagrees. Accordingly, just as in the natural order there is a certain natural repose, whereby a thing rests in that which agrees with its nature, for instance, when a heavy body rests down below; and again an unnatural repose, whereby a thing rests in that which disagrees with its nature, as when a heavy body rests up aloft: so, in the moral order, there is a good pleasure, according to which the higher or lower appetite rests in that which is in accord with reason, and an evil pleasure, whereby the appetite rests in that which is discordant from reason and the law of God.

The second reason can be found by considering the actions, some of which are good, some evil. Now pleasures which are joined to actions are more akin to those actions than concupiscences, which precede them in point of time.

Therefore, since the concupiscences of good actions are good, and of evil actions, evil, much more are the pleasures of good actions good, and those of evil actions evil.

Reply Obj. 1. As stated above (Q. XXXIII, A. 3), it is not the pleasures which result from an act of reason that hinder the reason or destroy prudence, but extraneous pleasures, such as the pleasures of the body. These indeed hinder the use of reason, as stated above (*ibid.*), either by contrariety of the appetite that rests in something contrary to reason, which makes the pleasure morally bad, or by fettering the reason; thus in conjugal intercourse, though the pleasure be in accord with reason, yet it hinders the use of reason, on account of the accompanying bodily change. But in this case the pleasure is not morally evil, as neither is sleep, by which the reason is fettered, morally evil, if it be taken according to reason; for reason itself demands that the use of reason be interrupted at times. We must add, however, that although this fettering of the reason through the pleasure of conjugal intercourse has no moral malice, since it is neither a mortal nor a venial sin, yet it proceeds from a kind of moral malice, namely, from the sin of our first parent; for, as stated in the First Part (Q. XCVIII, A. 2) the case was different in the state of innocence.

Reply Obj. 2. The temperate man does not shun all pleasures, but those that are immoderate, and contrary to reason. The fact that children and dumb animals seek pleasures does not show that all pleasures are evil, because they have from God their natural appetite, which is moved to that which is suitable to them.

Reply Obj. 3. Art is not concerned with all kinds of good, but with the making of external things, as we shall state further on (Q. LVII, A. 3). But prudence and virtue are more concerned with operations and passions than art is. Nevertheless "there is an art of making pleasure, namely, the art of cookery and the art of making unguents," as stated in the *Ethics.*[3]

ARTICLE 2. *Whether Every Pleasure Is Good?*

We proceed thus to the Second Article: It seems that every pleasure is good.

Objection 1. Because as stated in the First Part (Q. V, A. 6), there are three kinds of good, the virtuous, the useful, and the pleasant. But everything virtuous is good, and in like manner everything useful is good. Therefore also every pleasure is good.

Obj. 2. Further, that which is not sought for

---

[1] Aristotle, x, 1 (1172ª28); cf. below, A. 2.
[2] Aristotle, *Soul*, III, 3 (427ª21).
[3] Aristotle, VII, 12 (1153ª26).

the sake of something else, is good in itself, as stated in the *Ethics*.[1] But pleasure is not sought for the sake of something else; for it seems absurd to ask anyone why he seeks to be pleased. Therefore pleasure is good in itself. Now that which is predicated of a thing considered in itself, is predicated of it universally. Therefore every pleasure is good.

Obj. 3. Further, that which is desired by all, seems to be good of itself, because "good is what all things seek," as stated in the *Ethics*.[2] But everyone seeks some kind of pleasure, even children and dumb animals. Therefore pleasure is good in itself, and consequently all pleasure is good.

On the contrary, It is written (Prov. 2. 14): *Who are glad when they have done evil, and rejoice in most wicked things.*

I answer that, While some of the Stoics maintained that all pleasures are evil,[3] the Epicureans held that pleasure is good in itself, and that consequently all pleasures are good.[4] They seem to have thus erred through not discriminating between that which is good absolutely, and that which is good in respect of a particular individual. That which is good absolutely is good in itself. Now that which is not good in itself may be good in respect of some individual in two ways. In one way, because it is suitable to him by reason of a disposition in which he is now, which disposition, however, is not natural; thus it is sometimes good for a leper to eat things that are poisonous, which are not suitable absolutely to the human temperament. In another way, through something unsuitable being esteemed suitable. And since pleasure is the repose of the appetite in some good, if the appetite reposes in that which is good absolutely, the pleasure will be pleasure absolutely, and good absolutely. But if a man's appetite repose in that which is good, not absolutely, but in respect of that particular man, then his pleasure will not be pleasure absolutely, but a pleasure to him; neither will it be good absolutely, but in a certain respect, or an apparent good.

Reply Obj. 1. The virtuous and the useful depend on accordance with reason, and consequently nothing is virtuous or useful without being good. But the pleasant depends on agreement with the appetite, which tends sometimes to that which is discordant with reason. Conse-

quently not every object of pleasure is good in the moral order, which depends on the order of reason.

Reply Obj. 2. The reason why pleasure is not sought for the sake of something else is because it is repose in the end. Now the end may be either good or evil, although nothing can be an end except in so far as it is good in respect of such and such a man; and so too with regard to pleasure.

Reply Obj. 3. All things seek pleasure in the same way as they seek good, since pleasure is the repose of the appetite in good. But, just as it happens that not every good which is desired, is of itself and truly good, so not every pleasure is of itself and truly good.

ARTICLE 3. *Whether Any Pleasure Is the Greatest Good?*

We proceed thus to the Third Article: It would seem that no pleasure is the greatest good.

Objection 1. Because nothing generated is the greatest good, since generation cannot be the last end. But pleasure follows on generation, for the fact that a thing takes pleasure is due to its being established in its own nature, as stated above (Q. XXXI, A. 1). Therefore no pleasure is the greatest good.

Obj. 2. Further, that which is the greatest good cannot be made better by addition. But pleasure is made better by addition; for pleasure together with virtue is better than pleasure without virtue. Therefore pleasure is not the greatest good.

Obj. 3. Further, that which is the greatest good is universally good, as being good of itself, since that which is such of itself is prior to and greater than that which is such accidentally. But pleasure is not universally good, as stated above (A. 2). Therefore pleasure is not the greatest good.

On the contrary, Happiness is the greatest good, since it is the end of man's life. But Happiness is not without pleasure, for it is written (Ps. 15. 11): *Thou shalt fill me with joy with Thy countenance; at Thy right hand are delights even to the end.*

I answer that, Plato held neither with the Stoics, who asserted that all pleasures are evil,[5] nor with the Epicureans, who maintained that all pleasures are good,[6] but he said that some are good, and some evil; yet, so that no pleasure be

---

[1] Aristotle, I, 6 (1096ᵇ14).
[2] Aristotle, I, 1 (1094ᵃ3).
[3] See Augustine, *City of God*, XIV, 8 (PL 41, 412).
[4] See Cicero, *De Finibus*, II, 3 (DD III, 507); Augustine, *City of God*, XIV, 2 (PL 41, 403).

[5] See Augustine, *City of God*, XIV, 8 (PL 41, 412).
[6] See Cicero, *De Finibus*, II, 3 (DD III, 507); Augustine, *City of God*, XIV, 2 (PL 41, 403).

the sovereign or greatest good.[1] But, judging from his arguments, he fails in two points. First,[2] because, from observing that sensible and bodily pleasure consists in a certain movement and generation, as is evident in satiety from eating and the like, he thought that all pleasure arises from generation and movement; and from this, since generation and movement are the acts of something imperfect, it would follow that pleasure does not have the character of ultimate perfection.—But this is seen to be evidently false as regards intellectual pleasures. For one takes pleasure not only in the generation of knowledge, for instance, when one learns or wonders, as stated above (Q. XXXII, A. 8, Reply 2), but also in the act of contemplation, by making use of knowledge already acquired.

Secondly, because by greatest good he understood[3] that which is the supreme good absolutely, that is, the good itself apart from as it were, and unparticipated by, all else, in which sense God is the Supreme Good; but we are speaking of the greatest good in human things.[4] Now the greatest good of everything is its last end. And the end, as stated above (Q. I, A. 8; Q. II, A. 7) is twofold: namely, the thing itself, and the use of that thing; thus the miser's end is either money, or the possession of money. Accordingly, man's last end may be said to be either God Who is the Supreme Good absolutely; or the enjoyment of God, which denotes a certain pleasure in the last end. And in this sense a certain pleasure of man may be said to be the greatest among human goods.

Reply Obj. 1. Not every pleasure arises from a generation, for some pleasures result from perfect operations, as stated above. Accordingly nothing prevents some pleasure being the greatest good, although every pleasure is not such.

Reply Obj. 2. This argument is true of the greatest good absolutely, by participation of which all things are good; therefore no addition can make it better. But in regard to other goods, it is universally true that any good becomes better by the addition of another good. However it might be said that pleasure is not something extraneous to the operation of virtue, but that it accompanies it, as stated in the *Ethics*.[5]

Reply Obj. 3. That pleasure is the greatest good is due not to the mere fact that it is pleas-

ure, but to the fact that it is perfect repose in the perfect good. Hence it does not follow that every pleasure is supremely good, or even good at all. Thus a certain science is supremely good, but not every science is.

ARTICLE 4. *Whether Pleasure Is the Measure or Rule by Which to Judge of Moral Good or Evil?*

We proceed thus to the Fourth Article: It would seem that pleasure is not the measure or rule of moral good and evil.

Objection 1. Because "that which is first in a genus is the measure of all the rest."[6] But pleasure is not the first thing in the moral genus, for it is preceded by love and desire. Therefore it is not the rule of goodness and malice in moral matters.

Obj. 2. Further, a measure or rule should be uniform; hence that movement which is the most uniform, is the measure and rule of all movements.[7] But pleasures are various and multiform, since some of them are good, and some evil. Therefore pleasure is not the measure and rule of morals.

Obj. 3. Further, judgment of the effect from its cause is more certain than judgment of cause from effect. Now goodness or malice of operation is the cause of goodness or malice of pleasure, because those pleasures are good which result from good operations, and those are evil which arise from evil operations, as stated in the *Ethics*.[8] Therefore pleasures are not the rule and measure of moral goodness and malice.

On the contrary, Augustine, commenting on Ps. 7. 10, *The searcher of hearts and reins is God,* says:[9] "The end of care and thought is the pleasure which each one aims at achieving." And the Philosopher says[10] that "pleasure is the architect, that is, the principal end,[11] in regard to which, we say absolutely that this is evil, and that, good."

I answer that, Moral goodness or malice depends chiefly on the will, as stated above (Q. XX, A. 1), and it is chiefly from the end that we know whether the will is good or evil. Now the end is taken to be that in which the will reposes;

---

[1] See Aristotle, *Ethics*, x, 2 (1172^{b}28); Plato, *Philebus* (22; 60).
[2] See Aristotle, *Ethics*, x, 3 (1173^{a}29); Plato, *Philebus* (53; 54).
[3] Cf. Aristotle, *Ethics*, I, 6 (1096^{b}10); Plato, *Republic* (506).
[4] Cf. Aristotle, *op. cit.* (1096^{b}34). [5] Aristotle, I, 8 (1098^{b}25).
[6] Aristotle, *Metaphysics*, x, 1 (1052^{b}18); cf. *Physics*, IV, 14 (223^{b}13).
[7] Aristotle, *Metaphysics*, x, 1 (1053^{a}8); cf. *Physics*, loc. cit.
[8] Aristotle, x, 5 (1175^{b}24); cf. VII, 14 (1154^{a}18; ^{b}6).
[9] *Enarr. in Ps.* (PL 36, 103).
[10] *Ethics*, VII, 11 (1152^{b}2).
[11] St. Thomas took *finis* as being in the nominative, whereas it is the genitive—Τοῦ Τέλους; and the Greek reads, "He (i.e., the political philosopher), is the architect of the end."

and the repose of the will and of every appetite in the good is pleasure. And therefore man is judged to be good or bad chiefly according to the pleasure of the human will; for that man is good and virtuous who takes pleasure in the works of virtue, and that man evil who takes pleasure in evil works.

On the other hand, pleasures of the sensitive appetite are not the rule of moral goodness and malice; for food is universally pleasurable to the sensitive appetite both of good and of evil men. But the will of the good man takes pleasure in them in accordance with reason, to which the will of the evil man gives no heed.

Reply Obj. 1. Love and desire precede pleasure in the order of generation. But pleasure precedes them in the order of the end, which serves as a principle in actions; and it is by the principle, which is the rule and measure of such matters, that we form our judgment.

Reply Obj. 2. All pleasures are uniform in the point of their being the repose in something good, and in this respect pleasure can be a rule or measure. Because that man is good, whose will rests in the true good, and that man evil, whose will rests in evil.

Reply Obj. 3. Since pleasure perfects operation as its end, as stated above (Q. XXXIII, A. 4), an operation cannot be perfectly good unless there be also pleasure in good; for the goodness of a thing depends on its end. And thus, in a way, the goodness of the pleasure is the cause of goodness in the operation.

QUESTION XXXV

OF PAIN OR SORROW, IN ITSELF

(In Eight Articles)

WE have now to consider pain and sorrow, concerning which we must consider (1) Sorrow or pain in itself; (2) Its cause (Q. XXXVI); (3) Its effects (Q. XXXVII); (4) Its remedies (Q. XXXVIII); (5) Its goodness or malice (Q. XXXIX).

Under the first head there are eight points of inquiry: (1) Whether pain is a passion of the soul? (2) Whether sorrow is the same as pain? (3) Whether sorrow or pain is contrary to pleasure? (4) Whether all sorrow is contrary to all pleasure? (5) Whether there is a sorrow contrary to the pleasure of contemplation? (6) Whether sorrow is to be shunned more than pleasure is to be sought? (7) Whether exterior pain is greater than interior? (8) Of the species of sorrow?

ARTICLE 1. *Whether Pain Is a Passion of the Soul?*

We proceed thus to the First Article: It seems that pain is not a passion of the soul.

Objection 1. Because no passion of the soul is in the body. But pain can be in the body, since Augustine says (*De Vera Relig.* xii),[1] that "bodily pain is a sudden corruption of the well-being of that thing which the soul, by making evil use of it, made subject to corruption." Therefore pain is not a passion of the soul.

Obj. 2. Further, every passion of the soul pertains to the appetitive power. But pain does not pertain to the appetitive, but rather to the apprehensive part; for Augustine says (*De Nat. Boni,* xx)[2] that "bodily pain is caused by the sense resisting a more powerful body." Therefore pain is not a passion of the soul.

Obj. 3. Further, every passion of the soul pertains to the animal appetite. But pain does not pertain to the animal appetite, but rather to the natural appetite; for Augustine says (*Gen. ad lit.* viii, 14):[3] "Had not some good remained in nature, we should feel no pain in being punished by the loss of good." Therefore pain is not a passion of the soul.

On the contrary, Augustine[4] places pain among the passions of the soul, quoting Virgil (*Æneid,* vi, 733):

"Hence wild desires and grovelling fears
And human laughter, human tears."
(*Trl.* CONINGTON.)

I answer that, Just as two things are requisite for pleasure; namely, being joined to good and perception of this union, so also two things are requisite for pain; namely, being joined to some evil (which is in so far evil as it deprives one of some good), and perception of this union. Now whatever is joined, if it does not have the aspect of good or evil with respect to the being to which it is joined, cannot cause pleasure or pain. Hence it is evident that something under the aspect of good or evil is the object of pleasure or pain. But good and evil, as such, are objects of the appetite. Consequently it is clear that pleasure and pain belong to the appetite.

Now every appetitive movement or inclination consequent to apprehension, belongs to the intellectual or sensitive appetite; for the inclination of the natural appetite is not consequent to an apprehension of the subject of that appetite, but to the apprehension of another, as stated in

[1] PL 34, 142.   [2] PL 42, 557.   [3] PL 34, 385.
[4] *City of God,* XIV, 8 (PL 41, 412).

the First Part (Q. VI, A. 1; Q. CIII, AA. 1, 3). Since then pleasure and pain presuppose some sense or apprehension in the same subject, it is evident that pain, like pleasure, is in the intellectual or sensitive appetite.

Again every movement of the sensitive appetite is called a passion, as stated above (Q. XXII, AA. 1, 3), and especially those which tend to some defect. Consequently pain, according as it is in the sensitive appetite, is most properly called a passion of the soul, just as bodily ailments are properly called passions of the body. Hence Augustine[1] calls pain in particular a kind of "ailment."

Reply Obj. 1. We speak of pain of the body, because the cause of pain is in the body, as for instance when we suffer something hurtful to the body. But the movement of pain is always in the soul; for "the body cannot feel pain unless the soul feel it," as Augustine says on Ps. 86. 10.[2]

Reply Obj. 2. We speak of pain of the senses not as though it were an act of the sensitive power, but because the senses are required for bodily pain, in the same way as for bodily pleasure.

Reply Obj. 3. Pain at the loss of good proves the goodness of the nature, not because pain is an act of the natural appetite, but because nature desires something as good, the removal of which being perceived, there follows the passion of pain in the sensitive appetite.

ARTICLE 2. *Whether Sorrow Is the Same as Pain?*

We proceed thus to the Second Article: It seems that sorrow is not pain.

Objection 1. For Augustine says[3] that "pain is used to express bodily suffering." But sorrow is used more in reference to the soul. Therefore sorrow is not pain.

Obj. 2. Further, pain is only in respect of present evil. But sorrow can refer to both past and future evil; thus repentance is sorrow for the past, and anxiety is sorrow for the future. Therefore sorrow is quite different from pain.

Obj. 3. Further, pain does not seem to follow save from the sense of touch. But sorrow can arise from all the senses. Therefore sorrow is not pain, and extends to more objects.

On the contrary, The Apostle says (Rom. 9. 2): *I have great sorrow* (Douay,—*sadness*) *and continual pain* (Douay,—*sorrow*) *in my heart,* thus denoting the same thing by sorrow and pain.

[1] *City of God,* XIV, 7 (PL 41, 411).
[2] *Enarr. in Ps.* (PL 37, 1110).   [3] *City of God, loc. cit.*

I answer that, Pleasure and pain can arise from a twofold apprehension, namely, from the apprehension of an exterior sense, and from the interior apprehension of the intellect or of the imagination. Now the interior apprehension extends to more objects than the exterior apprehension, because whatever things come under the exterior apprehension, come under the interior, but not conversely. Consequently that pleasure alone which is caused by an interior apprehension is called joy, as stated above (Q XXXI, A. 3); and in like manner that pain alone which is caused by an interior apprehension, is called sorrow. And just as that pleasure which is caused by an exterior apprehension is called pleasure but not joy, so too that pain which is caused by an exterior apprehension is called pain but not sorrow. Accordingly sorrow is a species of pain, as joy is a species of pleasure.

Reply Obj. 1. Augustine is speaking there of the use of the word, because pain is more generally used in reference to bodily pains, which are better known, than in reference to spiritual pains.

Reply Obj. 2. External sense perceives only what is present; but the interior knowing power can perceive the present, past and future. Consequently sorrow can regard present, past and future, but bodily pain, which follows the apprehension of the external sense, can only regard something present.

Reply Obj. 3. The sensibles of touch are painful, but only in so far as they are disproportionate to the apprehensive power, but also in so far as they are contrary to nature; but the objects of the other senses can indeed be disproportionate to the apprehensive power, but they are not contrary to nature, save as they are subordinate to the sensibles of touch. Consequently man alone, who is an animal perfect in knowledge, takes pleasure in the objects of the other senses for their own sake; but other animals take no pleasure in them save as referable to the sensibles of touch, as stated in the *Ethics.*[4] Accordingly, in referring to the objects of the other senses, we do not speak of pain in so far as it is contrary to natural pleasure, but rather of sorrow, which is contrary to joy. So then if pain be taken as denoting bodily pain, which is its more usual meaning, then it is contrasted with sorrow, according to the distinction of interior and exterior apprehension; although, on the part of the objects, pleasure extends further than does bodily pain. But if pain be taken in a wide sense, then it is the genus of sorrow, as stated above.

[4] Aristotle, III, 10 (1118[a]16).

ARTICLE 3. *Whether Sorrow or Pain Is Contrary to Pleasure?*

We proceed thus to the Third Article: It would seem that sorrow is not contrary to pleasure.

Objection 1. For one of two contraries is not the cause of the other. But sorrow can be the cause of pleasure; for it is written (*Matt.* 5. 5): *Blessed are they that mourn, for they shall be comforted.* Therefore they are not contrary to one another.

Obj. 2. Further, one contrary does not denominate the other. But to some, pain or sorrow gives pleasure; thus Augustine says[1] that in stage-plays sorrow itself gives pleasure; and that "weeping is a bitter thing, and yet it sometimes pleases us."[2] Therefore pain is not contrary to pleasure.

Obj. 3. Further, one contrary is not the matter of the other, because contraries cannot be together at the same time. But sorrow can be the matter of pleasure; for Augustine says (*De Pœnit.* xiii)[3]: "The penitent should ever sorrow, and rejoice in his sorrow." The Philosopher too says that, on the other hand, "the evil man feels pain at having been pleased."[4] Therefore pleasure and pain are not contrary to one another.

On the contrary, Augustine says[5] that "joy is the volition of consent to the things we wish; but sorrow is the volition of dissent from the things we do not wish." But consent and dissent are contraries. Therefore pleasure and sorrow are contrary to one another.

I answer that, As the Philosopher says,[6] contrariety is a difference in respect of a form. Now the form or species of a passion or movement is taken from the object or term. Consequently, since the objects of pleasure and sorrow or pain, namely, present good and present evil, are contrary to one another, it follows that pain and pleasure are contrary to one another.

Reply Obj. 1. Nothing hinders one contrary causing the other accidentally, and in this way sorrow can be the cause of pleasure. In one way, in so far as from sorrow at the absence of something, or at the presence of its contrary, one seeks the more eagerly for something pleasant; thus a thirsty man seeks more eagerly the pleasure of a drink, as a remedy for the pain that he suffers. In another way, in so far as, from a strong desire for a certain pleasure, one does not shrink from undergoing pain, so as to obtain that pleasure. In each of these ways, the sorrows of the present life lead us to the comfort of the future life. Because by the mere fact that man mourns for his sins, or for the delay of glory, he merits the consolation of eternity. In like manner a man merits it when he does not shrink from hardships and difficulties in order to obtain it.

Reply Obj. 2. Pain itself can be pleasurable accidentally in so far as it is accompanied by wonder, as in stage-plays; or in so far as it recalls a beloved object to one's memory, and makes one feel one's love for the thing, whose absence gives us pain. Consequently, since love is pleasant, both pain and whatever else results from love, in so far as they remind us of our love, are pleasant. And, for this reason, we derive pleasure even from pains depicted on the stage, in so far as, in witnessing them, we perceive ourselves to conceive a certain love for those who are there represented.

Reply Obj. 3. The will and the reason reflect on their own acts, since the acts themselves of the will and reason are considered under the aspect of good or evil. In this way sorrow can be the matter of pleasure, or vice versa, not *per se* but accidentally; that is, in so far as either of them is considered under the aspect of good or evil.

ARTICLE 4. *Whether All Sorrow Is Contrary to All Pleasure?*

We proceed thus to the Fourth Article: It seems that all sorrow is contrary to all pleasure.

Objection 1. Because, just as whiteness and blackness are contrary species of colour, so pleasure and sorrow are contrary species of the soul's passions. But whiteness and blackness are universally opposed to one another. Therefore pleasure and sorrow are so too.

Obj. 2. Further, remedies are made of things contrary. But every pleasure is a remedy for all manner of sorrow, as the Philosopher declares.[7] Therefore every pleasure is contrary to every sorrow.

Obj. 3. Further, contraries are hindrances to one another. But every sorrow hinders any kind of pleasure, as is evident from the *Ethics.*[8] Therefore every sorrow is contrary to every pleasure.

On the contrary, The same thing is not the cause of contraries. But joy for one thing and sorrow for the opposite thing proceed from the

---

[1] *Confessions,* III, 2 (PL 32, 683).
[2] *Ibid,* IV, 10 (PL 32, 697).
[3] Contained among the works of Augustine (PL 40, 1124).   [4] *Ethics,* IX, 4 (1166b23).
[5] *City of God,* XIV, 6 (PL 41, 409).
[6] *Metaphysics,* X, 4 (1055a3).

[7] *Ethics,* VII, 14 (1154b13).   [8] Aristotle, X, 5 (1175b16).

same habit; thus from charity it happens that we *rejoice with them that rejoice*, and *weep with them that weep* (Rom. 12. 15). Therefore not every sorrow is contrary to every pleasure.

I answer that, As stated in the *Metaphysics*,[1] contrariety is a difference according to form. Now a form may be generic or specific. Consequently things may be contraries in respect of a generic form, as virtue and vice; or in respect of a specific form, as justice and injustice.

Now we must observe that some things are specified by absolute forms, for instance, substances and qualities; but other things are specified in relation to something extrinsic, for instance, passions and movements, which derive their species from their terms or objects. Accordingly in those things that are specified by absolute forms, it happens that species contained under contrary genera are not contrary as to their specific nature; but it does not happen for them to have any affinity or fittingness to one another. For intemperance and justice, which are in the contrary genera of virtue and vice, are not contrary to one another in respect of their specific nature; and yet they have no affinity or fittingness to one another. On the other hand, in those things that are specified in relation to something extrinsic, it happens that species belonging to contrary genera are not only not contrary to one another, but also that they have a certain mutual affinity and fittingness. The reason of this is that where there is one same relation to two contraries, there is contrariety; for example, to approach to a white thing, and to approach to a black thing, are contraries; but contrary relations to contrary things implies a certain likeness, for instance, to recede from something white, and to approach to something black. This is most evident in the case of contradiction, which is the principle of opposition; because opposition consists in affirming and denying the same thing, for example, white and not-white, while there is fittingness and likeness in the affirmation of one contrary and the denial of the other, as, if I were to say black and not white.

Now sorrow and pleasure, being passions, are specified by their objects. According to their respective genera, they are contrary to one another; for "one pertains to pursuit, the other to avoidance, which are to the appetite what affirmation and denial are to the intellect."[2] Consequently sorrow and pleasure in respect of the same object, are in opposition to one another

according to species; but sorrow and pleasure in respect of objects that are not opposite but disparate, are not opposed to one another according to the aspect of species, but are also disparate; for instance, sorrow at the death of a friend, and pleasure in contemplation. If, however, those diverse objects be contrary to one another, then pleasure and sorrow are not only not specifically contrary, but they also have a certain mutual fittingness and affinity; for instance to rejoice in good and to sorrow for evil.

Reply Obj. 1. Whiteness and blackness do not take their species from their relationship to something extrinsic, as pleasure and sorrow do; therefore the comparison does not hold.

Reply Obj. 2. Genus is taken from matter, as is stated in the *Metaphysics*,[3] and in accidents the subject takes the place of matter. Now it has been said above that pleasure and sorrow are generically contrary to one another. Consequently in every sorrow the subject has a disposition contrary to the disposition of the subject of pleasure, for in every pleasure the appetite is viewed as accepting what it possesses, and in every sorrow, as avoiding it. And therefore on the part of the subject every pleasure is a remedy for any kind of sorrow, and every sorrow is a hindrance of all manner of pleasure; but chiefly when pleasure is opposed to sorrow specifically.

Hence the *Reply to the Third Objection* is evident.—Or we may say that although not every sorrow is specifically contrary to every pleasure, yet they are contrary to one another in regard to their effects; for one has the effect of strengthening the animal nature, while the other results in a kind of discomfort.

ARTICLE 5. *Whether There Is Any Sorrow Contrary to the Pleasure of Contemplation?*

We proceed thus to the Fifth Article: It would seem that there is a sorrow that is contrary to the pleasure of contemplation.

Objection 1. For the Apostle says (II Cor. 7. 10): *The sorrow that is according to God, worketh penance steadfast unto salvation.* Now to look at God pertains to the higher reason, whose act is to give itself to contemplation, according to Augustine (*De Trin.* xii, 3, 4).[4] Therefore there is a sorrow contrary to the pleasure of contemplation.

Obj. 2. Further, contrary things have contrary effects. If therefore the contemplation of one contrary gives pleasure, the other contrary

---

[1] Aristotle, x, 4 (1055ª3).
[2] Aristotle, *Ethics*, VII, 2 (1139ª21).
[3] Aristotle, VIII, 2 (1043ª5); cf. VI, 12 (1038ª6).
[4] PL 42, 999, 1000.

will give sorrow, and so there will be a sorrow contrary to the pleasure of contemplation.

Obj. 3. Further, as the object of pleasure is good, so the object of sorrow is evil. But contemplation can have an aspect of evil: since the Philosopher says[1] that it is unfitting to meditate of certain things. Therefore sorrow can be contrary to the pleasure of contemplation.

Obj. 4. Further, any work, so far as it is unhindered, can be a cause of pleasure, as stated in the *Ethics*.[2] But the work of contemplation can be hindered in many ways, either so as to destroy it altogether, or so as to make it difficult. Therefore in contemplation there can be a sorrow contrary to the pleasure.

Obj. 5. Further, affliction of the flesh is a cause of sorrow. But, as it is written (Eccles. 12. 12) *much study is an affliction of the flesh.* Therefore contemplation admits of sorrow contrary to its pleasure.

On the contrary, It is written (Wisd. 8. 16): *Her,* that is, wisdom's, *conversation hath no bitterness, nor her company any tediousness; but joy and gladness.* Now the conversation and company of wisdom are found in contemplation. Therefore there is no sorrow contrary to the pleasure of contemplation.

I answer that, The pleasure of contemplation can be understood in two ways. In one way, so that contemplation is the cause, but not the object of pleasure; and then pleasure is taken not in contemplating but in the thing contemplated. Now it is possible to contemplate something harmful and sorrowful, just as to contemplate something suitable and pleasant. Consequently if the pleasure of contemplation be taken in this way, nothing hinders some sorrow being contrary to the pleasure of contemplation.

In another way, the pleasure of contemplation is understood so that contemplation is its object and cause, as when one takes pleasure in the very act of contemplating. And thus, according to Gregory of Nyssa,[3] "no sorrow is contrary to that pleasure which is about contemplation"; and the Philosopher says the same.[4] This, however, is to be understood as being the case properly speaking. The reason is because sorrow is of itself contrary to pleasure in a contrary object; thus pleasure in heat is contrary to sorrow caused by cold. But there is no contrary to the object of contemplation, because contraries, as apprehended by the mind,

are not contrary, but one is the means of knowing the other. Therefore, properly speaking, there cannot be a sorrow contrary to the pleasure of contemplation. Nor has it any sorrow joined to it, as bodily pleasures have, which are like remedies against certain annoyances; thus a man takes pleasure in drinking through being troubled with thirst, but when the thirst is completely driven out, the pleasure of drinking ceases also. Because the pleasure of contemplation is not caused by one's being quit of an annoyance, but by the fact that contemplation is pleasant in itself, for pleasure is not a generation but a perfect operation, as stated above (Q. XXXI, A. 1).

Accidentally, however, sorrow is mingled with the pleasure of apprehension, and this in two ways; first, on the part of an organ, secondly, through some impediment in the apprehension. On the part of an organ, sorrow or pain is mingled with apprehension, directly, as regards the apprehensive powers of the sensitive part, which have a bodily organ;—either from the sensible object disagreeing with the normal condition of the organ, as the taste of something bitter, and the smell of something foul,—or from the sensible object, though agreeable, being so continuous in its action on the sense, that it exceeds the natural habit, as stated above (Q. XXXIII, A. 2), the result being that an apprehension which at first was pleasant becomes tedious.

But these two things cannot occur directly in the contemplation of the mind, because the mind has no corporeal organ; and so it was said in the authority quoted above (*on the contrary*) that intellectual contemplation has neither bitterness, nor tediousness. Since, however, the human mind makes use in contemplation of the sensitive powers of apprehension, to whose acts weariness is incidental, therefore some affliction or pain is indirectly mingled with contemplation.

Nevertheless, in neither of these ways is the pain thus accidentally mingled with contemplation contrary to the pleasure of contemplation. Because pain caused by a hindrance to contemplation is not contrary to the pleasure of contemplation, but rather is in affinity and in harmony with it, as is evident from what has been said above (A. 4); but pain or sorrow caused by bodily weariness does not belong to the same genus, and hence it is altogether disparate. Accordingly it is evident that no sorrow is contrary to pleasure taken in the very act of contemplation; nor is any sorrow connected with it save accidentally.

[1] *Metaphysics*, XII, 9 (1074[b]32).
[2] Aristotle, VII, 12, 13 (1153[a]14; [b]11); X, 4 (1174[b]20).
[3] Nemesius, *De Nat. Hom.*, XVIII (PG 40, 680).
[4] *Topics*, I, 13 (106[a]38); *Ethics*, X, 3 (1173[b]16).

Reply Obj. 1. The *sorrow which is according to God,* is not caused by the contemplation itself of the mind, but by something which the mind contemplates; namely, by sin, which the mind considers as contrary to the love of God.

Reply Obj. 2. Things which are contrary according to nature are not contrary according as they exist in the mind; for the notions of contraries are not contrary, but rather is one contrary the reason for knowing the other. Hence one and the same science considers contraries.

Reply Obj. 3. Contemplation, in itself, is never evil, since it is nothing else than the consideration of truth, which is the good of the intellect; it can, however, be evil accidentally, that is, in so far as the contemplation of a less noble object hinders the contemplation of a more noble object; or on the part of the object contemplated, to which the appetite is inordinately attached.

Reply Obj. 4. Sorrow caused by a hindrance to contemplation is not contrary to the pleasure of contemplation, but is in kindred to it, as stated above.

Reply Obj. 5. Affliction of the flesh affects contemplation accidentally and indirectly, as stated above.

ARTICLE 6. *Whether Sorrow Is to Be Shunned More Than Pleasure Is to Be Sought?*

We proceed thus to the Sixth Article: It seems that sorrow is to be shunned more than pleasure is to be sought.

Objection 1. For Augustine says,[1] "There is nobody that does not shun sorrow more than he seeks pleasure." Now that which all agree in doing, seems to be natural. Therefore it is natural and right for sorrow to be shunned more than pleasure is sought.

Obj. 2. Further, the action of a contrary conduces to rapidity and intensity of movement; for "hot water freezes quicker and harder."[2] But the shunning of sorrow is due to the contrariety of the cause of sorrow; the desire for pleasure however does not arise from any contrariety, but rather from the suitableness of the pleasant object. Therefore sorrow is shunned more eagerly than pleasure is sought.

Obj. 3. Further, the stronger the passion which a man resists according to reason, the more worthy is he of praise, and the more virtuous, for "virtue is concerned with the difficult and the good."[3] But the brave man who resists the movement of shunning sorrow is more virtuous than the temperate man, who resists the movement of desire for pleasure, for the Philosopher says[4] that "the brave and the just are chiefly honored." Therefore the movement of shunning sorrow is more eager than the movement of seeking pleasure.

On the contrary, Good is stronger than evil, as Dionysius declares (*Div. Nom.* iv).[5] But pleasure is desirable for the sake of the good which is its object, but the shunning of sorrow is on account of evil. Therefore the desire for pleasure is more eager than the shunning of sorrow.

I answer that, The desire for pleasure is of itself stronger than the shunning of sorrow. The reason of this is that the cause of pleasure is a suitable good, while the cause of pain or sorrow is an unsuitable evil. Now it happens that a certain good is suitable without any discordance at all, but it is not possible for any evil to be so unsuitable as not to be suitable in some way. Therefore pleasure can be entire and perfect; but sorrow is always partial. Therefore desire for pleasure is naturally greater than the shunning of sorrow. Another reason is because the good, which is the object of pleasure, is sought for its own sake, but evil, which is the object of sorrow, is to be shunned as being a privation of good. And that which is by reason of itself is stronger than that which is by reason of something else. Moreover we find a sign of this in natural movements. For every natural movement is more intense in the end, when a thing approaches the term that is suitable to its nature, than at the beginning, when it leaves the term that is unsuitable to its nature; as though nature were more eager in tending to what is suitable to it than in shunning what is contrary. Therefore the inclination of the appetitive power is, of itself, more eager in tending to pleasure than in shunning sorrow.

But it happens accidentally that a man shuns sorrow more eagerly than he seeks pleasure, and this for three reasons. First, on the part of the apprehension. Because, as Augustine says (*De Trin.* x, 12),[6] "love is felt more keenly, when we lack that which we love." Now from the lack of what we love, sorrow results, which is caused either by the loss of some loved good, or by the entrance of some contrary evil. But pleasure suffers no lack of the good loved, for it rests in possession of it. Since then love is the cause of

[1] QQ. LXXXIII, qu. 36 (PL 40, 25).
[2] *Meteorology,* I, 12 (348b36).   [3] *Ethics,* II, 3 (1105a9).
[4] *Rhetoric,* II, 4 (1381a21).
[5] Sect. 20 (PG 3, 717).
[6] PL 42, 984.

pleasure and sorrow, the latter is the more shunned according as love is the more keenly felt on account of that which is contrary to it. Secondly, on the part of the cause of sorrow or pain, which cause is contrary to a good that is more loved than the good in which we take pleasure. For we love the natural well-being of the body more than the pleasure of eating, and consequently we would leave the pleasure of eating and the like, from fear of the pain occasioned by blows or other such causes, which are contrary to the well-being of the body. Thirdly, on the part of the effect; namely, in so far as sorrow hinders not only one pleasure, but all.

Reply Obj. 1. The saying of Augustine that "sorrow is shunned more than pleasure is sought" is true accidentally but not per se. And this is clear from what he says after: "Since we see that the most savage animals are deterred from the greatest pleasures by fear of pain," which pain is contrary to life which is loved above all.

Reply Obj. 2. The case is not the same with movement from within and movement from without. For movement from within tends to what is suitable more than it recedes from that which is contrary, as we remarked above in regard to natural movement. But movement from without is intensified by the very contrariety, because each thing strives in its own way to resist anything contrary to it, as aiming at its own preservation. Hence violent movement is intense at first, and slackens towards the end. Now the movement of the appetitive part is from within, since it tends from the soul to the thing. Consequently pleasure is, of itself, more to be sought than sorrow is to be shunned. But the movement of the sensitive part is from without, as it were from things to the soul. Consequently the more contrary a thing is, the more it is felt. And then too, accidentally, in so far as the senses are required for pleasure and pain, pain is shunned more than pleasure is sought.

Reply Obj. 3. A brave man is not praised because, in accordance with reason, he is not overcome by any kind of sorrow or pain whatever, but because he is not overcome by that which is concerned with the dangers of death. And this kind of sorrow is more shunned than pleasures of the table or of sexual intercourse are sought, which latter pleasures are the object of temperance; just as life is loved more than food and sexual pleasure. But the temperate man is praised for refraining from pleasures of touch

more than for not shunning the pains which are contrary to them, as is stated in the *Ethics*.[1]

ARTICLE 7. *Whether Outward Pain Is Greater Than Interior Sorrow?*

We proceed thus to the Seventh Article: It seems that outward pain is greater than interior sorrow of the heart.

Objection 1. Because outward pain arises from a cause contrary to the well-being of the body in which is life, while interior sorrow is caused by some evil in the imagination. Since, therefore, life is loved more than an imagined good, it seems that, according to what has been said above (A. 6), outward pain is greater than interior sorrow.

Obj. 2. Further, the reality moves more than its likeness does. But outward pain arises from the real conjunction of some contrary, while inward sorrow arises from the apprehended likeness of a contrary. Therefore outward pain is greater than inward sorrow.

Obj. 3. Further, a cause is known by its effect. But outward pain has stronger effects; for man dies more easily of outward pain than of interior sorrow. Therefore outward pain is greater and is shunned more than interior sorrow.

On the contrary, It is written (Ecclus. 25. 17): *The sadness of the heart is every wound* (Douay,—*plague*), *and the wickedness of a woman is all evil.* Therefore, just as the wickedness of a woman surpasses all other wickedness, as the text implies, so sadness of the heart surpasses every outward wound.

I answer that, Interior and exterior pain agree in one point, and differ in two. They agree in this, that each is a movement of the appetitive power, as stated above (A. 1). But they differ in respect of those two things which are requisite for pain and pleasure; namely, in respect of the cause, which is a conjoined good or evil, and in respect of the apprehension. For the cause of outward pain is a conjoined evil contrary to the body, while the cause of inward pain is a conjoined evil contrary to the appetite. Again, outward pain arises from an apprehension of sense, and especially of touch, while inward pain arises from an interior apprehension, of the imagination or of the reason.

If then we compare the cause of inward pain to the cause of outward pain, the former belongs, of itself, to the appetite to which both these pains belong, while the latter belongs to the appetite indirectly. Because inward pain

[1] Aristotle, III, II (1118^{b}28).

arises from something being contrary to the appetite itself, while outward pain arises from something being contrary to the appetite, through being contrary to the body. Now, that which is of itself is always prior to that which is by reason of another. Therefore, from this point of view, inward pain surpasses outward pain. In like manner also on the part of apprehension, because the apprehension of reason and imagination is of a higher order than the apprehension of the sense of touch. Consequently inward pain is, absolutely and of itself, more keen than outward pain. A sign of this is that one willingly undergoes outward pain in order to avoid inward pain. And in so far as outward pain is not contrary to the interior appetite, it becomes in a manner pleasant and agreeable by way of inward joy.

Sometimes, however, outward pain is accompanied by inward pain, and then the pain is increased. Because inward pain is not only greater than outward pain, it is also more universal, since whatever is contrary to the body, can be contrary to the interior appetite; and whatever is apprehended by sense may be apprehended by imagination and reason, but not conversely. Hence in the passage quoted above it is said expressively: *Sadness of the heart is every wound*, because even the pains of outward wounds are comprised in the interior sorrows of the heart.

Reply Obj. 1. Inward pain can also arise from things that are contrary to life. And then the comparison of inward to outward pain must not be taken in reference to the various evils that cause pain, but in regard to the various ways in which this cause of pain is compared to the appetite.

Reply Obj. 2. Inward pain does not proceed from the apprehended likeness of a thing as from a cause; for a man is not inwardly pained by the apprehended likeness itself, but by the thing which the likeness represents. And this thing is all the more perfectly apprehended by means of its likeness as this likeness is more immaterial and abstract. Consequently inward pain is, of itself, greater, as being caused by a greater evil, because evil is better known by an inward apprehension.

Reply Obj. 3. Bodily changes are more liable to be caused by outward pain, both from the fact that outward pain is caused by a corrupting thing joined to it corporally, which is a necessary condition of the sense of touch; and from the fact that the outward sense is more material than the inward sense, just as the sensitive appetite is more material than the intellectual.

For this reason, as stated above (Q. XXII, A. 3; Q. XXXI, A. 5), the body undergoes a greater change from the movement of the sensitive appetite; and, in like manner, from outward than from inward pain.

ARTICLE 8. *Whether There Are Only Four Species of Sorrow?*

We proceed thus to the Eighth Article: It would seem that Damascene's (*De Fide Orthod.* ii, 14)[1] division of sorrow into four species is incorrect; namely, into acedia, distress, which Gregory of Nyssa[2] calls anxiety,—pity, and envy.

Objection 1. For sorrow is contrary to pleasure. But there are not several species of pleasure. Therefore it is incorrect to assign different species of sorrow.

Obj. 2. Further, repentance is a species of sorrow, and so are indignation (*nemesis*) and jealousy (*zelus*), as the Philosopher states.[3] But these are not included in the above species. Therefore this division is insufficient.

Obj. 3. Further, the members of a division should be things that are opposed to one another. But these species are not opposed to one another. For according to Gregory[4] "acedia is sorrow depriving of speech; anxiety is the sorrow that weighs down; envy is sorrow for another's good; pity is sorrow for another's evils." But it is possible for one to sorrow for another's evils, and for another's good, and at the same time to be weighed down inwardly, and outwardly to be speechless. Therefore this division is incorrect.

On the contrary stands the twofold authority of Gregory of Nyssa and of Damascene.

I answer that, It pertains to the notion of a species that it is something added to the genus. But a thing can be added to a genus in two ways. First, as something belonging of itself to the genus, and contained in it virtually; thus rational is added to animal. Such an addition makes true species of a genus, as the Philosopher says.[5] But, secondly, a thing may be added to a genus, that is, as it were, extraneous to the notion conveyed by that genus; thus white or something of the kind may be added to animal. Such an addition does not make true species of the genus, according to the usual sense in which we speak of genera and species. But sometimes a thing is said to be a species of a certain genus

[1] PG 94, 932.
[2] Nemesius,—*De Nat. Hom.*, XIX (PG 40, 688).
[3] *Rhetoric*, II, 9, 11 (1386b9; 1388a30).
[4] Cf. Nemesius, *loc. cit.* Cf. Diogenes Laertes, *De Vita et Mor. Philosoph.*, VII, 111 (DD 183); Stobaeus, *Eclogae*, II, 6.
[5] *Metaphysics*, VII, 12 (1038a5); VIII, 2 (1043a5).

through having something extraneous to that genus indeed, but to which the notion of that genus is applicable; thus a live coal or a flame is said to be a species of fire, because in each of them the nature of fire is applied to a foreign matter. In like manner we speak of astronomy and perspective as being species of mathematics, in so far as the principles of mathematics are applied to natural matter.

In accordance with this manner of speaking, the species of sorrow are assigned by an application of the notion of sorrow to something extraneous to it. This extraneous thing may be taken on the part of the cause or object, or of the effect. For the proper object of sorrow is one's own evil. Hence sorrow may be concerned for an object extraneous to it either through one's being sorry for an evil that is not one's own; and thus we have pity which is sorrow for another's evil, considered, however, as one's own;—or through one's being sorry for something that is neither evil nor one's own, but another's good, considered, however, as one's own evil; and thus we have envy. But the proper effect of sorrow consists in a certain flight of the appetite. Therefore the extraneous element in the effect of sorrow may be taken so as to affect the first part only, by excluding flight; and thus we have anxiety which weighs on the mind, so as to make escape seem impossible; hence it is also called perplexity. If, however, the mind be weighed down so much that even the limbs become motionless, which belongs to acedia, then we have the extraneous element affecting both, since there is neither flight, nor is the effect in the appetite. And the reason why acedia especially is said to deprive one of speech is because of all the external movements the voice is the best expression of the inward concept and desire, not only in men, but also in other animals, as is stated in the *Politics*.[1]

Reply Obj. 1. Pleasure is caused by good, which has only one meaning, and so pleasure is not divided into several species as sorrow is; for the latter is caused by evil, which happens in many ways, as Dionysius says (*Div. Nom.* iv).[2]

Reply Obj. 2. Repentance is for one's own evil, which is of itself the object of sorrow; therefore it does not belong to these species. Jealousy and indignation are included in envy, as we shall explain later (Part II-II, Q. XXXVI, A. 2).

Reply Obj. 3. This division is not according to opposite species, but according to the diversi-

ty of extraneous things to which the notion of sorrow is applied, as stated above.

QUESTION XXXVI
OF THE CAUSES OF SORROW OR PAIN
(*In Four Articles*)

WE must now consider the causes of sorrow, under which head there are four points of inquiry: (1) Whether sorrow is caused by the loss of a good or rather by the presence of an evil? (2) Whether desire is a cause of sorrow? (3) Whether the craving for unity is a cause of sorrow? (4) Whether an irresistible power is a cause of sorrow?

ARTICLE 1. *Whether Sorrow Is Caused by the Loss of Good or by the Presence of Evil?*

We proceed thus to the First Article: It would seem that sorrow is caused by the loss of a good rather than by the presence of an evil.

Objection 1. For Augustine says (*De viii. QQ. Dulcit.*, qu. 1)[3] that sorrow is caused by the loss of temporal goods. Therefore, in like manner, every sorrow is caused by the loss of some good.

Obj. 2. Further, it was said above (Q. XXXV, A. 4) that the sorrow, which is contrary to a pleasure has the same object as that pleasure. But the object of pleasure is good, as stated above (Q. XXIII, A. 4; Q. XXXI, A. 1; Q. XXXV, A. 3). Therefore sorrow is caused chiefly by the loss of good.

Obj. 3. Further, according to Augustine,[4] love is the cause of sorrow, as of the other emotions of the soul. But the object of love is good. Therefore pain or sorrow is felt for the loss of good rather than for an evil that is present.

On the contrary, Damascene says (*De Fide Orthod.* ii. 12)[5] that "the dreaded evil gives rise to fear, the present evil is the cause of sorrow."

I answer that, If privations, as considered by the mind, were what they are in reality, this question would seem to be of no importance. For, as stated in the First Part (Q. XIV, A. 10; Q. XLVIII, A. 3), evil is the privation of good, and privation is in reality nothing else than the lack of the contrary habit, so that, in this respect, to sorrow for the loss of good would be the same as to sorrow for the presence of evil. But sorrow is a movement of the appetite in consequence of an apprehension, and even a privation, as apprehended, has the aspect of a

---

[1] Aristotle, I, 2 (1253ª10).   [2] Sect. 30 (PG 3, 729).

[3] PL 40, 153.   [4] *City of God*, XIV, 7 (PL 41, 410).
[5] PG 94, 929; also Nemesius, *De Nat. Hom.*, XVII (PG 40, 676); cf. Q, XXV, A. 4.

being, and so it is called a being of reason. And in this way evil, being a privation, is regarded as a contrary. Accordingly, so far as the movement of the appetite is concerned, it makes a difference which of the two it regards chiefly, the present evil or the good which is lost.

Again, since the movement of the animal appetite holds the same place in the actions of the soul as natural movement in natural things, the truth of the matter is to be found by considering natural movements. For if, in natural movements, we observe those of approach and withdrawal, approach is of itself directed to something suitable to nature, while withdrawal is of itself directed to something contrary to nature; thus a heavy body, of itself, withdraws from a higher place and approaches naturally to a lower place. But if we consider the cause of both these movements, namely, gravity, then gravity itself inclines towards the lower place more than it withdraws from the higher place, since withdrawal from the latter is the reason for its downward tendency.

Accordingly, since, in the movements of the appetite, sorrow is a kind of flight or withdrawal, while pleasure is a kind of pursuit or approach, just as pleasure regards first the good possessed, as its proper object, so sorrow regards the evil that is present. On the other hand love, which is the cause of pleasure and sorrow, regards good rather than evil, and therefore, since the object is the cause of a passion, the present evil is more properly the cause of sorrow or pain than the good which is lost.

Reply Obj. 1. The loss itself of good is apprehended as an evil, just as the loss of evil is apprehended as a good, and in this sense Augustine says that pain results from the loss of temporal goods.

Reply Obj. 2. Pleasure and its contrary pain have the same object, but under contrary aspects; for if the presence of a particular thing be the object of pleasure, the absence of that same thing is the object of sorrow. Now "one contrary includes the privation of the other," as stated in the *Metaphysics*,[1] and consequently sorrow in respect of one contrary, is, in a way, directed to the same thing under a contrary aspect.

Reply Obj. 3. When many movements arise from one cause, it does not follow that they all regard chiefly that which the cause regards chiefly, but only the first of them. And each of the others regards chiefly that which is suitable to it according to its own character.

[1] Aristotle, x, 4 (1055^{b}18).

ARTICLE 2. *Whether Desire Is a Cause of Sorrow?*

We proceed thus to the Second Article: It seems that desire is not a cause of pain or sorrow.

Objection 1. Because sorrow of itself regards evil, as stated above (A. 1), while desire is a movement of the appetite towards good. Now movement towards one contrary is not a cause of the movement towards the other contrary. Therefore desire is not a cause of pain.

Obj. 2. Further, pain, according to Damascene (*De Fide Orthod.* ii),[2] is caused by something present; but the object of desire is something future. Therefore desire is not a cause of pain.

Obj. 3. Further, that which is pleasant in itself is not a cause of pain. But desire is pleasant in itself, as the Philosopher says.[3] Therefore desire is not a cause of pain or sorrow.

On the contrary, Augustine says (*Enchirid.* xxiv):[4] "When ignorance of things necessary to be done, and desire of things hurtful, found their way in, error and pain stole an entrance in their company." But ignorance is the cause of error. Therefore desire is a cause of sorrow.

I answer that, Sorrow is a movement of the animal appetite. Now, as stated above (A. 1) the appetitive movement is likened to the natural appetite, a likeness that may be assigned to a twofold cause: one, on the part of the end; the other, on the part of the principle of movement. Thus, on the part of the end, the cause of a heavy body's downward movement is the lower place, while the principle of that movement is a natural inclination resulting from gravity.

Now the cause of the appetitive movement, on the part of the end, is the object of that movement. And thus, it has been said above (A. 1) that the cause of pain or sorrow is a present evil. On the other hand, the cause, by way of principle, of that movement, is the inward inclination of the appetite, which inclination regards, first of all, the good, and in consequence, the rejection of a contrary evil. Hence the first principle of this kind of appetitive movement is love, which is the first inclination of the appetite towards the possession of good; the second principle however, is hatred, which is the first inclination of the appetite towards the avoidance of evil. But since concupiscence or desire is the first effect of love, which gives

[2] Chap. 12 (PG 94, 929).
[3] *Rhetoric*, I, 11 (1370^{b}15).   [4] PL 40, 244.

rise to the greatest pleasure, as stated above (Q. XXXII, A. 6), hence it is that Augustine often speaks of desire or concupiscence in the sense of love, as was also stated (Q. XXX, A. 2, REPLY 2); and in this sense he says that desire is the universal cause of sorrow. Sometimes, however, desire taken in its proper sense, is the cause of sorrow. Because whatever hinders a movement from reaching its end is contrary to that movement. Now that which is contrary to the movement of the appetite is a cause of sorrow. Consequently, desire becomes a cause of sorrow in so far as we sorrow for the delay of a desired good, or for its entire removal. But it cannot be a universal cause of sorrow, since we sorrow more for the loss of present good, in which we have already taken pleasure, than for the withdrawal of future good which we desire to have.

Reply Obj. 1. The inclination of the appetite to the possession of good causes the inclination of the appetite to fly from evil, as stated above. And hence it is that the appetitive movements that regard good are reckoned as causing the appetitive movements that regard evil.

Reply Obj. 2. That which is desired, though really future, is, nevertheless, in a way present, in so far as it is hoped for. Or we may say that although the desired good itself is future, yet the hindrance is held as present, and so gives rise to sorrow.

Reply Obj. 3. Desire gives pleasure, so long as there is a hope of obtaining that which is desired. But, when hope is removed through the presence of an obstacle, desire causes sorrow.

ARTICLE 3. *Whether the Craving for Unity Is a Cause of Sorrow?*

We proceed thus to the Third Article: It would seem that the craving for unity is not a cause of sorrow.

Objection 1. For the Philosopher says[1] that "this opinion, which held repletion to be the cause of pleasure, and division[2] the cause of sorrow, seems to have originated in pains and pleasures connected with food." But not every pleasure or sorrow is of this kind. Therefore the craving for unity is not the universal cause of sorrow, since repletion pertains to unity, and division is the cause of multitude.

Obj. 2. Further, every separation is opposed to unity. If therefore sorrow were caused by a craving for unity, no separation would be pleasant; and this is clearly untrue as regards the separation of whatever is superfluous.

Obj. 3. Further, for the same reason we desire the conjunction of good and the removal of evil. But as conjunction regards unity, since it is a kind of union, so separation is contrary to unity. Therefore the craving for unity rather than the craving for separation, should not be held as the cause of sorrow.

On the contrary, Augustine says (*De Lib. Arb.* iii, 23),[3] that "from the pain that dumb animals feel, it is quite evident how their souls desire unity, in ruling and quickening their bodies. For what else is pain but a feeling of impatience of division or corruption?"

I answer that, In the same way that the desire or craving for good is considered as a cause of sorrow, so must a craving for unity and love be accounted as causing sorrow. Because the good of each thing consists in a certain unity, according as, that is, each thing has, united in itself, the elements of which its perfection consists; hence the Platonists held that one is a principle, just as good is.[4] And so everything naturally desires unity, just as it desires goodness, and therefore, just as love or desire for good is a cause of sorrow, so also is the love or craving for unity.

Reply Obj. 1. Not every kind of union causes perfect goodness, but only that on which the perfect being of a thing depends. Hence neither does the desire of any kind of unity cause pain or sorrow, as some have maintained, whose opinion is rejected by the Philosopher,[5] from the fact that repletion is not always pleasant; for instance, when a man has eaten to repletion, he takes no further pleasure in eating, for repletion or union of this kind is contrary to rather than conducive to perfect being. Consequently sorrow is caused by the craving, not for any kind of unity, but for that unity in which the perfection of nature consists.

Reply Obj. 2. Separation can be pleasant either because it removes something contrary to a thing's perfection, or because it has some union connected with it, such as union of the sensible to the sense.

Reply Obj. 3. Separation from things hurtful and corrupting is desired in so far as they destroy the unity which is due. Therefore the desire for a such separation is not the first

---

[1] *Ethics,* x, 3 (1173^{b}12); cf. Plato, *Philebus* (31; 32; 42).

[2] Aristotle wrote ἔνδειαν, want; St. Thomas, in the Latin version, read *incisionem* (for *indigentiam?*)

[3] PL 32, 1305.

[4] Proclus, *Inst. Theol.,* prop. XII (DD LV); prop. XIII (DD LV).   [5] *Ethics,* x, 3 (1173^{b}14).

cause of sorrow, but rather the craving for unity.

ARTICLE 4. *Whether an Irresistible Power Is a Cause of Sorrow?*

We proceed thus to the Fourth Article: It would seem that a greater power should not be accounted a cause of sorrow.

Objection 1. For that which is in the power of the agent is not present but future. But sorrow is for present evil. Therefore a greater power is not a cause of sorrow.

Obj. 2. Further, hurt inflicted is the cause of sorrow. But hurt can be inflicted even by a lesser power. Therefore a greater power should not be reckoned as a cause of sorrow.

Obj. 3. Further, the interior inclinations of the soul are the causes of the movements of appetite. But a greater power is something external. Therefore it should not be put as a cause of sorrow.

On the contrary, Augustine says (*De Nat. Boni,* xx):[1] "Sorrow in the soul is caused by the will resisting a stronger power, while pain in the body is caused by sense resisting a stronger body."

I answer that, As stated above (A. 1), a present evil, is cause of sorrow or pain, by way of object. Therefore that which is the cause of the evil being present, should be accounted as the cause of pain or sorrow. Now it is evident that it is contrary to the inclination of the appetite to be united with a present evil; and whatever is contrary to a thing's inclination does not happen to it save by the action of something stronger. Therefore Augustine accounts a greater power as being the cause of sorrow.

But it must be noted that if the stronger power goes so far as to transform the contrary inclination into its own inclination, there will be no longer opposition or violence; thus if a stronger agent, by its action on a heavy body, deprives it of its downward tendency, its consequent upward tendency is not violent but natural to it.

Accordingly if some greater power prevail so far as to take away from the will or the sensitive appetite their respective inclinations, pain or sorrow will not result from it; such is the result only when the contrary inclination of the appetite remains. And hence Augustine says (*loc. cit.*) that "sorrow is caused by the will resisting a stronger power," for were it not to resist, but to yield by consenting, the result would be not sorrow but pleasure.

[1] PL 42, 557.

Reply Obj. 1. A greater power causes sorrow, as acting not potentially but actually, that is, by causing the actual presence of the corruptive evil.

Reply Obj. 2. Nothing hinders a power which is not greater absolutely, from being greater in some respect; and accordingly it is able to inflict some harm. But if it be in no way stronger it can do no harm at all; hence it cannot bring about that which causes sorrow.

Reply Obj. 3. External agents can be the causes of appetitive movements in so far as they cause the presence of the object; and it is thus that a greater power is considered to be the cause of sorrow.

QUESTION XXXVII

OF THE EFFECTS OF PAIN OR SORROW

(*In Four Articles*)

WE must now consider the effects of pain or sorrow, under which head there are four points of inquiry: (1) Whether pain deprives one of the power to learn? (2) Whether the effect of sorrow or pain is to burden the soul? (3) Whether sorrow or pain weakens all activity? (4) Whether sorrow is more harmful to the body than all the other passions of the soul?

ARTICLE 1. *Whether Pain Deprives One of the Power to Learn?*

We proceed thus to the First Article: It seems that pain does not deprive one of the power to learn.

Objection 1. For it is written (Isa. 26. 9): *When Thou shalt do Thy judgments on the earth, the inhabitants of the world shall learn justice;* and further on (*verse* 16): *In the tribulation of murmuring Thy instruction was with them.* But the judgments of God and tribulation cause sorrow in men's hearts. Therefore pain or sorrow, far from destroying, increases the power of learning.

Obj. 2. Further, it is written (Isa. 28. 9): *Whom shall He teach knowledge? And whom shall He make to understand the hearing? Them that are weaned from the milk, that are drawn away from the breasts,* that is, from pleasures. But pain and sorrow are most destructive of pleasure; since sorrow hinders all pleasure, as stated in the *Ethics*[2]; and (Ecclus. 11. 29) it is stated that the *affliction of an hour maketh one forget great delights.* Therefore pain, instead of taking away, increases the power of learning.

[2] Aristotle, VII, 14 (1154ᵃ18; ᵇ6); cf. x, 5 (1175ᵇ24).

Obj. 3. Further, inward sorrow surpasses outward pain, as stated above (Q. XXXV, A. 7). But man can learn while sorrowful. Much more, therefore, can he learn while in bodily pain.

On the contrary, Augustine says (*Soliloq.* i, 12):[1] "Although during those days I was tormented with a violent tooth-ache,—I was not able to turn over in my mind other things than those I had already learnt; and as to learning anything, I was quite unequal to it, because it required undivided attention."

I answer that, Since all the powers of the soul are rooted in the one essence of the soul, it is necessary that, when the intention of the soul is strongly drawn towards the action of one power, it is withdrawn from the action of another power, because the soul, being one, can only have one intention. The result is that if one thing draws upon itself the entire intention of the soul, or a great portion thereof, anything else requiring considerable attention is incompatible with it.

Now it is evident that sensible pain above all draws the soul's intention to itself, because it is natural for each thing to tend wholly to repel whatever is contrary to it, as may be observed even in natural things. It is likewise evident that in order to learn anything new, we require study and effort with a strong intention, as is clearly stated in Prov. 2. 4, 5: *If thou shalt seek* wisdom *as money, and shalt dig for her as for a treasure, then shalt thou understand learning* (Vulg.,—*the fear of the Lord*). Consequently if the pain be acute, man is prevented at the time from learning anything; indeed it can be so acute, that, as long as it lasts, a man is unable to give his attention even to that which he knew already. However a difference is to be observed according to the difference of love that a man has for learning or for considering, because the greater his love, the more will he retain the intention of his mind so as to prevent it from turning entirely to the pain.

Reply Obj. 1. Moderate sorrow, that does not cause the mind to wander, can conduce to the acquisition of learning, especially in regard to those things by which a man hopes to be freed from sorrow. And thus, *in the tribulation of murmuring,* men are more apt to be taught of God.

Reply Obj. 2. Both pleasure and pain, in so far as they draw upon themselves the soul's intention, hinder the reason from the act of consideration, and so it is stated in the *Ethics*[2] that "in the moment of sexual pleasure, a man cannot understand anything." Nevertheless pain at-

tracts the soul's intention more than pleasure does. Thus we observe in natural things that the action of a natural body is more intense in regard to its contrary; for instance, hot water is more accessible to the action of cold, and in consequence freezes harder. If therefore pain or sorrow be moderate, it can conduce accidentally to the facility of learning, in so far as it takes away an excess of pleasure. But, of itself, it is a hindrance, and if it is intense, it prevents it altogether.

Reply Obj. 3. External pain arises from hurt done to the body, so that it involves bodily change more than inward sorrow does. And yet the latter is greater in regard to the formal element of pain, which belongs to the soul. Consequently bodily pain is a greater hindrance to contemplation which requires complete repose, than inward sorrow is. Nevertheless if inward sorrow be very intense, it attracts the intention, so that man is unable to learn anything new: therefore on account of sorrow Gregory interrupted his commentary on Ezechiel (*Hom.* x *in Ezechiel*).[3]

ARTICLE 2. *Whether the Effect of Sorrow or Pain Is to Burden the Soul?*

We proceed thus to the Second Article: It would seem that it is not an effect of sorrow to burden the soul.

Objection 1. For the Apostle says (II Cor. 7. 11): *Behold this self-same thing, that you were made sorrowful according to God, how great carefulness it worketh in you: yea defence, yea indignation,* etc. Now carefulness and indignation (*indignatio*) imply that the soul is uplifted, which is contrary to being depressed. Therefore depression is not an effect of sorrow.

Obj. 2. Further, sorrow is contrary to pleasure. But the effect of pleasure is expansion, the opposite of which is not depression but contraction. Therefore depression should not be accounted as an effect of sorrow.

Obj. 3. Further, sorrow consumes those who are afflicted with it, as may be gathered from the words of the Apostle (II Cor. 2. 7): *Lest perhaps such an one be swallowed up with overmuch sorrow.* But that which is depressed is not consumed; rather, it is weighed down by something heavy, while that which is consumed enters within the consumer. Therefore depression should not be put as an effect of sorrow.

On the contrary, Gregory of Nyssa[4] and Dam-

---

[1] PL 32, 880.   [2] Aristotle, VII, 11 (1152[b]16).

[3] PL 76, 1072.

[4] Nemesius, *De Nat. Hom.,* XIX (PG 40, 688); cf. Q. XXXV, A. 8, Reply 3.

ascene (*De Fide Orthod.* ii, 14)[1] speak of "depressing sorrow."

I answer that, The effects of the soul's passions are sometimes named metaphorically from a likeness to sensible bodies, for the reason that the movements of the animal appetite are like the inclinations of the natural appetite. And in this way fervour is ascribed to love, expansion to pleasure, and depression to sorrow. For a man is said to be depressed through being hindered in his own movement by some weight. Now it is evident from what has been said above (Q. XXIII, A. 4; Q. XXV, A. 4; Q. XXXVI, A. 1) that sorrow is caused by a present evil; and this evil, from the very fact that it is contrary to the movement of the will, depresses the soul, since it hinders it from enjoying that which it wishes to enjoy. And if the evil which is the cause of sorrow be not so strong as to deprive one of the hope of avoiding it, although the soul be depressed in so far as, for the present, it fails to grasp that which it craves for, yet it retains the movement for repelling that evil. If, on the other hand, the strength of the evil be such as to exclude the hope of evasion, then even the interior movement of the afflicted soul is absolutely hindered, so that it cannot turn aside either this way or that. Sometimes even the external movement of the body is paralyzed, so that a man becomes completely stupefied.

Reply Obj. 1. That uplifting of the soul ensues from the sorrow which is according to God, because it brings with it the hope of the forgiveness of sin.

Reply Obj. 2. As far as the movement of the appetite is concerned, contraction and depression amount to the same, because the soul, through being depressed so as to be unable to attend freely to outward things, withdraws to itself, closing itself up as it were.

Reply Obj. 3. Sorrow is said to consume man when the force of the afflicting evil is such as to shut out all hope of evasion; and thus also it both depresses and consumes at the same time. For certain things, taken metaphorically, imply one another, which taken literally, appear to exclude one another.

ARTICLE 3. *Whether Sorrow or Pain Weakens All Activity?*

We proceed thus to the Third Article: It seems that sorrow does not weaken all activity.

Objection 1. Because carefulness is caused by sorrow, as is clear from the passage of the Apos-

[1] PG 94, 932.

tle quoted above (A. 2, obj. 1). But carefulness conduces to good work; and so the Apostle says (II Tim. 2. 15): *Carefully study to present thyself . . . a workman that needeth not to be ashamed.* Therefore sorrow is not a hindrance to work, but rather helps one to work well.

Obj. 2. Further, sorrow causes concupiscence in many cases, as stated in the *Ethics.*[2] But concupiscence causes intensity of action. Therefore sorrow does too.

Obj. 3. Further, as some actions are proper to the joyful, so are others proper to the sorrowful; for instance, to mourn. Now a thing is improved by that which is suitable to it. Therefore certain actions are not hindered but improved by reason of sorrow.

On the contrary, The Philosopher says[3] that "pleasure perfects action," while on the other hand, "sorrow hinders it."

I answer that, As stated above (A. 2), sorrow at times does not depress or consume the soul so as to shut out all movement, internal or external; but certain movements are sometimes caused by sorrow itself. Accordingly action stands in a twofold relation to sorrow. First, as being the object of sorrow; and thus sorrow hinders any action, for we never do that which we do with sorrow so well as that which we do with pleasure, or without sorrow. The reason for this is that the will is the cause of human actions, and consequently when we do something that gives pain, the action must of necessity be weakened in consequence. Secondly, action stands in relation to sorrow, as to its principle and cause; and such action must be improved by sorrow. Thus the more one sorrows on account of a certain thing, the more one strives to shake off sorrow, provided there is a hope of shaking it off; otherwise no movement or action would result from that sorrow.

From what has been said *the replies to the objections* are evident.

ARTICLE 4. *Whether Sorrow Is More Harmful to the Body Than the Other Passions of the Soul?*

We proceed thus to the Fourth Article: It would seem that sorrow is not most harmful to the body.

Objection 1. For sorrow has a spiritual being in the soul. But those things which have only a spiritual being do not cause a change in the body, as is evident with regard to the intentions of colours, which images are in the air and do

[2] Aristotle, VII, 14 (1154[b]11).

[3] *Ethics,* X, 4, 5 (1174[b]23; 1175[b]17).

not give colour to bodies. Therefore sorrow is not harmful to the body.

Obj. 2. Further if it be harmful to the body, this can only be due to its having a bodily change joined to it. But bodily change takes place in all the passions of the soul, as stated above (Q. XXII, AA. I, 3). Therefore sorrow is not more harmful to the body than the other passions of the soul.

Obj. 3. Further, the Philosopher says[1] that "anger and concupiscence drive some to madness," which seems to be a very great harm, since reason is the most excellent thing in man. Moreover despair seems to be more harmful than sorrow, for it is the cause of sorrow. Therefore sorrow is not more harmful to the body than the other passions of the soul.

On the contrary, It is written (Prov. 17. 22): *A joyful mind maketh age flourishing: a sorrowful spirit drieth up the bones;* and (*ibid.* 25. 20): *As a moth doth by a garment, and a worm by the wood; so the sadness of a man consumeth the heart;* and (Ecclus. 38. 19): *Of sadness cometh death.*

I answer that, Of all the soul's passions, sorrow is most harmful to the body. The reason of this is because sorrow is contrary to man's life in respect of the species of its movement, and not merely in respect of its measure or quantity, as is the case with the other passions of the soul. For man's life consists in a certain movement, which flows from the heart to the other parts of the body; and this movement is befitting to human nature according to a certain fixed measure. Consequently if this movement goes beyond the right measure, it will be contrary to man's life in respect of the measure of quantity, but not in respect of its specific character. But if this movement be hindered in its progress, it will be contrary to life in respect of its species.

Now it must be noted that, in all the passions of the soul, the bodily change which is their material element, is in conformity with and in proportion to the appetitive movement, which is the formal element, just as in every thing matter is proportionate to form. Consequently those passions of the soul that imply a movement of the appetite in pursuit of something, are not contrary to the vital movement as regards its species, but they may be contrary to it as regards its measure; such are love, joy, desire and the like. Therefore these passions conduce to the well-being of the body, though, if they be excessive, they may be harmful to it. On the

other hand, those passions which denote in the appetite a movement of flight or contraction, are contrary to the vital movement not only as regards its measure, but also as regards its species and therefore they are harmful absolutely; such are fear and despair, and above all, sorrow which depresses the soul by reason of a present evil, which makes a stronger impression than future evil.

Reply Obj. I. Since the soul naturally moves the body, the spiritual movement of the soul is naturally the cause of bodily change. Nor is there any parallel with spiritual intentions, because they are not naturally ordained to move such other bodies as are not naturally moved by the soul.

Reply Obj. 2. Other passions imply a bodily change which is specifically in conformity with the vital movement; but sorrow implies a change that is contrary to it, as stated above.

Reply Obj. 3. A lesser cause suffices to hinder the use of reason than to destroy life, since we observe that many ailments deprive one of the use of reason before depriving one of life. Nevertheless fear and anger cause very great harm to the body, by reason of the sorrow which they imply, and which arises from the absence of the thing desired. Moreover sorrow too sometimes deprives man of the use of reason, as may be seen in those who through sorrow become a prey to melancholy or madness.

QUESTION XXXVIII
OF THE REMEDIES OF SORROW OR PAIN
(*In Five Articles*)

WE must now consider the remedies of pain or sorrow, under which head there are five points of inquiry: (1) Whether pain or sorrow is assuaged by every pleasure? (2) Whether it is assuaged by weeping? (3) Whether it is assuaged by the sympathy of friends? (4) Whether it is assuaged by contemplating the truth? (5) Whether it is assuaged by sleep and baths?

ARTICLE I. *Whether Pain or Sorrow Is Assuaged by Every Pleasure?*

We proceed thus to the First Article: It seems that not every pleasure assuages every pain or sorrow.

Objection I. For pleasure does not assuage sorrow, except in so far as it is contrary to it; for "remedies work by contraries."[2] But not every pleasure is contrary to every sorrow, as stat-

[1] *Ethics,* VII, 3 (1147[a]15).

[2] *Ibid.,* II, 3 (1104[b]17).

ed above (Q. XXXV, A. 4). Therefore not every pleasure assuages every sorrow.

Obj. 2. Further, that which causes sorrow does not assuage it. But some pleasures cause sorrow, since, as stated in the *Ethics*,[1] "the wicked man feels pain at having been pleased." Therefore not every pleasure assuages sorrow.

Obj. 3. Further, Augustine says[2] that he fled from his country, where he had been accustomed to associate with his friend, now dead; "for so should his eyes look for him less, where they were not wont to see him." Hence we may gather that those things which united us to our dead or absent friends become burdensome to us when we mourn their death or absence. But nothing united us more than the pleasures we enjoyed in common. Therefore these very pleasures become burdensome to us when we mourn. Therefore not every pleasure assuages every sorrow.

On the contrary, The Philosopher says[3] that "sorrow is driven forth by pleasure, both by a contrary pleasure and by any other, provided it be intense."

I answer that, As is evident from what has been said above (Q. XXIII, A. 4; Q. XXXI, A. 1, Reply 2), pleasure is a kind of repose of the appetite in a suitable good, while sorrow arises from something unsuited to the appetite. Consequently in movements of the appetite pleasure is to sorrow, what, in bodies, repose is to weariness, which is due to a non-natural change; for sorrow itself denotes a certain weariness or ailing of the appetitive power. Therefore just as all repose of the body brings relief to any kind of weariness, ensuing from any non-natural cause, so every pleasure brings relief by assuaging any kind of sorrow, due to any cause whatever.

Reply Obj. 1. Although not every pleasure is specifically contrary to every sorrow, yet it is generically, as stated above (Q. XXXV, A. 4). And consequently, on the part of the disposition of the subject, any sorrow can be assuaged by any pleasure.

Reply Obj. 2. The pleasures of wicked men are not a cause of sorrow while they are enjoyed, but afterwards; that is to say, in so far as wicked men repent of those things in which they took pleasure. This sorrow is healed by contrary pleasures.

Reply Obj. 3. When there are two causes inclining to contrary movements, each hinders the other, yet the one which is stronger and more persistent prevails in the end. Now when a man is made sorrowful by those things in which he took pleasure in common with a deceased or absent friend, there are two causes producing contrary movements. For the thought of the friend's death or absence, inclines him to sorrow, while the present good inclines him to pleasure. Consequently each is modified by the other. And yet since the perception of the present moves more strongly than the memory of the past, and since love of self is more persistent than love of another, hence it is that, in the end, the pleasure drives out the sorrow. Therefore a little further on Augustine says that his "sorrows gave way to his former pleasures."[4]

ARTICLE 2. *Whether Pain or Sorrow Is Assuaged by Tears?*

We proceed thus to the Second Article: It would seem that tears do not assuage sorrow.

Objection 1. Because no effect diminishes its cause. But tears or groans are an effect of sorrow. Therefore they do not diminish sorrow.

Obj. 2. Further, just as tears or groans are an effect of sorrow, so laughter is an effect of joy. But laughter does not lessen joy. Therefore tears do not lessen sorrow.

Obj. 3. Further, when we weep, the evil that saddens us is present to the imagination. But the image of that which saddens us increases sorrow, just as the image of a pleasant thing adds to joy. Therefore it seems that tears do not assuage sorrow.

On the contrary, Augustine says that when he mourned the death of his friend, "in groans and in tears alone did he find some little refreshment."[5]

I answer that, Tears and groans naturally assuage sorrow, and this for two reasons. First, because a hurtful thing hurts yet more if we keep it shut up, because the soul is more intent on it; but if it be allowed to escape, the soul's intention is dispersed as it were on outward things, so that the inward sorrow is lessened. This is why when men, burdened with sorrow, make outward show of their sorrow, by tears or groans or even by words, their sorrow is assuaged. Secondly, because an action that befits a man according to his actual disposition is always pleasant to him. Now tears and groans are actions befitting a man who is in sorrow or pain, and consequently they become pleasant to him. Since then, as stated above (A. 1), every pleasure assuages sorrow or pain somewhat, it follows

---

[1] Aristotle, IX, 4 (1166[b]23).
[2] *Confessions*, IV, 12 (PL 32, 698).
[3] *Ethics*, VII, 14 (1154[b]13).

[4] *Confessions*, IV, 13 (PL 32, 698).
[5] *Ibid.*, 12 (PL 32, 698).

that sorrow is assuaged by lamentations and groans.

Reply Obj. 1. The very relation of cause to effect is contrary to the relation between the sorrowing man and his sorrow, for every effect agrees with its cause, and consequently is pleasant to it; but the cause of sorrow is disagreeable to him that sorrows. Consequently the relation of the cause of sorrow to the sorrowful is contrary to the relation of sorrow to its cause, so that sorrow is assuaged by its effect, on account of this contrariety.

Reply Obj. 2. The relation of effect to cause is like the relation of the object of pleasure to him that takes pleasure in it, because in each case the one agrees with the other. Now every like thing increases its like. Therefore joy is increased by laughter and the other effects of joy; unless they be excessive, in which case, accidentally, they lessen it.

Reply Obj. 3. The image of that which saddens us, considered in itself, has a natural tendency to increase sorrow; yet from the very fact that a man imagines himself to be doing that which is fitting according to his actual state, he feels a certain amount of pleasure. For the same reason if laughter escapes a man when he is so disposed that he thinks he ought to weep, he is sorry for it, as having done something unbecoming to him, as Tully says (*Tusc. Quæst.* iii, 27).[1]

ARTICLE 3. *Whether Pain and Sorrow Are Assuaged by the Sympathy of Friends?*

We proceed thus to the Third Article: It seems that the sorrow of sympathizing friends does not assuage our own sorrow.

Objection 1. For contraries have contrary effects. Now as Augustine says,[2] "when many rejoice together, each one has more exuberant joy, for they are kindled and inflamed one by the other." Therefore, in like manner when many are sorrowful it seems that their sorrow is greater.

Obj. 2. Further, friendship demands mutual love, as Augustine declares.[3] But a sympathizing friend is pained at the sorrow of his friend with whom he sympathizes. Consequently the pain of a sympathizing friend becomes, to the friend in sorrow, a further cause of sorrow, so that his pain being doubled his sorrow seems to increase.

Obj. 3. Further, sorrow arises from every evil affecting a friend, as though it affected one-self since "a friend is one's other self."[4] But sorrow is an evil. Therefore the sorrow of the sympathizing friend increases the sorrow of the friend with whom he sympathizes.

On the contrary, The Philosopher says that "those who are in pain are consoled when their friends sympathize with them."[5]

I answer that, When one is in pain, it is natural that the sympathy of a friend should afford consolation. The Philosopher indicates a twofold reason for this.[6] The first is because, since sorrow has a depressing effect, it is like a weight of which we strive to unburden ourselves, so that when a man sees others saddened by his own sorrow, it seems as though others were bearing the burden with him, striving, as it were, to lessen its weight; and so the load of sorrow becomes lighter for him, just as also occurs in the carrying of bodily burdens. The second and better reason is because when a man's friends condole with him, he sees that he is loved by them, and this affords him pleasure, as stated above (Q. XXXII, A. 5). Consequently, since every pleasure assuages sorrow, as stated above (A. 1), it follows that sorrow is mitigated by a sympathizing friend.

Reply Obj. 1. In either case there is a proof of friendship, namely, when a man rejoices with the joyful, and when he sorrows with the sorrowful. Consequently each becomes an object of pleasure by reason of its cause.

Reply Obj. 2. The friend's sorrow itself would be a cause of sorrow; but consideration of its cause, namely, his love, gives rise rather to pleasure.

And this suffices for the *reply to the Third Objection.*

ARTICLE 4. *Whether Pain and Sorrow Are Assuaged by the Contemplation of Truth?*

We proceed thus to the Fourth Article: It seems that the contemplation of truth does not assuage sorrow.

Objection 1. For it is written (Eccles. 1 18): *He that addeth knowledge addeth also sorrow* (Vulg.,—*labour*). But knowledge pertains to the contemplation of truth. Therefore the contemplation of truth does not assuage sorrow.

Obj. 2. Further, the contemplation of truth belongs to the speculative intellect. But the speculative intellect does not move, as stated in the book on the *Soul.*[7] Therefore, since joy and sorrow are movements of the soul, it seems that

---

[1] DD IV, 18.
[2] *Confessions,* VIII, 9 (PL 32, 752).
[3] *Ibid.,* IV, 14 (PL 32, 699).

[4] Aristotle. *Ethics,* IX, 4 (1166[a]31).
[5] *Ibid.,* IX, 11 (1171[a]20).   [6] *Ibid.*
[7] Aristotle, III, 9 (432[b]27). Cf. III, 10 (433[a]13).

the contemplation of truth does not help to assuage sorrow.

Obj. 3. Further, the remedy for an ailment should be applied to the part which ails. But contemplation of truth is in the intellect. Therefore it does not assuage bodily pain which is in the senses.

On the contrary, Augustine says (*Soliloq.* 1, 12):[1] "It seemed to me that if the light of that truth were to dawn on our minds, either I should not feel that pain, or at least that the pain would seem nothing to me."

I answer that, As stated above (Q. III, A. 5), the greatest of all pleasures consists in the contemplation of truth. Now every pleasure assuages pain as stated above (A. 1). Hence the contemplation of truth assuages pain or sorrow, and the more so the more perfectly one is a lover of wisdom. And therefore in the midst of tribulations men rejoice in the contemplation of Divine things and of future Happiness, according to James 1. 2: *My brethren, count it all joy, when you shall fall into divers temptations;* and, what is more, even in the midst of bodily tortures this joy is found as "the martyr Tiburtius, when he was walking barefoot on the burning coals, said: Methinks, I walk on roses, in the name of Jesus Christ."[2]

Reply Obj. 1. *He that addeth knowledge, addeth sorrow,* either on account of the difficulty and disappointment in the search of truth, or because knowledge makes man acquainted with many things that are contrary to his will. Accordingly, on the part of the things known knowledge causes sorrow, but on the part of the contemplation of truth it causes pleasure.

Reply Obj. 2. The speculative intellect does not move the mind on the part of the thing contemplated, but on the part of contemplation itself, which is man's good and naturally pleasant to him.

Reply Obj. 3. In the powers of the soul there is an overflow from the higher to the lower powers; and accordingly, the pleasure of contemplation, which is in the higher part, overflows so as to mitigate even that pain which is in the senses.

ARTICLE 5. *Whether Pain and Sorrow Are Assuaged by Sleep and Baths?*

We proceed thus to the Fifth Article: It would seem that sleep and baths do not assuage sorrow.

Objection 1. For sorrow is in the soul, while sleep and baths regard the body. Therefore they do not conduce to the assuaging of sorrow.

Obj. 2. Further, the same effect does not seem to follow from contrary causes. But these, being bodily things, are incompatible with the contemplation of truth which is a cause of the assuaging of sorrow, as stated above (A. 4). Therefore sorrow is not mitigated by the like.

Obj. 3. Further, sorrow and pain, in so far as they affect the body, denote a certain change of the heart. But such remedies as these seem to pertain to the outward senses and limbs, rather than to the interior disposition of the heart. Therefore they do not assuage sorrow.

On the contrary, Augustine says:[3] "I had heard that the bath had its name[4] . . . from the fact of its driving sadness from the mind." And further on, he says: "I slept, and woke up again, and found my grief not a little assuaged," and quotes the words from the hymn of Ambrose in which it is said that "Sleep restores the tired limbs to labour, refreshes the weary mind, and banishes sorrow."[5]

I answer that, As stated above (Q. XXXVII, A. 4), sorrow, by reason of its specific nature, is contrary to the vital movement of the body; and consequently whatever restores the bodily nature to its due state of vital movement, is opposed to sorrow and assuages it. Moreover such remedies, from the very fact that they bring nature back to its normal state, are causes of pleasure, for this is precisely in what pleasure consists, as stated above (Q. XXXI, A. 1). Therefore, since every pleasure assuages sorrow, sorrow is assuaged by such bodily remedies.

Reply Obj. 1. The normal disposition of the body, so far as it is felt, is itself a cause of pleasure, and consequently assuages sorrow.

Reply Obj. 2. As stated above (Q. XXXI, A. 8), one pleasure hinders another, and yet every pleasure assuages sorrow. Consequently it is not unreasonable that sorrow should be assuaged by causes which hinder one another.

Reply Obj. 3. Every good disposition of the body reacts somewhat on the heart, which is the beginning and end of bodily movements, as stated in the treatise *Motion of Animals.*[6]

---

[1] PL 32, 880.

[2] Dominican Breviary, August 11th, commemoration of S. Tiburtius.

[3] *Confessions,* IX, 32 (PL 32, 777).

[4] *Balneum,* from the Greek βαλανεῖον.

[5] Hymn II *Deus Creator Omnium* (PL 16, 1473).

[6] Aristotle, 11 (703[b]23).

QUESTION XXXIX

Of the goodness and malice of sorrow or pain

(*In Four Articles*)

We must now consider the goodness and malice of pain or sorrow, under which head there are four points of inquiry: (1) Whether all sorrow is evil? (2) Whether sorrow can be a virtuous good? (3) Whether it can be a useful good? (4) Whether bodily pain is the greatest evil?

Article 1. *Whether All Sorrow Is Evil?*

We proceed thus to the First Article: It seems that all sorrow is evil.

Objection 1. For Gregory of Nyssa (Nemesius, *De Nat. Hom.* xix)[1] says: "All sorrow is evil, from its very nature." Now what is naturally evil, is evil always and everywhere. Therefore all sorrow is evil.

Obj. 2. Further, That which all, even the virtuous, avoid, is evil. But all avoid sorrow, even the virtuous, since as stated in the *Ethics*,[2] "though the prudent man does not aim at pleasure, yet he aims at avoiding sorrow." Therefore sorrow is evil.

Obj. 3. Further, Just as bodily evil is the object and cause of bodily pain, so spiritual evil is the object and cause of spiritual sorrow. But every bodily pain is a bodily evil. Therefore every sorrow of the soul is an evil of the soul.

On the contrary, Sorrow for evil is contrary to pleasure in evil. But pleasure in evil is evil; hence, in condemnation of certain men, it is written (Prov. 2. 14), that *they are glad when they have done evil.* Therefore sorrow for evil is good.

I answer that, A thing may be good or evil in two ways: first considered absolutely and in itself; and thus all sorrow is an evil, because the mere fact of a man's appetite being uneasy about a present evil is itself an evil, because it hinders the repose of the appetite in good. Secondly, a thing is said to be good or evil on the supposition of something else; thus shame is said to be good, on the supposition of a shameful deed done, as stated in the *Ethics*.[3] Accordingly, supposing the presence of something saddening or painful, it is a sign of goodness if a man is in sorrow or pain on account of this present evil. For if he were not to be in sorrow or pain, this could only be either because he

does not feel it, or because he does not consider it as something unbecoming, both of which are manifest evils. Consequently it pertains to goodness, that, supposing an evil to be present, sorrow or pain should ensue. Therefore Augustine says (*Gen. ad lit.* viii, 14)[4] "It is also a good thing that he sorrows for the good he has lost; for had not some good remained in his nature, he could not be punished by the loss of good." Because, however, in the science of Morals, we consider things individually,—for actions are concerned about individuals,—that which is good on some supposition should be considered as good; just as that which is voluntary on some supposition, is judged to be voluntary, as stated in the *Ethics*,[5] and likewise above (Q. VI, A. 6).

Reply Obj. 1. Gregory of Nyssa (Nemisius) is speaking of sorrow on the part of the evil that causes it, but not on the part of the subject that feels and rejects the evil. And from this point of view all shun sorrow, since they shun evil; but they do not shun the perception and rejection of evil. The same also applies to bodily pain, because the perception and rejection of bodily evil is the proof of the goodness of nature.

This suffices for the *replies to the second and third objections.*

Article 2. *Whether Sorrow Can Be a Virtuous Good?*

We proceed thus to the Second Article: It seems that sorrow is not a virtuous good.

Objection 1. For that which leads to hell is not a virtuous good. But, as Augustine says (*Gen. ad lit.* xii, 33),[6] "Jacob seems to have feared lest he should be troubled overmuch by sorrow, and so, instead of entering into the rest of the blessed, be consigned to the hell of sinners." Therefore sorrow is not a virtuous good.

Obj. 2. Further, The virtuous good is praiseworthy and meritorious. But sorrow lessens praise or merit; for the Apostle says (II Cor. 9. 7): *Everyone, as he hath determined in his heart, not with sadness, or of necessity.* Therefore sorrow is not a virtuous good.

Obj. 3. Further, As Augustine says,[7] "sorrow is concerned about those things which happen against our will." But not to will those things which are actually taking place is to have a will opposed to the decree of God, to Whose providence whatever is done is subject. Since, then, conformity of the human to the Divine will is a condition of the rectitude of the will, as stated

---

[1] PG 40, 688.
[2] Aristotle, VII, 11 (1152[b]15).
[3] Aristotle, IV, 9 (1128[b]30).

[4] PL 34, 385.   [5] Aristotle, III, 1 (1110[n]18).
[6] PL 34, 482.   [7] *City of God*, XIV, 15 (PL 41, 424).

above (Q. XIX, A. 9), it seems that sorrow is incompatible with rectitude of the will, and that consequently it is not virtuous.

On the contrary, Whatever merits the reward of eternal life is virtuous. But such is sorrow, as is evident from Matt. 5. 5: *Blessed are they that mourn, for they shall be comforted.* Therefore sorrow is a virtuous good.

I answer that, In so far as sorrow is good, it can be a virtuous good. For it has been said above (A. 1) that sorrow is a good according as it denotes perception and rejection of evil. These two things, as regards bodily pain, are a proof of the goodness of nature, to which it is due that the senses perceive, and that nature shuns, the harmful thing that causes pain. As regards interior sorrow, knowledge of the evil is sometimes due to a right judgment of reason, while the rejection of the evil is the act of the will, well disposed and detesting that evil. Now every virtuous good results from these two things, the rectitude of the reason and of the will. Therefore it is evident that sorrow may be a virtuous good.

Reply Obj. 1. All the passions of the soul should be regulated according to the rule of reason, which is the root of the virtuous good; but excessive sorrow, of which Augustine is speaking, oversteps this rule, and therefore it fails to be a virtuous good.

Reply Obj. 2. Just as sorrow for an evil arises from a right will and reason, which detest the evil, so sorrow for a good is due to a perverse reason and will, which detest the good. Consequently such sorrow is an obstacle to the praise and merit of the virtuous good; for instance, when a man gives an alms sorrowfully.

Reply Obj. 3. Some things do actually happen, not because God wills, but because He permits them to happen—such as sins. Consequently a will that is opposed to sin, whether in oneself or in another, is not discordant from the Divine will.—Penal evils happen actually, even by God's will. But it is not necessary for the rectitude of his will, that man should will them in themselves, but only that he should not revolt against the order of Divine justice, as stated above (Q. XIX, A. 10).

ARTICLE 3. *Whether Sorrow Can Be a Useful Good?*

We proceed thus to the Third Article: It would seem that sorrow cannot be a useful good.
Objection 1. For it is written (*Ecclus.* 30. 25): *Sadness hath killed many, and there is no profit in it.*
Obj. 2. Further, choice is of that which is useful to an end. But sorrow is not an object of choice; in fact, "a thing without sorrow is to be chosen rather than the same thing with sorrow."[1] Therefore sorrow is not a useful good.
Obj. 3. Further, "Everything is for the sake of its own operation," as stated in the book on the *Heavens.*[2] But "sorrow hinders operation," as stated in the *Ethics.*[3] Therefore sorrow is not a useful good.

On the contrary, The wise man seeks only that which is useful. But according to Eccles. 7., *the heart of the wise is where there is mourning, and the heart of fools where there is mirth.* Therefore sorrow is useful.

I answer that, A twofold movement of the appetite ensues from a present evil. One is that by which the appetite is opposed to the present evil; and, in this respect, sorrow is of no use, because that which is present, cannot be not present. The other movement arises in the appetite to the effect of avoiding or expelling the saddening evil; and, in this respect, sorrow is of use, if it be for something which ought to be avoided. Because there are two reasons for which it may be right to avoid a thing. First, because it should be avoided in itself, on account of its being contrary to good; for instance, sin. Therefore sorrow for sin is useful as inducing man to avoid sin. Hence the Apostle says (II Cor. 7. 9): *I am glad: not because you were made sorrowful, but because you were made sorrowful unto penance.* Secondly, a thing is to be avoided, not as though it were evil in itself, but because it is an occasion of evil; either through one's being attached to it, and loving it too much, or through one's being thrown headlong thereby into an evil, as is evident in the case of temporal goods. And, in this respect, sorrow for temporal goods may be useful; according to Eccles. 7. 3: *It is better to go to the house of mourning, than to the house of feasting: for in that we are put in mind of the end of all.*

Moreover, sorrow for that which ought to be avoided is always useful, since it adds another motive for avoiding it. Because the very evil is in itself a thing to be avoided; while everyone avoids sorrow for its own sake, just as everyone seeks the good, and pleasure in the good. Therefore just as pleasure in the good makes one seek the good more earnestly, so sorrow for evil makes one avoid evil more eagerly.

Reply Obj. 1. This passage is to be taken as referring to excessive sorrow, which consumes the soul; for such sorrow paralyzes the soul, and

---

[1] Aristotle, *Topics,* III, 2 (117ᵇ30).
[2] Aristotle, II, 3 (286ᵃ8).   [3] Aristotle, X, 5 (1175ᵇ17).

hinders it from shunning evil, as stated above (Q. XXXVII, A. 2).

Reply Obj. 2. Just as any object of choice becomes less eligible by reason of sorrow, so that which ought to be shunned is still more to be shunned by reason of sorrow. And, in this respect, sorrow is useful.

Reply Obj. 3. Sorrow caused by an action hinders that action; but sorrow for the cessation of an action makes one do it more earnestly.

ARTICLE 4. *Whether Bodily Pain Is the Greatest Evil?*

We proceed thus to the Fourth Article: It would seem that pain is the greatest evil.

Objection 1. Because "the worst is contrary to the best."[1] But a certain pleasure is the greatest good, namely, the pleasure of happiness. Therefore a certain pain is the greatest evil.

Obj. 2. Further, Happiness is man's greatest good, because it is his last end. But man's Happiness consists in his having whatever he will, and in willing nothing evil, as stated above (Q. III, A. 4, obj. 5; Q. V, A. 8, obj. 3). Therefore man's greatest good consists in the fulfilment of his will. Now pain consists in something happening contrary to the will, as Augustine declares,[2] Therefore pain is man's greatest evil.

Obj. 3. Further, Augustine argues thus (*Soliloq.* i, 12):[3] "We are composed of two parts, that is of a soul and a body, whereof the body is the inferior. Now the sovereign good is the greatest good of the better part, while the supreme evil is the greatest evil of the inferior part. But wisdom is the greatest good of the soul; while the worst thing in the body is pain. Therefore man's greatest good is to be wise, while his greatest evil is to suffer pain."

On the contrary, Guilt is a greater evil than punishment as was stated in the First Park (Q. XLVIII, A. 6). But sorrow or pain belongs to the punishment of sin, just as the enjoyment of changeable things is an evil of guilt. For Augustine says (*De Vera Relig.* xii):[4] "What is pain of the soul, except for the soul to be deprived of changeable things which it was wont to enjoy, or had hoped to enjoy? And this is all that is called evil, that is sin, and the punishment of sin." Therefore sorrow or pain is not man's greatest evil.

I answer that, It is impossible for any sorrow or pain to be man's greatest evil. For all sorrow or pain is either for something that is truly evil, or for something that is apparently evil but good in reality. Now pain or sorrow for that which is truly evil cannot be the greatest evil; for there is something worse, namely, either not to judge that to be evil which is really evil, or not to reject it. Again, sorrow or pain for that which is apparently evil but really good, cannot be the greatest evil, for it would be worse to be altogether separated from that which is truly good. Hence it is impossible for any sorrow or pain to be man's greatest evil.

Reply Obj. 1. Pleasure and sorrow have two good points in common: namely, a true judgment concerning good and evil, and the due order of the will in approving of good and rejecting evil. Thus it is clear that in pain and sorrow there is a good by the removal of which they become worse; and yet there is not an evil in every pleasure by the removal of which the pleasure is better. Consequently, a pleasure can be man's highest good, in the way above stated (Q. XXXIV, A. 3); but sorrow cannot be man's greatest evil.

Reply Obj. 2. The very fact of the will being opposed to evil is a good. And for this reason, sorrow or pain cannot be the greatest evil, because it has an admixture of good.

Reply Obj. 3. That which harms the better thing is worse than that which harms the worse. Now a thing is called evil because it harms, as Augustine says (*Enchirid.* xii).[5] Therefore that which is an evil to the soul is a greater evil than that which is an evil to the body. Therefore this argument does not prove; nor does Augustine give it as his own, but as taken from another.[6]

QUESTION XL

OF THE IRASCIBLE PASSIONS, AND FIRST, OF HOPE AND DESPAIR

(*In Eight Articles*)

WE must now consider the irascible passions: (1) Hope and despair; (2) Fear and daring (Q. XLI); (3) Anger (Q. XLVI). Under the first head there are eight points of inquiry: (1) Whether hope is the same as desire or cupidity? (2) Whether hope is in the apprehensive, or in the appetitive power? (3) Whether hope is in dumb animals? (4) Whether despair is contrary to hope? (5) Whether experience is a cause of hope? (6) Whether hope abounds in young men and drunkards? (7) Concerning the order

---

[1] Aristotle, *Ethics*, VIII, 10 (1160b9).
[2] *City of God*, XIV, 6, 15 (PL 41, 409; 424).
[3] PL 32, 881.   [4] PL 34, 132.

[5] PL 40, 237; *De Mor. Eccl. Cathol.*, II, 3 (PL 32, 1346).
[6] Cornelius Celsus, in a work now lost; cf. Augustine, *Solil.*, I, 12 (PL 32, 881).

of hope to love? (8) Whether hope conduces to action?

ARTICLE 1. *Whether Hope Is the Same as Desire or Cupidity?*

We proceed thus to the First Article: It seems that hope is the same as desire or cupidity.

Objection 1. Because hope is accounted as one of the four principal passions. But Augustine in setting down the four principal passions puts cupidity in the place of hope.[1] Therefore hope is the same as cupidity or desire.

Obj. 2. Further, passions differ according to their objects. But the object of hope is the same as the object of cupidity or desire, namely, the future good. Therefore hope is the same as cupidity or desire.

Obj. 3. If it be said that hope, in addition to desire, denotes the possibility of obtaining the future good; on the contrary, whatever is accidental to the object does not make a different species of passion. But possibility of acquisition is accidental to a future good, which is the object of cupidity or desire, and of hope. Therefore hope does not differ specifically from desire or cupidity.

On the contrary, To different powers belong different species of passions. But hope is in the irascible power, while desire or cupidity is in the concupiscible. Therefore hope differs specifically from desire or cupidity.

I answer that, The species of a passion is taken from the object. Now, in the object of hope, we may note four conditions. First, that it is something good, since, properly speaking, hope regards only the good; in this respect, hope differs from fear, which regards evil. Secondly, that it is future, for hope does not regard that which is present and already possessed. In this respect, hope differs from joy which regards a present good. Thirdly, that it must be something arduous and difficult to obtain, for we do not speak of any one hoping for trifles, which are in one's power to have at any time; in this respect, hope differs from desire or cupidity, which regards the future good absolutely. Therefore it belongs to the concupiscible, while hope belongs to the irascible part. Fourthly, that this difficult thing is something possible to obtain, for one does not hope for that which one cannot get at all; and, in this respect, hope differs from despair. It is therefore evident that hope differs from desire, as the irascible passions differ from the con-

cupiscible. For this reason, moreover, hope presupposes desire, just as all the irascible passions presuppose the passions of the concupiscible part, as stated above (Q. XXV, A. 1).

Reply Obj. 1. Augustine mentions desire instead of hope because each regards future good, and because the good which is not arduous is reckoned as nothing, thus implying that desire seems to tend chiefly to the arduous good, to which hope tends likewise.

Reply Obj. 2. The object of hope is the future good considered, not absolutely, but as arduous and difficult of attainment, as stated above.

Reply Obj. 3. The object of hope adds not only possibility to the object of desire, but also difficulty; and this makes hope belong to another power, namely the irascible, which regards something difficult, as stated in the First Part (Q. LXXXI, A. 2).[2] Moreover, possibility and impossibility are not altogether accidental to the object of the appetitive power. For the appetite is a principle of movement, and nothing is moved to anything except under the aspect of being possible; for no one is moved to that which he thinks impossible to get. Consequently hope differs from despair according to the difference of possible and impossible.

ARTICLE 2. *Whether Hope Is in the Apprehensive or in the Appetitive Power?*

We proceed thus to the Second Article: It would seem that hope belongs to the cognitive power.

Objection 1. Because hope seems to be a kind of awaiting; for the Apostle says (Rom. 8. 25): *If we hope for that which we see not; we wait for it with patience.* But awaiting (*expectatio*) seems to belong to the cognitive power, which we exercise by looking out (*exspectare*). Therefore hope belongs to the cognitive power.

Obj. 2. Further, apparently hope is the same as confidence; hence when a man hopes he is said to be confident, as though to hope and to be confident were the same thing. But confidence, like faith, seems to belong to the cognitive power. Therefore hope does too.

Obj. 3. Further, certainty is a property of the cognitive power. But certainty is ascribed to hope. Therefore hope belongs to the cognitive power.

On the contrary, Hope regards good, as stated above (A. 1). Now good, as such, is not the object of the cognitive, but of the appetitive

---

[1] *City of God*, XIV, 3 (PL 41, 406).   [2] Cf. Q. XXIII, A. 1.

power. Therefore hope belongs, not to the cognitive, but to the appetitive power.

I answer that, Since hope denotes a certain stretching out of the appetite towards good, it evidently belongs to the appetitive power; for movement towards things belongs properly to the appetite, while the action of the cognitive power is accomplished not by a movement of the knower towards things, but rather according as the things known are in the knower. But since the cognitive power moves the appetite by representing its object to it, there arise in the appetite various movements according to various aspects of the apprehended object. For the apprehension of good gives rise to one kind of movement in the appetite, while the apprehension of evil gives rise to another; in like manner various movements arise from the apprehension of something present and of something future, of something considered absolutely, and of something considered as arduous, of something possible, and of something impossible. And accordingly hope is a movement of the appetitive power ensuing from the apprehension of a future good, difficult but possible to obtain; that is, a stretching forth of the appetite to such a good.

Reply Obj. 1. Since hope regards a possible good, there arises in man a twofold movement of hope, for a thing may be possible to him in two ways, namely by his own power, or by another's. Accordingly when a man hopes to obtain something by his own power, he is not said to wait for it, but only to hope for it. But, properly speaking, he is said to await that which he hopes to get by another's help as though to await (*exspectare*) implied keeping one's eyes on another (*ex alio spectare*), in so far as the apprehensive power, by going ahead, not only keeps its eye on the good which man intends to get, but also on the thing by whose power he hopes to get it, according to Ecclus. 51. 10: *I looked for the succour of men.* Therefore the movement of hope is sometimes called expectation, on account of the preceding inspection of the knowing power.

Reply Obj. 2. When a man desires a thing and thinks that he can get it, he believes that he will get it; and from this belief which precedes in the knowing power the ensuing movement in the appetite is called confidence. Because the movement of the appetite takes its name from the knowledge that precedes it, as an effect from a cause which is better known; for the apprehensive power knows its own act better than that of the appetite.

Reply Obj. 3. Certainty is ascribed to the movement, not only of the sensitive, but also of the natural appetite; thus we say that a stone is certain to tend downwards. This is owing to the inerrancy which the movement of the sensitive or even natural appetite derives from the certainty of the knowledge that precedes it.

ARTICLE 3. *Whether Hope Is in Dumb Animals?*

We proceed thus to the Third Article: It would seem that there is no hope in dumb animals.

Objection 1. Because hope is for some future good, as Damascene says (*De Fide Orthod.* ii, 12).[1] But knowledge of the future does not belong to dumb animals, whose knowledge is confined to the senses and does not extend to the future. Therefore there is no hope in dumb animals.

Obj. 2. Further, the object of hope is a future good, possible of attainment. But possible and impossible are differences of the true and the false, "which are only in the mind," as the Philosopher states.[2] Therefore there is no hope in dumb animals, since they have no mind.

Obj. 3. Further, Augustine says (*Gen. ad lit.* ix, 14)[3] that "animals are moved by the things that they see." But hope is of things unseen, *for what a man seeth, why doth he hope for?* (Rom. 8. 24). Therefore there is no hope in dumb animals.

On the contrary, Hope is an irascible passion. But the irascible power is in dumb animals. Therefore hope is also.

I answer that, The internal passions of animals can be gathered from their outward movements, from which it is clear that hope is in dumb animals. For if a dog see a hare, or a hawk see a bird, too far off, it makes no movement towards it, as having no hope to catch it; but if it be near, it makes a movement towards it, as being in hopes of catching it. Because, as stated above (Q. I, A. 2; Q. XXVI, A. 1; Q. XXXV, A. 1), the sensitive appetite of dumb animals, and likewise the natural appetite of insensible things, result from the apprehension of an intellect, just as the appetite of the intellectual nature, which is called the will. But there is a difference, in that the will is moved by an apprehension of the intellect joined to it, while the movement of the natural appetite results from the apprehension of the separate Intellect, Who is the Author of nature, and it

[1] PG 94, 929.   [2] *Metaphysics,* VI, 4 ($1027^{b}27$).
[3] PL 34, 402.

is the same with the sensitive appetite of dumb animals, who act from a certain natural instinct. Consequently, in the actions of irrational animals and of other natural things, we observe a procedure which is similar to that which we observe in the actions of art. And in this way hope and despair are in dumb animals.

Reply Obj. 1. Although dumb animals do not know the future, yet an animal is moved by its natural instinct to something future, as though it foresaw the future. Because this instinct is planted in them by the Divine Intellect that foresees the future.

Reply Obj. 2. The object of hope is not the possible as differentiating the true, for thus the possible ensues from the relation of a predicate to a subject. The object of hope is the possible as compared to a power. For such is the division of the possible given in the *Metaphysics*,[1] that is, into the two kinds we have just mentioned.

Reply Obj. 3. Although the thing which is future does not come under the object of sight, nevertheless through seeing something present, an animal's appetite is moved to seek or avoid something future.

ARTICLE 4. *Whether Despair Is Contrary to Hope?*

We proceed thus to the Fourth Article: It seems that despair is not contrary to hope.

Objection 1. Because "to one thing there is one contrary."[2] But fear is contrary to hope. Therefore despair is not contrary to hope.

Obj. 2. Further, contraries seem to bear on the same thing. But hope and despair do not bear on the same thing, for hope regards the good, but despair arises from some evil that is in the way of obtaining good. Therefore hope is not contrary to despair.

Obj. 3. Further, movement is contrary to movement; while repose is in opposition to movement as a privation of it. But despair seems to imply immobility rather than movement. Therefore it is not contrary to hope, which implies movement of stretching out towards the hoped-for good.

On the contrary, The very name of despair (*desperatio*) implies that it is contrary to hope (*spes*).

I answer that, As stated above (Q. XXIII, A. 2), there is a twofold contrariety in changes. One is in respect of approach to contrary terms, and this contrariety alone is to be found in the concupiscible passions, for instance between love and hatred. The other is according to approach and withdrawal with regard to the same term, and is to be found in the irascible passions, as stated above (*loc. cit.*). Now the object of hope, which is the arduous good, has the character of a principle of attraction, if it be considered in the light of something possible of attainment; and thus hope tends to that good, for it denotes a kind of approach. But in so far as it is considered as unobtainable, it has the character of a principle of repulsion, because, as stated in the *Ethics*,[3] "when men come to an impossibility they disperse." And this is how despair stands in regard to this object, and so it implies a movement of withdrawal. Consequently it is contrary to hope, as withdrawal is to approach.

Reply Obj. 1. Fear is contrary to hope, because their objects, that is, good and evil, are contrary; for this contrariety is found in the irascible passions, according as they are derived from the passions of the concupiscible. But despair is contrary to hope only by contrariety of approach and withdrawal.

Reply Obj. 2. Despair does not regard evil as such; sometimes, however, it regards evil accidentally, as making the difficult good impossible to obtain. But it can arise from the mere excess of good.

Reply Obj. 3. Despair implies not only privation of hope, but also a recoil from the thing desired, by reason of its being thought impossible to get. Hence despair, like hope, presupposes desire, because we neither hope for nor despair of that which we do not desire to have. For this reason, too, each of them regards the good, which is the object of desire.

ARTICLE 5. *Whether Experience Is a Cause of Hope?*

We proceed thus to the Fifth Article: It would seem that experience is not a cause of hope.

Objection 1. Because experience belongs to the knowing power; hence the Philosopher says[4] that "intellectual virtue needs experience and time." But hope is not in the knowing power, but in the appetite, as stated above (A. 2). Therefore experience is not a cause of hope.

Obj. 2. Further, the Philosopher says[5] that "the old are slow to hope, on account of their experience"; from this it seems to follow that experience causes want of hope. But the same

[1] Aristotle, v, 12 (1019^{b}30).
[2] Aristotle; *Metaphysics*, x, 4, 5 (1055^{a}19; 1055^{b}30).
[3] Aristotle, III, 3 (1112^{b}24).   [4] *Ethics*, II, 1 (1103^{a}16).
[5] *Rhetoric*, II, 13 (1390^{a}4).

cause is not productive of opposites. Therefore experience is not a cause of hope.

Obj. 3. Further, the Philosopher says[1] that "to have something to say about everything, without leaving anything out, is sometimes a proof of folly." But to attempt everything seems to point to great hopes, while folly arises from inexperience. Therefore inexperience, rather than experience, seems to be a cause of hope.

On the contrary, The Philosopher says[2] "some are of good hope, through having been victorious often and over many opponents," which seems to pertain to experience. Therefore experience is a cause of hope.

I answer that, As stated above (A. 1), the object of hope is a future good, difficult but possible to obtain. Consequently a thing may be a cause of hope either because it makes something possible to a man or because it makes him think something possible. In the first way hope is caused by everything that increases a man's power; for instance riches, strength, and, among others, experience, for by experience man acquires the possibility of getting something easily, and the result of this is hope. Therefore Vegetius says:[3] "No one fears to do that which he is sure of having learnt well."

In the second way, hope is caused by everything that makes man think that something is possible for him; and thus both teaching and persuasion may be a cause of hope. And in this way also experience is a cause of hope, in so far as it makes him consider something possible which before his experience he looked upon as impossible. However, in this way, experience can cause a lack of hope, because just as it makes a man think possible what he had previously thought impossible, so, conversely, experience makes a man consider as impossible that which hitherto he had thought possible. Accordingly experience causes hope in two ways, despair in one way; and for this reason we may say rather that it causes hope.

Reply Obj. 1. Experience in matters pertaining to action not only produces knowledge, it also causes a certain habit, by reason of custom, which renders the action easier. Moreover, the intellectual virtue itself adds to the possibility of acting with ease, because it shows something to be possible, and thus is a cause of hope.

Reply Obj. 2. The old are wanting in hope because of their experience in so far as experience makes them think something impossible. Hence he adds[4] that "many evils have befallen them."

Reply Obj. 3. Folly and inexperience can be a cause of hope accidentally as it were, by removing the knowledge which would help one to judge truly a thing to be impossible. Therefore inexperience is a cause of hope for the same reason as experience causes lack of hope.

ARTICLE 6. *Whether Hope Abounds in Young Men and Drunkards?*

We proceed thus to the Sixth Article: It would seem that youth and drunkenness are not causes of hope.

Objection 1. Because hope implies certainty and steadiness, and hence it is compared to an anchor (Heb. 6. 19). But young men and drunkards are wanting in steadiness, since their minds are easily changed. Therefore youth and drunkenness are not causes of hope.

Obj. 2. Further, as stated above (A. 5), the cause of hope is chiefly whatever increases one's power. But youth and drunkenness are united to weakness. Therefore they are not causes of hope.

Obj. 3. Further, experience is a cause of hope, as stated above (A. 5). But youth lacks experience. Therefore it is not a cause of hope.

On the contrary, The Philosopher says that "drunken men are hopeful";[5] and that "the young are full of hope."[6]

I answer that, Youth is a cause of hope for three reasons, as the Philosopher states in the *Rhetoric.*[7] And these three reasons may be gathered from the three conditions of the good which is the object of hope—namely, that it is future, arduous and possible, as stated above (A. 1). For youth has much of the future before it, and little of the past; and therefore since memory is of the past, and hope of the future, it has little to remember and lives very much in hope. Again, youths, on account of the heat of their nature, are full of spirit, so that their heart expands, and it is owing to the heart being expanded that one tends to that which is arduous; therefore youths are spirited and hopeful. Likewise they who have not suffered defeat, nor had experience of obstacles to their efforts, are prone to count a thing possible to them. Therefore youths, through inexperience of obstacles and of their own shortcomings, easily count a thing possible, and consequently are of good hope. Two of these causes are also

---

[1] *Heavens,* II, 5 (287^{b}28).
[2] *Ethics,* III, 8 (1117^{a}10).
[3] *Instit. Rei Militar.,* I, 1 (DD 660).
[4] Aristotle, *Rhetoric,* II, 13 (1390^{a}5).
[5] *Ethics,* III, 8 (1117^{a}14).   [6] *Rhetoric,* II, 12 (1389^{a}19).   [7] *Ibid.*

in those who are in drink—namely, heat and high spirits, on account of wine, and heedlessness of dangers and shortcomings. For the same reason all foolish and thoughtless persons attempt everything and are full of hope.

Reply Obj. 1. Although youths and men in drink lack steadiness in reality, yet they are steady in their own estimation, for they think that they will steadily obtain that which they hope for.

In like manner, in *reply to the Second Objection,* we must observe that young people and men in drink are indeed unsteady in reality, but, in their own estimation, they are capable, for they do not know their shortcomings.

Reply Obj. 3. Not only experience, but also lack of experience, is, in some way, a cause of hope, as explained above, (A. 5 ANS. 3).

ARTICLE 7. *Whether Hope Is a Cause of Love?*

We proceed thus to the Seventh Article: It would seem that hope is not a cause of love.

Objection 1. Because, according to Augustine,[1] love is the first of the soul's emotions. But hope is an emotion of the soul. Therefore love precedes hope, and consequently hope does not cause love.

Obj. 2. Further, desire precedes hope. But desire is caused by love, as stated above (Q. XXV, A. 2). Therefore hope, too, follows love, and consequently is not its cause.

Obj. 3. Further, hope causes pleasure, as stated above (Q. XXXII, A. 3). But pleasure is only of the good that is loved. Therefore love precedes hope.

On the contrary, The gloss commenting on Matt. 1. 2, *Abraham begot Isaac, and Isaac begot Jacob,* says,[2] that is, faith begets hope, and hope begets charity. But charity is love. Therefore love is caused by hope.

I answer that, Hope can regard two things. For it regards as its object the good which one hopes for. But since the good we hope for is something difficult but possible to obtain, and since it happens sometimes that what is difficult becomes possible to us, not through ourselves but through others, hence it is that hope regards also that by which something becomes possible to us.

In so far, then, as hope regards the good we hope to get, it is caused by love, for we do not hope save for that which we desire and love. But in so far as hope regards one through whom something becomes possible to us, love

[1] *City of God,* XIV, 7 (PL 41, 410).
[2] *Glossa interl.* (v, 5r).

is caused by hope, and not vice versa. Because by the very fact that we hope that good will accrue to us through someone, we are moved towards him as to our own good; and thus we begin to love him. Though from the fact that we love someone we do not hope in him, except accidentally, that is, in so far as we think that he returns our love. Therefore the fact of being loved by another makes us hope in him, but our love for him is caused by the hope we have in him.

Hence the *Replies to the Objections* are evident.

ARTICLE 8. *Whether Hope Is a Help or a Hindrance to Action?*

We proceed thus to the Eighth Article: It seems that hope is not a help but a hindrance to action.

Objection 1. Because hope implies security. But security begets negligence which hinders action. Therefore hope is a hindrance to action.

Obj. 2. Further, sorrow hinders action, as stated above (Q. XXXVII, A. 3). But hope sometimes causes sorrow, for it is written (Prov. 13. 12) *Hope that is deferred afflicteth the soul.* Therefore hope hinders action.

Obj. 3. Further, despair is contrary to hope, as stated above (A. 4). But despair, especially in matters of war, conduces to action; for it is written (II Kings 2. 26), that *it is dangerous to drive people to despair.* Therefore hope has a contrary effect, namely, by hindering action.

On the contrary, It is written (I Cor. 9. 10) that *he that plougheth should plough in hope . . . to receive fruit;* and the same applies to all other actions.

I answer that, Hope of its very nature is a help to action by making it more intense, and this for two reasons. First, by reason of its object, which is a good, difficult but possible. For the thought of its being difficult arouses our attention, while the thought that it is possible does not hinder our effort. Hence it follows that by reason of hope man is intent on his action. Secondly, on account of its effect. Because hope, as stated above (Q. XXXII, A. 3), causes pleasure, which is a help to action, as stated above (Q. XXXIII, A. 4). Therefore hope is conducive to action.

Reply Obj. 1. Hope regards a good to be obtained, and security an evil to be avoided. Therefore security seems to be contrary to fear rather than to belong to hope. Yet security does not beget negligence, except in so far as it lessens the idea of difficulty, by which it also lessens the character of hope. For the things in which a man fears no hindrance are no longer looked upon as difficult.

Reply Obj. 2. Hope of itself causes pleasure; it is by accident that it causes sorrow, as stated above (Q. XXXII, A. 3, Reply 2).

Reply Obj. 3. Despair threatens danger in war, on account of a certain hope that attaches to it. For they who despair of flight strive less to fly, but hope to avenge their death; and therefore in this hope they fight the more sharply, and consequently prove dangerous to the foe.

QUESTION XLI
Of fear, in itself
(*In Four Articles*)

WE must now consider, in the first place, fear; and, secondly, daring. With regard to fear, four things must be considered: (1) Fear, in itself; (2) Its object (Q. XLII); (3) Its cause (Q. XLIII); (4) Its effect (Q. XLIV). Under the first head there are four points of inquiry: (1) Whether fear is a passion of the soul? (2) Whether fear is a special passion? (3) Whether there is a natural fear? (4) Of the species of fear.

ARTICLE 1. *Whether Fear Is a Passion of the Soul?*

We proceed thus to the First Article: It would seem that fear is not a passion of the soul.

Objection 1. For Damascene says (*De Fide Orthod.* iii, 23)[1] that "fear is a power, by way of συστολή"—that is, of contraction—"desirous of vindicating nature." But no power is a passion, as is proved in the *Ethics.*[2] Therefore fear is not a passion.

Obj. 2. Further, every passion is an effect due to the presence of an agent. But fear is not of something present, but of something future, as Damascene declares (*De Fide Orthod.* ii, 12).[3] Therefore fear is not a passion.

Obj. 3. Further, every passion of the soul is a movement of the sensitive appetite in consequence of an apprehension of the senses. But sense apprehends not the future but the present. Since, then, fear is of future evil, it seems that it is not a passion of the soul.

On the contrary, Augustine numbers fear among the other passions of the soul.[4]

[1] PG 94, 1088. [2] Aristotle, II, 5 (1105^{b}28).
[3] PG 94, 929.
[4] *City of God,* XIV, 5 (PL 41, 408).

I answer that, Among the other passions of the soul, after sorrow, fear chiefly has the character of passion. For as we have stated above (Q. XXII), the notion of passion implies first of all a movement of a passive power—that is, of a power whose object is compared to it as its active mover, for the reason that passion is the effect of an agent. In this way, both to feel and to understand are said to be passive. Secondly, more properly speaking, passion is a movement of the appetitive power; and more properly still, it is a movement of an appetitive power that has a bodily organ, such movement being accompanied by a bodily change. And, again, most properly those movements are called passions which imply some harm. Now it is evident that fear, since it regards evil, belongs to the appetitive power, which of itself regards good and evil. Moreover, it belongs to the sensitive appetite, for it is accompanied by a certain change—that is, contraction, as Damascene says (cf. obj. 1). Again, it implies relation to evil, according as evil has a kind of victory over some good. Therefore it has most truly the character of passion; less, however, than sorrow, which regards the present evil, because fear regards future evil, which is not so strong a motive as present evil.

Reply Obj. 1. Power denotes a principle of action; therefore, in so far as the interior movements of the appetitive power are principles of external action, they are called powers. But the Philosopher denies[5] that passion is a power by way of habit.

Reply Obj. 2. Just as the passion of a natural body is due to the bodily presence of an agent, so is the passion of the soul due to the agent being present to the soul, although neither corporally nor really present; that is to say, in so far as the evil which is really future is present in the apprehension of the soul.

Reply Obj. 3. The senses do not apprehend the future; but from apprehending the present, an animal is moved by natural instinct to hope for a future good or to fear a future evil.

ARTICLE 2. *Whether Fear Is a Special Passion?*

We proceed thus to the Second Article: It would seem that fear is not a special passion.

Objection 1. For Augustine says (QQ. LXXXIII, *qu.* 33)[6] that "the man who is not distraught by fear, is neither harassed by desire, nor wounded by sickness"—that is, sorrow—"nor tossed about in transports of empty joys." Therefore it seems that, if fear be set

[5] *Loc. cit.* [6] PL 40, 23.

aside, all the other passions are removed. Therefore fear is not a special but a general passion.

Obj. 2. Further, the Philosopher says[1] that "pursuit and avoidance in the appetite are what affirmation and denial are in the intellect." But denial is nothing special in the intellect, as neither is affirmation, but something common to many. Therefore neither is avoidance anything special in the appetite. But fear is nothing but a kind of avoidance of evil. Therefore it is not a special passion.

Obj. 3. Further, if fear were a special passion, it would be chiefly in the irascible part. But fear is also in the concupiscible, since the Philosopher says[2] that "fear is a kind of sorrow"; and Damascene says (*De Fide Orthod.* iii, 23)[3] that fear is "a power of desire"; and both sorrow and desire are in the concupiscible part, as stated above (Q. XXIII, A. 4). Therefore fear is not a special passion, since it belongs to different powers.

On the contrary, Fear is divided with the other passions of the soul, as is clear from Damascene (*De Fide Orthod.* ii, 12, 15).[4]

I answer that, The passions of the soul derive their species from their objects; hence that is a special passion which has a special object. Now fear has a special object, as hope has. For just as the object of hope is a future good, difficult but possible to obtain, so the object of fear is a future evil, difficult and irresistible. Consequently fear is a special passion of the soul.

Reply Obj. 1. All the passions of the soul arise from one source, namely, love, wherein they are connected with one another. By reason of this connection, when fear is put aside, the other passions of the soul are dispersed; not, however, as though it were a general passion.

Reply Obj. 2. Not every avoidance in the appetite is fear, but avoidance of a special object, as stated. Therefore, though avoidance be something general, yet fear is a special passion.

Reply Obj. 3. Fear is in no way in the concupiscible part, for it regards evil, not absolutely, but as difficult or arduous, so as to be almost irresistible. But since the irascible passions arise from the passions of the concupiscible part and terminate in them, as stated above (Q. XXV, A. 1), hence it is that what belongs to the concupiscible is ascribed to fear.

[1] *Ethics,* VI, 2 (1139[a]21).
[2] *Rhetoric,* II, 5 (1382[a]21).
[3] PG 94, 1088.   [4] PG 94, 929; 932.

For fear is called sorrow in so far as the object of fear causes sorrow when present; and hence the Philosopher says (*loc. cit.*) that fear arises "from the representation of a future evil which is either corruptive or painful." In like manner desire is ascribed by Damascene to fear (*loc. cit.*), because just as hope is caused or arises from the desire of good, so fear arises from avoidance of evil, while avoidance of evil arises from the desire of good, as is evident from what has been said above (Q. XXV, A. 2; Q. XXIX, A. 2; Q. XXXVI, A. 2).

ARTICLE 3. *Whether There Is a Natural Fear?*

We proceed thus to the Third Article: It would seem that there is a natural fear.

Objection 1. For Damascene says (*De Fide Orthod.* iii, 23)[5] that "there is a natural fear, through the soul refusing to be severed from the body."

Obj. 2. Further, fear arises from love, as stated above (A. 2, reply 1). But there is "a natural love," as Dionysius states (*Div. Nom.* iv).[6] Therefore there is also a natural fear.

Obj. 3. Further, fear is opposed to hope, as stated above (Q. XL, A. 4, reply 1). But there is a hope of nature, as is evident from Rom. 4. 18, where it is said of Abraham that *against hope* of nature, *he believed in hope* of grace. Therefore there is also a fear of nature.

On the contrary, That which is natural is common to things animate and inanimate. But fear is not in things inanimate. Therefore there is no natural fear.

I answer that, A movement is said to be natural because nature inclines to it. Now this happens in two ways. First, so that it is entirely accomplished by nature, without any operation of the apprehensive power; thus to have an upward movement is natural to fire, and to grow is the natural movement of animals and plants. Secondly, a movement is said to be natural if nature inclines to it, even though it be accomplished by the apprehensive power alone, since, as stated above (Q. X, A. 1), the movements of the knowing and appetitive powers are reducible to nature as to their first principle. In this way even the acts of the apprehensive power, such as understanding, feeling, and remembering, as well as the movements of the animal appetite, are sometimes said to be natural.

And in this sense we may say that there is a natural fear; and it is distinguished from non-natural fear by reason of the diversity of its ob-

[5] PG 94, 1008.
[6] Sect. 15 (PG 3, 713).

ject. For, as the Philosopher says,[1] there is a fear of corruptive evil, which nature shrinks from on account of its natural desire of being; and such fear is said to be natural. Again, there is a fear of painful evil, which is contrary not to nature, but to the desire of the appetite; and such fear is not natural. In this sense we have stated above (Q. XXVI, A. 1; Q. XXX, A. 3; Q. XXXI, A. 7) that love, concupiscence, and pleasure are divisible into natural and non-natural.

But in the first sense of the word natural, we must observe that certain passions are sometimes said to be natural, as love, desire, and hope, but the others cannot be called natural. The reason of this is because love and hatred, desire and avoidance, imply a certain inclination to pursue what is good or to avoid what is evil, which inclination is to be found in the natural appetite also. Consequently there is a kind of natural love, while we may also speak in a certain manner of desire and hope as being even in natural things devoid of knowledge. On the other hand, the other passions of the soul denote certain movements to which the natural inclination is in no way sufficient. This is due either to the fact that sensing or knowledge is of the very notion of these passions (thus we have said that apprehension is a necessary condition of pleasure and sorrow),[2] and so things devoid of knowledge cannot be said to take pleasure or to be sorrowful. Or else it is because such movements are contrary to the very notion of natural inclination; for instance, despair flies from good on account of some difficulty, and fear shrinks from repelling a contrary evil, both of which are contrary to the inclination of nature. Hence passions of this kind are in no way ascribed to inanimate beings.

Thus the *Replies to the Objections* are evident.

ARTICLE 4. *Whether the Species of Fear Are Suitably Assigned?*

We proceed thus to the Fourth Article: It seems that the species of fear are unsuitably assigned by Damascene (*De Fide Orthod.* ii);[3] namely, "laziness, shamefacedness, shame, amazement, stupor, and anxiety."

---

[1] *Rhetoric*, II, 5 (1382ª22).

[2] Cf. Q. XXXI, AA. 1, 3; Q. XXXV, A. 1.

[3] Chap. 15 (PG 94, 932); also in Nemesius, *De Nat. Hom.*, XX (PG 40, 683); for the origin of this doctrine amongst the Stoics, cf. Diogenes Laertes, *De Vita et Mor. Phil.*, VII, 112 (DD 183); cf. also Stobaeus, *Eclogae* II, 6 (p. 584).

Objection 1. Because, as the Philosopher says[4] "fear regards a saddening evil." Therefore the species of fear should correspond to the species of sorrow. Now there are four species of sorrow, as stated above (Q. XXXV, A. 8). Therefore there should only be four species of fear, corresponding to them.

Obj. 2. Further, that which consists in an action of our own is in our power. But fear regards an evil that surpasses our power, as stated above (A. 2). Therefore laziness, shamefacedness, and shame, which regard our own actions, should not be put as species of fear.

Obj. 3. Further, fear is of the future, as stated above (AA. 1, 2). But "shame regards a disgraceful deed already done," as Gregory of Nyssa (Nemesius, *De Nat. Hom.* XX)[5] says. Therefore shame is not a species of fear.

Obj. 4. Further, fear is only of evil. But amazement and stupor regard great and unaccustomed things, whether good or evil. Therefore amazement and stupor are not species of fear.

Obj. 5. Further, philosophers have been led by amazement to seek the truth, as stated at the beginning of the *Metaphysics*.[6] But fear leads to flight rather than to search. Therefore amazement is not a species of fear.

On the contrary suffices the authority of Damascene and Gregory of Nyssa (Nemisius) (cf. obj. 1, 3).

I answer that, As stated above (A. 2), fear regards a future evil which surpasses the power of him that fears, so that it is irresistible. Now man's evil, like his good, may be considered either in his action or in external things. In his action he has a twofold evil to fear. First, there is the toil that burdens his nature, and hence arises laziness, as when a man shrinks from work for fear of too much toil. Secondly, there is the disgrace which damages him in the opinion of others. And thus, if disgrace is feared in a deed that is yet to be done, there is shamefacedness; if, however, it be in a deed already done, there is shame.

On the other hand, the evil that consists in external things may surpass man's power of resistance in three ways. First, by reason of its magnitude; when, that is to say, a man considers some great evil the outcome of which he is unable to gauge, and then there is amazement. Secondly, by reason of its being unaccustomed; because, that is, some unaccustomed

---

[4] *Rhetoric*, II, 5 (1382ª22).

[5] PG 40, 689.

[6] Aristotle, I, 2 (982ᵇ12).

evil arises before us, and on that account is great in our estimation, and then there is stupor, which is caused by the imagination of something unaccustomed. Thirdly, by reason of its being unforeseen; because, that is, it cannot be foreseen; thus future misfortunes are feared, and fear of this kind is called anxiety.

Reply Obj. 1. Those species of sorrow given above are not derived from the diversity of objects, but from the diversity of effects, and for certain special reasons. Consequently there is no need for those species of sorrow to correspond with these species of fear which are derived from the proper division of the object of fear itself.

Reply Obj. 2. A deed considered as being actually done is in the power of the doer. But it is possible to take into consideration something connected with the deed, and surpassing the power of the doer, for which reason he shrinks from the deed. It is in this sense that laziness, shamefacedness, and shame are numbered as species of fear.

Reply Obj. 3. The past deed may be the occasion of fear of future reproach or disgrace, and in this sense shame is a species of fear.

Reply Obj. 4. Not every amazement and stupor are species of fear, but that amazement which is caused by a great evil, and that stupor which arises from an unaccustomed evil. Or else we may say that, just as laziness shrinks from the toil of external work, so amazement and stupor shrink from the difficulty of considering a great and unaccustomed thing, whether good or evil, so that amazement and stupor stand in relation to the act of the intellect as laziness does to external work.

Reply Obj. 5. He who is amazed shrinks at present from forming a judgment of that which amazes him, fearing to fall short of the truth, but inquires afterwards. But he who is overcome by stupor fears both to judge at present, and to inquire afterwards. Therefore amazement is a beginning of philosophical consideration, but stupor is a hindrance to it.

QUESTION XLII
OF THE OBJECT OF FEAR
(In Six Articles)

WE must now consider the object of fear, under which head there are six points of inquiry: (1) Whether good or evil is the object of fear? (2) Whether evil of nature is the object of fear? (3) Whether the evil of sin is an object of fear? (4) Whether fear itself can be feared? (5) Whether sudden things are especially feared? (6) Whether those things are more feared against which there is no remedy?

ARTICLE 1. *Whether the Object of Fear Is Good or Evil?*

We proceed thus to the First Article: It seems that good is the object of fear.

Objection 1. For Augustine says[1] that we fear nothing "save to lose what we love and possess, or not to obtain that which we hope for." But that which we love is good. Therefore fear regards good as its proper object.

Obj. 2. Further, the Philosopher says that power and to be above another is a thing to be feared.[2] But this is a good thing. Therefore good is the object of fear.

Obj. 3. Further, there can be no evil in God. But we are commanded to fear God, according to Ps. 33. 10: *Fear the Lord, all ye saints.* Therefore even the good is an object of fear.

On the contrary, Damascene says (*De Fide Orthod.* ii, 12)[3] that fear is of future evil.

I answer that, Fear is a movement of the appetitive power. Now it pertains to the appetitive power to pursue and to avoid, as stated in the *Ethics,*[4] and pursuit is of good, while avoidance is of evil. Consequently whatever movement of the appetitive power implies pursuit has some good for its object, and whatever movement implies avoidance has an evil for its object. Therefore, since fear implies an avoidance, in the first place and of its very nature it regards evil as its proper object.

It can, however, regard good also, in so far as it is referable to evil. This can be in two ways. In one way, in so far as an evil causes privation of good. Now a thing is evil from the very fact that it is a privation of some good. Therefore, since evil is shunned because it is evil, it follows that it is shunned because it deprives one of the good that one pursues through love for that good. And in this sense Augustine says that there is no cause for fear, save loss of the good we love.

In another way, good stands related to evil as its cause, in so far as some good can by its power bring harm to the good we love. And so, just as hope, as stated above (Q. XL, A. 7), regards two things, namely, the good to which it tends, and the thing through which there is a hope of obtaining the desired good, so also does fear regard two things, namely, the evil

[1] QQ. LXXXIII, Qu. 33 (PL 40, 22).
[2] *Rhetoric*, II, 5 (1382ᵃ30).
[3] PG 94, 929.   [4] Aristotle, VI, 2 (1139ᵇ21).

from which it shrinks, and that good which, by its power, can inflict that evil. In this way God is feared by man, in so far as He can inflict punishment, spiritual or corporal. In this way, too, we fear the power of man, especially when it has been thwarted, or when it is unjust, because then it is more likely to do us a harm.

In like manner one fears "to be over another," that is, to lean on another, so that it is in his power to do us a harm; thus a man fears another who knows him to be guilty of a crime, lest he reveal it to others.

This suffices for *the Replies to the Objections.*

ARTICLE 2. *Whether Evil of Nature Is an Object of Fear?*

We proceed thus to the Second Article: It seems that evil of nature is not an object of fear.

Objection 1. For the Philosopher says[1] that "fear makes us take counsel." But we do not take counsel about things which happen naturally, as stated in *Ethics.*[2] Therefore evil of nature is not an object of fear.

Obj. 2. Further, natural defects such as death and the like are always threatening man. If therefore such evils were an object of fear, man would have to be always in fear.

Obj. 3. Further, nature does not move to contraries. But evil of nature is an effect of nature. Therefore if a man shrinks from such evils through fear of them, this is not an effect of nature. Therefore natural fear is not of the evil of nature and yet it seems to pertain to it.

On the contrary. The Philosopher says[3] that "the most terrible of all things is death," which is an evil of nature.

I answer that, As the Philosopher says,[4] fear is caused by "the imagination of a future evil which is either corruptive or painful." Now just as a painful evil is that which is contrary to the will, so a corruptive evil is that which is contrary to nature. And this is the evil of nature. Consequently evil of nature can be the object of fear.

But it must be observed that evil of nature sometimes arises from a natural cause, and then it is called evil of nature not merely from being a privation of the good of nature, but also from being an effect of nature; such are natural death and other like defects. But sometimes evil of nature arises from a non-natural cause, such

as violent death inflicted by an assailant. In either case evil of nature is feared to a certain extent, and to a certain extent not. For since fear arises "from the imagination of future evil," as the Philosopher says, whatever removes the imagination of the future evil, removes fear also. Now it may happen in two ways that an evil, considered as future, may not seem great. First, through being remote and far off; for, on account of the distance, such a thing is considered as though it were not to be at all. Hence we either do not fear it, or fear it but little; for, as the Philosopher says,[5] "we do not fear things that are very far off; for all know that they shall die, but as death is not near, they heed it not." Secondly, a future evil is considered as though it were not to be on account of its being inevitable, and so we look upon it as already present. Hence the Philosopher says[6] that "those who are already on the scaffold, are not afraid," seeing that they are on the very point of a death from which there is no escape; "but in order that a man be afraid, there must be some hope of escape for him." Consequently evil of nature is not feared if it is not apprehended as future; but if evil of nature that is corruptive is apprehended as near at hand, and yet with some hope of escape, then it will be feared.

Reply Obj. 1. The evil of nature sometimes is not an effect of nature, as stated above. But in so far as it is an effect of nature, although it may be impossible to avoid it entirely, yet it may be possible to delay it. And with this hope one may take counsel about avoiding it.

Reply Obj. 2. Although evil of nature always threatens, yet it does not always threaten from near at hand, and consequently it is not always feared.

Reply Obj. 3. Death and other defects of nature are the effects of the universal nature, and yet the particular nature rebels against them as far as it can. Accordingly, from the inclination of the particular nature arise pain and sorrow for such evils, when present, and fear if they threaten in the future.

ARTICLE 3. *Whether the Evil of Sin Is an Object of Fear?*

We proceed thus to the Third Article: It seems that the evil of sin can be an object of fear.

Objection 1. For Augustine says on the canonical Epistle of John (*Tract.* ix),[7] that by chaste fear man fears to be severed from God. Now

[1] *Rhetoric,* II, 5 (1383[b]6).
[2] Aristotle, III, 3 (1112[a]23).
[3] *Ethics,* III, 6 (1115[a]26).
[4] *Rhetoric,* II, 5 (1382[a]21).
[5] *Ibid.* (1382[a]25).
[6] *Ibid.* (1383[a]5).   [7] PL 35, 2049.

nothing but sin severs us from God, according to Isa. 59. 2: *Your iniquities have divided between you and your God.* Therefore the evil of sin can be an object of fear.

Obj. 2. Further, Cicero says (*Quæst. Tusc.* iv, 6)[1] that we fear when they are yet to come those things which give us pain when they are present. But it is possible for one to be pained or sorrowful on account of the evil of sin. Therefore one can also fear the evil of sin.

Obj. 3. Further, hope is contrary to fear. But the good of virtue can be the object of hope, as the Philosopher declares;[2] and the Apostle says (Gal. 5. 10): *I have confidence in you in the Lord, that you will not be of another mind.* Therefore fear can regard evil of sin.

Obj. 4. Further, shame is a kind of fear, as stated above (Q. XLI, A. 4). But shame regards a disgraceful deed, which is an evil of sin. Therefore fear does so likewise.

On the contrary, The Philosopher says[3] that "not all evils are feared, for instance that someone be unjust or slow."

I answer that, As stated above (Q. XL, A. 1; Q. XLI, A. 2), as the object of hope is a future good difficult but possible to obtain, so the object of fear is a future evil, arduous and not to be easily avoided. From this we may gather that whatever is entirely subject to our power and will is not an object of fear, and that nothing gives rise to fear save what is due to an external cause. Now human will is the proper cause of the evil of sin, and consequently evil of sin, properly speaking, is not an object of fear.

But since the human will may be inclined to sin by an extrinsic cause, if this cause have a strong power of inclination, in that respect a man may fear the evil of sin, in so far as it arises from that extrinsic cause; as when he fears to dwell in the company of wicked men lest he be led by them to sin. But, properly speaking, a man thus disposed fears the being led astray rather than the sin considered in its proper notion, that is, as a voluntary act; for considered in this light it is not an object of fear to him.

Reply Obj. 1. Separation from God is a punishment resulting from sin; and every punishment is, in some way, due to an extrinsic cause.

Reply Obj. 2. Sorrow and fear agree in one point, since each regards evil. They differ, however, in two points. First, because sorrow is

about present evil, while fear is of future evil. Secondly, because sorrow, being in the concupiscible part, regards evil absolutely; hence it can be about any evil, great or small. But fear, being in the irascible part, regards evil with the addition of a certain arduousness or difficulty, which difficulty, ceases in so far as a thing is subject to the will. Consequently not all things that give us pain when they are present make us fear when they are yet to come, but only some things, namely, those that are difficult.

Reply Obj. 3. Hope is of good that is obtainable. Now one may obtain a good either of oneself, or through another; and so, hope may be of an act of virtue, which lies within our own power. On the other hand, fear is of an evil that does not lie in our own power, and consequently the evil which is feared is always from an extrinsic cause, while the good that is hoped for may be both from an intrinsic and from an extrinsic cause.

Reply Obj. 4. As stated above (Q. XLI, A. 4, Reply 2, 3), shame is not fear of the very act of sin, but of the disgrace or ignominy which arises from it, and which is due to an extrinsic cause.

ARTICLE 4. *Whether Fear Itself Can Be Feared?*

We proceed thus to the Fourth Article: It seems that fear cannot be feared.

Objection 1. For whatever is feared is prevented from being lost through fear that; thus a man who fears to lose his health keeps it, through fearing its loss. If therefore a man be afraid of fear, he will keep himself from fear by being afraid, which seems absurd.

Obj. 2. Further, fear is a kind of flight. But nothing flies from itself. Therefore fear cannot be the object of fear.

Obj. 3. Further, fear is about the future. But fear is present to him that fears. Therefore it cannot be the object of his fear.

On the contrary, A man can love his own love, and can grieve at his own sorrow. Therefore, in like manner, he can fear his own fear.

I answer that, As stated above (A. 3), nothing can be an object of fear save what is due to an extrinsic cause; not however that which ensues from our own will. Now fear partly arises from an extrinsic cause, and is partly subject to the will. It is due to an extrinsic cause in so far as it is a passion resulting from the imagination of an imminent evil. In this sense it is possible for fear to be the object of fear, that is, a man may fear lest he should be threatened by

---

[1] DD iv, 26.
[2] *Ethics*, ix, 4 (1166ª25).
[3] *Rhetoric*, ii, 5 (1382ª22).

the necessity of fearing, through being assailed by some great evil. It is subject to the will, however in so far as the lower appetite obeys reason, and so man is able to drive fear away. In this sense fear cannot be the object of fear, as Augustine says (QQ. LXXXIII, *qu.* 33).[1] Lest, however, anyone make use of his arguments in order to prove that fear cannot at all be the object of fear, we must add a solution to the same.

Reply Obj. 1. Not every fear is identically the same; there are various fears according to the various objects of fear. Nothing, then, prevents a man from keeping himself from fearing one thing by fearing another, so that the fear which he has preserves him from the fear which he has not.

Reply Obj. 2. Since fear of an imminent evil is not identical with the fear of the fear of an imminent evil, it does not follow that a thing flies from itself, or that it is the same flight in both cases.

Reply Obj. 3. On account of the various kinds of fear already alluded to (REPLY 2) a man's present fear may have a future fear for its object.

ARTICLE 5. *Whether Sudden Things Are Especially Feared?*

We proceed thus to the Fifth Article: It seems that unaccustomed and sudden things are not especially feared.

Objection 1. Because, as hope is about good things, so fear is about evil things. But experience contributes to the increase of hope in good things. Therefore it also adds to fear in evil things.

Obj. 2. Further, the Philosopher says[2] that those are feared most, "not who are quick-tempered, but who are gentle and cunning." Now it is clear that those who are quick-tempered are more subject to sudden emotions. Therefore sudden things are less to be feared.

Obj. 3. Further, we think less about things that happen suddenly. But the more we think about a thing, the more we fear it; hence the Philosopher says[3] that "some appear to be courageous through ignorance, but as soon as they discover that the case is different from what they expected, they run away." Therefore sudden things are feared less.

On the contrary, Augustine says[4] "Fear is startled at things unaccustomed and sudden, which endanger things beloved, and takes forethought for their safety."

I answer that, As stated above (A. 3; Q. XLI, A. 2), the object of fear is an imminent evil, which can be repelled, but with difficulty. Now this is due to one of two causes: to the greatness of the evil, or to the weakness of him that fears. But unusualness and suddenness contribute to both of these causes. First, they help an imminent evil to seem greater. Because all corporeal things, whether good or evil, the more we consider them, the smaller they seem. Consequently, just as sorrow for a present evil is mitigated in course of time, as Tully states (*Quæst. Tusc.* iii, 30),[5] so too, fear of a future evil is diminished by thinking about it beforehand. Secondly, unusualness and suddenness increase the weakness of him that fears, in so far as they deprive him of the remedies with which he might otherwise provide himself to forestall the coming evil, were it not for the evil taking him by surprise.

Reply Obj. 1. The object of hope is a good that it is possible to obtain. Consequently whatever increases a man's power is of a nature to increase hope, and, for the same reason, to diminish fear, since fear is about an evil which cannot be easily repelled. Since, therefore, experience increases a man's power of action, therefore, as it increases hope, so does it diminish fear.

Reply Obj. 2. Those who are quick-tempered do not hide their anger; hence the harm they do others is not so sudden as not to be foreseen. On the other hand, those who are gentle or cunning hide their anger; therefore the harm which may be impending from them cannot be foreseen, but takes one by surprise. For this reason the Philosopher says that such men are feared more than others.

Reply Obj. 3. Bodily good or evil, considered in itself, seems greater at first. The reason for this is that a thing seems greater when seen in juxtaposition with its contrary. Hence when a man passes unexpectedly from penury to wealth, he thinks more of his wealth on account of his previous poverty; and, on the other hand, the rich man who suddenly becomes poor, finds poverty all the more disagreeable. For this reason sudden evil is feared more, because it seems more to be evil. However, it may happen through some accident that the greatness of some evil is hidden; for instance if the foe hides himself in ambush. And then it is true that evil inspires greater fear through being much thought about.

[1] PL 40, 23.　　　[2] *Rhetoric,* II, 5 (1382[b]20).
[3] *Ethics,* III, 8 (1117[a]24).
[4] *Confessions,* II, 13 (PL 32, 681).　　　[5] DD IV, 20.

ARTICLE 6. *Whether Those Things Are More Feared, for Which There Is No Remedy?*

We proceed thus to the Sixth Article: It would seem that those things are not more to be feared for which there is no remedy.

Objection 1. Because it is a condition of fear that there be some hope of safety, as stated above (A. 2). But an evil that cannot be remedied leaves no hope of escape. Therefore such things are not feared at all.

Obj. 2. Further, there is no remedy for the evil of death, since, in the natural course of things, there is no return from death to life. And yet death is not the most terrible thing of all, as the Philosopher says.[1] Therefore those things are not feared most for which there is no remedy.

Obj. 3. Further, the Philosopher says[2] that "a thing which lasts long is no better than that which lasts but one day; nor is that which lasts for ever any better than that which is not ever-lasting"; and the same applies to evil. But things that cannot be remedied do not seem to differ from other things except in point of their lasting long or for ever. Consequently they are not therefore any more to be feared.

On the contrary, the Philosopher says[3] that "those things are most to be feared which when done wrong cannot be put right, . . . or for which there is no help, or which are not easy."

I answer that, The object of fear is evil. Consequently whatever tends to increase evil contributes to the increase of fear. Now evil is increased not only in its species of evil, but also in respect of circumstances, as stated above (Q. XVIII, A. 3). And of all the circumstances, long-lastingness, or even everlastingness, seems to have the greatest bearing on the increase of evil. Because things that exist in time are measured, in a way, according to the duration of time. Therefore if it be an evil to suffer something for a certain length of time, we should reckon the evil doubled if it be suffered for twice that length of time. And, accordingly, to suffer the same thing for an infinite length of time, that is, for ever, implies, so to speak, an infinite increase. Now those evils which, after they have come, cannot be remedied at all, or at least not easily, are considered as lasting for ever or for a long time. And therefore they inspire the greatest fear.

Reply Obj. 1. Remedy for an evil is twofold. One, by which a future evil is warded off from coming. If such a remedy be removed, there is an end to hope and consequently to fear. Therefore we do not speak now of remedies of that kind. The other remedy is one by which an already present evil is removed, and of such a remedy we speak now.

Reply Obj. 2. Although death be an evil without remedy, yet, since it does not threaten from near at hand, it is not feared, as stated above (A. 2).

Reply Obj. 3. The Philosopher is speaking there of things that are good in themselves, that is, good specifically. And such good is no better for lasting long or for ever; its goodness depends on its very nature.

QUESTION XLIII

OF THE CAUSE OF FEAR

(*In Two Articles*)

WE must now consider the cause of fear, under which head there are two points of inquiry: (1) Whether love is the cause of fear? (2) Whether defect is the cause of fear?

ARTICLE 1. *Whether Love Is the Cause of Fear?*

We proceed thus to the First Article: It seems that love is not the cause of fear.

Objection 1. For that which leads to a thing is its cause. But "*fear leads to the love of charity*" as Augustine says on the canonical epistle of John (*Tract.* ix).[4] Therefore fear is the cause of love, and not conversely.

Obj. 2. Further, the Philosopher says[5] that those are feared most from whom we dread the advent of some evil. But the dread of evil being caused by someone makes us hate rather than love him. Therefore fear is caused by hate rather than by love.

Obj. 3. Further, it has been stated above (Q. XLII, A. 3) that those things which occur by our own doing are not fearful. But that which we do from love is done from our inmost heart. Therefore fear is not caused by love.

On the contrary, Augustine says,[6] "There can be no doubt that there is no cause for fear save the loss of what we love, when we possess it, or the failure to obtain what we hope for." Therefore all fear is caused by our loving

---

[1] *Rhetoric*, II, 5 (1382ª26).
[2] *Ethics*, I, 6 (1096ᵇ3).
[3] *Rhetoric*, II, 5 (1382ᵇ22).

[4] PL 35, 2049.
[5] *Rhetoric*, II, 5 (1382ᵇ33).
[6] QQ. LXXXIII, Qu. 33 (PL 40, 22).

something; and consequently love is the cause of fear.

I answer that, The objects of the soul's passions stand in relation to them as the forms to things natural or artificial, because the passions of the soul take their species from their objects as the aforesaid things do from their forms. Therefore, just as whatever is a cause of the form is a cause of the thing constituted by that form so whatever is a cause in any way whatever of the object, is a cause of the passion. Now a thing may be a cause of the object either by way of efficient cause or by way of material disposition. Thus the object of pleasure is good apprehended as suitable and conjoined, and its efficient cause is that which causes the union, or the suitableness, or goodness, or apprehension of that good thing, while its cause by way of material disposition is a habit or any sort of disposition by reason of which this conjoined good becomes suitable or is apprehended as such.

Accordingly, as to the matter in question, the object of fear is something reckoned as an evil to come, near at hand and difficult to avoid. Therefore that which can inflict such an evil is the effective cause of the object of fear, and consequently, of fear itself. But that which renders a man so disposed that a thing is such an evil to him, is a cause of fear and of its object, by way of material disposition. And thus it is that love causes fear, since it is through his loving a certain good that whatever deprives a man of that good is an evil to him, and that consequently he fears it as an evil.

Reply Obj. 1. As stated above (Q. XLII, A. 1), fear, of itself and in the first place, regards the evil from which it recoils as being contrary to some loved good; and thus fear, of itself, is born of love. But, in the second place, it regards the cause from which that evil ensues, so that sometimes, accidentally, fear gives rise to love; in so far as, for instance, through fear of God's punishments, man keeps His commandments, and thus begins to hope, while hope leads to love, as stated above (Q. XL, A. 7).

Reply Obj. 2. He, from whom evil is expected is indeed hated at first; but afterwards, when once we begin to hope for good from him, we begin to love him. But the good, the contrary evil of which is feared, was loved from the beginning.

Reply Obj. 3. This argument is true of that which is the efficient cause of the evil to be feared. But love causes fear by way of material disposition, as stated above.

ARTICLE 2. *Whether Defect Is the Cause of Fear?*

We proceed thus to the Second Article: It seems that defect is not a cause of fear.

Objection 1. Because those who are in power are very much to be feared. But defect is contrary to power. Therefore defect is not a cause of fear.

Obj. 2. Further, the defect of those who are already being executed is extreme. But such do not fear as stated in the *Rhetoric.*[1] Therefore defect is not a cause of fear.

Obj. 3. Further, men compete with one another from strength not from defect. But "those who contend fear those who contend with them."[2] Therefore defect is not a cause of fear.

On the contrary, Contraries are caused by contrary causes. But "wealth, strength, a multitude of friends, and power drive fear away."[3] Therefore fear is caused by lack of these.

I answer that, As stated above (A. 1), fear may be set down to a twofold cause: one is by way of a material disposition, on the part of him that fears; the other is by way of efficient cause, on the part of the person feared. As to the first then, some defect is, of itself, the cause of fear, for it is owing to some lack of power that one is unable easily to repulse a threatening evil. And yet, in order to cause fear, this defect must be according to a measure. For the defect which causes fear of a future evil is less than the defect caused by evil present, which is the object of sorrow. And still greater would be the defect, if perception of the evil, or love of the good whose contrary is feared, were entirely absent.

But as to the second, power and strength are, of themselves, the cause of fear, because it is owing to the fact that the cause apprehended as harmful is powerful that its effect cannot be repulsed. It may happen, however, in this respect, that some defect causes fear accidentally, in so far as owing to some defect someone wishes to hurt another; for instance, by reason of injustice, either because that other has already done him a harm, or because he fears to be harmed by him.

Reply Obj. 1. This argument is true of the cause of fear, on the part of the efficient cause.

Reply Obj. 2. Those who are already being executed are actually suffering from a present evil; therefore their defect exceeds the measure of fear.

[1] Aristotle, II, 5 (1383[a]5).
[2] *Ibid.* (1382[b]13).   [3] *Ibid.* (1383[b]1).

Reply Obj. 3. Those who contend with one another are afraid, not on account of the power which enables them to contend, but on account of the lack of power, owing to which they are not confident of victory.

QUESTION XLIV
OF THE EFFECTS OF FEAR
(*In Four Articles*)

WE must now consider the effects of fear: under which head there are four points of inquiry: (1) Whether fear causes contraction? (2) Whether it makes men suitable for counsel? (3) Whether it makes one tremble? (4) Whether it hinders action?

ARTICLE 1. *Whether Fear Causes Contraction?*

We proceed thus to the First Article: It seems that fear does not cause contraction.

Objection 1. For when contraction takes place, the heat and vital spirits are withdrawn inwardly. But accumulation of heat and vital spirits in the interior parts of the body dilates the heart with consequent endeavours of daring, as may be seen in those who are angered, while the contrary happens in those who are afraid. Therefore fear does not cause contraction.

Obj. 2. Further, when, as a result of contraction, the vital spirits and heat are accumulated in the interior parts, man cries out, as may be seen in those who are in pain. But those who fear utter nothing; on the contrary they lose their speech. Therefore fear does not cause contraction.

Obj. 3. Further, shame is a kind of fear, as stated above (Q. XLI, A. 4). But "those who are ashamed blush," as Tully (*Quæst. Tusc.* iv, 8),[1] and the Philosopher[2] observe. But blushing is an indication, not of contraction, but of the contrary. Therefore contraction is not an effect of fear.

On the contrary, Damascene says (*De Fide Orthod.* iii, 23)[3] that *fear is "a power according to συστολή,"* that is, contraction.

I answer that, As stated above (Q. XXVIII, A. 5), in the passions of the soul, the movement of the appetitive power is as the formal element while the bodily change is as the material element. Both of these are mutually proportionate, and consequently the bodily change assumes a resemblance to and the very character

of the appetitive movement. Now, as to the appetitive movement of the soul, fear implies a certain contraction, the reason of which is that fear arises from the imagination of some threatening evil which is difficult to repel, as stated above (Q. XLI, A. 2). But that a thing be difficult to repel is due to lack of power, as stated above (Q. XLIII, A. 2), and the weaker a power is, the fewer the things to which it extends. Therefore from the very imagination that causes fear there ensues a certain contraction in the appetite. Thus we observe in one who is dying that nature withdraws inwardly on account of the lack of power; and again we see the inhabitants of a city, when seized with fear, leave the outskirts, and, as far as possible, make for the inner quarters. It is in resemblance to this contraction, which pertains to the appetite of the soul, that in fear a similar contraction of heat and vital spirits towards the inner parts takes place in regard to the body.

Reply Obj. 1. As the Philosopher says,[4] although in those who fear the vital spirits recede from the outer to the inner parts of the body, yet the movement of vital spirits is not the same in those who are angry and those who are afraid. For in those who are angry, by reason of the heat and subtlety of the vital spirits, which result from the desire for vengeance, the inward movement has an upward direction, and therefore the vital spirits and heat concentrate around the heart, with the result that an angry man is quick and brave in attacking. But in those who are afraid on account of the condensation caused by the cold, the vital spirits have a downward movement; for this cold is due to the imagined lack of power. Consequently the heat and vital spirits abandon the heart instead of concentrating around it, the result being that a man who is afraid is not quick to attack, but is more inclined to run away.

Reply Obj. 2. To everyone that is in pain, whether man or animal, it is natural to use all possible means of repelling the harmful thing that causes pain by its presence; thus we observe that animals, when in pain, attack with their jaws or with their horns. Now the greatest help for all purposes, in animals, is heat and vital spirits. Therefore when they are in pain, their nature stores up the heat and vital spirits within them, in order to make use of them in repelling the harmful thing. Hence the Philosopher says[5] that when the vital spirits and heat are concentrated together within, they require

---

[1] DD IV, 28.   [2] *Ethics*, IV, 9 (1128[b]13).
[3] PG 94, 1088.

[4] Pseudo-Aristotle, *Problemata*, XXVII, 3 (947[b]23).
[5] *Ibid.*, XXVII, 9 (948[b]20).

to find a vent in the voice, for which reason those who are in pain can scarcely refrain from crying aloud. On the other hand, in those who are afraid the internal heat and vital spirits move from the heart downwards, as stated above (reply 1); and therefore fear hinders speech which ensues from the emission of the vital spirits in an upward direction through the mouth, the result being that fear makes its subject speechless. For this reason, too, "fear makes its subject tremble," as the Philosopher says.[1]

Reply Obj. 3. Mortal perils are contrary not only to the animal appetite, but also to nature. Consequently in this kind of fear, there is contraction not only in the appetite but also in the corporeal nature, for when an animal is moved by the imagination of death, it experiences a contraction of heat towards the inner parts of the body, just as when it is threatened by a natural death. Hence it is that "those who are in fear of death turn pale."[2] But the evil that shame fears is contrary, not to nature but only to the appetite of the soul. Consequently there results a contraction in this appetite, but not in the corporeal nature; rather, indeed, the soul, as though contracted in itself, is set free from the motion of the vital spirits and heat, so that they spread to the outward parts of the body, the result being that those who are ashamed blush.

ARTICLE 2. *Whether Fear Makes One Suitable for Counsel?*

We proceed thus to the Second Article: It would seem that fear does not make one suitable for counsel.

Objection 1. For the same thing cannot be conducive to counsel, and a hindrance to it. But fear hinders counsel because every passion disturbs repose, which is requisite for the good use of reason. Therefore fear does not make a man suitable for counsel.

Obj. 2. Further, counsel is an act of reason in thinking and deliberating about the future. But a certain fear "drives away all thought, and dislocates the mind," as Cicero observes (*De Quæst, Tusc.* iv, 8).[3] Therefore fear does not conduce to counsel, but hinders it.

Obj. 3. Further, just as we have recourse to counsel in order to avoid evil, so likewise do we in order to attain good things. But just as fear is of evil to be avoided, so is hope concerned with good things to be obtained. Therefore fear is not more conductive to counsel, than hope is.

On the contrary, The Philosopher says[4] that "fear makes men of counsel."

I answer that, A man of counsel may be taken in two ways. First, from his being willing or anxious to take counsel. And thus fear makes men of counsel. Because, as the Philosopher says,[5] "we take counsel on great matters, because therein we distrust ourselves." Now things which make us afraid are not evil absolutely, but have a certain magnitude, both because they seem difficult to repel and because they are apprehended as near to us, as stated above (q. xlii, a. 2). Therefore men seek for counsel especially when they are afraid.

Secondly, a man of counsel means one who is apt for giving good counsel, and in this sense neither fear nor any passion makes men of counsel. Because when a man is affected by a passion, things seem to him greater or smaller than they really are; thus to a lover, what he loves seems better; to him that fears, what he fears seems more dreadful. Consequently owing to the want of right judgment, every passion, considered in itself, hinders the power of giving good counsel.

This suffices for the *Reply to the First Objection.*

Reply Obj. 2. The stronger a passion is, the greater hindrance is it to the man who is swayed by it. Consequently, when fear is intense, man does indeed wish to take counsel, but his thoughts are so disturbed that he can find no counsel. If, however, the fear be slight, so as to make a man wish to take counsel without gravely disturbing the reason, it may even make it easier for him to take good counsel, by reason of its making him want to do so.

Reply Obj. 3. Hope also makes man a good counsellor, because, as the Philosopher says,[6] "no man takes counsel in matters he despairs of," nor about impossible things, as he says in the *Ethics.*[7] But fear incites to counsel more than hope does. For hope is of good things, as being possible of attainment, while fear is of evil things, as being difficult to repel, so that fear regards the aspect of difficulty more than hope does. And it is in matters of difficulty, especially when we distrust ourselves, that we take counsel, as stated above.

---

[1] Pseudo-Aristotle, *Problemata*, xxvii, 1, 6 (947[b]12; 948[a]35).

[2] Aristotle, *Ethics*, iv, 9 (1128[b]13).   [3] DD iv, 28.

[4] *Rhetoric*, ii, 5 (1383[a]6).

[5] *Ethics*, iii, 3 (1112[b]10).

[6] *Rhetoric*, ii, 5 (1383[a]7).

[7] iii, 3 (1112[b]24).

ARTICLE 3. *Whether Fear Makes One Tremble?*

We proceed thus to the Third Article: It seems that trembling is not an effect of fear.

Objection 1. Because trembling is occasioned by cold; thus we observe that a cold person trembles. Now fear does not seem to make one cold, but rather to cause a dessicating heat. A sign of this is that those who fear are thirsty, especially if their fear be very great, as in the case of those who are being led to death. Therefore fear does not cause trembling.

Obj. 2. Further, fæcal evacuation is occasioned by heat; hence most laxative medicines are generally warm. But these evacuations are often caused by fear. Therefore fear apparently causes heat, and consequently does not cause trembling.

Obj. 3. Further, in fear, the heat is withdrawn from the outer to the inner parts of the body. If, therefore, man trembles in his outward parts through the heat being withdrawn in this way, it seems that fear should cause this trembling in all the external members. But such is not the case. Therefore trembling of the body is not caused by fear.

On the contrary, Cicero says (*De Quæst. Tusc.* iv, 8)[1] that "fear is followed by trembling, pallor and chattering of the teeth."

I answer that, As stated above (A. 1), in fear there takes place a certain contraction from the outward to the inner parts of the body, the result being that the outer parts become cold; and for this reason trembling is occasioned in these parts, being caused by a lack of power in controlling the members. This lack of power is due to the want of heat, which is the instrument by which the soul moves those members, as stated in the treatise on the *Soul*.[2]

Reply Obj. 1. When the heat withdraws from the outer to the inner parts, the inward heat increases, especially in the inferior (or nutritive) parts. Consequently the humid element being spent, thirst ensues; sometimes indeed the result is a loosening of the bowels, and urinary or even seminal evacuation.—Or else such evacuations are due to contraction of the abdomen and testicles, as the Philosopher says.[3]

This suffices for the *Reply to the Second Objection.*

Reply Obj. 3. In fear, heat abandons the heart, with a downward movement. Hence in

those who are afraid the heart especially trembles, as also those members which are connected with the breast where the heart resides. Hence those who fear tremble especially in their speech, on account of the tracheal artery being near the heart. The lower lip, too, and the lower jaw tremble, through their connection with the heart, which explains the chattering of the teeth. For the same reason the arms and hands tremble. Or else because these members are more moveable. For this reason also the knees tremble in those who are afraid, according to Isa. 35. 3: *Strengthen ye the feeble hands, and confirm the trembling* (Vulg., *weak*) *knees.*

ARTICLE 4. *Whether Fear Hinders Action?*

We proceed thus to the Fourth Article: It seems that fear hinders action.

Objection 1. For action is hindered chiefly by a disturbance in the reason, which directs action. But fear disturbs reason, as stated above (A. 2). Therefore fear hinders action.

Obj. 2. Further, those who fear while doing anything, are more apt to fail; thus a man who walks on a plank placed high up, is likely to fall through fear; but if he were to walk on the same plank down below, he would not fall, through not being afraid. Therefore fear hinders action.

Obj. 3. Further, laziness or sloth is a kind of fear. But laziness hinders action. Therefore fear does too.

On the contrary, The Apostle says (Phil. 2. 12): *With fear and trembling work out your salvation,* and he would not say this if fear were a hindrance to a good work. Therefore fear does not hinder a good action.

I answer that, Man's exterior actions are caused by the soul as first mover, but by the bodily members as instruments. Now action may be hindered both by defect of the instrument and by defect of the principal mover. On the part of the bodily instruments, fear, considered in itself, will always naturally hinder exterior action, on account of the outward members being deprived, through fear, of their heat. But on the part of the soul, if the fear be moderate, without much disturbance of the reason, it conduces to working well, in so far as it causes a certain solicitude, and makes a man take counsel and work with greater attention. If, however, fear increases so much as to disturb the reason, it hinders action even on the part of the soul. But of such a fear the Apostle does not speak.

[1] DD iv, 28.   [2] Aristotle, ii, 4 (416ᵇ29).

[3] Pseudo-Aristotle, *Problemata*, xxvii, 10, 11 (948ᵇ35; 949ᵃ9).

This suffices for the *Reply to the First Objection.*

Reply Obj. 2. He that falls from a plank placed aloft suffers a disturbance of his imagination, through fear of the fall that is pictured to his imagination.

Reply Obj. 3. Everyone in fear shuns that which he fears, and therefore, since laziness is a fear of work itself as being toilsome, it hinders work by withdrawing the will from it. But fear of other things conduces to action, in so far as it inclines the will to do that by which a man escapes from what he fears.

QUESTION XLV
OF DARING
(In Four Articles)

WE must now consider daring, under which head there are four points of inquiry: (1) Whether daring is contrary to fear? (2) How is daring related to hope? (3) Of the cause of daring; (4) Of its effect.

ARTICLE 1. *Whether Daring Is Contrary to Fear?*

We proceed thus to the First Article: It would seem that daring is not contrary to fear.

Objection 1. For Augustine says (QQ. LXXXIII, qu. 31)[1] that "daring is a vice." Now vice is contrary to virtue. Since, therefore, fear is not a virtue but a passion, it seems that daring is not contrary to fear.

Obj. 2. Further, to one thing there is one contrary. But hope is contrary to fear. Therefore daring is not contrary to fear.

Obj. 3. Further, every passion excludes its opposite. But fear excludes safety; for Augustine says[2] that "fear takes forethought for safety." Therefore safety is contrary to fear. Therefore daring is not contrary to fear.

On the contrary, The Philosopher says[3] that "daring is contrary to fear."

I answer that, It is of the very notion of contraries to be farthest removed from one another, as stated in the *Metaphysics.*[4] Now that which is farthest removed from fear is daring, for fear turns away from the future hurt on account of its victory over him that fears it; but daring turns on threatened danger, because of its own victory over that same danger. Consequently it is evident that daring is contrary to fear.

Reply Obj. 1. Anger, daring and all the names

of the passions can be taken in two ways. First, as denoting absolutely movements of the sensitive appetite in respect of some object, good or bad, and thus they are names of passions. Secondly, as denoting besides this movement a straying from the order of reason, and thus they are names of vices. It is in this sense that Augustine speaks of daring, but we are speaking of it here in the first sense.

Reply Obj. 2. To one thing, in the same respect, there are not several contraries; but in different respects nothing prevents one thing from having several contraries. Accordingly it has been said above (Q. XXIII, A. 2; Q. XL, A. 4) that the irascible passions admit of a twofold contrariety: one, according to the opposition of good and evil, and thus fear is contrary to hope; the other, according to the opposition of approach and withdrawal, and thus daring is contrary to fear, and despair contrary to hope.

Reply Obj. 3. Safety does not denote something contrary to fear, but merely the exclusion of fear; for he is said to be safe who does not fear. Therefore safety is opposed to fear as a privation, while daring is opposed to it as a contrary. And as contrariety implies privation, so daring implies safety.

ARTICLE 2. *Whether Daring Ensues from Hope?*

We proceed thus to the Second Article: It seems that daring does not ensue from hope.

Objection 1. Because daring is in respect of evil and fearful things, as stated in the *Ethics.*[5] But hope regards good things, as stated above (Q. XL, A. 1). Therefore they have different objects and are not in the same order. Therefore daring does not ensue from hope.

Obj. 2. Further, just as daring is contrary to fear, so is despair contrary to hope. But fear does not ensue from despair; rather indeed despair excludes fear, as the Philosopher says.[6] Therefore daring does not result from hope.

Obj. 3. Further, daring is intent on something good, namely, victory. But it pertains to hope to tend to that which is good and difficult. Therefore daring is the same as hope, and consequently does not result from it.

On the contrary, The Philosopher says[7] that those who are hopeful are full of daring. Therefore it seems that daring ensues from hope.

I answer that, As we have often stated (Q. XXII, A. 2; Q. XXXV, A. 1; Q. XLI, A. 1), all passions of this kind pertain to the appetitive power. Now every movement of the appetitive pow-

---

[1] PL 40, 21; cf. qu. 34 (PL 40, 23).
[2] *Confessions,* II, 13 (PL 32, 681).
[3] *Rhetoric,* II, 5 (1383ª16).　　[4] Aristotle, X, 4 (1055ª9).
[5] Aristotle, III, 7 (1115ᵇ28).
[6] *Rhetoric,* II, 5 (1383ª3).　　[7] *Ethics,* III, 8 (1117ª9).

er is reducible to one either of pursuit or of avoidance. Again, pursuit or avoidance is of something either by reason of itself or by reason of something accidental. By reason of itself, good is the object of pursuit, and evil the object of avoidance. But by reason of something accidental evil can be the object of pursuit, through some good attaching to it, and good can be the object of avoidance, through some evil attaching to it. Now that which is accidental follows that which is by reason of itself. Consequently pursuit of evil follows pursuit of good, and avoidance of good follows avoidance of evil. Now these four things pertain to four passions, since pursuit of good pertains to hope, avoidance of evil to fear, the pursuit of the fearful evil pertains to daring, and the avoidance of good to despair. It follows, therefore, that daring results from hope; for it is in the hope of overcoming the threatening object of fear that one attacks it boldly. But despair results from fear, for the reason why a man despairs is because he fears the difficulty attaching to the good he should hope for.

Reply Obj. 1. This argument would hold, if good and evil were not objects ordered to one another. But because evil has a certain order to good, since it comes after good, as privation comes after habit, therefore daring which pursues evil, comes after hope which pursues good.

Reply Obj. 2. Although good, absolutely speaking, is prior to evil, yet avoidance of evil precedes avoidance of good, just as the pursuit of good precedes the pursuit of evil. Consequently just as hope precedes daring, so fear precedes despair. And just as fear does not always lead to despair, but only when it is intense, so hope does not always lead to daring, but only when it is strong.

Reply Obj. 3. Although the object of daring is an evil to which, in the estimation of the daring man, the good of victory is joined, yet daring regards the evil, and hope regards the good joined to it. In like manner despair regards directly the good which it turns away from, while fear regards the evil joined to it. Hence, properly speaking, daring is not a part of hope, but its effect, just as despair is an effect, not a part, of fear. For this reason, too, daring cannot be a principal passion.

ARTICLE 3. *Whether Some Defect Is a Cause of Daring?*

We proceed thus to the Third Article: It would seem that some defect is a cause of daring.

Objection 1. For the Philosopher says[1] that "lovers of wine are strong and daring." But from wine ensues the defect of drunkenness. Therefore daring is caused by a defect.

Obj. 2. Further, the Philosopher says[2] that "those who have no experience of danger are bold." But want of experience is a defect. Therefore daring is caused by a defect.

Obj. 3. Further, those who have suffered wrongs are usually daring, like beasts when beaten, as stated in the *Ethics*.[3] But the suffering of wrongs pertains to defect. Therefore daring is caused by a defect.

On the contrary, The Philosopher says[4] that the cause of daring "is the presence in the imagination of the hope that the means of safety are near, and that the things to be feared are either non-existent or far off." But anything pertaining to defect implies either the removal of the means of safety, or the proximity of something to be feared. Therefore nothing pertaining to defect is a cause of daring.

I answer that, As stated above (AA. 1, 2) daring results from hope and is contrary to fear. Therefore whatever is naturally apt to cause hope or banish fear, is a cause of daring. Since, however, fear and hope, and also daring, being passions, consist in a movement of the appetite, and in a certain bodily change, a thing may be considered as the cause of daring in two ways, whether by raising hope, or by banishing of fear; in one way, on the part of the appetitive movement, in another way, on the part of the bodily change.

On the part of the appetitive movement which follows apprehension, hope that leads to daring is roused by those things that make us estimate victory as possible. Such things regard either our own power, as bodily strength, experience of dangers, abundance of wealth, and the like, or they regard the power of others, such as having a great number of friends or any other means of help, especially if a man trust in the Divine assistance; hence "those are more daring with whom it is well in regard to godlike things," as the Philosopher says.[5] Fear is banished, in this way, by the removal of threatening causes of fear; for instance, by the fact that a man has no enemies, because he has harmed nobody, because he is not aware of any imminent danger; for those especially appear to be threatened by danger who have harmed others.

---

[1] Pseudo-Aristotle, *Problemata*, XXVII, 4 (948ª13).
[2] *Rhetoric*, II, 5 (1383ª28).   [3] Aristotle, III, 8 (1116ᵇ32).
[4] *Rhetoric*, II, 5 (1383ª17).   [5] *Ibid.*, II, 5 (1383ᵇ5).

On the part of the bodily change, daring is caused through the incitement of hope and the banishment of fear, by those things which raise the temperature about the heart. Therefore the Philosopher says[1] that "those whose heart is small according to quantity, are more daring, while animals whose heart is large are timid, because the natural heat is unable to give the same degree of temperature to a large as to a small heart; just as a fire does not heat a large house as well as it does a small house." He says also[2] that "those whose lungs contain much blood, are more daring, through the heat in the heart that results from this." He says also in the same passage that "lovers of wine are more daring, on account of the heat of the wine"; hence it has been said above (Q. XL, A. 6) that drunkenness conduces to hope, since the heat in the heart banishes fear and raises hope, by reason of the dilation and enlargement of the heart.

Reply Obj. 1. Drunkenness causes daring, not through being a defect, but through dilating the heart; and again through making a man think greatly of himself.

Reply Obj. 2. Those who have no experience of dangers are more daring, not on account of a defect, but accidentally, that is, in so far as through being inexperienced they do not know their own failings, nor the dangers that threaten. Hence it is that the removal of the cause of fear gives rise to daring.

Reply Obj. 3. As the Philosopher says[3] "those who have been wronged are courageous, because they think that God comes to the assistance of those who suffer unjustly."

Hence it is evident that no defect causes daring except accidentally, that is, in so far as some excellence attaches to it, real or imaginary, either in oneself or in another.

ARTICLE 4. *Whether the Daring Are More Eager at First than in the Midst of Danger?*

We proceed thus to the Fourth Article: It seems that the daring are more eager at first than in the midst of danger.

Objection 1. Because trembling is caused by fear, which is contrary to daring, as stated above (A. 1; Q. XLIV, A. 3). But the daring sometimes tremble at first, as the Philosopher says.[4] Therefore they are not more eager at first than in the midst of danger.

Obj. 2. Further, passion is intensified by an increase in its object; thus since a good is lovable, what is better is yet more lovable. But the object of daring is something difficult. Therefore the greater the difficulty, the greater the daring. But danger is more arduous and difficult when present. It is then therefore that daring is greatest.

Obj. 3. Further, anger is provoked by the infliction of wounds. But anger causes daring; for the Philosopher says[5] that "anger makes man bold." Therefore when man is in the midst of danger and when he is being beaten, then is he most daring.

On the contrary, It is said in the *Ethics*[6] that "the daring are precipitate and full of eagerness before the danger, yet in the midst of dangers they give way."

I answer that, Daring, being a movement of the sensitive appetite, follows an apprehension of the sensitive power. But the sensitive power cannot make comparisons, nor can it inquire into individual circumstances; its judgment is instantaneous. Now it happens sometimes that it is impossible for a man to take note in an instant of all the difficulties of a certain situation; hence there arises the movement of daring to face the danger, and when he comes to experience the danger, he feels the difficulty to be greater than he expected, and so gives way.

On the other hand, reason discusses all the difficulties of a situation. Consequently men of fortitude who face danger according to the judgment of reason at first seem slack, because they face the danger not from passion but with due deliberation. Yet when they are in the midst of danger, they experience nothing unforeseen, but sometimes the difficulty turns out to be less than they anticipated; therefore they are more persevering. Moreover, it may be because they face the danger on account of the good of virtue which is the abiding object of their will, however great the danger may prove; but men of daring face the danger on account of estimation only, which gives rise to hope and banishing fear, as stated above (A. 3).

Reply Obj. 1. Trembling does occur in men of daring, on account of the heat being withdrawn from the outer to the inner parts of the body, as occurs also in those who are afraid. But in men of daring the heat withdraws to the heart; in those who are afraid, however, it withdraws to the inferior parts.

Reply Obj. 2. The object of love is good ab-

---

[1] *Parts of Animals,* III, 4 (667ª15).
[2] Pseudo-Aristotle, *Problemata,* XXVII, 4 (948ª17).
[3] *Rhetoric,* II, 5 (1383ᵇ7).
[4] Pseudo-Aristotle, *Problemata,* XXVII, 3 (948ª8).
[5] *Rhetoric,* II, 5 (1383ᵇ7).   [6] Aristotle, III, 7 (1116ª7).

solutely, and so if it be increased, love is increased absolutely. But the object of daring is a compound of good and evil, and the movement of daring towards evil presupposes the movement of hope towards good. If, therefore, so much difficulty be added to the danger that it overcomes hope, the movement of daring does not follow, but fails. But if the movement of daring does ensue, the greater the danger the greater is the daring considered to be.

Reply Obj. 3. Hurt does not give rise to anger unless there be some kind of hope, as we shall see later on (Q. XLVI, A. 1). Consequently if the danger be so great as to banish all hope of victory, anger does not follow. It is true, however, that if danger does ensue, there will be greater daring.

QUESTION XLVI

OF ANGER IN ITSELF

(*In Eight Articles*)

WE must now consider anger; and (1) anger in itself; (2) the cause that produces anger and its remedy (Q. XLVII); (3) the effect of anger (Q. XLVIII).

Under the first head there are eight points of inquiry: (1) Whether anger is a special passion? (2) Whether the object of anger is good or evil? (3) Whether anger is in the concupiscible part? (4) Whether anger is accompanied by an act of reason? (5) Whether anger is more natural than concupiscence? (6) Whether anger is more grievous than hatred? (7) Whether anger is only towards those with whom we have a relation of justice? (8) Of the species of anger.

ARTICLE 1. *Whether Anger Is a Special Passion?*

We proceed thus to the First Article: It seems that anger is not a special passion.

Objection 1. For the irascible power takes its name from anger (*ira*). But there are several passions in this power, not only one. Therefore anger is not a special passion.

Obj. 2. Further, to every special passion there is a contrary passion, as is evident by going through them one by one. But no passion is contrary to anger, as stated above (Q. XXIII, A. 3). Therefore anger is not a special passion.

Obj. 3. Further, one special passion does not include another. But anger includes many passions, since it accompanies sorrow, pleasure, and hope, as the Philosopher states.[1] Therefore anger is not a special passion.

¹ *Rhetoric*, II, 2 (1378ª31).

On the contrary, Damascene (*De Fide Orthod.* ii, 16)[2] calls anger a special passion, and so does Cicero (*De Quæst. Tusc.* iv, 7, 9).[3]

I answer that, A thing is said to be general in two ways. First, by predication; thus "animal" is general in respect of all animals. Secondly, by causality; thus the sun is the general cause of all things generated here below, according to Dionysius (*Div. Nom.* iv).[4] Because just as a genus contains potentially many differences, according to a likeness of matter, so an agent cause contains many effects according to its active power. Now it happens that an effect is produced by the concurrence of different causes; and since every cause remains somewhat in its effect, we may say that, in yet a third way, an effect which is due to the concurrence of several causes has a certain generality, in so far as it contains many causes in a certain manner in act.

Accordingly in the first way, anger is not a general passion, but is divided with the other passions, as stated above (Q. XXIII, A. 4). In like manner, neither is it in the second way, since it is not a cause of the other passions. But in this way love may be called a general passion, as Augustine declares,[5] because love is the primary root of all the passions, as stated above (Q. XXVII, A. 4). But, in the third way, anger may be called a general passion, in so far as it is caused by a concurrence of several passions. For the movement of anger does not arise except on account of some pain inflicted, and unless there be the desire and hope of revenge; for, as the Philosopher says,[6] "the angry man hopes to punish; for he desires for revenge as being possible." Consequently if the person who inflicted the injury excel very much, anger does not ensue, but only sorrow, as Avicenna states (*De Anima,* iv, 6).[7]

Reply Obj. 1. The irascible power takes its name from *ira* (anger), not because every movement of that power is one of anger, but because all its movements terminate in anger, and because, of all these movements, anger is the most manifest.

Reply Obj. 2. From the very fact that anger is caused by contrary passions, that is, by hope, which is of good, and by sorrow, which is of evil, it includes in itself contrariety; and consequently it has no contrary outside itself. Thus also in mixed colours there is no contrariety except that of the simple colours from which they are made.

² PG 94, 932.   ³ DD IV, 27, 29.
⁴ Sect. 4 (PG 3, 697).
⁵ *City of God,* XIV, 7 (PL 41, 410).
⁶ *Rhetoric,* II, 2 (1378ᵇ4).   ⁷ 22ra.

Reply Obj. 3. Anger includes several passions, not indeed as a genus includes several species, but rather according to the inclusion of cause and effect.

ARTICLE 2. *Whether the Object of Anger Is Good or Evil?*

We proceed thus to the Second Article: It seems that the object of anger is evil.

Objection 1. For Gregory of Nyssa (Nemesius, *De Nat. Hom.* xxi)[1] says that "anger is as it were the sword-bearer of desire," in so far, that is, as it assails whatever obstacle stands in the way of desire. But every obstacle has the character of evil. Therefore anger regards evil as its object.

Obj. 2. Further, anger and hatred agree in their effect, since each seeks to inflict harm on another. But hatred regards evil as its object, as stated above (Q. XXIX, A. 1). Therefore anger does also.

Obj. 3. Further, anger arises from sorrow; hence the Philosopher says[2] that "anger acts with sorrow." But evil is the object of sorrow. Therefore it is also the object of anger.

On the contrary, Augustine says[3] that "anger craves for revenge." But the desire for revenge is a desire for something good, since revenge pertains to justice. Therefore the object of anger is good.

2. *Moreover,* anger is always accompanied by hope, and so it causes pleasure, as the Philosopher says.[4] But the object of hope and of pleasure is good. Therefore good is also the object of anger.

I answer that, The movement of the appetitive power follows an act of the apprehensive power. Now the apprehensive power apprehends a thing in two ways. First, by way of an incomplex object, as when we understand what a man is; secondly, by way of a complex object, as when we understand that whiteness is in a man. Consequently in each of these ways the appetitive power can tend to both good and evil: by way of a simple and incomplex object, when the appetite simply follows or adheres to good, or recoils from evil (and such movements are desire, hope, pleasure, sorrow, and so forth); by way of a complex object, as when the appetite is concerned with some good or evil being in, or being done to, another, either seeking this or recoiling from it. This is evident in the case of love and hatred; for we love someone in so far as we

wish some good to be in him, and we hate someone in so far as we wish some evil to be in him. It is the same with anger, for when a man is angry, he wishes to be avenged on someone. Hence the movement of anger has a twofold tendency: namely, to vengeance itself, which it desires and hopes for as being a good, and in which consequently it takes pleasure; and to the person on whom it seeks vengeance, as to something contrary and hurtful, which bears the character of evil.

We must, however, observe a twofold difference in this respect, between anger on the one side, and hatred and love on the other. The first difference is that anger always looks to two objects, but love and hatred sometimes look to but one object, as when a man is said to love wine or something of the kind, or to hate it. The second difference is, that both the objects of love are good, since the lover wishes good to someone, as to something agreeable to himself, while both the objects of hatred bear the character of evil, for the man who hates wishes evil to someone, as to something disagreeable to him. But anger looks to one object under the aspect of good, namely, vengeance, which it desires to have, and the other object under the aspect of evil, namely, the undesirable person, on whom it seeks to be avenged. Consequently it is a passion made up in a certain way of contrary passions.

This suffices for the *Replies to the Objections.*

ARTICLE 3. *Whether Anger Is in the Concupiscible Part?*

We proceed thus to the Third Article: It would seem that anger is in the concupiscible part.

Objection 1. For Cicero says (*De Quæst. Tusc.* iv, 9)[5] that anger is a kind of desire. But desire is in the concupiscible part. Therefore anger is too.

Obj. 2. Further, Augustine says in his Rule,[6] that "anger grows into hatred"; and Cicero says (*loc. cit.*) that "hatred is inveterate anger." But hatred, like love, is a concupiscible passion. Therefore anger is in the concupiscible part.

Obj. 3. Further, Damascene (*De Fide Orthod.* ii, 16)[7] and Gregory of Nyssa[8] say that anger is made up of sorrow and desire. Both of these are in the concupiscible part. Therefore anger is in the concupiscible part.

On the contrary, The concupiscible is distinct from the irascible power. If, therefore, anger

---

[1] PG 40, 692.   [2] *Ethics,* VII, 6 (1149[b]20).
[3] *Confessions,* II, 13 (PL 32, 681)
[4] *Rhetoric,* II, 2 (1378[b]1).

[5] DD IV, 28.   [6] *Epist.,* CCXI (PL 33, 964).
[7] PG 94, 933.
[8] Cf. Nemesius, *De Nat. Hom.,* chap. 21 (PG 40, 692).

were in the concupiscible power, the irascible would not take its name from it.

I answer that, As stated above (Q. XXIII, A. 1), the passions of the irascible part differ from the passions of the concupiscible part in that the objects of the concupiscible passions are good and evil absolutely considered, while the objects of the irascible passions are good and evil of a certain elevation or arduousness. Now it has been stated (A. 2) that anger looks to two objects: namely, the vengeance that it seeks, and the person on whom it seeks vengeance; and in respect of both, anger requires a certain arduousness, for the movement of anger does not arise unless there be some magnitude about both these objects, since "we take no account about things that are nothing or very minute," as the Philosopher observes.[1] It is therefore evident that anger is not in concupiscible, but in the irascible part.

Reply Obj. 1. Cicero gives the name of desire to any kind of craving for a future good,[2] without discriminating between that which is arduous and that which is not. Accordingly he considers anger as a kind of desire, since it is a desire of vengeance. In this sense, however, desire is common to the irascible and concupiscible parts.

Reply Obj. 2. Anger is said to grow into hatred, not as though the same passion which at first was anger afterwards becomes hatred by becoming inveterate, but by a kind of causality. For anger when it lasts a long time engenders hatred.

Reply Obj. 3. Anger is said to be composed of sorrow and desire, not as though they were its parts, but because they are its causes; and it has been said above (Q. XXV, A. 2) that the concupiscible passions are the causes of the irascible passions.

Article 4. *Whether Anger Requires an Act of Reason?*

We proceed thus to the Fourth Article: It seems that anger does not require an act of reason.

Objection 1. For, since anger is a passion, it is in the sensitive appetite. But the sensitive appetite follows an apprehension, not of reason, but of the sensitive part. Therefore anger does not require an act of reason.

Obj. 2. Further, dumb animals are devoid of reason, and yet they are seen to be angry. Therefore anger does not require an act of reason.

Obj. 3. Further, drunkenness fetters the reason; nevertheless it is conducive to anger. Therefore anger does not require an act of reason.

On the contrary, The Philosopher says[3] that "anger listens to reason somewhat."

I answer that, As stated above (A. 2), anger is a desire for vengeance. Now vengeance implies a comparison between the punishment to be inflicted and the hurt done; therefore the Philosopher says[4] that "anger, as if it had drawn the inference that it ought to quarrel with such a person, is therefore immediately exasperated." Now to compare and to draw an inference is an act of reason. Therefore anger, in a fashion, requires an act of reason.

Reply Obj. 1. The movement of the appetitive power may follow an act of reason in two ways. In the first way, it follows the reason in so far as the reason commands, and thus the will follows reason; hence it is called the rational appetite. In another way, it follows reason in so far as the reason denounces, and thus anger follows reason. For the Philosopher says[5] that "anger follows reason, not in obedience to reason's command, but as a result of reason's denouncing the injury." For the sensitive appetite is subject to the reason, not immediately but through the will.

Reply Obj. 2. Dumb animals have a natural instinct imparted to them by the Divine Reason, in virtue of which they are gifted with movements, both internal and external, like rational movements, as stated above (Q. XL, A. 3).

Reply Obj. 3. As stated in the *Ethics,*[6] "anger listens somewhat to reason" in so far as reason denounces the injury inflicted, "but listens not perfectly," because it does not observe the rule of reason as to the measure of vengeance. Anger, therefore, requires an act of reason, and yet proves a hindrance to reason. Therefore the Philosopher says[7] that those who are very drunk, so as to be incapable of the use of reason, do not get angry; but those who are slightly drunk do get angry, through being still able, though hampered, to form a judgment of reason.

Article 5. *Whether Anger Is More Natural than Concupiscence?*

We proceed thus to the Fifth Article: It would seem that anger is not more natural than concupiscence.

---

[1] *Rhetoric,* II, 2 (1378ᵇ12).
[2] *Tuscul.,* IV, 6 (DD III, 26).

[3] *Ethics,* VII, 6 (1149ᵇ1).   [4] *Ibid.* (1149ᵃ33).
[5] Pseudo-Aristotle, *Problemata,* XXVIII, 3 (949ᵇ17).
[6] Aristotle, VII, 6 (1149ᵇ1).
[7] Pseudo-Aristotle, *Problemata,* III, 2, 27 (871ⁿ8; 875ᵃ29).

Objection 1. Because it is proper to man to be by nature a gentle animal. But "gentleness is contrary to anger," as the Philosopher states.[1] Therefore anger is not more natural than concupiscence; indeed it seems to be altogether unnatural to man.

Obj. 2. Further, reason is divided against nature, for those things that are according to reason are not said to act according to nature. Now "anger requires an act of reason, but concupiscence does not," as stated in the *Ethics.*[2] Therefore concupiscence is more natural than anger.

Obj. 3. Further, anger is a desire for vengeance, while concupiscence is a desire for those things especially which are pleasant to the touch, namely, for pleasures of the table and for sexual pleasures. But these things are more natural to man than vengeance. Therefore concupiscence is more natural than anger.

On the contrary, The Philosopher says[3] that "anger is more natural than concupiscence."

I answer that, By natural we mean that which is caused by nature, as stated in the *Physics.*[4] Consequently the question as to whether a particular passion is more or less natural cannot be decided without reference to the cause of that passion. Now the cause of a passion, as stated above (Q. XXXVI, A. 2), may be considered in two ways: first, on the part of the object; secondly, on the part of the subject. If then we consider the cause of anger and of desire, on the part of the object, thus concupiscence, especially of pleasures of the table, and of sexual pleasures, is more natural than anger, in so far as these pleasures are more natural to man than vengeance.

If, however, we consider the cause of anger on the part of the subject, thus anger, in a manner, is more natural; and, in a manner, concupiscence is more natural. Because the nature of any man may be considered either as to the generic, or as to the specific nature, or again as to the particular temperament of the individual. If then we consider the generic nature, that is, the nature of this man considered as an animal, in this way concupiscence is more natural than anger, because it is from this very generic nature that man is inclined to desire those things which tend to preserve in him the life both of the species and of the individual. If, however, we consider the specific nature, that is, the nature of this man as a rational being, then anger is more

natural to man than concupiscence, in so far as anger follows reason more than concupiscence does. Therefore the Philosopher says[5] that "to punish," which pertains to anger, "is more natural to man than meekness"; for it is natural to everything to rise up against things contrary and hurtful. And if we consider the nature of the individual in respect of his particular temperament, in this way anger is more natural than concupiscence, for the reason that anger is prone to ensue from the natural tendency to anger, more than desire, or any other passion, is to ensue from a natural tendency to desire, which tendencies result from a man's individual temperament. Because disposition to anger is due to a bilious (*cholerica*) temperament; and of all the humours, the bile moves quickest, for it is like fire. Consequently he that is temperamentally disposed to anger is sooner incensed with anger, than he that is temperamentally disposed to desire, is inflamed with desire; and for this reason the Philosopher says[6] that a disposition to anger is more liable to be transmitted from parent to child than a disposition to desire.

Reply Obj. 1. We may consider in man both the natural temperament on the part of the body, and the reason. On the part of the bodily temperament, a man, considered specifically, does not naturally excel others either in anger or in any other passion, on account of the equability of his temperament. But other animals, in so far as their temperament recedes from this equability and approaches to an extreme disposition, are naturally disposed to some excess of passion, such as the lion in daring, the hound in anger, the hare in fear, and so forth. On the part of reason, however, it is natural to man both to be angry and to be gentle, in so far as reason somewhat causes anger, by proclaiming the injury which causes anger, and somewhat appeases anger, in so far as the angry man does not listen wholly to the command of reason, as stated above (A. 4, REPLY 3).

Reply Obj. 2. Reason itself belongs to the nature of man; therefore from the very fact that anger requires an act of reason, it follows that it is, in a manner, natural to man.

Reply Obj. 3. This argument regards anger and concupiscence on the part of the object.

ARTICLE 6. *Whether Anger Is More Grievous than Hatred?*

We proceed thus to the Sixth Article: It seems that anger is more grievous than hatred.

---

[1] *Rhetoric*, II, 3 (1380ᵃ6).
[2] Aristotle, VII, 6 (1149ᵇ1).   [3] *Ibid.* (1149ᵇ6).
[4] Aristotle, II, 1 (192ᵇ35; 193ᵃ32).

[5] *Ethics*, IV, 5 (1126ᵃ30).
[6] *Ibid.*, VII, 6 (1149ᵇ6)

Objection 1. For it is written (Prov. 27. 4) that *anger hath no mercy, nor fury when it breaketh forth.* But hatred sometimes has mercy. Therefore anger is more grievous than hatred.

Obj. 2. Further, it is worse to suffer evil and to grieve for it, than merely to suffer it. But when a man hates, he is contented if the object of his hatred suffer evil; but the angry man is not satisfied unless the object of his anger know it and sorrow from it, as the Philosopher says.[1] Therefore, anger is more grievous than hatred.

Obj. 3. Further, a thing seems to be so much the more firm according as more things concur to set it up; thus a habit is all the more settled through being caused by several acts. But anger is caused by the concurrence of several passions, as stated above (A. 1), but hatred is not. Therefore anger is more settled and more grievous than hatred.

On the contrary, Augustine, in his Rule,[2] compares hatred to "a beam," but anger to "a mote."

I answer that, The species and character of a passion are taken from its object. Now the object of anger and the object of hatred have the same subject; for, just as the hater wishes evil to him whom he hates, so does the angry man wish evil to him with whom he is angry. But there is a difference of aspect; for the hater desires evil to his enemy, as evil, but the angry man wishes evil to him with whom he is angry, not as evil but in so far as it has an aspect of good, that is, in so far as he estimates it as just, since it is a means of vengeance. Therefore also it has been said above (A. 2) that hatred implies application of evil to evil, while anger denotes application of good to evil. Now it is evident that to seek evil under the aspect of justice is a lesser evil than to seek evil to someone absolutely. Because to wish evil to someone under the aspect of justice may be according to the virtue of justice, if it be in conformity with the command of reason; and anger fails only in this, that it does not obey the precept of reason in taking vengeance. Consequently it is evident that hatred is far worse and graver than anger.

Reply Obj. 1. In anger and hatred two points may be considered: namely, the thing desired, and the intensity of the desire. As to the thing desired, anger has more mercy than hatred has. For since hatred desires another's evil for evil's sake, it is satisfied with no particular measure of evil, because those things that are desired for their own sake, are desired without measure, as the Philosopher states,[3] instancing a miser with regard to riches. Hence it is written (Ecclus. 12. 16): *An enemy . . . if he find an opportunity, will not be satisfied with blood.* Anger, on the other hand, seeks evil only under the aspect of a just means of vengeance. Consequently when the evil inflicted goes beyond the measure of justice according to the estimate of the angry man, then he has mercy. Therefore the Philosopher says[4] that "the angry man is appeased if many evils befall, whereas the hater is never appeased."

As to the intensity of the desire, anger excludes mercy more than hatred does, because the movement of anger is more impetuous, through the heating of the bile. Hence the passage quoted continues: *Who can bear the violence of one provoked?*

Reply Obj. 2. As stated above, an angry man wishes evil to someone in so far as this evil is a means of just vengeance. Now vengeance is wrought by the infliction of a punishment, and the notion of punishment consists in being contrary to the will, painful, and inflicted for some fault. Consequently an angry man desires this that the person whom he is hurting may feel it and be in pain and know that this has been brought upon him on account of the harm he has done the other. The hater, on the other hand, cares not for all this, since he desires another's evil as such. It is not true, however, that an evil is worse through giving pain, because "injustice and imprudence, although evil," yet, being voluntary, "do not grieve those in whom they are," as the Philosopher observes.[5]

Reply Obj. 3. That which proceeds from several causes, is more settled when these causes are of one kind; but it may be that one cause prevails over many others. Now hatred ensues from a more lasting cause than anger does. For anger arises from a disturbance of the soul due to the wrong inflicted, but hatred ensues from a disposition in a man by reason of which he considers that which he hates to be contrary and hurtful to him. Consequently, as passion is more transitory than disposition or habit, so anger is less lasting than hatred, although hatred itself is a passion ensuing from this disposition. Hence the Philosopher says[6] that "hatred is more incurable than anger."

---

[1] *Rhetoric*, II, 4 (1382a8).
[2] *Epist.*, CCXI (PL 33, 964).
[3] *Politics*, I, 9 (1257b25); cf. II, 7 (1267b4).
[4] *Rhetoric*, II, 4 (1382a14).
[5] *Ibid.*, II, 4 (1382a11).
[6] *Ibid.* (1382a7).

ARTICLE 7. *Whether Anger Is Only Towards Those to Whom One Has a Relation of Justice?*

We proceed thus to the Seventh Article: It seems that anger is not only towards those to whom one has a relation of justice.

Objection 1. For there is no justice between man and irrational beings. And yet sometimes one is angry with irrational beings; thus, out of anger, a writer throws away his pen, or a rider strikes his horse. Therefore anger is not only towards those to whom one has a relation of justice.

Obj. 2. Further, "there is no justice towards oneself . . . nor is there justice towards one's own."[1] But sometimes a man is angry with himself, for instance, a penitent, on account of his sin; hence it is written (Ps. 4. 5): *Be ye angry and sin not.* Therefore anger is not only towards those with whom one has a relation of justice.

Obj. 3. Further, justice and injustice can be of one man towards an entire class, or a whole community; for instance, when the state injures an individual. But anger is not towards a class but only towards an individual, as the Philosopher states.[2] Therefore, properly speaking, anger is not towards those with whom one is in relation of justice or injustice.

The contrary, however, may be gathered from the Philosopher.[3]

I answer that, As stated above (A. 6), anger desires evil as being a means of just vengeance. Consequently, anger is towards those to whom we are just or unjust; for vengeance is an act of justice, and to inflict injury is an act of injustice. Therefore both on the part of the cause, namely, the harm done by another, and on the part of the vengeance sought by the angry man, it is evident that anger concerns those to whom one is just or unjust.

Reply Obj. 1. As stated above (A. 4, Reply 2), anger, though it follows an act of reason, can nevertheless be in dumb animals that are devoid of reason, in so far as through their natural instinct they are moved by their imagination to something like rational action. Since then in man there is both reason and imagination, the movement of anger can be aroused in man in two ways. First, when only his imagination proclaims the injury, and in this way, man is aroused to a movement of anger even against irrational and inanimate beings, which movement

is like that which occurs in animals against anything that injures them. Secondly, by the reason proclaiming the injury; and thus, according to the Philosopher,[4] "it is impossible to be angry with insensible things, or with the dead," both because they feel no pain, which is, above all, what the angry man seeks in those with whom he is angry, and because there is no question of vengeance on them, since they can do us no harm.

Reply Obj. 2. As the Philosopher says,[5] metaphorically speaking there is a certain justice and injustice between a man and himself, in so far as the reason rules the irascible and concupiscible parts of the soul. And in this sense a man is said to be avenged on himself, and consequently, to be angry with himself. But properly, and *per se,* a man is never angry with himself.

Reply Obj. 3. The Philosopher assigns as one difference between hatred and anger, that "hatred may be felt towards a class, as we hate the entire class of thieves, while anger is directed only towards an individual."[6] The reason is that hatred arises from our considering a quality as disagreeing with our disposition, and this may refer to a thing in general or in particular. Anger, on the other hand, ensues from someone having injured us by his action. Now all actions are the deeds of individuals, and consequently anger is always pointed at an individual. When the whole community hurts us, the whole community is counted as one individual.

ARTICLE 8. *Whether the Species of Anger Are Suitably Assigned?*

We proceed thus to the Eighth Article: It seems that Damascene (*De Fide Orthod.* ii, 16)[7] unsuitably assigns three species of anger,— wrath, ill-will and rancour.

Objection 1. For no genus derives its specific differences from accidents. But these three are diversified in respect of an accident; for the beginning of the movement of anger is called wrath (χόλos), if anger continue it is called ill-will (μῆνις), while rancour (κότοs) is anger waiting for an opportunity of vengeance. Therefore these are not different species of anger.

Obj. 2. Further, Cicero says (*Quæst. Tusc.* iv, 9)[8] that "*excandescentia* (irascibility) is what

---

[1] Aristotle, *Ethics,* v, 6 (1134^{b}12).
[2] *Rhetoric,* II, 4 (1382^{a}4).
[3] *Ibid.,* II, 2, 3 (1378^{a}31; 1380^{a}5).

[4] *Ibid.,* II, 3 (1380^{b}24).
[5] *Ethics,* v, 11 (1138^{b}5).
[6] *Rhetoric,* II, 4 (1382^{a}4).
[7] PG 94, 933; also Nemesius, *De Nat. Hom.,* XXI (PG 40, 692); cf. the doctrine of the stoics in Stobaeus, *Eclogae,* II, 6 (p. 583), and Diogenes Laertius, *De Vita et Mor. Philosoph.,* VII, 144 (DD 183).   [8] DD IV, 28.

the Greeks call θυμῶσις, and is a kind of anger that arises and subsides intermittently"; while according to Damascene (*ibid.*) θυμῶσις is the same as κότος (rancour). Therefore κότος does not bide its time for taking vengeance, but in course of time spends itself.

Obj. 3. Further, Gregory (*Moral.* xxi, 5)[1] gives three degrees of anger, namely, "anger without utterance, anger with utterance, anger with perfection of speech," corresponding to the three degrees mentioned by Our Lord (Matt. 5. 22): *Whosoever is angry with his brother* (thus implying anger without utterance), and then, *whoever shall say to his brother, "Raca"* (implying anger with utterance yet without full expression), and lastly, *whoever shall say "Thou fool"* (where we have perfection of speech). Therefore Damascene's division is imperfect, since it takes no account of utterance.

On the contrary stands the authority of Damascene (*loc. cit.*) and Gregory of Nyssa (Nemesius, *De Nat. Hom.* xxi).[2]

I answer that, The species of anger given by Damascene and Gregory of Nyssa are taken from those things which give increase to anger. This happens in three ways. First, from the facility of the movement itself, and he calls this kind of anger "bile" (*fel,* χόλος) because it is quickly aroused. Secondly, on the part of the grief that causes anger, and which dwells some time in the memory; this pertains to "ill-will" (*mania,* μῆνις), which is derived from the verb to dwell (*maneo,* μένειν). Thirdly, on the part of that which the angry man seeks, namely, vengeance; and this pertains to "rancour" (*furor,* κότος), which never rests until it is avenged. Hence the Philosopher calls some angry persons "choleric" (*acutus,* ἀκρόχολοι), because they are easily angered; some he calls "bitter" (*amarus,* πικροί), because they retain their anger for a long time; and some he calls "ill-tempered" (*difficilis,* χαλεποί), because they never rest until they have retaliated.[3]

Reply Obj. 1. All those things which give anger some kind of perfection are not altogether accidental to anger; and consequently nothing prevents them from causing a specific difference of anger.

Reply Obj. 2. Irascibility, which Cicero mentions seems to pertain to the first species of anger, which consists in a certain quickness of temper, rather than to rancour (*furor*). And there is no reason why the Greek θυμῶσις, which

is denoted by the Latin *furor,* should not signify both quickness to anger, and firmness of purpose in being avenged.

Reply Obj. 3. These degrees are distinguished according to various effects of anger, and not according to degrees of perfection in the very movement of anger.

QUESTION XLVII

OF THE CAUSE THAT PROVOKES ANGER, AND THE REMEDIES OF ANGER
(In Four Articles)

WE must now consider the cause that provokes anger, and its remedies. Under this head there are four points of inquiry: (1) Whether the motive of anger is always something done against the one who is angry? (2) Whether slight or contempt is the sole motive of anger? (3) Of the cause of anger on the part of the angry person. (4) Of the cause of anger on the part of the person with whom one is angry.

ARTICLE 1. *Whether the Motive of Anger Is Always Something Done Against the One Who Is Angry?*

We proceed thus to the First Article: It would seem that the motive of anger is not always something done against the one who is angry.

Objection 1. Because man, by sinning, can do nothing against God, for it is written (Job 35. 6): *If thy iniquities be multiplied, what shalt thou do against Him?* And yet God is spoken of as being angry with man on account of sin, according to Ps. 105. 40: *The Lord was exceedingly angry with His people.* Therefore it is not always on account of something done against him that a man is angry.

Obj. 2. Further, anger is a desire for vengeance. But one may desire vengeance for things done against others. Therefore we are not always angry on account of something done against us.

Obj. 3. Further, as the Philosopher says,[4] man is angry especially with those "who despise what he takes a great interest in; thus men who study philosophy are angry with those who despise philosophy," and so forth. But contempt of philosophy does not harm the philosopher. Therefore it is not always a harm done to us that makes us angry.

Obj. 4. Further, he that holds his tongue when another insults him, provokes him to greater anger, as Chrysostom observes (*Hom.*

---

[1] PL 76, 194.   [2] PG 40, 692.
[3] *Ethics,* IV, 5 (1268ª18).
[4] *Rhetoric,* II, 2 (1379ª33).

xxii *in Ep. ad Rom.*).[1] But by holding his tongue he does nothing against the other. Therefore a man is not always provoked to anger by something done against him.

On the contrary, The Philosopher says[2] that "anger is always due to something done to oneself; but hatred may arise without anything being done to us, for we hate a man simply because we think him such."

I answer that, As stated above (Q. XLVI, A. 6), anger is the desire to hurt another for the purpose of just vengeance. Now unless some injury has been done, there is no question of vengeance. Nor does any injury provoke one to vengeance, but only that which is done to the person who seeks vengeance. For just as everything naturally seeks its own good, so does it naturally repel its own evil. But injury done by anyone does not affect a man unless in some way it be something done against him. Consequently the motive of a man's anger is always something done against him.

Reply Obj. 1. We speak of anger in God, not as of a passion of the soul but as of a judgment of justice, according as He wills to take vengeance on sin. Because the sinner, by sinning, cannot do God any actual harm. But so far as he himself is concerned, he acts against God in two ways. First, in so far as he despises God in His commandments. Secondly, in so far as he harms himself or another, which injury pertains to God, since the person injured is an object of God's providence and protection.

Reply Obj. 2. If we are angry with those who harm others and seek to be avenged on them, it is because those who are injured belong in some way to us, either by some kinship or by friendship, or at least because of the nature we have in common.

Reply Obj. 3. When we take a very great interest in a thing, we look upon it as our own good, so that if anyone despise it, it seems as though we ourselves were despised and injured.

Reply Obj. 4. Silence provokes the insulter to anger when he thinks it is due to contempt, as though his anger were slighted; and a slight is an action.

ARTICLE 2. *Whether the Sole Motive of Anger Is Slight or Contempt?*

We proceed thus to the Second Article: It would seem that slight or contempt is not the sole motive of anger.

Objection 1. For Damascene says (*De Fide Orthod.* ii, 16)[3] that "we are angry when we suf-

fer, or think that we are suffering, an injury." But one may suffer an injury without being despised or slighted. Therefore a slight is not the only motive of anger.

Obj. 2. Further, desire for honour and grief for a slight belong to the same subject. But dumb animals do not desire honour. Therefore they are not grieved by being slighted. And yet they are roused to anger when wounded, as the Philosopher says.[4] Therefore a slight is not the sole motive of anger.

Obj. 3. Further, the Philosopher gives many other causes of anger,[5] for instance, being forgotten by others; that others should rejoice in our misfortunes; that they should make known our evils; being hindered from doing as we like. Therefore being slighted is not the only motive for being angry.

On the contrary, The Philosopher says[6] that "anger is a desire, with sorrow, for vengeance, on account of a seeming slight done unbecomingly."

I answer that, All the causes of anger are reduced to slight. For "slight is of three kinds," as stated in the *Rhetoric,*[7] namely, "contempt, despiteful treatment," that is, hindering one from doing one's will, and "insolence," and all motives of anger are reduced to these three. Two reasons may be assigned for this. First, because anger seeks another's hurt as being a means of just vengeance; and therefore it seeks vengeance in so far as it seems just. Now just vengeance is taken only for that which is done unjustly; hence that which provokes anger is always something considered in the light of an injustice. Hence the Philosopher says[8] that "men are not angry if they think that they have wronged some one and are suffering justly on that account; for there is no anger at what is just." Now injury is done to another in three ways: namely, through ignorance, through passion, and through choice. Then, most of all, a man does an injustice when he does it from choice, on purpose, or from deliberate malice, as stated in the *Ethics.*[9] Therefore we are most of all angry with those who, in our opinion, have hurt us on purpose. For if we think that some one has done us an injury through ignorance or through passion, either we are not angry with him at all, or very much less, for to do anything through ignorance or through pas-

[1] PG 60, 609.   [2] *Rhetoric,* II, 4 (1382ª2).

[3] PG 94, 932.   [4] *Ethics,* III, 8 (1116ᵇ25).
[5] *Rhetoric,* II, 2 (1379ª9).   [6] *Ibid.* (1378ª31).
[7] *Rhetoric,* II, 2 (1378ᵇ13).
[8] *Rhetoric,* II, 3 (1380ᵇ16).
[9] Aristotle, V, 8 (1135ᵇ24; 1136ª4).

sion takes away from the notion of injury, and to a certain extent calls for mercy and forgiveness. Those, on the other hand, who do an injury on purpose seem to sin from contempt; therefore we are angry with them most of all. Hence the Philosopher says[1] that "we are either not angry at all, or not very angry with those who have acted through anger, because they do not seem to have acted slightingly."

The second reason is because a slight is opposed to a man's excellence, for; "men think little of things that are not worth much."[2] Now we seek for some kind of excellence from all our goods. Consequently whatever injury is inflicted on us, in so far as it takes away from our excellence, seems to pertain to slight.

Reply Obj. 1. Any other cause, besides contempt, through which a man suffers an injury, takes away from the notion of injury; contempt or slight alone adds to the motive of anger, and consequently is of itself the cause of anger.

Reply Obj. 2. Although a dumb animal does not seek honour as such, yet it naturally seeks a certain superiority, and is angry with anything that takes away from it.

Reply Obj. 3. Each of those causes amounts to some kind of slight. Thus forgetfulness is a clear sign of slight esteem, for the more we think of a thing the more is it fixed in our memory. Again if a man does not hesitate by his remarks to give pain to another, this seems to show that he thinks little of him; and those too who show signs of hilarity when another is in misfortune, seem to care little about his good or evil. Again he that hinders another from carrying out his will, without deriving thereby any profit to himself, seems not to care much for his friendship. Consequently all those things, in so far as they are signs of contempt, provoke anger.

ARTICLE 3. *Whether a Man's Excellence Is the Cause of His Being Angry?*

We proceed thus to the Third Article: It would seem that a man's excellence is not the cause of his being more easily angry.

Objection 1. For the Philosopher says[3] that "some are angry especially when they are grieved, for instance, the sick, the poor, and those who are disappointed." But these things seem to pertain to defect. Therefore defect rather than excellence makes one prone to anger.

Obj. 2. Further, the Philosopher says[4] that "some are very much inclined to be angry when they are despised for some failing or weakness of the existence of which there are grounds for suspicion; but if they think they excel in those points, they do not trouble." But a suspicion of this kind is due to some defect. Therefore defect rather than excellence is a cause of a man being angry.

Obj. 3. Further, whatever pertains to excellence makes a man agreeable and hopeful. But the Philosopher says[5] that "men are not angry when they play, make jokes, or take part in a feast, nor when they are prosperous or successful, nor in moderate pleasures and well-founded hope." Therefore excellence is not a cause of anger.

On the contrary, The Philosopher says[6] that excellence makes men prone to anger.

I answer that, The cause of anger in the man who is angry may be taken in two ways. First in respect of the motive of anger, and thus excellence is the cause of a man being easily angered. Because the motive of anger is an unjust slight, as stated above (A. 2). Now it is evident that the more excellent a man is, the more unjust is a slight offered him in the matter in which he excels. Consequently those who excel in any matter are most of all angry if they be slighted in that matter; for instance, a wealthy man in his riches, or an orator in his eloquence, and so forth.

Secondly, the cause of anger in the man who is angry may be considered on the part of the disposition produced in him by the motive mentioned above. Now it is evident that nothing moves a man to anger except a hurt that grieves him. But whatever pertains to defect is above all a cause of grief, since men who suffer from some defect are more easily hurt. And this is why men who are weak, or subject to some other defect, are more easily angered, since they are more easily grieved.

This suffices for the *Reply to the First Objection.*

Reply Obj. 2. If a man be despised in a matter in which he evidently excels greatly, he does not consider himself the loser thereby, and therefore is not grieved, and in this respect he is less angered. But in another respect, in so far as he suffers a greater indignity through being despised, he has more reason for being angry; unless perhaps he thinks that he is envied or insulted not through contempt but through ignorance, or some other like cause.

[1] *Rhetoric*, II, 3 (1380ª34).   [2] *Ibid.*, II, 2 (1378ᵇ12).
[3] *Ibid.*, II, 2 (1379ª15).   [4] *Ibid.* (1379ª36).
[5] *Ibid.*, II, 3 (1380ᵇ3).
[6] *Ibid.*, II, 9 (1386ᵇ12; 1387ᵇ 4).

Reply Obj. 3. All these things hinder anger in so far as they hinder sorrow. But in another respect they naturally provoke anger, because they make it more unbecoming to insult anyone.

ARTICLE 4. *Whether a Person's Defect Is a Reason for Being More Easily Angry with Him?*

We proceed thus to the Fourth Article: It would seem that a person's defect is not a reason for being more easily angry with him.

Objection 1. For the Philosopher says[1] that "we are not angry with those who confess and repent and humble themselves; on the contrary, we are gentle with them. Hence dogs do not bite those who sit down." But these things pertain to littleness and defect. Therefore littleness of a person is a reason for being less angry with him.

Obj. 2. Further, there is no greater defect than death. But anger ceases at the sight of death. Therefore defect of a person does not provoke anger against him.

Obj. 3. Further, no one thinks little of a man through his being friendly towards him. But we are more angry with friends if they offend us or refuse to help us; hence it is written (Ps. 54. 13): *If my enemy had reviled me I would verily have borne with it.* Therefore a person's defect is not a reason for being more easily angry with him.

On the contrary, The Philosopher says[2] that "the rich man is angry with the poor man, if the latter despise him; and in like manner the prince is angry with his subject."

I answer that, As stated above (AA. 2, 3), unmerited contempt more than anything else is a provocative of anger. Consequently deficiency or littleness in the person with whom we are angry tends to increase our anger, in so far as it adds to the unmeritedness of being despised. For just as the higher a man's position is, the more undeservedly he is despised, so the lower it is the less reason he has for despising. Thus a nobleman is angry if he be insulted by a peasant; a wise man, if by a fool; a master, if by a servant.

If, however, the littleness or deficiency lessens the unmerited contempt, then it does not increase but lessens anger. In this way those who repent of their ill-deeds and confess that they have done wrong, who are humbled and ask pardon, mitigate anger, according to Prov. 15. 1: *A mild answer breaketh wrath,* because, that

[1] *Rhetoric,* II, 3 (1380ᵃ13).
[2] *Ibid.,* II, 2 (1379ᵃ1).

is, they seem not to despise, but rather to think much of those before whom they humble themselves.

This suffices for the *Reply to the First Objection.*

Reply Obj. 2. There are two reasons why anger ceases at the sight of death. One is because the dead are incapable of sorrow and sensation, and this is chiefly what the angry seek in those with whom they are angered. Another reason is because the dead seem to have attained to the limit of evils. Hence anger ceases in regard to all who are grievously hurt, in so far as this hurt surpasses the measure of just retaliation.

Reply Obj. 3. To be despised by one's friends seems also a greater indignity. Consequently if they despise us by hurting or by failing to help, we are angry with them for the same reason for which we are angry with those who are beneath us.

QUESTION XLVIII
OF THE EFFECTS OF ANGER
(*In Four Articles*)

WE must now consider the effects of anger, under which head there are four points of inquiry: (1) Whether anger causes pleasure? (2) Whether above all it causes fervour in the heart? (3) Whether above all it hinders the use of reason? (4) Whether it causes taciturnity?

ARTICLE 1. *Whether Anger Causes Pleasure?*

We proceed thus to the First Article: It would seem that anger does not cause pleasure.

Objection 1. Because sorrow excludes pleasure. But anger is never without sorrow, since, as stated in the *Ethics,*[3] "everyone that acts from anger, acts with pain." Therefore anger does not cause pleasure.

Obj. 2. Further, the Philosopher says[4] that "vengeance makes anger to cease, because it substitutes pleasure for pain"; from this we may gather that the angry man derives pleasure from vengeance, and that vengeance quells his anger. Therefore on the advent of pleasure, anger departs. Consequently anger is not an effect united with pleasure.

Obj. 3. Further, no effect hinders its cause, since it is conformed to its cause. But pleasure hinders anger, as stated in the *Rhetoric.*[5] Therefore pleasure is not an effect of anger.

[3] Aristotle, VII, 6 (1149ᵇ20).
[4] *Ethics,* IV, 5 (1126ᵃ21).
[5] Aristotle, II, 3 (1380ᵇ4).

On the contrary, The Philosopher quotes[1] the saying that anger is

"Sweet to the soul as honey to the taste."[2]

I answer that, As the Philosopher says,[3] pleasures, chiefly sensible and bodily pleasures, are remedies against sorrow, and therefore the greater the sorrow or anxiety, the more sensible are we to the pleasure which heals it, as is evident in the case of thirst which increases the pleasure of drink. Now it is clear from what has been said (Q. XLVII, AA. 1, 3), that the movement of anger arises from a wrong done that causes sorrow, for which sorrow vengeance is sought as a remedy. Consequently as soon as vengeance is present, pleasure follows, and so much the greater according as the sorrow was greater. Therefore if vengeance be really present, perfect pleasure ensues, entirely excluding sorrow, so that the movement of anger ceases. But before vengeance is really present, it becomes present to the angry man in two ways: in one way, by hope, because none is angry unless he hopes for vengeance, as stated above (Q. XLVI, A. 1); in another way, by thinking of it continually, for to everyone that desires a thing it is pleasant to dwell on the thought of what he desires, and thus the imaginings of dreams are pleasant. Accordingly an angry man takes pleasure in thinking about vengeance. This pleasure, however, is not perfect, so as to banish sorrow and consequently anger.

Reply Obj. 1. The angry man does not grieve and rejoice at the same thing; he grieves for the wrong done, while he takes pleasure in the thought and hope of vengeance. Consequently sorrow is to anger as its beginning, while pleasure is the effect or term of anger.

Reply Obj. 2. This argument holds in regard to pleasure caused by the real presence of vengeance, which banishes anger altogether.

Reply Obj. 3. Pleasure that precedes hinders sorrow from ensuing, and consequently is a hindrance to anger. But pleasure felt in taking vengeance follows from vengeance.

ARTICLE 2. *Whether Anger Above All Causes Fervour in the Heart?*

We proceed thus to the Second Article: It would seem that fervour is not above all the effect of anger.

Objection 1. For fervour, as stated above (Q. XXVIII, A. 5; Q. XXXVII, A. 2), belongs to love. But love, as above stated (Q. XXVII, A. 4), is the

beginning and cause of all the passions. Since then the cause is more powerful than its effect, it seems that anger is not the chief cause of fervour.

Obj. 2. Further, those things which of themselves arouse fervour increase as time goes on; thus love grows stronger the longer it lasts. But in course of time anger grows weaker; for the Philosopher says[4] that "time puts an end to anger." Therefore fervour is not the proper effect of anger.

Obj. 3. Further, fervour added to fervour produces greater fervour. But the addition of a greater anger banishes already existing anger, as the Philosopher says.[5] Therefore anger does not cause fervour.

On the contrary, Damascene says (*De Fide Orth.* ii, 16)[6] that "anger is fervour of the blood around the heart, resulting from an exhalation of the bile."

I answer that, As stated above (Q. XLIV, A. 1), the bodily change that occurs in the passions of the soul is proportionate to the movement of the appetite. Now it is evident that every appetite, even the natural appetite, tends with greater force to repel that which is contrary to it, if it be present; hence we see that hot water freezes harder, as though the cold acted with greater force on the hot object. Since then the appetitive movement of anger is caused by some injury inflicted, as by a contrary that is present, it follows that the appetite tends with great force to repel the injury by the desire of vengeance; and hence ensues great vehemence and impetuosity in the movement of anger. And because the movement of anger is not one of recoil, which corresponds to the action of cold, but one of prosecution, which corresponds to the action of heat, the result is that the movement of anger produces fervour of the blood and vital spirits around the heart, which is the instrument of the soul's passions. And hence it is that, on account of the heart being so disturbed by anger especially those who are angry betray signs of it in their outer members. For, as Gregory says (*Moral.* v, 45)[7] "the heart that is inflamed with the stings of its own anger beats quick, the body trembles, the tongue stammers, the countenance takes fire, the eyes grow fierce, they that are well known are not recognized. With the mouth indeed he shapes a sound, but the understanding knows not what it says."

[1] *Ibid.*, II, 2 (1378[b]5).
[2] *Iliad,* XVIII, 109, 110 (trans. Pope).
[3] *Ethics,* VII, 14 (1154[a]27).

[4] *Rhetoric,* II, 3 (1380[b]6).   [5] *Ibid.* (1380[b]10).
[6] PG 94, 932; also in Nemesius, *De Nat. Hom.,* XXI (PG 40, 692); cf. Aristotle, *Soul,* I, 1 (403[a]31); also Plotinus, IV *Ennead,* IV, 28 (BU IV, 130).   [7] PL 75, 724.

Reply Obj. 1. "Love itself is not felt so keenly as in the absence of the beloved," as Augustine observes (*De Trin.* x, 12).[1] Consequently when a man suffers from a hurt done to the excellence that he loves, he feels his love for it the more, the result being that his heart is moved with greater fervour to remove the hindrance to the object of his love, so that anger increases the fervour of love and makes it to be felt more.

Nevertheless, the fervour arising from heat differs according as it is to be referred to love or to anger. Because the fervour of love has a certain sweetness and gentleness, for it tends to the good that one loves, and hence it is likened to the warmth of the air and of the blood. For this reason sanguine temperaments are more inclined to love; and hence the saying that love springs from the liver, because of the blood being formed there. On the other hand, the fervour of anger has a certain bitterness with a tendency to destroy, for it seeks to be avenged on the contrary evil; hence it is likened to the heat of fire and of the bile, and for this reason Damascene says (*loc. cit.*) that it "results from an exhalation of the bile whence it takes its name (χολή)."

Reply Obj. 2. Time, of necessity, weakens all those things the causes of which are impaired by time. Now it is evident that memory is weakened by time, for things which happened long ago easily slip from our memory. But anger is caused by the memory of a wrong done. Consequently the cause of anger is impaired little by little as time goes on, until at length it vanishes altogether. Moreover a wrong seems greater when it is first felt, and our estimate of it is gradually lessened the farther the sense of present wrong recedes into the past. The same applies to love, so long as the cause of love is in the memory alone; hence the Philosopher says[2] that "if a friend's absence lasts long, it seems to make men forget their friendship." But in the presence of a friend, the cause of friendship is continually being multiplied by time, therefore the friendship increases; and the same would apply to anger, were its cause continually multiplied.

Nevertheless the very fact that anger soon spends itself proves the strength of its fervour, for as a great fire is soon spent having burnt up all the fuel, so too anger, by reason of its vehemence, soon dies away.

Reply Obj. 3. Every power that is divided in several parts is weakened. Consequently if a man who is already angry with one becomes angry with another, by this very fact his anger with the former is weakened. Especially is this so if his anger in the second case is greater, because the wrong done which aroused his former anger will, in comparison with the second wrong, which is considered greater, seem to be of little or no account.

ARTICLE 3. *Whether Anger Above All Hinders the Use of Reason?*

We proceed thus to the Third Article: It would seem that anger does not hinder the use of reason.

Objection 1. Because that which presupposes an act of reason, does not seem to hinder the use of reason. But anger listens to reason, as stated in the *Ethics.*[3] Therefore anger does not hinder reason.

Obj. 2. Further, the more the reason is hindered, the less does man show his thoughts. But the Philosopher says[4] that "an angry man is not cunning but is open." Therefore anger does not seem to hinder the use of reason, as concupiscence does; for concupiscence is cunning, as he also states.[5]

Obj. 3. Further, the judgment of reason becomes more evident by juxtaposition of the contrary, because contraries stand out more clearly when placed beside one another. But this also increases anger, for the Philosopher says[6] that "men are more angry if they receive contrary treatment; for instance, honourable men, if they be dishonoured," and so forth. Therefore the same cause increases anger and aids the judgment of reason. Therefore anger does not hinder the judgment of reason.

On the contrary, Gregory says (*Moral.* v, 25)[7] that "anger withdraws the light of understanding, while by agitating it troubles the mind."

I answer that, Although the mind or reason makes no use of a bodily organ in its proper act, yet, since it needs certain sensitive powers for the execution of its act, the acts of which powers are hindered when the body is disturbed, it follows of necessity that any disturbance in the body hinders even the judgment of reason, as is clear in the case of drunkenness or sleep. Now it has been stated (A. 2) that anger, above all, causes a bodily disturbance in the region of the heart, so much so as to affect even the outward members. Consequently, of all the passions,

---

[1] PL 42, 984.
[2] *Ethics,* VIII, 5 (1157^b11).
[3] Aristotle, VII, 6 (1149^a25).
[4] *Ethics,* VII, 6 (1149^b14).   [5] *Ibid.*
[6] *Rhetoric,* II, 2 (1379^b4).   [7] PL 75, 724.

anger is the most manifest obstacle to the judgment of reason, according to Ps. 30. 10: *My eye is troubled with wrath.*

Reply Obj. 1. The beginning of anger is in the reason as regards the appetitive movement, which is the formal element of anger. But the passion of anger forestalls the perfect judgment of reason, as though it listened but imperfectly to reason, on account of the agitation of the heart urging to instant action, which agitation is the material element of anger. In this respect it hinders the judgment of reason.

Reply Obj. 2. An angry man is said to show his thoughts not because it is clear to him what he ought to do, but because he acts openly, without thought of hiding anything. This is due partly to the reason being hindered so that it is not able to discern what should be hidden and what done openly, nor to devise the means of hiding, and partly to the dilatation of the heart which pertains to magnanimity which is an effect of anger; hence the Philosopher says of the magnanimous man[1] that "he is open in his hatreds and his friendships . . . and speaks and acts openly."—Concupiscence, on the other hand, is said to lie low and to be cunning, because, in many cases, the pleasurable things that are desired, savour of shame and voluptuousness, in which man does not wish to be seen. But in those things that savour of manliness and excellence, such as matters of vengeance, man seeks to be in the open.

Reply Obj. 3. As stated above (reply 1) the movement of anger begins in the reason, and therefore the juxtaposition of one contrary with another facilitates the judgment of reason, on the same grounds as it increases anger. For when a man who is possessed of honour or wealth suffers a loss in them, the loss seems all the greater, both on account of the contrast, and because it was unforeseen. Consequently it causes greater grief, just as a great good, through being received unexpectedly, causes greater delight. And in proportion to the increase of the grief that precedes, anger is increased also.

ARTICLE 4. *Whether Anger Above All Causes Taciturnity?*

We proceed thus to the Fourth Article: It would seem that anger does not cause taciturnity.

Objection 1. Because taciturnity is opposed to speech. But increase of anger conduces to speech, as is evident from the degrees of anger laid down by Our Lord (Matt. 5. 22), where

[1] *Ethics,* IV, 3 (1124^{b}26).

He says: *Whosoever is angry with his brother;* and . . . *whosoever shall say to his brother, "Raca";* and . . . *whosoever shall say to his brother, "Thou fool."* Therefore anger does not cause taciturnity.

Obj. 2. Further, through failing to obey reason, man sometimes breaks out into disordered words; hence it is written (Prov. 25. 28): *As a city that lieth open and is not compassed with walls, so is a man that cannot refrain his own spirit in speaking.* But anger, above all, hinders the judgment of reason, as stated above (A. 3). Consequently above all it makes one break out into disordered words. Therefore it does not cause taciturnity.

Obj. 3. Further, it is written (Matt. 12. 34): *Out of the abundance of the heart the mouth speaketh.* But anger, above all, causes a disturbance in the heart, as stated above (A. 2). Therefore, above all, it conduces to speech. Therefore it does not cause taciturnity.

On the contrary, Gregory says (*Moral.* v, 45)[2] that "when anger does not vent itself outwardly by the lips, inwardly it burns the more fiercely."

I answer that, As stated above (A. 3; Q. XLVI, A. 4), anger both follows an act of reason, and hinders the reason; and in both respects it may cause taciturnity. On the part of the reason, when the judgment of reason prevails so far that although it does not curb the appetite in its inordinate desire for vengeance, yet it curbs the tongue from unbridled speech. Therefore Gregory says (*ibid.*): "Sometimes when the mind is disturbed, anger, as if in judgment, commands silence."—On the part of the impediment to reason because, as stated above (A. 2), the disturbance of anger reaches to the outward members, and chiefly to those members which reflect more distinctly the emotions of the heart, such as the eyes, face and tongue; hence, as observed above (A. 2), "the tongue stammers, the countenance takes fire, the eyes grow fierce." Consequently anger may cause such a disturbance that the tongue is altogether deprived of speech, and taciturnity is the result.

Reply Obj. 1. Anger sometimes goes so far as to hinder the reason from curbing the tongue; but sometimes it goes yet further, so as to prevent the movement of the tongue and other outward members.

And this suffices for the *Reply to the Second Objection.*

Reply Obj. 3. The disturbance of the heart

[2] PL 75, 725.

may sometimes superabound to the extent that the movements of the outward members are hindered by the disordered movement of the heart. Thence ensue taciturnity and immobility

of the outward members, and sometimes even death. If, however, the disturbance be not so great, then *out of the abundance of the heart* thus disturbed, the mouth proceeds to speak.